THE JOHN HARVARD LIBRARY

BERNARD BAILYN
Editor-in-Chief

THE NATURE
AND TENDENCY OF
FREE INSTITUTIONS

By FREDERICK GRIMKE

Edited by John William Ward

THE JOHN HARVARD LIBRARY

The Belknap Press of Harvard University Press

CAMBRIDGE, MASSACHUSETTS

1968

CONTENTS

INTRODUCTION

FREDERICK GRIMKE: THE DYNAMICS OF FREEDOM

WHEN, in 1834, George Bancroft remarked on the need for a book which described the nature of American democracy, a correspondent replied that "no dependence can be placed upon any treatise that has yet appeared which professes to discuss [the business of government]. You must draw upon your own resources, you must think, — and think alone." [1] The opinion was widely shared. Orestes Brownson thought no American had produced a "work on politics of the slightest scientific value." [2] George Sidney Camp, in the preface to his little book, *Democracy* (1841), dwelt at length on the anomaly that "in a democratic country, where self-government has been successfully exercised by the people for nearly three quarters of a century," there was no literature on democracy to which one might refer "the young democratic disciple." The result was that Americans "journey on, living in the rich experience and practical enjoyment of democratic freedom, but in entire and reckless indifference to its abstract principles." Camp accounted for the anomaly by observing, with mild wit, that the "chief speculators" of the day were "in merchandise and real estate." Having won independence, with a continent to conquer and a nation to make, Americans were content "with the practical results" of their political system, hardly inclined to "patient study of its abstract nature." We have been "all action," said Camp. "There has been no room for the thinker; he has been jostled one side." [3]

Historians have agreed. The single high moment in American political thought remains the Revolutionary and Constitutional period, but even there the brilliance of a John Adams or an Alexander Hamilton, a Thomas Jefferson or a James Madison spent itself on shaping institutions rather than making books. State papers, occasional essays,

1. W. S. Wait to Bancroft, October 15, 1834, cited in Arthur M. Schlesinger, Jr., *The Age of Jackson* (Boston, 1948), p. 309.
2. *The United States Magazine and Democratic Review*, 13 (August, 1843), 129.
3. George Sidney Camp, *Democracy* (New York, 1841), pp. 10, 13, 15.

and letters were their form, not the architectonics of speculative theory. Once the challenge of revolution had passed and the need for a national government had been met, the intelligence of Americans turned to fields other than political theory. Even the terrible crisis of a Civil War brought forth blood, not political imagination. After the founding of the republic, American political thought seems, as Herbert Croly put it, a career in "intellectual lethargy." [4] The result is that we have turned to outsiders, especially Tocqueville, for critical perspective on our practice.

Yet, there is an exception to test the rule. There was at least one American, Frederick Grimke, who decided to step aside from the practical affairs of everyday life and devote himself to an analysis of the underlying principles of American democratic practice. The result was *Considerations Upon the Nature and Tendency of Free Institutions* which appeared in two editions in the author's lifetime, in 1848 and 1856, and in a third, in 1871, after his death. The three editions are, however, no measure of the book's contemporary fame, only of the author's tenacity. *The Nature and Tendency of Free Institutions* received only passing comment upon publication and has been largely lost to sight since.[5] But, if one of the tests of American scholarship is

4. Herbert Croly, *The Promise of American Life* (New York, 1909), p. 50.
5. The only considerable contemporary notice of *The Nature and Tendency of Free Institutions* was a long, unsigned review in the *North American Review*, 144 [n.s., 69] (October, 1849), 440–469. The *Southern Quarterly Review* drew attention to Grimke's book twice: 22 [n.s., 6] (July, 1852), 253–254; 23 [n.s., 7] (January, 1853), 120–140; the first is a bare notice that Grimke's book, along with two others by Southern writers, had appeared; the second is an essay on South Carolina and John C. Calhoun's theory of "concurrent majorities" which takes the form of an essay-review of eight titles, ranging from Calhoun's *Disquisition*, Tocqueville's *Democracy in America* and Algernon Sidney's *Discourse Concerning Government* to Grimke's *The Nature and Tendency of Free Institutions*, but with almost nothing explicitly on Grimke, only the implicit compliment of closely paraphrasing portions of his argument at the outset of the essay. The first notice in the *Southern Quarterly Review* is anonymous; the second is signed with the initials "E.H.B.," and in the edition in the Harvard College Library someone has in pencil corrected them to "E.B.B." and attributed the review to "Edward B. Bryan, Esq."
   The reviewer in the *North American Review* was critical of the structure and the content of Grimke's work. From the tone of his review, it is obvious that he is a Christian conservative ("freedom lies, not in the absence of restraint, but in the power of obedience to God," p. 442) and hostile to the Democratic party of Jackson and Polk. Grimke read this review and wrote to his sister, Sarah, asking if she could discover the name of the author. He caught the olympian tone of the review when he said, "The author bestows great praise, and yet seems to give it unwillingly, as if none but a Bostonian could write a great work." (Frederick

its responsibility to the sources of our common life, then Grimke's book deserves to be restored to its proper place. It is a penetrating analysis of the theory and institutions of American democracy. It fairly deserves comparison with Tocqueville's justly famous work, *Democracy in America,* and is in certain ways superior. It is, in any event, the single best book written by an American in the nineteenth century on the meaning of our political way of life.

I

We know frustratingly little about Frederick Grimke. What hints we have might recommend themselves to the intuition of, say, Henry James, for whom a gesture or a phrase could reveal the significance of an entire life; so too, the collective story of the Grimké family deserves the rich imagination of a William Faulkner. But the historian of Frederick Grimke's life, restricted by the pressure of fact, can have little to say.

Born September 1, 1791, into the famous Grimké family of Charleston, South Carolina, Frederick Grimke was one of fourteen children of John Faucheraud Grimké and brother of Thomas Smith Grimké and Sarah and Angelina Grimké. Grimke's father, a jurist and legal historian, author of *The Public Laws of the State of South Carolina* (1790), had gone as a young man to England to study at Eton and then Trinity College, Cambridge (A.B., 1774), after which he studied law in the Middle Temple in London. A young American abroad as the Revolutionary crisis threatened, the father was active in representing the colonial cause in England. The outbreak of the Revolution interrupted his studies and brought him home. He fought in the Continental Army, rising to the rank of lieutenant-colonel, served in the state House of Representatives under the Articles of Confederation, and was a member of the state convention that ratified the Federal Constitution, which he supported. His chief work lay, however, in the law, and as the *Dictionary of American Biography* puts it, "he did his best

---

Grimke to Sarah Grimké, July 31, 1850, in the Weld-Grimké Correspondence, William L. Clements Library, Ann Arbor, Michigan.)

In twentieth-century American historical scholarship, there is only one article on Grimke and his book: Arthur A. Ekirch, Jr., "Frederick Grimké [*sic*]: Advocate of Free Institutions," *Journal of the History of Ideas,* 11 (January, 1950), 75–92. Grimke did not, in print or in his own hand in his correspondence, use the acute accent on the last letter of his name.

work as a legal compiler in the period of legal reform following the revolution."

Thomas Smith Grimké, Frederick's older brother, a graduate of Yale (A.B., 1807), a lawyer, was an important figure in the ferment of reform in the early nineteenth century. Deeply religious (he had originally intended to become a minister) and strongly nationalistic (as a state senator he opposed South Carolina on the tariff and upheld the federal government during the nullification controversy in 1832), Thomas Smith Grimké was actively involved in a wide variety of reform movements, from plans to simplify spelling and the support of utilitarian education, which he thought appropriate to a democratic society, to the temperance movement and the peace crusade. But it is Frederick's sisters, Sarah and Angelina, who are best known to history because of their place in the abolitionist movement and the crusade for women's rights.

The two movements were intertwined in the minds of the Grimké sisters from the start. Sarah, the elder, regretted she had not been born a man so she could become a lawyer; her life-long devotion to the ideal of equality for her own sex was inextricably involved with her struggle on behalf of the Negro for freedom from the repressive forces of society. At first, Sarah was the leader. Restive under the institutional forms of her inherited Episcopalianism, Sarah was converted to the Quaker faith after exposure to the Society of Friends on a trip to Philadelphia. Angelina followed her lead, but the social conservatism of the Philadelphia Friends satisfied neither.

The turning-point of their lives, and the point at which Angelina seems to have gone beyond her older sister and assumed the dominant role, came in 1835 when Angelina wrote a letter to William Lloyd Garrison, urging him to continue his good work, a letter which Garrison published in *The Liberator* (September 19, 1835). Sarah disapproved, as did the conservative Friends of the Philadelphia meeting, but there was no turning back for Angelina, and the next year she published her *Appeal to the Christian Women of the South,* a pamphlet which asked the women of the South to use their moral influence to destroy the terrible iniquity of slavery. Written by a Southern woman, the *Appeal* had an obvious attraction for Northern abolitionists; in the South it was publicly burned and Angelina was threatened with prison if she were ever to return to her native city and state. Sarah overcame her initial reluctance and followed the course of her younger sister; in 1836, she wrote an *Epistle to the Clergy of the Southern States.*

The Grimké sisters were now identified with the cause of radical abolitionism. After first addressing audiences composed only of women, both achieved great notoriety, at a time when women were supposed to be seen and not heard, as the first women to deliver speeches before a mixed audience. The need to defend their own right to speak made them inevitable leaders in the cause for women's rights as well as opponents of slavery. After Angelina married Theodore Weld in 1838, Sarah lived with her, partly to help her sister who was frail and in chronically poor health.

Most of what one can discover about Frederick Grimke is through his letters to Sarah which still survive.[6] Frederick followed his older brother, Thomas Smith Grimké, to Yale where he roomed in his senior year with Samuel F. B. Morse, the painter and inventor, and became a member of Phi Beta Kappa and senior orator of the Class of 1810.[7] He returned to Charleston where he studied and practiced law, and about the time of the death of his father in 1819 moved to Ohio, first to Columbus, then to Chillicothe. The reason for choosing Ohio remains obscure, but it seems that he was a "protege" of Thomas Worthington (1773–1827), "The Father of Ohio Statehood." [8] In any event, he quickly impressed those he met. "He has been in the state about eighteen months," wrote a young friend in the Governor's office, "and has received the distinguished appointment of President Judge of the Court of C.[ommon] Pleas — He is a man of fine talents." [9] Grimke's first position on the bench as a judge in the

6. Frederick's letters to Sarah are to be found, as already noted, in the Weld-Grimké Correspondence in the William L. Clements Library at Ann Arbor, Michigan. Henceforth, reference to them will be by date in the text.

Sarah's side of what must have been a rich correspondence is lost because Frederick's papers were destroyed in a "great fire" (January 20, 1861). Presumably, Grimke refers to a fire on April 1, 1852, which gutted the center of Chillicothe, Ohio, where he then lived as a bachelor in a hotel. In local lore that fire was remembered as "the great fire" and it destroyed the entire center of town, including the city's two hotels. B. F. Sproat, *The Great Fire, Chillicothe, Ohio, 1852* (Chillicothe, Ohio, 1944).

7. Ekirch, "Frederick Grimké: Advocate of Free Institutions," p. 76.

8. George I. Reed, ed., *Bench and Bar of Ohio* (Chicago, 1897), I, 20–21.

9. "W.," to Miss Abby B. Lyman (Litchfield, Connecticut), January 17, 1820,

Court of Common Pleas was by appointment to fill a vacancy, but in 1830 he was elected by the General Assembly to a regular appointment as presiding judge. In 1836, he was elected to the Supreme Court of Ohio, a position which he held until 1842 when he resigned to devote himself to study and writing, the major result of which six years later was *The Nature and Tendency of Free Institutions*.[10]

Thus far the record. The rest of what one may say about Frederick Grimke is largely a matter of inference and speculation. It is clear that his life struck others as modest and retiring. The author of a notice of *The Nature and Tendency of Free Institutions* in the *Southern Quarterly Review* wrote, "Mr. Grimke . . . has long been known in the South as a gentleman, at once of great ability and modesty; of an ability which would justify his claim upon general attention, yet of a modesty that shrinks from notice altogether."[11] Grimke's style of life, as a bachelor living in hotels, further suggests a certain withdrawal from the social life about him, and when, in *The Nature and Tendency of Free Institutions*, he describes the virtuous life of the judge, he sounds as if he were elevating his own inclinations to the level of principle. It is not expected, he wrote, that the judge "will mingle in all the gayety and frivolity of fashionable life. He is thus placed out of the way of temptation more than other men, and is insensibly beguiled into a train of conduct the most favorable for the practice of both public and private virtue."

Yet beneath Grimke's outward modesty, one may detect considerable ambition. That ambition is implicit in the "Preface to the Second Edition" of *The Nature and Tendency of Free Institutions* where he attacks the "vitiated taste for reading" which spurned knowledge for books which were "of a superficial or of an exciting character." The result was not only "to enfeeble the understanding and even to pervert the moral faculties," wrote Grimke, but "the mischief extends itself to the few who are possessed by a noble ambition. Their efforts are chilled by the mental dyspepsia which prevails around them when

in the Greene-Roelker Papers, The Cincinnati Historical Society, Cincinnati, Ohio. Mrs. Andrew N. Jergens, Jr., the librarian of the Cincinnati Historical Society, writes that "the 'W' signature in the letter to Miss Abby Lyman was apparently William Greene. William Greene was born January 1, 1797 in Warwick, R.I.; died March 23, 1883. In 1821 he married Abby Lyman."

10. Elliot Howard Gilkey, *The Ohio Hundred Year Book, A Handbook of the Public Men and Public Institutions of Ohio . . .* (Columbus, Ohio, 1901), p. 470.

11. *Southern Quarterly Review,* 22 [n.s., 6] (July, 1852), 254.

they stand in need of being powerfully braced by a healthful and invigorating influence."

Whether out of personal coldness or dissatisfaction with the "mental dyspepsia" of Chillicothe, Ohio, Grimke turned in upon himself, withdrew from political and social life, and in his ambition set himself the task of educating his contemporaries to understand the nature of their own society. But he did not do so sourly. He obviously enjoyed his hotel life. He wrote Sarah on April 22, 1857, after a new hotel had been built in Chillicothe after the great fire, "I am boarding in a hotel as formerly. You know Dr. Johnson told Boswell that a tavern was 'the home of human felicity.' " Or, again, in response to some "fine things" Sarah had said of him in one of her letters, Grimke wrote (March 13, 1858) that she had caused him to remember "the sentiment of Michael Angelo, who on being asked why he had never married, replied that his profession was his wife, and his productions his children."

If Grimke appeared cold to most people, he had an ambition and a passion he revealed at least to his sister, Sarah. He kept a book of "maxims" and once filled a whole letter to her (November 16, 1850) with sixty of them. Maxim "50" read, "Some persons have an appearance of reserve which is mistaken for coldness. Exactly the reverse is the case. Instead of too little, they have an excess of passion. The intensity of their feelings makes them use constant efforts to restrain them, and this to commonplace folks, gives them the appearance of coldness." Sarah must have recognized the character because she scored the margin beside this particular maxim. Nor did Grimke surrender the pride and ambition which led him to devote himself to a lonely life of writing. His contemporaries may have refused to recognize his worth but Grimke was willing to let the future judge. When he died in 1863, *The Nature and Tendency of Free Institutions* was virtually forgotten, but in his will Grimke set money aside for a final edition of his work with the instruction that a copy "be presented to the Congressional Libraries of the United States and the Confederate States, to each of the States, and to the chief Universities in each." [12]

Further, if Grimke felt stifled in the intellectual atmosphere of his time and place, he did not surrender to it. However provincial the details of his outward life, Grimke's inner life was intellectually rich

12. *The Historical Magazine*, 7 (April, 1863), 136.

and cosmopolitan. He was alert to the best contemporary European thought of his time and kept a considerable library of books, many of which he ordered directly from Paris. His letters to Sarah are full of suggestions for her reading. He had lavish praise for Comte's *Positive philosophy* ("The French mind has thrown off no greater work") and urged Sarah to "make an absolute *study*" of Harriet Martineau's translation, especially the last three books (December 18, 1854). On February 20, 1857, when he was only up to volume fourteen of a French edition of Sismondi's *History of France* in thirty volumes, he recommended the work warmly to Sarah; when she complained she did not have time to read so much, he lectured her on what one could get through if one only put aside four hours a day for reading. At the same time, Grimke was alert to the thought and writing of his own country. He recognized the value of Robert Baird's *Religion in America* (1844), yet criticized it justly as being far from a "philosophical" work; "it is altogether a work of detail" (April 22, 1857). He listened to lectures by the Transcendentalist, Theodore Parker, and wrote Sarah (April 24, 1853) that Parker's "distinction between the Reason and the Understanding is borrowed from Coleridge, who borrowed from the German School. But it is without any foundation."

 The Nature and Tendency of Free Institutions bears sufficient witness to the breadth of Grimke's reading; one need not multiply examples from his letters to his sister. The point is simply that Grimke, living in a small town in the Old Northwest when the region was barely out of the frontier state, brought a range of reference and comparative study to bear upon his analysis of American political institutions which is admirable and which may still stand as an example to students of American life. Writing to Sarah (May 30, 1858) about the poor state of medical knowledge, Grimke insisted, "Individual cases prove nothing." He carried the same attitude to his study of American political institutions, and studied the practices of the ancient republics and contemporary Europe as well as the constitutions of the several states in order to make his study a "philosophical" work and not merely the work of "detail" he thought Baird's book on religion to be.

 Yet, among all the subjects and through all the reading Frederick Grimke wrote about to Sarah, there was one topic he refused to confront: Negro slavery. Grimke accepted slavery on the basis of a belief in the racial inferiority of the Negro. His sisters did not agree with him and reticence on the subject was not mutual; it lay on Frederick's side alone. In a long letter (June 10, 1857), after Sarah had obviously responded to a re-reading of *The Nature and Tendency of Free Institutions* when it appeared in a second edition, Grimke wrote: "I feel very much concerned to think that my chapter on slavery has given you so much trouble. You adopted the true sentiment on reading it in the first edition. You remarked, 'I differ with you, but I admire a mind *which is true to its own convictions.*' You probably do not recollect that you have not written me a single letter during the last twelve months which has not contained something on the subject. The golden rule you laid down in 1850, is I believe the most reasonable, the most natural, and the most just which can be adopted."

Grimke's reluctance to write to Sarah about Negro slavery can be understood in many ways. First, simple tact: he had said all he had to say in *The Nature and Tendency of Free Institutions* and there was no reason to exacerbate the feelings of a sister for whom he obviously cared deeply. Second — a generalization of the first — his "convictions" were markedly different from those of the world of his sisters and Theodore Weld. Grimke did not believe in the power of moral persuasion; he was skeptical of plans to reform the world and suspicious of the personal motivations of reformers themselves. He would approach these matters obliquely, but he never confronted Sarah with them directly. For example, he wrote Sarah (August 17, 1855), "The picture drawn by Victor Considérant, in 'Destinée Sociale' is very flattering, and delightful to look upon; but this fair exterior all vanishes at the touch of experience. The extreme feebleness of our condition, the imperfection of our faculties, and our dependence for enjoyment, on events which we can in no way control, naturally, and necessarily, produce this effect. And as this is the case, we must submit to the disadvantages, which are a law of our being, and not endeavor to exaggerate them by any artificial plan of life." Grimke did not believe, as did the Transcendentalists whom he criticized in the person of Theodore Parker, that man had access through intuition to the truth. He was a skeptical man who insisted upon the hard facts of daily experience. He knew he shared little of the fervent hopefulness which had led his sisters by the route of the inner light to a millennial dream of a world governed by love and justice.

These two reasons, Grimke's tact and his desire not to challenge further the assumptions of his sister's life, are probably sufficient to account for his decision to avoid slavery and the Negro in his letters to Sarah. But there is a possible third reason. There was another brother among the Grimke children, Henry, and Frederick Grimke may have known what his sisters were finally to discover only after his death: there was, through Henry, a Negro line of descent in the Grimke family.

Henry appears fleetingly in Frederick Grimke's letters. Although Frederick was not a wealthy man, he advanced loans to his brother which went unpaid. "Poor fellow," Frederick wrote Sarah (April 22, 1857) after Henry's death, "it is only surprising that he should have lived so long, for as nothing contributes so much to longevity as the love of life, so nothing contributes so much to shorten it, as a distaste, and a disgust for life. In his letters to me, two or three years ago, he was fond of ruminating on death, as an effectual relief from all unhappiness. I thought I had diverted his mind from this melancholy mood, but his late letters to you show that he had again returned to it. To defects which never injured any human being but himself, he joined many virtues. To his faults then we will be 'a little blind; and to his virtues very kind.' "

How much Frederick knew of the "faults" of his death-obsessed brother, one cannot know; Sarah and Angelina discovered the truth only by chance after the Civil War. In addition to a distinguished line of white descent, the aristocratic Grimké family had a line of black descent, no less distinguished. Henry, in addition to a family by his white wife, had by Nancy Weston, a family slave, three sons, Archibald Henry, Francis James, and John Grimke. In his will, Henry provided that his Negro sons should be freed, and left them under the guardianship of their white half-brother, E. Montague Grimké. But five years later, their white brother tried to sell them into slavery, which led, in the flat understatement of Francis J. Grimke years later, "to some complications."[13] To escape slavery, Francis J. Grimke ran off and became the valet of an officer in the Confederate Army. After two years, on a visit to Charleston where the officer he served was stationed at a fort in the harbor, he was arrested and thrown into jail for some months. While Francis was recuperating after jail in the home of his slave mother, E. Montague Grimké, fearful that Francis would run off again, sold him to another Confederate officer whom he served as body servant until the end of the Civil War.

13. See the letter by Francis J. Grimke, January 24, 1887, which is reproduced by Carter G. Woodson, ed., *The Works of Francis J. Grimke,* 2 vols. (Washington, D.C., 1942), I, viii–ix.

After the war Francis J. Grimke and his brother, Archibald Henry, went North to school. Their brother, John, stayed behind in South Carolina with their mother. Francis and Archibald came finally to Lincoln University in Pennsylvania where a faculty member, impressed with their ability, wrote about them to Samuel Shellabarger, the congressman from Ohio, who in turn wrote a story about the Grimke boys for the press. Angelina Grimké happened upon Shellabarger's account in a Boston newspaper and bravely wrote to Francis and Archibald to discover whether they were freed slaves who took her family's name or were actually her relatives.[14] When they discovered that the boys were indeed their nephews, Angelina and Sarah visited them, acknowledged them, and assisted them in their further education.

Sarah and Angelina made their discovery after Frederick's death, so the rest may be quickly told. Francis J. Grimke went to Princeton Theological Seminary, became pastor of the Fifteenth Street Presbyterian Church in Washington, D.C., and trustee of Howard University. Archibald Henry Grimke went to Harvard Law School, practiced law in Boston, wrote biographies of William Lloyd Garrison and Charles Sumner, and was active in Massachusetts politics. In 1894, President Cleveland appointed him consul to Santo Domingo. Both brothers were unremitting throughout their lives in the struggle for full citizenship and rights for the Negro, and both sided with W.E.B. Du Bois in the struggle against the leadership of Booker T. Washington which led to the schism in the Negro movement in 1906 and to the founding of the N.A.A.C.P. in 1909.[15]

For Frederick Grimke, the ultimate irony in the story is that his own relatives provided living proof of the inadequacy of his belief that the Negro was incapable of seizing the advantages of freedom which, except for the Negro, he understood so well.

II

Since Grimke's title declares that his book will be a consideration of institutions in a free society, a convenient place to begin is with his

14. Benjamin P. Thomas, *Theodore Weld, Crusader for Freedom* (New Brunswick, N. J., 1950), pp. 256–260, tells Angelina's and Sarah's side of the discovery.
15. Woodson's "Introduction" to his edition of *The Works of Francis J. Grimke* provides a brief general account of Francis' life. For Archibald H. Grimke, see the *Dictionary of American Biography* and the account by his daughter, the poetess, Angelina W. Grimke, "A Biographical Sketch of Archibald H. Grimke," *Opportunity: A Journal of Negro Life* (February, 1925), pp. 44–47.

analysis of how the departments of government, institutions narrowly
conceived, do function. To do so is, however, only convenient, because Grimke conceives of institutions in a much wider sense. He sees
particular institutions as the expression of the general structure of
society which calls them into being. He is a sociologist of politics.
His sociology, in turn, implicates him in a consideration of the social
dynamics of history and an ultimate justification of free institutions
which involves no less than a theory of human nature. He is, finally, a
philosopher of politics. The three levels of analysis are not discrete,
of course; they interpenetrate each other on nearly every page he
writes, but one may separate them in order to grasp clearly what Frederick Grimke called "the dynamics of freedom."

The Political Institutions of Freedom

From the beginning, there have been in American political thought
two, implicitly antithetical views of the nature of a proper constitution and the security it provides against arbitrary power. The first
places emphasis on the form of government created by a constitution,
on the institutional arrangement of the departments of government;
responsible government is to be achieved by setting up a government
in which power is distributed carefully among the various parts in
order to check undue power by any one particular branch in the whole,
finely articulated, self-regulating system. In this view, checks against
arbitrary or irresponsible power are institutionalized within the government which the constitution creates. In the American experience,
it is the view one normally associates with the term, "checks and balances."

The second view puts emphasis not so much on the organization of
the departments of government created by the constitution but on
the creation of government itself, the process by which governments
are made, and unmade, and insists that the true check on the power
of government, on any one or all of the particular branches of government, lies always in the power of the people outside the doors of the
government. In this view, the measure of a good constitution is not
simply the form of government but the effectiveness of the process by
which the people out of government are constantly able to discipline
government by exercising the inalienable power which ultimately
sanctions all governments. In the American experience, it is the view
one normally associates with the term, "constituent power."

The remarkable thing about Grimke's analysis of how in the United States the institutions of government actually function is his clear recognition of the centrality of the constituent power principle. Although he devotes an individual chapter to each of the three major departments of government, the executive, the judiciary, and the legislature, and has interesting comments on each, his major point in each of these chapters is that the separation of powers in the frame of the American constitution works not because power is distributed within the government but because all branches of the government are, directly or indirectly, responsible to the will of the majority of the people outside the doors of government. To drive his point home, he devotes a further chapter to the question "Is the American Government a Balanced One?" His answer is that if one thinks in the traditional terms of a balanced constitution "in which the principal checks to power reside within the government, the American government is not a balanced one." But it is balanced in "a still higher sense" in that restraint upon government derives from the surveillance of the people who are outside the government and who control each of the powers parcelled out within the government only for the practical purpose of making more effective the various functions of government.[16]

Early in his book, Grimke remarks that "all the mechanical contrivances for balancing government are falling from our hands and can only be superseded by the engine of knowledge." What Grimke means by "knowledge" will, ultimately, take us to a consideration of his conception of the nature of man, the assumptions which lie at the base of his politics, but for the moment what is important is his observation that in a society where the people choose their rulers it is artificial and finally useless to pit power against power within the government since all power is, and should be, he insists, the servant of the people. Sovereignty, for Grimke, is a function of society, not a function of government.

The importance Grimke attaches to the responsibility of government to the people shows clearly in his discussion of the legislature and his logical preference for a unicameral rather than a bicameral system within the states. He accepts the division of the Federal

---

16. It is perhaps worth noting that in the second edition of *The Nature and Tendency of Free Institutions* Grimke added four pages to the beginning of the chapter, "Is the American Government a Balanced One?" (Book IV, Chapter VI), in order to emphasize the importance of the power of constituents over the departments of government.

government into a Senate and House since the national government was not meant to be, to use his favorite term, a "consolidated" government but a federation of states. But in the states, since the people elect both houses of the legislature by roughly the same qualifications, he points to the obvious fact that the check does not lie between the two but between each and its responsibility to the people. He admits that tradition may sanction the continuing existence of the division of the legislature into two branches, but he argues that in a democratic society the true check lies not in that division but in the fact that both branches are the creatures of a sovereign people. Likewise, in his discussion of the executive power, Grimke makes a virtue of a weak president on the ground that he will be more responsive to the will of the people.

The most interesting instance of Grimke's belief "that once a nation has entered upon the task of self-government it is bound to encounter all the perils which are incident to it" and of his confidence that these "perils" are "the means provided for preserving the integrity of the system" is to be found in his treatment of the judiciary and his rejection of the notion that the judiciary should be free from popular control. An independent judiciary, so important to the view that government should be controlled by the separation of powers and a system of checks and balances, represented the major obstacle to Grimke's reliance on the power of the people to control and make government responsible.

Grimke opens his chapter on the judiciary (Book III, Chapter VII) by disposing of the authority of Montesquieu who argued that the judicial branch was powerless. Anyone familiar with the thought of Grimke's time will recognize the boldness of the strategy and how free Grimke was, in rejecting Montesquieu, from accepted clichés about American political institutions. At least since Hamilton's use of the authority of Montesquieu in Federalist No. 78, those who wished to insist upon life tenure for judges and their independence from the vagaries of popular democracy had constantly invoked the authority of "the celebrated Montesquieu." Hamilton's use of Montesquieu was ingenious, if not ingenuous. What Hamilton wished to do in Federalist No. 78 was to convince the people of the state of New York that the organ of government closest to their will was that organ furthest removed from them in their electoral capacity, namely, the court. He did so by arguing that the court was responsible to the will of the constituent people as embodied in the Constitution and, in putting a negative to an act of the legislature, that the court was simply being responsible to the people over and above the heads of their agents, their directly elected representatives. To lend authority to his position, Hamilton added a footnote: "The celebrated Montesquieu, speaking of them, says: 'Of the three powers [the executive, the legislature, and the judiciary], the judiciary is next to nothing.' "

Grimke calmly sets Montesquieu, and Hamilton, aside by saying that in a monarchy where the king is sovereign and where the judges are appointed by the king this might be true, but in a democratic republic where the people are sovereign the judiciary "seems to possess a disproportionate share of power." If power is to be responsible to a free people, it must be responsible to the will of that people, so Grimke endorses the application of the principle of constituent power to all branches of government "indiscriminately" by arguing for limited tenure in the appointment of judges.[17] Grimke argues that a judge, whether appointed or elected, should hold office for a sufficient number of years to enable him to master the intricacies of his role in government, but not so long as to be insensitive to "the healthful influence of those opinions and feelings which grow up in the progress of every improving society." What Grimke obviously fears is a lag or a gap between the demands of the society and the attitudes of judges protected in their opinions by life tenure. The reason for his fear is the recognition, derived probably from his own experience on the bench, that the court is a legislative as well as a judicial body; that, as a later age would put it, judges make law.

Grimke repudiates the notion that the court simply applies the law to particular cases, the idea "commonly entertained," as he puts it, that "it is simply invested with the power of expounding the law." But, he points out, the "power of expounding comprehends a great deal and reaches much further than is generally imagined." Both the argument that the court is controlled by previous decisions and the argument that the court simply applies general principles to particular cases leave wide latitude for the particular judge. As much as Grimke admires the principle of *stare decisis* because it represents adherence to the accumulated experience of men, he observes that any particular

17. Although Grimke does, in his chapter on "The Judicial Power," refer to the Supreme Court, his discussion is restricted generally to the state courts. The reason derives from his reading of federal-state relations.

case may easily be arraigned under contradictory precedents. Or, if the court applies general principles, then the question is simply "principles determined by whom?" Inevitably, he argues, the judicial power is also a legislative power and dangerous precisely because the legislative function it performs "is a fact entirely hidden from the great majority of the community."

Grimke's handling of the judicial power represents his total commitment to the faith that the true "regulative principle" in society is to be found in "public opinion." At this point he confronts the question which Jefferson dismissed in his lighter moments with the suggestion that the nation should have a revolution every generation. Grimke solves the essential problem of how the people outside the doors of government are to make their will felt upon those who exercise power inside government by understanding what few in his time had yet come to recognize, the necessary place of the party in American politics.

Today it seems an unaccountable lapse in the general wisdom of the founding fathers that they paid no attention to the one institution that would make representative government actually work, namely, the party system. In the first generation, opposition to those in power, "the government," was understood only as the work of a "faction," a self-interested and disgruntled minority. The Federalists, during the Alien and Sedition crisis, came close to identifying opposition to governmental policy with treason, and Jefferson was not being simply politic in his famous first inaugural when he assumed that all Americans comprised one great party. The notion persisted into the age of Jackson. As *The United States Magazine and Democratic Review,* the organ of the Jacksonian Democratic party, put it in its first issue, "there does not exist in the people, with reference to its great masses, that irreconcilable hostility of opinions and leading principles which would be the natural inference from the violence of the party warfare in which we are perpetually engaged"; it assumed that all Americans would range themselves under "the broad and bright folds of our democratic banner" once Democrats had led them to understand the issues "rightly." [18] Neither did Grimke think there were "irreconcil-

18. *The United States Magazine and Democratic Review,* 1 (October–December, 1837), 1–2; the first issue of the *Democratic Review,* although dated "October–December, 1837," was actually published in January, 1838. See the publisher's "Note" at the front of the first volume.

able" divisions among the American people, but almost alone in his time he saw and defined the necessary function of party. Not even Martin Van Buren, one of the great builders of party organization, quite grasped the heart of the matter, as is clear from his *Inquiry into the Origins and Course of Political Parties in the United States* (1867).

What Grimke clearly saw was the necessity of party organization in a society committed to control by the people over the government. Unless some agency emerged to give institutional form to the amorphous shape of public opinion, then the principle of constituent power would fall victim to two opposite and undesirable extremes, either the sterility of an ideal incapable of practical implementation, or the violence of a revolutionary destruction of existing government whenever it proved irresponsible to the will of the people. "Popular parties," Grimke recognized, "are not only the natural result of elective government but, what is of much more consequence, they are abso- lutely necessary to uphold and preserve it." Grimke's point is that political institutions in a society where power resides in the people require a different kind of control than they do in a non-representative government. "In the artificial forms of government," he goes on to say, "a system of checks and balances is devised . . . to maintain each department in its proper place; but such an expedient would be futile and powerless where government means vastly more than the rule of the persons who fill the various public offices." Since the essence of free political institutions is to confer power upon the people, Grimke observes, "We want something more, therefore, than a scheme of checks and balances within the government. . . . We must contrive some machinery equally extensive for the purpose of controlling them." The development of the institution of the political party pro- vided the necessary "machinery" and, Grimke concludes, "popular parties very naturally, not to say necessarily, take the place of that curious system of checks and balances which are well enough adapted to a close aristocracy or pure monarchy, but which play only a sub- ordinate part in representative government."

For Grimke the "distinguishing feature" of American political in- stitutions was "that we may vary the paraphernalia of government as much as we please, but it still obstinately persists in every one of its departments to be a government based upon the popular will." The power of the "popular will" was not only the distinguishing feature of

American government, it was its distinguishing virtue, and Grimke wished his fellow countrymen to recognize that fact and its inevitable corollary, the necessity of party organization to provide an institutional voice for the popular will and to bring it to bear upon each and every office of government. He recognized that "the prevailing spirit of party" with its "eternal din and confusion" had led "zealous and patriotic individuals" to wish to do away with party politics. But he reminded such individuals that the "passions and fierce disputes" of party politics were "the only means in a society, not enlightened above what it falls to the lot of humanity to be, by which any signal change in the public policy of the state or the condition of the people can be obtained."

At this point, Grimke obviously faces the problem of defining the nature of public opinion to which political parties are to give voice, but before turning to his discussion of that problem, one must first consider one further check upon the power of government which bulks large in Grimke's discussion of the institutional arrangement of government, namely, the dual system of political authority which divides power between the national government and the several states. Although Grimke explicitly repudiates the arguments of John Taylor and demolishes John C. Calhoun's doctrine of nullification, he defends the autonomous power of the individual state to secede from the Union in order to defend its particular interest.

The purpose of Grimke's defense of the right of a state, as a last resort, to secede from the Union is to protect slavery. He is not, however, an apologist for slavery, nor a defender of the South in the reactionary style of a George Fitzhugh. Grimke can see no reasonable solution to the problem created by the South's "peculiar institution" and uneasily accepts it as a given fact of life, a necessity imposed, however unfortunately, upon society. In this respect, he is probably more characteristic of the general run of Americans, North and South, than benevolent abolitionists like his two sisters, on the one hand, or aggressive feudalists like Fitzhugh on the other. Grimke's grudging acquiescence to slavery as an institution results from his inability, or his unwillingness, to extend to the Negro his conception of the nature of man and of the consequences of freedom. He excludes the black man on the basis of a dubious theory of race. But, again, Grimke probably spoke for the majority of Americans in his time who celebrated freedom for themselves and denied it to the Negro.

The most that can be said for Grimke is that he was unable to imagine the extension of freedom to the slave. But at least he was candid. Although slavery and the Negro appear nowhere in the two chapters (Book IV, Chapters I–II) that deal with nullification and secession, in the midst of his discussion of classes in the United States (Book IV, Chapter IV) Grimke says, "But if one only knew how to deal with so difficult and delicate a subject" as Negro slavery, "if one only had the ability requisite to remove the institution without leaving worse consequences behind, there can be no doubt that it would be better that all the occupations of society should be filled by a free population exclusively." Lacking that ability, Grimke did not indulge in the cant that slavery was a good thing or that the South was better for it. "The men of the South," he wrote, "cannot reasonably contend that the institution of slavery is a benefit 'per se,' " and he scouted the notion, so dear to Fitzhugh, that the prevalence of "novel and startling doctrines in religion, morals and politics" in the North argued for a better ordered society in the South. Grimke found slavery itself repugnant, but accepted the conservative, pragmatic argument that the consequences of emancipation "in communities where the slaves are very numerous and of a race entirely distinct" from their masters were worse than the institution itself.

Since the Negro and slavery do not arise in Grimke's discussion of the place of the state in the federal system of national government, one might argue, as some have done for John C. Calhoun, that he was simply extending to its logical conclusion the classical liberal position of the protection of all minority interests against the intrusion of the power of the state and the tyranny of the majority. Yet, in the face of Grimke's acceptance elsewhere of equality and the will of the people, this seems unlikely and is made even more unlikely by the history of the text. The entire second chapter in Book IV on the right of a state to withdraw from the federal union, to secede, was added to the second edition of *The Nature and Tendency of Free Institutions*. In the first chapter of that book, on the "veto power" of the state to set aside obnoxious legislation by the national government, Grimke had, certainly to his own satisfaction, destroyed Calhoun's doctrine of nullification. Since at the same time he had, however reluctantly, ac-

cepted the necessity of the institution of slavery, he must have realized that he had left the slave South in an awkward position with no
way to defend itself. So, confident of his own reading of the Constitution, Grimke added to the second edition the second chapter which
argues for acceptance of the right of secession. The end he had in
view, however, was the preservation of the Union.

Grimke begins his discussion of the "veto power" of the individual
state with a review of the dual system of government in the federal
system whereby the individual citizen is subject to two sets of laws,
those of the particular state and those of the national government. "It
is the independent character of these two classes of government," he
says, "which has caused some eminent minds in America to doubt
whether the judicial power of the union extends to the determination
of the validity of the state laws when they conflict with the federal
constitution. It has been supposed that there could be no arbiter in
this case, and that the states, nay each of them separately, must necessarily possess a veto upon the decisions of the national tribunal."
He then directly confronts the notion put forward by John Taylor and
John C. Calhoun that when a single state challenged the constitutionality of a law Congress was required to call a constitutional convention to determine the issue. Grimke scouts this proposition on two
practical grounds: first, that it is clearly contrary to the amendment
process laid down in the Constitution itself; second, and more important, it would constitute a retrogressive step and destroy the achievement of a system of government where the laws act upon individuals
and not upon groups, however defined. But Grimke's two reasons are
only historical and practical. He cuts deeper into the issue by turning
the doctrine of nullification back upon itself.

If any one state may summon a convention because it challenges
the usurpation by the federal government of a power the state thinks
is reserved to it, then, Grimke points out, logically any other state
may do the same if it believes a state is exercising a power which is
delegated to the national government. The practical conclusion would
be, says Grimke, that "if a state has the right to veto a law of the federal government because it is not a delegated power, for the same reason will the federal government have a right to veto a law of a state
because it does not fall within the reserved powers." And he pointedly
asks the South if it believes that such laws as the exclusion of free men
of color, as in North and South Carolina and Louisiana, would sur-

vive the veto power of a northern state. The ingenious strategy of Taylor and Calhoun was, Grimke insisted, "a two-edged sword." Further, Grimke thought, Calhoun's argument in his *Discourse Upon the Constitution* was woven out of a "sophism." The fact that the Constitution was ratified by the several states no more meant that the national government could be undone by the act of a single state than a government created by individual citizens could be undone by the will of a single individual.

At this point Grimke faced the fact that he had denied the southern states any legal or political argument within the American system of government. So, inevitably, he confronted the ultimate and last resort, the right of secession, when a state thought its particular interests violated by the national government. Grimke affirms the right of secession, but arrives at his goal by a curious route. The heart of Grimke's argument is that, contrary to Taylor and Calhoun, the act of secession is not an assertion of the sovereignty of the state, but quite the opposite, "an unequivocal admission that the sovereignty does not reside in the state seceding." Since the federal union is a cession of power by the states singly to the states jointly, to use Grimke's formulation, there is no possible recourse to nullification by the single state. There is only withdrawal, which is the obverse of the exercise of sovereignty. "In the case of secession, instead of the constitution and laws being removed out of the way of the discontentèd state, the state itself removes out of the way." Grimke puts the matter this way to drive home the point at issue, that the individual state must defer to the sovereignty of the federal government so long as it remains in the union. The consequence was that "each state for itself, and for itself only, may withdraw from the union." A league of states against the sovereign power of the federal government would be an act of rebellion. Grimke wished to isolate the single state, force it to recognize that in the act of secession it was implicitly admitting it was not the seat of sovereign power, while he still defended its right to depart if it saw fit.

The conclusion of Grimke's argument for the right of secession was the hope that recognition of the right was the surest way to see that the right was not used. The individual state would instantly recognize the enormous disadvantages of "standing alone in the midst of a firm and compact league" and so defer secession until it was the last remaining option; at the same time, "open recognition of the right to

secede will render it disgraceful to embark in any scheme of concerted resistance to the laws while the state continues a member of
the Union." In the North, a frank avowal of the right of secession
would impose caution and restraint upon the national government.
"The public councils would be marked by more reflection when a
moral agency was substituted in the place of brute force."

With that sentence, Grimke reveals the heart of his trust, the belief
that the solution of the problems which threatened to rend the nation
North and South lay in calm considerations by reasonable men concerning the advantages and disadvantages of the Union. He drastically
underestimated the emotional appeal of an emergent southern nationalism or the mystique of the Union which Lincoln was to dramatize. His
own cool rationality could lead him, at the end of his chapter on secession, to envisage the time "when the same causes which led to the formation of the present Union will lead to the formation of two or more
Unions." He was wrong, of course, but not just because he underestimated the role of emotion in human affairs, but because he believed the
function of government was to serve the "interests" of society. The
principle of representation which gave constituents power over government was one way to see to it that government was responsible to
the interests of its constituents. The other was to divide "a country of
great extent" into "separate jurisdictions." "If this is not done, the
general and local interests will be confounded." But Grimke's defense
of the right of secession was possible for him only on the assumption
that reasonable men would probably refuse to use a right so obviously
against their interest. He trusted that the open affirmation of the
right of secession would serve to maintain the Union, not destroy it.

The Social Basis of Freedom

In the midst of his plea for an open avowal of the right of secession,
Grimke observed, "The European doctrine is that in matters of government it is necessary that statesmen should have both a secret and a
declared opinion. The maxim in America should be that the justest use
will in the long run most likely be made of every right where it is
clearly, frankly, and unreservedly admitted." Beneath the carefully
reasoned constitutional and legalistic arguments Grimke made against
the doctrine of nullification and for the right of secession lay a firm
commitment to the power of public opinion and an abiding trust in

the good sense of the average citizen. Baffled by what to do about slavery, he was still sure that if a solution ever were to be found it would be through "the moral force of public opinion which . . . silently introduces changes which would otherwise have disturbed the whole order of society." So Grimke's discussion of the nature of the federal government brings him, as did his discussion of the role of party politics in a free society, to the nature of public opinion. An exploration of his understanding of that question involves Grimke's view of the social forces that call certain kinds of political institutions into being; it involves a consideration of Grimke's notions about the social conditions that create a sound public opinion and that make freedom possible.

In his chapter on the difficulties in the way of arriving at a "science of government" (Book I, Chapter II), Grimke remarks that "writers on political philosophy have for the most part employed themselves in studying what is termed the mechanism of government, rather than unfolding the structure of society." He then distinguishes between "negative" and "positive" influences of society upon the institutions of government. The influence is negative when the population "is sunk in ignorance and apathy" and government assumes the character of "a self-existing institution"; it is positive when "the standard of popular intelligence is high and no impediment exists to the exercise of . . . popular authority." For Grimke, the United States was an instance of the latter, a society in which "the people may truly be said to create and uphold the government." To employ one of his further distinctions, a representative republic was the only "natural" form of government; all others were "artificial." The government of the United States was, he thought, the only example of true, natural government in the world. As a student of the forms of government, Grimke places considerable emphasis on social determinism and cultural relativism in his analysis of political institutions. But as a philosophical observer of politics, he insists upon an ideal standard against which all historical forms must be measured. That standard was the principle of constituent power; "the bars" to irresponsible exercise of power must be "truly without, and not within" the institutions of government. Or, in other words, government must be constructed so that it is responsible to the will of the people. In the United States of his time Grimke thought it was, and he was no mere chauvinist in saying so. If he thought his contemporaries were more given to reflection, if he thought the free institutions of republican politics were capable of still further improvement, it was not because Americans were better than other men; they were simply in a different "situation." Formerly, Grimke wrote, it may have been "sufficient to study the mere mechanism of government, but it is now necessary to look a great deal further and to take in the structure of society as a most important element in the character and working of the political institutions."

In his discussion of the English Constitution (Book II, Chapter VI), Grimke notes that "mixed government" is a consequence of the "mixed character" of the population. There are "permanent classes in society whose interests are opposed to each other," and the English constitution is an institutional recognition of the fact. Then Grimke goes on to say, "In a representative republic, the composition of society is exceedingly uniform." Or, as he had put it earlier: "there is more sameness, more uniformity of character, among the American people than among any other." The great problem facing European nations was how to achieve sufficient equality in social conditions to allow "just and equal rules" for all men in politics. But in America, Grimke observes, "this substantial requisite is already obtained." Here, "the principle of equality has thus found a natural support. It has not been the creature of the laws." So the period in which he wrote was for Grimke "the golden age of the republic" for the simple reason that "Americans commenced where other communities will probably leave off." The third estate might have to struggle with kings and nobles in Europe, but in the United States the people were "almost entirely . . . middle class."

"When I speak of a society which is democratically constituted," Grimke insists, "I do not intend merely a society which has democratic institutions; it may have them today and lose them tomorrow. I intend a society in which not only the political but the social organization is so advanced as to render free institutions the natural expression of the national will." The social organization which made freedom so easy to maintain in the United States was the simple fact that there were no classes in it. One need only read Grimke's chapter on "The Classes of Society" (Book IV, Chapter IV) to see how diffuse the concept of class was when applied to the United States. Grimke may begin by saying "the greater the number of classes the less powerful will anyone be," or that "society is balanced by the various classes of men," but he is not thinking of class in an economic sense. The "orders of men," as he puts it, comprise the "young and the old, the rich and the poor, capitalists and laborers, the rural and town population, professional men, and lastly, the parties of majority and minority." Generational differences are equal in importance to wealth for Grimke, and the division of rich and poor is not a social division but a personal one: "Industry, sagacity and enterprise, though they can be neither seen nor touched, compose at the present day the chief elements of wealth." That is to say, the existence of rich and poor derived from personal attributes, "the result of certain laws of our nature," and not from the chances in life determined by the structure of society. Likewise, the division between the rural and town population vanishes upon inspection. "The distinguishing feature then of American society," Grimke observes, "was that the *tiers état,* or middle class, is not confined to the towns but is diffused over the country." In Europe, the bourgeoisie was to be found only in the towns; in the United States "it comprehends in addition a vastly more numerous class, to wit, the country population," and Grimke thought that fact one of "infinite moment" in the study of American institutions. The final result was that in the United States "the middle class has swallowed up all other distinctions in the state." Little wonder that free institutions worked in such a society. It already enjoyed the luxury of a "tacit agreement" among all men.

Grimke celebrated the middle class not simply because America was a society where the "great majority of the people have so deep a stake in the protection of property and in the maintenance of those laws which guarantee personal liberty." The enveloping middle class made free institutions possible because it created shared consensus, and those free institutions in their turn reacted upon society and forced men to be free and prosperous. Ultimately, Grimke's analysis of the virtue of freedom is not that property creates freedom but that freedom creates property. So he is not simply confounding the difference between politics and society when he includes the "parties of majority and minority" in his description of classes. His category derives from the fact that in the United States the individuals who compose the majority and the minority are constantly passing from one to the other because the "middle class may be said fairly to represent the interests which are common to the whole society." The right to property extends to the "man worth a million as well as to one who possesses only two thousand dollars"; and since "the ambition of everyone is to move forward and to rise as fast as possible into the class of the rich," the rule of the middle class also represents the aspirations of those who "commenced life with little or no property." The United States was, in the pithy phrase of a later historian, a society of "expectant capitalists." [19] If parties existed in the United States to act as "the representatives of the various interests of the community," it was also true that Americans could allow parties to "magnify their respective differences" because the "only effect is to set in a more striking light the numerous points of agreement which exist among them."

At this point, Grimke sounds like little more than still another witness to the generally received notion that Americans are unconscious beneficiaries (or victims, as some prefer) of an unexamined consensus, an uncritical devotion to liberal and bourgeois values. Grimke *is* devoted to liberal values in politics, that is, to equality before the law, to equal participation in government through representative institutions, and to the protection of the right to property by the state. He is equally devoted to bourgeois values in society, that is, to sobriety, industriousness, and decency, the civic virtues which the individual citizen internalizes within his own personality in order to make possible freedom from external control. But Grimke is neither unconscious nor uncritical of his own position. He is not, to use the phrase of Louis Hartz, an irrational Lockean, if by "irrational" one means someone who is unconscious of the assumptions which underlie his values because he has not bothered to think about them. To be sure, Grimke is a "Lockean" in the vague and diffuse sense in which Professor Hartz uses the word in *The Liberal Tradition in America*, that is, as a summary reference to the social and economic values of classical, middle-class liberalism. But, more important, he is also a "Lockean" in a much more precise sense, a sense which derives from Locke's *Essay on Human Understanding* as well as the *Second Treatise on Civil Government*. Grimke's celebration of the middle class, his affirmation of the social and political values which we associate with Locke's political theory, derives from his acceptance of Locke's epistemology and his acceptance of Lockean assumptions about the nature of knowledge and about human nature. The ultimate value of freedom, Grimke insisted, was that it created the kind of character which made freedom possible.

19. Algie M. Simons, *Social Forces in American History* (New York, 1911), p. 210.

Freedom and Human Nature

When the first edition of *The Nature and Tendency of Free Institutions* appeared in 1848, a writer in the *North American Review* remarked that the book had no "outward intellectual form," that it lacked a discernible structure. "No analysis," wrote the reviewer, "at the commencement or close of the work, lays open to us the plan of arrangement which existed in the author's mind. . . . It is a series of sensible, deeply meditated essays, well worth reading, but which would have been far more satisfactory if brought before us as parts of a great whole. It is a quarry of thought, not a temple; a wheat-stack, not a loaf of bread." [20] Even if one did not know through Grimke's letter to Sarah asking for the name of the author that Grimke had reacted to this review, one would be confident Grimke took the criticism into account when he revised *The Nature and Tendency of Free Institutions* for a second edition. His first sentence in the "Preface to the Second Edition" may be read as a rebuttal: "My design in writing the present work has not been to produce a formal treatise in which the parts are made to hang together by certain prescribed rules of art, but to unfold a system of thought which will exercise the mind, and not the critical skill, of the reader." Yet Grimke did accept the stricture that his reader might need greater direction in arriving at a full comprehension of the "system of thought" he wished to unfold in his book. He followed his critic's advice and added to the second edition a new first chapter and a new conclusion (in addition to the new chapter on the right of secession). Since Grimke thought the addition of these chapters pointed more directly to the central theme of *The Nature and Tendency of Free Institutions*, they provide a convenient entry to the basic assumptions of his social and political thought, assumptions which do not emerge explicitly in the development of his argument. They are assumptions about the nature of man and the nature of knowledge which constitute Grimke's intellectual universe and make possible (and, perhaps, more comprehensible to us) all else he has to say about the nature and tendency of free institutions.

Grimke's new "Introductory" chapter begins with the assertion that "the existence of free institutions presupposes the existence of a highly civilized society," and there follows a lengthy speculation on the origin

20. *North American Review*, 144 [n.s., 69] (October, 1849), 440–441.

and development of civilization. The crucial moment for Grimke, the moment when men are no longer "impelled by mere instincts," is when an agricultural surplus draws men into exchange one with another. Two results follow. First, "the circle of their desires will be enlarged and the range of observation and experience proportionally extended. The occupations of society then become more complex and more diversified. Men begin to reflect." Second, "in addition to the inanimate objects with which they will have to deal, their own minds will become the subject of observation. Each individual in order to regulate his own actions will be compelled to make observation of the actions of others; and the range of observation widening with every increase of the population, the understandings of everyone will be sharpened whether they will or no." Commerce, the emergence of a market economy, the development of the notion of property, all these are important to Grimke, but all are secondary to the basic influence the development of society has upon man's mind; "it acts upon the mind by presenting it with abundant materials for reflection."

If one turns to Grimke's conclusion, "The Ultimate Destiny of Free Institutions," one will discover that his tempered hope for the "wise and equitable government of society" is presented and argued in precisely the same language. "The actions of men," writes Grimke, "depend upon two causes: the faculties of one kind or another with which they are endowed, and the circumstances which are external to them, including in the last not only the physical world but other intellectual beings, together with the institutions, public and private, in the country where they reside and even those of other countries wherever they are capable of exerting an influence upon them. On the joint influence of these two causes depends the whole conduct and behavior of men. . . . It is impossible to conceive that it should be otherwise, since all actions imply something beyond us, affecting our faculties and at the same time affected by them."

Even one casually acquainted with the sensational psychology of John Locke will recognize the accent of Grimke's language. Grimke takes from Locke the notion that men have certain "faculties," that all knowledge is the product first of experience of an external world and then of reflection within the conscious mind. The advance of civilization widens the experience of men and forces them to reflect. Free institutions advance the cause of civilization because they are a further development of the dynamic which underlies civilization itself: "free institutions lead to an association of people of all classes." By multiplying the relations among men and by putting men in the way of the experience of governing themselves, freedom develops the understanding and the need for reflection which finally makes freedom tolerable. Similarly, freedom once established is irreversible because through experience it has, in the strict Lockean sense, become understood. America's influence upon the rest of the world derives from the "material application" of the principle of freedom in the American system of government: "Until then, it is the subject of conjecture, but not an item of knowledge, no more than it is one of experience." Grimke is claiming no less than that "freedom" existed only in the realm of conjecture until realized in the action and experience of the United States; then, freedom enters human history as an item of knowledge.

Closely allied to Grimke's insistence on experience and the development of the understanding is his constant depreciation of imagination and emotion. In the "Preface to the Second Edition," where he deplores his time's "vitiated taste for reading," Grimke rejects books which are "exciting" because they do not serve a "genuine desire for knowledge," and "nothing," Grimke concludes, "contributes more to enfeeble the understanding and even to pervert the moral faculties." Grimke has chosen his words carefully here and they emphasize his ambition for his own book. Grimke, in his own tone as well as in the substance of his argument, presents a society of sensible and sober men who, through experience, reflect on ideas and are not led astray by vain imaginings and exciting visions. Throughout *The Nature and Tendency of Free Institutions*, the power which has allowed kings and priests to rule irresponsibly over men is the untutored condition of the masses whose imaginations are inflamed by what their understandings cannot comprehend. "Kingly authority," wrote Grimke at the end of his long book, "is undoubtedly founded on an illusion of the imagination." That illusion may once have had an "infinite advantage" at a time when it was necessary to create unity in society, "to control the imaginations of men by a supreme imagination." But no longer. Once "more homely faculties have been cultivated at the expense of the imagination, the illusion vanishes."

From the start to the end of *The Nature and Tendency of Free Institutions*, Grimke equates despotism and arbitrary rule with the imposition of the imagination, and freedom and republican institutions with the development of the understanding of men through the

experience which freedom forces upon them. Grimke was even suspicious of the remnants of the force of the imagination among a free
people: "I should not err if I were to say that it is to the over-exercise
of the imagination that the greatest defects are to be traced, even in
a country of free institutions." The people may still tend to surrender
their judgment to the "showy authority" of the state, but the cure
for that weakness comes "when they are cast upon their own resources
and compelled to grapple with business as a matter of serious concern."
So, if the office of the executive in a republican form of government is
not so "dazzling," that is its very strength: "It will not affect the imaginations of men so strongly, but it will acquire a firmer hold upon
their understandings."

At one point, in a discussion of the extension of the suffrage and the
participation of all men in the experience of government, Grimke asks
the question, "Why it is that the communication of political privileges
to a people imparts so much vigor and activity to their whole character?" Political freedom, he answers, "removes a feeling of degradation," but adds, "one can hardly say that the peasantry of Russia or
Austria realize this feeling since, having been habituated from time
immemorial to a state of subjection, they can hardly form an idea of
the value of the privilege" of participation in politics. The only way
to acquire the idea of freedom is through the experience of freedom.
So, Grimke concludes, "The great advantage arising from the free
communication of the privilege [of political participation] consists
. . . in its giving men new faculties and not merely new rights."

Grimke is making an extraordinary claim here. When he writes that
"the political institutions of the United States may be described as the
greatest experiment which has ever been made upon human nature,"
he is not simply speaking in the hyperbole of the patriot. He speaks
out of a rich tradition in Western thought which names experience as
the source of all knowledge. Free institutions enlarge the "bounds of
human experience" and through that enlarged experience effect no less
than a change in human nature. Or, as he puts it in the last paragraph
of his book, "The enjoyment of liberty in its highest degree has opened
a great volume of experience to the American people and this experience, not the possession of any natural qualities superior to those of
other people," is what has shaped the character of Americans. Grimke's
sober, empirical, and skeptical tone throughout his book should not
hide from us his enormous faith in the consequences of freedom for all

men. The only way to make a man fit for freedom is to give him freedom. He may have a notion of freedom, but he will not realize a true idea of freedom until his understanding grasps it through actual experience. If a Lockean in such an argument, Grimke is decidedly not the Locke of the *Second Treatise* with its emphasis on certain natural rights common to all men; he is the Locke of the *Essay on Human Understanding* with its constant emphasis on experience as the only valid source of knowledge.

At this point one could multiply examples indefinitely, but the reader may do so for himself. Whether discussing equality which breaks down barriers between men, political parties which stir men into activity, the voluntary principle in religion which makes each man personally responsible, the inefficacy of ideas derived at second hand through books and education rather than directly through experience — whatever his subject, Grimke has constantly in mind one assumption: "There is but one way in which that perception of what is useful and fit can be gained, but one way in which any sort of practical knowledge can be acquired, and that is by placing those for whom such knowledge is desirable in a situation where they will be sure to realize the consequences which will follow from pursuing opposite courses." Or, again, "Free institutions, if they do not find men absolutely fit for self-government, are . . . wonderfully adapted to make them so."

There was, of course, one group of men Grimke did not think freedom would make fit for self-government, black men held in slavery. Grimke generally did not accept intrinsic differences in human nature. He argued for a common nature which developed in different directions because it was exerted on different objects in its environment. But he excluded the Negro from participation in that common human nature on the grounds of race. "In a democratic republic," Grimke wrote, "the field of human life is more thoroughly laid open than it is anywhere else. All the ordinary motives to reflection are increased because the objects about which reflection is employed are multiplied. Individuals are thrown more upon their own resources. Each has more to do, more to quicken his exertion, more to kindle hope and yet sadden with exertion." Perhaps his own language brought the hopeless slave to mind, because Grimke immediately added: "If the slaves of the south did not belong to a race decidedly inferior to that of the white man, it would be the highest wisdom to manumit them."

One may say of Grimke's racism what Grimke said of David Hume's

inability to conceive of the separation of church and state and full religious freedom: "Our speculations of any sort hardly ever rise much
higher than the age in which we live." The best excuse for Grimke's belief in the racial inferiority of the Negro, in flat contradiction to his
general view of human nature, is to point out that he shared a view of
race pervasive in his time. The typology which divided mankind up
into "races" distinguished by innate and irreversible traits was the
dominant intellectual attitude toward race in the period in which
Grimke wrote. The purpose of typology is to classify phenomena by
certain defined characteristics but, as one student of race has put it,
"classification poses problems, it does not solve them." [21] But the
concept of race as Grimke put it to work was not to pose a problem, it
was to avoid a problem. It was used simply to exclude the Negro from
the benefits of freedom.

Grimke's treatment of the Negro represents the single departure
in his book from the logic of his own argument. Though he is otherwise skeptical of abstractions which assert a case without proving it,
he has his own abstraction, his own unexamined prejudice, behind
which he will not go. When confronted with the Negro, Grimke reverses the entire logic of his argument for freedom and deserts his
faith that the experience of freedom creates the character necessary
for freedom. When he asks, "How shall we emancipate from civil disabilities two or three millions of people without admitting them to the
enjoyment of political privileges also?" he answers by a further rhetorical question, "And yet how can this be done without endangering the
existence of the very institutions which are appealed to as the warrant for creating so great a revolution?" The answer to that question
might well have been the answer Grimke gave elsewhere: the only
way to make a man capable of freedom is to make him free.
But Grimke refused to extend this argument to the Negro, to claim
for the Negro, too, that freedom does not require in advance a certain
character, but, rather, that freedom in itself creates the character appropriate for the conditions of freedom.

III

Grimke's discussion, then, of the political institutions of freedom
takes him inevitably to the social context of freedom and, finally, to a

21. S. L. Washburn, "The Study of Race," *American Anthropologist,* 65 (June,
1963), 526.

justification of freedom which rests ultimately upon an implicit conception of the nature of man. To separate the three major dimensions of Grimke's argument may, however, do Grimke a disservice. It ignores the integrity of his argument, the way in which each of the categories affect each other. It neglects, to use Grimke's phrase, the "dynamics of freedom." So, finally, one may stand back a bit from Grimke's book and ask the question of his title, what is the general "nature" of free society and what is its future, its "tendency"?

Grimke had read *Democracy in America,* and in *The Nature and Tendency of Free Institutions* he has high praise for Tocqueville who, like Plato, "visited a foreign land with the single view of seeking instruction and who, to the fine genius of Plato, unites the severe analysis and calm observation of Aristotle." But such extravagant admiration did not lead Grimke to concur with all that Tocqueville wrote about American democratic society in the early nineteenth century. He thought Tocqueville misunderstood the nature of equality in the United States, and he did not share Tocqueville's apprehensions about the tyranny of the majority, what Grimke called the force of public opinion.

Tocqueville, in both his book on America and in *The Old Regime,* believed that the meaning of Western history lay in the inevitable spread of equality. "The gradual development of the principle of equality," he wrote, "is therefore a providential fact. It has all the chief characteristics of such a fact; it is universal, it is lasting, it constantly eludes all human interference, and all events as well as all men contribute to its progress." [22] In the first sentences of the "Author's Introduction" to the *Democracy,* Tocqueville wrote, "Among the novel objects that attracted my attention during my stay in the United States, nothing struck me more forcibly than the general equality of condition among the people. I readily discovered the prodigious influence that this primary fact exercises on the whole course of society; it gives a peculiar direction to public opinion and a peculiar tenor to the laws; it imparts new maxims to the governing authorities and peculiar habits to the governed." [23]

For Tocqueville, there was the danger that under the mortar of equality the articulated structure of society would be ground down

22. Alexis de Tocqueville, *Democracy in America,* ed. Phillips Bradley (New York, 1945), I, 6.
23. Tocqueville, *Democracy,* I, 3.

to identical and equal particles and that democratic society would run the risk of two opposite but related extremes, the anarchy of isolated, self-interested individuals, or mass conformity where each individual, thinking himself self-sufficient, but like all the others, would be psychologically unable to resist the tyrannous weight of the opinion of the majority of his equal fellows. Although Tocqueville thought equality was God's plan for human history, he did not think too well of the plan. His own image of the good society was one formed by the notion of a social hierarchy, a chain of being in which each member of the community belonged to a clearly defined place in the hierarchical order of things. "Aristocracy," he wrote, "had made a chain of all the members of the community, from the peasant to the king; democracy breaks that chain and severs every link of it." [24] The consequence of equality for Tocqueville was this shattering separation of man from man and the rupture of traditional social relationships and social obligations.

Grimke shared Tocqueville's belief that the movement from status relationships among corporate groups to contractual relationships among equal citizens was a great moment in history, and he used the same metaphor of the chain of being to describe it.[25] "A great revolution was effected in the structure of society when the inferior classes lost their dependence upon the higher, when the relations of patron and client, or lord and vassal, ceased. A new relation immediately sprung up. Instead of the dependence being all on one side, the two orders became mutually dependent on each other. Society began to assume the character of a great partnership among the members, instead of that series of ascending links in a chain, one end of which was fastened to the throne." But the social consequence, Grimke believed, was precisely the opposite of what Tocqueville feared.

Grimke did not, as Tocqueville seems to have thought all American democrats did, believe in actual equality among men, nor did he anticipate or desire such a consequence. The obvious question, then, was "why do legislators constantly inculcate the maxim that all men are equal?" For Grimke the answer was plain. First, heuristically, to act *as if* men were equal was the only way to achieve whatever degree

24. Tocqueville, *Democracy*, II, 99.
25. Both Tocqueville and Grimke spoke out of a rich tradition in Western thought, of course, and I do not mean to imply that the metaphor is Tocqueville's and that Grimke had it from him; see Arthur O. Lovejoy, *The Great Chain of Being* (Cambridge, Mass., 1936).

of equality was possible; second, pragmatically, "it is not in the power of government to make anything like an accurate discrimination between the inequalities of different men"; third, ideally, to treat all men equally as citizens would do away with artificial distinctions among men and allow the inevitable differences among men to emerge naturally and justly. "The utmost which the citizen can demand," concluded Grimke, "is that no law shall be passed to obstruct his rise and to impede his progress through life. He has then an even chance with all his fellows. If he does not become their equal his case is beyond the reach of society and to complain would be to quarrel with his own nature."

To make a simple distinction, equality for Grimke meant not equality of condition but equality of opportunity. "The same laws which declare that all men are equal give unbounded scope to the enterprise and industry of all. Neither family, nor rank, nor education confer any peculiar advantages in running the career which is now opened. In many respects they even throw obstacles in the way. Men without education, with ordinary faculties, and who commenced life with little or nothing are continually emerging from obscurity and displacing those who have acquired fortunes by inheritance. They constitute emphatically the class of rich in the United States. It is the principle of equality there which introduces all the inequality which is established in that country." Grimke's *beau ideal* was the man on the make who asked only that he be given a fair chance to show that he was considerably more equal than his fellows. The "broad and indiscriminate rule of equality" among citizens, he thought, "obliterates all artificial distinction and yet brings out in bolder relief all the natural inequalities of men."

Nor did Grimke fear that those who lost the race would turn to politics to gain what they lost in society; "as a large proportion of the envious are constantly rising into the ranks of the envied, a powerful check is imposed upon the revolutionary tendencies of the former. They cannot reach, nor after reaching will they be able to enjoy that which is the constant aim of all their efforts without lending an earnest and vigorous support to the laws under which they live." Grimke could say so, of course, only on the assumption that all Americans did have a common as well as a constant aim, that they shared the same goals, and, if failures, would blame themselves and not the social system. Grimke did think Americans shared what he called a "tacit consensus," and, because he esteemed the values which defined that consensus, he was not greatly disturbed that the opinion of the majority had an enormous influence upon the single individual. "No one," he wrote, "who is an attentive observer of human nature can fail to be struck with the amazing influence which the opinion of a multitude of men exercises over the mind. We can stand up and confront a single individual even though we are far from being right, but we recoil with a sort of dread from any opposition to the opinion of a great number." And, having described the reasons why this was so, Grimke accepted the consequence: we live in "a world where a system of opinions and conduct is already established and it does not seem unnatural, but rather a necessary consequence of the process by which human conduct is shaped that we should defer greatly to the standard of opinion which is erected," that we "should be compressed into a conformity with it, and that any revolt against it should be followed with a sense of dread and uneasiness."

Grimke recognized that the stability of American society derived from the simple fact that each individual internalized within his own personality the values of American society. Or, to put it another way, freedom from external control was possible because each individual controlled himself. The self-restraint which Grimke argued was the necessary corollary of freedom was present in American society because, through the force of public opinion, the people controlled each other, and so did not need to rely upon the coercive power of the state. "I think if anyone will follow carefully and minutely the workings of American society, he will find that the people are fully as much occupied in keeping each other in order as they are in checking the authority of their governments." And, he concluded, "it is only by doing the first that they succeed in doing the last."

At this point, Grimke might have rested in the conclusion that the values of the middle class were so pervasive in American society that they would be self-sustaining through "that invisible power which we term public opinion." But he was not content with so relativistic an answer. He wanted that public opinion also to be reasonable. Otherwise, he could hardly have been so untroubled by the impotence of the single individual in the face of majority opinion. "Public opinion only tends to be right in proportion as it resembles itself to the opinion of mankind," he wrote, and went on to say, "I cannot help thinking that this effect will take place in proportion to the number of men who are in the possession of liberty, and who, on that very account, are driven to habits of thought and reflection." Grimke's view of the nature of the development of understanding and reflection among men closed the gap in his argument for him. Liberty would drive men to become as thoughtful as men could be, so the opinion of the majority under the conditions of freedom would come as close to the dictates of reason as men could expect to come.

Grimke also thought that men had to be "driven to habits of thought and reflection" and the ultimate worth, as well as the ultimate safeguard, of freedom was that it drove men to think and reflect. Grimke had, in one respect, a rather low view of human nature. He did not think men would stir themselves; men would not better themselves or advance in understanding unless they were forced to do so. "The human mind," he wrote, "with all its capabilities of thought and action is wonderfully disposed to listlessness, so that it requires the most powerful incentives in order to rouse its dormant energies." The effect of freedom was to rouse the dormant energies of the people and force them to attend to their own interests. This was why "the growth of popular parties constantly keeps pace with the diffusion of industry and property. The diffusion of industry and property, by exercising the mind intently upon small things at first, exercises it earnestly and seriously upon important ones in the end." But it was, Grimke recognized, a serious and strenuous world: "Free institutions introduce heart burnings enough into society. But these only constitute a state of discipline by which men are rendered more wise, more prudent, and more just than they would otherwise be."

There is little of the sublime in Grimke's picture of democratic society. He envisions a society of prudent and sensible men, industrious and responsible, holding themselves in check and guarding their own interests by participating actively in the governance of their society. If the vision seems at times a little bleak, one should also remember that such men were free. Or, as Grimke would have it, freedom made such men, and they would continue to be free so long as they continued to accept the heavy burden freedom imposed upon them. Grimke's tempered hope was that the future was on their side. Like many of his contemporaries, Grimke was at times troubled by the assumption that all societies went through a cyclical pattern of growth, and that civilization was followed, inevitably, by decline and fall. But he thought the United States would escape that fatality and "falsify the maxim of Montesquieu that a nation after it has attained a certain height is compelled by some invincible law of its being to decline." He thought the United States would avoid the vices of excessive civilization and the catastrophe of dissolution because "free institutions are endowed with a faculty of self-preservation which is possessed by no other form of government." Freedom forced men to be energetic, imposed experience upon them and inevitably developed their understanding. Freedom perpetuated among men the energy which had started civilization on its course in the first place, and the ceaseless activity and the strenuous burden of freedom afforded, Grimke thought, "a reasonable assurance of the perpetuity of free institutions." Progress was not inevitable—not necessarily God's plan for the world —but it was possible. That was Grimke's cautious hope, and he wrote *The Nature and Tendency of Free Institutions* to enlarge the understanding of his fellow Americans so that it might become probable.

IV

There is always the danger in discovering a neglected figure from out of the past of paying him, in compensation, too great praise. There are good reasons, reasons which may appeal especially to scholars of the early nineteenth century, for rescuing Grimke from obscurity, but there is as much disservice in unstinted and indiscriminate praise as in simple neglect. It is easy to understand why Grimke's contemporaries may have turned away from and forgotten *The Nature and Tendency of Free Institutions*. Grimke's defense of slavery and his cool contemplation of the possible dismemberment of the Union relegated him to a past which blood and battle were supposed to have buried. The same coolness may still keep the modern reader at a distance. Grimke's greatest weakness derives from his greatest strength, his image of the nature of man. His depreciation of imagination and emotion provides a foreshortened image of man, one which does not take sufficiently into account man's capacity either for passionate irrationality or for selfless commitment to a good which transcends his particular, individual interest.

Yet Grimke's cool and sober voice should not hide from us his fervent hope for the possibilities of freedom. He may have derided utopian schemes of perfection built upon the benevolence of human nature, but beneath his skeptical and empirical style there lies a great act of faith, the faith that the only way to make men free is to give them freedom. He was too much of his time to extend that faith to the Negro, but we have not yet done so well that we may deride him for his failure. We may properly wish to enlarge the conception of human nature upon which we build our politics, but Grimke may still remind us of the basic premise upon which free institutions are built. Freedom is its own justification, and the only way to make men free is to make them free.

John William Ward

April 1968

A NOTE ON THE TEXT

THE first edition of Frederick Grimke's *Considerations Upon the Nature and Tendency of Free Institutions* appeared in 1848 (H. W. Derby and Co., Publishers, Cincinnati; A. S. Barnes and Co., New York). A "second edition corrected and enlarged" appeared in 1856 (Derby and Jackson, New York; H. W. Derby and Co., Cincinnati). A third, posthumous edition, provided for by Grimke in his will, with the shorter title *Nature and Tendency of Free Instititions,* appeared as Volume I in *The Works of Frederick Grimke in Two Volumes* (Columbus Printing Company, Columbus, 1871), which is one book divided internally into two volumes. Grimke made extensive additions and corrections for the second edition. There are minor changes in the third edition which I have consulted in the case of a dubious reading, but for the John Harvard Library edition I have preferred the second edition because it was seen through the press by Grimke.[1] I have, however, accepted the title of the third edition because it is shorter and more direct.

As Grimke says in his "Preface to the Second Edition," he added three new chapters, a new "Introductory" chapter and a new concluding chapter, "Ultimate Destiny of Free Institutions," as well as an important chapter, "The Right of Secession in the Confederate Form of Government" (Book IV, Chapter II). He also made extensive additions to chapters in the first edition which he does not describe in his preface to the second. I have indicated all substantive additions in footnotes where they occur. I have not, however, felt it necessary to call attention to changes (fifty-four of them) in a word or a phrase where the change is minor and does not affect the sense.

I have made other changes on my own. Where the sense points to an

1. The third edition was seen through the press by Grimke's sister, Sarah. In a letter, April 22, 1857, therefore after the second edition, Grimke sent Sarah a list of "errata" to be corrected in her copy, but the list is lost and one cannot say whether a change is Frederick's or Sarah's. (The Weld-Grimké Correspondence, William L. Clements Library, University of Michigan, Ann Arbor, Michigan.)

obvious misprint, I have silently corrected it; where, given the context, a word appears to be erroneous, but where the change would alter the sense, I have suggested the change in a footnote. Grimke used punctuation, especially the comma, with an abandon that is offensive to the modern eye and that often obstructs the movement of his own thought, so I have greatly reduced the amount of punctuation. He also used variant spellings and I have standardized his spelling, choosing the preferred modern spelling wherever it presented itself; where he writes "every where" and "no where," I have made them single words. One change perhaps deserves comment: Grimke, in accordance with the custom of his time and not simply because he believed in the racial inferiority of the Negro, wrote "negro" with the lower-case letter. I have capitalized it throughout.

Grimke provided footnotes to his text, and for notation used the asterisk, dagger, and double dagger. In what follows, footnotes so marked are Grimke's; all numerical footnotes are mine and are enclosed in brackets. Editorial additions to Grimke's notes are also enclosed in brackets. Grimke sometimes used brackets in his own text, and to avoid possible confusion I have reduced them to parentheses, so all material in brackets in the present edition is mine.

My major debt is to Miss Miriam Gallaher at the Center for Advanced Study in the Behavioral Sciences at Stanford, California, who did the painful job of collating the three editions of *The Nature and Tendency of Free Institutions* for changes from one edition to the next. Beside myself, she is probably the only person alive who has read all three. I am also grateful to Professor Bernard Bailyn for his patience, his criticism, and his sharp editorial eye. Mr. William S. Ewing, curator of manuscripts at the William L. Clements Library, the University of Michigan, was an ideal host; he laid out in advance of my visit to his Library all the materials he knew I would wish to consult. Mrs. Andrew N. Jergens, Jr., Librarian of the Cincinnati Historical Society, was most kind and ran down for me information which is perhaps minor, but which becomes important to an editor when he gets involved in a small note. Mr. Kenneth W. Duckett, Curator of Manuscripts at the Ohio Historical Society, Columbus, Ohio, was also helpful in responding to letters of inquiry. But, for many references, Mr. E. Porter Dickinson, the Reference Librarian of the Robert Frost Library at Amherst College, was my chief support; his infectious enthusiasm while on the hunt made even the small game I was after seem worth the trip. Finally, my thanks to Mrs. Rosa White and her staff in the Faculty Service Center at Amherst College who managed to transpose what I gave them neatly to the typewritten page.

J.W.W.

THE NATURE AND TENDENCY
OF
FREE INSTITUTIONS

---

by Frederick Grimke

PREFACE TO THE SECOND EDITION

My design in writing the present work has not been to produce a formal treatise in which the parts are made to hang together by certain prescribed rules of art, but to unfold a system of thought which will exercise the mind, and not the critical skill, of the reader. The two are distinct and often irreconcilable. The reader, quick in apprehension, will have no difficulty in seizing the governing principle which pervades the whole work and in marking the many important results to which it has conducted me. Another object which I have had in view, an indirect one to be sure, has been to *endeavor* to correct, as far as it is in the power of a single individual to do, the vitiated taste for reading which prevails in our country. Great numbers read from ennui, not from a genuine desire for knowledge. The consequence is that the works selected are either of a superficial or of an exciting character. But nothing contributes more to enfeeble the understanding, and even to pervert the moral faculties. The mischief extends itself to the few who are possessed with a noble ambition. There is no tribunal to which they can address themselves. Their efforts are chilled by the mental dyspepsia which prevails around them, when they stand in need of being powerfully braced by a healthful and invigorating influence.

By laying open a field of thought which is peculiarly American (although allied with all other knowledge) and which has, in an eminent degree, both a literary and a philosophical interest, I flatter myself that I may contribute, however little, toward giving a more fortunate direction to the general mind. They who have studied the history of Europe during the middle ages must have been struck with one remarkable fact, that there was no beginning even toward the formation of a literature, science and philosophy, strictly modern, until ancient literature, *etc.*, had ceased to be studied, and that there was no other way by which it was possible to create it. We call the period which succeeded the disappearance of ancient and laid the foundation of modern literature and philosophy the dark ages because the fermentation which the human mind underwent in this transition period did produce a temporary mental eclipse. The instruction afforded by this remarkable case is not that we should fall back into a state resembling the dark ages, but that we should search in the rich resources of our own history, our form of society, our civil and political institutions, for the materials on which to construct an American literature. Until we do, our authors will have none of the originality and raciness which give dignity and interest to mental speculations, and our population will continue to read only to assuage the pain of ennui.

Very material additions have been made to the present edition — a chapter on the great question of "the right of secession in a confederate government," another on the still more important question, "the ultimate destiny of free institutions." New matter has also been incorporated into the former chapters — ten or twelve pages in Chap. vii. Book I., and the same number in Chap. vi. Book II., and Chap. iv. Book IV.; about eight in Chap. vi. Book I., and Chap. i. Book IV. In Chap. i. Book II. and Chap. vi. Book IV., four pages, and in several other chapters from a third of a page to three pages.[1] The introductory chapter on our modern civilization has also been added to the present volume, and the numerous typographical errors in the former edition have also been endeavored to be corrected.

1. [Grimke's description of the "new matter" incorporated in the second edition is not complete. See "A Note on the Text."]

BOOK ONE

CHAPTER I | INTRODUCTORY [1]

THE existence of free institutions presupposes the existence of a highly civilized society. An examination, therefore, of their genius and tendency will very naturally be preceded by an examination of the origin and nature of civilization.

Civilization, then, is that state in which the higher part of our nature is made to predominate over the lower, and the qualities which fit men for society obtain an ascendency over their selfish and anti-social propensities. But as much the greater part of the human race have always been found at one period in an uncivilized condition, the question what has induced a change from one state to the other is not one merely of curious inquiry but of the highest philosophical interest.

History presents us with the earliest traces of civilization in those regions where the densest population existed. This is a striking fact and perhaps it may afford a clue to the solution of the difficulty. A population which is only tolerably full is inconsistent with the hunter state. One which is still more dense is inconsistent with the pastoral state. Any causes therefore which give a decided spring to the population are calculated to draw men from a savage into a civilized condition. When they have multiplied up to a certain point, the cultivation of the soil which was before only occasional and in particular spots becomes, from the necessity of the case, general. It is sure also to be continued from choice in consequence of the variety of desires it satisfies and the command it gives over both the moral and physical world.

But the difficulty still meets us, what in the first instance occasioned the increase of the population: for the hunter state will carry

1. [For the second edition, Grimke added this entire "Introductory" chapter.]

the population to a certain pitch, and the pastoral state will extend it still further. But although we speak of a hunter and a pastoral state, these must not be considered as indicating what are the exclusive, but what are the predominant occupations of the population. A tribe of shepherds, and even of hunters, is always addicted to some species of agriculture, as an agricultural people are always addicted to the raising of flocks.

Civilization, then, would most probably commence in a region which combined the advantages of a genial climate and a fertile soil. These assist in giving a predilection for the cultivation of the soil and in gradually superseding both the hunter and pastoral states. The multiplication of the population to a certain point is the necessary condition of the progress of civilization, and how to obtain that condition is the precise inquiry we are engaged in.

When the climate is favorable and the land rich, men will be attracted to agriculture as naturally as to any other pursuit. The relaxing influence of the climate will indispose to much activity, while the rudest cultivation, the mere scratching of the earth, will supply its fruits in tolerable abundance. But the diversity of productions among an agricultural people lays the foundation for a more extensive barter than can exist in the hunter or pastoral state. One neighborhood will exchange its products with another and by degrees a communication will be opened between the more distant parts of the community. The rude elements of trade will be introduced and ultimately a regular commerce will be commenced. Some parts of the country will be more easily approached by water than by land. Sometimes the rivers, at others the coasts adjacent to the sea, will afford the easiest channels. When society has advanced so far, the population cease any longer to be impelled by mere instincts. The circle of their desires will be enlarged and the range of observation and experience proportionally extended. The occupations of society then become more complex and more diversified. Men begin to reflect, to look more into the future, and to conform their actions to something like rule and system. Enterprise, though exceedingly limited, will be one feature of their character. The coasts of neighboring countries will be visited for traffic, as their own coasts had been explored before. And from that time we may date the rise of a regular commerce.

Even before this period, the inhabitants will be brought into such intimate communication that their social qualities will be distinctly developed, and those of an opposite character kept more in the background. In addition to the inanimate objects with which they will have to deal, their own minds will become the subject of observation. Each individual in order to regulate his own actions will be compelled to make observation of the actions of others and, the range of observation widening with every increase of the population, the understandings of everyone will be sharpened and improved, whether they will or no. Industry and enterprise will not be the only traits in the character of the population. There will be symptoms of intelligence visible everywhere. And this will give a fresh spring to activity in every department of life.

The point of time when the minds of men begin to be the subject of observation is the most important period in the history of civilization. The foundation is then laid for reflection in its most extensive signification. And it is for this reason that I have laid so much stress on the cultivation of the soil and the consequent increase of the population, as the last is the necessary condition of the growth of civilization. For then, not only are the desires of men multiplied and the means of gratifying them augmented, but the beings whose minds act upon and stimulate each other are also multiplied.

The notion of property in land is never fairly grasped until agriculture has made considerable progress. Among a tribe of shepherds, this notion is very indistinct; among one of hunters, it is still more faint. It is only fully developed when agriculture becomes the predominant pursuit. The foundation of the right is laid at the first dawn of civilization, but at that period it is not distinctly recognized simply because the occupations of the inhabitants imply a use in common and are incompatible with a division of the soil. When the land is cultivated, each individual tills the spot on which the accident of birth has placed him. The dominion over the land was once what the dominion over the ocean always is. The one was once in common, the other continues to be so. As there is no superior right of one individual over another to navigate the ocean, there was no superior right of one over another to cultivate the land. And yet precisely because there is no superior right, each individual is at liberty to make use of both. But the traversing the ocean by one vessel in a particular path is inconsistent with its being traversed by another vessel in exactly the same path at the same time. The use of a particular path on the ocean becomes for the time being exclusive. But more than this momentary use is necessary in the case of the soil; and precisely because, as in the former instance, there is no superior right of one over another to the use, and this demands occupation, and occupation, protection, the right of private property in the land comes to be as legitimately established as the right to a private use of the ocean.

As soon as the notion of property has sprung up laws are necessary to enforce it. A system of legislation will be necessary which, however rude and imperfect in the beginning, will give shape and consistency to the social organization and push onward the march of general improvement.

But although civilization will originate among a people who have a genial climate and a fertile soil, it may be transported to other regions and give rise to even a higher condition of society. For as it is not in consequence of any original difference in the faculties of men of different countries, at least where there is no difference of race, but only from a difference in the circumstances in which they are placed that some civilize themselves while others continue in their primitive state, there can be no obstacle to the introduction of the arts and refinement of the most cultivated people to every region where a foothold can be gained. This is a fine provision in the constitution of human nature. But for it, there is no reason to believe that northern and central Europe would have emerged from their barbarous condition. Britain, France and Germany were inhabited by barbarians until Roman civilization was introduced. These countries are now the seats of a civilization more complete and refined than existed among the people who first conveyed thither the first rudiments of laws and manners. The conquest of the Romans first, and the dissolution of the empire afterwards, produced a mixture of the people of all parts of the continent and caused the laws and manners, the arts and sciences of the people of Italy to penetrate into every quarter. No other or further account need or can be given of the matter. But for Roman civilization, London, Paris, Berlin, as well as St. Petersburgh, Copenhagen, and Stockholm, would at the present day be villages of straggling huts. There is not the least reason to suppose that those spots would be inhabited by a race so far advanced in the scale of civilization as the present population.

No people, so far as our information extends, has been known to civilize itself. The civilization of ancient as well as of modern Europe was of foreign growth. Nevertheless, as civilization must have commenced somewhere in order to be carried abroad, it is plain that some one people who were originally placed in singularly propitious circumstances did originally succeed in civilizing itself. The earliest records of history place the first civilization on the eastern coasts of the Mediterranean whence it has spread all over Europe.

The English and Americans are accustomed to talk of their Anglo-Saxon descent. This savors much of affectation, if it does not denote a defect of information. For if Roman civilization had not been planted in the island of Great Britain before the Saxon invasion, the English and their descendants would have been very little lifted above the condition of the Saxons who inhabited the shores between Holland and Denmark. There was no European people at that day more thoroughly barbarous. This is more particularly true of the Angles, the chief tribe of the Saxons, and from whom the island derives its name of England. The lawless and piratical life they led was absolutely inconsistent with the manners and habits which are so carelessly attributed to them. There was no way of even beginning the work of civilization but by breaking them up as a tribe and planting them among a people who had already made considerable advances. The English and Americans have no more reason to be proud of their Anglo-Saxon descent than the people of southern Europe have to be proud of their Vandal or Gothic descent. In every instance where barbarous tribes have invaded countries in which Roman civilization existed, they adopted and grew into the institutions and customs of the more cultivated people and built the fabric of society on that foundation. The mixture of the two people had precisely the same effect, only on a much larger scale, as the mixture and intermarriage of the various classes in modern society. The stock of Patrician blood would run out, the upper ranks would become enervated, if they were not constantly recruited from the Plebeian orders. Nothing is more common than to mistake a mere coincidence for an antecedence and consequence — that is, for cause and effect. Thus, although circumstances peculiar to Great Britain (its being an island for instance) have secured to the people a better social organization than in any other European country, its great advances have been ascribed to a cause purely accidental, merely because it is more open to common apprehension. There can be no doubt if the Franks or Burgundians, instead of the Saxons, had invaded the country, the march of civilization would have been the same.

The difference between the people of New England and of the Southern States of America has been supposed to arise from the fact that the former were descendants of the Saxons, the last of the Normans. This is another instance of confounding a coincidence with cause and effect. The cavaliers (who we will suppose were descendants of the Normans) first planted Virginia, but the great bulk of the emigration afterwards were of the same class as that to New England. The difference between the two people is attributable solely to outward circumstances. The climate of the South was more soft, the land richer, the institution of slavery was better adapted to the country, and these are abundantly sufficient to account for the difference of manners (for that is the only difference) between the two people.

We should know absolutely nothing of the Saxons for three hundred years after the invasion if it were not for Bede's history, and Bede himself was not born until A. D. 673.[2] When there is so great a blank, and a blank only attempted to be filled up by the most superstitious of writers, it is easy to talk of Anglo-Saxon civilization without fear of contradiction.

It is now two centuries and a quarter since the English people emigrated to North America. During that period their descendants have peopled it in every direction and have covered it with the triumphs of art and science, so that if by possibility the country should be subjugated there is no reason to believe that the laws, manners, and institutions would be extirpated. On the contrary, they would form the basis of any future superstructure which might be raised, even if the invaders were as completely barbarized as the Saxons of the fifth century.

The Romans were in possession of the island of Great Britain for four centuries. We should make a great mistake if we supposed that it was only the Roman armies which occupied it. Roman citizens of every class and occupation emigrated there, as the English did to America. If we did not know this to be the fact, it would be a most improbable supposition that Roman civilization did not exercise a decisive and permanent influence upon the whole frame of Saxon society.

2. [Bede (or, Baeda), 673?–735, English historian and Benedictine monk, called the "venerable Bede" or St. Bede; his *Ecclesiastical History of the English Nation*, originally in Latin, is the major contemporary source concerning the growth of Anglo-Saxon culture in England.]

the existing society, has given them a vantage ground to stand upon and enables them to talk of the wonders which Saxon institutions achieved. If the question as to the structure of the English language involved a mere critical inquiry, it would be unimportant; but it necessarily assumes a character of profound philosophical interest, as it is connected with the whole problem of European civilization, and with the still deeper problem, what nation, if any, that has risen up in the world has ever been known to civilize itself?

It is supposed that the bulk of the Roman population was expelled from the Island after the invasion of A. D. 406; that the Roman legion had been removed some time before, in order to protect the empire in another quarter, is certain. It is highly probable, also, that numbers of Roman citizens among the employees and civil officers of the government also withdrew; but that the entire Roman population and the population of mixed blood which had been growing up during a much longer period than has elapsed since the settlement of the United States also withdrew is absolutely incredible. For what was the Roman population at the commencement of the fifth century? It was composed of persons who were Britons by birth, although descended from Roman ancestors, and this poulation which had been growing up for twenty generations had become fastened to the soil by habit and interest as well as by early associations. If a thousand years hence, there shall be no authentic history of the dismemberment of Spain from her American colonies, no one would place any confidence in the random conjectures that the Creoles had in a body abandoned Mexico, Peru and Chile. The belief would be, as is the fact, that they nearly all remained in the country of their birth.

The Saxon conquest was not the work of a day. It proceeded more slowly than conquests usually do. The armies which entered the country at considerable intervals were too small to exterminate the inhabitants, even if they had desired to do so, although in the end they were sufficient to overcome the military force which they encountered. Nor could there be any motives to induce the Roman British population to retire when all other parts of the empire were suffering from the overwhelming inroads of still more formidable Barbarians.

Historians speak of the expulsion of the Moors from Spain. With as much reason might a historian living three centuries hence speak of the entire emigration from Ireland to America of the Gælic race. The Moorish kingdoms of Spain were very gradually destroyed; the last, the existing society, has given them a vantage ground to stand upon and enables them to talk of the wonders which Saxon institutions achieved. If the question as to the structure of the English language involved a mere critical inquiry, it would be unimportant; but it necessarily assumes a character of profound philosophical interest, as it is connected with the whole problem of European civilization, and with the still deeper problem, what nation, if any, that has risen up in the world has ever been known to civilize itself?

It is supposed that the bulk of the Roman population was expelled from the Island after the invasion of A. D. 406; that the Roman legion had been removed some time before, in order to protect the empire in another quarter, is certain. It is highly probable, also, that numbers of Roman citizens among the employees and civil officers of the government also withdrew; but that the entire Roman population and the population of mixed blood which had been growing up during a much longer period than has elapsed since the settlement of the United States also withdrew is absolutely incredible. For what was the Roman population at the commencement of the fifth century? It was composed of persons who were Britons by birth, although descended from Roman ancestors, and this poulation which had been growing up for twenty generations had become fastened to the soil by habit and interest as well as by early associations. If a thousand years hence, there shall be no authentic history of the dismemberment of Spain from her American colonies, no one would place any confidence in the random conjectures that the Creoles had in a body abandoned Mexico, Peru and Chile. The belief would be, as is the fact, that they nearly all remained in the country of their birth.

The Saxon conquest was not the work of a day. It proceeded more slowly than conquests usually do. The armies which entered the country at considerable intervals were too small to exterminate the inhabitants, even if they had desired to do so, although in the end they were sufficient to overcome the military force which they encountered. Nor could there be any motives to induce the Roman British population to retire when all other parts of the empire were suffering from the overwhelming inroads of still more formidable Barbarians.

Historians speak of the expulsion of the Moors from Spain. With as much reason might a historian living three centuries hence speak of the entire emigration from Ireland to America of the Gælic race. The Moorish kingdoms of Spain were very gradually destroyed; the last, whether this stock should be a Saxon one or not. If the Franks had possessed themselves of Britain and the Saxons of Gaul, the structure of society in the two countries would have been the same as it is now. Two things were necessary: that the barbarous tribes should be placed in contact with a civilized people, that they should live among them and learn from them, otherwise there would have been no beginning for the new race; and secondly, that Roman civilization should be so modified as to adapt itself to this mixed people. The sufferings, the distress, and anguish of mind which the people endured threatened for a time to disorganize all European society. But these causes were never sufficient to tear up by the roots Roman civilization. On the contrary, the multiplied adversities to which men in all the relations of life were exposed developed reflection and individual energy and constituted a training and discipline for the new society which rose up from the ruins of the old. In the seventh and eighth centuries, learning had made greater progress in England than anywhere else. On the Continent, profane literature had entirely disappeared. In England the schools were flourishing and Greek and Roman literature were sought after with unusual ardor, as the history of Alcuin, the intellectual representative of the eighth century, completely attests.[5]

Do physical causes exercise an important influence upon the human character? This has been a much debated question. But it is not difficult of solution. That difference of race produces a difference of character among nations can admit of no doubt. But difference of race proceeds from an original difference of structure, or organization, and is entitled to infinitely more attention than food, air, and climate. The difference between the Chinese and the people of Europe is so marked that it is impossible to mistake it. The Chinese attained to their present state of civilization when the people of Great Britain, France and Germany were in a savage condition. Education is universally diffused in China, and men of letters have a distinction which they possess in no other part of the world. But their education is confined within the narrowest limits imaginable, and their literature is mawkish and trifling in the extreme, without depth or originality. They are the most lettered and the most ignorant among civilized people. The Tartar conquest operated no change in society; for the Tartars adopted the institutions

5. [Alcuin (735?–804), English churchman and educator, disciple of Bede, who helped to establish the seven liberal arts, the *trivium* and *quadrivium,* as the curriculum for higher education in medieval Europe.]

and manners of the conquered people, as the Franks, Goths and Saxons adopted those which they found planted in Gaul, Spain and Britain.

In Africa, civilization never even begun to dawn, except on the Mediterranean coast which was peopled by a race totally different from the Ethiopian. The brain is the organ of the mind, and any sensible difference in its structure must exercise a corresponding influence upon the character. There is a great difference in this respect between individuals of one and the same nation. If we were to single out all the weakest minded persons in Europe and America and plant them somewhere as a nation, they would probably be little inferior to the Chinese or Hindoos. We could not well compare them with the Ethiopians because they would at least have the gloss of civilization, while the last are still addicted to the most savage habits. But it is still a problem whether this physical cause proceeding from race and the original structure of the brain may not be countervailed by moral causes. The physical organization undergoes great changes in a highly civilized society. The moral causes which then exert an influence act upon the mind; and yet they act less directly than where the discipline is of a purely mental character. If we could transfer half a million of Chinese or Hindoos to Great Britain or the United States, place them socially as well as politically on the same footing with the people of those countries, but prevent intermarriages except with the people of their own race, we might be able after the lapse of a great many generations to determine whether the structure of the brain and not merely the external manners is capable of alteration and improvement. No experiment of this kind has ever been made, nor probably ever will. It will then be forever a problem. For, although as I have remarked, moral causes would seem to be better fitted to act upon that part of our structure which is immediately connected with the mind than upon that which is only so remotely, yet it must be remembered that the mind, and consequently its physical organ, have a power of resistance as well as a principle of ductility, and this power might be absolutely fatal to any fundamental change in the intellectual faculties.

The consideration of physical causes has been generally confined to the influence of food, climate, and air. Climate undoubtedly exerts a powerful influence upon the character. The inhabitants of the frozen and torrid zones are distinguished from each other by the most decisive traits, nor could any human device bring about a resemblance between them. In the first, the extreme rigor of the climate causes the whole of life to be spent in efforts to battle against the elements. The beings who are condemned to this dreary abode are occupied with no other care than that of sustaining animal life. Their faculties are dwarfed and mutilated and their feelings benumbed by the terrible agents which act perpetually upon them. In the torrid zone, the character is powerfully affected, but not in the same way nor to the same extent. The extreme heat of the climate produces a lassitude which is unfavorable to any vigorous or sustained exertion. In the first case, the mind suffers from being overtasked in ministering to the bodily wants. In the second, it suffers through defect of capacity for exertion. But the inhabitants of the torrid zone are capable of rising much higher, both intellectually and morally, than the inhabitants of the frozen. The climate does not act upon them with such unmitigated severity as upon the inhabitants of the extreme North. Instead of a scanty subsistence, they have an abundance of food. Their numbers consequently increase greatly, society is fairly established among them, and the intercourse which takes place makes great amends for the want of other motives to mental exertion.

In the temperate zone, the differences of climate are not such as to prevent all the people who inhabit it from attaining a very high, though perhaps not an uniform, civilization. Where physical causes are not absolutely overbearing in their operation, as in the polar regions and near the equator, they are capable of being overpowered by moral causes and bringing all the people subjected to them to a near resemblance to each other. The difference between the people of southern and central Europe is not so great that it might not be overcome by the operation of the same moral causes acting upon both. The difference between the Italians and the English is not so great as between the Italians and the people of Ancient Rome. In the United States, the difference between the people of the North and South is not so great as it is between the people of France who inhabit different provinces in the same latitude.

The influence which moral causes exert will be best appreciated by singling out those classes in different countries which are most completely subjected to them. If the intellectual men in different parts of the temperate zone have in the chief lineaments of character a strong resemblance to one another, it must be attributed to the influence which moral causes have in moulding the mind and disposition. The eminent men from the south of France in the Chamber of Deputies do not differ materially from the eminent members of the British Parliament who are natives of Scotland. Guizot and Berryer are not more distinguishable from Brougham and Macaulay than they are from each other. There is greater difference of character between Mackintosh and Grattan than between Burke and De Tocqueville.[6] Education, absorbing occupations, pursuits which demand judgment and reflection, overcome the difference of climate where this is not extreme and assimilate men wonderfully to each other. What is true in the higher walks of life is true in the lower; and if the institutions, both public and private, are the same the different classes in both will nearly resemble each other. The French are no longer the fickle and vivacious people they were before the year 1789. They begin to feel that they have some stake in the hedge, some interest in public affairs, and this has produced a marked seriousness of character. Thus, if difference of climate which is so well calculated to produce a difference of temperament can make two nations appear to be of different races, a train of moral causes acting upon both may make them resemble each other. The eminent statesmen of England and the United States are very much the same sort of persons; but there is a very great difference between all of them and Richelieu or Mazarin, or Wolsey, and Strafford.[7]

6. [Francois Guizot (1787–1874), French statesman and historian, one of the leading intellectual exponents of the bourgeois monarchy of Louis Phillipe in 1830; Antoine-Pierre Berryer (1790–1868), a conservative Christian royalist in French politics; Henry Peter Brougham (1778–1868), born in Edinburgh, leader of the liberal party in British nineteenth-century politics; Thomas Babington Macaulay (1800–1859), English historian, also distingushed Whig member of Parliament; Sir James Mackintosh (1765–1832), leading Whig defender of the French Revolution against Edmund Burke who, after 1796, became hostile to French radicalism; Henry Grattan (1746–1820), Irish patriot who led the fight to gain legislative initiative for the Irish Parliament.]

7. [Armand Jean du Plessis, duc de Richelieu, Cardinal de Richelieu (1585–1642), chief minister of Louis XIII of France in which position he exercised autocratic power; Jules Mazarin (1602–1661), French statesman and Cardinal who served Richelieu and succeeded him (1642) as chief minister to the King and advanced his policies of the centralization of power in the King's hands; Thomas Wolsey (1473?–1530), English statesman and Cardinal of the Roman Catholic Church who, in 1511, was appointed privy councillor to Henry VIII and virtually controlled English foreign and domestic policy; Thomas Wentworth, first Earl of Strafford (1593–1641), English statesman who under Charles I as lord deputy of Ireland enforced the King's rule with harsh severity.]

I have observed that the bringing men into close communication with each other and establishing some sort of society in the first instance was probably the principal means of civilizing them. This influence is two-fold. It acts upon the manners by imposing a restraint on the excessive indulgence of the selfish and antisocial propensities; it acts upon the mind by presenting it with abundant materials for reflection. For the study in one form or other of the minds and character of others makes up the greatest and the most valuable part of human knowledge. But free institutions lead to an association of people of all classes. The civilization, therefore, is destined to be more thorough and uniform than in any other species of government. In most countries, civilization can hardly be said to be an attribute of all classes. The various orders are separated as widely as if they were inhabitants of different ages and countries. This condition of society could not exist in the United States, nor would it have existed in other countries if the civil and political institutions had originally been so modelled as to bring people of all ranks into a free and constant intercourse. No nation has ever been known to civilize itself, and the only way of civilizing the uncivilized orders of the same country is to bring them under the direct influence of those which are civilized. The thorough civilization of the people of the United States (when compared with that of other countries) is more than any other circumstance destined to render their institutions lasting, and thus to falsify the maxim of Montesquieu that a nation after it has attained a certain height is compelled by some invincible law of its being to decline.

Although a southern temperament may make men fickle, passionate, and fond of pleasure, it also induces a contemplative turn of mind. This is a marked trait in the character of a southern people. Free institutions turn this quality to account, and prevent the contemplative disposition from wasting itself, as among the oriental nations, in vague and unprofitable reveries. A vast field for active exertion is opened, and this mixture of the practical and speculative contributes to the formation of a very high order of mind. A most acute observer, De Tocqueville, has perhaps exaggerated when he declares that the men of the Southern States of America, "are both more brilliant, and more profound, than those of the North." We shall not err, however, if we say that they have both these qualities in as great perfection.

In every country which has run a career of long and uninterrupted prosperity there is a tendency to what may be termed excessive civilization. Extremes frequently meet and excessive civilization carries men back to the indulgence of the same propensities which characterized them in savage life. The same vices, only under different forms, invade every rank, and the community would be in danger of universal dissolution unless some terrible calamity occurred to give a rousing shake to society. But if there is a country in which no wall of partition exists between the higher and lower orders this catastrophe may be prevented without breaking up the framework of society. The upper ranks will be constantly recruited from that part of the population which being inured to industry possesses greater simplicity of habits. The great disparity which exists in the condition of different classes may seem unnatural, but it answers among many other wise ends this important purpose: it prevents luxury and effeminacy from taking complete possession of the ruling orders, and the whole community from running rapidly to decay.

The influence which food and air exercise is very small. In the frozen zone, the first acts powerfully, but it is only as connected with the climate. The meagre and scanty subsistence which the inhabitants obtain from the forests and rivers does there stunt the growth both of body and mind. But in the temperate zone the food, although very different in different regions, is on that very account better adapted to the various physical organizations. The inhabitants of a southern climate have larger and more powerful muscles than those of a northern, which would seem to show that a moderate diet is not unfavorable to the complete development of the animal structure. No people in the temperate zone has been known to abstain from the use of stimulating drugs, such as tobacco, spirituous liquors, tea and coffee. If any such had ever been known, it would probably be found that the strength and health of both body and mind was greatly improved and that the human frame attained a perfection which it had not anywhere else. But no experiment having ever been made, we are deprived of the only certain means of verifying the conjecture.

The present has been termed the age of physical civilization; and it is even supposed that literature and philosophy have already begun to decline. This, like many other general propositions, has at least the merit of containing something striking. Its fault consists in presenting an imperfect and incomplete view of the matter. There never was a period when men were so much addicted to those pursuits which minister to the comforts and enjoyments of life. There never was one when these were so widely diffused. The display of human activity in this direction, having been so little formerly and so immense now, the intellectual exertion which is actually made is thrown into the background, and to an inattentive observer the unprecedented progress which one pursuit has made seems to imply the decay of all others. I doubt whether there ever was a time of greater intellectual exertion in France, Great Britain, and Germany than during the present century. There is a fault common to the great majority of minds, even those of a high order. They can see nothing excellent, nothing eminently fine, in anything which belongs to their own time. It is not merely that the living envy the living, not the dead. It is because the best minds are slow in analyzing and appreciating what has not been analyzed before their time. I have known very excellent minds affect great admiration for what are sometimes termed "the wells undefiled of English literature," and yet great parts of the works so characterized are heavy and dull in the extreme. A tinge of melancholy frequently pervades the finest minds in a civilized country. They are saddened by the present, not by the past, and they endeavor to escape from everything around them by studies which most effectually deaden and extinguish the sentiment of the present. This is a topic which is too large for me to dilate upon now. The reader must be satisfied with the few hints I have thrown out. These will exercise his mind more than if I were to explain the merits of the great number of brilliant, profound, and original writers who have adorned the present century. Physical civilization lies at the foundation of all higher civilization. It constitutes the rudiments of moral and intellectual cultivation. An age distinguished for it denotes two things: first, that civilization is more thoroughly diffused than at any former period; and secondly, that preparation is making for the growth of a more various, profound, and original literature than before existed.

The general taste for physical civilization at the present day is an indication of a very important revolution in the structure of society. If we confine our views to its influence upon the social and political organization, we cannot place too high an estimate upon it. Whatever contributes to raise the general standard of comfort contributes to the development of the popular mind and creates an improved taste and capacity for free institutions. And accordingly, the two countries (Great Britain and the United States) in which physical civilization has attained the greatest perfection are the two in which civil and political freedom have made the greatest progress. Free institutions are endowed with a faculty of self preservation which is possessed by no other form of government. The reason of this is that physical civilization diffuses property, knowledge, and power; and by so doing conduces to the equal distribution of the physical and moral strength of the community.

So far from believing that physical civilization is inconsistent with intellectual cultivation, I am convinced that the more the former is spread the higher is the point to which the last will be carried. We must, at any rate, admit that physical civilization has something to do with the formation of the intellectual men who have adorned society. We cannot conceive of such minds as Locke and Burke, Montesquieu and Cuvier, growing up in a society where they at least were not surrounded with the comforts of life. Health is a corporeal advantage; yet some degree of it is indispensable to the prosecution of any intellectual enterprise. And as a wise man will not wantonly neglect his health, he will not willingly forego any other outward advantage which conspires to the same end. Physical civilization supplies the materials on which intellectual men act. If we figure to ourselves two countries, one of which is covered with log huts interspersed among palaces, the other filled with populous and well built cities, the truth of the remark will be obvious. In one the matter for reflection and study will be inexhaustible; in the other it will be sterile and unprofitable. All speculations in philosophy and literature may be said to be experiments upon the human mind. But it is impossible to make such experiments where the race of mankind is lifted very little above the condition of the brutes.

The more widely physical civilization is diffused, the greater will be the chance that superior minds will emerge from obscurity. When the progress of industry and the arts is so slow that a small proportion of the population is placed in easy circumstances, a great number of such minds may be said to perish annually, like seed sown upon a sandy soil. If on the other hand, the comforts of life are extended to the bulk of the population the greater will be the number of the educated, not merely of the educated at schools and colleges but of those who have encountered the severe intellectual discipline which follows. The number of those who will be thinkers and actors of the age will be greatly increased. Physical civilization may postpone the period of intellectual cultivation; but the longer it is postponed the more certain it is of giving birth to the highest exertions in every department of philosophy and literature. Even excessive civilization is not without some advantages. The mind becomes wearied with the eternal round of heartless enjoyment and is thrust upon its own resources for occupation. The apparent dearth of intellectual effort in the United States is remarkable. Never in any country has there been so much intellect in activity; in hardly any one has so little distinction been attained in the higher walks of learning. The reasons are obvious: 1st the widespread political institutions, together with the learned professions, absorb nearly all the talent of the country; 2d, this greatly retards the growth of intellectual men as a body. But until they become such, they feel as if they were placed in a false position to society when, in truth, it is society which is placed in a false position to them. When the minds devoted to speculation become numerous, the common sympathy which will animate them will be a bond of unspeakable strength, and there will then, probably, be no country which will exceed the United States in every department of philosophy, science, and literature. And there can be no well ordered commonwealth unless there is a full development of the intellectual as well as the active faculties. The first balances it and gives it a right direction, the second keeps it in motion. All the mechanical contrivances for balancing government are falling from our hands and can only be superseded by the engine of knowledge. Take away all the intellectual men who have figured in public life and in the learned professions, together with the influence which they have exerted upon other parts of society, and the United States would be a desert. But as the population becomes dense the demand for intellectual qualities will become more pressing and cannot be satisfied by the amount which is expended in public life and the professions. And this demand is in due time answered. For in the natural course of things, political life and the professions become crowded to excess, and the various departments of knowledge begin to be filled up.

CHAPTER II | GENERAL VIEWS AND DIFFICULTIES

OF THE SCIENCE OF GOVERNMENT

AMIDST the general progress which the human mind has made during the last two hundred years, there is one science which has remained nearly stationary, and that is the philosophy of government.* It is true that all our knowledge is deduced from facts; and it is equally true that it is not in our power to create any one of those facts. The principles which go to make up what we denominate a science are nothing more than the philosophy of facts; and until the facts are given we cannot find the principles. But it is remarkable that during the period I have referred to a wider range of facts has been laid open to human observation and scrutiny than in any period of similar duration in the history of our race. For if we commence with the year 1642, in the midst of the great struggle between liberty and power in Great Britain, and come down to the present day, we shall find that nearly all the great revolutions in human affairs which have sensibly affected the social organization, the structure of government, and the functions of rulers are crowded into that compass. The inquiry, therefore, is not only the most natural in the world but it forces itself irresistibly upon us, why, in the midst of so great and so general a movement of the human mind, the science of government has seemed to stand still. It can never be necessary to know all possibly existing facts, otherwise no part of knowledge would ever be brought to completeness.

Several causes may be assigned for the slow progress of the science. The first consists in its intrinsic difficulties. There is no branch of

* The intelligent reader is no doubt familiar with the distinction between art and science. The first is the result of our experience, however limited that may be. The second is the repository of those great principles which are deduced from all experience. The first therefore necessarily precedes the last. It contains the rule in the concrete while the last contains it in the abstract or in a philosophical form. In Quintilian's time, it was a question, whether oratory was a science or an art. At the present day, I presume, no one will deny that government is both an art and a science. [Note added to the second edition.]

knowledge which to so great an extent demands the application of abstract truth to particular facts; none in which the facts are so diversified and so difficult to reduce to general rules. The very circumstance, therefore, that the two last centuries have been so prolific of materials, that they have afforded such an immense accumulation of facts, creates an impediment. Without these we cannot proceed a step, and yet with them the greatest powers of analysis are baffled in the endeavor to trace out those principles which shall everywhere be regarded as forming the great elements of the science. I can easily imagine that very many of the most thoughtful minds, both in Europe and America, have occupied a whole lifetime in surveying with intense interest and an eagle eye the changes which society and government have undergone in the last sixty or seventy years, and yet have recoiled from the attempt to reduce into a system such a vast mass of experience.

The second reason which I would assign is that government is the science not only of what is and what ought to be but, in addition to these, of what may be made to be also. It thus unites in itself the difficulties of all other sciences, and conducts to inquiries more complicated than any one of them singly. We can create no new facts, but we may vary indefinitely the combinations of those which are already known. If it is a painful effort, therefore, to apply abstract truths to particular facts, the difficulty is very much increased when we desire to make an entirely new disposition of those facts; when, for instance, we wish to alter existing institutions and to give a new form to the whole or to some part of the government.

Another impediment to the advancement of the science has arisen from the extreme backwardness which both writers and statesmen have constantly discovered in speaking out all that they know and believe. It is supposed that there are a great many secrets in government which will not bear to be divulged to the generality of mankind. We have read of the secret and the open doctrine of the ancient philosophers. Some things they revealed to the multitude, while others were hidden from all but a select few. The same custom existed among some of the ancient fathers;* although it has been endeavored to be ex-

* "*Some* of the Fathers held that wholly without breach of duty, it is allowed to the teachers, and heads of the Christian church, to employ artifices, to intermingle truth with falsehood." Riboff. Programme of the Doctrine and Discipline of the Fathers. [The note was added to the second edition and I have been unable to identify the source. It would be interesting to do so because in the first edition, in-

plained and palliated by eminent ecclesiastical writers. But the practice was by no means confined to the ancients. It has existed from all time and has prevailed extensively, though not avowedly, among the philosophers and politicians of modern times. It is now beginning to fall into disrepute since what are termed the multitude are increasing so fast in knowledge and information that it is no longer an easy matter to keep any secrets and since, on that very account, the disclosure can be productive of no detriment. For although the first effect of finding out many things which were before hidden is to make us fear nothing, not even the most violent changes; yet the ultimate effect is to make us fear many things and to show us precipices and hindrances at every step which we take.

The last cause which I shall mention as retarding the progress of the science is that in many instances the minds which are particularly fitted to extend its bounds are withdrawn from speculation into the field of active life. Profound thought, the ability to take the philosophical view which belongs to things the most common and familiar, joined to a keen insight into men's character and dispositions, are necessary to penetrate into the principles of the science. But he who possesses these qualities is very apt to be won over to one or other of the great parties which share the mastery of the country. The field of speculation, the field of imagination, and the field of action divide between themselves the empire of man's exertions. No one has been able to compass one of these in a lifetime; while the sense of enjoyment which is derived from mixing in active life is so much greater than is afforded by abstract speculation that few minds have sufficient fortitude to forego the first for the sake of the more brilliant and durable fame which attends the last.

Writers on political philosophy have for the most part employed themselves in studying what is termed the mechanism of government rather than in unfolding the structure of society. This is often the cause of great infirmity in the most ingenious speculations since, without pursuing the last course, we can neither thoroughly decipher existing institutions nor see our way clearly in binding together the gen-

---

stead of "the ancient fathers," Grimke had written "the fathers of the African church." The source would allow one to judge whether the change was a simple slip in transcription between "ancient" and "African," or whether Grimke, because of his belief in the inferiority of the Negro race, wished to avoid the possibility that some reader might associate the ancient fathers of the Church with African Negroes.]

eral principles which are fairly deducible from them. All governments are to a great degree dependent upon the manners, habits, and dispositions of the people among whom they subsist. This connection is closer and more striking where the institutions are democratic; and as the American constitutions are the only example of the thorough establishment of such institutions it is no wonder the error I have referred to has prevailed so extensively in the old world. It is both our privilege and our misfortune that our knowledge is so completely bounded by our experience: our privilege, because we are withheld from a multitude of visionary and fruitless expedients to better our condition, and our misfortune, because we are sometimes inclosed in such a narrow circle of experience as to remove us from the contemplation of a world of new facts which are transpiring beyond us.

The reason then why it is of so much importance to examine and understand the structure of society, and not merely the machinery of government, is because at the present day more than at any former period the political institutions are molded by the manners. It is true, every form of government may strictly be said to depend upon the constitution of society — upon the social organization in which it has taken root. But this dependence is of a totally different character in different countries. In some, the manners exert a positive influence, while in others they have properly a negative influence only. In a commonwealth, where the standard of popular intelligence is high and no impediment exists to the exercise of that popular authority which rightfully springs from such a state, the people may truly be said to create and to uphold the government. On the contrary, where the population is sunk in ignorance and apathy, government assumes the character of a self-existing institution, for there is no power beyond to direct and control it. In one instance, the will of society impresses itself as an active power upon the institutions, both ordaining and controlling them; in the other, for defect of will, the government is simply permitted to be what chance or circumstances originally made it. The political institutions of Russia and the United States equally depend upon the social organization; but in the former the influence is negative, in the latter it is direct and positive. In the former, the people by their inaction contribute to rear the fabric of despotism; in the last, they have created free institutions. It follows that in proportion as the influence is of a positive character will the institutions incline to the form of free government: for there may be every degree of this influence, stamping the greatest variety upon different schemes of government. Thus the English people are distinguished for the enjoyment of a greater degree of liberty than the French; and the last have made such noble advances in the same career during the last twenty years as to place their government entirely in advance of the Spanish or Portuguese. Sometimes a positive influence is exerted upon one part of the government; one department undergoes a fundamental change while others remain untouched. In other instances, no great alteration is made; the theory of the government continues as before; but such is the stringency and force of that invisible agent which we term public opinion that the conduct and behavior of all public men, the tone and temper of the public administration, are materially improved.

The legislature is that department which is apt to be first molded by the direct intervention of the popular will. It becomes a representative body long before it occurs to anyone that it is possible to render the executive and judiciary elective also. The legislature seems to touch more extensively, if not more immediately, upon the interests of society than any other department and it is the first, therefore, to which development is given. The judiciary would appear to have quite as intimate a connection with the business, the daily transactions, of the people as the legislature; but as its functions are supposed to consist simply in making application of a set of ready made rules, and therefore to be inconsistent with the attainment of any substantive power, it does not engage public attention so early, nor attract so general an interest, as it is entitled to do.

One great end which legislators in constructing government have proposed to accomplish is so to adjust the parts of which it is composed that they may act as checks upon one another. This scheme has given rise to the theory of checks and balances. But hardly anyone has adverted to a balance of a very different kind, without which the structure of the government must forever be faulty and its practical working inconsistent with its theory. I allude to that great balance which in a society rightly constituted is maintained between the government and the power out of the government. It is owing to the great alterations which the social and political organization has undergone in very modern times that this new fact in the history of political philosophy has escaped attention; at any rate, that a precise and definite place has not been assigned to it by those who have treated of government. The elevation of the lower orders, the formation of a great middle class, a thing but of yesterday, the creation of a genuine public opinion have wrought changes in the composition of government corresponding with those in the structure of society. Because the legislative, executive, and judicial departments comprehend that share of authority which is organized and which assumes a visible and determinate form, it has sometimes been supposed that they contain the sum total of the political power of the community; but it is a matter for curious inquiry, to say the least, whether the outward force which sometimes resides in society, no matter whether we arbitrarily range it under the head of liberties and franchises, has not risen to the rank of a substantive power; whether, in short, it has not become a new wheel in the machinery of the government. Those departments do indeed exercise the administrative authority of the state and, if they were left to themselves and permitted to use power without a constant and active control on the part of the people, they would constitute the government in the largest signification of the word. The extent to which that control exists is the single circumstance which at first determines the form of any particular government and afterwards gives a direction to all its movements. If it is extremely feeble, the government will be a monarchy or oligarchy, in the most unrestricted sense; if it is moderate in its operation, the mixed form of limited monarchy, or a tempered aristocracy, will grow up; and if very strong, it will give rise to free institutions or a representative republic. If it could be conceived to be all powerful, it would not introduce the licentiousness of an unbridled democracy but would rather supersede the necessity of all government. Wherever democracy in its extreme form exists, the control of society at large is very small instead of being very great; and therefore it is that such a government never has more than a temporary existence; it soon degenerates into an absolute government.

As the power I have spoken of as residing out of the government and in the society represents for the most part a moral force, it may be supposed that I have assigned it too important a place in regarding it as a new wheel in the political machinery. But they who undertake to expound the ordinary theory of checks and balances do not rely so much on the physical force which is exercised by the departments of government separately, as upon a set of moral causes which are recognized as belonging to human nature and which, as they are known to operate upon men as individuals, are with equal certainty expected to act upon them when they are made public rulers. And with the same propriety, in order to form a just notion of that species of balance I have referred to as existing between the government and the power out of the government, it is not necessary to consider the people as constantly invested with an armed force. The general tendency at the present day is to substitute moral power in the place of physical force, not because it is more convenient, but because it is more efficacious. The profound tranquillity which has been enjoyed by the American government—a tranquillity so remarkable as to constitute a new fact in the history of society—will easily lead us to comprehend how a check exercised upon so large a scale may be of so great importance; how it is that an invisible but ever active power, which the term public opinion is of too narrow a meaning to give a competent idea of, may be sufficient to determine the form of the government, and after it is created to superintend all its movements. The tendency of which I have spoken may, at some future day, be carried so far as to render it doubtful which is the government proper, the official agents who administer the public affairs, or the more complex machinery which presides over them and retains each department in its proper sphere.

Writers have divided governments into various classes. The most usual division is into monarchy, aristocracy, and democracy. This classification has been adopted not merely in consequence of the different manner in which those governments are put together, but, proceeding upon a more comprehensive view and considering each of them as founded in certain general and fundamental principles of human nature, those writers have treated the classification as a philosophical one of the highest importance. It is sometimes difficult to distinguish between an historical fact and a philosophical truth. That governments have existed under every variety of form is an undoubted fact; and that their existence may be accounted for from well known causes is equally certain. But what would be thought of the ethical philosopher who ranged the virtues and vices under the same head because they all have their root in certain principles of human nature. The error in both instances is precisely the same. There can be but one legitimate form of government, although there may be ever so many varieties which force or accident has given birth to.

If I ventured to make a classification, it would be into the natural and artificial forms, considering a representative republic as the only example of the first and every other species as coming under the second division. By arranging a truth in the same list with a number of errors, it loses the distinct importance which belongs to it, and ceases to be regarded as a truth. The aim of the writer is necessarily imperfect and unsatisfactory. Even admitting that it were absolutely impracticable to introduce free institutions into every country, that does not prevent their being considered as the only legitimate form of government, no more than the impossibility, if it exists, of engrafting the arts and refinement which are found among the English and American people upon the wandering tribes of Africa or America forbids us from treating civilization and savagism not merely as different but as two opposite states. The great end to be attained by holding up some principles and some institutions as just and true and others as the reverse is to quicken and animate both individuals and states in their efforts to abjure the former and to cultivate the last. The ancestors of the English and American people roamed like savages through the forests of Britain and Germany and lived for centuries after under a stern and cruel despotism. The people whom Cæsar and Tacitus describe as clad in skins and sacrificing human victims seemed to have no fairer chance of being raised to the arts and civilization which their descendants have attained than the great majority of rude tribes now in existence. By regarding and habitually treating some actions and some institutions as right and others as wrong, we make a considerable step toward rendering the former attainable, since it is of the very essence of right that it is something which can be reduced to practice. The distinction then is no longer between the possible and the impossible, but between things practicable and things which are only difficult to be attained.

Government when not founded upon the will of the people is necessarily an imperfect institution because, failing in the commencement to represent their interests, it is almost sure eventually to be placed in direct opposition to them. Power where it is condensed in a comparatively small class of the community is obliged in self-defense to strengthen in all possible ways the influence and authority of that class, and, to the same extent, to detract from the importance of all other orders of men. It is not a reasonable answer to this to be told that abundant causes for the existence of such a mode of government may be found in the actual constitution of society in some countries since there is no form of vice, however gross and detestable, which may not be accounted for and justified in the same way. We recognize the correctness of the historical deduction, but reject the general principle which is sought to be derived from it.

The political institutions of a country may be viewed as fulfilling two distinct ends: the one to administer all public business, the other to bind society together, in other words, to uphold civilization. But distinct as these two offices are, that constitution of government which is best fitted to promote the one is also best calculated to advance the other. The wants and weakness of individuals give rise to the institution of government, and government, in turn, becomes the instrument of furthering the general improvement of society. The mere material interests which the public agents are appointed to superintend, the protection of property, the collection and disbursement of taxes, the guarding against foreign invasion, are not so absolutely connected with the moral and intellectual condition of the people but what we may suppose the former to be competently managed without any remarkable improvement in the latter. But it is certain that the right constitution of government, joined to an upright and enlightened administration of what we denominate public affairs, does contribute wonderfully to impart freedom, activity, and intelligence to the general mind; and it is still more true that the diffusion of intelligence, the spread of the arts and sciences, and the growth of a vigorous morality do produce a marked influence upon the working of the political machine. The wider the basis on which government is made to stand — that is, the more thoroughly it represents the interests of all orders of men — the firmer the purpose and the more unremitting the efforts of individuals in improving their condition. The most effectual way then of raising the intellectual condition of the people is to connect their interests so closely with their improvement that these may be mutually dependent on each other; to throw knowledge in the way of everyone, that it may become of daily use and indispensable application in both public and private affairs, so that men in pursuit of their daily avocations and government in the discharge of its official duties may be compelled to run the same career of improvement. In this way, the maintenance of civilization and the more direct aim which the institutions of government contemplate are both answered at the same time.

CHAPTER III | THE FOUNDATION OF GOVERNMENT,

AND RIGHT OF THE MAJORITY TO RULE

THE foundation of government is laid in the nature of man; and this fact, simple as it is, explains how civil institutions came to have a beginning and why it is that they have rightful authority to command. It is sometimes supposed that the most natural view would be to consider individuals as possessing, originally, the right of self-government. But that cannot be natural which contradicts the constitution of human nature. The mistake arises from overlooking, or confounding, the double nature of man. He has attributes which are peculiar to him as an individual; on the other hand he has innumerable relations to the beings who surround him. If we could suppose the former to swallow up his whole being, then it would be correct to say not only that self-government was originally the rule, but we should be driven to the conclusion that it is now the rule and must be so in all time to come. But as this is not the case, we are relieved from stating an unsound proposition and from following it up by the most mischievous consequences. In truth the difficulty does not so much consist in conceiving how a collective body of men should be subjected to the government of society as in imagining how such a body, constituting in its natural signification a society, should know no other rule than the government of individuals. To say that many thousands or many millions of men inhabit together the same region is to imply that they have a multitude of relations to each other and a system of interests which are common to all. No man can practice a duty or exercise a right without touching more or less upon the corresponding duties and rights of other men.

But as this view admits that man has a double nature, it may be inquired what higher and stronger reason there is why those attributes which make him the being of society should have the precedence; why, in fine, they should be entitled to rule over the individual, rather than the individual should be permitted to have control over society. And laying aside the impracticability and self-contradiction involved in this notion, the answer is plain that in society the whole of our nature may be completely unfolded, while out of it hardly any part is even tolerably developed. The scheme of self government, as it erects the will of the individual into the supreme arbiter of his actions, necessarily implies the violation by each of the rights of all, and would thus mutilate and destroy even the character of the individual, if it did not produce the utter extermination of the race.

It is no wonder, therefore, that men in all ages have instinctively taken shelter under some sort of political institutions. The imperfection of these institutions is a natural consequence of the very imperfect nature of man. This does not show that the scheme is wrong, but rather that its excellence is such that it cannot be carried thoroughly into practice. Imperfect as all human contrivances necessarily are, civil government has been found necessary to the supply of our wants, the protection of our rights, and to the lifting of our condition much above that of the brutes.

Several theories have been proposed to account for the first formation of government. Some writers consider it as a divine institution, while others suppose that it originated in compact. This compact, however, has been described very differently. Mr. Locke treating it as an agreement between the people and their rulers, while Hobbes and Rousseau suppose the agreement was simply among the people themselves.

There is this very important distinction between the exact and the moral sciences, that in the former a proposition is either altogether true or false, while in the last there may be, and very frequently is, a mixture of both truth and error. This renders it exceedingly difficult to deal with moral propositions. Truth and error may be combined in every proportion, and it is only where the balance inclines greatly to the one side or the other that we can be sure we are right in adopting a given view. But there is this great compensation resulting from this defect and the total dissimilarity between these two departments of knowledge, that in politics when we embrace an error we very often embrace a considerable portion of truth along with it. Thus, in those matters which vitally affect the interests and happiness of mankind, the understanding is hardly ever condemned to the dominion of absolute and unqualified error. If one side of a proposition were altogether true and the other altogether false, the adoption of the latter would give rise to something more than a theoretical error: it would produce consequences fatal to the peace and well-being of society. The advantage which flows from this complete dissimilarity between two leading departments of our knowledge is not seen in those abstract propositions which, whatever way they may be decided, affect practice very little. But it is strikingly displayed in that vast multitude of questions which are of daily occurrence in administering the complicated concerns of an established and regular community. That is to say, the advantage arising from the principle increases in exact proportion to its application to the actual affairs of men.

The two theories which I have referred to [that is, divine right and social contract theories] are an illustration of these views. The first, although exceedingly far fetched, has this much of verisimilitude, that the divine law constitutes the highest standard of right of which we can have any conception, and communities as well as individuals in all their schemes of action are bound to be guided by it. But if we were to interrogate a philosopher or mechanician as to the cause of the movements of some complicated machine and they were to refer it to the divine agency, we should derive no satisfaction from the explanation. In one sense the solution would be correct, since the Supreme Being is the author of everything. But no addition would be made to our knowledge. So with regard to government; what we want to know, and what we are immediately concerned in knowing, is the process, the human instrumentality, which has given rise to the institution. If we were satisfied with the sweeping answer, curiosity and inquiry into the operation of those secondary laws which determine the form of particular governments would be damped and we should make very little effort to improve an institution which was placed so entirely beyond our reach. Accordingly a doctrine which has the appearance of introducing the highest and justest rules into the conduct of political societies is the one which has been attended with the most mischievous consequences. The advocates of the "jure divino right" have, at the same time, been the most idolatrous worshippers of the absolute power of governments, while the plain and homely understandings who have rejected it have set themselves vigorously to work to extend the blessings of rational freedom and to build up fortresses against the encroachments of power.

The other theory, which places the foundation of government in compact, especially the view taken by Hobbes and Rousseau, approaches the truth much nearer. It is not absolutely incorrect even as an historical fact. Compact is the only legitimate basis upon which government can stand. And if anyone will turn his attention to the formation of the American constitutions he will find that the idea is carried into actual practice. With an example so complete and decisive, it would be a very lame answer to say, with an eminent writer, that if the American procedure was not followed at the first dawn of society where government, like the infant in the cradle, was the creature of circumstances, therefore it is not entitled to notice. No machine, no production of art or science which was the fruit of man's exertions, at the present day or a thousand years ago, could have any claim to originality if this view were correct. All must be referred to an infantile society, simply because the men who have since lived descended directly from that society.

There are two principles which preside over and give a direction to the actions of men: reflection and spontaneous feeling. And there is this fine provision in our nature that where the attainment of an important end is desirable, which cannot be completely compassed without the aid of reflection and yet the reflection is wanting, still there is a corresponding appetite or sentiment which enables us to feel our way. This, in a society which has made any considerable advance, is denominated common sense. In a rude one, it is called sagacity or instinct. Thus, in those communities which existed at a period anterior to written history, although we cannot conceive anything like a formal agreement to have been entered into, we can very readily suppose, indeed we are compelled to suppose, that the minds of all the adult males, however untutored, spontaneously and without any set purpose conspired to that end. That those communities were societies, that is, collections of men in the aggregate, is abundantly sufficient to authorize the supposition. Certain it is that in the rudest community at the present day, that of the North American Indian, I discern far more evidences of the prevalence of a common will as actuating the tribe than of the independent and uncontrolled will of the individual.

We talk of tacit or implied agreements even in jurisprudence, and give the same force and authority to them which we do to express ones. And with great reason. Our notions of right and wrong, of just and unjust, are not determined by our positive agreements, but the reverse. So much so, that the same force is sometimes given to that which ought to be as if it were actually declared to be. For the same reason, although we might not be able to find any trace in a primitive community of an express compact, we should discover far more evidences of that form of society which results from one than we should of the self government of individuals. In other words, the causes which lead men to society and suggest the formation of political communities for the management of the common interests are of such controlling efficacy that they act independently of any formal agreement. And if the contrivances of government are very imperfect at first, the same imperfection belongs to the whole sphere of individual action. Although in the most perfect form of society, that of a representative republic, men possess far more personal freedom than they do as members of a rude tribe, yet it would be very incorrect to say that they did not enjoy individual liberty in this last state.

Moreover, although societies of men may originally have been gathered by accident and civil institutions planted fortuitously, the difficulty of conceiving such a thing as a social compact becomes less with every advance of civilization and knowledge. No one supposes that the authority of government, even in Great Britain and France, stands upon the same uncertain foundation as in the reigns of Henry VII and Louis XI. The idea that some sort of agreement lies at the foundation of government is so inseparable from the human mind, so constantly present in every form of society, that it survives all the mutations which human affairs undergo and at length causes this compact to be reduced to practice in all its details. Thus at the present moment a convention is assembled in the most populous and powerful of the American states* for the purpose of forming a new constitution, and that convention was elected by the votes of all the adult males in the State.

Even in some of the European States there is a settled conviction at the present day, not only among the reflecting but with the great bulk of the population, that the promotion of the general weal is the only legitimate end of government. Obstacles may have to be encountered in realizing the idea; but the idea is predominant. I can easily imagine that all the adults of a society may assemble for the purpose of forming a constitution and yet this constitution be very imperfect. Still it would be literally true that the form of government was the creature of compact. The imperfection might be the result of some defects inherent in human nature or of circumstances which were uncontrollable.

That all governments stand at least upon the footing of an implied

* New York.

contract is of the greatest importance in politics. For then every advance in knowledge adds strength to the notion and ultimately converts the implied into a solemn and formal agreement. And as our inquiries in political philosophy are not bounded by the actual, but are chiefly concerned with what ought to be and what may be made to be, the theory of the social compact should ever be held up as constituting the firmest and the most rational foundation of civil institutions and as that scheme which all people and lawgivers should make continual efforts to approach, even if it should not always be attained.

Great difficulty is sometimes expressed with regard to the rule of the majority, a rule which evidently lies at the foundation of free government. The difficulty is in truth no greater in the case of communities than of individuals, each of whom has conflicting and contradictory interests, opinions, and feelings, and yet knows that it is necessary to pursue some determinate plan, not merely to act successfully but in order to act at all. And if one could conceive all the people of a state as composing parts of one mighty individual, this great being would be as much agitated and embarrassed by discordant views as political communities are. He would be obliged to be governed by the majority of reasons in favor of or against a proposed line of conduct. Difficulties of this kind afford matter for curious and subtle speculation, but they rarely disturb the judgment or interfere much with practice. To say that the rule of the majority is a rule of sheer necessity, and must prevail on that account, would be an imperfect explanation. But if we say that it resembles those great general laws which bind together both the physical and the moral world, which are only rendered necessary because they produce beneficial results, we then shed light upon the reason as well as upon the mode of its operation.

If in laying the foundation of government our design is to consult the common interests of the whole population, there is no alternative but the rule of the majority. If when the vote is taken, either among the citizens at large or in the legislative body which represents them, the will of the greater number did not prevail, the minority would be at liberty to act without rule, not merely as regarded themselves but in regard to the majority also, and in this way we should fall into the solecism of self-government where several distinct wills have power, not only to govern themselves in relation to their individual interests, but also to infringe in innumerable ways upon the general interests of the society. Even if we suppose that the majority should retire and form a separate government, a new minority would immediately appear, and this would be the case on every subdivision of the population, however minute it might be. The process, if continued, and it must be once it is commenced, will unfold the preposterous and mischievous effects which would flow from departing from the simple and intelligible rule I have referred to. When the population by repeated subdivisions was morseled into the smallest fractions which would admit of a majority and minority, there would in a country of twenty-one millions of people be no less than seven millions of distinct governments. And to be consistent the division must be pursued still further, for in each of those seven millions of Lilliputian bodies politic, there is one individual to disagree to everything. The effect would be to create ten millions and a half of such governments; or, as it would be absurd when these assemblies were each reduced to two persons, not to accord to them equal authority, there would ultimately be precisely the same number of governments as individuals, that is, twenty-one millions. It is needless to add that before the process had been repeated four or five times society would be delivered over to wild uproar and confusion.

The rule of the majority does not disappoint the design of government, which is to represent the interests of the whole community and not merely those of a part. On the contrary, it is the only principle which is calculated to secure the happiness and prosperity of the whole. The various opinions and views which are current in society evidently do not exist for the purpose of being carried literally into practice. Their great use consists in this, that they rouse inquiry, sharpen discussion, lead to extended and thorough examination, and thus, by eliciting the truth in the only way in which it can be elicited, produce the greatest attainable advantage to the whole community. Men's opinions and feelings may be the most diverse imaginable, but their interests cannot be so. The giving free scope to the first, and then subjecting them to the will of the majority, is the only way to give consistency to the last and of reducing to a system the complicated concerns of society. The keen and searching inquisition which in a democratic republic is made into all the schemes of public policy constitutes a species of experiment upon their value and practicability, without which no permanent benefit could be secured to the whole or to any part of society. Without this process, men would become mere automata in the pursuit of ends to which instinct, not an enlightened reason, prompted them. So that the existence of a majority and minority, and yet the supremacy of the former, instead of marring the great design of civil institutions contributes directly to advance it.

It may be laid down as a proposition, admitting of few exceptions, that whenever a majority is competent to take care of its own interests, it will also be competent to take care of those of the minority. This results from two circumstances; first, that all the prominent and substantial interests of the lesser will be included in those of the larger body; and, secondly, that parties in a republic, the only form of government in which the terms majority and minority are legitimate expressions, do not occupy the fixed position which they have in monarchy and aristocracy; on the contrary, the individuals composing them are constantly shifting places, some passing from the major into the minor, and others sliding from the minor into the major party.

The constant tendency in a republic is to the formation of a middle class as the predominant body in the community. The consequence is that so numerous a party as a majority cannot exist without being principally composed of that class. If the minority should be exclusively formed from it, a circumstance which cannot occur, the majority will at least draw the greatest proportion of its members from it. Now a middle class may be said fairly to represent the interests which are common to the whole society. The very rich and the very poor may be sure that their extravagant and unreasonable desires will not be consulted; but they may be equally certain that all their just claims will be regarded and that, notwithstanding the occasional gusts which blow over society, their solid interests will be as carefully and effectually watched as, humanly speaking, can be the case. It can hardly be otherwise, as this great middle class was originally formed and is constantly recruited from the ranks of those who commenced life with little or no property and as the ambition of everyone is to move forward and to rise as fast as possible into the class of the rich. Moreover, the laws which protect property in a democratic community are necessarily common to all who have property — to the man worth a million as well as to one who possesses only two thousand dollars.

It is then correct to say that in a country where free institutions exist all the great interests of the minority will be inclosed in those of the majority, that the public men who conduct the one party will in no important respect be different from those who conduct the other, and that the great variety of opinions which divide the community will not in the long run and in the general upshot of human affairs affect fundamentally or even sensibly the well being of the state.

There is no other alternative than a government based upon the will of the majority or some one of the artificial forms of government; and hereditary monarchy and aristocracy do not properly represent either a majority or minority. I speak now of pure monarchy and aristocracy. For by a partial combination of free institutions with the hereditary principle, the will of the minority may be introduced into some part of the government, but never that of the majority. The term minority is merely a comparative one. It is so intrinsically and not merely verbally. A party in the minority is said to exist in reference to another party in the majority because its opinions are formed in contradiction to those of the last. The minority may be said to spring from the majority. If in pure monarchies, as Russia and Spain, or in pure aristocracies, such as Venice and Genoa once were, there is no way of giving expression to the opinions and collecting the will of the majority, there cannot, properly speaking, be a minority. Limited or constitutional monarchies, as Great Britain and France, make some approach to the formation of these parties because a distinct element has found its way into the composition of the government. But monarchy and aristocracy in their naked forms are a species of self-existing government; although the notion of a social compact is never lost from the population, no more than the notions of right and wrong, the just and the unjust, are ever obliterated from the minds of the rudest people, yet these governments are upheld for the most part by superstition and fear and have power to perpetuate themselves without making any direct and declared appeal to any part of society.

But it is a very important step towards the formation of regular government when the institutions, or any part of them, come to be founded even upon the will of a definite minority. The end at which government should aim begins then to be seen in a clearer light. The mind is gradually weaned from the notion of the "jure divino" right of rulers. As a considerable part of the population participates directly or indirectly in the administration of the government, the exercise of political privileges by this part constitutes a school of instruction which spreads its influence over the whole community, so that if we compare the England and Scotland of the present day with what they were in the reign of Elizabeth, when, as has been finely said, the intelligent were "like gaudy flowers upon a putrid marsh," we shall find

that the well informed are now as one hundred to one at the former
period.

The moment that a considerable body of the people begin to exercise a visible authority in the state, the way is prepared for the ultimate rule of the majority. Men then begin, for the first time, to analyze
their ideas on political subjects. As public men are now restrained by
a force residing out of the government, as the party which wields the
popular branch of the legislature, although it is a minority out of
doors, is yet obliged to defer to the opinions of every part of the community, intelligent men, indeed persons of very ordinary sagacity,
naturally interrogate themselves, why an artificial distinction such as
the possession of landed property alone should be permitted to stamp
the character of citizenship upon the population; why, in fine, a
straight line should be drawn through society placing beyond the pale
of the political franchises great numbers of men of substantial condition and every way qualified to bear a part in the administration of
public affairs.

We may then make a more particular division of governments than
that contained in the first chapter. We may divide them into three
classes: 1st. One of self-existing governments, as absolute monarchy
and aristocracy. 2d. Governments which rest upon the will of a definite
minority of the population, of which limited or constitutional monarchies are an example; and 3d. Governments which represent the will
of the majority, of which the democratic republic is the only example.
The two first are mere subdivisions of the more general classification
into the artificial forms of government. Nor is the classification a refined one. On the contrary it is entitled to the strictest attention. For
the period when government succeeds in founding itself upon the will
of the clear minority marks a most important era in the history of
society. It denotes that a majority of the population, although politically passive, are yet intellectually active; and there is yet this further consequence flowing from it, that if the minority contain a large
proportion of the substantial people, their interests, opinions, and
feelings will more and more resemble those which are common to the
great bulk of the community. So that if government is not administered in the best possible manner, it will be infinitely better administered than in pure monarchy or aristocracy. I observe that in Great
Britain and France every year adds to the force of public opinion;
that the governing power no longer supposes that it is absolved from

paying attention to the sentiments and wishes of even the most inconsiderable class; but that, on the contrary, it makes great efforts to accommodate the legislation to the interests of every part of the community. One of the most remarkable circumstances attending the rule of the majority is that it is no sooner invested with power than it sets about imposing limitations to the exercise of its own authority. This is an invariable consequence wherever a real majority, as in the United States, and not merely a constructive majority, as in France during the revolution, have the supremacy; and it is evident that it affords the most unequivocal test imaginable of the right and the fitness of the majority to rule. There is nothing surprising in this disposition on the part of the popular power. The same fact is observable in the conduct of individuals. There are few persons, given to the slightest reflection, who do not on entering upon life form for themselves a set of rules intended to act as restraints upon their own conduct and to produce order and arrangement in the management of their private affairs. The merchant, the shopkeeper, the mechanic, all act in this way, and with fully as much judgment and discretion as men of the highest education. That these same persons when collected into a body should be suddenly bereft of a faculty of so much advantage in the pursuit of all their interests would be difficult to explain upon any principles which belong to human nature. Self-interest, which prompts to its exercise in the first instance, will elicit it in the other also. The change which society undergoes when it has passed from a rude to a highly civilized state does not imply that self-interest is extinguished, but that it has become more enlightened, takes in a great number of objects of gratification, and thus tends constantly to bring about an agreement between the general interests and the interests of individuals.

It would doubtless be a great improvement upon all ordinary systems of government and would conduce materially to a just and regular administration of public affairs if we could introduce among communities some principle which resembled the faculty of reflection in individuals. We should then succeed in imposing a control upon the passions and remove the greatest obstacle in the way of free government. But whenever we have advanced to that point where the majority possess the supremacy and yet consent to impose limitations upon their own authority, we may be sure that we have succeeded to a very great extent in introducing that principle into the institutions.

These limitations, or checks, may be divided into three classes: 1st. Where a restraint is imposed upon both the majority and minority. 2d. Where peculiar advantages are accorded to the minority; and 3d. Where the authority of the community is so distributed as to give rise to a compound system of majorities and minorities.

A written constitution is an example of the first class. It is an instrument which undertakes to form, upon reflection, a body of fundamental rules for the government of the community which shall be a convenient shelter against the temporary gusts of party feeling. Precautions are thus taken, on laying the foundation of the system, for securing the interests of every order of men, without reference to the fact whether they shall afterwards fall into the party of the majority or of the minority. Every article of such an instrument is an authoritative declaration in behalf of general liberty. Opinions may vary, circumstances may change, rendering it desirable for the moment to depart from some of these fundamental rules; but this great covenant stares them in the face and, although it is plain that it is physically possible to overleap the bounds which it has set, yet such is the power which the rule of right exercises upon the minds of men when it is recognized as a general principle of action that there is hardly any faction but what recoils from the attempt or, if it is ventured upon, is compelled to retrace its steps. And what is very remarkable, the difficulty increases in proportion as the electoral franchise is enlarged and the number of active citizens augmented; which is the reverse of what would at first be supposed to be the case. It is more difficult to maintain a good understanding among the members of a party which is very numerous than of one which is small. Admitting that a majority of the majority should be bent upon infringing some parts of the constitution in order to attain a desired end, there are always a numerous body of individuals of calm judgment and solid reflection who, although every way disposed to make sacrifices for the sake of keeping the party together, will never consent to sacrifice to a party what belongs to their country. These individuals stand aloof, or go over to the minority which, becoming the majority, gains the ascendancy and restores the balance of the constitution.

During the last twenty-five years we have witnessed repeated attempts by the legislatures of several of the American states to violate their respective constitutions and sometimes even that of the federal government. In every instance the attempt has been abortive. So many of the people have abandoned the party in power that it became utterly powerless in the accomplishment of its plans and, after a time, the whole community returned with renewed satisfaction to the wise and salutary maxims which had been handed down to them by their fathers.

The constitution of Ohio was framed in 1802 when the population was a handful. It has now become a populous and powerful community, so that it has outgrown its constitution as the man outgrows the clothes which he wore when a boy. Great inconvenience has been experienced in consequence of some of the provisions of that constitution; yet the people have submitted patiently to them because, although a majority has constantly during the last twenty years been in favor of an alteration, yet the time has not arrived when the constitutional majority of two-thirds could be obtained.

An example of the second class of checks is when the minority have a proportional representation in the legislative body. The constitution of the executive and judiciary is such as to preclude the adoption of this plan, but the legislature is composed of so many members as very readily to admit of it. As representation takes the place of an actual deliberation by the people in person, when all parties would have an opportunity to be heard, there is every reason why the same right should be recognized in elective government. But it is obvious the moment the door is opened to a representation of the minority in the legislative hall that a most important restraint is imposed upon the majority. Some persons cannot conceive the existence of a check unless it has a coercive force. But it is often of more efficacy in consequence of being deprived of this quality. The minority in its present position are placed more upon their good behavior, exercise their wits more in finding out solid and substantial reasons for the opposition which they make, and from the single circumstance that they do not aspire to command but only to persuade are enabled to exercise very great influence at those critical periods when extreme measures are about to be pursued and when the minds of men have become greatly exasperated. A seat in the legislature is the most commanding position which can be occupied in the government. There is no calculating to what extent public abuses are prevented and the laws modified by the agency of a minority, although it may be impossible to lay one's finger upon the precise period when either was done. The instances are nevertheless without number.

The division of the legislature into two chambers is another instance of checks. Where two chambers exist and the members hold their seats for different terms the more popular branch may alone represent the opinions of a majority of the people at any given period, while the more permanent one will reflect opinions which once had the ascendancy but which are perhaps passing away. Whether the arrangement is an advantageous one — whether it is wise to permit this conflict of living with dead opinions — is a problem not easy of solution. Nor is it necessary in this place to enter into an examination of it. But if the system is of doubtful utility, it more strikingly displays the disposition of the majority on laying the foundation of government to concede great and decisive advantages to the minority. All the American states, except Vermont,* have adopted the plan. At an early period the people of Pennsylvania established only one chamber, but very soon after added another.

In those countries where one chamber is composed of an hereditary aristocracy, as in Great Britain, or of an aristocracy for life, as in France, Holland, and Belgium, the institution is of an entirely different character. The creation of an upper house is not an advantage conceded to the minority of the society, but is a personal privilege conferred upon a very small body. No matter what opinions either the majority or minority may have, there stands this immovable bulwark until the period has arrived when public sentiment has acquired so much power as to control the conduct of the highest authority in the state.

In the federal government of the United States the advantage afforded to the minority is permanent. And this has arisen from the fact that the Union was formed by a convention of the states and not by the people of America, as constituting one aggregate community. The relative extent and population of these states are very different. But as they all held an independent rank prior to the formation of the constitution, it was impossible to do otherwise than to give all an equal representation in at least one branch of the legislature. This renders the structure of the government more complicated than that of the states. Neither a majority nor a minority of the general population are represented in the senate. The majority of the votes belong to a minority of the local population. But in that great confederacy of na-

---

* In Vermont a second chamber has recently been created. [Vermont adopted a bicameral legislature in 1836, Pennsylvania in its constitution of 1790.]

tions, over which international law now presides with nearly as much force as municipal law does over single states, large and small communities stand precisely upon the same footing and are entitled to equal consideration. Moreover the difficulty is almost entirely obviated in America by the uncommonly skillful construction of the two systems of government. The federal and state interests are completely separated from each other, by which the most important part of the business of government is left to the exclusive management of the states. The veto of the executive may also operate sometimes as a check in favor of a minority. This power may be exercised in favor of a majority in the nation against a majority in the legislature; or in favor of a minority in the nation against a majority in the legislature; or, lastly, in favor of a minority in the legislature against a majority in the same body; without the means of knowing, at the precise time it is interposed, what is the actual state of public opinion among the people. Its operation is very different at different times, but the immediate effect is always to defeat the will of a majority in the legislature. The institution presents a problem of as difficult solution as the one just referred to. The difficulty consists in balancing the probabilities for a long series of years in favor of the rectitude of the opinions of the executive against the corresponding probabilities in favor of a majority of the legislature.

The third class of checks, depending upon a more general distribution of the power of the community, is where a system of primary and secondary governments is established: one intended to preside over those interests which are common to all the parts; the other to administer those which are exclusively local. The perfect form of confederate government affords a full illustration of the plan, although it is by no means necessary that the community should be a confederacy in order to give rise to it. Every state of great extent would find it [in] its interest to create a set of local jurisdictions to manage the local interests which are necessarily beyond the reach of the central government. The scheme does not belong exclusively to a confederacy of states. But its utility is first suggested by the practice under that form of government. The local jurisdictions of departments and "arrondissements" in France and the separate legislatures of Sweden and Norway are examples, though imperfect ones, of the plan. The United States is the only country in which it has been carried to its full extent. And as the restriction upon the electoral franchise is so very slight, it is easy to determine which party does in fact constitute the majority of the people. The creation of a national and state government has produced a double system of majorities and minorities. For instance, the minority in the national legislature may be a majority in several of the state legislatures, and vice versa. The interests to be administered are not the same in the two. They are therefore kept distinct. Under one homogeneous government the party in the majority might rule over both.

But in the United States the scheme is not confined to the federal government, but is pursued in the separate governments of the states, each of which has created a system of local jurisdictions within itself to manage the local interests. The county and township jurisdictions, each with its board of officers attached, are examples.

It is unnecessary to refer to any further instances of the various checks and limitations which the majority constantly impose upon the exercise of their own authority. What has been said contributes abundantly to fortify the position that wherever a majority is capable of taking care of its own interests, it will for that very reason be capable of presiding over the interests of the minority. In the new states which are constantly springing into existence in America and whose constitutions are based upon the principle of universal suffrage, we find that every precaution is taken in the outset to impose limitations upon the power of the majority, wherever these are believed to be subservient to the general weal.

CHAPTER IV | CHARACTER AND OPERATION
OF ELECTIVE GOVERNMENTS

IF the extreme rigor of the rule that the majority is entitled to govern is thus tempered in practice by the intervention of so many and such powerful restraints imposed by the majority, it may be affirmed that the country which denotes such a condition of society, or anything which makes a near approach to it, is ripe for the establishment of free institutions. The right of the majority to govern depends simply upon its capacity for self government.

But the inquisitive observer, fearful of the fate of free institutions in proportion to the interest he takes in them, may inquire whether the unbounded freedom of thought and action which they engender is not absolutely incompatible with the firm authority which government should possess; and whether they must not eventually perish from the unceasing action of the very element in which they are destined to live. But it is that very freedom of thought and action, unbounded as it may be supposed to be, which gives being to public opinion; and without the influence of public opinion society would be a mere waste. Although Europeans look with so much distrust upon the American commonwealth, yet it is remarkable that everything which is valuable in their own societies has been brought about by the communication of a greater degree of liberty to the people. So far from weakening the bond which holds society together the effect has been to render it stronger. In Great Britain and France, in Prussia and Belgium, it is in exact proportion to the power which public opinion has acquired that the administration of government has become mild and enlightened and that a character of firmness and durability has been imparted to the institutions. It was at one time believed that public tranquillity could not be even tolerably preserved without the constant presence of a military force. The people were terrified into submission to the government, rather than won over to obedience to the laws.

It may be laid down as a maxim in politics that the employment of physical force is rendered necessary by the absence or deficiency of moral force. If there is a happy distribution of the last through society, there will be less occasion to resort to the former. If, on the other hand, the distribution is very unequal, the discontent will be great because the amount of liberty is small, and hence as a natural consequence inordinate authority will be condensed in the hands of the government. Now, it is public opinion above all other agents which contributes to produce a just equalization of the moral power of the community; and it is the freedom of thought and action which gives birth to public opinion. It was on the first dawn of a public opinion in England, or rather I should say in Europe, that Pym and Selden, Coke and Hampden were roused to make such bold and intrepid exertions in behalf of popular freedom.[1] Man feels strong when he is conscious that he is surrounded by a power which represents not his feelings merely but the feelings of mankind. Abundant compensation is thus made for that state of feebleness and isolation in which individuals who cherish noble ideas would otherwise find themselves placed in the midst of society.

It is not surprising that the freedom of the press has met with so much resistance in monarchial and aristocratical governments. The tribunal of public opinion when fairly erected is so formidable an adversary to the exercise of every species of arbitrary authority that it invariably succeeds first in subduing the tone and temper of the public administration, and ultimately the form of the political institutions. Chateaubriand declared to the ministers of Louis Philippe, "on the day you decree the liberty of the press, you die." And if this audacious speech was not verified, it is plainly because the elements of public opinion are now everywhere visible throughout France.

In a country where a fixed aristocracy exists some men are necessarily endowed with a much larger share of influence than others. A body of nobility and gentry have sometimes possessed more weight than all the rest of the community. This unequal distribution of power is a great hindrance to the formation of a public opinion which shall

1. [John Pym (1583?–1643) and John Hampden (1594–1643), important Puritan leaders, defenders of the rights of Parliament, who were largely responsible for forcing Charles I to convene the Long Parliament (1640); John Selden (1584–1654), jurist and scholar, reputedly the most learned man of his time, was an important defender of Parliament in its struggle with the Crown; Sir Edward Coke (1552–1634), the famous jurist, was the champion of the common law against royal prerogative.]

rule over all; but it is highly favorable to the creation of a particular or sectarian opinion within the class itself. When, however, the dispersion of knowledge and property has elevated that multitude of men who occupied the inferior ranks of society, public opinion rises up and threatens to beat down the narrow and exclusive opinions which before existed. The array of physical force which was before necessary, sometimes to quell insubordination among the masses, sometimes to curb the turbulence of the nobles, and at others to restrain the usurpations of the prince, gradually disappears. All orders of men begin to find their true relative position in society, and public order and tranquillity are preserved with remarkable regularity. From whence it is very easy to understand why it is that a just distribution of the moral power of the community supersedes, to so great an extent, the use of mere physical force. The old ranks may continue to stand, but they will stand like broken and defaced columns amid the new structure which is reared around them.

One striking property of free institutions is that they present fewer subjects of contention between the government and the people than any other scheme of civil polity. I have already pointed to two characteristic features of a democratic republic: a written constitution and the establishment of local jurisdictions, contrivances of great wisdom and utility. For by the first, the principal controversies which have shaken other communities are struck out of being; and by the last, a very large proportion of what may be described as the secondary interests of society are withdrawn from the arena of national contention and are deposited with domestic governments by which they will be managed in the most skillful and unobtrusive manner possible. Under such a system men are able to find very few subjects to quarrel about; and even if government has less ability to resist encroachments, there is also infinitely less temptation and opportunity to assail its rightful authority.

Not only however are the most dangerous controversies diminished; those which remain assume an entirely different character. They are unfit to be decided by force. The prerogatives of an hereditary monarch are so incapable of exact limitation that he may often attempt to push them to the uttermost; or the strictly legitimate exercise of them may be productive of infinite mischief to society. The single power of declaring war may occasion the imposition of taxes insupportably burdensome to the community. The legislature may be a close body, in no way entitled to the appellation of representative of the people, and much more disposed to favor the projects of the prince than to consult the solid welfare of the state. The questions which grow out of such a condition of things immediately suggest the idea of an appeal to force. But whether the legislature shall make internal improvements, charter banks, or encourage manufactures, however interesting and exciting they may be, are still questions which belong to a totally different sphere. They could not ever grow up in any other society than one which had been trained to the arts of peace and where men had been habitually given to reflection. Such questions recommend themselves to the understanding alone, and it will be an exceedingly rare occurrence if one drop of blood is ever shed in deciding them.

This explains why it is that in modern societies men are so much addicted to reflection. It is not because they are by nature superior to the men of former times. It is simply in consequence of the independent condition to which they have risen. The cares and anxieties of life are multiplied even more than its enjoyments. A vastly greater proportion of the people than at any former period are engaged in industrial pursuits. These demand the constant exercise of judgment, prudence, and discretion; and being accustomed to calculate the consequences of their actions on a small scale, they are enabled to transfer the same habit to a larger theater of action and thus to render the exercise of their political principles not merely harmless but essentially beneficial to the community. At one time no one could practice a trade in a city unless he belonged to the guild, and hardly anyone out of the ranks of the nobility and clergy was the proprietor of land. There was no school for reflection among the people because there was no opportunity for its application, either in the walks of private or public life. It follows that in a democratic republic where there is a more equal distribution of property and where industry, whether in town or country, is unfettered, the mass of the population must be more distinguished for reflection than anywhere else. Thus, in that form of government where this invaluable quality is most in demand it is freely supplied, and where it is least wanted it is sparingly produced.

If it were possible so to construct government as invariably to connect the interests of individuals with those of the public, we should form a system which would bid fair to endure forever. I speak now of the interests of individuals as seen and understood by themselves; for the real interests of private persons never can be inconsistent with the general weal. Now although it is impossible to realize this idea, in consequence of the great diversity in the faculties and propensities of different men and the different manner in which these are combined in individuals, yet experience demonstrates that it is easy to carry it a great deal further than was once believed practicable. Philosophers who have sketched ideal plans of a republic have failed, not so much because they have placed too high an estimate on human nature as because they have not allowed room for the operation of some very homely qualities out of which spring what we term patriotism and public spirit. If what makes the artificial forms of government so dear to the select few who participate in their administration is that their whole interests are wrapped up in the preservation of them, there seems to be no reason why we may not imitate the scheme on a still larger scale and cause the great body of the people to be deeply interested in upholding free institutions. There is no necessity for imagining the existence of any higher qualities than before in order to produce this effect. For admitting that we cannot render the motives of human conduct more general in the one case than in the other, yet by giving to them an infinitely wider scope in the last instance, we found ourselves upon the same principle of interest and thus communicate both more freedom and more prosperity to a greater number of people. If the superstition inspired by the artificial form of government is a prodigious support to their authority, there is a very similar but a still stronger feeling at work among the people who live under free government. They are alive to every attempt to impair it, not merely because they believe their institutions to be the best but because they are the workmanship of their own hands.

In whatever light we may cast the subject, it seems evident that representative government is the only one which is fitted to fulfill all the great ends for which society was established. Not only is the general condition of the population greatly elevated so as to render the care of its interests the chief aim of government, but a multitude of persons are actually employed in the public administration. Public magistrates of various kinds, periodically rising from the people and returning to the people, are dispersed over the whole country. The sentinels of liberty are so thickly planted as to keep perpetual watch and the complicated and widespread machinery of the government makes it an affair of great difficulty to break it up or to take it to pieces. In the artificial governments, the handful of men who rule over public affairs are staked to the preservation of power; in a republic, the great body of the people are heartily interested in the maintenance of freedom.

In the event of any great convulsion, occasioned by foreign war or intestine commotion, the advantage is greatly on the side of popular government. Free institutions so thoroughly penetrate with their influence every part of the community that although it may be possible to shake the government, the question will still arise, can you shake the society. In war there is a distinction between conquering the government and conquering the people; and a similar distinction is applicable in this instance. In a monarchy or aristocracy, the overthrow of the government by foreign or civil war has sometimes nearly obliterated the traces of civilization. In a republic, where the great body of the people are fairly brought within the pale of civilization, such a disaster can never occur. Such a people feel deeper concern for their institutions than the people of other countries, and yet they are not so completely dependent upon every vicissitude which may befall the government.

There is another advantage which free institutions possess. They lay the foundation for a great body of experience. It is of the highest importance that societies, as well as individuals, should be placed in a situation which enables them to make actual experiment of the utility of those diversified laws which the wants of the community render necessary. In hereditary government, the machinery is so delicate that this can seldom be hazarded without endangering the whole fabric. I do not now speak of that bastard sort of experiment — the fruit of vain and fanciful theories — but of that which founds itself upon an intimate acquaintance with everything which appertains to the substantial interests of the community. As experience in its most comprehensive signification, including observation, is the foundation of our knowledge, as all science, in short, is nothing but the condensation of human experience, there seems every reason why we should be able to avail ourselves of it in what concerns the positive interests of society as well as in what relates to matters of more curious inquiry. The most gifted understanding, when relying upon its own resources merely, will forever be too imperfect to grasp all the conditions which affect the determination of any given enactment. As the whole groundwork of the institution is different in a republic from what it is in any other form of government, the quantity of experience which is supplied is correspondingly large. For we then have a people in the genuine acceptation of the term. The laws and the whole course of the public administration take an entirely new direction. War, negotiation, and finance no longer absorb the whole attention of statesmen. Public affairs have then a different meaning affixed to them. The legislature embraces a vast scope of practical interests which, being more level to the capacities of all, call into requisition a great amount of popular talent; and as they who make the laws are the very persons who will derive advantage or suffer inconvenience from them, a most instructive school of experience is established in which all are compelled to learn something.

I observe that more laws have been passed by the British Parliament in the last forty years than in the three preceding centuries; that is, the laws have multiplied in proportion as the real business transactions of society have increased, and these have increased because so large an amount of the population have been raised to a higher condition than formerly. A similar change is very perceptible in France. But on the whole, I should say that the democratic element, although it appears in bolder relief in France than in Great Britain, was not making so great and so sure advances in the former as in the latter country.

One of the most remarkable features of American society is the facility with which changes are made in the fundamental laws, wherever experience has shown that there is an infirmity in some part of the system. A convention in any one of the American states, assembled for the purpose of making alterations in its constitution, creates no noise or confusion. All the deliberations are conducted to a close with the same regularity as the proceedings of an ordinary legislative body. At an early period there was a remarkable sensitiveness on this subject. Constitutions, it was said by those who had not entirely escaped from the European forms of thought, were sacred things and once ordained should never again be touched. As if every institution did not acquire sacredness by being perfected and better adapted to its original design.

A great revolution was effected in the structure of society when the inferior classes lost their dependence upon the higher, when the relations of patron and client, of lord and vassal, ceased. A new relation immediately sprung up. Instead of the dependence being all on one side, the two orders became mutually dependent on each other. Society began to assume the character of a great partnership among the members, instead of that of a series of ascending links in a chain, one end of which was fastened to the throne. From that period the people have been constantly gaining in intelligence and power, so that it is doubtful whether, in more than one European state, if the laws of primogeniture and entail had been abolished a century ago, society would not be completely prepared for the introduction of the elective principles into every department of the government. There is every reason to believe that those laws will sooner or later give way. The force of habit among a whole people is as strong as it is in individuals. It frequently survives the existence of the causes which originally induced it, but it cannot survive them forever when there are so many counter agents unceasingly in operation.

Two apparently opposite effects are produced by that alteration in the structure of society which I have described. Governments are rendered stronger and yet both the absolute and the relative power of the people is augmented. As it becomes more and more necessary to take counsel of public opinion with regard to every important measure, it might be supposed that government had lost strength. But inasmuch as a man mutilated in one part is not able to exert so much general power as a man who is perfect in all his members, so a government which relies upon the entire strength of society must necessarily be more efficient in proportion as that strength is developed. In all the European governments in which a legislative body exists, however inadequately it may represent popular opinion, there is notwithstanding an increasing anxiety to consult popular interests. Any important change in language denotes a corresponding change in the ideas of the age. And the comparative disuse in some parts of Europe of the term subjects, and the substitution of the term citizens, or people, is an unequivocal indication that new things have come to pass. Mr. Fox was the first statesman who accustomed the English ear to this mode of speech.[2] He knew well that the way to fasten an impression upon the mind was to give it a palpable form — to incorporate it into the dialect of the country. The crowned heads of Europe do not venture to sport with the lives and property of the people as formerly, simply because the people have acquired a weight in the political system which

2. [Charles James Fox (1749–1806), parliamentary spokesman for liberal reform.]

enables them to exercise a powerful, though it may be an indirect, control over all public affairs.

There are two properties inseparable from every well constituted government: the one a capacity to receive impressions from public opinion, the other a power of reacting upon society. There is no contradiction between the two things. On the contrary, the last is the natural consequence of the first. The use of public opinion is to inspire government with confidence, fortitude, and resolution whenever public affairs are well conducted, and to impress it with shame, distrust, and fear whenever the contrary is the case. Two forces act in different directions and yet both tend to the same result: the causing public men to exercise a more legitimate and therefore a more effective influence than they could otherwise do. The more government reposes upon public opinion the more susceptible it is of being acted upon and yet the greater is the facility it acquires of acting upon the community in difficult emergencies. I do not now suppose the case of general resistance to its authority, for the structure of representative government is such as to render it a guarantee against such a contingency. But I speak of those partial insurrections against the laws originating in local discontents and to which the best regulated society will be occasionally subject. European writers on public law, with nearly one accord, admit the right of resistance on the part of the people whenever government has clearly and flagrantly transcended its authority; and very properly so, for where the institutions contain no provision for displacing men who have bid defiance to all law and who have evinced a settled determination to render the public interests subordinate to their schemes of self aggrandizement, there is no other alternative but that of resistance. It constitutes an excepted case, but a case consecrated by necessity, by right, by the eternal laws of God and man. The deposition of Napoleon and Charles X in France, of Charles I and James II in England, stand upon this clear and undisputed principle. That of Louis XVI may admit of some hesitation, and yet it is exceedingly doubtful whether the scheme of constitutional or limited monarchy could have been achieved without it.

But in elective government the case cannot occur. The powers of all public functionaries are not only very limited, but they are themselves quietly removed before they have had an opportunity to commit any great mischief. And I cannot help thinking that the reason why America has been less subject to even partial insurrections than any other country is owing to this circumstance. The power which is reposed with the government is conferred by all the parts equally; and the notion that the will of the majority is entitled to command is so indelibly impressed upon both people and rulers that, wherever a conflict occurs between the laws which that majority have ordained and any particular section of the population, a degree of confidence, energy, and alacrity is infused into all public men which enables them to triumph speedily over all opposition, and that without depending to any degree upon the instrumentality of a standing army.

A democratic republic will then possess the two properties I have mentioned in greater perfection than any other form of government. It will possess a capacity of receiving impressions from without because it is the creature of the public will; it will have the power of reacting upon society, not only because it will be powerfully supported by public opinion, but because the disturbances which will occur can never in the nature of things be more than local. Twenty times more blood was shed in Paris on the memorable three days which closed the reign of Charles X than in all the insurrections which have occurred in the United States since the foundation of the government.

It is the time now to direct the attention of the reader to a very material distinction, already hinted at, between a representative republic and the artificial forms of government. In the first the political authority of the community is divided into three classes; the powers which are exercised by the government, those exercised by the people, and those reserved to the people. In pure monarchy, and aristocracy, there is but one class. The whole power is centered in the government. In the United States it is common to make two classes only; the second is left out. All the active power of the community is supposed to be conferred upon the government; and all its latent power to be lodged with the people, liable to be roused to activity whenever a convention is assembled for the purpose of forming a new constitution. But this is a very imperfect view of the structure of the American government. The powers actually exercised by the people are numerous and of great importance. I have no reference now to the distribution of authority between the federal and state governments. That does in reality give rise to a fourth class which it is not now necessary to notice.

First, if we could consider the various persons who are chosen to perform the duties of the great number of offices which exist in representative government as naked instruments, mere conduit pipes, to convey the opinions and to give an audible expression to the interests of the people, the truth of the observation would be clear. The conduct of the representative would then be invariably determined by the will of his constituents. It might even be doubtful whether the latter did not exercise all political power not reserved. If, on the other hand, there is a considerable approach to that scheme or arrangement, the truth of the proposition will be still more manifest. The active power of the community will be partitioned between the government and the people. The arm is the mere servant of the will. If an individual had no immediate power in moving it but was able to exercise an intermediate control which might be relied upon as certain in the great majority of instances, it would still be correct to say that he exercised an important agency in determining its movements.

The physician who is employed to cure disease or the lawyer who is engaged to prosecute a suit are the agents in either case of those who apply to them. Yet the connection is not as strict as between the elector and the representative, because in the case of the physician and lawyer the skill demanded of them depends upon a body of scientific knowledge, an acquaintance with which is impossible for those who have not made it a special study. More strictly is he denominated an agent who is selected to transact the private business of an individual. And although this trust will require judgment, sagacity, and industry, that is, the exercise of qualities which belong properly to the agent, yet his conduct so far as concerns the substantial interests of the principal will, in ninety-nine cases out of a hundred, be determined by the last.

There is this difference, however, between the two cases; that where one man employs another to transact his private affairs there is a singleness, a unity of purpose, which it is easy to impress upon the agent but which cannot be exactly imitated where, instead of one agent, there are hundreds, and instead of one principal, there are thousands. The distinction is one of great consequence, and yet it does not detract from the truth of the observation that the active political power which exists in a republic is partitioned between the public officers and their constituents. But the distinction points to a very important end which representative government is adapted to accomplish.

For, as in order to execute the joint will of a very numerous society it is indispensable that agents should be employed, these agents, whose number is very small when compared with the whole population, act as convenient instruments for separating the more prominent interests of society from those which are of less moment. Their commanding position naturally leads them, amid the great variety of discordant opinions which are afloat, even in a small section of the country, to distinguish between those which are of vital and general importance and those which are the offspring of temporary prejudices and local feelings. In this way, the multifarious business of an extensive community is brought under some systematic rules, and a character of oneness and uniformity is impressed upon the movements of the government.

But there are instances in which the relation of principal and agent exists in its utmost strictness. The opinions and views which the representative is appointed to carry out are not all of the same kind. Some are very complex; that is, they require a great many acts to be done and a variety of unforeseen circumstances to be taken into account; and there are others, pointing to a single end, which cannot be mistaken. In the last the will of the constituent may be impressed upon the deputy as completely as the stamp impresses its image upon wax.

The election of president of the United States is a remarkable example of this. On that occasion, a greater number of electors than ever was known in christendom are assembled, and although an intermediate body is chosen by them for the purpose of making the election, yet those secondary electors invariably vote for the person who has been designated for the office by the primary electors. The result is reduced to absolute certainty before the colleges of electors meet. Thus in a case where the electors are most numerous and where it was supposed impossible to produce anything like harmony of opinion, the agreement is most complete. And what is of still more importance, where the public officer is elected to preside over the whole population and to embrace the greatest diversity of views, a character of unity is most effectually impressed upon him. As the extent of country and the great number of the electors remove him to a great distance from the people and tend to weaken his responsibility, it is of great consequence to exhibit before his eyes an example of the facility with which public sentiment can be united to all leading public measures and of the equal facility with which he can either be made or unmade.

In order to determine with something like exactness the closeness of the relation which exists between the representative and the constituent, where the duties to be performed involve a multitude of acts, the most satisfactory method would be to ascertain what proportion of the laws enacted have afterwards been repealed, distinguishing between those cases where the repeal has taken place in consequence of the representatives having gone counter to the will of their constituents from those where it has been brought about by a change of opinion on the part of the people themselves. And I apprehend that cases falling under the first class would be found to be exceedingly rare. A repeal effected by a change in public sentiment is obviously an example of the strictness of the relation.

It is common to talk of the powers of government and the liberties of the people. But this is rather in analogy with the structure of the European communities than in accordance with the genius of free institutions. The people of the United States do enjoy a very large share of liberty, but its character is such as necessarily to endow them with a large amount of active power. Their power constitutes the guarantee of their liberties. When we consider that, until very recently, all Scotland contained no greater number of electors than an ordinary county in America; that the members of Parliament from the cities were deputed by self-constituted bodies composed each of thirteen persons; that a majority of the members of Parliament are now elected by a minority of the whole number of electors; that the throne, the aristocracy, and the ecclesiastical establishments exist without any direct dependence upon the public will; that the right to bear arms and the right of association are exceedingly restricted, we may form some idea of the importance of the distinction between popular power and popular liberty.

It is remarkable that the three great maxims on which republican government reposes were recognized, and formally promulgated by the Italian states of the middle ages:

1st. That all authority exercised over the people originates with the people.

2d. That all public trusts should return periodically into the hands of the people.

3d. That all public functionaries are responsible to the people for their fidelity in office.

And yet it would be a great mistake to suppose that the people of these states, from the highest to the lowest, had any more idea of free institutions than the philosophers of their day had of the theory of the terrestrial motions. We might with as much propriety rob Harvey of the credit of discovering the circulation of the blood and attribute it to physicians in the time of Cicero. For when we inquire who the people (the inseparable condition of the three maxims) were, we find that they were a mere handful of the population. In the Florentine state, the best modeled of those republics, with a population of more than a million, the electors never amounted to more than twenty-four hundred, sometimes to a much less number. And the cruelties practiced by those invested with authority were not excelled in any of the monarchial governments of even that day.

The artificial forms of government, by the oppression and inequalities of one sort or other to which they give rise, lacerate the mind, sour the temper, and goad to revenge. There is no escape from the ills they inflict. They are of yesterday, today, and forever. Free institutions introduce heart burnings enough into society. But these only constitute a state of discipline by which men are rendered more wise, more prudent, and more just than they would otherwise be. A vast field is left open to individual liberty, so that the mind, instead of being deprived of its elasticity and vigor, is incessantly braced to fresh exertions in order to turn all the difficulties of life to the best account.

CHAPTER V | THE PRINCIPLE OF EQUALITY —

TO WHAT EXTENT CAN IT BE CARRIED

IT was a great imperfection attending society before the invention of printing that there was no means by which human experience could be made thoroughly available at a subsequent period or in remote countries. It is not only important that knowledge should be diffused among the men of the present day; it is also important that their successes and miscarriages should be recorded and appreciated by those who come after them and by those who are separated from each other by the greatest distances. Printing has remedied this imperfection. It not only extends information; it extends the bounds of human experience since this is very properly understood to include not merely what is personal to the individual but whatever can be distinctly realized as matter of fact. Mere speculation does not move the great mass of mankind, but example, sympathy, imitation all have a wonderful influence in molding their dispositions and conduct. Those who live apart from each other are now initiated into the form of society, the habits of thinking and acting, and the actual working of the institutions which prevail among each. They are enabled to distinguish what is practicable from what is proposed as a merely plausible theory; and, as very nearly the same feelings beat in the bosom of all men, every important amelioration of the condition of our race in one country is regarded as a body of experience which may be made more or less available in all others.

This enlargement of the bounds of human experience, so as to take in what is transacted in distant countries as well as what is acted on the spot, is exemplified in the case of America. The political institutions of the United States may be described as the greatest experiment which has ever been made upon human nature. Their influence upon the European mind has already been immense. It is natural, therefore, that they should afford matter for deep contemplation and that they should excite intense interest wherever they are known.

No one has even the right to indulge in fanciful and visionary speculations as to the form into which the institutions of society may be cast. But where our researches are pursued with care, where they are bounded and limited on all sides by a long and instructive experience, they may be rendered highly instrumental in shedding light upon the two great problems in politics: what ought and what may be made to be. It is not necessary that intelligence should be diffused in exactly equal proportions among all the individuals composing a community in order to found free institutions. It is true, knowledge is power, in politics as well as in private life, and may be made the instrument of detriment as well as of benefit. And if the interests of the great bulk of the population are delivered over to the less numerous body who consist of the enlightened, it may seem difficult to escape from the conclusion that a species of moral servitude must be established, let us adopt what form of government we please. Why it is not necessary, therefore, that all the members who compose a democratic community should be raised equally high in the scale of intelligence, and what is the extent to which intelligence should and may be actually pushed are necessarily inquiries of great interest and importance.

In a commonwealth where the structure of society is such as to give rise to an uniformity of interests among the population, or to anything approaching to it, it will to a great extent supersede the necessity of an equal distribution of knowledge. There may be the greatest diversity of knowledge amid the greatest sameness of interests and without occasioning the least interruption to it. Knowledge is the instrument by which the interests of men are managed, but it is not itself, at least in its highest degree, one of those interests. And if in a state where the elective principle prevails this settled uniformity of interests is the result of causes which are inherent in the framework of society, public men will be disabled from interfering with the interests of others without dealing wantonly with their own. The same laws which govern the ruled govern also the rulers. The ability to act is restrained and limited by the principle of self-interest. And the administration of public affairs is obliged to take a direction conformable to the public welfare because the general welfare and private interests meet and terminate at the same point.

But this approach to an identity of interests among the whole community does diffuse knowledge to precisely the extent which is wanted: 1st. Because it renders the intercourse of all classes more

thorough and easy. 2d. Because it presupposes a tolerably equal distribution of property, and the diffusion of knowledge is inseparable
from that of property. Not that the elevated attainments of the intellectual class will become the common property of the whole people,
for that can never be; but that species of knowledge which has to do
with the material interests of this world will insinuate itself into the
minds of all. Our acquaintance with any subject is in proportion to the
concentration of the attention upon it, and the great bulk of the population, by having their attention constantly fixed upon that sphere
of ideas which encloses all their substantial interests, may be trained
to a degree of knowledge which will be more effectual for the purposes of society than the greatest learning and the profoundest attainments. What is lost in variety and comprehensiveness will be more
than made up by the practical and serviceable character of the knowledge actually acquired.

If in France before the revolution four-fifths of the landed property
of the kingdom was engrossed by the nobility and clergy, and if in
the United States there is no such artificial monopoly, but the division
of the soil has followed the natural direction which private enterprise
and industry gave to it, the great difference in the structure of society
in the two countries is sufficiently explained. All the moral causes
which in the last country now contribute to perpetuate the existing
state of society may be fairly deduced from this simple arrangement
in the beginning. The principle of equality has thus found a natural
support in America. It has not been the creature of the laws. These
assist in upholding it, by giving it a visible activity in public life, but
both it and the laws are the off-spring of circumstances which no legislature could have had power to alter.

Two inquiries of exceeding interest now present themselves: 1st.
To what extent is political equality dependent upon the natural or civil
equality of men, and to what extent can the last be pushed; 2d. If
political equality is itself the result of causes which are peculiar to
America and these causes should cease to act, or act with less force at
a future period, may not the political institutions and the form of government undergo in the progress of time an entire revolution. Each
of the propositions — the laws secure political equality and the laws
have sprung from a given state of society — are clear enough. But it
is important that our speculations should be built upon something
more than a barren generality, that, so addressing ourselves to the rea-

son of mankind, we may employ our own reason in throwing out hints for their meditation.

The distribution of property in any community will depend in some degree upon the amount of the population. In a state which is densely peopled there will probably be a very large class of rich and a still more numerous class of poor. Not that this proportion may not exist where the population is thin. For it was undoubtedly the same or even greater in the European states five hundred years ago than it is at present, although the population has more than trebled in that time. But in the one case there is at least a physical possibility of rectifying the proportion which does not exist in the other. Where there are large tracts of uncultivated land, human ingenuity and industry, with a very slight assistance from the laws, may succeed in placing private fortune more upon a level. But where the soil has been appropriated for centuries, the inequality which shows itself after a long period of commercial and agricultural activity must be ascribed in part to that very ingenuity and industry, and in great part, also, to the political institutions themselves.

But within certain limits, an increase of population may be highly favorable to the distribution of property. Capital and labor are augmented by it, and the supply of both affords the means of breaking up large estates into smaller parcels. It is only when the population becomes very dense that, on the one hand, capital accumulates to such a degree as to create a large class of rich and that, on the other, labor becomes superabundant, which gives rise to a still larger class of poor.

There are several causes which tend to counteract the increase of population when it has reached a certain degree of density. The mortality becomes greater, the births fewer, and the average age of marriage higher. But these changes do not all of them take place with anything like the regularity which might be expected. For instance, it appears to be certain that the mortality in Great Britain is much less than it has been at any preceding period, that it is less than it was when the population was only one half what it is now. Lord Brougham computes it at 1:58; Mr. Malthus at 1:51; while the census of 1839, taken since and the only accurate register which has ever been made, finds it to be 1:45. The two first would have been an enormously low proportion. The last is low and indicates a less mortality than in any country which ever existed and containing an equally dense population. Although the population has increased greatly within the last fifty years, yet the general standard of comfort throughout the island has improved in a still higher proportion. And although it cannot be true, as has been conjecturally estimated, that the average age of death, or the expectation of life at birth, has mounted up from sixteen to thirty-three years, it is plain that it must be greatly higher than it was sixty or seventy years ago.

But increase the population a few millions more and the mortality would then tell in a greatly increased ratio. Whatever may be the increase, however, and in spite of all the influences which have hitherto been brought to bear upon society, there is a tendency in every civilized community to such an augmentation of the population as is inconsistent with anything like an equal distribution of property. Even the equal partibility of inheritances only partially corrects the evil. Primogeniture was unknown in the Grecian or Roman commonwealths. In France it never prevailed universally. And in Spain, equal partibility was always the rule and primogeniture the exception. Yet in all these states there existed extreme inequality in private fortunes. The laws, the character of the government, may do much toward either promoting or preventing the disparity of estates. And it is one reason why free institutions are preferable to any other that they contribute to produce this last effect. But the inquiry of greatest moment is whether there are any laws of our nature which, independently of the political institutions or with every assistance which they may legitimately afford, can have power to establish and maintain anything approaching to an equality of private fortunes. It seems natural to suppose that when we are in possession of an advantage up to a certain degree that it may be pushed on to a still higher degree and so on indefinitely, and that cannot be an impossible state of society which only consists in the addition to actually existing facts — of facts of the same kind. And this would undoubtedly be a correct mode of reasoning if the new facts to be added did not depend upon the voluntary action of a vast multitude of persons among whom there exists the greatest diversity of dispositions.

In tracing the generality of individuals through life and observing how they conduct themselves and the vehement struggle to acquire property, it is remarkable how little difference we can discover between the capacities of those who succeed and of those who fail. Some move forward with amazing velocity to the end they have in view and heap riches upon riches; some lag behind and are only able through the whole of life to obtain a comfortable subsistence; while others continue in a state of painful destitution from the beginning to the end of their career. And yet but for the result, which to ordinary observation seems to set the stamp of superiority upon some, we should not be able in the majority of instances to perceive any adequate reason for so striking a difference. So far as the faculties of those individuals, either natural or acquired, are concerned, there seems to be no very material difference. But that there must be some difference in that undefinable quality which we term the disposition is clear: otherwise the consequences would not follow. We know too little of the individual man to be able to handle with anything like accuracy and discrimination the secret springs which actuate human conduct. A fine writer has remarked of the character of the emperor Napoleon that it has presented a problem to be studied. But in truth, the character of almost all the individuals we meet with, however obscure they may be and however limited their faculties, presents very nearly the same problem. Whoever was able to unravel the mind of the least of these would be able to decipher that of Napoleon at a glance.

Some men are roused and quickened by adversity, while the faculties of others are clouded and overwhelmed by it. Some are strengthened by prosperity, others are blinded and led astray by it. And as there is an endless variety in the working of these causes, arising from inconceivably small differences of temperament and the perpetual interference of what is termed accident, their successes and miscarriages will be marked by innumerable shades of difference too secret and too fine for our analysis. It seems certain, however, that until we can master man's nature it will be impossible to impress anything like an exact similarity of character upon individuals. And he who cannot take to pieces his own mind must necessarily fall infinitely short of that task. The division of labor which is introduced so extensively into every department of industry is both a consequence and a cause of the inequality in the fortunes and condition of individuals. But if that were banished from society, not the ten-thousandth part of the comforts and enjoyments of life would exist for anyone. To say that everyone should be his own builder, manufacturer, and cultivator, to declare that each one should be tailor, shoemaker, cook, would be very nearly the same as saying that there should be no houses, no decent and comfortable clothing, and a very scanty supply of food. There would be nothing to set in motion that immense mass of industry which now affords employment and subsistence to the multitudes of men. The population would be gradually drawn within the narrow limits of a savage tribe; the most opulent and flourishing community would be carried back to the primitive state of barbarism. The annihilation of industry as a system would involve the annihilation of all moral and intellectual culture.

At the same time, it is evident that the division of labor which bestows such countless advantages upon society cannot exist without giving rise to very great inequality among individuals. It is only necessary to consider any of the most inconsiderable of the objects of mechanical skill to be assured of this fact. The workman who is employed in the manufacture of knives or pins is condemned to an occupation which, turn the subject in whatever light we may, cannot possibly improve his fortune or elevate his faculties so as to place him on a level with the master manufacturer. Nor would it remedy the difficulty to divide the profits of the last equally among all the workmen. For even admitting that he would feel the same powerful stimulus as before in the prosecution of his business, now that the disposition of his own property was violently interfered with, and that the workmen would submit to the same patient and indefatigable industry without which the plan must fail, this distribution would only tantalize without satisfying the desires of anyone. What would be a splendid income for one man would, when divided among hundreds, be no sensible addition to their enjoyments. There must be some wise purpose intended in this constitution of society. It may be that in a civilized community this variety in the pursuits of individuals is absolutely necessary to maintain the mind in a sound and healthful condition; or it may be that employment and occupation without regard to the variety of pursuits to which they lead are indispensable to balance the mind and to restrain the animal propensities within due bounds. For without the division of labor there would not only be little or no variety, but the occupations would nearly all cease to exist. At the same time, it is clear that while some are engaged in the higher and more important part of the work, others must be engaged in the inferior and subordinate branches. So that to maintain civilization at all there must be inequality in the fortunes and condition of individuals. There is no escape from our human condition whatever may be the shape into which the elements of society are thrown.

If we suppose that the distribution of the incomes of capitalists would place so large a number of the operatives in an improved condition as to withdraw them from work, the supply of labor would be diminished, wages would rise, there would be more leisure, greater opportunities. But the high wages would, in a single generation, lead to an increase of the population, to a supply of the demand, and to a renewal of the old state of things.

The distribution of property by law, even if it placed everyone in comfortable circumstance, would paralyze the springs of industry. It would diminish the vigor and activity of those who had acquired much and increase the sloth and inertness of those who had acquired nothing. This equal division of fortunes would apparently tend to an equality of enjoyments, while an equality of industry and exertions, which is of far more consequence, would be overlooked. If all were placed in prosperous circumstances for one year, the next would witness the decline of great numbers, and in a few more there would be the same inequality as before. We would absurdly introduce equality for the purpose of bringing out inequality.

It would seem that not only our own infirmities but that the infirmities of those around us are absolutely necessary to goad anyone to exertion. They who propose the plan of distribution or, which is the same thing, to make the people work in common like so many galley slaves, forget that the true way of strengthening the public virtues is to nourish the private affections, and that to turn all our efforts exclusively in one direction would be to eradicate some of the best qualities of human nature. That is the best because it is the natural arrangement of society which gives full play to the faculties of all orders of men. If it is beyond our power to control the private affections — if we cannot make men love other men's children as they do their own — it must be equally impossible to control the exertions which are the fruit of these affections. The instinct which leads men to become the center of a family is as much a part of his constitution as that which leads him to society. To give an undue preponderance to one of these would not be the application of a new regimen to his conduct; it would be a vain attempt to alter the laws which govern his nature. All the private affections in reality conspire to the general weal. They introduce into the moral world the great principle of the division of labor. More industry and sagacity are exerted, a greater amount of both public and private virtue is developed than under any other government. To dislocate therefore any of the important springs of human conduct — to declare that one should have the mastery — would establish a state of society in which we should avail ourselves of only half the man.

If we could realize the views of Mr. Malthus and introduce into a population which was threatening to become crowded the general prevalence of the check to early marriages, it would be followed by some very salutary consequences. But to carry it as far as is desirable and so as to make it tell with a decisive and permanent influence upon society might be attended with very many disadvantages. The idea is that it would be an effectual way of elevating the condition of the masses because it would keep down the numbers and render the circumstances of the actual population more easy. Let us suppose then that the check had begun to operate in England about seventy years ago. Wages might now be so high as to cause every department of industry to languish. English manufacturers would have been undersold in every foreign market. Other nations would have been in a condition to supply the English people with every species of manufacture and every article of food. But the last would be deprived of the means of purchasing from other nations, and the consequence is that England may have been one of the poorest instead of the richest country in Europe. The more thin population which would now exist would be in infinitely worse circumstances than at present. In Norway, the check to early marriages exists in greater force than anywhere else, and it is a poor country and an abject population.

I know nothing which would confer more salutary and lasting benefits upon society than to raise the general standard of comfort of the population, provided it be done without producing effects which would counteract its operation. But to raise the standard of comfort in any European community as high as every lover of humanity would desire would be the same as to raise wages so high as to enable everyone to maintain his family in comfort and to give them an education. And the consequences would be the same as before. The country would be undersold in every article of production; every branch of industry would decline until a foreign population poured in to receive lower wages, when the standard of comfort would be again reduced. The plan would undoubtedly succeed if we could introduce it alike into all countries. But if it has entirely failed in any one, except to be taken notice of by way of comparison with the condition of some others, it would require the will of Omnipotence to accomplish it.

All human exertions to better the social organization must necessarily be bounded within certain limits. Something must be taken for granted as the elements of all our reasoning in politics as well as in other sciences. We cannot be permitted to construct ideas which a fertile imagination has suggested and which only approach toward being verified in part because they cannot be verified universally.

Let us suppose that all those who have succeeded in life and who are placed in good circumstances were to go among the poor and ignorant, open up all the secrets of their hearts, recount the whole train of circumstances which contributed to elevate their condition. I can conceive of nothing which for the time being would so much expand the bosoms of those who believed, either rightly or erroneously, that fortune had frowned upon them. But, first: the thing cannot be done. Such a fearless and unreserved revelation of one's whole thoughts and actions can proceed from none but angels. Second: the exposition of so great an amount of infirmities as the revelation would disclose and as would be shown to attend frequently the most enviable condition would cause the vicious and the ignorant to hug vice and ignorance still closer. The greater part would become more bold and confident than ever, since there was no such broad mark of distinction as had been imagined between the highest and lowest condition. And one great check to irregularities of conduct would be removed. The counselors and the counseled in such an enterprise are equally covered with all sorts of infirmities. And the true way to get rid of these is to proceed upon the belief that they do not exist or, at any rate, that they are only adventitious. In this way everyone will be nerved to a greater amount of exertion than would otherwise be the case. If those who are placed in what is termed low life could penetrate the gaudy exterior of high life, they would find as little enjoyment as in their own humble sphere. Wealth creates full as many disquietudes as it heals. Fortunately they are unable to lift the veil, for then, perhaps, all human exertions would speedily come to an end.

It may then be inquired, why do legislators constantly inculcate the maxim that all men are equal. And the answer is plain: first, because to teach and to act upon it is the only way of attaining equality to the extent to which it is actually attained. Second, because it is not in the power of government to make anything like an accurate discrimination between the inequalities of different men, and the attempt to do so would be to encroach upon those points in which there is no inequality. Third, because the principle of equality may very well be recognized as the rule among men as citizens, as members of a political community, although as individuals there may be great and numerous inequalities between them. The utmost which the citizen can demand is that no law shall be passed to obstruct his rise and to impede his progress through life. He has then an even chance with all his fellows. If he does not become their equal his case is beyond the reach of society, and to complain would be to quarrel with his own nature.

It cannot be concealed that a difficulty now presents itself which is entitled to particular attention. Here are two sets of ideas which do not quadrate with each other: equality proclaimed by the laws and inequality in fact. And as, notwithstanding the artificial distinctions which we may make between the individual and the citizen, the former may be disposed to carry all his prejudices, narrow views, and selfish interests into the arena of politics, it might be supposed that a scene of discord would be introduced which after lasting for a given period must terminate in the ascendancy of one or other of these rival principles. Hence the misgivings of many persons, otherwise possessing good sense and reflection in an eminent degree. If they do not believe, they at any rate doubt whether the undisguised recognition of the principle of equality in America is not destined to take entire possession of society and ultimately to level the whole fabric of its institutions. The masses are put in possession of the same privileges as the educated and the wealthy; and, in the event of a struggle between the two orders, will not numbers be sure to gain the advantage?

But the principle of equality is itself the parent of another principle which sets bounds to it and limits its operation in practice. The same laws which declare that all men are equal give unbounded scope to the enterprise and industry of all. Neither family, nor rank, nor education confer any peculiar advantages in running the career which is now opened. In many respects they even throw obstacles in the way. Men without education, with ordinary faculties, and who commenced life with little or nothing are continually emerging from obscurity and displacing those who have acquired fortunes by inheritance. They constitute emphatically the class of rich in the United States. It is the principle of equality there which introduces all the inequality which is established in that country. The effects are visible to everyone and are understood and appreciated by the most ignorant men. Everyone is a witness to the miracles which industry and common sagacity produce. No one distrusts himself; no one can perceive those minute shades of

character and disposition which determine the destiny of some individuals, making some rich and leaving others poor. All place an
equal reliance upon their own efforts to carve out their fortunes, until at length the period of life begins to shorten, when cool reflection
and judgment take the place of the passions; and whether they have
succeeded or failed, a new feeling comes over everyone — a disposition
to submit quietly to what is the inevitable because it is the natural
progress of things.

Thus as it is impossible among millions to say who in running the
career of wisdom, influence, or wealth will attain the goal, government very rightly establishes the broad and indiscriminate rule of
equality, and the very means which it makes use of to effect this object
obliterates all artificial distinction and yet brings out in bolder relief
all the natural inequalities of men. And as a large proportion of the
envious are constantly rising into the ranks of the envied, a powerful
check is imposed upon the revolutionary tendencies of the former.
They cannot reach, nor after reaching will they be able to enjoy, that
which is the constant aim of all their efforts without lending an earnest and vigorous support to the laws under which they live. And in this
way free institutions are saved from shipwreck by the thorough and
undisguised adoption of a principle which seemed calculated to produce precisely opposite effects. It affords a remarkable example of the
intimate union between two things apparently contradictory and to
what an extent the system of compensations exists in a country of free
institutions, by means of which the defects of one part are cured by
some effectual contrivance in another. Hence the surprise which has
been constantly expressed by Europeans, from the day the cornerstone of the American government was laid down to the present, that
although a degree of liberty has been communicated to the people utterly unknown at any preceding period, society exhibits more evidences
of happiness and prosperity than are visible anywhere else; that for
so large an empire wonderful tranquillity prevails; and that the political institutions instead of losing strength are in reality increasing in
solidity and firmness. There does exist in that community as much as
in any other a powerful control upon the unruly elements of society.
But this is not the result of an artificial system; the control is wider
in its operation than anywhere else and it is, for that reason, more effectual than in any other government.

They who entertain fears that the enjoyment of so much liberty in the United States will exert any other than a favorable influence upon the social organization and the political institutions should recollect that equality may be a regulative principle of the highest importance, without ever being pushed to anything like the furthest extent. The laws may presuppose the possibility of pushing it so far, just as the precepts of morality suppose that they may be carried in great perfection into the practice of an individual. The advantage of having some great principle constantly in view is that it will then be sure of having some influence upon some individuals and a very great influence upon all others. Human nature modifies and sets bounds to all laws, but in order to render the principle of equality efficacious as a regulative principle it is necessary to admit the abstract rule in all its universality. The more widely the rules of morality are circulated and the more earnestly they are insisted upon, the greater will be the number of those whose conduct will be formed by them; and the more thoroughly the maxim of equality is taught, the more numerous will be the persons who will strive to make themselves equal to the wisest and best. More vigor, enterprise, and intelligence will be imparted to everyone; and the moral force communicated to society will contribute to rectify the very disorders which are supposed to be inseparable from the recognition of the principle.

Although, then, the struggle for equality never can produce equality in fact, yet there is an immensely wide scope within which it may operate. If the wealthy and those who found themselves upon the advantages of family and rank feel themselves incommoded by this eternal jostling — this continued struggle of inferior classes to rise to their level — I can easily conceive that the inconvenience may be productive of very great advantage.

If the difference between the higher and lower classes in point of morals and intelligence is not so great as is supposed, if the former wear for the most part an outside show, the struggle for equality by unveiling them, by exposing their false pretensions, will apply a sort of coercive influence to compel them to act up to the duties of their station. They will at first endeavor to rid themselves of the inconvenience by descending to the level of the lowest — by imitating their manners and truckling to their prejudices. The effect will not be lasting; the plan cannot be carried out. And after vain efforts to reconcile qualities the most incompatible, they will be driven to the necessity of cultivating habits which, as they most become, so they are universally expected from them. If adversity contributes to elevate the human character and if the struggle for equality is to be regarded as a species of adversity which is constantly present with us, it cannot fail to exercise a salutary influence. The diffusion of property and education are not sufficient to produce the degree of reflection which is requisite to maintain free institutions. The acquisition of property, notwithstanding its manifold benefits, has a tendency to undo all that education has done. The affluent become too contented, too self-complacent, to be either virtuous or wise. The ever enduring struggle for equality is the only agent which, united with property and education, will conduce to the right ordering of society.

CHAPTER VI | THE ELECTORAL FRANCHISE

THERE are two plans upon which we may proceed in forming a constitution of government. By one, the political power is vested in a select number composing what is termed the aristocracy of wealth and talent. And to accomplish this the electoral franchise and the eligibility to office are both restricted. The advantages of the plan are supposed to consist in the greater stability of the public administration and the superior energy which the government will possess in suppressing every species of insubordination. The second plan opens the door wide to the electoral privilege and the admission to office. Doubtless the great problem in political science is to procure the greatest amount of liberty consistent with the greatest degree of public tranquillity. And as we are compelled to take for granted that a large portion of the vice and licentiousness which have characterized the people of former times will always be found in society, it may be argued that the first plan is the safest and most judicious; but the republics which flourished in Italy in the thirteenth and fourteenth centuries were modeled upon this plan and yet were a prey to the most atrocious violence and tyranny. For after this disposition is made of the political power the question still occurs: in what way shall the governors themselves be governed? A large share of authority is conferred upon the government for the purpose of preserving order, and yet this authority is without any effectual control. Opening the door wide to every species of political privilege is the most certain means of increasing the natural aristocracy and of combining vigor in the government with popular freedom. For it is remarkable that although in the Italian republics the public officers were generally elected for very limited terms, for six and sometimes for so short a time as two months, it imposed no check upon the exercise of the most arbitrary authority. The moral sense, the perception of the plain distinction between right and wrong, was wanting in the whole community. There was ample power and opportunity to render the principle of responsibility a powerful restraint upon the conduct of public men, but there was no adequate appreciation of that conduct; no more meaning was attached to the words just and unjust than belonged to them in the monarchical governments of western and northern Europe — a striking example of the important agency which the political institutions have in forming the manners and habits of different nations. In all those communities, the select few who were chosen to conduct the public administration were thoroughly trained to the requisite skill and intelligence, in the Italian republics to a much greater extent than in Great Britain and France, because at that day the electoral franchise was much less restricted in the former. If, then, we extend political privileges of every kind still further and convert the great body of the people into citizens, the conclusion is fair that the same skill and intelligence will be diffused among the whole population. Now, it is these very qualities which develop that moral sense — that quick perception of what is right or wrong in the conduct of public men — which I have noticed as being so deficient in the Italian communities. The men who held important posts in Genoa, Venice, and Florence were sufficiently instructed, in consequence of their situation, in everything which affected their own interests. But those interests were by set design placed in contradiction with those of the mass of the people. Impart to the latter the same privileges, and the contradiction will disappear. For inasmuch as these will feel an equally strong interest in the protection of their own rights and will possess the moral power to enforce them, public men will be compelled to conform their conduct more and more to this altered state of public sentiment. The standard of right and wrong will of necessity, and not from choice, have a just and definite meaning. No education can instill the moral sense in any individual. But a certain train of circumstances and the discipline to which these subject the actions of men are indispensable in order to develop it and keep it in constant activity.

In the history of society we may remark three distinct grades of liberty which have existed in different governments. The first is where freedom is confined to the governors. This is the case in pure monarchy and aristocracy. Although the governments of Russia and Denmark are in no sense free, yet the Danish and Russian nobility, at any rate, enjoy as much political liberty as the American people. But the Danish and Russian people enjoy none. The second is where the people are divided into active and passive citizens, the former possessing political liberty while the latter live securely in the enjoyment of civil liberty only. The British government is the fairest example of this class which has ever existed. The third is where all the people are full and complete citizens, possessing both civil and political privileges. This can only be the case in a country where free institutions are established.

It is not difficult to account for this great diversity in the structure of different governments. Society everywhere appears to have been at a very early period divided into distinct classes. This institution was by no means peculiar to Egypt and Hindustan. But the superstitious observances which were ingrafted upon it in those countries and the immobile character of the population which prolonged its duration have rendered it more striking than anywhere else.

The separation of the people into different orders lay at the foundation of the Grecian and Roman commonwealths. It may be distinctly traced in the history of all the modern European states, and vestiges more or less plain are discernible in the most of them down to the present day. The division of the population into nobility, clergy, burgesses, and peasantry constituted at one time the settled classification of society in England and Scotland. Some of the ancient charters and statutes even went as far as the Roman laws in forbidding intermarriages among some of the classes. Guardians were prohibited from "disparaging their wards by wedlock with persons of an inferior condition." An inferior caste was recognized into which the military tenants could not marry without degradation. It is not necessary to account for this from the fact that long after the Saxon conquest the Roman law composed the groundwork of the jurisprudence. The operation of the same general laws which gave rise everywhere else to the existence of fixed classes produced the same effect in England. No doubt now remains but what the institution originally grew out of conquest — probably out of successive conquests. The conquerers composed the superior, the conquered the inferior ranks. In the course of time the different races in England and Scotland were melted into one. And the progress of civilization in the other European states has in a great measure obliterated this as well as every other remnant of an antiquated society.

It is not the least remarkable of the circumstances attending the first settlement of the United States that the native population were so thin and so immensely inferior to the emigrants that it disappeared as fast as these advanced. If the country had been as fully peopled as Mexico, great difficulties would have presented themselves in the formation of that system of uniform institutions which now exist. The

Indian race would have been disfranchised, precisely as are the Africans in both the northern and southern states. They would have composed as distinct a caste as these last do. The distinction would have been nearly the same as prevails in Hindustan.

The most obvious idea which we can form of government is that it is an institution intended for the common benefit of the whole people. Nor is there any difficulty in realizing this idea where the population does not consist of different races. Mere varieties of the same race oppose no obstacle, as has been proved in America where one uniform system of laws causes these varieties to disappear in two or three generations. But where the community is artificially distributed into classes which possess unequal privileges, the term government loses its just signification. One part of the population is then forcibly elevated and another depressed; and civil society becomes an institution exclusively appropriated to the advantage of the former. The great body of the people live under but not in it.

The disposition which governments shall make of the electoral franchise is destined to exercise a more important influence upon human affairs than any other political regulation of which I am aware. And the reason is obvious. There is none which is calculated to produce so deep an impression upon the structure of society and at the same time to affect so fundamentally the form of the government. The tendency everywhere at the present day is to extend the privilege. For every enlargement of it increases the demand, by raising up a greater number of people who are fitted to exercise it. The improvement of the political institutions and the improvement of the population go hand in hand.

Why are the people in mass admitted to the electoral franchise in the United States is a problem which has constantly exercised my mind.[1] Wherever I cast my eyes I seemed to see evidence of its being a solecism in politics. If I walked the streets of city or town, for one tolerably informed individual I met with twenty who were the reverse. If I traveled on the highway the same fact was exhibited even more glaringly. The great majority of persons I met appeared to know nothing beyond the narrow circle of their daily occupations.

But there is another fact equally striking which presented itself

---

1. [For the second edition, Grimke added new matter from the start of this paragraph to the paragraph which ends, ". . . in what relates to intellectual cultivation," on p. 131.]

to my mind: although the number of the intelligent was in so small a proportion to the ignorant, the number of bad or improvident laws compared with those which were wise and salutary was in an inverse ratio. They were even greatly less than one in twenty. I observed that the greatest stability reigned in those matters which concerned the general welfare. I witnessed a great deal of party strife, but in taking an account of the legislation for any series of years I could not discover that there had been any material departure from one uniform system which had prevailed from the beginning. The constitutions of the different states did not appear to be the work of ignorant men; the whole code of civil and criminal law was modeled with as much judgment and ability as if none but the well informed had been the electors.

There are two forces necessary to conduct the affairs of society. 1st. A certain amount of intelligence. 2d. A certain amount of integrity or honesty of purpose. Now, admitting that so far as intelligence is concerned it would be expedient to entrust the whole administration of the government to that very small class who possess intelligence, yet as the possession of office is corrupting in a high degree the experiment must necessarily be a failure; that is, the affairs of government would be so conducted as to subserve the interests of those who enjoyed a monopoly of power and not the interests of the whole community. Some plan must then be fallen upon, even though it should be in many respects imperfect, in order to rectify this great defect in the composition of society. We cannot find the requisite qualities of intelligence and honesty of purpose always united in the same individuals; but if we can find the intelligence in one class and the honesty of purpose, though without the intelligence, in another, we may combine the two together, making one people of them, and thus answer the conditions of the problem we are in search of. It will be no answer to say that this will be done imperfectly. This is admitted; for every instrument of government must partake of the defect of the materials from which it is made. But it will be correct to say that the plan will be more efficacious than any other which can be devised. It may be objected that honesty of purpose is no more characteristic of the masses than it is of the intelligent; that it is even less so, a certain amount of intelligence being necessary to make up the character of integrity in its genuine signification; that the common people are as much addicted to the practice of overreaching each other in their dealings as any other class. This will also be admitted. But the material inquiry is whether they are, or in the nature of things can be, so much so in what concerns public affairs. A small number of men to whom the electoral franchise and eligibility to office were confined might very easily live upon the people. The taxes extracted from them would be sufficient to gratify the most extravagant desires and the most insatiable avarice. But it is impossible for the people to live upon the people. The taxes imposed are only sufficient to pay the small number who conduct the machinery of government, and the amount necessary for this must be derived from their labor. So far as regards the expenditure of public money the common people may be considered as possessing honesty of purpose in a political sense in a high degree. They are deeply interested in preventing the public revenue from being squandered. This integrity of conduct may be a negative quality, but it is not the less efficacious on that account. In politics, positive and negative qualities sometimes count for the same. It is the matter of fact we have to deal with, and it is clear that the interest of the people is identical with that of the public, for they are the public. But the interest of the office holders may be directly opposed to that of the public. It is self-interest which renders the former honest in political matters and it is the same quality which under the guise of a half courtly, half sanctimonious exterior helps to make the latter corrupt.

It is in this way that we may account for what would otherwise appear to be an anomaly in the institutions of the United States: the permitting all classes to exercise the electoral franchise. It would seem at first view that we should have regard not merely to the number but to the intensity of the wills intended to be represented. And this is true, provided this intensity of will or superior intelligence was free from the vice of selfishness and manifested itself in a due comprehension of the public interests and are inflexible in pursuing them. But as we cannot find the two elements combined in one class we are driven to the expedient of admitting all classes to participation in the electoral franchise. The power of control which is thus possessed by the governed over the governing is indispensable in order to obtain all the ends of good government.

The system contains within itself a self-corrective principle. The longer the people are habituated to the exercise of the franchise the more completely will they grow into it. In France, when the revolution broke out, no class possessed the right of voting for any purpose. None had any voice in constituting any one of the departments of government. The consequence was that the men of letters, the merchants, moneyed men, and principal tradesmen were the instigators and chief actors in that revolution. Had they been accustomed for a very long period to the exercise of the privilege, the government would have undergone a gradual reformation. In the three first volumes of Mr. Bancroft's history, the first rudiments of American institutions are set forth with great judgment, and perspicuity.[2] The historian deduces from the events he relates the important fact that whenever the people were left to themselves and were rid of the rule of royal or proprietary government their affairs were conducted with the greatest judgment and address. If anyone should say, "admit the great body of the people to the elective franchise, but exclude the lowest class," the answer is that in a community where there has been a pretty equal distribution of property from the beginning the mischiefs arising from the possession of political rights by even the lowest class will be altogether less than in a country where everything has commenced wrong and where the laws are studiously intent on condensing property in the hands of a few. The lowest class will not be of sufficient magnitude in the former to make any sensible impression upon the result of the vote. The United States are the first country which has made the experiment upon a large scale, and it is of infinite moment to pursue it until its practicability is fairly tested. The lowest class have a stake in the commonwealth as well as any other class; they are the most defenseless portion of the population; and the sense of independence which the enjoyment of political rights inspires in innumerable instances acts as a stimulus to the acquisition of property. If the experiment fails, if the intervention of the lowest class in the elections exercises too disturbing an influence upon the motions of the government, the expedient which has been adopted in the government of cities and towns may be easily resorted to. The difficulty would be exceedingly great, impossible I may say, of effecting a change now. The lowest class are for the most part laborers, but their wages are such as to enable them to live in great comfort; they are closely connected with the great class which stands above them, and the sympathy which exists between the two would not permit the enactment of any law which should exclude the former from their present position. But

2. [George Bancroft (1800–1891), *History of the United States* (Boston, 1834–1874), 10 vols.; Volume I appeared in 1834; Volume II in 1837; Volume III in 1840; Volume IV in 1852 after the first edition of Grimke's book.]

if a host of proletarians should rise up whose voice in the government was detrimental to the public interests, unfriendly to the maintenance of that order, regularity, and justice which makes up the true idea of a commonwealth, the feeling of sympathy would be lost and, as there would be no motive for continuing a rule after the reason for it had ceased, the great body of the commonwealth who will forever be the majority would unite in imposing some restriction on the electoral franchise.

One very important consequence follows from these views, that it will be necessary to enlarge the rule of eligibility to office in the same proportion as that for the electoral franchise. If one is without restriction, the other should be so also. The ground upon which the argument in the first part proceeds is that it is impossible to find in one class all the qualities which are requisite to good government. But if we can find them separately existing in two classes, we may by combining them into one class for political purposes attain the desired end. Although honesty in political matters may simply consist in an instinctive resistance of the general interest to the private interest of a few, yet if in practice the consequences are the same as if it proceeded from natural integrity of character the legislator will have attained all he has any right to expect. The public interest is promoted by honest views. If honesty of purpose is the moving spring, the end is attained in its greatest perfection. If, on the other hand, an interest in the general weal is the moving spring, the same political end is attained. As a substitute for a property qualification for office some have proposed to place the age of the candidate high, to require that they should be forty or forty-five before admission even to the legislative body. This is evidently impracticable unless we raise the requisite age of the voters also. It is they who determine the rule of eligibility to office, and it is very improbable that they would deprive themselves of the privilege. But there are very wise reasons why this restriction should not be imposed. It would lower instead of elevating the capacity of candidates for office. At present, electors are the persons elected, and these again fall into the body of electors. If the legislature then is a school of discipline for those who compose it, it is equally so for the electors. In this way a most advantageous influence is exercised upon the whole mass of the population. The consciousness that they are electors and that they may be elected to a place of trust sharpens the minds of individuals and even amidst the confusion of party politics rears up a much greater number of sagacious and well informed persons than might at first be supposed. If during the last seventy years all the citizens under forty had been debarred from the elective franchise or entering the legislative assemblies in America, there would have been less instead of more order in the conduct of public affairs, for the great mass of the population would have possessed less intelligence, sagacity, and prudence. Bacon has said that there is "but one mode of predicting political events, and that is by ascertaining the predominant opinions of the average of men who are under thirty." [3] We are enabled to do this in a clear, determinate, and legal way by endowing them with political privileges. It is for this reason that even in the constitutional monarchies of England and France the age of the electors and members of the legislature is placed so low. Some of the states which compose the Swiss confederacy have erred on the other side. The age in some is so low as eighteen and in others sixteen. The legislative assembly is the place where opinions are discussed and where alone materials can be collected for predicting as well as for providing for the future. It is very important that the opinions of the young should mingle with those of mature age. If inconvenience is experienced from the ardent character of the one, fully as much would be suffered from the narrow and obstinate prejudices of the other. The political prosperity of the United States, the stability in the midst of progress which the institutions exhibit, are attributable to the young and the old being admitted to the public councils. This has not given a predominance to the opinions of either. It has simply operated a fusion of the opinions of the two and has placed at the command of society all the genius and activity of the one, together with all the wisdom and ability of the other.

M. Chabrol, in his "Recherches Statistiques," calculates that nineteen twentieths of the people of France are dependent on their labor or personal exertions of some kind for their subsistence; in other words, that not more than one twentieth are in a condition to live upon their income merely. Tucker, in his work on the census of the United States, has made the same calculation for the people of that country. The knowledge of this fact M. Sismondi considers indis-

3. [It would be pleasant to establish a seventeenth-century precedent for the modern notion, "Don't trust anybody over thirty," but I have been unable to locate in Bacon's writings the words which Grimke attributes to him.]

pensable in order to make a wise and safe distribution of the political power.[4] If nineteen twentieths of the population are condemned to employments which do not permit the free and vigorous exercise of their understandings, is it not absurd, asks M. Sismondi, to endow all the people equally with the electoral franchise; in other words, to give nineteen times more power to the ignorant than to those who are capable of understanding the interests of the country. But we should commit a great mistake if we supposed that the calculation of M. Chabrol had the same meaning in all countries. Although in every country the number of those devoted to physical labor is nineteen to one, it will not follow that the condition of the class is the same in all. For instance, the majority of proprietors in the United States possess from eighty to two hundred acres of land, in France from six to ten, in Great Britain from fifteen to twenty five; nevertheless, the American proprietor is as dependent for his maintenance upon the cultivation of his farm as the French or English proprietor. But the maintenance of the former comprehends much more than that of the two last. In Great Britain the rural population composes one third, in the United States it is three fourths of the population. These circumstances place a wide distinction between the population of the United States and that of Great Britain or France. The proportion of the rural population is as great in France as in the United States but their condition is infinitely lower. Although nineteen twentieths of the American people are dependent upon their labor, yet if more than one half of this number are placed in an easy condition and have a revenue greatly superior to the same class in other countries, their labor will not be anything like so intense and humiliating. The condition of the majority of French proprietors is little better than of the English operatives; neither earn more than enough to satisfy the lowest animal wants. American proprietors, on the contrary, live in comfort, and a fair opportunity is afforded for the development of their understandings. For even where the education is of a limited character, the

4. [Gilbert de Chabrol (1773–1843), engineer and administrator, published a statistical survey of France in Paris in 1824; George Tucker, *Progress of the United States in Population and Wealth in Fifty Years as Exhibited by the Decennial Census from 1790 to 1840* (New York, 1843); Jean Charles de Sismondi (1773–1842), Swiss historian and economist, at first a follower of Adam Smith, who because of the effects of the industrial revolution in England became a critic of laissez-faire economics, especially in *Nouveaux Principes d'Economie Politique* (Paris, 1819).]

feeling of independence gives a spring to the intellectual faculties. The difference between the American and European laborer is as great as between the American and European proprietor. The American laborer earns from three pecks to a bushel of wheat daily; the average wages of even the English laborer during the last five centuries have been a little more than one peck.

M. Sismondi insists (*Etudes sur les Sciences Sociales, v.* 1, p. 54) that the most fortunate result which can be expected from an election by universal suffrage is that the choice will be a mean between all the differences, so that if there are nineteen ignorant electors for one well informed the legislative body will be nineteen twentieths nearer the ignorance of the one than the intelligence of the other. This, however, is contradicted by universal experience. The opinion of Brougham is more correct when he declares that "if universal suffrage were now established in Great Britain, not one peasant would be elected to Parliament." [5] Moral inability produces nearly the same results as physical inability. Those who are without knowledge, without ability or aptitude for public affairs, feel themselves instinctively and irresistibly impelled to lean upon those who have these qualities in some respectable degree. There never has been a legislative assembly chosen by the people which did not contain men of high character and superior endowments. In France, after the revolution of 1848, such men as De Tocqueville, Berryer, Thiers, Barrot, Dupin, Arago, *etc.,* were immediately elected to the legislative body. The same result has invariably taken place in the United States. Why this should be the case — why some men of superior merit are returned together with a greater number of inferior capacities, and why the first will be able to exert a decisive influence in the assembly — affords matter for curious inquiry: 1st. There is in all men a natural and instinctive respect for superior knowledge. It is not the result of reflection and therefore cannot be got rid of any more than our other instincts. 2d. The sharp edge of envy is taken off by the knowledge which the people have that the successful candidates owe their election to them. 3d. Everyone in the affairs of private life calls upon others to do what he cannot do or

5. [I have been unable to locate the exact source for the quotation in Lord Brougham's many articles and speeches, but the sentiment is characteristic; in *The British Constitution: Its History, Structure, and Working,* he wrote "What body of men would choose artisans or day-labourers to represent them, were the right of voting ever so general?" *Works of Henry, Lord Brougham* (London, 1861), XI, 82.]

do so skillfully himself: upon the lawyer in a legal controversy, upon the physician in sickness. 4th. These causes are greatly strengthened by a circumstance peculiar to political men. The public display which they make, the topics they debate, strike powerfully upon the imagination of the common people. They are not merely instructed, they are amused, and their feelings roused by the animating spectacle which public affairs present. But there is nothing to produce animation when the public arena is occupied by dull, ignorant men, any more than there is at the theatre where the actors have none of the inspiration of genius. Through these various instrumentalities, some men of ruling intellect are sure to be elected to an assembly which has to do with great affairs; and such men, for even stronger reasons than have influenced the electors, will exert a commanding influence upon the other members. Superior minds, in whatever sphere they move, give unity to the thoughts and actions of other men. Profound writers, the pulpit, the bar, the seminaries of learning, all contribute to this great end. If we survey the condition of a savage or half-civilized community, we find this principle of unity entirely wanting: everything which relates to the social, moral, and political regime is at loose ends. If we examine the condition of a civilized country, but in which internal commotions have for a time broken in upon the regular order of society, we find the same fact exemplified in a remarkable manner. If we look into the condition of the same country when enjoying tranquillity, we find a state of things entirely the reverse. Everything is in its place; the thoughts and actions of men are controlled by a principle of unity, and that principle of unity is contained in the moral and intellectual machinery which is in operation. The institution of government contributes greatly to this end; it binds up the scattered, incoherent thoughts and interests of men and makes them all tend to some common end. The use of representative government, as contra-distinguished from pure democracy, is not to reflect the vague and loose opinions of the millions of men who live under it, but to sift those opinions, to draw out what is valuable, and thus to give fixedness, consistency, and unity to the thoughts of men as well as to the plans of government. This want is infinitely more pressing in a country of great extent than in one of narrow dimensions. But even the small republics of Greece were obliged to invent some plan in order to get rid of the disorder which would have arisen from an assemblage of the people in person, such as vesting the senatorial body with the initiative, confiding the reduction of the laws to special committees or bureaus, and the appointment of a certain number of public orators. All these were representative bodies and helped to make compensation for the inherent defects of the system. Without some such expedients the legislative assembly would have been converted into a bedlam. A government which is representative throughout attains these ends in much higher perfection. It is not necessary nor even desirable that a country should employ all its eminent men in political affairs. There are other and higher occupations for the ruling minds who belong to it; higher, because the eminent political men of every country are themselves formed directly or indirectly by the great thinkers and writers in every department of knowledge. America so far presents the singular spectacle of a country whose eminent men have been formed by the great minds of other countries. It is fortunate, therefore, that she at least does not convert all her gifted citizens into public men. Provision will thus be made for building up a profound literature at home and preventing us looking abroad in order to obtain the great rudiments of knowledge. We shall then cease to be an eleemosynary people in what relates to intellectual cultivation.

The notion of a property qualification as necessary to entitle to a vote seems to be derived from feudal institutions. A very few instances of the same kind are to be found in antiquity. The feudal law so completely united every species of political right with dominion in the soil that, even after a regular representative assembly grew up, the right of suffrage as well as the capacity to hold office was made to depend upon the fact whether the persons were landed proprietors or not. In Great Britain a qualification of this kind is still necessary, a freehold in county and a leasehold in borough elections. In Scotland, until recently, none but tenants in capite, that is, persons who held immediately of the crown (whether really or constructively was immaterial), had a right to vote in county elections. For the most extraordinary part of the system was that it was by a fiction only they were so denominated. It was not necessary that they should have any interest whatever in the soil. They possessed the franchise on account of what, in technical language, is termed superiority. They were originally tenants in capite, but it was in the power of anyone to sever his superiority from his land, selling the last and yet retaining the former; the purchaser consequently acquiring the right to a vote. This was a strange anomaly at any time, but that such a law should be found standing in the midst of the light of the nineteenth century and in the most enlightened country of Europe is difficult to explain by any sensible mode of reasoning. It shows that the artificial governments alone are able to reconcile the most heterogeneous and contradictory things — can insist that the public safety demands that property and power should forever go together, and then throw away the principle as unmeaning and valueless and confer power upon those who have no property. The consequence of this state of things was the electorial franchise was much more restricted and the system of representation altogether more irregular than in either England or Ireland.

In France, since the creation of a house of deputies, a different plan has been adopted. The right to a vote depends upon the payment of a certain amount of taxes, varying at different periods from forty to sixty dollars for each individual. This presupposes the possession of property, but then it may be indifferently either real or personal. The tax must be a direct one, but even if there is any real distinction between what are termed direct and what are termed indirect taxes, the former are deemed equally applicable to both kinds of property. In America a property qualification was once necessary in all the state governments, and in the federal government the right to a vote for members of the house of representatives was the same as it was in each state for the most numerous branch of the state legislature. The laws, however, have undergone a total alteration in almost all the states. Universal suffrage is now the rule, a property qualification the exception; and the elections to the federal legislature are obliged to conform themselves to the changes made in the respective states.

The origin of a custom is never sufficient to determine its utility, nor to give us its true meaning at a subsequent time. Such changes take place in the frame of society in modern communities that an institution which was well enough adapted to a very imperfect civilization may lose its signification and become highly injurious at a more advanced period. It is true, it sometimes happens that an institution which was fitted to answer one purpose may, when that has ceased to exist, be found to answer some other end in a still higher degree. And, therefore, it cannot be stated as an universal proposition that if the original design has failed the institution should therefore be abolished. But it is still more necessary to guard against the opposite error and never to take for granted that the antiquity of an institution is what entitles it to the respect of mankind. The prejudice is sometime of advantage by correcting the precipitancy of innovation. But in the greater number of instances it only darkens and confuses the understanding and contributes to retain society in a stationary condition.

A property qualification has been defended in modern times on two grounds: first, that property is the chief thing which the laws have to deal with, and therefore it is fit that the privilege should be worn by those who represent the most important interests of society; second, that as a general rule the possession of property affords a surer test of a capacity for the judicious exercise of the electorial franchise than any other which can be devised.

To disseminate property is to disseminate power and, on the other hand, the diffusion of liberty gives rise to the diffusion of both property and power. And, as the true plan of balancing power is to prevent its concentration in the hands of a few, to distribute it as widely as possible, so the only mode by which we can contrive to govern the governors is to open the way to all classes of men for the acquisition of property. And the most effectual way of doing this is to extend the electorial franchise as widely as practicable. Neither the abolition of primogeniture nor any other enactment of the civil code has in the United States assisted so much in effecting a distribution of property as have the political institutions. So that even admitting as a general rule that it is fit power and property should go together, it cannot be wise to adopt a system, the direct effect of which is to prevent the growth and dissemination of property. Formerly, landed property constituted the principal capital of society. But the case is now very much altered. Industry, sagacity, and enterprise, though they can neither be seen or touched, compose at the present day the chief elements of wealth. No man, however affluent, can now tell with any degree of certainty how long his estate will continue to be enjoyed by his descendants, such is the rapidity with which the inert habits of those who are born rich permit property to crumble and such the corresponding activity with which those who are born poor acquire the ability to appropriate that property to themselves.

Why it is that the communication of political privileges to a people imparts so much vigor and activity to their whole character, is not difficult to account for. It removes a feeling of degradation, the invariable effect of which is to benumb and stupify the mind, if it does not produce worse consequences. It is true, one can hardly say that the peasantry of Russia or Austria realize this feeling, since having been habituated from time immemorial to a state of complete subjection they can hardly form an idea of the value of the privilege. But in all the constitutional monarchies of Europe where the electorial franchise is already extended to a part of the population, those who are excluded from its exercise are able to make a comparison of their situation with that of others, and a sense of their own inferiority is forced upon them.

The great advantage arising from the free communication of the privilege consists, then, in its giving men new faculties and not merely new rights. It enables them for the first time to realize a sense of degradation which they were before too much debased to feel. It places the great body of the population in the only condition in which it is possible to place them: where their understandings will be opened, their views enlarged, and their feeling elevated. Nothing can be conceived more dreary and monotonous than the time which is passed in the drudgery of supplying our animal wants, if there is nothing besides to give variety and interest to life. The beings who are condemned to this species of subterranean existence are never able to acquire the proper character of men.

Medical writers have observed that nothing contributes so much to produce mental aberration as the habit acquired by some individuals of brooding over one train of ideas. The mind which is exercised in this way is deprived of its healthful action; the balance between its different faculties is lost, and its strength gradually undermined. It is only in extreme cases that this takes place. But there is a condition of mind very similar to this which may be termed fatuity — an intellectual torpor which in some countries takes possession of whole classes, produced by the addiction to an exceedingly narrow round of pursuits and which prevents the natural play of the mental powers and affections. Long habit familiarizes the observer to this melancholy spectacle, but it is not the less an example of mental aberration, though in a much less degree than the state before described. Whoever has closely watched the countenances and behavior of the peasantry of most European countries when they arrive in the United States must have been struck with this characteristic mark. There is an obtuseness of intellect, a withered and sunken aspect, a bent and difficult gait which contrast strongly with the alert step and animated countenances of American agriculturists.

There are two modes of rectifying this unfortunate condition of society — education and the influence of free institutions. Education alone is not sufficient. The mind may take in the mere rudiments of knowledge and yet its faculties never be developed. The institutions under which we live, the social organization which encompasses us, are what give vitality and meaning to much the greater part of the knowledge which the bulk of mankind ever acquire. Liberty both imparts elasticity to the mind and supplies the materials on which it is chiefly exercised. For the general communication of an important political privilege breaks down the wall of partition between the different classes. Men of low degree are brought into association with those who possess superior advantages. The former are taught to have more self-respect, more confidence in themselves, and the wide range of general information which is now placed within their reach inspires the greatest inquisitiveness imaginable in regard to the conduct of public affairs in which they have now become actors themselves. All this, so far from withdrawing attention from their private pursuits, adds fresh vigor to their exertions simply because it supplies such a fund of variety to life. And thus this unexpected consequence follows: that in a country where no property qualification is attached to the enjoyment of political privileges, the number of people who possess property is the greatest. And wherever the qualification is highest, the less is the number of those who have property — a remarkable instance of the false train of reasoning to which the mind is frequently conducted by an obstinate adherence to what is called the ancient and established order of society.

There is an old maxim that the political institutions can never be made to rise higher than the manners. And a more pernicious one has never been incorporated into the book of politics. There is no difference in this respect between political and any other institutions. And if the maxim had ever been carried to anything like its full extent society would never have made a single step in improvement. For what are religion, education, and the body of conventional rules which preside over a community but so many institutions which, finding men ignorant and weak, lift them up and make them better and wiser. The true maxim is that the political institutions do exercise a most important influence upon the manners, and that every improvement of the former contributes to raise society to a higher level. And I am persuaded if some of the European governments I could name were resolved, manfully but circumspectly, to rid themselves of the prejudice that what has been must continue to be, and if they would impart a large share of liberty to the people, that it would redound to the strength and prosperity of both government and people.

There are several considerations in addition to those already suggested which go very far to show that a law which attaches a property qualification to the right of suffrage is unwise and without utility.

First. Public opinion is becoming more and more the great moving force of all governments. It is then of the utmost importance to inquire what part of the population it is which contributes to the formation of this public opinion. Is it certain that it is only the class of proprietors? Very far from it; there are great multitudes of people in Great Britain and France who are totally disfranchised and whose opinions and interests are of so much consequence as to render their influence, even when deprived of suffrage, of infinite importance whether for good or for evil. And this constitutes the test of the expediency of a property qualification. If whole classes who are disqualified have sufficient weight in society to bear a part in the formation of public opinion, it decides the question in favor of a liberal rule of suffrage. If those who have faculties to think and an abundant curiosity with regard to all public affairs are excluded from the privilege, they will succeed in spite of every effort the legislator may make in giving a direction to public opinion.

I venture to say that all the great measures of reform which have been set on foot during the last twenty years in Great Britain have been brought about in great part through the influence of that numerous body of active and intelligent citizens who are shut out from a direct participation in political power. But critical emergencies occur in all governments when the passions of different orders of men are violently inflamed and when what was before an invisible influence will come to wear a more palpable form. The whole class of disfranchised, composed in part of sagacious and otherwise well disposed people, will then resemble a foreign force rather than a body of orderly citizens and may imagine that in self-defense it is necessary to batter down existing institutions.

The British, and still more the French government, is placed in this position. Two hundred thousand electors in the last, where the adult male population is five or six millions, is too great a disproportion; and it is not surprising that the fear of a disputed succession or some other speck discerned upon the political horizon should produce so much apprehension among those who take the lead in public affairs. In Great Britain the reform bill extended the privilege considerably, but one thirty-fifth part of the population is much too small a proportion in a country where the standard of popular intelligence has been so much elevated during the last half century. I am not acquainted with all the views of the English Chartists, but so formidable a body of men could hardly have been banded together in that great community unless the electoral franchise was needlessly withheld from a very substantial part of the citizens and unless those who were so earnest in endeavoring to effect a reform had been animated by the characteristic good sense of the Anglo-Norman race. There is no necessity for acquiescing in the extreme views of Mr. Bentham or Major Cartwright; a wide field for profitable legislation is opened whether we adopt or discard them.[6] The Chartists have assuredly paved the way for further concessions at some future day. The present law of Parliamentary reform was talked about by the party in power and the party in opposition, by Pitt and by Fox, as far back as 1786, and was achieved nearly half a century after.

Second. A government which confines the electoral franchise within very narrow limits fails to avail itself of the strength and faculties of the whole of its people. It is like the strong man cutting off his right arm with his left. In the United States the enjoyment of the privilege by the great body of the people gives rise to order and tranquillity instead of tumult and insurrection. For an unmistakable test is thus afforded that all public measures follow the course which the majority have decreed. And there is nothing which is so much calculated to subdue the will and to produce an irresistible obedience to the laws as the knowledge that they are imposed by an authority which has the only legitimate title to command. This alone is an immense advantage to society; so that even admitting that public affairs are not, in every particular instance, conducted with as much judgment and discretion as we could desire, yet if on the average they are characterized by more prudence and good sense, a greater deference to the public weal than is discoverable in other governments, we may even afford to prize the flaw in the system for the sake of its general utility. Montesquieu said if the press were established in Constantinople it would diffuse

6. [Jeremy Bentham (1748–1832) and John Cartwright (1740–1824) both argued for universal manhood suffrage, as did the leaders of Chartism, the workingmen's reform movement (1838–1848), after the failure of the Reform Bill of 1832 to extend the suffrage to the laboring classes.]

light even in that region. And it has actually done so; and I observe that every enlargement of the electoral franchise in Great Britain has had no other effect than to produce a greater degree of public tranquillity. Invariably the introduction of free institutions, if it does not find a people already prepared for self-government, will in no long time render them so.

The general communication of the electoral privilege banishes the distinction of patricians and plebeians — a distinction which is quick in making its appearance whenever it has any root in the laws. All the parts of society are thus combined into one firm and compact whole, and the strength and prosperity of the entire nation are proportionally augmented. On the other hand, where the right is very much restricted two forces in the state are placed in opposition to each other: the legal and natural majority; the one conscious of the right, the other of power. The country is then sure to be torn by intestine divisions — divisions not created by a difference of opinion as to the ordinary measures of administration which may follow one direction or another without much affecting the public welfare, but divisions which are of fundamental import as pertaining to the rights of the people and the prerogatives of the government. It is not surprising, therefore, that even the extreme into which the people of the United States have run of introducing universal suffrage, or nearly so, so far from destroying the public happiness, as was predicted, has been chiefly instrumental in promoting it. The natural and the legal majority being rendered identical, the surface of society is frequently ruffled, but the existence of the institution is no longer jeopardized.

Third. It is a striking characteristic of human nature that whatever is rendered common and familiar loses on that very account its power over the imagination. Our feelings may be ever so much interested in the pursuit of an object, yet no sooner is it fairly attained than the charm of novelty begins to subside. The mind which was before tossed by contrary hopes and fears recovers its composure, and a state approaching even to indifference sometimes succeeds to one of excitement. This is as true in the world of politics as in any other human concern. The same hopes and affections are set in motion in both, and they are liable therefore to be raised and depressed by the same causes. A privilege which before it was granted was viewed as a mark of distinction is deprived of a good deal of its attraction when it is shared by millions.

The European governments discover the greatest alarm and the most unreasonable timidity whenever the subject of popular rights is touched. But we are not authorized to believe that there is so much danger to the political institutions from that quarter when there is the fact staring us in the face, and which no one can gainsay, that those governments which have extended the sphere of popular rights the farthest are the best administered and are at the same time favored with the greatest degree of public tranquillity. I would say to all those governments, if you are afraid of the temper and disposition of a people which is fast growing into manhood, if you feel alarmed at the intelligence and consequent weight which the people are everywhere acquiring, make haste to avert the mischiefs which are brooding over society by imparting to them as large an amount of freedom as is practicable. Make what is now a privilege and distinction the common property of a great number, it will then become cheap, common, and familiar. A state of popular excitement will not be perpetually kept up, and society will in no long time accommodate itself to the change. There is no difference by nature between Americans and the people of other countries, for the former were themselves Europeans originally. Their institutions have made them what they now are.

The electoral franchise has effected this important revolution in human affairs. Public measures are no longer decided upon the field of battle; hostile armies are now converted into political parties, and military captains into civil leaders. Changes in the public administration which years of civil war were unable to accomplish are now brought about silently and imperceptibly by the agency of the ballot box. If few are aware of the value of the mighty change which has taken place, or even of its existence, it is in consequence of causes to which I have already referred. Men cease to be moved by what has become the settled order of society.

But there is another benefit which the general possession of the privilege will confer. A people who enjoy a long period of uninterrupted prosperity are apt to become slothful and effeminate. The exercise of political privileges, by opening an arena for the operation of parties on the largest possible scale, keeps the minds of men in constant activity and wards off the approach of that listlessness and decay which have hitherto been the bane of society when it has attained a very high civilization.

There is this advantage from founding government upon the will of the majority: that if alterations are afterwards found expedient they will all originate with the same power. It is possible that at some distant period the public weal in the United States may require some modification of the right of suffrage. The true maxim in a republic is that every right should be placed in subordination to the general welfare. If then the right is ever restricted the change will be attended by this important advantage. It will be brought about with the consent of a majority of the people. This differs the institution fundamentally from what it is anywhere else.

It is not the mere abstract limitation of the right which is to be complained of. For none but males are now admitted, and, as to them, the age of twenty one is arbitrarily fixed upon as the commencement of the right. It is the restriction of the privilege by a section of the community (as in the European governments) which constitutes the chief ground of objection. It is remarkable that the Americans have constantly adhered to the principle that some other qualification than mere citizenship or residence is necessary in municipal elections. A property qualification of some kind is uniformly imposed in this instance. This is not only the case in the large cities; it is the general rule in all the smaller towns which are scattered over the country. If, therefore, it shall ever be deemed wise to impose a limitation upon the right of voting at the general elections, the transition will not be a violent one. It will simply be the application of a principle in one form to which, in another, the public is already habituated. Doubtless the qualification exacted at all charter elections interferes as much with the abstract principle of equal rights as would a similar restriction imposed upon the general voter. Yet there is at present a very general conviction of the propriety of the rule in the former case.

As to the mode of collecting the suffrages of the people, whether it should be "viva voce" or by ballot, I do not believe that the question is of so much importance as is generally supposed. In the early history of most communities, the former was probably the practice. But this was owing to the inability to write rather than to the simplicity of the manners. It is rarely a secret how anyone votes when the election is by ballot. Free institutions throw open the windows of society so wide as to unveil all political transactions. In the United States the vote of every elector in a county has been sometimes calculated with absolute precision beforehand. Cicero laments the disuse of the "viva voce" vote in his time. But in a period of deep gloom and adversity, such as existed when he wrote, the mind which is laboring under its depressing influence will lay hold of any circumstance to give color to its apprehensions. The ballot does not render the vote of anyone a secret; while at the same time it has this eminent advantage, that an election becomes less noisy and tumultuous in consequence. It is made to resemble the quiet and orderly transaction of private business.

When the electors are very numerous, it is fortunately impracticable to organize them on the plan adopted in France. There the electors form themselves into what are denominated colleges, into which no one not privileged to vote is admitted. The elections are thus freed from violence, but they are shrouded in darkness and are therefore subjected to the most sinister influence. Until 1830, the presidents of these colleges were nominated by the king, a circumstance which was understood to give them a decided advantage if they were themselves candidates — so sadly does a monarchical government disfigure free institutions whenever it attempts to imitate them.

The intermediate vote has been a favorite with some very able writers. Mr. Hume proposes it in his plan of a republic.[7] The experiment has been made in France on a more extended scale than was ever attempted in any other country. At one time, two intermediate bodies were interposed between the primary electors and the candidates so that three successive elections, by as many different bodies, each diminishing in number, were necessary to the election of the legislative body. The whole plan, however, was abandoned in 1817. In the United States, a scheme in some respects similar has been adopted in the election of the president and senators, and in most of the state governments in the election of judges and a few of the administrative officers. But in France, not only were members of the legislature elected by the intermediate vote but, what was infinitely worse, the electoral colleges who chose them were constituted for life. The small number

7. [Grimke refers to David Hume's essay, "The Idea of a Perfect Commonwealth," the last in the second volume of *Essays, Moral and Political,* first published in 1742. The first collected edition, *The Philosophical Works of David Hume* . . . (Edinburgh, 1826), 4 vols., III, 561–579, presents a slightly different version. Hume's "plan" was to divide Great Britain and Ireland (or any country of comparable size) into one hundred counties, each divided into one hundred parishes, and then to have property owners in each parish meet once a year to elect from among themselves a "county representative"; two days later, the one hundred county representatives would meet to elect from among themselves ten magistrates and one senator. The one hundred senators would, in the capitol, constitute the "whole executive power" of the commonwealth.]

of persons composing them, together with the permanent tenure of their office, rendered these colleges mere aristocratic bodies.

The election laws of France were at one time disfigured by another deformity. All those who paid a certain amount of taxes, seven hundred francs I think, were entitled to vote twice. In Great Britain the double and even the triple vote is allowed, but it stands on a slightly different footing. In France, the same elector might vote twice for a member of the chamber of deputies. In Great Britain, the same elector cannot vote twice in the same county, but he may vote in different counties if he has land of sufficient value in each. He may vote twice, and even oftener, for different members of the House of Commons. All such schemes are entirely inconsistent with the genuine spirit of free institutions and only serve to stave off, or to hasten the day, which sooner or later will come when a more just system will be established. Indeed, in France the plan has already been established. In Great Britain it [*i.e.,* the double vote] stands, notwithstanding the reform act of 1832.

It is a most valuable provision in the American laws that the elections are held in the townships or parishes. This contributes mightily to break the force of party spirit. The plan has been recently imitated in Great Britain. Formerly, the elections were held at but one place in each county. It is now held at several places. A similar arrangement has also been adopted in France. Instead of the elections being held by departments, they are held in the smaller subdivision of "arrondissements." The British and French plans are still imperfect. The American is thorough and goes directly to its object. In Europe, the plan is to diminish the number of electors instead of multiplying the places of election.

There is another difference between the British and French and the American elections. In Great Britain the polls were kept open for an indefinite period. In the celebrated Westminster election when Mr. Fox lost his seat, they were open for six weeks and were then closed only because the session of parliament commenced. The period is now restricted to one day in cities and boroughs, and to two in counties. In France, an election continues six days. In America, the polls are generally closed in one day, and nothing is more remarkable than the universal calm which immediately succeeds. The elections in America may be said to exhibit the extraordinary spectacle of prodigious excitement in the midst of the profoundest tranquillity.

CHAPTER VII | THE ELECTION OF THE PUBLIC OFFICERS

THERE is one property peculiar to representative governments which I do not remember to have seen noticed. It doubles the responsibility of the public agents. The persons who are elected to office feel a general responsibility in common with their constituents because the interests of both are substantially the same, and they feel an additional responsibility in consequence of the station which they are selected to fill. An association of individuals acting in common for their mutual advantage are compelled to listen to some other motives than self-interest, otherwise it would not be true that they acted in common. But the moment it is decided that all public measures shall be managed by deputies instead of by the people in person, a new and very important element is introduced into the government. The incentives to good conduct on the part of the representative are increased. The very self-interest which before stood in the way of each one acting effectually for the public good is made to operate advantageously upon the officer. He is no longer confounded with the crowd. He stands out to public view as one selected to discharge important duties. His constituents expect something more from him than they do from themselves, and his conduct is obliged to be more prudent and circumspect than it would otherwise be.

The corrupting influence of office has often been taken notice of. But it may be made to have a directly opposite effect. I have in repeated instances known individuals to make use of untiring efforts to obtain some public trust, the duties of which consisted in the most laborious drudgery in the performance of a mere round of clerical duties, and I have observed them closely after their object was attained. To see the singleness of purpose and the indefatigable industry which they applied to their new occupation, one would suppose that they had made discovery of some inexhaustible source of enjoyment which was unknown to anyone else. Before they were chosen, their conduct seemed to be without any definite aim. It was a bundle of expedients, not a system of action. They were not only not distinguished for intelligence, industry, or sobriety of demeanor, but seemed to be absolutely deficient in all. As soon as the public confidence was held out to them, all these qualities were suddenly waked up, and they were transformed into active and valuable citizens. In most countries, the greater part of these individuals would have been cut off from all opportunity of obtaining office. They would have occupied the place of passive citizens merely and not even have been admitted to the exercise of the electoral franchise. Thus, the extreme liberty which representative government imparts to the population carries along with it its own corrective. Of all governments it is the one which creates, if I may use the expression, the greatest amount of business transactions, and it is, therefore, the one which demands the greatest amount of business talent and industry.

It is very true that the separate interest which a public officer feels in the emolument and influence which office bestows may be so much enhanced as entirely to outweigh the interest which he has in the public welfare. The way to cure this defect is to distribute power as widely as possible, to assign moderate salaries to every place and to limit the duration of office. The distribution of power, by calling into requisition the abilities of a large proportion of the population, prevents anyone from acquiring undue influence and, by joining effective labor to almost every public employment, identifies the interests of the public with those of the officer.

The ancients never made a full discovery of the principle of representation, and accordingly their application of it was very feeble. The Roman commonwealth had recourse to another principle in the constitution of its legislative assemblies. Men were arranged into distinct orders and the votes were taken by classes instead of "per capita."

Thus, where a modern republic is chiefly intent on melting down the inequalities of different parts of the society by establishing the principle of representation, an ancient republic endeavored to perpetuate them by giving them full play. There is hardly an instance in antiquity of a legislative body which was elected. The senate of Athens may be an exception, though that is a question which is involved in great obscurity. In the Roman commonwealth, the comitia of the centuries and of the tribes constituted at successive periods the real legislature. The senate was regarded in the light of an executive magistracy, and the members who composed it, although they were elected by the people during the latter half of the republic, were not elected to the senate.

They had previously been chosen to some other office, and by virtue of this choice became senators for life.

The elective principle, however, was thoroughly practiced upon in framing the executive department. In the modern European states, the rule is reversed. The legislature, or one chamber, is elected, while the executive is an hereditary magistrate, and the judicial and all the subordinate administrative officers are appointed by him. The United States is the only country where the principle of representation has been introduced into every department of the government.

To procure an upright and enlightened appointing power is the chief desideratum in the formation of a commonwealth.[1] It is the final aim of all government and all other devices are but means to the attainment of it. In Great Britain this power is nominally a prerogative of the crown; in practice, it is exercised by the minister or some other public officer. Thus all the puisne judges are appointed by the chancellor, and it has been observed by an eminent English writer that the fitness of the persons thus selected, is "not only unquestioned, but unquestionable." [2] It was a maxim of the French economists that a legal despotism, if it were practicable, would be the best form of government. That is, the uncontrolled authority of one man of the greatest wisdom and virtue would conduce better than all other political contrivances to the attainment of public felicity. But if we were able to find one such man in society, we should for the same reason be able to find a great many others. The diversities of human character, great as they are, cannot in the nature of things be pushed to such an extreme as to present us with one individual rising supremely in virtue and intelligence above all others. We might, therefore, with much more reason desire that a great number of the citizens possessed these endowments, for although the wish would be as unavailing in the one case as in the other, the object of both is equally possible, while the last would indicate a more exact and comprehensive notion of the ends of civil government.

One reason why the selections by the English chancellor are so good is because that officer is not lifted so high as to be insensible to the in-

1. [For the second edition, Grimke added new matter from the start of this paragraph to the paragraph which ends, ". . . constrained and disposed to consult their interests," on p. 156.]
2. [In law, a "puisne" judge is a judge of lesser rank, as an "associate" judge of the superior court.]

fluence of public opinion, and yet is so independent as to be able to
resist the aberrations to which public opinion is occasionally liable. In
a republic it is impossible to make such a disposition of the appointing power. The arrangement is an artificial and accidental one and
cannot be introduced in such a government without subverting its
foundation. It is not merely because the character of the chancellor depends upon that of the Prince and that of the Prince upon chance, nor
that the existence of such an officer would be a solecism in a republic;
it would frustrate one of the great ends in the formation of a commonwealth, which is to identify the administration of government with the
interests of the people, and so to discipline them by an actual experience of this connection that the appointing power may be freed, not
for a season but forever, from the caprice of an individual. It is not
uncommon in a monarchy to find the civil rights of the citizens well
guarded, although the political abuses are both flagrant and numerous.
An assiduous care for some of our interests frequently withdraws the
mind from hardships and grievances of greater magnitude.

How to constitute the appointing power is then a question of the
deepest interest in representative government. There are two ends
which we desire to attain: one, to make government an institution for
the common weal; the other, to render public opinion as nearly conformable as possible with the public reason, that is, to reflect what we
may suppose to be the most enlightened views with regard to the common interests. These two ends are not easily reconciled, for government cannot be made an institution for the common benefit unless the
people participate in it. Their exclusion and the confinement of the
political power to a comparatively small number will be followed, in
the first instance, by a careless regard to their interests, and will lead
by successive steps to a fixed design to build up an authority so independent as to be inaccessible to attack or observation. On the other
hand, if public opinion which sets government in motion is not a reasonable and well informed one, the interests of the community may be
sacrificed, whatever may be the share which the people may have in
the direction of public affairs. These are the difficulties of the problem.
We want government to be instituted and administered by the majority; and yet we want public opinion, which reflects the sentiments
of that majority, to be both vigilant and enlightened. If we say that the
people are unfit to exercise the appointing power directly, and confide
it to the executive, or the executive and senate, or the legislative

body, the dangers will be only apparently lessened, for all these magistrates are themselves elected by the people and will partake more or less of the same character.

Is there then any impossibility in the nature of things, any impossibility under all circumstances and conditions of society, in causing public opinion and the public reason to be in conformity with each other? 1st. There is a very perceptible tendency towards something of this sort even in communities which are not the best regulated. This arises from a principle of human nature and is not at all dependent upon the mechanism of government. The most uncultivated men form to themselves a standard of excellence which they cling to until that period of life when the passions are silenced and their conduct and actions become less dangerous to society. It is for this reason that society everywhere exhibits a principle of progress and never of retrogradation. 2d. This feeling is so spontaneous and so little under the command of the will that it disposes the bulk of the population to look up to and to defer to the opinions of the superior classes. The ideal which is floating in the minds of the uncultivated, although not realized in themselves, is able to find a visible representative in some other part of society. The operation of these principles, as they lie at the foundation of all human improvement, lie also at the foundation of all the institutions of government. Let anyone try, if he can, to worship ignorance and depravity; he will find it is impossible, even if he is himself ignorant and depraved. Let anyone in the most obscure walks of life inquire what has induced him by daily toil and labor to better his physical condition; he will find that there has been a constant though vague desire to get beyond the narrow circle in which his physical wants are enclosed, hence the strong desire, the homely pride of the uncultivated, to lift their offspring by education above their own level. 3d. Without pretending to assert that there is no condition of society in which the two difficulties I have mentioned cannot be reconciled, we may at least affirm that if there is a country in which knowledge and property are widely dispersed, in which consequently private and public interests are nearly identified and the selfish affections do not swallow up the man, the problem can hardly be considered as insoluble. For conditions of society which differ from each other cannot afford the same results; if they did, they would not be different but similar states of society. Spain and Portugal, Naples and Russia, exhibit a social organization entirely variant from that of the United States or

Great Britain. It is only by ruminating on the things in which they agree and leaving out those in which they differ that the judgment is confused. The institutions of the two last countries are obliged to be different in character from those of the first by a principle no stronger than that which links the effect to its cause.

In what way is public opinion formed? The groundwork is to be found in the principle I have already noticed: the standard of action which everyone, high and low, forms to himself, and which always rises higher than his own conduct. Hence it is not true that none but the enlightened contribute to the formation of public opinion. The uneducated have a share in it, for all the fundamental notions of morality are as strongly impressed upon them as upon the superior classes and the hereditary monarch is visibly influenced, though never directly governed, by the opinions which pervade his peasantry. But public opinion, when it comes to be applied to the affairs of an extensive, wealthy, and densely peopled community, becomes a very complicated organ, for although it reposes upon a few simple principles these become greatly diversified in a highly civilized state. In such a state, public opinion may be defined to be the judgment which is formed concerning the rights, duties, and interests of the population in relation to the government, of the government to the population, and of the citizens to one another. If there is great diversity in the condition of the various classes, those rights, duties and interests will be seen under very different aspects, and there cannot, properly speaking, be any such thing as a public opinion. The term public reason will be employed to denote that there is another tribunal of still higher authority, although it may reflect the sentiments of a comparatively small part of the population. If, on the other hand, knowledge and property are pretty equally distributed, public opinion will not diverge materially from what is denominated the public reason. The diffusion of property alone may have this effect. For what is the consequence of a diffusion of property? It is to produce habits of business, industry, judgment, and reflection in the management of property, and the very means by which private comfort is attained contribute to discipline the understandings of the great majority of the population.

Notwithstanding these views, the subject still seems to be full of difficulty. The beings we meet on the highway, the operatives, common laborers, and menial servants seem to be incapacitated by nature, or by circumstances as strong as nature, from forming any the most general notions of the end of government, even so far as their own interests are concerned. But these beings have since the foundation of the American commonwealth actually taken part in the election of the executive and of both branches of the legislatures. The American legislatures are all elected by universal suffrage or by a rule nearly equivalent to it. On entering these assemblies, an unpracticed eye will be startled with the boorishness and apparent ignorance of many of the members; a calm observer will see nothing inconsistent with a skillful and orderly management of the public business; and a well informed one will recollect that the composition of these bodies is infinitely better than was that of the provincial estates, or even of the states general of France, and better than that of the English Parliament before the commencement of the eighteenth century. That there are great differences in the capacities of the members who compose the American legislatures is certain. How, then, is business conducted with regularity? How are laws passed to meet the complicated exigencies of such wealthy and populous communities? That they are so framed is a matter of notoriety. For if we examine the codes of those states, whether criminal, civil, or political, we will find that they make a more wise, exact, and judicious provision for the wants of all classes than is to be found anywhere else. If these codes were imitations of those of older nations, the difficulty would not be removed; for great skill would be requisite in making the proper selection. But when it is considered that there are great departures from any existing code, and that these are every year becoming wider, that experience is the foundation on which these laws are built, the difficulty is increased. He who can collect experience into a body and decipher its true meaning is the wisest man. If we admit, then, that a considerable proportion of those who compose these legislatures are incompetent to frame the laws, would it be an extraordinary circumstance that the smaller number who are able should execute the task? Does anyone at all acquainted with human nature expect to find a legislative body, however constituted, materially varying from this description? It is the character of both the English chambers, the Lords and Commons; that is, it is the character of those very bodies which might seem worthy of imitation, if the elective principle which prevails in a republic was abandoned. Not one fourth of the English Peers, or Commons, is able to grapple with the perplexing questions of foreign or internal policy which are submitted to them.

It appears, then, that there is a principle of human nature by which, when a number of persons are assembled to transact any important business, the task will be voluntarily yielded to those who have most skill and ability, although it will by no means follow that the presence of those who are deficient in these qualities can be dispensed with.

The application of these views to the electors, the class who choose the public officers, is obvious. The same result will take place as in a legislative body. Those who are incapable of forming a clear estimate of the part they are called upon to perform will be counselled and controlled by those of more intelligence, although it must not be inferred that the privilege should be confined to the last. Parents advise and guide their children, but the conduct of the parent as well as of the child is better on that very account. It is true, the electors are not collected into one body like a legislative assembly, and cannot act so directly upon one another. But they are parcelled into families, neighborhoods, and townships, and this presents the same or even a more advantageous mode of communication. Admitting, then, that among the common people the proportion of those who are capable of voting understandingly is only one to ten, that one will exert a marked influence. And how is it with the superior ranks: the proportion is not greater for, if an humble condition of life rears rough and ignorant men, wealth rears feeble and effeminate ones. Thus the majority in each class is powerfully acted upon by a small number. That the superior knowledge of the few will sometimes be turned to sinister purposes is certain, but this is a vice common to both classes and does not interfere with the views I have taken.

If the structure of society is such as to permit the establishment of representative government, no reason absolutely satisfactory can be assigned why some public officers should be elected by direct suffrage while others are chosen by a close body. If the principle of responsibility is the hinge on which republican government turns, it does not appear clear why a thorough application should be made of it in some instances, and an imperfect one in others. If the judges should be elected by a pre-existing body, it would not seem improper that the executive and legislative should be elected in the same way.

It is curious to trace the changes which have taken place in the appointing power in the United States. At first it was conferred upon the governor alone, as it is at the present day in Delaware. The next step was to vest it in the governor and council, and a third was to entrust it to the governor and senate. The taking the power from the governor was the commencement of a very important revolution. It broke the connection between him and the various civil officers of the state. It discarded the idea that the appointing power was an attribute of the executive magistrate. The transition was gradual; a council was created who divided the power with the executive. As the council was created for this express purpose, it may be said to have produced a new organization of the executive authority, and not merely a new disposition of the appointing power. The effect was to create a plural executive. In process of time, the power underwent a further change; it was distributed among a greater number, and this was important, as it gradually paved the way for more decisive changes which the structure of society rendered necessary. The next step accordingly was to confer the power upon the governor and senate. This was a more decisive change, for it divided the power between the governor and one branch of the legislature. It repudiated the maxim that the power was an attribute of the executive, whether the executive is a singular or a plural body. The reason of the change is to be found in the fact that in America after the revolution written constitutions were adopted. Writing teaches men to analyze their ideas, and causes their speculative opinions to correspond more exactly with the results of experience. By no device could the authority of the governor of a state whose institutions were democratic be made to resemble that of an hereditary magistrate. The legislature became at once the most important and imposing of the three departments. The power of appointment was not in the first instance devolved upon the whole body, but only upon one branch. The successive steps were not a departure from this design, but in furtherance of it, and prepared the way for its final accomplishment. But who can teach us how to create a governor and senate which shall be a thoroughly upright and impartial appointing power. Whether composed of illiterate or educated men, it would be subject to the vice of intrigue. The only approach to such an institution would be a body so permanent, and composed of members so affluent, as to render them inaccessible to the solicitations of unworthy candidates. But it would be only an approach, for no sooner was the system set in motion than the body would degenerate into an aristocratic cabal; an interest separate from that of the community would grow up, and offices would be disposed of by a system of favoritism. Representatives will act more circumspect than their constituents only when the trust confided to them does not present a powerful conflict between private and public interest. Do what we will, we cannot raise men so high by wealth or station as to render them wise and virtuous, but we may easily render them the reverse.

The third step which was taken was to devolve the power upon the entire legislature. This completed the design which we may suppose to have been originally contemplated, which was to despoil the executive, not in part, but in whole of the attribute. The various civil magistrates then ceased to be his agents and henceforward held by a tenure as independent as his own. But the system, although relieved of one inconsistency, fell into another equally glaring. If the appointing power is not an appropriate part of the executive authority, it is as little so of the legislative. By wresting the power from the governor and lodging it successively with bodies more and more numerous, the selections were apparently at least of a more popular character, and an approach was made to that plan to which everything was irresistibly tending, to wit, a direct appointment by the people.

The chief objection to all the plans which preceded is that they deprive us of the most effectual means of training the popular mind to self-government. Experience, personal experience of the importance of correct appointments, of the connection between them and the public weal, is indispensable to fulfil not in theory merely, but in practice, the design of representative government. We desire to have a disinterested and upright impartial appointing power. To procure that is to procure everything. And we immediately set about devising a scheme for excluding the bulk of the population; in other words, we exclude those for whom government is made. In some conditions of society this may be necessary; in others, the gradual transition from an appointment by a close body to a larger number may facilitate the final transference of the power to the people themselves. But it is supposed that it is impossible to get beyond one or two stages in this transition. The impossibility arises from perseverance in the plan of close appointment. By adhering to it inflexibly, we decree that it cannot be otherwise; we deprive ourselves of the only means of getting out of it. All knowledge is gained by experience; even that of a strictly speculative character is confusedly apprehended, unless we apply our own faculties to the subjects we undertake to deal with. In the affairs of government the proposition is true without any limitation. If the citizens have not a direct voice in the appointment of the public agents, they form a very inadequate notion of the purpose which those agents are intended to answer. They hear that certain functionaries are necessary in order to administer public affairs and they believe it, only because they are told so. They conceive government to be a species of self-moving machine, and although they are told that it is established to preside over their interests they apprehend this only in a vague and general way. Appointments are made, but as they are not made by themselves they conceive that they have only an accidental connection with their interests, and that they have no control over that connection. Thus admitting that popular appointments are practicable, they cannot be made so unless the power is brought into exercise. The danger of acting precipitately is not so great as is imagined. In a state habituated to free institutions, it is very slight. It might be otherwise in one which did not possess this advantage. In the former, experience would afford the rule; in the last, the rule would be the subject of conjecture. An enlightened ruler of one of the German principalities visited the United States about 1825 and was so struck with the reasonableness and good sense of confiding to the people the choice of those who make the laws, that he introduced an elective assembly into his dominions.[3] His people protested that they were incompetent to the task. He persevered, however, well understanding no doubt that the difficulties and exigencies of human life are the true school of human conduct. In the United States, where a great fund of experience has been acquired, I would, if necessary, force the appointment of the judges upon the people. I may have misgivings, but they are no greater than I have for the result of any human contrivance which has not been tested by actual experiment.

It appears that in the United States, the plan of electing the judges by a close body was retained long after it had been abandoned in the election of the executive and administrative officers. There must be a reason for this. Jurists are accustomed to distinguish between the question of fact and the question of right. An understanding of the first may shed light upon the last. In the American provinces, there was no order of nobility with which to compose a senate; there were no materials for creating an hereditary executive. The country, therefore, very naturally slid after no long time into a popular election of both. But the judges had always held for life, and this circumstance with-

3. [Karl Bernhard, Duke of Saxe-Weimar-Eisenach (1792–1862), *Travels Through North America, during the years 1825 and 1826* . . . (Philadelphia, 1826).]

drew them from the operation of the rule. The tenure for life had never been combined with a popular choice. The notion of responsibility is so closely connected with that of popular election that the moment the last is introduced it is united with a tenure for a term of years. The irregularity in the system continued in consequence of the extreme difficulty of overcoming the prejudice that the tenure of the judges must be for life. The governors had been generally appointed by the king, but there was now no king, and the senate had never been an hereditary body. Both chambers of the legislature, therefore, were elected by the people. The governor was with some exceptions elected in the same manner; not universally, because a vague notion still lingered in some of the states that a distinction must be made between his election and that of the legislative body.

His appointment had originally been different, and this circumstance contributed to keep alive the distinction. At present there is but one state in which he is chosen by the legislature.

I have alluded to the remark of a very eminent statesman (Lord Brougham) that the appointments to the bench in England were unexceptionable. But the same statesman, in his celebrated speech on the reformation of the law, declares that "it is notorious, whenever a question comes before the tribunals, upon a prosecution for libel, or any other political matter, the counsel at their meeting take for granted, that they can tell pretty accurately the leaning of the court, and predict exactly which way the consultation of the judges will terminate." [4] I doubt whether a like character can be given of the administration of justice in the higher tribunals of the United States, in those whose jurisdiction resembles that of the king's bench and common pleas. And I am persuaded that where this habitual bias exists, it must more or less affect the decision of those civil controversies in which the parties are of different political opinions. The same very able statesman speaks of "the incompetent judges" and "the slovenly administration of justice," as these are spoken of in the United States, in reference to some of the judges of the subordinate courts. In England, until 1809, no judge could hold court in the county in which he resided. In the United States, where no such prohibition ever existed, the judges often voluntarily decline sitting in their own county lest an unfavorable influence might be exercised upon them. The "black

4. [On February 7, 1828, Henry Peter Brougham brought before Parliament a detailed plan for the reformation of the law in a speech of six hours' length.]

book" confirms the observations of Lord Brougham.[5] It informs us that a Tory ministry never selects a judge from the Whig party, nor a Whig ministry one from the Tory party. This, the author remarks, "tends to lower the character of the judges in public estimation, by clearly evincing that politics, as well as legal fitness, have a share in ministerial promotion. It also instils into the minds of expectant judges, and of men already on the bench, a party feeling, fatal to strict justice, on political questions." An election for a limited time diminishes the temptation to run into the excesses of party. The prize is not of sufficient magnitude to overcome the natural sentiments of justice which, in order to have full play, only require that there should be no powerful provocative to depart from them. The judge elected for a term of years balances in his mind the uncertain advantage of retaining his place against the permanent advantage of maintaining his character. It does not follow that he will be re-elected, even if his party should continue in power. The principle of rotation in office never fails to exercise great influence in a democratic community and it reduces the tenure of office to a mere contingency. If the public officers were appointed for life, the prejudices which they originally contracted would cling to them without any countervailing motives to moderate them. Thus an election by the people, a tenure for a term of years, and rotation in office, which might be supposed to push the democratic principle to its furthest extreme, are the most efficacious means for restraining its disorders and for giving to public opinion a more just, active, and pervading influence. The legal ability which fits a man for the bench is very capable of being estimated by the generality of mankind. The capacity of the physician is much more a secret, and yet no one, in any condition of life, is at a loss to employ one eminent in that profession. Many may be unable to pay the best. But who the best are is a matter of notoriety in every town or neighborhood in which they reside. And for more obvious reasons this is the case of the lawyer.

As the connection between the interests of the great bulk of the population and the behaviour of all public officers is very close, it would be a grand desideratum to establish a thorough intercourse between candidates and constituents. Men of elevated character now recoil from anything which might seem to have the appearance of

5. [*The Black Book* (1820), an attack by English Radicals on the abuses of the unreformed House of Commons; there were many editions and the name became a generic name for exposures of the corruption of government.]

soliciting for office. But I observe in some parts of the country a corresponding disposition on the part of the people, an aversion to be caressed and tampered with by the demagogue. "I do not know (said a mechanic in one of our Southern cities) what these candidates proposed to themselves in paying such assiduous court to us the people. It will not deter us from exercising our judgment, but it may deprive them of our vote." I predict that the reaction of public men on the one hand and of popular sentiment on the other will give rise to a more healthful public opinion than formerly existed, and that the intercourse of the two classes will be of a more rational character. This would complete the security for the preservation of free institutions.

We may refer to an example which has only a partial application to the United States, but which is not the less instructive on that account. The remarkable solidity of the Venetian government, enduring as it did for a thousand years, is attributable to a circumstance which was peculiar to it among the other Italian states. The Venetian nobles engrossed the whole power, but they had no possessions on the mainland, no castles and strong fortresses in the country. They were shut up in a city built upon islands, in close contact, therefore, and under the constant observation of the other classes. They were unable to keep on foot large armies, to wreak their vengeance on each other, or to battle with the plebeians, as the nobles of Milan, Genoa, and Florence were accustomed to do. The disadvantage of their position led them to cultivate the good will of the plebeians who were accordingly governed with more equity and moderation than in any other Italian state. Very similar causes, although operating on a vast and comprehensive scale, give stability to the American republics. There is no political aristocracy, no baronies, no military retainers; the civil aristocracy are mixed indiscriminately, or, to repeat the expression, are shut up with the other classes, and are both constrained and disposed to consult their interests.

A property qualification for office has been retained in some of the American states even where it has been abolished in regard to the electors. In the Athenian constitution this species of qualification was at one period dispensed with, except where the office involved a pecuniary responsibility. In the United States, the rule is reversed. Property qualification is in some states required to entitle to a seat in the legislative body when it is not demanded of the administrative officers. But in the place of that qualification, another requisite, much more effectual, is substituted. The officer must give security for his fidelity in office. This reconciles the claims of the rich and the poor, and at the same time attracts to the public service the talents and industry of all orders of men.

In England, knights of the shire originally represented the counties in the House of Commons. They were the lesser barons, in other words, an inferior order of nobility. And although this chamber is no longer modeled upon that plan, a property qualification is still required of candidates. But by the act of 1838 this may be either of personal or real property.

It is a great objection to a high property qualification that it confines the competition for office to the rich exclusively. The rich only can afford to practice bribery, and hence the English elections have been corrupt to a degree utterly unknown in the United States. Thus, this remarkable consequence, and one not at all calculated upon, has taken place: that in those countries where the eligibility to office as well as the electoral franchise have been most restricted, the greatest corruption and licentiousness have prevailed; and where both have been thrown open to nearly the whole population the elections are the most orderly and the most free from sinister influence. The rich will forever put forth the lower qualities of human nature, unless they are controlled by those who are placed in circumstances of less temptation. A rich man going to attend an election where none but rich men can elect or be elected is like the twenty thousand nobles who used to march upon Warsaw to choose a chief magistrate. The extreme variety which characterizes the pursuits of the Americans, the diffusion of education, the unobstructed intercourse of all classes and, above all, the operation of the institutions themselves disperse knowledge in every direction and render the property qualification useless.

The duration of the term of office is a matter of still graver consideration. It is indispensable to the faithful administration of the government that responsibility should be a vital and active principle, not a mere form. And the only way to accomplish this is by guarding against a too permanent tenure of office. Those are the wisest institutions which render it the interest of the officer to consult the public good. A system which succeeds in reconciling these two apparently contradictory things is well calculated to beget habits of rectitude and good conduct which a mere conviction of the propriety of such habits would be insufficient to instill. And it then becomes as difficult to lay down these habits as it was originally to take them up. Doubtless there is an intrinsic connection between morality and self-interest. All the seeming exceptions to this rule arise either from some disturbing influence to the conduct of the individual who is called upon to act, and to which he is not a party, or else they arise from self-interest not being properly understood. That scheme of government, therefore, which endeavors as well as it can to combine duty with interest conforms best to the original design of our nature, and tends greatly to the preservation of public morality.

It may be supposed if the duration of office is short that it will lead to instability in the public councils. But there is such a thing as too great stability as well as too great instability in government. This may seem to be a paradox and therefore requires explanation. A government, in order to pursue any plan of public policy with constancy and vigor, must be invested with power. But power is of two kinds, personal and political, and the last may be raised to so high a degree as to be transformed into the former, to become, in other words, a mere personal authority in the chief of the state. Nevertheless all public measures will be characterized by the greatest stability and uniformity. There is more simplicity in the management of public affairs, fewer cross purposes to overcome, where government is at liberty to consult its own separate interests, than where it is employed in administering the vast and complicated interests of a free and intelligent people. In one sense the governments of Russia, Prussia, and Austria possess this property of stability in a pre-eminent degree. The monarchs of these countries wield an independent authority. No obstacle stands in the way of their designs so long as they keep within tolerably reasonable bounds. There is a singleness of plan, an unity of purpose, belonging to such governments which cannot in the nature of things be possessed by one into which the popular element is infused. Thus in Great Britain, where the political power of the community is shared to a considerable extent by representatives of the people, public measures vary more than they do in the governments of eastern Europe. And yet, in another and still higher sense of the word, the government of Great Britain does undoubtedly possess more stability than any European government of ancient or modern times. The stability of power and the stability of the government are, therefore, by no means the same thing. The changes of administration and the changes of public men in Great Britain and the United States are more frequent than anywhere else, and yet the institutions possess greater stability than do those of any other country and they possess it in consequence of and not in spite of these changes.

The enjoyment of an independent authority by public rulers has been the principle incentive to all the criminal enterprises which have ever afflicted society. From time immemorial, power has been firmly secured in the kings and nobility who have ruled the European states, and the consequence is that from the Christian era down to the peace of 1815 Europe was the theater of the most atrocious and sanguinary wars. Since this last period, the popular power, the real effective public opinion in Great Britain, has at least doubled. The public weal has therefore greater firmness and consistency, notwithstanding the changes of administration have been more frequent than before. If the President of the United States and the members of the Senate were hereditary officers and the House of Representatives elected for a long term, it is more than probable that America would have embarked in frequent wars, when experience has demonstrated that the prosperity of the country demands that peace should be its permanent policy. And the vigor with which warlike enterprises would have been prosecuted would have impressed upon the government precisely that character of stability which is so much admired by unthinking individuals. A system which was even productive of considerable instability in the ordinary measures of government would be greatly preferable to this. It would protect the state from infinitely worse mischiefs. The Americans, like most people who enjoy an uncommon share of prosperity, frequently complain of the fluctuation in the public measures. They complain because they are not able to grasp all the minor as well as the more important advantages of fortune.

The compensation afforded to the public officers should be sufficient to insure competent ability, and should not go beyond this. High salaries create a separate interest in the office, independent of the interests of the people. On the other hand, low salaries render officers careless in the discharge of their duties, and the people themselves become gradually reconciled to a feeble and bungling administration of the laws when they know that the reproach lies at their own door. The legislator therefore must have sufficient judgment to strike a mean between the two things. Moderate salaries are one means of enforcing responsibility. And as this is the hinge on which free institutions turn, it is fit that we should avail ourselves of every device which is calculated to give strength to it. Moreover, moderate salaries enlist in the service of the state the abilities of persons in the middle walks of life. As the rich can best afford to dispense with a high reward, it might be supposed that this plan would cause them to be the principal candidates for office. But such is not the case. Moderate salaries chill and enfeeble their ambition; they do not gratify the ardent and impatient desires of the rich. But they contribute to raise solid usefulness from obscurity, and the officer who obtains an important post finds himself disabled in every effort he makes to leap beyond the bounds of his legitimate authority. In the United States far the greater part of all public employments are filled by men in moderate circumstances.

The number, as well as the nature, of the public offices in a republic will depend upon the fact whether it constitutes one aggregate community or has the form of a confederate government. I say the form, because in every extensive and populous state it would be of the highest advantage to imitate the plan of domestic or local jurisdictions, even though the government is not composed of states which were originally distinct and independent.

A territorial division of the state of some sort is an arrangement known to every civilized nation. Even the most centralized government cannot dispense with it since it is the only way by which the public authority can be present everywhere at the same time. The principle on which the division was originally founded was very different from what it is now. Most of the European states were at one time divided into feudal baronies. These inferior governments have long since disappeared. They are now merged into consolidated governments. But other divisions have been substituted in their place, whether known as departments, circles, or shires. These districts sometimes occupy the same ground which was once marked out as the domain of a feudal sovereignty. Accident has determined their extent but not their use. When the authority of the central government was feeble, these inferior jurisdictions usurped nearly all power. Now that that authority is strong, they serve to convey it through all parts of the country.

But the principle on which this division depends is very different in different countries, even at the present day. In some the power which is set in motion in these smaller compartments flows from the central government as its source. In others the central authority is itself the creature of the lesser governments, and these continue, after the establishment of the former, to exercise a larger share of the power which originally belonged to them. The United States afford the most perfect example of this plan. Accidental circumstances gave rise to it. The states were independent sovereignties when the federal constitution was formed, so that this precise arrangement cannot be adopted where all the parts of society are melted into one homogeneous community. But there is no more interesting problem in government than to determine how far it is practicable to introduce the principle of the plan into all communities, no matter whether they have the confederate form or not. Not merely because this arrangement leads to a more convenient and efficient administration of public affairs, but because it is doubtful whether the maintenance of free institutions in any state of considerable extent does not absolutely depend upon it. The establishment of local jurisdictions gives a new direction to the whole course of legislation. Civil government is only a generalization of the principles on which the affairs of society are conducted. But generalization may be pushed to such an extent as to make us lose sight of very important interests which, although they are themselves capable of generalization, are yet incapable of being ranged under the same class. By effecting a separation of those interests which are common to the whole society from those which are local or sectional, these last are brought distinctly into view — they are forced upon the public attention.

In most countries legislators have occupied themselves exclusively with those large and ponderous questions which further the aggrandizement of the nation rather than its solid prosperity. Even the Emperor Charlemagne was impressed with this fact, and gave vent to the frank declaration that it was impossible for one central government to superintend the affairs of an extensive community. Princes are forward enough to tell the truth when they are not placed in a situation which obliges them to act upon it. But what was true during so early a period as the ninth century when society was everywhere in a rude condition must be still more true in the nineteenth century. For the affairs of every civilized state have become so complicated and so minute that they cannot be administered with the requisite skill and ability by a central legislature merely. Convenience alone would suggest the propriety of a territorial division and the creation of domestic jurisdictions, if not as extensive as those of Scotland and Ireland before their union with England, yet much more so than the departments of France.

But what at first may be a rule of convenience leads directly to consequences of still greater importance. It lays the foundation of the great principle of the distribution of power and reconciles two apparently opposite qualities — popular freedom with vigor and efficiency in the government. No matter how popular the mode of electing the public officers is, yet if in the United States there were no domestic jurisdictions to preside over the local interests the government would be republican in form only.

I know nothing which is more calculated to arrest the attention of the philosophical inquirer as well as of the lover of freedom than the new character which has been impressed upon the business of legislation in the United States. The state governments are confined exclusively to the care of the local interests, and this complete sequestration of those interests from everything which appertains to the national administration causes them to be more thoroughly studied and appreciated than could otherwise possibly be the case. There is no security that legislation will be for the people unless it is by and through the people. Nor any security that it will be by and through the people unless the subjects of legislation are brought so near as to be matter of immediate interest and constant observation.

The legislatures of the American states have applied themselves more diligently and effectively to the care of the substantial interests of the people than it has been in the power of a single legislature in any other country to do. If there is ground of complaint, it is in consequence of the excess of legislation. But it is impossible to have enough of any good thing without having a superfluity. Experience, which becomes a great instructor wherever the system of representation is thoroughly introduced, will assuredly correct this defect.

We will suppose that, on an average, one month will be sufficient for the legislative sessions of the states and that five months will be consumed by the national legislature. Thirty-four months then are required in order to legislate advantageously for the national and domestic interests, a period nearly three times the length of the year. In Great Britain, with a population considerably larger than that of the United States, Parliament sits on an average only six months. If we make a further allowance for the unnecessary consumption of time by the American legislature and for the fact that the United States is in a state of greater progress than any other country, it is still evident that the time employed by the British legislature is altogether too short to permit of an effective administration of the public interests in the sense in which the term is now understood. If the country were more extensive, and the population greater, six months would still seem sufficient. Necessity would compress the immense mass of public business into that short space, and the public mind would become habituated to it as the natural and reasonable period. The defect arises from having a single legislature to preside over the interests of twenty-seven millions of people. Nor will the defect ever be apparent so long as the system continues to exist. The human mind possesses a wonderful ductility in accommodating itself to any set of habits which have been fastened upon it. Thirty years ago the American people were thoroughly persuaded that they got along well enough without canals and without the employment of steam by land or water. And it was with the greatest reluctance that they embarked in the plan of internal improvements. The first project of a canal, on an extensive scale, was literally carried through the legislature by storm amid the most virulent and formidable opposition. And it is not improbable if the position in which the American states were placed after the Revolution had not given rise to the confederate form of government that the public would have been completely reconciled to the establishment of a single legislature where thirty now exist.

There is nothing peculiar to America rendering so much more time necessary to the successful administration of the public business than in any other highly civilized community, unless it is the single circumstance of its free institutions. For although society is in a state of progression, yet it is so only in consequence of these institutions. There is no country which contains more wealth, a more thorough civilization, and more general intelligence. It is then in the condition of one of the oldest, instead of one of the newest, nations on the earth. And it may be said with great truth that there is more room for progress and improvement in every state of continental Europe, if there were only the ability and opportunity to set it in motion. In Russia and Denmark the legislative body is nothing more than a council nominated by the king. No doubt these councils seem to transact all the requisite business, and the machinery of government goes on regularly from year to year without any great feeling of inconvenience. Nevertheless the disproportion, in point of efficiency, between those mock legislative bodies and the British Parliament is nearly as great as between the last and the combined legislatures of the United States.

There may be an inconsistency in erecting a government for one aggregate community and then morseling the public authority by distributing it among a number of lesser governments. There is no inconsistency, however, if the plan is the result of the natural economy of society. The principle on which it is founded may be discerned everywhere, even in those governments where it is intended that the national power should be the most firmly consolidated. The departments of France, the corporate cities of Great Britain, are in reality lesser governments enclosed within a supreme government. And the only question is whether the principle may not be advantageously pursued much further wherever constitutional government exists, without reference to the fact whether the state is one or is composed of distinct members.

A people who constitute an undivided community would possess this advantage over the plan adopted in the United States: that the creation of domestic jurisdictions, being the act of the whole instead of the parts, there would be less danger that they would exercise a disturbing influence upon the central authority. One is so much accustomed to consider the American government as a system "sui generis," as deriving its meaning and utility from the originally independent existence of the parts, that it is supposed no system bearing an analogy to it is practicable in any other community. The mind is so habituated to consider cause and effect in the precise order in which they first presented themselves that it becomes difficult to break through the association and to make application of our experience where the principle is the same and the collateral circumstances only are different.

It is plain enough that the independent character of the states could not be preserved if they had not power to superintend the domestic interests. But these interests do not acquire the character of domestic ones in consequence of the federal form of the government. The same reasons for regarding them in that light would have existed if no such government had been created. In other words, if the American commonwealth had originally constituted one homogeneous community the central authority would have been entirely inadequate to the management of them, unless powers not exactly the same but resembling those which now exist were distributed among a set of local jurisdictions. The effect of the progress of civilization is not to diminish but to increase immeasurably the whole business of society; and unless this is skillfully and judiciously divided among a class of lesser governments, the institutions, however carefully modelled at first, must ultimately sink beneath the immense power condensed in a single government. The example then which America holds out is chiefly valuable not because it proves the utility of the confederate form of government, but because it teaches us that in order to maintain free institutions in their true spirit it is necessary to make an extensive distribution of the powers of society, and that without any regard to the circumstances which give rise to the formation of the government. It presents a great problem in political philosophy and not merely an incidental question in the history of one particular set of institutions.

Even in the consolidated government of France, long after the extinction of its feudal sovereignties, as late indeed as the reign of Louis XV, a plan in many respects resembling the American once prevailed. The provincial legislatures, or particular estates as they were called to distinguish them from the general estates, or national congress, possessed very considerable local powers. Independently of the inferior civilization of France when compared with that of the United States at the period when this system existed, and which necessarily prevented it from working anything like as well, there were several vices attendant upon it. It is only necessary to refer to two: 1st. The very imperfect responsibility of the deputies to those provincial legislatures to their constituents. 2d. The power which they acquired after the abolition of the States General, if indeed they did not exercise it before, of granting supplies for the whole kingdom and not merely such as were necessary to defray the expenses of the provincial governments.

The same plan of local governments existed in the ten Flemish provinces when they were a part of the Austrian empire; and it is even more firmly established in both the Dutch and Belgian monarchies, notwithstanding the limited territory of each of them. That the system in these two last instances does not perform its movements with anything like the same precision as in the United States is not the fault of the system, but arises from a defective basis of representation and from the imperfect responsibility of the provincial officers to the local population.

There is no foundation for the opinion that the existence of these domestic jurisdictions weakens the force of the central authority. On the contrary, this last is less embarrassed in the administration of the national interests. That the formation of a system of lesser governments constitutes a deduction from the whole mass of powers which would otherwise be deposited with the central government is evident. For that is precisely the purpose for which they are created. But as the sphere within which the former move is distinctly defined and the duties allotted to it are more simple than before, it is enabled to act with more promptitude and energy. Like the man who is intent on accomplishing some important design and whose attention is distracted by a variety of other pursuits, by ridding himself of all care for the last, he can prosecute the former without interruption.

A central government, armed with extensive powers, stands much more in need of checks than of provocatives to the exercise of its authority. And if the establishment of local jurisdictions gives greater force to public opinion and raises up obstacles to the exertion of too much power, it is not the less valuable on that account. I have heard many persons express admiration of the wonderful energy with which the British government prosecuted the wars which grew out of the French Revolution. But if the expense had been defrayed by taxes and loans not resorted to, the people would have seen that their substantial interests were placed in direct opposition to the enterprises of the government. It was only because this fact was hidden from their view that those wars were sustained with such amazing enthusiasm. The just fear of unpopularity would have prevented public men from embarking in such an unnecessary contest. And although this fear would have been regarded by some persons of very high notions as crippling the power of the government, yet it would only have crippled it in order to make the people strong. The same obstacle has constantly existed to the prosecution of similar enterprises by the American government, and the simple effect has been to accelerate the national power and prosperity to a degree absolutely unprecedented. And yet in a necessary war there is no government which would be supported with so much enthusiasm and would put forth so much power as that of the United States. But more than ninety-nine out of a hundred of the wars which have ever taken place have been unjust and unprofitable wars. And if the machinery of a system of local governments contributes indirectly to diffuse the popular will through every part of the country and disarms the central government of the power to do mischief, it is not the less deserving of our admiration on that account.

But there is another view of the great advantages of that system which is not apt to be thought of: the maintenance of the public authority at home — the inculcating a general obedience to the laws is the principal object — the final aim indeed — of civil government. If that is attained, everything else will go right. But the system of local governments contributes directly to the promotion of this end. It brings the authority of the laws nearer to everyone. The government which undertakes to preserve order is not removed to a great distance — is not regarded with an unfriendly eye — as if it were constantly intermeddling with the interests of a people with whom it had no direct sympathy. On the contrary, each individual feels as if he were surrounded by an authority, in the creation of which he himself bore a part and which yet, somehow or other, is more vigilant and active and imperative than any other.

Thus, as the family and the school train men in order to turn them out in the world afterward, so the domestic governments create a species of moral discipline on a still more extended scale. They educate their own people to obedience to the laws and then deliver them over to the national government. The authority of the last, instead of being weakened, is redoubled by this preparatory discipline.

Another advantage of the plan of local governments is that it prevents geographical parties from exerting an inordinate influence in the national councils. These parties will inevitably make their appearance in every country of considerable extent. It is not desirable to extinguish them, but only to place them at a distance where their reasonings will be heard and their passions not felt. By creating local jurisdictions, geographical parties are enclosed within geographical limits and are not brought into eternal collision at the heart of the government. Although such parties are actually found on the floor of the American Congress, yet if the state governments did not exist they would have displayed a front infinitely more formidable and would have either jeopardized the integrity of the union or the existence of free institutions. At present a vast amount of legislative power is withdrawn from the national assembly and circumscribed within bounds so clearly defined as to be not only harmless, but to produce a skillful and orderly administration of the public interests. Although Great Britain is of very small extent when compared with the United States, yet if, when the Scotch union took place, a compact had not been formed securing to Scotland its ecclesiastical and civil institutions forever, geographical parties would instantly have appeared and would have had an influence fatal to the public prosperity. Although the separate legislature of Scotland was abolished, the effect of the union was to declare all its former acts to be permanent and thus to compel all future legislation to take a direction conformable to them. It was the next thing to perpetuating the existence of the Scotch parliament. For want of this wise precaution, when the union with Ireland * took place, a formidable geographical party has been kept alive in that island, to the great annoyance of the peace of both countries, and producing heart burnings which never can be cured until England consents, or is compelled, to be just to Ireland.

What amount of power should be deposited with the local jurisdictions, where the confederate form of government is not established, is a question as novel as it is interesting. Doubtless, it would be necessary to adopt some medium between the comprehensive legislation of the American states and the meager authority which is exercised by the French departments. The American states are complete governments within themselves, having unlimited power of taxation, except as to imposts on commerce, with an authority equally extensive over the whole field of civil and criminal jurisprudence. Education, private and public corporations, internal improvements, all lie within the scope of their jursidiction. They have a written constitution, a regular legislative assembly, an executive magistrate, and a corps of administrative officers, together with a judicial system unsurpassed by that of any other country. No one would desire to make any alteration in this admirable plan of government, for it has not only contributed to a most wise administration of public affairs, it has done more: it has hastened the march of civilization. If it were impossible in the case of a consolidated republic to obtain the medium I have suggested, it would be better to adopt this system. But that there is such a medium

* The articles of union between England and Ireland did, *in terms*, guarantee to the last her laws. But there were in truth no Irish laws to guarantee. As early as the reign of Henry VII, all the statutes made in England were declared of force in Ireland, and from that period to 1782 no subsequent law could even be proposed to the Irish Parliament without the consent of the English Privy Council. This last disability was removed only eighteen years before the union. [Note added to the second edition.]

is clear from the examples I have referred to of the particular estates of France and the provincial legislatures in the Belgian and Dutch governments; examples which, however imperfect, are nevertheless highly instructive inasmuch as they present the existence of the system in monarchical governments to which they are much less adapted than to countries where free institutions prevail. It is clear, also, from the various plans which were proposed in the convention which framed the American constitution, some of which seem to have proceeded upon the idea that the United States composed one aggregate community and were modeled upon the hypothesis.

A certain number of deputies then will be sent to the national and to each of the local legislatures. As regards the first, shall the whole country constitute one electoral district, or shall each of the local divisions compose one, the people voting by general ticket; or shall these divisions be subdivided into districts, each containing the population which entitles it to one member? The first plan may be dismissed as absurd. It has never been thought of, even in those European monarchies where the principle of representation has been introduced. The electors would be completely confounded in looking over a vast extent of country for several hundred individuals whom each was to vote for, and no choice could be understandingly made. The central government, or its managers, would choose for them.

But even if a selection in the genuine sense could be made, there would be no representation of the minority. The party in the majority would wield the power of the commonwealth without control, without the corrective influence which an antagonist party is so well calculated to exert. The minority might approach to within one or two hundred of the majority, among two or three millions of votes, yet the last would elect every member. Even in the consolidated governments of Great Britain and France, therefore, the country is divided into electoral districts, which is a plain acknowledgment that even where there are no local governments there should be local representatives. The justice and utility of recognizing in some mode or other the local interests is forced upon society even where the form of government seems to forbid the idea. The arrangement which nature makes of human affairs sometimes rides over all the laws which are intended to counteract it.

With regard to the two other modes of election, by general ticket in each of the great local divisions, or by electoral districts carved out of those divisions, the reasoning which has already been employed is equally applicable to show that the latter is greatly to be preferred, whether the elections are to the national or the local legislatures.

In England, as before remarked, knights of the shire were originally the representatives from the counties. The shires were local divisions of the kingdom, and the knights of each shire deputed one of their own number to Parliament. The continuance of these Parliamentary districts has survived the artificial state of society from which it sprung and contributes in an eminent degree to the freedom and independence of the legislative body. It is this mode of election which has given rise to the question so often agitated: is the member elected the representative of the whole state, or of the district which chooses him? Which is in some respects similar to another question which might be put: whether man is an individual or a member of society. The answer would be nearly the same in the two cases. Man is both an individual and a citizen; and the deputy is a representative of his district and at the same time of his whole country. And as that system of private conduct which most effectually consults the welfare of the individual conduces most to the prosperity of the community, so that system of public conduct which most truly advances the interests of one part of the country is certain to redound to the advantage of the whole. But inasmuch as men do not always see things as they really are, as ignorance, prejudice, and egotism lead them so much astray in whatever regards the public interests, the system of domestic government is contrived in order to prevent the interference of sectional with the national interests. And thus the question, is the deputy the representative of his district or of the country, is of infinitely rarer occurrence in the United States than it would be if the population composed one aggregate community. Election by districts mitigates the rigor of the rule that the majority are entitled to govern. It draws the bond of responsibility closer and it breaks the force of party spirit. The first has been sufficiently explained.

Where local legislatures are created, the effect is that the national interests are not represented in them, nor are the local interests represented in the national assembly. This is the general tendency of the plan, though as the boundary between the two jurisdictions cannot be drawn with exact precision exceptions will necessarily occur. The responsibility of the deputy to the local legislature will be stronger because, if his constituents are local, so also are the interests which he represents. The responsibility of the deputy who is sent to the national legislature will be more complete: because, although his constituents are local, the interests which he represents are exclusively national. Where this distribution of the powers of government is established, this further effect takes place. As the responsibility of a legislative body is in an inverse ratio to the number of its members, after a certain point is reached, so also the responsibility of the members is greater where those to whom they are immediately accountable do not compose a great multitude. The representative of a district is constantly exposed to the gaze of his constituents. He might hide himself among two or three millions of people. He cannot do so among fifty or an hundred thousand.

Whatever contributes to afford a clear insight into public affairs and enables everything to be seen in its true light abates the violence of party spirit. Whatever shrouds them in mystery and causes them to be seen confusedly gives force to party spirit. The representative is the instrument of communication between his constituents and the world of politics and whatever causes his conduct to be distinctly surveyed causes the system of public measures to be more easily grasped and more generally understood.

MANY persons of great intelligence, and who are inclined to look with a favorable eye upon the progress which society is everywhere making, when they behold the scene of strife and contention which parties in a republic give rise to recoil from it with dismay and are instantly disposed to take refuge in what they denominate strong government. Nevertheless, it is most certain that the distinguishing excellence of free institutions consists in their giving birth to popular parties and that the annoyance and inconvenience which these occasion to individuals, both in public and private life, are productive of incalculable advantage. It is a great mistake, with our knowledge of constitution of human nature, to suppose that society would be better ordered if its surface were a perfect calm.

The democratic principle has come into the world not to bring peace, but a sword; or rather to bring peace by a sword. One may easily conceive of an individual that his various faculties may be so evenly balanced as to give rise to the justest and the most consistent scheme of conduct. And one may liken the state to some huge individual and say that the rival views and opinions of different parties conspire to the same end; that when these are free to give utterance to their sentiments, a similar equipoise takes place among all parts of society, and that something like a regular system takes place in the conduct of public affairs.

The human mind, with all its capabilities of thought and action, is wonderfully disposed to listlessness, so that it requires the most powerful incentives in order to rouse its dormant energies. And the condition of the great majority of mankind is such that none but those sensible interests which touch them on every side can be relied upon as the instrument of moving them. By giving a full play and a favorable direction to these, we succeed in imparting activity to the disposition. And this being attained, a great amount of thought and reflection is sure to be developed among the great bulk of the population. Party spirit at bottom is but the conflict of different opinions, to each of which some portion of truth almost invariably adheres; and what has ever been the effect of this mutual action of mind upon mind, but to sharpen men's wits, to extend the circle of their knowledge, and to raise the general mind above its former level. Therefore it is that an era of party spirit, whether religious, philosophical, or political, has always been one of intellectual advancement. A powerful understanding may be sufficiently stimulated by the study and investigation of abstract truth: but the diffusion of knowledge in the concrete seems to be indispensably necessary to produce this effect among the great majority of mankind.

The existence of parties in a republic, even noisy and clamorous parties, is not therefore a circumstance which should be regarded as inimical to the peace and welfare of the state. It should rather be received as a special and extraordinary provision for furthering the interests and advancing the intelligence of the most numerous class of society. By creating an arena on which all men may be active and useful, we are certain of attracting an incalculably greater number to the pursuit of industry and knowledge than would be possible under any other state of things. The growth of popular parties constantly keeps pace with the diffusion of industry and property. The diffusion of industry and property, by exercising the mind intently upon small things at first, exercises it earnestly and seriously upon important ones in the end.

The true theory of popular parties then consists in multiplying the employments of private individuals — in increasing the active industry of the whole community. The regular deportment and habits of reflection which these produce counteract the vicious tendencies of the system and operate as a safeguard against the extreme excesses and the violent revolutions which occur in other countries. As the interests of private persons under this system become more and more identified with those of the state, each one has a desire and a motive for understanding and taking part in public affairs. The question in human affairs is never whether any particular arrangement shuts out all mischief and inconvenience, but only whether it excludes the greatest practicable amount; and not of one kind merely, but of all kinds. Thus, although in a democratic republic a vastly greater number of people take part in politics than under any other form of government, the minds of a vastly greater number are exercised by some healthful and useful occupation which not only inspires sagacity and energy but communicates a character of seriousness and reflection to the whole population. The weak side of human nature is thus constantly propped up and strengthened. The bickerings and animosities of parties are not extinguished; but there is, notwithstanding, a greater degree of public tranquillity than would otherwise exist.

Popular parties are not only the natural result of elective government but, what is of much more consequence, they are absolutely necessary to uphold and preserve it. It is too common to regard certain arrangements of society as a sort of necessary evil and thus very imperfectly to comprehend their true design and the important agency which they have in securing the public welfare.

As the political institutions in a republic are of a totally different character from what they are in monarchical or aristocratical government, there is a corresponding difference in the machinery which sets each of them respectively in motion. In the artificial forms of government, a system of checks and balances is devised to secure the influence of the public authority and to maintain each department in its proper place; but such an expedient would be futile and powerless where government means vastly more than the rule of the persons who fill the various public offices. In a republic a substantive part of the political authority is designedly communicated to the whole population. We want something more, therefore, than a scheme of checks and balances within the government. As the forces which are set in motion are so much more extensive, we must contrive some machinery equally extensive for the purpose of controlling them. And thus popular parties very naturally, not to say necessarily, take the place of that curious system of checks and balances which are well enough adapted to a close aristocracy or pure monarchy, but which play only a subordinate part in representative government.

In a despotism parties have no existence. Factions there may be, but not parties. In all the other artificial forms of government, the constitution of parties is more or less imperfect because they are overborne by an extraneous influence which disables them from faithfully representing opinions. In a democratic republic, the people themselves compose all the existing parties. Hence opinions are not only submitted to examination, but they are submitted to the examination of those who are immediately affected by them. But the greater the number of persons who are consulted with regard to any measure which has an important bearing upon their interests, the greater is the probability that it will be adjusted with a view to their common welfare. The process may be tedious and circuitous, but this is an advantage since it will cause a greater amount of reflection to be employed. Moreover, when opinions have to pass through a great number of minds before they are reduced to practice, society does not experience a violent shock as it does upon their sudden and unpremeditated adoption. Factions stir the passions of men, but parties introduce the conflict of opinions.

It would appear, then, that the wider the arena on which parties move, the more numerous the persons who compose them, the less dangerous are they to the state; which is the reverse of the conclusion to which the great majority of men are inclined to lean.

The absence of parties in a country of free institutions would imply the existence of unanimity on all occasions. But in the imperfect condition of man unanimity would not be desirable. As in the individual, one faculty is set over against another in order to elicit the greatest amount of judgment, wisdom, and experience; so the mutual encounter of rival opinions in different sections of society constitutes a discipline of the same character on a much larger scale. Unanimity, which has the appearance of being the only rightful rule, would, if it were conceivable, render society absolutely stationary. Man is not born with knowledge, and all the useful or noble qualities which he ever exerts are the offspring of variety, not of uniformity. Constituted as human nature is, there would be no virtue without some conflict of interests and no wisdom without some conflict of opinions.

And this supposes a very important fact in the history of society; that although the majority rule, the minority by virtue of the naked power which belongs to opinions are able to exert an indirect and yet very decisive influence upon the course of public affairs. This influence is so great that no one who has been accustomed to examine the workings of society in different countries can fail to have been struck with the repeated instances in which the opinions of a minority have triumphed over those of the majority, so as ultimately to become the settled and established opinions and to transform the minority into the majority. And this, notwithstanding the civil institutions may not have been very favorable to the rise and growth of parties.

Among the important changes in the scheme of public policy which have taken place in Great Britain in very recent times may be enumerated the abolition of the slave trade, the amelioration of the criminal code, the introduction of more liberal principles into commerce, the reformation of the civil jurisprudence, catholic emancipation, and parliamentary reform. In each of these instances the new opinion commenced with an exceedingly small party and encountered in its progress the most solidly established authority. If the triumph has not been complete, it is certain to become so in consequence of the strong ground which these very efforts have enabled popular parties to stand upon. So far from a minority not exercising a very marked influence upon the conduct of public affairs, the instances will be found to be exceedingly rare in any country where opinions are able to make themselves felt in which a minority have not succeeded, if the cause it espoused entitled it to be victorious. This fact would seem to show that so far as effective and permanent influence is concerned, it is of little consequence whether an enlightened scheme of policy is first suggested by the minority or the majority. The fact that it is enlightened gives it a claim to success and that success is almost infallible.

Among the important movements which have taken place in American society may be noticed the Revolution, the establishment of the federal constitution, and the ascendancy which the Republican party attained in 1801. Each of these revolutions commenced with an inconsiderable band, which ultimately won its way to public confidence, and totally reversed the position of parties. The Declaration of Independence was only carried by one vote. The freedom of the colonies might have been rightfully asserted half a century prior to 1776. But although the struggle of opinions may be more protracted than that of armies, it always terminates in more decisive results. As to the second of those revolutions, the establishment of the confederate form of government, it was at one time deemed absolutely impracticable. Governor Pownall in his work on the administration of the colonies, written about the time of the celebrated convention at Albany, declared that they had no one principle of association among them and that their manner of settlement, diversity of characters, conflicting interests, and mutual rivalship forbid all idea of an union.[1] And Dr. Franklin, who was one of the commissioners to that convention, declared that an union of the colonies was absolutely impracticable — or

1. [Thomas Pownall (1722–1805), *The Administration of the Colonies* (London, 1764); the Albany Congress was in 1754.]

at least without being forced by the most grievous oppression and tyranny. The acutest observers and the most experienced statesmen underrated the force with which opinions are armed when they are pursued with a steady and unfaltering resolution.

The third revolution was the natural consequence of the others. The two first acted upon the political institutions and remodeled the government. The last acted upon the manners and brought the laws and the structure of society into harmony and agreement with each other.

I will mention but two instances in the history of the state governments in which the opinions of a party greatly in the minority have finally prevailed and obtained an almost unlimited ascendancy. These are the amelioration of the criminal code and the establishment of a system of internal improvements. Each of these enlightened schemes originated with a very small party — the one in Pennsylvania and the other in New York. And they have not only conquered all opposition in those states but have extended their influence over the whole union.

The struggle of new with old opinions will be more tedious in an old than in a new country. The abolition of the laws of primogeniture and the simplification of the code of civil jurisprudence did not occupy much time in the United States. In Great Britain it is only within a few years that the second has been even partially accomplished. The first may not be effected in half a century or more.

Thus, whenever the general state of public opinion is least prepared for an important change in the existing institutions, that is, whenever agitation, discussion, and the encounter of rival opinions is most necessary and will be productive of most advantage — by developing a great amount of observation and experience — the struggle of a new opinions is the longest protracted; and wherever these qualities already exist in great perfection, the contest is short and soon brought to a close.

As soon as the period arrived when Congress had authority to abolish the slave trade, it was abolished. The debate on the subject is not one of the memorable debates in the American legislature. But it is one of the most memorable which has taken place in the British Parliament during the last half century.

It is curious to notice the manner in which parties deal with each other and to watch the process by which opinions are communicated from one to the other. For parties would be without meaning and with-

out utility if they were eternally to battle with each other with no
other result than the alternate loss and acquisition of power. The desire to obtain the ascendancy may be the moving spring which actu-
ates each, but fortunately this spring cannot be set in motion in a
country of free institutions without rousing a prodigious amount of reflection among a very large portion of the population. Doubtless the
true use of parties is very far from being to administer provocatives
to demagogues to gratify their private ambition. Their selfish views
may be necessary in order to animate them in the pursuit of certain
opinions. But the moment these opinions are promulgated they are
subjected to a searching examination in all parts of society because
they are felt to have a practical bearing upon the substantial interests
of all. The true office of parties then is to elicit and make manifest the
amount of truth which belongs to the tenets of each, so that the great
body of the people who belong to no party save the party of
their country may be both easily and understandingly guided in the
path they pursue.

In the progress of the struggle which takes place between parties,
they will often be very equally balanced, and each will for a time al-
ternately acquire the ascendancy. The first time that the party which
before had been habitually in the minority attains a decided preponderance is felt as a presage of permanent success. The new opinions
are then deemed to be practicable. Old associations are broken and a
new impulse is given to the new party. The party which had been accustomed to carry everything falls back into the minority, and this example of the instability of power sets every one a thinking and, even
amid the strife of politics, produces more prudence and moderation.
The party in the minority, and now discarded from power, is at first
disposed to cling to its most extreme opinions. Its pride has
been wounded and its ambition disappointed. It has no idea of turning to any sets of opinions upon compulsion. But a popular party contains a vast number of individuals whose temperaments, modes of
thinking, and opportunities of information are often exceedingly different and whom it is impossible to fashion as you would a close body
into one unalterable form. Reflection, sooner or later, takes the place of
passion. And as the attachment of individuals to their own independent
opinions is often much stronger than to the opinions of a party, every
assurance is afforded that the new and enlightened opinions which
have been introduced into the public administration will not only be

the rule for the party in power but that they will spread their influence more or less over the men of all parties. Everyone soon sees that there is really no such thing as compulsion in representative government and that if a system of policy has fairly won over a majority of the suffrages of twenty millions of people a very considerable portion of truth, to say the least, must belong to that system. They recollect that as no one man can represent the whole of humanity, so no one party can represent the whole truth in politics. Thus the minds of many who were most obstinately set in the opposite direction are gradually opened to the reception of new opinions. They begin to declare, for the first time, that some very important changes were necessary to secure the well being of the state. Great numbers openly go over to the opposite party; some from settled conviction, others from a sort of instinctive feeling that all was not right before. This gives additional strength to the majority which, when it does not advance merely novel opinions but appeals to truth and to the judgment of mankind, is sure to retain the supremacy for a considerable period. Everything then becomes fixed and settled.

But this very fixation of everything, so delightful to those who have been tormented by anxiety and tossed by contrary hopes and fears, is not to last forever. This state of repose is often as fatal to the maintenance of free institutions as the ill-regulated ambition of parties. Prosperity corrupts parties as well as individuals. The long enjoyment of power persuades those who have possessed it that it can never be wrested from them. Abuses, though not perhaps of the same kind, break out again. These abuses gain strength gradually. They are fortified by the prejudices which the prescription of time creates, as well as by the self-interest and cupidity of the leaders of party. Any attempt to root them up is regarded as before as an attempt to change fundamental usages and to tamper with the vital interests of the community. Then commences a new struggle very much resembling the former; the same circle of opinions will be described as in the former revolution. Everything will again be set right without shedding one drop of blood, without the employment of any other instrumentality than the simple dropping of the ballot. But it may happen that the new opinions which now spring up will not be entitled to as entire confidence as in the former revolution. In the progress of the controversy, each party will cause some portion of its own opinions to be adopted. The issue will not be so decisive. A new party, or probably an old party with views greatly modified, will succeed to power and will preside for another term of years. It is in this way that all parties find themselves, somehow or other, represented in the state—some virtually, others potentially; and although the government is frequently exposed to the most formidable power by which it can be assailed, that power is exercised so steadily and yet so silently as to overturn nothing and yet to revolutionize everything.

There is another very curious inquiry connected with this subject, one which unfolds a very instructive chapter in the history of human nature. I believe it will be found on a close observation that parties in a republic in great numbers of instances originate in, and are nourished by, secret rivalships in private life; and that although questions of state policy serve to designate them and to give them an outward form, those questions are in great part laid hold of in order to give force and effect to feelings of a very different kind. If the history of every hamlet and neighborhood in the United States were written, this fact would be found verified with wonderful exactness. But it is not necessary that we should be acquainted with the chronicles of all. It is enough to seize the events which pass under our own observation. What takes place in a few will differ in no material respect from what transpires in all.

This is a view of the subject which is not only exceedingly curious, as affording an insight into the workings of human nature, but is highly instructive, as it sheds great light upon the formation and composition of parties.[2] It is generally supposed that individuals connect themselves with parties upon political grounds; that is, that they are influenced by a persuasion of the propriety or impropriety of certain public measures. This is a great error. Numbers enter into these associations from motives which are of a purely personal or private character. And this is true equally of the common people and of the higher classes. In speaking of motives of a personal character, however, I do not at all refer to the preference which is felt for a particular leader; for this is generally of a negative character. It may help to decide the turn which parties sometimes take, but falls entirely short of the view to which I wish to direct the attention of the reader. To a very great extent, parties are formed and changed in consequence of

2. [For the second edition, Grimke added new matters from the start of this paragraph to the paragraph which ends, ". . . necessary to sweep away public abuses," on p. 182.]

the position in private life which individuals occupy. Anyone who has lived in any town in the United States long enough to make an accurate observation of the structure of society and the dispositions of the people who inhabit it must have noticed that there is a constant tendency towards what may be called the supremacy or precedence of certain individuals or families. These will, perhaps, be composed of the old residents, of the merchants, of professional men, etc. As adherents of these will always be found a number of the inferior classes, so that it cannot be termed a merely aristocratical party. Two circumstances, however, in the progress of time contribute to weaken or entirely to break up this association: 1st. Where any body of men, no matter how wide or how narrow the sphere of their influence may be, has maintained a certain degree of precedence for a considerable time, those who compose it become confident in themselves and annoy others by making show of their influence. 2d. In the great majority of towns under twenty thousand there will be a lack of talent in this body, owing either to the circumstance that the long enjoyment of a fixed position in society diminishes the motives to exertion or that there is not now enough for the strenuous action of mind upon mind. Either of these causes, and, of course, both combined, lead very naturally to the crumbling of the party and to the formation of new opinions and a new party. I visited several parts of the United States during the administration of James Monroe. Parties could not be said to be extinct, but they were feeble and inactive. In every town and village, and I may add neighborhood, a predominant and complacent influence was exercised by certain families or individuals on the principle I have suggested. I visited or obtained accurate information of most of these some years afterwards when parties were distinctly formed. These parties were termed political and in outward appearance had no other character. But political disputes only gave occasion to them and afforded a plausible ground for open hostility when, in truth, the actuating motives were of a strictly personal character, and it was the individuals who were arrayed against one another. Everywhere it was the new men against the old; very often the talented and the ambitious against the supine and unintelligent. In many instances, it was the reverse; it was the radical, the ignorant, the persons jealous of any influence which overshadowed them, no matter how rightful that influence was, who battled against superior talents and long continued influence. In many instances whole counties and districts of country were revolutionized, the new men succeeding to the old. In others, the new men did not succeed in obtaining the mastery but they notwithstanding wrought a great change in the habits and mode of thinking of other people, for even ineffectual opposition may have a very advantageous influence. It wakes up those against whom it is directed; it leads them to soften or correct their defects; otherwise they cannot maintain the victory they have won. In hardly any instance were political questions the springs which brought about these changes. One body of men simply felt uneasy in the subordinate position which it seemed to occupy. In general conversation and in public meetings questions of public policy were seized as the ruling motives; in private conversation it was otherwise. There people freely declared that political questions were of very inferior moment compared with the annoyance which was daily experienced in private life from the complacent rule of a clique which could show no intrinsic title to respect.

It is of great importance that these views should be thoroughly studied by everyone. Public controversies are not everything, even in politics. Every community requires, if I may so express myself, to be occasionally ventilated, and this can only be done by operating upon the secret and more delicate springs which work the machinery of society. We thus gain a clearer insight into the origin, character, and fluctuation of parties. It is as necessary to study the physiology of society in order to understand the workings of government as it is to study the physiology of man in order to penetrate the character of the individual. The changes I have referred to are periodical. They take place about every generation. The reason is obvious: a period of twenty or thirty years is necessary to confirm the authority of any body of men, and until it is confirmed it is not very troublesome to anyone. Those who are growing into manhood then unite with the discontented among the older men. If this view does not present a very flattering picture of human nature, it at least shows that through the instrumentality of some very harmless agents important changes in the structure of society are brought about silently and peacefully. A democratic community will not therefore be so liable to those terrible shocks which in other countries are necessary to sweep away public abuses.

If we suppose that there are two or three men in a neighborhood who possess considerable influence, whether arising from family connections, wealth, or any other of the advantages of fortune, this at once lays the foundation for rivalship in its most secret forms. Envyings and heartburnings insensibly grow up. This is a fact we are bound to know, only to draw instruction from it. This rivalship gradually extends to the connections of each, to their friends and acquaintances— to all those who may be disposed to take refuge under the influence of one rather than of the others—until at length the whole neighborhood is involved in their disputes. One perhaps acquires a decided ascendancy, and in a few years this disproportioned influence incommodes great numbers of people in all the walks of private life. Many immediately declare that they can see no reason why so much importance should be ascribed to anyone who does not possess either eminent virtue or ability; and they set themselves to work more vigorously than ever in order to abate so great a nuisance. At the same time political questions are discussed and agitated everywhere, and regular parties in the state are organizing. Each of these neighborhood clans connects itself with one or other of those parties as the chance of success in their private views may dictate. The democratic party is understood to be the one which is most favorable to the equal rights of the citizens, and all the opponents of this mimic aristocracy in a country neighborhood ally themselves with that party.

The influential man does not always put himself forward as a candidate for office. He feels that this would be to create envy among his own dependants — that it would be a dangerous test of his capacity and wisdom. But he brings someone forward who leans upon him and who, if not the most capable, will be the most available man. And party politics now having two faces, the most available will generally be the most incompetent man. This mixture of private views with the political questions of the day will sometimes render the machinery of parties very complicated and difficult to understand. And it will cause oscillations among parties when they were least expected. But we will suppose that the democratic party prevails. The influence which was before so serious an annoyance and the subject of so much complaint in private is then greatly diminished. Someone whose connection with the wealthy will be less obvious and whose reliance upon the masses will be closer is elected. He also may be nicknamed an available man — that is, a man whose face is smoothed — or a practical man, which means a man with a single idea. At any rate the personal weight and importance which political promotion gives him and the bright prospects which everyone beholds opening in his path concur to clothe him with a very enviable share of influence. Or, if he also has been merely put forward to further the private schemes of others the same effect is produced. A new influence is raised up in the neighborhood to act as a counterpoise to that which before prevailed. But in a few years the same annoyance is felt in consequence of the ascendancy of this new party. Men begin then to exercise a bolder spirit of inquiry than they were willing to trust themselves with before. They see no reason why wealth or any other fortuitous advantage should give claim to precedence in society. The new favorite perhaps owed his elevation to personal motives and private views. But he is perhaps not fully sensible of this; or, at any rate, it does not readily occur to him that after being elected to a public station of considerable responsibility he has any other vocation than to attend to the public business. He separates the end from the means and congratulates himself with the reflection that now a public trust is confided to him he will be at liberty to act with a single eye to the people's interests.

After an interval more or less long during which there will be great fermentation in the ranks of both parties, some new man will be selected who will reflect the feelings as well as the political opinions of those who elect him. His success is almost certain, for the private aims and secret prejudices which were originally set in motion have been continually gaining strength. And in order that the successful candidate may now well understand the line of conduct which he is expected to pursue, what were before regarded as motives, which might well enough influence without determining public conduct, are erected into opinions on which full as much stress is laid as on any of the questions of public policy. This gives a deeper movement to the workings of parties. All sorts of opinions are now hazarded; men approach inquiries which before were only touched lightly and by stealth. The fault with the public man now is that he runs into the opposite extreme. He takes his constituents literally at their word and acts out his part even to exaggeration. He is intent only on gratifying his spleen; he indulges in personal invectives, in gross and indecent assaults. He has brought himself to believe that the public business is not merely of secondary importance, but that it is of hardly any importance whatever. He administers provocatives enough to the bad passions, but neglects and mismanages public business. The consequent derangement of political affairs is now more or less felt by the people in their private interests. Moreover, they are mortified in finding that some portion of the disgrace which their favorite has incurred attaches to themselves. Numbers then confer together, but in such a way as to avoid if possible the notice of the opposite party. They consult in private how it may be possible, with the least noise and inconvenience, to remove the present incumbent and to elect someone of prudence and discretion, even though his talents should be as moderate. A majority, perhaps, are candidly of this opinion; but a considerable number still cling to their personal views as being the true index of public opinion, and without the aid of this body it will be impossible to effect anything. Without their votes the majority will fall back into the minority. All the private consultations are then hushed up, and the differences which produced them are forgotten for a time. The party displays a bold and decided front at the polls, and re-elects the former man. But the blow which is to crush him is already struck. His enemies are gathering strength. They even feel envious of him that he is in a condition to display so much more energy than themselves. The minority of the party feel that it would be absurd that the majority should constantly yield to them. Besides, the new fashion of thinking begins to infect themselves. They regard their favorite with coldness simply because so many people are disposed to discard him. They even permit him to feel this in order that he may so act toward them as really to deserve their cold treatment.

During all this time, and while these changes succeed each other with more or less rapidity, the utmost inquisitiveness is excited among all orders of men. The connection which has taken place between politics and private manners brings the former more completely within the reach of everyone. It seemed impossible before to gain admission to state secrets so as to have any notion of the complex machinery by which government is worked, simply because there was so little to stir the feelings and through that medium to rouse the understanding.

This difficulty is in a great measure removed; and in spite of the eternal wrangling of parties, or rather in consequence of it, a greater amount of knowledge, a keener sagacity, and juster views are created than would otherwise exist. Those who had formerly been invested with influence and who imagined they were the hinges on which society turned look on with amazement to find public affairs conducted as well as when they took the lead. They observe that an entire revolution has taken place in the disposition and management of society.

They ascribe this to envy, and doubtless envy had a great part in bringing it about. But in human affairs the inquiry is not always what is the cause of any particular change so much as what is the character of the change itself. It is a great compensation for the existence of bad passions and propensities, when we cannot be without them, that they may ultimately be subservient toward rendering human nature better than it was before.

Through the instrumentality of the cause at which I have merely glanced in order to set the reader a thinking, knowledge has been diffused and power and influence in both public and private life have been more evenly balanced in every township and county of an extensive country. These views contribute to explain a remarkable fact in the history of parties in America. Taking any considerable series of years, it is surprising to find how often parties have been very equally balanced. The see-saw politics of some of the states seems even to be a reproach to them. But beneath this outside appearance there is always something to ponder upon. For if, on whichever side the scale of power inclines, the equilibrium of influence in every village and neighborhood is disturbed, the only way to restore it is by throwing more weight into the opposite scale, and thus the oscillations of parties may be almost as frequent as the annual elections. As soon as one party obtains a decided predominance, new rivalships grow up. A multitude of passions and desires (independent of the political controversies of the day) are set in motion for the purpose of displacing it or diminishing its authority.

Hence another apparently singular phenomenon, that individuals of the most opposite political predilections and of the greatest difference in point of character and mind are habitually ranged in the same party. It would be deplorable if it were not so. And although one party is sometimes foolish enough to arrogate to itself all the virtue and talents in the community, yet there is in truth a very equal distribution among the men of all parties.

Another and equally curious fact may be noticed, that parties often seem to exhibit a mere struggle between the ins and outs. But if the power which is brought to bear upon political affairs is adjusted and regulated by the power and influence which are distributed in private life, and if this affects human happiness more than all other causes put together, the struggle may conduct to very important ends. I have already said that in a republic parties take the place of the old system of balances and checks. The latter balance the government only, the former balance society itself.

Frequent changes of the public officers are a consequence of these vicissitudes among parties. But it is of the greatest importance in a country where the electoral franchise is extensively enjoyed that as large a number of the citizens as practicable should be initiated into the mode of conducting public affairs, and there is no way by which this can be so well effected as by a rotation in office; and the direction which party disputes take affords the opportunity of doing it. If it were not for this, public employments would be continued in the same individuals for life, and after their death would be perpetuated in their families. But public office of even an inferior grade is a species of discipline of no unimportant character. It extends the views of men, trains them to the performance of justice, and makes them act for others as well as for themselves. It thus binds together the parts of society by the firmest of all bonds and makes it tend constantly to a state of order and tranquillity in the midst of the greatest apparent disorder. If men were less quarrelsome, if an easy good nature was all that moved them, they would not be inclined to change their public officers as often as the interests of society demand. The detriment which would follow would be much greater than any which their quarrels produce.

It has been supposed that where these changes are frequent the persons elected must for the most part be inexperienced and incompetent. The fear lest this should be the case is wisely implanted in our nature. It holds us back when we are about to run into an extreme. The feeling is as much a part of our constitution as any of its other tendencies and must be strictly taken into account in every calculation which we make as to the general working of the system. But public office itself creates to a great extent the very ability which is required for the performance of its duties. And it is not at all uncommon when individuals have been snatched up from the walks of private life to fill responsible stations to find that the affairs of society are conducted pretty much upon the same principles and with as much skill and intelligence as before. Habits of order and method are soon imparted to the incumbent, and they constitute the moving spring of all effective exertion, either mental or physical.

In a republic, the rise and fall of parties are not merely revolutions in public life, they are revolutions in private life also. They displace some men from office, but they alter the relative position of a much greater number in private life. Political controversies afford an opportunity for parties to develop themselves, and these controversies do very often present a legitimate field for discussion. But they do not contain everything; they do not express the whole meaning of parties. A given scheme of public policy may affect very remotely the substantial interests of the population; but the jostling of men in private life is a perpetual source of uneasiness and discontent, and they seek to relieve themselves by an alliance with party because as individuals they are powerless, while party associations are strong.

The views and actions of men may be the most narrow and selfish imaginable, and yet they may terminate in consequences of the most beneficial character. The prominent men of each party exert themselves to carry extreme measures; a great multitude of private individuals intend to acquire some advantage unseen, but not unfelt, over their neighbors. The fall of a party at such a time, like a sudden stroke of adversity, quells the pride of the politician and inculcates prudence, caution, and forbearance in private behavior.

The reason why the workings of party are so much more ramified and extensive in a republic than in any other form of government is easily explained. In monarchy and aristocracy the bulk of the people are spectators, not actors, and the operation of parties is necessarily confined within a narrow circle. But free institutions presuppose that the mass of the people are active not passive citizens and parties not only regulate the conduct of the handful of men who preside over public affairs, they regulate also the conduct of the millions who, although out of the government, yet constitute the springs which set the government in motion. If this were not the case, if there were no regulative principle to shake society as well as to act upon the government, there would be no way of maintaining free institutions. Men who hold office may be punished for misconduct, but how is it possible by legal enactments to punish whole parties? When, however, a party is tumbled from power, the individuals composing it lose caste — lose some portion of that consideration which before attached to them. If this produces more boldness and recklessness in some, it promotes more reflection and prudence in others.

CHAPTER IX | A REPUBLIC IS ESSENTIALLY A
GOVERNMENT OF RESTRAINT

No one who is an attentive observer of human nature can fail to be struck with the amazing influence which the opinion of a multitude of men exercises over the mind. We can stand up and confront a single individual even though we are far from being right, but we recoil with a sort of dread from any opposition to the opinion of a great number. Many causes concur to produce this effect.

First. If the individual feels awed by the presence, it is because he is conscious that they are rendered strong by being in a body.[1] This must necessarily be the case. Men are physically stronger when they act together and they are morally stronger when they sympathize together. The phenomenon then is easily explained. The principle even shows why the individual is awed where he is in the right and the multitude clearly in the wrong. That multitude, so far as physical injury is concerned, is as strong as before; so far as moral injury is concerned, it is not near so strong, but it is much stronger than the individual. Their sympathy with one another is still a weapon of offense against those who do not share in that sympathy. The individual then feels his weakness because, the sentiment of sympathy being a principle of his own nature, he is left without support when he is entitled to the strongest. The first feel their strength as before, simply because sympathy is a principle of moral, as an actual union is of physical, strength. The principle manifests itself in another shape. When an individual is conceived to represent a multitude, no matter whether it is an enlightened or an unenlightened multitude, his presence to a certain extent conveys an impression of their presence and produces a similar effect.

The institution of patron and client which prevailed in Rome for so long a time is an illustration of the same principle. Individuals sur-

1. [For the second edition, Grimke added this paragraph and the next.]

rounded themselves with retainers, not merely to add to their physical power but to increase their moral influence. The same custom was introduced into the Republics of Florence and Genoa in the middle ages, and gave an artificial weight and importance to those who adopted it. Even in England traces of the same custom are closely discernible as late as the beginning of the sixteenth century. The practice of having a numerous body of retainers and giving them badges or liveries was not put an end to until 1509 in the reign of Henry the seventh. Even where no such custom exists, we can still perceive indications of a disposition moving in the same direction. Everywhere we see men allying themselves with other men, not merely openly as with parties but tacitly with other individuals in order to inspire themselves with confidence and to give countenance to their behavior. In a democratic community where individuals fear each other so much, the custom is difficult to be established, but the weapon of ridicule is wielded by cliques and coteries as the most convenient mode of attack.

Second. The notion of right and wrong is implanted in all men. That we should feel distress and anxiety when we do wrong requires no explanation; for this is running counter, if not to our propensities and passions, yet, at any rate, to the governing principle of our conduct. To say that we feel an immoral action to be wrong, whatever may be the allurements with which it is accompanied, is the same as to say that the sense of right is felt to be the authoritative principle, and that any departure from it fills us with uneasiness and apprehension.

But, in the second place, the training and formation of the human character are conducted in youth when the mind is feeble and without much observation and experience. We, therefore, emerge into a world where a system of opinions and conduct is already established and it does not seem unnatural, but rather a necessary consequence of the process by which human conduct is shaped, that we should defer greatly to the standard of opinion which is erected, and our deportment (not so far as regards the fundamentals of morality, but as regards those actions to which are affixed the appellations fit and unfit, proper and improper, reasonable and unreasonable) should be compressed into a conformity with it, and that any revolt against it should be followed with a sense of dread and uneasiness. And this more especially as so large a proportion of this class of actions affect other men, and carry along with them not merely the force of opinion but that of authority.

If it should be said that the presence of such a force constantly acting upon the faculties of men and holding them in check must frequently have a disturbing influence upon their actions, this will be admitted; but there is, on the whole, much greater security for the preservation of a tolerably right standard than if everyone felt himself independent of the opinions of all. This singleness in the character of the rule gives unity to those numberless actions which are isolated and prevents their being drawn too exclusively in the direction of self-interest.

Each individual is apt to view himself from a point different from that where he is viewed by others. His horizon is more limited than theirs, not because he has fewer or feebler faculties or because he has less correct notions of right, but because in the case of the individual these notions are liable to be obscured by feelings and interests which, although they may be common to all, are obliged to be kept under and restrained when they come to think and act in a body. There is a high probability, therefore, that the opinion of an individual as to his own conduct is biassed, and an equal probability that the sentiment of the body is impartial. The mere apprehension that this may be the case hangs like a perpetual weight upon each one and renders him, to say the least, more thoughtful and circumspect than he would otherwise be. He is thus better enabled in those instances where he is in the right and they in the wrong to appeal from their judgment to the judgment of mankind.

That class of actions which are generally denominated selfish carry for the most part their own antidote along with them. That they are selfish constitutes the great protection of the community against their inroads. For it will be easily seen that if there were the same sympathy with others in the gratification by them of their lower propensities, as there is in their noble and disinterested actions, the former would gain the mastery and society be converted into a bedlam. However men may act therefore in particular instances, both the secret and the declared opinion of everyone is obliged to be on the side of right. And this opinion is even fortified by self-interest when self-interest comes to be viewed from the proper point. For although the private interest of the individual may sometimes seem to coincide with the commission of wrong when it is abstracted from all regard to his relations with others, yet it can never do so when these relations are taken into the account. Now, our relations with others, if they do not create, at least modify that whole circle of interests which we denominate private. I do not now speak of those actions which spring from the lower propensities but of those which are employed by everyone in the improvement of his outward condition. The pursuit of an absolutely separate interest by some would consequently break in upon the private interests of all others; while at the same time it is equally clear that a regard for the rights of all others is the only guarantee that our own will be preserved. Here then, also, what is termed the general opinion is obliged to take a direction favorable to the common weal and unfavorable to the selfish views of individuals. In this way the opinion of all is brought to bear upon each; and hence it is that in a democratic republic, where the government appears to be wanting in authority, and individuals to possess unbounded freedom, what is termed public opinion is armed with so much power, inspires so general a respect for the laws and so much terror on the infraction of them. In what is termed strong government society is divided into fixed classes, one of which sits in judgment upon all the others. But it is far less probable that the opinion of a class should represent the opinion of mankind than that the combined sentiment of a whole community should do so. The laws having consecrated that class as a separate interest have to that extent confounded the opinion of right with that of interest.

It would appear, then, that liberty is essentially a principle of restraint. It is true, if others are free while I am not the principle operates unequally—the restraint is on one side. But if I am admitted to the enjoyment of the same privilege, my actions will impose a check upon the conduct of others and their actions will impose a corresponding check upon me, and the influence of the principle will be more or less felt throughout the whole of society. The exercise of unrestricted freedom by all, when all are free, is a self contradiction. It supposes a power in each to invade the rights of all others, in which case liberty would fall to the ground and no one be free. The possession of the privilege then by all limits its exercise in practice and men are restrained and controlled precisely because they are free. My liberty of action is an habitual restraint upon the conduct of others when they attempt to invade my rights, and their liberty is in similar circumstances a restraint upon me. It would not therefore be strong enough to say that, where free institutions are thoroughly diffused, it is the evident interest of everyone to impose a restraint upon his actions. It would be still more correct to say that the constitution of society renders it necessary that he should do so.

The walks of private life furnish us with a fine illustration of this important principle. The youth looks forward to the time when he will arrive at manhood with feelings of delight and exultation. His imagination paints it as the introduction to a state of unalloyed enjoyment. But he has no sooner entered upon the world than he finds himself hampered and controlled on every side by a multitude of other beings who have acquired the same freedom as himself. The restraint which he met with under the parental roof was nothing when compared with the iron weight which now presses upon him; and although no one can claim to be his master, so that physically his actions may be freer than ever, yet he finds what before he very imperfectly understood, that the moral force which men exercise upon each other in society is the sharpest and most powerful of all kinds of restraint.

Now, free institutions produce an effect of precisely the same character and on a much larger scale. They advance the whole population to the condition of political manhood. If they do not confer anything like the enjoyment which was anticipated, they give rise to what is still more valuable: they multiply the cares and interests of life and teach to the great majority of men habits of prudence, of reflection, and of self command. That they do not produce this effect in all instances, and in very few to the extent which is desirable, is no answer to the view here taken; nor does it afford any good reason why we should never speak above our breath when we are discoursing of the benefits of liberty. That there is a marked tendency to the production of the effect I have noticed is an important fact, since it shows that if liberty is power, it is also a principle of restraint. And if a general acquaintance with the manner in which the principle operates will contribute to strengthen this tendency, we have abundant reasons for speaking out all that we know.

When I make reference to the mighty influence which the opinion of a multitude of men exercises over the human mind, I do not shut my eyes to the fact that the principle may operate sometimes, nay, that it does very frequently operate, so as to have a sinister and very pernicious influence by giving an undue authority to associations and particular sections of society. I am aware that in this way a party, nay, even a clique, whether in public or private life, may acquire such do-minion for a time as to incommode and afflict great numbers of other men. Parties collect the opinions of a multitude into one focus and make them appear like the judgment of an invisible being. They have been able therefore sometimes to oppress the most upright individuals and even to countenance acts of insurrection against the public author-ity. No one has ever mastered a general principle until he is cognizant of all the leading exceptions to it. The argument in favor of free in-stitutions, therefore, never proceeds upon the ground that they are exempt from imperfection, but that they are more so than any other form in which government has been cast, as much so as we dare ex-pect from any scheme which human ingenuity may invent.

That invisible power which we term public opinion only tends to be right in proportion as it resembles itself to the opinion of mankind. And I cannot help thinking that this effect will take place in pro-portion to the number of men who are in the possession of liberty, and who on that very account are driven to habits of thought and re-flection. The parties and cliques which spring up in a republic, how-ever noisome and hurtful they may be in some respects, may con-tribute to further this important end. For:

First. They either presuppose, or they excite to, an abundance of curiosity, observation, and inquiry. Instead of one or two great eminences and all the rest of society a dead level, we have a great many eminences, helping about as well as human imperfections will permit to lift the great body of the population to a higher condition.

Second. These parties, associations, and cliques become so nu-merous in a republic that they thwart, counteract, and control one another. Their frequent discussions and wrangling lead directly to the detection of each other's impostures and serve to correct the aberrations into which the different sections of society are perpetu-ally falling. By modifying and limiting each other's views and opin-ions, public opinion is brought more and more into an accordance with the voice of mankind. It is an immense boon to society when, if any-thing is transacted in society which is prejudicial to its interests it shall at any rate not be done in a corner; that all who act for the public, or upon the public, in order to acquire any influence are compelled to act openly. The so doing is the recognition of the existence of a tribunal of opinion above themselves which sooner or later rejects all their false and pernicious opinions. Perhaps the majority of persons of intelligence and observation—all who have carefully pondered upon the experience which they have had of human nature and from it deduced general results—instead of being perplexed by the exceptions are sufficiently convinced of the wholesome influence which free institutions exercise. The only question with them may be whether it is ever expedient to speak out so loud as to be overheard by the masses.

It is not necessary to scan American institutions with a very critical eye to perceive, that notwithstanding the great amount of liberty which is set afloat and the inflammable character which this liberty sometimes possesses, that there is somehow or other a sort of self-regulative principle residing in the society which tends to keep everything in its proper place, that this principle can nowhere else be so distinctly traced, and that it is entirely different from the formal authority which the government wields. And as there is no reason for supposing that there is anything very mysterious about the matter when all the machinery of society is openly exposed to our observation, the fact, however novel, must admit of explanation, and what explanation so natural as is to be found in the restraint which the very enjoyment of liberty causes every individual and each member of society to impose upon one another? It is the partial distribution of the privilege, not the communication of it to all classes, which has occasioned so much disorder and insubordination in society. Rights and duties are reciprocal. My rights in relation to others are the foundation of their duties towards me, and their rights give rise to a set of corresponding obligations on my part. Hence we may say, in a general way, that the equal communication of liberty, by enlarging the circle of duties in the same proportion as it widens the sphere of rights, tends constantly toward the introduction of a principle of restraint which reaches more or less every part of society. Not that the American people are naturally better than the people of other countries, but that the political and social organization renders it the interest of a greater number to respect and obey the laws, and that this feeling of interest operates in such a way as to have not merely a persuasive but a coercive influence. Not that there are not many evils incident to American society, but that there are fewer than in other governments, especially when we take into account those secret and uncomplained of grievances which are smothered by the hand of power, or which are made to appear insignificant amid the dazzling glare of the throne and aristocracy. Lord Coke has said of the court of

star chamber that "the right institution, and orders thereof, being observed, it doth keep all England in quiet." [2] And if such extravagant
and unfounded notions could be entertained at that period, we may be
permitted at the present day to search through society for some more
homely and yet more active and diffusive principle of order.

There are two opposite plans of introducing order and good government into society. The one consists in arming the civil magistrate with
a very large share of authority and thus making everyone feel as
if an enemy were at his door. The other, not unmindful of the importance of clothing the public functionaries with ample power, is
yet chiefly intent on enlarging the sphere of popular rights. It expects
to fortify the authority of government in this very way. The first is the
plan of almost all the European governments; the second is that of the
American republic. By pursuing the last, we add an additional force
to society — we cause the people to control each other as well as to be
controlled by the authority of the laws. The working of the same principle may be observed in one or two of the European communities, but
it manifests itself in exact proportion to the degree in which popular
liberty has grown up.

It is not placing an undue estimate upon free institutions, therefore, to say that in a republic the distribution of justice and general
administration of the laws will be attended with more weight and
authority than in either monarchical or aristocratical government.
The fact is of the greatest consequence since it enables us to draw
so near the solution of the very difficult problem, how to reconcile
popular liberty with political power. The experiment was deemed
perilous in the extreme until the firm establishment and thorough
working of American institutions, when what was once a brilliant
theory began to wear the character of a regular and well-compacted
system. Sir James Mackintosh was perhaps the first English statesman who clearly descried a principle of order in this new community.
The living under such institutions for a considerable period might beget habits of acting which would insure their perpetuity was very
nearly the remark of that enlightened man. Many intelligent Europeans still hesitate. The difficulty of the experiment may be at an

2. [Sir Edward Coke (1552–1634), eminent English jurist, champion of the
Common Law. The "star chamber" was the meeting place of the King's councilors
in Westminster, taking its name from stars painted on the ceiling; arbitrary and
secret in its proceedings, it has since become a synonym for any oppressive tribunal.]

end in America, but they feel unable to calculate the exact amount of influence which American institutions may exert upon their own. They therefore prefer to exercise the obvious duty of patriotism rather than to seem precipitate in espousing the most salutary principles. There is nothing so difficult and irksome as the taking up a line of conduct, however wise and reasonable it may be, provided it is something entirely foreign to our former habits. Its claim to respect only increases the awe which its novelty is calculated to inspire; but the plan once entered upon, it is amazing how fast the difficulties vanish and how easily the new habit sits upon us. What is true of an individual is, for obvious reasons, still more true with regard to a community.

If in Great Britain and France there exists at the present day more public order, as well as a firmer and more regular administration of the laws, than at any antecedent period, I do not know to what cause we must ascribe it unless it is to the infusion of a greater amount of popular freedom into the institutions of the two countries. Invariably, a wise and liberal communication of liberty has the effect of appeasing instead of inflaming the passions. But more than this, where the population only feels the pressure of their government, they are apt to herd together like miserable sheep; they are unconscious of any other danger than that which stares them in the face and take little or no account of each other's actions, although these exercise so wide and so constant an influence upon the public weal. I think if anyone will follow carefully and minutely the workings of American society, he will find that the people are fully as much occupied in keeping each other in order as they are in checking the authority of their governments. It is only by doing the first that they succeed in doing the last.

In a democratic republic, public opinion is a thing of more comprehensive import than it is anywhere else and it is made to bear more extensively upon delinquents, public or private. In the artificial forms of government, the force of society is wielded by the few. It is an iron armor worn by a class set apart. The consequence is that although the great bulk of society stand in awe of it, they also most cordially detest it, since whatever we fear we also hate, and whatever we both hate and fear we endeavor to beat down, openly if we can, furtively if we must. But in a country of free institutions, I discern a marked difference in the feeling of all classes where crime has been committed or insurrection set on foot. The guilty persons, as soon as they have time to reflect, are conscious that they are under the ban of public opinion. They whisper to themselves, "it is not a privileged class who seek to trample upon us; it is our fellow citizens whom we have arrayed against us; the judgment of mankind will condemn us." Such very nearly was the exclamation of one of the actors in an American mob. This species of awe has a wonderful effect in crumbling to pieces the stoutest league which was ever formed. The insurgents soon feel themselves to be powerless, their weapons drop from their hands, they fall off one by one and seek to hide themselves from public view. The general truth of these remarks is abundantly confirmed, not only by the few instances of civil commotion which have occurred in the United States, but by the remarkable facility with which they have been suppressed.

This subject is obviously one of great and of increasing interest and very naturally suggests many other very important views. In the first place, it must be admitted that hardly any instance of insubordination to the laws occurs in the United States but what we hear complaint of the indecision and backwardness of the public magistrates at the commencement of the affair. Whenever any circumstance is observable in the political history of this country which is different from what takes place elsewhere, there is, to say the least, a high probability that there is some adequate reason for it, and that it is not necessary to suppose, because the precise mode of executing the laws which is practiced in other governments is not adopted there, that therefore the American police is very defective or that it is infected with the same spirit of licentiousness which is displayed in other parts of society. The complaints which are uttered, the uneasiness which takes possession of all classes lest the laws should not be executed, are themselves unequivocal symptoms of the soundness of public sentiment and of the operation of that moral force which is of so much consequence in guarding the peace of society. In the second place, this apparent laxity in enforcing the laws is in great part attributable to the few public disturbances which take place and to the fact that they are invariably of a local character. The American police, if I may use the expression, have not got their hand in — they have seldom had the opportunity to become initiated into the practice of using brute force. An insurrection does not, as in other countries, threaten to sap the foundations of the government and to carry desolation into the heart of society. The Americans can afford, therefore, to proceed with a little more caution and deliberation than other governments. It is the strong, not the weak, who are most sparing of their strength.

Third. This caution is the result of another circumstance which is equally calculated to engage our attention. It springs from a conviction which, whether openly expressed or not, is constantly felt, that one side is not necessarily altogether in the right and the other altogether in the wrong. The Americans have got to acting upon this principle as one of some appreciable value and do not permit it to remain as a barren and unfruitful maxim in the code of ethics. It pervades both public and private society in all their ramifications, and yet the supremacy of the laws is firmly upheld.

Fourth. This wise prudence, this apparent slowness to act, causes less mischief to be done and restores order more speedily and effectually than if a detachment from a standing army were commanded instantly to shoot down the rioters. The shocking enormities of the French Revolution were not put an end to until the middle class took matters into its own hands and, by intervening between the two extreme parties, was enabled to exert both more prudence and more resolution. The great difference between the two countries is that in America the population is almost entirely composed of this middle class. That is done constantly and silently and by way of prevention which in France could only be effected after the two parties had shed torrents of blood.

A habitual desire to avoid, if practicable, all extreme measures is eminently favorable toward rousing reflection and inspires all who would make opposition to the laws with a sense of insecurity and distrust in themselves. They see that the moral and physical force of society are against them and they very soon learn that the forbearance which springs from humanity is invariably coupled with bravery, and that it is the invariable precursor of the most resolute and determined behavior. The government which is strong enough to use forbearance in every act of authority is sure to gather all the strength which the occasion demands. No band of men, however imposing it may be, can maintain a conflict of any duration with the public authority unless it can go beyond itself and derive support from public opinion.

Various conjectures have been hazarded in order to account for the remarkable order and tranquillity which have existed in the United States. The most plausible are those which ascribe it to the exemption of the country from foreign war and to the incessant occupation which the several departments of industry afford to the population. But in truth these are only auxiliary circumstances, very well fitted to give full play to the operation of some other principle, but insufficient of themselves to account for the phenomenon. Very opposite effects have frequently taken place. A season of peace has sometimes been highly favorable to the growth of internal dissensions and conspiracies of every kind. In the Italian republics of the thirteenth and fourteenth centuries, the period of their greatest prosperity, the suspension of foreign war was invariably the signal for reviving the most implacable disputes within. The various branches of industry offered an inexhaustible fund of occupation to the people, for Italy was then the greatest agricultural country in Europe and was also the principal seat of commerce and manufactures. But in examining the constitutions of those states we find that no higher political privileges were accorded to the people than are possessed in most of the monarchical governments now existing, and not near so high as are enjoyed by the English commonalty.

The Italian nobles looked upon government as an institution made for their benefit, and spent the lives and property of the citizens to gratify their personal ambition. The liberty which they possessed was not met by a corresponding liberty in other parts of society. The people were held in restraint, but there was no principle of restraint to operate upon the superior classes. Too little freedom in one quarter leads directly to too much power in another, and the very natural consequence is an eternal conflict between the different orders of society. The foreign wars which have scourged the European states have been the effect rather than the cause of the discontents and unequal condition of the population.

The wisest plan then, perhaps the only practicable one in the end for all countries, is that pursued in America: to communicate equal rights to the people—to throw them indiscriminately together instead of dividing them into fixed orders. They are then compelled to associate freely, and this ultimately ripens into a confirmed habit. Individuals and classes then act as a perpetual restraint upon each other. They are brought to an easy understanding of all these difficulties and interests which under a different constitution of society lead to interminable feuds. Doubtless people incommode each other very much in a country of free institutions, but this is the secret of the good effect which takes place. They are made to act as watches upon each other, to consult each other's temper and disposition, to balance the great advantage of acting from reflection. They become keenly alive to each other's faults, simply because they have so deep a stake in each other's conduct. A new force is applied to society which acts in detail and not merely in the gross and which, by regulating the conduct of individuals in the first instance, succeeds ultimately in regulating that of the masses. The machinery may be very imperfect after all, but it is the best which is placed in our power. Free institutions are the only instrument on a large scale for elevating the general condition of the people because they are the only species of government which is capable of being converted into an instrument of moral and not merely of political discipline for all classes.

As the preservation of order, the maintenance of the laws, the causing one part of society to be just to all others are the great end of civil institutions, it is plain that unless the republican form contains some active principle of restraint which shall take the place of the consolidated authority exercised by other governments it will be no better than monarchy or aristocracy.

The tendency to reflection has been noticed as one of the striking characteristics of modern societies. Everything seems to depend upon the cultivation of this quality. Reflection is what distinguishes the civilized man from the savage, and it is reflection which makes some men lovers of order, while others are vicious and disorderly. In the midst of civilization, we are always surrounded by some remains of barbarous life. The great desideratum in politics is how and to what extent we can get rid of them. Now the principle of equality is eminently calculated to teach habits of reflection. First, it makes men depend very much upon themselves, taxes their own resources, and obliges them to make exertions which they would otherwise never put forth. Second, it brings them more into contact with each other and thus multiplies their mutual relations since all our efforts to better our own condition have an immediate reference to others; and whatever multiplies the relations of man to man enlarges the whole field of observation and gives more both to think and to act upon. It may be that at some future day it will not be necessary for some men to be vicious in order to compel others to be virtuous. The principle of equality may cause jostling enough among men to keep them in order, without that wild license which not only makes them touch at every point but causes them to trample on each other.

I cannot help thinking that they who suppose when the population of America has grown to its full complement it will be exceedingly difficult to uphold free institutions have magnified the danger arising from that source, or rather, that they have mistaken the influence which that circumstance will exert upon the destiny of the country. The denser the population becomes, the more will the people be brought into close proximity with each other and the more rigorous will be the control which they will mutually exercise. This may be regarded as a law of society which, unless it is countervailed by other circumstances, is certain and invariable in its operation. It is a wise provision and one productive of the most salutary consequences; the check increases in intensity in proportion to the need which we have for it. More tranquillity prevails among the European communities than when their population was one third or one fourth of what it is now. To refer to the general progress of civilization would be reasoning in a circle, for the progress of civilization is itself in great part attributable to the increase of the population. The vast empire of China where civilization has been stationary as far back as history goes seems to show that the density of the population is not merely not adverse to the maintenance of tranquillity, but that it is highly favorable to it. The form of civilization is greatly below what exists in Europe and the United States, but it is superior to that which exists in the South American states.

I know few things better calculated powerfully to arrest our attention than the fact that during two years (I think 1835 and 1836) there was not a single execution in London. London is itself an immense community and that amid such discordant elements, such an eternal jangling of interests, such a craving of all sorts of wants and desires, so much order and tranquillity should be maintained is, to say the least, a striking fact in the history of society. Nor is this state of things an accidental one. The diminution of crime for a series of years before had been very regular. The convictions for murder and for assaults with intent to murder were for a period of ten years commencing with 1816 no more in London than they were in New Orleans during the same time. The population of the one was not more than thirty-five thousand, of the other a million and a half. In the United States, it is in the thinly settled states of the west and southwest that outrages are most frequently committed and the authority of the laws set at defiance. Those states, without doubt, contain an exceedingly sound population; but great numbers of the profligate emigrate to them because they know they will be less exposed to the surveillance and control of others than they would be amid the fuller population of the older states. If it should be said that this state of things is owing to a defective administration of the laws, it may be answered that this defect would be cured by a more numerous population. Public opinion is the most effectual auxiliary in the execution of the laws; but public opinion is necessarily feeble where the settlements are to a considerable extent composed of wandering adventurers. Those states are rapidly passing through the same purifying process which all the others have gone through. They will ultimately contain as sound, because they will contain as dense, a population as other parts of the union.

The reason, then, why the control which the parts of society exert upon each other is more stringent and more active as the population increases is obvious. Individuals and collections of individuals are placed more completely within reach of each other and have a more immediate interest in each other's conduct. No one can then exercise his faculties or perform any action, however insignificant, without affecting many others. Each individual acts as a sentinel upon his neighbor and thus, through the co-operation of all, the private interest of each is rendered as consistent as possible with the interest of all.

There are then two sorts of control existing in society; the one a control on the part of the government, the other of the people upon each other. The last is a most important element in the social organization at the present day.

Free institutions give force to both species of control. The principle of equality which pervades them brings individuals into closer juxtaposition, and the check which these habitually exert upon one another's behavior not only familiarizes them to the authority of the government, but greatly interests them in upholding it, since the laws are only intended to accomplish what the great majority of private persons are aiming at, but which they are too feeble to effect.

BOOK TWO

CHAPTER I | WRITTEN CONSTITUTIONS

THE formation of a written constitution is one of the most decisive steps which has been made toward the establishment of free institutions. It implies the exercise of reflection in its highest degree, an ability to frame the most comprehensive rules, and to make application of them to the actual affairs of men. Most governments are easily enough initiated into the art of governing the people, but a written constitution is a scheme by which the governors themselves are proposed to be governed. The commencement of this very important movement is of recent date. We cannot carry it further back than the era of the American Revolution. For although a few examples have been handed down to us from antiquity, and one or two attempts of the same kind are recorded in European history prior to 1776, the difference are so numerous and so fundamental that we are not entitled to range them in the same class with the American constitutions. It sometimes happens that a mere difference in degree between two things is so wide as to place an absolute distinction between them and to render them opposite instead of resemblances of one another. The constitutions of antiquity confounded what we would characterize as political ordinances with the acts of ordinary legislation. This was the case in the code of the Roman decemvirs, and it was equally so in the systems introduced by the Athenian and Spartan lawgivers. One design of a written constitution is to define the boundary between political and civil laws. For as it is not intended that the two should have an equally authoritative character, it is not intended that they should have an equally durable form. This incongruous mixture of two things so different was therefore an infirmity. It showed that the mind had not yet got so far as to be able to analyze its ideas in matters of government, no matter whether this analysis is the product of great learning or whether it is the result of a long course of experience. Not to estimate the difference between two things is not to understand the nature of one of them at least, and so to make one or both occupy an unfit place in the system which we construct.

This subject has given occasion to very important discussions in France since the establishment of constitutional monarchy; and it has sometimes required the efforts of the most enlightened French statesmen to prevent the error I have alluded to from being committed in "the charte." [1] Once settle the relative powers of the different departments of governments and the office of the legislative body will be plain enough. Its power will be better guarded and yet will be more full and ample than it would otherwise be. The varied exigencies of society, the unforeseen changes which take place in human affairs, the slow accumulation of that wisdom which flows from experience, all demand that once the orbit within which the legislature is to move is marked out a large and liberal discretion should be given to it in the enactment of laws.

But that which places the greatest imaginable difference between the constitutions of antiquity and those of the United States is that the former were in no sense the offspring of the popular will while, on the contrary, the latter have emanated directly from the people. The same may be said of those European states which now have written constitutions. Those constitutions have been the gift of some self-constituted lawgiver, or have been imposed by bodies of men who very imperfectly represented the supreme authority of the state.

The constitutions of antiquity showed clearly enough that there were among the citizens some individuals of contemplative and cultivated minds. But they indicated nothing further. They afforded no evidence that those great truths which lie at the foundation of all just and legitimate government were seized and appreciated by the people at large; or rather they afford incontestible proof to the contrary. A conjectural plan of government is as easily drawn up as any other composition; which is one reason, perhaps, why many otherwise enlightened understandings affect to treat all such works very lightly. A constitution which deals in certain preconceived general principles,

1. [Grimke refers to the French Constitution of 1830 which, after the revolutionary overthrow of Charles X, established the constitutional monarchy of Louis Philippe.]

and seeks to mold the affairs of men into a conformity with them, is very different from a system of government which undertakes to arrive at the knowledge of fundamental maxims by availing itself of a vast fund of experience and observation existing among the people themselves. The American constitutions were for this reason a really difficult and arduous achievement. The difficulty did not consist in the degree but in the extent of intellect necessary for the occasion. A plan of government in which the popular will has had a direct agency presupposes a very wide diffusion of intelligence, and this at once stamps upon the undertaking both a practical and a comprehensive character. Lord Somers and his colleagues, who took the lead in the Revolution of 1689, Benjamin Constant and Lafayette who took the lead in the kindred Revolution of 1830 were the real thinkers and actors on those occasions.[2] But Hamilton and Madison, equally great names, who took the lead in the formation of the American constitution, were but spokesmen of the popular will. Hence the profound and impressive debates which took place at that time in popular assemblies; and hence the necessity which was felt of laying before the public a full exposition of the proposed plan of government. The letters of Publius are, in this respect, perfectly unique.[3] No similar production is recorded in the history of ancient or modern civilization.

Some of the remarks I have made are applicable with still more force to the attempts which have been made by individuals of ingenious and powerful understandings to frame schemes of government for a whole people. We might as well tear out of the volumes of Plato, Harrington, or Mr. Hume the plans of a republic which they conceived and ordain them as constitutions as to call Mr. Locke's and the Abbe Sieyès' efforts by that name.[4]

2. [Lord John Somers (1651–1716), English jurist and statesman who presided at the forming of the Declaration of Rights (1688) and established the legality of the accession of William and Mary; Benjamin Constant (1767–1830), French-Swiss writer and political theorist, liberal supporter of constitutional monarchy and civil liberties, one of the major actors in the July Revolution (1830) in France; Marquis de Lafayette (1757–1834), French hero of the American Revolution, leader of the moderate party in the French Revolution of 1789 and 1830.]

3. [The *Federalist Papers* were published over the pseudonym, "Publius."]

4. [John Locke drafted a model constitution, "The Fundamental Constitutions for the Government of Carolina" (1669), which, although formally adopted by the Lords Proprietors of Carolina, was never put into practical effect; Emmanuel Joseph Sieyès, French revolutionist and statesman, who prided himself on his logical and systematic drafts for constitutions, helped to write the French Constitution of 1791 and for the year VIII (1799) under Napoleon.]

Nor is there any reason for surprise that the popular mind and not merely the popular will should have so direct an agency in the formation of a constitution of government as is manifestly the case in America. If the mere addition which a life of the closest study and the greatest learning makes to the mind of the highest capacities is not so great as the knowledge which is possessed by the man of the most untutored understanding, a fact of which there can be no doubt, there is nothing unnatural in the supposition that the plainest men when they are placed in a situation favorable to the acquisition and realization of a large amount of political experience, should not only be equal to such an undertaking but that without their cooperation no such undertaking can be understandingly executed.

Some persons, eminent for their intelligence, have occasionally hazarded the assertion that there is no force in constitutions on paper and that we should be as well without them. Admitting that it is fair thus to withdraw the mind from the all-important consideration that a constitution which is the work of the popular mind marks an entirely new era in the history of society, no opinion can well be conceived which is more completely behind the age in which we live.

The reasoning which has been relied upon to sustain this strange assertion would be equally conclusive to prove that there is no force in written laws. And yet it is plain that without written laws society would be a scene of discord and confusion. The occasional violation of a constitution would not even help to prove the assertion. The laws are repeatedly violated and yet no one lays his head upon his pillow without feeling a wonderful sense of security under their protection. Even the English "magna charta," an instrument far less comprehensive in its scope and possessing therefore much fewer guaranties than an American constitution, was repeatedly violated, but it constituted a landmark amid all the troubles of the day, and the English monarchs were compelled to ratify and reratify it until it acquired a weight and authority which no one was strong enough to throw off.

The precise and definite form which writing gives to our ideas renders it an indispensable auxiliary in reducing those ideas to practice and in spreading their influence over an extensive country. If instances are to be found where communities have been governed with considerable wisdom without written constitutions, this is either because there has been some approach to one, some resemblance to an instrument which, however imperfect, has acquired the sanction of successive generations of men, or such communities have lived in close fellowship, have been bound in an intimate alliance with others which had written constitutions, and were moreover obliged by the league of which they were members to owe allegiance to a federal constitution. The first is the case of England, the second that of Connecticut and Rhode Island. But all three of these examples prove that there is great force in written constitutions.

A written constitution is a repository of tried and experienced truths with an authoritative sanction accompanying it, capable of being appealed to in all times of party conflict when the minds of men are tormented by the danger of civil commotion and when every means which is calculated to fix reflection and to steady the public mind is of so much importance to the peace of society.

In every department of life it has been found that the collection of human experience and wisdom into some visible organ capable of making a sensible and durable impression on the mind was the only way to give a fixed and permanent direction to the actions of men. It cannot be otherwise then with civil government where the body of rules which are adopted has this additional advantage, that it is the result of a deliberate compact between the members of the community. It would be much more reasonable to assert that there was no utility in a system of religious doctrines, or a system of education, in a code of jurisprudence, or in the rules which are adopted for the army and navy, than to affirm that there is no force in a body of fundamental ordinances for the government of the state.

We may pronounce of a country in which a written constitution has been framed by delegates chosen by the people, that it is from that very circumstance placed entirely beyond the reach of monarchical or aristocratical institutions. A change in the structure of society so thorough and so decisive is absolutely incompatible with the existence of either of those forms of government. But this change may take place although the great body of the people are not advanced to the highest pitch of intelligence or to anything like an equal degree of intelligence. The system of common schools has existed in New England for more than two hundred years, and yet great inequalities still exist, and will forever exist, in the capacities of the men who inhabit it. But as there is a certain limit beyond which knowledge must not advance in order to insure the existence of any one of the artificial forms of government, so there is also a limit beyond which knowledge need not advance in order to insure the establishment of free institutions.

Those rules which govern the interests of large collections of men are never so recondite as those which are obtained by the study of the individual alone. And if we examine the history of any of the great revolutions which have changed the condition and destiny of the human race, it will be found that the leading ideas — those which presided over the whole movement — were the simplest imaginable. Let us take, for an example, the Protestant reformation. The principles with which the great reformer set out and which were his constant weapon from the commencement to the close of the controversy were so plain, so homely, so easy to be understood and handled by the unlettered man that men of refined learning were puzzled to find out how it was possible to create so great and so general a movement through the instrumentality of such trifling propositions. The public debates which took place throughout Germany seemed to turn upon mere truisms and puerilities. And yet these apparent puerilities could not be battered down by the greatest amount of learning which was brought to bear upon them.

It is the same with all the important and salutary revolutions which take place in civil society. The governing ideas are few and easily comprehended because they contain general truths; and the truths are general because they have reference to the interests of large collections of men. A highly intelligent man who had been a member of the American legislature remarked to me that "he must give up all his notions as to the incompetency of farmers to legislate for the community. They have both more sagacity and more information than I had at all calculated upon."

The establishment of constitutional government in the United States has given a decided impulse to the public mind in Europe. Ten or twelve of the European states have adopted written constitutions. But none of them rest upon the same firm foundation as in America. A written constitution emanating from the popular will, while the government was monarchical or aristocratical in character, would be a solecism in politics. Neither of those governments could possibly survive the establishment of such an instrument. If not immediately annihilated, they must speedily fall to decay. Men, whatever their physical strength may be, must at least have a fit atmosphere to breathe in. So that we must either say that the diffusion of knowledge is incompatible with the solid interests of mankind, or that monarchy and aristocracy are incompatible with the existence of constitutional government in its legitimate sense. There cannot be two inconsistent rules at one and the same time for the government of a community, the one founded upon the general interests, the other upon some particular interests only. One or the other must give way, and it is easy to see which will ultimately have the advantage amid the general spread of knowledge which we witness in the nineteenth century. Where resides the moral power of the community, there also will be found to reside its physical power. The maxim that power is constantly sliding from the many to the few is false in a republic. The tendency is directly the reverse. The maxim is true only where the political institutions are unfavorable to the development and spread of knowledge and where every contrivance has been employed to render the affairs of government complicated and mysterious in the extreme, and so to impress the popular mind with a conviction, not only that it has no right but that it has no sort of ability to bear any part in them.

But however imperfect the European constitutions may be, they are a great step toward the establishment of regular government. No event which has occurred in that quarter of the globe affords more signal evidence of the general advance of society. A written constitution never adds to, but always subtracts from, the power which previously existed. It is not only an open recognition of certain general principles favorable to liberty, but it is obliged to make a definite application of these principles. What was obtained when the community was struggling for freedom can with difficulty be recalled when it has arrived at greater maturity. For a written constitution, together with the body of new laws which it gives occasion to, acts directly upon the manners, diffuses more inquisitiveness and information, and inspires all classes with a greater degree of self-confidence. The ability to guard the institutions is derived from the influence which the institutions have themselves created. There may be still more progress, but there will rarely ever be a retrograde movement.

The French "charte" is the most remarkable of the European constitutions. It was wrested from the king. And this indicates, at least, that knowledge and liberty have acquired sufficient strength to make a vigorous protest against the unlimited authority of kings. The leading men in the kingdom were obliged to fall in with this movement in order to sustain their own influence, but they have contributed, however unwillingly, to strengthen the popular will. The "tiers état," a name which once startled the ear, has become a body of acknowledged importance in the state.

The European governments had all grown by piecemeal. The fragments of which they consisted were put together as force or accident determined. Not representing the public will, the people were at a loss to discover the title which their rulers arrogated to themselves. There was no way of solving the difficulty but by having recourse to an authority from above. Hence the doctrine of the "jure divino" right of kings to rule. The minds of men were then filled with all sorts of superstition, and the prince whose privileges flow from so exalted a source seems alone entitled to place a construction upon them. Elizabeth told the English Commons that they must not dare to meddle with state affairs; and Charles XII of Sweden told the senate that he would send his boot to govern them. Constitutional government has effected the same revolution in politics which the progress of physical science has produced in religion. Both have banished superstition, the one from the domain of government, the other from that of religion. The human mind can no more get back to the notion of the divine right of kings than it can get back to fetichism and idolatry.

A popular constitution is necessarily a restraint upon the majority, so that that form of government which it has been supposed would be most exposed to the inroads of licentiousness is the one which is most strongly secured against them. For as a written constitution is obliged to contain an exact distribution of the powers of the various departments, the persons who fill those places cannot separate themselves from the rule which created them and say, because they are temporarily and for certain purposes the majority, that therefore they are the majority for all purposes and for all time to come. Do as we will, the moment we establish a popular constitution we are compelled to afford a substantial security to the minority against the majority. It could not be a popular constitution unless it contained provisions for securing the rights of all classes without reference to the fact whether either shall afterward fall into the party of the majority or into that of the minority. And although it is plain that it is physically possible to overleap the bounds set up by the constitution, yet so firm is the hold which this solemn covenant has upon the minds of everyone that the most ambitious and unprincipled men recoil from the attempt. When this has become the settled habit of thinking among the people, their feelings and imagination come in aid of their convictions of right. The constitution becomes a memorable record, and the fancy clothes it with additional solemnity. If the altar and the throne become objects of veneration in monarchical government, the altar and the constitution become objects of equal veneration in a republic. In those rare instances when attempts have been made by the state legislatures in America to violate their constitutions, there has been a redeeming virtue among the people which has either compelled the majority to retrace their steps or, by converting the minority into the majority, has brought the constitution back to its pristine spirit.

If there were no such instrument, parties would do very much what the exigencies of the moment dictated. For how would it be possible to argue upon the constitutionality of any measure when there was no constitution in existence. The alarm may be given of a contemplated violation of some fundamental right, but how can the people be made to understand this? A written constitution affords the only plain test. Some of its provisions may be the subject of dispute, but in the great majority of instances it will be a clear and most important guide in judging the actions of all the public functionaries.

The express and the implied powers in a written constitution are sometimes identical.[5] This is a distinction which deserves great consideration for from it very important consequences follow. The express powers are identical with the implied whenever the former would be unmeaning and inoperative unless laws were subsequently passed to carry them into effect. Without the aid of these laws which are referred to the head of implied powers, the express powers would be a nullity. This is evident from the 8th section of the 1st article of the constitution of the United States. All the powers therein delegated to the legislature are express powers, and yet not one can be exercised without passing laws. It is different with regard to the powers which are conferred upon the executive. These, for the most part, may be executed without the intervention of any laws. This is evident from the 2d and 3d sections of the 2d article.[6] Some, perhaps, all, the pow-

5. [For the second edition, Grimke added new matter from the start of this paragraph to the paragraph which ends, ". . . will the bulwarks of liberty be guarded," on p. 218.]

6. [Article I, Section 8, gives Congress the power "to lay and collect Taxes, Imposts and Excises, to pay the debts and provide for the common Defence and general Welfare of the United States" with the provision that all duties, excises, and imposts "shall be uniform throughout the United States"; Article II, Section 2, Clauses 1–3, deal with the powers and duties of the President; Article II, Section 3, with the initiative of the President in recommending legislation and the execution of the laws.]

ers there enumerated may be modified by the legislature. For instance, the power of removal from office may be forbidden under certain conditions, but they are all substantially exercisable without any acts of legislation. This is the case, also, with the powers conferred upon the judiciary. Some of these powers also may be modified by the legislature, while the most important part of them execute themselves and render it unnecessary to resort to any implied powers. This important difference between the legislative and the other two departments contributes greatly to enlarge the powers of the former, as the field within which the implied powers may be exercised is never precisely determined. On the other hand, there is this compensation for reducing to the character of implied powers all those which are wielded by the legislature, that those which are possessed by the executive and judiciary, being complete without the intervention of any laws, these two departments are protected against the assaults of the legislature. If, then, it were possible to reduce to the character of express powers all those which are conferred upon the legislative, in analogy with those conferred upon the executive and judiciary, a very important step would be made towards improving the whole structure of government. That this may be effected to a great extent cannot be doubted. A very important movement has been lately made in this direction by some of the American states. It is no objection that it will render constitutions a little more voluminous. A constitution is faulty when, by going into detail, its provisions are ambiguous. But when the opposite effect, that of greater clearness and precision, is attained, the objection loses its force. If in the federal government the powers which appertain to the legislature are all of the character of implied powers, this is true in a still higher sense in the constitutions of the states. The former does contain an enumeration of the powers which are proper to be exercised by the legislature, although none can be exercised without the aid of the implied powers. But the state constitutions generally do not even contain this enumeration. They simply create the legislative power, and then leave it free to act as the public exigencies and its own discretion may dictate. The reason of the distinction is obvious. The federal constitution is one of strictly limited powers, limited not merely in respect to the constitution making power but as regards the state governments. It was necessary, therefore, to make a specification in gross of its powers in order to separate them from those of the states. But there are powerful reasons, as I shall presently show, why a state constitution should be as well guarded in this particular as the constitution of the Union.

One use of the veto of the executive is to protect him against the usurpations of the legislature, but another and still higher use is to protect the community against those usurpations. One reason why the executive, although a single individual, may succeed in the exercise of this power is that he is armed with an extensive patronage. This clothes him with great authority and enables him when he acts with fidelity to rally the sound part of the community. One reason why the veto is generally dropped in the state constitutions is that it is impossible, even if it were consistent with the genius of free institutions, to create an executive with very extensive patronage; another is, that the states are not so extensive as to foster powerful local interests. Thus, the necessity of the veto is accompanied with a corresponding necessity of strengthening the magistrate who exercises it; and, on the other hand, in proportion to its inutility is the difficulty of rendering it authoritative.

It may be supposed that in an extensive country like the United States executive patronage would be so great as to enable the chief magistrate to exercise the veto improperly. Doubtless this will sometimes be the case. In every human institution we always make allowance for occasional aberrations, as we do in the most perfect machinery. But there is an antidote to the evil. Where universal suffrage is established, the amount of patronage, though great as regards the executive, is very small when compared with the number of the electors.

In a limited monarchy, the absolute veto is conferred upon the king in order to protect him against the usurpations of the legislature which represents the sovereignty; in other words, he is himself made a branch of the legislative power, for to give him the absolute veto is to confer upon him legislative power. In a republic the written constitution guards him against those encroachments for his powers are clearly defined. But if the powers of the legislature are all of the nature of implied powers, which cannot be defined, it may be necessary to invest him with the qualified veto, the danger of usurpation not being as where there is no enumeration of either the express or implied powers. This would seem to afford an argument for giving the veto to the governor of a state for, as I have observed, the list of implied powers in a state government is vastly more extensive than in the federal and the danger of encroachments on the community is as great, although there may be little danger of invading the prerogatives of the governor. There are, however, two ways of protecting society against the usurpations of the legislature. One in the manner I have just indicated, the other by circumscribing the authority of the legislature, that is, by inserting limitations in the state constitutions on the exercise of every power which is intended to be withheld from the legislature and express grants of every one which is intended to be exercised. There is a marked tendency in this direction in the state constitutions which have lately been framed. The prohibition of contracting a public debt unless authorized by vote of the people, first inserted in the constitutions of Rhode Island and Iowa and since in those of New York and Ohio; the provision that special charters shall not be granted; that the legislature shall not authorize the suspension of specie payments; that the stockholders in a corporation shall be individually responsible, contained in the 8th article of the constitution of New York, and the whole of the 14th section of the 7th article of the same constitution are remarkable examples. Of the same character are the 4th, 5th, 15th, and 16th sections of the 3d article, and the 4th and 11th sections of the 6th article, and most of the provisions in the bill of rights, or 51st article.[7] Indeed, it is remarkable that until recently the restrictions upon the legislative power for the most part have been carefully placed in the bill of rights. The great importance of controlling the department by express limitations did not command public attention. Notwithstanding, however, that the constitution of

7. [In the New York State Constitution of 1846, article VIII deals with individual liberty; Grimke must mean the whole of the fourteen sections of article VII since each of them carefully hedges the legislature's power to create or discharge debts. Article III, Sections 4 and 5, deals with the equitable apportionment of legislative districts; Section 15 says that no bill shall be passed unless by a majority of all members; Section 16 forbids omnibus legislation by asserting that no private or local bill "shall embrace more than one subject." Article VI, Section 4, deals with the organization of judicial districts and Section 11 allows for the removal of a Justice of the Supreme Court or of the Court of Appeals only by a two-thirds vote of the Assembly and a majority of the Senate. There is no "51st article." Since Grimke refers to the bill of rights he probably means to refer to the first article which is largely an enumeration of the right to trial by jury, free speech, religious worship, and such rights that we associate with a bill of rights. For a full text of these articles and sections, see *The Federal and State Constitutions, Colonial Charters, and Other Organic Laws of the States, Territories, and Colonies Now or Heretofore Forming the United States of America*, 59th Congress, 2nd session, Document No. 357 (Washington, 1909), V, 2653–2692.]

New York has so far exceeded any other in the precision and comprehensiveness of its restrictions upon the legislature, the veto of the governor is retained. It will probably be retained until experiment has ascertained all the cases in which exact limitations may be imposed. When these are exhausted, when all the implied powers are converted into express powers, it may be dropped.

It would seem, then, that the veto is only conferred upon the executive in consequence of the imperfect character of the limitations imposed upon the legislature. If society can be protected against the predominance of local interests, against the improper exercise of implied powers by express limitations, these will be much more efficacious than the veto. Even in the federal government, what an amount of mischief may have been averted if precise provisions in relation to a bank, to the tariff, to internal improvements, *etc.,* had been inserted. Nothing but experience could disclose where the weak points of the system lay. But the difficulty of availing ourselves of this experience in the federal government is infinitely greater than in those of the states. It is exceedingly difficult to obtain amendments in the former. The veto will therefore be retained there after it ceases to be employed in the latter.

An immense advantage will arise from this scheme of strict limitations, independently of its dispensing with the veto. It will, to a great extent, close the door upon party dissensions. If anyone reflects upon the various questions which have agitated the people of the states and kindled so fierce a spirit of party, he will find that they are nearly all attributable to the defect of the state or of the federal constitutions in defining the attributes of the legislature. If a state constitution merely creates this department and is almost entirely silent as to its powers, the door is immediately opened to the most unbounded discussion as to the propriety of various acts of legislation. If the federal constitution does contain an enumeration of its powers, and this is wanting in the requisite precision, an endless controversy is kept up, not merely as to the expediency, but as to the constitutionality of various laws. A few words in the one case, a few lines in the other, would have prevented the mischief.

It would appear, then, that so far from its being true that constitutions are sacred and should never be touched, that they partake of the character of all human institutions, and should be open to amendment. It is not in the power of the finest genius to draw up a constitution which shall be perfect at the time, much less which shall be so in all time to come. Time and experience are indispensable to develop the true character of the powers which are marked out and to reveal the secret flaws which have prevented the exact working of the system. England was convulsed with civil wars or ruled with a rod of iron until the Revolution of 1688, when some precise limitations were imposed upon the power of government. And yet these limitations do not contain as much as is contained in the bill of rights of some of the American states. So far is it from being true that written constitutions are of no avail that the British constitution derives all its efficacy, all its healthful activity, from those written provisions which were made about the time of the Revolution. It may be said that that nation is not yet prepared for an entirely written constitution. But given the fact that a nation is thus prepared and then, the more exact and the more comprehensive are its provisions in relation to the legislative power, the more securely will the bulwarks of liberty be guarded.

A constitution is open to alteration by the same power which enacted it. The sovereign authority residing in the people is necessarily inalienable. It cannot be extinguished because there is no human power superior to itself to have that effect. To assert that a constitution is of so sacred a character that it can never again be touched would be to return to the European notions of government. A constitution, however, may provide in what way alterations shall be made so as to get rid on the one hand of the difficulty which would arise from one generation attempting to bind all others and, at the same time, to secure that the future generation which does make alterations shall be the people themselves and not their rulers.

All the American constitutions contain provisions of this kind. But as it rarely happens that a constitution will require to be entirely remodeled, a way is provided by which particular amendments may be made without the necessity of assembling a convention. In some states the proposed change must be deliberated upon, and agreed to by two thirds of two successive legislatures; in others it is after a vote of two thirds of two successive legislatures submitted to the people at their annual elections. In Pennsylvania a majority of two successive legislatures is sufficient for this purpose. All these plans are substantially alike. By the first, it is the legislature which makes the alteration. But the members have been chosen by the people with a direct view to the question of change or no change. In Ohio, Vermont, and New Hampshire, alterations can only be made by a convention which in the former must be authorized by a vote of two thirds of the legislature, in the second by a vote of two thirds of a council of censors. But this vote cannot be taken oftener than once in seven years. And in New Hampshire the votes of the people are taken every seven years by the selectmen and assessors as to the expediency of calling a convention.

The design of all these plans is to secure that alterations shall be made in so solemn and deliberate a manner that there shall be no question but what they have emanated from the people.

In France it is a settled maxim that "the charte" can never be altered, that there is no power whatever competent to touch it. This seems to savor strongly of the school of Sir Robert Filmer.[8] But in reality it is a disguised departure from the doctrines of that school. "The charte" has shaken the power of the king and nobility. The danger of alteration, therefore, arises from that quarter. The notion of its inviolability is a check upon them, but it is not a check when popular sentiment calls loudly for some additional safeguard to liberty. Thus, the charte was remodeled in 1830 when provisions of vital importance to Frenchmen were inserted.

In Great Britain the maxim is that Parliament is the sovereign power. But I imagine that no parliament would dare to meddle with any of those fundamental enactments which secure English liberty. In 1689 it was deemed fit that "the convention" which seated William on the throne and passed the celebrated "act of settlement" should be composed of the members who had sat in the two preceding Parliaments.

Government, like every other human interest, is the subject of experience and therefore capable of improvement. We are bound, therefore, in devising a system of civil policy to avail ourselves of the same helps and resources which give strength and security to every other institution.

Society is not resolved into its original elements by the call of a convention to alter the constitution.[9] There is no instant of time in the transition from the old to the new state of things when there is not a subsisting government. Until a new constitution is ordained, the citizens are bound by the old. But a strange imagination exists among some persons that whatever the people have power to do, they have

8. [Sir Robert Filmer (d. 1653), apologist for the divine right of kings in *Patriarchia; or, The Natural Power of Kings* (1680).]

9. [For the second edition, Grimke added new matter from the start of this paragraph to the end of the chapter.]

also the right to do. It is not that such persons are at all friendly to the exercise of licentious power, but they can see no way of separating right and power where there is no positive or organized authority to limit and control the last. First, then, a distinction must be made between the power of voting and the power of executing. A convention might declare all existing marriages null, bastardise the children, confiscate the property of every one at death, authorize theft and murder, *etc.*; but it is plain that it would not have power to carry these ordinances into effect. This distinction between the power of declaring and the power of executing has been repeatedly illustrated in the history of all the European governments, even those which have possessed the most solidly established authority. The English Parliament, armed with all the powers of a convention, was not able in the reign of Mary to exterminate the Protestants; it was not able in the succeeding reign to abolish either the Catholic or Puritan religion. The French monarchs, prior and subsequent to the time of Henry the great, although they employed every instrument both physical and moral, were unable to exterminate the Huguenots.[10] That sect survived every effort to subdue them, and are now a powerful and influential body in the kingdom. No monarch ever possessed more absolute authority than Charles V and Philip II of Spain, yet they were unable to execute their edicts among the people of the low countries. This people annulled their edicts and became sovereign themselves.

Second. A constitutional convention has not the right to do everything which it has the power to do. Individuals every day have the opportunity to kill others, but they have not the right to do so. That an individual may be punished, and that a nation or the majority is dispunishable, makes no difference; for it will be conceded that if there were no means of punishing an individual, as there frequently are not, his guilt would be precisely the same and his right without the shadow of foundation. There is no possible way, therefore, by which we can make right and power convertible terms. It is in vain to say that these are extreme cases and therefore prove nothing, for they do indeed prove everything which is proper to be proved. They destroy the notion of universality as a part of the rule, and they therefore destroy the rule itself. They may also prove that the same principles which falsify

10. [Henry "the great" was Henry IV (1553–1610), King of France (1589–1610), who abjured Protestantism to maintain his rule and hoped to solve the Protestant-Catholic dispute in France by the Edict of Nantes (1598), a policy of toleration for Protestants.]

the rule in some particulars operate throughout the whole system of legislation and may be calculated upon with precision. But it may be said that there are many questions about which there is no such general opinion of right and justice as to render the enactments of a convention at all uniform, that this opens the door to a certain latitude of judgment, and that within this debatable field it is free to declare what is right and has power to enforce its decrees. This is admitted: there must be many questions about which a difference of opinion will prevail among persons of equal integrity and capacity. It is, however, a great boon gained to society when all those questions which are not debatable *in foro conscientiæ* are withdrawn from the field of controversy. This happens more certainly in a society democratically contituted than in any other. It is a fine observation of Mr. Hume that events which depend upon the will of a great number may be calculated upon with much more certainty than those which depend upon the will of a single individual or of a small number of persons. Events which are dependent upon a great number are governed by general laws, laws which are common to the species; those which depend upon one or a small number are subjected to the caprice or momentary disposition of the individual. The reason, then, why the advantage I have indicated appertains to a society democratically constituted is that the will of a great number, and upon that great number public events then depend, is consulted. No one has ever heard of a provision inserted in any American constitution or law which did violence to any of the fundamental rules of morality. Individuals may be guilty of a violation of them constantly; and, therefore, while we place no confidence in any calculation we may make as to what they will do, we may rely with great certainty upon a calculation as to the conduct of a very large body of men. But when I speak of a society which is democratically constituted, I do not intend merely a society which has democratic institutions; it may have them today and lose them tomorrow. I intend a society in which not only the political but the social organization is so advanced as to render free institutions the natural expression of the national will. In such a community, the greater the number whose opinions are taken, the greater the probability that those opinions will be reduced to unity; in other words, that the incoherent views which are entertained by some will be swallowed up in the opinions of a great number. For to say that they are incoherent is to say that they do not reflect the opinions which are common to the whole.

CHAPTER II | THAT IN A REPUBLIC THE GOVERNORS

AND THE GOVERNED ARE IDENTICAL

AND DIFFERENT

SOME persons find exceeding difficulty in comprehending how the people who govern should be one and the same with the people who are governed. The simplest and the most general notion which we ever form of government is that it is an institution established to preside over society, to maintain the supremacy of the laws, and to resist all efforts from without to shake and undermine its influence. To accomplish this it would seem to be necessary that government should possess an independent authority, that it should be armed with a power which could not be wrested from it at the very time when it was most important to employ it. Self government, or a democratic republic, which presupposes that the governors and the governed are one and the same, appears then to be a solecism in politics. It seems to contain an inherent principle of decay, and on that account to be the least eligible form of government which can be adopted. The notions which we frame to ourselves on all subjects, but especially on politics, are so much determined by the forms of thought which have previously existed that it is always a work of difficulty to break up old associations and to persuade the mind that any remarkable change in the institutions of society can be easily accomplished, much less that it would be both safe and advantageous.

The actual operation of popular government relieves us from the difficulty which has been suggested. For there, parties in the majority and minority immediately rise up. And as the former is entitled by right and by necessity to the supremacy, an example is afforded at the outset of a presiding power in the state which is distinct from that of the whole of society. Thus, if a small number of persons when compared with the entire population are disposed to be vicious and to violate the private rights of any individual, inasmuch as the administration of the laws is deposited with a much larger number, a check upon the conduct of the former is created which operates with certainty in ninety-nine cases in a hundred. And if we suppose that a still greater proportion — a proportion which constituted nearly or even quite a majority — were so inclined, still, if the distribution of property is such that the major part of the citizens have some allotment, some stake in the hedge, their interests will outweigh the propensity to commit mischief. And the sense of interest, combining with the operation of the laws after civil government is fairly established, redoubles its authority and in the course of no very long time beguiles the understandings of all men — the educated and the illiterate, the honest and the depraved — into the belief that there is indeed an inherent power residing in the government which can in no way be confounded with the local and discordant opinions which prevail without.

Nor, even if the unanimous consent of the people were admitted to be necessary to the first institution of government, would there be any great difficulty in obtaining it. Even the most abandoned men shrink from a public exposure of their hearts. Nor are crimes ever committed from habitual disposition, but from sudden impulse or powerful temptation which cannot well exist at the time when a popular convention is deliberating upon the form of government which shall be established. Nor, if it were otherwise, would it alter the case, since the worst men are as deeply interested in the maintenance of the general body of laws as are the best. They would not be able to commit any crime unless their own lives were protected up to a certain point. Their persons would not be safe as soon as they discovered a disposition to commit violence upon others. This is the reason why what is vulgarly termed "lynch law" is so abhorrent to offenders as well as to all lovers of law and order. Once established as a rule and the mere suspicion that a crime was committed or about to be committed would lead to summary punishment, while the penalty inflicted might be out of all proportion to the character of the offense. "Give me a fair trial," said a miserable creature whom I once knew summarily dealt with. "If I have broken the laws, I am entitled to justice."

Instances have come under my observation where individuals who freely voted for the establishment of a constitution afterwards rendered themselves amenable to the laws which were passed in conformity with that constitution. And I recollect two instances of individuals, members of a legislative body, who assisted in the enact-

ment of laws which punished forgery and perjury with great severity
and each of whom was afterwards the victim of one of those laws.
Few men assist in passing sentence upon themselves. But all men are,
somehow or other, irresistibly impelled to create the tribunal which is
destined to punish them if they are guilty.

So far we have considered government chiefly in its simplest form:
the government of the people in person. But it is not practicable to
conduct the affairs of a large state in this way. Almost all the ancient
commonwealths were of small size. The Grecian states were none of
them larger than an American county. Attica, the most famous, was
of no greater extent than Ross county, in Ohio. Indeed, city and state
were synonymous terms with the Grecian lawyers. By the government of a state, they intended the government of a city. Even in the
Roman commonwealth, the governing power was for a long time in
theory, and almost always in practice, confined to the walls of the city.

But when the elective principle is introduced, the machinery of the
government becomes more complicated. Those administrative officers
who were before appointed by the people are invested with additional
authority. And the legislative body becomes at once the most important and the most imposing of all the institutions of government.

There is no good reason why a popular constitution should not be
established in a simple democracy as well as in a representative government. In both, the minority require to be protected against the
majority. But the idea of a written constitution does not readily suggest itself unless the state is sufficiently large to occasion the introduction of the elective principle into general practice. The fundamental ordinances of the ancient lawgivers were of a totally different character, not merely in their origin but in their purport, from the American
constitution. They were like the ordinary acts of legislation which are
intended to restrain the people, whereas one great design of a constitution is to restrain the government.

The adoption of such an instrument, then, may appear to be a
source of weakness, but in reality it is a source of great strength to the
government. The individual whose conduct is marked by most propriety, no matter whether from internal or external motives, acquires
most power in the circle within which he moves. And a representative
government which moves within the ample but well defined jurisdiction marked out for it acquires unspeakable influence from that circumstance. And although the original intention in framing a written

constitution was to supply the grand defect which existed in all preceding governments, to-wit, the absence of a control upon the governors, yet it operates with equal efficacy in restraining the rest of society. The existence of such an instrument, then, is another addition to the apparatus of the government, giving it an air of greater solemnity, investing its proceedings with a more regular and decisive authority, and thus contributing practically to separate in the minds of everyone two ideas which are at bottom the same, to-wit, the idea of the people as governors and of the people who are governed.

Various reasons have been assigned for the division of the legislature into two branches. The plan appears to have been unknown among the republics of antiquity. Where two chambers did exist, one possessed powers of a different character from those of the other and therefore the cooperation of the two was not necessary; or else, one acted as a deliberative body merely, with at the utmost the power of initiating measures, while the other possessed the legislative power proper. Feudal institutions, which gave rise to a baronial nobility, seated by the side of growing and powerful cities, introduced the scheme as it exists in modern states. The population of the towns was of too much importance to be overlooked while at the same time the barons were too haughty and jealous to permit the representatives of those towns to have seats among themselves. The legislative body therefore became separated into two bodies, occupying at first the same hall, but afterward sitting in two when the practice of public debate took the place of the private conferences and rendered it impossible to conduct the proceedings at different ends of even a large apartment. And although the reason for this arrangement has ceased to exist, the institution is still preserved. Perhaps we may be able to assign to it an office distinct from that which has been ascribed to it and say that although it has the appearance of being more out of place in a democratic republic, where the subordination of ranks does not exist, than in any other form of government, yet, inasmuch as two chambers render the machinery of legislation more complex than one alone and communicate to the government a more imposing character than it would otherwise wear, this division of the legislative body may assist, although indirectly, in upholding the public authority and in maintaining order and tranquillity throughout the state. It is no objection to an institution that it exercises an influence over the imaginations of men, provided this influence does not interfere with the useful and legitimate purposes which were designed to be answered but, on the contrary, contributes to carry them out more fully.

A regular system of jurisprudence would appear to be as essential to a people living under the simplest form of popular government as for any other community. The eternal principles of justice are not of man's creation, and they have on that account an authority which no man is at liberty to deny or disparage. A code of jurisprudence is nothing more than an exposition of those principles so far as they apply to the affairs of society. But the existence of such an instrument is hardly known until after the state has passed from the simplest form of democratic rule and has assumed the character of a representative government. The people when sitting in judgment personally cannot with any convenience make application of those principles of law requiring, as they do, the most concentrated attention and the exercise of an undisturbed judgment. Indeed, such principles have the appearance of being out of place where the form of government presupposes that there is no superior authority behind the judicial magistrates. We hear of the Roman or civil law. But no one has ever heard of Grecian law. The organization of the Grecian tribunal was exceedingly unfavorable to the growth of a regular system of civil jurisprudence. The principal court was composed of six or eight thousand people, and the decisions of such a tribunal must necessarily be vague and conjectural. Nor did Roman law make any progress until the judicial power passed from the popular assemblies of the comitia and became exclusively vested in the representative magistrates termed prætors. It is not until the reign of Hadrian, in the commencement of the second century, that jurisprudence began to wear the character of a regular system, such as it is known at the present day. The division of labor was then consummated. The judicial power was lodged with certain magistrates, set apart for that purpose, who were obliged to act upon some fixed, general rules. And the collection of those rules into a body constitutes in great part the foundation of the civil law. In the time of the emperors the prætors were not an elective magistracy, but the special character of the duties they were assigned to perform, after a beginning had been made, was far more favorable to the growth of a regular system than the tumultuous meetings of the comitia. In addition to which an absolute government in a highly civilized country is very willing to purchase an unlimited political authority by establishing exact rules of justice in what concerns the civil relations of men. If it were not for some principle of virtual representation at least, neither law nor civilization would ever make any progress.

But what the appointing power effects is accomplished still more fully by the elective power. In no country in the world has jurisprudence acquired a more regular and systematic character than in the United States. The perfection which it has attained constitutes its only objection. All the leading principles on which it reposes have been so thoroughly ramified and rendered so flexible with the professional man in their application to new cases, that the science no longer presents the same attraction as formerly to minds of a highly intellectual cast. We may say of the law what has been said of mathematics, that it has become an exhausted science. But this regular growth of a body of laws with appropriate tribunals and magistrates to administer it, the natural result of the introduction of representative government, has a wonderful effect in giving to the institutions an appearance of complexity and in surrounding them with an air of authority which only contributes to carry out the design for which they were originally created. These institutions are the workmanship of the people. And yet between the people and the government is interposed a vast and complicated machinery, difficult to break through, and which inculcates and enforces among the whole population the notions of right, of obligation, of justice, more effectually than the decrees of the most absolute government could do.

The extent of county over which the government presides assists in keeping up the delusion, in persuading people that there is an authority residing in the government totally independent of the popular will — if that can be called a delusion which has its origin in the most settled principles of human nature and which only contributes to heighten the reverence for the laws and to maintain order and tranquility throughout the land.

Even where the territory is only of tolerable extent, government is called upon to act through the medium of a host of functionaries in a great number of particular instances. And this acting in detail repeatedly and on such an infinity of occasions, without any perceptible interference from without, separates the notion of governmental authority from that of the popular will, augments the authority of the former, and enables it to exercise an easy empire over the minds of men. And yet it possesses this influence only in consequence of being founded upon the popular will and on the condition of making itself eminently useful to society.

When men are called upon to act openly in face of the world, their actions are naturally more guarded and circumspect than where they are free from so wholesome a control. This is the case even though the sense of right should be supposed to be no stronger than on other occasions. For when they come to deliberate in public, each one finds that the interests of others have an intimate relation with his own, and that, do as he will, their opinions will entitle themselves to equal consideration with his. This is the case in the simplest form of democratic government where all the citizens meet together to consult upon public affairs. But the effect is increased where the elective form of government is established. In the first instance, the whole population constitute the public. The actors and the spectators, the delinquents and the judges are indiscriminately mixed. The restraint therefore is not complete. Hence the tumultuous assemblies in the Grecian republics. In the second case, the legislature, executive, and judges, together with the whole body of administrative officers, constitute at any one time only a fraction of the population. The government and the public are separated from each other in order that the last may bear with greater weight and a more defined authority upon the first. The keenness of the observers is heightened, and the conduct of the actors is more circumspect. Those who are invested with public trusts of any kind find that they are no longer able to bury their motives and disguise their actions amid a vast and heterogeneous assembly. The circumstances in which they are placed rouse a feeling of responsibility to other men and this in its turn awakens reflection and a sense of justice. But the circumstances in which men are placed constitute a very large part of their education through life. And this sense of justice and this habit of reflection, although originally induced by external causes, may in progress of time become very important springs of action. If all those public functionaries were accustomed to act as simple members of an immense assembly, called together on the spur of the occasion, they would be carried away by every temporary delusion and their actions would seem in their own eyes worthy of condemnation only when it was too late to correct them.

This is the reason why what we term public opinion acquires so much force and wears so imposing an authority in representative government. That portion of the population which gives being to it is far more numerous, the public much more extensive, than in any other form of government; while at the same time, the public officers of every grade stand apart and distinct from that public and are therefore subjected to a constant and active supervision from without; and, if the separation of the two has the effect of heightening the sense of responsibility and increasing the capacity for reflection in the former, it has the same influence upon the people. These are also placed in new circumstances which are eminently calculated to promote thought and inquiry. And although the persons who fill the three great departments of the government and all the administrative officers are but the agents of the people, yet this people now view the conduct of the former from a point different from that at which they view their own. They expect and demand better things than they would from themselves. And the constant working of this principle, in spite of all the tendencies to licentiousness of opinion, ultimately communicates to both the public and the government more calmness and moderation and a disposition to view things not merely as they are, but as they should be. It frequently happens that on the proposal of an important public measure popular feeling seems to run in one direction, while the representatives of the people are disposed to take a different course. The discussion which takes place in the legislative body gives rise to discussion out of doors. The people and their representatives have time to compare notes, and instead of a high state of feeling and exasperation a greater degree of reflection is produced. So that when the final vote has been taken in the legislative body it has received the most cordial approbation from the men of all parties. The settlement of the Oregon controversy is an instance of this.[1] It is a memorable proof that the question of peace and war is coming to be viewed in a manner totally different from what it was formerly and that the American people and government are deeply impressed with the notion that to preserve peace is to maintain civilization. The institutions of government in a republic have some other office to perform besides that of giving occasion to the exercise of political power. They beget habits of reflection and disseminate a spirit of inquiry throughout the land. Nor are

1. [Oregon, originally the name for the Pacific Coast region west of the Rockies, north of California, and south of Alaska, was the subject of dispute between the United States and England for many years until the peaceful settlement of their rival claims in 1846.]

those protracted debates which take place in the legislature and which are so much the subject of criticism abroad without their use. They allow time for public opinion to ripen and bring the people and their representatives into harmony with each other. Half a century ago the treaty negotiated by Mr. Jay, although it was exceedingly advantageous to the United States, created a degree of agitation which shook the confederacy to its very center.[2] The institutions were then young; the people had not grown into the new circumstances in which they were placed. Time, and the consequent increase of population which it was predicted would develop in ten-fold strength the mischiefs then experienced, has had a contrary effect. A dispute which in 1795 may have kindled a bloody and unprofitable war was in 1846 easily adjusted upon the same principles on which sagacious men of business act in settling their private controversies.

In a democratic republic of considerable extent the electors are so numerous that each feels himself like a drop in the ocean. So that the more the number of active citizens is increased, the greater is the power of the state and yet in the same proportion is the importance of each individual diminished. The governors and the governed are in reality one and the same, but so exceedingly small is the share of influence which falls to each person that everything seems to go on without any cooperation on his part. The movements of the political machine seem to be directed by an unseen hand and to be conducted with as much regularity and precision as in the most consolidated governments. The difference between the two cases is that in the former it is a mere illusion, while in the last it is all reality. But the illusion which is practiced upon the imagination, instead of detracting from the weight which the governed possess in the character of governors, adds greatly to it. Each one of the citizens is of importance, and yet if it were possible for him to realize this — to believe that he was of so much consequence that his participation in the government was necessary to

2. [Jay's Treaty (1794) settled a number of serious disputes between the United States and Great Britain which derived from the terms of the Treaty of Peace of 1783, chiefly the determination of the northeast and northwest boundaries of the United States and the evacuation of forts still held by the British in the West in violation of American sovereignty. But the treaty said nothing about freedom of the seas and the right of a neutral to trade in non-contraband goods to and between enemy ports, as the United States in the war between Great Britain and France. Ratification of the treaty was a party matter, with the Federalists for and the Republicans against, and passed the Senate with a bare two thirds majority (20–10), June 22, 1795.]

the general weal — public affairs would meet with constant hindrances instead of proceeding with order and regularity. It is because each one does act, and yet so acts that his voice appears to be drowned in that of the public, that so much alertness and energy are combined with so much prudence and circumspection in the management of public affairs, and that one of the most difficult problems in government — that of conciliating the rights of each with the interests of all — approaches as near solution as, humanly speaking, is possible. It is in those countries where the electors are few that the government feels most apprehensive and is in danger of the most frequent revolutions. So that so far is the notion that the governors and the governed may be one and the same from being a paradox in politics, the more completely we succeed in practice in carrying it out, the more secure is the government and the more prosperous and powerful are the people.

The same sense of feebleness and insignificance which each citizen feels as an elector is more or less experienced by him when he desires to be a candidate for office. Although the elective form of government has the effect of multiplying the public employments, yet these are after all so few when compared with the great number of persons who are eligible to them that not one in a thousand dares flatter himself that he will be the successful candidate, or if he is that he will be able to retain his place beyond the short period for which he is at first elected. This has one good effect. In spite of many untoward influences acting in an opposite direction, it lessens the self importance of individuals and puts everyone on his good behavior.

Thus, in a republic, men demand that the utmost equality should prevail. They establish free institutions and thus open the way to all the offices and emoluments in the state. But they have no sooner done so than they find themselves crowded and incommoded in every effort to acquire the object of their ambition. If they lived under a monarchical or aristocratical government, they would have been obliged to contend with those who had the advantages of rank or fortune on their side. Those advantages are now annulled, but the number of those who are eligible to offices is multiplied more than a hundred fold and the obstacles in the way of acquiring them, although of a very different kind, are yet fully as great as in any other form of government. But those institutions which have raised up so many barriers to the ambition of all popular candidates, and contracted their hopes and expectations within the narrowest possible dimensions, are the workmanship of the people themselves. They have neither the right, therefore, nor any the least disposition to quarrel with its operation. This is one reason why in the United States the profoundest tranquillity prevails after the elections. Up to the time when they are held all is excitement and agitation. But they are no sooner closed than the whole population seeks repose. The same institutions which extend liberty to all establish the empire of public opinion which, representing the sentiments and interests of all classes, presses with an irresistible weight upon the whole community, giving security to the government and contentment to the people. All is brought about by the votes of a majority of the citizens, and to this majority all parties are habituated by a sense of interest as well as from the necessity of the case to pay unlimited deference.

Thus, although the electoral franchise is extended to the utmost so that the government is literally wielded by the people, yet between the people and the organized authority of the state there is interposed a machinery which, as it is viewed by each individual, has an air of sanctity and importance which gives additional force to the public will. It is illusion. The institutions are the direct and legitimate offspring of the popular vote. Each citizen contributes to the formation of public opinion but once it is formed it represents a whole and presses with an undivided weight upon each. So each individual of the majority contributes to make up the million and a half of votes which decide the election of the American president. But that majority is then viewed in the aggregate and so acquires an easy empire over the imaginations of all.

But this is not all. As it is only a small number of the people who can fill the public offices at any one time, as it is a still smaller number who can ever succeed to the highest, the government and the people seem to be still more separated from one another. All the public officers are mere agents of the people. But they are as one to thousands. They are set apart for the performance of special duties and are all clothed with a greater or less degree of authority. Although chosen for short periods and constantly watched by the searching eye of public opinion, yet the separation is made, and this is sufficient to impress upon the laws an air of authority which commands respect from the whole population. Moreover, there is no time when the public offices are vacant. The persons who conduct public affairs are continually shifting, and yet the government seems to be immortal. There is nothing more worthy of admiration than those numberless contrivances which exist in a society by which a system of compensations is established and the irregularities of one part are corrected by an unforeseen influence in another. The process is noticeable in the individual man and is equally observable in that collection of men which we denominate a community.

I do not see why so great difficulty should be felt in conceiving that the people who govern and the people who are governed may be one and the same when the principal design of civil government is to bring out and to represent those qualities which are common to all. The individual may crave many gratifications, and pursue a great number of ends which appertain to his private interests. These may not interfere with the public weal; they may even contribute directly to promote it. But wherever there is a conflict, inasmuch as all have a right, if one has, to run athwart the public interest, while at the same time the attempt by all to exercise the right would annul it for each, it becomes a matter of necessity and does not altogether depend upon reflection that all learn to distinguish more or less carefully between those interests which are peculiar to each and those which are common to all.

But although it is not left to reflection to make the distinction in the first instance, yet, as reflection is powerfully awakened by enlarging the sphere of popular rights, it has a great deal to do with the matter afterward. In the great majority of mankind the formation of habits of reflection must necessarily depend upon the exercise which their minds receive from the daily occupations which engage them. The contrivance of means toward the attainment of the ends they are in pursuit of, the balancing of advantages against disadvantages, and the anxieties of all kinds which are consequent upon this employment of their faculties makes them reflective in spite of themselves. It has been observed that the Americans are the most serious people in the world. And the remark is undoubtedly just. They are not the gravest, but they are the most serious people. For there is a very wide difference between gravity and seriousness. The former may be the result of vanity or dullness or a frigid temperament. The last always implies thoughtfulness. It is a fine remark of Schiller that the serene and the placid are the attributes of works of art, but that the serious belongs to human life.

But in a democratic republic the field of human life is more thoroughly laid open than it is anywhere else. All the ordinary motives to reflection are increased because the objects about which reflection is employed are multiplied. Individuals are thrown more upon their own resources. Each has more to do, more to quicken his exertion, more to kindle hope, and yet to sadden with disappointment. When we look over the vast agricultural population of the United States and observe that it is almost entirely composed of proprietors, the reason why there is so much activity and yet so much reflection, so much stir and yet such perfect tranquillity, is apparent. Proprietors are charged with the entire management of a business which in other countries is divided between two or three classes. They are rendered thoughtful and circumspect because they have so much to engross their attention and to tax their exertions. If the slaves of the south did not belong to a race decidedly inferior to that of the white man, it would be the highest wisdom to manumit them. The abolition of slavery would have the same effect as the abolition of the laws of primogeniture. It would melt down large properties into farms of a reasonable size. The number of proprietors would be greatly increased, and so would the number of those who would be trained to habits of independent exertion. The agricultural population of the United States are the conservators of the peace and the great balance wheel of the constitution.

In a country where free institutions exist, not only is the sphere of individual exertion enlarged, the amount of business transacted by private individuals increased, but the interests which are common to all are also increased. If the effect were only to animate the cupidity of individuals, to sharpen the appetite for self-gratification, and thus to nourish an universal egotism, it would run counter to all the ends for which civil government is established. But we cannot well enhance the importance of anyone's private business without placing him more in connection with others, compelling him to cooperate in their exertions and causing them in their turn to be instrumental in his. If in America the rural population is for the most part composed of proprietors, and in the towns the trades are thrown open to all and not confined to colleges of artisans, there must be a constant tendency toward the creation of a system of common interests since a great majority of the people have so deep a stake in the protection of property and in the maintenance of those laws which guarantee personal liberty. Governmental regulation of one kind or another becomes more and more necessary. And this necessity is realized by a very great number of people. So that although men escape from the restraint which the ar-tificial forms of government impose, they find themselves when living under free institutions, surrounded by all sorts of restraints. The great difference between the two cases is that in the last the restraint is im-posed for the common benefit of all and with the free consent of all.

But this does not prevent the operation of that illusion to which I have constantly referred. Government has a vast and complicated business to transact, ever increasing with the increase of the popula-tion, so that the management of public affairs in the single state of New York is far more intricate and weighty than it was in the great empire of Charlemagne. The intervention of the governors stands out in bold relief as something distinct from and totally independent of society. The people of that state created their government and lend it a free and unanimous support. And yet, there is hardly one of them perhaps on hearing pronounced the words "people of the state of New York" in a simple indictment, but what feels as if an immense but undefinable authority was impending over him.

The property which elective government possesses beyond any other of representing those interests which are common to the whole population has this further effect: it tends to correct the idiosyncrasy of individuals. So that contrary to all expectation there is more same-ness, more uniformity of character, among the American people than among any other. In other countries the inequality of rank, the inequal-ity in the distribution of property, together with innumerable influ-ences springing from these, produce the greatest diversity of char-acter. The Americans enjoy more freedom than any other people, but if the structure of society is such that all are obliged to conform to some common standard, this freedom will simply terminate in ren-dering the manners and modes of thinking of all more alike.

Foreigners, in noticing the commanding authority which the will of the majority impresses upon American society, object to it and even liken it to the awe which is inspired by monarchical government. But the two things are of an entirely different character. That ma-jority after all reflects pretty much the substantial interests and the leading opinions of all. It could not be a majority of the people if it did not produce this effect. Parties may afford to magnify their re-spective differences, if the only effect is to set in a more striking light the numerous points of agreement which exist among them. Moreover, if the superstitious submission which prevails in a monarchy contrib-

utes to fortify monarchical institutions, the authority which public
sentiment exercises in a republic has a mighty efficacy in giving force
and durability to free institutions. It is very true that if in the United
States anyone is so wicked or so unwise as to entertain views favorable
to the establishment of monarchical or aristocratical government, he
dare not give utterance to them. But it is very certain that this species
of despotism which is exercised over the minds of men, by causing public sentiment to run in one channel places the institutions and the
manners in harmony with each other and gives strength and consistency to the first.

Thus, under whatever aspect we may view representative government, the same idea presents itself of an invisible authority residing
in the state which only represents the will of the people and yet, in
the imaginations of all, the high and the low, the rich and the poor, is
clothed in a form which exacts as unlimited obedience to the laws as
any other government. Perhaps this phenomenon is only a manifestation of that tendency which the human mind constantly dis-
covers, of figuring to itself some ideal standard of law and justice
which, although it may never be attained, yet acts as a powerful regulative principle in controlling the actions of man. This ideal cannot be
found in the partial and half-formed opinions of individuals. It is
therefore endeavored to be obtained from that character of unity
which the collective authority of all stamps upon society. We may occasionally notice something of the kind even in the artificial forms of
government, where the prince has pushed his authority to such an excess as to rouse a general popular sentiment for the time being. During
the celebrated three days in Paris a rumor was given out by the leaders
of the popular party that a provisional government was formed. Sentinels were stationed before one of the hotels where Lafayette, General Gérard, and the Duke de Choiseul met, and when anyone came
to the door these sentinels would say, the government is in session.[3]
This idea of a government, the historian says, gave ten-fold force and
energy to the popular cause and decided the revolution in its favor.
But in the democratic republic of the United States, this notion of
government, this abstract representation of law and justice, has a

3. [In the July Revolution of 1830 in France, Lafayette, Claude-Antoine-Gabriel
de Choiseul (1760–1838) and Étienne-Maurice Gérard, Marshal of France (1773–
1855), signed a public proclamation in the city of Paris establishing a provisional
government.]

legitimate foundation. It, therefore, takes firmer hold of the imaginations of men and prevents the occurrence of those dreadful commotions which have convulsed France and other countries. It not only prevents any rival notion from springing up, it prevents any rival institution from planting itself in the country.

There is an institution in America which is something new in the history of the civilized world and which proves with what facility the notion of the governors and the governed being one and the same may be carried into practice. The religious establishments are all supported by the voluntary contributions of the respective congregations. It was a prevailing idea at one time, even in the United States, that if the state did not take religion under its own care the religious sentiment would fall to decay. Entirely the reverse has been found to be the case. There is no country in the world where the attention to religion is so marked and so universal as in the United States. The sum which is voluntarily contributed is greater than is collected in any European government except Great Britain; and the amount which is paid to those who perform the actual duties is larger than in any other without any exception whatever. So far from infidelity overspreading the land and everyone doing what seems right in his own eyes, the restraint which religion exercises is more manifest than anywhere else. Society is singularly exempt from the scornful hate and the pestilential breath of the infidel.

In this instance the governors and the governed are the same; the institution is on an exceedingly large scale for it embraces a great majority of the population. And the interests with which it has to do are of unspeakable magnitude as they involve all our hopes hereafter and constitute the chief ties by which society is held together. For religion lies at the foundation of all our notions of law and justice. Nor is there the least reason to believe that free institutions can be permanently upheld among any but a religious people.

It is curious to note the working of this principle, that the governed may govern themselves, in some of its minute ramifications. There was a custom in Connecticut at one time (probably still existing) which permitted juries in all cases to retire to consider of their verdicts unattended by any officer charged to keep them together. When the judge of the federal court first visited the state for the purpose of holding a term he was startled at this custom, and was so convinced that the laws could not be impartially administered under it that he expressed a determination to banish it from the tribunal over which he presided. But a previous residence in the state would have satisfied him that the verdicts of juries in no part of the world were more free from suspicion — more unexceptionable in every respect — than in Connecticut. Too active an inquisition into the actions of men frequently puts them upon doing the very things which were intended to be prevented.

There is a controversy depending in England at the present day between the bench and bar on one side and the press on the other. The press undertakes to report the proceedings of the courts in important public trials while they are in progress, and the bench and bar deny the right to do so, maintaining that such a practice is calculated to forestall the public mind and to influence the verdicts of juries. This controversy commenced, or at any rate assumed a threatening aspect, in the time of Lord Ellenborough.[4] That eminent judge, anxious no doubt to hold the scales of justice with an even hand, gave it to be understood that unless the practice was desisted from the most severe and exemplary measures would be adopted. This was repeatedly proclaimed during the trial of some very important criminal cases, but I believe without effect. Now I do not pretend to say which side is in the right, relatively to an English population, but I do not believe that any harm has resulted in the United States from the freest publication of similar trials during their progress through the courts. As all trials are public in America as well as in England, whatever is transacted within the walls of the court house is immediately spread abroad by the multitude of listeners who are present. And as from imperfect apprehension, want of tact, or a variety of other causes, representations widely differing from each other will be made of the proceedings, the publication by a journal which employs a reporter for the purpose of taking down the evidence, so far from prejudicing the public mind and turning the course of justice aside, may contribute to correct all the erroneous notions which are afloat. It may be laid down as an invariable maxim that the good use of an institution will be in proportion to its constant and familiar use.

It is at a comparatively recent period that the comparison of handwriting has been submitted to the jury. The old rule which deferred the examination to the court exclusively has been changed, and the

4. [Edward Law Ellenborough (1750–1818), conservative British jurist, Lord Chief-Justice (1802–1818).]

reason assigned for the change is that the persons who composed the jury formerly could not write. As this is no longer the case, the court now derives great assistance from the judgment which is exercised by the jury on this difficult matter. Juries are able to govern themselves although they are no longer subjected to the rigid control of the court.

The freedom which females enjoy is another remarkable trait in American society. In Roman Catholic countries, indeed in Protestant European communities, nothing of the kind is observed. It may have been supposed, proceeding lamely from a knowledge of what had been to the conclusion what would be, that so much liberty would give rise to great licentiousness. The reverse is the case. In no country is the purity of the female character better preserved. In order to give to the laws of morality a controlling influence upon our actions, it seems indispensably necessary that we should share to some degree, even in youth, in the responsibility which attaches to those actions. And this can only be accomplished by a delicate mingling of the two things, freedom and restraint.

The liberty of the press is another example. It was once predicted that a press without a licenser would produce infinite licentiousness in conduct and opinions, and that the authority of the government, if not violently overturned, would be secretly undermined by the incessant action of so powerful an agent. All such conjectures have been entirely falsified. In no country is the press so powerful for good, in none is it so powerless for evil as in the United States. If it were strictly guarded and only circulated opinions by stealth, the appetite for change would be constantly whetted. The most startling doctrines would gain credence, simply because they were forbidden. By abolishing the office of licenser, the monopoly of the press is broken down. Opinions are harmless because being free they mutually correct each other. Great multitudes of persons pride themselves upon holding opinions the most adverse to the public safety when it is a privilege to promulgate them, whether that privilege is conferred by the laws or is only obtained by stealth. Take away the privilege and the appetite for all sorts of dangerous novelties gradually wears itself out; for what is novel today becomes threadbare tomorrow, and juster and more sensible views on all subjects will be more likely to make their way among the whole population because the disturbing influence of the passions will be less instead of greater.

If anyone supposes that it has been any part of my design to inculcate the notion that free institutions are a panacea for all the evils which are incident to society, he will be greatly mistaken. No one can be more pressed down with a conviction of the vices and infirmities which cling to human nature, whatever may be the form in which the institutions are cast. All I have aimed at is to show that the democratic form of government is free from the objections which have been made to it, that without pretending to anything like perfection it is, on the whole, the best form of civil polity which can be devised, the one which is best fitted to bring out the greatest amount of good qualities both in the individual and the citizen.

I have, therefore, endeavored to show that representation, which in the beginning is an institution by the people, comes, in process of time and through the instrumentality of causes which are immutable in their operation, to be an institution over as well as by the people. That it is the people who give being to this whole system, and that thus the governors and the governed may be identical and yet different.

CHAPTER III | SOVEREIGNTY OF THE PEOPLE —

IMPORT OF THE PHRASE

IT is certain that free institutions do not render men so perfect but what they may commit great mistakes in the exercise of the privileges which are committed to them. It is equally true that in that form of government men are often led away by the grossest delusions and are persuaded even to travel beyond the bounds which the great law of morality has prescribed. The term "sovereignty of the people" is one of those which has been subjected to a most fatal misconstruction. Because in a republic the political authority of the state has been removed from the insecure foundation on which it formerly rested, because the will of the people has been substituted in the place of hereditary rule, it is sometimes supposed that this new power possessed unlimited attributes and that it was free to make any disposition which it pleased of the rights of any part of the community. The "juro divino" right has been repudiated, and yet another maxim has risen up in its place equally terrible to humanity and destructive of the very interests which free institutions are designed to protect. There is no power on earth, the people no more than the prince, which can be conceived to be absolved from the eternal principles of justice. To assert the contrary would be to deny the existence of some of the most fundamental laws of our being — of those laws which stamp upon all human actions a character of right or wrong. Such laws are not mere arbitrary rules without any dependence upon some governing principle and free at any time to be taken up or laid down. They are a part of our original constitution, as much so as any of our intellectual faculties or appetites but with a far higher authority. There is a rule then which is superior to what is sometimes called the will of the people and which obliges them to the observance of rectitude with as high, although with no higher, authority than it binds the consciences of private individuals.

Right and physical power are not correlative terms. Right and moral power would be more nearly so. It is supposed, however, that there is a wide distinction between the conduct of individuals and of a whole nation, that inasmuch as the former may be restrained by positive laws they have neither the power nor the right to commit injustice, that on the other hand as there is no power actively to control the will of the people they have from the necessity of the case both the power and the right to do as they please. But some things are here too hastily taken for granted. There is, properly speaking, no way of preventing the actions of individuals any more than of a whole people. Actions may be punished after they are committed, but the most absolute monarch is obliged to permit his subjects to be free until they have acted. A physical necessity compels him to do so. All the people cannot be jailors of all the people. If, then, because the state is at liberty to do as it pleases, it has the right also; for the same reason, private persons have the right to commit murder or any other heinous offence. If it should be said that as the latter may be punished afterward, this at any rate places an entire distinction between the two cases, the truth of the proposition might be admitted. But it would nevertheless be a surrender of the whole ground of argument by making the distinction an incidental instead of an intrinsic and necessary one.

But even here, there is an important step in the reasoning which is taken too hastily. Nations may be and frequently (perhaps I should say universally) are punished for their misdeeds. Sometimes they are punished by other nations. At others they are cruelly scourged by intestine divisions. France, in the reign of Louis XVI, was visited by the heaviest misfortunes, and these misfortunes may be traced directly to the corruption which had spread like a leprosy over those classes of society which had the management of public affairs. These misfortunes first fell upon the royal family, the nobility, and the clergy because the abuses committed in those quarters stood out in bold relief and shocked the common sense of mankind. The people, whom the general progress of knowledge had silently lifted into some importance, began to feel their own strength. But they put forth this strength by committing all sorts of enormities. And they in their turn were visited by the most frightful calamities: 1st, by foreign wars occasioned by the excesses of the revolution; 2d, by furious parties in the bosom of France which after revenging themselves upon each other delivered over that fine country to the wildest uproar and confusion until at length these parties were themselves extirpated by a military despot. And this new power, having fulfilled the end for which it was appointed by Providence, was suddenly overthrown, leaving behind a warning to all nations that neither kings nor people can commit crimes with impunity. Charles I of England and his infatuated ministers were punished by the people; the people were then punished for the violence of which they were guilty by the re-establishment of the royal power in the full plenitude of its authority. James II persuaded himself that this counter-revolution had lasted long enough to show that the prerogatives of the crown were consolidated for all time to come and he acted upon this belief. He and his adherents were driven into exile, and it was not until all orders of men abjured the maxim that might gives right that any approach was made toward the establishment of regulated freedom.

Illustrations might be drawn from the history of the United States, though in that country they are not exhibited on anything like so large a scale because the American people have never imagined that they possess the omnipotent authority attributed to them by slavish demagogues. There is a watchfulness and circumspection now visible in the conduct of nations, the result of the growing reflection of the age, which holds them back when they are about to leap too fast and so prevents the occurrence of a world of mischief. But whenever the legislatures of the American states, acting upon the assumed will of the people, have betrayed the trust confided to them and passed laws which infringed the great rules of justice, misfortunes of one kind or another have been the invariable consequence. I believe if anyone were to set himself upon making a searching and critical examination into a subject which at first sight seems to be confused and mystified by the great variety of agencies which are simultaneously at work in society, it would be found that nations are even more certainly punished for their misdeeds than individuals.

But it may be said in reply to these views, which if true are of so great importance, that when calamities are the consequence of the unlawful acts of governments or people, great numbers of innocent persons are involved in the suffering which overtakes the guilty. But,

First, This is no answer to the argument which is, that the guilty are sure to be punished sooner or later.

Second, The same circumstance occurs in the punishment of private individuals. We cannot put to death or imprison any man without afflicting more or less numbers of persons who are dependent upon or in some way connected with him. We cannot do so without frequently casting a blight over the reputation and happiness of family and friends. This is an invariable dispensation of Providence. And it is doubtless so ordered because in every such instance some shadow of blame or reproach, although not immediately visible to the public eye, does in reality fall upon persons who are not openly guilty or not guilty of the same identical fault.

The maxim, "the king can do no wrong," has been ingrafted into the monarchical constitutions of Europe because it has been supposed that such governments were founded upon opinion. In other words, as the authority of the prince is a fiction, it is necessary to prop and support it by a fiction. Wherein, then, will a nation be the gainer by the establishment of a democratic form of government, if it shall be declared that the people can do no wrong? It will be to maintain that their authority is a fiction and that it can only be upheld by a fiction. Human affairs will be a prey to as much disorder as ever. For as the people can never in any country of even tolerable extent personally take part in the public administration, society will be ruled by factions. And the maxim that right and power are convertible terms will be made to defeat itself in practice by substituting in the place of the will of the people the will of a mere fraction of the state. I believe that the greater the amount of power which is communicated to a whole nation, or, to speak with more precision, the greater the proportion of the population by whom political power is exercised, the greater will be the probability that the laws will be just and wise and that their administration will be impartial; and "vice versa," the fewer the number of citizens who possess political rights, the less the probability that the course of legislation will be characterized by an observance of the great principles of justice.

When the whole authority which appertains to government is concentered directly or indirectly in the people, as in the American commonwealth, the national power is the strongest; for then, not only is the will which moves the strongest, but the instruments by which it moves are most readily subservient to a common end. Such a community if it chooses to put forth its strength is equal to almost any achievement. If it never does exert its power to anything like the extent of which it is capable, it is in consequence of the self-limiting tendency which great popular power invariably has. For, consider for whom and upon whom this power is to be exercised. It is not enough to consider by whom it is exerted without taking into account the manner in which it is obliged to operate, as we would do in the case of any other government whose character we were desirous of sifting.

Now in a democratic republic the laws are made by the people and for the people, and they act directly upon the people. And when this is the case it becomes, not impossible to be sure, but exceedingly difficult to consult the interests of the few to the prejudice of the many. The theory of such a government is that the common interests of the whole community shall be consulted. But what does this phrase, common interests of the whole community, mean? It signifies undoubtedly that the rights of all the citizens shall be equally guarded and respected. It is where the privileges of A or B are violated for the benefit of C or D that we say injustice is done to individuals. It is when the interests of one body of men are trampled upon for the advantage of another body that injustice upon a still larger scale is committed. So that if the government is so constructed as not merely to give the ability but to render it the interest of the law-giving power to protect the rights of all, the probability is greatly increased that the rule of right will be the standard, that the laws will be in accordance with the eternal principles of justice. Not because men living under such a government are naturally more disposed to the observance of rectitude than any other men, but simply because there is no way by which any considerable number of people can obtain justice for themselves but by consenting that justice shall be administered to others also. It is a circumstance of great importance, however, that although there may be no original difference between men in this respect and that human nature is strictly the same everywhere — the same in Massachusetts and Ohio as in Italy or Turkey — yet that the habit of living under such institutions for any considerable period and the consequent experience of the unspeakable benefits which in the long run accrue to everyone contribute powerfully to fortify men in the pursuit of the rule of right, to incline them spontaneously, and not merely upon compulsion, to act correctly, and thus to raise the general standard of the manners, as well as that of the laws. And although minds which are disposed to look upon the dark side of everything, or minds which are fretful and discontented because they cannot jump immediately to the fulfillment of all their desires or realize some preconceived theory of their own, may make all sorts of objections to such a constitution of government, yet it is not the least of the excellences of such a system that it possesses the two-fold property of allowing the fullest latitude to the expression of private discontent and yet of controlling it in such a manner that it shall do no harm to any part of the machine.

Thus, the more thorough the establishment of free institutions, the greater is the chance for the maintenance of just laws and the preservation of public tranquillity; for the interests of each become more nearly identical with the interests of all, and the rights of each are only a reflection of the rights of all. But we must distinguish between a people who have a democratic character and democratic institutions and a people who have democratic opinions only. The last may rush headlong into all sorts of excesses and with difficulty escape the yoke of the most galling tyranny. The first is protected from such calamities because it is the capacity for freedom, and not the possession of it, which is able to effect an advantageous distribution of the political power of the community. The one was the condition of France during the revolution, the other is that of the United States.

I have spoken of a democratic republic as the form of government in which the greatest amount of power resides. And persons who are captivated by appearances may suppose that this is a mistaken view. It may be argued that the United States have never put forth anything like the amount of power which has been wielded by Great Britain or France. But the possession and command of power are not the same with the actual exercise of it. I suppose that if we could imagine the American republic to be animated and borne along by some one predominant idea, as was the case with France and England in the gigantic wars of the French Revolution, more strength, more resources, and a greater degree of enthusiasm would be called into requisition than was the case in either of those instances. My argument has been purposely directed to show that where the greatest amount of power resides in the nation, it will necessarily be attended with a self-limiting tendency; that the incapacity, or rather the want of inclination, to exert itself will continue no longer than is proper; that if the solid interests of the state demand military effort, it will be made; and that if this species of exertion does not become the habitual practice of the nation, it is because the greater the power, the more it is drawn into a direction favorable to the development of the interior interests of the state and unfavorable to the concentration of power in the government alone. In other words, if we would carry national power in its genuine sense to the highest possible pitch, we must make every man a citizen, but by so doing we render the wanton and useless expenditure of this power inconsistent with the common welfare and therefore inconsistent with the maintenance of just and equal laws. If we were to suppose the United States attacked by a confederacy of all the potentates of Europe for the express purpose of extirpating free institutions (an event, the opportunity for doing which has now passed over), I imagine that the amount of both moral and physical power which would be put forth by the nation would exceed anything of the kind of which history gives an account.

In the case of Great Britain and France, if the people possessed a higher degree of power, that is, if the national strength were intrinsically greater, less outward display would be made of it; the resources of those states would not be wasted in the maintenance of vast military and naval establishments; the productive labor of those communities would have taken a direction less fitted to captivate the imagination but infinitely better calculated to promote their solid prosperity. When we speak of one nation as very powerful, in contrast with some others, we ordinarily but inconsistently enough mean that the structure of society is such as to enable a ruling caste to command the lives and fortunes of the major part of the population; that is, we view what is in reality a capital defect in the institutions as a system of strength; we put a part in place of the whole, and because this disposition of the national strength is so imposing in appearance and bears with such an enormous weight upon the mass of the population, we conclude that the nation is more powerful. Doubtless, if we were to imagine the vast resources of the United States placed under the command of a military despot and the minds of men to be moved by an irresistible impulse, the national grandeur, as it is falsely termed, might be carried to the highest conceivable point. But the effective strength of the country would decline and the moral energy which now animates the people would be speedily extinguished. As such a scheme of government would commence in injustice, it could only maintain itself by all sorts of injustice and the laws would cease to be guided by the great rule of right because the nation had become weaker instead of stronger. The formation of written constitutions by the people themselves is an incontestible proof that they believe there is such a rule; that it is superior to the mere commands of men; and that it has authority to govern in all public affairs as well as in the private relations of society. Constitutions which are originally designed to be a restraint upon the government operate necessarily in a popular commonwealth as a restraint upon the people also. An individual who voluntarily places himself in a situation which disables him from doing wrong gives proof of his superiority. He only who is strong enough to be wise can afford to be just. And the same is true of a whole nation.

There is this difference between a convention exercising the supreme power of the people and an ordinary legislative body: the former enter upon the trust committed to them with a conviction that they are dealing with fundamental principles. The questions, what is right, what should be declared as rules, not temporarily but for all time to come, are less embarrassed by the fleeting opinions of the day. And the ordinances which are framed have something of the absolute character of abstract truths. Hence no people would insert in their constitution any provision which was manifestly immoral or unjust, though the same could not be said of a legislative assembly. All the things which it may or may not do cannot be written down in the constitution. And so a field of limited extent is still left open to exercise the judgment and discretion of the legislature.

But may not this body transgress the bounds which have been marked out by the constitution and pass laws which, to use a term which is strictly an American one, are unconstitutional? May it not do so in compliance with the will of its constituents, the people? And it is very certain that all this may be done. But in the United States the instances are exceedingly rare where it has actually been done. In almost every case where an alleged violation has occurred, it has afforded subject matter for fair argument and debate on both sides, or the legislative act complained of was passed improvidently and was subsequently repealed. The states of New Hampshire, New York, Maryland, Ohio, Kentucky, Illinois, *etc.*, passed laws which were adjudged by the supreme court of the union to be unconstitutional, and those states immediately retraced their steps, although in one instance that tribunal went the length of decreeing that a prospective law impaired the obligation of contracts, and to the extreme length of declaring that although such laws were not within the scope of state jurisdiction it was competent to the federal legislature to pass them; and yet I confess it is exceedingly difficult for me to conceive how it can be competent to any legislative body to violate a fundamental rule of morality.

The admission of Texas might seem to be an exception to these remarks. It is certain that it was viewed by one party as an express violation of the federal constitution. But as that instrument does not contain an enumeration of the cases in which the treaty-making power may be exercised, the question is necessarily attended with great difficulties. Certainly it behooves a free people to guard against a too great extension as well as a too narrow limitation of the power. The authority by one government to accept an offer from another government of a transfer of itself so as to be incorporated with the former appears at first blush to be too great an one to be confided to one department of the legislature. And as the most natural disposition which can be made of this right is to deposit it with the entire legislature, we are free to do so when the constitution is absolutely silent upon the subject. It will hardly be supposed that the English people are unreasonably latitudinarian in their notions of legislative power. The tendency is rather the reverse. The disposition is to guard scrupulously the prerogatives of the crown. The term treaty-making power has even a more indefinite meaning in that country than it has in the United States and might seem therefore to swallow up every interest which concerned the foreign relations of the state and which was not absolutely confided to the legislature. We might well suppose that the cession or exchange of European territory lay fairly within the scope of the treaty-making power. And yet it is the opinion of the greatest English statesmen that no such cession or exchange could be made unless it were concurred in by both houses of Parliament.

There is no direct warrant for this interposition of the legislative authority. It can only be made out by admitting that the transfer of European territory belonging to England is theoretically within the treaty-making power, and yet insisting that it is not within its spirit. Nor does it alter the aspect of the American question that because the treaty-making power in Great Britain is vested in the King alone, it is therefore necessary to guard against its exercise in so novel a case by subjecting his action to the control of the entire legislature. The question still turns upon, what is the theory of the British constitution and where is the authority for limiting the treaty-making power in one particular case? Nor does it affect the argument that British statesmen hold that such a compact must at least originate with the King. The difficulty still recurs, by what authority is the treaty-making power curtailed in a government where it seems to be least ambiguous and least open to construction? The difficulty is similar to another which occurs under the American constitution. The treaty-making power is conferred without limitation on the president and senate. Would a treaty by which the United States were bound to lay a duty upon certain articles of export be valid? The clause which forbids such an impost is contained in the article which limits the legislative power. There is no limitation whatever in the article which confers the treaty-making power. The settled construction, however, in America is that a duty upon exports would be unauthorized in any shape whatever — in other words that in order to give effect to the spirit of the constitution we must transfer a limitation from one part to another part to which it has properly no relation whatever. And if this construction is well-founded, there can be no doubt but what the construction put upon the treaty-making power in the admission of Texas is also well-founded.

The "unions" of England and Scotland, and England and Ireland were brought about by separate acts of the parliaments of the respective countries.[1] The three governments acted upon the presumption that it was not enough to appoint commissioners to treat; in other words, that the measure did not properly fall within the treaty-making power, and that therefore the legislative power must be appealed to. The unions, therefore, were decreed by separate acts of the English and Scotch, and the English and Irish parliaments, and the proceeding was by bill as in all other acts of legislation.

There is a very interesting problem which the power of altering constitutions presents in America. When the deputies of the people have assembled for this purpose and have not been bound by any specific instructions, is society resolved into its original elements? Can the mass of society be treated as mere "tabula rasa" so that the whole body of laws and institutions can be, not only prospectively, but retroactively, annulled? If, for instance, numerous private associations have grown up under the protection of the former laws, can they be swept away without regard to the deep and permanent injury which would be done to great multitudes of private persons? This power has been contended for in one state convention, but it was instantly rejected, although the population of that state was at the time perhaps the most democratic in the union — a remarkable proof to what an extent the American people are impressed with the notion that might does not give right, and how deeply all orders and parties are

---

1. [For the second edition, Grimke added this paragraph.]

convinced that the great rules of morality and justice are not a gift by men, but a gift to men.[2] It is admitted that the authority of all public officers may be instantly abrogated by a constitutional convention and the argument that the analogy should be pursued through every species of private association which the laws had created would appear to have some color. Nevertheless, the distinction has been rigidly adhered to and the contrary doctrine been proclaimed as both immoral and anti-republican. If this were not the case, there would be nothing to prevent a convention from annulling all marriages and so introducing a host of mischiefs which no time could cure. I do not pretend to say that instances may not occur of associations which are semi-political and semi-civil in their character and which may be abolished by an "ex post facto" constitutional ordinance. But there must be a great and overruling necessity to authorize it to be done. The mischief intended to be remedied must be so glaring as to shock the common sense of mankind.

What I have been most intent upon showing is that the American people have been scrupulously jealous of their own power, that they have endeavored to guard against the idea that might gives right, and have thus given to the term "sovereignty of the people" an interpretation which it has received in no other commonwealth, either of ancient or modern times.

2. [Grimke may have had in mind Rhode Island after Dorr's rebellion of 1841–1842.]

RELIGIOUS toleration has produced tranquillity in the Christian world, and if toleration could also be introduced into the affairs of government it could not fail to exercise a similar influence. But it does not very readily appear how this can be done. It is not necessary that religious sects should act; at least it is not necessary that they should act beyond the sphere of their own societies. All that is necessary in order to render religious toleration complete is to permit all denominations to enjoy freedom of thought and to make such regulations within themselves as are conformable to their own creed and discipline. But the case is very different in the world of politics. It is made up of political parties, and of one or other of these parties is the governing power of the community composed. In other words, the government must be wielded by the majority, and this majority is not only obliged to act but to act beyond itself, to make rules for others as well as for itself, to preside, in short, over the interests of the whole community. There is then a wide distinction between religious and political parties which seems to place insuperable difficulties in the way of introducing political toleration.

If it is possible, however, to contract the sphere within which parties, even the party in the majority, are permitted to act; if, without questioning the authority of this last to go beyond itself and to make rules for others, the occasions on which it exercised this right were diminished both in number and importance, it is not impossible that we might succeed in introducing into political affairs a spirit of toleration which would exercise upon governments an influence very similar to that which religious toleration has exercised upon religious sects.

For that it is not at all necessary for a religious party so to act as to impress its authority upon others is a maxim of very recent date, and is an effect of the very general progress which the human mind has made during the last hundred years. Religion at one time was regarded as one of the chief, if not the chief, political concerns of the state. Religious parties did constantly act and act so effectually as to affect the life, liberty, and property of the citizen. The system of intolerance seemed calculated to perpetuate itself, and so long as it lasted the most enlightened understandings were borne down by the innumerable obstacles which stood in the way of religious toleration.

It was easy to frame a plausible argument in defense of this state of things. It might be said that from time immemorial religious and political questions had been so mixed that to attempt to separate them would be to do violence to both religious and political interests, would, at any rate, undermine the authority of government, if for no other reason simply because the minds of men had constantly run in that channel; that when there was a multitude of sects in the state their religious tenets would exercise a powerful influence upon their political opinions; that this would lay the foundation for intestine dissensions which would rend the whole community; that the only cure was to give unity to religion, to establish it by law, and to exclude all dissenters from the privileges which were enjoyed by the favored sect; that in this way the unity of the government would be preserved and its authority rendered inviolable. The inference then would be a necessary one that government could no more avoid acting in religious matters than it could avoid the duty of defending the state against foreign invasion. Arguments, in some respects similar, might now be employed to show the impropriety of political toleration.

The Pope at a very early day became one of the most considerable potentates of Europe. Religious dogmas of one kind or other exercised complete dominion over the minds of men, and other princes, in order to maintain tranquillity among their own subjects and to preserve an equilibrium of power abroad, believed that it was necessary to add to their political a very large share of ecclesiastical authority also. Through all the ramifications of society, in public as well as in private life, religious and political opinions were so interwoven that it seemed impossible to separate them. A war might be waged by the head of the church for the avowed purpose of imposing the most absurd and impious rites upon other nations, and if, as might naturally be expected, numerous adherents of these rites still lingered among those nations, their governments might persuade themselves that it was necessary to suppress freedom of religious opinion at home in order to deal a successful blow upon the enemy abroad. This was the first occasion of religion becoming an engine of government in the modern European states and of the universal introduction of religious intolerance. And as religion was thus erected into an affair of state, a further consequence took place that ecclesiastics very generally became the statesmen of Europe.

The destruction of the papal power — the gradual decline of all the Italian commonwealths which for centuries composed the most civilized part of the European continent — the employment of men in civil life in all public affairs — and above all the general progress of knowledge, industry, and freedom have contributed to reverse the old order of things. A separation has actually been effected between the political interests of the state and the religious doctrines which are taught.

The tendency of modern society, then, is to withdraw religion from the arena of politics, to put all sects in the possession of privileges which were formerly usurped by one, so that it shall no longer be necessary, nor even possible, for government to extend its legislation over some in order to promote the aggrandizement of others. The freedom of thought which has grown up everywhere, at the same time that it has disarmed the civil magistrate of a most dangerous authority, has created such a multitude of sects that it would sometimes be impossible to bestow power upon one without oppressing a very large majority of the population. It is not in consequence of any speculative notions as to the justice and humanity of the principle of toleration that it has gained ground so rapidly: the change has been brought about by a total alteration in the structure of society. The popular will which reflects religious as well as political opinions has gradually insinuated itself into the councils of all governments until it has itself become a power of formidable import. It has attained this influence either directly by virtue of the principle of representation, or indirectly through the instrumentality of public opinion. In the former case, the utmost freedom of opinion is obliged to be accorded to all religious sects.

There are two ways of imitating this system in the region of politics. One is by extinguishing the cause of political disagreement; the other, by rendering it the settled interest of all political parties to tolerate each other's opinions respectively. The first plan would seem to be impracticable, but it is not so. Both plans are adopted in the

United States which, being the only country where complete religious toleration has been established, it is natural should also be the one in which the nearest approach has been made to the assertion of political toleration.

A written constitution, framed by representatives of the people, locks up and forever withdraws from the field of party strife almost all those questions which have been the fruitful source of discord among other communities. For almost all the civil commotions which have occurred in the European states have been caused by a disagreement about questions which are no longer open to debate in America. The constitution, with the approbation of men of all parties, has placed them beyond the reach of the government. The authority appertaining to the political departments is also strictly limited, and thus a large class of powers which other governments have been in the habit of dealing with without any control cannot be exercised at all. In the same way as religion is withdrawn from the political world and has given rise to religious toleration, the fundamentals of government are also withdrawn from all interference with by party and all men agree to think and to act alike with regard to them.

As to those subjects which are left open to controversy, a great approach has been made, though in another way, toward the establishment of political toleration. In the first place, everyone is free to think and to speak as he pleases; and in the second place, the minority, so far from being excluded from the government, are entitled to a representation in exact proportion to their numbers. This is of the greatest importance because this body are thus placed in a situation where they may not only think and speak for all purposes, but where the exercise of so enviable a privilege may ultimately enable them to act for all purposes. It is very easy to construct a legislative body so as to represent only one interest in the state. It may be hereditary or for life, in which case it would wield an undivided influence and there would be no effective and practical toleration for other classes; or the electoral franchise may depend upon so high a qualification as to produce an effect similar in its operation. Very different, however, is the case in the United States. The legislative assemblies are composed of men of all parties, and although in politics the governing authority cannot deliver itself from the necessity of acting, yet so much freedom is enjoyed by the members who compose those assemblies that political questions borrow light from all parties. I believe if we were to take any considerable series of years, it would be found that the leading measures which have been adopted in the United States have been the fruit of the joint exertions of all parties; that they have been ultimately so arranged as to reflect in part the opinions of the majority and in part those of the minority. And thus the spectacle is no longer presented of one fixed and immovable interest engrossing the whole power of the state.

The introduction of the principle of political equality is another step toward the establishment of the most complete toleration. Men are obliged to recognize the liberty of others in order to maintain their own. The same revolution is effected in politics as was formerly brought about in religion. The multiplication of sects was so great as to deprive any one of them of a predominant influence and so excused government from investing it with exclusive privileges. This first suggested the notion that toleration was not only just, but that it was eminently expedient. The great diversity of opinions, so far from being an obstacle in the way of religious toleration, was the means of establishing it. But the same causes which have multiplied religious have also multiplied political opinions, so that there is no possible way by which one party can be free without permitting all to be free.

The confederate form of the American government adds additional force to the principle of political toleration. The country is divided into a number of separate and to most purposes independent governments. And it is a consequence of this arrangement that all political opinions are not subjected to the control of a central legislature. The affairs of government are divided into two classes: one of which comprehends the federal interests, the other the domestic interests of the states. And this second class may again be divided into as many subordinate ones as there are states composing the confederacy. If this system were not adopted the local interests would be subjected to the jurisdiction of a single legislature which could not adapt itself to the diversified wants of so extensive a country, and so the laws might follow one undistinguishing rule for communities whose pursuits were ever so different. But now, the governing party in the national councils may or may not be at any one time the governing party in a majority of the states. The effect, in other words, is not merely to permit the people of each section of the country to exercise freedom of thought and speech, but to carry their opinions into practice — to frame their laws in conformity with their own wishes, instead of being governed by the general majority of the whole country. As all religious sects are tolerated and placed in the possession of equal rights because religion is divorced from government, so all local parties, however numerous, are tolerated and have an equal share of power because the administration of the state governments is wholly disconnected with that of the confederacy.

Political toleration, then, is not a solecism in politics: it is actually incorporated into American institutions, though, like all other great blessings, they who possess it are least sensible of its existence.

Political toleration is carried to a much greater extent in the United States than is religious toleration in many of the most enlightened European governments. For let us consider what the term religious toleration imports, even in England. It does not mean that all sects are placed upon an equal footing. All sects are permitted to enjoy their religious opinions and to adopt what forms of worship they please, but only on condition that they pay the tithe which is collected for the support of the established clergy. That is to say, all dissenters from the state religion are punished for the exercise of the rights of conscience. It is not necessary to recur to the fact that certain oaths are still imposed upon all dissenting ministers and that one class of dissenters is forbidden to hold some of the highest offices in the state. The assessment upon all denominations equally for the support of an established hierarchy makes a wide and important distinction between religious toleration in England and political toleration in the United States. And although all political parties in the latter are taxed for the support of government as it is administered by the majority, yet there is after all a wonderful coincidence in the line of policy which is advocated by both parties. The points of agreement are a hundred-fold greater than those in which they differ. The latter acquire importance from standing out as exceptions to the general rule. They only contribute to keep up some animation in society where otherwise all would be dull and monotonous. Besides, there is no party established by law. The laws which are passed by the majority are the supreme rule, but the majority today may be the minority tomorrow. But in England a powerful religious party is established by law, nor is there any way of moderating its influence through the occasional ascendancy of other opinions. Its privileges are exclusive and permanent and depend in no manner upon the exercise of the popular will. The injustice which is thus done to a very large and enlightened portion of the English people is plain enough. But it is still more glaring in the case of Ireland where dissenters from the established church are an immense majority of the whole population.

CHAPTER V | MONARCHICAL GOVERNMENT

WHAT is the foundation of that illusion which has caused such multitudes of people in all ages to yield a willing and implicit obedience to the rule of a prince? A weak man or woman, nay a child, once seated upon the throne exercises a dominion over the imaginations of men which the longest time, the greatest reflection and experience, seem unable to conquer. This vast and disproportioned influence of one individual above millions seems an anomaly in the history of human nature. It cannot be ascribed to a persuasion among the community of the eminent advantages which spring from such a disposition of the political power. A considerable fraction of the community may have this persuasion in great strength, but to suppose that the community as a body reasoned in this way, that they proceeded upon any settled and deliberate view of the utility of the plan, would argue the existence of so high a degree of reflection as to give rise instantaneously to representative government. That fraction of the community who are so persuaded are only so in consequence of their observing the operation of some other very different principles which rule over the mass of mankind. They notice the superstitious feeling which ignorance engenders; they then notice the idolatrous attachment of superstition to every species of authority and still more to the gorgeous ensigns of authority. One may observe the workings of a similar principle in the government of private families. Children very generally believe their parents to be superior to other men and women. It is not until they become adults (and very often not then) that they are disabused of this prejudice. Some observation and experience are necessary to this end. But it is obvious how much this feeling contributes to the establishment of parental authority; it is equally obvious how much a similar and equally mysterious principle contributes to the government of mankind.

The peasant who ascends a lofty mountain is instantly struck, no matter how untutored he may be, with the grandeur and sublimity of the scene before him. A vague notion of infinity is irresistibly thrust upon his mind, although he knows that the vast surface beneath him is composed of alternate patches of wood and cleared land exactly like those in his own neighborhood. So when he confusedly calls to his recollection the vast population in which he lives, called a state or community, he dwindles into insignificance in the comparison, although that vast body is only made up of men and women like those in his neighborhood. In the first instance, a being beyond the world is suggested; in the second, a being beyond himself and yet not out of society. In both instances the notion of unity seems necessary in order to give support to his vague notion of immensity and to make tolerably comprehensible what would otherwise be beyond the reach of his faculties. The conviction of the existence of a governor of the universe very naturally takes possession of him; the notion of royalty as the impersonation of the state is thrust upon him with nearly equal force.

In a republic men all descend into the plain; they are no longer overpowered by the indistinct notion of immensity. The understanding gains the ascendancy and they are enabled to form more just notions on all subjects. Their religion which was at first the creature of impulse and therefore easily fabricated into some form of superstition becomes both more rational and more devout. In like manner they are better able to survey calmly and one by one the men and things which make up the great community in which they live. The feeling does not leave them entirely, but it now becomes subservient to very important ends and is made to promote their own interests as men and citizens. Each individual has the sense of personal independence, not merely as applied to himself but as applied to all other individuals, more and more impressed upon him because the point from which he now views everything is more favorable to cool analysis and to setting everything in its proper light. But the reverberation of an authority from without still reaches him. He hears of millions of other people who are associated with him under the same government. Of these millions perhaps he never saw a thousand, perhaps not even an hundred. The existence of those beings on that very account makes a profounder impression upon his mind. On an analysis, perhaps it will be found that it is the notion of immensity which is gained by the view (the more indistinct the more imposing) of a vast population which serves to cherish and to uphold the notion of royalty. The king is regarded as the special representative of that vast population. He becomes the state itself; so that if we can give to the terms "state," "people," sufficient unity, republican rule will exercise as potent an influence over the imaginations of man as monarchical rule.

Doubtless, it would be as impossible to create the rule of an hereditary monarch in the United States as it would be to carry physical science back to the condition in which it was before the time of Bacon, and for precisely the same reason. For want of a rational system of experiment and observation, phenomena the most simple and the most easily explained now were subjected to the most crude and fanciful speculations. Superstition reigned over physical, as it still does in many parts of the world, over political science. Actual experiment and observation have dissolved the superstition in the first instance, and it is possible that the sturdy good sense of the nineteenth century will go a great way toward undermining it in the last. The doctrine of occult causes was precisely akin to the political illusion of which I have spoken.

Where the people are immersed in ignorance, they feel themselves incapacitated to take any part, even the most indirect, in public affairs. This feeling cannot be shaken off, for knowledge is power in every department of human life, and wherever there is great ignorance the desire and the power to will effectually are both wanting. This state of things, for the time being at least, withdraws all political power from the masses and reposes it in the hands of those who either by rank or education are lifted to a higher condition. Power is thus transferred easily and without noise or violence to a very small portion of society. But whenever a set of institutions come to represent the opinions and feelings peculiar to a class, those opinions and feelings will not be understood by those who are out of the class. The modes of thinking and acting among the former will begin to wear an air of mystery which time will only increase, until at length the whole machinery of what are termed great affairs will be absolutely unfathomable by the multitude.

The great men will then begin to quarrel among themselves for the mastery. The most warlike or the most crafty will obtain it. In the event of a vacancy to the succession, he will possess himself of the crown. A new revolution will then take place. Before, the high places in the government and the lustre which surrounded them overpowered the imaginations of the people. They paid a sort of instinctive obedience to the prince; which is the same as to say that a great power had risen up in support of the throne. Now, also, it is not against the assaults of the people that he stands in need of protection, for they are already overawed; it is against the assaults of the other great men. But the same sentiment of obedience, so undefined and yet so enthusiastic, constitutes an impregnable barrier against those assaults also. The great men in the state soon discover that although out of their own limited circle nothing is understood concerning state affairs, yet that this very ignorance has given birth to a power which none but themselves have to fear. As soon as one of their number is made chief, as soon as he is fairly seated on the throne, the reverence of the multitude is directed toward him and withdrawn from all others. The spell even begins to take possession of their own ranks. A sentiment of superstition in one part of society is converted into an universal conviction of right. The throne is fortified from within and without; it is equally guarded against the violence of the multitude and the conspiracies of the nobles.

In the progress of time, it may be a very long period, the number of those who are placed in independent circumstances will be greatly augmented. Rich landed proprietors, great merchants, and opulent manufacturers spring up, and this will give birth to a new class, formed out of intermarriages between the families of the nobility and those of rich commoners and which is denominated the gentry. Still later, education is extensively diffused; the press, although it should be under some restraint, spreads intelligence; a higher and wider civilization takes place. A popular branch is added to the legislature or, if one already exists, greater influence and authority are conferred upon it. A remarkable crisis now occurs. The lustre which surrounds the throne seems to be more dazzling than before. Notwithstanding the spread of intelligence and the general elevation of the popular mind, its power appears to be firmer and more durable than ever. The class of the rich and influential have been swelled to a great magnitude, and this class for the most part lends its support to the throne rather than to the people.

Patronage, which supersedes the rough and irregular exercise of power, gives the monarch great influence among this class. Offices are multiplied in proportion as civilization advances. And in addition to all this, great numbers of people among the middle class, fearing more from the turbulence and licentiousness of popular freedom than from the exercise of the royal prerogatives in a limited monarchy, array themselves on the side of old institutions. A great party is for the first time formed, composed of persons whose opinions are founded upon the most mature and deliberate reflection. They would have more freedom imparted to the institutions of government, if they could only see their way clearly through the process which leads to it. They do not believe it can be done without endangering the whole system. Russia and Austria may be considered as illustrations of the first period; France and Great Britain of the second. Prussia must be regarded as trembling between the two.

The second period may be of indefinite duration. The country is then filled with wealth and intelligence; civil liberty seems to be secured to all conditions of men; a great middle class has been created, holding the balance of power in the state and yet constantly inclined, whether from temperament, habits of reflection, or views of ambition, to throw the weight of its influence in favor of the superior classes. But, inasmuch as reflection has been roused and a disposition to think and ponder upon the men and institutions which surround them has been developed in a great multitude of minds, it is plain that the artificial and unnatural principles on which government originally hinged are beginning to be probed and comprehended, and that the great mysteries of government, in order to be unveiled, only wait for an opportunity favorable to calm and deliberate action. And when this is the case, as all knowledge is progressive and even contagious, it will be difficult to predict with anything like certainty how long the institutions will be permitted to stand still, or how soon the hand of a thorough and yet judicious and temperate reform may fall upon them.

When this interesting period has arrived, great numbers of men will unite in order to obtain important changes in the government; associations will be formed with this avowed design, the majority of whose members will perhaps be composed of citizens who are politically disfranchised and yet consisting of so large a portion of those who are not as to give great weight and authority to the opinions of the whole body. A majority of that part of the middle class who do possess political privileges will be roused and will recoil at every attempt of this new party, until at length the spirit of reflection which has silently prepared the way to every species of salutary improvement has effected a reconciliation between parties, when much will be conceded and yet some substantial advantages will be obtained by the great movement party. This revolution will be repeated at successive intervals until at length the entire body of what may be justly termed the middle class are admitted to the electoral franchise and rendered eligible to office, when all further changes will cease, not merely because none other will be wise, but because the moral force of society will be arrayed in defense of what has been gained and in opposition to any further change. Before this revolution is accomplished, the notion that the middle class comprehends none but persons who have an interest in landed estate will naturally be discarded. The citizens who possess personal property will be placed upon an equally favorable footing; nay, the rule will perhaps be made still wider and everyone of good character and who contributes to the support of government will be admitted to the electoral franchise. For so long as any one of those who go to make up the effective strength of the state is excluded, government not only commits great injustice to a numerous class of the people, but it deprives itself of a powerful support to the laws.

There is a fourth period which may occur, one deeply interesting to the cause of humanity and to the final success of free institutions. The acquisition of so many blessings, the enjoyment of such delightful tranquillity, both in public and private life, may lead to too much repose and inactivity. Sloth and voluptuousness may overspread the land and the institutions may fall in the midst of the greatest prosperity. It is true society will be more completely protected against the disaster than at any preceding period. As the distribution of wealth will be more equal, the moral force of society will be better balanced, the means of recruiting the superior ranks from the classes below them will be more abundant than ever. Still, all this may not be sufficient. It may be necessary for society to go backward in order again to spring forward. For the dissolution of an old and worn-out society has sometimes the effect of breathing a new spirit into the whole population. All classes and conditions are then confounded together. The rich and the powerful are tumbled from their enviable position; they are brought down to the level of the obscure and humble who now begin to run a new race for all the advantages of fortune. This is a provision inherent in the constitution of every community which has become effete with luxury and corruption. There may be no way of revivifying the elements of society and of imparting fresh vigor to the population but by passing them through the ordeal of a terrible adversity. But the experiment will be quite new when any nation shall have traveled to the utmost limit of the third period. As the institutions will then have a sort of self-preserving faculty and will contain powerful antidotes to the evils just indicated, we do not know whether any further revolution will be necessary. The high probability is that it will not; and this is the last term — the final consummation of our hopes.

ONE of the most remarkable properties of the English government is the faculty which it possesses of accommodating itself to alterations in the structure of society. The theory of the constitution is pretty much the same as it was in the reigns of the Tudors but its practical working is totally different. The social organization has undergone a great change during the last seventy years and this has made a deep and lasting impression upon the political institutions. The king, the nobility, and the ecclesiastical hierarchy occupy the same relative position to each other, but they do not occupy the same position toward the people. This power of adapting itself to the altered condition of society is one of the most valuable qualities which a government can possess. It is next in importance to positive changes in the composition of the government.

The revolution I have spoken of has been silent but progressive. It has effected an entire change in the modes of thinking of all public men and has wrought a corresponding change in the system by which public affairs are conducted. The prerogatives of the king and aristocracy are the same as formerly, but the people have been steadily advancing in strength and importance; and how is it possible to employ power against the powerful? As the general improvement of the population and the consequent amelioration of the manners has imparted a new character to the temper and dispositions of individuals, so the inability under which public men find themselves of exerting even an acknowledged authority renders that authority in great part merely nominal; and the administration of the government in practice no longer agrees with what the theory imports.

There are only two ways of effecting alterations in the political institutions. The one is by sudden leaps, the other by slow and insensible advances. The first is sometimes attended with so much violence and confusion as to endanger the existence of the entire fabric. The second, although it avoids this evil, has, nevertheless, a tendency to postpone the most wise and salutary changes to a period far beyond that when society is ripe for their introduction.

Montesquieu said of the British government that it was a republic in disguise; which shows what inadequate notions this eminent writer had formed of a republic. But it is not at all improbable that it will become at some future day, not perhaps very distant, a republic in reality and not one merely in disguise. When I perceive the great bulk of the people growing to the full stature of men, and when I observe that in every contest between liberty and power the advantages gained have been constantly on the side of the people and never on that of the government, I see causes in operation which are not only sufficient to bring about this result but which seem to lead straight forward to its accomplishment.

But how is it possible without sudden leaps to get beyond the point which has already been reached? How, in other words, without creating an universal revolution can the structure of the government be changed fundamentally? It is through the instrumentality of that invisible but powerful agent which we term public opinion that a spirit has been breathed into the institutions. But public opinion does not construct, it only influences and modifies. It may, step by step and without noise and confusion, affect the working of the machine, but this is very different from taking the machine to pieces, very different from abolishing the royal power and the House of Lords and substituting in their place an elective chief magistrate and senate.

This is an obstacle and a formidable one in every attempt to alter the composition of an ancient government. Society in Great Britain is ripe for the introduction of free institutions, if there were no other system already in existence. The existence of that other system, with the vast patronage and influence appended to it, has a powerful tendency to counteract the force of public opinion, and renders it a work of infinite delicacy to make any radical alteration whatever.

But the process I have described may continue so long as to give rise to further changes of the same character, and by molding the minds of men after a different fashion of thinking may have power sufficient to overbear the influence of the throne and aristocracy. In this way, what would have been an abrupt and violent leap at an early period of society may become an easy transition at a more advanced stage. Everything depends upon the shock which the mind receives. We do violence to the political institutions only when we do violence to inveterate habits of thinking. But if old associations are broken in upon, there is no room for committing violence in any quarter. I think it cannot be doubted that the footing on which the electoral franchise, parliamentary representation, religious toleration, and the freedom of the press now stand in Great Britain would, in the reign of Elizabeth, have been regarded as a much greater movement than would at the present day the entire reconstruction of the executive magistracy and the House of Lords. Although the second appears to involve a more direct and positive interference with established institutions, it does not run counter to the genius and tendency of the age: it would therefore give much less shock to the understandings of men.

It is a remark of Mr. Hume that there was in his day a constant tendency toward a diminution of the personal authority of the King. This fact has been still more observable since Mr. Hume wrote. And the reason why it is so is very obvious. The amount of real business which falls under the management of the executive becomes so vast and multifarious with the advance of society that no one man, much less a king, can attend to the one hundredth part of it. The consequence is that the whole of this business has been gradually transferred to an executive board. So long as it was possible to conceal the cause of this change from general observation, the King continued to retain the dazzling influence which the vulgar apprehension ascribes to him. But now that this cause is apparent to everyone, the royal and the executive authority have ceased to be even nominally the same. For not only is the King totally unable to discharge this huge mass of business, but ministers do not even hold their places at his will. The direction of public affairs was formerly a very simple concern. The gratification of the King's pleasures and ambition comprehended the whole. And although some share of business talent could not well be dispensed with, yet as public transactions consisted for the most part of war, negotiation, and intrigue, the imaginations of the people very naturally figured the King as incomparably the most prominent actor upon the stage. But the case is very different now. Intellectual ability, extensive information, indefatigable industry, are all absolutely necessary to any tolerable success in the management of public affairs. The English statesman nowadays has to deal chiefly with the interior interests of a densely peopled and highly civilized community. War, which formerly employed the whole attention of the state, is becoming a mere episode in its history. It is impossible for any monarch, however ignorant or bigoted he may be, to misunderstand the import and bearing of this great revolution in human affairs. With regard to the lords, I have in another chapter alluded to the process which seems destined to bring about the decay of their power and influence. Wealth constitutes the soul of an aristocracy. Other qualities may add lustre to the institution but it is wealth, exclusive wealth, which gives it a firm hold and a commanding authority in society. But riches are now obtained by such a multitude of individuals that they can no longer be the foundation of a privilege. What was once the chief element of an aristocracy is now a great element of popular power. The same causes which conspired to create an hereditary order are now at work to enfeeble it. The English nobility are no longer the haughty and powerful barons who formerly lorded it over the commons. They are simply among the most polished and affluent gentlemen of the kingdom, guarded for the present by a sort of conventional respect, but no longer wielding a formidable authority over the rest of the population.

The French have very recently made a fundamental alteration in the institution. The peerage is no longer hereditary. An event which seventy years ago would have startled the public mind throughout Europe has been brought about with as much facility and has created as little sensation as an act of ordinary legislation. It is true, the English nobility are a much wealthier body than the French. But the English commons are wealthier than the French "tiers état" in a still greater proportion. The materials for constructing an aristocracy are more near at hand in England than in France, but the uses of the institution would seem to be more apparent in the latter than in the former country.

An aristocracy is of two kinds. It may be so numerous and engross so large a share of the landed property of the country as to form a component and very substantial part of the whole population. This was at one period the case in almost every European state. It has ceased to be so everywhere except in Russia and Poland. Or it may consist of so small a number that the only way to compensate for its want of strength and to preserve it as a distinct order in the state will be to make the entire members a constituent part of one branch of the legislature. This is the case in Great Britain, except so far as regards Scotch and Irish peers, a certain number of whom are elected by their own order to seats in the House of Lords. Scotch and Irish peers are not so numerous as to prevent their sitting in one chamber along with the English peers, but political considerations, growing out of the union of the three countries, have given rise to the present arrangement.

But where a nobility compose so very small a part of the population and yet are endowed with such extensive political authority, the incongruity between the natural influence which belongs to them as well-educated gentlemen and the artificial privileges heaped upon them must strike everyone of the least reflection, no matter how familiarized he may have become with such a state of society. To remodel the institution, therefore, or to dispense with it altogether, would do no violence, would cause no disturbance to the public tranquillity. As the change would be strictly in accordance with the ideas of the age and would but second a movement which is in full progress, so it would affect but a mere handful of men. And there are probably no persons in the British empire more observant of the course of events, more thoroughly convinced that the day is approaching when it will be impossible to oppose their authority, even nominally, as a counterpoise to the commons than the nobility themselves.

While the active political authority of the king and nobility has been gradually decreasing, that of the commons has been as constantly advancing. The same cause, the dispersion of knowledge and property, has produced these opposite effects. But as the people rise in the scale of intelligence (even though we confine the meaning of people to that powerful body called the middle class) in proportion as they participate, although indirectly, in the affairs of government, they are brought to a clearer understanding of everything which appertains to the machinery of government and have a closer insight into the character and motives of all public men. Things which were before regarded as mysterious in the highest degree and which were never approached without a feeling of awe are now handled and touched and become thoroughly familiar to common apprehension. Wealth originally gave privileges to a few hundreds, but it has now given intelligence to the million, and this enables the commoner to stand upon something like an equal footing with the nobleman. Men are never able to take exact gauge of each other's dimensions until they are made to stand side by side of one another; when those qualities which were before so much magnified by the mist through which they were seen assume their due proportions and the individual man is valued more for what he possesses and less for what he can make display of. The characters of

public men appear grand and colossal only in consequence of the il-
luminated ground on which they are exhibited.

There is one branch of the British legislature in which very great
alterations may be made comformable with the genius of the age without immediately affecting the absolute theory of the government, although these alterations may ultimately disturb the whole balance of
the constitution and lead by an easy transition to fundamental
changes in the structure of the government. The House of Commons
is elected by the people, but to what extent it shall be the genuine representative of the popular will depends upon the high or low qualifications of the members and the restrictions imposed upon the electoral
franchise. If the qualifications in both instances were lowered, the
power of the people would rise in proportion. Now there is an evident
tendency in that direction at the present day. The Reform Bill, which
is one of the most memorable acts of the British Parliament, has gone
a great way toward altering the relative influence of different parts of
the government.[1] But the achievement of one reformation renders
the necessity of others more easily discernible, and very frequently
paves the way for a change of the greatest magnitude which had not
before been dreamed of. The basis of representation, in all human
probability, will continue to be enlarged until the House of Commons
has acquired such a preponderant weight as to make everyone see
the extreme incongruity of a legislative body which fairly represents
all the substantial interests of the state standing in intimate connection with two institutions which have no immediate dependence upon
the public will. It is true the concurrence of the House of Commons
will be necessary to any further reform of Parliamentary representation. Indeed the laws which are designed to effect that object must be
supposed to originate in the popular branch. And it may be said that
it will be the evident interest of the members to oppose every plan by
which the field of competition for their own seats shall be widened, or
by which the numbers of their constituents shall be so multiplied as
to render them less easily manageable by either intrigue or bribery.
These considerations did not prevent the passage of the act of 1832.
Public opinion when it has acquired a certain amount of strength acts
upon the mind with as much force and as absolute certainty as the
most powerful motives of self-interest. The temper and dispositions of

1. [The Reform Bill of 1832 reduced qualifications for the suffrage in the interest of the middle class and enfranchised about 800,000 voters.]

men become inflamed, as well as their understandings enlightened. The new fashion of thinking becomes contagious, and takes possession of society without anyone being aware whither it is carrying him. Indeed the causes which lead to any great changes in the structure of society are never under the immediate control of men. They determine the will, instead of the will determining them.

It is through the operation of a great many causes, the diffusion of knowledge and property, the growth of public opinion, the creation of a great middle class in society, and the giving to the representatives of the people a distinct voice and commanding influence in the legislature, that the public mind may be irresistibly conducted to a change in the fundamental laws by which the officers of every department of the government will be rendered strictly responsible. There is no good reason why the chief magistrate and the senate should continue to be hereditary when the popular body has become so numerous and so powerful as to swallow up the distinction of classes. The creation of a king and nobility may be said to have been originally owing to the inordinate influence which the imagination exercises over the minds of men at an early stage of society. But reflection, the most striking characteristic of the present age, is a wonderful extinguisher of the imagination in all affairs of real life.

It must be admitted that the principle of virtual representation, which is incorporated into British institutions, has been more successful than in any other government which has existed. But even if it were possible to perpetuate the system, it has many intrinsic defects. The great advantage of actual representation consists in its fixing the attention of all classes upon the conduct of public men. It thus initiates the people into an acquaintance with the practical working of the system and founds their attachment to government upon their interests. Virtual representation is without these advantages. However powerful public opinion may be, and although it may prevent acts of injustice in the gross, yet it cannot reach them in detail. The system of public measures and the conduct of public men are made up of an infinite number of acts, each of which may be inconsiderable and yet the aggregate of incalculable importance. When the rulers of the state are not subjected to a strict accountability, they become a law to themselves; they create a standard of opinion within their own circle which necessarily weakens the force of that general opinion whose office it is to watch over the actions of all the functionaries of government. It is true there is a species of adventitious authority attached to all human institutions which, after all, must come in for a very large share in the government of mankind. But the American experiment has demonstrated that free institutions possess this quality to as great extent as either monarchy or aristocracy. The popular mind clothes all the symbols and insignia of a legitimate authority with the same sort of veneration and respect which contribute to uphold the artificial forms of government.

There is one circumstance which might be supposed to stand in the way of all interference with the fundamental laws and to prevent any alteration in the existing theory of the government. The middle class are, in effect, the governing class in Great Britain. By them everything must be done. And it may be insisted that when this class reflect upon the perfect security which they now enjoy, they will be unwilling to exchange it for an untried state of being; that they will be more strongly impressed with the advantage which a system of institutions, in part artificial, has in producing domestic quiet and inspiring an instinctive obedience to the laws. They may fear that all industrious occupations which now confer comfort and independence upon them may be interfered with, if they give countenance to any further changes, no matter how just and how beneficial in many respects those changes may be. In short they may be convinced that if royalty and aristocracy are evils, they are at any rate necessary evils in the government of an ancient society. There is, no doubt, force in these considerations, but they presuppose, and rightly too, a high degree of reflection among that class; and it is this reflection which, on the one hand, constitutes a guarantee against the mischiefs which are apprehended and, on the other, is a sure presage of very material changes in the structure of the government. These changes will only be postponed to a period when they will cease to be regarded as a revolutionary movement and will appear to be a natural transition of the institutions into a position already prepared for them. They will be preceded by a very important measure, one which will place all the members of the middle class upon the same footing and give them all an equal voice in the government. For, although I have represented the middle class as holding the balance of power, yet it is not the entire body, but only a part, which possesses this influence. Not all the middle class are comprehended in the list of voters. The qualifications of electors might descend much lower and take in a very numerous and substantial part of the population which is now left out. Moreover, the possession of personal as well as real and leasehold property might be made a qualification. When these two measures, so natural and so easy of adoption, are actually accomplished, the danger to society will no longer seem to consist in taking down a part of the government in order to reconstruct it, but rather in permitting it to stand as it is, not representing the popular will, and yet the popular will possessing all power and authority.

As I have already remarked, there is no class of men who have a more distinct appreciation of the very general progress which knowledge, industry, and morals have made among the English people than the nobility themselves; none which is more thoroughly sensible of the goal whither things are tending.

Mixed government, of which the English is the most complete model, proceeds upon the principle that there are two permanent classes in society whose interests are opposed to each other: the higher and lower orders.[2] It proposes, therefore, to secure a distinct representation to each so that the two shall act concurrently and yet each possess a veto upon the acts of the other. The legislature is divided into two chambers; one composed of an order of nobility, the other of deputies of the people. In addition to this, an hereditary monarch is placed at the head of the system. And it may be asked, where is the necessity of this arrangement when the great bulk of the population are already represented? It is in consequence of the mixed character of the population. In a representative republic, the composition of society is exceedingly uniform: there is no order of nobility; a character of consistency and homogeneity is impressed upon it from the beginning. But in a state differently constituted there must be some additional contrivance in order to give this character of unity to the whole government. It is supposed that an hereditary monarch, holding his title independently of the two great classes, will answer this purpose. It may even be supposed that he will answer it better in a highly advanced state of society than in one which has made little progress in knowledge and refinement. In the former, both classes are powerful; in the latter, the nobility alone are so. In the first, he will be not merely disposed but compelled to act as arbiter between the two orders; in the last, he will endeavor either to render the nobility subser-

2. [For the second edition, Grimke added new matter from the start of this paragraph to the paragraph which ends, ". . . in the British Isles," on p. 284.]

vient to his designs or, failing in this, he will be engaged in a perpetual conflict with them. In either event, the interests of society would be endangered. It is not surprising, therefore, that nations which have made great progress in cultivation and among whom knowledge is widely diffused should obstinately cling to the office of king long after the state of society in which it originated has passed away.

There is an additional reason for the continuance of the institutions in an advanced state of society. The popular class itself becomes divided into two great classes, the middle and the plebeian class. Each of these grows in magnitude as the society advances; so much so that the order of nobility loses its original character as a component part of the society, although it retains its place in the government. The great object now is to bridle the unruly and licentious habits of the plebeian class, and the authority of a king, added to that of the nobility, is thought to be necessary for that purpose. If the power of the nobility had not declined, there would be no danger of their using the plebeian class in order to curb the independence of the middle class. But the fact that they retain their place in the government, while their personal authority is diminished, enables them in conjunction with the commons to exercise just so much influence as is necessary to check the encroachments of the plebeian class. An invasion of the rights of the commons, now that these have become formidable from their wealth, would be an invasion of their own, unless they could make the whole body of plebeians instrumental in designs against the middle class. But this they are disabled from doing. And as the king was at first entrusted with the sword in order to keep peace between the nobility and the people, he is now entrusted with it in order to keep peace between the two orders into which the people itself is divided. The standing army of Great Britain is kept up solely for this purpose. It is part of the system of internal police, only designed for the whole kingdom as the constabulary force is designed for a town or county. There is this difference, however, between the old and new order of things. In the first, there was danger of encroachments of the nobility upon the people and of the people upon the nobility. In the last, the danger apprehended is all on one side; it is of encroachments of the plebeians upon the middle class. May there not, then, be danger in the further progress of society, of an oppressive exercise of power as against the lower classes? If all other orders, king, nobility, and commons, are leagued together against them, may they not ultimately be driven to the wall and one half of the population be subjugated by the other half? But in truth, the change is highly favorable to great moderation in all parts of the society. Instead of a powerful patrician class and a handful of commoners, we have a handful of patricians, and a vast body of commoners. Power has been displaced from the position it formerly occupied. The influence of the middle class has been prodigiously augmented and that of the nobles proportionally diminished. Not only has power changed hands, but the new power which has risen up is of an entirely different character from that which it has superseded. The commons are too feeble, singly, to embark in any schemes detrimental to the public interests; they are too numerous to make it an object to do so. But their strength in the aggregate enables them to exercise a decisive influence and authority over other parts of the society. The intervention of the nobility in the disputes between the commons and the proletarians has ceased to be necessary. For, 1st, there is a stronger bond of connection between these two classes than between the nobility and the plebeians. 2d, the exercise of force in the name of the commons is productive of less exasperation than its exercise by the nobility. The great use of the commons at present is to temper the power which the nobility might be disposed to exercise against the plebeian class. 3d, as the population has become more homogeneous since the decay of the personal authority of the nobles, it is a system of general order which is now sought to be preserved, and that end is best attained where the authority which presides over the public welfare represents the general will of the community and not merely the particular interests of a class. When political power was very nearly divided between the nobility and the commons it was necessary, in addition to the means which each possessed for protecting its own interests, that a third power, an hereditary monarch, should be instituted to prevent any excess of power by either of the conflicting orders. And when the popular body became divided into two classes, the intervention of this third power was still deemed necessary in order to compose their dissensions. But when in the further progress of society the middle class entirely overshadows all others and absorbs all influence and all effective power, the personal authority of the monarch is also enfeebled. It is then that a government in which the commons are represented by an executive magistrate and two chambers in the legislature becomes abundantly strong to quell insurrection and insubordination to the laws. The experiment of the American government is full of instruction on this subject. The utmost vigor and decision have been displayed by both the federal and state governments in suppressing tumult and disorder. A government which knows that it represents the opinions and interests of the great body of the people is necessarily a strong one and goes straightforward to its end, without any of those misgivings which perplex the holders of a less legitimate authority.

Mixed government, then, may be described as the transition state from pure monarchy to representative government. We must not consider it as the form in which the institutions are destined to be permanently cast. The most eminent English statesmen of both parties are accustomed to pronounce it the best without any qualification. But there is a wonderful proclivity even among the most enlightened minds to believe each step in the progress of society to be the best and the final step. This law of our nature is not without its use. Each step may be one of indefinite duration. It is important, therefore, to render it popular, so that society may not go back instead of moving forward. The force of public opinion is thus arrayed in favor of each successive advance, and when further change becomes desirable society is prepared for it by reason of the progress it has already made. And this leads to other and still more important views in relation to this matter. For a considerable period prior to each step in advance, there is a general fermentation among the minds of men. New opinions and doctrines are freely discussed and resolutely proclaimed. A close observer of English society at the present day, one who has noticed the wide extent to which liberal opinions are circulated among all classes, will find more cogent reasons than those suggested by mere theoretical propriety why the existing form of society is not destined to last forever. If popular intelligence and power continue to make much further progress, it will be impossible to preserve the *sentiment* of monarchy and aristocracy in its pristine force. It may be supposed that the commons will be disposed to uphold the existing frame of government from a conviction that it is the best on the whole; and undoubtedly in this event it will be maintained. But what shall we say, if among that very class, opinions of an opposite character are widely diffused? The commons may battle against the opinions of any other class, but they cannot make war upon their own. What is now the subject of frequent discussion will become matter for familiar everyday conversation. The principles which hold together the old fabric are already shaken, but the blows will be so constant that it may ultimately be undermined. An illusion of the imagination cannot be kept alive by reasoning upon it when the creature of the imagination becomes himself the reasoner. A close body, like the ancient priesthood of Egypt and Hindustan, might persuade others to accept their impostures, but they never accepted them themselves. And whenever any error or imposture is thoroughly penetrated by the popular mind, it is sure to be assailed on all sides until it loses its force upon the imagination. When the secret can no longer be kept, because so many are let into it, there is an end of its influence upon society. A profound and original writer,* in exposing the unsoundness of what is termed "the development hypothesis," remarks that it is impossible to travel by railroad or steamboat without hearing the freest discussion of this question. If a doctrine so abstruse and so far removed from the ordinary pursuits and speculations of men has become the subject of bold and unreserved discussion, it is not surprising that political questions, which however abstract are mingled with all the affairs of men, should be made the subject of general and familiar conversation.

In that form of society to which I have supposed the present current of events is tending, it will be unnecessary to disturb the question of universal suffrage. Every department of government in the United States was representative before universal suffrage was introduced. A moderate qualification for the exercise of the elective franchise would be consistent with the interests of that great body denominated the commons or middle class, but the artificial structures of king and nobility will be entirely inconsistent with those interests.

The system of patronage which has taken such deep root in the British government depends for its existence upon the institutions of king and nobility. There is no subject which has more deeply engaged the attention of enlightened men in that country, ever since the memorable resolution introduced into the House of Commons in the early part of this century that the influence of the crown has increased, is in-

---

* "Footsteps of the Creator"— By H. Miller. [Hugh Miller (1802–1856), *The Foot-prints of the Creator; or, the Asterolepis of Stromness* (London, 1849), a defense of Christianity and a rejection of the potential atheism of the pre-Darwinian "development" school because of its rejection of a radical difference between man and the rest of the natural creation; the third London edition was reprinted in the United States (Boston, 1850) with a foreword by Louis Agassiz.]

creasing, and ought to be diminished. It has exercised the minds of great numbers who had hitherto kept aloof from such speculations. The Black Book of England, a work of unimpeached authority, lets us into an acquaintance with the curious machinery by which this patronage is so wielded as to enable a small number to domineer over the great body of the people. I shall notice a few instances only: 1st. Almost all offices in the West Indies, both civil and judicial, are discharged by deputy, the principal residing in England. 2d. Pluralities exist to an enormous extent, both in state and church. 3d. Nine hundred and fifty-six pensioners and placemen receive the immense sum of £2,788,907. 4. Sinecures exist for life, with reversions sometimes to persons in the cradle, to the amount of £1,500,000. 5. Many offices even in Great Britain are discharged by deputy. 6. From the returns of 1833, there were sixty members of the House of Commons holding offices and receiving emoluments from civil appointments, sinecures, etc., exclusive of eighty three holding naval and military commissions. And there are so many as eighty five members who enjoy church patronage. 7. The vast patronage of the church of which the king is head and to the principal offices in which he appoints. 8. The firm and irresponsible tenure of the whole body of civil officers. The power which this confers, the important agency it has in binding to the crown a vast organized corps interested in holding all sorts of abuses, is equally evident.

The patronage of the American president is not only small in comparison with that of the British king, but is of a totally different character. Real duties are annexed to all the offices which are dispensed by the former. If the president appoints with a view to his re-election, the influence emolument conferred on the persons appointed is inconsiderable. The tenure by which he holds his trust is short, so is that of his appointees. Both are placed on their good behavior from a consciousness of the insecurity of their places. But the king has an army of officers for life, for not one in twenty go out on a change of administration. The fluctuation of offices in America is a source of security to the institutions, independently of the good effect it has in introducing so large a part of the population to an acquaintance with public affairs. The displacement of a number of civil officers in the United States is simply an application of the principle of rotation which takes place in the election of the president himself. The blind and arbitrary rule of the choice by lot is superseded by one which is clear and intelligible.

Removals may undoubtedly be made from improper motives, and I know nothing which would impart to political affairs so lofty a character as that all the good which is done to society should be done from perfectly pure motives. If this cannot be accomplished, the next thing most desirable is to make sure that the good should at any rate be performed. The great principle in the American government is that power should never be conferred on the best man which in the hands of the worst would be liable to abuse. Hence the rule which establishes a moderate tenure of office for the executive and members of the legislature, and the same rule runs through the appointment of all the subordinate administrative officers. If I were asked what is the secret spring which actuated the leaders of parties in the United States in the selection of a president, I should say it was the desire to elect the man who was most approachable. Men of moderate talents are much more so than men of superior endowments. But from the choosing men of moderate talents and of unexceptionable character flow a great number of consequences which are of inestimable advantage. A patrician class is dispersed as soon as it shows itself, while the power of the middle class is strengthened and consolidated. And with the frail materials we have with which to erect government of any kind, or under any circumstances, we can never do so well as by reposing the political power with that class chiefly.

English writers speak of the ease with which their government sustains an enormous patronage. But it would be more correct to speak of the ease with which a well organized system of patronage may be made to sustain government. For what is it we intend when we speak of the ability of monarchical government to sustain patronage? It simply means that the system of patronage is so firmly fenced in, so thoroughly supported by the rich and powerful, that it becomes a self-perpetuating institution, producing quiet because it stifles without removing discontent. The feature which is most calculated to produce alarm is the very thing which hides the vices of the system from view.

The corrupting influence of patronage is less in a republic than in a monarchy. 1st. Because the power and emoluments bestowed are greatly inferior. 2d. Because they are so insecure. 3d. Because real duties, duties which demand unremitted attention and industry, are attached to all offices. 4th. The candidates are greatly more numerous in popular than in monarchical governments, so that the people exercise a perpetual check upon each other. 5th. The list of public offices is exceedingly diminutive when compared with the number of the electors. 6th. The multitude disappointed and interested in voting against the chief magistrate, when he is a candidate a second time, is so much more formidable than that of the appointees. These circumstances render the mischiefs of patronage in a representative republic much less than the theory of such a government would lead us to suppose. The executive dispenses offices to the people and to the people he is indebted for his election. Yet this patronage is comparatively impotent in securing his re-election. The number dissatisfied, in conjunction with the still greater number who have no expectation of obtaining office, is so immense that it is doubtful whether one chief magistrate in ten will be re-elected. The practice of electing for one term has grown up since executive patronage has been vastly enlarged. It may be supposed that the public interests will be damaged by not re-electing an officer who has already acquired a competent knowledge of public affairs. But in proportion as the institutions of a country are matured and perfected, less talent is requisite for conducting them. Public business becomes organized into a regular system and little is left for the incumbent unless he has the temerity to depart from that system. To the stability of office is substituted the stability of a complicated system, easy to administer and yet difficult to break in upon.

I have observed that the system of patronage in Great Britain contributes mightily to strengthen the power of the king and aristocracy. But there are some circumstances which, independently of the growing authority of the commonalty, have a contrary tendency, and not the less so that they are of a more hidden character and act silently and imperceptibly upon the government. That the defects of a government should gradually lead to an alteration in its structure will not appear surprising, but that its excellencies should have the same effect is still more surprising and would not be apt to strike the mind of any but a close observer. A very great change has taken place in European society in very modern times in the habits and manners of what are called the superior classes. Formerly crimes and every species of disorder were committed by the men who belonged to those classes, fully as much as by those who filled the inferior ranks. In modern times, and more particularly in Great Britain, outrages against life and property are almost entirely confined to the lowest walks of life. This change in the manners is one reason why society is so much more easily governed than formerly. Crimes are now strictly personal and are no part of the habitual conduct of the governing class. This, to all appearance, confers a great advantage upon that class. It does so in reality for a very considerable period. It evidently gives popularity to the government of that class and wins over to it the obedience of all other orders. But it is also evident that the more the manners of the higher ranks are likened to those of the middle class, the greater is the authority and influence which the last acquire. The middle class in England and Scotland are more distinguished for energy, sagacity, and information than any other class during any period of European history. That the substantial excellencies of their character should be copied by those who wield so much political influence is not so much a compliment (for with that we have nothing to do) as a recognition that that class have certain elements of public and private virtue which, when they have full play, make up the whole of public and private prosperity. But if these are the qualities most essential both in public and private life, they are the very ones which are the best fitted to govern mankind. And as the commonalty are a numerous and powerful body and the aristocracy a small one, it may happen that the whole effective authority of the state may slide, not from any set purpose or preconceived design, but insensibly and quietly, into the hands of the former; and then it must be admitted, it would not be a work of great difficulty so to change the institutions as to make their outward form correspond with the genius which animated them. Perhaps it would be more correct to say that it would not only not be difficult, but that it would be the end to which society would straightforward tend as not only the most natural but as affording in the altered condition of the social organization the most effectual means of giving strength and stability to the institutions.

There is another circumstance which is calculated to arrest our attention. A great change has taken place in the manners of European courts. The regime, the domestic police, if I may so express myself, of the princely mansion, is totally different from what it was formerly. Never were the manners so thoroughly dissolute, so corrupt, as in the time of Louis the Fifteenth of France, and Charles the Second of England. Nothing of the kind is witnessed at the present day. The French Revolution of 1789 revolutionized the manners of the French court, and Napoleon was the first monarch who introduced something like decency and propriety in the princely household. The English Revolution, a century earlier, effected the same thing in that country. The manners which formerly prevailed, and which were supposed to be peculiarly adapted to a court, would not be tolerated at the present day.

The cause of this great change is evidently to be found in the power which public opinion has acquired. The prince and the nobles who were elevated so high as to be exempt from its control are now made directly responsible to it. But what has given being to this public opinion? Evidently the rise of that great class whom we denominate the commonalty, whose habits of life are for the most part alien to anything like unbridled licentiousness and whose numbers add great weight and authority to the new law which is imposed upon society. Thus the prince, as well as the nobleman, finds himself involuntarily copying after the manners and habits of the middle class. The exterior may be more refined, but the ground work is the same. This singular and unexpected consequence, however, follows from this revolution in the manners. Kingly power and grandeur strike the imagination with infinitely less force than formerly. The very fact that the monarch was lifted so high as to be absolved from all restraint, that he was not only not amenable to the laws, but not amenable to those conventional rules which preside over the manners of a civilized society, gave an imposing air to everything which pertained to his office. How this should happen, how he who was set so high, whose conduct should be so just, and his manners so unexceptionable, should be polluted with so many vices seemed to be inexplicable; and the fact that it was inexplicable imparted additional mystery to the royal authority. That so startling a contradiction should exist, and no one be able to answer why it was permitted, acted like a charm upon the imagination of the masses. Kingly power was not only a great office, but more than that it was a great mystery. The heathen mythology exercised a sovereign mastery over the popular mind, although the gods were tainted with every species of vice. The human mind could probably give no other explanation of this anomaly than that if they were not lifted so high as to be absolved from all the laws which govern mankind they would partake of the character of men, and would cease to be gods.

Thus in proportion as princes mend their manners and practice those virtues which give dignity to the individual in whatever station he is placed, in the same proportion do they contribute to break the spell which inspired unlimited obedience among all classes. If to come down to the level of those homely virtues which adorn their subjects has become the fashion of the day, a fashion not arbitrarily taken up but imposed by the irresistible course of events, the notion may gradually insinuate itself into the minds of those subjects that government is not a grand mystery, nor the prince an impersonation of the deity; that as it is now for the first time a received maxim in politics that government should be administered for their advantage, that advantage would be most certainly attained by the appointment of responsible agents by themselves. Once a delusion of the imagination is broken up, men begin to reason, and although I do not undertake to predict what form the institutions will assume an hundred or even fifty years hence, yet there is nothing inconceivable, nothing unreasonable in the supposition, that within the shortest of those periods a firm, wise, and vigorous representative government may be established in the British Isles.

There is, then, a very general conviction that the present state of things cannot last forever — that royalty and aristocracy cannot stand secure amid the light of the nineteenth century. When this is the case, the revolution is half accomplished. The middle class at a future day need not say to the king and his ministers, you may squander the wealth of the state, provided you will protect us against the assaults of the lower classes. For they will be able to protect themselves as effectively and with infinitely less expense; while at the same time, innumerable abuses and deformities in the system which have no other use than to prop up an exceedingly artificial form of government will be extirpated.

CHAPTER VII | THE LEGISLATIVE POWER

THE great defect of what is termed pure democracy as distinguished from representative government consists in this, that the former is without an established system of laws. The momentary and fluctuating will of the people constitutes the law on every occasion — which is the reason why that form of government is the worst except despotism. Nor does there at first sight seem to be any reason why there should be any pre-established ordinances to bind the people when they assist personally at every public deliberation. Their will constitutes the law because there is no superior human power behind them to draw them back when error is about to be committed. For error, politically, is out of the question. Every such assembly is itself a convention of the people. Its last declaration, as it is the freshest expression of the public will, is also a full expression of the sovereign power of the state.

But there is no democratic republic which has existed in which the inconveniences, not to say the manifold evils, which spring from such a scheme of government have not been felt. There is not one which has not departed widely from the theory on which it professed to be founded. Solon drew up a body of laws for the Athenian state and Lycurgus one for Sparta. But this departure from the naked theory of democratic government was not a step taken in favor of representative government. It was the introduction of a capital feature of monarchical government. It was a recognition in disguise of the one man power. Nor was the case very different with the Roman decemvirate. Commissioners sent abroad to make a selection from the laws of other countries, and exercising their own judgment as to what ordinances would be adapted to the Roman community, is very different from a convention assembled among the people for whom the new code is to be framed, drawing instruction from a deep and careful survey of the form of society which lay before them and suiting the laws exclusively to their domestic interests.

Fortunately for most nations which have been inclined to establish popular government, the extent of territory has opposed an insurmountable obstacle to carrying out the naked theory of democratic government, while the extent and diverse character of the population have been equally fatal to the attainment of a predominant influence by one or two individuals. It becomes impossible for the people to assemble in mass and still more so for them to perform the duties which appertain to an executive and judicial magistracy. This compels the adoption of the principle of representation in every one of the political departments. Representatives, when convened under this plan as a legislative body, pass laws from time to time as the exigences of society require, until at length these laws become so numerous and the chief part of them so adapted to the leading and permanent interests of the population that they lose the character of mere temporary regulations and are erected into a system of fixed rules for the government of the community. That is, they acquire a higher dignity and greater importance than they had before, notwithstanding they are not passed by the people but by the people's deputies. The restrictions imposed upon the law-making power increase its solemnity because they require a more exact and undivided attention to the duties which appertain to it than would be possible in an assembly of millions or thousands convened on one day and dispersed the next. For in the first place, in a country of wide extent and whose people are fitted for self-government, there will very naturally if not necessarily be a constitutional ordinance prescribing the duties of the legislator and the limits of legislation. And in the second place, representatives acting on behalf of others, in order to give any intelligible account to those who have deputed them, are obliged to proceed with considerable care in the preparation and consideration of bills. The laws are no longer carried by acclamation but are conducted through a long and tedious process; and the language in which they are expressed is endeavored to be made precise and perspicuous in order that the constituent may understand how the deputy has discharged his duty.

Thus representation which was at first intended to cure one defect in democratic government, that is, to facilitate the transaction of public business, comes in process of time to cure all defects by substituting, as nearly as humanly speaking can be done, a government of laws in the place of one of force. The people are the real law-givers, the members of the legislative body their agents only; and yet, in consequence of the double machinery which is employed the laws are made to reign supreme over the people themselves. For not only is the passage of all laws attended with certain solemnities and published in a form which renders them accessible to everyone, there is another circumstance which contributes to impress upon them the character of a system. The greater the number of persons for whom the laws are made, the greater must be the generality of the rules which they will contain. It is not difficult to legislate for a small number of individuals, or for a considerable number collected in a small space, by particular enactments. But there is no way of legislating for millions inhabiting an extensive country, but by very general laws. We then make abstraction of everything peculiar to the individual and take account only of those circumstances in which they all agree.

It is in proportion as the laws acquire this character of abstract general rules that they are fitted to exercise authority over the minds of men; and that in proportion as the territory is enlarged and the population multiplied the restraint which is imposed upon society is augmented. To reconcile a high degree of freedom with a due authority on the part of government is one problem which political philosophers have proposed to themselves. If we take refuge in monarchical or aristocratical government, we do indeed arm the public authority with a mighty power, but it is at the expense of popular liberty. If we have recourse to democratic government, we do not succeed in introducing a noble and generous freedom into the community while at the same time we detract materially from the authority of the laws. Representative government which is then the only alternative is also the most natural direction which the institutions can take, the one which promises to answer all the desired ends as well as we are permitted to expect.

Government, in order to fulfill the notion of a wise and useful institution, should aim to connect the private welfare of individuals with the public good of the state. To lose sight of the former — to suppose that the proper idea of government was that it had regard exclusively to public affairs and took little account of men's private interests — would be to form a very inadequate conception of it. The political institutions are an accessory to a great end, rather than the end itself. To permit the various occupations of individuals to be conducted with freedom and security is the final aim to which they should tend. But in the pure form of democratic government, the legislative, executive, and judicial powers would all be wielded by the same persons in mass; encumbering everyone with such a multiplicity of public business that their private affairs would go to ruin; and the people would cease to be men in their efforts to become citizens, when the maxim should be, that in order to become citizens it is first necessary to become men. And in such a constitution of society the public interests also would fall to decay as there would be wanting that concentrated attention which is indispensable to a skillful management of them. Representation, by applying the principle of the division of labor to the affairs of government, overcomes these difficulties. By collecting into a general system those rules which are intended to preside over the common interests, it gives additional authority to the laws; by abstaining from intermeddling too often and too minutely with the actions of individuals, it gives security and contentment to the people.

There is another view equally important. Men, even in the prosecution of their private business, have separate and selfish interests which they are ever intent upon gratifying. In a legislative assembly composed of a vast multitude, public and private interests would be confounded. The elective principle, without intending any such thing, effects a separation of the two. The number of private ends which are sought to be gratified will be diminished as the assembly diminishes, not only because the number of individuals exposed to the temptation is reduced but because the power of gratification is less. With no more wisdom and fully as much selfishness as the great majority of mankind, the members of this body are now placed in a situation where their attention will be more exclusively fastened upon the public interests, and one also which exposes their conduct more than ever to the scrutiny of other men. The people say to their deputies, as we are physically precluded from looking after our private ends we will, in revenge, observe your conduct more strictly. The deputies, on the other hand, although it may conflict with their private ends, are obliged to assume a character of earnestness and of devotion to the public business. They endeavor to place before themselves a standard of right by which to shape their conduct. A representative body, in other words, to make use of a homely phrase, operates as a strainer in separating the good from the bad qualities of individuals. It brings the public interests out in bolder relief, and weakens the cupidity of private persons.

An assembly so constituted is eminently favorable to reflection, not merely among its own members but among the community at large. The distribution of property and knowledge in modern times has created a wide basis for government to stand upon. But as it has multiplied the number of persons who have an interest in public affairs, it has increased the intensity of party spirit. The legislative body has stated times for convening; it does not meet like the popular assemblies of antiquity on every gust of wind which may blow over the commonwealth. Between the first ebullition of public feeling and the time appointed to deliberate, six months or more may elapse. This interval is eminently favorable to reflection, not merely because it gives opportunity to so many minds to calculate the consequences of a proposed line of action, but because time itself has a sedative influence, and calms the most agitated passions. Or if we suppose that some event of very exciting character has occurred when the legislature is on the eve of assembling, the set forms of proceeding to which such a body is addicted and to which it becomes singularly attached enable it easily to postpone the final determination for months, or even "to the first day of the succeeding session." The people willingly acquiesce in this delay on the part of their deputies when they would not listen to it in a tumultuous assembly of themselves. The claim to the whole of Oregon would have been carried by acclamation in a popular meeting when first proposed. But as the question had to be deliberated upon in a representative body whose responsibility was increased because they were acting for others and not merely for themselves, it was held under consideration for three years. And the manner in which it was finally adjusted, although so different from what was at first expected, met with a more hearty and unanimous approval from the American people than almost any other public measure which has been adopted.

Thus representative government is highly favorable to reflection, both in and out of the legislative body. It no longer speaks to itself alone, as was formerly the case. So far as regards the mere form of deliberating, the assembly sits within the four walls of the capitol. But for all important purposes the whole state may be considered as an extension of those walls. If there is any species of information which is widely disseminated, it is that which relates to what is transacted in those walls. This is conveyed not once and in one form only, but repeatedly and in every variety of shape so as to gratify the utmost inquisitiveness and to rouse the attention of the most censorious observer of public affairs. It has been finely remarked that one office which men of high intellectual endowments perform is to act as instruments of communication between the intellectual world and society at large. And a representative body, with all its imperfections, performs a service of a very similar character.

There is no one circumstance in the history of modern communities which more strikingly displays the great changes which have been wrought in the general structure of society than the manner in which business is now conducted in a legislative body. There was a time, and that not very remote, when such an assembly did not pretend to deliberate upon, or in any sense of the word to conduct, the public business in person, but devolved the whole burden upon a handful of individuals. Thus the Scotch Parliament which was composed of the three estates of the clergy, nobility, and burgesses never sat except on the day of meeting and the day of adjournment. On the first, it made choice of a committee, styled, "lords of the articles," which was composed of three persons from each of the estates. And this committee drew up all the bills and transacted the whole business. On the day appointed for the adjournment, these bills were submitted in mass to the Parliament and were all on that same day either approved or rejected. There was no free, open investigation, no debate, no account taken either one way or the other, of the serious consequences which might result from the proposed laws. Very similar was the mode of proceeding in the boasted Italian republics. The law was no sooner proposed than the votes of the different orders were immediately taken. It is very easy to understand what otherwise seems to be a riddle, how it came to pass that a legislative body, whether composed of one or more chambers, sat in one apartment. As there was no discussion, none of that bold and inquisitive spirit which now finds its way into such an assembly, as, in short, everything was conducted in silence, the several estates or orders might very conveniently meet in the same hall. The mode of conducting the legislative proceedings in France was even worse than in Scotland or Italy. Madame de Sévigné, in her letters, has given a very animated description of the fashion of doing business.[1] The canvassing the demands of the crown, the inquiry whether any and what taxes should be imposed, was not made in the legislative halls, but was carried on at the table of the nobleman who had been

1. [Marie de Rabutin-Chautal de Sévigné (1626–1696), French woman of letters whose correspondence of more than 1,500 letters is a major source for the history of taste and manners of her time.

commissioned by the king to preside over the estates, or provincial legislatures, and everything was carried by acclamation.

If there is any danger at the present day, it is of running into the opposite extreme. But it is better to err on that side. A superfluity of debate is infinitely better than none at all, or even than too little. It affords unequivocal evidence of two things: 1st, that the interests of the great body of the people have grown to be something; and 2d, that the deputies of the people are compelled to set themselves earnestly to work in order to acquire a competent knowledge of public affairs. In every deliberative assembly there are always a few individuals who stand out prominently above their fellows and succeed in fixing public attention. But it would be a great mistake to suppose that the speeches of other members of inferior endowments were unworthy of notice, that they were to be regarded as empty and prosy harangues. It not unfrequently happens that the reputation of a public speaker is not so much owing to his intellectual power as to some external advantages. Some men succeed full as much in consequence of their physical as of their mental organization. And one is often perplexed on reading the speeches of a leading member to account for the fame he has acquired. The speeches of some other members are as full of good sense and contain views as just and as comprehensive. Nevertheless, it is the fashion to regard these last as intruders into the debate and as hampering the public business by their everlasting "longeurs."

It is the population residing beyond the walls of the state house who in our modern societies constitute the real and effective audience, and to them a sensible speech is always interesting, although the voice of the speaker may be unmusical and his manner ever so ungainly. It was remarked of one of the most eminent statesmen America has produced * that while he sat in the House of Representatives he gave marked attention to the speech of every member. There was hardly an instance, he observed, when he did not derive instruction, or when new views were not suggested to him by the speeches of persons of even inconsiderable reputation. There was more wisdom in the observation than would at first strike the mind. The habit contracted by this eminent statesman gave him a thorough insight into the workings of other men's minds and was one cause of the remarkable intellectual ability which he himself displayed. Doubtless there is a rea-

---

* William Lowndes [(1782–1822) Congressman from South Carolina, noted especially for his calm and dispassionate manner of speaking in the House].

sonable share of egotism to be found in every large assembly of men. But even egotism may sometimes become our instructor. For as it supposes a desire to obtain the public approbation, and as that approbation is very insecure unless there is substantial merit, the representative even in his efforts to attract the notice of his constituents is obliged to make himself acquainted with the merits of the questions he undertakes to discuss. And as I have already observed, even if the speeches are unnecessarily prolix, there is an incidental advantage attending their delivery; they keep the public mind in abeyance and contribute by their very defects to cool the feelings and mature the judgment. It might be supposed that the danger would be on the other side, that the country would be kept in a state of feverish excitement in consequence of the inflammatory harangues of demagogues. But the day of inflammatory harangues is gone by when the competition for public speaking becomes so great as it necessarily is in a country of free institutions. Like everything with which we become abundantly familiar, those harangues pall upon the appetite and make us ardently desire to hear something truly brilliant. In ninety-nine cases in a hundred, the inflammatory speaker succeeds in enflaming none but himself.

Shall the legislative power be divided? shall it consist of two or more branches? is one of those questions which the human mind hardly ventures to debate any longer. Public opinion everywhere and in every form of government, except the absolute, has determined it in the affirmative. In the ancient commonwealths, in the limited monarchies of modern Europe, and in the United States, the division of the legislature has been regarded as an axiom in politics. An institution which is founded upon long-established custom and which has apparently adapted itself to almost every form of society has on that very account a strong claim to respect. This claim, however, must not be looked upon as absolutely decisive; for it is a fact of as ancient and as universal notoriety as any other which falls under our observation, that the human mind is wonderfully disposed to accommodate itself to what it finds to be the established order of things. Here are two principles set over against each other, a consideration which should make us exceedingly careful, but which should by no means dissuade us from a critical examination of the subject.

The distribution of society into classes was, doubtless, the foundation of the division of the legislative body. Where this classification did not exist, or where the inferior classes occupied an exceedingly insignificant position in the state, the legislature was seldom a plural body. Thus, in the earlier stages of English history, the great council was composed of the wise men or barons only, holding their seats not by virtue of an express authority delegated to them but by a tenure as firm and as independent as that of the king.

Society in its rude beginnings is held together chiefly by the force of the imagination. Where there is an immense disparity in the condition of the upper and lower ranks, where the first possess nearly all the property, the superstitious reverence which this circumstance inspires irresistibly invests them with the legislative authority. But in proportion as society advances and a different distribution of property takes place, whether this is occasioned by the civil wars of the barons which crumble their property or by the growth of trade and industry which raises up an entirely new class, this superstitious feeling loses its hold upon the mind. The appropriation of nearly all the property by the barons conferred upon them an exorbitant authority in comparison with the great majority of the population, and the gradual division of this property, whether in fee or in lease, afterward transfers some portion of that authority to other parts of society. A class below the nobility makes its appearance first in the towns and afterward in the country, and this class finally succeeds in obtaining a distinct and independent position in the community. While this new class is imperceptibly growing to manhood, the rivalry and disputes between the king and nobility reveal its importance and enable it actively to assert a power which lay dormant before. The people have now got to be something, because their intervention in the controversies of the day may be turned to account by one or other of the parties. They now elect their own representatives, and this gives occasion to another chamber of the legislative body.

But on a further advance of society the change becomes more marked and important. The barons dwindle into a mere handful. They cease to be even virtually the representatives of the community. Their weight in society is personal, rather than that of a class. If at an early period their number is small, this is compensated by their possessing the entire moral power of the state. At an intermediate stage their numbers and wealth are both diminished, but not so sensibly as to deprive them of their claim to constitute a separate branch of the legislature. At a still later period, their number is not only reduced but their wealth becomes insignificant when compared with that of the aggregate of the population. The division of the legislative power then loses its original meaning: it no longer stands upon the same foundation as formerly. And it becomes not merely matter for curious but for strictly legitimate inquiry whether the plan shall be preserved. Society may have undergone great alterations so that the causes which led to a particular political arrangement may have ceased to operate, and yet others may have sprung into existence which equally demonstrate its utility. Perhaps the very prejudices which surround an ancient institution may help us to ward off some other infirmity to which we will be exposed in constructing a new system.

In an old and established government there is this difficulty, the division of the legislature was not the result of any set design. Society fell into the arrangement at a period when circumstances controlled men instead of their controlling circumstances. The institution grows into an usage which incorporates itself with the habits of thinking of everyone. This gives it so firm a hold upon the imagination that the legislator hardly feels as if he had power, much less has he the inclination, to interfere with it. In a new society and new government, the case is different. If there is no regular classification of society, no subordination of ranks, and the principle of representation is introduced, and yet the division of the legislature has been copied from older states, its entire want of adaptation either annuls its influence or the influence which it has is of so vague and doubtful an appearance as to withdraw public attention altogether from the consideration of it.

De Lolme is almost the only writer who has undertaken to examine this question.[2] The reasoning is very ingenious. "Whatever bars," he says, "a single legislature may make to restrain itself can never be, relatively to itself, anything more than simple resolutions; as those bars which it might erect to stop its own motions must then be within it, and rest upon it, they can be no bars." This is undoubtedly true if the members hold their seats by hereditary right or where, being elected, the tenure is long and the electoral franchise exceedingly restricted. But where the entire legislative body is chosen by popular

2. [Jean Louis de Lolme (1740–1806), Swiss political writer who for political reasons emigrated to England where he published *The Constitution of England* (London, 1771). The passage Grimke cites is slightly misquoted and is from Book II, Chapter III, "The Division of the Legislative Power."]

suffrage and for a limited period, a new principle rises up and takes the place of those bars, to wit, the responsibility of the members to their constituents. The condition which De Lolme was in search of in order to restrain the legislature is then found. The bars are truly without, and not within, the body. De Lolme, although investigating a general principle, confined his attention exclusively to British society where from time immemorial the distinction of ranks existed; nor did he frame to himself any just conception of a commonwealth where privileged orders had no place, and where the responsibility of the members shall be so direct and immediate as to create an inevitable check upon their conduct.

From this view, it would seem to follow that the question, shall the legislature be divided? depends upon the mode of election and the tenure of the members; in other words, upon the provision which is made in the system for giving effect to the principle of responsibility and not upon the nature of the power which is exercised. In most of the European states the legislative body is composed of a class of nobles and of deputies chosen by the people, and as these two orders are supposed to have contrary interests, each is protected against the encroachments of the other by both possessing coordinate authority and consequently the right to veto the acts of each other. No such reason exists in a democratic republic. Indeed, one great design of that form of government is to unite together, as far as is practicable, the different classes of which society is composed instead of inventing devices for keeping them asunder. It is on that very account that the principle of representation is introduced into every department of the government. All the members of the legislative assembly are elected, and the reason is not very apparent why they should be distributed into two any more than into three or four chambers. This incongruity between the institution and a democratic form of society may be productive of one or other of two results. It may give rise to much confusion and inconvenience in the working of the government, or its tendency to produce that effect may be neutralized by the otherwise skillful structure of the body; the dead principle may be countervailed by the living one with which it is incorporated. When the last is the case, the institution degenerates into a mere formal arrangement which is preserved simply because it is found to be part of an old-established system. If no glaring inconvenience is perceived, people very easily persuade themselves that the institution is not only wise but that it is an indispensable part of the machinery of free government.

Other reasons, however, than those I have referred to may be assigned for this mode of organizing the legislative body. It may be argued that it is calculated to introduce more reflection into the public deliberations than would be the case if the body were a single one. The United States is the only country which affords much light upon this part of the subject. So far as regards the state governments, and I purposely confine myself to them at present, it is by no means certain that experience justifies the conclusion. Perhaps on a very close and attentive observation it would be found that the division of the body has been productive of increased violence and exacerbation, although in ways which are at first calculated to elude observation; or it may be that a predominant idea having once taken possession of the mind its influence is not easily weakened by all the observation which we have made.

In order to execute this plan of accompanying every legislative measure with a greater degree of reflection, it would seem to be necessary that the mode of electing the two chambers should be different, or that at least the terms for which the members of the two are chosen should be of different duration. In both respects there is little or no discrimination in much the greater part of the state governments. In Maryland the senate was formerly elected, like the president of the United States, by a college of electors. But this feature in the old constitution has been superseded by the ordinary and more natural plan of direct choice. In Massachusetts, New Hampshire, North and South Carolina, a property qualification is necessary to entitle to a seat in either house. And the amount of property necessary for a senator is double that which is requisite for a representative. But in the great majority of the states no distinction exists. In Virginia a property qualification is indeed demanded of both senators and representatives, but the qualification is the same in both instances and is none other than is required of the electors themselves.

As to the duration of the term, in some states senators and representatives are elected for the same term. This is the case in Maine, Massachusetts, New Hampshire, Connecticut, Rhode Island, New Jersey, North Carolina, Georgia, and Tennessee. In Maryland senators are elected for six years. In Delaware, Mississippi, Arkansas, and Illinois, for four; but in these states the sessions of the legislature being biennial, the four years is equivalent to two terms only. In Virginia, South Carolina, Kentucky, Louisiana, and Missouri they are elected for four years and the legislature meets annually. In Pennsylvania, Indiana, and Alabama, they are elected for three, and in New York, Michigan, and Ohio, for two. And in these six last states the legislature also sits annually. The only states in which representatives are chosen for two terms are South Carolina, Louisiana, and Missouri.

All this shows an exceeding variety in the mode of composing the two chambers, or at least in the outward form which they are made to assume, and indicates, moreover, that the notion of giving to senators a more independent tenure than to representatives in order to create a balance between the two bodies was often entirely lost sight of, and in no two instances thoroughly carried into practice. The division of the legislature was copied from older communities in which a regular subordination of ranks existed. But in America, there was no similar classification of society and the materials for constructing an upper house on the European model were entirely wanting.

In some of the states candidates for the senate must have attained a higher age than those for the house. But the distinction in this respect is so small as to create no material difference in the constitution of the two chambers. In no state does there appear to have been the least design to create a council of elders. But the scheme of a plural body having been adopted, it was necessary to give color to it by creating a distinction, however unimportant it might be. Age undoubtedly, in the great majority of men, contributes to extend the circle of their ideas and to mature the judgment. It would be difficult to fall upon any precise rule, applicable to all men, as there is not only a very great difference in the natural faculties of individuals, but a great difference also in the ripening of different minds which possess equal power. Forty-five has been supposed to be the earliest period at which, in the average of men, the judgment is thoroughly matured and the knowledge and experience which have been previously acquired may be made available to the business of public life. But in no state except Kentucky is a higher age than thirty required in order to entitle to a seat in the senate. In most of the states the candidate need not be more than twenty-five; and in Connecticut, New York, New Jersey, Rhode Island, and North Carolina, persons who have attained twenty-one years are eligible to either house. The provisions on this subject also show how very imperfectly the scheme of balancing one body against the other has been accomplished. In some respects the age of five and twenty is more unfavorable than twenty-one. The young man just arrived at majority is apt to be more diffident, to distrust his own powers more than he would if four or five years older. At five and twenty we feel more confidence, a greater degree of self-assurance, even though there should be less ability to second our efforts. I am not sure, therefore, but what the constitutions of Rhode Island, New York, New Jersey, and North Carolina have adopted the wisest plan. A man at twenty-one may be both more discreet and better informed than one at twenty-five. A man at twenty-five is sometimes superior in both respects to one at forty-five. Instead of establishing an unchangeable rule, the best plan is to defer the matter to the electors and enable them to exercise their judgment in making the selection. Legislation in the United States is not, as in some other countries, an affair which is exclusively engrossed by the nobility and gentry. It is a matter in which the great bulk of the population have a deep stake and in which consequently they are made to take an active part. Their observation and experience, although not affording an unerring guide, will ever prevent them from going very wrong.

There is another feature in which the upper and lower houses of the American legislatures differ. The last is invariably the most numerous body. But where the constitution of the two is in other respects substantially the same, this difference is little more than an arrangement of detail. One can easily conceive of an upper house composed of so few and of a lower of so great a number of members as to create a complete antagonism between them. This was the case in the Athenian commonwealth where the senate consisted of one or two hundred and the popular assembly of eight thousand. It was so, also, in the Roman State where the senate contained three hundred and the comitia of the centuries, or tribes, twenty or thirty thousand. But the disparity in point of numbers, as well as in other respects, is so inconsiderable in the American states that if there is any efficacy in an upper house, it is doubtful whether it is not attributable to the name rather than the thing. We call it an upper house, figure it to ourselves as the most dignified body of the two, and thenceforward a firm conviction takes possession of the mind that it must perform some office distinct from and of superior utility to that performed by the other house. In the English government the House of Peers is a less numerous body than the House of Commons; the former consisting of four hundred and thirty-nine and the last of six hundred and fifty-eight members. But the different operation of these two bodies does not arise in the smallest degree from that circumstance. It is not the fewness of the number but the fewness of the class which renders the House of Peers a totally different body from the House of Commons. The former represents itself; the last represents millions. So that if the upper house were the most numerous body of the two, and yet the constitution of both was in other respects precisely the same as at present, the operation of the system would be the same.

Copying after English precedents, the American governments have sometimes sought to establish a difference in the functions as well as in the composition of the two chambers. Thus, in some of the states, money bills can only originate in the lower house. This is an arrangement which is obviously without meaning or utility in the local governments. It has accordingly been dropped in the constitutions of Connecticut, Rhode Island, New York, Ohio, Illinois, Michigan, and Arkansas. The members of both chambers are equally representatives of the people, and no very solid reason can be assigned why any bill should not be permitted to originate in either. One thing is certain that, notwithstanding the efforts which have been made to create an artificial distinction between the two bodies, they remain essentially the same. This it is which constitutes a distinguishing feature of American institutions; that we may vary the paraphernalia of government as much as we please, but it still obstinately persists in every one of its departments to be a government based upon the popular will. In other countries, the different structure of these departments is occasioned by great diversities in the organization of society. The difficulty is how to retain these, and yet to obtain so much uniformity in the character of the population as to dispense just and equal rules to all men. In America, this substantial requisite is already obtained, and American legislators can therefore afford to make experiments as to the mere outward form which their institutions shall wear. America may copy after Europe; but the great problem is, can Europe copy after America?

The materials then for constructing an upper house, such as they exist in Europe, are entirely wanting in America, and I have doubted (for it is perhaps impossible to pronounce an opinion absolutely decisive when the question is of taking down an old, not of erecting a new, institution) whether it was worthwhile to adhere to the principle of a division of the legislature in the state governments. The difference, however slight, in the tenure by which the members of the two chambers hold their seats causes them sometimes to represent different parties; and this reflection of opposite opinions lays the foundation of a spirit of rivalry and animosity which impedes the progress of business during a whole session. A single body having the public eye intently fixed upon it, and not distracted by the shuffling and the maneuvering of two chambers, would feel a more thorough because a more undivided responsibility to its constituents. The true office of a minority consists in its influencing, not governing. If the legislature consisted of a single chamber, the predominant party would abstain from those extreme measures which it is now driven to vindicate in consequence of the equally extreme measures which are defended by the chamber of the minority. Each dares the other to do as it says; each obstinately clings to its own opinions, because each knows that neither can possibly be carried, and in this way both have in repeated instances endeavored to fly from the responsibility which they owed to society.

This is the reason why the veto of the governor on bills passed by the legislature has been abolished in nearly all the American states. That power was at one time supposed to answer the same purpose as the division of the legislature: to maintain a salutary check upon that assembly. But experience has demonstrated that it is as well, if not better, to place the legislative body in a situation where it will feel the undivided weight of the responsibility imposed upon it.

It sometimes happens that although the duration of the term for which senators and representatives are chosen is the same that the two chambers still reflect the opinions of different parties. This circumstance is ascribable to various causes. Sometimes it is in consequence of the mere difference of the number of members which compose the two chambers. The districts in which senators are elected will naturally be larger than for representatives. And although the qualifications of the electors may be the same in both, yet where parties in the state are pretty evenly balanced a different territorial division will give rise to different results in the selection of the members. This was recently the case in Tennessee where senators and representatives are elected for the same term. The melancholy spectacle was presented of one house obstinately refusing to go into an election because, on joint ballot, the vote would be unfavorable to the predominant party in the house. It is a striking proof of the soundness of public opinion in America that where a course of conduct of this character has been pursued, one so alien to the genius of free institutions, it has terminated in the overthrow of the refractory party. The ballot box at the succeeding election has converted the majority into the minority. But in none of the other nine states where the term of senators and representatives is the same, do I recollect to have heard of such unjustifiable proceedings. This conduct, and other of a similar character, has been confined to those states where the duration of the term is different.

There is one of the American states in which until recently the legislature was composed of a single chamber. This is Vermont. And it is certain that in no state has the course of legislation been more uniformly marked by good sense and propriety; in none has there been a more watchful attention to the interests of the people. At an early period, the legislature of Pennsylvania was also a single body. This arrangement was altered before there had been sufficient time to test the experiment. The brilliant repartee of Mr. Adams in answer to Dr. Franklin, who was in favor of a single chamber, captivated the minds of men and was decisive of the question at a period when the fashion of thinking in America was so much molded upon European institutions.[3]

3. [At the Pennsylvania Constitutional Convention, Benjamin Franklin is supposed to have carried the motion for a unicameral legislature with a story "which compared a legislature with two branches to a loaded wagon with a team at each end." *The Works of Benjamin Franklin* . . . , ed., Jared Sparks (Boston, [1840]), I, 409. In a short chapter on Franklin in *A Defence of the Constitutions of Government of the United States* . . . (London, 1787), John Adams has Franklin tell the story but renders it quite differently, adapting it to his own preference for bicameralism, and has the two teams at the front and the back of the wagon working together to get the loaded wagon down a dangerous slope. But in Adams' telling, the story is so confused that it hardly qualifies as "brilliant repartee." Perhaps Grimke had in mind what Adams then puts in the mouth of James Harrington (1611–1677), English political philosopher, author of *Oceana* (1656): "O! the depth of the wisdom of God, which, in the simple invention of a carter, has revealed to mankind the whole mystery of a commonwealth." *The Works of John Adams*, ed. Charles Francis Adams (Boston, 1850–1856), IV, 390.

There is no sure evidence that Franklin actually did use the anecdote of the wagon and the two teams of horses. He did use another anecdote against two chambers in the legislature: "Has not the famous political fable of the snake with two heads and one body, some useful instruction contained in it? She was going to a brook to drink, and in her way was to pass through a hedge, a twig of which

De Lolme attributes the wise and circumspect conduct of the English Parliament to its division into two chambers. But the theory of the constitution was precisely the same in the times of the Tudors and Stuarts as when De Lolme wrote. At the latter period, England enjoyed a considerable share of internal tranquillity because the people, having risen in importance, had become a sort of make-weight in the government. During the two former periods, the government was little better than a despotism and the laws were frequently the most iniquitous imaginable. So great a revolution, the theory of the constitution remaining the same, can only be accounted for by supposing that some equally important change had taken place in the structure of society and consequently in the practical working of the government. And this change consists in nothing less than the gradual elevation of the popular body and the creation of a well defined tribunal of public opinion which, impressing its authority powerfully upon the whole system, has maintained each department in its proper place. These are the bars which have been erected to fence off the encroachments of the legislative power. The condition which De Lolme demanded is obtained. The bars are not merely without the chambers; they are without the entire body and are much more effectual than any curious adjustment of the interior mechanism of the government.

I have in a preceding chapter alluded to the very important balance which is maintained between the government and the power out of the government; and the British constitution, at the time De Lolme wrote, and still more at the present day, affords an instructive example of it. Construct government as you will, if it is afterward left to itself and permitted to command its own motions the power it wields may be distorted to any purpose. But if there is a corresponding power — a presiding influence without — which subjects it unceasingly to the action of public opinion, even a faulty arrangement of the parts will be corrected. The English chambers no longer encroach as they formerly did on each other's rights, nor on the rights of the people, because the popular body has become the first estate in the realm and holds in check both the king and the nobility as well as the commons. This is

---

opposed her direct course; one head chose to go on the right side of the twig, the other on the left; so that time was spent in the contest, and, before the decision was completed, the poor snake had died of thirst." This homely political fable was printed in the *Federal Gazette*, November 3, 1789 (*The Works of Benjamin Franklin*, ed. Sparks, V, 166–167), but whether Adams responded to it, I do not know.]

the simple explanation of the difficulty; and if one born under the Henrys could rise from his grave, he would be struck with amazement at finding that British councils were conducted with so much more skill and wisdom than formerly and that public men, in spite of the selfish interests which fill their bosoms, are placed under a restraint from which the most powerful standing army could not deliver them.

In the times of the Tudors and Stuarts, not to go back to a still earlier period, the legislative power was divided as it now is. But under those princes the country was either ruled by a stern and rigorous despotism, or it was a scene of incessant broils. At the present day a species of virtual representation has been established in both houses of Parliament which, although it falls far short of an actual representation, has had power sufficient to work a most striking alteration in the conduct of public affairs.

De Lolme also attributes the remarkable solidity of the crown in Great Britain, in part, to the division of the legislature. But this is a circumstance which is not peculiar to that country. The same thing is observable of all the kingdoms and principalities of northern and central Europe, in some of which there is no proper legislative body; in some the legislative body consists of a single chamber, and in others of more than two chambers. The compact and vigorous authority of the royal power in Russia, Austria, Prussia, Sweden, and Denmark is quite as remarkable as it is in Great Britain and affords a strong contrast to the feeble condition of the crown in Spain and Portugal, in both of which there are two chambers modeled after the English system.

This singular stability of the royal power throughout the greater part of the kingdoms of Europe, a circumstance of apparently evil omen to the growth of popular power but in reality favorable to it, is mainly ascribable to the fact that the most absolute monarchs are insensibly accommodating themselves to the new ideas of the age. They are more restrained and are therefore permitted to be more secure. A king is compelled not so much to truck and huckster to the great men who surround the throne, as to cultivate the good will of the people. The close intercourse which now exists between all the European communities has created a sort of informal league between them; and one member, although far behind some of the others in civilization, is powerfully acted upon by the institutions which exist in those others. Although the condition of society is such that no powerful middle class exists, as in Great Britain, to control the government, yet public opinion in Great Britain, in France, Belgium, Holland, and throughout nearly all Germany exercises a potent extra-territorial influence and is insensibly begetting habits of thinking and acting among princes totally different from what they were accustomed to formerly. This influence has even penetrated the Turkish empire, and the sovereign is accordingly a wiser and more discreet ruler than were most of the English Henrys. He has consented to do what they never dreamed of — to draw up an instrument imposing limitations upon his own authority, to appoint a commission to digest a code of jurisprudence after the plan of the celebrated code civil of France, and to establish a system of public schools for the education of the people. The influence has obviously come from abroad and, without indulging in any idle notions concerning the progress of society, we may reasonably figure to ourselves a day when each of the European states will bear a resemblance to the various districts or provinces of one great commonwealth, and when the fashion of copying after those which have attained the highest civilization will be even stronger and more general than it is at the present day. I know that when the most absolute sovereign of the north of Europe is concerting measures to introduce jury trial into his kingdom, that there is a power at work which belongs to the age, not to the individual.

I would not be understood as maintaining that there are not good reasons for the division of the legislature in the European states, nor that this arrangement may not have been productive of advantage. Given a constitution of society in which a regular subordination of ranks exists and is firmly upheld by the laws, and it may be wise for a time, the duration of which it is difficult to calculate, to place the privileged order in a separate chamber. But there are other causes which have contributed to the wisdom of English councils and the general security of civil liberty which are absolutely overwhelming in comparison of the division of the legislature. And perhaps the period is approaching when it will be advantageous for both government and people that some different disposition should be made of that department so that, even if the plan of dividing it is adhered to, it may at any rate be placed upon a wider foundation.

I have also in treating of American institutions confined myself to the domestic government of the states. And there does not appear to be any convincing reason why the division of the legislative power should be retained in them, other than that the institution has been incorporated in the general habits of thinking and that an institution which is upheld by the imagination is sometimes as formidable and as difficult to be removed as any other.

But the national government presents an entirely different case. It is a federal and not a consolidated republic; and the most obvious way of executing this plan and maintaining the separate existence of the states was to establish two chambers of legislation, in one of which the people of the states should be treated as co-equal sovereignties and therefore entitled to the same number of representatives. An upper house was thus constructed, which instead of being composed of a body of nobles consisted, like the lower house of representatives, of the people. But the apportionment of these representatives is different from what it is in the lower house.

This plan of constructing a senatorial body is entirely new. The chamber of nobles in the German diet bears no resemblance to it, as the members hold their seats "de jure" and not by election. The American system, in this respect, may be said to constitute the transition state from the artificial structure of the upper house in all the European states to the more simple and direct plan of founding it like the other house upon an equal representation of the people. The system may exert an unspeakable influence upon other communities as it demonstrates the practicability of composing a senatorial body of other materials than an order of nobility, and shows that a house so composed may possess as great stability, and display as much wisdom and firmness as any privileged body which has ever existed. The plan may suggest new views to the enlightened minds which help to control the destinies of other countries.

But I am treating of free institutions generally, and not merely of the particular form in which they have been cast in the American union. The separate and independent existence of the members of the American confederation was an accidental circumstance. The republican form of government cannot be maintained in a country of considerable extent without the establishment of local or domestic jurisdictions; but it may well exist although those jurisdictions should not possess the extensive powers which belong to them in the United States.

The question then presents itself directly — is there any solid reason for distributing the legislative power in a simple republic into two chambers? — and I am of the opinion that there is, so far as regards the national assembly only. As in such a form of government the local jurisdictions would emanate from the aggregate authority of the state, instead of the central government emanating from them, the parts would neither be sovereign states nor would they contain an unequal population. As a census is now taken in the United States for the purpose of apportioning the representation in the lower house to the population, so in a simple republic a census would have the double effect of varying the limits of the several compartments and adjusting the representation equally among all. There would then be no reason for constructing an upper house upon the principle which governs the composition of the American senate. There would be no reason for so doing, even if the territorial divisions were ever so unequal; but as these divisions would not contain sovereign states, there would be no motive for making them unequal at the commencement and of course none for permitting them to become so after the government had gone into operation. They would be created for the purpose of administering the local interests, pretty much on the same plan as these interests are administered by the state governments of America, because in an extensive country a single legislature, whether its character be national or federal, cannot either easily or advantageously superintend the vast amount of business which properly falls under the cognizance of government. I have in another chapter declared that it would be a mistake to suppose because the republic was a simple and not a confederate one that therefore domestic jurisdictions could be dispensed with. Their use would be the same as that of the local governments in America, but the mode of constructing them would be different. In the United States, not only are the domestic legislatures a necessary part of the machinery of the government, but it would be impossible to get along without a great number of still lesser jurisdictions, subordinate to and enclosed within the state governments, such as county and township jurisdictions. And the same would be the case in any other community, provided the form of government were republican.

We cannot expect that all the republics which may hereafter exist will be composed of independent states. Some may spring up in Europe out of the consolidated governments which now exist. At any rate the question cannot be avoided, shall the legislative power in a simple republic be divided?

I have said that I incline to the opinion that, so far as regards the national legislature alone, it should be. But my reasons are directly opposite to those which are assigned by De Lolme. He would divide the legislature in order to make one chamber control the other. This is the exterior bar to which he refers; not a bar exterior to the whole body and residing in the society, but a bar exterior to each chamber and therefore imposed by each upon the other. In a democratic republic this principle of control is superseded by another of far more efficacy, because of more comprehensive influence: the responsibility of the entire body to the people who elect it. The bars are then not merely exterior to each chamber, but they are exterior to the whole body and act with a force which is in constant activity. The defect now is the reverse of that of which De Lolme complains. The bars are too strong, instead of too weak. The control is too stringent, instead of being too easy. In other words, as the legislators are the mere agents of the people and elected for a short period, not merely will they be constantly subjected to the influence of public opinion in all their deliberations, which is a most happy circumstance, but there will be a constant tendency to the formation of a counterfeit public opinion also, which in times of great party excitement it may be difficult to distinguish from the other. This will unavoidably be the case in a country of wide extent. In order to condense public opinion, as it is termed, caucuses and cliques will be formed, and these may very imperfectly represent the opinions of the people. Public associations are the genuine offspring of free institutions, but it is not all associations which are entitled to this character. A knot of busy, active politicians will sometimes succeed in robbing other people of their opinions, instead of representing them. It becomes very important, therefore, to place the legislative body in a situation where it will be enabled to distinguish the real from the constructive majority and to protect the community from the machinations of the last. By dividing the body, the proceedings are attended with a greater number of forms and with more solemnity. The discussions will be more thorough, the time consumed will be longer; add to which, dividing the body is like creating two bodies. The authority and influence attributed to it will be doubled and all these circumstances will not only contribute to a clear perception of what is the genuine public sentiment, but will give to the body, or to one chamber at least, ability to resist the influence of the counterfeit representation without. It is, therefore, not with the view of detracting from the authority of the legislature but of adding to it and atoning for its weakness that I would divide it. Doubtless it seems to be too strong when it is carried away by the misguided passions of a part of the population who cause their voices to be heard above those of a majority of the people. But this is a symptom of weakness, not of strength, since it exhibits the body as a prey to the artifices of those who are not its real constituents.

I have said that there are two essential properties of good government: first, a susceptibility of receiving an influence from without, of being acted upon by society; and second, a corresponding power of reacting upon that society. It is in order to conciliate these two opposite ends that I would, in a country of wide extent where it is difficult to collect and mature public opinion, divide the legislative body.

But it does not follow that it is necessary to pursue the same plan in constructing the legislative power of the domestic governments. The great principle of responsibility has superseded the check which one chamber formerly exerted upon the other. And that principle should never be modified, unless it is necessary in order to render the responsibility more strict. Money bills could only originate in the lower house because the constituents of the lower house were the persons upon whom the weight of taxation fell most heavily. The possession of the privilege was an effectual check upon the proceedings of the upper house. But where both chambers are composed of representatives of the people and the territory is of no greater extent than the American states, there does not appear to be any good reason for distributing the members into two chambers, unless it is that the plan is already identified with all the notions which have been formed of regular government, and that it is sometimes as difficult to root up an idea as it is to build up an institution. Vermont had a single chamber until 1836, and the business of legislation was conducted with the greatest wisdom and prudence. The see-saw legislation, the refractory conduct pursued by the legislatures of other states, were unknown because the simple character of the body took away the temptation and the ability so to act.

The allusion to the plan of local governments suggests another view of great importance. There is a division of the legislature which proceeds upon a totally different plan from that contemplated by De Lolme and Montesquieu and which is much more efficacious than the old scheme. It consists in a division of the power, and not merely of the body. American institutions afford the only fair example of this plan. The legislative power, in this great commonwealth, is not devolved upon one body; it is divided between the national assembly and the thirty legislatures of the states. The powers which appertain to the domestic interests of the states are separated from those which relate to their exterior interests, and thus an arrangement which was originally intended to answer one purpose has the effect of answering another equally important. The care of the national interests is entrusted with the Congress, that of the local interests with local assemblies; so that whatever might be the constitution of these thirty-one bodies, whether they were each composed of a single or a double chamber, the legislative power would be effectually divided. This arrangement is productive of far more important results than a mere division of the body. It is true we may call it a division of the body. We may say that the whole legislative power of the union is confided to sixty-two chambers. But we should then lose sight of the principle on which the division is made as well as of the manner in which it operates. It would be correct to say that in Sweden the legislative body was distributed between four chambers. But in America it is the power which is distributed. And although there are sixty-two chambers, yet these do not act coordinately, but each of the thirty-one legislative bodies exercises powers which are distinct and independent of those of the others.

This disposition of the legislative power in America constitutes a deduction from the power which would otherwise be exercised by the national assembly. It erects still stronger and more numerous bars against the enterprises of the legislature and these bars are all without and not within the body. It does not merely balance power, it absolutely withholds it. If the whole mass of authority which is wielded by the national and state legislatures were delegated to one assembly, all the other bulwarks of freedom would be undermined. The political power of the community would be completely centralized. The minds of men would be distracted by the vast amount and the complex character of the business which would be transacted at a distance so far removed from their observation. Public affairs would become a great mystery, and whenever that is the case government is in a fair way of acquiring inordinate power. But under the present admirable arrangement, public business like all other knowledge is classified and distributed, so as on the one hand to protect against usurpation, and on the other to secure an orderly administration in every part of society.

A republic has been defined to be a government of laws but, as Rousseau has well remarked, a government may be one of laws and yet be exceedingly imperfect in its construction. It must be one of equal laws in order to fulfill the plan of republican government. Society has undoubtedly secured one great advantage when public affairs are conducted upon some fixed and regular scheme and where general rules are laid down for the government of individuals. This is better than to have everything dependent upon the arbitrary will and caprice of a handful of public rulers. Moreover, when this first step is taken better things are in prospect and only wait a favorable opportunity to be introduced. But there may be the most orderly arrangement in a system of government and yet the system may act very unequally upon different parts of society. The laws may set out with taking it for granted that there is a radical and permanent distinction between different classes of society and, when this is the case, the whole course of the subsequent legislation will be directed to uphold this distinction. In nearly all the European states the executive is a hereditary magistrate and the legislative body, or one chamber at least, is composed of the nobility. That this should be so is in those communities regarded as among the most settled principles of wise government. If the laws did not originate the system, they everywhere confirm and support it. These communities may be said to be governments of laws. All public business is conducted with great precision and regularity. But this does not prevent the system from bearing with immense inequality upon different parts of society. The influence which such a scheme of government exerts is not always direct; it may operate circuitously through many subordinate channels, but still affecting materially the manners and consequently the character of the legislation. Thus in Great Britain, where the nobility are a small fraction of the population when compared with the middle class, Parliament in no act of ordinary legislation ever avows the design of making a formal distinction between the two. But the influence and power of the former are upheld in a great variety of ways, by an overgrown church establishment, by the creation of monopolies, by the structure even of the House of Commons which admits persons principally who belong to the class of gentry and who are therefore more or less connected with the aristocracy proper. All this inspires a general taste for aristocratic distinctions, long after the nobility have ceased to appropriate to themselves one half of the power and property of the community. The government of France is one of laws, but the House of Deputies only possess one third of the legislative power and represents only two hundred thousand persons in a population of thirty-five millions.

There is another difficulty which meets us: although the laws do not accord any fixed immunities to one class, there will still exist great inequality in the conditions of the citizens. The same laws applied to all will operate unequally upon some. A tax proportioned to the income of individuals may reduce some to poverty while it leaves other in affluence. The state invites all the citizens to enter the halls of legislation or to fill other important posts. Accidental circumstances, natural infirmity of mind or body, or some other of the disadvantages of fortune may prevent numbers from profiting of the invitation, while it will conduct others to wealth and distinction. We may alleviate if we cannot cure the defects of the first kind; we may take care that taxation shall never bear with inordinate weight upon the poor. But there is no way of rectifying the last species of imperfection, if an inequality which is stamped upon all created beings can be called an imperfection. But government has no right to exaggerate the inequalities which actually exist among men and to create distinctions which would not otherwise take place. All men are not born equal, but all men are born with an equal title to become so, and government has no right to throw impediments in the way of making that title good. The high standard of popular intelligence in the United States is not owing to education alone. It is in great part ascribable to the absence of that mighty weight which presses upon the faculties of men in the middle walks of life, when they live in a state in which aristocratic distinctions lie at the foundation of the government.

The government of the United States comes as near the idea of a government of equal laws as any we dare expect to see. The laws are made by the people, and they are consequently made for the people. There may be great difference in the legislation of two countries although the laws are the same in both. For instance: laws which are designed to protect property affect but a small proportion of the population where property is monopolized by a few, as is the case in Russia and Poland and as was the case in France before the Revolution when nearly three fourths of the land was appropriated by the clergy and nobility. Something of the same kind may be observed in countries much more enlightened than Russia or Poland. For instance: the law of perpetual entail exists in Scotland and Germany so that in the former much more than one third of the land is tied up forever, the wholesome restraint which the English courts have imposed upon English estates being unknown. Scotland is under a government of laws, but those who are protected by the laws are a privileged class.

This constitutes a leading distinction between the legislation of the United States and other countries. The Americans commenced where other communities will probably leave off. Property is more equally distributed than anywhere else. The laws, from the necessity of the case, are obliged to be more equal than anywhere else. But this lays the foundation for more important changes in their character. They will become more enlightened, less encumbered with subtle and unmeaning fictions, because they will acquire a greater degree of simplicity; and they will have this simplicity because being enacted by the people they will be more thoroughly adapted both to their wants and their comprehension.

Thus, although America derived the elements of its jurisprudence from England, material changes have been made especially during the last thirty or forty years. And when in 1828 the British Parliament entered upon the great work of reforming the civil code, the laws of the American states furnished the pattern after which it was obliged to copy. In the laws of one or other of the American states are to be found almost every material improvement which has been made, and a still greater number which may have been advantageously inserted in the new code.

The criminal codes of the American states are stamped with the same distinguishing features as the civil. The two go hand in hand because the subject matter of both is closely connected. The temptations to violate the rights of property are increased in proportion as property is confined to a few. And thus this new result will take place that in a country where nearly everyone is interested in the acquisition and secure possession of property, the laws will be more humane than in those where property is distributed to a few.

As to the mode of proposing the laws to the legislative body for its adoption, this has been very different in different countries and in the same country at different times. In the European states, formerly, the executive possessed the exclusive privilege of propounding what laws were proper to be enacted. The manner in which the initiatory step is now taken in some of those states indicates a very great change in the relative authority of the two departments. The power of proposing the laws when vested exclusively in the executive gives him complete command over the motions of the legislature. This body was at one time regarded as a mere appendage to the executive. The last was in reality the supreme legislative tribunal. In course of time this apparently slight change took place. The legislature addressed the king in the form of petition as to what law they wished to be passed. This gave the former a more active part in their formation but still fell very short of the appropriate office of a legislative assembly. The executive was still regarded as the ultimate arbiter of all public measures. In England, a further change took place. Bills were drawn up in general terms and the judges performed the task of framing them into laws. But this was not done until the session of Parliament was closed — a strange practice, if we did not know that all human institutions in their immature state wear a strange and uncouth character. The judges at that period were dependent on the king and the shape given to the laws was not always what was intended. This practice indicated very clearly, however, that something like system and regularity was beginning to be introduced into the transaction of business. It was the forerunner of still more salutary changes. Accordingly, in no very long time, Parliament asserted the exclusive right of originating and framing the laws. The legislature then began to assume the character of an independent body. The prerogative of the king was transformed into a negative upon the laws after they had passed through the two houses, instead of being exercised at the first stage of the proceedings.

A similar change has been brought about in the French government. The right of the king to propose the laws, which was retained in the "charte" of 1814, is abolished by that of 1830 and the power may be exercised indifferently by the king, the Chamber of Peers or the Chamber of Deputies. But it is not so in the constitution of Holland or Belgium, though in so many respects they are copied after the English model, and underwent a revolution in the same year that the new provision was inserted in the French constitution.

In the United States this power of initiating the laws could at no period be exercised by the executive, for the legislative power, both in the national and state governments, is vested solely in the general assembly of each. The privilege which is conferred upon the president and governors of suggesting such changes as they may deem beneficial is of a totally different character from the power of propounding the laws as it is understood in European language.

There are two customs which exist in the French and English governments, which may be regarded as relics of the ancient prerogatives of the executive. The one is the speech made from the throne at the annual meeting of the legislature; the other consists in the right which ministers have to seats in that body, either "de jure" as ministers as in France, or by virtue of an election as in Great Britain. Wherever the executive is a hereditary magistrate, the last is an exceedingly advantageous arrangement because it brings him within reach of the legislature and subjects him to the immediate action of public opinion. The theory of the constitution places him beyond it; the practice draws him insensibly within the circle of its influence. But the speech which is made at the opening of the legislative body is a wise regulation whether the executive is an hereditary, or an elective magistrate.

When we read the instructive and business-like communications of the president to Congress and of the governors to the state legislatures, the observation that they are the broken relics of a formidable prerogative of kingly power may appear to be new, yet such is undoubtedly the case. The American custom, however, is of unmixed benefit to the community. Some centuries hence, another Montesquieu or Millar will set about exploring American institutions which will then acquire additional interest from being covered with the rust of antiquity, and in poring over the history of the country will fasten upon very many things as worthy of deep attention and study which in consequence of their familiarity elude the observation of Americans at the present day.[4] Existing institutions are often more difficult to decipher and thoroughly understand than those of a remote age. They are mixed up with so much which is apparently familiar and with so much which is really extraneous that it demands a severe and comprehensive analysis to disentangle the last and to give to the former their just place. But when institutions grow old, things which were once familiar become striking facts and whatever was extraneous has dropped off and fallen into oblivion; so that time operates the same analysis with re-

4. [John Millar (1735–1801), Scottish philosopher and historian, one of the earliest advocates of what is today known as economic determinism, whose *Historical View of the English Government* (Dublin, 1787) was one of the first constitutional histories of England.]

gard to an ancient system of government which it requires the utmost thought and reflection to effect in relation to an existing one.

The custom of sending to the legislature a communication, containing a clear account of the state of public affairs, not only maintains friendly relations between the two departments, it tests the capacity of the chief magistrate and makes it his ambition to obtain exact information of everything which affects the condition and future prospects of the community over which he presides. The more the minds of public men are turned in this direction, the less the danger of their meditating schemes unfavorable to the general weal. And doubtless one reason why America has enjoyed such unexampled tranquillity is that the administration of public affairs has assumed a thoroughly business-like character. Men of the finest understanding have been repeatedly governors of the states: Jefferson and McKean, Griswold and Clinton, McDuffie and Everett, without mentioning many others who belong to the same class.[5] If these men had been nurtured under a Spanish or Portuguese government, or in an Italian republic, their minds would have been subjected to a discipline the most unfavorable imaginable and their public conduct would have taken a totally different direction. When in reading American history one comes across such a character as Aaron Burr, it seems as if we had encountered a being who properly belonged to another sphere. He also possessed faculties of a high order, but he stands alone in one respect: he appears never to have realized what all other Americans find it impossible to forget, that he was born and educated in a country of free institutions. He seems to be a man of Venice or Genoa, rather than one of New York.

The communities in which the executive messages are most full and comprehensive are the very ones which possess most liberty, so much has the custom deviated from the institution out of which it sprung. In monarchical states where we might expect the executive to dictate minutely what should be done, he says little or nothing. And in a republic, where from his authority being exceedingly limited we might expect him to say very little, he traverses the whole field of inquiry and

5. [Thomas McKean (1734–1817), Governor of Pennsylvania; Matthew Griswold (1714–1799), Governor of Connecticut under the Articles of Confederation, and Grimke may refer to his son, Roger (1762–1812), later Governor of Connecticut; George McDuffie (1790–1851), Governor of South Carolina; De Witt Clinton (1769–1828), Governor of New York; Edward Everett (1794–1865), Governor of Massachusetts.]

appears to feel as deep an interest as if the state were his property and the people his subjects. Nothing can be more jejune than a king's message, while few documents are more instructive and satisfactory than the messages of the American president and governors. The king fears to show himself upon an arena where he would find so many private citizens his superiors. A few words are sometimes understood to be a sign of wisdom and with kings it becomes an universal maxim that they are so.

The establishment of a written constitution necessarily introduces a great change in the character and functions of the legislative body. The effect is to create a division of the legislative power between the people and the ordinary legislative assembly, another contrivance much more efficacious than the distribution of the last into two chambers. The people exercise their share of authority when assembled in convention; they ordain fundamental rules for the government of all the departments; or when collected at the polls they ratify or reject proposed alterations in the existing constitution. Sometimes a constitutional charter adds to the powers of the legislative body, but in a great majority of instances it diminishes them. In the former case, it would perhaps be correct to say that there was a displacement or new arrangement of the powers of the ordinary legislative body. Thus, in a republic, the authority to declare war is delegated to this assembly, but it has been taken from the executive. The same amount of legislative power as before may be delegated, but a very important part is wrested from one department in order to be deposited with another.

But it is more important at present to notice those powers which are entirely withdrawn from the legislative assembly and retained by the people. The freedom of religion and of the press, the organization of the political departments, trial by jury, the qualifications of electors and of candidates for office are a few of them. The legislature can no longer intermeddle with these matters, though the people in convention may make what disposition they please in regard to them. The noblest efforts have been made in France to introduce constitutional liberty. But the liberties of no people can rest upon a solid foundation unless the constitution is the work of their own hands. The revolution of 1830 was occasioned by the daring interference of the king with the freedom of the press and the law of elections, matters which should be carefully locked up by the constitution. The most exciting controversies, those which have caused nearly all the insurrections which have taken place, are precisely those which a popular constitution withdraws from the cognizance of a legislative assembly. A constitutional ordinance severs, if I may so say, the conventional from the legislative power. It marks out a limited field for the exercise of the last. The temptation and the ability to usurp power are not absolutely diminished, but they are greatly repressed.

There is another division of the laws into those which relate to the manners and those which have a direct reference to the rights of persons and property. In the first rudiments of society, a code of jurisprudence is very apt to touch extensively upon manners. The community then bears a strong resemblance to the family and the government to the government of a family. The progress of society produces the same change in the laws which a knowledge of the world produces in the character of individuals. It enlarges the field of observation and inquiry, and places in an insignificant light many actions to which the utmost importance was attached. All laws are the result of a process of generalization. But when the community has grown from a city or an inconsiderable territory to an extensive and populous state, it becomes impossible to regulate private manners minutely and yet to preserve the system of generalization. The codes of some of the Germanic tribes, the Franks, and the Burgundians, interfered extensively with the manners. The blue laws of Connecticut are also a remarkable example of the same species of legislation, though it is a great mistake to suppose that laws of that character were confined to that province. Similar regulations, only not so numerous nor carried to so great an extent, were adopted in others. They were not even confined to the northern provinces, but were in force in some of the southern also.

Sumptuary laws were very common among the ancient commonwealths. They even lay at the foundation of the government of Sparta. But Sparta was smaller than a moderate sized American county and this system of legislation gradually gave way after intercourse with the other Grecian states had produced a higher civilization, and given rise to more liberal modes of thinking.

The Oppian law enacted at Rome was one of the most remarkable of this class of laws.[6] It imposed severe restrictions upon the dress of females, forbade ornamental apparel, and the legislature which con-

6. [During the second Punic War, Oppius (213 B.C.), a tribune of the people, carried a law to curtail the luxuries of Roman women; see Tacitus, *Annals*, III, 33, 34.]

vened for the purpose of deliberating whether it should be continued in force drew around the Roman forum a mob of women as formidable as the band of men which in 1780 collected under the banner of Lord George Gordon to intimidate the British Parliament.[7] The city of Rome, however, was the real Roman commonwealth; the Italian provinces occupied the place of dependences, rather than that of integral parts of one state.

But the list of such laws after all was not very extensive. It would have been an endless task to legislate for the manners and morals of the people. As positive regulations could not reach them, the matter was left to the discretion of the censor. But what the laws have not power to do, it is plain no individual will attempt, and this part of the duty of the censor was not very strictly performed.

It is sometimes difficult to draw a distinct line between the two classes of actions to which I have referred. Life, liberty, and property are the subjects which the laws principally deal with. Yet in some highly civilized countries duelling has not always been punished; the reason of which is that the manners have been too strong for the laws. In some countries men fight in obedience to the manners; in others, they abstain from fighting, also in obedience to the manners. As the punishment of death has no terror for the man who in order to escape death seizes the last plank in a shipwreck from a weaker man, so it has no terror for the man who persuades himself that even an imaginary disgrace is more intolerable than death. But duelling is a relic of aristocratic institutions. It follows, therefore, that in proportion as the principle of equality gains ground and becomes thoroughly incorporated with the fashion of thinking, the custom will disappear. The manners are then made to correct the manners. Equality has a wonderful influence in laughing out of countenance all fanciful notions. It is absurd to expose our own lives when a grievous injury has been done to us. It is worse than absurd when we have only been affronted. I observe that in the southeastern states, where the principle of equality has gained ground so fast and where in consequence the minds of men have been driven to reflection, the custom is falling into disrepute.

Some governments permit theatrical entertainments while others

7. [Lord George Gordon (1751–1793), leader of Protestant demonstrations against the removal of civil disabilities from Roman Catholics; the Gordon riots in London (June 2–7, 1780) resulted in injury or death to about eight hundred people.]

prohibit them altogether. The legislature of Connecticut has resisted every effort to introduce them. Although these exhibitions in some respects afford an innocent and even noble recreation, yet the sum of their influence is deemed as pernicious as any of those actions which immediately affect the persons or reputation of others. New Haven is as large as New York was in 1776 when the latter had a regular theatrical corps. But if it were as large as New York now is, or as large as Boston, it may be doubted whether the legislature would be enabled to persevere in its excellent intentions. The creation of domestic governments in the United States has this advantage: it enables particular sections of the country to adapt the laws to the manners, instead of being involved in the consequences of one general and sweeping system of legislation.

If the inquiry should still be pressed: why do legislators for the most part confine their attentions to those actions which immediately affect life, liberty, and property and leave untouched a very large class of others which have a very important, although it may be an indirect, bearing upon the public happiness? the following observations may be made, in addition to those which have been already suggested:

If there were no laws, actions which are now visited with a penalty would not go unpunished. The great benefit arising from a regular code of laws and a corresponding system of procedure consists in the restraint which these impose upon private revenge. For this would then pass all bounds and punish too much. The influence of the laws is such that it substitutes reflection in the place of passion. And with regard to those actions which affect others indirectly but do not assume any tangible shape, although the laws do abstain from punishing them, yet they are most certainly punished. But inasmuch as the punishment is applied to a different class of actions, it assumes a different character. Acts of violence were before followed with violence; and vices in the manners are followed by a countervailing influence of the manners. Hatred, envy, and ingratitude are exceedingly prejudicial to public as well as to private happiness; and they are visited in private life with a penalty as certain as that which the law inflicts upon delinquencies of a graver kind. The state undertakes to punish these because individuals would exceed all bounds if punishment were left to them. And it abstains from noticing the former because it could neither punish so generally nor so judiciously as when the punishment is left to the silent but searching operation of opinion. Murder and robbery are very far from being driven from society by the severest laws, but they are rendered much less frequent than they would otherwise be. So, although the worst passions still infest society, yet without the punishment which now constantly attends them, the most civilized community would be turned into a pandemonium.

I cannot leave this subject without noticing a species of legislation which has lately made its appearance in some of the American states and which has in a remarkable manner arrested public attention both at home and abroad. I allude to the license laws, laws which are intended, if possible, to extirpate the use of intoxicating liquors. These seem to partake of the character of sumptuary regulations and therefore to be an interference with subjects which are properly withdrawn from the care of the civil magistrate. But I hold that they constitute an exception to the rule.

It was not until public attention was particularly drawn to this matter that anyone was aware to how great an extent the commission of crimes was to be traced to the use of spirituous liquors. Still less did persons of even considerable reflection form any conception of the influence which the practice of moderate drinking, as it is termed, has in confusing the judgment, blunting the moral sense, and souring the temper. But it is evident that a vast portion of misconduct, want of judgment, feeble, irresolute, and contradictory actions, which were supposed to be unaccountable and were not regarded as of great importance, are attributable to this cause and have shed a most baneful influence upon society. This is a matter, therefore, which, even if it wholly concerned the manners, has an importance which belongs to no other of a similar class. And the efforts which have been made by the people of New England, Tennessee, and New York are symptoms of an exceedingly sound state of public opinion. It is because the people have themselves taken this matter into consideration that it possesses so much importance. In some countries, legislation by the people suggests the notion of licentiousness, of a predatory spirit. Here is a remarkable example, the most remarkable I am aware of, to the contrary. Without the cooperation of the people, it would be a herculean task to lift the popular mind; but with their cooperation everything good and useful may be accomplished. If the laws which have been passed in some of these states should remain unrepealed, they will be a lasting monument of the wisdom and virtue of the people. I am inclined to think that they will constitute the most memorable example of legislation of which we have any record, not so much in consequence of their widely salutary influence, as because they argue a degree of self-denial and reflection which no one before supposed to belong to the masses. Let no European after this indulge in the fanciful notion that the people are incapable of self-government. As a single act, it is the most marked proof of a capacity for self-government of which I have any knowledge.

Nor would it materially weaken the force of the reasoning if these laws were repealed. That they have been proposed by the popular mind, that they have enlisted a powerful and numerous class in their favor, is decisive of the soundness of public opinion. If two millions and a half of people hold opinions which are eminently favorable to morality and good government, and three millions hold opposite ones, the influence of the first will be felt beyond all comparison before that of the last. It would afford matter for curious and instructive inquiry if we could ascertain the exact influence which government and the laws on the one hand, and the manners and habits of a people on the other, exercise respectively on society.[8] The laws are the offspring of the manners, and yet when the former are fairly established and have acquired authority from long usage they exert a distinct and additional influence upon society.

1st. If there were no government and laws, there would be a voluntary association or associations similar to those voluntary conventions and societies which now spring up in the community and which are employed in diffusing information relative to public affairs. But admitting that a large proportion of the population would be disposed to fall in with every measure which reason and good sense suggested, there would always be a number who would not be so disposed. Even if all assented at first, there would be numerous instances of disobedience when those measures were to be carried into execution. The disturber of the public peace, the flagrant violator of private rights, would claim an exemption on the ground that the resolves of the association were not laws, had no authoritative sanction, and the exercise of private judgment on the part of some would be as effectual in annulling as the exercise of the same judgment on the part of others in maintaining them. So far, then, as one, and that a considerable portion of society

8. For the second edition, Grimke added new matter from this sentence to the sentence which ends, ". . . in which the task has been performed," in the middle of the second paragraph on p. 326.

was concerned, laws, that is, coercive enactments, would be indispensable to the peace of society.

2d. But there are an infinity of other questions which would arise in every extensive community besides those which bear directly upon the public tranquillity. Dissent with regard to these would be very common, even among those who were agreed as to the necessity of fixed rules in respect to the last. There would then be no system of measures; everything would be thrown into confusion; the sense of a common interest, which might be sufficient to uphold the former, would operate in a contrary direction with regard to the latter. The total want of authority in carrying into effect the civil regulations of the association would undermine its authority in executing the criminal resolves. Infractors of public and private rights, perceiving the confusion which existed in one part of society, would acquire boldness and activity in the perpetration of their deeds. The other part of society would lose confidence in their authority, simply because they were conscious of a disobedience on their own part to measures not of the same sort, but originating in precisely the same species of authority. Civil government, then, has a two-fold influence, 1st, in controlling the population and, 2d, in controlling those who undertake to govern. Society could not exist without coercive enactments to prevent crimes, **and** the authority which the laws acquire in restraining these is very naturally transferred to all the political and civil regulations of the community and thus carries one principle of obedience through all ranks of society. We see frequent opposition to every species of civil enactment and very little to the laws which punish crimes. The first are intended to guard the rights of the highest as well as the lowest classes; the second are made especially to restrain the lowest. But the society is compelled to arm the first with the same authority as accompanies the last; otherwise the principle of obedience would be weakened at its source. The manners, the rules of conventional conduct, would be sufficient to prompt to the prohibition of very many acts, but they would be powerless in executing the wishes of the society and equally powerless in commanding or forbidding others to be done. Men are thus irresistibly led from society to government; the manners and the laws act reciprocally upon each other, and in the progress of time the two are so intimately blended that it is impossible to distinguish the exact influence which each exercises in molding the habits and conduct of individuals.

3d. It is in this way that the rule of the majority, a rule indispensable to the existence and well being of society, comes to be firmly established. The majority cannot win the minority to obedience to the laws unless they also obey them. In numberless instances, individuals among the majority would desire to escape from the operation of the laws, but they cannot do so without breaking the bond which runs through the whole of society. They are compelled to adhere to the great principle of obedience in order to maintain their own authority. They might command the physical force of society, but physical force is impotent when it is not accompanied with the opinion of right. This opinion, or sense of right, is like the self-possession and resolution of a small man which make him an overmatch for a strong man who does not possess those qualities. Moreover, so many among the majority would be inclined to escape from the enactment of the laws (the poor, for instance, from the payment of taxes) that the majority would dwindle into a minority; universal disobedience to a great part of the civil enactments would take place and the criminal laws, having no sanction, would also be trampled under foot. The manners and the laws again act mutually, the one upon the other; the maintenance of great principles is discovered to be identical with self-interest. The first as being better defined, and more easily appreciated, is laid hold of as of immutable obligation and the sense of interest is ultimately swallowed up in the sense of justice. Every law carries with it a title to be obeyed, because one law contains as full an annunciation of a great principle as all the laws combined, and to deny the authority of one is to deny the authority of all. By multiplying the laws, we only multiply the application of a principle, but we cannot multiply a principle for that is indivisible.

4th. The laws are a reflection of the manners. The manners give birth to the laws, but when the manners are incorporated in the laws they acquire great additional authority. Legal enactments reduce to unity the great diversity of opinions which exist and relieve the mind from the irksome task of perpetually inquiring into the reason of the laws. The value of the principle consists in this, that a great majority of the citizens are instinctively and habitually led to regard the law as the supreme rule of conduct. After a system of laws is established, the manners cannot be preserved unless there is an adherence to the laws: the manners then become the powerful ally of the civil magistrate and public order and tranquillity are insured.

5th. The wider the influence of the manners, the wider will be the influence of the laws; that is, the greater the number of people who will contribute to the formation of what we term public opinion, the stronger will be the authority of the government. Wherever, then, it is in our power to mold the institutions on the democratic model, the standard of both laws and manners will be elevated. In a democratic republic the manners have necessarily a more extensive influence than in any other form of government. Public opinion, therefore, has a more direct influence upon the execution as well as upon the formation of the laws. In most countries the laws are devised by the few. The opinions of the many and the few are thus placed in an antagonist relation to each other. In England and Scotland, the manners have infinitely more influence in shaping the laws than in Spain and Portugal. English institutions contain a stronger infusion of republican notions and the laws are infinitely better obeyed than in Spain and Portugal. In the United States the spirit of obedience is still stronger, as is shown by the fact that no standing military force has ever been kept up. But as a general rule the laws are somewhat in advance of public opinion. The wider the sphere of their influence, therefore, the more powerfully will they act upon the manners, and the manners will be rendered more and more auxiliary to the execution of the laws.

6th. Constitutions and laws, then, are not mere parchment barriers. The instances in which they are violated are to those in which they are obeyed as one to ten thousand. But the reason why this is so deserves particular consideration. As a general rule the constitution and laws are obeyed because it is felt to be right that they should be. But this opinion of right derives great strength from the fact that each law and each clause in a constitution is the result of a mental analysis which has already been gone through with. He who can give us an analysis of his ideas is listened to with more respect than he who can give us only his loose thoughts. But singular as it may appear, the great majority of mankind are even more affected with the result of an analysis than with the analysis itself. It wears a more imposing character, 1st, because it presents them with the idea in a form too large for their apprehension. They are unable to comprehend the analysis while at the same time they possess sufficient discernment to perceive that the end it leads to is the result of a mental operation. 2d. A constitution and code of laws are each a system of rules, and all men, the learned as well as the unlearned, are wonderfully affected with this notion of system. Each article in the one, and each enactment in the other, flows from some common principle; each part lends a sanction to every part, so that the sum total of authority which is possessed by the whole is greater than that of the parts. The constitution and the laws are, for the most part, an impersonation of the manners, and yet they acquire an authority so totally distinct from the manners that to speak of the two as identical would appear to the common mind a violation of the rules of good sense.

7th. The cooperation of the laws and the manners is, then, evident. But there are a great number of instances in which the laws have a peculiar efficacy in giving a direction to the manners. It is sometimes even necessary to force a law in order to bring about a given result. The first law which laid the foundation of the system of internal improvement in New York, the grand canal, was carried through the legislature by storm.[9] The enactment of some laws is vehemently resisted for a long time although the public opinion is in favor of them. The manifestation of public opinion is not clear and decisive until they are actually passed: they then show a title to obedience as well as to respect. The desired reform becomes more instead of less popular. It then represents a definite number of people who derive support from a mutual sympathy and who, through the medium of the same principle of sympathy, gradually impart their opinions to a still wider number. If any of the American states succeed in abolishing the traffic in spirituous liquors, it will be on this principle. At first public opinion is only half muttered; its expression is only found in detached masses of men, although the aggregate of opinions of these masses would represent a decided majority. The law combines them, gives unity to the opinions of all, and the authoritative sanction thus afforded to them secures the triumph of the reform. As a first step toward bringing the Russians within the pale of civilized Europe, Peter I made an ordinance prohibiting them from wearing their beards. In no very long time the disuse of the custom became not only popular but fashionable. There was great opposition in France and many of the American states to the repeal of the law of primogeniture. In the last the law has so entirely molded the manners and set the fashion that even desires which are unrestrained follow the rule of equal partibility. In France the same effect would follow if the law had not controlled desires as well as regulated the course of descent.

9. [The reference to the "grand canal" is to the Erie Canal.]

8th. The institutions of a country not only ought to be, but they necessarily are in advance of the popular intelligence. 1st. They must be so because they are the work of the more intelligent class of community even where intelligence is widely diffused. A constitution of government, a code of jurisprudence, institutions for the education of the people, *etc.*, all demand information, together with powers of analysis and generalization to which the common mind is incompetent. 2d. They ought to be lifted above the common run of opinions for the same reason. The intelligence displayed in those various institutions, taking advantage of the capacity for improvement among the common people and presenting constantly to the view some permanent standard of action, pushes them forward, stimulates them to thought and reflection, and induces habits of conduct every way superior to what they would otherwise have attained.

The civil and political institutions, nevertheless, represent all classes. They represent the more enlightened because they are the work of their hands; they represent all other classes because they are designed to regulate their conduct toward each other and toward the government. They contain what they desire they should contain, although they are unable to give account to themselves of the manner in which the task has been performed. And if a fraction only of the three millions entertain different opinions, the majority agreeing with the two millions and a half, and only hesitating as to the expediency of positive legislation, we make sure of one of two things, that such laws will be passed at some future day, or the public opinion will be so searching and so powerful in its operation that they will be unnecessary.

There are a multitude of subjects on which the legislative power may be exercised which it would be unprofitable to recount in detail. Some of these will be more particularly noticed under distinct heads. The important modification which this department undergoes in consequence of the existence of a written constitution, the abolition of a chamber of nobility, and the distribution of the power between a national and local legislatures are things which it is of most consequence to keep in view. When the operation and influence of these are fairly grasped, it will be easy to understand the character and functions of the legislature in a country of free institutions, whether the form of government is that of a simple or a confederate republic.

For instance: what a variety of subjects are withdrawn from the national legislature in America in consequence of the existence of the state governments. This plan is attended with two important advantages. It alters the whole character of legislation. The domestic affairs of the population which outweigh in number and importance all others become the subject of chief importance, while at the same time more judgment and skill are devoted to those interests than could be the case if they were all superintended by a central government. In the second place, the immense deduction which is made from the power of the national legislature prevents its being brought in perpetual collision with popular rights. As the whole amount of public business which is transacted in a country of free institutions is incomparably greater than in any other, the danger of introducing a complete system of centralization would also be greater if the legislative authority were not distributed among two classes of government.

At one time it was believed in America that the power to make internal improvements, not merely military and post roads but every other kind of roads and canals, might well be exercised by Congress. The power was regarded as a sort of paternal authority which would be engaged in dispensing benefits to the whole population and from which therefore no political evil need be apprehended. But reflecting and clear-sighted statesmen thought they could discern behind this paternal authority the germ of a power which, if it were permitted to take root and spread, would give rise to a system of centralization which would fritter away the authority of the states and therefore be detrimental to popular freedom. They therefore opposed the exercise of the power even where the state consented; and very consistently, for consent cannot give jurisdiction. A state cannot surrender a power to the federal government which the constitution has withheld. To do so would be to disarrange the whole system and to alter the balance between the national and state governments. The school whence those opinions emanated was at one time derisively termed the Virginia school of politics, but with great injustice, for these opinions have been productive of unspeakable blessings to the American people. It should rather be denominated the American school of politics, as it is a genuine representation of the mode of thinking which should be familiar to everyone in a country of free institutions. All experience shows that there is more danger from a too lax, than from a strict, construction of the constitution.

Everyone may have read the interesting and graphic description of the solemn mission which was deputed by New York to Washington city for the purpose of engaging the general government to embark in those public improvements which the state has itself executed in much less time, and with so much more skill and judgment than if they had been left to a central government. The state distrusted its own ability to construct these works. This was one motive. Another probably was that it would avoid the responsibility of laying the taxes necessary to defray the expense. But the mission to Washington met with an insurmountable obstacle. The federal government at that time was administered under the auspices of that Virginia school of politics to which I have referred, and for the first time in the history of nations a government was found which openly avowed that it was unwilling to augment its own power. Fortunate result, in every aspect in which it can be viewed. The states have escaped a system of centralization which would inevitably have impaired their just authority; and the great state which first projected the plan of internal improvements on a broad scale has succeeded beyond all expectation in the execution of its gigantic works. The series of years of unparalleled activity in every department of industry which followed has gradually enlisted every other state in the same scheme, and difficulties which seemed too great for the resources of any single state have been easily overcome by all.

This is one among many instances of the advantages resulting from a division of the legislative power between a national and local legislatures.

A striking example of the effect which a popular constitution has in altering the character of the legislation is afforded by the disposition which has been made of the war-making power in the American government. It has been taken from the executive and confided to the legislature alone. It is true that this arrangement may be adopted in a government where such a constitution is unknown. In Sweden, at one time, the states or diet had the exclusive power of declaring war. And at present they possess a veto upon the resolution of the king. But a popular constitution makes sure of abridging the power of the executive and, what is of still more consequence, it provides for the creation of a legislative body which shall really, not nominally, represent the public will. The legislative power is the power to make laws, and the law which gives rise to a state of war is one of the most important which can be enacted. War was formerly made without any solemn declaration, and on this account, perhaps, the power was supposed to fall within the appropriate sphere of executive jurisdiction. Devolving the power upon representatives of the people is a step taken in favor of civilization, not merely in one nation but among all nations. The power will be used with infinitely more caution. "War," says Mr. Burke, "never left a nation where it found it." It not only alters the relations between the belligerents; it produces the most serious changes in the internal condition of each. It annuls "ipso facto" some of the laws which were before of force; it renders necessary the passage of new ones, affecting immediately the pursuits of private individuals, and very frequently entails the heaviest calamities upon all classes of society. The law of war, therefore, has been attributed to the executive in consequence of that confusion between the functions of the different departments which always takes place in the early history of governments and which, once established, it is so difficult to remove.

It is true that in Great Britain and France the supplies are voted by the legislature and the bill must originate in the chamber in which the deputies of the people sit. But this sometimes is a very inadequate security against the prosecution of wars of ambition. The structure of the government must conspire with the social organization to throw discredit upon such wars and to put them entirely out of fashion. If the manners exercise a powerful influence upon government, so also does government exert a like influence upon the manners. A hereditary monarch and an order of nobility necessarily possess an amount of influence which cannot be measured by the mere formal authority with which they are invested. This influence too generally begets tastes and habits incompatible with the maintenance of peace as the permanent policy of the country. These will extend more or less over every part of society and give tone to the deliberations of the popular branch. Although, therefore, the two states I have named, as well as Belgium and Holland, are better protected than other European communities against unjust and impolitic wars, in consequence of the steady and vigorous growth of a middle class, the protection is very far from being complete. The crown and aristocracy still wield a disproportioned influence and overshadow the deliberations of the more popular body by contributing to prevent it from containing a genuine representation of that middle class. The only wise plan, therefore, is to confide the war-making power to the legislature and to compose this body of representatives of the people. If this disposition of the power will not prevent republics from waging unjust wars, it will at any rate render such wars much less frequent.

In those governments where the popular representation is very slender, the right of petition is regarded by the people as one of the dearest they possess. In those where there is no popular branch of the legislature, it is the only means by which the people can cause themselves to be heard. In the democratic republic of the United States, this right has not the same use. The people have no need to petition a body which is created by themselves and reflects their own opinions. Nevertheless, it is there considered more sacred, and is more extensively employed than in all other governments put together. And I am persuaded that its importance is increased instead of being diminished in proportion as the institutions assume a popular character. In absolute monarchies, such as Turkey and Russia, the right is almost entirely confined to the redress of individual grievances. An obscure individual is permitted to carry his complaint to the foot of the throne, for this does not at all affect the solidly-established authority of the monarch. It only places that authority in bolder relief. But in a republic the right acquires a far more comprehensive character: it becomes an affair of large masses of men who desire, in an authoritative but peaceable manner, to impress their opinions upon the governing authority. The opinions of an individual may sometimes be treated lightly; the opinions of whole classes are always entitled to notice. They are often indications of the propriety of some change in the legislation for which the majority will not be prepared until public opinion has been thoroughly sounded; or they may denote some new movement in society which, whether for good or for evil, should have the fullest publicity in order to be appreciated at its real worth. The great current of thought which is constantly bearing the mind forward is quickened or interrupted by a great number of lesser currents whose depth and velocity must be measured in order that we may determine our reckoning.

Petitions in the United States are of various kinds. Sometimes they contain the private claim of an individual upon the government. Sometimes they relate to the interests of agriculture, manufactures, and commerce. And in a few instances they have been made to bear upon the political institutions themselves. The memorials accompanying the second class of petitions have often displayed consummate research and ability and have shed a flood of light upon the subjects they have handled. It would be endless to refer to all the instances in which these compositions have sustained this high character. Two may be mentioned as samples: the memorial of the chamber of commerce of Baltimore on "the rule of 1756," and the report accompanying the memorial of the merchants of Boston in relation to the tariff; the first from the pen of William Pinkney, the second from that of Henry Lee.[10] These papers are profound and elaborate disquisitions upon subjects which have greatly perplexed both American and European statesmen.

As the legislature is immediately responsible to the people, it is of the utmost consequence that every channel of communication should be opened between the two. In this way public opinion will exert a steady and salutary control upon public men; and public men will endeavor to make themselves worthy of the trust confided to them by the display of eminent ability and the acquisition of information relative to the condition and interests of their state and country. In absolute government the right of petition is an affair of individuals only; in a democratic republic it is one means by which the government and the people are more closely bound together and the responsibility of the representatives rendered more strict. The views and opinions which prevail in different parts of an extensive community are necessarily very various; and the true way to reduce them to anything like uniformity is to give free vent to the opinions of all. Notwithstanding the exceeding diversity in the modes of thinking of individuals, we may lay it down as a safe general maxim that they are all in search of one thing, truth, and the mutual action of mind upon mind, although it at first increases the sharp points in each one's character, ultimately brings all to a better agreement. It is one distinguishing feature of American institutions that the robust frame of the government permits it to wait the slow process through which opinions

10. [Grimke refers to William Pinkney (1764–1822) of Maryland who published January 21, 1806, a "Memorial on the Rule of the War of 1756. . . . The Memorial of the Merchants and Traders of the City of Baltimore." It is reprinted in Henry Wheaton, *Some Account of the Life, Writings, and Speeches of William Pinkney* (Boston, 1826), pp. 372–396. The memorial is a brief against the seizure of American ships by the British Navy. Great Britain argued its right to interdict trade between the United States and France on the basis of precedent derived from 1756 during the Seven Years' War (1756–1763).

Henry Lee, *Report of a Committee of the Citizens of Boston and Vicinity, Opposed to a Further Increase of Duties on Importations* (Boston, 1827), generally known at the time as the "Boston Report."]

pass, without being at all incommoded, whereas most other governments too easily persuade themselves that opinion is noxious because it is new, and strive therefore, by force or by influence, to stifle it in its birth.

As to the stated meeting of the legislative body, I am of opinion that as a general rule it should be annual. In seven of the American states the session is biennial; but an annual meeting, accompanied with the limitation of the time during which it should sit, would be preferable. The indirect advantages which accrue from a political institution are sometimes as important as the immediate end which is intended to be accomplished. Thus the appropriate office of a legislative assembly is to pass laws for the government of the community; but there are certain incidental benefits, growing out of the meeting of the body, which are of inestimable value. We stand in need of every help and device by which to promote the intellectual communication of different parts of the country or state. As is the general standard of intelligence, so will be the character of the assembly which emanates from the people. To frame enlightened laws, experience, judgment, and information are all necessary. It is the necessity of exercising the understanding about the material interests of this world which raises men so much above the condition of the brutes. I would therefore employ every means in my power to advance the standard of popular intelligence. The capital where the legislature sits constitutes the center of information of the whole state. It may be a very imperfect contrivance, after all, for collecting the scattered rays of thought from abroad. The assembly may contain a great deal of ignorance and a great deal of presumptuousness, but it very often contains a considerable amount of sterling ability and good sense. I think it will not be doubted that if Congress had been the sole legislative body in America, civilization and intellectual improvement of every kind would not have made anything like the progress which they have during the last sixty years; so true is it that an institution which was originally designed to perform one office often succeeds in performing many others equally important.

The capital is the focus of general information. It is the place where the most important courts sit. Great numbers are attracted there from various motives. But I observe that the men who can impart knowledge, who can stir the faculties of other men, invariably command most attention in the private assemblages which take place there. Individuals of very superior minds, and who think they feel a sufficiently powerful stimulus from within to the attainment of mental distinction, may underrate the benefits which indirectly flow from the assembling of thirty legislative bodies. They are not aware of the influences which have given their own minds a firm ground to stand upon and a wide field for observation and inquiry. They are still more insensible to the advantages which the general mind receives in this way. Yet, it is most certain that the high standard of popular intelligence in the United States is in great part attributable to the annual meeting of the legislative assemblies.

In those states where the legislature sits biennially, there are doubtless some good reasons for the arrangement. The business to be transacted may be so small as not to require annual meetings, or the state may be burdened with debt and may nobly resolve to adopt every practicable plan of retrenchment rather than be unfaithful to its engagements.

As to the basis of representation, that is, the principle on which the legislative body should be elected, the rule in America differs greatly in different states. But notwithstanding this variety, it may be affirmed that the United States have made a much nearer approach to a regular plan than is observable in any other country. In Great Britain, the apportionment of the representatives has always been arbitrary. It is less so now than before the act of 1832. There are not so many flagrant discrepancies as formerly, not so many populous cities unrepresented, nor so great a number of unpeopled boroughs. But there are immense inequalities notwithstanding. Not only is a majority of the House of Commons elected by a part only of the substantial population, but it is elected by a minority of the legal electors. In France, the rule is attended with more regularity. The Chamber of Deputies is composed of four hundred and fifty-nine members who are elected by so many electoral colleges. These colleges are nothing more than assemblages of the qualified electors for the purpose of making the choice. They bear that name, instead of the simpler one of the polls so well understood in England and the United States, because the election is not conducted in public but has much the character of a secret meeting.

The number of "arrondissements" or territorial divisions next in size to those of the departments is four hundred and fifty-nine also. The colleges are composed of the voters in each of these, so that each "arrondissement" sends one member to the chamber of deputies. There is great inequality in the population of these territorial divisions. But notwithstanding this, there is less inequality in the apportionment of representatives than in Great Britain. The principal difference between the two countries as regards the composition of the popular chamber consists in this: in France, the basis of representation is less arbitrary; but in Great Britain, the number of persons who possess the electoral franchise is much greater in proportion to the whole population than it is in France; so that the House of Commons is a more popular body than the House of Deputies. The population of Great Britain and Ireland is not as large as that of France by five or six millions, but the electors are four times more numerous in the former. In order to found a popular body, both principles should be combined. The apportionment of the representation should be as equal as is practicable, and there should be a liberal rule for the exercise of the right of suffrage.

Representation may be proportioned to the gross amount of the population, to the number of electors, to the number of taxable inhabitants, or the basis may be a compound one, of taxation and population; for these various rules have all been followed in the different American states. In addition to which there is a fifth plan which has been adopted in the federal government and in a few of the southern states. The representation in Congress and in the lower houses of Maryland, North Carolina, and Georgia, is determined by adding to the whole number of free persons, three fifths of the slaves. In the composition of the federal senate, the rule, as I have already remarked, is necessarily different from all these. But so far as regards the state governments, the same reason does not exist for making the rule of apportionment different in the one house from what it is in the other. Yet there is considerable diversity in this respect. For instance: in Massachusetts, New Hampshire, and North Carolina, representation in the senate is based upon taxation; while in the lower house it is in the two former based upon the number of electors. In Rhode Island, South Carolina, and Georgia senators are distributed by a fixed rule among different districts, without making allowance for a variation in the population or taxation; while in the second, representatives are according to a mixed ratio of taxation and population; and in the first in proportion to the population, with this exception, however, that each town or city shall always be entitled to one member at least. In one respect, the rule in Connecticut and Virginia is different from what it is in the other states. The representation in both houses proceeds upon an arbitrary, or at least conjectural, rule. In the former, the senate is composed of twelve members chosen by general district, and the number of representatives from each town is declared to be the same as it was prior to the formation of the constitution, with this exception, that a town afterward incorporated shall be entitled to one representative only. In Virginia, so many senators and representatives are distributed among different sections of the state without any power in the legislature to alter the apportionment. In a majority of the states, the composition of the two houses is the same, being based in both either upon the gross amount of the population or the number of the electors.

But notwithstanding the great variety of plans which are adopted in the several states, the basis of representation, either for the senate or the house, is in every one of them far more equitable than it is in any other country.

The plan which appears to be most conformable to the genius of free institutions is to make population the basis of representation. 1st. The most populous will, as a general rule, be the most wealthy districts also. 2d. Where this is not the case, a representation of property interferes with the great principle of equality, as much as if we were to give to some men a quarter or half a vote, and to others a whole vote. If of two districts containing an equal population, one sends a single member and the other, in consequence of its superior wealth, sends two members, the men of the last have what is equivalent to two votes when compared with the first.

But the existence of slavery raises up a new rule in the southern states of America and one which contributes greatly to complicate the question. The most wealthy will never be the most populous districts where slaves are not counted as persons. If they are counted as property, there is nothing to correspond with them as persons. In other words, the very thing which is regarded as property is itself population. Shall these half persons, half things, form the basis of representation for freemen, although they have no representation themselves? It must be recollected, however, that this species of inequality will exist to some extent wherever the gross amount of the population affords the rule, whether that population is wholly free, or in part composed of freemen and in part of slaves. There is no way of avoiding it altogether but by making the number of electors the basis of representation. There are only five states, however, in which this rule is adopted. But the number of electors and the number of the people are of course very different. The former are male adults only; the latter include both sexes and all ages. Is there, then, more injustice in a representation of slaves than in one of infants? It may be said that whether we make the electors or the whole free population the basis, the distribution of representatives will be the same for all parts of the country; that is, that the electors are everywhere in the same proportion to the population. It is not the less true, however, that some persons are made the basis of representation who are not themselves entitled to vote. Now the thing which forbids their voting, to wit, want of capacity, is the very thing which has induced all wise legislators to interdict the right to slaves. Moreover, the proportion of adult males to the whole population may not be the same in all the non-slaveholding states. This proportion is different in an old from what it is in a new country. And it is, for the same reason, different in one of the new and growing states of the American confederacy from what it is in older ones; — different in Indiana and Illinois from what it is in Massachusetts and Connecticut. And when we consider that it is not the whole number of slaves, but three fifths, which ever enter as an element into the basis of representation, the rule adopted by the federal government and three of the states has neither the character of novelty or of harshness. The same remarks may be made in reference to the plan of basing representation in one house upon taxation, to that of basing it generally upon the number of taxable inhabitants, and to that of assigning one senator to each town in the state. The first is the case in New Hampshire, the second in Pennsylvania, and the third in Rhode Island. Neither the amount of taxation nor the number of taxable inhabitants correspond with the number of the electors. Minors and females will frequently be subject to taxation. And the Rhode Island as well as the Virginia plan designedly rejects both the rules of population and that of the number of electors.

But I am of the opinion that the rule of federal numbers will ultimately be abolished in the three states I have named, although probably never in the federal government. I observe that in all the new states which have been formed to the south, the ratio of federal numbers has been rejected. This is the case even in Louisiana, the only state except one where the slaves outnumber the whites. As the old states have exercised a great and salutary influence upon the new, the new will probably in their turn exercise a like influence upon the old. Their experience will be a sort of double experience; that which their ancestors who emigrated from the older states handed down to them, and that which they themselves have acquired.

But there is a stronger reason. The tendency everywhere manifest, to incorporate thoroughly the principle of equality into the political institutions, will operate to produce this effect. The democratic principle will not lead to the emancipation of the blacks, for this would be to place the most democratic part of society in immediate association with them. But it will lead to the abolition of a representation of slaves in the state governments, since that places different parts of the white population on an unequal footing.

The English government, says De Lolme, will be no more when the representatives of the people begin to share in the executive authority. But when we consider how the executive authority in that government is constituted, that the king possesses numerous attributes which properly belong to the legislature and that without any direct responsibility to the people, it would be much more correct to say that the constitution will always be in jeopardy unless the representatives of the people succeed in appropriating to themselves some of his vast prerogatives. The tendency of the legislature to become the predominant power in the state is visible in all the constitutional governments of the present day. But far from rousing apprehension, it is an unequivocal symptom of the progress of regular government. This tendency in Great Britain is more marked at the present time than when De Lolme wrote; it was much more so in his day than during the reign of the Stuarts, or during those of William or Anne. The same changes have occurred in France. No monarch now dare go to the legislative hall to pronounce, as Louis XV did, the dissolution of the only body which served as a counterpoise to the throne. The whole kingdom quaked and was petrified by that memorable discourse because the body to whom it was delivered had not been lifted up by the people and was therefore unable to assert the rights of the people. The changes which have taken place both in Great Britain and France, so far from endangering the executive authority, have given it strength; so far from filling those countries with confusion, have promoted public tranquillity.

The preponderance of the legislative over the executive department is the natural consequence of the system of representation. In a highly civilized community in which the system is sure to make its appearance in one form or another, a larger amount of legitimate business falls to the legislature than to the executive; and that department which transacts the greatest amount of effective business for society is sure to acquire the largest share of authority. We must quarrel with the principles of representation therefore, or admit that when the people have risen in importance, kings must part with very many of the prerogatives which have been attributed to them.

But if the legislature is destined to become the most influential body in the state, will not the balance of every constitution be overthrown? The balance of no constitution is upheld at all times by precisely the same means. On the contrary, an adjustment which may have been skillful and judicious at one period may afterward become very faulty, because illy adapted to the structure of society. If this has undergone material changes, it is most likely that the machinery by which we propose to maintain the constitutional balance will undergo a corresponding change. If at the present day the only way by which an equilibrium of authority in the British government is preserved is by denying in practice powers which are theoretically ascribed to the king, it is plain that the day is not very distant when the theory of the constitution will be brought into a much nearer conformity with the practice. For the disguised and silent transference of power from the executive to the legislature is, in a highly advanced society, the certain forerunner of a formal and legalized appropriation of it by the latter.

In a representative government the legislature gains strength, while the powers of the executive either fall into disuse or are distributed among a great number of administrative officers. But the responsibility of the legislature to the whole community is also increased. We cannot then adopt the opinion of De Lolme, but should rather insist upon it as an undeniable truth that when all efforts to diminish the power of the king have become unavailing the British constitution will be no more. Every scheme for widening the basis of representation is a step in disguise toward lessening the regal authority. The reform act of 1832 strengthened the legislature and saved the constitution; and other reform acts will certainly be passed which will humble the powerful but add strength and security to the government.

The preponderance of the legislative power is the striking fact in the history of the American governments, both national and state. No communities, to say the least, have been better governed. And it is but the other day that one of the greatest English statesmen declared that "there was no reason why this system should not endure for ages." It is true, all human institutions are after all very imperfect. All fall infinitely short, not only of what is conceivable, but very far short of what is practicable. Let us cherish what we have as the only means of extending the limits of the practicable. Some future generation may be able to do what now seems impossible: to resolve the great problem of the social, as the present have resolved that of the political, equality of men. All that is necessary to this end is to cause all men to obey the precepts of virtue and to become educated. It is clear that there is no absolute impracticability in the first; and although the last, in the extended sense in which I use the term educated, is now totally inconsistent with the multiform, subordinate, and laborious employments of society, yet I am persuaded that if the first is ever accomplished the second will be made to follow through instrumentalities of which we can only obtain an indistinct glance.

The opinion of Montesquieu is more plausible, because it is more vague and ambiguous than that of De Lolme. The English constitution, says Montesquieu, will be no more when the legislative becomes more corrupt than the executive. But to this term, corrupt, we are entitled to give a more extended meaning than is generally attributed to it. A legislative body is corrupt when its members procure their seats by bribery and other sinister practices. This was the case when Montesquieu wrote and it is to be feared that it is too much the case now. But a legislative body is still more corrupt when exercising not merely the ordinary legislative power but, representing the sovereignty of the state, it permits, century after century, the grossest inequalities in the representation without adopting some plan of remedying them. A legislative body is corrupt when, holding the relation of guardian to a sister island, it permits the most wanton oppression to be practiced upon large bodies of men because their religious creed was not the same as its own. All these things, and many more, were practiced and undertaken to be justified when "the spirit of laws" was written. And yet the English constitution, as it then existed, was the *beau ideal* of government with Montesquieu. It is one advantage of free institutions that they discountenance certain political vices by putting them out of fashion. Time out of mind there has been a constant tendency to exaggerate the vices of the weak and to extenuate those of the powerful, because the powerful lead the fashion. And if the British Parliament has relaxed its severities toward Ireland, has opened its doors to Catholics, and placed the representation in other respects on a more equitable footing, we must not conclude that it has become more corrupt, that it has usurped power, although these things do in reality increase the power of the legislature and render it more than ever a counterpoise to the executive.

BOOK THREE

CHAPTER I | RELIGIOUS INSTITUTIONS

THERE is an argument in favor of an established church, contained in Mr. Hume's *History of England,* which on account of its extreme ingenuity is entitled to great consideration. He admits that almost all the arts and sciences which administer to the instruction of mankind may be safely left to the voluntary efforts of those who undertake to teach them; but he contends that religious doctrines constitute an exception to the rule. This eminent writer supposes that the violent and immoderate zeal of different sects, each striving by every art and device to gain proselytes to its cause, will be productive of interminable contention and that in this way the tranquillity and good order of the state will be deeply affected. He proposes, therefore, as the only cure for the evil, to give one sect the supremacy; in other words, to create an established church. But the mischief which Mr. Hume was desirous of curing lies much deeper than in the mere number or the discordant opinions of different sects. It is to be traced solely to the mixture of politics and religion. It is the officious interference of the civil magistrate with religion, and the unbecoming interference of religious sects with state affairs, which whets the spirit of proselytism and furnishes incentives additional to, and foreign to, those which the spirit of Christianity suggests to enslave the minds of men. By giving one sect a religious establishment, religion is converted into an engine of government, and instead of curing we only give a different direction to the mischief. The zeal of religious parties is more inflamed by withholding from them privileges which are bestowed upon the established church than would be the case if all were placed upon an equal footing. To be placed under the ban of public opinion, to be subjected to some disability or disadvantage which does not attach to other men,

is a powerful and not always a commendable motive for making unusual exertions to diminish the influence of the last. There is no effectual plan, therefore, of doing justice to all sects and reconciling the
great interests of religion with those of the community but dissolv-
ing the connection between church and state and so administering civil
affairs that no sect in the propogation of its doctrines shall draw to
itself any part of the authority which appertains to government.

Our speculations of any sort hardly ever rise much higher than the
age in which we live. The use of all our knowledge is to be employed
about the actual phenomena which are submitted to us; and it is the
phenomena which surround us which rouse in us all our aptitude for
thinking and supply all the information which we are able to attain.
Books give us the history of the past, while all philosophical speculation has reference to the present. But to be successful in our inquiries
we must witness the development, up to a certain point, of the events
which are submitted to us. In no other way can we make any sure
calculation of the results. The superiority of some minds to others often
consists in the opportunity afforded to take advantage of the favorable
point of view.

When Mr. Hume wrote, religious establishments had existed from
time immemorial, and yet religious quarrels and religious conspiracies had constantly disturbed the peace of society. Neither the Edict of
Nantes nor the English act of toleration extinguished them.[1] If he
had lived at the present day and witnessed the great advantages
which have attended the abolition of a state religion in America his
views would have been more just, because more comprehensive, and
he would have been led to a different conclusion. Warburton would
not even then have been convinced.[2]

The late Dr. Arnold, however, a most able and estimable man, in
an appendix to his lectures on history, has insisted upon the right and
the duty of the state to take the affairs of religion under its superintendence.[3] His notions of the office and functions of the civil magistrate are such that he would have government ordain the maxims of
religion as laws on the same principle that it makes any other enact-

1. [Edict of Nantes (1598), promulgated to restore internal peace to France by
defining the rights of French Protestants, revoked by Louis XIV in 1685.]

2. [William Warburton (1698–1779), English Bishop and writer who was famous for his arrogance and prejudice.]

3. [Thomas Arnold (1795–1842), father of Matthew, preacher, educator, and
classical historian.]

ments for the regulation of the citizens. If the public weal requires the imposition of taxes by a legislative body, for the same reason is it supposed that the public weal demands that the cardinal rules of religion should have the same authoritative sanction affixed to them.

These are the views of a man who hated every species of oppression and who was sincerely and thoroughly devoted to the good of his fellow creatures. But although he can in no sense be said to have been wedded to a sacerdotal caste, yet it is evident that the institutions under which he lived exercised a powerful influence upon him and communicated a tincture to all his opinions upon this subject. The plan of which he has given a sketch (for it is attended with such inherent difficulties that it will only admit of a sketch) is met by two arguments which it is difficult to answer because they are both deduced from experience, and from experience on a very broad scale. And first, it is an undoubted fact that there is as strong a sentiment of religion and morality pervading the American people as exists among any other, and much stronger than among the great majority of nations who have had a state religion. In the second place, it will be admitted that if people would voluntarily consent to pay their taxes, or if they would faithfully comply with all their private contracts and abstain from the commission of personal injuries, there would be no necessity for the intervention of government by the appointment of tax gatherers and the establishment of courts of justice. This is not the case, however, in matters of this kind, but it is so in all religious concerns. Men do actually discharge their religious duties, not as well as could be desired but infinitely better than when the state interferes to exact the performance of them. The very reasons therefore which render it incumbent on the state to interpose for the protection of one set of interests lest they should fall to decay prompt it to abstain from intermeddling with another set lest they also should fall to decay. It is immaterial whether we call one class secular and the other religious interests; we may call both secular or both religious, but it will not follow that the actions which fall within these two classes should be subjected to the same discipline. The true theory then is that, inasmuch as religion creates a relation between God and man, the religious sentiment is necessarily disturbed by the intervention of the civil magistrate.

It is not necessary to notice the intrinsic difficulties which would attend the scheme of Dr. Arnold if it were attempted to be put in practice. Shall the maxims of religion which are proclaimed by the civil magistrate as laws be subjected to the interpretation of Catholics or Episcopalians, of Presbyterians or Unitarians? Every attempt to prop up religion by such a feeble instrumentality would end in covering religion with dishonor.

There is another view which may be taken in reference to Mr. Hume's plan. The clergy of an established church, from their position in society and their acquaintance with much of the literature and philosophy of the day, have much to do with the education of youths. Now, it is an undoubted fact that the progress of religious inquiry is closely connected with that of philosophical inquiry, that freedom of thought in the one contributes to enlightened views in the other, and that the true way to promote knowledge is to extend the utmost latitude to all kindred pursuits. If it were only a question with regard to the progress of knowledge among the clergy themselves, this view would be of importance; but when it is recollected that they stand at the head of the schools of education, and thus assist in training to thought and speculation all the minds which are destined to figure in society in any way, the question becomes one of still greater magnitude. For although an ecclesiastical establishment with freedom of worship to dissenters is greatly preferable to the supreme dominion of one sect, yet the evil is only mitigated, not cured, in that way. In place of the authority of the law giver, the influence of the law giver is substituted. And no one need be told that the influence of government has a wonderful efficacy in repressing the efforts of the human mind, as well among those whom it takes under its patronage as among those whom it discards from its countenance and favor.

The plan of curing the dissensions of religious sects by giving monarchical rule to one of them is akin to the error which prevails in politics that it is necessary to confer supreme authority on a prince or body of nobles in order to extinguish civil dissensions. Whereas, the true maxim is that the peace of society is never in so much danger as when authority of any sort is consolidated and never so well guarded as when it is dispersed. Power may be condensed in ecclesiastical as well as in political institutions, and the scheme on which the American people have proceeded in religious affairs is only an amplification of the great principle of the distribution of power. It is a mistake to suppose that if some sects are disfranchised they are therefore deprived of the ability to do mischief. On the contrary, their zeal and activity are increased, and their efforts are sure to take a direction prejudicial to the public tranquillity. We seek to shut them out from all interference with political questions by endowing one denomination with extraordinary privileges, and they are thereby more completely drawn within the vortex of politics. In other words, because religious parties are disconnected with the state it does not therefore follow that they are disconnected with the political world. The sect between which and the state an alliance is formed, or which stands in the relation of dependent to the state as its head, will naturally exercise its influence in favor of the government, and the dissenting sects will throw their influence in the opposite direction. These behold their own government as the author of the disabilities under which they labor and only wait for a favorable opportunity to crush an authority so unnatural and so revolting to all persons of good sense. Ireland is an example on a great scale, and the American commonwealth, before the thorough dissolution of the connection between church and state, is an example on a small one. And even in England from the commencement of the French Revolution to the present day, political disputes have derived much of their acerbity from the same source. It is easy to see that all questions of parliamentary reform receive a complexion from the views and influence of the dissenting sects. It is equally easy to perceive that many other projects of a still more sweeping character, and which are only smothered not destroyed, are engendered by the same cause.

It is now proved that the greatest interest which can occupy the mind of man — that which is fitted above all others to engage his attention from the age of puberty to the grave — may be entirely withdrawn from the care of the civil magistrate, and that both religious and secular interests will be thereby subserved. The plan of an established church was at one time adopted in all the American states, except Pennsylvania and Rhode Island. The nature of the establishment was, to be sure, not the same in all. In Massachusetts, Connecticut, New York, Maryland, Virginia, and South Carolina, the connection between church and state was as strict as in Great Britain. In the others it existed in a modified form. In all of them this connection has been entirely dissolved; in the greater part, soon after the Revolution. But it was not until the year 1816 that it was thoroughly put an end to in Connecticut; and not until the year 1833, that the finishing blow was given to it in Massachusetts.*

* *Religion in America*, by R. Baird, pp. 115, 116. [Robert Baird, *Religion in America; or, An Account of the Origin, Relation to the State, and Present Condition of the Evangelical Churches in the United States. With notices of the Unevangelical Denominations* (New York, 1844).]

Men of all denominations in every one of these states — those who were most opposed to the introduction of the new system — now acknowledge that it has been productive of great benefit to both church and state. There is more religious harmony and consequently a greater degree of political tranquillity because simply there is nothing to pamper the power of one sect and to provoke the hostility of others. As the connection wherever it exists is established by the laws, the sects who feel themselves aggrieved will take an active part in all political elections for the purpose of delivering themselves from the burden of which they complain. Thus, in Connecticut where the Congregational sect was the favored one, all other denominations, Episcopalians, Baptists, Methodists and Universalists, united themselves closely together in order to uproot the laws, and after years of struggle, which occasioned painful heartburnings in every part of society, they at last succeeded in gaining a majority in the legislature and acquiring that Christian liberty to which all men are entitled. So in Virginia, after the Revolution: all the dissenting sects combined to influence the elections, as it was only in that way that the Episcopal, which was the established, church could be deprived of the authority and privileges which had been conferred upon it. The debate, which resulted in the dissolution of church and state, was one of the most stormy which has occurred in the Virginia legislature.

This great question as to the political constitution of the church agitated the German reformers at the commencement of the reformation. They were exceedingly anxious to get rid of the supremacy of princes in everything which related to the interests of religion. But they could conceive no way of doing this but by placing themselves under the dominion of an ecclesiastical hierarchy. Vain and fruitless expedient, for an ecclesiastical hierarchy will ever terminate in an alliance between church and state. It was reserved for the American states to solve this difficult problem. And the religious institutions of this country may be said to be the last and most important effort which has been made in completing that great revolution which commenced in the sixteenth century.

I have alluded to the unfavorable influence which an ecclesiastical establishment has upon the progress of knowledge and the general freedom of thought. This influence is very striking in everything which concerns the political interests of the state. The ministers of an established church look with singular complacency upon the abuses which have crept into the state since to question or discountenance them would be to impair materially the authority which assists in upholding themselves. Civil government is as much the creature of improvement as any other human interest, and whatever operates as a restraint upon inquiry raises up obstacles to this end, the more formidable as those who create them are insensible of their influence. The alliance between the government and a powerful and influential priesthood enables secular princes to defy public opinion. The minds of men, pressed by the combined weight of superstition and authority, are slow to find out anything wrong in a system to which they and their ancestors have been habituated, and people soon persuade themselves that the king has the same right to govern the state which God has to govern the world.

Many causes may contribute to counteract this influence. No nation is permitted in the nineteenth century to sit securely locked up in its own institutions without receiving numerous influences from abroad. The communication between the people of different countries is more constant now than it was between the people of the same country a century ago. In Great Britain it is in spite of, not in consequence of, the connection between church and state that the general mind has been borne onward in the march of improvement. The existence of an established church has produced what Mr. Hume was desirous of avoiding; it has multiplied the number of dissenters from the Church of England so that instead of being an inconsiderable body as formerly they now stand, in England and Wales, in something like the proportion of six millions to nine millions. And it is not improbable that the growth of their numbers, joined to the superior energy which they possess, may at some not very distant day bring about the same revolution and by the same means as was accomplished in Connecticut and Virginia.

The clergy of the established church in England were at the head of the party which first stimulated the American and then the French war. There was but one of the English prelates who voted against the first; the Bishop of Llandaff was the only one who declared himself in opposition to the second.[4] The African slave trade — the barbarities of which are so shocking to every mind of humanity — was vindicated in Parliament by nearly the whole body of prelates, so that Lord Eldon was heard to declare that a traffic which he had learned to believe was

4. [The prelate who opposed measures in the House of Lords against the American colonies was Jonathan Shipley, Bishop of St. Asaph.]

the most infamous in which human beings could engage could hardly be so inconsistent with the principles of Christianity.* It was the bench of bishops who opposed most vehemently the reform bill, an act demanded by every consideration of prudence, not to say of justice and equity, and the only possible objection to which is that it did not go far enough. If we inquire what body of men have been most luke-warm in the cause of popular instruction, who most hostile to the noble efforts of Romilly and Mackintosh to ameliorate the provisions of the criminal code, the answer is the same: it was the clergy of the estab-lished church who exerted themselves directly or indirectly to thwart these improvements.[5]

It is clear, then, that the clergy of an established church, in conse-quence of their close connection with the crown, the elevated position which they occupy in the state, and their power of influencing the peo-ple, may become an engine in the hands of government capable of be-ing wielded as effectually as the army or navy.

That the principle of religion is absolutely necessary to hold together the elements of civil society is a proposition which will be doubted by few. It is so, not merely as has been supposed because it presides over a large class of actions of which the civil magistrate cannot take cognizance, but because it lies at the foundation of all our notions of right and prevents in innumerable instances the commission of crimes which are punishable by the civil magistrate. Indeed it is doubtful if human affairs were delivered over to the conduct of beings in whom the religious sentiment was not the master principle whether the terms civil magistrate and laws would have any signification, and whether the uni-versal licentiousness which would prevail, involving, as it must, both magistrate and citizen, would not disable any community from uphold-ing institutions which were calculated to redress and punish crime.

It may be supposed that if the religious principle is of so great im-portance to the well being of society that it should in some way or other enter as an element into the general legislation, and admitting that an established church is as inconsistent with the spirit of Christian-ity as it is with the genius of free institutions, yet that there are a num-ber of ways in which the laws might interfere in order to secure the

---

* Black Book, pp. 6 and 7. [John Scott, First Earl of Eldon (1751–1838), Lord-Chancellor, of whom the *Dictionary of National Biography* says, "his normal atti-tude towards innovations of all kinds was one of determined hostility."]

5. [Sir Samuel Romilly (1757–1818), Sir James Mackintosh (1765–1832): both active in English legal and penal reform.]

observance of religious duties. But it is not in the power of human legislation to reach all the actions of men, and although this might be thought to be a great defect in the constitution of human nature yet in reality it is a wise provision, calculated to strengthen the religious sentiment and to cultivate a pure and genuine morality. For if the laws were to overshadow the whole circle of human actions, men would be converted into mere automata, religion into an empty ceremonial, and nothing being left to the natural impulse of the heart, the fountain from which the laws derive their chief strength would be dried up.

It is, to be sure, difficult to determine always what are the exact limits of legislation — to distinguish between those actions with which government should interfere and those which it should let alone. But although the precise boundary between the two is invisible, yet in practice it is easy to find it. Something must go behind the laws which cannot therefore be itself the subject of legislation.

A very eminent writer, and one of the greatest statesmen France has produced, Benjamin Constant, is opposed to an established church, but he believes it to be necessary that the clergy should be salaried by the government. This is one step in advance of the other European states, for it is not the clergy of one but of all denominations who are intended to be provided for. Great ideas seldom spring up in the mind more than half-formed. The understandings of the wisest men are in a state of continual pupilage. And here is one of the most powerful and enlightened advocates of civil and religious freedom who desires in the mildest manner possible to cement the religious interests of the people with their political institutions. He who is master of my income possesses an influence over my actions, and if he is clothed with political power he possesses something more than influence — he possesses authority. Benjamin Constant supposes that the clergy will not be adequately rewarded unless the state interposes to provide for them. And yet in America, where the voluntary principle is universally introduced, the ministers of religion are much more liberally paid than in France. The amount raised for this purpose in the United States, with a population of twenty millions, is nearly eleven millions of dollars. In France, the population of which is thirty-two or three millions, it is not much more than nine millions of dollars. The compensation which the American clergy receive is larger than is paid in any state of continental Europe. It is double what it is in Austria or Russia and quadruple what it is in Prussia.

The plan proposed by Benjamin Constant has been incorporated into the constitutional "charte" of 14th August, 1830. In some respects it resembles the system which formerly prevailed in two of the New England states. Both plans may be characterized as a species of modified connection between church and state. In Massachusetts, the parish or township imposed the taxes necessary to the support of the clergy. In one respect, this is infinitely preferable to the French system; for in the first, the duty of defraying the expense was devolved upon the local jurisdiction where the church was situated; while in the last, being collected by the government, a system of universal centralization is established both in church and state. But in another respect, the French system is most entitled to approbation, for it distributes the reward among all Christian sects, while in Massachusetts it was reserved for ministers of the Protestant faith exclusively. The Massachusetts scheme was a relic of those institutions which were planted during the early settlement of the colony when the Presbyterian church was the established religion. The Constitution of 1780 effected a great change in this respect. The funds collected, instead of being appropriated to the support of one denomination, were reserved for that sect to which the majority of voters in the township belonged. But the minority, however large, were thus compelled to support a clergyman of a different faith than their own and were frequently deprived of the building which they had themselves erected. Like the English system the people were obliged to maintain a clergyman to whose creed they were conscientiously opposed. It was not until 1833 that this last remnant of superstition was obliterated and the union of church and state finally terminated in America.

An established church is in no way subservient to the interests of religion or the good government of the state. It does not allay the feuds between rival sects; it only inflames their zeal. It is surprising when Mr. Hume had advanced so far as to admit of toleration to all dissenters that the same process of reasoning had not conducted him to the end and persuaded him that if such happy consequences were the fruit of removing some part of the unnatural restraint imposed by the civil magistrate, that still more salutary effects would follow from removing it altogether.

An ecclesiastical hierarchy does not contribute to the promotion of religion among either people or clergy. Its tendency is directly the reverse. It lays the foundation for wide-spread irreligion and immorality. The cost of the church establishment in England is as great as in all the states of continental Europe put together. But a large proportion of the clergy have no more connection with their congregations than if they resided in America. They receive the stipend and employ deputies for a pitiful sum to perform the duty. Nor can it be otherwise when the abominable system of pluralities prevails so extensively and when the minister is entirely independent of his congregation for his salary and may not even be the man of their choice. The church establishment costs about forty millions of dollars, and out of this enormous sum not half a million is paid to the four thousand two hundred and fifty-four curates who are for the most part employed to do the real and effective duty. Not only have the congregation of the established church no voice in the choice of their minister, the right of presentation is as much the subject of traffic as the public stocks or any other commodity in the market. The consequence is that immorality and licentiousness prevail to a fearful extent among a large proportion of the English clergy. The mere ceremonial of religion is substituted in the place of religion itself and may be said to constitute the system of modern indulgences by which men purchase for themselves an exemption from reproach, a system which does not differ essentially from that preached in the sixteenth century but simply conformable to the fashion of this day as the other was to the age of Leo the tenth. So that unless a second Luther appears, the day may not be distant when persons in whom the religious sentiment is not extinct may set themselves about inquiring whether in order to be religious it may not be necessary to abstain from going to church. In the United States, although there is much connected with this matter which is calculated to make a thoughtful mind ponder, yet it cannot be doubted (since we have the testimony of impartial Europeans) that the observance of religious duties is more strict and the conduct of the clergy more free from reproach than in the great majority of the European states. Indeed it may be doubted whether if there were no vicious clergymen there would be any infidels.

The ecclesiastical establishments of Europe and the United States, then, present this difference: that in the former, the clergyman is independent of his congregation for his place and salary, while in the latter he is entirely dependent upon it for both. The American system is productive of one mischief. The minister is sometimes obliged to wink at many improprieties among his congregation in order to retain his popularity. But there is no way of avoiding this but by encountering still greater difficulties. Any scheme is preferable to one which would give us a fox-hunting, card-playing clergy, or a clergy which could afford to be slothful and idle because they were opulent. In the European system corruption commences at the fountain head. Men cannot deliver themselves from it, if they were so disposed, and the new habits of thinking which are inculcated by the example of those in high places render them indifferent about doing so even if they were able.

In an American congregation I can always discern some persons who are sincerely religious. But the minister is equally dependent upon all the members of his congregation, upon those who desire to see him true to the faith as well as upon those who would have him countenance a lax and fashionable morality. Some compromise must take place between these two different classes. Those who are indifferent do not wish to separate themselves from the rest of the congregation in order to choose a minister more to their taste. This is (most generally) the very last thing they would desire. Independently of the increased expense they would incur, and independently of the odium which would follow from an open rupture, there is that sense of justice among the great majority of mankind that they respect virtue wherever it is to be found and admire nothing so much as a fearless and unwavering performance of duty, even though it may interfere with their own practice. I observe among an American congregation a very general willingness on the part of those who are indifferent to religion to defer to the opinion of those who are sincere. They distrust their own judgment and feel as if they had no right to command where they had never learned to obey. The influence which is exercised in these ways is highly salutary. The clergyman feels that his moral power after all depends upon the religious part of his congregation; and those of his hearers who would have had things conducted after a different manner — who perhaps joined the congregation to promote their worldly interests — are at last persuaded that if religion be true, religion must be preached. All parties are in this way made better than they would otherwise be. The sagacious clergyman with his eye ever intent upon the action of so many apparently contradictory motives, and not wishing to dash the prospect of doing good, but rather to make everything turn up for the best, does not relax the strictness of his preaching, but dismisses that tone of authority which is so prevalent among the clergy of an established church. He uses the most straightforward and yet the most gentle means to accomplish his object. He renders the good, better, and wins over many who would be irritated, perhaps forever alienated, by a contrary course. So true is it that a fashionable clergyman is not, therefore, a popular one, that I have known many instances in the United States of pastors dismissed by their congregations for levity and unbecoming manners, and very few where they were dismissed in consequence of a fearless and upright discharge of their duties.

In France, not only are the clergy dependent for their salary upon the government; they are dependent upon it for their places. The league between church and state is even closer than in Great Britain. In the last the minister collects his own tithes; in the first, government receives and disburses the taxes which are imposed for this purpose. The king of France nominates the archbishops, thirteen in number; he also nominates all the bishops. Both these orders of ecclesiastics receive canonical investiture from the pope and make solemn oath to the king as a condition precedent to entering upon the discharge of their functions. The bishops, on the other hand, nominate all the inferior clergy; but these nominations, with some exceptions, are submitted to the king, who may either reject or ratify them.

Another remarkable feature in this system consists in the control which the crown exercises over the clergy of the Protestant church. This church is presided over by the ministers, by consistorial assemblies, and by synods. But the election of a pastor, although it is made by the consistory, must receive the approbation of the king in order to be valid; and although the synods may make regulations relative to church discipline and doctrine, yet their decisions are obliged to be submitted to the king for his approval. Nor have the synods liberty to assemble without the permission of the government. The state is not satisfied with being the head of one church; it is the head of all. It reigns supreme, not merely over the predominant sect but over all sects. Like the Grecian and Roman commonwealths, it takes all denominations under its guardianship and establishes all by law. Doubtless this state of things is greatly to be preferred to that which formerly existed when this fine country was as much distracted by religious strife as it was by political dissensions. The step which has been taken toward the promotion of religious freedom is immense. And if government does interpose at all in ecclesiastical matters, it may be said with a good deal of justice that inasmuch as the clergy of all denominations are provided for by law all denominations should come under the supervision of the law.

But the introduction of the voluntary principle which now prevails universally in America is a prodigious step in advance of what any other government has attempted. It is a system "sui generis," and has grown up silently and steadily without attracting much observation from abroad. Nevertheless, I regard this complete severance of church and state as the "chef d'œuvre" in ecclesiastical government and as redounding more to the political tranquillity of the state than any single civil regulation which has ever been made. The connection between all secular and religious interests is strengthened just in proportion as the connection between government and church is weakened.

The rise of a sacerdotal caste in the United States seems to be forbidden by the great multiplication of sects. Religious and civil liberty are both protected by the same means. The unbounded freedom of thought which pervades every class of society creates the greatest diversity of opinions, and the influence which is possessed by any one sect is modified and controlled by the influence of all others. Each wants to be free, but none can succeed in obtaining freedom unless all are permitted to enjoy it.

When one surveys the vast establishments of our Bible, missionary, and other societies, when one considers the princely revenues which are received by some of the churches, in one instance almost vying with those of an eastern prince, the thought may very naturally cross the mind of one who is least disposed to take exception to anything because it is not in conformity with his preconceived notions, whether all these things may not ultimately terminate in raising up an ecclesiastical hierarchy similar to what exists in most other countries. Religion was everywhere first preached in simplicity, but wealth and prosperity, in numerous instances, corrupted the clergy who sought to conceal this deplorable change from the multitude by assuming more pomp, arrogating more authority, and causing the unintelligibleness of their doctrines to keep even pace with the degeneracy of their manners. It is in this way that a sacerdotal caste, as distinguished from an independent religion, has been established in so many countries. Nor do I pretend to assert that there is any absolute certainty the United States will be saved from this destiny, nor that the approach to it may not even be more gradual and more concealed from public observation than it has been anywhere else. One way to guard against a public evil is to persuade everyone that its existence is possible. The watchfulness and circumspection which are thus created present innumerable obstacles in the way of those who might be disposed to abandon the simplicity of religious worship in order to build up a gorgeous fabric of superstition.

When we consider that not only are powerful religious associations constantly springing up in the United States but that government and religious sects do not stand upon the same vantage ground, there might seem to be an additional reason for feeling alarm. The state is forbidden by all the American constitutions from intermeddling with religion, but the clergy are not forbidden to interfere with the affairs of state. They are not only at liberty to inculcate political doctrines from the pulpit, but under the federal and most of the state constitutions they are eligible to seats in the legislative body and may hold other important offices. An immunity, however, is not of equal advantage to all unless all are equally able to turn it to account. The clergy and the laity may be placed on the same footing, so far as regards the mere possession of a privilege, but they may not be able to exercise it with the same facility. Now I observe among the people generally a marked disapprobation of everything like political harangues from the pulpit. I observe an equally general disinclination to elect ministers of the gospel to civil offices. The constitutional ordinance which prohibits the government from interfering with religion is founded upon the notion that religion is something beyond and above human legislation, and that to mix the two incongruously together would be to do violence to both. No class is more sensible of this than the clergy themselves. They feel that to mingle in the disputes of political parties is to desert a strong for a weak position; that although an inflammatory harangue from the pulpit or a seat in the legislature may give them a temporary or local popularity, yet they lose in the same proportion in point of weight and influence as clergymen. The consequence is that no class of men are so unambitious of political preferment, and (with very few exceptions) it is with exceeding caution and distrust that they venture to touch upon the political questions which divide the community.

But it is the great multiplicity of sects in the United States which constitutes the chief security against the growth of an ecclesiastical hierarchy. The same causes which act upon political parties act upon religious sects. Whenever one party in the state is disposed to carry things with a high hand and to arrogate to itself an exclusive authority, the alarm is instantly given and hostile opinions grow up which tend to counterbalance its authority. And as soon as one religious sect gives promise of becoming an aristocratic body, other denominations vie with each other in calling back the minds of men to the pure doctrines and manners which originally distinguished the Christian community. It even happens sometimes that two or more sects are formed out of one. An incompatibility of views, arising out of causes similar to those I have mentioned, produces a schism in a whole denomination and leads to a still greater multiplication of sects. We have seen a remarkable example of this in the United States within a few years. The three most numerous sects, the Presbyterians, Baptists and Methodists, have been rent in twain in consequence of dissensions among themselves. And although the interpretation given to some doctrines or a desire to effect a change in some form or other of church government and discipline have been put forward as the causes of these disagreements, I think I can discern behind them some other more powerfully operating motives. Thus to take a single example: although the new-school separated from the old-school Presbyterians chiefly in consequence of objections to the doctrine of the necessity of the will, which the latter maintained, a doctrine which probably no argument will ever shake, yet it is possible for a religious sect to build up a well-compacted system of doctrines and then, forgetting that this after all constitutes but the skeleton of religion, to fall down and worship it instead of worshiping religion. I think I observed a strong desire on the part of those who seceded to introduce more warmth into religious exercises and a more practical manner of teaching and expounding the truths of Christianity.

If I could fasten upon any causes which will arrest this multiplication of sects, I might then be able to discern the existence at some future day of a sacerdotal caste in America. Extreme indifference to religion, if it pervaded all classes, would undoubtedly have this effect. The institution would degenerate into a mere form and then a pompous ceremonial. The priesthood would acquire power in proportion to the little interest which the general population felt in religion. And the manners of men would be molded into the form best calculated to fortify the worldly authority of the clergy. Where an universal indifference prevailed, there could be no incentive to diversity of opinion, and the distinction of sects would cease.

Will the same causes which threaten everywhere to demolish the idea of kingly rule be equally fatal to the notion of a single ruler of the universe? Is the unity of the Governor of the universe so allied with that of a human governor that if all traces of the last should be obliterated religion would be in danger of being undermined? If it be true that in other countries what are termed the enlightened classes are infidels at heart and only profess religion because they believe it is a check upon the masses, what will be the consequence when the thorough dissemination of instruction renders the great majority of the people well informed? I predict that if ever the spread of equality is fatal to the notion of unity in religion, it will not give rise to a plurality of gods; it will sweep all religion from the face of the earth, and satan will be literally unchained to turn earth into hell. I cannot but believe that when the North American continent contains a population of one or two hundred millions, all speaking the same language, and impelled by an irresistible curiosity to make inquiry into everything, that when the sameness of manners and sameness of dialect have opened free access to everyone's thoughts and schemes, it will exert an influence such as has never been witnessed upon the progress of knowledge, the social organization, and the religious institutions. But I am of opinion that the diffusion of equality will be fatal to the worldly authority of priests and that the right modeling the authority of civil magistrates will add wonderfully to the reverence for God. I find that the greater the range of inquiry of a single mind, the more diverse the objects which it takes in, the more certain it is of arriving at some general and presiding truths. There is nothing, therefore, in the diversified views of religious or political sects which is hostile to the notion of a Supreme Governor of the universe.

It is true, until very modern times, the popular mind was unaccustomed to meddle with the subject of religion. Now it approaches that as well as every other interest belonging to man and grapples with religious creeds with the same freedom which it employs in attacking political opinions. The unlimited range of inquiry subjects every institution to the most fearless and unscrupulous examination. Is there not danger, then, not that a passive indifference, but an universal unbelief may seize upon the minds of men and succeed in thoroughly rooting out the principle of religion?

There are some things which it is not in the power of man to accomplish, although these things have to do with his own interests exclusively. He cannot alter the structure of the human understanding, nor extirpate the affections of the heart. In every estimate or conjecture which we may form of the destiny of our race, we are safe in reposing upon these as undeniable truths. We can make no certain calculation in regard to individuals so as to say what their conduct will be under particular circumstances; but with regard to the race of mankind, we may predict with absolute certainty. We are obliged to believe that the religious sentiment will never be extinguished upon the same, although not any higher, ground than that which convinces that insanity or idiocy will not be the lot of the human species, or that the private affections and desires which have animated the heart since the first formation of man to the present time will never be eradicated.

CHAPTER II | INSTITUTIONS FOR THE EDUCATION OF
THE PEOPLE

THE great use of popular education, in a political view, consists in its incapacitating the people for any other than free institutions. Education tames ambitious men and presents new motives and a new theater of action. It trains the people to a due sense of their weight in society, gives them new habits, new modes of thinking, and a different style of manners. In this way they not only acquire a decided taste for such institutions — they become morally unable to adopt any other. When the great bulk of the population is uneducated, a few men of ill-regulated ambition, banded together, may wield an irresistible influence in the community, but where popular instruction is widely disseminated, the additional power which is imparted to the mass acts as a perpetual counterpoise to this ambition. If the man who craves after public distinction is well informed and expert in debate, so also will be the sons of the people. The former may set himself about studying the people and may calculate upon success in proportion to his adroitness in moving their prejudices, but the latter acquire an equal facility in diving into the depths of all his motives. Those qualities which were dangerous when confined to a few will be of unspeakable advantage when dispersed among a very numerous body. Education, then, is a constituent part of the plan of free institutions.

In some countries politicians who are bent upon their own aggrandizement acquire an exaggerated notion of the importance of striking upon the imaginations of the people. But this is an instrument difficult to use where a system of popular instruction is introduced. Knowledge, information, habits of reflection, especially where these are employed about the daily business of life, act as a wonderful damper upon all flights of the imagination. Nothing is more amusing and at the same time more instructive than to witness the awkward behavior of some men of untaught or unteachable minds in a country where the people have acquired an elevated position. They want to imitate the great men of other countries, but for want of acquaintance with the temper of the times every step they take places them in a false position and reveals difficulties which they are unable to surmount. They become entangled in the web they had woven for others. If they move onward, they perhaps make themselves amenable to the laws; if they falter and stumble, they are the subject of scorn; if they make good their retreat, they are covered with ridicule. It is from constant experience of the unsuitableness of those arts of ambition which were formerly so successful that the active spirits in a democratic community are gradually inured to new modes of thinking and acting. They acquire a clearer insight into the scope and aim of the institutions under which they live. They strive to render themselves eminently great by being eminently useful. And as this opens in the paths of eloquence, learning, and every species of intellectual effort, an almost boundless field of ambition, the altered temper which they acquire communicates an influence to others. The example once set is soon erected into the fashion, is incorporated into the national manners, and becomes the standard of conduct for succeeding generations. So true it is that the diffusion of education both elevates the people and tames the ambition of public men. No man in the United States dreams of running the career of Cromwell or Bonaparte. Intellectual distinction, capacity for business, large and generous views of patriotism are the aim of everyone, even in those countries where the noise of this revolution is just beginning to be heard. Such statesmen as Guizot, Brougham and Lowndes now rise up in society and take the place of the Richelieus and Straffords of former days. The power which it is necessary to confer upon public men is not so great as it was because the people are now able to do for themselves a great many things which were once obliged to be devolved upon others; and the authority which is exercised by government is wonderfully tempered in practice in consequence of the course of discipline which the minds of all public men have to pass through.

This alteration in the structure of society which is brought about solely by the elevation of the popular mind is full of important consequences. As it sets bounds to the personal influence of ambitious men, it presents a natural obstacle to the introduction of monarchical or aristocratic institutions and disposes all the artificial governments to imbibe some of the spirit and temper which belong to free institutions. In the early stages of society the authority of a few men of commanding character may be highly salutary, although that authority may not be strictly bounded. But the employment of this instrument ceases with the advancement of society, at least where that advancement is general and not confined to the superior classes. In other words, when popular instruction is diffused the authority of goverment is abridged because the people are then able to stand by themselves.

It is no inconsiderable argument in favor of a system of general education that it tends greatly to preserve the identity of the language among all classes of the population and consequently to maintain civilization. Where no such system exists in a country of only tolerable extent, the people of different districts very soon fall into the use of different dialects which by and by become distinct languages. The simplest elements of education, the knowledge how to read and write, uphold the standard of the language and by so doing maintain the standard of the laws and manners. Newspapers, which are the genuine fruit of education, exercise the same influence. The unexampled circulation which these journals have reached in the United States is undoubtedly one reason why the uniformity of the written and spoken language is so well preserved. If then we do not confine our view to the present inhabited part of the United States, but consider that all North America is destined to be peopled from the Anglo-Norman stock, the benefits resulting from a thoroughly diffused education are incalculable. The present territory of the union will easily contain one hundred and fifty millions of people, and the use of a common tongue among this vast population will exert a mighty influence upon the progress of society. For as the difference of languages is one of the greatest obstacles to the diffusion of civilization, the doing away with this difference will cause a greater amount of civilization to bear upon the ruder and less cultivated portion of this great commonwealth. And as the influence of America upon Europe will be prodigiously augmented, the nations of the old world will be brought more and more within the circle of American civilization. People who speak the same language look upon each other in some sort as members of one family. Those who speak different languages are sometimes very little disposed to regard each other as fellow creatures. The easy communication and sympathy which the prevalence of one common dialect introduces is singularly favorable to the spread of all sorts of improvement. The minds of Great Britain are now chiefly exerted for the people of Great Britain. Those of France and Germany for the people of those countries. But if all Europe spoke one common tongue, the intellect of any one country would be an addition to the stock of general intelligence. If the people of the American States had spoken different languages, there would perhaps have been no union; at any rate the advance of knowledge and civilization would have been materially retarded. The influence which has been exerted upon European society in consequence of French or English, the language of the two most enlightened nations of that continent, being spoken in all the great capitals, is very perceptible to anyone whose attention has been drawn to the subject. More intelligence and a greater amount of civilization have been introduced into St. Petersburg and Hamburg, Copenhagen and Stockholm, Vienna and Berlin, and the effect has been felt more or less in the remotest provinces of those countries. But it would be very difficult to calculate the amazing influence which would have been exerted if all Europe had spoken one language.

Before the American territory is peopled with one hundred and fifty millions it will probably be divided into distinct confederacies, and the identity of the language will contribute powerfully to a good understanding among those separate communities. It is the maintenance of one civilization, not the maintenance of one union, which we are most deeply interested in. Identity of language in some degree takes the place of an actual equality among men. The Scottish highlanders and lowlanders were until a very recent period like two distinct nations inclosed within the same nation. The spread of the English language among both has broken down the barriers which separated them as completely as if they had been distinct orders of men. The laws, the manners, and the intelligence of the more cultivated districts were quickly diffused among all when all were enabled to understand each other. Nothing contributes so much to the action of mind upon mind as placing men on an equality; nothing so much to civilization as this action of mind upon mind; and nothing so much to the maintenance of free institutions as the equal diffusion of civilization.

Leibnitz conceived the idea of an universal language, but he did not carry the thought further than to suggest the practicability of a language which should be common to the learned. He did not venture to propose to himself the idea of all the nations of a great continent containing one or two hundred millions of people possessing a lan-

guage which should be the familiar dialect of all classes.* Nevertheless, it would be an achievement of infinitely greater importance to
the progress of the human understanding. Profound and inquisitive
minds derive the materials upon which they work chiefly from the
unlearned; and the unlearned derive their incitements to exertion
from the learned. The observation and analysis of the minds of other
men is the foundation of much the greatest part of human philosophy,
and the broader the field of vision, the more exact and comprehensive
will be the results. One of the principal impediments to the progress
of knowledge consists in the extensive prevalence of what may be
termed class opinions in the different systems of thought. These opinions were originally taken up from a narrow view of human nature, and
many of them are gradually discarded by the learned themselves,
but a great number are still preserved because they render philosophy
a sealed book. If we compare a Chinese or Hindoo system of laws or
of ethical science with works of the same kind which have come down
to us from Greece and Rome, and if we run a comparison between
these last and similar productions of English or American origin, we
shall be made aware of the wholesome influence which has been exerted upon some of the most important human interests by opening a
wide field for observation and inquiry. The attrition of the popular
mind does not merely render a system of philosophy or of laws more
level to the common apprehension; it renders all human speculation
more solid, coherent, and comprehensive.

Small and insignificant beginnings often give rise to important consequences and influence the destiny of generations through the longest lapse of time. The system of common school education, which
originated in New England when the colony was a mere handful, has
now spread over nearly all the American states and has contributed
more than any other cause to preserve the identity of the language, to

---

* Leibnitz, in "Nouveaux Essais de l'entendement," B. IV., ch. VI., hints at the
possibility of inventing a universal language. But in his letters to Mr. Oldenburg,
he contemplates only the construction of a philosophical language. [Gottfried Wilhelm von Leibniz (or Leibnitz) (1646–1716); his major philosophical work,
Nouveaux Essais sur l'Entendement Humain (Paris, 1703), is an extended dialogue
with John Locke and follows the order of argument in Locke's *Essay on Human
Understanding*; it was not published until 1765. Henry Oldenburg (1615?–1677),
natural philosopher and man of letters, born in Germany, came to England about
1640, one of the charter members of the Royal Society (1660) for which, as secretary, he carried on a large international correspondence. Grimke added the note to
the second edition.]

advance civilization, and to bind those republics together in a firm and beneficent union. When this system is introduced among a population of fifty or a hundred millions, it will present a spectacle from which the whole race of mankind will be able to derive instruction.

It has been supposed that government has properly nothing to do with the education of the people, that it is an affair which concerns the private citizen exclusively, and does not fall within the province of the legislator. But the maxim, "laissez nous faire," must not be interpreted in such a way as to destroy its own value. The whole body of laws, the direct design of which is to promote the good government of the community, the civil, criminal, and commercial codes, all interfere necessarily with the behavior of individuals; yet, it is admitted that they do not lie within the range of the maxim. I do not know that any precise line can be drawn between those actions which affect the public weal and those which have a relation to private persons only. For as no system of legislation can avoid interfering to some extent with the conduct of individuals, so there is no scheme of private conduct but what may affect the whole community. It is not because there is any exact and definite distinction between the two classes of private and public actions that government is bound to interfere in one instance and yet to abstain in another. It depends upon who can most effectually and most advantageously, for both government and people, preside over the one and the other.

Governments, in many instances, originated colleges and other institutions of learning and benevolence. Government first set on foot newspapers. By anticipating the existence of these important instruments of science and information, the time was hastened when the people appropriated them to their own use. There are some subjects which fall under the superintendence of government in the early stages of society which cease to belong to it when a people have risen up. And there are others where the care exercised by government becomes more intense in proportion as free institutions take root.

There is one sure test which may be applied to all such questions, one, however, which is not capable of being employed in any but a democratic republic. This test is afforded by the rule of the majority; not the majority of today or tomorrow, but the majority of a considerable series of years. We may be quite sure that if the people themselves agree that government shall undertake the management of a particular interest, and adhere to this agreement after long experience of its effects, the arrangement is a wise and salutary one. It is possible for the majority temporarily to oppress the minority. But it is a much more difficult matter than is generally supposed for it to persist in so doing. It is impossible in a country of free institutions, in a country where the electors number three millions, to present any such prominent distinctions in the circumstances of different classes as to insure the rule of a fixed majority, if it is disposed premeditatedly and of set purpose to run counter to the substantial interests of the minority. Any such effort will forever terminate in converting the minority into the majority. It may frequently happen that on the first proposition of a most wholesome and beneficial law, the minds of many men may be taken by surprise, and that it will require a good degree of reflection on their part to be convinced of its propriety. That the majority have agreed to it; that is to say, that a body of individuals, no way distinguishable in their habits and condition of life from the great body of the minority have given their consent to a particular enactment is strong "prima facie" evidence of its reasonableness; and if this enactment remains in the statute book for a considerable period, it is almost conclusive evidence of its wisdom. I observe that at the present day, in New York and in all of the New England states but one, there are laws prohibiting the sale of ardent spirits. One can hardly imagine a case where the interference of government with private conduct is more direct and imperative than it is here. But it is very difficult to conceive any case where private conduct is capable of exercising a deeper and more extensive influence upon the public weal. These laws have been too recently passed to enable us to say with certainty whether they will stand. I am disposed to think that ultimately they will prevail; that although there may be fluctuations of public opinion leading to their alternate repeal and re-enactment, they will in the end conciliate the minds of the great bulk of the population and bear down all opposition.

The difficulty, then, of distinguishing in theory between those things which the civil magistrate should take under his jurisdiction and those which should be left to the discretion of private individuals is resolved in practice by the simple rule of the majority. Where government is truly the representative of the people, we can afford to trust it with the doing of many things which under other circumstances it would be desirable to place beyond its reach. Where it is a self-existing authority, it is too prone to intermeddle with private conduct; it seeks to thrust itself into every corner of society because its own influence is increased in proportion as the people are rendered dependent. But this is a mistake which can rarely be committed in a republic where those who are affected by the laws are themselves the authors of the laws.

It is remarkable that while Mr. Hume is in favor of a strict super-intendence of religious interests by government that he would leave every other department of instruction to the voluntary and unassisted efforts of individuals. In America the rule has been entirely reversed. There, the people claim the interposition of their state governments in securing a system of popular instruction, while they deny the right or the utility of interfering in any degree with religion. And this system has been attended with incalculable advantages to both govern-ment and people. It is the existence of an established church which in England has opposed so many obstacles to the introduction of a system of popular instruction. A fear has been constantly felt by Episcopalians lest, in that course of training and discipline which the minds of youth undergo at school, opportunity might be taken to in-still notions unfavorable to the doctrines of the Church of England; while on the other hand dissenters of all denominations have taken a totally opposite view and have concluded that there was even greater probability that principles adverse to their own particular creeds might be insinuated into the minds of their children. A system of common school education established in England and headed by an ecclesi-astical hierarchy might have so many bad features as to counterbal-ance the good of which it would be otherwise productive; while the same system in America, originated by representatives of the people and superintended by them, would be fraught with unmixed advan-tage. A country in which free institutions are sought to be perpetuated presents a strong case for the interposition of the government in every-thing which concerns popular instruction. The system of common school education is applied to the formation of the mind at a period of life when it is too feeble to originate any scheme of mental dis-cipline for itself. And the great object is so to train the youth of the country that when they come to be men they may render themselves useful members of the great commonwealth in which they live. And it is a consideration of great importance that where the population of a country is well instructed, the interference of the legislator is unnecessary in a multitude of instances where it would otherwise be demanded.

When education is widely diffused the whole population is introduced into active and useful life at a much earlier period than could be the case if the means of instruction were limited and difficult to be obtained. This necessarily constitutes an immense accession to the strength and resources of the state. The great body of the people then become not merely the bone and sinews of the community, they become its soul and its vivifying principle. Lord Bacon, like Cicero, complains that men who have obtained a tolerably advanced age are frequently withdrawn from public usefulness when their influence and counsels would be most profitable to the public. This great man would not have had so much reason to indulge in this lamentation if, instead of the brutish and ignorant population by which he was surrounded in the beginning of the seventeenth century, he had lived in the midst of an instructed people. In the United States a very considerable part of the business of society falls under the management of young men. The liberal professions, the legislative assemblies, all the branches of trade, of manufactures and the mechanic arts derive immense accessions from their exertions. And it is perhaps one reason why all these pursuits have caught so liberal a spirit and are freed from the cumbrous forms and antiquated usages which hang around them in other countries. The effect is similar to that which is produced by the substitution of free in the place of slave labor. General education imparts general freedom of thought. And this freedom of thought is the parent of vigorous exertion, of self-reliance, of that thorough sense of responsibility which causes everyone to walk alertly and yet cautiously over the difficult paths of life.

Until recently, no one was eligible to the French House of Deputies until he was forty. This fact sheds an abundance of light upon the social organization in France. The laws are a pretty sure index of the manners, and where we find the age of political majority raised so high we may be very certain that the age of civil manhood is also high, and that both the minds and characters of individuals are slow in maturing. In some countries, the hour glass of life is more than half run out before the faculties of men can be made available and effective for any part of the business of society. At present, the age of admission into the House of Deputies is thirty years, and contemporary with this alteration of the constitution a great change took place in reference to popular education. Formerly, the government appropriated twenty-five thousand dollars for that purpose. At present, twenty-five millions are granted. More than forty-two thousand schools are maintained by the state, the departments, and the cantons, while at the same time, the private schools have also been augmented. For although the laws are an index of the manners, yet in a country where a system of artificial institutions has existed for a very long period government may, nowithstanding, originate the most important improvements and thus bring about a change of the manners themselves. The whole number of pupils at school in France is very nearly three millions, and the cost of primary instruction alone is estimated at two and a half millions of dollars.

In the United States, it is very common to see men by the time they are thirty already established in some useful and profitable employment. At that age we see them conducting with judgment and ability an extensive practice as lawyers or physicians or embarked in the most difficult branches of trade. It is evident that such a constitution of society must contribute materially to augment both the moral and physical resources of the community, and that it must be equally instrumental in giving strength and solidity to the political institutions.

Those persons who are prone to look upon the dark side of human nature and to magnify the licentiousness of the present age would derive great instruction from looking into the interior of society as it was only one hundred and fifty years ago, and that among some of the most enlightened European states. The system of common or parochial schools was established in Scotland in 1696. Fletcher of Saltoun, the celebrated Scotch patriot and a person eminently distinguished for soundness of judgment and purity of character, writing about this time, draws the following vivid picture of the general state of manners in that country: "There are at this day in Scotland (besides a great many poor families provided for by the church boxes, with others who, by living on bad food, fall into various diseases) two hundred thousand people begging from door to door. These are not only no way advantageous but a very grievous burden to so poor a country. And though the number of them be perhaps double to what it was formerly by reason of the present great distress, yet in all times there have been about one hundred thousand of these vagabonds who have lived without any regard or subjection to the laws of the land or even to those of God and nature: fathers incestuously accompanying with their own daughters, the son with the mother, and the brother with the sister. No magistrate could ever discover or be informed which way one in a hundred of those wretches died, or ever that they were baptized. Many murders have been discovered among them, and they are not only an unspeakable oppression to poor tenants (who, if they give not bread or some kind of provision to perhaps forty such villains in one day are sure to be insulted by them), but they rob many poor people who live in houses distant from any neighborhood. In years of plenty, many thousands of them meet together in the mountains where they feast and riot for many days, and at country weddings, markets, burials, and other like public occasions they are to be seen, both men and women, perpetually drunk, cursing, blaspheming, and fighting together." [1]

This state of abject poverty and wild disorder cannot be attributed to the density of the population. Scotland, at the close of the seventeenth century, contained hardly a million of inhabitants. By the census of 1841 it contained more than two millions and a half. But at the former period the Scotch were destitute of education; destitute, therefore, of those moral capacities which could alone lay open to them the resources of nature. At present they are among the best educated people in Europe, and the condition of the country is totally changed from what it was when Fletcher wrote. In the place of a lawless band of marauders, traversing the country and inflicting all sorts of injuries upon unoffending people, we have, from one end of the country to the other, a shrewd, active, and industrious population, the great bulk of whom possess a very reasonable share of the comforts of life and live in a state of strict subordination to the laws. Doubtless, we may find very great defects in the social organization of any country, and the disposition to magnify these may even sometimes be a favorable symptom of the general soundness of society. It may indicate that a very high standard of excellence is constantly held up by everyone, which, although it can never lead to the attainment of all which is conceivable, yet is the only means of reaching so much as is actually attainable. But to make any comparison between the moral and indus-

1. [Andrew Fletcher (1655–1716), known as "Fletcher of Saltoun," *Two Discourses Concerning the Affairs of Scotland Written in the Year 1698* (Edinburgh, 1698), the second of which proposed sweeping measures of social reform to cure Scotland of beggars and vagrants.]

trial state of Scotland in the seventeenth century and its condition since the system of parochial schools has been matured and borne its fruit would be to forego the use of our faculties. We might as well institute a comparison between the annals of bedlam and those of New England or Ohio.

What will be the effect, ultimately, of placing men so much on an equality as the general diffusion of knowledge supposes is an inquiry at once novel and interesting. The great qualities which we admire in the eminent men who take a lead in public affairs are in very great part formed by their power of acting upon other men. But this power depends for its exercise very much on the structure of society. A state which contains a handful of intelligent and sagacious individuals, all the rest of society being condemned to a state of intellectual inferiority, presents the most favorable opportunity for the development of those qualities. Men who are surrounded by the ignorant feel a stimulus to exertion, in one walk of ambition at any rate, the force of which it is difficult to calculate. Under such circumstances they are inspired with a wonderful degree of assurance, resolution, and self-command: mighty agents in counterfeiting as well as in making great qualities. But if we contrive to scatter knowledge and so to multiply the number of independent thinkers among the people themselves, much of this artificial stimulus to an artificial greatness is taken away. It becomes then a much more difficult matter to manage men, less easy to control their wills so as to render them subservient to the designs of ambitious leaders. In such a condition of society, the aspiring man sees a great number of sagacious individuals, not merely in the sphere in which he moves, but interposed between himself and the people, and in the ranks of the people themselves. His power is by little and little frittered away, until at last it becomes doubtful whether there will any longer be opportunity for the display of those qualities which have hitherto attracted so large a share of the public attention.

And admitting that this will be the consequence, it is clear that society will be infinitely the gainer, not merely because qualities which depend so much for their formation on the ignorance of other men must necessarily contain a great deal that is factitious and superficial, but because the community as a body will be rendered wiser and stronger and the political institutions be made firmer and more durable.

There is one inconvenience attending society when knowledge is widely circulated and the principle of equality consequently gains strength — the feeling of envy is apt to pervade all classes of men. Everyone seems to forget that although the dispersion of knowledge does in truth break down many of the distinctions which before existed between individuals, that it cannot destroy the natural inequality which the God of nature has stamped upon different minds. Everyone, however, fancies that he is capable of everything. All want to be great, and yet are too indolent to make themselves wise. And as chagrin and disappointment must follow the indulgence of such vain hopes and pretensions, men instantly fall into the deplorable vice of detracting from the merit of those who have run before them in the attainment of reputation. If they cannot reach the object of their ambition, the next most desirable thing is to prevent others from obtaining it. In a barbarous or half-civilized community men slay each other to make room for themselves. In a highly-civilized one, they rarely go further than to wish the death of each other.

But although this is to a considerable extent the character of every society where knowledge is diffused and people are placed pretty much on a footing of equality, yet it is attended with so many compensations that a wise man is not at liberty to desire a change. We must avail ourselves of every spring of improvement which is planted in human nature. If we cannot rely solely upon the noble ambition of excellence for its own sake, we may very reasonably tolerate some other qualities of an inferior kind, provided they are productive of effects any way similar. Our nature is so admirably adjusted that even our defects are often converted into instruments for our improvement. But there is this very important distinction to be made: that we intend our virtues shall redound to the good of society, whereas we intend no such thing with regard to our vices. These are made to produce results without our knowing it through the interposition of an overruling providence. Root out envy from the human bosom and we take away one of the strongest incentives to all sorts of exertion, from the lowest, the mere acquisition of wealth, to the highest, the perfectionment of our moral and intellectual nature.

In surveying the extensive provision which is made in America for the promotion of popular instruction, the inquiry may very naturally be made: what is to be the result of the plan if it is not turned to some account reaching beyond the years of puberty? The system of common school education gives the ability to read and write, but the possession of this ability is one thing and the application of it after leaving school is another and very different thing. In other words, even admitting that the whole youth of the country are taught those important arts, what will it profit them if, after the acquision is made, it is not employed in getting knowledge? The ability to read and write is merely mechanical — it is only a means to the attainment of an end. If the means is possessed and yet the end totally neglected, in what respect is society better off than when this mechanical art was entirely withheld from the general population?

I imagine, however, that when the matter is considered attentively, the deficiencies of society will be found to be much less than this view supposes and I have purposely placed it in the strongest possible light. It is true, when we take a survey of some of the best educated communities, the United States and Holland for example, we are struck with the unintellectual character of the masses. But the fault is in ourselves: we compare the condition of these masses with that of the most cultivated class, instead of comparing it with the condition of those masses prior to the diffusion of education. In pursuing the first course we are disappointed, perhaps even shocked; in adopting the last, we will find that our most sanguine expectations are realized. Reading and reflection, unless carried beyond a certain point, cannot be productive of what we term striking results; and yet when employed short of this point, they may have a decidedly intellectual influence. There is in reality much more read by the people than is generally supposed, only it is not visible to those who live in the full blaze of knowledge. The single fact that a greater number of newspapers are circulated in the United States than in the whole of continental Europe is pretty good evidence that the Americans turn the ability to read to some practical purpose. The reading of the daily journals is an occupation to which the most accomplished minds are addicted for they contain, with all their demerits, a great part of the history of the times in which we live. They do not contain this information in the gross, as is the case in works professedly historical, but they present the transactions and events of the day minutely and in detail; and although the narrative is on this account less imposing, it is doubtful whether it is not more instructive. This species of reading, although it produces in some a disrelish for any other study, has a contrary effect with others. It whets the appetite for knowledge, opens up the connection between those things which are contained in the newspapers and the ten thousand other things which can only be alluded to by them. A great many persons among the mechanical, agricultural, and commercial classes are thus beguiled into habits of reading who would never otherwise have taken up a book. Newspapers first created a general taste for reading, and reading is of great assistance in grasping and analyzing the information which newspapers contain. The profitable use which may be made of these journals is in exact proportion to the general stock of knowledge which individuals possess. Facts related by them, which a casual observer would pass over as signifying nothing, may with minds of reading and reflection possess a great deal of meaning and conduct to very important conclusions.

The system of popular education has many negative advantages which are not inferior to the positive benefits which it bestows. The training of the hearts of youth is very properly confided to the domestic circle, but intellectual occupation, the acquisition of the mere rudiments of learning, exercises a decidedly moral influence upon the character. If it only to some extent shuts out the temptation to vice, it prevents the lower appetites from gaining the mastery.

In Sismondi's *History of the Italian Republics* (iv, 193) we have some insight into the state of popular education in the republic of Florence in the fourteenth century.[2] The city then contained one hundred and fifty thousand inhabitants. In the territory beyond the city, there were about seven hundred thousand. From eight to ten thousand children learned to read, twelve hundred learned arithmetic, five or six hundred logic or grammar. In Scotland, at the present day, one eleventh of the whole population go to school. In New England and New York, this proportion is about one fourth or one fifth, in other words, three fourths of the children between five and fifteen years of age go to school. The proportion then in Florence, which was greatly advanced beyond any of the other Italian states in this as well as in every other respect, was surprisingly small. It was only about the eightieth part of the population. It is exceedingly small, even when compared with England, where one in nineteen, or with Ireland where one in thirty-two, of the whole population are trained to the first rudiments of education.

The moral influence exerted upon society in these different communities has been in about the same proportion as the diffusion of edu-

2. [Jean Charles Léonard Simonde de Sismondi (1773–1842), *History of the Italian Republics in the Middle Ages* (Paris, 1809–1818), 16 vols.]

cation. It was less in Florence than in Ireland, less in Ireland than in England, and in England less than in Scotland, New England, or New York. The register of crimes shows this fact very conclusively. The number of criminals in Ireland is about one in five hundred; in England, one in nine hundred and sixty; in Scotland, New England, and New York, out of the city, one in about five thousand. We have no materials from which to form any exact calculation as to Florence. But we do know that it contained an exceedingly disorderly population and that it was a scene of the most sanguinary civil feuds during the period to which I have referred. The riots of an American city are a mere episode in the history of the country; those of Florence were barbarous in the extreme, were fomented by the chief citizens, and were of so frequent occurrence as to constitute the principal part of its annals.

There is still a difficulty, however, connected with this subject which demands attention. All the people cannot be expected to be educated. Even admitting that with the munificent provision which is made for the establishment of schools in New England, New York, and Ohio, all the males receive the first rudiments of learning, it would be going too far to suppose that all will get much further than those rudiments and become well informed. We will probably have in those sections, and ultimately throughout the whole country, a better instructed people than have ever existed. But very many will still remain wrapped up in ignorance. The number of the electors then will be much greater than that of the educated. Whereas, the theory of democratic institutions seems to require that all who exercise the right of suffrage should be at least tolerably instructed. In other words, the administration of public affairs in America, both in the federal and state governments, gives rise to a multitude of questions of great magnitude and complexity which cannot be understandingly apprehended without information and reflection. Nevertheless, the people are either directly or indirectly invested with the whole power of deciding upon these questions; and yet, numbers are very ignorant in relation to them. How are we to reconcile this plain discrepancy between the demand for knowledge on the one hand and the lack of it on the other? The difficulty is startling at first view. It is one which has constantly exercised the minds of the most thoughtful and judicious men in the United States.

In the first place, then, it must be recollected that a like analogy runs through every department of human affairs; that political knowledge is like every other kind of knowledge; that it is subject to the same rules which apply to all other human interests; and that if a slight observation does disclose the strangest incongruities, greater attention will reveal a system of compensations by which the mischief is in a great degree neutralized. In the whole circle of human interests there is hardly an instance where theory and practice are united to any great extent. It is one of the most striking and beneficent provisions in the constitution of our nature that the combination of the two is not always necessary in order to act efficiently and correctly; that on the contrary, our conduct may be determined with the utmost promptitude and regularity without our being able to analyze our thoughts, that is, without our comprehending the process by which we are impelled to act. The commonest laborers will skillfully apply all the mechanical powers without understanding their nature. Millions of men are engaged in the processes of manufactures without any insight into the world of knowledge of chemistry and natural philosophy which their occupations seem to imply. Many who successfully and skillfully pursue the professions of law and medicine are unacquainted with the philosophy of those sciences. There are no subjects upon which a greater amount of thought and learning have been employed than upon theology and ethics; yet the religious and the moral are to be found among the unlearned as well as among the enlightened. The analogy may be traced through every interest appertaining to human life. Indeed, if the ability to act were dependent upon knowledge of the machinery by means of which we act, our condition would be more deplorable than that of the brutes.

It is worthy of observation, also, that on all the important questions which agitate a civilized community, a wide difference of opinion exists among the enlightened as well as among the uninstructed. The utmost which we can reasonably demand is that public affairs should be conducted by those whose vision is the keenest and most comprehensive and whose intentions are the most upright.

But even such minds are constantly ranged upon different sides. Perhaps the difficulty is more apparent than real. It may be that it is the egotism and narrow views of politicians which give an importance to questions to which they are not entitled, and that those who are uninstructed, by being less ambitious and consequently more impartial, serve to moderate the ultra views of politicians of all parties. A great nation may do great injustice to itself by imagining that its substantial interests are dependent upon the existence of a central bank or the enactment of a high tariff. Public men feel as if they must have a wide field opened on which to make a display of their abilities, and such questions present the opportunity, although the advancement of the country in riches and power would not be sensibly affected one way or the other whether such schemes were adopted or discarded.

But although the difficulties which beset free institutions are great, it is plain that there is no way of elevating the great mass of the population but by disseminating the benefits of education. If the mischiefs complained of are not cured, they are at any rate greatly abridged. The question is not whether the social organization and the political institutions of a representative republic are preferable to such a picture as our imaginations may draw, but whether they are not the best which we can reasonably hope to attain; whether they do not present a state of society infinitely better than that of Spain, Italy, or Russia, better even than that which exists in Great Britain where the laws and the manners have a fairer aspect and a more wholesome influence than in any other European state only because they approach nearer to the model which the American commonwealth has set up.

CHAPTER III | MILITARY INSTITUTIONS

THERE is no fact in the history of our race more striking than its addiction to military pursuits. From the earliest period and in every form of society, whether barbarous or civilized, war has been one of the habitual occupations of mankind. It might almost be supposed that it answered some necessary want of our nature and that the propensities which lead to it were as much entitled to be considered a part of the original constitution of man as any of those which rule over his ordinary actions.

The least insight into human nature apprises us of the great variety of faculties which are planted in our constitution. Qualities which tend to raise the species to a condition almost above humanity are immediately associated with others which sink it to a level with the brutes. And it is plain that if the former were not capable of exerting a control over the last, the human mind would be a mere jumble of contradictory properties, each acting with the force of a separate instinct and giving rise to actions the most incoherent and unmeaning imaginable.

It is true, war is sometimes productive of beneficial effects. In the absence of any more powerful stimulants, it scourges the lazy elements of society, brings to light some dormant spring of improvement, and gives a totally different direction to human affairs from what was intended. If our bad qualities are not controlled by ourselves, a higher power has ordained that they shall be instrumental of good in some other way. By rendering it necessary for individuals to act under circumstances of the greatest peril and amid the most deplorable calamities which can fall upon society, war calls out some of the noblest qualities of our nature, inspiring some with a lofty patriotism and self-denial and training others to humility, resignation, and fortitude. If conquering Rome had not penetrated a great part of Europe, and if the hordes from the northern and central part of that continent had not in turn penetrated Italy, it may be doubted whether civilization would have made much progress up to the present day beyond the confines of the Italian peninsula. Christianity and Roman civilization lie at the foundation of our modern civilization, and I do not see how it would have been possible to diffuse one or the other if there had not been that complete mingling of races consequent upon the Roman conquests and the irruptions of the barbarians. I believe that if it had not been for those events, the inhabitants of Britain, France, Germany, and Prussia would have continued down to the present time the same wandering and barbarous tribes which they were in the times of Cæsar and Tacitus. That there was no spring of improvement within is demonstrated by the fact that they had remained in a stationary condition for more than two thousand years. If then there had not been some powerful causes set in motion from without, there is every reason to believe that those countries which have made such prodigious advances in knowledge and in all the arts of life would still be inhabited by an ignorant and barbarous race.

The subsequent wars which have prevailed among the European states have probably contributed to produce an effect of a similar character. Doubtless the guilty individuals who fomented them were only animated by a desire to gratify their selfish ambition, and they have been subservient to ends which they neither desired or contemplated. I will only take as an example the wars which scourged Europe from the commencement of the French Revolution to the general peace in 1815. Assuredly no one can take a survey of European society before and since that period without noticing the immense progress which has been made in knowledge, industry, and the arts, and the corresponding improvement which the social and political organization has undergone in that quarter of the globe.

The influence which these wars have exerted is similar to the effect produced in the United States by breaking down the distinction of ranks. Civilization has circulated more freely in consequence of the last, and the wars of the French Revolution, by contributing to break down the barriers which separated the European states from each other, have brought the inhabitants of all to a more intimate acquaintance and connection than existed before. The intercourse of all kinds which now takes place, political, commercial, and personal, between different communities is greater than it once was between the people of the same country. Civilization is contagious; the manners of a cultivated people exercise an amazing influence upon others which are less advanced, and the European nations which were once distinguished by the greatest inequalities in this respect are gradually assuming the character of one great commonwealth of civilized states.

These views conduct to others equally important. Historical works which, for the most part, contain a narrative of foreign and intestine wars would have been doubly instructive if their authors had constantly drawn the attention of their readers to the difference of races. I imagine it would be found that this difference lay at the bottom of nearly all those wars. China whose population is greater than that of all Europe has, with very inconsiderable exceptions, enjoyed profound tranquillity for more than two hundred years. During the same period, the European people of the same country, as well as of different countries, have been tearing each other to pieces. Let us take as an example a single historical work: Sismondi's *History of the Italian Republics*. What a flood of light would this profound and eloquent writer have shed upon the times of which he treats if he had throughout the whole work directed the attention of his readers to the original diversity of races and to the very slow process by which they were fused into each other. The mixture of Goths, Vandals, Lombards, Normans, and Saracens with the Italian population produced a total disorganization of society and made men of the same district, and even living within the walls of the same city, implacable enemies. I have no reference now to the times immediately succeeding the invasion of those hordes; for then it is plain enough, without the historian pointing to it, that the incongruous assemblage of peoples of different civilizations was a fruitful cause of disorders. I allude to periods much later, to the twelfth, thirteenth, and fourteenth centuries, when the descendants of all these various races inhabited Italy and when, notwithstanding intermarriages between them, the original lineaments of character had not disappeared. The same view might be taken of the intestine troubles of Spain, France, and Great Britain. We know that it is not much more than one hundred and fifty years since the Saxon and Norman population in this last country could be considered as completely amalgamated, and that the amalgamation of the Gaelic population of the highlands of Scotland with that of the rest of the country dates from a much more recent period.

This suggests another important view which is, that in proportion as the various races have been melted into each other in the same country, in proportion as they have tended to form one homogeneous population, the character of war became gradually changed. The different people no longer inhabited the same country, but belonged to different countries. Hence in very modern times, instead of domestic wars we have had foreign wars. The extraordinary uniformity of character in the population of the United States has undoubtedly been one great cause of the unprecedented tranquillity it has enjoyed at home. It is not merely that this sameness of character presents fewer points of actual difference, but it has led to a thorough intercourse between men of all classes and between those inhabiting different parts of the country.

No nation is composed of a greater variety of races than the United States. But the English type is predominant above all others. The emigrants who flock thither are from the most civilized parts of Europe. Although for the most part they belong to the inferior classes of society, their minds are more ductile on that very account — more capable of receiving impressions from the manners and institutions which surround them. They behold a high standard of civilization existing in the country. Their natural instincts impel them to imitate it since in no other way can they compete with the native inhabitants in the acquisition of comfort and independence. The older emigrants adhere to their own language. After a certain period of life it is difficult and irksome in the extreme to learn a new language. But their descendants do not find the same difficulty. Their dispositions and organs are more pliable. The intercourse between all parts of the population is so great that they insensibly acquire the language of the country and learn to regard that of their ancestors as a foreign tongue which is now both useless and unfashionable. This obstacle being surmounted, intermarriages take place. Their transactions of business lie with the natives, much more than with their own countrymen. American courts are opened to them when they have any difficulties to adjust. They must converse with their lawyers in English in order to make themselves understood. Their interests no less than a desire so natural to the human heart, to imitate those who have wealth, power, and intelligence, conspire to weld them thoroughly to the institutions among which they live. So that in process of time the English type promises to be not merely the predominant but the universal one.

The distinction of race may be regarded in a two-fold aspect, as it arises from physical or moral causes. When we speak of difference of race, we generally have reference to some variety of conformation and habits which has been wrought by physical causes. But there may be a difference superinduced by moral causes. For instance, independently of the varieties which have been noticed by philosophical writers, the political institutions of different countries may differ so widely from each other in their structure and influence as to render nations who have sprung from the same stock as alien to each other as if they had emerged from totally distinct tribes. And so also, the institutions of the same country may act so unequally upon different parts of the population as to create great diversity of habits, manners, and modes of thinking and so to estrange from each other men inhabiting the same country. It is in the power of governments then to create artificial races among their own population. Monarchical and aristocratical institutions, together with an imposing ecclesiastical hierarchy, may contribute to perpetuate distinctions long after the original lineaments of race have disappeared. So long as this is the case, the seeds of intestine war exist; and whatever foments intestine war acts in one way or another as a provocative to foreign war. Soon after the breaking out of the French Revolution, the party in the ascendancy waged war against some of the European governments in order to prevent their interference in re-establishing the odious privileges which divided one part of French society from another. And when strong government was established, war was still waged in order to keep down the insubordination of men of all parties at home.

There is one part of the policy of the American government which is entitled to great praise. I allude to the laws for the naturalization of foreigners. I will not stop to inquire into the propriety of a little shorter or a little longer residence in order to entitle to citizenship. The main design of the plan, which is that of a speedy naturalization of foreigners, is marked by the soundest wisdom. These laws have been regarded as something entirely new in the history of governments. And it is true that they do differ materially from the laws which exist in the European states. But they are pretty much the same as those which prevailed prior to the establishment of American independence. Similar laws were passed by the mother country for the purpose of encouraging emigration to a country which had a vast extent of fertile land and too few inhabitants to cultivate it. America, although its population is now greater than that of many of the kingdoms of Europe, has still an abundance of unoccupied land. The same reasons, therefore, which lead to the original enactment of these laws would prompt to their continuance.

But without denying that these laws offer strong inducements to emigration, it is doubtful whether the emigration would not be nearly as great without them. The immediate temptation to the inhabitants of densely-peopled countries to emigrate arises from the prospect of bettering their condition. The desire to become proprietors when before they were serfs, to acquire comfort and independence and so to raise their offspring reputably when otherwise they would have been sunk low in the scale of society, not to mention the absolute cravings of want among great numbers which make them satisfied with merely wages sufficient to uphold life; all these motives conspire to bring great crowds of people to the new world. Although they might not be admitted to the possession of political privileges for fifteen or twenty years after their arrival, they would enjoy freedom of religion and a larger share of civil liberty than falls to the lot of any European people.

But it is of infinite importance to assimilate as speedily as possible all parts of the American population, to melt down all the different races into one race and thus to produce the greatest harmony and agreement between the manners and the political institutions. This is a more powerful and convincing reason for the enactment of the naturalization laws of the United States than would be the mere desire to encourage emigration. Examine all history from the earliest records down to the present time and it will be found that the presence of different tribes in the same country, and yet separated from each other by unequal privileges and consequently by dissimilar habits, has been the most fruitful source of internal dissensions and civil disturbances. We know that the Roman patricians and plebeians were not originally different classes of the same people, but that they were in reality two different people, that they assumed the relation of different classes only in consequence of the laws which kept them asunder after they were incorporated into one commonwealth, and that Rome enjoyed no tranquillity until the laws were repealed. When this was effected the two people were easily melted into one, and a character of unity and solidity was imparted to the political institutions. If you traverse Italy or Germany, you will find vestiges everywhere of the same policy which guided Rome in its infancy. A close examination would probably disclose many traces still unobliterated of similar laws growing out of similar circumstances in almost all the large kingdoms of Europe. It was therefore a fine idea of the American government to begin at the beginning — to take speedy and effectual measures for fusing into one the diverse tribes of which its population would be composed. A monarchy or aristocracy may suppose that it is greatly for its interest to impose severe restrictions upon its foreign population, or even to make aliens of one part of its native population, as has been too often the case. But a republic is deeply concerned in smoothing as far as practicable all the inequalities and unevennesses which obstruct the intercourse of society, that so the political institutions may be adapted to the whole people and the whole people be made heartily interested in upholding those institutions. In 1708 an act was passed by the English Parliament for the naturalization of all Protestant aliens.[1] The *reasons* urged were that it would encourage industry, improve trade and manufactures, and repair the waste of the population by war. But one of the *motives* was to counterbalance the power of the landed aristocracy. The objection was that the new citizens would retain a fondness for their native country and, in time of war, act as spies and enemies, that they would insinuate themselves into places of trust and profit, become members of Parliament and by frequent intermarriages effect the extinction of the English race. The act was repealed in 1711. In 1751 another bill was introduced but failed. It was strenuously supported by Wm. Pitt (Chatham) and other enlightened members, but fell through in consequence of the same narrow and bigoted views which were urged in 1708.

Great numbers of people who now emigrate to America are Catholics and fears are entertained lest they should exercise an untoward influence upon the rest of the population. But these fears are without foundation. The institutions of the United States will protestantize the Roman Catholic religion, for Protestantism is a vigorous protest against both religious and political superstition, and whatever contributes to check the one contributes equally to check the other. Maryland was settled by Catholics, yet it is certain that the Protestant population have exerted a much more powerful influence upon them than they have exerted upon the Protestants. I can observe no difference in the manners and modes of thinking of the people of this state from

1. [For the second edition, Grimke added new matter from this sentence to the end of the paragraph.]

what I observe in other states. So true it is that in everything which addresses itself to the reason, the true policy of government consists in permitting the utmost latitude of thought and the freest exercise of conscience. To pursue an opposite course would be to fill a country with dissensions, perhaps civil war, which has hitherto enjoyed unparalleled tranquillity.

The risk which America has to encounter in the absence of those causes which ordinarily produce heartburnings and jealousies in other communities arises from the institution of slavery. There is no danger of any serious and lasting contest between the white and the black race. But it is possible for the white man of the North to fight the white man of the South through the black race. Such is the perversity of human nature that it will sometimes create differences where nature has made resemblances, and a diseased imagination may convert the white man of the South into a being of different race in order to enable him of the North to indulge in a misguided fanaticism.

But the security against this danger is after all very great. It consists in the substantial identity of the white population of the North and South which, although a gust of feeling may occasionally obscure the horizon, will force itself upon the attention of everyone and cement the two sections of the country until the natural period of their separation has arrived. A certain degree of zeal, of even enthusiasm, is always necessary to set the mind a-thinking and to enable it to apprehend the bearings and consequences of any important measure. It must never be supposed because passion and feeling mingle in public disputes that they are going to run away with the understandings of people. That passion and feeling only act as a healthful stimulus to the faculties, and by producing greater intensity of thought may ultimately conduct to conclusions very different, perhaps totally the reverse of those which were at first seized. There is a species of intelligence which is bottomed upon good sense and a sound judgment which is eminently unfavorable to an overindulgence in fanaticism. And there are no people who as a body are more distinguished for this same intelligence than are the people of the North.

The reader may suppose that I have lost sight of the subject on which this chapter professes to treat. Such is not the case however. But it is my desire to present a different view from what is usually taken. In other words, it is no part of my design to describe either the military institutions of any particular country or to make inquiry what system would most conduce to promote the power and aggrandizement of a nation. My object is the reverse: it is to examine very briefly those causes which have hitherto given rise to foreign and civil wars, and more especially to consider the train of events and that constitution of society which at the present day give promise of checking the propensity to war. For although war may have its uses, yet these uses may in the progress of time be exhausted. Not that there is any probability that wars will absolutely cease to be waged by nations, but the tendency of public opinion everywhere is such as to discountenance the practice. Not only do the interests of communities impel them in an opposite direction but, what is of infinitely more consequence, the understanding, the conviction that such is the case, is continually gaining strength. Foreign wars, so far as they are occasioned by the unequal civilization of different states, may become less frequent when civilization is more evenly diffused, not because the power of different nations will then be more equally balanced, for the reverse may be the case, but because a more equal civilization in all produces a superior civilization in each, and a high state of civilization, such at any rate as exists in our modern world, is absolutely incompatible with the habitual pursuit of war. So also civil wars may become much less frequent in consequence of the more thorough civilization which will exist among the population of the same state. For then the interests of different parts of the state will somehow or other be found to be better adjusted to each other and will more seldom be brought into violent conflict.

If, hitherto, appeals to the humanity and good sense of nations have been insufficient to put an end to the atrocious practice of war, a train of causes may be set in operation by the Governor of the universe which will accomplish the same end. The people of Europe may at least be made to see and to feel that their interests are identified with peace; and as the control of popular opinion upon the actions of the government is continually gaining ground, the same sense of interest which disinclines the people to war may disable rulers from making it.

When these causes have been in operation for a considerable period, when the wisdom which is learned from experience has had time to produce some sensible alteration in the habits of thinking prevalent among men, the moral sense will be powerfully and effectually awakened. It is amazing with what facility the human mind will reconcile itself to customs the most abhorrent to reason and the most revolting to humanity; and it is equally surprising how easily it may be weaned from them when new circumstances have arisen to produce a clear judgment and a sound state of feeling. For in what respect does the killing in war — in war which is not absolutely in self-defense — differ from private murder except that in the former case a great multitude of people have leagued together to do the deed and, by so doing, have organized among themselves a species of public opinion in order to drown remorse and to absolve from condemnation?

An almost total exemption from war is one of the memorable things in the history of the American republic. One war of short duration in a period of nearly seventy years is a phenomenon without a parallel in the history of European society.* It is true, America is removed to a distance from the great theater of modern wars. But the vast countries of South America are near at hand and present an arena for warfare much more tempting to that sort of cupidity which formerly impelled both people and governments to fall upon the weak and defenseless in order to aggrandize themselves. Rome, when it made war upon all the nations of Italy, was a more unequal match for them than the United States would be against all South America. But Rome and the United States have been placed in very different periods of the world.

But whatever may be the causes which have produced so marked and so general a disinclination to war among the American people, it was of the greatest importance that the experiment of peace as a part of the permanent policy of a state should be fairly made. The experiment has proved that an abstinence from military pursuits is not only consistent with the highest civilization, the greatest national power, and the most enduring prosperity, but that it contributes directly and powerfully to the furtherance of these ends. It has proved that the passion for war bears no resemblance to any one of those natural instincts which are planted in the constitution of man for the purpose of stirring up and quickening his higher faculties, and that it may be easily counteracted by principles which possess much greater force.

The true secret of the steady adherence to a pacific policy on the part of America is to be found in the inconsistency of any other policy with the maintenance of free institutions. The moment it was determined to establish a republican form of government, it became neces-

* The Mexican war has occurred since this was written.

sary to throw away military pursuits. For war is the most effectual instrument which can be employed to undermine public liberty.

But even though we should admit that the policy pursued by the United States is attributable to the peculiar position in which it was placed, the example may be of unspeakable importance in its influence upon other nations. An experiment made under one set of circumstances may suffice to show that it may be made under all circumstances. For the circumstances are a mere accident, while the experiment itself is conformable to the interests of every civilized nation on the globe.

A new state of things seems to be growing up in the European world, entirely variant from the old, and although it does not entitle us to predict the total destruction of this last, yet promises to make some approach to it and distinctly indicates that the tendency to peace is one of the predominant characteristics of the present age.

First, then, I observe that since the peace of Paris which closed the unexampled wars of the French Revolution, princes have made efforts such as have never before been known to cultivate a good understanding among themselves. It is immaterial whether this combination has been formed for the purpose of checking the progress of the democratic principle, so visible everywhere. Princes very often intend to do one thing and the course they are compelled to pursue insures the accomplishment of another and totally different thing. The fact that such a concert does exist is inconsistent with the continual wars which once prevailed in that part of the world. And if it is adhered to for another thirty years by the principal European powers, it may eventuate in very important consequences. It has created a counter-revolution to the French Revolution, and this counter-revolution only stands in need of time in order to render it successful. For in the second place, the democratic principle instead of losing is constantly gaining ground. Crowned heads are afraid of their subjects and combine in order to secure their own authority; and the steady growth of industry and popular intelligence which is the consequence of this pacific policy is all the time adding to the moral power of the people and placing in their hands, instead of in those of their rulers, the means by which alone peace can ever become the permanent policy of Europe. For, in the third place, the prodigious impetus which has been given to every department of industry within the last thirty years is directly calculated to render the middle class the predominant class in society.

When it has fairly become so, the disinclination to war will be nearly as manifest as it is in the United States; not, perhaps, because the people of one period are intrinsically better than those of another, but because in the vehement and obstinate pursuit of their own interests they have become insensibly inured to habits of peace and realize what the mass of an European population was not formerly in a situation to do, the importance of making peace the fundamental policy of the state.

When the embargo was laid by the American republic in 1806, it was for the first time authoritatively announced to the world that war is inconsistent with the prosperity of a free state. And when in 1833 the industrious classes in France protested against war with the United States, it was for the first time authoritatively announced by an European people that it is inconsistent with the interests of even a monarchical state. Military pursuits, then, are irreconcilable with the highest degree of national prosperity. War contributes to alter the relative distribution of both property and power. It takes property from the industrious classes in order to bestow it upon a very different order of men or, what is worse, it causes the destruction of wealth without any retribution whatever. I know of but one instance which seems to form an exception to this view. During the wars which grew out of the French Revolution, Great Britain did not appear to suffer materially. On the contrary, there were evident symptoms of a regular advance in wealth. Every department of industry was alive and active. The maritime ascendancy of the nation enabled it to open new channels of commerce and to protect its vessels in almost every quarter of the globe. This is the favorable view of the subject. But the true question is, what would have been the condition of the country if the expenses of the war had been defrayed by taxes collected within the year? Instead of this being done, a debt has been created so overwhelming that no one dare believe that it will ever be paid and which, whether it be paid or not, will equally postpone the disasters of the war to a period far beyond its termination. For if, on the one hand, a national bankruptcy will dry up the income of great multitudes of people, on the other, the reimbursement of the debt will trench so largely upon capital as to shake to its foundation the commercial prosperity of the country. When either of these events occur, we will be able to form an adequate idea of the influence of war in disturbing the natural distribution of property.

Similar views are applicable to the question of the distribution of power. Property and power are invariably connected. Whatever affects the disposition of the first affects that of the last, whether as between different classes of the people or as between the people and the government. War, more than all other circumstances put together, assists to condense power in the hands of a few. Its effect upon the distribution of power is more immediate and decisive than it is upon property.

It is not difficult to follow the process by which this revolution is effected. Impending danger, at home or from abroad, may alarm the mass of peaceful citizens, but it inspires the ambitious with resolution and boldness. If the crisis is at all doubtful, if either civil or foreign war seems to be brooding, a vague sense of patriotism persuades people that it is right to confer ample power upon government to beat down the evil, and a large military force is raised. But the use of this instrument, where liberty is not most solidly guarded, is apt to give an exorbitant authority to the government. The imaginations of the people are intoxicated by the pomp and circumstance which are introduced upon the theater of public affairs. They lend a disproportioned importance to those who are the principal actors, and are led, step by step, to intrust a larger and larger authority to public rulers. The army becomes an end instead of a means; war is provoked when peace might easily have been maintained. And whether in consequence of the altered modes of thinking which everyone then adopts as to the general tendency of war, or through the instrumentality of the army itself, the way is prepared, if not for the conquest of the people, at any rate for greatly abridging their liberties.

It is not surprising, therefore, that the great mass of the American people should feel such an aversion to war. There is no instance to be found where this sentiment has been anything like so general or so strong. The nation no sooner goes to war than it sets about framing expedients by which to obtain peace. It is not from fear of the enemy, for no country possesses both the "materiel" and "personnel" of war to a greater extent. But the nation fears itself and would put away the temptation to acquire a dangerous greatness. Hitherto the disinclination to military pursuits has been so great among all parties that it is not easy to form an estimate of the consequences if there should be anything like a general change in the tone of public sentiment. Military men have been bred in civil pursuits or have lived during the greater part of their lives in a state of profound peace. Their character consequently partakes more of that of the citizen than of the soldier. If they are introduced into political life, they find themselves entangled in the complicated network of our free institutions, and the last thing which a soldier president dreams of is to employ the army for the purpose of perpetuating his power. But let public opinion run for any considerable period in an opposite direction, let military pursuits become more popular than trade, agriculture, and manufactures, and I, for one, would desire to hide myself from contemplating the countless evils which would be the consequence. For as no nation ever was endowed with such a capacity for doing good, none has ever been endowed with such a capacity for inflicting evil.

It is impossible to foretell with any accuracy what will be the issue of those immense political assemblages which are constantly held in every part of the United States. The effect may be to discipline two vast armies which will ultimately take up arms and tear each other in pieces. The experience which we have had of domestic violence in some of our large cities proves that it would not be an impossible thing to embroil parties to such a degree as to occasion the most disastrous civil wars. On the other hand, the people may become so familiarized to peaceful assemblages, and so habituated to reflect upon the widespread ruin which would be the consequence of a resort to arms, that the greatest political excitement may always terminate, as it has hitherto done, in merely affecting the ballot box. On the issue of this experiment are suspended the destinies of this great republic.

The disposition to reflection is one of the remarkable characteristics of the men of the present day.[2] Two circumstances have contributed to awaken it. 1st. The prodigious development of industry. Commerce, agriculture, and manufactures are now conducted on so immense a scale and interest so great a number of minds that they have to a great extent superseded the practice of war. 2d. The men of the present day have more individuality, if I may so express myself, than at any former period. The first circumstance supplies materials on which reflection may exercise itself. The second develops the faculty itself. For by rendering individuals more dependent upon themselves and less dependent upon a class, they are thrown upon their own resources and exercise more caution, prudence, and judgment in their behavior. And when this habit has been established in private life, it is

---

2. [For the second edition, Grimke added this paragraph and the next.]

very naturally and even necessarily transferred to the scene of public affairs.

When I was a young man, I have heard older persons relate that in their time it was expected that at all dinner parties the guests should not only be of good cheer, but that they should drink until they were merrily drunk. The custom had been of time immemorial and not to conform to it was considered as an indication of a poor spirited fellow. This practice is now unknown among anything like good company. It is banished to the night cellars and other haunts of the dissipated. I also observed that a great many other changes had taken place in the manners; that for ten duels not more than one was fought now. I concluded that there must be some general cause for so great a change, and I traced it to the strong habit of reflection which had grown up. I found that the alteration in the manners showed itself in public life also, and I will only refer to one or two examples. At the time when the struggle between the Union and the nullification parties was at its height, when the exacerbation of feelings was so intense that the least circumstance, a look or a gesture might lead to a sanguinary conflict, the leaders of those parties entered into a formal agreement that not only should no wanton insult be offered by any individual of one party to any individual of the other, but that the most active and vigilant precaution should be taken to prevent any occurrence which might by possibility lead to it. During the extreme excitement of feeling which preceded the presidential elections in Tennessee in 1844, a similar agreement was entered into by the two parties in Nashville.

Nothing is more common than to see politicians pursue a line of conduct which they intend shall advance their own influence and authority and which, nevertheless, terminates in setting bounds to both. What the leaders of the parties often design to effect by these political meetings is to promote their own selfish aims, to obtain office immediately, or to prepare the way for their elevation at the first favorable moment. If endowed with ambition, resolution, and self-command, they may be disposed to wink at the most offensive conduct on the part of their adherents in order to bring matters to extremities. By embroiling the two parties in a civil dissension, they would render themselves more necessary to their respective partisans. But the course which they are insensibly impelled to pursue, once they have fairly entered upon the career of public debate, is calculated to give an entirely new turn to affairs. Civil war rarely makes its way through the medium of public debate. Discussion and reasoning on such an extended scale presuppose a wide diffusion of information and a very general disposition to reflection among the great mass of the people, both of which are greatly assisted by listening to these debates. The independent condition in which the bulk of the population are placed, their educated habits, and the strong masculine sense which the two conjoined produce impart to them a strong appetite for public discussion. When the plan of holding these conventions was first introduced, the public mind seized upon it with avidity as something which it had long been in search of. For nothing presents so imposing and animating a spectacle as do these assemblages since they bring into play a living instead of a merely fictitious sympathy. The love of strong sensation is an universal trait in the human character and it finds vent in this way. Hence political assemblages may be said to constitute the amusements of the American people. The crowds who attend them desire to hear public affairs talked over and reasoned about. And the leaders of parties are compelled to follow this bent of their disposition. However incompetent a great number of the speakers may be, their ambition is at any rate directed into a new channel. They strive to make display of their information, to show their acquaintance with the political history of the country, to grapple with the most difficult problems of legislation. Every step they take only raises up fresh obstacles in the way of civil war. An intellectual cast, in spite of themselves, is given to the whole machinery of parties, and, instead of those dark conspiracies and acts of desperate violence which have been so common in other countries, the efforts of these politicians simply terminate in curbing their own ambition and in making the people more deeply sensible than ever of the deplorable consequences of civil insubordination. The European kings raised the privileges of the towns in order to use them in bridling the power of the nobility. The result was that the towns succeeded in checking the power of both kings and nobility.

It is one great advantage of these meetings that they bring the country and the town population into contact and association with each other. Political conventions which were once held only in large cities are now equally common in the agricultural districts. The meeting may take place in the county town but vast numbers from the country flock to it. I have known twenty, thirty, fifty thousand people assembled on these occasions. Now the rural population are the natural balance of the city population. In other countries, in consequence of the want of combination among the former and their destitution of the means of instruction, the inhabitants of the towns have had things all their own way. But in the United States the means of instruction are imparted to all parts of the population, and political conventions afford the most favorable opportunity for concert and united efforts.

The military institutions of the United States stand upon a different footing from what they do in Europe. In the European states an army is kept up, ostensibly to provide against the contingency of foreign war, but with the further design of maintaining the authority of government at home. That which is the principal end among the nations of the old world is not even a subordinate end in America. The government of the United States relies upon the people themselves for the preservation of order. And that this reliance has not been misplaced, an experience of nearly seventy years amply testifies.

This very remarkable difference between the military institutions of these nations is the natural and necessary consequence of the difference in their civil institutions. As in the United States the government is the workmanship of the people, by the people is it most naturally preserved; but as in the old world it is a sort of self-existing institution, it is driven to rely upon its own resources for the maintenance of its authority. The European princes complain that obedience to the laws cannot be insured unless they are placed in possession of an imposing military force. And how can it be otherwise, when the laws are neither made by the people nor for the people. In Italy and Spain when a murder has been committed, persons who are spectators of the deed flee instantly in order that their testimony, if possible, may not be used against the criminal. So detestable in their eyes is the whole apparatus of government that they involuntarily shrink from lending assistance in the detection or condemnation of the criminal. And the same feeling seizes everyone on occasion of those civil disorders which are infractions of the law upon a much larger scale. The army is the king's, not the people's, and let the king take care of himself seems to be the language of the spectators.

In the United States an insurrection against the laws in which a majority of the people should be embarked is an event which cannot take place. In the European states it has frequently occurred and would happen still oftener, if the few did not grasp a weapon of powerful efficacy in repressing popular grievances. In the United States the militia, which is only a collection of the citizens, constitutes the reliance of government in suppressing disturbances whenever the ordinary police is not sufficient for the purpose.

The difficulty of creating a militia in the European states arises from the extreme repugnance of those governments to permit the people to have arms. The permission, wherever it exists, is regarded in the light of a privilege and is accompanied with the most odious restrictions. The celebrated statute of William and Mary, generally known as the Bill of Rights, allows persons "to have arms for their defense, suitable to their condition and degree, and such as are allowed by law." The words which qualify the privilege are provokingly ambiguous, and were doubtless intended to be so in order to wait a more favorable opportunity for asserting the full authority of government. Accordingly, the statute of George III, c. 1 and 2, authorizes justices of the peace to seize arms whenever they believe them to be in possession of persons for dangerous purposes.

Now one can conceive of a militia to whom arms were never intrusted except when they were actually called into service, but it would be a militia without a soul. The single circumstance that the American government feels no jealousy whatever as to the carrying of arms by private individuals sheds a flood of light upon both the civil and military institutions of the country. In truth, there is no such institution as a militia in the proper signification of the term in any European state. It is the offspring of free government and can only exist in conjunction with it. In Great Britain, by an act passed in the reign of George II, a certain number of the inhabitants, selected by ballot, were to be organized as a militia for successive terms of three years. They were to be annually called out, trained, and disciplined for a certain number of days, and the officers to be appointed among the lords, lieutenants of counties, and the principal landholders. But this force was only intended as auxiliary to the regular army, and the whole scheme has been long since abandoned. The plan of training and disciplining the whole adult population, in peace as well as in war, has never been entertained except in the United States. The national guard of France approaches the nearest to it. In theory, it is composed of the entire adult male population, but in practice it is otherwise.[3] The disinclination of the great majority of the lower classes to leave the employments on which they depend for subsistence has established a sort of dispensation for them from this service, so that the national guard rather resembles the uniform companies than the ordinary militia of the United States. It is very much the same in Great Britain. The militia there simply means the yeomanry, a body of men organized in each county but selected from among those who are known to be well affected to the government. The election of their own officers by the national guard has not grown out of the revolution. The practice was introduced by Louis XI.

As is often the case where what was once a privilege has become the common property of all, the people in some of the American states appear to set very little value upon their character as soldiers. Public opinion appears to have undergone a very great change with regard to militia duty. In Massachusetts, Maine, and Vermont, compulsory drills became so unpopular that they were at length abolished. In Massachusetts, the sum of fifty thousand dollars is annually appropriated to any number of the militia, not exceeding ten thousand, for voluntary duty a certain number of days in every year. In Maine, the militia system is retained by continued enrollment of all who would be bound at her call to come forth for the support of the laws or the defense of the soil. In Vermont, the laws requiring militia drills have been repealed, and in their place has been substituted an enrollment similar to that for jury purposes of all who under the old system would have been liable to militia service. The militia system is retained in these states as the only effective military force, but the frequent mustering deducted so much time from the civil pursuits of the people that it has been dispensed with. They only who compose the substantial power of the commonwealth can afford to abstain from making continual display of it.

3. [For the second edition, Grimke added new matter from this sentence to the end of the paragraph.]

CHAPTER IV | INSTITUTION OF THE PRESS

THE press is a component part of the machinery of free government. There would be an inconsistency, then, in arguing whether it should be free. It is the organ of public opinion, and the great office which it performs is to effect a distribution of power throughout the community. It accomplishes this purpose by distributing knowledge and diffusing a common sympathy among the great mass of the population. Knowledge of some sort or other all men must act upon in the ordinary affairs of life in order to render their exertions fruitful of any result. Political society, which connects men together while living in the most distant parts of an extensive country, is in need of a still wider range of information. It would be correct, therefore, to say that the freedom of the press was to knowledge what the abolition of primogeniture was to property: the one diffuses knowledge as the other diffuses property.

If we inquire why in most countries so much power is concentered in the hands of government, the answer is, plainly, that knowledge is condensed in the same proportion. If we could suppose it to be uniformly diffused, government would cease to be a power; it would become a mere agency. For although it would be necessary to confide exclusive trusts to the public magistrates in order to conduct the joint interests of society, yet the extent and activity of public opinion would give control to the power out of the government. This is an extreme case, and an extreme case is the most proper to illustrate the intermediate degrees where the shades of difference are so minute as to run into one another.

If in a state where representative government was established we should suppose the press to be suddenly annihilated, the political institutions would not long preserve their character. As there would be no superintending control anywhere and no acquaintance with what was transacted in public life, the affairs of state would soon be involved in the deepest mystery. Knowledge would be confined to the men who were the chief actors upon the stage of public life, and the very necessary authority which had been conferred upon them in order to further the public welfare would be converted into a mere engine of power. Usurpation would be heaped upon usurpation. Society would at first be a scene of infinite confusion. During this period there would be many violent struggles between liberty and power. But as a state of disorder can never be the permanent condition of any community, the contest would terminate in the consolidation of power. And this vantage ground once obtained, the population would easily be molded so as even to cooperate in carrying out the designs of the governing authority.

If the press were extinguished, the great principle on which representative government hinges, the responsibility of public agents to the people, would be lost from society except in those few instances where the duties to be performed were confined within so narrow a circle as to render them the subject of as direct supervision as the affairs of private life. The parish and the township officer would continue to be watched and controlled until the revolution I have described established a system of universal centralization and wrested the power of electing even those officers from the people.

These views afford a sufficiently clear illustration of the truth of the observation that the principal function which the press performs in a political view is to equalize power throughout all parts of the community.

The power which opinions exert upon society is in direct proportion to the intrinsic value they possess and to the publicity which they acquire. Both these circumstances are affected by the condition of the press which gives impulse to thought and free circulation to opinions. The action of mind upon mind sharpens the faculties and kindles enthusiasm; and the extent to which an opinion prevails indicates the number of persons whom it interests and the degree of concert which is established among them. A thought wrapped up in the bosoms of a few individuals can never acquire importance, but when it engages the sympathy of a great multitude it becomes more than a thought: it is then a new power added to public opinion.

What we term public opinion is not the opinion of any one set of men, or of any particular party, to the exclusion of all others. It is the combined result of a great number of differing opinions. Some portion of truth often adheres to views and speculations which are apparently the most unreasonable, and it is the true side which they present that goes to swell and to make up the sum of public opinion. Not that this is always the case — not that it is the case in any particular instance — but the tendency is constantly in that direction.

Very important consequences follow from this in a political point of view. The mixture of so many opinions, causing light to be shed upon each, contributes to moderate the tone of party spirit. However irreconcilable the views of parties may appear to be, a free communication cannot be established between them without producing a visible influence of each upon all. The press in its efforts to widen the breach and to make one opinion predominant is compelled to make all opinions known and creates the very process by which all are sought to be rectified. The free exposition of the views of parties constitutes a sort of lesser experience which supersedes the necessity of actual experiment as a means of testing the utility of each. The public administration is prevented from running rapidly from one extreme to another, and in spite of the machinations of all sorts of parties the people are insensibly drawn to the defense and adoption of wiser and more wholesome measures. Political contentions in a monarchy or aristocracy are like those personal rencounters in which one party is beaten to the ground. But the war of opinions is not conducted after this manner, for there the weaker side often rises from the conflict with redoubled strength.

Opinions may be even absolutely absurd and preposterous, and yet may contain a sort of negative truth. A system of religious belief founded upon the grossest superstition may simply signify to the men of other sects that their practices are totally at war with the pure doctrines which they profess to teach. So it is said that in some parts of the United States individuals are to be found who have a predilection for monarchical government. Such fanciful notions cannot put out the light of the nineteenth century, but they may read a very instructive lesson to the men of all parties. They may signify to many who espouse free institutions: "Your conduct is inconsistent with the noble sentiments you profess to admire. Your designs are the most selfish and unpatriotic imaginable, and you would leave no stone unturned in order to compass them. If this were not so, our opinions could not stand up for a moment. In America, at least, they would never have gained entrance into a single bosom." Thus the existence of error often leads to a clearer sight of the truth, and the wide dissemination which the press gives to opinions increases the intensity of the light by which all parties are enabled to see their sentiments reflected.

The facility with which opinions are promulgated might seem to be unfavorable to stability in the public councils. And if it were so, it would be preferable to the complete despotism of one opinion over all others. But all change, which is the result of liberal inquiry, invariably leads to stability, for this never consists in the inflexible pursuit of one line of policy, but in listening to suggestions from all quarters and causing the public administration to rest upon the widest foundation possible. Certain it is that although this may never be the design of those who stand at the head of public affairs, yet in a democratic republic the existence of the press, somehow or other, insures that it shall sooner or later be brought about.

In France during the reign of the Bourbons, and in England in that of the Tudors, one set of opinions ruled the state, and it was ruled with a rod of iron. In America, where one party has never been able to succeed to the extent of an extreme opinion, the public administration, although wearing occasionally the appearance of fickleness, has in the main preserved a character of remarkable consistency. It has been made firm only at the cost of being enlightened.

The press may then be regarded as an extension or amplification of the principles of representation. It reflects the opinions of all classes as completely as do the deputies of the people. The difference consists in this, that it has the ability to influence without that of compelling. And there is this advantage attending it, that it is in constant activity before the public mind, and does not like the legislative body speak only periodically to the people. Checks in government, as I have before remarked, are of two kinds: positive and indirect. The European states afford instances enough of the first; the American republic exhibits a great example of the second. Public opinion is the great preventive check of civil society, and wherever it is firmly established the necessity of a recourse to the system of positive checks is to the same extent diminished.

When Cecil, the celebrated minister of Elizabeth, established the first newspaper in England, he little thought that he was creating a powerful counterpoise to that throne of which he was an idolator. To disseminate information with regard to the movements of the Spanish armada, and thus to assist the country in making a vigorous and concerted resistance to a foreign enemy, was his design. The most exaggerated accounts were circulated with regard to the Spanish armament, terror was spread among the inhabitants, and Lord Burleigh, who had reflected maturely upon the moral influence which the press was cal-

culated to exert, fell upon this expedient as a certain means of relieving the public mind from anxiety and inspiring it with resolution. The
journal which he called into being diffused information far and wide,
corrected the misrepresentations which were afloat, and produced
union and combination among all parts of the population. But the
plan has resulted in a vast and complicated system by which the rights
of the people are protected from invasion by their own government. A
new engine was created which has contributed materially to effect all
the great changes which have since taken place in favor of civil liberty.
In 1821, there were twenty-four millions of newspapers annually sold
in Great Britain. In 1827, there were twenty-seven millions circulated
in the United States.

The process by which this great revolution has been brought about
is very obvious. The press has given a voice to an immensely numerous class of the population who before composed a mere lifeless and
inert body but who now contribute essentially to the formation of what
we term public opinion. A single newspaper may be very barren and un-
interesting, but the sum of all the information which is in this way
brought to bear upon the public mind is incalculable. What we stand
in need of is information, and not merely the result of information. The great mass of mankind acquire knowledge with surprising
facility when it is communicated in detail. Facts thus presented
have a distinctness which gives them an easy admission to the mind,
and the conclusions which are deduced are both more comprehensive
and more practical. The sagacious and inquisitive spirit of very obscure
men in the inferior walks of life frequently stirs the public mind on
questions of the greatest interest to society. Such persons often suggest hints and anticipate improvements which men of cultivated understandings, and more intent upon past history than upon the character and genius of their own age, would not have had the boldness to
adopt. Perhaps it would not be too much to affirm that almost all the
great revolutions in human affairs may be traced to this source. The
wealthy and educated, having attained the goal of their ambition, have
nothing further to desire. Their views and exertions are confined to
their own order. If such is the case with the men who occupy a
lower position in society, if they also are intent upon advancing their
own interests, we at any rate make sure when activity is imparted to
them that all orders of men in the state shall be taken care of. But
to give activity to the great classes of society is in effect to connect

them together, to form substantially one class, and to create a system of opinions and interests which shall be common to the whole population. Accordingly in the United States men of all conditions are found associated in endeavors to extend education, to promote public improvements of every kind, and above all to further the interests of religion and morality. The great advantage which the towns formerly possessed over the country consisted in their superior intelligence and greater ability to combine for any public purpose. But the dispersion of knowledge by means of the public journals has placed the city and the rural population on nearly the same footing — another example of the influence of the press in producing an equal distribution of both knowledge and power throughout the community.

The freedom of religion, of suffrage, and of the press, which has been introduced into some countries, was brought about by the very reasonable complaints of men who occupied an inferior position in society. The learned and the educated consulted their books, interrogated history; they paused, they doubted, they refused, until at last public opinion grew to be too strong. Suddenly a great change was effected in the political institutions and, as government was thenceforward made to stand upon a broader foundation than before and to interest all classes in its preservation, those who had predicted that the most fatal consequences would follow from such innovations were surprised to see their calculations falsified and to find that every interest which pertained to society had acquired additional stability.

The political press in the United States has a different character from what it has anywhere else. As there are no privileged classes, it is emphatically the organ of popular opinion. Society is divided into parties, but they are all parties of the people. The moment the people drew to themselves the whole political power, public disputes began to wear a new aspect. They ceased to be the feuds of distinct orders of men and became the quarrels of members of one of the same family. And it is needless to add that this was not calculated to lessen the acrimony of political dissensions; on the contrary, it has greatly increased it. But there is this compensation for the mischief: that instead of the terrific assaults of two hostile combatants upon one another, the power of the press is broken up into small fragments, and we have only a war of skirmishes.

The journals of no country surpass those of the United States in ribaldry and abuse. But a great part of what we term public discontent is in reality only private discontent in disguise. Our private troubles we do not care to divulge because hardly anyone can take an interest in them; they are deposited among the secrets of the human heart. But the burden is too great, and everyone endeavors to find out some circuitous means of giving vent to them. As soon, therefore, as the exciting topics of political controversy begin to agitate the public, the fiery elements of the character are seen to burst forth. All those private discontents which originated in envy, personal animosity, neighborhood bickerings, the finding one's self placed in a false position to the rest of society, in fortune, reputation, or understanding immediately disclose themselves and give a bitterness and vulgarity to public disputes which do not properly belong to them. Men throw the mantle of politics over their faces and fight each other in masks. The consequence of this state of things is that private character and personal conduct of almost every kind are the subject of attack beyond anything which is known elsewhere.

So long as legislators are reduced to the necessity of governing by general rules, society must in part be regulated by the rival passions and propensities of individuals. They who narrowly scan American society may believe that it is in danger of being universally overrun by backbiting; and what in its vulgar form is party politics but backbiting reduced to system?

But this melancholy infirmity like many other defects is designed to have a salutary influence. In private life it assumes the character of a regulative principle by which, in the absence of any better corrective, men succeed in keeping each other in order. Nor is its influence in public life less conspicuous, for there also it contributes to put everyone upon his good behavior. If the American journals were exclusively the organs of the refined and educated, their tone would undoubtedly be more elevated. But it must be recollected that the groundwork of the human character is pretty much the same in all classes. People living in polished society have passions and propensities as well as the common people, only in the former case they are not put forth with so much nakedness. It may then be inquired whether it is not one capital object of all institutions, whether in private or public life, to draw a veil over the bad side of human nature so as to hide from view the selfishness and deformities of the character. And the answer is plain: such is the object wherever the concealment does not have the effect of protecting from censure and rebuke the vices which are in disguise.

As all the parties which exist in the American republic originate among the people and are essentially popular parties, it follows that the press is a censorship over the people, and yet a censorship created by the people. There would, consequently, be no meaning in the office of a censor appointed by the government. That institution is superseded by the very nature of the American press. Where a censorship is established by the political authority of the state, it is applied to restrain one class of publications only. No one ever heard in a monarchical or aristocratical government of any attempt to forbid the circulation of writings which were calculated to increase the influence of the prince and nobility. The utmost indulgence is extended to them, while a rigorous control is exercised over every appeal in behalf of popular rights. Popular licentiousness is bridled, but there is no restraint upon the licentiousness of men in power. There is but one way of remedying the defect and that is by causing the press itself to perform the office of censor; in other words, to grant such absolute freedom to all the political journals that each shall be active and interested in detecting the misrepresentations and impostures of the others. There is a real and formidable censorship of the press in America, but the institution is in and not out of the press. The consequence is that the efforts of all parties are most vehement and untiring, and yet more harmless and pacific than in any other country.

I shall conclude this chapter with two reflections. The first is a very obvious one: it is that the existence of a free press is not alone sufficient to inspire a people with a just sense of liberty and to cultivate in them those qualities which are necessary to the establishment and maintenance of free institutions. The press was free in Denmark, Sweden, and Prussia until very modern times. It is nearly so in China. But in all these countries the moral power to set in motion this vast engine is wanting. The Prussian and Danish youth may be as well educated as the American, but the Prussian citizen is not half so well educated as the American citizen.

The second reflection is that the press must not be regarded merely as the representative of political opinions. The dissemination of information in the daily journals, in magazines, pamphlets, and books on a variety of subjects interesting to the popular mind withdraws the attention of the people from a too intense devotion to party politics and educates them to be both men and citizens.

THERE is a fine observation of Adam Smith, in the *Theory of Moral Sentiments,* relative to the formation of ranks. He remarks that where there is no envy in the case we sympathize more readily with the good than with the bad fortune of individuals; and, as much envy cannot be supposed to exist among the great mass of common people, they feel a real delight in beholding the prosperity and luxury of the rich, and in this way the foundation of an aristocracy is laid. The observation is neither recondite nor farfetched; on the contrary, it is both solid and ingenious and is founded in the deepest insight into human nature. The same idea seems to have struck Bonaparte when he was revolving the plan of establishing the "legion of honor." He was struck with the curiosity which the populace exhibited in surveying the rich uniforms and decorations of the dignitaries who surrounded him. There was always a crowd in the neighborhood of his residence to witness the show. "See," said he to those who objected to the unpopularity of the institution, "see these futile vanities which geniuses disdain. The populace is not of their opinion. It loves those many-colored cordons. The democrat philosophers may call it vanity, idolatry. But that idolatry and vanity are weaknesses common to the whole human race, and from both great virtues may be made to spring." In order to the existence of an aristocracy, it is not merely necessary that there should be great inequality in the distribution of wealth; it is necessary, also, that this condition of society should fall in with the prevailing tastes and prejudices of the people. A privileged class may be created by dint of force, but to maintain its existence for any considerable time it must somehow or other interweave itself with the affections and sentiments of the people.

But Adam Smith does not direct the attention of his readers to another fact of still greater importance, inasmuch as it prevents the rise of a privileged class or prepares the way for its extirpation after it has been established. We may very easily suppose a state of society in which the common people, being lifted to a considerable share of independence, will feel more self-respect and have less admiration for outward show and splendor; at any rate, in which the envy of which Adam Smith speaks will stifle that sentiment of admiration. About the time he wrote commenced that extraordinary prosperity of the English nation which has continued with little interruption to the present day and which has given a prodigious impulse to all sorts of industry, to commerce, manufactures, and agriculture. But the effect has been to raise up from among the ranks of the people, once so poor and humiliated, a formidable class whose wealth eclipses that of the nobility. And a further consequence is that the sympathy which was before felt in the fortunes and reputation of a privileged body is now engrossed by an exceedingly numerous class of the population. The envy of which Adam Smith speaks now begins to show itself. The people feel that they are able to rival the aristocracy in wealth and intelligence, and they envy the exclusive privileges which are accorded to that aristocracy. I think I can discern many symptoms of a loosening of the hold which the institution once had upon the popular mind. As the absence of envy among a thoughtless and ignorant people contributed to the formation of ranks, an opposite cause may tend gradually to undermine their influence. The institution has already ceased to be hereditary in France and some other countries. The curious trait of character which Bonaparte observed in the French populace has been wonderfully modified by some other circumstances.

In the United States there is no foundation upon which to build an aristocracy. Landed property is very equally distributed, and the laws prohibiting primogeniture and entails prevent its accumulation beyond a very limited period. It is the greatest nation of proprietors which has ever existed. One may observe signs of the same love of splendor and outward show which are visible among the people, for, as the French ruler remarked, it is common to the whole race of mankind. Nevertheless, the feeling is different from what it is in other countries. Instead of making people contented with their own condition and satisfied with beholding the splendor and outward show which others make, it renders everyone uneasy and restless and goads them to unceasing exertions to procure to themselves some of the advantages of fortune.

As it is the effect of free institutions to take power from the superior ranks and to add power to the popular body, in the progress of time these two classes change places. The aristocracy is converted into the democracy and the democracy into the aristocracy; for there where the political power resides will reside also the aristocracy. What was once the governing power becomes the subject body. Hence, in popular government, one may observe a general disposition not only to pay court to the people but to imitate their manners, and to fall down to the level of their understandings.

Declamatory talent takes the place of genuine eloquence, superficial views of profound thinking. It may also be said that the people set the fashion in every respect. And if it were not for a tendency in an opposite direction, if the people were not making constant efforts to elevate themselves, the condition of society would be melancholy in the extreme. For the true democratic principle does not consist in letting down the highest in the land to the level of the lowest, but in lifting the greatest possible number to the highest standard of independence and intelligence. Although those who endeavor to ingratiate themselves with the people are intent upon advancing their own interests, they somehow or other succeed in giving an impulse to popular improvement. Foreigners suppose that the democratic institutions of America are calculated to degrade the character of all public men and to lower the general tone of intellectual and moral excellence. But it is important to look to ultimate and permanent results and not merely to immediate consequences. Candidates for office are doubtless, in numerous instances, led to the employment of arts and the cultivation of qualities which are unfavorable to the growth of a sturdy and manly virtue. But independently of the fact that these qualities would under any other form of government be found to exist, only under different forms and with more mischievous tendencies, the great desideratum is obtained — that of bringing about an association among the different orders of men of which the state is composed. The superior man may for the time being be lowered, but the inferior man will be sure to be elevated. The opportunities which most of the candidates have enjoyed in some degree, their pursuits in after life, their addiction to politics, even if it be only the superficial part of the science, enable them to impart some things to the people which the people are very inquisitive to learn and the knowledge of which would be otherwise withheld from them in consequence of their daily occupations. The general intercourse which is thus established gives the most ordinary mind some tolerable insight into public affairs, initiates the uninstructed into the conduct of public men and the import of the public measures, so that the mind the most captious and the least disposed to estimate free government at its true value must see upon reflection that the advantages springing from this order of things greatly preponderate over the mischief which is incident to it. It is impossible to produce as general an intercourse among all classes as is desirable without incurring the mischief. But the intercourse gives to the popular understanding a very important discipline. Curiosity is the first step in the acquisition of knowledge; rouse that among a whole people and you possess yourself of the master-key to their faculties. The common people even form exaggerated notions of the advantages of information after listening to repeated conversations and discourses of public men. A strong and general taste for education is diffused among them, and in progress of time a new people grows up which is able to detect the hollowness of those artifices which were before employed to gain its favor. The evil is corrected by that same instrumentality which it was supposed would augment and perpetuate it. Doubtless politicians are bent upon promoting their own interests in their efforts to win the good will of the people. But somehow or other, public and private interests are inseparably connected. Providence has wisely ordered that there shall be no way by which men can substantially and permanently advance their own interests without advancing that of others. The lawyer, the physician, the merchant, are all chiefly intent upon lifting themselves in the scale of society, but they cannot do so without scattering benefits around them and lifting the condition of others as well as of themselves.

Wealth and refinement, when they are not confined to a separate order, are not necessarily unfavorable to a high standard of intelligence and morals; on the contrary, they may be made highly instrumental in the promotion of both. If this were not the case, the condition of a free people would be the most hopeless imaginable, for they are destined to make the most rapid advances in the acquisition of riches.

Let us walk through the apartments of the rich man and survey the interior economy of his house. We can only obtain a lively and correct picture of society by examining the minute and delicate springs which govern it. The first thing which strikes us is the number of persons who compose the household. Besides the family proper, the easy circumstances in which he is placed enable him to employ several persons to attend to the various offices of the house. There is at once the introduction of a principle of order and regularity. The larger the family and the more numerous the occupations the greater the necessity for rules by which to govern it. The very subordination in which the members of the household are placed is favorable to a system of discipline in every part. The head of the family is constrained to exercise a certain degree of authority, and this authority is chiefly displayed in the maintenance of order and arrangement in each one's occupations. The education of his children is one of the first things which engages the attention of a man placed in independent circumstances. If he has not been educated himself, his heart is the more set upon it on that very account. This contributes still further to introduce the elements of good morals into the bosom of the family. If there is refinement and luxury and even ostentation, there are also some powerfully counteracting principles in operation. The authority of the head of the family cannot be maintained, the obedience of his children cannot be easily won, if he breaks through the rules of morality and sets an example which is at war with all the precepts which he undertakes to inculcate. There cannot be one code of ethics for parents and another for children. The consequence is that children will impose a restraint upon parents, as well as parents upon children. And however ineffectual the former may sometimes be, yet in the great majority of instances it will exercise a marked influence upon the interior economy of the household. Individuals make great efforts to acquire property in order that they may live in what they term elegance; and they have no sooner succeeded in their desires than they find themselves surrounded by beings whose appetite for novelty and splendor is even stronger than their own. The only way to maintain a due authority in their families, without which everything would run to confusion and there would be neither elegance nor enjoyment for anyone, is to introduce a system of rules for the government of the family. And these rules, to have any effect, must somehow or other connect themselves with the principles of morality. And when that is the case, the wealth which was amassed in order to enable its possessor to live independently and free from control is the means of creating an active control in the bosom of private families. Manners, that is, good breeding and civility, are one of the attendants upon a well-ordered, domestic society, and this creates a new bond of connection not only between the members of the family but between them and the great society out of doors. And it is very easy to see, even from this rapid sketch, how the acquisition of wealth may contribute to elevate the general standard or morals and intelligence in the community.

But the man placed in independent circumstances has a great variety of relations to society at large. He walks abroad and he finds other men engaged in enterprises of private and public improvement. If he were a subject under a monarchical government, he would perhaps lend his fortune to aid in conducting a foreign war. If he belonged to the order of nobles in an aristocracy, he would expend it in furthering his own aggrandizement and that of his order. But he is simply the citizen of a republic in which different modes of thinking prevail and he is absolutely unable to free himself from their control. His whole conduct, whether he will or not, is governed by laws as fixed and determinate as those which guide the actions of men in less easy circumstances. He becomes the member of various societies for the promotion of knowledge, the diffusion of benevolence, the amelioration of the face of the country in which he lives. All this is calculated to give him great influence, but this influence is bounded by the very nature of the enterprises in which he embarks, for they contribute directly to the distribution of property and knowledge among other men. He can only attain weight and consequence in society by efforts which tend to elevate the condition of those who are below him. So that in a country of free institutions, the acquisition of wealth by individuals may be decidedly favorable to the cultivation of both public and private virtue, at the same time that it can hardly fail to promote the intellectual improvement of the whole population.

The influence of property is necessarily modified by the structure of society and the character of the institutions which prevail at different times. At an early stage of civilization a military aristocracy makes its appearance. There is then little wealth and that little is condensed in the hands of a few. To this succeeds a species of baronial aristocracy in which there is more wealth but the distribution is as unequal as before. And when free institutions are established both these forms are superseded by the dispersion of knowledge and property. The title then ceases to be a distinction. It is shared by so many that there is no possible way of causing wealth to enter as an element into the structure of the government without at the same time giving supremacy to the popular authority. In the Italian republics of the middle ages, the term, nobleman, signified simply one who was the proprietor of land. In Florence alone mercantile wealth was able at one time to dispute this title with the possessors of the soil.

In the United States where the distribution of wealth is more complete than in any other country, one may remark a difference in the groundwork of society in different parts of the union. In New England, a species of ecclesiastical aristocracy, if I may so express myself, once prevailed. But the growth of commercial and manufacturing industry has modified that state of society without at all impairing the force of the religious principle. The term "merchant princes" is still more applicable to the merchants of Boston than it was to those of Florence. In the South, a sort of baronial wealth exists, but two circumstances have concurred to prevent its assuming the character of a political aristocracy. The laws of primogeniture and entail have been swept away so that a new distribution of property takes place at every successive generation. And although wealthy proprietors have a great number of dependents or retainers, yet this class, possessing no political privileges themselves, are unable to confer any upon those who are masters of the soil. There is, in other words, this peculiarity attending the cultivation of the soil in the South, that tillage is performed by a class different from and inferior to the proprietors. Such an aristocracy, although it may confer personal independence, cannot create political authority. In the middle states, where there are no such distinctive traits in the composition of society, an aristocracy of parties may be said to predominate. Party spirit accordingly rages with more violence in these states than in any other part of the country.

But notwithstanding these differences, there is an infinitely greater uniformity of character among the people of America than is to be found anywhere else. As M. de Tocqueville remarks, there is less difference between the people of Maine and Georgia who live a thousand miles apart than between the people of Picardy and Normandy who are only separated by a bridge. So it is said that people inhabiting different districts in the kingdom of Naples are entirely strangers to each other. And when two gentlemen from the city of Naples lately visited the Abruzzi in quest of information as to the natural productions of the country, they found there many medicinal plants growing in the greatest profusion which the Neapolitans were regularly in the habit of importing from foreign countries.

The leading fact in the history of American civilization undoubtedly consists in the very equal distribution of the landed property of the country. And this is owing to the circumstances in which the country was found when it was settled by Europeans. The population was so thin and so entirely below the standard of European civilization that it quickly disappeared and left the whole field of enterprise open to the whites. This is a fact quite new in the history of society. Two effects immediately followed, each having an important bearing upon the character of these settlements. First, two distinct races, one the conquering, the other the conquered, were not placed side by side of each other to nourish interminable feuds and to obstruct the quiet and regular growth of free institutions. Second, if the country in 1607 had contained as dense a population as Italy at the foundation of the Roman commonwealth, if it had only contained as full a population as Spain, Gaul, or Great Britain when they were subdued by the northern tribes, the territory in all human probability would have been found divided among numerous chiefs and petty nobles and the colonists would most certainly have accommodated themselves to this condition of society. The new proprietors, instead of vacant land, would each have acquired cultivated estates, together with a retinue of serfs and vassals, from whom the most ample revenue might be drawn. This would have been so gratifying to the adventurous spirits who emigrated, some of whom were connected with the best families in England and their notions consequently tinged with the modes of thinking then prevalent, that the distribution of property would have become very unequal and would have been perpetuated to this day. But as it was, the whole country was a wilderness; the high and the low had to begin the world by turning laborers themselves. There were no great estates cultivated and adorned and ready to be taken possession of, no body of retainers who might help to form an European aristocracy. All men were compelled to begin at the beginning. Men were from the first trained in the school of adversity and hard labor. The land was obliged to be sold and cultivated in small parcels in order to give it any value. Its treasures were a thing in prospect only, depending upon what should be done hereafter and not upon what had been done already. To rent it was almost impossible since the product was not more than sufficient to reward the labor of the cultivator.

Two effects followed from this: the land was pretty equally divided and the agricultural population, instead of being divided into the two classes of proprietors and renters, assumed almost universally the single character of proprietors. That this has contributed to give an entirely new direction to the political institutions and the whole social economy of the state must be obvious to everyone.

When the colonies were severed from the mother country, an immense body of vacant land was claimed by the respective states. This was ultimately ceded to the federal government and the system established by that government for the sale of this land has insured a still more uniform distribution than existed before the Revolution.

Similar causes influence the growth and municipal government of the American cities. Neither the aristocratic "regime" of the Roman "commune" which prevails in the south of Europe, nor the gothic system of tradesmen and artificers which grew up in the middle ages and still prevails in central Europe, could well be introduced. It was the country people who founded the villages and continued to replenish them until they became large cities. These, when collected on the present sites of New York, Philadelphia, Baltimore, etc., found themselves in a state of as complete dependence as the rural population.[1] The foundation of equal privileges was laid and took the place of that equal division of the soil which prevailed in the country. Nothing at all resembling the close corporations which have existed in Europe, even in Scotland and Holland, has ever been known in America. That in Edinburgh, a city containing one hundred and thirty thousand inhabitants, the city council should have been a self-existing body, perpetuating itself by filling up vacancies in its members, and that the member of Parliament should be chosen not by the men of Edinburgh but by this same city council is a monstrosity which could hardly gain belief if we did not know as a historical fact that such was the case up to the year 1832. M. Guizot, in his admirable work, *De la Civilization Francaise* (v. 5, ch. 18), has drawn a comparison between the rise of the cities in the south of France and of New York, Boston, *New Haven*, and Baltimore.[2] If he had pointed out the striking contrast which exists in the municipal "regime" of these two very different species of "communes," he would have afforded most solid instruction to his European readers.

But whatever may have been the beginnings of society in America,

1. [In all editions, Grimke writes "dependence," but in the context the sense would seem to require "independence."]

2. [Why Grimke should have italicized "New Haven" escapes me, unless it is the filial piety of a son of Yale.]

if the country is destined to make prodigious advances in wealth, will not aristocracy ultimately show itself? Will not society, even more than in other countries, contain a very large body of wealthy individuals who will attract to themselves an unreasonable share of influence? And if we mean by an aristocracy a class of rich individuals, such will undoubtedly be the case. But when we call them individuals and say that they will be exceedingly numerous, we point to two circumstances which will limit their power and cast the institution, if institution it can be called, in a different form from what it has assumed anywhere else. There would be no meaning in democracy if it did not open up all the avenues to distinction of every sort, and we may with much more reason hold up such a condition of society as exhibiting the "beau ideal" of the democratic form of polity.

For aristocracy may be divided into two totally distinct kinds, a civil and a political aristocracy. The first is the very natural consequence of the unobstructed progress of the population in wealth, refinement, and intelligence. The second is the workmanship of the laws which, proceeding in a course directly opposite, undertake to mold society into a form most favorable to the condensation of power and property in the hands of a few and, by so doing, gives an artificial direction to the political authority of the state. In the United States a political aristocracy is unknown, but as the country has advanced with unexampled rapidity in the acquisition of wealth and the diffusion of knowledge a civil aristocracy is everywhere apparent. If there are' any causes which condemn one part of society to great inferiority to another part, if slothfulness, want of a wholesome ambition or vicious habits make some men the natural enemies of this admirable state of things, Providence has very wisely ordered that an antidote commensurate with the evil should pervade the system: that the class to whom influence belongs, having themselves sprung from the people, should know how to temper moderation with firmness, and not be able to bear down upon any class with the weight of a titled aristocracy.

The civil aristocracy which I have described may be said to consist of the learned professions, of capitalists, whether belonging to the landed, the commercial, or the manufacturing classes, and of all those associations whose efforts are directed to the furtherance of public or private prosperity.

The profession of the law differs from that of medicine in this particular. Lawyers are called upon to make display of their knowledge in public, and this circumstance invests them with a sort of public character. They wear more nearly the character of a corps or class. Moreover, their pursuits have a close affinity with all political questions, which cannot be said to be the case with the members of any other learned profession. The professors of medicine whose services are performed in private and whose position in society is necessarily more isolated endeavor to make compensation for these disadvantages by establishing everywhere colleges and universities dedicated to instruction in their particular science. The colleges which were at one time established in England for teaching the civil law and the inns of court in London, a rival institution for teaching the common law, have nearly fallen to decay. In the United States, medical colleges are very numerous, but no college of jurisprudence exists. And yet the science of law is divided into fully as many distinct branches as is that of medicine, to each of which a professor might be assigned and thus give rise to the establishment of law as well as of medical colleges. Lawyers, however, seem to be satisfied with the share of public attention which the nature of their pursuits attracts to them.

Although the efforts of the clergy are all in public, yet each minister stands alone in the performance of his duties. And they seek to relieve themselves from this disadvantage in two ways: first, by establishing, like physicians, seminaries devoted to teaching their own system of doctrines; and secondly, by the institution of ecclesiastical assemblies of various grades, sometimes embracing the whole clergy of one denomination throughout the country, sometimes the clergy of one state, and sometimes of districts only in the same state. The first, under the names of general conventions, assemblies, or conferences, transact the business common to all the members of a denomination throughout the country. The second and third classes attend to those matters which concern the churches of one state or of one district. And all contribute to bind together the members in one league and to give them a just weight and influence with the whole lay population.

The strength of the natural aristocracy of a country depends upon the worth and intelligence of the members who compose it. Neither wealth nor any other adventitious advantage are of any moment unless they tend to the cultivation of these two master qualities. And it is because the acquisition of wealth in the United States does actually tend in this direction that its influence is so beneficial. The civil aristocracy becomes so numerous and so powerful that it is impossible to found a legal or political aristocracy. But it has been supposed that the popular sentiment in America is unfriendly to intellectual distinction. And yet a very fair proportion of men of eminent endowments have been elevated to office. This envy of intellectual distinction which has been ascribed to the people, if it does exist, indicates at any rate that that species of distinction is appreciated and coveted by them. Men envy in others those qualities which confer respect, and in so doing give no slight evidence that they are themselves ambitious of the same distinction. It is the first step in the intellectual progress of a nation. When the population is an inert, ignorant mass, it has no envy because it has no inward spring of improvement. Moreover this jealousy of talent, although it may for a time cast very eminent men into the shade, is sometimes attended with very great advantages to themselves. The revolution which brought Mr. Jefferson into office found the great body of American lawyers enrolled in the ranks of the Federal party. They were consequently very generally excluded from office. This withdrawal from the noisy field of party politics caused them to devote themselves more exclusively to their profession and the consequence was that the legal profession attained an unparalleled eminence during the twenty-five succeeding years. American jurisprudence was built up into a compact and regular science, and acquired such a commanding influence that it became a sort of make weight in the constitution.

The revolution which lifted General Jackson to office confounded all the former distinctions of party. Lawyers were therefore appointed to office without regard to the particular party to which they had before belonged. The taste for public life which has in consequence been imparted to them has been in the same proportion injurious to the profession. The present race of lawyers are not equal to their predecessors. It must be admitted, however, that this state of things is not without its advantages also. As lawyers are now very generally introduced into public life, they are less exclusively addicted to the technical forms of their profession and this contributes to enlarge and liberalize their understandings. The great work of forming jurisprudence into a regular and well-defined system having been accomplished, the community can afford to let them mingle freely in public transactions in order that they may impart the influence of their own habits of business to other classes and, at the same time, bring back from those classes some portion of their varied and diversified views.

There are two ways by which mankind have hitherto been governed: the one by a fixed authority residing in a select class, the other by a sense of common interest among all the members of the society. In the first, the imagination may be said to be the ruling principle of government; in the second, we avail ourselves of the same simple machinery by which all other human interests are managed, good sense, a love of justice, the conviction that the interests of the individual are, after all, identified with the public welfare. The idea with European statesmen is that a government fashioned after the first plan will possess a greater degree of impartiality — that it will be more completely freed from the influence of parties. But inasmuch as the structure of society in modern times is constantly tending to weaken the influence of the imagination upon all the business concerns of society, the time may very speedily come when there will be no choice as to the form of government which shall be adopted.

Nor is it true that a government which is absolved from a dependence upon parties is more impartial on that account. Parties are simply the representatives of the various interests of the community, and these interests will never be able to attain an adequate influence unless they can make themselves felt and heard. Doubtless monarchical and aristocratical governments may be very impartial in one respect. They may be so strong as to turn aside from the claims of all parties. But as no government which is not founded upon men's interests can administer those interests with skill and success, so no government which is not animated by popular parties can ever be made to understand those interests. It is only since the rise of parties in Great Britain and France that public affairs have been conducted with anything like impartiality.

CHAPTER VI | THE INSTITUTION OF SLAVERY

THE institution of slavery has an entirely different character in the United States from what it possessed in the ancient commonwealths. In these, the servile class occupied very nearly the same position as the inferior ranks in the modern European states. They might not only be freed, but they were afterward capable of rising into the ranks of genuine freemen. At Rome, after the second generation, their blood was considered sufficiently pure to gain them admission to the senate. As slaves were most generally brought from barbarous countries, the restraint imposed before the manumission was favorable to the acquisition of habits which would fit them to be freemen. But before manumission, they filled a number of civil occupations which at the present day are assigned exclusively to freemen. Even the professions of physic and surgery, notwithstanding the doubts suggested by Dr. Mead seem at one time to have devolved upon them.[1] Thus the servile class of antiquity may be regarded as a component part of the general population, connected with all other classes by numerous links and recruiting the ranks of the last with citizens of hardy and industrious habits.

This great difference in the relative condition of freemen and slaves in modern and ancient times arises from the fact that in the last the two classes were composed of one race, while in the United States they belong to distinct races./This renders the whole question of slavery at the present day difficult in the extreme. [The light of the nineteenth century very naturally stimulates the mind to inquiry, nay, imposes upon it the duty of making an examination. And yet, the problem presented for solution — "Is it practicable to do away with slavery?" —

1. [Probably the famous Dr. Richard Mead (1673–1754) of London who, in 1723, delivered an oration at the College of Physicians which was "for the most part a defence of the position of physicians in Greece and Rome, showing that they were always honoured. . . . Conyers Middleton attacked the oration, and maintained that the physicians of Rome were slaves." (*Dictionary of National Biography*, XXXVII, 184).]

is surrounded with difficulties so numerous and of so grave a character as almost to baffle the best-directed efforts we can make. For how shall we emancipate from civil disabilities two or three millions of people without admitting them to the enjoyment of political privileges also? And yet how can this be done without endangering the existence of the very institutions which are appealed to as the warrant for creating so great a revolution? In some of the American states, the colored population might constitute a majority of the electors. Where this was the case, the plan would simply terminate in raising up a black republic. For although it should be possible to overcome the prejudice of caste among the whites, yet the still greater difficulty of overcoming it among an inferior and unenlightened order of men remains to be disposed of. The probability is that long before the colored population could become educated and informed, if such an event may be deemed possible, the whole management of public affairs would fall into their hands, or, by a combination between them and the worst part of the white population, the political power would be divided between the two. The extraordinary spectacle would then be presented of a highly enlightened people voluntarily exerting itself to turn the tide of civilization backward — for assuredly, if the scheme succeeded, society would return to the barbarous condition which it has cost the human race so many ages of toil and suffering to emerge from. In Haiti the whites are a mere handful and create no jealousy. In the British West Indies, the property qualification which is imposed upon voters continues the black race in a state of political servitude, so that the experiment in neither has produced any result which can shed light upon the most difficult and perilous part of the undertaking. In the United States universal suffrage, or very nearly so, is the rule. It would then be impossible to make a distinction between the two races without running into direct contradiction with the principles with which we had set out. How could we refuse to impart the benefit of those institutions whose existence is the very thing which has suggested the change? And yet on the other hand, how could we consent to commit violence upon those institutions by placing them in the power of a race who have no comprehension of their uses?

The earnest and extended inquiry which this great question has given rise to cannot fail to be attended with advantage. If there is any plan by which the institution of slavery can be gotten rid of, that plan will be suggested through the instrumentality of discussion. If there is no practicable mode of abolishing it, the freest inquiry will have the effect of confirming the public mind in that conviction. In either case, the tranquillity and welfare of the state will be better secured than where everything is seen through the twilight medium of doubt and ignorance. The great advantage of discussion consists in this: that by engaging a number of minds in the investigation of a particular subject that subject is no longer viewed from one position only. The point of observation is continually changed and the conflict of so many opinions, each of which contains some portion of truth, ultimately elicits the whole truth. Before the press had roused the human understanding to vigorous and earnest inquiry on all subjects, society was full of all sorts of exclusive opinions and exclusive institutions, each of which was pent up in a narrow circle and defended from the approach of any improvement. That was formerly and to a very great extent is still the condition of much the greater part of the civilized world. Force, disguised under one form or other, was once the principal means resorted to, to set things to rights. But in America the discovery has been made that the agency which is most powerful and most comprehensive in its operation consists in the moral force of public opinion which acting incessantly and in every direction silently introduces changes which would otherwise have disturbed the whole order of society.

When the same object is seen under different aspects by different minds, the most partial views are acquired in the first instance. Nevertheless each one, uninstructed in the process by which opinions are gradually matured, is vehement in the promulgation of his peculiar dogmas, not because they are true, but because they are his. This is the danger which society runs in that intermediate period when opinions are yet in a state of fermentation and before time and reflection have been afforded to separate what is true from what is erroneous. This danger is diminished, instead of being increased, in proportion as the spirit of inquiry becomes more free and independent. For then, to say the least, the shades of opinion are so infinitely varied that the advocates of one and the same plan are frequently obliged to pause in order to come to an understanding and compromise among themselves. Half-formed and sectarian opinions are very apt to produce sinister feelings and designs. This diminishes their influence still more and prevents their acquiring an exclusive authority in the community. In the non-slaveholding states of America, the population is universally opposed to slavery. Public opinion, however, is so justly tempered that the party which desires to carry out the extreme measures of the abolitionists constitutes a small minority. But opinions which are even tinctured with sinister views ought never to be disregarded on that account. Our enemies always tell us more truth than our friends and they are, therefore, frequently the best counsellors we can have.

There is another danger to which society is exposed. In times when schemes of public improvement are agitated, the spirit of philanthropy is sure to be awakened. This is more particularly the case where these schemes are intended to affect private manners. But a well-informed understanding is as essential to the execution of any scheme of philanthropy as is a benevolent disposition. The two put together make up the only just and true idea of philanthropy. Not only a correct discrimination between the possible and the impossible, but a wise and cautious adaptation of means to ends in everything which is practicable are necessary to insure success. Without an enlightened understanding, there is no governing principle to guide; and without benevolence, there is no motive power to give vigor and effect to our actions. Hence, when these two qualities, each exerting a prime agency in the constitution of man, are dissociated or not properly balanced, all our efforts become abortive or mischievous. They become so simply because we have not acted up to the genuine notion of philanthropy.

In a country where free institutions are established and unlimited freedom of discussion exists, this danger is increased since everyone then persuades himself that he is in duty bound to give utterance to his opinions, and that if these opinions are only conceived in a spirit of benevolence they must necessarily be entitled to command: thus reversing the whole order of our nature and making the feelings an informing principle to the understanding, instead of the understanding acting as a regulative principle to the feelings.

On the other hand, this danger is greatly countervailed by the very causes which give occasion to it. An unbounded freedom of thought and inquiry being exercised by all, those who hold contrary opinions are equally earnest in the promulgation of them. And even if the views on either side are pushed to an extreme, as they probably will be, the incessant disputation which takes place gradually wears out and exhausts the feelings and enables the understanding to take clearer and more comprehensive views of the whole field of inquiry.

There are three errors to which philanthropists (those of the unphilanthropic are without number) are chiefly exposed:

First. By fastening attention upon some one defect in the social organization and giving it an undue importance, they weaken the sentiment of disapprobation with which other defects, equally glaring and mischievous, should be regarded. This forms no part of their design but it is the inevitable consequence of the course they are driven to pursue. Great multitudes of persons who are entirely free from the stain which is endeavored to be wiped out, but who are overrun by other vices or infirmities equally offensive to genuine morality, join the association of philanthropists. They do so because this presents one common ground upon which people of the most contradictory opinions and habits in other matters may meet; and because, by combining with the philanthropic in a philanthropic design, they withdraw public attention from their own defects, nay, they even seem to make amends for them and to purchase the privilege of persevering in them by lending their efforts to a single undertaking whose avowed object is to ameliorate the condition of mankind. Hence, the extraordinary spectacle which is frequently presented that a party dedicated to a benevolent purpose is, notwithstanding, crowded by persons whose designs are the most sinister imaginable and whose feelings are nothing but gall and bitterness.

Second. There is another mistake into which philanthropists are apt to fall. In every society which has attained a high civilization there are always numbers of persons who, from a variety of causes too indefinite to be described, are discontented with the social organization amid which they reside. No matter whether this proceeds from temperament or ill-fortune of one kind or another, from disappointed ambition in any favorite end, whether in the walks of public or private life, or from being placed in a false position to the rest of society, the fact is so, and it exercises a deep influence upon human actions. Such persons seek to administer opiates to their troubled feelings by brooding over the infirmities and binding up the wounds of others. The somber and melancholy interest which pervades all their actions impresses them with a character of earnestness and sincerity which irresistibly commands respect. The opinions of this class of persons are never to be shunned, for as human nature is constituted it seems impossible to sympathize with the sufferings of others unless we have been made to suffer much ourselves. We should avail ourselves of the feeling, but join to it an enlightened understanding that so we may be more intent on relieving the infirmities of others than of curing our own.

The present has been correctly termed the age of eclecticism in mental philosophy. It is so in every department of thought. The tendency in everything connected with the knowledge or the interests of man is to draw light from every quarter; not to consider different opinions on the same subject as forming distinct systems but, rather, as all conspiring to form one consistent and comprehensive scheme of thought.

Third. There is frequently among philanthropists a want of tact in distinguishing between the practicable and the impracticable. This causes the path they would follow to be strewed with numerous difficulties and temptations. I do not use the word "tact" in its vulgar signification, as importing mere adroitness or empirical dexterity, but as simply denoting an ability to make application of our theories to the practical affairs of men. In this sense it may be said to be the consummation of all our knowledge. But it implies a wide observation and a profound acquaintance with the history and constitution of man. It is well when actions which abstractedly have a character of benevolence have in practice an opposite tendency to describe them as they are; and it is equally proper, when words which exercise such dominion over one half of mankind have usurped a foreign or ambiguous meaning, that we should call them back to their appropriate signification.

The man of the highest faculties, and who devotes them exclusively to improve the condition of his species, on being placed in society immediately finds himself pressed with this difficulty. On the one hand there is a rule of right which, in consequence of its being a rule, is in theory conceivable of universal application. On the other hand stands the fact that in spite of all the efforts of the individuals who have preceded him a vast amount of poverty, suffering, and vice exists everywhere. As the causes which produced this state of things were beyond his control, so no remedies which he will apply can have more than a partial application. Is he to stop short, to abate his exertions? Not at all. There is a wall of adamant somewhere, over which he cannot leap, and which yet he is unable to discern. He should, therefore, endeavor to make constant approaches to it as if it were nowhere, but at the same time never to part with the conviction that it does actually exist. This will diminish the force of his exertions, since within the bounds of the practicable there is more than enough to give employment to the most active benevolence. But it will render those exertions more enlightened and therefore more efficacious. There is another thing which he may do and one which is neglected above all others. He may in his own person afford an example that the rule of right, not in one particular only but in all, is carried to the furthest extent of which it is capable. It is because we fail to do this that all our efforts to improve the manners of others fall entirely short of the mark. Nor can I conceive anything better calculated to exercise a powerful influence upon the actions of other men than a genuine example of purity of life, if it were to be found, even though it should never assume to intermeddle with the conduct of others.

These three circumstances contribute to corrupt the manners by rendering some abuses more prominent than others which are equally or more deserving of animadversion; and by investing the last and the men who practice them with an air of authority which no ways belong to them. 2d. The moral sense is perverted by making our own uneasiness and discontent the prime mover of our actions. For then it only depends upon accidental circumstances whether the individual shall plunge into dissipation, become the victim of misguided ambition, enlist in the ranks of the soldiery and throw himself into an association, the novelty of whose enterprises will create strong sensation and prevent the mind from preying upon itself. 3d. The judgment is obscured by a failure to know and to appreciate the very thing which a being of limited capacities is bound to be acquainted with: the extent to which he may carry his exertions and consequently the means which should be employed for that purpose. So that they who undertake to instruct and improve mankind, and who suppose that the very nature of their vocation places them beyond the reach of public opinion, very frequently find that they are equally obnoxious to it and that they themselves stand greatly in need of instruction and improvement.

The term slavery has sometimes an odious meaning attached to it, and yet it deserves very grave consideration whether the distinction between what we call slavery and some other forms of servitude is not for the most part an artificial one. The former denotes in its highest degree the relation which exists between master and servant, or employer and employed. The immature faculties of children give rise to a similar relation. The disabilities of both a moral and physical character under which menial servants and the great body of operatives in every civilized country labor give rise to the same connection. What avails it to call these by the name of free if the abject and straitened condition in which they are placed so benumbs their understanding as to give them little more latitude of action than the slave proper? In an investigation of so much importance, it is the thing, not the name, we are in search of. It is true, it would be infinitely desirable to cure all these inequalities in a society where servitude does not ostensibly exist, as well as in one where it is openly recognized. But in order to do this we must be able to regulate invariably the proportion between capital and labor, which would imply on the part of the legislator a complete control over the laws which govern the increase of population. Nor is it certain then that we should be able to succeed since there are so many inequalities in the faculties, disposition, and temperament of individuals as to give rise to every conceivable diversity of sagacity and exertion, from the feeblest up to the most strenuous and energetic.

It is vain to say that what is termed the institution of slavery contradicts the whole order of Providence, for society everywhere exhibits the most enormous disparities in the condition of individuals. Nor is it possible to conquer these disparities unless we abjure civilization and return to a state of barbarism.

That one race of men should be inferior to another is no more inconsistent with the wisdom of Providence than that great multitudes of the same race should labor under the greatest inferiority and disadvantages in comparison with their fellows. We know not why it is that so many wear out life in anguish and sickness, nor why a still greater number are cut off in the blossom of youth. We are only permitted to conjecture that if it were not for these inequalities the little virtue which has place in the world would cease to exist anywhere.

The institution of slavery when it is imposed upon the African race may simply import that inasmuch as the period of infancy and youth is in their case protracted through the whole of life, it may be eminently advantageous to them if a guardianship is created to watch over and take care of them. Amiable and excellent individuals have descanted upon the ill treatment and severity of masters. But no one has been bold enough to rise up and tell us all he knows. Domestic society in all its relations, if its secrets were not happily concealed from public observation, would as often exhibit mischiefs of the same character. Perhaps it may be asserted that every new country has to a great extent been peopled by young persons who at home were surrounded by influences of one kind or another with which they were not satisfied. There is always a limit at which the most downright and headlong philanthropy is fain to halt and that stopping place is the inmost chamber of domestic life, although there it is that the foundation of all the virtues and vices of our race is laid. It would not do to lift the veil here, else it might show us how little genuine virtue exists and thus cast a blight over the exertions of philanthropists, as well as take away from the authority with which they speak. It is painful to think that a great part of mankind are driven to talk much of the defects of others, in order to convey an impression that they are free from any themselves.

It must never be forgotten that no institution can stand up amid the light of the nineteenth century without partaking greatly of its influence. As the species of servitude which formerly existed in all the European states has been wonderfully modified in some by the surrounding institutions and the general amelioration of the manners, the system of slavery which prevails in the southern states of the American union has received a still more decided impression from the same quarter. In the eastern division of Europe where money rents are unknown, where even the metayer plan of cultivation had not been introduced, but the system of serf labor is almost exclusively established, the treatment which the laborers receive is not near so humane as that of the American slaves.[2] In Austria, the "Urbarium of Maria Theresa" still continues to be the "magna charta" of the peasantry.[3] Nevertheless the absolute authority which landed proprietors exercised over them has been very imperfectly removed. In 1791 the peasantry of Poland succeeded in obtaining a new charter of liberties. But it was only in name, and their condition has not materially improved. During the last half century, laws, customs, and manners have undergone a great change. But this change is nowhere so perceptible as in the United States. It is not surprising, therefore, that intelligent foreigners should have been so struck with the fact that the condition of slaves in America is altogether more eligible than that of free laborers even in the western division of Europe. It is impossible to communicate an impulse to the institutions of society in one part without causing it to be felt in every part. And for a very obvious reason, that every species of moral influence acts upon an institution not as a dry sys-

2. [The "metayer plan of cultivation" is the cultivation of the land for a share of its yield, as in American share-cropping.]

3. [Maria Theresa (1717–1780), Queen of Bohemia and Hungary, a Habsburg recognized in Austria. "Urbarium" is assumed to be a latinization of the German word for "arable," *urbar*, and is used to denote legislation concerning labor services throughout the Habsburg Empire.]

tem, but goes to the bottom and affects the manners and dispositions of the beings who set it in motion.

Thus the institution of slavery, growing up with the manners and partaking of the spirit which animates free institutions, may be gradually so molded as to acquire a still more favorable character. It may become in effect a mere branch of the domestic economy of the household, differing from others in no one respect except the nature of the occupations to which it is devoted. In the Roman common-wealth the treatment of slaves was cruel in the extreme. Branding, the torture, slitting the ears and noses, and crucifixion were employed for the most trivial offenses. It has been reserved for the people who first established free institutions to introduce also the only humane system of slavery which has ever existed.

M. Sismondi, in his *History of the Italian Republics* (v. 7, p. 68, n.), remarks that it was not due to Christianity to have abolished slavery. And he mentions several instances (v. 8, pp. 160, 226 and 157) where the captives taken in the wars of those republics were indiscriminately reduced to slavery. And this as late as the commencement of the six-teenth century. But in the last passage he qualifies the remark by say-ing: "That it is not to the Roman church that we should accord this high praise." For Christianity is the parent of philanthropy and the parent of those institutions which in America have abolished the bar-barous system of slavery once in vogue and reared up an institution differing from it to precisely the same degree that the political institu-tions differ from those of the European commonwealths.

The influence of race is a subject which has recently engaged the attention of philosophical inquirers. It may be that the light which has been shed upon it is still too imperfect to enable us to solve all the difficulties which meet us. But it would be a great mistake to suppose that the inquiry is in no way connected with the question of slavery in the United States. On the contrary, it is the single circumstance which renders the inquiry difficult in the extreme, both as regards mas-ter and slave. Philanthropists, in treating the subject, desire to deal in the most abstract propositions imaginable; but it is of infinite im-portance to make application of these principles in order to ascertain whether they are not limited and qualified by an extensive range of experience and observation. It is certainly very remarkable that Eu-rope is the only one of the four continents which has been thoroughly civilized. And Europe is the only one which is exclusively inhabited by the Caucasian or white race. It is equally remarkable that through-out Africa no trace has ever been discovered of civilization except where the white race has penetrated. The ancient commonwealths of Egypt, Cyrene, and Carthage were not, as some people suppose, composed of Ethiopians. They were all three settlements from Arabia, Ionia, or Phoenicia. The black race do not appear to have possessed even the faculty of imitating, so as to build up any institutions resembling those which were transported to their soil. This race still continues wrapped up in that immovable state of barbarism and inertia which existed four thousand years ago. Denmark, Germany, France, and England were inhabited by barbarians only two thousand years since and, yet, through the instrumentality of causes which have acted upon Africa as well as upon Europe, the latter has been reclaimed and the fabric of civilization which it has built up exceeds in beauty and variety the model from which it was taken. According to all the laws which have hitherto governed the progress of civilization, Africa should have been civilized as early as Europe. We can give no further account why it has not been than that there is an inherent and indelible distinction between the two races which retains one closely within a certain limit, and permits the other to spring far beyond it. To deny the distinction is not a mark of philanthropy, but rather a defiance of those laws which have been imposed by the Deity and which are no more inconsistent with his benevolence than innumerable physical and mental differences which exist among individuals of the same race.

The revolution in Haiti dates back half a century, a period of sufficient duration to ascertain something of the capabilities of the Negro race. Two generations of freemen have come upon the stage in that time. But we can nowhere discern any distinct trace of European civilization. The inert and sluggish propensities of this people have already created habits which preclude all hope of any substantial advancement. If they had found the island a wilderness, it would now be covered with wigwams. Instead of the strenuous industry which carries the white man forward in the march of improvement and makes him clear up the forest with as much alacrity as if he were subduing an empire, the Negro is satisfied if he can appropriate one or two acres of land. All he cares for is to obtain just enough to satisfy the wants of animal life. He has the name of freeman only: for liberty is of no account unless it absolves us from the yoke of our own propensities and vices which are far more galling and degrading than any physical disabilities whatever.

I differ with those who suppose that the worst effects of emancipation will be disclosed immediately. On the contrary, I believe that they will be developed very gradually and that the impediments to the introduction of order and industry among the blacks will become more instead of less formidable with the progress of time. On the establishment of the new system in the British West Indies, the novelty of the situation in which the blacks found themselves placed infused for a time an unwonted ardor and alacrity into their exertions. But this soon died away. They have fallen back into their natural apathy. It is impossible to induce a race to make strenuous exertions to better their condition when they are satisfied with a mere garden patch to sustain animal life. In the small islands of Barbados and Antigua, where there is hardly a foot of uncultivated land, they have been obliged to labor. But in Jamaica, where a great proportion of the soil is still uncleared and where consequently it has been an easy matter for the Negroes to obtain one or two acres apiece, they manifest the same disposition as in Haiti to squat themselves down and to drag out a mere animal existence. It is no wonder, therefore, that the plan of importing laborers from abroad was at one time seriously agitated in Great Britain, nay, carried into effect; nor that after being abandoned it should again be revived at the present moment. The experiment so far has been anything but successful. It seems to be impossible to train this emasculated race to the hardy and vigorous industry of the white man. To have made slaves of them originally was a deep injustice. To introduce them into the society of whites and to leave them to contend with beings so greatly their superiors is a still more flagrant injustice. Even if there were not an incontestable distinction between the two races, still if there is a total defect of sympathy, arising from causes which it is impossible to remove, all efforts to melt them into one people must fail. The statesman is bound to take notice of all those secondary principles which are planted in our nature and which exercise so wide and permanent an influence upon human conduct. He must make allowance for them as the mechanic does for the operation of friction. If he fixed his attention exclusively upon certain primary laws which do indeed lie at the foundation of human society but which are so greatly modified in their operation, he runs the risk of losing every advantage which may be derived from either the one or the other. No one supposes that the prejudices of kindred can be conquered or, if it were possible, that it would conduce to the welfare of society. They constitute an important part of our structure and are no more to be disregarded than are those general principles which rule over extensive associations of men. Yet the affections of kindred confine our attention and views within a very narrow circle and consequently modify all our conduct beyond that circle. The same analogy is visible throughout the whole economy of human nature. It is therefore the part of sound wisdom to gather up all these inequalities and to assign to each its appropriate place.

The philanthropic association which planned the colony at Liberia were fully aware of the truth of these principles. They, therefore, made it a fundamental regulation that white people should not be permitted to settle there. One can easily conceive that immense advantage might be derived from the presence and influence of the white race. But this is only on the supposition that that influence would be of the most unexceptionable character. And as it is not allowable to make this supposition, wise and discerning men have determined to effect a complete separation of the two races. The settlement at Liberia is one of the most remarkable schemes in which human enterprise has engaged, even in an age distinguished above all others for noble and generous undertakings. But the philanthropy which planned it was obliged to take into consideration the distinction of race as constituting one of those secondary principles of our nature which influence human conduct in spite of all that we can do.

We may say that a difference of color and of physical organization are to be regarded as accidental circumstances only. But accidental circumstances exercise a very wide influence upon the actions of men. The particular period when we were born, the institutions under which we live, the country which bounds our views and engages our patriotism, were all of them accidental circumstances originally. But as soon as they exist they cease to be accidents or subject to our will. We may have been born at another period of the world, or in another country, have been nurtured under totally different institutions, when our habits, our character, and our whole scheme of thought would have taken a different direction. If in all those particulars our lot has been most fortunate, let us use our privileges discreetly and not trample under foot the blessings we enjoy, because we cannot mend the works of the Deity according to our own crude conceptions.

As the distinction of color is not at all dependent upon climate, there is every reason to believe that a meaning was intended to be attached to it. Doubtless, it was intended to signify that there is a difference in the intellectual structure of the two races and that it is the part of true wisdom, therefore, to keep them apart. The physical make and constitution of individuals of the same race are frequently of so great consequence as to give a coloring to the whole of life and to stamp an impression upon their conduct in spite of themselves.

There is one class of philanthropists who would have us consider men as merely disembodied spirits and as entirely freed from the incumbrance of matter — a generous error, if the narrow and one-sided views in which it originates did not lead to consequences of an entirely opposite tendency and afford a striking example of the untiring operation of the lower part of our nature upon those who fancy they are the most completely lifted above it. We are never more in danger of sensualizing our whole being than when we believe we have attained the highest degree of illumination. The founder of the Moravian sect wished to introduce some of the obscene rites which are practiced in the Brahminical religion of Hindustan. The Quakers of New England, at an early period, entered the places of public worship and danced stark naked. It is but the other day that an association of perfectionists was announced in the city of New York which proclaimed the right and the duty to practice promiscuous concubinage. It requires but one step of false and detestable reasoning to stride over the gulf which separates virtue from vice. If we have attained perfection, there is no way of manifesting it so decisive as to practice all the things which are denominated vices in order to prove that we are incapable of contamination from them.

It has been predicted that when the population of the southern states of the American union has attained a certain degree of density, slavery will disappear. It is remarkable, however, that the existence of the institution has nowhere hitherto depended upon the greater or less compactness of the population. It existed in the holy land, in India, and in Italy for centuries after the population had reached its maximum. And on the other hand it disappeared from the northern states of America and from most of the European communities while the population was very thin. In England, the final blow which was given to the institution may be said to have been in the reign of Charles II when the population of the whole island was not greater than that of the two states of New York and Ohio at the present time.

There is one circumstance, however, which at this period is calculated to have great influence upon the existence of the institution. The present is beyond all comparison the most commercial age which has been known. Nations do not live within themselves as formerly. Each is striving to produce as large an amount of surplus commodities as possible in order to exchange them for the superfluity of other nations. And as there is no doubt but what the labor of the freeman is, as a general rule, more efficient than that of the slave, a nation which employs slave labor will labor under great disadvantages when it goes into the market of the world and finds that the price of every species of produce which is not a monopoly one is regulated by the supply of those nations which obtain it at the least cost. The nation which employs the cheapest labor will command the market. It may be true, therefore, as applicable to the present state of the world, that when the population of the southern states of America has acquired a certain density, the labor of slaves will be less profitable than that of freemen. And when this is the case it would seem, still proceeding upon general principles, that the slaveholders will be the persons chiefly instrumental in effecting the abolition of the institution.

But lest we should proceed too fast, there are here a good many things which must be taken into consideration. When we talk of the density of the population in a region where slaves already constitute a great proportion of the laborers, we must mean a density occasioned by the multiplication of the whole people and not merely of the freemen. Our calculations, therefore, must be founded upon the supposition that the community will be able to avail itself of the labor of those who have been emancipated to the same extent as before and with the additional advantage of finding their exertions more strenuous and effective than ever. This at once lays open the source of all the difficulties which attend the abolition of slavery in the United States. For is it quite certain that the labor of the free black will be more or even as productive as the black when a slave? I imagine that the reverse is the case and that although the labor of the white man, when free, is altogether more efficient than when he is a slave, precisely the contrary is the case with the Negro. None of these difficulties attended the abolition of slavery in Europe. Freemen and slaves were of the same race; and the last, after they were emancipated, slid by an easy process into the position of the first. Maryland and Kentucky may abolish slavery, but the effect will be not so much to get rid of slavery as to get rid of the African race altogether. Persons born after a certain period will be declared free and in the intermediate period the slaves who might give birth to this race of freemen will be disposed of in the southern market. The number of slaves in New York, at the first census of the United States, was more than twenty-one thousand. The number of colored persons in the state should now be somewhere about eighty thousand, if the increase was only equal to that of the slaves, and this independently of the great number of colored freemen and fugitives from labor who have gone from the southern states. The aggregate number of colored freemen should have been greatly above one hundred thousand. But the census of 1840 makes it fifty thousand and twenty-seven. Either a great part of the original stock of slaves have been sold, or the free institutions of the United States are singularly unfavorable to the growth and prosperity of this portion of the population.

The efforts which any class of men will put forth for the purpose of bettering their condition will be in proportion to their own ideas of the standard of comfort, not to the notions which other people have formed of it. If the man is endowed with strong moral energy, his exertions will be vigorous. The circle of his hopes and desires will be enlarged. It requires but little food and raiment to satisfy our mere animal wants and little toil, therefore, if these are all which bound our exertions. It is the disposition to go beyond this limit, the desire to acquire the faculty of enjoyment and not merely some of the things which administer to enjoyment in its lowest form, that has given occasion to that immense mass of industry which is now wielded and which has covered Europe and North America with thriving and powerful communities.

Now, if we suppose that the American Negroes on being emancipated will fall into the inert and sluggish habits which characterize their race throughout Africa, in Jamaica, in Haiti, that they will be content with a few acres of ground upon which to seat themselves and to vegetate in a condition little above that of the brutes, we cannot make the same calculations as if the country were peopled by the white race alone. The population may be numerically dense and yet in reality thin. And I do not see how it is possible to avoid making the supposition.

All history bears witness to the existence in the Ethiopian of a character totally dissimilar to that of the white man. And the former, equally with the last, is thoroughly convinced of the fact. "Black man is nothing by the side of white man," was the exclamation, says Mr. Park, of the Negroes on witnessing some very indifferent exhibitions of skill at Pisania.[4]

This then is the great difficulty which is to be encountered in the United States. There is no doubt but what the labor of the white man, when free, is more productive than if he were a slave, and this whether the population is dense or thin. But the reverse is the case with the Negro. His services when placed under the controlling guidance of the white man may be rendered very valuable, but when left to himself he invariably falls into habits totally incompatible with strenuous and vigorous exertion. I remember a few years ago remarking to an intelligent individual who was active in promoting the formation of a Fourier association that the great objection to the plan of a system of common labor and property was that it destroyed the incentives to exertion. His reply was a sensible one. He said he did not suppose it would answer as a general rule for society, but that from long observation he had become acquainted with a fact, perhaps new, but one of great interest and importance in the history of the individual: that there are always a number of persons scattered through the community who, from causes difficult to discern or explain, felt themselves to be too feeble and inert to take the management of any business into their own hands and more particularly their own business; that such persons would show themselves alert and active in attending to the affairs of others but lost their self-command and labored under a confusion of judgment as soon as they set about managing their own. He maintained that it was to relieve this class of persons from the weight which constantly hung over them and which cast a blight over all their exertions that such associations were formed; that they constituted the exception, not the rule for society. And is it at all incredible or inconsistent with the benevolence of the Deity that qualities which are inherent in numbers of individuals of our own race should belong to an entire race? Are the members of Fourier associations withdrawn

4. [Mungo Park (1771–1806), the famous English explorer of Africa. Pisania was a small town, an English trading post, on the banks of the Gambia River which was the starting and ending point of Park's travels. In the American edition of *Travels, in the Interior Districts of Africa* . . . (New York, 1813), there is a decription of the town on p. 21; the remark, "black men are nothing," appears on p. 259.]

from the pale of humanity on that account? No more than is the African race.

There is nothing which the human mind so much delights in as to generalize its ideas. The faculty of doing so is the highest which belongs to man. To be able to deduce a great truth from a given number of facts is alike flattering to human ambition and serviceable to the cause of general knowledge. But at the same time that the legitimate exercise of this faculty is of great advantage, the unskillful and imperfect use of it is often of exceeding detriment both to morals and knowledge. To fasten upon a few isolated facts, or upon facts ever so numerous, and to bind them together in the same class with others facts to which they bear some resemblance but from which they disagree substantially is not in any degree to subserve the cause of knowledge; and if our efforts are designed to have an application to the practical affairs of men they denote something worse than an error of judgment. They are noxious and mischievous in the extreme. But it is this extreme fondness for constructing general propositions, this worship of abstract ideas, if I may so express myself, which constitutes the besetting sin of very many of the associations which have sprung up recently. Because some people are exceedingly good and benevolent, perfectibility is possible. Because some men are not so active and energetic when working alone as when united into an association, all men should be herded together in associations. Because the white and the black man have one generic name, from that name are deduced the most absolute and sweeping propositions.

But in the event of the whites multiplying to such an extent as to fill up all the occupations of society, to become the sole operatives and agricultural laborers everywhere, what will be the condition of the blacks? They would be gradually deprived of their little possessions which would become more and more valuable with the increasing density of the population. The whites would have the means to purchase them and the blacks would be unable to resist the temptation to sell. Or if we suppose that a considerable number continued in the employments in which they were engaged before their emancipation, what still are their prospects? The accounts which we have of the abject condition of the lower classes in Europe are enough to sicken the heart and almost to cause minds which are not powerfully fortified by reflection to despair of the cause of humanity. A vigorous writer in the *Boston Quarterly Review* for 1840, on surveying the deplorable condition to which the white laborer is doomed by the operation of the inexorable laws of population, concludes that it is idle to talk of the evils of slavery when American slaves are placed in a far more eligible condition than any class of European laborers; that there are certain mischiefs in the social organization of every free community as now constituted, and that it is incumbent upon all enlightened men and lovers of humanity to probe the mischief to the root.[5] And he proposes that the property of all deceased persons should fall to the state to be distributed among the population. The views which this writer took of the condition of the lower classes was for the most part correct, but the remedy he proposes would be utterly powerless. If, however, there is among all intelligent observers such an unanimous opinion as to the abject condition of the white laborer when the population has attained a certain density, what must be the condition of the African when he is placed in close and death-like encounter with beings so greatly his superior? If that period were suddenly to come upon us now, the most extraordinary revolution would take place in the opinions of philanthropists. They would take ground precisely opposite to that which they now occupy. They would cry out against the cruelty and injustice which would be done to the blacks by emancipating them; they would, if true to their principles, inculcate the duty of maintaining a guardianship, the yoke of which would then be so easy and so desirable to bear.

The probability is that the same fate which has overtaken the Indian race would be that of the Negroes. The process of extinction would be more gradual, but it would be sure. The Ethiopian disappeared before the march of civilization in Egypt, Cyrene, and Carthage. And the more thorough civilization of the United States would assuredly bring about the same result.

It is evident, then, that difficulties of the greatest magnitude surround this question. Now, there are few obstacles which a powerful and enlightened people cannot overcome, if it can be made to see them clearly. But long familiarity with the institution of slavery is apt to beget partial and indistinct views among slaveholders as well as among abolitionists. I do not suppose there is any danger that the blacks will ever gain the ascendancy. They never succeeded in expelling the whites who founded so many commonwealths on the Barbary

5. [Grimke refers to Orestes A. Brownson's famous article, "The Laboring Classes," *Boston Quarterly Review*, 3 (July, 1840), 358–395.]

Coast. On the contrary, they were themselves driven to the wall. And what has been the fortune of communities founded by an Asiatic race will be the fortune of those which have been founded by the Anglo-Norman race in the United States. Insurrections would take place among the liberated blacks. And they would be quelled. But humanity recoils from contemplating the stern and inexorable justice which would have to be dealt out in so terrible an emergency.

Two alternatives seem to present themselves: to transport the African race bodily to some other country, or to retain them in their present condition. The first would be literally a gigantic undertaking; or rather, we may regard it as an impracticable one. Independently of the violent shock given to every species of industry by the sudden withdrawal of such a multitude of laborers, the expense would surpass the resources of the slave states, even if those resources were unaffected by the deduction of such an immense mass of labor from the soil. The mere cost of removal would completely exhaust them. To transport a number sufficient to keep down the annual increase and to continue this plan until the country were emptied would be beyond the ability of the southern states. The Moors of Spain and the Huguenots of France were expelled, not removed. And the expulsion in neither instance was anything like complete. The Moors and Huguenots had effects to take with them to enable them to begin life again. The first had a kindred race on the neighboring shores of the Mediterranean who were glad to receive them. The second were welcomed in every Protestant community throughout the globe. The state incurred no expense. It lost a body of valuable citizens, but the laws of population soon filled up the void. These cases differ widely from the present. Not that the analogy fails in every particular, but that when we sum up the difficulties on both sides they are incomparably greater in one case than in the other.

If then it is impossible to melt the two races into one; if to transport one of them is impracticable and to emancipate it would be an act of injustice and inhumanity, there is but one alternative: to retain the institution of slavery. We are never masters of the circumstances under which we were born. We may desire a change in every one of them. But the wise and inscrutable decrees of Providence have ordered otherwise, and we can in no way fall in with its designs so completely as by accommodating ourselves to difficulties which cannot be surmounted; in other words, by acting up to the rule of right in every situation in which we may be placed, and this not merely where our duties are plain but where they lead us over a dark and difficult way. To attempt to beat down an institution because we were not consulted as to its establishment is to arrogate an authority which does not belong to us. But we may convert that institution into an instrument of good. We may apply to it the same rules of justice and humanity which are applicable to every other part of the economy of society.

The men of the South find themselves born under an institution which they had no hand in creating — which their fathers did not assist in building up, but vehemently protested against when it was introduced by the mother country. Their course is plain. If it cannot be removed, to employ the same judgment and discretion in the management of it as are due to every other institution which is placed beyond their control. The relation of parent and child is the most extensive and important which exists. The relation is different in degree, but not in kind, from that of master and slave. Parents by harshness and severity may, and probably in great numbers of instances actually do, cause the fairest and gentlest virtues to wither in the blossom when, by tender and judicious treatment, they may have reared men and women who would have been ornaments to society. And although all our exertions to produce a different conduct may be of no avail, although we may not even have the right to intermeddle with the private relations of others, yet the duty of parents to act otherwise stands as firm and unalterable as ever, and this notwithstanding the innumerable crosses to which they are subject in the management of their household. Precisely the same is the case with the master. Great numbers of parents in all parts of the world are compelled to make use of the labor of their children, in tillage, in manufactures, in every species of employment. A very large proportion in densely peopled countries do actually task them to occupations, the recital of which makes us shudder. And if this be an evil inseparable from the density of the population, so that all efforts to extirpate it will be ineffectual, it affords another example of those uncontrollable circumstances under which we were involuntarily born, but one which far surpasses in magnitude the institution of slavery as it has hitherto existed in the United States.

CHAPTER VII | THE JUDICIAL POWER

MONTESQUIEU has said that the judiciary is the weakest of the three departments of the government. There are few general maxims which do not admit of some limitation — there is hardly one which does not demand this limitation in order to be true. The observation of Montesquieu is perfectly correct in reference to some particular forms of government. In hereditary monarchy, where the executive is a self-existing authority from which all appointments flow, in an aristocracy, where the legislative and executive authority is condensed in a body of nobles, the judicial power is necessarily feeble. But in a democratic republic where the legislative and executive power is strictly bounded on all sides, the judicial may become a very imposing department. Its relative if not its absolute strength is then increased, for while the other two departments have been deprived of some of their most important attributes the judicial power retains very nearly the same position and character which it before held. It even seems to possess a disproportionate share of importance, which is probably the reason why some of the state constitutions of America have substituted the tenure of a term of years in the place of a tenure for life. By so doing, the great principle of responsibility is applied to all the departments indiscriminately. As the power of impeaching the chief magistrate and of punishing in some way equally effectual the various administrative officers of the government is not deemed a sufficient reason why they should hold their places for life, it has not been deemed sufficient with regard to the judges.

The judiciary does not deal so directly nor so frequently with political questions as do the other departments. But it does sometimes deal with them, and that too definitively; in addition to which it extends its authority over a vast multitude of private transactions, many of which receive a hue, more or less distinct, from the political disputes of the day. If then the judges are appointed for life, they may have the ability to act upon society, both inwardly and outwardly, to a greater degree than the other departments. For when we talk of political authority we must distinguish between the abstract power which belongs to the body and the active authority which may be wielded by the members. If, for instance, the deputies to the legislature are never the same for any two successive years while the judges are elected for life, then, although the legislative authority of the state may be ever so great, yet still the power and influence of the judges may be greater than that of the deputies.

Courts of justice may well be described as an institution framed for the express purpose of putting an end to the practice of private war. The legislature is well fitted to make general rules for the government of the people and the executive to keep watch over the public safety. But without the instrumentality of the judicial tribunals which act in detail and not merely in the gross, society would be a prey to perpetual civil dissensions. Disputes between private individuals are occurrences of every day. The manifold relations which men have to each other in a thriving and cultivated society multiply them greatly. These disputes have relation to the most valuable interests of society: life, liberty, and property. And to have devised a mode by which they may be quietly appeased is one of the greatest achievements of modern civilization. In a state of imperfect civilization, the quarrels of individuals frequently assume a formidable shape and become matters of the gravest public interest. The injured parties interest first their relatives and friends, then the neighborhood, and finally whole districts of country are involved in the ferment. A dispute respecting the boundary of lands, or a mere personal trespass, is kindled into a furious insurrection which nothing but a military force can subdue. An institution, therefore, which goes to the bottom of the evil and takes up each case as it arises, separately and in detail, and which is so constructed as to inspire a very general confidence in its impartiality and integrity necessarily occupies a very important place in the complicated apparatus of government.

It is curious to mark the successive steps by which the practice of private war has been finally put down; how, from the most confused and discordant elements, a regular system for administering justice has sprung into existence. The trial by ordeal and judicial combat which make such a figure in the codes of the European states at an early period were the first rude attempts to mitigate the custom of private war. There may be said to be this natural foundation for the combat, that all ignorant people when they are offended immediately feel like fighting; and for the ordeal, that all superstitious people have faith in the determination by lot. But it would be a great mistake, as an admirable writer* has remarked, to suppose that these customs were calculated to fortify or to continue the practice of private war. On the contrary, they were designed to have an opposite effect. The legislator said to the injured party: if you insist upon revenging yourself, you shall at any rate do it according to certain forms and in the presence of the public. The secret pursuit, the midnight murder of an enemy, were thenceforth put an end to. The pecuniary compensation was a step still further in advance. Although at first it was at the election of the injured party whether he would accept it, in time it came to be absolutely binding upon him. And thus the practice of even regulated warfare was completely checked. When we read in some of the most ancient European codes of the trial by ordeal, of judicial combat, and of the "wehrgeld," we are apt to regard them as anomalies in the history of society of which no just and satisfactory account can be given.[1] They were undoubtedly relics of a custom still more barbarous, but the true view is to consider them as the first feeble efforts which were made to rid the community of the practice of private war. The duel was substituted in the place of private assassination and in progress of time the relations of the murdered man were compelled to receive a pecuniary compensation, instead of revenging themselves by the murder of the criminal or his family.

Although the pecuniary mulct excites surprise when we read of it in the history of the middle ages, it has notwithstanding occupied a considerable place in the criminal codes of some of the most enlightened modern states. In that of Ohio, passed so late as 1809, it makes a part of the punishment of every felony except four. There was this difficulty attending this system, under the Salic and Ripuarian laws,[2] that the delinquent having no property might be unable to pay the

---

* Guizot's "Civilization Francais," I, p. 365. [Francois Guizot (1787–1874), French statesman and historian; his major work, *General History of Civilization in Europe* (London, 1829–1832), 6 vols., was never completed and covers principally the civilization of France up to the fourteenth century.]

1. ["Wehrgeld": the payment of money for having slaughtered a man, what Grimke here calls "pecuniary compensation" or the "pecuniary mulct."]

2. [*Lex Salica* (c. 508) and *Lex Ripuaria* (early seventh century), two important codes of law for the Frankish group of German tribes.]

fine. What then should be done? Montesquieu says that he was placed out of the pale of the law and the injured party was permitted to redress the wrong. But this was not the course resorted to by all the German nations. Some of them imposed outlawry, banishment, transportation, or slavery. The laws of Ohio avoided the awkward predicament of the Salic and Ripuarian codes by combining the penalty of imprisonment with that of the fine; so that the maximum of the first would alone be sufficient, if the circumstances of the criminal made it necessary to abstain from the fine. The existence of the pecuniary composition in the American laws and in the Saxon, Salic, and Ripuarian codes marks two totally different states of society. In the last it denoted a feeble effort to get rid of the lawless violence which everywhere prevailed; but in the other it was a step from one regular mode of procedure to another still more regular, but more humane and judicious. In other words, it constituted the transition state from the system of capital punishments to the scheme of penitentiary discipline. There was another difference still more striking. The Germanic tribes held fast to the notion that a crime was an offense against an individual. They were not able to raise themselves to the higher conception that it was an offense against society, much less that it was an infringement of the laws of God. Hence the fine was never so high but numbers to whom revenge was sweet could afford to pay it; hence also it was not paid to the state, but was given to the injured person, or in case of homicide to the relations of the deceased.

The whole course of modern jurisprudence runs counter to such ideas. A crime is not merely regarded as an infringement of private rights but as a violation of the great rules of morality, so much so that the private injury in the most flagrant cases is merged in the public offense. For it is the chief design of legislators at the present day to impress everyone with so deep a sense of the heinousness of crime that the guilty man shall both regard himself and be regarded by the community as an outlaw from society. In this way the remorse of conscience is added to the physical punishment which is inflicted. For want of such just notions, society was formerly a prey to the wildest disorders. For as long as the license to commit crime could be purchased at a price, the power of conscience was necessarily very feeble. The license was regarded as a privilege, instead of as a badge of disgrace. The life and reputation of man seem to be cheap until he is raised high in the scale of civilization. He becomes more accustomed to the degradation of his own existence and views the existence of others as being equally degraded with his own.

I do not mean to give any opinion as to the propriety of compelling the criminal to make additional satisfaction to the injured person or, in the case of felonious homicide, to his relations. But this should never be enjoined as the chief end of punishment. If the plan is adopted, it should never in the graver offenses be by way of fine. The delinquent should be condemned to hard labor in the penitentiary and that labor be made available to the widow and children who had been deprived of their support. There are even then some difficulties in carrying out the plan in detail. The murdered man, for instance, was perhaps so worthless that, instead of sustaining, he was sustained by his family. At the same time, therefore, that the public punishment cannot be dispensed with, there is no room for compensation to private individuals. And although cases will occur where the degree of private injury can be easily ascertained, there will be others where it will be exceedingly difficult to compute it in advance, since no one can determine how long the murdered man may have lived and may have been able and willing to maintain his family. The laws in modern times never give the fine to an individual, except in those cases where there is the least propriety in so doing, that is to say, to the base informer.

The judiciary is considered by Montesquieu as a branch of the executive power. That there are resemblances between these two departments is certain, and that the points of resemblance between the two are different at different stages of society is also clear. But it is necessary to trace the gradual rise of both in order to ascertain in what respects they differ and in what they agree. A proposition may sometimes be true as an historical fact and yet untrue as a principle. And the reverse may also be the case. In the former instance, the business of the political philosopher is to make use of the fact only so far as it may be the means of eliciting the principle.

At an early period of society, the king, or chief of the nation, by whatever name he was known, dispensed justice in person. It would be correct to say that the judiciary then formed a branch of the executive authority. But the great multitude of controversies, both civil and criminal, which grow up with the progress of civilization put an end to this arrangement and cause it to be superseded by another. The executive magistrate has neither the time nor the ability to attend to the ten-thousandth part of the controversies which are perpetually springing up in an industrious and densely populated country. He is obliged to employ a great number of subordinate agents, and this immediately introduces new combinations and a new element of power into the government.

What was originally regarded as an arrangement of convenience turns out to be an important step in the advancement of society. These deputies of the king render themselves so useful to the community and acquire in consequence so large a share of influence that they are no longer viewed as his dependents. The administration of the laws by a class of men set apart for that purpose raises the whole body of judicial magistrates to an independent position in the state, and not only renders it unnecessary but absolutely forbids that the executive magistrate should take part in judicial proceedings. James I was the last British monarch who ventured to take a seat on the bench and he was reminded by the judges that he had no business there — no right to give counsel and advice on the trial of any cause.

But as the judges still continue to be appointed by the king and to hold their places at his pleasure, the next important step is to render them irremovable after they are commissioned. And this was not effected in Great Britain until the act of settlement in 1689, nor even then completely until the first year of George III. In France, at one time, the tenure of the judges went beyond anything known in England. The office was hereditary. It was the absolute property of the incumbent, capable of being disposed of by sale or devise. And we know that Montesquieu, the celebrated writer, made sale of his when he retired into the country to write *The Spirit of Laws*. At present the tenure is the same as it is in Great Britain.

These changes are afterward followed, though at very long intervals, by another of still greater importance. The executive not only ceases to be judge, but he loses the power of appointment. The same causes, the general spread of intelligence, and the complicated transactions of society which gave the judges so independent a position in the community, act with even more force upon another department. The legislative body, the more immediate representatives of the people, attains an entirely new rank and importance, and the appointment of the judges is devolved upon it. And if when these were nominated by the king, it was correct to say that the judiciary was a branch of the executive power, with equal reason may we assert that it has now become a branch of the legislative department. But suppose that the chief magistrate, and the members of the legislative assembly are themselves elected by the people for limited terms, we shall not be at liberty to make either the one assertion or the other. In the early stages of society, the king is literally the sovereign, and it is by virtue of this attribute that he then centers in himself the powers of both the other departments. He is not merely judge; he is supreme legislator also. In proportion as the state becomes strong, he becomes weak. He is deprived of his prerogatives one by one in order that they may be distributed by the real sovereign, the people, which now for the first time, makes its appearance upon the stage. The government then assumes the character of a regular system. Three distinct departments are created by one common power, neither of which can lay claim to any part of the sovereignty of the state.

But there is one sense in which the judges may be said in a very advanced state of society to exercise a very important share of the executive authority. When the chief magistrate is elected for a short term and none of the subordinate officers are chosen by himself, his power is so greatly abridged that he is known by the name rather than by the functions he exerts. The decisions which he makes are not one in a hundred to those which are made by the courts, and to these tribunals are attached officers who carry into immediate execution the orders which they receive. This is the case in all the state constitutions of America which afford the most perfect models of government that have ever been established. In Ohio, for instance, the judges are perpetually active, while the executive, having little or nothing to do, is almost inert. If the executive officers of the courts were only appointed by the courts, we might say that the judiciary had usurped nearly all the executive power of the state.

The independence of the judiciary has been considered as a fundamental principle in government. But by that term is understood in Great Britain and France, and even in the United States where European ideas sometimes contribute to modify the institutions, a tenure for life. And yet the same arguments which are employed to vindicate the propriety of this arrangement may be used with nearly equal force to show that the executive and the legislative body should hold their places for life. In some respects there would be even greater propriety in establishing this rule in the latter than in the former case. For the chief magistrate and the popular deputies stand in the midst of the party conflicts of the day, and if we wish to protect them from the storms of political life that so their judgments may not be swerved from the path of rectitude by the changeable currents of opinion, no way would seem so effectual as to withdraw them from this influence. There may be the most solid reasons why in a monarchical government the judges should be independent, in the English sense of the term, and yet these reasons may be inapplicable in a republic and not have sufficient force to lay the foundation of a general maxim. That only is entitled to the dignity and value of a maxim which, although it may not be applicable to all circumstances and to every condition of society, is yet applicable to the most perfect disposition of the subject matter which we have to deal with.

In Great Britain and France the executive magistrate is a hereditary officer and the appointment of the judges is vested in him. The only plan, therefore, of creating anything like an independence of him is to make the tenure of their office permanent. The only alternative is between removability at the pleasure of the king and a tenure for life. The last plan has been adopted in order to produce an effect which in a country of free institutions is unnecessary and out of place. As the station which the king holds is so far removed from the wholesome influence of public opinion, the judges, if dependent upon him, might be subservient to his worst designs. The influence of the crown would be felt everywhere, in the walks of private life as well as in political affairs. So great an authority centered in one person might render him the preponderant power in the state. By breaking the link of connection from the moment the appointment is made, there may be good ground to expect that the judges will feel a due sense of responsibility to the community which they are appointed to serve.

For what we intend, or should wish to intend, when we reason in favor of the independence of the judges is that they should be freed from the control of any individual, that they should not be subjected to any species of personal influence. But this by no means implies that they should be independent of the society or community whose interests they are designed to administer. The two things have been constantly confounded, although in reality they differ from each other in most respects. If in the United States the appointing power was a hereditary body or one elected for life the analogy would hold. It would then be necessary to render the judges independent of that power in order to secure their dependence upon and responsibility to the people. But if the appointing power is itself chosen by the people for a short term, a tenure for a limited period may not only be compatible with the independence of the judiciary, it may be the true way of reconciling that independence with a due sense of responsibility. If the term independence of the judiciary does necessarily mean an emancipation from the control which electoral government imposes, the people of America would be led to pull down the whole fabric of the institutions which they have constructed in order to introduce so salutary a principle into all departments.

Nothwithstanding the independence of the judiciary, as understood in Europe, is an anomaly in some of the American constitutions, there are some circumstances which have caused it to work well in practice.

First. The pursuits of a judge are of a highly intellectual character, and all intellectual pursuits exercise a favorable influence upon the character. They have a decidedly moral tendency. Although the investigation of legal questions may not contribute to open and invigorate the understanding so much as some other mental occupations, it assists powerfully in strengthening the moral qualities. The duties which the judge is called upon to discharge consist in the application of the rules of morality to the affairs of real life, and are therefore calculated to impress his whole behavior with an air of seriousness and conscientiousness. To be called to act as umpire in the numerous and important controversies between individuals, to sit in judgment upon the life and reputation of a fellow being, to hold the scales of justice with a firm and unfaltering hand: these are duties of no common import, and except in natures very illy formed are every way fitted to purify and elevate the character. The judge, too, is removed from the scene of party conflicts, nor is it expected that he will mingle in all the gayety and frivolity of fashionable life. He is thus placed out of the way of temptation more than other men, and is insensibly beguiled into a train of conduct the most favorable for the practice of both public and private virtue.

Second. The system of judicial precedents acts to a considerable extent as a check upon the conduct of judges. As it is necessary that there should be rules to restrain private individuals, so it is also necessary that there should be a law to restrain the court, and precedents constitute that law. The respect for cases which have already been adjudged, although it should never be carried so far as to render them absolutely binding, prevents any marked or habitual dereliction of duty. The profession are apt to be keenly attentive to both the motives and the reasons of the bench when it undertakes to overthrow a decision which has grown to be a principle; and in this way a system of responsibility is created which in the case of all other public functionaries can only be brought about by short terms of office.

These views are of considerable importance in surveying this interesting question in all its parts. But they rather show that there are some compensatory contrivances incident to the system than that the system is as perfect as it may be made. The theory of compensations is sometimes of inestimable value. It is even our only resource where the structure of society is of so fixed a character as to give us a very limited control over the political institutions. But if these contrivances will not always continue to act with effect, if they do not cure all the defects which it would be desirable to reach, above all if the society in which we are placed presents entirely new materials, it may be the part of wisdom to endeavor to reconstruct in part a system which has grown up under other and very different circumstances. To permit it to stand forever in the same position would be a confession that what we term compensations are something which makes amends for our own want of foresight and ability rather than for any inevitable fault in the system itself.

Public opinion in America was at one time universally in favor of the independence of the judiciary. In some parts of the union there are at present many individuals of the greatest intelligence who are firmly attached to the scheme. They believe that the most untoward influences may be brought to bear upon the administration of justice unless this is inserted as a fundamental principle in the government. My own opinion is that once a nation has entered upon the task of self-government it is bound to encounter all the perils which are incident to it, and that these perils, numerous as they are, are among the means provided for preserving the integrity of the system. A nation which has once fairly entered upon this arduous career has overcome the principal difficulty; all other obstacles will be surmounted as the people grow into the system. Perhaps many of the mischiefs which now incommode society are a consequence of the rubbing together of old and new ideas. But when the new ideas become a thing of familiar apprehension and of daily exercise, the minds of men will take a wider survey of the whole field of experiment and acquire more confidence in the results which may be expected. And this increase of confidence will add strength to the institutions — will give them the very support which they stand in need of. Nothing throws so many obstacles in the way of self-government as a denial of the right and ability of the people to engage in it. If on the other hand these are frankly conceded and all intelligent men lend their assistance in carrying out the plan, everything will go easy.

An election for a term of years may be necessary to enable the mind of the judge to keep pace with the general progress of knowledge and more especially to make him acquainted with the diversified working of the institutions under which he lives, in the administration of a part of which he is engaged but all parts of which are thoroughly connected. A public officer may be wonderfully skilled in all the mysteries of his profession and yet lag miserably behind the age in which he lives. It is a great mistake to suppose that because the judges are called to expound the principles of an abstruse science that they should be insensible to the general movement of the age and country in which they are born; that they should live in society and come perpetually in contact with the practical concerns of men and yet be unaffected by the influence of public opinion. There is a very wide difference between being drawn from the path of rectitude and duty by every temporary gust of party spirit and submitting the mind to the healthful influence of those opinions and feelings which grow up in the progress of every improving society. The first unhinges the mind; the last refreshes and invigorates it. There is no public magistrate whose mind will not be enlarged and liberalized, whose views will not be rendered both more wise and just, by catching something from the influence of that public opinion which constitutes to so great an extent the regulative principle of society. There is no art or calling or profession which is not greatly modified in practice through the instrumentality of this influence. But when the judge is sure, provided he commits no technical violation of duty, that he will retain his station for life, he is very apt to regard himself as entirely absolved from this control. And although he may not outrage the law in a single instance, he may give evidence of the narrowest views and the most rooted bigotry which, although unperceived by himself, will give a tinge to the whole administration of justice. There is always a vast amount of large and enlightened views, and these popular ones too, pervading every society in which free institutions are established which do not deserve to be treated as mere algebraical quantities; for although they do not exactly constitute the principles of any particular science, they surround every science and profession which have to deal with the interests of men and afford light and assistance at every step which we take.

But the chief argument in favor of a limited tenure of office is derived from the peculiar character and functions of a court of justice, so different from what they appear to be in theory and so different from what they are actually supposed to be from a cursory observation. Such a tribunal does in effect partake to a great extent of the character of a legislative body. The idea commonly entertained is that it is simply invested with the power of expounding the laws which have been ordained by another and a distinct department of government; and this office it does undoubtedly perform. But this power of expounding comprehends a great deal and reaches much further than is generally imagined. It at once communicates to a court of justice the double character of a legislative and judicial tribunal. This is inevitable and arises from the inherent imperfection which attends all human institutions. It is not in the power of any collection of men formed into a legislative assembly, however fertile in resources their understandings may be, to invent a system of ready-made rules which shall embrace all, or anything like all, the cases which actually occur. The consequence is that a judicial tribunal which has been created with the avowed design of applying the laws as they are made finds itself engaged in an endless series of disquisitions and reasonings in order to ascertain the precise rule which is applicable to any particular case. The innumerable contracts, voluntary dispositions, and delinquencies of individuals are perpetually giving a new form to private controversies and present new views and new questions to the examination of the court. However full and however minute the code of laws may be in its provisions, a vast field is still left open for the exercise of the reasoning powers and the sound discrimination of the judges. The cases of the "first impression," as the lawyers term them, are as numerous now as when Marshall and Kent took their seats upon the bench.[3] It is not a reproach to the legal profession that this should be so; it is merely a curious and interesting fact in the history of jurisprudence that the exigencies of society, the ever varying forms into which

3. [James Kent (1763–1847), important American jurist, appointed judge of the supreme court of the State of New York in 1798; John Marshall (1755–1835), fourth Chief Justice of the United States in the Supreme Court, appointed in 1801.]

the transactions of business are thrown, should ramify to such an endless extent the rules which regulate the conduct of individuals. Perhaps it is no more than happens to every other department of knowledge, for every conquest which science makes, every fresh accession it receives, only presents a new vantage ground whence the mind can see further and take in a wider scope than it did before. But in jurisprudence, the experiments which are made are infinitely more numerous than in any other science, and this contributes to modify and to attenuate to a wonderful extent the rules which have been made and the principles which have already been adjudged. For every question which arises, every case which is tried, is a new experiment which lays the foundation for new views and new analyses, and which the finer and more subtle they are the more they escape from the grasp of general principles and the greater the discretion which is conferred upon the courts of justice.

It is sometimes supposed that all the decisions which are now made, all the rules which are declared, are mere deductions from some general principles which had been previously settled. But how far back, and by whom, were these principles settled? Not by the legislature. The greatest genius which had devoted itself exclusively to the task would be incompetent to its performance. Hence the laws are comparatively few, while the books of jurisprudence are immensely voluminous. The human mind is able to invent very little. Its true employment consists in the observation and analysis of phenomena, after they have been developed, and in then binding them together into classes. And as this process of development in the case of jurisprudence is constantly going on, after as well as before the legislature have passed the most comprehensive laws, the functions of the judge, do what we will or turn the question in whatever aspect we please, are compelled to bear a very close analogy with those of the law-making power. If all the rules which are now declared by the courts are mere corollaries from the statute book or from previous adjudications, the same may have been said one or two hundred years ago, and then what is the meaning of that vast accumulation of learning which then exercised and still continues to exercise human ingenuity? Admitting that there are some sciences where a few elementary truths being given, the whole mass of subordinate principles may be readily evolved from them — a proposition which may require further investigation before it is admitted — yet this cannot be the case with jurisprudence which does not deal with abstract propositions simply, but with a state of facts where the question is perpetually recurring — what does human experience prove to be the wisest rule which can be adopted? or what does it prove to be the wisest construction of a rule already in existence?

Profound writers, and among others Leibnitz and Dugald Stewart, have supposed that jurisprudence might be reduced to a regular and exact science in which all our conclusions may be deduced with absolute rigor and with the force of demonstration from certain previously established principles.* But to the question, how numerous shall these principles be, the most acute understanding can give no satisfactory answer. In every department of moral science, in order to be able to range a case under any particular principle we must first go through a process of analysis more or less tedious. The principle may be taken for granted and yet its applicability be determinable only after much investigation. If it is not only applicable to the whole extent but requires to be modified, a thing of common occurrence, the foundation is immediately laid for a host of other principles, equally authoritative and each claiming to control all the cases which can be brought under it, until at length, the process of analysis being pushed still farther, these principles give way before others still more numerous which assume to be the guide because they are more exactly applicable to a given state of facts. So that, admitting the great value of what are termed general principles — and hardly anyone will deny it — what a wide field is notwithstanding opened to human ingenuity in tracing out the fine analogies which may connect a given controversy with an elementary truth. How different may be the judgments of

* In "Nouveaux Essais de l'entendement," b. iv. chap. vii, Leibnitz says that jurisprudence and medicine differ widely in this respect; that in the former, we can deduce all our conclusinons from certain general principles; that we want few books therefore, but in medicine we cannot have too many. But medicine depends upon our physical structure, jurisprudence upon both our physical and moral structure. Medicine is adapted to the constitutions of individuals, jurisprudence to collective societies of men. The last, therefore, must be the most complicated; it must require as much experience and observation and therefore as wide an induction of facts and as full a collection of those phenomena which we call *cases*. And, therefore, it is that law books have always, in the age of Tribonian as well as that of Kent, been more numerous than medical works. [Tribonian (d. 545?), Roman jurist who compiled the *Corpus Iuris Civilis* under Justinian I; James Kent, *Commentaries on the American Law* (New York, 1826–1830), 4 vols.; Dugald Stewart (1753–1828), Scottish philosopher and leading figure in the Scottish or Common Sense school of philosophy. Grimke added the note to the second edition.]

different minds equally astute and ingenious when exercised upon precisely the same state of facts. The functions of the court will still be resembled to those of a legislative body. There will be ample room for the operation of sinister motives which will both warp the judgment and blind the moral vision. And the position which I have endeavored to enforce will be true: that if it is not wise to confer a permanent tenure of office upon the executive and legislative, it should not be conferred upon the judiciary, and the more so because the legislative functions which the last perform is a fact entirely hidden from the great majority of the community.

It is remarkable that some very enlightened minds should be so wedded to the independence of the judiciary when in the nature of things men must sometimes be elevated to the bench who are deficient in both the moral and intellectual qualities which are requisite and when the only remedy which can be applied consists in re-eligibility. I, for one, protest against the adoption of a principle which would secure an incompetent or badly-disposed judge in the possession of his place for thirty or forty years because he committed no flagrant violation of duty. It is not always a reflection upon the wisdom of the appointing power that an improper person has been elected. Very excellent lawyers have sometimes made indifferent judges and lawyers not the most eminent have sometimes become very distinguished judges. Nor are the moral qualities of the man always sufficiently developed to assure us what his future conduct will be if he is placed for life in a situation of even tolerable ease. The experiment however must be made, and our only alternative is to provide a plan by which an unworthy or ignorant judge may be removed, as well as a fit one be continued in office. And admitting that no scheme will be entirely successful in accomplishing either the one or the other, I do suppose that none which can be invented will so well answer all the ends which we are in search of as an election for a moderate term of years.

The purity of character and the eminent learning of the English judges have always been the subject of commendation, and certainly it does not become anyone who is not furnished with the most exact information to detract from this high praise. That the English judges as a body have been superior to those of the states of continental Europe may be conceded, but at the same time it is clear that there may be numberless improprieties and aberrations from the strict path of duty which the exceedingly technical character of the English system of procedure would entirely conceal from the public eye. Moreover, the English bench is connected with the aristocracy. The two institutions are glued together. And whenever society is distributed into distinct classes, it is difficult for those who are out of a particular class to penetrate into its interior so as to observe and understand everything which is transacted within it. It is only incidentally that we are able to catch anything which sheds light upon the manners of English judges.

The peculiar interest which attached to the life of Savage caused his biography to be written by one of the most remarkable men of the day who has related the very extraordinary behavior of the judge who sat upon the trial.[4] An eminent Englishman, in his sketch of Lord Ellenborough, has detailed the high-handed course which that eminent judge pursued on the trial of some very important state cases.[5]

In France, where the tenure of the judges is the same as in Great Britain, it has always been the custom for suitors to visit the judges. The practice, to say the least, does not look well. It may not be attended with any improper influence. But a violation of decorum is often a stepping stone to the commission of some graver fault. The system of bribery, once universally in vogue, may have been entirely abandoned, but an intelligent traveler who lately attended the trial of a case in a French court tells us that he saw the judge who presided driving the splendid equipage in which a few days before the successful suitor traveled to the assizes.

Indeed if one were disposed to look to England to furnish us with a body of experience which would help to decide this interesting question, we might find arguments in favor of the absolute dependence of the judges as decisive as those which are employed on the opposite side of the question. For the chancellor, the judges of the admiralty and of the ecclesiastical courts are removable at any time, and yet these mag-

4. [Richard Savage (d. 1743), minor poet and notorious figure of eighteenth-century England; Dr. Samuel Johnson included the "Life of Savage" (1744) in his lives of the English poets. The judge was Sir Francis Page, known by contemporaries as the "hanging judge."]

5. [Edward Law, first Baron Ellenborough (1750–1818), lord chief justice of England. Grimke probably refers to Henry Peter Brougham, *Historical Sketches of Statesmen Who Flourished in the Time of George III*, 3rd ed. (London, 1842); Ellenborough had violently attacked Brougham from the bench when Brougham was acting as counsel for James Henry Leigh Hunt against the charge of libel against the Prince of Wales (December 9, 1812).]

istrates have been in every respect equal to their brethren of the common-law courts.

The judicial system of the American states differs in many respects from that established in Great Britain. As civil government is not understood to exist for the purpose of creating a splendid and imposing pageant of authority, all the institutions are made to administer in the most easy, effectual, and unostentatious manner to the practical wants of the community. To cause justice to be dispensed thoroughly, extensively, and with the least cost and parade has been the governing idea in the organization of the courts. It is not enough to possess such tribunals unless they are completely within the reach of everyone who has a complaint to make before them. England and Wales with a population of eighteen millions have about twenty judges assigned to the superior courts. The United States, with a population a little larger, have more than two hundred.

I take no account in the enumeration of the county courts, courts of request, and other subordinate tribunals which are established in the former country, since the business transacted by them all falls within the jurisdiction of justices of the peace in America whose numbers amount to many thousands. I simply confine myself to those courts which in the two countries exercise a corresponding jurisdiction. The disparity there is immense, and it is a fact full of interest and instruction. No man who is not clad in an armor of gold can gain entrance into the English court of chancery and no man can litigate effectually in the king's bench, or common pleas, unless his circumstances are very independent. Very different is the state of things in the United States. Local courts, of a high as well as of an inferior jurisdiction, are established throughout the whole country and amply compensate by their intrinsic utility for the want of pageantry and show. But this consequence follows, that however easy it may be to select twenty men with splendid salaries to occupy very imposing stations in the government, it may be a matter of very considerable difficulty to induce two hundred to accept office where the duties are unremitting and arduous, the salaries low, and where the occupation, although of an intellectual character, is yet seldom sufficiently so to fill the mind and to gratify a high ambition. The law being an exhausted science, so far as regards the leading principles, the business transacted by the courts becomes one chiefly of detail, not requiring faculties so high as formerly but demanding more patience and assiduity and a greater degree of tact in the performance of the duties. What is sought after in America, and what should be the object of pursuit in every other civilized state, is a judicial system which shall do the business, the whole business, and nothing but the business, and this in the most prompt and effectual manner practicable. And this end cannot be attained without the establishment of numerous courts of superior jurisdiction and without therefore running the risk of sometimes procuring incompetent persons to act as judges. The average number of court days in all the six circuits in England (exclusive of London) is one hundred and thirty-five. The average number in each of the fifteen circuits in the single state of Ohio, whose population is not more than two millions, is one hundred and sixty-three. It is no wonder that want of time to try the case was assigned as one reason for proceeding by impeachment, rather than by indictment, against the late Lord Melville.[6] That the risk incurred in selecting proper persons to set upon the bench in America has turned out to be much less than was calculated may be matter of surprise, but that it will always exist to some extent is a decisive reason why the judges should be chosen for a term of years. Even in England, we are assured upon very high authority that not more than twenty lawyers can be found competent to fill the place of "puisne" judge. But if the courts were more numerous and the demand for ability greater, there can be no doubt that the supply would keep pace with it and that there would be no more difficulty in obtaining two hundred than there is now of obtaining twenty judges.*

At the present day the tenure for life is abolished in nearly one half of the American states. The term of office varies considerably in different parts of the Union. In Pennsylvania it is fifteen years, while in Vermont it is only one year. In the greater number the period is seven years. So far as we may judge from the books of reports, I do not know that any courts have given evidence of more solid and extensive learning than those of New Jersey where the duration of the office under both the late and present constitutions is eight years. And Indiana,

6. [Henry Dundas, first Viscount Melville (1742–1811), impeached but finally acquitted by the House of Commons in 1805 for misuse of public funds during his tenure as First Lord of the Admiralty.]

* During the Cromwellian Revolution in England, the professors in the universities were removed and dissenters appointed in their place. On the restoration of Charles II, the new incumbents were found to be so entirely competent to the discharge of their duties that no thought was entertained of removing them. They all retained their places. [Note added to the second edition.]

where the system is the same, furnishes the example of a very young community immediately springing forward in this career of improvement. The decisions of her supreme court are also marked by uncommon ability and learning.

In Pennsylvania, the system has been recently adopted, but there is every reason to believe that her courts will continue to maintain the high reputation which they have hither enjoyed. In Connecticut, it is quite remarkable that before the independent tenure was introduced and when the elections were annual, the bench was eminently distinguished for the learning ability and integrity of the members who composed it. I believe I do not exaggerate when I say that five or six of the judges who sat in her superior court prior to the constitution of 1818 would have done honor to any of the courts of Westminster hall. By causing the administration of justice to penetrate every part of the community, the conduct of the judges in America is submitted to a more thorough observation and scrutiny by the public at large than in any other country. And as it is the people, and none but the people, who are interested in the upright and impartial administration of the laws, an unworthy man who has fortuitously wriggled himself into office will stand an uneven chance for re-election.

For what period shall the judges be elected? is a question to which different minds may give different answers. Nor is it very important what the precise period shall be. Once the system of responsibility is established, we have made sure of the ruling principle which is to guide in the constitution of the courts and the greater or less exactness with which it is applied is a matter of minor consideration. I should say that the term should not be less than five, nor more than ten years. One reason why the members of the legislative body are elected for so short a period as one or two years is to introduce the great body of the citizens to an acquaintance with public affairs and to cultivate in them an ability to take part in their management. Free institutions are a security for the preservation of liberty only because they lay the foundation for that discipline of the character which enables us to know and appreciate what liberty is. But the law is a science which no more than theology or medicine can be made the study of the great bulk of the people. It is necessarily the exclusive pursuit of a small number whose training and education both before and after they are admitted to the bar is obliged to take a direction which conspires to a single end. The legislature is a numerous body; the free and discursive character of the debate and the large dimensions which very many questions assume force upon the mind of almost every member some tolerable acquaintance with their purport and bearing. But a single controversy at the bar in order to be grasped may demand the most minute and painful attention of even the professors of the science; so much so that it is not at all uncommon for a lawyer who has been present but not engaged in a particular trial to feel himself at a loss if he undertakes to give a distinct account of the testimony and of the precise legal questions which were mooted. It is not because the law is a cabalistical science that it is full of perplexity; it is because it deals so much in detail and because it is impossible to get rid of this detail when we are obliged to apply our knowledge to the multifarious transactions of human life. The general principles by which the mercantile body conduct their affairs are pretty much the same everywhere; yet how much caution, attention, and sagacity are sometimes necessary in settling a long and intricate account, even where no difficult, legal question intervenes. I would, therefore, make the tenure of the judges long enough to induce lawyers of competent ability to abandon the profession in exchange for that office; while at the same time, I would not make it so long as to absolve the judges from a strict responsibility to the community. I would rather increase the salaries than part with the dependent tenure.

The manner in which the laws are administered, the exterior deportment of the bar and bench, are a matter of very great importance. The business habits which are acquired by an experience of some years insure promptitude, skill and dispatch in the decision of legal controversies. The trial of cases is conducted with ease, order, and regularity. The confidence of suitors is greatly and justly increased by this circumstance. Instead of altercations between the judge and the advocate which so much disturb the regular course of business and detract from the weight of the court, everything proceeds in an even and regular manner. Integrity of purpose is not of more consequence than ability, for without knowledge there is no room for the exercise of integrity. A judge may intend very well in the general and yet be unable to mean anything distinct when it becomes all important for him to act and to make his integrity apparent in the things which he does. The term of office, therefore, should be long enough to enable the public to make a fair trial of the ability and moral qualities of the incumbent, and not so long as to prevent a removal in a reasonable time if he is deficient in either.

I have referred to the system of legal precedents as constituting a salutary check upon the conduct of judges. It now becomes necessary to approach this subject more closely and to explain distinctly the view I have taken in order that we may be able to understand, in its full extent, what is the force and operation of precedents. But if anything is said which goes to qualify the proposition I before laid down, the reader must not therefore run away with idea that there is contradiction. Political philosophy has to encounter the same difficulties which beset jurisprudence. Our principles have to be constantly modified, but they are not therefore to be dispensed with.

When one considers the vast amount of adjudged cases which are already reported in the United States alone, it is obvious that the utmost attention and patience may be necessary to decipher them when they are appealed to as rules or as mere guides in the determination of particular cases. They will be a very ineffectual check upon one who is unable to seize their import and to appreciate them for exactly what they are worth. The principles of jurisprudence in almost every one of its departments have been so exceedingly ramified by the multitude of similar or very nearly similar controversies that the shades of difference between different precedents are often so minute as to hold the judgment in suspense as to which should be relied upon. And yet they may conduct to totally different conclusions in a given case. The consequence is that a very considerable proportion of the cases which are actually decided might be determined either way with a great show of reason and with a like reliance upon precedents in either case. This observation will startle the general reader, but it will not fail to be comprehended by the learned and experienced jurist. Nor is it more remarkable than what is daily exhibited in all courts of justice, to wit, the appearance of lawyers of known integrity on different sides of a case, each arguing with zeal and perfect conviction for the correctness of the views he advocates. Persons who are imperfectly informed believe that this practice is totally inconsistent with the uprightness which should belong to the members of any profession. Others look upon it as something which can be explained in no way whatever. But in truth it is not imputable to dishonesty, nor is it incapable of reasonable explanation. It is a natural consequence of the nature of the science which having to deal with an infinity of detail necessarily runs out into an infinity of deductions and conclusions which perpetually modify and cross each other. Independently of a number of cases which are settled out of court by the advice of the profession, and of a number which might be equally settled in the same way, there are still a greater number where the principles appealed to on either side are very evenly balanced.

But this very important consequence follows: that in many cases where the distinctions are fine and the authority of precedents is half obliterated, an ill-disposed judge may cast his prejudices into the scale in order to decide the controversy without his motives being suspected by anyone, or if suspected, without the possibility of being detected. The judge who has a competent share of the pride of human opinion, the lawyer who believes that jurisprudence is a science "par excellence," a science of strict and immutable rules, may demur to these views, but I am satisfied they will gain the assent of a majority of both the bench and the bar. And if they are well founded, they afford powerful reasons why the judicial tenure should not be for life. By submitting the conduct of the judge during a limited period to the observation of the public in those instances where his motives and reasons will be apprehended, the probability is less that he will on any occasion free himself from the restraint which a sense of duty should invariably impose upon him. The public feel as if they had no right to scan the conduct of a public magistrate who has a freehold right to his office. He is protected from all intrusion of this kind except where he is guilty of some open delinquency. An election for a term of years removes this indisposition on the part of the public to observe the course which the administration of justice takes. The judge, sensible that his actions are the subject of attention and not knowing to what extent this scrutiny may be pushed, becomes more circumspect in his conduct; and as it is difficult to impress two contradictory habits upon anyone, whether public or private individual, his conduct will more readily conform to that one which is dictated equally by self-interest and by a regard to duty.

I have not yet adverted to another and a deeply interesting question: whether the judges should be elected directly by the people or by an intermediate authority. The last is the plan adopted in the great majority of the American states as well as in the government of the union. But the intermediate body which appoints is not the same in all these instances. In Maine, Massachusetts, and New Hampshire, the appointment is made by the governor and council. In eight states, as well as in the federal government, the executive and senate appoint. In rather more than one half of the states, the election is made by the two branches of the legislature. Delaware stands alone in this respect for the governor has the sole power of appointment.

The great object to be obtained in organizing the courts is to select persons who are every way qualified to discharge the duties. But the qualities which are requisite in a judge are different in many respects from what are demanded in any other public officer and the selection is proportionally more difficult. It is not because the ability of the people to make a fair choice is distrusted that this power has been delegated; it is because they are supposed not to have the opportunity of forming a correct judgment. The seat of government is the place where information from all parts of the state is collected and where abundant materials exist for forming a proper estimate of the qualities of candidates. Members of the legislative body are properly elected in districts in which they reside and these districts are of so convenient a size that the qualifications of the candidates are under the immediate observation of the electors. With regard to the governor, whose duties in most of the states are few, it is not necessary that he should be versed in any particular science, though no species of learning or accomplishment is amiss in any public officer but adds greatly to his reputation and gives illustration to the state over which he presides. The case of the judges differs materially from both these classes of public officers. The learning and accomplishments which are demanded of them are of such a character that the great body of the citizens are neither desirous nor have any interest in acquiring them. As an individual therefore of the soundest judgment and the fairest intentions, who has not within his reach the information upon which he desires to act deputes another to act for him, so the American people for similar reasons have delegated to agents immediately responsible to them the difficult task of selecting fit persons to preside in the courts of justice. That an individual voluntarily avails himself of the intervention and services of another is proof of his liberty, not of his constraint, and that a whole people should proceed upon the same obvious and rational views may denote the exercise of the most enlightened freedom.

It must not be imagined that in every instance where the public authority is delegated the power of the people is therefore abridged.

Rousseau was mistaken in supposing that wherever the people act through the instrumentality of agents they are free only during the moments of the election, that the choice being made, power has departed from them not to be resumed until the return of another election. This may be true to a greater or less extent in the artificial forms of government where so many of the magistrates not being elective, but holding by hereditary title, wield an authority which counterbalances that of the people and so effectually controls public opinion. But in a democratic republic, it is precisely the reverse. As the principle of responsibility runs through all the institutions, no one can escape from it in order to shelter himself under an independent authority. It is true that construct government as we will, there will always be a tendency in some part or other to elude the control of public opinion. But where the great body of the institutions is sound, the utmost degree of exactness and theoretical propriety may be a matter of indifference: like an individual possessing a fine constitution and robust health and who does not take every sort of precaution against changes of the weather, a people in the full possession of free institutions need not guard themselves too tenderly against every possible contingency. The intervention of a jury in all common law trials renders such extreme scrupulousness less necessary in the constitution of the judiciary than in that of the other departments.

But a great revolution has just been effected in one of the American states. The new constitution of New York has ordained that the judges of all the courts shall be elected directly by the people. This I regard as one of the greatest experiments which has ever been made upon human nature. This single feature in that constitution stamps the convention which framed it as the most important which has ever sat in America since the formation of the federal constitution. Nor can it be viewed as a hasty or visionary scheme, since the assembly which planned it was composed of an unusual number of able men, of men who united in a high degree all the qualities which are necessary to make up the character of wise and enlightened statesmen: experience, sagacity, and information and a desire to innovate for the sole purpose of reforming. No public measure which has been adopted in America has so powerfully arrested my attention or given me more painful anxiety. The conclusion to which I have come, forming my judgment from the general character of the population, is that if the experiment does not succeed the people will cheerfully retrace their steps. But I am strongly inclined to think that it will succeed. There is such a thing as making an institution succeed, however much it may appear to run counter to the received opinions of the day. This repugnance may be the only obstacle to success. If the people of New York persevere in the immense exertions which they have hitherto made to educate themselves, and if in consequence a thorough conviction is imbibed, not merely as something gained from others but as realized by themselves, that an upright and enlightened administration of justice is indispensable to the protection of their interests, I cannot doubt that the experiment will succeed. Mischiefs will exist and precisely of the same kind as those which now trouble the community: the disposition to centralization, the effort on the part of political leaders to control public opinion, the substitution of a constructive majority in place of the real majority. But with a state of society such as is fast growing up from the operation of causes which I have referred to, I can easily conceive that these evils may be warded off as effectually, and perhaps more so, than under the old system. So important a movement can only be regarded at present as an experiment, and it has been most justly remarked of the Americans that they possess the faculty of making experiments in government with less detriment to themselves than any other people.

But anyone who was attentive to the circumstances under which the New York convention assembled and who watched throughout the course of the proceedings must be sensible that there is a soundness of public opinion in that state which will prevail upon the people to retract, if the experiment is not successful. It should be observed, however, that the same constitutional provision exists in the state of Mississippi and has been in operation for more than ten years. Even this experiment is too recent to enable us to pronounce a decisive opinion upon. The scale upon which it is made being so much smaller than in the other case, the plan has attracted very little public attention. But if it does succeed in both these states — if it succeeds in New York alone — it will probably be adopted throughout the greater number of the American states. And I predict that it will then be the parent of more important changes in both government and society than have been brought about by any other single measure.

The theory of the judiciary cannot be well understood unless we take into consideration the uses of jury trial, an institution which exercises so wide and salutary an influence upon the administration of justice.

First. The juries act as a check upon the conduct of the judge. He discharges his most important functions not only in the presence of, but with the cooperation and assistance of his fellow citizens. The jury are not chosen as in the Roman commonwealth from a patrician body; they are taken indiscriminately from the great mass of the people. The responsibility is consequently increased; his deportment and actions are not merely observed by the spectator, they are narrowly watched by those who participate in the trial and to whom is committed the ultimate determination of the issue. Benjamin Constant proposed that the juries should be selected from the class of electors, that is, from among those who pay a tax of from fifty to sixty dollars. And this is now the law. In Great Britain the qualifications of jurors are also very nearly the same as those of the electors. But the latter being much more numerous than the French electors, the jury is a more popular body. In America, the same reasons which led to the adoption of a liberal rule of suffrage have also augmented the number of persons qualified to act as jurymen.

Second. The institution of the jury introduces the great bulk of the people to an acquaintance with the practical working of the laws, interests them in their faithful administration and contributes to train them to an ability for self-government. "He only," it has been said, "is fitted to command, who has learned to obey"; he only is fitted to take the lead, who has already passed through the subordinate ranks.[7]

Third. The intervention of the jury helps to mitigate the extreme rigor of general rules, to give effect to the import of general maxims and yet occasionally to make allowance for that infinite variety of shades in human transactions of which the laws cannot take cognizance.

Fourth. Juries stand in the place of impartial spectators and are therefore well calculated to act as umpire in settling controversies among their neighbors. This is an office which could not be so well performed by a pre-existing tribunal. As I have already observed, it is an inestimable advantage which we derive from a regular judicial establishment that it extinguishes the motives for private war, the most

7. [The proverb can be traced back to Plato and in English is at least as old as John Florio, *First Fruits* (1578): "Who hath not served cannot command."]

deplorable of all the calamities which can visit society. This benefit, however, would not be so perfect if it were not for the jury whose composition is such as to inspire general confidence in the fairness of all law proceedings.

Fifth. The intervention of a jury gives publicity to trials. The disuse of the institution on the continent of Europe, consequent on the introduction of the Roman law, was the cause why the proceedings in a court of justice became secret. As long as the "prodes homines," the jury, were a necessary part of the machinery, judicial investigations were a matter of curiosity to the public. As soon as they were dispensed with and the whole evidence was collected in the form of depositions, legal controversies gave rise merely to a discussion of technical points and the public no longer felt an interest in them. The halls of justice were thenceforth abandoned to the judge and the advocate. What was once a custom soon became a law, and at the present day trials are for the most part conducted in secret throughout the greater part of continental Europe.

The non-introduction, or rather the partial introduction of the civil law into England, accounts for the preservation of jury trials there and for the remarkable publicity which law proceedings have always had. The fifty-fifth section of the French constitution of 1830 declares that the trial of criminal causes shall be conducted in public, except in those instances where publicity would be injurious to decency and good morals, and the court is bound to announce that as a reason for sitting in private — a very remarkable state of society when it was reserved for a constitutional ordinance to provide that the halls of justice should be thrown open to the inspection of the public. But jury trial was unknown in France until the revolution; it is no part now of the procedure in civil cases. Its introduction in criminal trials is the reason why they have been rendered public. Not only was the examination in secret, but there could be no cross-examination, for the only person entitled to ask questions was the judge. It is but recently that this unnatural custom has been put an end to, and that counsel in behalf of the prisoner have been permitted to assist in the examination. In Scotland, where the civil law has from time immemorial constituted the foundation of the jurisprudence, juries were unknown until 1815 in any but criminal cases. They were then for the first time introduced as an experiment into one of the civil courts of Edinburgh, and they are now a constituent part of the procedure in the court of sessions. The practice of conducting trials in public secures two distinct and very important ends. It operates as a safeguard against corruption and it prevents the administration of justice from becoming odious to the people. In some parts of Europe the criminal magistrates and officers are regarded with detestation and horror. They are looked upon as the instruments of an infernal tyranny whom the innocent shun and even shudder to approach. This is not the feeling in Great Britain or the United States. As the proceedings are conducted openly, the public may be said to take part in them. The fate of the criminal may be deplored, but everyone feels that he is condemned rather by the public voice than by the sentence of the judge.

There is one respect in which the institution of jury trial has been disadvantageous. It has caused the rules of evidence to be more strict than they would have otherwise been. The manner in which this has been brought about is very easily explained. The composition of juries originally and for centuries after the institution took its rise was such as not to permit the committing to them any evidence which might by possibility be misinterpreted or misapplied. Certain rules were consequently adopted which shut out every species of testimony which in order to be rightly used would demand a degree of caution and discrimination which could not be expected in the persons who made up the jury. The evidence excluded (and which was denominated incompetent) might shed abundant light upon all trials if it were confided to persons of judgment and good sense. But the condition of European society was generally low and juries necessarily partook of the same character. The consequence is that the rules of evidence have been gradually molded into a system so exceedingly artificial and complex that in the endeavor to correct one mischief another equally dangerous has been incurred. A great deal of truth has been shut out in order to prevent some falsehood from gaining entrance. And this system, having once taken root, has been continued long after the state of things which occasioned it has passed away. The constitution of American society is such that juries are every way competent to the management of that testimony which is now declared inadmissible. By the Belgian code, lately promulgated, the only persons who are absolutely excluded from giving testimony are the parties, relatives in the direct line, and husband and wife.

At an early period of society, the human mind does not dare to trust itself with any but the roughest and the most general rules. It feels an utter inability to enter into long inquiries, to compare and to balance a great many items of testimony in order to elicit the truth from the whole instead of from a part. For fear of doing wrong, it shuts itself up within a narrow circle, although the effect is to preclude a great deal of information and knowledge. But as society advances, the vision becomes more clear and distinct and the rules which are framed for the conduct of every department of life are rendered more free and liberal.

The Livingston code of Louisiana, as originally drawn up, excluded none as witnesses except attorneys and Catholic confessors.[8] Parties, however, were admitted with this limitation: their evidence could not be proffered by themselves, but must be demanded by the opposite party, by the court or by the jury. In England and New York efforts have recently been made to annul the distinction between competency and credibility: to permit parties and persons interested to testify in all cases, leaving their credit to be determined by the jury. And what sensible reason can be given why parties should be permitted to testify in one form of proceeding and not in another? In chancery suit and not on a common law trial? When the grand jury ("jury d'accusation") was introduced in France, the experiment for many years was deemed absolutely hopeless. It was found impossible to make the members understand the distinction, between the finding of a true bill and a sentence of conviction. They supposed that the first involved the last and often refused to find bills where there was the strongest "prima facie" evidence of guilt. No such misapprehension exists among the English or American grand juries. Still less would there be any misunderstanding with an English or American traverse jury as to the relative weight of the testimony, some part of which was unexceptionable and another open to examination, for the daily transactions of life, their ordinary business avocations, thoroughly initiate them into this manner of viewing and employing testimony.[9] I think there can be little doubt that in no long time a more liberal system will be established and that everyone will be convinced that it conduces to a much more enlightened and satisfactory administration of justice.

8. [Edward Livingston (1764–1836), jurist and stateman, who in 1821 was appointed to prepare a new code of laws and criminal procedure for the state of Louisiana where he was then a member of the legislature; the code was not adopted, although it brought Livingston international fame.]

9. [A traverse jury is one impaneled to try a civil or a criminal case; or, a trial jury as distinguished from a grand jury.]

The admission of the testimony of all those persons who are at present excluded (and I know of no case which should form an exception) would diminish the number of suits, and in those which were tried would cause the truth to be elicited more promptly and successfully. Greater solemnity would be imparted to all judicial proceedings when the evidence of persons who knew all about the transactions was thoroughly sifted, instead of applying, as is now the case, to witnesses who know very imperfectly or only by piecemeal. If a defendant in a criminal prosecution were in all instances examined, real delinquents would feel more terror of the law and innocent persons would have greater respect for it.

Whether the rule of unanimity or that of a majority should prevail in the finding of a verdict is a question which has been much debated in France since the introduction of jury trial in 1789. The rule of the majority has been constantly adopted there. By the law of 1789, this majority was fixed at 8:4. By that of 1791, at 9:3, and by that of 1835, at 7:5. And recently a proposition for another change has been discussed in the House of Deputies, but I am not informed what the result has been. M. Isambert says, if the English rule of unanimity had been adopted in France such men as Bailly, Lavoisier, and Malesherbes would never have been condemned.[10] The greater part of the judgments of the revolutionary tribunal were made by a fraction. M. Fermot has calculated, that where the majority is 7:5, the probability of error is as 1:4, indifferently in favor of and against the accused.[11] Where it is 8:4, the chance of error is 1:8, and where unanimity is required it is 1:8000. These are calculations which should make Englishmen and Americans prize the rule of unanimity even more than they have done. For although in the even tenor of ordinary times there should be as little probability of error under the French as under the English and American rule, yet, when the ele-

10. [François-André Isambert (1792–1857), French jurist and statesman, best remembered for his role in the abolition of slavery in the French colonies, who wrote widely on the history of French law; Jean Sylvain Bailly (1736–1793), who, as mayor of Paris, allowed the National Guard to fire upon a demonstrating crowd (July 17, 1791) and was later convicted and sent to the guillotine for having contrived the "July Massacre"; Antoine Lavoisier (1743–1794), French chemist, guillotined during the Reign of Terror; Chrétien Guillaume de Malesherbes (1721–1794), French statesman, defender of Louis XVI at his trial, who was arrested as a royalist and sent to the guillotine.]

11. ["M. Fermot": Grimke probably means Pierre de Fermat (1601–1665), the French mathematician.]

ments of society are greatly disturbed and the minds of men are heated by party spirit, the jury and the unanimity of the jury are the shield of the innocent. Unanimity is attended with this advantage: it compels to more discussion and deliberation among the jury. The verdict which in practice is very generally the verdict of a majority is the result of a more patient examination and is therefore more likely to be unexceptionable. In Scotland, the rule of unanimity prevails in civil and yet not in criminal cases: the reverse of what one would suppose should be the case. But the employment of the jury (composed of fifteen) in criminal trials dates very far back and was a distinguishing feature of Scotch institutions; whereas, the jury of twelve in civil causes was copied directly from England; the court in which the experiment was first made was presided over by an English barrister and nothing seemed so natural as to establish the English rule of unanimity.

One of the greatest difficulties which attend the administration of the law is the exceedingly technical character which the system has acquired. This is the chief of the popular objections which are ever made to it, and I am persuaded that it had great influence in carrying forward the plan of judicial reform in New York. The objection may be ill conceived and yet the reform may prove to be salutary. For let us analyze our ideas. Does this character of technicality arise from the fact that the legal profession have been in the habit of following a principle, or has it arisen from an adherence to precedents? If the first is the case, the law differs in no respect from any other pursuit in which the exercise of mind is demanded, from the practice of medicine down to the most inconsiderable of the mechanic arts. One cannot conceive of administering justice in a civilized community except upon some previously established rules. But this difficulty presents itself: that where a science deals so extensively and yet so much in detail with the practical interests of men, as is the case with the law, principles which were at first broad and clearly distinguishable become in the course of time exceedingly ramified, and our distinctions are then so fine that it is almost impossible to found a conclusion simply upon a rule of abstract justice. When this is the case, a new course is adopted as subsidiary to finding the principle. The question then raised is, what does human experience as tested by a great number of adjudications prove to be the best mode of applying the law in those countless instances where the rule of right in the abstract seems to be indifferent? As jurisprudence is eminently an experimental science, it is very important to ascertain to what extent a system of practice contributes to the public weal. Now, in innumerable instances, precedents are looked to because the abstract principle is so shadowy that it cannot be explored and, yet, it is of infinite consequence if we can to cling to some rule which has a near affinity to a principle, while at the same time a number of years of experience may bring the matter to a test and enable the legislator to ascertain whether any and what changes will be advantageous. The frequent revisions of the laws in the American states is one effort to attain this end. And there is a further plan which would recommend that it should be made the duty of the judges to make annual reports as to the working of specified parts of the system.

In administering this technical science then, the inquiry is, are we following a principle or only a precedent? If the former, how do we obtain the principle? When it is asked, is it right to murder or steal? the answer is plain enough. If it is asked, ought B to pay A a sum of money he borrowed from him? the answer also is plain. But the instances are without number where our principles become so dim that we are warned to pursue a new direction in order to find them. We are enabled to discover what is useful by knowing what is right, and we are enabled to find out what is right by understanding what is truly useful. The two are never disjoined.

But whatever may be the cause of the exceeding technicality of the law, whether it arises from the adoption of principles or the adoption of precedents or from both together, as is undoubtedly the case, there is no possible way of avoiding it; nor is there any one science, profession, or art to which the same difficulty does not adhere. It is more apparent in the case of the law than in any other calling because the science is applied in such infinite detail to the actions of men, and because this application is to so great an extent the subject of popular observation. That is to say, the very thing which stamps upon the law its character of excellence and utility, its application to the infinitely diversified affairs of society, is the foundation of the objection and the open and public administration of it is what gives occasion to the complaint. If the law were applied as sparingly as it is in despotic countries, it would lose this character of complexity immediately. It is in proportion as civilization advances and the institutions become free that our knowledge becomes both more full and more minute and that every profession or art which springs from knowledge becomes more difficult in the management. This is doubtless a wise dispensation of Providence: that in proportion as the temptation to abuse our power or our liberty increases, new bulwarks may be raised up to restrain our actions.

But in what I have now said, I do not mean to be understood that a great deal may not be done to free the law from the artificial character which it has acquired. On the contrary, I am persuaded that a field is here opened in which wise and judicious minds may perform inestimable good for society. The abolition of the distinction between competency and credibility would go a great way. And the abolition of the various forms of action at common law and the substitution of one simple form, as in chancery proceedings — these two alone would sweep away a multitude of refined and artificial rules which now incumber the practice. But what I do mean to say is (and I know the exceeding difficulty of propounding or conceiving two things which appear to conflict, although in reality one only qualifies the other) that do as we will, make what disposition we please of jurisprudence, it is absolutely impossible, even if it were desirable, to free it from its character of technicality. This is a quality which will forever belong to it, so long as it has any pretension to the character of a science and so long as it is understandingly and uprightly administered. If we suppose all our present legal institutions destroyed, the courts abolished, the books of law burned, society a mere "tabula rasa" to begin again, new tribunals established with directions to have no reference to any existing elementary works or precedents, a system would nevertheless in process of time grow up quite as technical as that which now exists. One single circumstance, and yet one which cannot be dispensed with, would insure this: to wit, the commanding that the decisions of all the higher tribunals shall be reduced to writing and published. English law never assumed a decidedly technical character until this important safeguard was interposed between the courts and the public. And what, in the case supposed, will be the consequence of this admirable practice, independently of its operation as a check upon the courts? — that the minds of the profession will immediately fall into a train of generalization. Certain fundamental principles will be grasped, a classification of them will be made as applicable to different departments of the law, other principles subordinate to them will be seized, principles within principles, as in all other sciences, and yet the last not evolved from the first but only classed under them after the induction is made. The amount of business will increase, the pile of precedents will also increase, an abundance of elementary works will be written, embodying the decisions and rendering the law more scientific in form and yet more approachable and more intelligible to the profession. The same process will be gone through as heretofore. A fabric will be erected, vast, complicated, and full of labyrinths to the ignorant, and yet differing in no one respect from any other system of knowledge except in its more extensive application to the actual business of men.

For what are technical rules? It is of the utmost importance to distinguish between what is artificial and what is technical. Every rule which is artificial is technical, but very many are technical without being artificial. A technical rule, then, is nothing more than a general principle. When we begin with it, in the case of A or B, there is nothing intricate about it; it is more like a simple statement of the circumstances of the case. But the case of A or B soon comes to be the case of thousands, each varying in some particulars. Then our difficulty commences. The mind is compelled to look further, to extend its principles more and more, and yet at the same time to be minute and ever on the watch in its examination. As the research will embrace objects entirely new, a new class of ideas will be formed and new names will be given to them. Or, as is very commonly the case, old and well understood words will be used and yet the connection in which they are found, although the most natural imaginable, will instantly give them a character of abstruseness. For instance, the words "remainder" and "condition" are ordinary English terms familiarly used in common life. And yet what an infinite fund of learning is attached to them, of which there is no possible way to get rid without encountering difficulties infinitely more formidable than those which are complained of. No man not a physician can understand the language of a physician. No man not a mathematician or chemist or political economist can understand them. Nay, no man not a mechanician, a horticulturist, or agriculturist can go but a very little way along with those who have devoted themselves to these pursuits and have made them the subject of direct application to the affairs of life. The language of every one of these persons is highly technical because having bent their minds upon one particular pursuit they have obtained new ideas, have learned to classify them, and have given them appropriate names. How, then, should there be such exceeding difficulty in understanding why the law is and forever must be a technical science? No one can feel a greater interest than myself in seeing what is artificial in the law swept away, but no one is more sensible of our utter inability to give it any other character than that of a technical science.

The law applied to land titles in Virginia and to the military districts in Ohio is a remarkable example how vain all our efforts must be to communicate to any branch of jurisprudence a phraseology which shall be other than technical. This part of the law is almost exclusively the creation of the courts of Kentucky. It grew up when these courts were in their infancy, when there was no previously accumulated learning to help to give it a technical air, and in a state which was less disposed than any other to adopt any part of the refined system which prevailed in England, and other states. It is the only state, I believe, in which there existed a positive prohibition not only to the reference to English reports as authority, but against reading them at all in court. The state of society was simple; the community was composed of farmers; the foundation of titles was different from what it was anywhere else, so that it could borrow no assistance from the real property law of Great Britain. Everything was favorable to the building of a system which, if possible, should be free from technicality. But it was found absolutely impossible to effect this. The simplest elements of title, a warrant, an entry, and a survey, familiarly apprehended by all the settlers and called by those names as soon as the process of legal investigation commenced, were recognized in every case, and yet in cases so endlessly diversified that a system of classification and of rules become speedily necessary in order that a court of justice should not be converted into the bed of Procrustes. For technical rules are adopted not to obstruct, but to further the regular and just administration of the laws. This system, so perfectly unique in its principles and yet reduced to so much precision, is a monument of the wisdom and ability of the courts of Kentucky. It has now nearly performed its office, that of settling land titles, and will hereafter be regarded by those who are fond of looking into the history of laws and institutions as a remarkable instance of the fertility of the human mind and of its capacity for framing general rules, even where the materials are the most scanty.

I can imagine one way in which the popular institutions of the United States may succeed in modifying, perhaps in entirely overthrowing, the vast system of technical jurisprudence which is now in use. The profession of the law may come to be regarded as an aristocratic institution. The path to it may be laid open by admitting everyone who pleases to practice, as is the case in some of the states with the medical profession. This by itself would effect very little, for so long as a learned and enlightened system was upheld by the courts it must be appealed to by all practitioners and the license to plead would be an empty privilege. The lawyer must still show his ability in order to succeed. But in addition to this arrangement the judges may be selected not from the class of jurists, but like members of the legislature from the citizens indiscriminately. This last movement would at once sweep away all use of precedents, for it would be impossible to construct them. The law would cease to be a science or a branch of knowledge. The administration of justice would be likened to that of a Mohammedan judge who founds his judgments upon the circumstances of each particular case as it arises, who professes to be guided by the dictates of good sense merely, and whose appreciation therefore of the value of experience, as well as his notions of right and wrong, are the most crude imaginable.

But first, there is less probability that the profession in the United States will be regarded as an aristocratic institution than there is [in] any other country. Lawyers do not compose a distinct corps. They are not collected in one great city as is pretty much the case in England and Scotland. They are dispersed over the whole country, and are not distinguished by any privileges from the general mass of citizens. I shall take occasion, hereafter, to notice more particularly this very remarkable feature of American society.

Second, as regards the scientific character of the law and the use of precedents, or what is the same thing, the appointment of persons to administer justice who shall be capable of analyzing their ideas, of forming an intelligible exposition of their judgments, and then causing their opinions to be recorded, there is no way of dispensing with these things unless we resolve to go back to a state of society different in so many respects from the high civilization which now exists. We desire to free the law from its technicality and we remove all check upon the judge. We wish to make the principles of law familiar to all the citizens, and we adopt a procedure which forbids that there shall be any principles whatever. The Mohammedan judge does as he lists; he acknowledges the authority of no rule nor the value of any experience. He is absolved from all regular control, and the public have no insight into the motives or reasons of his judgment. What we term precedents are in reality a great volume of human experience, and it is upon the wisdom which is gained by experience that free institutions are built and by which they must be preserved. Indeed the system of precedents is peculiarly adapted to a democratic commonwealth which seeks to establish equality and demands that the same rules, wherever applicable, shall be applied to all the citizens equally.

The absence of all reports of adjudged cases was a great defect in Roman law.[12] It led first to a nearly arbitrary exposition of the law by the prætors. Second, to a recourse to the opinions of the lawyers as to what the law was. The edicts of the prætor are an example of the first. This officer on entering upon his duties (and the election was annual) published an edict, or little code, containing the rules by which he intended to be governed in the decision of cases. It was understood that he could not depart from the enactments of the twelve tables, but the power of expounding the laws opens a wide field to construction when it is not guarded by the force of precedents. The meaning of those laws was constantly tortured and all sorts of subtleties invented in order to introduce new rules of interpretation. The prætor could not depart from the provisions of his own edict: this was inviolable during the year he was in office. But this was no security for the permanence and stability of the law under succeeding prætors. And it was not until the time of Hadrian that a perpetual edict was established. When I say was established, I mean only to state the fact and not to engage the reader in the unprofitable controversy whether this was the result of a positive decree of that emperor or was brought about by the silent operation of other causes. The English common law was never rendered authoritative by an act of Parliament. Hugo, in his history of the Roman law, declares that the annual edicts of the prætors afforded the means of harmonizing the legislation with the spirit of the times.[13] It was one step, but a most dangerous one in that direction. The spirit of the times could not be so fluctuating as to require a new edict every year, and the Roman legislature was constantly in session. The reports of adjudged cases, which constitute the

12. [For the second edition, Grimke added new matter from the start of this paragraph to the end of the chapter.]

13. [Gustav Hugo (1764–1844), *Lehrbuch der Geschichte des römischen rechts* . . . (Berlin, 1790), which went through many editions and appeared in a two-volume French translation in 1822.]

crowning glory of English and American jurisprudence, perform this office without opening the door too wide to construction. The respect for adjudged cases becomes a habit; they are of general notoriety to the profession because they are in print and any eminent departure from them is viewed with extreme jealousy; while on the other hand, as no judgment is absolutely binding (except in a few specified cases) unless between parties and privies, no positive impediment is thrown in the way to prevent a reconsideration of the principle in future cases. The collection of the opinions of eminent civilians was the next contrivance to help the defect arising from the want of law reports, but it was inadequate to this purpose. A compilation of this kind will cover an exceedingly small part of the ground comprehended within the list of adjudged cases. The Pandects or Digest was a work of this character, but it afforded a very feeble light in the administration of the laws compared with the English and American reports and the learned treatises which are founded upon them. The last not only announce a greater number of leading principles, but these are so ramified as to shed light upon a still greater number of subordinate ones.

BOOK IV

CHAPTER I | ON WHAT IN AMERICA IS SOMETIMES

TERMED THE VETO POWER OF THE STATES

IT seems difficult, at first view, to assign any reason completely satisfactory why the judiciary should be the final arbiter in determining upon the constitutionality of the laws. For if we say that the courts are the expounders of the constitution, it may be answered that the enactment of a law involving a constitutional objection is itself an exposition of the constitution and that, if the judges by repeated adjudications decide one way, the legislature by repeated enactments reaffirming its own construction, may decide another. The difficulty does not consist in attributing to the judges the right to decide, since whenever a constitutional question is involved the court must give a construction; it consists in making that tribunal paramount and supreme. It is perfectly correct to say that the judiciary is invested with the power of applying the laws, but whether it has a right superior to the legislature in expounding them does not appear so clearly. Nevertheless it is this very power of applying the laws, distinguishable as it is from that of expounding them, which has enabled the courts to assert and maintain the exclusive right of expounding them and caused them to be regarded as the natural and ultimate arbiter in all such questions. The legislature declare the construction of the constitution; the judges not only make declaration of their construction but, in addition to this, they carry that declaration into execution. For the various executive officers, marshals, sheriffs, etc., together with the "posse comitatus," are appended to the courts, not to the legislature. Now it is plain that that tribunal which is able to decide the law and also to carry its judgment into immediate execution must ultimately acquire the supremacy. When, therefore, the question is asked why is the judiciary the tribunal of dernier resort? the obvious answer is that its office as such is the natural and necessary consequence of the manner in which the government is constituted. The question confounds two entirely different things, the theoretical propriety of the arrangement with the plain matter of fact that it does exist. Even if we were to admit that the first is open to debate, upon the second the door to discussion is closed. The legislature in America bears to the courts the same resemblance which the present national government has to the old confederation. The present government acts upon persons, the latter acted for the most part upon states only. And the reason why this last did so act was that (with a single exception) it was unprovided with courts to enforce the execution of its resolves. The national legislature now in existence, like the state legislatures, passes laws affecting the community at large, and the judiciary executes its decisions upon all the individuals in the land. The courts never arrogate to themselves the imposing authority of making general declarations. They act only in detail, and yet it is the exercise of this more humble duty which has rendered them the undisputed arbiters in construing the constitution. Humility and modesty in private life often procure a high authority and reputation for those who practice them; and it is fortunate when governments can avail themselves of the same salutary tendencies in order to strengthen the authority of the laws and to maintain order and tranquillity in the state.

Notwithstanding the right to which I have referred sometimes affords matter for disputation in America (for although discussion is the proper office of the understanding, its place is often usurped by the feeling) yet nothing has struck foreigners with more admiration than the firm establishment and general recognition of the principle in America. It is a necessary consequence of the introduction of free institutions. For a constitutional chart is itself an act of legislation. It is the supreme law of the land. To determine therefore upon the constitutionality of a law is not more improper than the construction of any other enactment in which a question of constitutionality is not involved. It does not place the judge higher than the lawmaker; it only maintains the supremacy of the sovereign legislature, the people.

And if the original propriety of this arrangement should be questioned (its existence as a matter of fact being admitted), it may be answered that all our knowledge is more distinctly apprehended when it is in the concrete than when it is clothed with an abstract and gen-

eral form. The legislature view the law in its general features. The
courts deal with it in detail and in its application to a particular case.
It is not because the judges have mental powers superior to the legislature that the duty of deciding is devolved upon them; it is because the
form which the question assumes, distinct and unembarrassed by any
extraneous matter, facilitates the process of analysis, and it is by this
process alone that we are able to give precision to our ideas and certainty to our conclusions.

But this power of deciding constitutional questions has a much wider
application than I have yet supposed. The state courts decide upon the
validity of state laws in reference to their own constitutions. The courts
of the union do the same in reference to the federal constitution. But
the supreme court of the United States is also the tribunal of last resort
for determining the validity of state laws whenever these conflict with
the federal constitution. And this, also, is a consequence of the structure of the government. The introduction of the perfect form of confederate government, its substitution in the place of the imperfect
form which formerly existed, has produced a corresponding change in
the constitution of the courts and given a new direction to the exercise
of judicial power. As the laws of the union do not operate upon states
but upon individuals, the decisions of the courts do not act upon governments but upon persons.

One of the most striking features in the American government is
the double system of representation which it contains. It is a great
achievement to introduce the elective principle into all the departments
of a consolidated government, to render the executive and judiciary as
well as the legislature elective. But the American is not a consolidated
but a federal government. Separation has, therefore, been made between the general and local interests. Each have been deposited in
distinct governments, and the principle of representation has been
established in both. The states are not mere municipal corporations,
deriving their existence and franchises from the central government.
Their separate jurisdiction is secured by the same instrument which
created the confederacy and is therefore equally fortified against attack. It is the independent character of these two classes of government which has caused some eminent minds in America to doubt
whether the judicial power of the union extends to the determination of
the validity of state laws when they conflict with the federal constitution. It has been supposed that there could be no arbiter in the case,

and that the states, nay, each of them separately, must necessarily possess a veto upon the decisions of the national tribunal.

Mr. Hume, in a short essay "on some remarkable customs," has stated as a singular fact that the legislative authority in the Roman commonwealth resided in two distinct assemblies: the comitia of the centuries, and the comitia of the tribes, acting independently and not concurrently, each having a veto upon the acts of the other and a right to carry any measure by its single authority. And this example has been relied upon, together with other views, by the able author of *New Views of the Constitution* in support of the veto power of the states.[1] But the American government is a government "sui generis," and it is not safe to resort to other political systems for the purpose of finding analogies. Admitting the fact to be as stated by Mr. Hume, there are some very important differences between the Roman and the American plans. The two comitia were parts of one and the same government and not institutions of two distinct governments. Conquering Rome annihilated all the confederacies which once existed in Italy, the Tuscan, Volscian, *etc.,* and substituted in their place one homogeneous government. Second, the two legislatures were not distinct bodies in the same sense as the English Houses of Lords and Commons are, but were composed of nearly the same persons, only in one the vote was collected by classes and in the other "per capita." Third, they did not always preside over the same interests. A similar organization of the legislative power has taken place in every country where civilization has made slow progress and where the melting down [of] the various classes of society into one body has been the work of time. In England, at one period, the nobility, burgesses, and clergy taxed their own order separately. Those assemblies did not act concurrently as is the practice now; each voted separately and did not wait for the concurrence or disapproval of the others to its own bills.

But inasmuch as the two Roman comitia did frequently vote upon the same subject matter, upon the question of peace or war, for instance, there is a difficulty even greater than in the case just referred to. There is no part of history which is more obscure than is the con-

1. [John Taylor (1753–1824), *New Views of the Constitution* (Washington, 1823), a Jeffersonian argument for the strict construction of the Constitution and for limitations upon the power of the Federal government in opposition to the nationalistic program of John Marshall.]

stitutional history of Rome. Things which were plain enough to contemporary writers, which involved no contradiction whatever and which are therefore not related with precision but even with carelessness, are full of perplexity at the present day; nay, were so at the time Livy wrote. That two legislative assemblies should exist, each possessing an independent jurisdiction upon the same matter and each therefore armed with authority to undo immediately whatever had been resolved by the other, involves so glaring an inconsistency that we are compelled to believe that there must be something further in the case which, if it could be seized, would at once dispel the difficulty. Such a theory of government, if there were nothing further, would lead to absolute inaction. The vote of the last assembly ought to decide the matter, but there could be no last if each was absolutely independent and could incessantly revoke the bills passed by the other. On the other hand, if there was a stopping place, the vote in the last decided the matter and gave to that body alone the supreme legislative authority.

We know that the plebian assembly were at first confined to legislate about matters which concerned their own order. Afterward they procured the privilege of deliberating, and deliberating only, on all matters which affected the general interests. If prior to 372, a proposition was discussed in both assemblies and was carried by the vote of the centuries in contradiction to that of the tribes, it could hardly be said that those two bodies acted independently. For the proceedings in the first were only like the proceedings in one of those voluntary conventions which are so common in America. It might deliberate and resolve, but it had no power to carry any measure into effect. It had in other words no real power of legislation. This constitution of government is a very common thing even in modern societies. The French tribunate in the Abbe Sieyès' constitution, and which existed for several years, was merely a deliberative body. So also the Danish, Prussian, and Russian councils deliberate but do not enact. A still more remarkable example is afforded by the Germanic legislature. It is composed of three chambers, the princes, electors, and deputies of the towns. But the last, although it may discuss, is never admitted to vote. An example on a small scale is exhibited in the American Congress where the delegates from the territories enjoy the full privilege of debate but have no right to vote on any question.

In the course of time the two Roman assemblies shifted their positions. The popular body which before met to deliberate only acquired complete legislative authority: precisely as would be the case in the Germanic confederation if free institutions were introduced, when the deputies of the people would exercise the entire legislative power leaving it free to the other orders to meet and deliberate if they chose. If this revolution were to take place, if the art of printing did not exist, or through some calamity or other all public records and histories were lost or mutilated, the same puzzle would exist as in the case of the Roman comitia and from the same causes. Suppose that the same catastrophe should happen to American institutions and that two or three thousand years hence someone were to read this passage in the very able speech of Mr. Calhoun on his resolutions: "the powers not delegated are reserved, against the judiciary as well as against the other departments." If no copy of the constitution could be found, nor any document which shed light upon the subject, he might suppose not only that the proposition was true, which it undoubtedly is, but that it proved the existence of a veto power on the part of the states even as against the determination of the supreme court of the union. But with a copy of the constitution in his hand, he would find that that court was by irresistible implication clothed with the power of deciding upon the constitutionality of state laws and that what he had taken to be the statement of a fact was the statement of the view of an individual.

But the most remarkable circumstance is that in the debates which recently took place the existence of a veto power, on the part of the states, was taken for granted. Its advocates did not confine themselves to showing that there would have been propriety in so organizing the government. They asserted that its existence was an undoubted fact. And such is the exceeding fertility of the human mind, not merely in finding reasons for what it conceives ought to be but in converting its conceptions into reality, that numbers of people in one part of the union, who had never dreamed of the existence of such a power, began to hesitate. It may be allowable to doubt where one is obliged to search in the dark caverns of antiquity for materials to guide our judgments. But the institutions of the United States are open to the apprehension of everyone. If what they ought to be admits of discussion, what they really are is matter of history.

The extreme novelty, not to say the alarming tendency, of such a power in a country where infinite pains have been taken to establish regular government compelled those who advocated it* to assume that Congress were bound to call a convention to amend the constitution whenever a single state dissented to a law as unconstitutional. In this way the mischief of civil war, which would otherwise be inevitable, was sought to be avoided. But in order to attain this end the assumption went still further. It was insisted that when the convention assembled the proposition should be, not to insert by way of amendment the limitation upon the power of the federal government which a single state had contended for, but to insert the power claimed and actually exercised by Congress with the consent of every state but one. Everyone will perceive the immense difference which is made by only changing the form in which the question is put. In the one way, the constitution will be amended by a very small minority of the states; in the other, it can only be effected by a very large majority. Now admitting that Congress may sometimes transcend its powers and that this way of proceeding would arrest it, the inquiry properly is not what would be the effect in one or two instances, but what would be the effect in all time to come and in the numberless instances in which the states, encouraged to resistance, would succeed in paralyzing the operations of the government? Is there not, so far as we proceed upon any known principle of human nature, infinitely more security in the vote of a majority of Congress and three fourths of the states than in a very small minority of both? We may admit that there are certain dormant powers residing in every community and that the right to resist an intolerable tyranny is one of them, but this does not permit us openly to recognize the existence of a wild excess of power and to insert it as a standing provision in the constitution of the government.

* *New Views of the Constitution*, by John Taylor; and Calhoun's speech, 1832–3. [Grimke's reference to "Calhoun's Speech, 1832–3" is confusing because Calhoun was not in the Senate in 1832. He resigned the vice-presidency on December 28, 1832, having been elected senator from South Carolina on December 10, but did not take his seat in the Senate until January 4, 1833. Grimke probably refers to Calhoun's speech against Jackson's "Force Bill" against the threat of nullification of a tariff bill by South Carolina in 1832, a speech in which Calhoun rejected the right of the Supreme Court to adjudicate conflicts between a state and the national government and claimed for the individual state the right to determine the extent of powers reserved to it under the Constitution. See "Speech on the Revenue Collection Bill (Commonly Called the Force Bill), in reference to the Ordinance of the South Carolina Convention, delivered in the Senate, February 15th and 16th, 1833," in *The Works of John C. Calhoun*, ed. Richard K. Cralle (New York, 1853), II, 197–262.]

The mode of calling a convention to amend is one of the parts of the constitution which is least liable to misinterpretation. It can only be assembled with the consent of two thirds of the states or two thirds of both houses of Congress. The effect of the doctrine in question would be to give this power to a single state. Not that this view would be taken by its advocates, for our own arbitrary conceptions are able to give shape and form to almost anything. It would still be insisted that two thirds of congress or two thirds of the state legislatures must concur in calling a convention. But if two thirds or a majority in either case were convinced of the constitutionality of the law in existence, it is plain that a convention could only be assembled by the authority of the single dissenting state. For there is no way in which we can conceive of a legislative body acting, at any rate of its having a right to act, but by persuasion of the correctness and lawfulness of what it does. To assert that it is bound to call a convention against its most settled convictions is to assert that it is bound to call one upon compulsion. Nor can any human ingenuity make it otherwise.

It is an established maxim in American institutions that the government can no more concede an ungranted privilege than exercise an ungranted power. To concede a privilege is to communicate a power and is guarded with the same caution as the usurpation of authority. If it had been intended that a convention should be assembled, not only when two thirds of Congress were convinced of the expediency of so doing, but upon the complaint of a single state, the constitution would have said so in plain words. There cannot be a shadow of doubt upon the subject. The two cases are totally distinguishable from each other. Each affords a specific occasion for acting, and to suppose that the one was intended to involve the other would argue a confounding of two things, unnecessary, improbable in the extreme, and full of mischief. But to have inserted in plain language the provision contended for would have been so startling that every member of the convention would have recoiled from it. Strange as it may seem, therefore, there is no possible way of claiming the existence of any such power, except upon the ground that it has been absolutely omitted in the constitution. It is impossible to defend usurpation by law, but it is often possible to argue plausibly against law.

Not only has the constitution forbidden the exercise of the veto power by refusing to grant it and by prescribing a mode of amendment absolutely inconsistent with and repugnant to its exercise, it has closed the door upon all controversy by creating a tribunal which shall be the ultimate judge in all controversies between the state and the federal governments. On the 13th June, 1787, in the convention which framed the constitution of the United States, it was moved by Mr. Randolph and seconded by Mr. Madison that the jurisdiction of the national judiciary shall extend to all questions which involve the national peace and harmony. The resolution was passed and was embodied by the committee which had charge of it in the precise and definite language in which the power is clothed in the third and sixth articles of the constitution as ratified. Now I do not pretend to say that a doubt may not still be raised, for it is possible for an ingenious mind to doubt everything. But when I observe that the constitution and the laws made in pursuance of it are declared the supreme law of the land, anything in the constitutions and laws of the states to the contrary notwithstanding, and when I observe that the exclusive right to expound the law in these cases is conferred upon a federal tribunal, I am compelled to believe that there can be at least no solid foundation for doubt.

The celebrated author of the Virginia resolutions and report admits that the supreme court of the Union is the tribunal of last resort whenever the validity of a state law asserting the existence of an unconstitutional power in the states is called in question. The construction of that clause which prohibits the states from issuing bills of credit, *etc.*, he declares is referred to that tribunal. This is in effect a surrender of the whole ground of argument, for the prohibitions on the power of the states are as much a part of the constitutional compact as are the limitations on the power of the federal government. And if it be true that in all questions which relate to the boundary of power between the two governments there is no common umpire, and neither has the right to decide, there is no reason for ascribing supreme authority to the court in the one case which does not equally exist in the other.

There is an interesting problem in government which may be thus stated: when is it that two political powers in the state being set up, one against the other, their mutual rivalry will lead to a just balance of authority and conduce to a successful administration of public affairs? And the answer is that this adjustment of the parts of government will be safe whenever these two rival authorities are compelled to act concurrently and when they are controlled by some common authority which is superior to both. The various departments, the legislative, executive and judiciary, have rival interests, but they are amenable to one common power and they cooperate in carrying out one plan of government. So on a smaller scale, the court and the jury are set up against each other with power in each to overrule, "ad infinitum," the determination of the other. But they are bound by one common ligament to the people and combine in administering the same laws. The Roman tribunate may be mentioned as an example of the same class. It was, like the senate and the "comitia," a constituent part of one and the same government.

In the artificial forms of government, only one of these conditions is complied with; the three departments conspire in the administration of the same system but their responsibility to a common constituent is very imperfect. And the consequence is that one usurps nearly all power or an interminable conflict exists between them. In proportion as the popular power is raised and pure monarchy is transformed into limited or constitutional monarchy, the responsibility becomes direct and positive and the departments are more easily retained within their respective spheres. The walks of private life afford a similar analogy. How is it that so many thousand individuals, all armed with propensities and desires which constantly stimulate them to run counter to the general interests, are so restrained as to produce anything like tolerable tranquillity in society? The tribunal of public opinion which represents those interests controls them all and produces regularity of behavior in those numberless instances which the laws would never reach.

It would have been wonderful then if the American people, after establishing free institutions, had so far spoiled the original design as to create a counterbalancing force to the system in the sectional and particular interests of one member of the confederacy. Circumstances may occur which would render it meritorious in a state to remonstrate and to take high ground in order to induce a change in the public measures. But it must be a very extraordinary case — a case which must make the law for itself — which would justify civil war. There may be secrets in public as well as in private life, and a state which resists the laws of the union may calculate on the length it may go in order to procure a compromise, and may at bottom determine to go no further. But the statesman who should draw the sword, if compromise failed, would incur the transcendent ignominy, as well as merit, of going into battle without his shield. No man has a right to be brave at the expense of his patriotism.

In the Germanic confederation there was a tribunal in some respects resembling the supreme court of the United States. The chamber of Wetzlar, or Westphalia, possessed exclusive jurisdiction in deciding upon disputes between members of the empire. But it had no power to execute its decisions. The laws operated not upon individuals but upon states, and a sentence of the supreme judicial tribunal had no higher effect. The consequence was that it became necessary to resort to force, and to this end the empire was divided into circles the entire military force of which was at the disposal of the emperor to enable him to execute the sentence of the court against a refractory member. Under the new constitution of 1815, a different organization took place. If the rights of one state are invaded by another state, the injured party must choose one of three members of the diet selected by the defendant; or if the defendant neglect to select, the diet is bound to name them. And the court of final resort, in the state of the member thus chosen, decides the case. And if the party against whom the judgment is pronounced does not obey, a military force is resorted to, to coerce submission. There does not appear to have been any judicial tribunal either under the old or the new constitution for the purpose of settling disputes between the states and the confederacy. The diet, or national legislature, seems to have possessed this power. The American system stands alone amid the institutions of the world. And although it was a natural consequence of the adoption of the perfect form of confederation, yet as this species of government is a work of the greatest refinement and the result of a very high state of civilization, the organization of the national judiciary may be pronounced one of the greatest achievements which political science has made.

There is a tribunal of another European state which it is curious to notice in consequence of its novel mode of procedure, although it is never called to decide upon the conflicting rights of different governments. The court of errors, or of cassation, in France, is the highest judicial tribunal in the kingdom. And the principle on which until recently it proceeded was this, if the judgment of an inferior court was reversed, the case was sent back to be tried again. If the court below persisted in its error and the cause was again appealed and the court above reaffirmed the judgment before pronounced, it was sent back a second time. But if the inferior court still persevered in its error, the decree of the court of cassation no longer afforded the governing rule. The legislature was then appealed to, to settle the law by a declaratory act. But the absurdity of the scheme, the temptation which it held out to the local tribunals to resist the judgment of the highest court and to unsettle all the principles of law, produced so much mischief that in 1837 the English and American procedure was adopted, and the determination of the court of cassation is now final and absolutely binding upon all other tribunals.

It is not uncommon to meet with this odd combination of liberty and power in monarchical government. The system of monarchical rule is itself a compensation of errors where if the weight presses too much in one part it is carelessly relaxed or altogether removed in another part. The most remarkable example of this is contained in "magna charta," which authorizes the barons to pursue and to kill wherever found the monarch who presumes to violate any of its provisions. It legalizes civil war all over the land, and England was accordingly a scene of confusion and violence for more than two centuries afterward. It is to the regulated liberty which free institutions introduce that we must look for a salutary restraint upon the actions of men and as the only means of giving supreme authority to the laws.

The reason why no tribunal like the supreme court of the United States is known in monarchical or aristocratical governments is because too much instead of too little power is condensed in the political institutions. The king and nobility having acquired an extravagant share of authority, there is no way of subjecting their public acts to the scrutiny of a regular legal investigation. Questions cannot arise because, as there is no popular constitution, the right is all on one side. The establishment of such a system as the American is a sure indication that the odious maxim of the sovereignty of the government is abjured and that of society substituted in its place. Then for the first time questions arise between government and the members which compose it, for the same fundamental ordinance which is obligatory upon the one is obligatory upon the other. The notion that public rights are unsuited to such a mode of proceeding grows out of the idea that they are of too high a dignity to be submitted to the same examination as private rights. The notion, then, is anti-republican in the extreme. All public as well as private rights are rights of the people. Formerly government was not amenable to any tribunal while private citizens were. But as soon as the basis on which government rested was changed, the moment that its whole authority was referred to the consent of society, the rights of government and those of its members were placed upon the same footing. The constitution of the United States does not imitate "magna charta" — the makeshift of a semibarbarous age — and authorize one member of the confederacy to place its veto upon the most solemn acts of the government. It does not, in order to settle a question of right, first unhinge the notions of justice, but fortifies the one by guarding and maintaining the other. It submits national and state controversies to the calm and patient investigation of a tribunal which, as it represents both parties, is eminently adapted to compose the angry feelings of both.

There is infinite convenience in administering the government where the public authority is made to act directly upon individuals. The laws are then executed with promptness and facility. But it is not for the sake of convenience merely that the plan is adopted. There is another and a higher end which is designed to be effected and that is to banish civil war, to preserve internal tranquillity, in short, to uphold civilization itself. The form which all questions take, their submission to a judicial instead of a political tribunal, is an immense advantage to the cause of free institutions. And admitting what must be admitted, that every human tribunal however skillfully contrived must be subject to error, yet all who have had any experience of human affairs will see the great importance of having some tribunal of dernier resort, some tribunal, in other words, which shall be able to speak with authority after it has deliberately examined and decided.

There is a peculiarity in the form of confederate government established in America which sheds great light upon this subject and points to the supreme court of the union as the most fit tribunal to decide upon questions of controverted jurisdiction. The national government is not represented in the states, but is itself a mere representation from the states. Senators are elected by the local legislatures, the president and representatives are chosen by the people of the states and not by the people as composing one aggregate community, and the judges are chosen by the two first and from the districts in which they reside. But there is no similar representation of the national government to be found in the executive, legislature, or judiciary of the states. Now all confederacies are not constructed in this manner, nor was there any absolute necessity why the American should have been so. But a little reflection will show that it contributes materially to promote one very important object, and that is the complete separation of the powers of the two classes of government, the national and the state.

Before the union of Scotland and Ireland with England, independently of the fact that there were no local executives like the governors of the American states, the two former countries being presided over by the king of England, this officer as representing the central government appointed the members of two estates in the Scotch parliament, the nobility and bishops, and nominated a certain proportion of the lords of articles, by whom the real legislative business of Scotland was transacted. In Ireland, until within a few years before the union, no law could even be propounded to its Parliament until it had received the previous assent of the English Parliament. The case in both instances was the reverse of what it is in the United States. The federal head was effectively represented in the local governments while, on the other hand, those governments were not represented by the national executive, legislature, or judiciary. Or, to take another example: the provinces of Holland are a confederacy in a much more strict acceptation than was the British government, for there is a more complete separation of the local from the general interests. Each province has its own legislative assembly, and one chamber of the states general, or federal legislature, is composed of representatives chosen in the provinces. But the provincial governments differ exceedingly from the state governments of America. They are intended to administer the local interests and should, in order to carry out this design, represent exclusively the local population. But this is not the case. Not only is the number of the members of the Chamber of Deputies and of the electors who choose them fixed by the federal executive, but he nominates the members who compose the upper house in every one of those provincial legislatures.

The American government would have resembled the Dutch if the plan of a constitution presented to the convention by Mr. Hamilton had been adopted. The plan proposed that the governors of the states should be appointed by the federal government and that they should have a negative upon the laws passed by the state legislatures. The federal government would then have been effectually represented in the state governments. The same object would have been accomplished in another form if the plan advocated by Mr. Pinckney and Mr. Madison had been accepted. This proposed that the national legislature should have power to negative all laws of the state legislatures, not merely such laws as were repugnant to the federal constitution but all laws which appeared improper. There would still have been this difference between the American and the Dutch and former British confederacy: that in the former the states are represented in every department of the national government, whereas in the second they are very imperfectly represented, and in the last they were not represented at all. There would have been much stronger reasons, therefore, in the first than in the two last instances for creating a supreme tribunal to decide upon the conflicting rights of the two classes of government and vesting the appointment of its members in the federal head. Those plans, however, and others of a similar character, were avoided and the constitution adopted is accordingly the only example of the perfect form of confederate government which has anywhere been known. It fulfills the three indispensable conditions of that species of government. First, there is a complete separation between the general and local interests. Second, the laws operate upon individuals, not upon governments. And, third, the federal head is a mere representation of the states, but has no power to intermeddle in their domestic legislation. This mode of constructing the government determined the character and jurisdiction of the tribunal of last resort. It was a judicial tribunal: 1st. Because the laws were designed to act upon persons. 2d. Because the process of analysis by which the unconstitutional feature in a law is detected is more completely reached in that form of proceeding. 3d. Because the constitution and character of such a tribunal necessarily shuts out the influence of party feelings, so fatal to the firm and just appreciation of what is right. The members of this tribunal were appointed by the federal government because that government is made up of a representation from the states and is in no way represented in the state government. And if ingenious minds should still seek to raise objections and insist that a jurisdiction of the kind conferred upon the supreme court savors too much of political power, it may be answered: 1st. That this constitutes one of its chief recommendations. 2d. That political power must necessarily be wielded by some one or more of the citizens and that the members of the court are alike citizens with the members of any other department. 3d. That it is infinitely desirable to break up political power as much as possible, to distribute it among several tribunals, instead of condensing it in one.

We may illustrate the great advantage which is derived from giving to all the movements of the government the greatest simplicity imaginable by an institution which prevails in America and which is now sought to be imitated in all the constitutional monarchies of Europe. The popular elections are not conducted in counties, much less in larger divisions of districts, but in the townships or parishes. Instead of assembling a vast multitude of people on one spot to engage in broils and fights, this army of electors is cut up into minute parcels, each of which is separated from the other by miles. The force of party spirit is broken, and when the election is over universal tranquillity is established. This is an emblem of American institutions in the general which undertake to compass the most important end in the easiest manner possible. The organization and procedure of the supreme court of the union is an application of the same principle to things apparently different but which are in reality the same. We want an institution which shall have power to protect us against the rage of party spirit in those cases where party spirit would be most fatal, an institution which shall be able to appease the sharpest discontents among the states by the employment of calm judgment and reflection. The reaching rights of this ponderous character through the simple and unostentatious forms of the law is, as I before said, the chief recommendation of the system. If it savors of political power, this power is at any rate morseled into small fragments, is only employed in detail, and on occasions where there is the least temptation to render it subservient to political ends. And although we may not be authorized to say that it is the best conceivable plan, we are well justified in declaring it the best practicable one.

The constitution of the United States is a compact. Every popular constitution is both a compact and a delegation of power, whether the government be a consolidated or a federal one. In the first, the compact is between the people, and the delegation of power is by them; in the second, the compact is between the members of the confederacy, and the delegation of power is by them only. And when the constitution is framed, the government created represents the joint authority of the states. This different mode of proceeding does not render the authority actually granted less binding in the one case than in the other. It alters the structure and form of the government, but the compact, or constitution, is equally obligatory in both. And as in an aggregate community neither the citizens, nor even a majority of the people can go beyond the compact and interpose a veto upon the acts of the government, so in the confederate government neither a single state nor a majority of the states have any right to do the same thing. No one ever heard that when government was acting within the legitimate sphere of its jurisdiction, the jurisdiction itself should be questioned because the measures pursued were not agreeable to everyone. If there were no discontent in the state, government would be unnecessary. Civil institutions are appointed for the purpose of melting down the idiosyncrasies of different parts of society; and it is not merely from a noble self-denial but from a sense of evident interest that men are ordinarily persuaded to lend their support in upholding the influence of these institutions.

The division of the territory of the United States into distinct states was an accidental circumstance, but the advantage which has sprung from it is not accidental. If the people of America had composed one aggregate community it would have been the height of wisdom to imitate the present plan, to have created local governments with complete jurisdiction over the local interests and a central government to preside over the common interests. The scheme is in effect carried out to a considerable extent in the individual states. The counties and townships are lesser jurisdictions inclosed within a larger one, administering their domestic affairs skillfully and economically because they are not mixed up and confounded with the general interests of the state. And if this form of civil polity was the result of a constitutional compact at the first foundation of the government, the counties and townships would possess complete sovereignty within their respective spheres which could only be alienated or altered in the mode prescribed by the constitution. For the sovereignty of the parts of which the community is composed does not depend upon the time when they became sovereign, but upon the fact that they are so. Nor is it possible for ingenuity to frame further objections and insist that the parts would in that case be the offspring of the central authority, whereas in the confederate government the central authority is itself but an emanation from the parts. For in both instances the form of government is the offspring of the voluntary consent of the parts: only in the one, the parts are more numerous, as they are made up of individuals; in the other, they are composed of states, or separate collections of individuals.

Now if in a state government thus constructed, the original compact should appoint a tribunal for the purpose of settling constitutional disputes between these two sets of government, no one of the parts could object to its jurisdiction and interpose its veto because the law complained of did not equally benefit all the parts. Nor could it do so even if the law declared to be valid were in reality invalid, since in theory such a supposition would be itself unconstitutional, while in practice it would undermine all authority — that of the parts as well as of the whole.

It is remarkable that those who advocate the veto power of the states have taken for granted the existence of a power which is nowhere recognized in the constitution and at the same time deny the jurisdiction of the supreme court which is contained in language as unequivocal as could be desired, as unequivocal as that which confers jurisdiction on any other department. So much do times of high party excitement confound all our notions of justice and make shipwreck of the most settled principles of government. As a large part of our opinions and beliefs are not absolutely determined by the objects with which they deal but are modified by the structure of mind and the temperament of each individual, it is perhaps surprising that uniformity of opinion does exist to as great an extent as is actually the case. But in order to correct those aberrations in which we are so liable to fall upon all political questions, it is of great importance to view them at a time when the judgment will be least liable to be perverted by any disturbing influence. The doctrine of the veto power of the states was for the first time proclaimed in the case of The Commonwealth *vs.* Cobbett.[2] At a time when party spirit ran high, C. J. McKean ventured to express the opinion that it was the duty of Congress to call a convention whenever a state protested against a law as unconstitutional.[3]

2. [Grimke added this sentence to the second edition.]

3. [The case of Commonwealth *vs.* Cobbett was the trial in 1797 by the Commonwealth of Pennsylvania against William Cobbett for libel against the Spanish ambassador, Don Carlos Martinez de Yrujo, when Spain was closely allied to France at the time the United States was bitterly divided domestically between Federalists who favored England and Republicans who favored France, which is the context of Grimke's remark that "party spirit" ran high. "C. J. McKean" is undoubtedly Thomas McKean (1734–1817), chief justice of Pennsylvania and later governor, who was Cobbett's enemy. Action against Cobbett was going forward in the federal as well as the state courts and Cobbett appealed for dismissal of the suit by Pennsylvania on the grounds that the federal court constituted a superior jurisdiction. Chief Justice Thomas McKean rendered the decision of the court during the December term, 1798, and ruled that in the case of conflict between a single state and the federal government ("all the other states") that neither the state nor the federal government was competent: "There is no provision in the constitution, that in such a case the Judges of the Supreme Court of the *United States* shall control and be conclusive; neither can the Congress by a law confer that power." For the text of McKean's decision, see A. J. Dallas, *Reports of Cases Ruled and Adjudged in the Several Courts of the United States, and of Pennsylvania* . . . (Philadelphia, 1799), III, 467–476.]

This singular opinion was easily molded by the fertile genius of John Taylor into a regular system and has been defended by other minds of equal vigor and fertility as the panacea for all the irregularities in our system of federal government.

The United States is not the only country in which geographical features have made their appearance.[4] The southern provinces of France have for a long time shown a disposition to counteract the legislation of the kingdom because it was deemed too favorable to the northern provinces. At the very period (1833) when geographical parties in the United States threatened the Union, two parties in France of the same character and founded upon the same principles were arrayed against one another. In 1834 was drawn up the celebrated manifest of the southern provinces demanding that the kingdom should be intersected by a line east and west, separating the vinegrowing from the non-vinegrowing provinces, and that south of this line the customs should be abolished. The then minister, M. Thiers, declared that "he had given great consideration to the subject, but in endeavoring to consult the interests of Bordeaux, I should do violence to those of Lyons. In attending to the complaints of Elbouf, I must sacrifice the interests of Havre." The vinegrowing constituted the predominant [interest] in the south, but it was not the predominant interest in the kingdom nor the exclusive pursuit in the south. As the north was not an exclusively manufacturing, the south was not an exclusively agricultural region. The government of the minority, then, would be subject to more abuse than that of the majority. But I return to a consideration of the veto power of the states.

If in America a single state in consequence of its possessing this power can compel Congress to assemble a convention whenever it supposes a power not delegated is exercised, there must be a corresponding right on the other side whenever a state assumes a power which is not reserved; otherwise the equilibrium of the system would be destroyed. On this subject, Taylor and Calhoun are silent. We will then suppose that in this case Congress will be obliged to call a convention as well to protect the rights of the other states as its own authority. The question in that convention will be not whether the constitution shall be so amended as to delegate a given power, but whether it shall be so

---

4. [For the second edition, Grimke added new matter from the start of this paragraph to the paragraph which ends, ". . . was not a consolidated republic," on p. 502.]

amended as to reserve it. The discontented state derives every advantage in the first instance from the singular mode of propounding the question; but it loses this advantage in the second. The question is so framed with the express intention of enabling a small minority of states to overrule a large majority. But this small minority which in the first instance determined the question adversely to the federal government will now decide it adversely to the discontented state. But much the greater number of questions which have arisen between the two jurisdictions have related to powers assumed by the states as reserved. The consequence is that by this novel construction of the constitution, the rights of the states would be placed in jeopardy. As all the powers reserved are not enumerated, it would be peculiarly necessary to call a convention to determine whether the power exercised by the state was usurped or reserved. And the right of North Carolina, South Carolina, and Louisiana to regulate the ingress of free people of color would be decided against them. This would also be the case with regard to constitutional provision in Indiana prohibiting the immigration of the same persons, for it is certain that three fourths of the states could not be found to declare that these powers were part of the reserved rights. The same disposition would have been made of the Dartmouth college case, the laws of Kentucky suspending the payment of debts, and those of Massachusetts, Rhode Island, and Maine prohibiting the sale of spirituous liquors, for they might be supposed to interfere with the delegated power of Congress to permit their importation. The two writers I have referred to contend for a new and unheard of power but do not seem to be aware that the rule which permits it would operate in contrary directions; that if a state has a right to veto a law of the federal government because it is not a delegated power, for the same reason will the federal government have a right to veto a law of a state because it does not fall within the reserved powers; and that the same consequences will follow the assembling of a convention in which by the same mode of propounding the question the right would be authoritatively and finally settled against the state.

It must not be supposed that no case can be conceived where a power is assumed to be reserved which does not raise the question whether it is delegated. For 1st. A power prohibited to the states cannot have that effect. 2d. A power neither directly prohibited to the states nor reserved may be assumed before any law has been passed by Congress.

3d. If the delegated powers presuppose the existence of the reserved, the reserved equally supposed the existence of the delegated. Nor does the non-enumeration of all the reserved render it necessary to propound the question always in the same form, for a considerable number are enumerated and the enumeration of the delegated is ipso facto a designation of the reserved. It will be remarked that the question is between the authority of a single state and the joint authority of the other states. If it were between the state and some depository of power created by itself alone, the presumption might be that an authority not delegated had been exercised, for the two would stand in the relation of inferior and superior. But there is no such relation between a state and the Union. Each of the other states is the equal of the one which complains, and jointly they are its superior because the constitution was the result of a joint act and not the act of a single state. The presumption, therefore, is that the power is not reserved and not that it is one not delegated.

The greater the number who concur in doing an act, the more of a popular character is stamped upon it; but that is on the supposition that it is actually done. The merely making provision that several shall concur to render an act valid is something very different from their actually concurring: for if they do not, the consequence is that the measure adopted, instead of enlisting a greater number than a majority, may enlist one that is much less. The rule that requires a number greater than a majority is only adopted in order to preserve the old order of things. For this reason, it is very sparingly used because all legislation supposes alteration. The moment it is employed to introduce a new state of things it becomes mischievous. And that is the old state under which a government had hitherto been uniformly administered, and that the new which would overturn the old. If the unconstitutional doctrine of calling a convention were put in practice, it would follow that whichever asserts a power inconsistent with the established order of things is bound to show its validity. If a state attempts to impair the obligation of contracts by violating the visitatorial power in a collegiate institution (1), or by enacting a law suspending the collection of debts (2), or by an insolvent law discharging the debt (3), or by imposing a tax on packages of goods imported in the hands of the merchant (4), or by laws abolishing the duties (5), or by laws annulling the fugitive slave act (6), the question appropriately submitted to a convention would be, shall the right assumed be deemed a reserved one? Shall a declaratory amendment be passed to that effect?*

There is another view of great importance. I have considered the scheme as a two-edged sword, as operating equally against the states and the federal government. But in truth it would operate very frequently against the states, even where the convention was consequent upon the veto of a state and the question was, shall the power be delegated to the Union. Vermont and Massachusetts have vetoed the fugitive slave law. If a convention were assembled for the preposterous purpose of delegating the power to pass the law, it would be very difficult to obtain the votes of three fourths of the states in the affirmative. If the same course had been pursued in 1836–7, when the act prohibiting the circulation of incendiary papers by the mail was passed, a declatory amendment delegating the power to pass the act could not have been procured. If one of the non-slaveholding states had vetoed as unconstitutional the act admitting Missouri into the Union, the constitutional number of the states could not have been found to vote in the affirmative, shall the power be delegated to the national legislature. It will be observed that the right asserted does not depend upon the fact whether the law may or may not be executed within the territory of the discontented state, nor upon its ability to oppose any actual resistance to its execution: it is sufficient that a state protests against any law and Congress is immediately obliged to assemble a convention. If in 1802 any one of the states had protested against the constitutionality of forming new states out of territory acquired since 1789, a convention would not have delegated the power. Or, if the protest had been against the acquisition of territory by treaty, Louisiana may not have been purchased. Great Britain would have seized it during the war which was soon after rekindled between herself and France. It was to prevent this catastrophe that Napoleon consented to part with it. Even Mr. Jefferson declared he was not satisfied that the United States could accept the cession unless the people inhabiting the territory voluntarily submitted to live under the American government. He saw no difficulty in the alienation or division of the sovereignty by the people themselves, but he saw great difficulty in an alienation or division by the government which presided over them. But there is no intelligible

* 1. New Hampshire. 2. Kentucky. 3. New York and Louisiana. 4. Maryland. 5. South Carolina. 6. Vermont.

way of dealing with a question of this sort unless we suppose an anterior consent, tacit or implied, to the alienation, or the joint consent by the people of France and Louisiana to the same. Any other interpretation would throw into confusion the boundaries of every state on the face of the globe.

It would appear, then, that the operation of the system under the present and only true construction of the constitution is more favorable to that wise and just spirit of compromise which should forever preside over the counsels of a federal republic. Taylor and Calhoun suppose that the veto will always be interposed by a southern state and that that state will always be triumphant. But the scheme would be equally fatal to the southern and northern states.

The two authors I have referred to suppose that because the American states entered separately into the confederacy and separately ratified the constitution, the government of the Union is the agent of the individual states. All constitutional government is strictly an agency; in a democratic aggregate community it is the agent of individuals; in a confederacy it is the agent of states. But although individuals form the first, they do so jointly and, therefore, no one individual can unmake it; and for the same reason, although states formed the last, they did so jointly, and no one state has power to take it to pieces. It is immaterial whether the joint power which created and the government and constitution which were created were all one act or successive acts. The existence of the joint power is undeniable; otherwise we fall into the absurdity of supposing that one individual made the one and one state the other form of government. It follows, therefore, that as the sovereignty in the former resides in individuals jointly, in the last it resides in states jointly. This separates the sovereignty in both instances from the agency and renders it as easy to find it in one form of government as in the other. The sovereignty resides in those who make the government: in aggregate community, in the people jointly, in a confederate government, in states jointly. In the former, the sovereignty is not lodged in individuals because they voted per capita, nor in the second does it reside in the states separately because they also voted per capita. For all this was necessary to be done in order to render the act in each instance a joint one. This gives rise to a division of sovereignty, though this sometimes creates confused notions, as it seems to import a division of the faculty of sovereignty at one and the same time, instead of a division between two distinct political beings. The first is impossible, the second is easily understood. The states jointly, not the government, are sovereign as regards the federal interests; the states singly, as regards their domestic interests. Nor is there any difficulty in conceiving how a state should be sovereign as to some things and not sovereign as to others; the difficulty is the other way, in conceiving how a state should be solely sovereign over other states. If there is any act of sovereignty, it is in the creation of a government or in the alteration of it after it is created. The joint power of the states is as distinguishable from the government as the joint authority of individuals in an aggregate community is distinguishable from the government they create. No single state framed the constitution, nor has a single state power to alter it. It was framed by the states jointly, each voting separately, for there is no other device by which a joint act can be made to originate, and the concurrence of three fourths, not the voice of one, is necessary to alter it. It follows, therefore, that the sovereignty is partitioned between the states jointly and the states individually. For as it would be contradictory to say that a joint association could act in the capacity of a single member, it is contradictory to say that a single member can act in the capacity of a joint association. For the same reason that the states jointly cannot alter the constitution of a state, no single state can alter the constitution of the Union. It is contended that this renders the states sovereign as to the reserved and not sovereign as to the delegated powers. And how should it be otherwise? The reserved powers are simply those powers which belong to each state separately. Over these it must be supreme, because they have never been alienated; over the last it cannot be, because they were created by the states jointly. The reserved powers are placed in the constitution, but it is for the express purpose of separating them from the body of federal powers. If the objection were, this makes the states separately sovereign as to the reserved and separately not sovereign as to the delegated powers, its futility and want of meaning would be apparent; but by making use simply of the word states, in both instances, an ambiguity is created which gives rise to a confusion of ideas. If the objection were, this makes the states separately sovereign as to the reserved and jointly not sovereign as to the delegated powers, its falsity would be immediately seen. By using the word states in both instances without qualification, that hazy state of mind is created which is most favorable to the admission of every kind of error.

The argument in the *Discourse on the Constitution* is woven out of a sophism. The states are said to have formed the constitution separately, but with *concert* and *mutual understanding*. The infirmity of the argument would be flagrant, if something *resembling* a joint act were not alluded to. Hence, those words of half meaning are employed. The appropriate terms compact or united wills are not used, though so much stress is afterwards placed upon the first in passages where it is not of more importance that they should be used. The reason is obvious; the frailness of the reasoning would be instantly seen if that precise and unequivocal language were employed. States may with concert and mutual understanding agree to establish separate constitutions. Very different is the case where a compact is entered into for the formation of a single constitution for the whole. In the last the constitution is by irresistible implication the result of the joint will of the states thus united. The argument of Taylor and Calhoun is this: the states separately sent delegates to the convention; in the convention the vote was taken by states, and each state separately ratified the constitution; therefore, the constitution was ordained by the states separately as completely as were their domestic governments. The argument has an air of plausibility, especially when connected with the words "with concert" and "mutual understanding"; for these by their ambiguous import contribute to hide the sophism which lurks beneath. They are not inconsistent with the formation of either a federal or a state government. But they do not explain with precision the foundation on which a federal government rests. The states did separately send delegates to the convention, the vote in the convention was taken by states, and each state separately ratified the constitution, as each party to a treaty separately ratifies it. It will not be denied that a federal government may be established by the joint will or authority of the members, and a little reflection is sufficient to convince us that it is impossible it should be established in any other way. In subsequent parts of the *Discourse,* "compact" and "contract" are frequently used. The reason is obvious; the author is there engaged in considering the violations of the constitution, and to represent that instrument as having been framed merely with concert and mutual understanding would be language too loose and ambiguous to answer the purpose there intended. That the vote in the convention was taken by states and that the states severally ratified the constitution does not prove that all was not done by the joint will of the states, for the joint will of separate states can only be ascertained in this way. It merely proves that the population was not an aggregate one and that the government was not a consolidated republic.

To hear some persons talk of the federal government of America, one would suppose that it was a foreign government seated in a remote country, presiding over the general interests of the states, and yet without any visible connection with or dependence on them. One would hardly recognize a government which derived its whole being from the states and which was constantly recruited and supported by them.

There is one way in which I can conceive that an important revolution may be effected in the structure of the supreme court. The judges may be appointed for a term of years and the marshals may be elected by the people of the respective states. The relation which the judges bear to the federal government will not be changed, the bond which now connects them will not be broken, but it will be materially weakened. The wisdom and authority of the judges will be in some degree eclipsed, not only in their own eyes but in the eyes of all those who are called upon to assist in executing a judgment. I think I can already discern symptoms of a reluctance in those state courts whose judges are elected for a term of years to touch a constitutional question, if it can be avoided; a disposition which is in every way commendable as it does not necessarily imply a shrinking from duty, but may produce much more caution than would otherwise be observed. There is an important rule on this subject, which is, that every law is "prima facie" to be deemed constitutional and that the reasons to show the reverse must be very convincing. But the duty of judges in America is peculiar: they may have to decide upon two conflicting laws, or two conflicting constitutions, when the "prima facie" presumption cannot be presented with so much distinctness. The result, however, may be the same; more prudence and caution will be observed in weighing the arguments on both sides. The court will more readily retract an erroneous judgment when it is less accessible to that pride of opinion which makes it desire on all occasions to give an example of consistency with itself, even at the expense of inconsistency with the rule of right.

CHAPTER II | THE RIGHT OF SECESSION IN THE

CONFEDERATE FORM OF GOVERNMENT [1]

THIS is an entirely new question in political philosophy. No confederate government has ever provided for the emergency. In America the constitution is equally silent upon the subject. It provides for amendments, but amendments imply the continued existence of a constitution, whereas secession is a partial dissolution of it. Nor do the 9th and 10th amendments affect the question, for these merely guarantee to the states the exclusive control of their domestic interests and presuppose the continued existence of the two governments, state and federal, instead of the extinguishment of one of them.

States, before they form a confederate government, are distinct and independent communities, and the question very naturally arises whether the entering into a compact of this nature necessarily forbids a withdrawal from it. The determination of this difficult and interesting question renders it necessary to examine the principles which lie at the foundation of the confederate form of government.

If the individuals composing an aggregate society establish a consolidated government, whether that government is republican, aristocratical, or monarchical, a part of the society have not the right, they have not even the ability, to secede. Such a government comprehends a defined and undivided territory, the territory inhabited by all the people within it; and there is a plain inconsistency in supposing that some of the people may be politically out of the government while territorially they are within it. Territory and government, where the community is homogeneous, are corresponding and convertible terms. If independent states enter into the same form of government, they will be subjected to the same disability. They will have created an aggregate society and erased the existence of separate peoples. Although the former boundaries of their respective territories may be traced,

1. [For the second edition, Grimke added the entire chapter.]

their population is completely merged. In half a century a new people have grown up, total strangers to the original lines of demarcation and absolutely knowing but one country and one government. Although the boundaries of the states occupied by their ancestors may be preserved in tradition or record, the political geography of the country is altered, the moral boundaries of the population are obliterated, and secession would be a solecism.

These difficulties do not exist where independent communities enter into a confederacy. Each separate state is an aggregate community: its people, therefore, cannot withdraw their allegiance from it in any other way than by removal. But if a state secedes, the people who inhabit it are instantly placed, both politically and territorially, without the federal government. A confederate, as such, possesses no territory. In the case of secession, therefore, the laws would at one and the same time cease to operate both territorially and politically over the state withdrawing. The great difference, then, between a consolidated and a federal government is that in the first, there are no parts, or if originally there were, they are merged; in the second, the parts continue to have a distinct existence.

The soundness of a principle is said to consist in its operating both ways, and a mind fertile in resources may inquire whether if a people composing one aggregate community, whose territory was either inconveniently large or inconveniently situated, were to divide the state into two states, first receiving the vote of the new state in favor of this arrangement, and that this last proceeded to organize a separate government, it may be asked whether it would be competent for the people inhabiting the old division to annul the compact and to reabsorb the new state into itself. The answer is that it would not, the reason of which is that, in the case supposed, there is a double compact giving birth to two distinct governments. The dismemberment of Massachusetts by the erection of Maine is an example. The consent of the people, as composing one entire community, was first obtained and then the separate vote of the newly contemplated state. But in the formation of a federal government by independent states, the vote of the states is alone taken; the vote of the people as forming one aggregate community is not and cannot be. In the first case there is a double compact, in the second a single one. The principle therefore would be misapplied. In order to render the analogy complete, the hypothesis should be that the people, composing one aggregate community, carved out of the territory distinct, local or municipal governments, but without any regard to the consent of the local population and consequently without forming any compact with it. In this case it would be competent for the former to annihilate those local jurisdictions. Their formation is only a mode of administering the government, not a contrivance for severing it. The erection of departments, provinces, or districts is an example. They all stand upon the same footing. The greater or lesser extent of authority possessed by some of these domestic jurisdictions makes no difference in principle between them. It is not the extent but the nature of the power, the source whence it is derived, which determines where there is a similitude or difference between them. And as it is competent for a state which is a member of the confederacy to extinguish the municipal governments within its territory, it would be competent for a people composing one undivided empire to annihilate any of the local governments upon its surface. There is no necessity for the reservation of the right. It springs from the charter and constitution of the society. The same is true of a confederate government formed by independent states. It is the creature of a single, not of a double, compact, and each state for itself, and for itself only, may withdraw from the union. The right flows by irresistible implication from the original structure of the society. But although a formal recognition of it is unnecessary, I am by no means satisfied that it would be unwise to insert it. For the minds of men are as much moved by magnitudes in the moral as in the physical world. Whatever protects us from the delusions of the imagination, or from the effect of a train of inconsequential reasoning in matters pertaining to political society, is as much to be valued as the deliverance from a present calamity.

I have spoken of a single in contradistinction to a double compact. The distinction is of great importance. Some writers in treating of the social compact regard it as a contract between the government and the people, while others with much more reason consider it as a contract between the people themselves for the establishment of a government. If both took place, it would be a double compact. So in the division by an aggregate community of the territory into local governments, the compact is single, and in the formation of a central government by independent states the same is the case. The compact in the one is between the individuals composing the society; in the other, between the states. Where a people have established a single government they may alter or abolish it, for that government is an agency. Where they have established local or municipal jurisdictions, they may annihilate them; and where independent states have entered into a confederacy, any one of them may secede from it. The reason of the last will not be so readily apprehended, for it may be supposed that, as in the first and second, a majority of the people would be necessary to exercise the powers described, in the third, a majority of the states would be necessary to annul the central government as regards even a single member. But the two things are *diverso intuitu*. In the two first, the original organization of the government is effected by the majority; in the last, it is effected by the separate vote of each state. The principle of the majority is entirely foreign to the constitution of a federal government. It only begins to play a part after it is set in motion. It is an instrument in the administration of the government, not in laying its foundation. So that the analogy fails, and we are brought to the same conclusion that each state, each member of a confederacy, may for itself, but for itself alone, abdicate and silently withdraw from the confederacy.

First. It has been attempted to deduce the right of secession from the hypothesis that the sovereignty is inalienable and indivisible. The argument may be thus stated: the sovereignty originally resided in the states; it is incapable of alienation or division; therefore, the right of secession is a perpetually subsisting right. This opinion is, however, without foundation, and I have therefore called it an hypothesis. Those who maintain it regard it as a settled and fundamental maxim of government. Even if it were so, it would not be applicable, for secession does not imply the exercise of sovereignty, but the reverse, as I shall presently show.

A striking thought sometimes crosses the mind with the rapidity of lightning and its novelty and brilliance forbid a rigorous examination of it. But analysis is the only test of the validity of any opinion. Our knowledge is so multifarious and lies in such confused heaps in the mind that nothing is clear until it is reduced to its simple elements. When we assert that the sovereignty is inalienable or indivisible, we in effect impose limitations upon the sovereignty, which is a contradiction; we annul the very principle upon which the proposition rests; we take from the sovereignty its most capital attribute in the very sentence which is intended to give it the most extensive signification. Once the notion of sovereignty is admitted, it follows as an unavoidable consequence that it has power to do at least what will contribute to the well-being of the nation in whom it resides. Emergencies may occur which would render it highly desirable that one people should come under the government of another. If we say that the former is unable to do so — unable to merge its sovereignty in that of the latter — we in effect declare that it has not the capacity of self-preservation; that it is deprived of the choice of means for furthering so important an end, and yet sovereignty has no meaning unless it supposes the power of making this choice. Scotland and Ireland merged their sovereignty in that of England by the acts of union, and it is certain that if the United States had been a consolidated instead of a federal government, it would have been competent for the people of Texas to ask to be incorporated into it. It would have been so if, instead of a republic, the United States had been an unlimited monarchy like China or Russia. When in the reign of Elizabeth the people of Holland made overtures to the English nation to become united to it, as Wales is to England, it was an exercise of that very sovereignty which belongs to every independent people.

The dogma of sovereignty, if pursued in all its ramifications and followed out in all the consequences to which it leads, is full of absurdity. The people of France have undoubtedly transferred all sovereignty over Louisiana to the United States, and although it may be said that this was a renunciation of sovereignty over a colony and not over themselves, yet, first, the fact is certain (which is all I care for) that the sovereignty has been alienated, has been displaced from where it once resided, and that it cannot be recalled. Secondly, we can form no conception of sovereignty unless it is attached to all the people living under the same government. The mere distance of the parts of an empire from each other can make no difference in the principle if there is any force in it. But to render the view still clearer, the French nation, instead of ceding Louisiana, may have ceded a part of European France. In this case, there would be absolutely no ground to stand upon in maintaining the dogma of the indivisibility of the sovereignty. Either the sovereignty did not reside in the French nation, or if it did they would by the cession have alienated it *in perpetuo*. In the whole range of political philosophy, I know of no opinion which has been seen in so confused a manner and which, perhaps on that very account, has been seized with so much avidity. By the treaty of Vienna, Genoa was ceded to Sardinia, Finland to Russia, Norway to Sweden. In all those instances, the sovereignty over the people was irrevocably transferred to other nations. The sovereignty in neither Persia [n]or Turkey resides in the people, but it would be absurd to say that the prince and sultan in whom it resides are incompetent to alienate it, or that the progress of knowledge and the advancement of popular power may not gradually displace it from where it is now lodged and deposit it with the people. Knowledge is power, especially in the political world. Where that resides, the sovereignty is to be found. Writers on political philosophy do not limit the maxim to one form of society, but extend it without distinction to all; and therein they have reason, and argue at least consequentially, for the power to alienate must depend upon the faculty of sovereignty, not upon the body in whom it resides.

In a confederate government, the states composing it always reserve to themselves certain rights, and it may be supposed that in that case there can be no alienation of sovereignty. But in the English and Scotch union, where the merger was almost complete, Scotland reserved various rights to her people, the ecclesiastical establishment, the judicature, and private law, *etc*. And on the cession of the District of Columbia a similar course was pursued, but the sovereignty over the residue was forever alienated. It is incapable of being resumed, except with the consent of the United States. In the instances of Norway, Genoa, and Finland, the sovereignty was transferred; in that of Scotland and the District of Columbia it is divided. If the United States had been a consolidated government and without any representation of the people, the annexation of Texas would also have operated as a complete alienation of the sovereignty if it were without any reservation, and with it would have been a division. Some very excellent minds are ready to admit that there may be a division, while they are unprepared to admit that there can be an alienation. The keen mind of Rousseau saw clearly enough that unless the indivisibility of the sovereignty was admitted, the dogma of inalienability must fall to the ground. He has, therefore, declared peremptorily, "that sovereignty is inalienable and indivisible." For it will be evident on reflection that there is no difference in principle between the two. A division of the sovereignty is *pro tanto* an alienation.

On entering into political society, the individuals composing an aggregate community may make an entire surrender of their rights to the joint society created, or they may reserve to themselves a portion of those rights. The bill of rights of every state constitution in America is a reservation of this character, but this does not prevent the transfer of the sovereignty over the residue to the people of the state as composing one homogeneous community. The celebrated maxim, therefore, to which I have referred is as untrue as it would be injurious. It is one of those generalities which are so fascinating to the mind because they seem to condense a great deal of knowledge in a very small compass. It has no foundation in reason because it assumes to set bounds to the sovereignty; it has none in fact because the course of human affairs has repeatedly contradicted it.

The author of *New Views of the Constitution* argues that there are only two ways in which it is conceivable the sovereignty of the states forming a confederacy can be alienated: to the people in the aggregate, or to the government; and as there is no aggregate people in such a community and as those who administer the government are only agents, he concludes that in the formation of the federal constitution of America no alienation has been made. The objection is easily answered. There is a third mode which may be and actually has been adopted. The alienation was by the states separately to the states jointly.

When individuals unite to form a government, each conveys to all. When states do the same, each also conveys to all. Not merely does the administration of the government appertain to this newly created power, but the government itself, the federal authority, resides in the states jointly. That the American states entered separately into the confederacy and separately ratified it does not contradict, but is in exact agreement with this view. For how can the concurrence of all be ascertained but by taking the vote of each separately upon the question whether they do concur? No other device can be imagined by which this consent can be effected. The states are, by the supposition, separate and independent communities, and we wish to ascertain whether they concur in lodging a vast mass of power in a joint association and displacing it from the separate jurisdictions where it before existed. It is clear that every act done up to the time when the new power is actually created must be separate; otherwise the states would be a joint association before the compact creating them such would have been made. The consent of each is then necessary to create the joint society of states and when this is effected a large amount of power which before resided in the states separately is made to reside in them jointly. Nor does it vary the matter whether the consent was given before or after the formation of the constitution. When several act together, the consent of each is necessary; for how could it become the act of all, if it were not the act of each? A treaty which is separately ratified by two or more nations is the joint act of both, precisely because it is the act of each. It would not be more effectually the act of both if each had given full power to its ambassadors to make the treaty, consenting to be bound by their acts, and waiving all ratification. The separate consent of each would still be necessary to this agreement. But that the treaty would be the fruit of a joint not of a single authority is manifest; for the consent of all the parties, not the will of one, would be necessary to unmake it. And yet the ratification by the American states after the constitution was formed is supposed, by the ingenious author I have referred to, to prove that it was the act of each and not the act of each and all, between which there is the greatest imaginable difference. That it was not the act of a majority of the states but of the states unanimously does not prove that it was the act of each separately, for the consent of each would be necessary to make the act of a majority binding.

In a consolidated republic the united wills of individuals make the constitution, although the vote of each is taken, and in a confederate republic the joint will, not the will of any one member, makes the government, although the vote of each is also separately taken. In those private associations which reflect the image of a large state on a small scale, each member has entered separately, but its constitution is a joint act: every exercise of authority is from the necessity of the case joint and not several; all effective power over the subject matter within its jurisdiction resides in the association, not in the government set up by it nor in the agents appointed to administer it, but in the joint society to which the separate wills of individuals have given birth. In like manner, in a federal government the sovereignty over the common interests is transferred by each, not to the government but to the states jointly. No other supposition is admissible; nor does it require any metaphysical acumen to perceive that power may reside in states jointly as well as in states separately. That the consent to make the transfer and the transfer itself are *uno flatu* need not puzzle us, for such is the case in every species of political transaction.

Second. Secession is not the exercise of an act of sovereignty, but the reverse. Between it and the veto of a state there is a clear and broad distinction. Secession is an unequivocal admission that the sovereignty does not reside in the state seceding. An act of sovereignty removes officers, abolishes offices, alters constitutions, extinguishes the powers exercised by the government. In the case of secession, instead of the constitution and laws being removed out of the way of the discontented state, the state itself removes out of the way. This is a plain recognition that it is not vested with sovereignty over the federal government, has no right to assume it, and that it is obliged to succumb to it. It is precisely like the emigration of individuals from a country whose government is a consolidated one, who become discontented with the condition in which they are placed or with the institutions under which they live, and remove to another country. They are aware that as individual members of society they have no right to control the government. Instead of assuming to do so, they quietly withdraw from it. A confederate government being the result of a joint compact between the members and not the act of any one singly, the veto would be the usurpation of a power which cannot belong to a single member. It would transform a joint into a single government. Secession admits the incompetency of the seceding state to do so, and instead of bending the government to its will, it is compelled to bend to the will of the government. Great mistakes have been committed from confounding secession with the veto. They are entirely different from each other, as the preceding observations sufficiently show.

There are different forms of confederate government, and it may be supposed that the question whether the right of secession exists cannot be decided without having regard to the precise form which is adopted. The Amphyctionic, Achæan, Italian, and German confederacies were all different. The Achæan had this peculiarity, that the states composing it were obliged to adopt the same domestic institutions as well as to submit to one uniform rule of federal legislation. The former and present confederations of the United States were also very different. There is one circumstance, however, in which they all agree, and that is in possessing a common federal jurisdiction, distinct from the jurisdiction which each state possesses within its own territory. They were all governments, although the amount of power which was wielded by the federal head varied in all. Thus the former and present confederacies of the United States were constitutions; otherwise they would not have been governments. We term both federal unions in order to distinguish them from the consolidated form of government. The principal feature in which they differed was in the operation of the laws. In the first, these as a general rule acted upon the states, but not universally, for they were sometimes executed upon individuals. On the other hand, the laws as a general rule operate upon individuals, but not without exception. There are some instances in which they operate upon the states directly. There is one feature, however, in which these two governments resemble each other and that is in the binding and obligatory force of all the federal laws upon all the people. The mode in which these laws are executed cannot vary the obligation to obey them. In both, Congress was the source whence these laws emanated, in some instances executing them through the instrumentality of agents appointed by the central power. The disposition and arrangement of the federal authority presents a question of more or less convenience in the administration of the government, but does not affect the validity and supremacy of the laws.

When the federal government depends upon the states for the execution of the laws and they are not executed, the delinquent member may be coerced into obedience by the whole force of the confederacy. But the coercion of a state implies the coercion of the individuals composing it, and thus we are led to the same conclusion, that every form of confederacy is a constitution and government, that the laws are equally obligatory upon the citizens, and that the distinction between them consists in the more or less perfect machinery which is employed to enforce them. In all there is a division of the sovereignty, one portion being retained by the states separately and the residue alienated, not to the central government, but to the states jointly. The distinction, then, so far as it affects the right of secession, is not between the more or less perfect form of federal government, but between a federal and consolidated government. This is the only test in our power in order to determine when the right of secession exists.

Very imperfect notions were entertained, even under the former confederacy, of the structure and attributes of the state governments. In the debates of the convention (Yates notes, p. 184), Mr. Madison says, "the states at present are only great *corporations,* having the power of making *by-laws*." [2] "The states *never* possessed the essential attributes of sovereignty. These were always vested in Congress." He then compares the states to the counties of which they are composed

2. [Robert Yates, *Secret Proceedings and Debates of the Convention Assembled at Philadelphia, in the Year 1787, for the Purpose of Forming the Constitution of the United States; from Notes Taken by the Late Robert Yates, Esquire, Chief-Justice of New York* . . . (Richmond, 1839).]

and argues that as the counties are not sovereign the states cannot be. If so fine a mind could err so greatly with regard to the appropriate authority of the states, it will not appear surprising that very inadequate notions are entertained at the present day. From one extreme political writers have plunged into another.

A great principle can never depend for proof of its validity upon examples, since these may contradict some other principle of equally high authority. But where the example has been deduced from the principle, and could not have existed without it, it is of wonderful use in testing its value. It is then a direct corollary from the principle and not merely a happy illustration of it. The confederation of 1778 was broken up by secesssion. The articles on which it was founded provided that no alteration should ever be made unless with the unanimous consent of the states who were parties to it. The states were not unanimous in the change which substituted another ordinance and converted the government into the present confederation. Rhode Island and North Carolina rejected the scheme and may have remained out of the Union to the present day. Eleven states thus seceded from the old confederation. If it should be said that these states did not secede because the new government erected in place of the old was itself a federal union, the answer is that any change of the articles, much more the radical change which led to the formation of a new government, was absolutely prohibited unless the consent of each state was obtained. Indeed the futility of the objection will be manifest on a very little reflection. If two or more states were now to assemble in convention, or if all the states were so to assemble, and by a majority of votes should form a different federal government, it would be absurd to say they had not seceded because the form of polity which they had established had one or more features in common with the former. But if in order to test the bearing of the objection, we should admit it to be well-founded, the difficulty still exists. The states of North Carolina and Rhode Island then seceded. Their right to remain out of the new union was never disputed; it was openly and unequivocally admitted. The Congress under the new government never dreamed of coercing them into an adherence to it, but dealt with them as independent nations; and as I have before observed, they may have continued to this day separate and independent states.

There is another difficulty which presses upon us and which creates more than a doubt whether the states composing a confederation are mere corporations or municipal bodies, like the provinces and departments of a consolidated government. The states of Rhode Island, New York, and Virginia, in ratifying the constitution, expressly reserved the right to secede. The first declared "that the powers of government may be reassumed by the people, whenever it shall become necessary to their happiness." The second made a declaration in precisely the same language. Rhode Island entered the Union a considerable time after New York and copied the language which had been used by the New York convention. The ratification of Virginia declared that "the powers granted under the constitution, being derived from the people of the United States, may be resumed by them, whenever the same shall be perverted to their injury or oppression." No language can be more precise and unequivocal. Each of these states declare that although on entering into the confederacy a division of the sovereignty was made between the states jointly and the states separately, this partition was not inconsistent with a withdrawal from the Union and that the right to secede was reserved to the states respectively. No tribunal is erected or contemplated in order to determine the course of action of the states when the crisis arrives. The question whether the trusts conferred upon the federal government have been perverted, or in the unqualified language of New York and Rhode Island whether "the happiness of their people would be promoted" by a resumption of the powers granted, is not submitted to any tribunal under the federal government. The supreme court of the United States is never alluded to. Its interference is by necessary implication precluded. No such disposition could possibly be made of the matter. A judicial tribunal is unable to determine a question of expediency; it is only adopted to adjudicate cases where the naked question of right is presented. The constitution has skillfully guarded the peace of the confederacy while the states remain in it by referring the constitutionality of the laws to the supreme court. But what causes shall be of sufficient magnitude to induce a state to withdraw altogether from the operation of the constitution and laws, and by thus withdrawing to avoid all conflict between state and federal jurisdiction is, from the necessity of the case, submitted to the state itself. This is the undisguised avowal of the three states I have referred to; it is equally so of the whole Union which accepted these declarations as conformable with the fundamental principles of a confederate government and thereby ratified them. As one member of a federal union cannot possess any higher federal right than is enjoyed by all, the inference is direct that even if the right of secession were not an inherent attribute of confederate states, it is at least reserved to every American state. The time has gone by when we can conceal the truth from a persuasion that the knowledge of it may be abused. The discovery will assuredly be made, and if made in the midst of a settled and determined opposition to its promulgation, all the institutions of society, and not one merely, will be in jeopardy. The European doctrine is that in matters of government it is necessary that statesmen should have both a secret and a declared opinion. The maxim in America should be that the justest use will in the long run be most likely to be made of every right where it is clearly, frankly and unreservedly admitted.

The value and importance of the principle I have been endeavoring to unfold will be appreciated when it is recollected that in every community whose population comes to be spread over a wider and wider arena, a diversity of views, habits, and customs will necessarily grow up over which the laws can very imperfectly preside. Even Charlemagne who wielded the power of one of the most consolidated governments which ever existed was compelled to declare that "it was impossible for the central authority to watch over every interest with all the care which was desirable or to retain every one in the path he should follow."

All writers on public law agree that in the event of intolerable oppression the people are justified in making resistance to the government. The terms in which this proposition is conceived are very remarkable. 1st. The cases which will authorize so violent a departure from the settled order of things are not enumerated and defined. The principle is expressed in language the most general and ambiguous. 2d. The idea of a tribunal to sit in judgment upon the controversies which may lead to revolution is not entertained, but is directly repudiated. 3d. The maxim is proclaimed in governments which are supposed to possess an absolute and self-existing authority. The principle is attended with dangers of the greatest magnitude, and yet we can discover no way of escaping from it. The great desideratum then is to be able to contrive some expedient which will exempt us from this stern necessity, which will substitute peaceable in the place of violent revolution. The aggregate form of government does not admit of this remedy; the confederate does. Instead of forcible resistance to the federal head, instead of unlawful attempts to annul the laws of the Union while the member is within it, that member is at liberty quietly to depart while others retain their position in the confederacy. This is one of the most important attributes of a federal government. Secession is the instrument happily substituted in the place of open hostility to the laws. So that in the confederate form of government the law itself provides against those great emergencies which in other countries are said to make the laws for themselves.

The great risk which will be incurred by the seceding member, the disadvantageous position in which it will be placed, standing alone in the midst of a firm and compact league, will operate as a powerful check upon its conduct and will prevent recourse to such an extreme measure unless it can be justified before the bar of public opinion. At the same time, the open recognition of the right to secede will render it disgraceful to embark in any scheme of concerted resistance to the laws while the state continues a member of the Union. The explicit recognition of the right will also operate as a salutary restraint upon the central government. If one or two states seceded, they would inevitably be the losers; it would be staking everything upon the cast of a die. But if several threatened to do the same, the confederacy would be in danger of being deprived of so much strength and importance that every measure which prudence and calm judgment could suggest would be adopted to avert so great a calamity. The public councils would be marked by more reflection when a moral agency was substituted in the place of brute force. Rhode Island and North Carolina were resolute in their opposition to the present constitution, and for a time refused to enter into the Union. Congress pursued towards them the same course which it did towards the European states: it treated them as independent nations, and applied to them the laws relative to discriminating duties. This contributed greatly to change their resolution. They entered the confederacy, one of them two years after it was formed, and motives still more powerful will deter either from now seceding. The right of secession, then, is a weapon of defense of great efficacy in the hands of the states, but it supposes one still more efficacious in the hands of the federal government. The advantages of union are so manifold, the position of a member when isolated is so insignificant and when united with others so commanding, that nothing but the greatest injustice or the most irreconcilable diversity of interests will occasion the exercise of the right. Instances of secession are accordingly very rare. Two of the states composing the Boetian confederacy seceded, and the dismemberment of the provinces of Holland and Belgium may perhaps be regarded as similar. They were united in one confederacy in 1814 and were disunited in 1830 by the withdrawal of Holland. The rupture was occasioned in part by an irreconcilable difference in the religious creeds of the two peoples and in part by the improper interference of the central government with the education of the people.

The principle of representation is one of the finest expedients which has been devised for perfecting the machinery of government. In a country of great extent it is ineffectual unless it is combined with another principle of equal importance. This consists in dividing the territory, if it has not previously been divided, into separate jurisdictions and investing each with complete control over its domestic interests. If this is not done, the general and local interests will be confounded. The last can be but imperfectly represented or understood, and yet will be subjected to the same undistinguishing majority which rules over the national interests. The principle of representation would then fail to answer the end it was intended to reach. The United States, in consequence of the great extent of country, presented greater obstacles than any other country to the solution of the difficulty, and it is the one in which the nearest approach has been made to that solution. But it by no means follows that the confederate form of government may be carried to any extent, that there is no limit to the number of states which may be combined in one union. It would be more correct to say that there is a limit, although happily it is difficult to define it. It is like a great many other interests appertaining to society in which the rules are certain enough, and yet the precise circumstances under which they are applicable are difficult to predict. The time will certainly come when the same causes which led to the formation of the present Union will lead to the formation of two or more unions. The institution of government, as I remarked in a preceding chapter, is an experiment to classify, to reduce to unity, the diversified rights and interests which spring up in society. But the generalization may be pushed so far as to trespass upon the interests of the parts in spite of the machinery of the local governments. The time, however, must not be anticipated. Union is itself one means of overcoming geographical differences and harmonizing geographical parties. These parties were appealed to in the convention of 1787 and in the succeeding state conventions as opposing insuperable difficulties to the formation of a federal constitution. In the period which has elapsed, no country has been so happy and prosperous, none so free from civil dissensions, none which has so well succeeded in reconciling a large amount of liberty with the requisite energy in government.

CHAPTER III | THE EXECUTIVE POWER

IT is more difficult to form a distinct idea of the executive than of any other department of the government. In some countries it comprehends nearly the whole authority of the state, not to be sure dispensing with laws but usurping to itself the sole power of ordaining them. In absolute monarchies the prince is legislator, judge, and ministerial magistrate. The permanence of the executive is doubtless one reason why in the majority of governments it has been the most imposing authority. The minds of men are more strongly impressed with the notion of government when its image is constantly before them than by the occasional or periodical exercise of authority by a legislative body, the members of which are disbanded during a great part of the year. The political institutions of a state may be said to perform two distinct offices: first, to hold society together, to maintain civilization; and secondly, to administer the interests of that society. The last implies a mere agency, a delegation of power by the members to conduct the affairs of the community with judgment and discretion. Nor is the first at all inconsistent with the same notion of delegated authority; on the contrary, the various elements of which society is composed, its diverse population and different interests, are never so firmly cemented together as where government represents the will of the people. But this is a character which it has seldom acquired. The institution of a prince, termed by way of eminence the executive magistrate, has been deemed necessary almost everywhere to bind together the parts of society and to give a character of unity to the authority of the state. It is this notion of unity perpetually revolving in the mind, in matters of government as well as religion, which gives a shape to the political institutions and enabled the prince to center in himself nearly all power. The gradual and unobstructed progress of society, wherever it takes place, at length sets bounds to this state of things. As civilization advances, public affairs become so unwieldly and complicated that it is physically impossible for one mind to preside over them, much less to administer them in person. The prince communicates his authority to subordinate agents in order to relieve himself from the burden, but by so doing he step by step diminishes his influence, loses his prerogatives, and prepares the way for more regular institutions. He appoints judges and administrative officers to do thoroughly what he had been able very imperfectly to perform. A legislative body soon after makes its appearance, at first only representing constructively the society in which it is assembled. And as this body will necessarily have a close connection with all those affairs which are immediately superintended by the ministers of the crown, it ultimately acquires a considerable control upon the crown itself. It at first influences, but in the progress of time it absolutely determines the appointment and removal of those ministers. The prince, in order to relieve himself from the cares of public business and to have more time to devote to the gratification of his pleasures or ambition, assists in raising up a host of officers in the state; by so doing he causes a larger proportion of the people to be trained to the understanding and management of public affairs, and without intending any such thing creates a counterpoise to his own authority. Through the operation of the same causes which speedily give birth to some species of legislative assembly, the judges no longer expound a code of laws enacted by the sole authority of the king. The legislature is at first permitted sparingly to interfere with such high matters, but in progress of time it is enabled to speak out audibly and intelligibly and the judges are then freed from a servile dependence upon the executive magistrate. He retains the power of appointment, but as soon as it is made a new relation is established between the judges and the community at large and they are declared irremovable at his pleasure. Their responsibility becomes both more strict and more extensive, and the laws are consequently administered in a much more enlightened manner than before. The powers which are thus gradually wrested from the king are not extinguished, but they are deposited in other hands where they are even amplified and strengthened. The commonwealth gains in power much more than the monarch loses. In order that the increasing demand of the state for the services of its citizens may be fully answered, knowledge and education are sought after by everyone. And thus at length that invisible but powerful authority which we denominate public opinion comes to preside over every movement of the government and to fulfill more completely than ever the notion of unity which continues to float in the mind, whatever may be the mutations which the political institutions undergo.

It is through a circuitous process, then, that a gradual separation of the executive from the legislative and judicial authority takes place and that three distinct departments are created. But this separation is hardly ever complete. The same difficulty which we have to encounter in every other branch of knowledge meets us with redoubled force in political philosophy. The principles are given but the facts do not all agree, or the facts are given but the principles which we look to do not exactly correspond. The limits, however, which are drawn around the human mind, even in matters of this kind, are never so absolutely fixed but what we may sometimes escape from the dilemma. It is often possible by the application of principles which do not strictly correspond with the facts to produce an alteration in the facts themselves, to give rise, in other words, to an altered condition of society, and then the disagreement will in great part disappear.

The thorough introduction of the elective principle into the government effects a separation of the different departments from each other. This is a natural and a very important consequence of the establishment of representative government. Where public officers are chosen by the people, it is with a view to the performance of some prescribed duty and the exercise of some precise and definite power. But as soon as a practical and determinate end is sought after, the functions of the different officers lose all the vagueness and ambiguity which before hung over them. The prince consulted materially the interests of society when he laid down some of his prerogatives, although it was only for the sake of his convenience. But the people go straightforward to the same end as soon as they possess the electoral franchise in its full extent. A feeling of convenience also determines them to remold the institutions. But as this view to convenience has reference to the general good, to the practical affairs of society, the work is performed more completely by them.

As the prince is not elected but is a hereditary magistrate, the powers with which he is clothed have been determined by accident only. Hence his prerogatives are neither adjusted by any distinct rules nor to the actual exigencies of society. His title commenced at some remote period when society was full of noise and confusion — when the human mind was not sufficiently instructed nor the interests of the community sufficiently developed to give any determinate character to his functions. At first by dint of superstition or force, afterward by means of the vast influence which his strong position enables him to command, he succeeds in maintaining the most extravagant and contradictory powers, and this long after society is prepared for an entire change in the structure of his office.

When not merely the public officers who fill the various departments are elected, but in addition to this the entire system of government is founded upon a written constitution, the opportunity and the power to effect a separation between these departments are both increased. The experience which has been previously acquired, the adaptation which each part of the government has obtained in practice to one appropriate end and no other, are seized by those who assemble in the constitutional convention and suggest certain fundamental rules by which to give fixation and stability to the plan. A constitution is indeed only a generalization of the diversified rights, duties, and exigencies of men in society. And when the generalization is made upon reflection and deliberation—when it is brought to bear upon matters which have been the subject of actual experiment, it is necessarily more distinct as well as more comprehensive.

It has been proposed to elect the president of the United States by lot. This mode of choice is thought to be peculiarly adapted to a democratic republic which presupposes that all the citizens stand upon an equality. This is to take a one-sided view of the matter, a course which is always attended with error. The great principle of equality demands that all the citizens should have free liberty of choice in selecting persons capable of managing their affairs. We attribute to them equal rights, and straightforward adopt an arrangement which overthrows the most important of those rights. We start with the principle of liberty, and then inconsistently introduce a principle which causes the actions of everyone to be controlled by a rigid necessity. The principle of equality does not require that all the citizens should succeed in turn to the presidency, for that is an impossibility, but it does require that all should be equally eligible. Now the only way in which it is possible to reconcile this right with that of free choice is by the establishment of the elective principle. If there were any inconsistency between the two, it is plain that the former should yield to the latter as being of superior importance. But in truth there is no inconsistency. The right to hold office would be a frivolous and unmeaning one if it were not combined with the principle of election. That cannot be called a right whose existence is absolutely dependent upon blind chance or an irreversible necessity. That only is a right in society which springs from the free consent of society. It is because the principle of election is calculated to carry to perfection all the other rights of mankind that it is made the corner stone of a republic, and it is because the lot would confound and subvert those rights that it should be rejected.

If in a community of twenty millions of people the chief magistrate, legislature, and judges were chosen by lot, it is evident that the selection would in the greater number of instances be very unfortunate. That it might be so would be a sufficient objection, but that it would necessarily be so is an insuperable one. Offices are created because they are indispensable to the management of the public interests, to the well-being of society. But the office is an empty thing, a mere abstraction, unless it is filled by someone who is competent to discharge the duties, and integrity, ability, and experience are all necessary to fulfill this design. A state, then, which is founded upon republican principles, which undertakes to procure the greatest happiness of the greatest number, is entitled to the services of those citizens who possess these qualities. That the elective principle will not invariably secure this advantage is no objection to it, but that it does actually attain it to a much greater extent than any other system which has been devised is a conclusive reason why it should be adhered to.

In order to avoid the difficulties which attend the lot, it has been proposed to combine with it the principle of free choice, as in the case of the Venetian doge. Hillhouse's plan, the earliest which was presented to the American public and the parent of all others, contemplated the election of president by lot from among the senators.[1] A plan, presented twenty-five years later, proposed that he should be

---

1. [James Hillhouse, *Propositions for Amending the Constitution of the United States; Submitted by Mr. Hillhouse to the Senate, on the Twelfth day of April, 1808, with his Explanatory Remarks* (New Haven, 1808). In an attempt to exclude "all *cabal* and *undue influence*" by those seeking the office of President, Hillhouse's plan was that the President of the United States "be taken by lot from the Senate, and is to hold his office for one year." In 1808, the proposal derived from a fear of party spirit and was an attempt to get an executive officer free from the influence of party. In 1830, Hillhouse's proposal was reprinted as an "appendix" to *Propositions for Amending the Constitution of the United States, Providing for the Election of President and Vice-President, and Guarding Against the Undue Exercise of Executive Influence, Patronage, and Power* (Washington, 1830), which seems to have been directed against the power of Andrew Jackson.]

chosen in the same way from members of the House of Representatives. This, to be sure, reversed the Venetian scheme in which the doge was elected by forty-one nobles, they themselves having been appointed by lot. The two plans, however, are substantially the same; in both there is a combination of choice and chance. But there is no arrangement in which the lot enters as an element which is not objectionable. The lot might fall upon some senator or representative who was eminently unfit for the station. The manner in which the fortunate individual succeeded to the chief magistracy would be exposed to the same objection as exists to monarchical government. The prince reigns by accident and the selection of the president would be determined by accident also. The community would be unable to profit by the lessons of experience; it would not have the power on a succeeding occasion to cure the error which had been committed. The lot might fall successively upon those who had not the requisite qualifications.

The objections to a free and untrammeled election are the very argument I should employ in favor of it. They who propose the lot have fastened their attention upon the prevailing spirit of party. It is to prevent the eternal din and confusion which it occasions that they have presented this plan. Zealous and patriotic individuals they are, for they wish to attain all the good which is attainable, but they are not sufficiently appraised of the means through which alone this desirable object can be reached.

It may be very important that the president of the United States should be chosen by a party. Parties, whatever may be the exterior form which they wear, almost always contain the elements of great improvement. They are among the instruments which are appointed to push the race of mankind forward. The heated passions and fierce disputes through which they sometimes cause themselves to be heard are the only means in a society not enlightened above what it falls to the lot of humanity to be by which any signal change in the public policy of the state or the condition of the people can be attained. In elective government, public men may be said to be the representatives of the ideas of the age as well as of the grosser interests with which they have to deal, and to give those ideas a visible form is the most certain way of commanding public attention and of stimulating inquiry.

It would be a noble undertaking, if it were practicable, to separate the mischievous qualities of parties from the good they contain, to suppress the one and retain the other. But that is impossible as men are now constituted. To endeavor to rid ourselves of the anxieties and sufferings of life would be an attempt to free society from the most wholesome discipline to which it is at present subjected. No important end can be attained, perhaps none is worthy of being attained, unless it is through some sort of difficulty and danger. These are not merely to be viewed as obstructions in the way which it requires some strength to overcome, but as constant monitors to remind us of our own imperfections while we are endeavoring to rectify those of others. The innumerable annoyances of which party spirit is the occasion are planted in the walks of public life in order to exercise a similar influence. That we complain of them may be only a proof that they have the desired effect. That the lot would contribute to banish parties from the commonwealth, instead of being a recommendation, therefore, is a solid and conclusive objection to it.

Men undoubtedly take upon themselves a difficult task and involve themselves in a great many troubles when they undertake to elect the highest officers in the state. But it is the only way by which the people can be trained and habituated to the practice of self-government. If public affairs go wrong, they cannot say it is government which has done the mischief and we will revolt and overturn the existing authority, but they are brought after a painful and instructive experience to understand that they are themselves the direct authors of the public distress and that they alone have the power to remedy it. Thus a great number of petty misfortunes have the effect of averting an enormous evil.

The popular election of the American president has not been productive of the mischiefs which were anticipated. Instead of wild disorder and misrule, it has been eminently favorable to public tranquillity. This is a necessary consequence of the elective principle as it is applied in the United States. By communicating the electoral franchise freely and at the same time distributing into small fragments the bodies which exercise it, the ability to do mischief is very much abridged. The machinery which sets in motion the elections is like the machinery of a federal government. It acts upon the whole mass and yet through springs so numerous and so fine as to combine all the strength of a consolidated government with all the freedom of a popular one. The share of power which each individual exercises is so small that he is constantly reminded of his insignificance and does not boast of his importance, while the principle of the majority is so imposing and authoritative in its influence as to command instant and universal obedience to the laws. It may, indeed, be laid down as a maxim in politics that the danger to the institutions is diminished rather than increased in proportion to the enlargement of the electoral franchise.

Representative government imposes a check upon the electors as well as upon the elected. It is not apt to be viewed in this light. The accountability of the public officer to his constituents was the thing to which public attention was directed when free institutions were first established. That was a novelty before. No man, it is true, ever ventured to deny that he was under an obligation to consult the welfare of the people over whose interests he presided, but amid the contradictory elements of monarchical and aristocratical government the principle could never be made to have a practical operation, much less to assume the supreme authority to which it is entitled. A responsibility, however, on the part of the public agents cannot exist in full vigor without creating a counter principle of equal strength and efficacy. The numerous magistrates who are created, the regular system of administration which grows up in spite of the popular character of the institutions, stamps upon the government a degree of authority which either wins or compels the obedience of all. Not only is the responsibility of the citizens to the public increased, but what is of more consequence, the responsibility of each to the whole society is heightened.

The public officer is made responsible to the people for the very obvious reason that their interests are involved in every act of his public life. A perception on their part of what is advantageous for the public weal is necessary to place the officer in that relation. Unless this condition is admitted, the whole theory of representative government falls to the ground. Nor is it necessary to entertain any fanciful views with regard to popular intelligence in order to suppose that this condition may be fulfilled. There is but one way in which that perception of what is useful and fit can be gained, but one way in which any sort of practical knowledge can be acquired, and that is by placing those for whom such knowledge is desirable in a situation where they will be sure to realize the consequences which will follow from pursuing opposite courses. It is supposed that if the lot is established we shall get rid of all the noise and confusion of elections, that everything will go on smoothly, that the officer will feel greater pride in the discharge of his duties when he occupies an independent position than when he was a candidate and obliged beforehand to shape his conduct so as to meet all sorts of contradictory opinions. But this extreme smoothness of public affairs I have constantly observed to be inconsistent with much progress in society, and to be invariably followed by commotions and disturbances afterward. These commotions are the compensations of a bad system of government and have been the only means by which European society has been prevented from falling into the sluggish and inert condition of a Chinese population. Popular elections not only afford employment to the superabundant activity of the people, but they create innumerable checks upon the conduct of public men. They thus act by way of prevention in warding off great mischiefs, instead of encountering them after they have arrived by calamities still more formidable. It is a great mistake to suppose that public men would possess more integrity, patriotism, or knowledge if they were less interfered with. The mistake would be fully as great if we were to suppose that the people would be more peaceable and orderly, or anything like as inquisitive and well informed on public matters, or indeed on any matters whatever, if the lot were substituted in the place of elections. I am so persuaded of the utility of the last, so well satisfied that the advantages which they procure could be obtained in no other way, and these advantages accrue not merely in spite of but in consequence of the inconveniences which are complained of, that I would dispense with even more of the ease and comfort of individuals if that were necessary in order to retain them. I know no other plan by which it is possible to keep alive the intelligence of the great bulk of the adult population, none by which it is possible to give activity to the popular mind, and at the same to exercise it upon subjects which shall have interest and importance enough to lift it above the narrow round of ordinary pursuits. I know of no other plan by which it is possible to maintain the integrity, industry, and activity of public men. An eminent physician has said that life and bodily health are forced states. And so are intellectual and moral health. Many hard and disagreeable things are necessary to preserve the former, and annoyances, privations, and inconveniences of one kind or other are equally necessary to preserve the latter. There is hardly anyone but what would pass away life in a state of careless ease if he were permitted. In youth we are constrained to do otherwise by the superintending hand which guides us, and in manhood we are driven to exertion and to the pursuit of laudable ends not less by the wants of life than by the constant interference of others with every plan of conduct which we may pursue. The elective system only carries out this part of the economy of human nature; the difficulties and temptations with which it surrounds both the electors and the candidates may force a state of moral and intellectual culture, but after it is obtained it becomes the natural state. And everything then goes on more easily and quietly than it would in any other society. For I do not find that public affairs in the United States have been reduced to less system, that they have been conducted in a less orderly manner or with a view to the attainment of objects of less magnitude and importance than in other countries. On the contrary, I believe that in consequence of the conflict of parties the public will has been more steadily directed to the advancement of the public weal than in any other country. The disputes and contentions of parties have been favorable to that unity of purpose which is demanded in all human affairs. The more frequent and varied these disputes are, the more they help to strip both public men and public measures of whatever is adventitious about them. The former are observed more readily, and the analysis of the latter becomes easier.

It is not surprising that the popular election of chief magistrate in the United States has never led to any political disturbance. The elective principle cures the mischiefs which have been apprehended from the contests of parties. The lot would deprive us of the most valuable means for maintaining free institutions. It would annul the use of experience or render its application impossible. It would cut asunder the bond which now connects the representative with his constituents and would remove the check which the exercise of the elective franchise imposes upon the electors themselves. It would be better that the lot should be applied to the choice of any other officer than that of president, for in this the election is on so large a scale that it raises the minds of the people above the narrow and contracted views which they are sometimes prone to take of public affairs. It gives them large objects to look at and thus refreshes their feelings and expands their minds.

There is the greatest imaginable difference between the election of a king of Poland and of the American president. It was precisely because there were no parties of the people in Poland that that unhappy country was filled with confusion whenever the time of election came round. The body of nobles who were masters of the landed property had thereby a mortgage upon the understandings of the people. Factions there were, but parties had no existence. It was not because the prize was so high; it was because the election was managed by a close body that Poland was a prey to every species of intrigue and violence. Parties are unfavorable to civil commotion, while factions engender and support them, one reason of which is that parties in any country of tolerable extent are so large that in order to enable them to act they must be subdivided into still smaller parties, into bodies so numerous as to render intrigue or intimidation very difficult, whereas factions concentrate immense power in a small compass. The principle of the distribution of power is applied in the one case but not in the other. Thus in the United States the people assemble at ten or fifteen thousand places to vote for a president, and in Poland the election was conducted by a ferocious band of nobles all armed and collected upon one spot. The experiment of electing the chief magistrate has succeeded in America because it has operated in a manner different from what was expected. It has succeeded because the election is in effect by the people and not by the electoral colleges.

The unity of the executive power is regarded as a fundamental principle in political science. In this, there is a striking distinction between antiquity and our own times. It is remarkable that almost all the capital rules of government have undergone a revolution in modern times. In the ancient commonwealths the principle of representation was applied to the executive but not to the legislature. A hereditary nobility which has made a figure in the modern European states was unknown to the ancient. And the constitution of the executive presents us with a third example of the great diversity between the old and new systems of government. A plural executive was considered by the ancient lawgivers as indispensable to the right ordering of a state. In the Spartan commonwealth there were two kings, in the Athenian the archons, at Rome two consuls. The elevation of the great body of the people in modern times has given birth to the principle of representation as applied to the legislative body. A hereditary nobility is the offspring of feudal institutions, and to the decay of those institutions we may trace the unity of the executive power. The chieftain who centered in himself the greatest amount of authority, who was able to bridle the ferocity of the other barons and to impose an iron arm upon their will, usurped the supremacy under the title of king.

De Lolme is the most vigorous defender of the unity of the executive, and his views are entitled to great attention. This indivisibility of the executive authority, he says, fulfills two very important and apparently opposite conditions. Power is more easily confined when it is one, while at the same time it is placed more completely above the reach of assault. But a train of reasoning which is suggested by the frame of the English constitution may be very inapplicable to other forms of government, still less may it be entitled to rank among the fundamental principles of the science. If our design be to establish regal government, if we determine to create an executive magistrate with vast powers and prerogatives, it is certain that we will produce one effect. The prestige and luster which will surround the office, independently of the positive authority which is conferred upon it, will make a powerful impression upon the imaginations of the people. They will be awed to obedience to a bad as well as to a good government. The throne will acquire great stability; conspiracies to overturn it will rarely be formed. Although it may be free from the wholesome interference of public opinion, it will at any rate be placed above the assaults of ambitious men. But these are all consequences of the artificial character which is at the outset communicated to the executive, and unless its imposing prerogatives are an inseparable condition from its existence, we are not obliged to leap to the general conclusion that therefore the executive should be one. For if, on the other hand, we intend to establish a republican form of government, the executive will be elective; the precise authority assigned to it will be settled by a constitutional ordinance and not be left to stand upon the debatable ground of opinion. The office will be less dazzling, but it will on that very account be less open to attack. It will not affect the imaginations of men so strongly, but it will acquire a firmer hold upon their understandings. It will be protected by a real force, instead of by an invisible agency, and will secure the obedience of the people by the practical benefits it dispenses.

In these two examples, the structure of the government is totally different, and yet results in some respects similar may take place but without any regard, so far as we can yet see, to the fact whether in the last the executive is a single or a plural body.

The second position of De Lolme, that the executive power is more easily confined when it is one, is as a general proposition more questionable than the first. The condensation of power is the chief circumstance which renders it formidable and difficult to be restrained. And it is for this reason that free governments proceed upon the plan of distributing power as the most certain means of controlling it. The splendid attributes which are ascribed to a hereditary prince overpower the minds of the great majority of mankind; the people are incapacitated from making resistance to the most alarming exercise of authority, or from rectifying the most inveterate abuses, for a feeling of superstition has taken possession of them, and they feel as if they were ruled over by a force superior to society. And when to this is added the physical power which is placed at the command of this single individual, it is obvious that if he is restrained it must be by some compensatory contrivance totally independent of the unity of the executive, and indicating perhaps that there is a faulty rather than a wise constitution of that department. I speak now of the unity of the executive as understood by De Lolme whose reasoning is founded upon the notion of a hereditary monarch, although his views are conceived with a design of laying the foundation of a general principle. So difficult is it for even the finest understanding to analyze its ideas that the argument is a defense of the unity of the executive as the only way of maintaining the hereditary principle, rather than a defense of the first for the sake of establishing a principle of universal application. The subordinate end is made to take the place of the superior one, a very common error when the mind has fastened upon one set of phenomena and is determined to deduce all the principles of a science from them alone. It was after the usurpation of Octavius Cæsar, when the executive authority which was before divided came to be centered in the hands of a single individual, that it was found impossible to set bounds to it. The theory of nearly all the European governments, so far as regards the constitution of the executive, is the same now that it was centuries ago. And yet history shows that it was absolutely impossible to control it in England in the times of the Stuarts and in France under the reign of the Bourbon princes, not to go back to periods still more remote when it swallowed up every other authority.

What has occasioned the remarkable change which has taken place in very modern times? Not the recognition and establishment of the maxim of De Lolme, for that was the cornerstone of government when all Europe was filled with the most frightful tyranny. Causes of a very different character must have given rise to this revolution. It can only be ascribed to the growth of a new power in the state, to wit, that which is represented by the popular will. And that this new power will acquire still more influence and ultimately succeed in modifying the whole constitution of the executive is as certain as any event which is the subject of human speculation. It was formerly sufficient to study the mere mechanism of government in order to explain the phenomena of government, but it is now necessary to look a great deal further and to take in the structure of society as a most important element in the character and working of the political institutions.

All the tendencies of society at the present day, all the new forces which are created within it, are unfavorable to the condensation of power in any department of the government. This was not the case until very modern times. When De Lolme wrote the English House of Commons was just beginning to acquire a due weight in the constitution; the people were making slow but steady advances in the acquisition of knowledge and property; public opinion, for the first time in the history of society, showed signs of becoming a power of commanding influence in the state. All these agencies have received a wonderful accession of strength during the last seventy years, and begin to press with an enormous weight upon the executive authority. In other words, the power out of the government more nearly balances the power within, and produces the two opposite effects of confining and yet giving stability to the regal authority. This is evidently attributable to the altered structure of society and not to the unity of the executive.

There is this difference between a monarchy and a republic: that in the former, the government is more simple as a whole and yet very complicated in its parts; while in the latter, it is exceedingly complicated as a whole and yet very simple in the construction of its parts. In a republic, power is not condensed in any single institution as in a monarchy. It is divided among a great number of offices. When, for example, the chief magistrate is elected, his term of office short, his powers greatly abridged, the executive department will not be so complex and artificial a contrivance as it is in a hereditary government. It may even be a matter of very little importance whether it is composed of one or more members. Its original structure in other and more important respects is such as necessarily to confine it within its appropriate sphere. And the same power which confines it also protects it.

In modeling the executive department in a republic, a double plan is pursued. Certain attributes which were before regarded as inseparable from it are extinguished; the hereditary principle, the right to create peers, the absolute veto, the authority to dissolve the legislative body are all annihilated; they are deposited nowhere. The residue of the power is then divided between the officer who still maintains the title of executive and other departments or offices, some portion being extinguished as to him but yet remaining in other parts of society.

But two plans may be pursued in distributing power. A certain amount of power may be conferred upon two or more individuals to be jointly exercised by them, or the power itself may be divided, that is, lodged in different institutions and not merely distributed among several persons all holding the same office. Examples of the first were common in the ancient commonwealths. The executive authority was confided to two or more, but all composed one body. The French directory, and afterward the consulship when composed of three members, and the governor and council in some of the American states are instances of the same arrangement. The executive power is exercised by a plural body. The German, Swiss, and American confederacies are examples of the second plan. The executive authority is not divided among a number of persons all composing one body or one department, but is distributed among a great number of institutions. In the German and Swiss confederacies this power, so far as regards one class of objects, the exterior relations of the members of the confederacy, is deposited with the general diet which in both is a numerous body, and as regards the local interests of each of the members, it is sometimes confined to a plural and sometimes to a single executive. In the American government the same power is apportioned between the president and the thirty states. For it is plain that if the United States were a hereditary and consolidated monarchy the entire authority which is possessed by the state executives would be wielded by a single individual. This might also be the case if it were one aggregate community and yet a republic. But it would fall very far short of the true notion of a republic which absolutely requires not only that the public authority should be divided among several persons, but that it should be distributed among a number of sections or local departments. And although we may view the American confederacy as composed of several distinct governments rather than as parts of one system of government, yet it is neither necessary nor advantageous to do so; not necessary, because the same or a similar scheme must have been adopted if the country had not been accidentally divided into distinct colonial provinces; and not advantageous because a scheme analogous to the present is indispensable to the maintenance of free institutions. By taking the view I have just adverted to, the mind fastens upon a circumstance entirely accidental and loses sight of the principal point to be gained in constructing a democratic republic, whether it be composed of one homogeneous people or of several distinct peoples, and that is to subdivide the executive authority, to make such a disposition of it that it shall no longer be the inalienable attribute of one man, and thus to falsify the maxim of De Lolme.

Or in order to make the train of reasoning still clearer: we must not suppose that the principal design in founding the American government was to preserve the identity of the states and to make a merit of necessity by assigning to them very extensive powers. The prime object was to establish a government thoroughly republican, and there was no way of effecting this but by abridging the immense power which would otherwise have been exercised by the political departments and no way of accomplishing this but by dividing power, not only among several persons, but among several bodies. The government may have been a confederacy of monarchies, as in the German league, or a confederacy of aristocracies. The principal design, then, would have been to unite the whole for the sake of defense, to consult the exterior rather than the interior interests of the parts. But the American system went a great way beyond this, and it became necessary to retain the state governments in order to subtract power from the central government and to render the creation of a republic even possible. And although the American government is generally viewed as a system in which the federal authority superintends the external and the states the internal interests, yet the true view is to consider it as a whole in which the principal design was to consult and secure the interior prosperity and welfare of all the parts, and the division into local jurisdictions was an accessory, indispensable to carrying out this design.

Where the whole executive authority of the commonwealth is distributed among several distinct departments, or jurisdictions, three plans may be adopted. The whole or the greater part of the administrative officers appertaining to each of those jurisdictions may derive their appointment from one person who will thus be constituted the chief magistrate in regard to one class of interests; or the power of nomination only may be conferred upon him, subject to the approval or rejection of one or both chambers of the legislative body; or their appointment may flow from an entirely distinct source, in which case they will all, from the highest to the lowest, be independent of each other as well as of the head of the state. The first is the plan of monarchical government, whether absolute or limited. The second is the theory of the federal; and the third is that of the state governments of America. On either of these three plans, however, it is evident that the maxim that the executive should be one loses great part of its force. Thus, if the German confederation were presided over as formerly by the emperor, all federal appointments might flow from him, while all the administrative officers in each of the states would hold under some magistrate or council which was established in each, none of these magistrates or councils having any dependence upon the chief of the confederacy. The confederate form of government is then a device for breaking up the power of the different departments. It is not a mere arrangement of convenience. Convenience, or even necessity, may have determined it in the first instance, but the result is that a much greater amount of liberty is introduced into the state. The character and not merely the form of government is altered.

But the state governments of the United States afford the most remarkable example of an entire departure from the maxim that the executive should be one. In most of them the governor has no participation whatever in the appointment of the other executive or administrative officers. There is in truth no way of constructing free government without doing violence to that maxim. Executive power, as it is understood by all writers on government, implies the appointment of the whole host of administrative officers by a chief magistrate. This is an authority too large, too vague, and too dangerous to be confided to any one individual. We are compelled to divide and to subdivide the power in order to uphold another principle of still greater value and importance, the responsibility of the public agents to the people. The European governments proceed upon the plan of conferring enormous power upon a single executive, and then the difficult problem is presented, how shall this unnatural authority be controlled? The American governments get rid of the difficulty by getting rid of the problem. The executive power is distributed between the president and the thirty state governors, or it is in part devolved either upon the people themselves or upon agents appointed by them. And this arrangement, while it causes all public business to be conducted with a greater degree of exactness and regularity, imposes numerous and powerful checks upon the exercise of the power. The plan which is the most natural, the one which falls in best with the convenience of society, will be sure to be the best constructed. The effect may be to spoil the beauty of a favorite theory and to render what was once a cardinal principle of government a mere formal arrangement or a matter of detail. But it will not be the less valuable on that account.

In the federal government of America, it is only a small proportion of the public officers who are elected by the people. Not to mention officers in the army and navy, as well as foreign ambassadors, officers of the customs, heads of departments, the judges, the attorney general and district attorneys, together with the marshals, are all appointed by the president and Senate. The postmasters of higher grade are appointed in the same way; those of an inferior grade are appointed by the postmaster general. The president and members of the House of Representatives only are elected by the people, and the Senate by the state legislatures. In a democratic republic this at first appears to be a novel arrangement. But the confederate form of government naturally, if not necessarily, leads to a system of centralization within itself. And hence the importance of local jurisdictions becomes more manifest in order to prevent the whole authority of the state from being swallowed up by a single government. To centralize the powers of the federal government seems to be the only way of preventing the two jurisdictions, the national and the domestic, from being confounded and ultimately running into each other. The same reason does not exist in a consolidated government, for there all the public officers may be elected by the people. But what more particularly deserves attention in the structure of the American federal government is that those officers whose administration is central, the president and members of the legislative body, are chosen in local districts, while those whose administration is local are appointed by a central authority. It is not so in the state governments where nearly all the administrative officers are elected by the people. For there is no danger in the domestic governments that any rivalship will grow up between their public officers and the state authority.

Thus the federal government still clings to the system of patronage, while almost all the state governments have since 1789 gradually introduced the elective principle in the appointment of civil functionaries. The consequence is that the relative position of the two governments toward each other is different and the balance between the two materially altered. Federal politics now create the only existing parties of moment and these parties not only rule in the national councils, but control the local parties within the states. And the only question is whether by controlling their local politics they will finally succeed in controlling their local interests also. There can be no objection to the natural influence of general politics within the states, for that contributes to fasten more closely the bond which connects the national with the local interests, but when to this natural influence is added the artificial strength derived from the patronage of the federal government, a doubt is suggested whether the state jurisdictions will retain the independent position which was originally assigned to them. It is this patronage which creates the system of centralization in the federal government and which not only raises up two great parties but, subordinate to them, the local parties in the states.

In a democratic republic, then, there are two apparently opposite tendencies, the one to a distribution, the other to a centralization of power. As soon as the elective principle is extensively introduced it leads directly to the creation of local jurisdictions as the only way of connecting firmly the constituent with the representative. The advantages which they procure are not thoroughly realized until the population comprised within them have become habituated to the management of their own affairs. The experience then acquired inculcates all the skill and ability which are requisite. But as there will be a residuum of power left after the institution of these local authorities, to wit, that which represents the state as a collective whole, the notion of a central government forces itself upon the minds of the most democratic people. And the question then is how to avail ourselves of the great benefit of such a government without introducing a system of centralization also.

When the constitution of the United States was established the state governments were all differently modeled from what they are now. The administrative officers in each were by no means so generally elected by the people as they are now. The constitution of New York at that day vested the power of appointment in a council; that of Pennsylvania conferred it absolutely upon the governor whose authority in that respect closely resembled that of the British monarch. And the other state governments tended more or less to the same system. Important changes have been made since that period in many of these states, while in the new states which have since risen up the elec-

tive principle greatly predominates. Thus, at the time the federal constitution was established, state patronage contributed to balance the
patronage of the national government, that is, created state parties on
a large scale, and armed them with great influence. Those parties then
absorbed a corresponding share of public feeling and served to break
the impetuosity of the national parties. Perhaps if the system since introduced had existed in 1789, it may, so far as regards some of the public officers, have been copied after in framing the federal constitution.

The executive power is commonly defined to be the authority to
carry the laws into execution. But the constitution of nearly all the
European governments shows the widest possible departure from this
idea. The institution is made to correspond to the name, not the name
to the institution. The power of declaring war and of making treaties,
which are devolved upon the prince without the participation of any
other department, signify a great deal more than the right to execute
the laws. They amount to the declaration of a new law for the community, and appertain more properly to the legislative department.
The creation of an order of nobility, or the adding to their number, has
no shadow of connection with executive power. It is not merely the
creation of a new and a fundamental law, but it influences the making
of all laws which shall be subsequently passed. How these attributes,
together with the vast patronage which the appointing power implies,
came to be associated with the notion of executive power may be gathered from the observations made in the commencement of this chapter.
In a society which has not attained a high civilization, men are governed more through their imagination than their reason. That mysterious principle of our nature which in some respects is even stronger
in the common race of mankind than it is among the educated, and
which makes them figure to themselves a higher standard of excellence
than can be found in real life, affords the explanation of this phenomenon. It is for this reason that regal power exists in the greatest vigor
in the most imperfect form of society — in Russia, Turkey, and Persia,
than in Great Britain, France, and Belgium. When the masses are very
ignorant and a prey to all sorts of superstition, they are the most disposed to take refuge, from a sense of their own degradation, in the
creation of an ideal phantom of sovereignty which commands their
obedience because it enchains their admiration. The throne with its
immense and imposing prerogatives gives to this brilliant image a
visible form and existence. It seems to the imaginations of the people

that the further the source of all political power was removed from themselves, the nearer was its approach to the supreme fountain of law and justice. And an institution which has once fairly acquired this preternatural authority is in a condition to retain it long after society is prepared for a thorough and permanent change. The executive power will still comprehend a great number of attributes which do not properly belong to it.

Even where the chief magistrate is deprived of the war and treaty-making powers and the right to create one chamber of the legislative body, the interpretation put upon the executive power, that it is the authority to carry the laws into execution, must be received with very great caution. It will have some semblance of truth if we intend to describe the power as it exists in some particular countries, instead of defining it as it belongs to a regular and well constituted government. Nor will it ever be rigorously true except in theory, for in practice the execution of the laws is reposed in a great multitude of officers scattered over a wide extent of country whose official transactions cannot be understood, much less superintended, by a single individual. The advance toward a state of general and not merely of high civilization, the increase of the business transactions of society, necessarily sets bounds to the executive authority. The public interests become so diversified and complicated as to require the laborious attention of many thousand officers where a handful was before sufficient. This produces two effects of great importance. It first separates the administrative officers from the chief magistrate; he continues to appoint them, and yet the duties performed by them are removed from his inspection. It then disconnects entirely their offices from his and alters the theory as well as the practice of the government. It is needless to add that this last change is never brought about except in a democratic republic. As the chief magistrate can neither execute the laws in person nor see that they are executed by such a multitude of agents, the idea is sooner or later suggested that the great majority of the administrative officers have in reality no connection with him. He is consequently deprived of the power of appointment, and the theory of the government is then made to correspond exactly with its practice. But this is the result of time and is only brought about by great reflection and by a minute as well as extensive experience of public affairs.

I observe, in the new constitution of New York, an arrangement which is not to be found in any other state constitution. The administrative department is separated from the executive proper and is classed under two distinct heads, "administrative" and "local officers." An arrangement of the parts of a constitution may sometimes be a matter of detail, but in this instance it is the result of a strict logical analysis and indicates that the true notion of executive power has been seized and thoroughly appreciated. The effect is to disconnect, more clearly than has ever been done before, the administrative officers from the chief magistrate; in other words, to produce a division of the executive power.

In some of the state constitutions, under the head of executive power, the language is, the "chief" executive power shall be vested in a governor. This is the case in the constitution of Mississippi where all the other executive officers are, as in New York, made to derive their appointment directly from the people. The election of the principal of those officers, however, is prescribed in the article which defines the executive power. In New York, the word "chief" is omitted; but the distribution of power which would seem to render the employment of it very natural is actually made, and so the use or rejection of the word is even less than a matter of detail.

In some of the state constitutions, the appointment of some of the administrative officers is ranged under the head of executive power, while others are placed apart and under no distinct head whatever. This is the case in the constitution of Ohio. The office of secretary of state is created by the article which defines the executive power; while those of treasurer and auditor are placed under no distinct head. On the other hand, in the constitution of Kentucky the offices of secretary of state, of attorney general, district attorneys and sheriffs are ranged under the head of executive power; while the state treasurer and printer are to be found in the article which confers judicial power. The two last officers, being elected by the legislature, would more naturally have been placed under the legislative department. This very confusion, however, which is to be found in many of the other state constitutions, is an unequivocal proof of an entire change in the structure of government in America. The convention of New York have adapted the arrangement and phraseology of the constitution to this change and by so doing have communicated to a very important principle of government a degree of clearness which it did not before possess.

At one time the chief magistrate was regarded as very much the state itself. But when he came to be divested of prerogatives which have no shadow of connection with the executive power he ceased to be viewed in that light. A great change took place in the ideas of men of all classes. The responsibility of the administrative officers, which was before referred to him as their chief, is now referred to the people. The term "subordinate" when applied to these officers is then used to denote the relation which they hold to the community, not to indicate their dependence upon him. In other words, responsibility to the people is substituted in the place of accountability to one individual.

And yet the reasons for divesting the chief magistrate of the power of appointment are not so strong in a republic as in a monarchy. Where he holds by a self-existing title, there would seem to be a greater necessity for rendering the appointment of the other executive officers independent of his control than where he is elected by the people and his responsibility to them is immediate. But a dependence of the public officers upon the community, however consistent with the interests of society, would be totally incompatible with the genius of monarchy. It would cease to be monarchy from the moment the change was effected, and the prince himself would fall into a dependence upon the new appointing power whether that was composed of agents of the people or of the people themselves. The federal and a few of the state governments have endeavored to reconcile the two plans by pursuing a third which combines some of the features of both. The power of appointment is wrested from the chief magistrate, but he retains the power of nomination. This is sometimes viewed in the light of an absolute power of appointment. And this is correct so far as regards the political party from which the nominee is selected, but no further. The control which the body to whom the nomination is made possess over the appointment may not always be discerned because in the great majority of cases it acts as a preventive check, deterring the officer from the nomination of persons whom he would otherwise select. But there are many instances in which its direct operation has been distinctly shown. Presidents have sometimes so conducted on these occasions as to persuade the impartial among their own party that they did not so much "believe in the rule of the majority, as in the rule of him who had obtained the majority"; and the Senate have been compelled to perform the austere but patriotic duty of rejecting persons who were eminently unfit for the station which they were named to fill.

There are many defects in this system, however, notwithstanding the control of the Senate. The person nominated may, in common acceptation, be both capable and honest, so that he could not be rejected with any show of reason. And yet his dependence upon the president for renomination, or for a continuance in office for a single week, will be very apt to impel him to a course of conduct which will be completely subservient to the personal ambition of that officer. He may, perhaps it is not too strong to say that he will, inevitably, be nominated with a view to that result. This greatly mars the plan upon which the executive authority is constituted, which proceeds upon the idea that as the president is himself elected, he may be as much confided in in making nominations as in the performance of any other duty. The design in both instances is that he should act as the representative of the people. But there is this difference between the two cases, that in one the president simply influences the opinions of men, in the other he acts directly upon their will and determines their actions. The effect is in some degree to counterbalance his responsibility to the people. For if he can place in lucrative situations a multitude of persons who are bound to him by the powerful motives of interest, he is possessed of an authority entirely foreign to any which the elective principle contemplates. He is provided with an instrument of no mean force in promoting his re-election. The original design of the government so far fails because one great defect of the monarchical regime is attached to it. The prince holds his station independently of the will of the people, and the president is armed with a power which may insure his re-election in spite of well-founded objections to his administration. Thus the principle of representation is made to defeat itself. The political institutions are themselves converted into instruments for corrupting both public officers and people.

There are but two plans by which this defect can be cured. The one is to cause all or the greater part of the administrative officers of the federal government to be elected by the people in the districts where their offices are located, precisely as in the state governments; the other is to declare the president ineligible a second time. The first plan would carry the division of the executive further than it is now; the second would render the president comparatively powerless in the dispensation of the patronage which is attributed to him.

It may be supposed that if the first plan were pursued the effect would be to confound the authority of the two governments, to obliterate the boundary which now separates them, and to make the citizen forget that he was as much bound in allegiance to the national as to the state government. It is true that the president is himself elected by the people of the states and not by the people of the United States, and so are members of the Senate and House of Representatives. And these elections not only take place in each state separately but in the third instance they are conducted in local districts and on the same plan that members of the state legislatures are chosen. The election of president has also been sometimes held in electoral districts. It is at any rate always conducted in minute subdivisions, smaller even than those of counties. But the chief magistrate of the union is stationed at the seat of government where all his duties are centered. It is there only that we are familiar with him as one exercising political authority. Congress holds its sittings at the same place. It is to this spot that all its proceedings are referable. This contributes to keep these parts of the machinery of the national government in activity before the public eye and to draw a broad line of discrimination between it and the state institutions. But if the whole corps of administrative officers were chosen in the same way, it might be to be feared that they would lose their separate identity since their functions are necessarily performed in local districts within the states and not at some central point. It may be apprehended, if this scheme were adopted, that the centripetal force of the federal government would be much weakened, that the love of union and the spirit of patriotism which takes in the whole country would be extinguished. The power of nomination may originally have been conferred upon the president because it was supposed to be an attribute of the executive authority. That may not be its true character and yet it may fulfill another purpose of still higher importance.

The power which the imagination exercises upon the opinions of men is a thing not to be absolutely neglected, at any rate when it comes in aid of any of the legitimate objects of government. But it has never been found that the minute division of the state authority, the creation of county, township, and city jurisdictions, relaxes the bond which holds together the parts and connects them with one presiding authority — that of the state. On the contrary, the bond is made firmer and stronger. The complete centralization of the appointing power does indeed affect the imaginations of men sensibly because it sets in motion a power which is beyond themselves, but the communication of the same power to the people gives it a more palpable connection with their interests and in the end produces a more durable if not a more vivid impression upon them. Instead of referring the authority of the state to one individual, it is made to represent the joint power of the whole society, a thing equally mysterious and invisible in its operation and yet constraining the actions of men with a force almost irresistible. The delinquent in America, whether his crime be of a political or a private character, as soon as the officer pronounces the words, "I arrest you by the authority of the state," delivers himself up. He quails before an authority which means so much and which only speaks through an humble individual whom he has himself been instrumental in electing. More is gained than can ever be lost by founding government plainly and directly upon the interests of the people. The practical working of the system will gradually inculcate the requisite skill and experience and, while the influence of the imagination will still count as something, powerful motives will be added to render the people prudent and circumspect in the selection of the public officers. I should not err if I were to say that it is to the over-exercise of the imagination that the greatest defects are to be traced, even in a country of free institutions. Like the children of the rich who believe that they will be abundantly taken care of by others, the people, when the management of their interests is placed far from them, are disposed to concede everything to the showy authority which presides over public affairs. But when they are cast upon their own resources and are compelled to grapple with business as a matter of serious concern, they are taught to be more cautious and wise in every step which they take. In America the population increases so rapidly, generation crowds upon generation so fast, that society may be said to be still in a state of fermentation. It is (contrary to the opinions of European writers) when the population becomes dense and society is thickly planted with the sentiments of public liberty, when long and inveterate habit has rendered republican rule both firm and durable, that a due estimate will be placed upon the political institutions.

We have no reason to believe that public officers in Great Britain are selected with more judgment than in the American states. To take one example — that of justices of the peace, who are so numerous that the aggregate amount of business transacted by them is of immense consequence to the community. These magistrates do not exercise in the first country the very important civil jurisdiction which they do in the last. But they possess some other powers of considerable magnitude and their criminal jurisdiction wholly exceeds anything which is known in the United States. For they can sentence to almost unlimited imprisonment, and even to transportation for seven and fourteen years. In England they are appointed by the lords lieutenant of counties, a class of officers who are totally irresponsible. In the United States they are almost universally elected by the people of each county or township. These officers perform their homely but useful duties very much to the satisfaction of the public, although their jurisdiction in some of the states extends to one hundred dollars and a very great amount of money consequently passes through their hands. But in the British kingdom, the malpractices of these magistrates of one kind or another have been so flagrant and notorious as to engage the attention of the leading men in Parliament. Lord Brougham when in the House of Commons dilated upon them with much severity, although there was every disposition on his part to soften the censure which they deserved.

I am aware that although the president's patronage exercises a disturbing influence upon the domestic politics of the states, this is in some degree counteracted by another effect. By strengthening and consolidating two great national parties, the sectional jealousies, the narrow and contracted views which mere state politics would create, if not swallowed up, are at any rate mitigated and kept more out of view. The domestic jurisdictions are prevented from tearing each other to pieces by placing them on an arena where one common sympathy, one mutual interest, may animate equally the citizen of Georgia and the citizen of Ohio. These are effects of no light moment, and if they can be brought about in no other way than by clothing the president with the vast patronage he now enjoys, it cannot be doubted that the evils incident to the system are amply compensated. But national parties must exist, and will ever have a commanding influence, since the questions with which they deal are so weighty and of such general interest to the whole country.

I am persuaded that a genuine devotion to the national interests and a generous patriotism would not be lost to the community, even if a considerable portion of the administrative officers of the federal government were elected in the states. The two governments would be more identified in interest than before, and the execution of the laws by a federal officer would be accompanied with the same authority which attends the execution of state laws. It is the operation of the laws upon individuals which gives efficacy to the system of confederate government. The laws of the United States are in truth laws of the states and, admitting that there is never unanimity in their enactment, there is as seldom unanimity in the passage of state laws. And yet there is rarely any resistance to the execution of a state law in those counties whose representatives have voted against it. The state is an aggregate of counties, as the nation is an aggregate of states. And although in the first the parts are carved out of the whole, while in the last the whole is formed out of the parts, yet the whole cling as tenaciously to the local divisions of counties and townships as they do to the larger division into states. Hardly any of them would submit to the unbroken central authority of the state more than it would to the authority of a consolidated national government. The existence of those minor jurisdictions accordingly is coeval with the foundation of the state governments. Logically, if not chronologically, it would be correct to consider the states as originally issuing from the settlement in townships and counties, rather than the reverse. This is so true that if the states in which they have subsisted from time immemorial were to undertake to abolish them, public opinion would be as much shocked as if the national government were to invade the undoubted rights of the states. Those lesser jurisdictions then contribute to bind together the parts of which the states are composed. And the existence of the larger jurisdictions of the states, so far from weakening the authority of the central government, adds strength to it on the same principle that the division of the judicial power between the judge and the jury increases the effective authority of the former. The judge is relieved from the performance of duties which, although the least difficult in themselves, are the most apt to engender heart-burnings in society. And the federal government is in like manner relieved from responsibility in so many matters which engage the attention and feelings of the people that its authority has more freshness; and where it does act, it has the advantage of greater vigor and alacrity. I am not disposed therefore to think that the election of one class at least of the administrative officers of the federal government would subtract in any degree from its legitimate authority.

Cases may arise where there will be a collision between the authority of the state and federal governments. And to guard against the consequences flowing from this, there is one class of officers whose appointment might well remain as it is. The attorney general, district attorneys, and marshals, as well as the judges of the federal courts, might continue to hold under the president and Senate. The share of patronage thus devolved upon the chief magistrate would not be great, and would do no harm even if it were unattended with one particular advantage. Perhaps it is not certain that the laws would not be as faithfully and energetically executed if the district attorneys and marshals were elected by the states. Instances have already occurred where these officers have resigned in consequence of some temporary obstruction to the discharge of their duties, and their unwillingness to make efforts to surmount the difficulty. For the officer is nothing unless he can clothe himself with the armor of public opinion. The instances of resistance to the execution of state laws have certainly been more numerous than of resistance to the laws of the union. The executive officers of the former as well as of the last have notwithstanding invariably triumphed. But if there is any uncertainty whatever, that is a sufficient reason for retaining the appointment of those officers as it is now. An experiment with a more numerous class of public agents will shed great light upon the practicability of extending it still further.

Postmasters are the most numerous class of civil officers appertaining to the federal authority. They outnumber all others put together. Their duties are essentially of a local character, that is, are confined to certain territorial divisions within the states. I see no good reason, therefore, why if a convention were now called to frame a constitution of government the appointment of these officers might not be devolved upon the people, precisely as is that of members of the House of Representatives. The scheme seems to run counter to our notions of theoretical propriety, but that is the most which can be said of it. This notion of preserving a certain symmetrical arrangement no doubt had great influence with the conventions which first organized the state governments. The power of appointment seemed at that day to be peculiarly an attribute of the executive, and almost all the states conferred the right of nomination, at least, upon the governor. A great change has been effected in almost all the old states, and in the new hardly any trace of the system can be discerned. Yet the conduct of all public business is, to say the least, as orderly, upright, and intelligent as it was under the old plan. There is no possible way of making free institutions succeed but by training the popular mind to habits of self-government, to make it feel and realize the consequences which ensue from any mistake in the management of public business. And even if we should admit that the frequent elections acted as a provocative to party spirit, this would be no argument against them. No great good ever was obtained but by contending with great difficulties.

Experience, however, seems to prove that popular elections are highly favorable to public order. We may account for this unexpected fact in a variety of ways. First, public jealousy is very much softened when place and emolument are not confined to a close body but are laid open in reality, and not merely in name, to free competition. Second, there is a principle of human nature almost universal in its operation that once the desires of the mind are fairly gratified, they lose their attraction and have no longer the same power to stir the passions. Third, the more equal distribution of power which popular elections necessarily introduce gives rise to a more equal distribution of benefits also. Men are no longer favored by classes or sections, for all classes and sections participate in the management of public business. Fourth, the popular mind becomes infinitely better educated than under the old system. I am aware of the silly affectation of perpetually underrating the present in comparison with the past, no matter at what period of time the present may be placed. But I believe I have not been an inattentive observer of the progress of society; at least I have endeavored to make it a chief object of my thoughts, and I think I can discern very visible marks of improvement, both moral and intellectual, in every part of America. The two countries which in very recent times have been most convulsed by party spirit and which have been a prey to all sorts of crime and immorality are Spain and Portugal. An election which in America makes very little noise beyond the district or county, and which as soon as it is over leaves everything behind tranquil, renders those countries scenes of perpetual strife and disorder.

In the event of a constitutional amendment which would refer the election of postmasters to local districts, there are several important checks upon their conduct which would be retained by the federal government. First, they would be commissioned by the president of the United States on the same principle that state officers who are chosen in territorial divisions of the states are commissioned by the governors. Second, they would be governed by the federal laws, which would not only mark out the election districts but which would prescribe all the duties to be performed. Third, they would be amenable to the federal courts. And fourth, their transactions would all be referable to the seat of government, so that in the event of any charge against them they might be suspended by the president. A president would be apt to be very cautious in the exercise of this power of even temporary displacement where the public officer did not hold directly under him. The present system holds out temptations which very few public magistrates can withstand. It invites the president to treat all the administrative officers like the men upon the chess board and to use them for no other purpose but to play the old fashioned game of politics. The plan proposed would contain abundant checks upon the conduct of those officers, while it would create a powerful and most salutary restraint upon the actions of the president.

I believe there are few presidents who would not greatly prefer to be relieved from the annoyance and heart-burnings which these appointments create. As long as the authority exists, no one holding the station feels at liberty to turn away from the arbitrary exercise of it. The party, if not the public generally, expect that changes for political ends will be made. The constitution and laws have thrown out a challenge to that effect which the chief magistrate dare not decline, although he would cheerfully part with the prerogative in order to be delivered from the eternal clamor and the despotic dominion of cliques. At present he makes changes just as caprice dictates, but he is first rendered a capricious being by having so unnatural an authority cast upon him.

There is a difficulty with regard to the removal of public officers which has pressed upon the minds of thinking men. If an officer is elected by the people and is guilty of gross misconduct, while at the same time the period for another election does not come around until a year or two afterward, in what way shall we deal with him? One way of curing the difficulty is to make him give security for his good conduct. But this may not always be sufficient; he may commit more mischief than can be compensated by any bond which can be taken. The Italian republics of the middle ages endeavored to get rid of the difficulty by electing their officers for exceedingly short terms, sometimes for six months and sometimes for only one. It was believed at that day that there was no possible way of reconciling the two principles of responsibility and election but by rendering the duration of the office so limited that the officer would hardly have time to commit any flagrant delinquency. They required no bond and they not only never removed before the expiration of the term, but it was held to be a fundamental principle that there could be no trial for misconduct until that term had elapsed. These difficulties are all easily avoided in the state governments of America. They are met in a very plain and effectual manner. In Ohio, county treasurers are removable by the county commissioners without waiting for the tedious process of a trial and conviction. So also the governor of the state, upon being impeached, ceases for the time being to be governor, and in the meantime the president of the senate supplies his place. In New York, the treasurer of the state and other administrative officers may be suspended by the governor whenever there has been a violation of duty. These provisions which seem never to have suggested themselves to the Italian politicians are perfectly familiar to the Americans. The officer has been elected by the people. No magistrate, therefore, should have power to deprive him of his office. But there is every propriety in suspending him for the time being. If he is ultimately removed, it is only upon conviction by a tribunal of the people.

In the great majority of instances, the bond taken from the federal officers would be sufficient to insure the faithful performance of their duties as is the case with the state officers. The same system throughout, which has been adopted in the state governments, might with equal advantage be introduced into the federal government. It would act as a check upon both the president and the administrative officers while we should also get rid of the corrupting influence of executive patronage.

I place reliance upon the plan of distributing the power of appointment among the people, not merely because it best agrees with the genius of free institutions, but because I do not believe that the ineligibility of the president a second time will reach the mischiefs which it is so desirable to remedy. Where the desire of re-election cannot be gratified, a new passion will take its place. The chief magistrate will become deeply interested in the choice of his successor. The ambition of living even after we are dead is one of the most powerful springs of human conduct and unfolds itself in every variety of form in our progress through life. Before feudal institutions had firmly planted the hereditary principle in government, kings were as ambitious of being instrumental in the choice of their successors as if it were a matter of personal interest to themselves. The Roman emperors, even when there was no question of kindred in the case, were as desirous of this reputation as they were of extending the limits of the empire. The American president will always be surrounded by powerful and aspiring men who will seek to ingratiate themselves in his favor, and to some of whom he may be under inestimable obligations in prosecuting his plan of administration. He will strive to live in the person of his successor.

There is another consideration of great importance. As free institutions delight to lift up the man of the humblest pretensions to the most exalted station, they also teach the man who has attained the highest honors that he does not tarnish the luster of his reputation by afterward accepting an inferior station. In two instances have ex-presidents consented to fill offices of inferior grade.[2] It is the man who ennobles the office and never the reverse. The precedent has only to be set when it will be generally followed, especially where the retiring president is in the vigor of life and in the full possession of his faculties. The experience of one who has seen so much of public life in all its allurements and anxieties may be full of instruction to those who are just entering on the stage of public life. This presents a powerful motive of interest, as well as of ambition, to engage the president in the choice of his successor. He may be the future ambassador of the nation, or he may aspire to any other office to which his extensive fame and abilities recommend him. He may have retired from the presidency, very creditably to himself, a poor man. Instead of a pension, which free governments never bestow, he will be ambitious of earning a reward by being in some way useful to his country. But it will be impossible for him to lose sight of the influence which party connection will have in promoting his desires.

A political arrangement which is destined to further one chief end generally succeeds in answering some other subordinate ones. The complete centralization of the power of appointment gives unbounded sway to the government of the majority. But if this power is distributed among the districts where the officers are located, the extreme rigor of the rule that the majority is entitled to govern is very

2. [After he was President, John Quincy Adams was elected as representative to the Twenty-second Congress (1831) and was returned for eight successive terms. For the second instance, Grimke may have in mind James Madison who was elected to serve as a delegate to the Virginia Constitutional Convention of 1829.]

much mitigated without substantially impairing its force. The various administrative officers, also, will be chosen by those who have the best opportunity of judging of their capability. For, as I have before remarked, free institutions, if they do not find men absolutely fit for self-government, are somehow or other wonderfully adapted to make them so.

Doubts, however, will still suggest themselves to even the most intelligent minds. It will be inquired how it is possible to succeed in the government of a mighty population if the chief offices in the state are not surrounded by something of the prestige of authority. If the hereditary principle is dispensed with and the prerogatives of royal power are abolished, what plan can be fallen upon to atone for this diminution of the authority of government, unless it is by centering the whole power of appointment in the chief magistrate? In what way can we keep alive the notion of unity as an attribute of the government, a notion which has hitherto been of so much efficacy in the government of mankind? If we are bound to take notice of the good qualities of human nature, it may be said that we are equally bound to take notice of its bad qualities. And while all statesmen from the earliest times have been convinced that the chief desideratum of government was to place all sorts of checks upon popular feeling, shall the American government part with the only one which is left and one which is merely indirect in its operation? Even if these objections have not been sufficiently considered in different parts of this work, I feel so firmly persuaded that the system of patronage cannot always maintain its ground that I would even make a merit of necessity and forestall the period when it will fall into disuse. There is a strong current of public opinion running against it. And I have constantly observed that whenever there has been a very general and decided tendency to any great movement in society, it has been sure to be brought about; and what is of equal importance, it has been accompanied with safeguards and compensatory contrivances which were entirely overlooked. There may be particular or local tendencies to change and these never tell anything. But any event, the tendency to which is of so general and marked a character as to stamp an impression upon the age or country, is sure to take place and to succeed.

I observe that a very great change has taken place in the mode of procuring appointments. Formerly, one or two individuals in a state arrogated the right to dictate to the president the nominations he should make. It was one way of subserving their own private ends. Most generally it was with a view to strengthen their political connections. But sometimes the motives which governed them were purely personal. I knew one instance where an individual of some influence procured the appointment of a near relation of his enemy in order to bind the former to his own interests and to inflict a deadly blow upon the last. The appointment was absolutely unexceptionable; a better could not have been made. But the example was of pernicious influence.

Within fifteen or twenty years a very great change has taken place in the management of this matter. A public man, no matter what his influence may be, feels constrained to defer considerably to the opinion of the people among whom the appointee is to reside and to discharge his duties. Recommendations are drawn up, and even if the persons designated are not altogether to his liking he feels himself in duty bound to second them. This change in the mode of operation of the system is a sure indication that the system itself is on the eve of being changed.

The system of patronage belongs properly to monarchical government. It is not adapted to the genius of a republic. Cecil was the first European minister who seems to have been aware of its importance as an engine of government.[3] He announced it as a maxim in politics that the nation must be governed through, not by, the Parliament. James I was the first king who acted upon this maxim by seducing a Parliamentary leader from the popular cause and making him prime minister.[4]

The rise of this system in monarchical government is an infallible proof that a great change is taking place in the working of the institutions. It denotes that the government is passing by insensible degrees from absolute to limited monarchy. All absolute monarchs reign by dint of force or superstition. They may be obliged, as Mr. Hume remarks, to "truck and huckster" to some particular men, but the great

3. [Robert Cecil, Earl of Salisbury (1563–1612), statesman, secretary of state to Queen Elizabeth and James I.]

4. [Grimke's use of the term, "prime minister," in relation to James I is anachronistic since it came into usage only in the eighteenth century. He probably has in mind Sir John Savile, a leader in the House of Commons and opponent of the court who was made a privy counsellor and later baron; David Hume observed, "This event is memorable; as being the first instance, perhaps, in the whole history of England, of any king's advancing a man on account of his parliamentary interest, and of opposition to his measures." *The History of England* (Oxford, 1824), VI, 102.]

bulk of the community are ruled by fear or superstition. If in a society thus organized, a train of causes can be set in motion which will rouse the popular mind to activity and spread knowledge and industry throughout the land, a more direct communication will be opened between the people and the government. Public opinion will be something, as in after times it will grow to be everything. The prince will be obliged to throw away the coarse instruments of government which he had before employed. As men can no longer be driven by force, he will resort to the seductive influence of patronage. And this is undoubtedly a great improvement upon the old system, inasmuch as it supposes that men are endowed with free agency, that they must be governed by some sort of persuasion addressed to their understandings, even though it should be through their interests.

This mode of governing a community may be denominated the transition state from absolute to limited monarchy. Its continuance may be of indefinite duration, as it possesses a faculty of self-preservation greatly beyond the old system. It may last so long, but in a greatly mitigated form, as to render it also the transition state from limited monarchy to free institutions. It may raise up so large a body of educated people and independent thinkers as to create an effectual counterpoise to the throne and aristocracy. The American government commenced where all other governments had left off, and if here and there the federal government exhibits features of a monarchical character, it must be attributed to the absence of all experience in modeling a republican government upon so extensive a scale.

There is one circumstance, however, which has tended greatly to diminish the mischiefs of patronage in the United States. This is the immense disproportion between the number of offices and number of the electors. The influence which the system of patronage exerts evidently depends upon the number of persons who can be gained over, and this depends upon the number of active citizens, not meaning thereby the number of adult males, but the number of those who are admitted to the enjoyment of political rights. We do not talk of patronage as applied to the brute, unformed mass of a Turkish or Russian population. They are easily governed without the employment of this delicate but powerful instrument. The king of France appoints to one hundred and thirty-eight thousand offices, the aggregate salaries of which amount to forty millions of dollars. The president of the United States "nominates" to fifteen thousand, the salaries of which amount to five millions of dollars. There is not merely a great disparity between the number of lucrative places to be disposed of in the two countries but, what is of infinitely more importance, there is an immense disproportion between the number of offices and the number of citizens who can be influenced in this way. One hundred and thirty-eight thousand public officers, with two hundred thousand electors only, discloses a patronage literally gigantic when it is contrasted with fifteen thousand officers and three millions of electors. The reform act of Great Britain which has increased the number of electors from three hundred and forty thousand to eight hundred and thirteen thousand has in the same proportion diminished the power of the British monarch. The American president cannot nominate to office more than one in every two hundred of the electors. The king of France has the absolute disposal of so many places that he can present more than every second man in the kingdom with one apiece. The effect of the one system is to train a vast corps of civil officers in the service of the government; that of the other is to create an independent body, and one vastly more numerous, out of the government. And this view alone is abundantly sufficient to show how greatly mistaken they are who have run a parallel between the European monarchs and the chief magistrate of America.

There is a circumstance of an entirely different character which does increase the power of the American president and one which is peculiar to representative government. The immense development of the democratic principle, a thing of yesterday, without entering as a distinct element in the composition of the government, cripples incalculably in practice the effective power of the French and English monarchs. The structure of society and the political institutions are not in complete harmony with each other. In the United States it is the reverse, and the predominance of the popular power may be said both to limit and to fortify the authority of the chief magistrate.

For the true notion of political power does not consist in contesting and running counter to the general interests, but rather in founding itself upon the general will and so placing at the command of government a greater amount of both physical and moral energy than it would otherwise be able to employ. But nothing contributes so much to give strength and influence to a public officer as the confidence and support of a free people. It is more than equivalent to the obedience of a great army. Free institutions do not detract from the legitimate authority of any public magistrate, but they do give a new direction to ambition and insensibly habituate the most aspiring genius to fasten all hope of acquiring a brilliant and lasting reputation upon the ability to advance the solid prosperity of the state. And the untrammelled authority which may be exercised to carry out so noble a design is as truly power as are the prerogatives of any potentate on earth. This new direction of power is one of the most marked characteristics of the age. Even the emperor Napoleon, who lived amid elements little calculated to inspire such feelings, was obliged to take refuge in one monument which he had constructed for the public welfare. "I shall go down to posterity," he exclaimed, "with the code of laws in my hand." And although this code was in no sense the work of his hands but was drawn from the profound writings of Pothier and other eminent jurists, yet circumstances enabled him to call it into being and one can easily pardon, nay greatly admire, the vanity which seeks in any degree to associate itself in part with those who have been the real benefactors of mankind.[5] On a more recent occasion, an English king, William IV, placed himself at the head of the party which contended for Parliamentary reform. Elizabeth countenanced the establishment of newspapers, but little thought that this was the first step toward raising up a new power in the state. And a subsequent monarch ratified "the mutiny bill" without exactly deciphering the consequences which would follow from it. But William IV well understood the import of the bill which introduced Parliamentary reform and manfully leaped to the conclusion that although it circumscribed his authority it added wonderfully to his influence. The institutions of a democratic republic help to render that the habitual temper of public men which in other countries is only an occasional burst of magnanimity.

I have noticed one change which very gradually takes place in monarchical government: the substitution of patronage as an instrument of power in the place of superstition and fear. There is another equally remarkable, and one which is every way calculated to arrest the attention of an inquisitive mind. The regal and the executive authority which are originally united in one person in progress of time come to be entirely separated from each other. They may both continue ostensibly to be exercised by the head of the state, but in practice, in the actual administration of public affairs, the tendency is to

5. [Robert-Joseph Pothier (1699–1772) historian of French law.]

disconnect them entirely. This is an event which contributes to break the force of the royal authority and to nullify the maxim, "the king can do no wrong," by introducing something like a regular responsibility into the management of the public business. It hastens the passage from absolute to limited or constitutional monarchy and facilitates the ultimate transition to free institutions.

Two causes may be assigned for this important change. First, that diminution of the personal authority of the king which invariably takes place in a community which has attained a high civilization. So many and such powerful interests then spring up to obscure the luster of the throne that the officer ceases to exercise the magical influence which he formerly had upon the minds of men. In the meantime, the power and importance of the other departments are as regularly advancing. They attract to themselves a large portion of the influence and respect which were before exclusively bestowed upon the monarch. The words of Louis XIV, "the state, why I am the state myself," come to be regarded as an empty ebullition of vanity rather than as a treasonable expression.

In the second place, the duties appertaining to the executive become, as before observed, so intricate and demand the exercise of so much ability, industry, and information as to be absolutely unmanageable by a single individual. A regular board of executive officers then takes the place of those pompous and luxurious functionaries who were the mere servants of the king. The members of this board will continue to be nominated by him, but the business devolved upon them will be so complicated and difficult as not even to be understood by the prince. This will give to the board a distinct character and importance which, in process of time, will ripen into something more than a nominal independence of him. The importance of the principal is not always increased by the ability of the agents he employs. It is often the reverse. The relation which the executive officers ultimately bear to the community is so much more extensive than to the king that they may even act as a counterpoise to his authority.

The seats which ministers have in the legislative body contribute to consummate this great change in the constitution of the regal power. The arrangement was originally intended to give support to the throne. But in a highly civilized community the legislature is sure to acquire the supremacy and turns all the instruments of the crown to its own advantage. By placing the chief members of the ministerial board in the popular branch of the legislature (as is most usually the case), they are brought into immediate contact with the representatives of the people, are subjected to the direct control of public opinion, and are sure to be displaced whenever the majority is decidedly against them. Thus, by a slow but irresistible process, the executive is effectually separated from the royal power. The prince is a hereditary magistrate, the people have no voice in his appointment; but to compensate for this unnatural arrangement, he loses the executive functions. The persons who exercise them are virtually appointed by the representatives of the people. It is not surprising that an English premier should prefer a seat in the House of Commons to one in the Lords, for as nothing can deliver ministers from the omnipotent control which public opinion exerts, they are certain by acting in conjunction with it to add to the weight of their authority.

By the act of settlement of twelve and thirteen of William III it was declared that no person holding an office or place of trust should be eligible to Parliament. This provision was afterward altered so as to exclude persons holding pensions and to vacate the seat of any member of the House of Commons upon his appointment to office. He was, however, immediately re-eligible. Instead of being incapacitated from holding a seat by a fixed constitutional provision, it was referred to the people themselves to determine whether under the circumstances he should again be elected. This change has been disapproved of by some eminent writers, but it is plain that the ordinance, as it was originally penned, would have increased instead of diminished the power of the crown. The admission of members of the executive to the hall of legislation has a decidedly democratic tendency. It brings them within speaking distance of the people, and when that is accomplished much of the mystery and statecraft which would otherwise surround public affairs is dissipated. It has had another very decided advantage. It has led to the practice of appointing ministers from among distinguished commoners, rather than from among the nobility. The king makes a merit of his dependent situation by courting popular favor and relying upon it as his chief support.

The compelling ministers, then, to appear in presence of the representatives of the people and to show their hands is a contrivance for breaking the power of the crown. By bringing the conduct and views of the king himself under the notice of a legislative assembly, it makes him indirectly a representative of the people. If we could suppose the

British monarch to be brought upon the floor of the House of Commons, the effect would be instantaneous in diminishing the luster of the office. It would almost annihilate his personal authority and in no very long period he would become an elective magistrate like the president of the United States. By placing members of the executive board there, his authority is to a certain extent preserved, but the executive and regal power are completely separated. Instead of the king governing the people through Parliament as an instrument, Parliament and the people control the king through the instrumentality of ministers.

Thus in proportion as government approaches to anything like perfection, there is a constant tendency to a division of the executive power. If there is no fundamental ordinance to bring about this result, the vast expansion which the whole framework of society acquires, the entire change which takes place in the social and political organization, become a law to the government and even in a country where monarchical institutions have existed time out of mind mold the authority of the chief magistrate into a new form. The maxim that the executive should be one is true only in despotic government.

In the United States the executive officers are not eligible to Congress, and the reason is apparent. There is no hereditary prince whose authority it is desirable to limit by breaking it in pieces. The people choose the chief magistrate; he holds his office for a short period, his salary is small, his powers few, and his responsibility to the people is immediate. It is unnecessary then to subject him or the other members of the executive board to the same species of control as in the British government. For the authority which they exercise is circumscribed by other and more effectual means. In a hereditary monarchy we are obliged to cut in two the office of chief magistrate, leaving the kingly authority to the monarch and erecting ministers into an executive board; and in order to give them a substantive authority distinct from his they are introduced upon the floor of the legislature. But there is no necessity for the last in a republic. A much more exact distribution of the executive power than this implies is made by the fundamental laws. If in the former government the personal influence of the king is diminished, this is the very object sought after by the institution. But in a republic we do not attempt to detract from the influence of the president, since being permitted to deal with his office by fixed laws at the first organization of government, there is no occasion for any compensatory contrivances afterward.

In France, since the reconstruction of the government, the same plan is adopted as in Great Britain and the same consequences have followed from it. Ministers are named by the king, but they must act in conformity with the will of the deputies. The system of public administration must have the sanction of public opinion in order that they may be secure in their places. In the former country, however, they are by virtue of their office entitled to a seat in the legislative body and are at liberty to pass from one chamber to the other for the purpose of explaining their views. In both these respects they differ from the English ministers who must be elected in order to have a seat and can only appear in the chamber of which they are properly members. That part of the French plan which permits ministers to appear in either chamber is an improvement on the English. If ministers are selected from the peers, it makes sure of bringing them into immediate contact with the deputies of the people.

In Great Britain and France, ministers go out of office in obedience to the will of the legislature, in the United States to that of the president. It may then be supposed that the force of public opinion is stronger in France and Great Britain than it is in the United States. The case is entirely the reverse, however. In the two first countries, ministers are appointed by the crown; they are brought into the legislature to weaken the authority of the king who would otherwise be beyond the reach of public opinion, as he is already beyond the reach of the laws. But the president is himself the creature of public opinion, and the reason why his secretaries do not abdicate on a change of parties in the legislature is because public opinion is strong instead of being weak, so strong as to render their influence comparatively null, notwithstanding their continuance in office. But these two contrary practices are both indications of weakness in the executive power. Only in limited monarchy the king not merely submits to it but is obliged to make confession of it. If his ministers were not entitled to seats in Parliament, there would be no occasion to remove them.

This notion of a double character as belonging to the head of the state, this distinction between the functions of the governing and the executive power, was doubtless revolving in the mind of the celebrated Sieyès, when he drew up his plan of a constitution in 1799. And it was a capital feature of that plan to carry out the distinction more precisely and thoroughly than had ever been done before. The chief magistrate, with the title of grand elector, was to be maintained in princely splendor; he was charged with the appointment of all the administrative officers of the state, who were thenceforth declared irremovable by him. He was to be elected by a close body of two hundred members, denominated the constitutional jury. Although living in splendor like a hereditary prince and surrounded with all that luster which is calculated to captivate the imaginations of the people, he was not permitted to exercise himself any part of the executive authority. His authority was strictly confined to the appointment of the executive officers.

This was to resemble the system of government to those mechanical contrivances fashioned by the hand of man which perform all their movements in exact compliance with the impulse originally given to them. But political institutions possess more or less a self-determining power which perpetually interferes with any artificial rules which the lawgiver may prescribe. The great defect of this, as of most other theoretical plans of government, was that it proposed by a set of curious and complicated contrivances to check one part of the government by another, and this at a period when the power out of the government had grown to such magnitude and importance as to demand the chief consideration. The mere internal mechanism of the government was once everything; its relation to the social organization almost nothing. Very different is the case now. A scheme of government in order to have any chance of success must connect itself, in some way or other, with the popular will. How much more simple, and how much more effectual for France, is the present arrangement where a House of Deputies is elected immediately by the people and exercises a complete control upon the appointment of ministers. The effect is to establish practically, and not merely theoretically, a division between the regal and the executive power. When the structure of government is rendered very artificial, it becomes in the progress of time unadapted to the condition of society. But if it only has the merit of simplicity, no matter how incomplete it may be, it acquires the faculty of accommodating itself to the progressive change without. As the popular strength and intelligence are developed, so will be the political institutions also. It may be no difficult matter to enlarge the electoral franchise gradually so as to create a million of electors of the

House of Deputies. But how can such odd and grotesque contrivances as the mute legislative body, the grand elector, and the constitutional jury be improved, unless it is by abolishing them? The most complex and artificial contrivance ever devised was proposed by one of the profoundest minds France has produced, at a time when above all others society was least prepared to receive it.

The scheme of a double cabinet, which originated in the court of Frederick, Prince of Wales, proceeded from an effort on the part of the heir apparent to escape from the wholesome control of Parliament.[6] This control, in the reign of George II, was beginning to assume a regular form and to be regarded as an important feature in the constitution. It was not unnatural, therefore, that the king should feel uneasy under a restraint from which every other European monarch was free. Hence this attempt to raise up one set of ministers among the court to thwart and humble another set who had come in through Parliamentary influence. But it was in vain to resist the current of public opinion which was silently effecting a separation between the regal and the executive power; and notwithstanding renewed efforts, in the early part of the reign of George III, to maintain the prerogatives of the crown unimpaired and to render the whole ministerial board dependent upon it, the control of Parliament over the appointment of ministers has been thoroughly established and is at this day regarded as a fundamental principle of the constitution. No finer illustration can be found in all history of the constant tendency of public opinion in a limited monarchy to bring about a separation of the kingly and executive power.

In Great Britain, the separation of the regal and executive office has only been brought about by the gradual rise of the Commons. And the same will be the case in France. But the French "tiers etat" is not yet as powerful a body as the middle class in Great Britain and therefore does not exert as sensible an influence upon the movement of the government. Abbe Sieyès' constitution, at the same time that it deprived the grand elector of the power of governing, annulled the authority of the second legislative chamber by taking from it the right of debate and by rendering the basis of representation exceeding narrow and confined. The grand elector was only placed in the system to keep alive a pageant which might subdue men to obedience through the influence of the imagination, and yet he is robbed of all the attri-

6. [Grimke added this paragraph to the second edition.]

butes which are calculated to have that effect. But the governing idea of the plan is very visible: to cut in twain the executive power and to bestow the largest share of authority upon those who have the management of the real business of society.

In the state governments of America the idea which was floating in the mind of the Abbe Sieyès has been carried into practical operation. But all the other institutions are framed in harmony with this arrangement. The governors are elected not to direct the movements of the government, but simply to keep watch, to see that all is right, and upon any critical conjuncture to ring the alarm bell to the legislative assembly which is dispersed during the greater part of the year. Government in those communities is so plainly founded upon the interests of men that it has been found the easiest thing imaginable to dispense with all the trappings and insignia with which the chief magistrates of even the German states surround themselves. As the real and effective business of the state is transacted by the legislature and judiciary, there, accordingly, has the active authority of the state been deposited. And as every agent upon whom power is conferred may be tempted to abuse it, the basis of representation is rendered so wide as to create a strict responsibility to all orders of men and not merely to one class. The chief magistrate is there placed like a sentinel upon the highest position to give warning of any approaching danger. There is no blind, mechanical contrivance, as in the constitution of 1799, by which each department is expected to act as a check upon the others and, without any presiding power without, to keep the whole in order. Free room is allowed for the development of public opinion; since it is upon public opinion after all that all legitimate government must rest. Without public opinion, in other words, without the elevation of the great body of the people to a condition which will enable them to obtain some insight into the management of public business, responsibility would be a dead, instead of a living and active, principle.

The American system has answered the desired purpose, and it may be termed the "beau ideal" in politics. It has demonstrated that all the great ends for which civil government is established may be attained without the employment of those curious and artificial contrivances which render men unfit for self-government simply because they hide government from their observation. By rendering men free, by satisfying all their wants, so far as it is in the power of human institutions to do, it has removed out of the way the prime cause of all public discontent, and has thus guarded against the dangers to which both government and society are exposed.

Perhaps with the help of so instructive an experience, it may be found an easy matter to balance the government of the most extensive community upon the same plan. The fact that no commonwealth formed upon the same model had ever before existed gave rise to the belief that none such could exist. The firm persuasion that a thing is impossible often creates a real and invincible obstacle to its attainment. And as the imagination has a wonderful influence upon all our opinions, we get rid of its disturbing influence and of the notion of impossibility where we have the example of thirty states (many of them singly more populous and powerful than Venice, Genoa, or Florence in their palmiest days) in which the elective principle is thoroughly introduced and where the political institutions possess both more consistency and firmness than has been witnessed anywhere else.

The absolute veto is one of the attributes of the executive in monarchical government. The design in creating the office of king we may suppose to have been to raise up someone who should occupy the place of mediator between the higher and the lower ranks. Hence the office is rendered hereditary in order to clothe it with the greatest possible influence. Originally the king had no occasion to exercise the veto because he had the initiative of all measures. But after the transition of the legislative assembly from a mere council to the rank of an independent body, his situation became very different. The legislature was then able to run counter to his views, and he was consequently endowed with a corresponding power to ward off the attack and to protect his own prerogative. But in the course of time an entire change takes place in the nature of his office. The executive authority gradually falls into his hands. And this places him in a still more advantageous position for acting as a mediator between conflicting parties. For a hereditary monarch can hardly be said to belong to any of the parties in the state. This complete independence of all of them exempts him from all interest in any question of party politics; and if his personal influence is undermined in consequence of so many rival powers growing up around him, his ambition is less provoked to indulgence and his prejudices have less room to show themselves. He therefore not only removes his ministers, but refrains from the exercise of the veto in order that he may conform as much as possible with the views of the legislature. This is the last term, the final aim, to which the veto tends in the progress of monarchical government. It becomes, in other words, a dormant power in practice as soon as the legislative and executive boards meet upon the same floor and are obliged to cooperate in devising plans for the public welfare.

In the earlier stages of that form of government, the prerogative is employed to compose the dissensions of the patrician and plebeian classes or as a defensive weapon against assaults upon the executive. But those two classes are at length succeeded by another, the great middle class, which itself conciliates the rival interests of the other two by containing a tolerably faithful representation of the opinions of both. This class, then, occupies the place of umpire which the king before held, and having drawn to itself, by its commanding influence in the legislature, a complete control over the executive board, it ceases to meddle with the prerogatives of the king.

In a republic, the chief magistrate is an elective officer. He is chosen by the party in the majority because he belongs to it. He is, therefore, designed to be its representative and is expected to speak its sentiments. For this reason the exercise of the veto may be more frequent than in a monarchical government. And it is because the political institutions are more instead of less democratic that this will be the case. The authority of the king is so independent of public opinion, he is so completely exempted from all party connection, that he will readily assent to any measures proposed by the legislative body provided they do not trench upon his prerogatives. But the president is altogether the creature of public opinion. He has no prerogatives. His authority consists in exercising the power which the majority of society have conferred upon him. His ambition is to represent and to give effect to the will of that majority.

But here a difficulty occurs: the president is elected for four years, the popular branch of the legislature for two, while one third of the Senate retires every two years. The majority which elected the president, therefore, may not be the majority two years after he is chosen. The exercise of the veto, then, at that period, may seem to contradict the public will while in reality it may be in accordance with it. It presents a doubtful case, a case in which a wise magistrate may well pause to reflect in order that he may be saved from the reproach of too hastily giving in to every measure which a temporary majority may favor and the still greater reproach of contradicting the settled and well understood opinion of a permanent majority of society. If he were a hereditary officer and these doubts were very perplexing, the true way to solve them would be to ratify the proposed law. He would then make sure of conforming himself in some degree to the public will since one chamber of the legislature is elected, although the electoral franchise may be very restricted. The president in aiming at the same result, that is, in seeking to find the real majority, may be driven to pursue an exactly opposite course. If the king should refuse to ratify a law when his consent should have been given, the mischief is without remedy. For his veto is absolute. But if the president does the same and thus contradicts the unmistakeable will of the public, the legislature may place their veto upon his or, if the majority is not sufficiently large to do this, he may be quietly displaced in a year or two after. It is very remarkable that very few instances have occurred of the rejection of a law by the president which has not met with subsequent approbation. That is, if we may judge from the succeeding election of president. But as the patronage which is at present attached to the office gives him a great advantage in molding public opinion, we must beware of speaking too positively on the subject. We cannot be sure what would have been the result if that patronage had not been created.

But it is obvious that the exercise of the veto must necessarily have a more democratic tendency in a republic than it is possible for it to have in a monarchy. In a republic parties take the place which is occupied by classes in monarchical government. The advantage of this is that as the great body of the citizens will be admitted to the enjoyment of the electoral franchise no parties can well exist which are not of a popular character. The great object is to make even the suspensive veto represent the opinions of at least a large body of the community. In a monarchy it might represent the opinion of a single individual. The electoral franchise is usually so restricted that there is no way of certainly ascertaining how large a portion of the community is enlisted for or against a particular measure. In France, whose population is thirty-four or five millions, two hundred thousand electors are a very feeble representative of the public will. Either the majority or the minority of the deputies chosen by them are an equally feeble representation of the parties whose sentiments they undertake to speak. In elective government, properly so called, the basis of representation is so wide that both the great parties which divide the country are essentially of a popular character. And thus where the veto is in accordance with the vote of the minority, it has the merit of founding itself upon the opinions of a very large section of society, an advantage which it can only accidentally possess in monarchical government. And it is for this reason that the veto is suspensive, not absolute in its operation. The design is to prevent the chief magistrate from contradicting the clear and unequivocal expression of the public will. Armed with the absolute veto, he might persist in its exercise, whatever was the strength of the majority against him; or what would be more common, he might refrain from exercising it when the public good very clearly demanded it. The suspensive veto enables him to make efforts to find out what the public will is. And if two thirds of the legislature annul his veto, it becomes impossible for him to run counter to the declared opinions of a majority of the people. Do what he will, however, he must act in obedience to the wishes of a popular party and that party, whether in the majority or minority, must compose a very considerable portion of the legislative assembly.

It has been proposed, as one means of insuring a system of enlightened legislation that the consent of two thirds or three fourths of the legislature should be required to the enactment of all laws. Great inconvenience and mischief, however, would be the consequence of this. In the first place, a very large proportion of the laws are not of sufficient importance to require it. 2d. It might have the effect of delivering the legislative power permanently into the hands of the minority. Now it is never the design in representative government to make the government of the minority the rule, but only the exception to the rule, so that in a few isolated cases the majority in the country may be sought through the minority in the legislature. The invariable rule of two thirds would be better adapted to monarchical than to republican government. In the last, every law is an experiment submitted to the people, and it is often very desirable that this experiment should be gone through with in order that the effects of any given measure may be distinctly understood and that public opinion may be firmly united one way or the other. The temporary inconvenience is overbalanced by the benefit attending it.

To avoid the mischiefs arising from the invariable rule of two thirds, it has been proposed to subject only those laws which affect interests of great magnitude to this ordeal. But it is impossible to discern beforehand what laws will possess this character. Many enactments derive great importance from the circumstances or the particular crisis when they are made. The suspensive veto is intended to reconcile all these difficulties. It may be described as a power, or rather as a duty, which renders it incumbent on the chief magistrate to inform the legislative body when the measure about to be adopted is of so grave a character as to require a reconsideration and to render it expedient that two thirds of the members should concur in its enactment. If the clause in the constitution were couched in terms signifying this, the veto would not have been thought of any more than one talks of the veto of the jury upon the opinion of the court, or that of the court upon the jury, although the effect is the same, leading sometimes to a change of opinion on the part of the court and sometimes to a change on the part of the jury. The president simply says to the two chambers: you are in the heat of the battle; you would not, therefore, trust yourselves with the power of deciding precipitately when the emergency is such as to demand a reconsideration. I am, it is true, not entirely removed from the conflict. But the independent position in many respects which I hold and my election by the people at large instead of by a district or single state impels me, whether I will or no, to form a judgment which doubtless will sometimes be erroneous, but which may in the great majority of instances be conveniently relied upon. This is the reason why the constitution vests the whole legislative power in Congress. The chief magistrate is not considered as a third estate. He is, therefore, not permitted as in the European government to have a part in the enactment of the laws. His office is simply to notify the legislature when a measure is of so great importance as to demand a reconsideration and a vote of two thirds.

There is another circumstance which differs the exercise of the veto power in the American government very materially from what it is anywhere else. In Great Britain and France, the legislative power constitutes the sovereignty and is competent to change the constitution. In the United States it is otherwise; the sovereignty resides in the people, and none but a convention of the people have authority to change the constitution. In the European states the king may prevent any fundamental alteration in the government however wise and beneficial it may be. In the United States no constitutional change can be made by a mere law, and the president has no opportunity of defeating the public will in this important particular. The veto, even the suspensive veto, is unknown to a constitutional convention because the forms under which it assembles, the rules which are necessary to be observed before it can be called together, presuppose that consideration and reconsideration on the part of the community which are indispensable in handling matters of so grave a character. It is easy to adopt the rule of two thirds or three fourths in this instance when it would be impracticable or highly inconvenient to do so in the ordinary business of a legislative body. The king may persist in maintaining the vast prerogatives which were conferred upon him centuries ago, although material changes in the structure of society have occurred to render them desirable. This power is absolutely denied to the president. If in monarchical government it is necessary to confer so great an authority upon the crown in order to enable it to protect its prerogatives from the assaults of other branches of the legislature, no such reason exists in a republic because the powers of the chief magistrate are placed beyond the reach of the legislative body.

There is another view which is entitled to great attention. Every law alters more or less the existing state of things. It is intended to effect a change in some measure or measures which were themselves brought about by the act of a majority. But it is quite otherwise in almost all other communities where government is a self-existing institution, never representing the majority, often not even the minority of what may be termed the substantial population. So that in the United States, whether the veto be exercised or not, we know that the old state of things, if it is permitted to continue, or the new, if it actually takes place, have both been effected by a clear majority of the community. The great desideratum, in other words, is that the legislation of the country shall be based upon the will of the majority; and in the only instance where this rule is departed from, the laws in being still stand as the expression of a majority of but a few years antecedent, to which is added the vote of any number less than a mere majority of both chambers of the existing legislature. We make sure that the veto shall never represent the mere arbitrary will of a single individual, that the chief magistrate, whatever his personal wishes may be, cannot free himself of an alliance with public opinion.

In the compound republic of America there may be a further use in vesting a qualified veto in the president. Notwithstanding the utmost care in separating the domestic policy of the states from the national jurisdictions, they will sometimes conflict. Geographical parties will occasionally make their appearance, influencing the course of legislation and demanding the interposition of an umpire in order to compel them to be just to each other. Senators are elected by the states and representatives by districts comprised within the states. But the president is elected by the united suffrages of the whole. Although, therefore, there might seem to be an incongruity in setting up the will of an individual to control that of the legislature, yet if the mode of election is such as to render that individual a more exact representative of the community as a whole than the members of the legislature, the incongruity will immediately disappear.

The disparity between one man and the two or three hundred members who compose the legislative body is the circumstance which strikes the mind with so much force and makes it appear both unnatural and unjust to array the opinions of the first in opposition to those of the last. But this is a very imperfect way of making a comparison between the two things. When one considers the immense disproportion between the handful of representatives who make up the legislative assembly and the twenty millions who compose the community, the disparity in the first instance ceases to make any strong impression, not because it is not greater than in the second but because the difference between one man and two or three hundred men is so little when both are compared with the whole population that the disparity in the first instance is reduced to insignificance. And as no one considers the legislature a defective institution because it contains an exceedingly small fraction of the community, for the same reason no one can consistently maintain that the office of chief magistrate is absurdly contrived because it sometimes interposes the opinions of a single individual to counteract the wishes of that small fraction.

The power which the English House of Commons possess to grant or withhold the supplies has been regarded as an mportant check upon the enterprises of the executive. But this check has no application in a republic; the constitution of the executive presents no occasion for its exercise. To declare war and to make treaties are the exclusive prerogatives of the king in a monarchical government. In the United States, the war-making power belongs to the legislature, and the treaty-making power is under the control of the Senate. A refusal on the part of the legislature to make the necessary appropriations would interpose an obstacle to measures which had originated with itself, or to which one chamber was a party, instead of creating a restraint upon the executive power. The necessity of conferring the absolute veto upon the prince has been argued from the nature of the office. It is necessary, it is said, to enable him to defend himself against the assaults of the legislature. He may refuse his signature to a law in the passage of which the legislature is deeply interested in order to coerce it into some other measure, which will be favorable to the prosecution of his own plans. Such an adjustment of the powers of government is unnatural in the extreme. Representative government, therefore, proceeds upon totally different principles. It is not the executive but the whole community who are interested in the question of war. The power to declare it is therefore intrusted with the legislative body. Even in Great Britain, the check which has been so much relied upon no longer possesses the same efficacy as formerly for the Commons have acquired so much importance as to make itself in practice a party to every declaration of war.

But there is this great defect in monarchical government, that not only is the direct authority of the king very considerable, but the fashion of thinking prevalent in a court has a wonderful influence in shaping public sentiment. A war, therefore, may have the approbation of a great majority in the legislature although it is clearly repugnant to the interests of the people. The elevation of the middle class in Great Britain has done much to rectify this unnatural state of things, but it cannot accomplish everything as long as there is a powerfully disturbing force in some other part of society, at any rate, not until that middle class is thoroughly and genuinely represented.

In the United States there has been a marked disposition of late years to elevate men of moderate talents to the presidency. And this has been regarded as a circumstance of deep omen to the future and as indicating a retrograde movement in society. But there is no reason why we should take this view of the matter. The election of such men, where there is no question of their integrity and patriotism, may not only be very consistent with the public welfare but it may have a distinct and very important meaning which it is our duty to decipher. I have generally observed that where a community is undisturbed by revolution, a tendency of public opinion in one direction, no matter how singular it might appear to be, was an indication that there was a defect somewhere which required to be rectified and that this tendency was one means of rectifying it. There is no necessity for supposing that there is any such thing as a grovelling propensity among the

American people to search among the descending rather than among the ascending ranks of society for candidates for the presidency. The man of commanding talents is not sought after because he represents too faithfully one part of society and, by so doing, fails to represent all other parts. On the other hand, the man of moderate abilities, the man who has no very strong and salient points of character, by failing to represent any one part exclusively succeeds more fully in representing the whole.

There is another compensation for the disadvantage of excluding superior men from the first office in the government. A great writer of antiquity has remarked that the Grecian commonwealths were absolutely compelled to the employment of the ostracism in consequence of the despotic control which popular favorites exercised. The American government has no need of resorting to any such instrument. But a president who possesses pre-eminent abilities has a sort of magical control over his party. He may retain the influence he has acquired, notwithstanding he has committed the greatest faults. The man whose fame has never made any noise, the moment he is guilty of any serious blunder begins to feel the foundation on which he stands tremble. Instead of molding public opinion to his wishes, public opinion controls him and stops him in the commencement of his career. The selection of men of moderate talents may have been fallen upon as an expedient to subserve the selfish interests of a party. But of all plans, it is the one least calculated to promote that object.

CHAPTER IV | THE CLASSES OF SOCIETY

No one man — no one class of men — is able to represent all the attributes of humanity. It is a fine provision, therefore, and not a defect that society should be composed of a great number of classes, alike distinguished for the variety of their pursuits and the still greater variety of faculties which they exert for the common benefit. The greater the number of classes the less powerful will any one be, the distance which separates them will be less, and the influence which they exercise upon each other will be proportionably increased. The ultimate effect of a great number of differences will be to produce more uniformity, a greater identity of interests and opinions among the whole. It may then be said that society is balanced by the various classes of men.

But what is it which gives a distinct character to this great variety of classes? Evidently, the communication of freedom to all. So that the enjoyment of a privilege which European statesmen have fancied would open the door to a countless train of disorders may not only carry with it an antidote to those disorders but may be productive of the most direct and positive advantages.

Among the various orders of men, we may enumerate as most prominent the young and the old, the rich and the poor, capitalists and laborers, the rural and the town population, professional men, and, lastly, the parties of majority and minority.

No one who has been an attentive observer of public events can have failed to observe that society is frequently subject to periodical revolutions of public opinion and that these revolutions, somehow or other, correspond with the growth of successive generations. In the United States this important and very interesting fact has been more distinctly manifested than anywhere else. In 1776, one of these revolutions took place; in 1801, a second; and in 1829, a third.[1] It would seem that they depend to a great extent upon the present generation

1. [Grimke refers to the American Revolution, the election of Thomas Jefferson, and the election of Andrew Jackson.]

which, after the lapse of twenty or thirty years, rises up to take the place of the older and that the younger men of the community exercise a very sensible influence upon the whole course of public events. This influence may be for good or for evil, but as a philosophical fact it is entitled to great attention.

As in every society of even tolerable duration, a fresh generation arrives at manhood every year and every day as much as every twenty-five years, it may be supposed that the influence of these successive populations one upon the other is greatly exaggerated. And doubtless such would be the case if the term influence did not import two things: agents capable of acting and a material upon which they may act. Now the laws and institutions of every country are not only intended to endure much beyond a year, but it is absolutely necessary that they should do so in order that there may be any experience of their character and a subject matter for public opinion to exert an influence upon. But this we may say, that the constant succession of one generation to another breaks the force which would otherwise be exerted after a lapse of years. Something is achieved every year toward the advancement of society, but that there is a marked influence after more distant intervals is a fact which forces itself upon the attention of everyone.

In a well constituted community this influence will be advantageous. It is in this way that provision is made for renewing the elements of society and modifying old institutions by the action of new and more liberal opinions. As this influence in a democratic republic is not stifled by the power residing in the government, it is gradual and never leads to those violent changes which in other countries threaten the dissolution of society. Instead of a French or an English revolution, the result of the accumulated abuses of centuries, society passes by an easy transition to new tasks, new habits, and an improved social organization.

Very important conclusions may be deduced, in reference to particular countries, from the fact whether the average duration of life or mean age of death is high or low. In England it is said to be as high as twenty-five or twenty-seven. In the United States, it is probably as low as sixteen. For it depends principally upon the rate of increase of the population. If this is rapid and consequently the births numerous, the average duration of life will be comparatively low since the majority of deaths occur in infancy.

In New England, taken separately, I presume that this average is considerably above sixteen. A society, however, in which the mean age of death is high will be apt to be led and controlled by those who are past middle age and, where it is low, men under that age will come in for a large share of offices and of public favor. Men who are past middle age constitute a larger proportion of the population in the first instance than they do in the second. Thus where the population is nearly or quite stationary, society will be most controlled by those whose views are most stationary; and where it increases with most rapidity, it will be apt to be controlled by those whose feelings and opinions are most easily modified. There is a natural foundation then for the existence of a movement and a conservative party. The first may wish to move too fast, the last may be averse to move at all. The mixture of these two classes so as to insure that each shall have a due degree of influence is the great desideratum. In the western states of America, the population increases faster than in any other part of the world. The movement party, therefore, has a tendency to become the predominant one. This tendency, however, is in a great measure counteracted by another circumstance. The institutions are all taken from the older states. They embody the experience and opinions of an old class of men. They transfer the influence of that class into younger societies. The laws and institutions may be modified but the fundamentals of government are adhered to tenaciously by all.

But whatever may be the rate of increase of the population and the proportion between the young and older men of a country, a very great deal will depend upon the nature of the political institutions. The United States and Russia are the two countries in which the population increase most rapidly. But the aspect of society in the two is very different.

Free institutions introduce men at an early period upon the active theater of life. They hasten the period when they shall take part in political affairs because they hasten the time when they shall engage in the pursuits of civil life. The last constitute a state of preparation for the first. If a greater degree of enthusiasm is imparted to the character of public men, a greater amount of experience is acquired at an early age and the judgment is sooner matured than in those countries where men are not permitted to meddle with the interests of others, and hardly with their own, until the age of thirty or forty.

But it is not merely the part which the younger men of a country taken in the active business of society which is important to be considered. The influence of the feelings and opinions which are acquired by men in youth upon their after life is of great consequence also. Both species of influence are dependent upon the nature of the political institutions. In aristocratical and monarchical government the period of youth is to a great extent one of subjection and rigid discipline from which the mind does not escape until the feelings and opinions have been completely molded. And the generation which has emerged from it know no other rule than to act the part which their fathers did by them, to maintain their youth in a state of the strictest discipline, and to transfer similar habits and modes of thinking to the walks of public life. But in a democratic republic, although there is no unnecessary relaxation of parental authority, the feelings and opinions which are acquired in youth are permitted to expand freely, and they therefore spread their influence upon the whole of the subsequent period of life. In such a community education has a meaning which it has nowhere else. It then becomes the duty of the government to take care that the elements of instruction shall be imparted to the whole people. In other words, as every new generation after certain intervals gives a fresh impulse to society, it is of great importance that this new movement should be controlled by a corresponding share of intelligence. Without free institutions the mind would be motionless and society inanimate. With free institutions, but without a widely-diffused intelligence, the impulse which would be communicated would be more likely to be for the worse than for the better.

The most general division of society is into the superior and inferior classes. This is a distinction which we have no reason to believe will ever be effaced. The different degrees of sagacity, energy, and opportunity which fall to the lot of individuals will forever create a wide difference in their respective fortunes. The only effect of an agrarian law would be, for the time being, to convert the whole of society into a dead level where there would be neither knowledge, or industry, or active virtue. Our efforts to elevate all men would only terminate in sensualizing all. Instead of lifting the lower classes higher, we should procure the abasement of all classes. The improvement of our condition, whether intellectual or physical, depends infinitely more upon our own independent exertions than upon all other circumstances put together. One condition is indispensable: that the laws should not render property inalienable or in any way obstruct its circulation, that it may be won by those who have industry, activity, and judgment to win it. In the United States, neither the wealthy nor the merely independent class is composed of those who inherited property, but of those who commenced life with little or nothing.

The existence, then, of two very large classes is the result of certain laws of our nature which have a fixed operation whatever may be the form of government. And the true inquiry is not whether either can be gotten rid of, but whether the influence of the one upon the other is not part of the machinery by which the welfare of society is designed to be promoted. American institutions have existed a considerable period under circumstances calculated to give activity to the exertions of everyone. And yet even in America we can discern a well-defined line between the higher and lower orders of men. Free institutions do not obliterate the distinctions; on the contrary, they are eminently favorable to the accumulation of wealth in private hands since they add to the natural gifts of some the further advantages of opportunity and the protection of a system of laws which is equal and invariable in its operation. It is like the addition of a new faculty to some men. The resolute, the enterprising, and the industrious move forward with rapidity, while those who are differently organized or whose will is subdued by causes which are almost inscrutable to observation remain in the background, less prosperous, less fortunate in every respect, but not the less fitted to perform a very important part in the machinery of society. The most valuable qualities may belong to men in the inferior walks of life although, do what you will, these qualities may never be made to tell in the improvement of their condition. And it is the express design of free institutions to give to this class a position and weight in the commonwealth which no other form of government has ever accorded.

It will be readily conceded that the superior class exert a salutary control and influence upon the inferior. But it is not so easily perceived that the influence which the last exercise upon the former is equally important. The two orders of men represent two antagonist forces; the action of one upon the other prevents either from running away with the power of the community, and establishes a powerfully regulative principle which, although it is independent of the laws, yet constantly cooperates with the laws.

It may then be inquired where is the difference between a democratic republic and the artificial forms of government. The last are founded upon a classification of men, and the preceding views suppose that each class plays a very important part in society and that the influence of both is necessary to give system and regularity to the movements of the government. And this simple statement, which I have purposely adopted, is sufficient to explain the very wide difference between the two cases. In monarchy and aristocracy, the superior class is placed in the government and the inferior thrust out. In a republic all classes are admitted to the enjoyment of political franchises. The influence therefore which is capable of being exerted by the one class upon the other, and of both upon the government, is totally different in the one instance from what it is in the other.

To talk of the influence of the inferior classes will seem out of place, perhaps even absurd, to those who figure everything which is low and vulgar as belonging to them. Even if this were the case, their agency might be very important. If they imparted nothing positive to the rest of society, they might at any rate act as a check upon the excesses, the splendid vulgarity, if I may so term it, of the higher orders. If one effect of wealth and refinement is to corrupt and sensualize the rich and at the same time to make the acquisition of political power more easy of attainment by them, and if we cannot get rid of wealth without destroying all incentives to industry and enterprise, the only alternative is to raise up a class which will be too numerous to be bought and which will be constantly interested in watching the movements of the class above them. This control will be negative in its operation at first, but it cannot exist long without compelling this class to the cultivation of more wisdom, moderation, and virtue than could possibly be the case if they had the whole field to themselves. Providence never intended the inferior classes to be mere instruments for the gratification of the power and ambition of the wealthy, but rather to act as a corrective of the great defects which are incident to the enviable situation of the last, to prevent unbridled licentiousness from taking entire possession of the community, and, by putting the refined and the educated on their good behavior, to make them exert in their turn a salutary control upon the ignorant and unenlightened. No control is effectual if it is all on one side. It must be mutual. It is then more than a control; it is a positive benefit.

In surveying the walks of private life, one is frequently struck with the numbers of individuals whose tempers are soured and who seem to be every way uneasy in their condition. An air of pleasantry may be assumed and is almost universally so when men meet in companies, but a close and practical observer will easily penetrate through this thin disguise. The cause of this discontent is that all have defects and infirmities and yet the defects and infirmities are not the same in each, or at least manifest themselves in different forms. This causes individuals to run against and to incommode each other. If the infirmities of all were the same, there would be much more placidity of temper, for each would then cordially sympathize with each and, although these infirmities led to much vice and ignorance, they would be tenderly cherished because there was no one to frown upon them. There would be less discontent perhaps, but this advantage would be greatly counterbalanced by the injury done to man as a rational being. An easy good nature would take possession of everyone and this would terminate in a species of mere animal enjoyment or in a state of absolute vacuity of mind. By coming into contact with and incommoding each other, individuals for the first time hear of and are made to realize their defects. Great numbers are put upon all sorts of exertion to cure them and to raise themselves in the scale of intellectual beings. Now precisely the same process and with the same good effects is witnessed in the action of the different classes of society upon each other. If all were alike, all superlatively prosperous and happy, or if the reverse were the case, society would become a barren waste.

If then the agency of the inferior classes is so important as a check upon the superior, the institution of slavery must be attended with some disadvantages. Its tendency would seem to be to lead to what we may term an unbalanced state of society. Slaves have no personal or political influence whatever, and the higher orders are thus freed from a restraint upon their actions which is beneficial in the highest degree.

Doubtless they who live in a state where the institution is established suppose that their condition is peculiarly fortunate; they may even persuade themselves that society is better balanced than it would otherwise be, inasmuch as it is exempt from the turbulence and insubordination which frequently take place among the class of free laborers. But as in private life there would be no domestic happiness or morality without numberless cares and anxieties, perhaps even adversities, so there would be no public virtue and felicity without very many trials of the same kind. It was the dissolution of the old form of society in Europe, the breaking up the system of servitude, which gave rise to the middle class and caused the whole frame of society to be better adjusted than it was before. We may go further and say that this revolution gave birth to the superior ranks and substituted in the place of a boorish, ignorance, and turbulent aristocracy a class which is in a high degree distinguished for its urbanity and intelligence. There would be no superior class in Europe at this day, in the proper acceptation of the term, if it had not been for the disfranchisement and consequent influence of the classes below them.[2] The European states in which the higher ranks are most polished, most enlightened, and at the same time most numerous are those in which the greatest amount of civil and political liberty is accorded to the bulk of the population. Much discomfort and annoyance may be experienced in a society so constituted, but that very discomfort and annoyance are the source of nearly all the blessings which have fallen to our modern communities.

In many respects the Negro slavery which exists in the southern states of America is not open to these objections. Slaves there do not fill up, as in the commonwealths of antiquity and the European states of the middle ages, nearly all the departments of industry. There is a very numerous class of freemen occupying the middle and inferior walks of life. But if one only knew how to deal with so difficult and delicate a subject, if one only had the ability requisite to remove the institution without leaving worse consequences behind, there can be no doubt that it would be better that all the occupations of society should be filled by a free population exclusively.

The men of the south cannot reasonably contend that the institution of slavery is a benefit "per se." But they may well insist that the character which it has assumed among them is totally different from what it is anywhere else; and that as it is impossible to emancipate in communities where the slaves are very numerous and of a race entirely distinct from their own without producing the most disastrous consequences to both masters and slaves, it becomes not so much their right as their duty to maintain the institution. They may also insist that there are many compensations attending the system, not withstanding the disadvantages under which it otherwise labors; that slaves are kept under a domestic surveillance like the children of a

2. [In the context, Grimke's sense would seem to call for "enfranchisement" rather than "disfranchisement."]

family, each master superintending the behavior and actions of those who compose his own household, that in this way innumerable infractions of the laws are prevented which other communities are only able to punish after they have been committed. I observe that the people of the north are sensible of the disadvantage of their situation in this respect. They accordingly make prodigious exertions to educate themselves and to raise the lower classes to the level of the middle class. They have gone a step further than this. Experience has taught them that the use of ardent liquors is one of the most fruitful causes of crime and of every other species of disorder; they have, therefore, made immense efforts to exterminate the practice. They hear it defended in a great many plausible ways: that it contributes to good cheer and conviviality. The people of New England and New York have turned all these specious arguments in their minds, and have found that after all infinitely more mischief than good is the consequence of the habit, that the indulgence in it, whether by the rich or the poor, whether moderately or in excess, almost invariably disturbs the judgment and clouds the moral faculties. This, as has been remarked in a preceding chapter, argues an uncommon degree of reflection among a class to whom reflection has not been usually ascribed. For it is among the great body of the population and not among a select few that these just sentiments prevail; and even if this body do not actually constitute a majority so as to insure the enactment of corresponding laws, it is at any rate so large as to demonstrate the existence of a sounder and healthier condition of society than has ever existed before. I cannot help thinking that the control of a popular class which is distinguished for such rare intelligence and virtue cannot but be salutary in a high degree, that it will contribute essentially to a well balanced society, and that it may even be difficult to foresee all the good effects which will ultimately spring from it.

It has been noticed as a characteristic difference between the northern and southern people of the United States that among the former all sorts of novel and startling doctrines in religion, morals, and politics are constantly propounded, while among the last, opinions on all those subjects have acquired a degree of fixedness and uniformity which it is uncommon to meet with in the oldest settled communities. This difference is supposed to indicate a better social organization in the south than in the north and to afford a proof that if education has been the means of imparting more knowledge to the northern people it has been at the expense of bewildering them and of filling society with all sorts of mischievous opinions. This view is very incorrect, however. Inquisitiveness and a reaching after knowledge of any sort, the desire to form independent opinions upon all subjects and the ability to discuss them argues a development of the popular mind which should never be treated too lightly. If there were no crude and half-formed opinions in the world, there would never be any thoroughly matured ones. The speculations which are constantly afloat in a society where information is widely diffused constitute the philosophy of the people. They not only give an impetus to the popular mind, but they rouse and set in motion the cultivated understandings of the country. The germ of almost all the great truths in philosophy and politics may be traced to the working of the popular mind.

It has been supposed that democratic institutions give too much control to the inferior classes, that they favor inordinately the elevation of persons of indifferent character and low attainments. But in practice the effect does not take place to anything like the extent which has been predicted. The tendency to it is counteracted by two causes: first, by the consciousness which is ever present to the great majority of uneducated men and from which they are never able to free themselves, that they are unequal to the higher offices in the state. This feeling, in spite of all the encouragement which is given to popular ambition, may be calculated upon with as much certainty as any other propensity which influences the actions of men. It is even desirable sometimes to overcome it, to draw men of humble acquirements into the walks of active life in order that free institutions may answer the end for which they were designed, that is, to make the faculties of men of all conditions as available as possible to the public service. Second: it is counteracted by the jealousy which ignorant men entertain of each other. They are only occasionally brought into contact with the enlightened, but they live in perpetual juxtaposition with one another. They are accordingly more incommoded by each other than they are by the superior classes and feel a greater degree of envy of any remarkable good fortune which may fall to the lot of their own number.

I think, however, that I can at present discern symptoms in all parts of the United States of a decided movement in the opposite direction. The dispersion of knowledge in a democratic community multiplies the numbers of the well-informed to such a degree that the members of this class begin also to incommode and interfere with one another. So many of this class are necessarily disappointed in obtaining office that they very soon lay schemes for selecting candidates among the class below them, and once the example is set these new favorites are not backward in availing themselves of such good fortune. The former may not be actuated by any liberal or patriotic views; they probably wish to make a merit of their disappointment or, by forming a close alliance with the masses, to lay the foundation of their own advancement at a future day. Nevertheless, the course they adopt is without any intention on their part productive of great advantage to society. The elevation of persons of even ordinary capacity to places of trust and responsibility stimulates them to exertion and frequently awakens dormant qualities which were never suspected to exist. The minds of all are improved by being made conversant with interests which look much beyond the farm or the shop.

Thus the educated and influential set on foot a revolution which gradually undermines their own importance, but it is only accomplished by raising a great number of men in the inferior walks of life to their own condition, in other words, by creating a counterpoise to their own selfishness and ambition. The great works of internal improvement which have been executed in the American states were debated and matured in assemblies composed for the most part of ordinary farmers.

The town and the rural population constitute another division of the classes of a community. These two orders of men no longer live apart from each other with habits and manners as distinct as if they were separated by different ages. This change is much more remarkable in the United States than in any other country. Free institutions, which commence by individualizing men, ultimately tend to draw them closer together. The greater the amount of personal independence which each one enjoys, the more numerous are his wants and the stronger is the desire and the aptitude for society.

Civilization commences in the towns, for it is only by congregating together that men learn to defer to each other's wants and are led to cooperate in plans which are calculated to promote their common interests. The city constitutes a nucleus of civilization around which the country population gathers; and the more frequent the communication between the two the more rapidly will the whole population advance in every species of improvement. In some countries, burdensome and vexatious imposts are levied upon the trade between the towns and the country. I do not know how far the necessities of any particular government may render this mode of taxation desirable, but it is certain that it creates a very serious impediment to a free and liberal intercourse between the two classes; nor is the degree of this impediment measured merely by the amount of the number of duties which are levied but goes greatly beyond. Any obstruction to a communication between two classes whose habits and manners were originally different lays the foundation for still greater differences and keeps them wide apart for centuries.

Although the people of the United States are eminently an agricultural one, yet in no part of the world is there such a disposition to build towns. The town and the country have constantly advanced hand in hand. The same causes which give rise to a distribution of the political power of the community produce also a more exact distribution of the population. The growth of the cities is not determined by the residence of a court and nobility, or by any other causes equally artificial, but takes the course which is most natural and therefore most favorable to the general prosperity. And although foreign commerce will always rear some very large towns, it may be predicted with certainty that internal commerce will build up a still greater number nearly as large, and that in America there will always be a more equal balance between the town and country population than in any other state which does not possess the advantage of free institutions. The effect of a thorough intercourse between these two great classes is to diffuse intelligence, to render the civilization more uniform, and to cause a more exact equilibrium of power among the whole. This operates as a protection against those violent revolutions which take place in other countries where the cities, having acquired the supremacy, are in a condition to lord it over the whole country.

A city presents an organized force somewhat resembling that of an army, and unless the country population is raised to a level greatly above that of the European peasantry it cannot exert the influence which naturally and legitimately belongs to it. The French revolution offers a striking example of this fact: the city of Paris ruled with absolute sway over the provinces because the provinces were composed of an abject population. In the United States, the people of the country are always willing to obey a summons which calls them to suppress an insurrection in the towns, and their conduct on the very few occasions where their services have been necessary has been alike distinguished for humanity and bravery.

A prime object of political institutions should be to neutralize the power of great masses and thus to ward off even the approach of revolution; and the most certain way of effecting this is by dispersing knowledge and property among the whole population. The laws of France restrict the electoral franchise within such narrow limits as to give an undue preponderance to the towns. The qualifications are so high and the division of the soil so minute as to place the great majority of the electors in the towns. Bustle, activity, and enterprise are characteristics of the towns; while to the rural population belong greater simplicity of manners, more hardihood of character, and a peculiar aptitude for cool reflection. By establishing a close communication between these two classes, the whole population is bound together by one common interest and the general standard of character is greatly elevated.

Capital and labor give rise to another division in society, not materially different from the classification into the higher and lower orders, but pointing more directly to the causes which in a thriving and industrious community lead to the distribution. The relation of lord and serf at one time swallowed up all other distinctions and paved the way everywhere for the establishment of aristocratical or monarchical government. On the other hand, the existence of the two great classes of capitalists and laborers is an infallible indication of a tendency toward an improved condition of society. In the United States, these two classes not only compose the population of the towns — they compose also the population of the country. Agriculture in that community has become a great trade. The division of the soil, while it is unfavorable to the acquisition of political power by a few, procures independence to a very large number. The proportion between laborers and capitalists is, as everywhere else, determined by the principle of supply and demand, but the condition of the two classes is greatly modified by the influence of free institutions.

The struggle between capital and labor is one of the most striking facts in the history of modern communities. The forces of society seem to have taken an entirely new direction. Instead of efforts to acquire political power which must necessarily be confined to a few, the great effort of everyone now seems to be to acquire property. Two good effects flow from this: 1st, the political institutions enjoy more repose

— the government is not so much endangered by the cabals and con-spiracies of the few as was formerly the case; 2d, by interesting so great a number in the acquisition of property, the value of property is generally felt and the population are insensibly trained to habits which best fit them for self government.

In the United States, the struggle between capital and labor pre-sents a much more difficult problem than it does anywhere else. For if the class of laborers outnumbers that of capitalists, and the present system of nearly universal suffrage prevails, may not the public tran-quillity — nay, the very being of government be endangered?

The struggle may be harmless so long as the reward of industry is so liberal as to allow a competent share to both classes. But when the population has doubled and trebled, the condition of the laborer will no longer be so fortunate; for although capital will also have accumu-lated, yet the objects upon which it can be employed will not have in-creased in the same proportion, and the double effect of an augmented competition among both capitalists and laborers will necessarily re-duce the amount of the products of industry and cause a much less quantity to be partitioned among the two classes. The condition of both will be altered for the worse, but that of laborers much more so than of capitalists. The last may be able to live in comfort while the first may be reduced to a mere subsistence. The struggle will then become infinitely more intense than it has yet been. It may give rise to formidable associations among laborers to raise their wages and, if these efforts are not successful, it may lead to serious riots and insur-rection, or the ballot box may be resorted to as a more peaceful and effectual means of curing the supposed evil. Laborers may outnum-ber all other classes and by the simple exercise of the right of suffrage may cause the laws to be shaped to suit their own wishes. This is pre-senting the dark side of the picture and it is necessary to view a ques-tion of so much interest and magnitude in every possible aspect so as to form a valuable opinion of what is to be the future destiny of a country hitherto so fortunate in its career, and to find out if certain evils are necessarily incident to a state in which free institutions are established; whether there may not be some way of alleviating them — whether they are not attended with many compensations — whether, in short, they may not be turned into advantages.

The reason why the struggle between capital and labor presents so threatening an aspect in the United States is that laborers are placed in a much more advantageous condition than in any other country.[3] They stand higher in the scale both physically and morally. They have on this account a more resolute and independent character. The very circumstance which renders their condition so enviable is regarded as ominous of the future tranquillity of the country. We thus look into the future from a wrong point of view. We suppose that the demand for laborers will never be counterbalanced by the demand for employment, or that the present independent feeling of laborers will continue even after their condition is changed. As society advances, there is a constant tendency to a fall of wages. This is inevitable, whether we ascribe it to the increase of the number of laborers or to the increased difficulty of procuring the means of subsistence. The vast extent of cultivable land in the United States will retard the fall, but come it must whenever the population has attained the density of that of France or Great Britain. Nature will then impose a powerful check upon passions which would otherwise be ungovernable. For I have constantly observed that poverty, straitened circumstances, the humility of feeling which these create have a wonderful effect in subduing the will and producing a submission to circumstances which are beyond our control. It would be infinitely better if the present independent condition of laborers could be maintained. But if the fall to lower wages at a period more or less distant is unavoidable, the mischiefs which now threaten society will wear a different aspect; and I do not see how it can be denied that the safeguard to the institutions will be as strong as it is now, and that it will increase in intensity exactly in proportion as it is needed. Discontent will be much more common, but it will not be accompanied with the same degree of power as now. The laborer will have much more cause to complain; but 1st. the change in his condition will be brought about by certain laws of society which neither he, nor anyone else can control. 2d. The same causes will enfeeble his will and deprive him of the effective power to do mischief. Outbreaks will be much more common and they will of course take place among a much more numerous body of men, but they will be powerless compared with what they would be if laborers possessed the same independent condition as at present. 3d. There is a constant tendency as society grows older to an augmentation of capital and an increase of the number of capitalists.

3. [For the second edition, Grimke added new matter from the start of this paragraph to the paragraph which ends ". . . will ultimately assume," on p. 595.]

All those institutions which embody wealth and power will become stronger so that not only will the ability to invade property be diminished, but the ability to protect it will be increased. I predict that the civil aristocracy which will grow up in the United States will be more powerful, more intelligent, and more pacific than any political aristocracy which has ever existed.

The originally equal distribution of the soil in the United States is a circumstance which has never been sufficiently appreciated. It explains the secret of the private comfort and well being of the population, and it may be regarded also as the hinge on which turns the stability of the institutions. The soil of Ireland is distributed among less than one thousand proprietors. Ohio with very nearly the same area and one third of the population is divided among two hundred thousand. It is obvious that this great disproportion, in the one case, be- tween the numbers of the people and the distribution of the soil must exert an influence literally immense upon the condition of the people, upon their manners, character, and powers of exertion; and that it must to the same extent affect the structure and the whole machinery of government. Ireland is an extreme case, but the same causes which have produced so striking a disproportion in the division of property there have acted with more or less force in every other European state. All have commenced the rudiments of life in the savage state and all have submitted at one period or another to the dominion of a foreign enemy who have camped down among them and parcelled out the soil among the chiefs of the army. In England and Scotland, in France and Spain, in Italy and Germany the effect of these revolutions is percepti- ble at the present day. And if the question were asked, what has ren- dered possible the establishment of free institutions in the United States and what has rendered their existence so precarious in Europe, the decisive and the satisfactory answer would be the originally differ- ent distribution of the soil has produced these opposite results.

The distinguishing feature then of American society, that which differs it from all others either ancient or modern, is that the *tiers état,* or middle class, is not confined to the towns but is diffused over the whole country. In Europe it comprehends the bourgeoisie, in the United States it comprehends in addition a vastly more numerous class, to wit, the country population. This is a circumstance of in- finite moment in the study of American institutions. It has made a pro- found impression upon them already and may exert immense influ-

ence upon the future destinies of the country. Until in Europe the
middle class is composed of both the great divisions of the population, the cause of free institutions will be involved in great uncertainty. 1st. Because until then the population cannot be said to be
fairly amalgamated. It is not necessary that the population should
all be melted down into one class, but it is necessary that there should
be a certain degree of uniformity in order to prevent an incessant conflict of interests and opinions and to make the institutions of government something more than the representative of a section of society.
2d. Until then, the middle class will not be sufficiently strong and enlightened to command that respect which silently and without the
employment of force molds the institutions to its own purpose. The
revolution which annihilated the legislature and elevated Napoleon
III to the throne could not possibly have taken place if France had
contained a powerful middle class. No individual can have power to
take to pieces the government if the population who live under it can
agree among themselves; and this is impossible where the inequalities
of society are so great and so numerous as to create the greatest diversity of opinions and interests. That merely tacit understanding
which takes place among the members of a community in which there
prevails great uniformity of condition imposes an instant check upon
all attempts to revolutionize the government. The artificial institutions of monarchy and aristocracy are resorted to for the single purpose of repressing those great disorders which grow out of the inequalities among the different parts of the population. A standing army,
then, becomes part of the regular police. It is only a more thorough
organization of the constabulary force. If it took from the Christian
era to the French Revolution to create a *tiers état* in the towns alone
in continental Europe, how long will it take to create one among the
rural population? In private life, an individual entitled to respect
generally commands it. The same is true in political society. Where a
strong middle class makes its appearance, it does not stand in need
of a standing army to protect it. It may even give control of the army
to the executive. No one attempts what is impossible, but at the utmost
what is only improbable.

Are there any causes in operation in the United States which are
calculated to diminish the numbers and to weaken the influence of the
middle class? I have alluded to the difficulty of procuring food and
the consequent fall of wages which takes place when a country becomes densely peopled and the greater part of the arable land has been

appropriated. There is another circumstance, however, which is beginning to exercise a powerful influence upon European society. Within the last fifty years a great revolution has taken place in the whole system of industrial pursuits, in agriculture, manufactures, and commerce. The tendency everywhere is to the creation of vast capitals and the extermination of small ones. An infinitely greater net produce can be obtained from the soil where it is cultivated in large farms than when it is divided into small ones. As the population residing on and supported by it is much less, the expense of cultivation is much less also. The employment of a large capital and the application of those improvements which none but the wealthy proprietor can command enables him to sell cheaper, as a moderate profit upon such a capital produces more riches than the same profit upon a small capital. The effect of this system has been to expel from the soil the former cultivators and to introduce in its stead the system of day labor. Until within the last fifty years, the English laborer lived on the soil which he cultivated — it was his permanent home. It is very different now. The cultivation is almost entirely performed by day laborers who are dismissed whenever there is no occasion for their services and who are consequently without employment during the greater part of the year. In England the agricultural laborers only amount to about 1,061,000. This great revolution has not been unnoticed by writers on political economy, but the comprehensive genius of Sismondi* first pointed out its connection with some of the most important problems in political philosophy. The same revolution, but with still greater effect, has taken place in manufacturing industry. Vast numbers of laborers, driven from the soil, are collected in the towns where manufacturing establishments have grown up. Their wages are very moderate and they are liable on every disaster of trade to be left in a state of destitution. Immense capitals are employed in these manufactures. Formerly fifty thousand dollars was considered an ample capital. At present less than half a million is not considered adequate to the successful prosecution of the business. The larger the capital, the cheaper can the proprietor afford to sell. The same amount of profit which on a small capital would only maintain his family will yield an immense income on a large one. The constant tendency, then, is to the creation of colossal fortunes in the hands of a few and the consequent creation of a vast army of proletarians.

The introduction of industrial pursuits first broke up the feudal

* *Economie Politique.*

system and established the metayer system of cultivation. It has now almost completely broken up this and introduced the system of day labor. The lower classes have been freed from the direct control and authority of the landed proprietor, but they are placed in a state of greater dependence than ever. Instead of living on the soil where the means of subsistence was assured to them during the year, or rather for life, they are now employed and dismissed at the pleasure of the proprietor. It is difficult to predict what will be the result of this system, so entirely unknown either in ancient or modern times. An overwhelming mass of proletarians has been created both in town and country, and although a corresponding increase of the enlightened classes and the concentration of wealth and power in the hands of landed, manufacturing and commercial capitalists renders it as easy, or even easier, to govern the masses than formerly, yet it is evident that the system may be pushed so far as to cause its own ruin. The extermination of small capitals on the land, in manufactures, and commerce may cause the middle class to dwindle into insignificance. The class of proletarians may be augmented indefinitely; they may be driven to despair; their overwhelming numbers may enable them to combat successfully against the most solidly established authority.

This is the unfavorable side of the picture, and it is necessary to understand what is possible in order to comprehend the probable, or even the present. But there are two remarkable circumstances connected with English society which show that there is a power of resistance somewhere to this extreme state of things. The first is that the wages of labor have varied very little during the last five hundred years.* A peck of wheat a day has been the average during the whole of that period. The extraordinary improvements which have been made in the science of agriculture and which have kept pace with the increase of the population have retarded the fall of wages. It is true that a peck of wheat a day may be a very insufficient reward to the laborer when he is only employed six months in the year, although in consequence of the fall of price in all manufactured products he may be able to purchase with it more of the necessaries of life. The operatives in manufacturing establishments, however, are not subjected to this disadvantage. They are hired during the year. The second circumstance which is entitled to our attention is presented in the British income tax returns of 1812 and 1848. From these it appears that there has

* Malthus' *Political Economy*.

been an increase of the number of moderate and a comparative diminution of colossal fortunes.

	1812.	1848.
Between £ 150 and £ 500,...............	30,723	91,101
500 and 1000,...............	5,334	13,287
1000 and 2000,...............	2,116	5,234
2000 and 5000,...............	1,180	2,586
5000 and upwards,............	409	1,181†

M. Sismondi has not noticed these two circumstances. The mind to which new and striking views are presented is very apt to run them out to extreme consequences. Nor is this to be regretted. They would not make so strong and distinct an impression if they were not pushed to extremity, nor would those circumstances which contribute to modify them be so easily found out. The consideration of what is possible, as I before remarked, sheds light upon the probable and even upon the actual.

The employment of immense capitals in every department of industry is the secret of the commercial prosperity of England. The complete centralization of capital causes all commodities to be produced and sold cheaper, and compensates, in some degree, for heavy taxation and the increasing difficulty of obtaining food. But it is doubtful whether the great mass of the population are placed in more favorable circumstances. The number of the poor, instead of diminishing, is augmented by the increase of riches. Never was industry productive of such brilliant results and never was the class of proletarians more numerous.

This system is evidently springing up in the United States. There is the same tendency to the employment of great capitals in every department of industry. It will be a very long time before the system

† Nat. Intelligencer, March 20, 1851. [Grimke does not define his categories precisely here in relation to the figures he presents, but if by "colossal fortunes" he means incomes of more than five thousand pounds, then his figures actually show a slight increase in the proportion, from 1.029% in 1812 to 1.042% in 1848. If, however, he means the two highest categories, those making more than two thousand but less than five, plus those making more than five, then there is a decline from 3.996% in 1812 to 3.322% in 1848. But, then, his "moderate" group needs to be designated because the two groups which comprise those making more than five hundred pounds but less than two thousand show a decline from 18.736% in 1812 to 16.334% in 1848, as does the single group making between one and two thousand pounds, from 5.321% in 1812 to 4.615% in 1848.]

attains its maximum, but to the political philosopher, one or two hundred years are but as a single day. There are some circumstances, however, which will contribute to counteract the effects of this system. 1st. The general standard of comfort is higher than it has ever been in any other country, and inveterate habit will render it very difficult to depart from it. 2d. The principle of equal partibility prevails in the descent and devise of estates. Equal partibility, however, may be carried so far as to create an immense army of proletarians or it may terminate in an opposite result. Great capitalists may purchase a multitude of these small estates and the system of great landed properties may ultimately be introduced. The principle of equal partibility, however, will be applied to these large properties also, and they will be crumbled in a few generations into small fragments. The desirable medium may in this way be attained, and the high standard of comfort, together with the alternate creation and destruction of overgrown estates, may place the great mass of the population in more advantageous circumstances than anywhere else.

M. Sismondi is silent with regard to the condition of the French population. This arises from the adoption of an exclusive theory, the strength of which might seem to be impaired by admitting any important exceptions to it. The theory is entitled to great attention, but it is indispensable to be acquainted with the whole ground on which we travel. France affords a very instructive lesson. There is the same tendency there as in other countries to the employment of large capitals in manufactures and commerce, but it is otherwise in agriculture, and agriculture constitutes the occupation of the great majority of the population. The rule of equal partibility has prevailed for more than half a century. The number of proprietors has consequently augmented prodigiously. According to M. Dupin, France in 1834 contained twenty-four millions of proprietors in a population of thirty-two millions.[4] Such is the number inscribed on the public registers. A very ingenious writer insists that as the report made by M. Guion to the Chamber of Deputies the same year shows that the land is incumbered with a debt contracted by proprietors to the amount of thirteen thousand millions of francs, those who owe this debt are only

4. [Probably Baron Charles Dupin (1784–1873), geometer and statistician who wrote prolifically on the French economy.]

nominally proprietors.* The mortgagees of the land may ultimately swallow up these innumerable small properties. The fact, at any rate, shows the wretched condition of the agricultural population and that the division of the soil and the cultivation of it by those who reside on it has not been more favorable to the general comfort than the opposite system of large farms and large capitals. More than twenty millions of this people can neither read nor write; twenty-two millions earn only from six to seven sous a day; and of the twenty-four millions of proprietors, twelve or fourteen millions have not always even coarse bread to subsist on. It would seem that neither the English system, which aims to produce the greatest amount of net income, nor the French, which is directed to the production of the greatest amount of gross produce, have succeeded in placing the great bulk of the population in a state of even tolerable independence. Here are two opposite experiments proceeding simultaneously in two countries, separated only by a narrow channel, and the result in each has been to produce a vast army of proletarians.

If we suppose then that all the overgrown estates in Great Britain and Ireland were broken up and sold in small parcels, there is no absolute assurance that the condition of society would be permanently ameliorated. The effect of the division of property is to give a fresh stimulus to the population. The abolition of the laws of primogeniture and entail would almost necessarily produce this great change. Properties would be subdivided every generation, and the British peasantry and operatives might be reduced to the same fare of black bread as the French. In applying these views to the United States, we must again revert to the circumstance to which I before alluded. The division of the soil was originally, and continues to be, incomparably more equal than in any European country. This original difference in the structure of society combined with the high standard of comfort, each acting upon and contributing to fortify the other, may forever ward off the existence of either the French or the English system. And when we add to this the influence of those political institutions which grew up at the very foundation of their society, habits absolutely indelible may be grafted upon the whole population. As the experiment stands

* P. Considerant, *Dest. Soc.*, v. 1, p. 152. [Victor Prosper Considérant (1808–1893), *Destinée Sociale* (Paris, 1837), 3 vols., mainly a digest of the socialist writings of Charles Fourier.]

alone in the history of human nature, the results may be different from what they have been in any other country.

I have now pointed out some of those general causes which impede the regular march of society and which raise or depress the condition of the various classes. But there are some circumstances of a more hidden character which act with more or less force upon multitudes of individuals whatever may be the structure of society and however wide the arena of exertion may be. Thus, in the United States, where it is strictly correct to say that the great bulk of the population belongs to the middle class, there are very great diversities in the condition of individuals. It is because these circumstances are confined to individuals and do not characterize classes that it is difficult to unravel them. The history of the individual has never been written. The character and habits which are common to classes are easily seized and appreciated, those which belong to individuals are indefinitely diversified and we search in vain for a clue to guide us to some general rules.

It is not necessary to inquire why in the great majority of countries one half, sometimes a much greater proportion, of the population is in straitened or destitute circumstances. But why in the United States, where the field of exertion is almost unbounded, there are the greatest diversities in the condition of individuals is a problem for the inquisitive mind to ponder upon. The present may be termed the golden age of the republic: there is not the least reason, so far as physical comfort is concerned, that as a whole anything better will succeed. It is the first time in the annals of mankind that the wish of Henry the Great has been realized, "that every man had a piece of meat to put in his kettle." Do the differences I have alluded to arise from difference of capacities, taking capacities in its most detailed signification as denoting good understanding, acquired ability, shrewdness, manners, acquaintance with the world, etc.; or, second, from a difference in the affective faculties or of constitution, health, temperament; or, third, from difference of opportunities; fourth, from difference of organization, disposing some instinctively to exertion and inclining others to love of pleasure, repose, and inaction; fifth, from so many having little or nothing to begin life, the families to which they belong being numerous and leaving little to be divided; sixth, or from receiving so much as to corrupt their character, and enfeeble their exertions?

To trace the operation of these causes, not only singly but in their complication with one another and with a multitude of others so minute as almost to elude scrutiny, would be the work of a lifetime. To trace their operation in a society of ten or fifteen thousand would be impossible without a close and minute knowledge of the individuals who compose it. But how shall we obtain this knowledge in a society of millions? The human countenance and manners, even in the commonest individuals, draw over the mind and character such a disguise that it is difficult to penetrate the interior. Persons the most dissimilar in understanding, in affective faculties, in organization, constitution, and health frequently wear pretty much the same face and demeanor, and yet a difference in any one of these respects, not merely in the broadest signification but a difference of shade only, may give a direction to the whole of life.

Is there any way of legally removing the great inequality of property? Can those who accumulate wealth be considered as appropriating to themselves the just proceeds of the labor of others? And if they can, would those others appropriate these proceeds to themselves, or would they, for want of the industry and energy which set labor in motion, cease to be produced at all? These are all inquiries of great nicety as well as of great moment in determining what is to be the nature of the struggle between capital and labor and what the form which the institutions of society will ultimately assume.

I am very far from regarding the struggle between capital and labor as of ill omen to the future prosperity and well being of a country. It is a pretty sure indication that the laborious classes have risen in intelligence and importance and that they, as well as capitalists, are enabled to exercise some judgment as to the standard of comfort which befits them. It is this very struggle which permits the former to maintain something like a respectable and independent station. The man distracted by poverty has no time to look beyond his mere animal wants; the man who obtains due wages feels his faculties unbound. He can look around him and gather up some of the information which is scattered about. He feels new motives to a regular and virtuous conduct and is rendered an active and useful citizen instead of being a brute machine. If this introduces a new element into every calculation which has for its object the determining the proper amount of wages due to the laborer, so much the better. It cannot be doubted that capitalists enjoy a great advantage in this respect in consequence of their superior intelligence, that this intelligence does count for something, and although the relation between the supply and the demand of labor is the over-ruling principle, yet that like all other general principles it is capable of being greatly modified in practice. There is every reason, therefore, why, if the class of capitalists are raised in the scale of intelligence, the class of laborers should be also. For when we speak of the struggle between capital and labor, we necessarily intend something more than the mere fortuitous or customary adjustment of the two by causes independent of any human control; we intend that the judgment is exercised and that active efforts are made use of by both parties in every contract of service. To denounce the struggle between capital and labor, therefore, would be in effect to lament over the improved intellectual and moral condition of the lower classes. But this we cannot do consistently. If there is any one object which every man, philanthropist, patriot, or statesman has at heart, it is to diffuse education as widely as possible and to lift the greatest number of men possible to the rank of intelligent beings. That there must be a limit to our efforts is obvious, but when one compares the condition of the lower classes, even in Europe at the present day, with what it was two centuries ago, it is evident that infinitely more may be effected in this respect than any human sagacity would have predicted. That laborers and operatives are able to exercise some judgment as to the amount of wages which are justly their due, that, in other words, the struggle between capital and labor is not a struggle all on one side, is every way favorable both to the prosperity and the tranquillity of the country. It gives to the community a body of more effective laborers and tempers the misguided feelings which would otherwise take possession of them whenever a season of distress occurred to interrupt their enjoyment as well as that of capitalists. The reflection which their improved habits impart to them draws them back whenever they are in danger of running into excesses.

It must not be supposed because people are poor that they are therefore rendered insurgent and revolutionary. In order to produce this effect they must, as a general rule, be able to connect their disadvantageous condition with the hand of government as its cause. Poor people, as a class, are fully as much disposed to be orderly as people in a higher condition. Prosperity of any kind administers so many provocatives to the passions that it requires to be counteracted by powerful motives of self-interest. A humble condition and the constant occupation which it renders necessary are apt to have a subduing influence upon the temper and character. It is when government undertakes to make discriminations prejudicial to the inferior classes that they are most disposed to acts of insubordination. Doubtless the institutions of America are environed with many difficulties, and it is in order to lessen the weight of these that I desire to see the great body of operatives raised as high as practicable in the scale of society. The contest between capital and labor will then not be settled by brute force on the one side or by superior adroitness on the other, but will be conducted with some degree of judgment and caution and will terminate, in the great majority of instances, in a compromise advantageous to both parties. What are termed "strikes" are by no means uncommon in the United States. Sometimes there is no well-founded cause for complaint, and then workmen recede from their demands and return quietly to their occupations. But the reverse is frequently the case, and then each party concedes something to the pretensions of the other. A new agreement is made which, without sensibly impairing the productiveness of capital, adds something to the comforts of laborers and smooths all those difficulties which had for a time suspended their accustomed occupations. But capitalists will forever possess one advantage over laborers. They can afford to lie idle for six months, or even longer; while the last, having accumulated little, are obliged to depend upon their regular wages. And this advantage increases just in proportion as combinations among laborers become most dangerous, that is, in proportion as the population becomes more dense. It is fortunate, therefore, that as society advances to the period when the circumstances of so great a number will be very much straitened, there should be some causes in operation calculated to raise the standard of both physical and moral comfort and to present the only natural corrective which exists to an absolute redundancy of the population.

I observe that it is not unusual in the United States for workmen to specify their grievances in writing and to cause them to be published. This circumstance is no small indication how much that class are elevated in the social scale. To be able to analyze our thoughts and to frame reasons for our conduct in any important conjuncture is precisely that sort of mental ability which it is so desirable to encourage in order to temper the passions of the multitude by the exercise of calm judgment and reflection.

And the practice of giving publicity to these complaints is particularly worthy of commendation. It affords very strong evidence that those who complain are themselves convinced of the justice of their complaints and that they are willing to put them to the test of an open and manly avowal. Instead of those secret combinations which were formerly so common, and with regard to the merit of which no impartial person could form any judgment whatever, workmen who set themselves up in opposition to the exactions of their employers feel themselves under an obligation to sustain their conduct by a fair and intelligent exposition of their case. The public is for the most part an impartial spectator in affairs of this kind; it is not apt to be moved by inflammatory appeals when these appeals, however common, are made by distinct bodies at different intervals and never comprehend at any one time any considerable class of the population. I cannot refrain from copying one of those memorials which expresses the justest sentiments in language of the greatest terseness and brevity. The journeymen house carpenters in one of our cities made a strike for the ten-hour system, and this is what they say in their statement: "We are flesh and blood; we need hours of recreation. It is estimated by political economists that five hours labor per day, by each individual, would be sufficient for the support of the human race. Surely, then, we do our share when we labor ten. We have social feelings which must be gratified. We have minds which must be improved. We are lovers of our country and must have time and opportunity to study its interests. Shall we live and die knowing nothing but the rudiments of our trade? Is knowledge useless to us, that we should be debarred the means of obtaining it? Would we be less adept as workmen? Would the trade of which we are members be less respected or useful? Or would the community of which we are members suffer less because we were enlightened?"

We need not fear any ill consequences from the influence of the class of working men when we find them capable of taking such just and liberal views, views which denote that they have a true perception of their own rights and that they desire so to use them as to make them subservient to the common weal. We should rather hail this influence as the symptom of an exceedingly sound and healthful condition of society. It is fit that the relations which this class bear to the class of capitalists should be adjusted by these two parties instead of by appeals to governmental regulation. An European community may be obliged to resort to the last course. But wherever the first is pursued, we may be sure of two things: that the class of working men has risen greatly in the scale, and that there is a high probability the affairs of society will continue to be conducted in a peaceful and orderly manner.

Even admitting, therefore, that the inferior classes should come to predominate in the United States while the present laws of suffrage continue to exist, it does not therefore follow that the country is to be converted into a bedlam. On the contrary, there is every reason to believe that things will continue pretty much in the same even tenor which they have hitherto held. In progress of time, there will be both a more numerous class of rich and a more numerous class of poor. But the middle class will forever outnumber both the others. The distribution of the rural population, so different from what it is in any other country, insures this, whatever may be the growth of manufacturing industry. It is to the exertions of this class that the operatives in England are indebted for the amelioration of their condition. And it is upon the permanent influence of this class that we are entitled to fasten all our hopes of the future in America.

If we were to suppose the operatives of the manufacturing establishments to constitute a majority of the electors and even a majority of the legislature, what laws could they pass which would better their condition? To make a division of incomes between the capitalists and themselves would instantly annihilate capital and would render the condition of the last unspeakably wretched. If the income of all the rich was equally divided among all who were not rich, it would not amount to a week's support to each. And admitting that there would be a large number who were incapable of foreseeing these consequences, there would be a still larger number who would clearly discern them.

The ignorance of the ignorant is rarely so great as to blind them to the perception of the few elementary principles on which their own interests hinge. After making every allowance, therefore, for those popular excesses to which society in whatever form it may be cast will forever be occasionally liable, I cannot help thinking that the enjoyment of political liberty by the inferior classes, instead of being a hindrance to good government, will assist in promoting it. Nor is there the least probability that these classes will ever compose the majority in the American legislatures. There are certain laws of human nature, the operation of which may be calculated upon with nearly as much certainty as those which preside over the physical world. Every man would gladly be his own lawyer and his own physician, and, whenever occasion required it, show himself master of every other department of knowledge. It would save a great deal of expense and would administer mightily to human vanity if such could be the case. But the impossibility of the thing is so manifest and is so universally felt that, although all professions should be laid open to general competition as are already all other branches of knowledge, the great majority of people will apply to those who have skill and experience and would consider it the greatest misfortune in the world to be cut off from their advice and assistance. The same is the case with matters of government. The most ignorant men may desire to become legislators; their interest and ambition would seem to be as much gratified in this way as by becoming their own lawyers and physicians. But a desire which as soon as it is formed is sure to be smothered by an overwhelming sense of deficiency can never have any effect.

It is not merely as a political privilege that the electoral franchise is so valuable; the influence which it exerts upon the general manners is inestimable. It causes men to respect and to defer to each other's opinions. It accustoms those who are invested with any species of influence, whether of a political or a merely civil character, to use it equitably and prudently; and it disposes those who are any ways subject to this influence to regard it not as an odious privilege, but as a source of peculiar benefit to themselves. Doubtless the very general enjoyment of the electoral franchise in the United States is one reason why the system pursued in the management of manufacturing establishments is placed upon a so much more advantageous footing than in any other country. By learning to respect others, we are made acquainted with their interests, and this respect then becomes something more than a dead formality. Not merely are the operatives in these establishments better fed and clothed but they are treated much more as reasonable beings. Their education and religious instruction are considered as having some place in the economy of these institutions.

The enjoyment of political privileges by men in the inferior walks of life is in reality the only way of effectually conciliating the interests of all classes. It may be said that as the management of public affairs requires skill and information of a particular kind, it should be devolved upon those who have time and opportunity to acquire them on the same principle as a division is made of all the other pursuits of society; that inasmuch as the mechanic and the farmer do not undertake to interfere with each other's calling, nor either to dictate to the physician or the lawyer as to the right way of applying their information and experience, there would be the same propriety in confining the whole business of government to a class set apart for that purpose. The two things are in truth very properly compared, and it is because they are similar that the management of political affairs is not conferred upon a particular order of men; although the professions and trades are exercised by those who have skill in them, yet all who have need of legal or medical assistance are free to choose their own physician and lawyer. If this were not the case, if a monopoly were established in favor of a few select practitioners, the same skill would not be exercised by them and the public would lose all confidence in their ability and integrity. The perfect freedom of choice which every individual enjoys does not prevent the various professions and trades from being separated from each other. And the same is the case with political affairs. The right of choosing their own rulers does not convert the whole population into lawgivers or judges, nor interfere in any degree with the weight of such public men as are remarkable for their talents and information. The division of labor in America is in this respect as strict as it is in any other country. The institutions may fit a greater number for political employments, but the employments themselves are distinct from any other pursuits as they can well be made. If the citizens did not enjoy the right of voting for their public officers, if a monopoly of all public trusts were created in behalf of a few, there would be no effectual check upon the conduct of public men. They would do pretty much as they pleased and, instead of being overawed by public opinion when their actions were reprehensible, they would themselves create public opinion and compel all others to yield obedience to it.

The dark side of the picture, as I have termed it above, supposes that the operatives and laborers may become so numerous as to control the elections and ultimately to undermine the most wholesome and the most solidly-established institutions. The error consists in supposing that what is possible is therefore probable and that whatever is probable may be strictly reduced to practice; whereas, the probable is subject to as determinate laws as the certain. We do not always will to do what we desire, for the motives to human action are derived from without as well as from within; moreover, we find innumerable ob-

stacles in the mere will of other individuals. And although, if we are
the majority, there is a physical possibility of bending their actions to
suit our purposes, yet invariably in practice a limit is imposed upon
our efforts. The moral possibility must be taken into the account
fully as much as the physical, and although the laws which govern
the first are more undefined, more dimly seen, than those which govern
the last, yet the difficulties which surround any novel and violent enterprise are not on that account lessened but are, in the greater number instances, very much increased. So far as the history of human
nature is handed down to us in the history of the various communities
which have existed, we find that in no one instance have a majority
of men ever accomplished those things which they may be supposed
to have desired to do; and this is calculated to suggest the thought
whether moral hinderances do not, in fact, impose as insurmountable
obstacles to action as physical ones, although when we view each in
the abstract we say of the former that they are something which can
invariably be overcome, and of the latter that they can never be.
What is the reason that whole peoples have lived for centuries under
despotic governments, although those who desire a change constitute
an immense majority? The change could be easily effected if there
were only the determined and the united will. Moral obstacles then, it
would seem, are absolutely insurmountable sometimes, even when
the physical impediments are capable of being removed.

There must be some wise reason for this constitution of our nature.
When we deal with the actions of other men, when we meddle with the
institutions which preside over them as well as over ourselves, we require a good deal of knowledge in order to see our way clearly, a good
deal in order to carry us successfully through and still more in order to
inspire us with the requisite assurance and self reliance. The want of
these presents as real obstacles to human conduct as any physical
impediments and we may, therefore, calculate with as absolute certainty upon part of the actions of whole communities as we do upon
the happening of physical events.

We will suppose that a large majority of the members elected to
the American legislatures was composed of day laborers and operatives and that the favorite scheme with these two bodies was the
passage of an agrarian law — not one like the Roman which confined
itself to an equal distribution of the public domain and exacted an adequate rent for it, but one which contemplated an equal division of all

the property already in the possession of individuals and the result of their independent exertions. These bodies would no sooner have met than the spectacle would be one so repugnant to the common sense of mankind (including in the term, mankind, all those who belong to the class elected) as to frustrate in the very beginning all schemes which had been set on foot. For what can be conceived more unnatural than that a considerable part of the population of any civilized community should cut themselves off from all communication with the educated and enlightened, that they should refuse to listen in any respect to the counsel and assistance of those whose superior opportunities pointed them out as indispensable guides in every public emergency, and that they should so act for the express purpose of committing an act of gross injustice to all proprietors of land and personal property in the country? I venture to say that the exceeding awkwardness which those legislative bodies would feel in finding themselves placed in so unheard of and so startling a position would strike with impotency every resolution which may have been formed: I go further and say that this single consideration proves that no such bodies ever will or can be elected in America.

The most plausible supposition that we can make is not that the day laborers and operatives should elect representatives from their own body, but rather that they should choose from among the other classes persons who had some pretensions to education and some acquaintance with the general run of public affairs and who, having little stake in the public weal, should be every way inclined to fan the embers of public discontent in order to gain a name in the world. In the first instance, we introduce into the legislative halls members who would feel themselves absolutely powerless at the outset in the discussion or concoction of any measures whatever. In the second we introduce persons there whose advantages of one kind or other place them in near communication with the enlightened and influential. But these men's actions will be governed by some fixed laws. They only differ from other men in being very discontented; and discontent and envy, we know, often drive men to do many things which they feel to be wrong. This feeling, the consciousness that they stand in a false position to society, cannot be shaken off; it will introduce an element of discord into all their actions. In order to act with vigor and promptitude they will be obliged to make efforts to conciliate public opinion. They either fall to the ground on every encounter with members who are superior in moral and intellectual accomplishments, or they seek to win both sides by pursuing a middle course.

The third and the most rational supposition we can make is that the class to which I have alluded, although never so numerous as to elect anything like a majority of the members, will always have sufficient influence to cause their interests to be represented, that they will even sometimes send members who will entertain the same ultra view as themselves. If they did not, it would be to be feared that ultra views on the other side would take possession of society. No harm but, on the contrary, very great benefit will be the consequence. There are many problems in the social organization which remain to be settled and which can only be settled by the mutual and earnest cooperation of all classes. But a revolutionary movement invariably jeopardizes everything; it is sure to be followed by a reaction, and after an interval more or less considerable men are compelled to begin anew, to set out with reflection and a due regard for the rights of all others. If anyone should still insist that these considerations are not sufficient to show that the evils of universal suffrage will not be averted, I have no objection, but rather prefer that this apprehension should constantly press upon the mind of everyone. It is, as I have often repeated, a most wholesome provision of our nature that our apprehension of the mischief which may ensue from our own conduct should have a perpetual influence upon us. The feeling in great part supplies the place of reflection where this is deficient. My desire is never to pursue the analysis to the utmost limit for fear of impairing the strength of that feeling; or to speak more correctly, I am denied the ability to do so because it would interfere with an essential part of the machinery of society.

Professional men constitute another division of the classes of society. The influence they exert is immense, nor is it easy to conceive of a well-balanced society unless they were a constituent part of the population. The intellectual men of a country are the hinges upon which society turns, and the members of the three learned professions necessarily compose a very large part of the class of intellectual men.

It is a fortunate circumstance that some degree of knowledge and education is absolutely necessary to even the physical well-being of society. If such were not the case, it is doubtful whether men would ever have made any advances in intellectual improvement worth naming. The three professions grow immediately out of wants which are common to all mankind; and as they render study, information, and mental discipline essential to those who practice them reputably and successfully, they serve both to diffuse and to perpetuate knowledge. But these professions are either directly or indirectly connected with all other departments of science, and this lays the foundation for a general system of education and creates a fourth profession: the teacher, whether in schools, academies, or universities. It is a fine provision, therefore, in the constitution of society that our physical wants and the passions which grow out of them render necessary the employment of our higher faculties; and that the more those wants and passions increase in strength and become dangerous to the state, the more certain is the tendency and the encouragement to knowledge. Without knowledge, or at any rate without the influence which knowledge imparts, men would be condemned to a condition very little above that of the brutes, and with power infinitely greater than that of the brutes to injure and torment each other. As the individual who exercises all his faculties has the best balanced mind, so a society in which education is widely diffused and knowledge is permitted to have its rightful authority is sure to give rise to the best balanced community.

The influence which professional men are capable of exerting upon the rest of the population will depend in a great degree upon the manner in which they are distributed through the state. There is the greatest difference imaginable in this respect between the legal profession in the United States and Great Britain. In the former lawyers are scattered over the whole country, while in England and Scotland the greater part congregate in London and Edinburgh. I do not now speak of attorneys, but of barristers, the correlative of which in America is the term lawyers. Attorneys in Great Britain practice a trade rather than a profession, and a trade so mischievous in many respects that it is not surprising the abolition of the order should have entered into the plan of the commissioners who were appointed under the act for the reformation of the law. The offices of attorney and barrister are for the most part performed by the same persons in the United States. Where this is not the case, where the business is of such an amount as to render necessary a division of labor, a partnership is formed, one member of which devotes himself to the duties of an attorney and the other to those of barrister and counsellor. The existence of a partnership, however, is no evidence that the duties are separated, for the instances are much more common where both the members practice equally in the different walks of the profession. There is at any rate no such class known as the corps of attorneys. The lawyer is responsible for all the business which he transacts or is connected with; there is no race of jobbers behind his back whose conduct is withdrawn from his supervision and almost veiled from the rest of the community.

The very equal distribution of lawyers among the population is a remarkable feature of the social organization in the United States and is attended with the most salutary consequences. Something similar to it may be observed in France where the system of local courts is now established; but the difference between France and the United States in this respect is as great as between France and Great Britain.

The intellectual influence which professional men exercise is twofold. They apply much learning and sagacity to the subjects with which they are particularly conversant, and this insures the existence at all times of a certain amount of knowledge in the community. The lawyer assists in protecting our property and personal rights from invasion, the physician preserves our health, and the clergyman teaches and unfolds those truths without which all other truths would be impotent and valueless. In order to accomplish these tasks, the best endowed minds in each profession are obliged to bring a very considerable body of scientific information to bear upon the practical interests of men. This gives to that information a tangible character and introduces even unprofessional men to a very tolerable acquaintance with it. The clergyman and the lawyer appear before the public in the discharge of their professions. The practice of the physician is necessarily of a private character, being confined to his office or to the sick chamber, which is doubtless one reason why there is less general acquaintance with the science of medicine than with either law or divinity, although it is not more abstruse than the two last and although the great majority of mankind have so great a desire to pry into its secrets. But the acquisition of any one branch of knowledge is an easy introduction to a fund of general information on other subjects. The intelligent clergyman, lawyer and physician will not be satisfied with a knowledge of their respective callings; they will each strive to go beyond in order to render themselves both more useful and more respectable. Hence, professional men are apt, as a general rule, to be the best informed class in the community.

Now it is obvious that the location of lawyers in the United States, the fact that they are distributed through the whole population instead of being congregated at one spot, gives them a great advantage in spreading not only the benefits of their profession but in diffusing the information which they have acquired; and it is productive of equal advantage to all other men by exposing them to an influence which, however imperfect, must necessarily count for something in raising the general standard of improvement.

It is easy to estimate the different degree of influence which is exerted by the members of the legal profession in the United States and Great Britain, when one considers that their location in the former is not a consequence merely of the confederate form of government which would very naturally assemble a certain number within each of the states. But their dispersion within these as is wide as it can well be conceived to be. Lawyers are established at every county town or seat of justice, frequently in several towns in the same county, and as the counties are reduced greatly below the size of English counties, they are much more extensively distributed than would be the case in Great Britain if English barristers were addicted to the same custom. In the United States it is not at all uncommon to meet with lawyers in towns of three or four thousand inhabitants who are as profoundly conversant with their profession and whose intellectual endowments are to the full as high in every respect as can be found among the leading men of the same profession in cities of three or four hundred thousand. It needs no argument to show the multiplied advantages which spring from this arrangement of society. A very large proportion of the population are present from time to time at the debates which take place in the halls of justice; nor are the persons who make a figure in these removed to a great distance during the rest of the year, so as to impress other men with a notion that there is something so mysterious and beyond their faculties to comprehend in the learned profession of the law that they may not aspire to educate their sons to the same pursuit.

But lawyers exercise a political as well as an intellectual influence upon society. The acquaintance which they have with the laws of their country is necessarily greater than that of any other class, and this points them out as among the fittest persons to be elected to the legislative body. But this affords an additional reason why they should be distributed as equally as possible among the rest of the population.

By mixing much with all other classes they acquire a knowledge of their habits, an insight into their interests, and a degree of tact in both which could be gained in no other way. I am not at all insensible to the counter influence which is exerted upon their character. Much of this is undoubtedly mischievous, but in the aggregate the influence is of incalculable benefit to society.

Where lawyers are congregated together at the capital city, they soon acquire the "esprit de corps" which either unfits them for political pursuits or, if they do take part in them, disposes them to be arbitrary in their conduct and to deal with public opinion as if it were governed by the rigid rules of their profession. British lawyers when elected to Parliament have almost always disappointed public estimation. Brougham is the only remarkable exception to the contrary of which I am aware. Even Erskine and Jeffrey appeared to be out of their element in the House of Commons, though it is clear that they were equaled by a very few of those who were conspicuous for their talents or influence.[5] The reverse is the case in the United States; eminent lawyers have always been among the most distinguished members of Congress. Such men display no lack of ability from their first entrance into the legislature. This only can be accounted for from some difference in their previous training, and I know of no other difference but this: that the position which they occupy in society necessarily forces upon them a very general acquaintance with the political history and interests of their country, and that the discipline which their minds have received from the abstract science of the law acting upon the body of information thus acquired renders their views both more comprehensive and more practical than those of most other men.

I have mentioned the majority and minority in enumerating the different classes of society. But these two grand divisions of the community not only comprehend all inferior divisions but serve to regulate their conduct and to bring the actions of all into some sort of general agreement.

5. [Henry Erskine (1746–1817), lord advocate, who had the contemporary reputation of having "never opened his mouth in the House of Commons," *Dictionary of National Biography*, XVII, 411; Francis Jeffrey (1773–1850), the critic, but also lawyer and lord advocate whose "parliamentary career was hardly a success," *Dictionary of National Biography*, XXIX, 274.]

THE French "charte" differs from the American constitution, fully
as much in the source from which its authority is derived as in
the character of the government which it undertakes to establish. It
was not the act of a popular convention. An assembly of that kind
has never been witnessed except in America. And yet the popular
will in France did manifest itself so far as to obtain some decided advantages on the side of liberty. Magna Charta was wrested from the
English kings by the barons alone. The Chamber of Deputies which
assisted in procuring the French "charte" was elected by eighty-
seven thousand citizens. The provisions, therefore, which are intended
to guard the rights of the subject are altogether more comprehensive
and systematic in the last. The character of a political constitution
will then depend upon the degree of elevation which the popular mind
has attained. In the thirteenth and fourteenth centuries, the English
commonalty had acquired little or no weight; in France at the present
day, the "tiers état" compose a body whose opinions and interests every
French statesman is compelled to consult; and in America, the middle
class has swallowed up all other distinctions in the state. The constitutions of each of these three countries at these various epochs partake
exactly of the character of society in each. In England, civilization had
made feeble advances among any class at the date of the great charter; in France, in 1830, it had made very considerable progress; in
the United States, it is more widely diffused than in any other country.

A constitution of government which has been extorted from a prince
is an important event in the history of a nation. It indicates that very
considerable changes are taking place, or have already taken place,
and it smooths the way for more important alterations in future. If
power has a tendency to increase, so also has liberty; and if the last
can succeed in advancing to a certain point, it is almost sure of mak-

ing further conquests. Thus a charter of privileges constitutes a vantage ground upon which to stand in defense of regular government. It may be the work of a week or a day, but into that short interval an immense mass of experience and wisdom may be crowded. As such an instrument will possess an openly recognized authority, it will be resolutely appealed to by the oppressed. It has been wrested from the monarch of right and is, therefore, entitled to greater respect than the power which it has displaced.

Public opinion in England had acquired so much authority in 1688 that the revolution was a bloodless one. In France, in 1830, the popular will had been so much strengthened by the deliberate and repeated concessions made to liberty that it cost little more effort than in England to effect a revolution. A constitution, therefore, however imperfect it may be as to the source from which it emanates, or the provisions it contains, is a great step in the progress of government. It shows that public opinion has acquired some appreciable weight and that it is in a fair way of becoming an important element in the constitution of society. The way is prepared for the acquisition of liberty on a still wider scale, the public mind begins to be trained after a new fashion, the thoughts of men are occupied quite as much with the interesting subject of their own rights as with the prerogatives of the king and nobility. Thus, although the English nation made a very feeble beginning, yet as they begun early they have run ahead of every other European state.

An unwritten or partially written constitution, like the English, may have this advantage. If the community is not prepared for the thorough introduction of free institutions and is yet capable by single efforts at different intervals to make considerable approaches in that direction, the form of government may be made ultimately to reach a higher standard and to acquire greater consistency, if for a time a wise and prudent forbearance is observed as to some things. To set forth "in extenso" the maxims of liberty when popular opinion was weak would be to endanger the whole undertaking. It is because liberty and power have so seldom been brought into direct conflict in Great Britain that the former has silently acquired so much influence.

On the other hand, it cannot be doubted that the establishment of a form of government which is greatly in advance of the manners may be a powerful instrument in molding society and lifting the people to a higher condition. A remarkable example of this is afforded in America where the introduction of the most enlightened institutions and laws into the western states, at the earliest possible stage, keeps the minds of men in one track and trains the whole population to the same habits and manners as prevail among the oldest members of the confederacy. It is the most striking instance I am aware of, of the immense control which the political institutions may be made to have upon the social organization.

France, like these new states, commenced the fabric of a constitution amid the light of the nineteenth century and after a struggle the most trying and momentous which any nation has undergone. It was not a time for sudden and irregular leaps. That day had passed by, the period had arrived when in order to bind together the confused elements of society an entire system of government must be adopted. The sufferings endured by the whole population during the revolution were a necessary preparative to this end. Adversity, when it is not pushed to the extent of benumbing the mind, has a wonderful effect in collecting and balancing it, and the griefs and distresses which men of all classes had endured brought about that degree of reflection which was necessary to the establishment of regular government. As the States General had been abolished nearly two centuries before, there had been no opportunity for public opinion gradually to mold the institutions into a conformity with the altered structure of society. For a legislative body not only performs the office of making laws, it fulfills another office of equal importance: it opens a communication between the government and society at large, maintains an exact equilibrium between the manners and the institutions, and carries both to a higher pitch than could possibly be the case otherwise. The throne and nobility in France had domineered so long and had acquired such formidable strength that there was no way of proving that they might be controlled but by first breaking them in pieces. On the opening of the States General in 1789, powers the most discordant were for the first time placed side by side of each other, without any fixed position in the state and therefore without any distinct recognition of their authority on the part of society. The "tiers état" had gathered strength and risen into influence before anyone was aware of its existence, so that the whole kingdom was startled from a dream when the Abbé Sieyès with a single dash of the pen proclaimed that a new power had risen up in the state. This mixture of heterogeneous elements, this encounter of so many hostile interests and pretensions, necessarily led to a bitter conflict: for where all was undefined, what individual or class could have influence sufficient to impose just and precise limitations upon the rights of all? No party could do it, for parties neither understood themselves nor each other. They were placed in collision by a train of unforeseen and uncontrollable events, and some equally imperious law of necessity must deliver them from their situation. This collision was indispensable in order to inspire a knowledge of their relative rights and wisdom sufficient to moderate their lofty pretensions. The struggle which took place disclosed clearly the existence of a great middle class in France and proved that this class must sooner or later become a coordinate power in the state. The consulate and the empire succeeded an anarchy of many years, as the protectorate of Cromwell and the arbitrary government of Charles II succeeded to the English civil wars. The absolute rule which was imposed in both instances only suspended for a while the spirit of liberty. The military triumphs of Bonaparte and Cromwell, and even the careless gaiety of Charles's court, relieved the minds of men from the tormenting anxieties which had harrassed them and gave rise to a species of good feeling before there was any union of interests. This second stage of the revolution in France contributed to balance the understandings of men; for it not only showed them the peril of both extremes into which they had run, but it closed a period of considerable duration and one eminently fraught with matter of reflection for all classes. Certain it is that the deplorable excesses into which France had fallen and the opposite calamity of absolute government prepared the way for the establishment of regulated liberty whenever the opportunity should present itself.

In 1799, the Abbé Sieyès drew up the plan of a constitution, but it failed because it was neither accommodated to the old nor to the new order of things. A grand elector as chief magistrate without any administrative functions, a legislative body without the power of debate, a conservative jury, or censorial body, sovereign and irremovable, but endowed with authority to depose all other officers, were things entirely new in the history of society. The value of the experiment consisted in its proving the worthlessness of mere theory and in disposing the minds of men to fall back upon some simpler and more practicable scheme of government.

Two apparently opposite conditions are required in a political constitution, that it should give stability to the institutions and yet render those institutions susceptible of further improvement. No government can be permanently secured against assault from without unless it is capable of being acted upon by the regular and gentle influence of public opinion. Nor is it difficult to conciliate the two ends I have pointed out since government after all must rest upon opinion of some sort or other, and the wider its influence, the more enlightened it becomes, the nearer is the approach which it makes to what we denominate public opinion and the greater the strength which is imparted to the institutions. The tendency to improvement is as much a principle of our nature as is the attachment to law and order, and the existence of a wise frame of government, like any other enlightened body of ideas, suggests new hints and causes any imperfection to be easily detected and remedied. If most constitutions have failed in giving stability to the government, it is because they have contained so little provision for giving activity to the principle of improvement. That of Great Britain, notwithstanding its imperfectly constituted House of Commons, has permitted very great freedom of opinion and has consequently contributed mightily to elevate the general standard of intelligence. The extension of the electoral franchise, therefore, in 1832, was effected without occasioning any shock to old ideas and with infinite advantage to the just authority of government. The wisest plan is always to place the institutions somewhat in advance of society, yet this is a plan from which European statesmen generally recoil as one fraught with trouble and insecurity to the community. The general population must not only attain a certain degree of intelligence, it must acquire a certain rank, a positive authority in the state, before it is deemed prudent to accord any privileges to it. Yet there is no truth more important and more obvious at the present day than that the political institutions are among the chief instruments at our command for raising the general standard of the manners. To place government upon a liberal foundation, to give to the great majority of adults some stake in the hedge, is one way of impelling men to rise above their mere animal wants and of connecting them in reality, and not merely in name, with the general weal. And if the cultivation of the popular mind is a thing of so much consequence, what can be better calculated to promote it than a system of institutions which act as a perpetual discipline and set everyone a thinking because their knowledge and their interests are then so closely connected? The free institutions of the United States, so far from being based upon a general system of education, preceded it by half a century in the middle and southern states. Those institutions for a long time atoned for the want of a system of popular instruction. The plan of education is not now as complete in some of those states as it is in several of the European monarchies. The idea seems first to have been suggested to the American mind that youth is not the only season for learning, that the whole of life is a school, and that the information which men acquire, the subjects of thought with which they become conversant after they have attained to manhood, are a more severe exercise to the mind than all that has been previously learned.

There is no maxim, therefore, more unsound and mischievous than that which teaches that the institutions of a country can never rise higher than the manners. If this maxim had been acted upon in Great Britain and France, the inhabitants of both would be in the same condition they were in, in the first century. Roman civilization and Roman institutions were planted in both countries when the people were in a half-savage state and gave the first start to Britons and Saxons, to Gauls and to Franks.

In every civilized country a large proportion of the laws is in advance of the condition of the great bulk of the population. This is the case with the body of civil law, the code which regulates private rights; nor can it well be otherwise, for although this species of laws originates with those who take the lead in public affairs, it is difficult as a general rule to adapt them to that class only. For instance, those rules which determine the title and transference of estates have an indiscriminate application to men who have small as well as to those who have large properties. But when we come to the system of political law, the case may be widely different. The reasons for holding to an equality of political rights may be equally strong, but they are not near so apparent as those which lead to an equality of private rights. Government in most communities is regarded as something totally distinct and apart from society; it is viewed as the guardian, not as the representative, of the citizens. Hence a rigorous control is exercised over political rights at the very time that the most just civil regulations are in force.

The accident of birth gives to one man the exclusive right to govern. The same circumstance determines the constitution of one branch of the legislature, and the electoral franchise and the qualifications for office are then easily disposed of by a power which is deemed to be beyond the interference or comprehension of the people. Thus those institutions which are capable of exercising the most powerful and durable influence upon society are frequently found to be the least enlightened. Very much the same code of civil law which was framed under the Roman emperors exists in the democratic republic of Louisiana. Such a code might well be administered under a form of government purely monarchical, for the prince cares little about the equality of men among themselves provided he is lifted immeasurably above them all. But in Louisiana, as in Ohio and Kentucky, free institutions as well as an enlightened code of jurisprudence were introduced at an early day, and the effect is seen in the thorough diffusion of civilization and the high standard of popular intelligence. The political laws, then, act more thoroughly upon the social organization than does a mere body of civil regulations, and the reasons are stronger why they should always be considerably in advance of the population.

The French constitution of 1799 annihilated the regal authority and the privileges of the aristocracy, and yet failed to create a popular branch of the legislature. The electoral franchise was not employed to elect any of the public officers, but simply to create a body from which the government might select; and very soon after this grotesque form of a constitution was proclaimed even that privilege was taken away.

If public opinion in some of the European states should continue to gain strength, as it has done during the last half century, it is not at all improbable that the office of king will finally give way and be superseded by systems of government which will be both wiser and stronger because they will enlist the support of a so much larger portion of the population. I can easily conceive that the day may come, and that it may not be very distant, when the superior classes will feel it to be their interest to cooperate with the rest of the citizens in the most fundamental plans of reform. Every concession which those classes have hitherto made has been for the sake of securing peace and tranquillity to themselves, and this is a feeling which increases in strength in proportion to the diffusion of popular intelligence. The king gets tired of wearing the crown when he must either consent to be a mere automaton or to be stretched upon a bed of thorns. The nobility become wearied with a perpetual struggle for the maintenance of privileges which have no longer any root in the interests or affections of the people. The expression of an eminent English statesman recently, "we must work up our institutions after a more democratic model," if uttered in the House of Commons a century ago, would have been as startling as the invocation of the "tiers état" by the Abbé Sieyès. Nevertheless, the sentiment, like many others which are never uttered above a whisper by Englishmen, is full of meaning at the present day and speaks in a way not to be mistaken to the personal interests as well as to the intelligence of the higher ranks.

France has now a house of commons as well as Great Britain, and it is chiefly upon the influence which will be exercised by it that we must rely for any great advance in popular intelligence and liberty. As soon as government makes any even tolerable provision for giving expression to the popular will, all the artificial institutions begin to be in danger. Two forces are then in existence, one of which is constantly tending to the acquisition of more authority, while the other is as constantly declining in both power and influence.

The European governments will undoubtedly experience immense difficulties in reconstructing society and in consequence of not possessing one advantage which America has. They are mostly consolidated states. The state governments of the United States perform this admirable office: they serve, if I may use the expression, as breakwaters against the authority of the central government, morseling the whole power which is wielded by the community into smaller fragments, and thus contributing essentially to the maintenance and solidity of free institutions. In one respect the condition of France is better than most of the European communities, although incomparably inferior to that of the United States. She has a regular system of departmental administration in which the people participate to a considerable extent and by which they have been disciplined to some knowledge of self-government. The notion of a confederate government, which was perpetually revolving in the minds of French statesmen during the early part of the revolution, shows the value which was set upon this species of government as auxiliary to the introduction of free institutions; but how to make the leap, any more than how to make the leap from two hundred thousand to six millions of electors, is the great, the tormenting problem. The people may in a general sense be ever so well prepared for representative government, that is, they may be educated and informed, but if the entire authority of the state is wielded by a single government, no matter whether it be republican in form, the institutions will stand upon an insecure foundation.

The territorial division of France created at one period immense obstacles to the formation of regular government. The feudal principalities which existed during the middle ages were the source of constant disorders, and their extinction and reunion with the crown were of the utmost importance to the prosperity of the nation. On the other hand, the municipal jurisdictions of departments, arrondissements, and communes which have superseded them are of the greatest advantage. They effect a distribution of power and yet do not disturb the action of the central government. This organization of the power of the state has then a shade of resemblance to the division of America into states, counties, and townships. Each department has an executive officer or governor, termed the "prefect," and he is assisted by a council composed of from three to five members who transact the details of business. In addition to this there is a general council of the department consisting of twenty-five members. But the powers of this mimic legislature are exceedingly limited when compared with those of the state legislatures of America. It has this advantage over the other council, that it is an elected body and has the privilege of choosing its president and secretary; whereas, the council of the prefect, as well as the prefect himself, are appointed by the king.

The arrondissements which are about the size of an American county are also presided [over] by an administrative officer. Attached to each is a council with powers resembling those of county commissioners in the American states. And as the general council of the department legislates concerning those interests which are common to the arrondissements comprised within it, the arrondissement besides disposing of its own local business superintends the general interests of the cantons and communes.

The government of communes is not confined as in Great Britain to city corporations, but is extended over the rural as well as the town population. This is a fine arrangement; each commune is a nucleus of civilization, a school in which as in the American townships the people are gradually initiated into the practice of self-government. And this salutary influence, thus extended equally over the whole surface of the state, may become an important means of elevating the country as well as the town population. France has the skeleton of free institutions, and it remains for time to determine whether it is possible to communicate an animating soul to this skeleton. The officers of the communes, the mayor and council, were never properly speaking a popular body until recently. During the reign of Louis XVI, government usurped the power of appointing them. Up to 1771 they were elected, but the election was not placed upon the same liberal footing as at present. The number of persons who now exercise the electoral franchise is not as large as in the incorporated towns of the United States, but it greatly exceeds the number of national electors in France, and is larger than that of any electoral body out of America. For by a "comte rendu" made by the minister of the interior in 1839, it appears that two millions eight hundred and eighty thousand one hundred and thirty-one persons voted at the communal elections, that is, more than fourteen times as many as the national electors.

Great Britain contains no local jurisdictions at all resembling those of the French departments, arrondissements, and communes. The islands of Jersey, Guernsey, and Man, with their separate parliaments, are too inconsiderable and too much detached from the body of the community to form exceptions to the remark.

A system of lesser governments, as I have had occasion repeatedly to remark, whether the government is a consolidated or confederate one, is indispensable to the thorough and orderly management of the local interests. That no inconvenience is felt for the want of them is no proof of their inutility. Mankind have a wonderful ductility in adapting themselves to circumstances. If a Frenchman had been asked in the reign of Louis XIV whether any inconvenience was experienced for want of a national legislature or of a regular system of courts, he doubtless would have answered, no, that everything was in the hands of the grand monarch who was competent to take charge of the most weighty and the most minute interests of society. The French departments are about the size of Rhode Island and Delaware; they are eighty-six in number, a territorial division which seems to have existed at a very early period. For in the ninth century France had eighty-six districts. Similar institutions have existed at one time or another in every state, but they have not answered the same end in all countries. In some they have been made completely subservient to the centralization of power, while in others they enjoy a sort of independent authority and contribute to distribute power. If the departments were fewer and their privileges more extensive, while at the same time the arrondissements and communes were retained as a part of the system, a plan of local administration would be introduced which could not fail to be advantageous. The very general taste which prevails in England for a country life, the residence of so large a number of intelligent and influential proprietors upon their estates during a considerable part of the year, compensates in a small degree for the absence of local governments. But the effect is incomplete so long as the institutions contain no provision for training the popular mind to habits of self-government.

The French Revolution which threatened to destroy everything terminated in reforming everything. No man assuredly would have made such a revolution with the uncertain chance of procuring a better state of things. But the laws which rule over human affairs are frequently placed beyond the reach or even comprehension of individuals and when lawgivers and statesmen cease to govern wisely and beneficently, a superior power interposes and overrules all the plans and enterprises of the enlightened as well as the ignorant.

Among the great benefits which the revolution has conferred upon France, we may enumerate the following. It has caused the abolition of feudal services and feudal tribunals as well as the antiquated system of corporate bodies. It has elevated the condition of the communes and other municipal bodies. It has given birth to a representative assembly, reorganized the judicial system, abolished the privileges of the clergy and nobility, diminished the personal authority of the king, separated the regal from the executive authority, diffused education, established the freedom of the press, suppressed entails and primogeniture, introduced trial by jury in criminal cases, and caused such trials to be conducted in public. It has armed the tribunal of public opinion with ten-fold authority, augmented the numbers and power of the middle class, given rise to a better organization of the departmental authorities, compelled the abolition of the conscription, and gradually inclined the minds of men to the quiet pursuits of peace. It has been the means of introducing a system of order and accountability into the administration of the finances, rendered the debates of the peers and deputies public, abolished the hereditary quality of the peerage, provided a regular and legal mode of punishing all public officers, supplanted the uncouth and heterogeneous laws and customs which existed in the provinces by an uniform and enlightened code of jurisprudence. It has, consequently, given rise to habits of reflection and imparted to all classes a more independent tone of thinking and speaking, and for the first time introduced a written constitution into an European community.

These constitute material and radical changes in the framework of society, and yet, it seems as if nothing were done, so much remains to be accomplished. A nation in this respect is like an individual. Every step in advance which the latter makes enlarges the circle of his horizon, and the progress which a people have made in reforming its condition unfolds new wants and makes all deficiencies more striking and palpable. But the more unsatisfied it is with the position it has already attained, the greater the hope for the future. When M. Guizot, one of the finest minds France has produced, made to the Chamber of Deputies the following declaration, certainly the most remarkable which has yet fallen from any European statesman, that "it was impossible not to recognize in American society, and by consequence in its influence, principles of justice, of humanity, of regard for the well being of man which have been wanting in the greater part of the communities which have been great and powerful in the world," he pronounced a sentiment which has relation to America but which was listened to with profound emotion in France and over all Europe. That a statesman high in authority in a monarchical government should give utterance to such an opinion is a sure indication that the human mind is not standing still in the old world; it reveals to us that thoughts are perpetually crossing the minds of the most elevated men in that quarter which look to something not merely as better but as practicable. The course of events with its irresistible current is bearing forward all opinions, and conquering minds which seemed least disposed to submit to its influence. In former times, it was no part of the business of an European statesman to concern himself with schemes for the improvement of society. Their interests seemed to lead in a totally different direction. The ignorance and helplessness of the great mass of the population rendered the influence of public men more conspicuous, and they felt no desire to part with an advantage which was so cheaply and so easily secured. Lord Brougham, when in the English House of Commons, was the first European statesman who devoted himself systematically and earnestly to the improvement of the condition of the people. Mr. Burke prided himself chiefly for his exertions on East India affairs, but Lord Brougham, with a mind equally comprehensive, will go down to posterity with "the plan for the education of England" in his hand.

The superior social organization of the British community above that of France has been sometimes ascribed to an inherent difference of character. But what is meant by an original difference of character? It is easy to understand its meaning when the comparison is between two races, between the white and the Ethiopian or the white and the Mongolian. But when the race is the same there must be some other way of accounting for the difference. The minds of men are formed to so great an extent by outward circumstances that the greatest diversities of character may very well grow up among the same race. Some nations, like some individuals, are not masters of those circumstances at as early a period as others. But, as soon as they are, many hidden qualities begin to develop themselves. Emigrants from among the peasantry and artisans of continental Europe are continually arriving in the United States. They have none of the quickness and ductility of mind which belong to the American character. But their descendants, after a few generations, cannot be distinguished from the original population. They are trained in a new school and are subjected to the influence of a new set of moral causes. The descendants of the English and Dutch in New York, of the Swedes and Finns in Delaware, of the English and French in South Carolina are all pretty much the same sort of people, about equally distinguished for sagacity, industry and intelligence — a memorable fact, and which should teach all European statesmen that the only effectual way of elevating the condition of the people is "to work up their institutions after a more democratic model."

The freedom of the press, the establishment of the representative assembly, the creation of even two hundred thousand electors, and the abolition of a hereditary nobility are immense achievements for civil liberty in France. The foundation is at any rate laid upon which to build all sorts of liberal institutions. A very considerable share of the political power is now deposited with the middle class, and it is easy to foresee that this class, in spite of the subdivision of the soil, will increase and acquire still greater importance. It is the first time in the history of France that any regular scheme of government, any scheme which combines liberty and power in something like due proportion, has been established, thereby affording unequivocal evidence that great changes have been wrought in the structure of society since the revolution.

In all human probability the electoral franchise will be further extended, for although two hundred thousand electors are a great boon to a country which but the other day was a military despotism, yet this number is grossly disproportioned to the substantial population. No one is entitled to vote unless he pays a tax of three hundred francs. If the qualification were lowered and the electors raised to a million, there is no reason to believe that "France would be blotted out of the map of Europe." On the contrary, there is every reason to believe that she would for the first time find her true position among the nations of the earth. Great Britain and Ireland, with a population of less by six millions, have as many as eight hundred thousand electors. France commenced with fifty thousand. The number was enlarged to one hundred thousand, then to one hundred and fifty thousand, and finally to the present amount. Experience has shown that the surest guarantee of public order is to be found in the cooperation and influence of the substantial population, and that the moment a government divorces itself from all care for the interests of the people it legalizes within its own bosom a power which will allow it no rest.

The plan of indirect suffrage, or of choosing by a body intermediate between the primary electors and the candidate for office, has been repeatedly tried in France but was finally abandoned in 1817. The principal objection to it is that it reduces the number of the last electors to so inconsiderable a number as to render them a close body instead of a popular assemblage. Hence they were denominated "electoral colleges," an appellation which grates harshly upon an American ear. An electoral body chosen directly by the people may be fit enough to make a single appointment, for public opinion will then be sure to influence the determination of the body, but an electoral college removed by one or more gradations from the people invariably degenerates into a mere clique or school of intrigue. The effect is to annul the control of the popular will and to render the chamber of representatives as irresponsible as the electors.

But the most extraordinary part of the plan was that the colleges were chosen for life, that the king nominated an officer to preside over them, and that their proceedings were conducted in secret. Vain effort to reconcile the worn-out idea of a by-gone age with the institutions which belong to an improving society. There is but one way in the nineteenth century of curing the dissensions of a civilized state and communicating order, regularity and strength to the government, and that is by giving to the people a direct and palpable interest in their institutions.

France with two hundred thousand electors has made a much nearer approach to constitutional government than when the primary electors amounted to two or three millions, but the actual choice was made by a few close bodies collected in different parts of the kingdom. All sorts of contrivances have been fallen upon for the purpose of endowing government with a certain amount of strength and of conciliating at the same time the popular will. But statesmen everywhere will be compelled to have a recourse to the very simple plan of founding government plainly and directly upon the interests of the people.

In the Roman commonwealth the plan of arranging men into classes according to their various professions and trades was at one time industriously pursued. The comitia of the centuries, the then legislative body, was organized in this manner. But to marshall the various orders of men into distinct classes and yet to make sure that one or two of these classes should decide the vote was the very way to prevent a reconciliation of the interests of all. This assembly was accordingly superseded by another legislative body, the comitia of the tribes, in which the members voted "per capita." This is the true way of preventing classes from being arrayed against each other and of giving unity and vigor to the public will. Nothing is more common in America than to find individuals of the same class or occupation enrolled in different parties. Our opinions, when they are free to express themselves, do not depend upon the callings we pursue but are modified by numberless other causes. But the moment we draw men up in classes and make this arrangement a fixed political institution in the state, we diminish the chance of uniting the interests of all. The "esprit de corps" starts up and disposes the members of different classes to look upon each other with a hostile eye. The Roman and the French commonwealths were never so prosperous as after all circumlocution in the mode of voting was abolished.

The constitution of France, in its general outlines, is modeled after the British. The chief points of difference are that in France (by the law of 1831, now incorporated into the "charte" as provided for by its sixty-eighth section) peers can only be created for life and no endowment of property can be bestowed upon them. There is also in the ordinary acceptation of the word no ecclesiastical establishment. Religion may be said to be established by law, but no one sect has a preference. The clergy of all denominations are equally provided for by the government. The life tenure of the peerage, however, throws that body into a greater dependence upon the king than is compatible with constitutional monarchy. The only remedy short of the abolition of the order is to cause those members who sit in the House of Lords to be elected by the general body of nobility instead of being placed there by the king. There is much more reason for adopting this plan in France than in Scotland and Ireland. The French nobility are exceedingly numerous, amounting to several thousands, while the nobility of Scotland and Ireland are a very small body each. Moreover, the institution would more quietly and gradually give way to a different and better organization of the upper house. The tenure for life is one step toward this end. But without the intermediate preparation I have indicated, the transition from a privileged body to a senatorial assembly would be more abrupt and violent than would be desirable.

It has been supposed that the minute division of the soil in France was unfavorable to the formation of a middle class. That such a class does exist however is certain, from the fact that there are two hundred thousand persons, the least wealthy of whom can afford to pay a tax of three hundred francs. These two hundred thousand persons with their families will give nearly a million of individuals. There are not many countries in Europe where so large a proportion of the population is placed in more independent circumstances. Something more besides primogeniture and entails is requisite to prevent the creation of small properties. In Italy where the eldest son succeeds to the estate, the division of the soil is carried further than in France, yet it is surprising how large a number of proprietors in the former can afford to lease their land even upon the metayer system of cultivation and at the same time live comfortably upon their proportion of the produce. The number of idle persons is larger in Italy than in France. The younger sons are disinherited, feel little or no incentive to exertion, and live as they can upon the pittance doled out to them by the eldest brother. Land in Italy and a great part of France can bear to be divided into smaller estates than in northern and central Europe because the productions of the soil are monopoly ones and therefore give monopoly prices. Certain it is, however, that the abolition of primogeniture and entails in France, by placing men more on an equality, has driven them to greater self-exertion. Large properties give rise to a larger surplus, but for the same reason they create a host of laborers both in the town and country. If there is no class in France so rich as the country gentlemen of England, there is none so poor as the manufacturing population of the latter country. The views with regard to both countries have been doubtless exaggerated. The subdivision of the soil in France is not so general as is represented, nor are large properties in England so universal as is sometimes supposed. A large proportion of the land which belonged to the French "noblesse" before the revolution has got back into their hands and very extensive farms are common throughout the northern part of the kingdom. The majority of the French population live in the country, the majority of the English inhabit the towns. The employments of the people and the means of subsistence which they derive from these employments may, after all, be as much divided in the one country as in the other. The location only of the poorer class in each may be different. In France this class will be found principally in the country; in England it is congregated in the towns.

Up to the time of the revolution, it was the king and nobility who were set over against each other for the purpose of maintaining the equilibrium of the government. Now it is the "tiers état" and the king. The middle class have figured greatly in all the revolutions which have occurred since the reign of blood. It was that class which was chiefly instrumental in closing the period of anarchy. It was the same class which ruled during the memorable three days of 1830 and succeeded in establishing constitutional monarchy. The "charte" of Louis XVIII was an act of mere grace; that of the present king was fairly extorted by public opinion. Indeed, when one considers that all the revolutions in Europe, in Germany and Italy as well as in France, have been accomplished chiefly by that class, it is evident that very important changes have taken place in the structure of society, that there is, in other words, a very general tendency toward depositing some part of the active power of society in an entirely new quarter. When this state of things has lasted long enough to exert a positive influence upon the manners and to persuade all public men that in order to govern securely as well as wisely, it is not enough to defer in some small degree to public opinion, but that it is necessary to enlist its active cooperation in the administration of the government, the difficulties which have hitherto obstructed the progress of enlightened institutions will be in a fair way of being overcome. For admitting that it should never be possible to carry out the plan of the American government in its full extent, so as to make the public will in its genuine signification the moving spring of government, yet unspeakable advantage will be procured to all orders of men by communicating to the middle class a political weight corresponding with the rank which it has attained in society. The unbalanced governments stand in need of some such support, of some mediatorial power, which standing between the two extremes, the highest and the lowest classes, shall control the excesses of the last and make it the interest of the first to be just to all parts of society.

CHAPTER VI | IS THE AMERICAN GOVERNMENT

A BALANCED ONE?

IF by a balanced constitution we intend one in which the principal checks to power reside within the government, the American government is not a balanced one. The materials are happily wanting with which to construct a political system of that character. There is no order of nobility, no hereditary prince, no ecclesiastical establishment. These are necessary elements in the composition of what is ordinarily understood by a balanced government. There is no commonalty as distinct from the rest of the population. The people are not divided into active and passive citizens; the electoral franchise is enjoyed by all, and the government is thoroughly elective in all its branches. The political institutions, though destined to perform different functions, have one character and conspire to one common end. As they are not the accidental growth of circumstances but have been formed with design, the power which created them continues afterward to uphold them and to regulate their movements. So that the American government, although not a balanced one in the European acceptation of the term, is so in a still higher sense. None of the departments possess a self-existing authority, none exercise an independent will of their own, for they are all controlled by a great outward force which resides in the community.

Political checks are of two kinds, those which exist in the society but are exterior to the government, and those which are inserted in the government and which for the most part compose that organized body which we denominate the political system.[1] The first is of two kinds: it may consist either in that omnipresent control which the public reason or public opinion exercises, or in the more delicate and complicated control which several governments united together in a common league

1. [For the second edition, Grimke added new matter from the start of this paragraph to the paragraph which ends, ". . . better able to control their movements," on p. 631.]

exert upon each other and upon the central authority. The second class of checks is also two-fold; they are either such as exist by virtue of a self-derived and independent authority possessed by some or all the departments of the government, or such as are created by the deliberate act of the community. The two classes may be characterized, the first as perfect and the second as imperfect checks, the reason of which will readily appear. The first represents the moral force of an entire community; the second represents the isolated strength of the bodies themselves. If the last do more than this, it is because in the societies where they exist the first species of checks acts with more or less force. This is a distinction of the utmost importance; the not making it is a source of the greatest error and confusion. For instance, if on surveying the structure of the English government in which two of the departments exist by a self-derived authority, we were to assert that the happy balance of the constitution was attributable to that circumstance, we should commit a fatal mistake. The balance of the constitution, the adjustment of the various departments to each other, is in spite of, not in consequence of, the self-existing authority which those departments possess. The public will, or public opinion, is more potent and more pervading than in any other government, ancient or modern, except the United States. That this affords the explanation is obvious, as I have observed in preceding chapters, for until public opinion had grown to be a great power in the state, England was no better and often not as well governed as many of the continental states at the present day. And the adjustment of the political departments, in other words, the balance of the constitution, has kept pace exactly with the growth of that public opinion.

I have considered the second class of checks as of two kinds: those which possess an authority independent of the community, and those which are created by the community. An hereditary monarch and hereditary nobility are examples of the first, and the various departments of political power in a representative government of the second. I have characterized both as checks of an imperfect kind, but for different reasons. The first act from an impulse within; if they borrow any authority from abroad, it is accidental and is no part of their original constitution. The second, being created by the community, do on that very account possess, and possess designedly, a still larger share of this borrowed authority. It is only because it is borrowed, that is, derived from the power which creates the first class of checks, that it is not of so high a character as these; it is the same in kind, but inferior in degree. The question, which is the best of these subordinate checks, may be viewed in two lights. Each may be best under certain conditions, that is, best relatively. But to the question, which is the best absolutely, that is, of two societies, each of which possesses the system of interior checks appropriate to it, which will be best governed? the answer must be the last. In other words, the states of continental Europe, from Naples and Portugal to the Baltic, have not been as well governed as the United States. And although we should endeavor to escape from this way of viewing the question by saying that those states have a very imperfect social organization and that the social is the parent of the political organization, yet this would be reasoning in a circle and contributes to fortify the position that I have taken. The checks which exist in those governments are comparatively feeble because there are inherent causes which prevent them from being otherwise.

Where the check consists in the exercise of a power independent of the society, it may be viewed in two lights. It will represent the body in which it resides, or it may represent the body and together with it a portion of society, more or less considerable, which do not belong to it but whose interests are similar. The last species of representation, however, will be merely virtual. France, with the exception of the interval between 1815 and 1848, Poland and Hungary, all the Italian and German kingdoms, etc., are examples of the first. Great Britain is the only fair example of the second. One and a very important cause of this difference is to be traced to the small body of nobility in the last and its disproportionate size in the former. In Great Britain, the number is about four hundred and fifty; in France, Poland, and Hungary, it was from two hundred thousand to half a million. In these three states the nobility had not only exclusive titles but they had exclusive privileges also. Their interests, therefore, were set in direct contradiction to the rest of society. In Great Britain, the privileges of the body are few and inconsiderable. The nobility there represent not only their own order, but they represent virtually the whole body of gentry and landed proprietors. They do not represent the entire landed interest, not the numerous class of farmers, for instance, because the interests of the two are not the same. At the present day the English nobility may be said also to represent virtually and to some extent the manufacturing and mercantile classes. Trade and industry which for the first time became popular after the establishment of the commonwealth has now become fashionable, and the fortunes of numbers of the nobility are now embarked, directly or indirectly, in manufactures and commerce.

When two or more bodies with rival interests are placed in opposition to each other, the design is to prevent each from pursuing a separate interest of its own. It is intended that they shall mutually control one another. The course which they will actually pursue under these circumstances, says an eminent writer (Brougham), will be a mean between the extreme wishes of each. It will be a diagonal and not in the direction of one side of a parallelogram. The illustration is a happy one and is a conclusive answer to the theory of Jeremy Bentham that all checks are ineffectual. But why will this be the result of so disposing different bodies? It must either be from a calculation of the ability of each to resist an encroachment on its rights, or from a calculation of the superior ability of that power which exists out of the government, but is ever ready to enter into it when any derangement of the system occurs. The last affords the clue to the efficacy of those checks which are inserted in the government. For it is obvious that it is impossible to construct two or more political departments whose power shall be so skillfully proportioned that each shall be a counterpoise to the other, much less to two others combined. But if a powerful check exists outside of the government, although it is habitually of a preventive character and only occasionally active, the knowledge that it may be roused at any moment will discourage all attempts of one department to invade the rights of the others. The passage of the "reform act" in 1832 and the repeal of the corn laws about sixteen years later are memorable examples of this. These are the two most important acts which have been passed by the British Parliament within the last hundred years. They both run counter to the opinions and prejudices of the nobility becuse they contributed to fortify the power of the middle class. But public opinion run with so mighty a current, the commonalty of England took so decided a stand, that a refusal to concur in their passage would have endangered the existence of the body. Indeed, the reasonings of all those who insist on the efficacy of the system of interior checks imply the exercise of a check beyond and above these. But not one has noticed it as a distinct fact; all consider the last as merely subservient to the checks within the government instead of as a distinct and independent counterpoise differing both in kind and degree from every other species of checks.

In a half civilized or in a civilized but unsettled state of society, the knowledge which individuals have that each stands ready to protect himself does not prevent insults and perpetual combats. But when society has so far advanced that a well-defined public opinion has grown up, such occurrences fall wonderfully into disuse, although the motives and occasions for them are greatly multiplied. It is precisely the same with rival bodies of men. As society advances, public offices become more lucrative and dazzling, the incentives to ambition are heightened, and the desire of encroachment is greater; but this very advancement gives birth to a public opinion whose circumference is constantly enlarging and which exerts a more and more searching influence in every part of society. There is no other way in which we can account for the irregular action of the same checks at different periods in the history of the same government: how it is that at one time they exert little or no influence, at another have even a pernicious tendency, and at a third act with precision and efficacy. What we are accustomed to call a healthful operation of these checks is nothing more or less than the omnipresent control of a power which is external to the political departments and which, for that very reason, is better able to control their movements.

In order to illustrate the different structure of the American and European governments, we will suppose two associations of individuals, each composed of one thousand persons. In one, the members are for the most part in good circumstances, possess a competent share of intelligence, and elect their own officers. In the other, a large proportion of the members are in an exceedingly dependent condition, enjoy none of the advantages of education, and are unable to form to themselves a true notion of the qualities which make up the character of a citizen. In this society, the principal officers perpetuate themselves in office and have power to appoint such other subordinate ones as they please. The machinery by which the business of these little societies is transacted may be the same, that is, the various functions and duties which the officers of both perform may be nearly alike, yet it is obvious that there will be the greatest difference imaginable in the amount of personal influence and positive authority which will be exercised in the two cases. In one, the officers will govern the members; in the other, the association will govern itself. This original difference in the constitution of the two societies will give a totally opposite direction to their future destiny. The various officers in each may occupy the same relative position to each other, but they will stand in very different relations to the members. In one, the introduction of a thorough system of responsibility will prevent encroachments upon the rights of the members; in the other, the officers will continue to check and balance each other's authority, but they will be uncontrolled by any force of sufficient authority to prevent a combination against the interests of the society.

What is true within so limited a sphere is still more true when we come to consider the large scale on which civil government is constructed. There are then such an infinity of objects to manage, the interests of society become so numerous and complicated, that the machinery by which public affairs are set in motion may be easily concealed from those who are most deeply concerned in understanding all about them.

Free institutions afford to the mind the very assistance which is desirable; they facilitate the process of analysis which it is so necessary to employ in order to have any tolerable insight into what are usually termed state matters. The exercise which the mere enjoyment of the electoral franchise gives to the mind produces that effect. Few are so little inquisitive or so much absorbed in the cares of life as not to be led to form their own notions of the character of public men, of the general tenor of public measures, and thence by an easy step to gain some acquaintance with the practical working of the government.

The great objection to the plan of checking one part of the government by another is that it is impossible to give to the various departments sufficient power to produce this effect without endowing them with so much as to enable them to rule over society, instead of society ruling over them. And although one may figure to himself the greatest licentiousness as the consequence of the opposite plan, yet this licentiousness, I imagine, will generally be found to proceed from some defect in the character and manners of the superior classes rather than from any natural proneness to insubordination on the part of the people. If we could suppose the numerous body of the French noblesse in the reign of Louis XVI to have consented to alter their character so far as to view with unmingled satisfaction the prospect of establishing a constitutional government, if we could suppose them to have lent themselves sincerely and unreservedly to the plans of the enlightened leaders of the "tiers état," the revolution would have been unnecessary. Now I do not blame men for having modes of thinking and habits of acting conformable to the system in which they and their ancestors had been nurtured. I only speak of the fact, the ease with which unheard of calamities may have been warded off and the blessings of civil liberty secured, if the influential and the high in rank had voluntarily consented to lay aside those hateful privileges which they now do so well without and which few of them would recall if they were able. The same may be said of England in the time of Charles I. And we may go further and say that if the nobility and gentry of that country, in spite of the habits in which they have been bred, could be supposed to take the same natural view of the office of civil government which is entertained in America, if we could only suppose them to lay aside the antiquated notion that the populace can only be ruled by strong government and that there can be no strong government without a prince and nobility, the transition from hereditary to elective government might be made without occasioning any shock to society. And if this view be correct the consequences to which it leads are of the utmost importance to all governments. It shows that the introduction of enlightened liberty is unembarrassed by those extreme difficulties with which it has hitherto been surrounded. The proposition is not an abstract one that if a thing is willed to be done, it will surely be done; for of all things, nothing is more dangerous than to meddle with abstract propositions when we have to deal with the actual affairs of men. But the proposition is, that if a thing is willed to be done, and if that thing is nothing more than a scheme of civil polity such as has existed quietly and securely for a great number of years in one community, and if the best faculties and the sincere desires of the influential are made to cooperate with the will to do, that the thing will not only come to pass but that it will work so far beyond expectation that all men will wonder why it should have been postponed to so late a period. And if this reasoning is correct several very important conclusions would seem to flow from it: that there is no community whatever, provided only it be entitled to the appellation of civilized, which will not admit of the infusion of a much larger amount of liberty than was supposed practicable; that there is no necessity why the transition from monarchy or aristocracy to elective government should be violent and abrupt; and that invariably it is fully as much in consequence of the want of intelligence among the superior classes as of ignorance among the lower that the most important reforms of government are ever postponed to a day when there seems to be no other alternative. I have in another place spoken of the great benefit which is procured to the cause of regular government by delaying the steps by which it is finally achieved; the advantages which are thus gained are unobserved and occasion no alarm while they add to the ability to obtain still greater. But this is only upon the supposition that to any plan of reform which was at once thorough, comprehensive, and effective, we should be unable to gain the influence and cooperation of the great body of intelligent men in the country. On the same principle, in other words, that if anyone had risen up in the reign of Elizabeth, or so late as the time of George I, and proposed the formation of religious, benevolent, and educational institutions like those now existing in Great Britain, the plan would have been derided as chimerical and as fraught with little or no value. Yet it is most certain that the spread of these associations at the present day marks one of the most memorable eras in the history of the human race. They may more than anything else contribute to falsify the notion so generally prevalent that there is a point to which the civilization and prosperity of a nation may rise after which it is necessarily doomed to decline. So that in speaking of things which are impracticable, we must distinguish between those which are rendered so in consequence of some imperious law of our nature which cannot be gotten rid of, and those which would be practicable if men would only consent to make an active use of the faculties with which they are actually endowed.

Thus, if the great body of intelligent men in Great Britain, on surveying the manifold abuses which exist in every part of the government (abuses which they never deny, except when challenged to admit them): an ecclesiastical establishment which wrings a princely support to itself from all other sects; a national debt which can never be redeemed; a prince whose vast and unnatural prerogatives conciliate public approbation either in consequence of their antiquity or of the seductive patronage which enlists a great multitude of the influential in their support; a nobility, a handful of well-educated gentlemen, yet possessing an absolute veto upon the representatives of the people; a chamber of representatives a majority of whose members are elected by less than one half of the electors, the electors themselves with qualifications unnecessarily restricted; a judicial establishment so expensive and so inadequate to the wants of the community as to shut out men of moderate property or to beggar them if they enter the halls of justice — I say, if on contemplating these things and a great multitude of others which indirectly grow out of the system (and to detail which would be to run over innumerable transactions of public and private life), the enlightened men of all England were with one accord to devote themselves to the establishment of free institutions, there would not be as much difficulty as in bringing about the revolution of 1689. The difficulty would be overcome by the simple act of making such a resolution. When we talk of the shock given to society in consequence of any material change of the government, we mean the shock occasioned to the superior classes only. The placing King, Lords, and Commons in the constitution for the purpose of balancing each other was never attended with the desired effect until very modern times. But for another circumstance they may have continued to stand side by side of each other as in the reigns of the Henrys and Stuarts, each struggling for the mastery and filling all England with disorder and misrule. It is the influence of the popular will which now maintains them within their proper spheres.

It may, indeed, be laid down as a maxim of universal application that the system of interior checks can never be relied upon where there exists no power external to the government to act upon all the departments and to maintain each in its proper place. And this necessary condition can only be attained where free institutions are established; not merely because these presuppose the existence of a power without which has authority to command, but because the parts of which government is then composed have so much simplicity, and such an intimate connection with the community without, that the influence of public opinion is both easy and certain in its operation. As government is then framed with design and deliberation, the share of authority allotted to the various departments will be adapted to the functions which they are intended to perform, and these will have a precise and immediate relation to the interests of the community. Government after it is built up will not be left to the scramble of ambitious men, for the power which created it will be in constant activity and will continue to preside over each act of the public administration. Encroachments by the executive upon the legislature or by the legislature upon the executive will no longer be viewed as an affair in which public officers are concerned; they will be regarded as invasions of the rights of the whole body of society. In the artificial forms of government, the several departments of power represent distinct and contradictory interests in the state, and not the state itself. And the idea of balancing the authority of one by that of the others is the necessary consequence of a society so organized. Not that in that form of government there are not as strong and even stronger reasons for checking them all by some other influence. But no such influence can grow to maturity where the original constitution of the departments is such as to endow them with a self-existing authority.

If the inquiry is made in what way the controlling power out of the government is made to operate in America, the answer is that in framing the institutions precautions are in the first instance taken to prevent any of the departments from obtaining an undue ascendancy. The powers of all are materially abridged. Instead of a chief magistrate clothed with immense prerogatives and an order of nobility possessing exclusive privileges, the executive is chosen for a short term and is intrusted with a very moderate authority. Instead of a chamber composed of hereditary nobles, both branches of the legislature are elected, although the principle on which the choice is made is not the same in both. All the public agents are thus made directly responsible to the people. Not only is the power which is conferred upon the government less, but the means of controlling it are greatly increased. Instead of one department being accountable to another, they are all rendered accountable to the community; and although this might seem to lead to licentiousness and to give rise to the most unbalanced government imaginable, yet in practice it is found that the greater the number of persons who are interested in the exercise of political privileges, the greater is the number who prize the advantages of regulated liberty and of public order, that so far from the laws being weak and inoperative, they command a ready and almost universal obedience.

Nor is it difficult to explain the reason why this should be so. If there were no self-interest, there could be no general interest. But if we would, we could not contrive a society better calculated to augment the number of persons who have some private interest at stake than one in which free institutions are established, none in which so great a number of persons are interested in the protection of property. But this protection can no more be obtained for private than for public rights unless the authority of the law is supreme. This notion is forced upon the observation of everyone; it is not left to be worked out as a problem in ethics, by those who have acquired a refined education. The right to property as well as all other private rights is from the earliest period of life indissolubly connected with the maintenance of the laws.

Government, then, becomes a personification of the law, and individuals no more think of rising up in rebellion against it than they do of abjuring any of the other obvious advantages of life. Exceptions there will necessarily be, but it is with general and permanent results that we have to deal, and it would seem to be almost a self-evident proposition that the greater the number of individuals who have interests to be protected and whose situation and habits enable them to appreciate the connection between those interests and the authority of the government, the greater will that authority be. Foreigners on arriving in the United States are frequently surprised to witness the even tenor with which the administration of the law is conducted in the most remote parts of the country. They learn that all the public officers are elected, and yet they see these officers exercising an authority as complete as they had ever witnessed in Europe. Whether they walk the streets of the largest cities or penetrate into the interior, they find the same system in operation, the same rigorous and impartial dispensation of justice, and after reflection they come to the natural conclusion that if the people voluntarily created the government and passed the laws, they must not only be interested in upholding them but more than all other people in the world they must be disposed to lend an active assistance in their execution.

If, then, we desire to strengthen the arm of the civil magistrate and to give to the government the greatest possible authority, what plan more likely to produce the effect than to give force and importance to the popular will? For even if the class of the disorderly increase as society grows older, the class of those who are interested in the maintenance of public order will assuredly increase still more. In the large cities of America the police are invariably more strict, more alert, more resolute in the performance of their duties than in the small towns or country districts. The officers are elected by the people, but this only adds to the weight of their authority.

Thus the American government is, in the strictest sense, a balanced one, but the principle on which this balance is adjusted is different from what it is elsewhere. The political departments are as numerous and perform duties very similar to those which are performed in other countries but, possessing no inherent and independent authority, the idea of balancing the one against the other would be futile unless a new motive power had been introduced, a power which because it resides without and not within the government both controls and strengthens the exercise of political power.

As public opinion is indispensable in order to give efficacy to this great principle, the extent of that public opinion, the number of people who contribute to form it, and who are in turn themselves affected by it, is a matter of great consequence. In some countries, so limited is the range of intelligence and information that both opinion of right and opinion of interest help to fortify instead of controlling power. If, in a country of twenty or thirty millions of people, one or two hundred thousand make up all the active citizens of the state, this affords no proof that a much larger number are not entitled to be placed upon that footing, but it indicates how very small is the force which is brought to bear upon the solid and compact machinery of the government. It also indicates that the millions who are left out in the formation of public opinion may be disposed at one time to combat on the side of power, and at another to run into the opposite extreme of licentiousness.

There is no better way of arriving at a fair estimate of the force and extent of public opinion in any country than by ascertaining the number of public journals which are circulated in it. Even though the majority of these should not be conducted with great genius and ability, it would afford no objection to this view, but rather the reverse. It is a proof that what is termed public opinion does not comprehend the highly educated merely, but that it extends to a great number of people in the descending ranks of society who, although they may not be gifted with learning or eloquence, yet have a very ready apprehension of those things which most deeply affect their interests and are capable of forming a very sensible estimate of the manner in which government is administered.

The number of newspapers and other journals published in Great Britain and Ireland is five hundred and fifty-five. On the whole of continental Europe it does not exceed twelve hundred, while in the United States they amount to nearly two thousand. Doubtless they are cheaper in the last than in any other country. Their cheapness brings them within the reach of the great mass of the population, and they are cheap because it is more profitable to supply a large number of effective demanders at a low price than a small number at a high one; and from this circumstance a very important consequence follows, that a great proportion of those classes who in other countries are mute and inanimate spectators of public events are raised to the condition of active and intelligent citizens. The circle of public opinion is wider, the principle of responsibility more stringent and efficacious, and the influence which is brought to bear upon the government is increased tenfold. Government is intended to restrain society, and yet society is intended to restrain the government, and the first species of check is not lessened but is greatly increased by enlarging the basis of popular power.

The establishment of local governments in the United States constitutes another class of checks very different from what exists in any other country. In order that the popular will may exercise an influence both salutary and effective, it is not enough that power should be divided in the first instance between the people and the government; it is necessary that it should be distributed among different jurisdictions. A consolidated government, although republican in its structure, would be an object too large for ordinary apprehension and would be removed to too great a distance to be watched and controlled by the people. The federal and state governments act as checks upon each other. They exercise distinct powers; and so do the King and Parliament, but, in the first case, these powers are enclosed within different spheres and do not act in conjunction. The force of the check, therefore, does not depend in any degree upon the interests or ambition of those who hold office, but is exerted whether they will or no. The two governments are not only confined to the management of different affairs but are placed upon different theaters, and it may be supposed that on that account this form of government does not very readily afford a notion of what is understood by a system of checks, nor does it indeed in the ordinary acceptation of the term. But it is for that very reason more deserving of attention. Those who wield the political authority of these different communities are not brought into immediate contact, so that the will of one may directly control that of the others. But it will be admitted that if the original constitution of Lords and Commons were such that neither could well move out of the position assigned to it, the check would be much more complete than it could otherwise be. It would be so because so much was made to depend upon the structure of the institutions themselves and so little upon the personal views and ambition of individuals. A check does not lose that character because it is more comprehensive in its operation, but is the more entitled to the appellation on that account. The constitution of King, Lords and Commons approaches much more nearly the idea of a system of checks and balances since the revolution and the various ordinances which followed it than in the reign of Henry VII or Charles I. The same is true of France. The king, the legislature, and the judiciary, since the constitutional "charte" of 1830, are infinitely better restrained than in the reign of Louis XIII, for so feeble was the control upon the royal power at this last period that a single decree was enough to abolish the legislative body.

The establishment of the local jurisdictions of America, then, gives efficacy to the influence of public opinion. The men of Ohio would have a world of business to attend to if they were called to watch the management of affairs in every other part of the country. But it is no very difficult matter for them to give an eye to everything which is transacted within their own borders, nor for the men of the twenty nine other states to do the same. The confining the domestic interests of these communities within a comparatively narrow sphere not only renders those interests more readily appreciable, but it gives a fairer opportunity to become acquainted with the working of the central government also since its powers are rendered both fewer and more simple than would otherwise be the case. In other words, the force of public opinion which is brought to bear upon the central government is increased in the same proportion as that which acts upon the state governments.

Not only is this the case, but the authority which these various governments exercise over the population is more full and extensive also. If the influence of public opinion is brought nearer to the government and therefore falls upon it with more weight, for the same reason the authority of government is brought nearer to every part of the population and therefore exerts a more constant and palpable influence upon it. Thus the American government is truly a balanced one, but the system is "sui generis." The checks are not only more numerous, more widespread than in any other community, the power out of the government is not only as great as it can consistently be made, but it is so distributed as to create a countervailing power on the part of the government which renders the institutions both freer and stronger.

CHAPTER VII | THE INFLUENCE

OF AMERICA UPON EUROPE

A TRAIN of accidental causes no doubt assisted in the establishment of free institutions in America. But now that they have grown to maturity, their influence is in no way dependent upon circumstances. The thinly-peopled country of which the first emigrants took possession, its seclusion from the disturbing influence of foreign politics, presented the golden opportunity. But when this novel experiment had succeeded, its power of reacting upon other communities was, like any other system of conduct, dependent upon the ordinary principles of human nature. The minds of men became more interested in the inquiry, what these institutions gave promise of, than how they came to be put together. It is like the case of an individual in whom a happy train of incidents has awakened great powers; once these are matured, his influence, whether for good or for evil, is independent of fortuitous circumstances.

The influence of one nation upon the manners and institutions of another is no new fact in the history of society, but the way in which this influence operates is different from what it formerly was. Conquest, the incorporation of one people into another, the exercise of authority in some form or other were the chief instruments in establishing this influence. America is the first instance in which the institutions of one country have been permitted to spread their influence abroad without the intervention of any force — without even the desire to employ any. It is consequently the first instance in which a deep and general impression has been made upon the manners and habits of thinking of other communities. In order that one people should exert a decided influence of this kind, there must be some point of approach, some easy way of opening a communication between the two. The wide commercial intercourse which subsists between the United States and Europe affords in part this necessary condition. That species of communication is the most constant and the most general which can well take place. It engages a greater number of persons and, what is of more importance, it brings the American people into a close correspondence with that part of the European population, the middle class, upon whom the strongest and the most lasting impression is likely to be made. It is because the United States is almost exclusively composed of this class that its commerce has attained such an unexampled growth. The country presents a greater number of effectual demanders for commodities than any other. But commerce cannot well advance the prosperity and social condition of one nation without communicating some portion of these benefits to others. It will improve the condition and rouse the faculties of all who partake in that commerce. The influence abroad of the Grecian and Roman commonwealths was next to nothing because their commerce was so exceedingly limited. Commerce multiplies the numbers of the middle class and creates a community of feelings and opinions between different people, how widely soever they may be separated from each other. My first proposition then is, that American commerce has assisted, directly or indirectly, in promoting the growth of the middle class in more than one country in Europe.

Here, a question very naturally presents itself: why should American institutions exert a more marked influence upon Europe, than European institutions exert upon America? The answer has already been hinted at. Under any [of] the most tolerably favorable circumstances, the tendency of most communities is one of progress rather than of retrogradation. Circumstances of one kind or other, foreign conquest or long-continued civil commotions, may check this tendency for a time, but it is sure to reappear and to become the rule not the exception in the history of a nation's life. But if the middle class constitute the great bulk of the population in the United States, and if this class, in consequence of its favorable position, is enabled to make rapid and substantial advances in everything which concerns individual and social well being, its influence or the influence of the community it represents will be proportionally great abroad. It will be so not merely in consequence of the numbers who go to make up this influence, but because of the number upon whom it is fitted to act.

Now, the form of government established in the United States (one peculiarly adapted to a country in which the middle class predominate) is the most striking event of the age. It excites the inquisitiveness of all classes in other countries, of the common people because such a scheme promises to lift them higher in the scale, and of the speculative because having worked so well in practice the doubts which have troubled them so much are in a great measure resolved. There are symptoms, not to be mistaken, that this new system is exercising the minds of the thoughtful and enlightened in every part of Europe more than at any preceding period.

Free institutions contribute to produce uniformity in the manners and laws, and this again contributes to produce a more uniform civilization. But the unequal civilization of different parts of the same country is the most fruitful source of all the disorders to which society is liable. A system, therefore, which is calculated to repress licentiousness in one part and too much power in another is no longer regarded as a startling theory. Sober and discreet individuals everywhere put to themselves the question whether the time is not coming when there will be no other alternative than such institutions or a frightful conflict between liberty and power, and whether it would not be the part of true wisdom to ward off by forestalling the evil day?

Morality, knowledge, the prevalence of good manners denote what we term civilization; and as these are all set in motion by freedom of thought, the more widely freedom of thought is diffused, the more powerful will be the impulse given to civilization. A community which exhibits cultivation and refinement only in the higher ranks can exert no sensible influence upon the mass of the population in another country, but when a people are lifted so high as to be within reach of the superior classes, and yet not so high as to be alienated from the inferior, a door of communication is opened with both. And this explains more precisely the reason why America is destined to exert a more marked influence upon European institutions than it is possible for Europe to exert upon American institutions.

What, then, it may be inquired, is to be the ultimate effect? Are the European states destined to be republicanized? That is not a necessary consequence. The existing governments may be greatly improved without possessing the perfection or, we may say, without having the precise character which the American constitutions have. It may be admitted that it will be difficult to arrest the progress of free inquiry if, after liberty has gained any great advantage, the authority of government is found to be firmer and yet the people are rendered happier. Wild license may be checked, perhaps totally suppressed, but it is not easy to set bounds to any general movement of the human mind. As soon as in any European state the middle class have become the influential one, and this is, perhaps, already the case in more than one or two, it indicates that the tribunal of public opinion is fairly erected there, and this is very nearly the same as to say that such a state is ripe for free institutions, although these may not in every instance be modeled after the same plan.

Difference of languages among different nations has hitherto created great impediments to the exercise of any general influence of one upon another. Governments have acted upon each other, but the people have found no channel of communication. Thus different languages have contributed to form and to perpetuate dissimilar manners and institutions, and these in their turn have caused the people of different countries to look upon each other as belonging to different races. A taste and a capacity for free institutions places all more nearly upon one common ground, creates a sort of universal language intelligible to all, and brushes away those distinctions which had drawn a line of separation between them.

The construction of a system of government like the American, one which is thoroughly representative in all its parts, may not be exactly entitled to the appellation of a discovery, but it approaches so nearly to the character of one as to render the dispute little more than verbal. The new application of a great principle may be quite as important and display as much fertility of invention as the discovery of the principle itself; or rather, the discovery cannot be said to be complete and perfect as long as any material application of it remains to be found out. Until then it is the subject of conjecture, but not an item of knowledge, no more than it is one of experience.

We see a plain illustration of this in all those sciences which have reference to the physical world. Great laws of the human understanding may be discovered, and the discovery necessarily terminate there. But a principle in mechanics, in chemistry, *etc.*, may be almost null until it is applied. Until then it may be thought over, but cannot be said to be fairly grasped. Newton transferred the principle of gravitation from the terrestrial to the celestial world, and the application is justly regarded in the light of a discovery. Very frequently the problem presented is not, does a certain agent exist? for that may be a matter of general notoriety, but whether an untried and therefore unknown application of it is practicable. The finding out this application is a real discovery, more or less important in proportion to the importance of the application. Almost all the discoveries in physical science present us with the application of some previous knowledge. To deny on that account that they were discoveries would be to erase from the history of the mind the entire list of discoveries to which it lays claim. Fulton made discovery of the application of steam. It was this application which substituted a principle in the place of a mere fact.

Prior to the existence of the American government, the plan of representation had been applied, however imperfectly, to one political department but never to all in the same government. The Americans transferred the principle to the entire system of government as Newton transferred the principle of gravity to the whole material universe. And as in chemistry, the mixture of two substances will often produce a third, differing in all its qualities from either of the others, so a new combination of two political elements may produce a result different from any before witnessed.

If we admit that the American government is a valuable scheme, then the two great problems which it has solved are: first, the practicability of conferring the electoral franchise upon the great body of the people; and secondly, of making all the political departments elective. And if this scheme is not entitled to the name of a discovery, it comes so near to one, as I before remarked, that the dispute is little more than one of words. For what questions are there in political philosophy which press with so much weight upon the minds of all thinking men in Europe as the very two to which I have referred? What other questions are there which by them are still considered as debatable and unsettled? One has no right to quarrel with those who are disposed to view these questions in that light, but once admitted that they are settled, although it should be for America alone, and the system is assuredly raised to the rank of a discovery.

The introduction of written constitutions into some of the European states is the first instance I shall notice where the influence of American institutions abroad is clearly visible. France, Belgium, Holland, as well as some of the German and Italian states, have resorted to this species of fundamental ordinance by which to balance and regulate their governments. Prior to the formation of the American constitutions there was not a single example to be found. A written constitution, however imperfect, will never be a change for the worse and can hardly fail to be one for the better. But it is very doubtful whether, if some powerful influence from abroad had not occurred to furnish hints to the thoughtful, a single European state would at this day be in possession of such an instrument.

As a happy suggestion, concurring with favorable circumstances or bending circumstances its own way, has frequently had power to change the fortunes and alter the destiny of an individual, the striking example of a wise and yet novel system of government in one community rouses great multitudes of people in others to new views and may give an entirely new direction to their future career.

It is a fine observation of John Taylor, of Caroline,* that constitutions or political laws are intended to restrain governments as civil laws are intended to restrain individuals. It is because the former are so efficacious in producing the effect intended that the public men of Europe made so much resistance to their introduction. They apprehended that whatever power was subtracted from the government would constitute an addition to the ill-regulated power of the masses, and that full vent would be given to the worst passions and the most unbridled licentiousness. But this is a great mistake, for a constitution, as I have before remarked, acts as a double restraint; it is a restraint upon the people to fully as great an extent as it is upon the government. And what may appear still more surprising, it is more stringent, more efficacious in its operation in both respects when it is ordained by the people than when it is a grant from the ruling authority.

Until the formation of a written constitution the great majority of mankind make no distinction between the will of the government and the will of the community. The two are considered identical. What the former commands is deemed to be lawful and what it forbids to be unlawful. Thus, although there is a well defined rule for the observance of the people, there is no law by which we can arraign the government. Hence the maxim, "the king can do no wrong," a maxim which, although professing to be applied to one person, yet cannot well subsist without rendering all public men less amenable to public opinion than they would otherwise be.

Government in many communities bears a close resemblance to the ecclesiastical system of antiquity. A thorough separation was effected

* *Tyranny Unmasked*, p. 255. [*Tyranny Unmasked* (1822) was a pamphlet and an attack on the protective tariff which would render government independent of the people for support and, so, tyrannous because there would be no effective check against it.]

between religion and morality. That a dogma was incredible, that it shocked human belief and ran counter to all the precepts of virtue, only served to recommend it. The highest notions were formed of the priesthood when it could make things the most incongruous stand together. In the same way, dogmas in government which contradict the common sense of mankind acquire a hold upon the mind because there is no rival authority to dispute their rectitude.

America has also exerted an influence upon the structure of the legislative authority in Europe. When the American constitutions were established, Great Britain was the only state in which there was even the semblance of a representative chamber. The plan upon which the legislative body in Europe was originally formed was that of representation of estates, not of persons. This at one period was the case in England, and in Scotland it continued to be so until the union. The same system is still preserved in the Swedish monarchy. This plan invariably denotes a rude and uncultivated society. For independently of the very imperfect manner in which these estates are represented, such a scheme of government exhibits the community as divided into distinct tribes or clans rather than as composing one aggregate community. Hence a legislative body which represents citizens, not classes or orders, is one of the finest expedients for correcting the numberless discrepancies in the manners, customs, and modes of thinking of different sections of society. The creation of the French House of Deputies has assisted greatly in bringing about this result in that country as much as the formation of its celebrated civil code. Both conspire to the same end. The one establishes a uniform rule for the government of men in their civil relations, the other renders them one people as regards their political interests.

The plan of popular representation is still very imperfect in all the European states. But that a great impulse has been communicated to the public mind in that quarter, and that this dates from the establishment of free institutions in America and has kept pace with them are undoubted facts and the very ones I am intent upon showing.

As soon as the antiquated system of a representation of estates in one chamber of the legislative body begins to give way, a very important step is taken toward discarding it altogether. A chamber of nobles may exist for a considerable period afterward, but in several of the European kingdoms a hereditary peerage has been abolished, and this is a second and very decisive step toward a thorough reorganization of the legislative authority. A house of lords is a remnant of the old scheme of dividing men into classes. In order ever to get rid of it, it is important in the first instance to do away with the hereditary principle. This shakes the institution without producing any convulsion. It deprives the nobility of a large share of the prestige which before surrounded them, and by weakening the hold which they had obtained upon the imagination of the people renders it easier to reconstruct the whole institution. By going thus far, say European legislators, we follow the example of Solon who gave the people not the best laws, but the best which they are at present capable of bearing.

Senate is a term the meaning of which had been almost lost from the political world until it was revived in the United States. Several of the European states, copying after America, now designate the upper house of the legislative body by the name of senate. There is "power in words," and however short these bodies may fall of the American Senate, the change of name is an index of a very material revolution in the state of public opinion. National Assembly, the name given to the French legislature in 1789 in the place of that of "general estates," was no further important than as it indicated which way the strong current of public opinion was running and served as a rallying sign to gather the friends of liberty together. But this was importance enough. It foreshadowed the rise of the present House of Deputies.

How long the British community will deem it expedient to retain the House of Lords we can form no conjecture. The spread of popular intelligence contributes to weaken its authority and, yet, this very diminution of authority assists for a time in fortifying the institution. How long the opposite working of one and the same principle will last, we are unable to predict. Popular intelligence, carried to a certain point, acquires the double character of a conservative as well as of an innovating agent. It is where the disorders of society become so frightful as to baffle all efforts to reform that it assumes the last character exclusively. The immense influence which public opinion has acquired in the present century puts both king and nobility very much upon their good behavior. So far from committing outrages upon the popular will, they become more and more disposed to fall in with, nay, even to succumb to it. The abolition of the institution of a hereditary chamber is thus indefinitely postponed because the practical working of the system is such as to refer nearly all the legislative power to the House of Commons.

But so many causes are in operation to elevate the popular mind and to cause public opinion to be the representative of the middle class, and not as formerly of the nobility and gentry, that the same revolution which banished the Gothic system of a representation of estates in one chamber is silently undermining it in the other. If the House of Peers were to stretch its authority so far as the theory of the constitution supposes, it would be in immediate danger. The history of the events which attended the passage of the reform act goes very far to show this. Chartism has been silenced, but it is difficult to conceive how there can have been so decisive a manifestation of opinion as that association indicated unless there had been some general movement in other parts of society. Chartism, no more than the House of Lords, can be triumphant, because the triumph of an extreme opinion would involve the demolition of all others, when the use of opposing opinions is to limit and correct one another. But we may with propriety assert that the opinions of that body of men were powerfully instrumental in rousing the legislature to enter upon the task of reform, and that these occurrences afford very strong evidence that the notion of free institutions has taken deep hold of the public mind.

Municipal reform is another department of legislation in which America has exercised an influence upon Europe. Until a recent period the government of the towns in Great Britain, especially in Scotland, was wielded by a close aristocracy. In the latter, the town councils were self-existing bodies and supplied all vacancies in their own number. In England and Wales the government of the towns was not so thoroughly defective, but there were faults enough to call for the most speedy and extensive reform. The commissioners who were appointed in 1833 to inquire into the state of the municipal corporations of England and Wales conclude their very able report by declaring that these bodies "neither possessed nor deserved the confidence of his majesty's subjects, and that a thorough reform must be effected in them before they become what they ought to be, and might become useful and efficient instruments of local government." The act of 1835 carried out the views of this remarkable paper, and the system of municipal government throughout Great Britain for the first time resembles very nearly that which has constantly existed in the United States. Amid the agitation of the human mind in the nineteenth century, amid the bold and independent spirit of inquiry which has seized all classes and is bent upon sifting every question of political right, the composition of the most inconsiderable local jurisdictions becomes a matter of the gravest importance.

In France similar alterations have been made in the structure of the communes. Two years prior to the revocation of the Edict of Nantes, their privileges were greatly curtailed. But a portion of the inhabitants still participated in the choice of some of the officers. At present, as I have already had occasion to notice, the communal electors in all France amount to nearly three millions. Men are first taught to manage their private affairs because they are the first which are brought close to their view. The intimate relation which exists between the inhabitants of a commune resembles the association of a family, and the transition is easy from the management of their private business to that of the corporation. When they are fairly initiated in this they begin to look beyond and discover that the prosperity of these local jurisdictions is linked in numberless ways with the prosperity of the whole state. The knowledge which they acquire by exercising their minds upon a new theater, so far from interfering with their private pursuits, renders them more skillful and more prudent in the conduct of their public affairs. The observation of this fact as forming a striking feature in American institutions and manners has caused those institutions to exert a wide and extensive influence upon European society.

The spirit of reform has penetrated even the Austrian government. An edict has been proclaimed this year (1846) which abolishes all guilds, corporations, or jurauda of trades and professions, leaving everyone to follow whatever business he chooses. Butchers, bakers, and keepers of public houses are alone excepted. These guilds, corporations, and jurauda are so entirely unknown in America that the inhabitants of that country have great difficulty in even understanding the import of the terms.

There are some institutions which appear to be of secondary importance, but which on a close examination and viewed as parts of an extensive system are found to be of primary value. The plan adopted in the United States for collecting the votes at all popular elections is an example. The minute division of the electoral districts which are established for that express purpose elude our attention in consequence of their extreme familiarity. Yet it is this very circumstance which renders the plan valuable. If we say that a mere regard to convenience was sufficient to have suggested the idea, the question still recurs: whose convenience is consulted? And as the answer is that it is the convenience of the electors, that is, of the people, which is sought to be promoted, the whole plan is indicative of the elevated position which the popular body in America occupy. Behind a rule which appears to be one of mere detail, we find concealed a principle of the highest magnitude.

In the United States the votes for a member of Congress are sometimes given at sixty or seventy places in the district. In those states where townships exist, the votes are collected in them; in those where there is no such territorial division, they are collected in parishes; and in those where there are neither townships nor parishes, artificial districts are created under the name of "precincts." This is a great convenience to the country population, and this regard for the convenience of individuals is attended with immense public benefit. The presence at the polls of the substantial class of citizens is insured. The industrious, the orderly, the reflecting are punctual in their attendance. Little time is consumed in going to and from the polls, and the private business of no one is interrupted. The assembling of a great multitude at one spot would lead to infinite confusion, to riots, intoxication, and every species of disorder. It is a remarkable trait in the human character that when people are abroad and collected in considerable numbers they not only feel themselves licensed, but they even feel under a sort of obligation to take liberties which they would not dream of at home. Until very recently some English statesmen were accustomed to congratulate themselves on the advantages of this plan. Writers of the liberal party insisted that the periodical bursts of popular feeling which took place at the hustings were indispensable to keep alive the spirit of liberty and to countervail the influence of the king and aristocracy. Popular opinion, it was said, wore an air of more authority in consequence of these tumultuous assemblages. There is great force in this view, but it is doubtful whether the plan was not attended with some disadvantages so great as even to counterbalance all the good which might be expected from it. It is doubtful whether great numbers of well-disposed persons, those who were sincerely desirous of tempering the authority of the government by an admixture of more of the popular element, were not driven to take refuge in that very authority from the greater evils which impended in another quarter. The effect was to fortify the influence of the crown and aristocracy rather than to introduce those staid and orderly habits which fit men for self government. At any rate, I observe that the party which magnified so much the advantage of collecting the whole votes of a county at a single spot have abandoned it and adopted the American plan. In conformity with a provision contained in the reform act of 1832, the counties are divided into a number of smaller districts or precincts in which the votes are taken. There is another advantage attending this plan: the polls are not kept open for six or eight weeks as formerly. In analogy to the American laws on the same subject, they are kept open two days in the counties, and but one in the cities. The course of legislation in France has followed the same direction. The elections, instead of being holden at the chief town of the department, are held separately in the arrondissements. Thus the polls are opened at four hundred and fifty-nine, instead of at eighty-six places only. This number, however, is below that which exists in many of the American states taken singly. In Ohio it is more than double. For every arrangement of detail in matters of this kind is an indication of something important lying at the bottom. Ohio has three hundred thousand electors and all France has only two hundred thousand.

In another respect the French legislature have likened the electoral system to that of the United States. There is no distinction, as in Great Britain, between members from counties and from cities. The representation is proportioned to the amount of the population, not its locality. If a city is large enough to send one or more deputies, the elections are held for it exclusively as in the United States, but not because it is a city. The consequence is that a majority of the deputies cannot, as in Great Britain, be returned by a minority of the electors. The separate representation of boroughs and counties is another relic of the antiquated system of representation by estates. The members do not compose different bodies as formerly; the veto is transferred from the estates to the electors who choose.

A national bank was established in the United States in the year 1790. It continued to exist, with the exception of a short interval, until 1835. The most striking and original feature in the plan consisted in the organization of branches in all the chief cities. But it is remarkable that at the very time Congress were engaged in deliberating upon the law which terminated the existence of the institution, the British Par-

liament were busily employed in modeling the Bank of England upon
the same plan. The act of 1833 which renewed the charter authorized
the establishment of branches in various parts of the kingdom. And it
cannot be doubted that if it be wise to create an institution of this kind
the advantages of which it is capable should be diffused over the whole
country. It is but the application of the great principle of distributing
power and privileges. The operation of this principle is witnessed in
all the political institutions of the United States. It is equally displayed in all those institutions which are of a mixed character or which
are semipolitical and semicivil. There are two ways of distributing
power; one is by rendering all the associations who exercise it independent of one another; the other, by creating a single institution
and causing its benefits to be spread over as large a population as possible. The first plan guards as well as humanly speaking can be done
against the condensation of power. But the second may have a totally
different effect from the one intended. And where this is the case it is
plainly anti-republican. It is true the more an institution scatters its
agents, the more it is exposed to the scrutiny of the public eye. This
acts as a check upon it. But the check may be insufficient notwithstanding; the tendency to centralization where all the officers are parts
of one and the same corporation may still be too strong. A national
bank was an experiment in America and the plan of creating branches
was a fine idea. It is no wonder, therefore, that it was first seized by
France and afterward by Great Britain. One design of the institution
in America was to act as a check upon the over-issues of the local
banks. But in order to compass this end, it would be necessary at the
present day that it should wield an enormous capital. And this leads
to the inquiry whether it is ever wise to endow an institution, half
civil and half political, with so great an influence; or, as a corporation
of this character must necessarily be conducted by beings of similar
capacities and passions with those who preside over the local institutions, whether it would be prudent to risk all at one stake instead
of diminishing the chances of a great loss by the multiplication of
banks.

The bank of the United States was on the eve of bankruptcy in 1819.
In 1835 it became totally bankrupt. The refusal of Congress to re-
charter it may have this good effect. It may compel the state governments to adopt some effectual plan for preventing the disorders of
their own currency. So long as a national bank was looked to as the

great regulator of state issues, it did not occur to anyone that it was possible to place the local institutions upon any other than the precarious foundation on which they had previously stood. But it is plain that if it is possible to secure the fidelity of the first, it must be equally so to secure that of the last. Thus the disuse of a national bank may now have the same effect which its establishment was originally intended to have. One design was to make it act as a check upon the issues of other banks, but these have multiplied to such an extent as to render the check totally insufficient; while at the same time the multiplication of local banks is an indication that these have become institutions of the people and not of a separate moneyed interest, and we have the same security that they will be governed by the same wholesome laws which pervade every other part of society. I do not know that any device will be completely effectual to guard against their misconduct and to prevent the fatal revulsions to which the community is exposed. And yet they are so thoroughly incorporated into the habits of the American people that it would be a herculean task to abolish them. We cannot do with them, yet we cannot do without them. The bank of England stopped payment from 1797 to 1817. Notwithstanding the control which it exercised over the provincial banks was more complete than that possessed by the bank of the United States over the state banks, yet in 1825 more than seventy banks out of London were crushed by the temporary pressure of that year. And 1814, 1815, and 1816 (says a distinguished writer*), "a greater destruction of bank paper took place than had ever previously been known, except perhaps at the breaking up of the Mississippi scheme in France." [1] The notion that banks have contributed materially to further the prosperity of the country has had great influence

---

* M'Culloch. *Statistical View of Great Britain*, vol. 2, p. 29. [John Ramsay McCulloch (1789–1864), statistician and political economist, *A Statistical Account of the British Empire*; it was first published in London in 1837 in eight volumes, but Grimke used the two-volume London edition of 1839.]

1. [The "Mississippi scheme" was the enterprise of John Law (1671–1729), born in Edinburgh, controller-general of French finance (1720). Having established a useful and successful bank in France, Law prevailed upon the Duke of Orleans, then regent, to make over to him and his associates the entire territory of Louisiana (August, 1717). Because the territory was drained by the Mississippi River, Law's company received its popular name. Ultimately, the whole of the non-European trade of France as well as the royal mint fell into the hands of Law's company and it became practically the sole creditor of the state. Shares in Law's system reached a speculative high in 1720 when a radical devaluation of the value of bank notes precipitated a panic and the crash of Law's financial empire.]

in reconciling the American people to them. Everyone feels as if they were somehow or other connected with that prosperity. And this is undoubtedly the case. But it may be that they stand in the relation of effect and not of cause. The Americans do not believe that they have explored and mastered every department of political knowledge, but they do believe that the circumstances in which they are placed have permitted them to make more constant and earnest endeavors to do so than it has fallen to the lot of any other people to be able to make.

The amelioration of the criminal code is one of the most decisive marks that I know of, of the general progress of society. It is an indication of a high state of civilization, in contradistinction to a merely high state of refinement. In no country have so great efforts been made in this department of legislation as in the United States. And these have had a very perceptible influence upon the European states. It has been said with great force that the humane treatment of animals can in no sense be regarded as a duty toward them, for duty imports a relation to intelligent and conscientious beings; but it is most clearly a duty toward ourselves and other men. Every species of brutality, toward whomsoever it may be exercised, adds strength to the lower part of our nature which stands in need of checks instead of provocatives to its exercise. And when such treatment is exhibited toward criminals and is sanctioned by the laws the fountain of morality is poisoned at its source; the whole community is involved in a species of guilt. The desire of witnessing exhibitions of cruelty and suffering we should characterize as unnatural, as a deformity in the human character, if it were not so general. But no matter what it proceeds from, whether from an instinctive curiosity to know everything which affects our common nature or, as is most probably the case, from a desire to hide and to suffocate our own infirmities and vices, it invariably terminates in corrupting the whole of society. On this account, the amelioration of the criminal code of a country has a much more extensive bearing than at first appears. Even if it were attended with no absolute diminution of crime and had but little influence upon the band of criminals, it contributes mightily to purify the moral atmosphere of society and to make other men more humane and more virtuous than they would otherwise be.

The system of penitentiary discipline in the American states has almost entirely superseded capital punishments, the pillory, branding, etc., and it has commanded an unusual share of attention from the public men of Europe. Commissioners from England, France, and Prussia visited the country in order to become thoroughly acquainted with it and to make reports to their own governments. The eastern penitentiary at Philadelphia, the most remarkable institution of the kind then existing, attracted their notice in a particular degree. I believe all of these commissioners concurred in the opinion that the plan adopted there answers all the ends of punishment better than any other which has been fallen upon. In England it was immediately carried into effect. The secretary for the home department to whom this interest is confided issued a circular in 1837 directing all the prisons of the kingdom to be placed upon that footing. I have no exact information as to the course which has been pursued in France and Prussia. It is exceedingly important that the efficacy of the plan of entire seclusion which is adopted in the Pennsylvania penitentiaries should be thoroughly tested; it has not been introduced in the other states and the public mind is in great hesitation as to its propriety. The experience of the English public will, therefore, contribute greatly to settle this difficult and interesting question.

When Dr. Rush and other eminent men in Pennsylvania ventured the opinion that cruel punishments increased instead of lessening the number of crimes, people were exceedingly slow in comprehending how this could be the case.[2] And yet no experiment which has been made upon human nature has been more decisive than the substitution of mild in the place of severe punishments. The ferocity which used to be practiced toward criminals roused their ferocity the more; they were converted into a band of soldiers who believed that they were of right called upon to make war upon the unnatural institutions of society.

In England criminals were executed by thousands where they now are by dozens. Romilly and Mackintosh, as illustrious for their virtues as for their intelligence, commenced the work of reform. No great alterations were made for some time, but a powerful impulse was given to the public mind and that was enough to insure ultimate success. Sir Robert Peel threw the whole weight of his influence into the scale; he procured the abolition of capital punishment in a great number of instances. For more than a century prior to 1827, every species

2. [Benjamin Rush (1745?–1813), American physician, signer of the Declaration, active in many reform movements, including penal reform.]

of forgery had been punished with death. The various statutes on this subject have been one by one repealed. In the first year of the present queen, the last hand was put to the work by abolishing the punishment in the only two remaining cases. In the three years ending with 1836, no execution for any offense took place in London. But not only has the number of executions diminished greatly but, what is of much more importance, the commitments for offenses which were once punished capitally have also decreased.

It was, I think, in the year 1836, also, that the American custom of permitting counsel to all accused persons was for the first time introduced into England. The reader is familiar with the anecdote told of Shaftesbury. This statesman had a powerful understanding, but as a speaker he was awkward and hesitating. While speaking on this question he became embarrassed and was thrown off his guard by some trifling circumstance, but recovering himself he appealed strongly to the good sense of the House, demanding what must be the condition of the prisoner, forsaken by everyone and yet perhaps innocent, when he who stood up as a member of the most illustrious assembly in the world was so easily abashed and confused.

The bill, however, did not pass. The plan seemed to be unworthy of attention at a time when it was the common sentiment that accused persons did not stand within the pale of humanity. It is only ten years ago that Lord Lyndhurst succeeded in procuring the passage of a bill which permits counsel to prisoners in felonies as well as in treason.[3] The French government had preceded the English in the work of reform. The emperor Napoleon was so much struck with the reasonableness and humanity of the American law that he caused a similar provision to be inserted in the criminal code. It had been said in England that the judge was the prisoner's counsel, a saying which comports little with our knowledge of the human heart. A judge would not be very apt to err in summing up the testimony, and yet I recollect a trial which took place a few years before the late act of Parliament when a prisoner, arraigned for a capital offense, corrected the judge who delivered the charge upon a matter of fact, on which the whole issue depended.

3. [John Singleton Copley, Lord Lyndhurst (1772–1863), son of the American painter and lord chancellor. In 1836, "he was the means of carrying the valuable bill for authorising the defence by counsel of prisoners in criminal trials." *Dictionary of National Biography*, XII, 186–187.]

It is very common in the United States to hear the remark, "all our jurisprudence has been borrowed from England." But I am persuaded that if anyone would be at the pains to examine the codes of the several states he would find that the diversities between the English and American law were both striking and numerous. The alterations which have been made at any one time are perhaps inconsiderable, but when we sum up the whole, the aggregate is very imposing. I am not sure but what the differences are as great as between the common and the civil law. Roman law was the "substratum" of English law. It could not be otherwise, for the Saxons who settled in Britain were among the most barbarous of the European tribes, while on the other hand the Romans were a highly civilized people and their institutions of every kind had existed uninterruptedly for four centuries. But the Roman law was modified by the new customs and altered condition of society which grew up gradually after England became an independent state. A similar revolution has taken place in American jurisprudence. Very great changes have been wrought directly by the operation of the political institutions, and a still greater number indirectly by the manners and by the habits of business consequent on those institutions. The abolition of primogeniture and entails is one example among many of the first; the abolition of fines and recoveries, the disuse of real actions, and the simplification of the modes of conveyance are instances of the second. The speech of Henry Brougham on the reformation of the law, although the most remarkable effort which has been made to remold English law and to give it a more democratic character, contained very few suggestions which had not long before been anticipated in America. The commissioners who were appointed under the resolution offered by that great statesman made elaborate reports on each department of the law, and so striking are the similarities in some instances, even in detail, between the changes proposed by them and the actual state of American law that one might be inclined to suppose that the codes of some of the American states were before them at the time. Mr. Humphreys, an English lawyer, has written an able and instructive work on real property.[4] But its great merit consists not in an exposition of what the law is, but in pointing out

4. [James Humphreys (d. 1830), legal writer and liberal reformer, *Observations on the Actual State of the English Laws of Real Property, with the Outline of a Code* (London, 1826).]

various important changes which should be made, many of which have long since been introduced in America.

The "procedure" of the courts of justice makes up a very important part of the jurisprudence of a country. I shall notice a few differences between the English and American law. A few are enough to set the intelligent reader athinking. English writers have remarked that the way to an English court was over a bridge of gold. In America it has been supposed that this is true only of the court of chancery. But I find that in the king's bench the expense of recovering so small a sum as twenty-five dollars, even where no defense is made and judgment goes by default, was not less than seventy dollars prior to the late reform acts. The constitution of the courts, however unexceptionable it may be in theory, may dwindle into insignificance if the practical working of the system is attended with such enormous expense as to bar the entrance to them.

The time which is allotted to the hearing of causes is a matter of equal importance. In England, the average number of days set apart for this purpose in the six circuits is two hundred and eighty-five. In the single state of Ohio, the average number in each of the fifteen circuits is one hundred and fifty-two, independently of the terms of supreme court. The business transacted in those fifteen circuits corresponds exactly with that which is transacted by English judges on their circuits, with the addition in the former instance of complete chancery jurisdiction. The population of England is more than fifteen millions, that of Ohio is two millions. The pressure of business in the English courts is so much beyond the ability of the judges to transact that great numbers of suitors are necessarily precluded from appealing to them. This defect has to some extent been lately rectified by referring the trial of cases of small amount to tribunals similar to those of American justices of the peace, and by obliging counsel in the higher courts to make a statement in writing of the facts in controversy and the points relied upon. This frequently cuts short the whole matter and the case is settled summarily and satisfactorily. This practice is of familiar occurrence in many of the courts of the American states.

The difference between English and American jurisprudence (a difference which is visible both in the civil codes and the codes of procedure of the two countries) arises from this circumstance: that in the latter, the laws are made by the representatives of the people and are accommodated to the wants and exigencies of the people; in the former, the laws are viewed as parts of an artificial and complex system, and to interfere with them extensively might have the effect, although indirectly at first, of displacing in some part or other the authority of the government.

I believe there is but one of the American states in which land is not liable, precisely like personal property, to the satisfaction of all debts. And in that one it is capable of being reached, although the process is a little circuitous. A sweeping reformation of this kind is of more moment than a hundred other enactments which sometimes engage the attention of the curious and learned inquirer. We may pardon the human mind for its obliquities when it is condemned to grope its way in the dark; and when we learn that the reason why, originally, certain creditors could only extend one half of the debtor's land was because the king might want the other half in his wars, we make allowance for the uncouth notions which everywhere prevailed in the middle ages. But the law has continued to exist long after England has been blessed with a succession of wise statesmen and enlightened lawyers. The cause of the difference between the two countries, then, must be sought in the fact that in America the people are very generally landed proprietors and that in England the case is otherwise. A law which exempts real property from the payment of debts is not so much a civil as it is a political regulation. It contributes to fortify the authority of a landed aristocracy.

When we learn that in two of the three English courts of common law the practice of the profession is a strict monopoly, that in the common pleas none but sergeants are permitted to practice, and that in the exchequer the business is confined to four attorneys and sixteen clerks, as the practitioners in that court are denominated, this may not strike all minds alike. Some will view it as a mere arbitrary rule and as a matter of indifference one way or the other; others will regard it as an arrangement adapted in some way or other to institutions different from their own and therefore not to be tried by the same standard. But others will take the plain and direct view of the matter and, considering courts of justice as established for the express purpose of adjusting the numerous controversies which arise in every civilized community, will conclude that an institution which confines the transaction of legal business to a few privileged persons will be fatal to the ambition of others, will render those who do manage it less

the old world. A few instances are abundantly sufficient to suggest matter for thought and to lead the reader to the recollection of a much greater number.

A remarkable instance has just occurred in Scotland, and this revolution consists simply in the introduction of what in America is termed the "voluntary principle" in religion. At the head of this movement stands Chalmers who, notwithstanding the reasoning he had employed to vindicate the customs of primogeniture and entails, yet takes the lead in weakening indirectly the hold which they have obtained upon the public mind. For all the institutions of society which are any ways of a kindred character are intimately connected, and whatever contributes to strengthen or to lessen the authority of one has a similar effect upon all. To introduce liberal and enlightened notions into some of these, therefore, and to resist vehemently their influence in others is to run counter to the end we propose and to neutralize the good we effect by the ill we leave behind. Doubtless, one reason why American congregations are able to compensate their ministers so handsomely is because the repeal of all laws which fetter the transmission of property has given an unwonted energy to individual enterprise and increased the number of those who are in independent circumstances.

At the date of the American Revolution nearly all the states had an ecclesiastical establishment similar to that of England and Scotland. The introduction of the voluntary system was one of the fruits of that revolution. The scheme was a new one. In Europe it was predicted that religion would fall to decay. So powerless is the mind in forming its conclusions when it is left without the help of experience. The support afforded to religion in the United States is larger than in any European state except Great Britain; the professors of religion are numerous and public order and morality, to say the least, are as well preserved as in any other part of the world.

In France, the disproportion between Catholics and Protestants is much greater than in Great Britain, yet the plan of an established church has been dispensed with. All sects are placed upon an equal footing. But as government makes provision for the clergy, the change can only be regarded as one step, though a very important one, toward the complete dissolution of the connection between church and state.

The Catholic church was mainly instrumental in building up our modern civilization. If it became corrupt, it was in consequence of the absolute supremacy which it attained. To prevent the like corruption from visiting the Protestant church, there is no way but to accord equality to all sects.

But the revolution in Scotland is in a particular degree fitted to engage the attention of the statesman as well as of the religious man. The opinion has been general in Europe that the people were no more capable of taking care of their political than of their religious interests. If the experiment in Scotland succeeds (of which no one has any doubt), the notion will very naturally insinuate itself into the minds of all enlightened men that self government is not impracticable in political any more than it is in religious affairs.

I have heard persons of great good sense insist that the voluntary principle was nugatory in its operation so far as regarded the choice of the clergymen, that there is no congregation in America in which the nomination is not determined by a very few influential members. But the knowledge which these members have, that it is in the power of the congregation to overrule them, will forever prevent any abuse of their influence. It cannot happen as in Scotland that ministers highly offensive to the congregations should be thrust upon them, and thrust upon them because they were thus offensive.

Popular education is another of those public interests upon which America is likely to exercise an important influence upon Europe. Perhaps no material changes will be made in the plan of instruction. But the true idea of popular education is that the system should be administered by and through the people as well as for the people. In other words, the management by the people is itself a chief element in the scheme of popular education.

America affords a practical illustration of the close connection between education and government. But it does so because the former is throughout of a popular character. Whenever monarchical government draws to itself all authority and establishes a complete system of centralization, the good which was intended for youth is in great part undone for men. If the system of popular education never can be complete until free institutions are introduced, this is an argument for and not against their introduction.

What we ordinarily term a plan of popular instruction is one adapted to the minds of youth, but, if this is not followed up by a system which confers independence of thought in after life, the faculties and knowledge which were acquired at schools and academies will become inert and fruitless. The governments of Prussia, Denmark, and Holland may continue their well-devised schemes of education for an indefinite period; but if their youth, on entering upon the world, are unable to make application of their knowledge, they can never become as enlightened citizens as the men of New England and New York. It is not improbable, however, that the system of education prevailing in these countries will gradually change the political institutions. One of them is already converted into a constitutional government. And there are very clear symptoms that both the others are on the eve of becoming so.

America is above all others the country of private associations. These societies had existed elsewhere before, but they were never applied to such an infinite diversity of subjects as in the United States and they were almost invariably connected with some sort of influence in church or state. In America they are altogether of a popular character and are consequently both more numerous and more effective than in any other community. They supply the want which the mind feels for the employment of its faculties after the schools are left, and the discipline which they impart helps to prepare men for the theater of political life. Associations, religious, benevolent, political, literary, and industrial, abound in every state. They may be regarded as bulwarks for all time to come against the corruption of the manners, the usurpations of the government, and the decay of popular liberty.

If I desired to contrive a plan by which individual freedom and the general interests of the people might be easily conciliated with the just authority of the government, I would set about the formation of private associations. Government is never so able to exert and to maintain the influence which of right belongs to it as when the citizens voluntarily submit themselves to a discipline, the effect of which is to spread knowledge, industry, and benevolence throughout the land. The present has been termed the age of licentiousness. It less deserves the name than any preceding age. Nor would it ever have been so characterized if the venality and vice which exist were not seen in contrast with so many and such striking monuments of benevolence and morality. These associations which are fast springing up in every country are alone sufficient to redeem the age from the imputation. Doubtless they will never exterminate vice and ignorance, but they will assist mightily in setting bounds to them.

We need not inquire whether the notion of popular associations has been borrowed by other countries from America. At the present day the spread of an institution, the application of it to new and unthought purposes, is much more important than the question where it originated. The diversified forms which these associations have assumed in the United States and the multiplied advantages which have accrued from them have rendered them popular abroad, have indeed produced a profound impression upon the European mind. Mr. Pitt succeeded in suppressing a debating society in London at a time when such societies existed in every town in America.

The example which America has set in endeavoring to make peace the permanent policy of the country is destined to exert great influence upon the European communities. There is no more unequivocal proof of a sound and healthful condition of society than a general repugnance to warlike pursuits. This state of feeling indicates many things:

First. The existence of habits of reflection among classes of people who were before supposed to be deficient in that quality.

Second. The prevalence of more exact notions of justice and morality than have usually been popular.

Third. That the population are so addicted to the pursuits of industry as to render war incompatible with their plainest interests.

The war which has just burst out may seem to contradict these views, but it affords complete illustration of their truth. For never in the history of any nation has there been so deep and so general a manifestation of public feeling in opposition to military pursuits.

The war was sprung upon the people when they least expected it. It was a false step in politics, soon to be retrieved and never again to be repeated. Nor would the contest have continued one month if peace could have been procured. But being commenced and overtures of peace being refused, it did not strike people generally that there was any other way of prosecuting it than according to the old-fashioned plan of inflicting heavy blows upon the enemy in order to bring him to terms. The Americans have been so long inured to the arts of peace, so unaccustomed to wearing a military armor, that they not unnaturally prosecuted the war on the same principles which have been followed by other civilized states. But what I wish particularly to notice is that the conflict has only existed seven months and already an entirely new system of operations is proposed. This is to abandon all notions of an offensive war; and even for defense to occupy the line assumed as the boundary between the two states and to concentrate the small military force which will be necessary in that direction exclusively. This plan is even proposed by a military man who has displayed the greatest genius for war and whose ambition and interest would seem to consist in prolonging the contest.[6] It is one of the most signal proofs I am aware of how completely the character of the soldier in the United States is swallowed up in that of the citizen. The plan is a fair index of the genius and dispositions of the American people. It has made a deep impression upon men of all parties and all classes and will afford instruction in any future difficulty in which the country may be engaged.

I know no spectacle more sublime than was witnessed during the pendency of the Oregon controversy: the presentation of addresses from all parts of Great Britain to the American people in favor of peace. Mr. Pitt and his immediate successors exerted themselves to make war the habitual occupation of the people. At the very same period the United States were earnestly engaged in maturing a scheme of administration which should render peace the settled and inflexible policy of the country. This system had never before been pursued by any civilized nation. And I cannot help thinking that when the fruits of this policy were distinctly seen in the unparalleled prosperity of the United States, it exercised very great influence upon the European states. The Pitt policy has lost ground. It is not merely considered vicious, but what is sometimes of more consequence in what concerns the manners, it has fallen out of fashion. Peace societies in England, Scotland, and America made the noblest exertions during the late difficulty to maintain peace. It may be said that the masses, the substantial population in both countries, leagued themselves together with a sort of tacit understanding that their respective governments should be withheld from going to war.

It is not difficult to understand the cause of the great influence which America exercises upon Europe; it is equally easy to understand the way in which it operates. When we learn that more than one hundred thousand Europeans annually arrive in the United States, we

6. [Grimke probably refers to General Zachary Taylor who, after the fall of Monterey, was "for adopting a boundary line that would include enough territory to pay all just American claims, and standing there on the defensive." Justin H. Smith, *The War with Mexico* (New York, 1919), I, 282.]

know that the unoccupied land is not all that constitutes the attraction; we know that the noise of American institutions has gone abroad, that their influence has spread over millions who avail themselves of every opportunity to take shelter under the shade of those institutions. I do not perceive that these people ever show a disposition to cling to the habits and prejudices amid which they were reared but, on the contrary, that the feeling is one of congratulation at being delivered from their influence, that the most substantial and intelligent among them fall in with American notions and lend a ready and cordial support to American institutions. I know, then, that the influence is on one side; that it is America which acts upon Europe, not Europe upon America.

The channels through which this influence finds its way are so numerous that it would be difficult to count them up. There are probably two millions of persons in the United States who have relatives, friends, or correspondents in Europe. If we had access to the epistolary communications which constantly pass between them and could read the vivid and yet simple picture which is frequently drawn of American institutions, we would be able to form a more just and complete idea of the power which they exercise than in any other way. This would be sufficient to solve the mystery and to let us understand not only why such crowds are drawn to the American shores, but why so deep an impression is made upon the population which remains behind.

The commercial correspondence is necessarily immense, nor will letters upon business be written without very frequently affording an insight into the curious machinery by which so wide an arena has been opened to man's exertions and such a mass of unfettered industry has been set in motion. This species of correspondence only serves to confirm the speculations and conclusions contained in letters written professedly to impart information; and Europeans very naturally put the question to one another — sometimes in a whisper, sometimes out loud — why, if so great prosperity and so much public order are the fruit of free institutions in America, the same institutions may not be made to work equally well in Europe since Americans are only Europeans or of European descent. No other example of self-government is to be found, and the obvious inference is that it is the institutions which have made them what they are. But as soon as the people of the old world begin to interrogate one another, although it should be only in a whisper, as to the causes which have given birth to this new form of society, it is clear that they have placed themselves under an influence from which they cannot afterward escape. That an important change has been produced in the mode of thinking of Europeans on all those questions which pertain to the social organization is, I think, certain. The precise amount of influence which will be exerted upon the political institutions it is impossible to calculate.

America is also made known to the European world by books of travels. Within the last twenty-five years travelers to the United States have been incomparably more numerous than at any preceding period. The greater part have been persons of enlightened understandings, and the most enlightened are precisely those who have done most justice to American institutions. At the head of this class, at the head, indeed, of the European mind, stands De Tocqueville who, like Plato, visited a foreign land with the single view of seeking instruction and who, to the fine genius of Plato, unites the severe analysis and calm observation of Aristotle. With powers of generalization absolutely unrivaled in the department of political philosophy, he seized the clue to American institutions and taught Europeans to view them in a totally different spirit from what they had been accustomed to. He taught them that those institutions were neither to be slighted as something gross and familiar to the common apprehension, nor to be viewed as a startling paradox in government. Writing for Europe, not for America, he felt the weight of the task which had fallen upon him. He readily conceived that although ancient institutions were not to be shaken to the ground in a day, yet that by a wise, skillful, and delicate survey of his subject, mingled occasionally with doubts as to the absolutely unexceptionable character of American institutions, truths of which no one could be directly persuaded might be gradually and profitably insinuated into the minds of all. This work has spoken with a weight and authority which belong to none other treating of the institutions of a foreign country.

American works have contributed to the influence which is exercised upon Europe. Although these works for the most part are not addressed to the philosophical mind, they are calculated to have a wide circulation among the general run of readers. Works, historical, statistical, and economical, afford a clear insight into the working of American society. They are easiest of apprehension to general readers, and yet open an unlimited field of inquiry to profounder understandings. There are certain pauses in the history of the human mind when it leaves off philosophizing and speculating for a season in order to recollect itself and to set in order the vast pile of materials which have accumulated in the interval. The age prior to Bacon's was one of those periods, and this is another. The revolution wrought by that great man in the mode of philosophizing has laid open a vast range of inquiry in physical science, and this enlargement of the bounds of physical science has communicated an impulse to all other branches of knowledge. It has shaken all and yet perfected none. An infinity of new views is perpetually crossing the mind without time being allowed for arranging them and binding them together as a whole. The literature and philosophy of the present age, eminently tentative in their character and superabounding in materials for thought, make it probable that we are on the eve of an intellectual revolution similar to that of the seventeenth century. The superficial character of the literature which prevails in America and to some extent in Europe, sometimes dealing in matter of fact and sometimes venturing upon speculations the most mysterious and fanciful, may be only the prelude to that revolution. I believe anyone who pays close attention to the character of mind of a very numerous class of readers, both in Europe and America, will find that there is something besides ennui or the mere desire to gain a respectable share of information which is at work, and that even where the surface of society gives evidence of nothing positive, there never was a period when the human mind was so deeply stirred.

The rank which the United States has now attained as one of the three great powers of Christendom has invested American institutions with that sort of prestige which gives title to unquestioned influence abroad. A nation, no more than an individual, is [not] proclaimed great until it is able to move the will as well as the understandings of others. The great danger is lest the will should run away with the understanding and that a nation untrue to itself should engage in acts of external violence, inconsistent with its own prosperity and with the welfare of mankind at large. America has hitherto avoided this snare. Peace has made her both powerful and prosperous, nor is it possible for her to continue to uphold free institutions unless peace is her cardinal policy. Occasional interruptions there may be; her ascendancy will soon be such as to place her beyond the reach of these if she holds a strict guard upon herself. What I most desire to inculcate is that peace, as the habitual policy of the country, as the policy which it of choice marks out for itself, is indispensable to the enjoyment of genuine freedom and to the maintenance of that great influence which it exercises upon Europe. An individual does not strengthen his moral and intellectual nature in order to give full play to the lower appetites. No more will a nation do so which is mindful of its true interests. The utmost amount of power which a community is able to acquire is never more than enough to set in motion the springs of improvement within and to dispense the blessings of civilization to its own population. So that the influence of a nation abroad is never so great as when it is least intent upon asserting it and when its whole efforts are directed to the development of its own resources.

In surveying the changes which have taken place in the laws, manners, and social organization of some of the European states, it is impossible to say how much is due to the separate influence of America. It is very remarkable, however, that they have all been crowded into the space of the last fifty or sixty years. Even in the absence of any definite facts on which to hinge, the presumption would arise that America has come in for a large share of the influence which has produced these changes. Certainly the European commonwealths were on the advance when the American frame of government was established. For the growth of industry had given an impulse to knowledge and the spread of knowledge was step by step lifting the bulk of the population to a higher level and making men somewhat better acquainted with their rights and interests. I will not quarrel with the European reader (if any such there should be) who believes that there is exaggeration in these pages, confident that after some reflection he will recur to very nearly the same views, and that what he at first regarded as exaggeration will only be viewed as an effort to render more distinct truths which in substance are correctly set forth.

CHAPTER VIII | ULTIMATE DESTINY

OF FREE INSTITUTIONS [1]

IN contemplating the great improvement which society and the art of government have undergone in very modern times, the inquiry instantly presents itself: is there a probability that this improvement will continue, to what extent can it be carried, and have we a reasonable assurance that it will be permanent? These are problems of great importance and require a distinct and clear examination. There is this great difference between physical and political science. In the first, all we can do is to observe and collect the facts and to elicit the principles which govern them and which are constantly the same. In the physiology of society and government, the facts and therefore the principles are subject to variation. But this gives rise to a double progress in the last. In physical science every department has made rapid strides during the last century. This improvement consists in a more thorough and exact acquaintance with the laws of the physical world. If the improvement which took place in the political science were of the same character, and none other, all the accession which it would have received would consist in a more thorough and orderly redaction of the principles which had governed society up to that period, for all the improvement in physical science consists in a more complete knowledge of physical phenomena. These phenomena existed always precisely as they do now, but they were not perceived and thought out, so that we were ignorant whether they existed. But in the political world, the facts, the phenomena, are not always the same; they have varied greatly, although these variations are themselves limited within certain bounds. Beyond these they cannot go in consequence of the radical sameness of the human organism at all times and all places. But this variation is something entirely different from anything which occurs in the physical world, and it gives rise to what may be termed a

1. [Grimke added this entire last chapter to the second edition.]

system of secondary laws of political society. The physical world also has a set of primary and secondary laws, but the difference consists merely in the character of inferiority of the last to the first, for the phenomena on which both depend existed always precisely as they do now. But the phenomena on which the secondary laws of political society depend did not exist always, but have been revealed to our observation in very modern times. Hence the double improvement, that is, the improvement additional to that in physical science which takes place in political science. Not only is an improved method introduced, but an improved state of facts on which to found an improved method corresponding with it. The astronomy of Newton and the physiology of Liebig lay open to our knowledge phenomena which always existed but which required thought and penetration to bring to light.[2] The political work of De Tocqueville reveals not only new laws, but an entirely new class of phenomena. Indeed, when we speak of the improvement of society and government we convey this idea. No change, no improvement which we know of, has taken place in the phenomena and laws which govern the planetary motions; all was perfect from the beginning. But a visible and marked improvement has taken place in both the social and political organization within a hundred years.

The chief obstacle to a successful investigation of this subject is the belief that, unless some state of very high perfection is attained, all efforts to reconstruct society and government so as to render them stable and permanent and to endow the last with both the ability and disposition to rule wisely and justly must be abortive. In considering the limit to which society may go, we must at the outset discard all idea of any radical and fundamental change in the character of men and boldly avow that this unchangeable character of human nature is the inevitable consequence of the infirmity and defects, physical and moral, of individual man; for as society is made up of individuals and all its institutions are administered by them, everything must partake of that infirmity and those defects.

We may figure to ourselves two ends as worthy of attainment in political society. 1st. The elevation of the whole population to a very high standard in the scale of physical, moral, and intellectual being;

2. [Justus von Liebig (1803–1873), German organic chemist; an English translation of his major work, *Organic Chemistry in Its Application to Agriculture and Physiology*, appeared in London in 1840.]

or 2d, the elevation of so considerable a number as to ensure their own good conduct and, as a consequence, the wise and upright government of those whose advancement beyond a certain point is never attained. The first is impracticable; all schemes to bring it about must be abortive for they would prove in the end inconsistent with the existence of an elevated class in any part of society. The steady and regular augmentation of the middle class may accomplish the second. The diffusion of property and knowledge will capacitate them for this position, and the conviction which long and painful experience may force upon every other part of society, that that class have the fairest title to govern, will clothe them with that weight and respect which are so necessary in order to exert a legitimate influence over other men. This will take place not in consequence of any optional or arbitrary determination on the part of the population, but in consequence of certain laws of human nature which operate steadily and invariably. "If universal suffrage (says an enlightened writer) were introduced this day into England, not a single peasant would be elected to Parliament." We may conceive of a society subsisting so long under the influence of these elements that even the lower classes may have common sense and judgment sufficient to discern that to break it up would make shipwreck of their interests. For reflection, which is a prominent characteristic of the superior classes in the present age, has increased greatly among the lower. It must also be borne in mind that although the last are inferior in all the advantages of fortune to the first, they perform a very important part in checking them and restraining their actions within certain limits. It is doubtful if in the imperfect condition of our nature, which requires restraints from above and below, we could succeed at all without this instrumentality. If the reformation I have referred to, a reformation falling infinitely short of any utopian plan, is deemed chimerical, we have only to compare the condition of every European country in the first fourteen centuries with what it is at present. The same proportion of advancement would give us as a state of society as eligible as I have supposed.

First. The faculties, propensities, and passions of men are on an average the same which they always were, and yet the influence of civilization is such as to produce very perceptible differences in their actions at different periods. It might be supposed that the offspring of those who have lived in a highly civilized society might after several generations have their physical organization so much changed as to give rise to different propensities, or to propensities so materially modified as to amount nearly to the same thing. We know nothing of the laws which govern our physical organization, but observation and experience militate strongly against the supposition and seem to prove that these propensities can be no further altered than by giving them different objects on which to expend themselves. Domitian, Nero, and Commodus, as well as Trajan and the two Antonines, were descended from ancestors born in a highly civilized society. The conflict between our selfish and social propensities, the constant predominance of the former in consequence of our feeble condition which causes nearly the whole of life to be spent in devising means of improving even our physical state, are a great obstacle in the way; for the selfish propensities, the propensities which are personal to us, are as necessary to the advancement of the individual as the social propensities are to that of the race. And although among great numbers the passions may be gratified otherwise than in acts of cruelty, rapacity, an insurrectionary spirit, and lawless disorders, there will always be a large body, increasing with the advance of civilization, who will be depressed to a very low point in the scale and whose dispositions will be marked by great ferocity.

In order to test the practicability of elevating the whole population to a high and equal level, for it would be of no importance to place all on a level unless that level imported a highly eligible condition, we will suppose that all the land of a country were now to be divided equally among individuals and that the proportion allotted to each should be two hundred acres, for less would be insufficient to rear and educate a family. The plan would be encompassed with all sorts of difficulties. 1st. The common sense, sagacity, judgment, and habits of industry of different men are exceedingly different even in the homely occupation of improving their physical condition. 2d. Even if the country were already cleared, the demand for labor to cultivate it would far exceed the supply. For by the supposition, all the men above twenty-one are proprietors; nor would it be possible to establish any other rule, as our design is to elevate all and we cannot effect this unless all, at the period of manhood, are permitted to enter upon life with an equal facility of bettering their condition. Each individual, then, has a tract of land given to him, and at the outset he finds himself totally unable to cultivate more than the tenth part of it, for the great majority of laborers, at present, are above twenty-one and none of them could be hired to perform work for others when they had more of their own than they could attend to. But we will for a moment suppose that the experiment is successful. The comfortable circumstances in which everyone is placed will give a prodigious stimulus to population. The unmarried, who would have waited until they could in the ordinary course of things acquire the means of subsistence, will now marry. Numerous families will be the consequence; the land will be partitioned among a greater number, and in a few generations the division of the soil will be carried to such an extent as to mar the whole scheme and to forbid all idea of elevating the whole mass to the station which was contemplated. Society will retrograde and will continue to do so until it reaches the lowest point in the scale. Two circumstances will contribute to hasten this downward progress. The number of children of different families will be very unequal. This difference will occasion large possessions to be engrossed by some while others are confined to a meagre subsistence or become paupers. The skill, industry, and aptitude of individuals for their calling will also be very different, and this will contribute still more to hasten the retrograde march. The original division into proprietors and laborers will be re-established, and we shall neither secure to each an equality of property nor succeed in lifting all to a high level. When we speak of elevating the whole population, we must mean morally and intellectually as well as physically. I have supposed two hundred acres to be the least quantity which would be required to attain this end. No one would have the means of educating a family nor the opportunity of devoting a considerable part of life to the acquisition of knowledge with less. But I have made no mention of the other classes, merchants, manufacturers, artisans, etc., whose agency is so necessary to attain anything like a high state of even physical civilization. I have separated one thing from another in order to render the analysis more striking and complete. Without the intervention of those classes everyone would be obliged to build his own house, to manufacture and make his own clothing, to construct all the tools and implements of agriculture, which would absorb so much time, if time were possible, as instantly to arrest all progress and to blast the fruit of what had already been made. Or if we suppose the separate existence of those classes, all idea of a distribution of property is at an end. It is physically possible, for the moment, to make a division of the soil, but we cannot make a division of the qualities which are necessary to the prosecution of other departments of industry. We cannot decree that the skill and dexterity of A and B, acquired by a long apprenticeship to a calling and sharpened by natural aptitude and sagacity, shall be distributed to C and D. The reader will fill up the outline with the numerous suggestions which will crowd upon him, confirmatory of the view I have taken. Our nature is as it is. The constitution of society is the result of that nature, and we must make up our minds to submit to it, if we would do anything valuable and useful to advance it.

To what extent may we consider the beings who now live in the most civilized societies, Great Britain and the United States, for instance, as radically the same, as endowed with the same appetites and propensities as those who acted a part in the proscriptions and massacres of Marius and Sylla, in the atrocities of the French revolution, and in numberless enormities and cruelties which disfigure the history of England down to the revolution of 1688? Although nothing of the kind now appears on the surface of society, it does not follow that the same passions do not exist. They may be disguised or diverted into a different channel, and yet be ready to break out if any unhappy conjuncture should occur to give a violent shock to the institutions. For it is clear that unless our structure is radically altered, those passions and propensities must be found at bottom the same. In a state of profound tranquillity there is but one way of ascertaining the fact, and that is by studying and analyzing the characters of men in private life and, as far as we are able, in public life also. To pursue this inquiry vigorously, it would be necessary to draw aside the curtain which conceals the most secret thoughts and transactions, so secret that if any application were made to individuals it would be in the power of each, and that with the greatest plausibility, to exclaim against such unjust imputations. But the philosophical inquirer must not be deterred by such difficulties from at least stating the fact and leaving it to individuals who have sufficient acuteness and observation to make the application to all but themselves; and in this way, already so familiar to everyone, we shall succeed in comprehending all the individuals of the species; the problem will be solved with the unanimous consent of all but without any knowledge on their part of the result. He is the true friend of mankind who pursues the truth fearlessly, and he may be sure he has attained it when the assent which is given to his deductions is a secret, not an avowed one. Everyone who has the skill to unravel these subjects will be convinced that the same heart-burnings and envyings which have ever existed exist now, and that these malignant passions have been the sole cause of all the cruelties, massacres, and judicial murders which pollute the page of history. The annals of other countries and other times wear a foreign and antiquated air. They are regarded as the recital of strange things, and the reader has neither the disposition nor the ability to make a direct and immediate application of what they record to the men and transactions of their own times.

I must now refer again to what I have said of our original structure. Our nature is made up of qualities which are eminently social and also of qualities which are selfish, that is, personal to ourselves. If the last are not the foundation of the first, they open free scope to them and render them more pleasurable and agreeable than they otherwise would be. The laws of society, then, are like the laws of the physical world: the same centripetal and centrifugal forces reign over both and by their united operation both worlds may be maintained in harmony. But there is this difference: the selfish propensities are much stronger than the social and, unless they can find a sufficient number of objects on which to exhaust themselves, they almost invariably interfere with the other set of qualities. They are stronger than these because they are necessary to the existence of the race which the last are not. The procurement of the means of subsistence is felt as a first and imperious want, without which all other wants would be valueless because they could not be gratified. This is the first occasion on which the order and harmony of society is disturbed. But man, besides partaking of the qualities of the lower animals, is also an intellectual being, and this, although it affords an opportunity for conciliating the two rival qualities of his nature, opens in reality a greatly extended arena to the operation of his selfish propensities. For the gratification of all those wants which to subsistence adds comfort, to comfort affluence, to affluence respect, to respect influence, and to influence power are for the most part selfish or personal to ourselves. And yet the gratification of all these is necessary to the perfectionment of the individual and to any considerable progress of society itself. But the exceeding difficulty of maintaining a just equipoise between these two contending principles will be evident to everyone who reflects upon our feeble and imperfect condition. Our selfish wants, both the higher and the lower, are so urgent and so multiplied that it seems as if they must forever obtain the mastery and encroach more and more upon our social being. All the efforts to gratify the wants I have enumerated, and many subordinate ones which I have not enumerated, are directed without any immediate regard to the welfare of society. All of them are like instincts, acting without premeditation or, if accompanied with this in some individuals, lending additional force to them.

It is very true that a state of things may be supposed in which this constitution of our nature would not be inconsistent with the maintenance in their utmost vigor of the dispositions which lead men to society. Society is itself a collection of individuals. If each member succeeded in providing for his well being both physical and moral, all, that is, society, would attain the same end; and the greater the intensity with which each one prosecuted his own interests the greater the probability that the last end would be accomplished. For, by the supposition, the faculties of all would be directed in channels the united influence of which would make up the happiness of all.

But this state of things, although there is a constant tendency to approach it, can never be realized. The difficulties in the way are so numerous that it is impossible to enumerate them all. A few are sufficient. In the first place, life is commenced at a period when the faculties are immature, when there is a total want of experience and observation, and when the passions are so strong as to threaten to swallow up the whole being. Mistakes of all kinds are constantly made so common as never to be noticed. And yet these are incurable in consequence of the inherent defects I have referred to. 2d. Even in the adult, the faculties, both intellectual and affective, are extremely imperfect while at the same time there is the greatest imaginable inequality among different individuals. 3d. The constant increase of the population multiplies these difficulties and renders them more obstinate. The more favorable the condition of the society, the easier the means of subsistence; the stronger is the impetus given to the population. And as this increase is gradual and the inconveniences it produces take place silently and unobservedly, men are by little and little familiarized to them, and ultimately forget the high standard of comfort which they once presented to themselves. This fails to operate as a check upon a further increase. Reflection has ever exerted a very imperfect influence in this matter, although there are very perceptible differences among different peoples. But these differences are insufficient to prevent the greatest inconveniences and mischiefs among all and, when combined with the other causes to which I have alluded, they present the most formidable obstacles to the realization of that utopian scheme of society which is so easily imagined precisely because it is so unnatural. All the circumstances I have referred to spring from certain inherent principles of our nature which can only be changed by a radical change in our organization.

Can it be matter of surprise when millions of beings are collected in one community that there should be an infinite deal of jangling, disorder, and confusion, and that the good order of society and the wholesome control of government should be perpetually threatened? The great majority of these beings, in a country the most happily favored, are struggling for a comfortable subsistence. This sets in motion a host of passions which, by this straitened condition, are disarmed of the power to do any immediate mischief, but not sufficiently so to prevent society from being infested with a multitude of domestic evils. When we come to the classes above, not so numerous and yet formidable enough, we perceive the same defects of character, the same inequalities, the same passions and propensities, but all greatly heightened in consequence of the more complicated struggle in which they are engaged. The constant interference of so many and such imperious desires prevents society from assuming that fair aspect which it would be so delightful to look upon and, at first view, it seems as if it would be better if we were unable to form the conception of such a picture, if our reason did not assure us that it is only by having an ideal standard before us that we are impelled to make efforts to attain what is really practicable.

In the preceding observations, I have represented human nature as it is. I have supposed our wants, desires, and propensities to be a necessary part of our structure and as having been implanted for the wisest purposes, to lead us in the first instance to even physical exertion, and afterwards to the employment of our higher faculties. I have spoken of the existence of different classes of society as inconsistent with the scheme of perfection which we may form to ourselves and yet as indispensable to the maintenance of a condition much raised above that of the lower animals, as indispensable, in fine, to the maintenance of civilization in any part of society. But when to the wants and appetites of the class which is struggling for subsistence are added the more numerous and the more complicated wants and desires of the superior classes, all armed with a greater degree of strength and influence than among the inferior ranks, we must not be surprised if society never exhibits a perfectly quiet aspect nor if it is sometimes torn by the most bitter and cruel dissensions. I have represented everything as depending upon certain fixed principles which may assume different forms among different people as operating unerringly within certain limits, although these limits are not everywhere the same. This it was necessary to do in order to answer two inquiries proposed in the commencement of this chapter: [1st.] To what extent can social improvement be carried; is it possible to effect the elevation of all to a high and uniform level? 2d. Although the advancement of all to a high point in the scale of physical, moral, and intellectual excellence is impracticable, may not the social and political organization with or without our contrivance be so ordered as at least to insure a wise and equitable government of society? This is the only alternative remaining. It is entirely distinct from the other and must be constantly kept separate from it, otherwise we shall be unable to extricate ourselves from the confusion of ideas which two things compatible in theory and yet incompatible in practice will occasion. Up to a certain point, the two are closely connected. The wise, prudent, and upright administration of public affairs depends upon the moral and intellectual elevation of the population, but it cannot depend upon the equal elevation of all. If it did, our destiny would be most stern indeed, for we should be unable to avail ourselves of a contrivance visible in every other part of creation, the making compensation for defects in one part by the possession of counterbalancing advantages in another. I venture to lay it down as a maxim in political philosophy that the institutions may be skillfully contrived and wisely and happily administered, although all classes are not wise and virtuous, nay, although a large proportion are lamentably deficient in these qualities. The principle alone may so outrun the growth of those principles which are calculated to elevate and improve the race and to call out its good qualities as to retain a great number in ignorance, poverty, and bad habits; while there may be a larger number than has hitherto existed in any known country on whom those incentives will act powerfully and invariably. In this way only can we gain a glimmering of light in the dark path we are pursuing and be prevented from tormenting ourselves with the belief that because all manner of good is not attainable, none is worth pursuing. If we are able to succeed to the extent which I have indicated as practicable, the benefit to the class which is excluded from the advantages of property, intelligence, and education will not be less than to the more fortunate classes. The former will be governed with more wisdom and prudence than is practicable under any other scheme of society.

The actions of men depend upon two causes: the faculties of one kind or another with which they are endowed, and the circumstances which are external to them, including in the last not only the physical world but other intellectual beings, together with the institutions, public and private, in the country where they reside and even those of other countries wherever they are capable of exerting an influence upon them. On the joint influence of these two causes depends the whole conduct and behavior of men. Diminish the influence of one and you alter or annihilate the influence of the other. This law prevails among societies, governments, and nations, as well as among individuals. It is impossible to conceive that it should be otherwise, since all actions imply something beyond us, affecting our faculties and at the same time affected by them. In the general, the fact is admitted by everyone; it is the precise appreciation of facts and the rigorous application of them which is so difficult to be attained.

Thus a vast deal depends upon the circumstances in which an infant society, growing up to be a great nation, is placed: its position on the globe with respect to climate, or its position in relation to other nations, the state of the country in which they are placed, the period when its members began to congregate as a society, the institutions which had previously shaped their conduct, and the causes which originally led to their formation. As an individual born today in Sparta or Athens will be very different from what he would have been if born two thousand years ago, a society growing up in one country at one period may be very different from what it would have been if planted in another country and at another period. This will be the case after making every allowance for the remarkable sameness of organism which prevails among the human species. That organism is not an unit, but is a collection of the most diversified faculties and hence results the apparent anomaly that, notwithstanding the sameness in the groundwork of the human character, the actions of men are so different. If powerful incentives or uncontrollable circumstances are applied to some faculties, while others are acted upon feebly, the conduct of the individual will be very different from what it would have been if the state of the case had been exactly reversed, if those faculties and propensities which are powerfully stimulated and developed in one direction lay dormant, and those which are feebly influenced were very strongly acted upon. In the same way, the aptitudes, capacities, and habits of some nations may be shaped by outward circumstances, very different from those which surround other nations, and their life and destiny may be very different. When the institutions of a country, happily circumstanced, are matured and consolidated, they become a cause external to other nations and may powerfully influence their conduct.

There is no knowing to what extent this part of the machinery of society may be carried in modifying the character of individuals and nations. The field within which it may operate is very large, although we may be assured that the fundamental organization of our nature forbids all idea of making men gods. The general principle is this: if strong incentives are applied to call out the better qualities of human nature, they will be called out among great numbers; and if the incentives to vice, idleness, and disorder are also enfeebled, a still greater number will be powerfully acted upon. The whole scheme of punishment proceeds upon the idea that the actions of men may be rendered different from what they would be by the presentation of motives which are external to them; not merely that the conduct of those who have already violated the law will be changed, but that a much greater number will be deterred from mischievous habits and abandoned courses. And when in addition to this the circumstances which surround individuals and societies are such as to present strong positive motives to the formation of good habits, there is not a probability but a certainty that they will be formed among great numbers. All this is true if men are endowed with good as well as bad qualities, of which, I suppose there will be no question. The beginnings of society in the United States are very remarkable. If we compare them with the early history of every other country, ancient or modern, the contrast is very striking. The first centuries in the annals of Greece, Rome, France, Great Britain, *etc.*, exhibit a scene of eternal warfare, domestic, civil and national. The circumstances which surrounded the people of the first country were very different from those which surrounded the people of the four last. The first were born at a period when civil and religious liberty ran high; they planted themselves in an empty country, remote from the theater of European contention and free from any disturbing causes within. The land was uncultivated and habits of industry and frugality were imposed upon them; their private institutions were not subjected to the control of any authority without, and for the first time in the history of the world organised a system of common schools. They were so remote from England that she meddled very little with their political institutions; the members of which they were composed were so much on an equality that they established a republican government. The effect of all these causes, acting from without, was the formation of certain habits which became a new cause and an additional incentive to further improvement. Domestic government was maintained with great strictness and purity. The offspring of people thus trained were, of course, more susceptible than themselves to external influences; they obeyed the discipline prescribed to them; a character of industry, energy, and intelligence has been handed down from generation to generation; and from these elements has arisen a nation in whom the possession of these qualities in a much higher degree is not only conceivable but practicable, [who are] yet perhaps more remarkable for them than any other.

To the question proposed in the commencement of the chapter, will the improvement which has taken place among all civilized nations continue to advance? the answer must be that it will. No nation has ever been known to recede unless some overwhelming calamity from without has violently arrested its progress. The principle of progression is the rule, that of retrogradation the exception. The reason why this is so is obvious. Progress implies something higher and therefore something desirable. It would not be something higher unless it were also desirable. This ensures at any rate a certain tendency at all times to advancement. But the gratification of the appetites and propensities in all stages of society is also desirable, and this undoubtedly will disturb the regular operation of the first principle. But it is only where these appetites and propensities are in excess, for the moderate, that is, the natural, gratification of them is not only consistent with the development of the higher part of our nature but contributes to it. On the other hand, the gratification of our higher faculties to any degree is not detrimental but serviceable to society. Hence, where the circumstances by which individuals are surrounded are at all favorable, there is always a disposition to leap forward. If they are alike favorable to all, this tendency will be general; if only to a part of society, it will take place in that part; and it will be correct to term Great Britain, France, Germany, as well as the United States, highly improving societies, although this improvement is not the same in all parts of their populations. Nor can it be doubted that if it were carried not to some imaginable point, but to a degree perfectly practicable, institutions might be established in those countries where they are not already which would provide, not during a few generations but permanently, for the wise and equitable government of all classes. This is the only reply we can make to another question proposed in the opening of the chapter, To what extent may social and political improvement be carried? It cannot be carried to anything savoring of perfection, and yet it may be carried indefinitely because it may take an indefinite time to reach the point which is attainable. It may be carried so far, at least, as to ensure a steady, impartial, and judicious administration of the government, and this will be an inestimable acquisition and a reasonable compensation for that radical infirmity of our nature which forbids all idea of attaining a state of great perfection.

With regard to the great problem, what is to be the ultimate destiny of free institutions, we can only offer probable conjectures, not certain opinions. In the body of this work, I have represented these institutions as eminently favorable to the development of the faculties of the greatest number of men and to the advancement of both civil and political freedom. Apprehensions of their instability will perpetually cross the mind. But these I have described as a wise provision inserted in our nature and as contributing mightily to ward off the very mischiefs which are apprehended. The stronger they become and the greater the number who entertain them, the stronger will be the resisting force of society, the greater its ability to arrest disorder of all sorts before it has gone to extremities.

[I.] But first, it is remarkable that in proportion to the amount of popular freedom which has been breathed into governments which are not republican in their structure, the more stable they have become and the more prudent and circumspect has been the conduct of all public functionaries. This is remarkably exemplified in the case of Great Britain, a government which neither commanded the undivided force of its people nor ruled wisely and judiciously until a large share of popular liberty was engrafted upon it. This change dates from the revolution which placed William III on the throne, and it has become more and more marked every reign since. There is, indeed, this mischief attending a government whose institutions are partly free and partly not free, it is rendered preternaturally strong and is able to postpone further reforms which would be advantageous at an earlier day. I do not intend to pronounce an unqualified opinion against mixed government, but it should be regarded only as a temporary state and not as political writers have viewed it, as the standing model of government. The remarks which I have made in respect to the English government may be applied to the French, though their correctness there will not be readily perceived. There can be no doubt, although the executive is styled emperor, which seems to denote the exercise of monarchical authority in its greatest plenitude, that the government is administered with vastly more prudence and discretion than under the reigns of Louis XIV or Louis XV. This is due to the reforms which were executed between 1789 and 1799 which still exercise immense influence upon the opinions of the people and the conduct of the government. Nor can it be doubted that the empire is only a provisional state and will sooner or later be succeeded by a constitutional government in which public and private rights will be more firmly established than they were between 1815 and 1848. The revolution of 1848 is an illustration of all I have said. The difference between it and the revolution of 1789 is entitled to the deepest attention. In the last, the monied men, merchants and principal tradesmen, and men of letters were the chief actors. In 1847, it was the reverse, and this can only be ascribed to one or other of two circumstances — either the abuses were not near so hideous and alarming, or the frightful calamities which were brought to everyone's door during the first revolution sunk so deep into the minds of men and exercised their reflection so powerfully that they recoiled from the commission of any atrocities and cruelties. In either event, it is evident that the general manners have undergone a great regeneration. The middle class in Paris is now the predominant class, and it understands its interests infinitely better than when, as in 1798, it was just emerging into importance. It is composed of two hundred thousand proprietors, rent holders and tradesmen, and of one hundred thousand clerks, the interests of all of whom are mutually interwoven and who have so just a sense of these interests as not to dare to jeopardize them, if it is possible to avoid it, and yet exert so decided an influence upon the government as to constrain it to act within the bounds of a constitutional monarchy.

II. Free institutions best fall in with the natural desire of improvement. They afford scope and opportunity to a greater number to lift themselves in the scale of physical and intellectual improvement. It is not merely because they afford a wider arena to the exertions of all;

this is a necessary condition, but it is not the moving spring. Such institutions are fatal to the authority of prejudices and opinions which spring up in a society legally divided into classes and which impose an invincible spell upon the faculties of men. It was not until after the French Revolution that industry became popular in France. There were some symptoms of a tendency in this direction in the time of Louis XV.* These only concurred with innumerable other causes to hasten the revolution. They were too feeble to render industry really popular, until the authority of opinion was completely demolished by the thorough reform in the groundwork of society which afterwards took place. It was not until then that the Gothic system of corporate bodies of tradesmen endowed with exclusive privileges was abolished, as well as the regular course of apprenticeship, companionship, etc. These hung like a dead weight upon the industry of France, not only confining it within the smallest possible compass, but imposing for centuries an universal belief that the settled order of things could not be departed from. It was not until after the English revolution in the time of Charles I that a like change was effected in the opinions and habits of men. Then, for the first time, it became customary for the gentry to bind their sons as apprentices to the merchants.† This at once rendered industry both popular and fashionable, and from that period dates the prodigious impetus to popular intelligence and popular power in that country. The complaint now is that industry has become too fashionable;‡ that both nobility and gentry have entered into competition with the middle ranks of society; that their fortunes are embarked in commerce, in vast manufacturing establishments, or in enterprises not less costly for the improvement of their estates. In the reign of Louis XV, the only kind of industry which was permitted to the impoverished noblesse was that of blowing glass. This did not imply the use of their hands, and it was manual labor which was supposed to degrade the man. The objection that industry has become too fashionable discloses one of its chief merits. Although in very many instances the higher classes in Great Britain, France, Germany, Italy, etc., do superintend the employment of their capitals, in a greater number they are placed at the command of the classes below them. They

* Reign of Louis XV, by De Tocqueville. [Grimke must mean *L'Ancien Régime et la Revolution* (Paris, 1856).]

† Clarendon. [Edward Hyde, Earl of Clarendon (1609–1674), English statesman and historian.]

‡ Sismondi.

thus contribute to fructify and invigorate every branch of industry. But the chief advantage of this consists in its introducing habits of order, economy, and industry among an idle and turbulent aristocracy as well as among an idle and vicious populace. It has aided in melting down differences of opinion which were apparently irreconcilable, and has caused the higher classes to partake of the qualities of the lower and the lower to partake of those of the higher. If England ever becomes a republic, that is, if the principle of representation is carried into every department of the government, the new form which industry has assumed, foreign as it may seem to the subject, will be principally instrumental in bringing it about.

III. Free institutions cause a greater number of beings to be civilized than could possibly be the case otherwise. This follows from the preceding remarks. The rise of a powerful middle class is the most striking fact in the history of modern society. But the whole meaning of the fact is contained in the observation that free institutions extend civilization to a greater number of individuals than any other form of government. The more thorough the civilization of a country, the more completely it pervades every part of society, the more orderly and contented will be the population, the more singleness of purpose will be imparted to the government. This results from the greater harmony among the elements of which society is composed. It is only because the public cannot agree among themselves that one man or a few men are able to seize the supreme power. A close league among a comparatively small body is sufficient to overpower the efforts of a disunited multitude. This effect of a more or less thorough civilization of all parts of society is entitled to great attention. It is greatly promoted in the first instance by the freedom of the institutions, but more than all other things it contributes ultimately to give them durability and strength. "I found the crown rolling in a gutter, and only put it on my own head," said the first emperor Napoleon; nor could it be otherwise when the lawlessness of the feudal system first, and the uncontrolled despotism of kingly authority afterwards, crushed every germ of popular improvement. There is at present a strong middle class in France, not strong enough to rule, but strong enough to influence the notions of the government. It is that class which has consented to the elevation of another Napoleon, and by so doing may be considered as saying to him: *there is a body of anarchists in our midst, small compared with the body of the population, but firmly leagued together. We can-*

not afford to be ever on the watch, and ever under arms, to resist their machinations. The mere title of emperor will operate as a spell upon the imaginations of these beings. In order to pursue unmolested our private occupations, under the title of emperor we make you the chief of police of this troubled country and thereby design to augment the constabulary force of the kingdom. If you abuse the trust, we will abandon our occupations and expel you. This you know, and your knowledge is, humanly speaking, a guarantee for the fulfillment of that trust. Such is the unhappy condition to which a nation is subjected when it is partly free and partly not free.

IV. A greater degree of reflection is instilled into men of all classes and their conduct is consequently more cautious and prudent. It is reflection which enables men to control their appetites and passions, to exercise self-command, to foresee the mistakes they will inevitably commit if they pursue a certain line of conduct. This office it performs, not from any persuasion on their part that such conduct is abstractly right and proper, but from a perception of the consequences which will ensue if they follow the impulse of passion and prejudice. The mere diffusion of property diffuses reflection. The possession of property is a something, and that too of no inconsiderable importance, on which the affections, hopes, and aspirations of the great majority of men in a republic are fixed. Their interests, and not any imaginary qualities of mind, render them in the first instance reflective and, by and by, reflection swells these interests to a greater magnitude and causes them to be guarded with still more judgment and discretion. We are thus delivered from the necessity of supposing that men must possess very elevated qualities in order to be reflective. To be so in a very high degree they must possess these qualities, but they are not demanded in the ordinary vocations of life; they are not necessary to the bulk of mankind in their conduct, either in private or public life.

These considerations, together with many others in the preceding part of this work to which the reader will recur, afford a reasonable assurance for the perpetuity of free institutions. But we cannot speak with absolute certainty. An excessive growth of the population alone may disappoint these expectations. I say may, for it need not necessarily have this effect. China is more fully peopled than any other country on the globe, and yet the institutions established twenty-five hundred years ago have subsisted without alteration to the present day, and it has enjoyed profound tranquillity during a vastly longer

period than any other country.* It is not because the form of government is regal, for all the European kingdoms have been torn with
dissensions and involved in the most cruel wars during the same period.
The high standard of comfort to which the people of the United States
have been habituated may repress the excessive growth of the population. We see this exemplified already. The average age of marriage in
this country is twenty-five; in Ireland, it is twenty. The Irish have
been familiarized to a very low standard and they enter recklessly
upon marriage without any prospect of being able to maintain a family.
The mere habit of living under free institutions contributes powerfully to fortify their spirit. The Americans are the only people who
have been able to make a fair beginning, and that is all-important.
They have never lived under any other than free institutions;† they
have no prepossessions in favor of any others, nor are there any materials for the construction of them. But it may be inquired whether
the rule of universal suffrage will be always adhered to! Although the
numbers and importance of the middle class should always secure
to them the ascendancy, will not a formidable body of proletarians in
the process of time rise up and constantly disturb the regular movement of the government? I have already suggested that the American
people have long been familiarized to a limitation of the right of suffrage, not merely in the large cities, but in hundreds of smaller towns
throughout the country. The principle is then already recognized as
one which is both just and practicable. It is so recognized because
it has been ordained by the majority in those cities and towns, and
the same species of power, the majority of the people in the states, may
give it a wider application. The will of the majority is a wonderful
sedative to the disturbances of society. The only reason why the legislatures of the states do not carry the rule of limitation beyond their
municipal governments is that the middle class is so numerous as to
render the action of any other comparatively harmless. But I predict
that if the time ever arrives when the danger to the institutions becomes imminent, from the banding together of the lowest class, the
right of suffrage will be limited. The maxim of equality is a great regu-

---

* From 1650 to 1850.

† The colonists did pretty much as they pleased, although they were an appendage
to a monarchy. Adams' *Defence*. [John Adams, *A Defence of the Constitutions of
Government of the United States of America* (London, 1787).]

lative, but not a constitutive principle of society; a distinction of great importance in the political world, when it ceases to perform the first function it ceases to be a principle in the construction of the government.

It is not probable that the hereditary principle will be ever introduced into a country where free institutions have taken deep root. The materials for founding an order of nobility will be wanting; the prejudices against it will be deep and difficult to eradicate, and the natural aristocracy of the country will be so numerous and powerful that they cannot be brought to agree in vesting the supremacy in a close body. An oligarchy only would be practicable, but this, of all the forms of aristocratic government, is the most difficult to establish. It has never succeeded to any extent worth mentioning, except in Venice where the natural aristocracy were only as one in a thousand to what it will be in the United States. Take away the overgrown estates of the English nobility and you annihilate them; destroy the illusion which has grown up during a long tract of time and which has persuaded the nation that it is an order superior to any other, and you undermine its authority; render them as numerous as the great landholders of America and you introduce the democratic principle into the body and fritter away its power. It has been said, and with great justice, that the people themselves may be persuaded of the expediency of establishing one or other of the artificial forms of government, that viewing the political institutions as ordained for their advantage alone they may consider monarchical or aristocratical government as on the whole best adapted to promote their interests. This has been said in countries which have never known any other form of civil polity, and in which immemorial usage has so long swayed public opinion that it is very difficult to form any other notions. Opinions are sometimes more difficult to be eradicated than institutions. All I mean to say is that where the course of human affairs has drawn the opinions of men in an opposite direction, where the manners, the laws, the distribution of property, and the form of government have all partaken of the genius of republican government, it will be exceedingly difficult to lay a foundation for aristocratical or even mixed government to rest upon. There is great difference between permitting such a government to stand when it is already existing and calling it into being in opposition to inveterate and deep-seated opinions.

The difficulty is as great with regard to an hereditary chief magistrate as with regard to an hereditary nobility. Kingly authority is undoubtedly founded on an illusion of the imagination. This illusion may be of infinite advantage in some periods of society when it is necessary to give something like unity to the discordant materials of which it is composed and to control the imaginations of men by a supreme imagination. But if in the first rudiments of society and for centuries after opposite opinions have prevailed, if more homely faculties have been cultivated at the expense of the imagination, the illusion vanishes and the foundation on which we would build is taken from under us. The question is no longer, is regal government expedient; it is, is it possible.

The idea of an elective is still more incongruous than that of an hereditary monarchy. The condition of society which imposes a king as a necessary evil presupposes a state of things entirely at war with the exercise of popular power. It is for this reason that the elective principle may in a monarchy be employed in the choice of representatives, but never of the prince himself without introducing greater disorders than those attempted to be cured.

We must then discard all idea of lifting the whole body of the people to a very high standard in the scale of physical and intellectual improvement, but the social organization may at least be carried to such a degree of improvement as to insure wise institutions and a prudent and judicious administration of public affairs. And when time and inveterate habit have confirmed these institutions, they may acquire a self-existing authority which will perpetuate them. The problem of government is not at all different from the problem which is presented to every individual in private life. He is born into the world without any choice on his part; from the commencement of adult age he finds himself surrounded by inconveniences, physical, moral, and social, which he did not create and which are too widespread and obstinate for him to control. After a few years experience he is brought to accept this as something which is inevitable; and as it is inevitable, he does not recoil but falls upon a plan of life which will enable him to overcome these obstacles and to avail himself of the good which is invariably mixed with the evil. The enjoyment of liberty in its highest degree has opened a great volume of experience to the American people, and this experience, not the possession of any natural qualities superior to those of other people, *may* bring them to see that the manifold inconveniences which beset society are of precisely the same character with those which they encounter in private life: that they are indestructible, but not unmanageable, and that the plainest maxims of common sense powerfully urge them to cling to the eminent advantages which they possess and to venture upon no devious and untried paths.

INDEX

INDEX

INDEX

THE JOHN HARVARD LIBRARY

The intent of
Waldron Phoenix Belknap, Jr.,
as expressed in an early will, was for
Harvard College to use the income from a
permanent trust fund he set up, for "editing and
publishing rare, inaccessible, or hitherto unpublished
source material of interest in connection with the
history, literature, art (including minor and useful
art), commerce, customs, and manners or way of
life of the Colonial and Federal Periods of the United
States . . . In all cases the emphasis shall be on the
presentation of the basic material." A later testament
broadened this statement, but Mr. Belknap's inter-
ests remained constant until his death.

In linking the name of the first benefactor of
Harvard College with the purpose of this later,
generous-minded believer in American culture the
John Harvard Library seeks to emphasize the impor-
tance of Mr. Belknap's purpose. The John Harvard
Library of the Belknap Press of Harvard University
Press exists to make books and documents
about the American past more readily
available to scholars and the
general reader.

A History
of Civilizations

===

FERNAND BRAUDEL

A HISTORY OF
CIVILIZATIONS

TRANSLATED BY RICHARD MAYNE

ALLEN LANE
THE PENGUIN PRESS

ALLEN LANE

THE PENGUIN PRESS

Published by the Penguin Group
Penguin Books USA Inc., 375 Hudson Street,
New York, New York 10014, U.S.A.
Penguin Books Ltd, 27 Wrights Lane,
London W8 5TZ, England
Penguin Books Australia Ltd,
Ringwood, Victoria, Australia
Penguin Books Canada Ltd, 10 Alcorn Avenue,
Toronto, Ontario, Canada M4V 3B2
Penguin Books (N.Z.) Ltd,
182-190 Wairau Road, Auckland 10, New Zealand

Penguin Books Ltd, Registered Offices:
Harmondsworth, Middlesex, England

This work was first published in France in the collected works of S. Baille, F. Braudel, R.
Philippe, *Le Monde actuel, histoire et civilisations*, librairie Eugène Belin 1963
First published in France as *Grammaire de Civilisations*,
Les Editions Arthaud 1987
First published in America 1994 by Viking Penguin,
a division of Penguin Books USA Inc.

1 3 5 7 9 10 8 6 4 2

LIBRARY OF CONGRESS CATALOGING–IN–PUBLICATION DATA
Braudel, Fernand.
[Grammaire des civilisations. English]
A history of civilizations / Fernand Braudel ; translated by Richard Mayne.
p. cm.
Includes index.
ISBN 0-713-99022-8
1. Civilization—History. I. Title.
CB78.B73 1993
909—dc20   93-30639

Printed in the United States of America
Set in 12/14 pt Lasercomp Bembo

Contents

━━━

List of Maps

Translator's Introduction

BY RICHARD MAYNE

=====

Anyone new to the work of the late Fernand Braudel may need not one Introduction but four: first, to the man himself; then to the *Annales* group of French historians he represented and helped to lead; thirdly, to the present book; and finally to its translation.

I

'For us he is a prince,' wrote Georges Duby of the Collège de France in 1967, when Fernand Braudel was sixty-five. Like many a fairy-tale hero, he had been born in a village – Luméville, in the Meuse province of north-western Lorraine.

Here were the same rows of large adjoining houses (containing barn and stable as well as living quarters) with their backs turned on the gardens behind, but their massive barn doors opening directly, at the front, on to the broad streets, *les rues à usoirs*, cluttered on both sides with carts, harrows, ploughs, dungheaps. The houses were roofed with the curved tiles known as 'Roman' tiles, although it is not thought today that this Lorraine tradition has anything to do with Rome . . .

I confess that during my travels, which tend to create illusions, I have dreamed of a Europe starting on the banks of the Somme, the Meuse or the Rhine and stretching away to Siberia and distant Asia. Such thoughts came to mind because, from the Rhine to Poland, I kept coming across the same rural architecture as in the Lorraine countryside of my boyhood: the same clustered villages, the same open farming, the same cornfields, the same triennial rotation, the same images . . .

No doubt if one were to be spirited back into a French farmhouse of, say, the 1920s, one would have plenty of cause for complaint. Working the land was hard, and there was no end to it, despite a deceptive freedom. One had a choice, yes, but only between equally backbreaking kinds of work. Nevertheless, people did not complain to each other, whether about the lack of running water (it had to be fetched from the well or the village pump), or about the poor light at night (no electricity), the drab clothes, only occasionally renewed, or the lack of conveniences and distractions to be found in the towns. Everyone had enough to eat, thanks to the kitchen garden, to the fields, which now included potatoes as a crop, thanks to preserved fruits and vegetables, butcher meat on Sundays and the family pig, which was usually killed and eaten at home. But can I count as a reliable source my own childhood memories?

Like Alsace, Lorraine has suffered over the centuries from invasion and annexation. Perhaps on account of its frontier position, it has been a home of French patriotism. Joan of Arc came from Domrémy-la-Pucelle, Maurice Barrès from Charmes-sur-Moselle; Verdun was its major battlefield; the double-barred Cross of Lorraine was the emblem of General Charles de Gaulle. 'I love France,' wrote Fernand Braudel, 'with the same demanding and complicated passion as did Jules Michelet; without distinguishing between its good points and its bad, between what I like and what I find harder to accept.' But France was not his only love. 'I have loved the Mediterranean with passion,' he wrote elsewhere, 'no doubt because I am a northerner like so many others in whose footsteps I have followed. I have joyfully dedicated long years of study to it – much more than all my youth.'

The son of a teacher, as a student he went to the Lycée Voltaire in Paris, near the Père Lachaise cemetery, and then to the Sorbonne, where he took his degree in history in 1923. His first teaching post took him south, across the Mediterranean to Constantine in Algeria. For a young man, the experience was rewarding.

I have been fortunate enough to find myself all my life on the side of tolerance. I am comfortable with it. But I cannot claim any personal credit on that account. I only really discovered the Jewish question for instance in Algeria, in 1923, when I was already over twenty years old. For the next ten years, still in Algeria, I was living in a Muslim country where I learnt to understand and respect Arabs and Berbers.

Was it there that he also began to consult local archives? He was later able to say, of those from the former Government General building in Algiers – 'a rather odd collection of Spanish documents' – 'I have read the entire collection.'

Braudel returned to Paris in 1932, to teach at the Lycée Condorcet in the rue du Havre near the boulevard Haussman, and then at the Lycée Henri IV in the Latin Quarter behind the Panthéon. But after three years he was off again – this time to the other side of the world.

In 1934, a new university was founded in Brazil, the state-supported Universidade de São Paulo, incorporating the historic Faculdade de Direito or Faculty of Law as well as other existing institutions. And in 1935 Fernand Braudel joined the new venture for a three-year stint in its Faculty of Arts.

This too was a heady experience. 'Living in Brazil,' wrote Braudel, 'I met black people in an atmosphere that reminded me of *Gone with the Wind*.'

Before 1939, when Latin America was still semi-colonial, only a few actors seemed to occupy the small stage of political life and culture, at the same time as they dominated the peaceful world of business. Charming, likeable, and cultivated, they owned hundreds, thousands of acres, as well as the richest of libraries. Some of them were veritable Renaissance princes, just the type to captivate a journalist, traveller or intellectual from Europe. On the eve of the Second World War, however, they already gave the impression of being a social anachronism. They bore immense responsibilities – one in charge of almost all British capital in Brazil, another the representative of something like the Dearborn Chemical Society, another running public finance, governing a State or trying to become President of the Republic, and yet another a General risen from the ranks. But they all seemed to rule, as it were, from the inner sanctum of their thoughts and their libraries, as if in an unreal universe. They believed in the virtues of culture, civilization, and reason.

They seemed to belong to the liberal and aristocratic mode of nineteenth-century Europe, in an atmosphere of benevolent despotism, or perhaps enlightened paternalism.

And at the same time, outside their charmed and firmly closed circle, there were new men, industrialists and immigrants who had made their fortune. They were beginning to achieve astonishing economic success; and only their children would acquire a certain polish.

As well as observing Brazilian society, Fernand Braudel had by this time been working for some years on the research for his massive thesis on the Mediterranean. Already in 1932 he had visited Palermo – only to find that 'the Archivio di Stato and the Archivio Comunale had closed their doors, and I was only able to spend a few days in the former and view the outside of the huge registers of the latter'. He made up for this disappointment in 'the rich Biblioteca Comunale'; but like all research workers he had to face other setbacks, including a ban on photographing documents in the invaluable Ragusa Archives, where he worked in 1935. This, he noted, 'made my research a hundred times more difficult'.

Far worse difficulties lay ahead. In 1938, Braudel returned to Paris and became a member of the prestigious postgraduate Ecole Pratique des Hautes Etudes. Working again in the Latin Quarter, he was once more well placed to use the French Archives Nationales, the Bibliothèque Nationale, and the document collections in the Ministry of Foreign Affairs. Research further afield posed problems. 'I could do no more than take cognizance, from a distance, of the German, Austrian, and Polish archives. My intention was to supplement the many published works available by taking samples from documents in the archives.' But, as he put it, 'circumstances' prevented this. War broke out in 1939, and in 1940 France fell. Fernand Braudel was serving as a lieutenant on the Rhine frontier and became a prisoner of war.

Is there any Frenchman after all who has not asked himself questions about his country, whether at the present time or in particular during the tragic hours through which our destiny has repeatedly taken us as it has run its course? Such catastrophes are like great rents in the canvas of history, or like those gaping holes in the clouds glimpsed from an aeroplane, plunging shafts of light at the bottom of which we see the earth below. Yawning disasters, gaping chasms, plunging tunnels of gloomy light – there is no shortage of these in our history. To go no further back than the nineteenth century, we have had the fateful dates 1815, 1871, 1914. And then there was 1940, when the knell tolled for us a second time at Sedan: when the drama of Dunkirk was played out in the indescribable disorder of defeat. It is true that in time even these monstrous wounds heal, fade, are forgotten – according to the iron law of all collective life: a nation is not an individual or a 'person'.

I have lived through some of these disasters. Like many other people, I was brought face to face with these questions in that summer of 1940 – which by an irony of fate was gloriously hot, radiant with sunshine, flowers and *joie de vivre*. We the defeated, trudging the unjust road towards a suddenly-imposed captivity, represented the lost France, dust blown by the wind from a heap of sand. The real France, the France held in reserve, *la France profonde*, remained behind us. It would survive, it did survive.

So did Fernand Braudel – and so did his fighting spirit. He spent the next five years as a prisoner at Lübeck in Germany, until the end of the war. But in captivity, astonishingly, he wrote most of his Mediterranean thesis – partly, he said, as a 'direct existential response to the tragic times I was passing through'.

All those occurrences which poured in upon us from the radio and the newspapers of our enemies, or even the news from London which our clandestine receivers gave us – I had to outdistance, reject, deny them. Down with occurrences, especially the vexing ones! I had to believe that history, destiny, was written at a much more profound level.

When the war was over and Fernand Braudel returned to France, he put the whole thesis into shape, and successfully defended it before the examiners in 1947. Two years later, it was published as *La Méditerranée et le monde méditerranéen à l'époque de Philippe II* – and it made his name. By the time of his death in

1985, he had been elected to the Académie Française; but he was also famous among historians and general readers far beyond the frontiers of France, and he held honorary degrees from universities all over the world.

Well into his eighties, he wrote and published steadily. In 1963 came *Grammaire des civilisations*, the original of the present book, part of *Le Monde actuel: Histoire et civilisations*, whose other two parts were by Suzanne Baille and Robert Philippe. In 1966 came a thoroughly revised and enlarged edition of *La Méditerranée* (translated by Siân Reynolds as *The Mediterranean and the Mediterranean World in the age of Philip II*, 1972 and 1973). In 1967, Braudel published *Civilisation matérielle et capitalisme* (translated by Miriam Kochan as *Capitalism and Material Life, 1400–1800*, 1973). He followed this in 1969 with a collection of articles, *Ecrits sur l'histoire* (translated by Sarah Matthews as *On History*, 1980). Next, in 1979, came the three-volume *Civilisation matérielle, économie et capitalisme, XVe–XVIIIe siècle* (translated by Siân Reynolds as *The Structures of Everyday Life*, 1981, *The Wheels of Commerce*, 1982, and *The Perspective of the World*, 1984). Fernand Braudel's last large-scale work was *L'Identité de la France*.

I have come rather late in the day [he wrote] to my home ground, though with a pleasure I will not deny: for the historian can really be on an equal footing only with the history of his own country; he understands almost instinctively its twists and turns, its complexities, its originalities and its weaknesses. Never can he enjoy the same advantages, however great his learning, when he pitches camp elsewhere. So I have saved my white bread until last; there is some left for my old age.

There was more than enough. Fernand Braudel the perfectionist was still working on the book when he died. It was seen through the press by his widow Mme Paule Braudel, and published in 1986 (English translation by Siân Reynolds as *The Identity of France*, two volumes, 1988 and 1990). The year 1987, finally, saw the second French edition of *Grammaire des civilisations*, the last of Fernand Braudel's books to be translated into English.

II

As an historian, then, Fernand Braudel was not without honour, even in his own country. As a prophet, pioneering a new kind of history, he found a less ready response. In the last public lecture he gave, at Chateauvallon on 20 October 1985, he said: 'People I like tell me not to be "unreasonable, as usual". Do you think I've heeded their advice?' His listeners appreciated the irony, for what made him seem unreasonable to some traditional historians was the breadth of his approach to the past.

Despite the fact that his thesis on the Mediterranean had been accepted by the examiners,

without drum and trumpet and with a thousand nice-sounding words in my ear, I . . . was excluded from the Sorbonne in 1947. When I defended my thesis that year, one of the judges suavely said to me: 'You are a geographer, let me be the historian.' I was named indeed to the Collège de France in 1949, but the Collège is and always has been marginal to the University. In the same year I was designated to chair the history section of the national programme of teacher certification (*président du jury d'agrégation d'histoire*) but only by the individual will of Gustave Monod, Director General of Secondary Education, who in an effort to reform this venerable system of competition was eager to turn the house upside-down. I was not remiss in my duties but, in 1954, I was ousted, and the Sorbonne took the operation back into its own hands. If, in those years, Lucien Febvre and I were included in the commissions of scientific research, to which we were elected by the *entire group* of French historians, we were a minority in them: heading the list came the right-thinking persons, and one year, indeed, I was blackballed by the electors.

Braudel could have said, with Racine's Phèdre, *'Mon mal vient de plus loin.'* The dispute with the Sorbonne dated back at least as far as 1929, when Lucien Febvre and Marc Bloch had founded in Strasbourg the *Annales d'histoire économique et sociale.* Although its first editorial committee included two Sorbonne professors, neither was an orthodox historian: one, Albert Demangeon, was Professor of Human Geography, and the other, Henri Hauser, was Professor of Economic History. Of the rest, one was an archivist at the French Foreign Ministry, one a professor of sociology at Strasbourg, one a professor of Roman history there, one a professor of political economy at the Faculty of Law in Paris, one a professor at the Paris School of Political Science, one a Deputy Governor of the Bank of France, and the last the Belgian expert on economic history, Henri Pirenne.

As its title implied, the *Annales* sought to broaden the scope of historiography, introducing economic and social concerns alongside politics and diplomacy. 'Nothing could be better,' wrote Bloch and Febvre in their first Introduction, 'than for each person, concentrating on a legitimate specialization, laboriously cultivating his own back yard, nevertheless to force himself to follow his neighbour's work. But the walls are so high that, very often, they hide the view . . . It is against these deep schisms that we intend to raise our standards.'

'It is certain,' wrote Fernand Braudel, looking back,

that they were conscious of labouring towards an absolutely new and even revolutionary history. Their means were relatively simple. History was for them one human science among others. Without even standing on tiptoe, the historian could glimpse the fields and gardens of the neighbouring disciplines. Was it so complicated, then, so extraordinary, to set out to see what was happening there, to plead in favour of a community of the human sciences, despite the walls that separated them from one another, and to regard them as necessary auxiliaries of history? To think that the historian might be able to render service for service? An exchange of services: such was and such is still, I believe, the last and profoundest motto of the *Annales*, its only rallying cry.

Today, when historians have revealed so many more facets of the past, and cross-fertilized historical disciplines once firmly divided into constitutional, political, diplomatic, military, economic, social, and cultural studies, such a slogan may seem superfluous.

But in 1929 the cry was new, and the programme it called for seemed aberrant or ludicrous to traditional historians, perhaps too ambitious even for the partisans of the new current of thought . . .

The task of the two Strasbourg professors was crystal clear: to go out among the other disciplines, return with the booty, and set forth again on the quest of discovery, demolishing obstructing walls at each occasion. To pounce on their opponents, moreover, seemed the best defence.

In Strasbourg, those opponents were nicknamed '*les Sorbonnistes*'.

That name, as Professor Gertrude Himmelfarb has pointed out, 'lost some of its sting when the *Annales* moved from Strasbourg to Paris'. But although Lucien Febvre joined the Collège de France and Marc Bloch was appointed to a chair at the Sorbonne, neither had escaped what Braudel called 'the Sorbonne's wary surliness'. Bloch had been defeated as a candidate for the Fifth Section of the Ecole Pratique des Hautes Etudes in an election that Braudel denounced as 'shameful', and he had been 'side-stepped' by the Collège de France. He won his Sorbonne professorship only because, as Braudel put it, 'there simply was no other candidate sufficiently qualified to seek to succeed Henri Hauser in the chair of economic history, the only chair of economic history in the French university system'.

In that same year, 1937, Braudel joined the editorial committee of the *Annales*. He described it, nostalgically, as

a small group that could be contained with ease – despite the advent of the 'new men', Henri Brunschwig, Ernest Labrousse, Jacques Soustelle, and myself – in Lucien Febvre's combined salon and office in the rue du Val-de-Grâce, known to us intimately as 'le Val'.

Marc Bloch did not survive what Braudel called 'the heinous gash of the Second World War': as a member of the French Resistance he was shot by the Nazis in 1944. But the *Annales* continued. It had already gone through two changes of name, being known for a time as the *Annales d'histoire sociale* and for a time at the *Mélanges d'histoire sociale*; and in 1946 it adopted a still more ambitious title

– *Annales: Economies, Sociétés, Civilisations*. By now, Braudel had become one of its leading lights, and from 1956 to 1968 he was virtually its editor.

It was certainly a new period [he wrote]. But the second *Annales* genera-tion added nothing essential to the lot of ideas put into circulation by the first. None of us newcomers, Charles Morazé, Georges Friedmann, and I, contributed any really new idea or concept to the existing arsenal of theory . . . It is a fact that a whole new generation of historians chose their 'thesis subjects', that is, their line of future work and endeavour, within the framework of *Annales* thought. I therefore envisage that period as one of translation into practice, as a time of confrontation of the *Annales* model with the huge reality of history, through a blossoming of admirable works all related to one another, although dispersed across time and space.

Scholars associated with the *Annales* at the time included some cited in the present book – not only historians such as Henri-Irénée Marrou, Alphonse Dupront, Joseph Chappey, and Lucien Goldmann, but also the structuralist Roger Bastide and the anthropologist and sociologist Marcel Mauss. As Gertrude Him-melfarb said of the *Annalistes*, 'under the editorship of Fernand Braudel their journal became the most influential historical organ in France, possibly in the world. It has also proved to be remark-ably innovative. Going well beyond the more traditional forms of economic and social history, it now derives both its subjects and its methods from anthropology, sociology, demography, psychology, even semiotics and linguistics.' 'It aims similarly,' as the American anatomist of the *Annales* Traian Stoianovich has said, 'at the "demasculinization of history" and at the development of a history of women, of youth, of childhood, of oral cultures, of voluntary associations, of non-Western civilizations, of nonconsensual cultures.'

In practice, Fernand Braudel and the *Annales* cast their net wider still. In their quest for 'total history' they included geography, climatology, physics, biology, religion, mythology, navigation, and much else, not forgetting literature and the cinema. In *La Méditerranée*, for example, Braudel referred not only to the Sardinian novelist Grazia Deledda's *La via del male* (1986) and *Il Dio dei viventi* (1922) and to books by Gabriel Audisio, Jean Giono, Carlo Levi, André Chamson, and even Lawrence Durrell, but also to Vittorio De Seta's 1961 film *Banditi a Orgosolo*.

The authority of the *Annales* scholars had been greatly strengthened after the Second World War by the addition to the Ecole Pratique des Hautes Etudes of a Sixth Section. This, in the words of Traian Stoianovich, 'was conceived as a graduate but non-degree-granting centre at which scholars associated with the *Annales* journal and other distinguished or promising scholars would train advanced students and carry on discourse with them in the methods and problems of social and economic history, of economics, and of the behavioural or communications sciences. Set up under the Section almost from the start were a new Centre de Recherches Historiques under Braudel and a Centre de Recherches Economiques under Charles Morazé.'

Allowed to be born [as Braudel added] only because the Ecole des Hautes Etudes, like the Collège de France, did not have the right to grant university degrees, the Sixth Section developed, slowly and with difficulty, as a marginal institution equipped only for the purpose of research. That it knew how to turn this restriction into its strengh, into the basis of its autonomy, and into the very motor of its expansion, is another matter. In any case, the more successful it became the more opposition and hostility it met from the traditional University – along with, it is true, examples of exceptional friendship.

In 1963, a new Maison des Sciences de l'Homme was established, initially scattered, but gathered together in 1970 in a single steel-and-glass building with Braudel as President Administrator.

This institution at its inception [wrote Braudel] was the last refuge to which we resorted only after the University had blocked our plan for an experimental faculty of economic and social sciences. Yes, we were heretics until almost 1968, ever more numerous and stronger perhaps but compelled, willy-nilly, to fight ceaselessly for each concession.

The troubles of May and June 1968 changed everything ... By an irony of fate, this was for me the Establishment period. After collapsing at one blow in 1968, the citadel of the Sorbonne was divided into a dozen different institutions of higher learning. From the reforms that followed, a new life began to take hold, and more than one innovation was meritorious. As a conclusion to these reforms, the Sixth Section in 1975 lost its numerical rank and honoured name, to become the Ecole des Hautes Etudes en Sciences Sociales, with degree-granting rights.

So the *Annales* group, as Braudel suggested, had in a sense become the Establishment. As such, they in turn faced criticism, not only from those they had once challenged. 'The lay reader,' wrote Professor Arthur Marwick, 'will find *Annales* a rather forbidding journal: like any other learned journal, it does not try to fulfil the necessary historical role of communication with the wider audience, society as a whole ... In *Annales* discourse statistical tables abound, their precise significance not always being made very clear (save that, allegedly, they demonstrate a solid structural base); flow charts and diagrams, too, sometimes seem designed more to impress than to illuminate; visual sources are sometimes reproduced as if they spoke for themselves (which, of course, they never do).'

More serious were three further points that Marwick stressed: 'a hostility to, and neglect of, political history; a concentration on medieval and early modern history, with a general avoidance of industrial and contemporary societies; and an attempt, not always completely comprehensible to the uninitiated, to annex stucturalism to history.'

Few of Marwick's mild reproaches applied to Fernand Braudel. But in the last paragraph of the second edition of *La Méditerranée*, written on 26 June 1965, he confessed:

I am by temperament a 'structuralist', little tempted by the event, or even by the short-term conjuncture which is after all merely a grouping of events in the same area.

Earlier, he had called events 'crests of foam that the tides of history carry on their strong backs'. And the last words of his unfinished *L'Identité de la France* were:

Men do not make history, rather it is history above all that makes men and thereby absolves them from blame.

It was Braudel's apparent detachment from more immediate human concerns that led Professor Geoffrey Elton to write in 1967 that *La Méditerranée* 'offers some splendid understanding of the circumstances which contributed to the shaping of policy and action; the only things missing are policy and action. There is a clear and admirable sense of life, but how those lives passed through history is much less clear.'

It was a criticism with which Braudel was already familiar. He had already distanced himself from the 'over-simple theories' and 'sweeping explanations' of Arnold Toynbee and Oswald Spengler. He was equally dismissive of any historian who too slavishly adopted Marxist social models, which had been 'congealed in their simplicity and given the value of law'. But he was aware that his own view of '*la longue durée*', the long term, might be called 'Olympian'.

The question is frequently put to me, both by historians and philosophers, if we view history from such a distance, what becomes of man, his role in history, his freedom of action?

Gertrude Himmelfarb put the question very pertinently, pointing out that in 1940, when Braudel was a prisoner of war, exclaiming, 'Down with occurrences', and working on his long-term history, 'Europe was being convulsed by the passions of a single man.'

Yet, in his own way, Braudel had already acknowledged what might be called 'the Hitlerian paradox'. In *La Méditerranée* he had written:

That is not to say that this brilliant surface is of no value to the historian, nor that historical reconstruction cannot perfectly well take this micro-history as its starting-point ... To put it another way, history is the keyboard on which these individual notes are sounded ... I would conclude with the paradox that the true man of action is he who can measure most nearly the constraints upon him, who chooses to remain within them and even to take advantage of the weight of the inevitable, exerting his own pressure in the same direction. All efforts against the prevailing tide of history – which is not always obvious – are doomed to failure.

Indeed, as Traian Stoianovich put it: 'Braudel may be a structuralist by temperament, as he claims, but his structuralism is that of a poet, painter, theatrical director, or music conductor . . . In the work of such an historian, even geographic entities such as the sea may be "raised to the rank of historical personages" (as Lucien Febvre remarked). For this historian, the world is theatre . . . In the final analysis, however, the director must return to the actors, without whom there would be no theatre.'

Braudel was familiar with the technical problems that this caused. In 1963 he had asked:

Is it possible somehow to convey simultaneously both that conspicuous history which holds our attention by its continual and dramatic changes – and that other, submerged history, almost silent and always discreet, virtually unsuspected either by its observers or its participants, which is little touched by the obstinate erosion of time?

He found an answer by measuring time on three scales or levels: the quasi-immobile time of structures and traditions (*la longue durée*); the intermediate scale of 'conjunctures', rarely longer than a few generations; and the rapid time-scale of events. Each was represented in one of the three parts of *La Mediterranée*, as he explained:

The first part is devoted to a history whose passage is almost imperceptible, that of man in his relationship to the environment, a history in which all change is slow, a history of constant repetition, ever-recurring cycles . . .

On a different level from the first there can be distinguished another history, this time with slow but perceptible rhythms. If the expression had not been diverted from its full meaning, one could call it *social history*, the history of groups and groupings . . .

Lastly, the third part gives a hearing to traditional history – history, one might say, on the scale not of man, but of individual men, what Paul Lacombe and François Simiand called '*l'histoire événementielle*', that is, the history of events . . . It is the most exciting of all, the richest in human interest, and also the most dangerous. We must learn to distrust this history with its still burning passions, as it was felt, described, and lived by contemporaries whose lives were as short and as short-sighted as ours.

III

As may be seen later in the present book, Fernand Braudel was by no means short-sighted, whether looking to the future or to the past. But he had long perceived the need to shift focus at will, from one scale or type of history to another. As long ago as September 1936, he had set out some of his essential ideas in a lecture to the São Paulo Institute of Education.

Its subject was 'The Teaching of History', and it began by asking how to turn the 'educational story' into a 'tale of adventure'. The secret, said Braudel, was simplicity – not

simplicity that distorts the truth, produces a void, and is another name for mediocrity, but simplicity that is clarity, the light of intelligence. Find the key to a civilization: Greece, a civilization of the Aegean, from Thrace to Crete – and not a Balkan peninsula. Egypt, a civilization that tamed the Nile.

His model, he said, was Henri Pirenne, 'the foremost French-language historian today'. To be understood, avoid abstract terms. To hold the attention, 'let history have its dramatic interest'. Teaching history meant above all knowing how to narrate it.

Moving from research to teaching history is like moving from one watercourse to another . . . Take care that your teaching is not guided by your preferences as a research worker. I insist on that. It would be a dereliction of duty to talk to students only about firms, cheques, and the price of wheat. Historiography has slowly gone through various phases. It has been the chronicle of princes, the history of battles, or the mirror of political events; today, thanks to the efforts of bold pioneers, it is diving into the economic and social realities of the past. These stages are like the treads of a stairway leading to the truth. Do not omit any of them in the presence of students.

These principles came to mind some twenty years later, when Fernand Braudel found himself in the thick of the French secondary-school reforms that indirectly gave rise to the present book. History teaching was one of their targets. Since 1945, it had been divided chronologically along the students' career in the lycée, beginning with Mesopotamia and Ancient Egypt and ending, in the top two classes, with so-called 'contemporary history': 1789–1851 in the last class but one (*première*), 1851–1939 in the final (*terminale*) class. From 19 July 1957, the syllabus was pushed back one year, so that 1789–1851 was taught in the last class but two (*seconde*) and 1851–1945 in *première*, while *terminale* was devoted to studying 'the main contemporary civilizations'. These were divided into six 'worlds': Western, Soviet, Muslim, Far Eastern, South-East Asian, and Black African.

This reform was largely the work of Gaston Berger, then Director of Higher Education, who also initiated what later became the Maison des Sciences de l'Homme. But the breadth of the new subject – to include gleanings from 'neighbouring social sciences: geography, demography, economics, sociology, anthropology, psychology' – clearly showed the influence of the *Annales* and of Fernand Braudel. Not unexpectedly, it aroused considerable resistance. Two years later, in 1959, the geographical specification was modified: 'the civilizations of the contemporary world' now included only five regions, since the Far East and South-East Asia were amalgamated into 'the Indian and Pacific Oceans', while a final section was added to cover 'the major problems of today'. More significantly, the period 1914–45 was brought back into the first term of the *terminale* class.

It was a setback, but not a defeat. The new syllabus was close enough to Braudel's ideas to spur him to write the present book –

partly, perhaps, to forestall any further backtracking. The *Annaliste* Maurice Aymard was right to call it 'a fighting book'. Originally published as the central and most controversial part of a collective work with Suzanne Baille and Robert Philippe, *Le Monde actuel: Histoire et civilisations*, it was aimed primarily to support the new history being taught in *terminale*. As Braudel wrote in 'By Way of Preface' below,

It seems to me essential that at the age of eighteen, on the brink of preparing for whatever career, our young people should be initiated into the problems of society today, the great cultural conflicts in the world, and the multiplicity of its civilizations.

Unfortunately, despite his victory at university level, Braudel eventually lost the battle of the secondary schools. Already in 1964, Maurice Aymard, newly appointed to a provincial lycée North of Paris, found to his surprise that the teachers' council had decided that Braudel's book was 'too hard for the students'. In 1965, moreover, the Ministry of Education further truncated the 'civilizations' syllabus. As Maurice Aymard put it, 'In the midst of decolonization, at the very moment when the newly independent States were gamely trying to write their own history, a decree dated 10 August 1965 purely and simply eliminated "the African world".'

In 1970, Braudel's book was discreetly withdrawn from sale; and soon afterwards the secondary school syllabus was altered again, freeing the top forms from an innovation that had disturbed too many old habits, and restoring old-fashioned narrative 'contemporary history', 1914–45. The syllabus now taught 'new history' to the junior classes and traditional history to the seniors. It was the reverse of what Braudel had proposed. As he told his audience at Chateauvallon in 1985,

I find it appalling, abominable, that students should be questioned in the baccalauréat about the period from 1945 to 1985 as is done today. I'm sure that if I were an examiner I should fail any historian at the baccalauréat! And if I were examining myself, I'd fail myself too!

But the present book is more than just a weapon from a battle that Fernand Braudel lost. Written between the first and second editions of *La Méditerranée* and before the first volume of *Civilisation matérielle*, it forms a solid part of his *oeuvre*, his work as a whole. During the 1960s, it was translated into Spanish for university students and into Italian as a pocket book, regularly reprinted. In 1987 it was reissued in France, shorn of its pedagogic apparatus but with a Preface reproduced from an article by Fernand Braudel in the *Corriere della Sera* in 1983. That second French edition is the version translated here.

IV

Translating Fernand Braudel into English is a task that compels respect and requires ingenuity. Professor J. H. Plumb has accused Braudel's translators of destroying the original's distinctive sparkle; and Braudel himself admitted that

It is no small task to adapt my not uncomplicated style to the vigorous rhythms of the English language.

I agree. The quotations from Braudel in this Introduction I have left in their respective translators' versions, without attempting embellishments of my own. The book itself I have treated more freely, in two respects.

Madame Paule Braudel has been kind enough to say 'Your translation is free, like all good translations', and to call it 'rapid and lively, as befits a work of this sort'. I am very grateful for the compliment, as I am for Mme Braudel's meticulous assistance throughout the task. Any errors or infelicities that remain are my own, save for possible misprints; and I should be glad to correct them in any future edition.

There is a second sense in which this is a 'free' translation. Had Fernand Braudel lived to see this book republished, he would surely have wanted to rewrite it. In his Preface to the English edition of *La Méditerranée* he declared:

I would not have wanted to reissue the book without thoroughly revising it.

For ten years, he was asked to 'adapt' the present book for a wider public; and although he never refused to do so, he always postponed the task. But, as Mme Braudel has said, 'it is unusual to translate in 1993 a book that is a reflection on the world of 1962'. For this reason, mainly by changing tenses, I have very hesitantly adjusted the text – a form of gentle *remuage*, as in the maturing of champagne. I hope that this delicate operation has merely, as it were, helped shift the sediment towards the cork for easy extraction. I am encouraged to think that Fernand Braudel would not have objected too strongly: he himself added some pages to the book – mainly on Sino-Soviet relations – for the Italian translation.

What struck me, continually, while working on the text, was how little updating it really needed – and how prescient Fernand Braudel was. I happened to be completing the chapter on the Soviet Union and its centrifugal tendencies just when the plot against Mikhail Gorbachev was hatching. It was as if Braudel were looking on. Not to say 'I told you so', for that was never his manner; but reminding one reader, at least, in those dangerous moments, how *la longue durée*, in the hands of a master, can help explain the most dramatic convulsions in the past, the present, and the future.

By Way of Preface

One word from François Mitterrand, in a speech on 16 September 1982, was enough to revive the debate about history teaching. It was no doubt only waiting to flare up again.

It is an old debate, but one which is always popular and leaves nobody unmoved. It interests the public, more than ever devoted to history, and the politicians, obliged to keep up to date; it interests the press and, above all, the teachers of history. It is an old debate, and promises no surprises; yet its scope is continually broadening. It offers shelter to every conceivable cause. They all take cover at the sound of gunfire, like well-trained troops.

In principle, the debate concerns only the curricula of the primary schools (about which, strangely, very little is said) and those of the secondary schools (which are mentioned more often than they are studied). It concerns also the disaster – or so-called disaster – of these schools as measured by our children's allegedly scandalous results. But could these results have been perfect? Have they ever been? In 1930 or thereabouts, an historical review was pleased to print a large collection of schoolchildren's howlers. And yet, at that time, orthodox teaching relied on the sacrosanct Malet-Isaac textbook, which so many polemicists praise today.

Finally, critics attack the various ways in which history itself has developed. For some, traditional history, faithful to narrative and indeed a slave to it, overloads the memory, weighing it down needlessly with dates, with the names of heroes and with the lives and deeds of notabilities. For others, 'the new history', seeking to be 'scientific', dealing with the long term and neglecting events, is supposedly responsible for catastrophic didactic failures, involving at the very least unpardonable ignorance of chronology. This dispute between Ancients and Moderns has done a great deal of harm. In a discussion which is about teaching, not scientific theory, it conceals problems and failings instead of shedding light on them.

Is the problem really so complex? You have before you, in the secondary school, first children and then adults. At some point, necessarily, their teaching has to change, in history as in other subjects. The question is how the things to be taught should be spread over the successive – and very different – school years. At the beginning, the pupils are children: at the end, they are adults. What suits the former will not suit the latter. The curriculum must be divided; and this requires an over-all plan, a choice of priorities and needs, and a guiding intelligence.

For children, I have always recommended simple narrative, pictures, television series and films – in other words, traditional history improved, adapted to include the media with which children are familiar. I speak from experience. Like all the academics of my generation, I was for a long time a *lycée* teacher; and, as well as the top forms assigned to me, I always asked to take also the most junior class, with children aged ten to twelve. They make a delightful, spontaneously spellbound audience, to whom one could show history unfolding as if with a magic lantern. The main problem is to help them, in the process, to discover a sense of perspective, of the reality of past time, its direction and significance, and the successive landmarks which first gave it a recognizable shape. I am appalled if a pupil of average ability does not know where Louis XIV comes in relation to Napoleon, or Dante in relation to Machiavelli. A feeling for chronology, gradually acquired, should help to dispel confusion. But plain narrative should also open out quite naturally into spectacular scenes, landscapes and panoramas. We are in specific places – Venice, Bordeaux, London. And as pupils come to understand time, they need to learn vocabulary, so as to be precise about words, ideas and things. Plus some key concepts: a society, a State, an economy, a civilization. All of which should be done as simply as possible.

Require familiarity with essential dates; show when prominent, important, or even hateful people lived. Put them in their context.

And now we have crossed the dividing-line: we face young people, freer perhaps than we were at their age, yet less happy; rebellious, when in fact it is society, the world and life today that are changing around them – the real source of their movements, their constraints and their outbursts. They may be less intellectual, less bookish, than we were when we finished our apprenticeship, but they are just as intelligent, and certainly more inquisitive. What account of history are we to give them?

The absurd curricula enforced in France inflict on the next-to-top form 'The world from 1914 to 1939', and then on the top form 'The world since 1939'. Twice the vast world is to be studied; but a world of politics, wars, institutions and conflicts – a prodigious mass of dates and events. I defy any historian, even those with photographic memories, to guarantee to pass an examination on this mass of often trivial facts, one after another without rhyme or reason. I have before me the latest textbook on *The Present Day* – the best of the bunch, I am told. It seems to me useful and well produced, but disappointing. It contains not a word of any value on capitalism, on economic crises, on the world's population, on civilizations outside Europe, or on the underlying causes of conflicts rather than just the conflicts themselves.

Why this scandalous state of affairs? Because of an absurd decision taken by the French Ministry of Education. Personally, as I have always said, I should have introduced 'the new history' only in the *very top form*. The new history deliberately draws upon a number of the social sciences which study and explain the contemporary world and seek to make sense of its confusion. And it seems to me essential that at the age of eighteen, on the brink of preparing for whatever career, our young people should be initiated into the problems of society and the economy today, the great cultural conflicts in the world, and the multiplicity of its civilizations. To take a simple illustration, they should be enabled to read a serious daily newspaper and understand what they read.

But no: the new history has been placed or planted in the junior forms, where it has clearly played havoc. What else could have been expected?

In fact, the two kinds of history have both been misplaced, one in the lower forms of the *lycée*, the other at the top, with mutually damaging results. The ensuing confusion has been compounded by the liberties that teachers have taken since 1968: with the best will in the world, they have stressed one part of the curriculum to the detriment of another. Owing to such haphazard choices by a succession of teachers, some pupils have gone through their whole school careers without hearing about one or another important period in history. This hardly helps them to follow the thread of chronology.

Unhappily, the history taught to our children has suffered the same fate as their mathematics or their grammar. Why teach in bits and pieces a subject which is a *whole*? Especially to ten-year-olds who will never master elementary calculus or will very rarely, and only much later, tackle higher mathematics. The study of linguistics has ravaged grammar like a wild boar's snout burrowing through a potato field. It has cloaked it in pedantic, complicated, incomprehensible language which is also quite inappropriate. The result? Grammar and spelling have never been so badly neglected. But anomalies like these should not be blamed on linguistics, higher mathematics or the new history. They do what they have to do, without worrying about what can or cannot be taught at various ages. The blame lies, in fact, with the intellectual ambitions of those who draw up school curricula. They want to go too far. I am delighted that they are ambitious for themselves. But for those in their charge they should try to be simple, even – and especially – when this is difficult.

I wonder how much this debate can interest a non-French reader. Yet, if one really considers it, what is at stake is of immense importance, and cannot be ignored. Who can deny the violence that has stemmed from history? Of course, historians have no business fabricating dubious national myths – or even pursuing only humanism, which I myself prefer. But history is a vital element in national self-awareness. And without such self-awareness there can be no original culture, no genuine civilization, in France or anywhere else.

Introduction:
History and the Present Day

These preliminary pages seek to explain what the new history curriculum requires of students in the senior forms. Logically, they had to figure here, at the beginning of the book; but for teaching purposes they belong elsewhere. Ideally, in fact, they should be read towards the end of the second term, when the first part of the course has been completed and serious study of the great civilizations is about to begin. By that time, students will already be more familiar with philosophical terminology and debate. There is a case, however, for tackling the subject, at least initially, here and now.

The new history curriculum for the senior forms poses difficult problems. It amounts to a survey of the contemporary world in all its confusion and complexity, but made intelligible in various ways by an historical approach which may involve any of the kindred social sciences – geography, demography, economics, sociology, anthropology, psychology, etc.

It would be pretentious to profess to explain the present-day world. All one can hope is to understand it better by a variety of means. Your curriculum offers three such methods.

First, the present can partly be understood by reference to the immediate past. In this brief look backwards, history has an easy task. The first part of your course, therefore, covers the dramatic and often brutal days and years that the world has experienced since the outbreak of the First World War in August 1914, and continuing to the present time. These upheavals have shaken and shaped the twentieth century, and in countless ways they affect our lives still.

By themselves, however, the events of yesterday cannot fully explain the world of today. In fact, in varying degrees, the present is the outcome of other experiences much longer ago. It is the fruit of past centuries, and even of 'the whole historical evolution of humanity until now'. That the present involves so vast a stretch of the past should by no means seem absurd – although all of us naturally tend to think of the world around us only in the context of our own brief existence, and to see its history as a speeded-up film in which everything happens pell-mell: wars, battles, summit meetings, political crises, *coups d'état*, revolutions, economic upsets, ideas, intellectual and artistic fashions, and so on.

Clearly, however, the life of human beings involves many other phenomena which cannot figure in this film of events: the space they inhabit, the social structures that confine them and determine their existence, the ethical rules they consciously or unconsciously obey, their religious and philosophical beliefs, and the civilization to which they belong. These phenomena are much longer-lived than we are; and in our own lifetime we are unlikely to see them totally transformed.

For an analogy, consider our physical environment. It certainly changes: mountains, rivers, glaciers and coastlines gradually shift. But so slow is this process that none of us can perceive it with the naked eye, unless by comparison with the distant past, or with the help of scientific studies and measurements which go beyond mere subjective observation. The lives of countries and civilizations, and the psychological or spiritual attitudes of peoples, are not so seemingly immutable; yet generation succeeds generation without really radical change. Which by no means lessens – far from it – the importance of these deep, underlying forces that invade our lives and indeed shape the world.

The recent and the more or less distant past thus combine in the amalgam of the present. Recent history races towards us at high speed: earlier history accompanies us at a slower, stealthier pace.

This early history – long-distance history – forms the second part of the course. To study the great civilizations as an explanatory background to the present means stepping aside from the headlong rush of history since 1914. It invites us to reflect on history with a slower pulse-rate, history in the longer term. Civilizations are extraordinary creatures, whose longevity passes all understanding. Fabulously ancient, they live on in each of us; and they will still live on after we have passed away.

Recent and remote history, then, are the first two keys to understanding the present. Finally, the course provides a third. This involves identifying the major problems in the world today. Problems of every kind – political, social, economic, cultural, technical, scientific. In a word, what is required goes beyond the double historical approach already outlined: it means looking at the world around us to distinguish the essential from the peripheral.

Normally, historians work and reflect on the past; and if the available documentation does not always enable them to grasp it completely, at least they know in advance, when studying the eighteenth century for instance, what the Enlightenment led to. This in itself greatly enhances their knowledge and understanding. They know the last line of the play. When it comes to the present day, with all its different potential dénouements, deciding which are the really major problems essentially means imagining the last line of the play – discerning, among all the possible outcomes, those which are most likely to occur. The task is difficult, hazardous, and indispensable.

Condorcet, the eighteenth-century *encyclopédiste* whose best known work was his *Sketch for an Historical Tableau of the Progress of the Human Spirit*, thought such a task legitimate. Serious historians today also defend forecasting – with some courage, given its risks. In 1951, a world-famous economist, Colin Clark, used the statistics then available to predict the probable scale of the future economy. In 1960, Jean Fourastié calmly discussed *The Civilization of 1980*, which in his view determined – or should have determined – the policy to be followed at the time he wrote. A very precarious 'science', which the philosopher Gaston Berger has called 'prospective', claims to specialize in forecasting the near future – the 'futurible', to use a frightful word beloved of certain economists. The 'futurible' is what now can legitimately be described in the future tense – that thin wisp of tomorrow which can be guessed at and very nearly grasped.

Such proceedings are sometimes mocked. But although they may be only half-successful, they at least offer an escape route from the confusion of the present day, looking ahead to identify the biggest problems and try to make some sense of them. The world of today is a world in evolution.

The accompanying map shows the probable distribution of the world's population in the year 2000. It contains food for thought. It should make clear among other things that no planners – and planning means the attentive and 'prospective' study of today's major problems – can do their job properly without such a map (and many other documents) in their mind's eye. It certainly corroborates the remark by Félix Houphouët-Boigny, President of the Ivory Coast Republic, that planning must take different forms in Asia and in Black Africa, because poverty in Asia must cope with over-population, whereas in Black Africa under-population is the challenge.

History, a house of many mansions

It may seem surprising that history should be open to such diversions and speculations – that it should seek, in a word, to be a science of the present, and of a present which is ambiguous, at that. Is it not going astray? Is it not, like the wolf in the fable, putting on false clothing stolen from other social sciences? We shall return to this question at the beginning of Part II. By then, the problem should have been clarified, for it is a problem relating to time itself, and the nature of time will have been broached in the course of studying philosophy.

The obvious multiplicity of the explanations that history provides, the gaps between different points of view, and even their mutual contradictions, together form a *dialectic* which is specific to history, and based on the different varieties of time which it

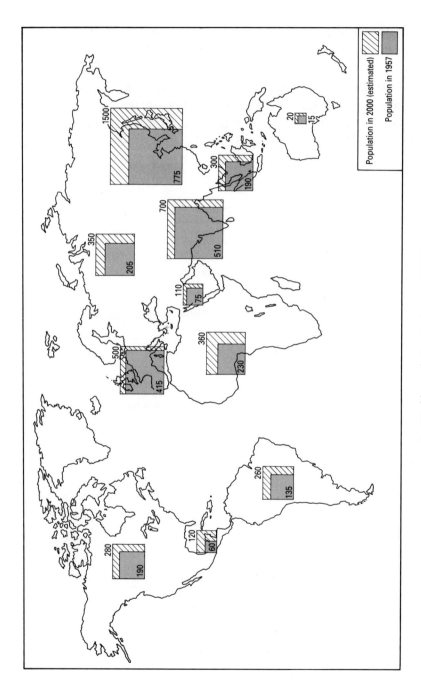

1. *World population in the year 2000*

describes: rapid for events, slower for periods, slower still, even sluggish, for civilizations. For any particular study one can choose a particular variety of time. But any attempt at a *global* explanation – like the history of civilizations – needs a more eclectic approach. One must consult many different snapshots of the past, each with its own exposure time, then fuse times and images together, rather as the colours of the solar spectrum, focused together, combine at last into pure white light.

I. A History of Civilizations

1. Changing Vocabulary

It would be pleasant to be able to define the word 'civilization' simply and precisely, as one defines a straight line, a triangle or a chemical element.

The vocabulary of the social sciences, unfortunately, scarcely permits decisive definitions. Not that everything is uncertain or in flux: but most expressions, far from being fixed for ever, vary from one author to another, and continually evolve before our eyes. 'Words,' says Claude Lévi-Strauss, 'are instruments that people are free to adapt to any use, provided they make clear their intentions.' In the social sciences, in fact, as in philosophy, there are wide and frequent variations in the meaning of the simplest words, according to the thought that uses and informs them.

The word 'civilization' – a neologism – emerged late, and unobtrusively, in eighteenth-century France. It was formed from 'civilized' and 'to civilize', which had long existed and were in general use in the sixteenth century. In about 1732, 'civilization' was still only a term in jurisprudence: it denoted an act of justice or a judgement which turned a criminal trial into civil proceedings. Its modern meaning, 'the process of becoming civilized', appeared later, in 1752, from the pen of the French statesman and economist Anne Robert Jacques Turgot, who was then preparing a universal history, although he did not publish it himself. The official début of the word in print occurred in 1756, in a work entitled *A Treatise on Population* by Victor Riqueti, Marquis of Mirabeau, the father of the celebrated revolutionary Honoré, Count Mirabeau.

He referred to 'the scope of civilization' and even 'the luxury of a false civilization'.

Oddly enough, Voltaire omitted the useful word 'civilization' from his *Essay on the Customs and Spirit of Nations* (1756), although as the Dutch historian Johan Huizinga remarked, 'he is just the man to have conceived the notion . . . and first outlined a general history of civilization'.

In its new sense, civilization meant broadly the opposite of barbarism. On one side were the civilized peoples: on the other, primitive savages or barbarians. Even the 'noble savage' dear to Jean-Jacques Rousseau and his disciples in the eighteenth century was not regarded as *civilized*. Without a doubt, the French at the end of the reign of Louis XV were pleased to see in this new word the image of their own society – which at a distance may still appeal to us even today. At all events, the word appeared because it was needed. Until then, *poli* (polite), *policé* (organized), *civil* and *civilizé* had no corresponding nouns. The word *police* rather connoted social order – which distanced it somewhat from the adjective *polite*, defined in Furetière's 1690 *Universal Dictionary* as follows: 'Used figuratively in ethics to mean civilized. To civilize: to polish the manners, make civil and sociable . . . Nothing is more apt to civilize a young man than the conversation of ladies.'

From France, the word 'civilization' rapidly spread through Europe. The word 'culture' went with it. By 1772 and probably earlier, the word 'civilization' had reached England and replaced 'civility', despite the latter's long history. *Zivilisation* took root in Germany without difficulty, alongside the older word *Bildung*. In Holland, on the other hand, it met opposition from *beschaving*, a noun based on the verb *beschaven*, to refine, ennoble or civilize, although the word *civilisatie* did later appear. 'Civilization' encountered similar resistance South of the Alps, where Italian already had, and soon used in the sense of 'civilization', the fine old word *civiltà*, found in Dante. Deeply entrenched, *civiltà* prevented the intrusion of the new word, but not the explosive arguments that came with it. In 1835, Romagnosi tried in vain to launch the word *incivilmento,* which in his mind signified 'civilizing' as much as 'civilization' *per se.*

In its travels round Europe, the new word 'civilization' was accompanied by an old word, 'culture'. Cicero had used its Latin equivalent, as in *'Cultura animi philosophia est'* – 'Philosophy is the cultivation of the soul.' It was now rejuvenated, and took on more or less the same sense as civilization. For a long time, indeed, the words were synonyms. At the University of Berlin in 1830, for instance, Hegel used them interchangeably. But at length the need to distinguish between them began to be felt.

Civilization, in fact, has at least a double meaning. It denotes both moral and material values. Thus Karl Marx distinguished between the *infrastructure* (material) and the *superstructure* (spiritual) – the latter, in his view, depending heavily on the former. Charles Seignobos remarked: 'Civilization is a matter of roads, ports, and quays' – a flippant way of saying that it was not all culture. 'It is all that humanity has achieved,' declared Marcel Mauss; while for the historian Eugène Cavignac it was 'a minimum of science, art, order and virtue'.

So civilization has at least two levels. Hence the temptation felt by many authors to separate the two words, culture and civilization, one assuming the dignity of spiritual concerns, the other the triviality of material affairs. The difficulty is that no two people agree on how the distinction is to be drawn: it varies from country to country, and within one country from period to period, and from one author to another.

In Germany, after some confusion, the distinction finally gave culture (*Kultur*) a certain precedence, consciously devaluing civilization. For the sociologists A. Tönnies (1922) and Alfred Weber (1935), civilization was no more than a mass of practical, technical knowledge, a series of ways of dealing with nature. Culture, by contrast, was a set of normative principles, values and ideals – in a word, the spirit.

This explains a remark by the German historian Wilhelm Mommsen which at first sight strikes a Frenchman as strange: 'It is humanity's duty today [1851] to see that civilization does not destroy culture, nor technology the human being.' The first part of the sentence sounds bizarre to French ears because for us the word 'civilization' takes precedence, as it does in Britain and the United States, whereas in Poland and Russia culture is more highly prized, as it is in Germany (and through German influence). In France, the word 'culture' retains its power only when it denotes what Henri Marrou has called 'any personal form of the life of the spirit'. We speak of Paul Valéry's culture, not his civilization, because the latter word more usually refers to the values of the group.

There remains one further complication, greater than all the rest. Since the year 1874, when E. B. Taylor published *Primitive Culture*, British and American anthropologists have tended more and more to use the word 'culture' to describe the primitive societies they studied, as against the word 'civilization', which in English is normally applied to modern societies. Almost all anthropologists have followed suit, speaking of primitive cultures as compared with the civilizations that more developed societies have evolved. We shall make frequent use of this distinction in the course of the present work.

Fortunately, the useful adjective 'cultural', invented in Germany in about 1850, suffers from none of these complications. It applies, in fact, to the *whole* of the content of a civilization or a culture. One can say, for example, that a civilization (or a culture) is the sum total of its cultural assets, that its geographical area is its cultural domain, that its history is cultural history, and that what one civilization transmits to another is a cultural legacy or a case of cultural borrowing, whether material or intellectual. Perhaps, indeed, the word 'cultural' is *too* convenient: it has been called barbaric or ill-formed. But until a replacement is found, it remains indispensable. No other, at present, fits the bill.

In about 1819 the word 'civilization', hitherto singular, began to be used in the plural. From then onwards, it 'tended to assume a new *and quite different* meaning: i.e., the characteristics common to the collective life of a period or a group'. Thus one might speak of the civilization of fifth-century Athens or French civilization in the century of Louis XIV. This distinction between singular and plural, properly considered, raises a further substantial complication.

In the twentieth century, in fact, the plural of the word predominates, and is closest to our personal experience. Museums transport us in time, plunging us more or less completely into past civilizations. Actual travelling is more instructive still. To cross the Channel or the Rhine, to go south to the Mediterranean: these are clear and memorable experiences, all of which underline the plural nature of civilizations. Each, undeniably, is distinct.

If we were asked, now, to define civilization in the singular, we should certainly be more hesitant. The use of the plural signifies, in fact, the gradual decline of a concept – the typically eighteenth-century notion that there was such a thing as civilization, coupled with faith in progress and confined to a few privileged peoples or groups, humanity's 'élite'. The twentieth century, happily, has abandoned a certain number of such value-judgements, and would be hard put to it to decide – and on what criteria – which civilization was the best.

This being so, civilization in the singular has lost some of its cachet. It no longer represents the supreme moral and intellectual value that it seemed to embody in the eighteenth century. Today, for example, we more naturally tend to call some abominable misdeed 'a crime against *humanity*' rather than against *civilization*, although both mean much the same thing. We feel somewhat uneasy about using the word *civilization* in its old sense, connoting human excellence or superiority.

In the singular, indeed, civilization now surely denotes something which all civilizations share, however unequally: the common heritage of humanity. Fire, writing, mathematics, the cultivation of plants and the domestication of animals – these are no longer confined to any particular origin: they have become the collective attributes of civilization in the singular.

This spread of cultural assets which are common to all humanity has become phenomenal in the modern world. Industrial technology, invented in the West, is exported everywhere and eagerly adopted. Will it unify the world by making everywhere look alike – the same ferro-concrete, steel and glass buildings, the same airports, the same railways with their stations and loudspeakers, the same vast cities that gradually engulf so much of the population? 'We have reached a phase,' wrote Raymond Aron, 'where we are discovering both the limited validity of the concept of civilization and the need to transcend that concept . . . The phase of civilizations is coming to an end, and for good or ill humanity is embarking on a new phase' – that of a *single* civilization which could become universal.

Nevertheless, the 'industrial civilization' exported by the West is only one feature of its civilization as a whole. By accepting it, the world is not taking on Western civilization lock, stock and barrel: far from it. The history of civilizations, in fact, is the history of continual mutual borrowings over many centuries, despite which each civilization has kept its own original character. It must be admitted, however, that now is the first time when one decisive aspect of a particular civilization has been adopted willingly by all the civilizations in the world, and the first time when the speed of modern communications has so much assisted its rapid and effective distribution. That simply means that what we call 'industrial civilization' is in the process of joining the collective civilization of the world. All civilizations have been, are being, or will be shaken by its impact.

Still, even supposing that all the world's civilizations sooner or later adopt similar technology, and thereby partly similar ways of life, we shall nevertheless for a long time yet face what are really very different civilizations. For a long time yet, the word civilization will continue to be used in both singular and plural. On this point, the historian is not afraid to be categorical.

2. The Study of Civilization
Involves All the Social Sciences

===

To define the idea of civilization requires the combined efforts of all the social sciences. They include history; but in this chapter it will play only a minor role.

Here, it is the other social sciences that in turn will be called in aid: geography, sociology, economics and collective psychology. This means four excursions into very contrasting fields. But, despite initial appearances, the results will be seen to tally.

Civilizations as geographical areas

Civilizations, vast or otherwise, can always be located on a map. An essential part of their character depends on the constraints or advantages of their geographical situation.

This, of course, will have been affected for centuries or even millennia by human effort. Every landscape bears the traces of this continuous and cumulative labour, generation after generation contributing to the whole. So doing, humanity itself has been transformed by what the French historian Jules Michelet called 'the decisive shaping of self by self', or (as Karl Marx put it) 'the production of people by people'.

To discuss civilization is to discuss space, land and its contours, climate, vegetation, animal species and natural or other advantages. It is also to discuss what humanity has made of these basic conditions:

agriculture, stock-breeding, food, shelter, clothing, communications, industry and so on.

The stage on which humanity's endless dramas are played out partly determines their story-line and explains their nature. The cast will alter, but the set remains broadly the same.

For the expert on India, Hermann Goetz, there are two essential Indias. One is humid, with heavy rainfall, lakes, marshes, forests and jungles, aquatic plants and flowers – the land of people with dark skins. It contrasts with the dryer India of the Indo-Gangetic plain, plus the Deccan plateau – the home of lighter-skinned people, many of them warlike. India as a whole, in Goetz's view, is a debate and a tug-of-war between these two contrasting areas and peoples.

The natural and man-made environment, of course, cannot predetermine everything. It is not all-powerful. But it greatly affects the inherent or acquired advantages of any given situation.

To take inherent advantages, every civilization is born of immediate opportunities, rapidly exploited. Thus in the dawn of time, river civilizations flourished in the old world: Chinese civilization along the Yellow River; pre-Indian along the Indus; Sumerian, Babylonian and Assyrian on the Euphrates and the Tigris; Egyptian on the Nile. A similar group of vigorous civilizations developed in Northern Europe, around the Baltic and the North Sea – not to mention the Atlantic Ocean itself. Much of the West and its dependencies today, in fact, are grouped around that ocean, rather as the Roman world of former times was grouped around the Mediterranean.

These classic instances reveal above all the prime importance of communications. No civilization can survive without mobility: all are enriched by trade and the stimulating impact of strangers. Islam, for instance, is inconceivable without the movement of its caravans across the 'dry seas' of its deserts and steppes, without its expeditions in the Mediterranean and across the Indian Ocean as far as Malacca and China.

Mentioning these achievements has already led us beyond the

natural and immediate advantages which supposedly gave rise to civilizations. To overcome the hostility of the desert or the sudden squalls of the Mediterranean, to exploit the steady winds of the Indian Ocean, or to dam a river – all that needed human effort, to enjoy advantages, or rather to create them.

But why were some people capable of such achievements, but not others, in some places but not others, for generations on end?

Arnold Toynbee offered a tempting theory. All human achievement, he thought, involved challenge and response. Nature had to present itself as a difficulty to be overcome. If human beings took up the challenge, their response would lay the foundations of civilization.

But if this theory were carried to the limit, would it imply that the greater the challenge from Nature, the stronger humanity's response? It seems doubtful. In the twentieth century, civilized men and women have taken up the forbidding challenge of the deserts, the polar regions and the equator. Yet, despite the material interests involved, such as gold or oil, they have not yet settled and multiplied in those areas and founded true civilizations there. A challenge, yes, and also a response: but civilization does not always follow – at least until improved technology makes the response more adequate.

Every civilization, then, is based on an area with more or less fixed limits. Each has its own geography with its own opportunities and constraints, some virtually permanent and quite different from one civilization to another. The result? A variegated world, whose maps can indicate which areas have houses built of wood, and which of clay, bamboo, paper, bricks or stone; which areas use wool or cotton or silk for textiles; which areas grow various food crops – rice, maize, wheat, etc. The challenge varies: so does the response.

Western or European civilization is based on wheat and bread – and largely white bread – with all the constraints that this implies. Wheat is a demanding crop. It requires field use to be rotated annually, or fields to be left fallow every one or two years. Equally, the flooded rice-fields of the Far East, gradually spreading into low-lying areas, impose their own constraints on land use and local customs.

Responses to natural challenges thus continually free humanity from its environment and at the same time subject it to the resultant solutions. We exchange one form of determinism for another.

A cultural zone, as defined by anthropologists, is an area within which one group of cultural characteristics is dominant. In the case of primitive peoples, these may include not only their language but also their food crops, their marriage ceremonies, their religious beliefs, their pottery, their feathered arrows, their weaving techniques and so on. Defined by anthropologists on the basis of precise details, these zones are generally small.

Some cultural zones, however, cover much larger areas, united by characteristics common to the group and differentiating them from other large communities. Marcel Mauss claims that the primitive cultures surrounding the vast Pacific Ocean, despite the obvious differences and immense distances between them, are all part of a single human or rather cultural whole.

Naturally enough, following the example of the anthropologists, geographers and historians have taken to discussing cultural zones – this time with reference to advanced and complex civilizations. They identify areas which in turn can be subdivided into a series of districts. Such subdivision, as we shall see, applies essentially to large civilizations: these regularly resolve themselves into smaller units.

Western civilization, so-called, is at once the 'American civilization' of the United States, and the civilizations of Latin America, Russia and of course Europe. Europe itself contains a number of civilizations – Polish, German, Italian, English, French, etc. Not to mention the fact that these national civilizations are made up of 'civilizations' that are smaller still: Scotland, Ireland, Catalonia, Sicily, the Basque country and so on. Nor should we forget that these divisions, these multi-coloured mosaics, embody more or less permanent characteristics.

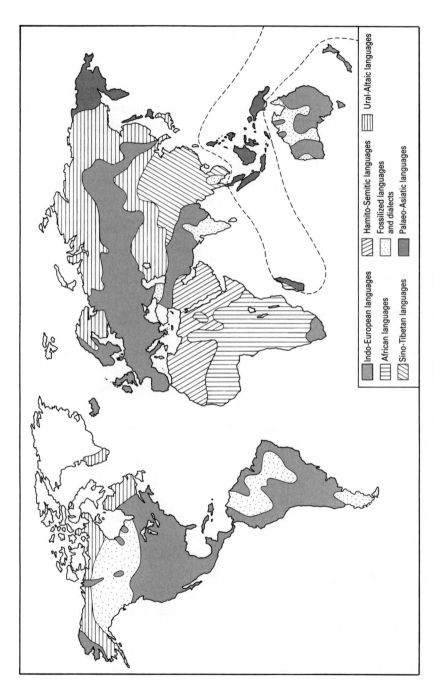

2. *Linguistic map of the world*

Indo-European languages

African languages

Sino-Tibetan languages

Hamito-Semitic languages

Fossilized languages
and dialects

Ural-Altaic languages

Palaeo-Asiatic languages

The stability of these cultural zones and their frontiers does not however isolate them from cultural imports. Every civilization imports and exports aspects of its culture. These may include the lost-wax process for casting, the compass, gunpowder, the technique for tempering steel, a complete or fragmentary philosophical system, a cult, a religion or the song about Marlborough that went the rounds of Europe in the eighteenth century: Goethe heard it in the streets of Verona in 1786.

The Brazilian sociologist Gilberto Freyre once made a list of all that his country had received pell-mell from Europe – then very distant – in the last decades of the eighteenth century and the first five or six of the nineteenth. It included brown beer from Hamburg, the English cottage, the steam engine (a steamship was already plying the *baia* of San Salvador in 1819), white linen summer clothes, false teeth, gas lighting and – ahead of all of them – secret societies, notably Freemasonry, which played so big a role in Latin America at the time of independence. A few decades later came the philosophical system of Auguste Comte, whose influence was so marked that traces of it can be detected there even today.

The example of Brazil is one among many. It shows that no cultural frontier is ever completely closed.

In the past, cultural influences came in small doses, delayed by the length and slowness of the journeys they had to make. If historians are to be believed, the Chinese fashions of the T'ang period travelled so slowly that they did not reach the island of Cyprus and the brilliant court of Lusignan until the fifteenth century. From there they spread, at the quicker speed of Mediterranean trade, to France and the eccentric court of Charles VI, where hennins and shoes with long pointed toes became immensely popular, the heritage of a long vanished world – much as light still reaches us from stars already extinct.

Today, the spread of cultural influence has attained vertiginous speed. There will soon be nowhere in the world that has not been 'contaminated' by the industrial civilization that originated in Europe. In North Borneo (which with Sarawak was under British rule until 1963), a few loudspeakers used to relay radio programmes from Communist China and Indonesia. Their listeners understood nothing of what the broadcasts were saying, but the rhythms they heard very soon affected their traditional music and dancing. How much greater is the influence of the cinema, especially from Europe and America, on the tastes and even the customs of countries on the far side of the world.

No example, however, could be more telling than an experience described by the American anthropologist Margaret Mead. In her youth she had studied a Pacific island people whose life she had shared for several months. The war brought them into unexpected contact with the outside world. After the war, Margaret Mead returned and wrote a book in which she movingly described what had happened, with photographs showing many of the same people as they had been and as they were, totally transformed.

Such, again, is the dialogue between civilization and civilizations of which we shall hear so much in this book. Will the ever faster spread of cultural influence remove the frontiers between civilizations that were once so firm in world history? Many people fear – and some rejoice – that they will. Yet, however avid civilizations are to acquire the material adjuncts of 'modern' life, they are not prepared to take on everything indiscriminately. It even happens, as we shall see, that they stubbornly reject outside influence. This is why, now as in the past, they are still able to safeguard characteristics that everything seems to threaten with extinction.

Civilizations as societies

There can be no civilizations without the societies that support them and inspire their tensions and their progress. Hence the first inevitable question: was it necessary to invent the word 'civilization' and encourage its academic use, if it remains merely a synonym for 'society'? Arnold Toynbee continually used the word 'society' in place of 'civilization'. And Marcel Mauss believed that 'the idea of civilization is certainly less clear than that of society, which it presupposes'.

Society and civilization are inseparable: the two ideas refer to the same reality. Or, as Claude Lévi-Strauss put it, 'they do not represent different objects, but two complementary views of a single object, which can perfectly well be described by either term according to one's point of view.'

The idea of 'society' implies a wealth of content. In this it closely resembles that of civilization, with which it is so often linked. The Western civilization in which we live, for example, depends on the 'industrial society' which is its driving force. It would be easy to characterize Western civilization simply by describing that society and its component parts, its tensions, its moral and intellectual values, its ideals, its habits, its tastes, etc. – in other words by describing the people who embody it and who will pass it on.

If a society stirs and changes, the civilization based on it stirs and changes too. This point is made in a fine book by Lucien Goldmann, *The Hidden God* (*Le Dieu caché*, 1955), which deals with the France of Louis XIV. Every civilization, Goldmann explains, draws its essential insights from the 'view of the world' it adopts. And in every case this view of the world is coloured, if not determined, by social tensions. Civilization simply reflects them like a mirror.

The age of Jansenism, Racine, Pascal, the abbé de Saint-Cyran and the abbé Barcos, whose fascinating letters Goldmann has rediscovered, was as *The Hidden God* shows an impassioned moment in the history of France; and the tragic view of the world that prevailed then had originated with the parliamentary upper middle classes, disillusioned by the monarchy with which they were at odds. The tragedy of their fate, their awareness of it, and their intellectual ascendancy all combined to imbue the period with their own dominant mood.

In a quite different spirit, Claude Lévi-Strauss also identifies civilizations with societies when he argues the difference between primitive and modern societies – or, as most anthropologists put it, between cultures and civilizations. Cultures in this sense are societies

which produce little disorder – what doctors call 'entropy' – and tend to remain indefinitely as they originally were: which is why they look to us like societies that lack both history and progress. Whereas our societies (those that correspond to modern civilizations) ... are powered by a difference of electrical pressure, as it were, expressed in various forms of social hierarchy ... Such societies have managed to establish within them a social imbalance which they use to produce both much greater order – we have societies that work like machines – and much greater disorder, much less entropy, in relations between people.

For Lévi-Strauss, then, primitive cultures are the fruit of egalitarian societies, where relations between groups are settled once and for all and remain constant, whereas civilizations are based on hierarchical societies with wide gaps between groups and hence shifting tensions, social conflicts, political struggles, and continual evolution.

The most obvious external sign of these differences between 'cultures' and 'civilizations' is undoubtedly the presence or absence of towns. Towns proliferate in civilizations: in cultures they remain embryonic. There are of course intermediate stages and degrees. What is Black Africa but a group of traditional societies – of cultures – embarked on the difficult and sometimes cruel process of fostering civilization and modern urban development? African cities, taking their models from abroad in a style now international, remain islands amid the stagnation of the countryside. They prefigure the society and the civilization to come.

The most brilliant societies and civilizations, however, presuppose within their own borders cultures and societies of a more elementary kind. Take, for example, the interplay of town and country, never to be underestimated. In no society have all regions and all parts of the population developed equally. Underdevelopment is common in mountain areas or patches of poverty off the beaten track of modern communications – genuinely primitive societies, true 'cultures' in the midst of a civilization.

The West's first success was certainly the conquest of its countryside – its peasant 'cultures' – by the towns. In the Islamic world, the duality remains more visible than in the West. Islamic towns were quicker to arise – were more precociously urban, so to speak – than in Europe, while the countryside remained more primitive, with vast areas of nomadic life. In the Far East, that contrast is still the general rule: its 'cultures' remain very isolated, living by themselves and on their own resources. Between the most brilliant cities lie tracts of countryside whose way of life is almost self-sufficient, at subsistence level, and sometimes actually barbaric.

Given the close relationship between civilization and society, there is a case for adopting the sociological mode when looking at the long history of civilizations. As historians, however, we should not simply confuse societies with civilizations. We shall explain in the next chapter what we believe the difference to be: in terms of the time-scale, civilization implies and embraces much longer periods than any given social phenomenon. It changes far less rapidly than the societies it supports or involves. But this is not yet the moment to go fully into that question. One thing at a time.

Civilizations as economies

Every society, every civilization, depends on economic, technological, biological and demographic circumstances. Material and biological conditions always help determine the destiny of civilizations. A rise or a fall in the population, health or illness, economic or technological growth or decline – all these deeply affect the cultural as well as the social structure. Political economy in the broadest sense is the study of all these massive problems.

For a long time, people were humanity's only major implement or form of energy – the sole resource for building a civilization by sheer brawn and brain. In principle and in fact, therefore, an increase in the population has always helped the growth of civilization – as in Europe in the thirteenth, sixteenth, eighteenth, nineteenth and twentieth centuries.

Just as regularly, however, when the population grows faster than the economy, what was once an advantage becomes a drawback. Such was the case, undoubtedly, by the end of the sixteenth century, as it is today in most underdeveloped countries. The results in the past were famines, a fall in real earnings, popular uprisings and grim periods of slump: until epidemics and starvation together brutally thinned out the too-serried ranks of human beings. After such biological disasters (like that in Europe in the second half of the fourteenth century, with the Black Death and the epidemics that followed it), the survivors briefly had an easier time and expansion began again, at increasing speed – until the next setback.

Only industrialization, at the end of the eighteenth century and the beginning of the nineteenth, seemed to have broken this vicious circle and made even surplus people valuable again, able to work and live. As the history of Europe showed, the growing value and cost of human labour, and the need to economize on employees, encouraged the development of machines. Classical antiquity, intelligent as it was, had no machines to match its intelligence. It never really tried to acquire them. Its failing was that it possessed slaves. Imperial China, flourishing long before the eighteenth century, very intelligent and technically skilful, nevertheless suffered also: it had too many people. They cost very little, and performed almost all the tasks required by an economy virtually lacking animal power. As a result, although China enjoyed a long lead in matters scientific, it never crossed the threshold of modern science and technology. That privilege, that honour, that profit it left to Europe.

Economic life never ceases to fluctuate, at intervals sometimes long and sometimes short. Good times and bad times succeed each other; and societies and civilizations feel their effects, especially when the upturn or downturn is prolonged. The pessimism and disquiet that were widespread in the late fifteenth century – what

Johan Huizinga called *The Waning of the Middle Ages* – reflected a marked recession in the economy of the West. European Romanticism, likewise, coincided with a long economic recession between 1817 and 1852. The expansion in the mid-eighteenth century (from 1733 onwards) saw some setbacks (for instance on the eve of the French Revolution); but in general at that time economic growth placed the intellectual development of the Enlightenment in a context of material well-being, active trade, expanding industry, and growing population.

Whether in boom or slump, economic activity almost always produces a surplus. The expenditure, or squandering, of such surpluses has been one of the indispensable conditions for luxury in civilizations and for certain forms of art. When today we admire architecture, sculpture or portraits we are also contemplating, not always consciously, the calm pride of a city, the vainglorious folly of a prince or the wealth of a *nouveau-riche* merchant banker. In Europe from the sixteenth century onwards (and probably earlier), the ultimate phase of civilization wears the emblem of capitalism and wealth.

So civilization reflects a redistribution of wealth. Civilizations acquire different characteristics, first at the top and then among the mass of the people, according to their way of redistributing wealth, and according to the social and economic machinery which takes from the circulation of wealth whatever is destined for luxury, art or culture. In the seventeenth century, during the very hard times of Louis XIV's reign, there were very few patrons except at Court. Literary and artistic life was confined to this small circle. In the lavish, easy-going economic climate of the eighteenth century, aristocracy and bourgeoisie joined with royalty in spreading culture, science and philosophy.

But luxury, at that time, was still the privilege of a social minority. The civilization underlying it, that of modest workaday life, had very little share in it. And the ground floor of a civilization is often its crucial level. What is freedom – what is an individual's culture – without enough to live on? From this point of view the much-maligned nineteenth century, that boring century of the *nouveaux riches* and the 'triumphant bourgeoisie', was the harbinger (if not yet the exemplar) of a new destiny for civilizations and for the human personality. While the population rapidly increased, more and more of its members were able to enjoy a certain collective civilization. No doubt the social cost of this transformation – unconscious, admittedly – was very heavy. But its advantages were great. The development of education, access to culture, admission to the universities, social progress – these were the achievements of the nineteenth century, already rich, and full of significance for the future.

The great problem for tomorrow, as for today, is to create a mass civilization of high quality. To do so is very costly. It is unthinkable without large surpluses devoted to the service of society, and without the leisure that mechanization will no doubt soon be able to offer us. In the industrialized countries, such a future can be envisaged not too far ahead. The problem is more complex in the world as a whole. For, just as economic growth has made civilization more accessible to some social classes than to others, it has similarly differentiated various countries in the world. Much of the world's population is what one essayist has called 'the foreign proletariat', better known as the Third World – an enormous mass of people, many of whom have yet to earn a bare living before they can enjoy the benefits of their own countries' civilization, which to them is often a closed book. Unless humanity makes the effort to redress these vast inequalities, they could bring civilizations – and civilization – to an end.

Civilizations as ways of thought

After geography, sociology and economics, we must finally turn to psychology. With this difference: that, as a science, collective psychology is less self-confident and less rich in results than the other social sciences so far considered. It has also rarely ventured along the paths of history.

Collective psychology, awareness, mentality or mental equipment? It is impossible to choose among them. Such uncertainties about vocabulary show what a youthful science collective psychology still is. 'Psychology' is the expression preferred by Alphonse Dupront, a great specialist in this field. 'Awareness' refers only to a phase of development, generally the final phase. 'Mentality' is obviously more convenient. Lucien Febvre, in his excellent *Rabelais*, prefers to speak of 'mental equipment'. But the words matter little: they are not the problem. In every period, a certain view of the world, a collective mentality, dominates the whole mass of society. Dictating a society's attitudes, guiding its choices, confirming its prejudices and directing its actions, this is very much a fact of civilization. Far more than the accidents or the historical and social circumstances of a period, it derives from the distant past, from ancient beliefs, fears and anxieties which are almost unconscious – an immense contamination whose germs are lost to memory but transmitted from generation to generation. A society's reactions to the events of the day, to the pressure upon it, to the decisions it must face, are less a matter of logic or even self-interest than the response to an unexpressed and often inexpressible compulsion arising from the collective unconscious.

These basic values, these psychological structures, are assuredly the features that civilizations can least easily communicate one to another. They are what isolate and differentiate them most sharply. And such habits of mind survive the passage of time. They change little, and change slowly, after a long incubation which itself is largely unconscious too.

Here religion is the strongest feature of civilizations, at the heart of both their present and their past. And in the first place, of course, in civilizations outside Europe. In India, for instance, all actions derive their form and their justification from the religious life, not from reasoning. The Greeks were astonished by this, to judge from an anecdote reported by Eusebius, Bishop of Caesarea (265–340): 'Aristoxenus the musician tells the following story about the Indians. One of them met Socrates in Athens and asked him to describe his philosophy. "It is the study of human reality," replied Socrates. At which the Indian burst out laughing. "How can a man study human reality," he asked, "when he knows nothing of divine reality?" '

Siniti Kunar Chatterji, a contemporary Hindu philosopher, gives the following well-known illustration of humanity's inability to fathom the immense mystery and unity of the supernatural. 'We are like blind people who, feeling this or that part of an elephant's body, are severally convinced that one of them is touching a pillar, another a snake, a third something hard, the fourth a wall and another a brush with a flexible handle – according to whether they are in contact with a leg, the trunk, a tusk, the body or the tail.'

By comparison with this deep religious humility, the West seems forgetful of its Christian sources. But, rather than stress the break that rationalism has supposedly made between religion and culture, it is more to the point to consider the coexistence of laicism, science and religion and the serene or stormy dialogue in which, despite appearances, they have always been engaged. Christianity is an essential reality in Western life: it even marks atheists, whether they know it or not. Ethical rules, attitudes to life and death, the concept of work, the value of effort, the role of women and children – these may seem to have nothing to do with Christian feeling: yet all derive from it nevertheless.

Since the development of Greek thought, however, the tendency of Western civilization has been towards rationalism and hence away from the religious life. That is its distinguishing characteristic, and something to which we shall return. With very few exceptions (certain Chinese sophists, and certain Arab philosophers in the twelfth century), no such marked turning away from religion is to be found in the history of the world outside the West. Almost all civilizations are pervaded or submerged by religion, by the supernatural, and by magic: they have always been steeped in it, and they draw from it the most powerful motives in their particular psychology. This is a phenomenon we shall have many opportunities to observe.

3. The Continuity of Civilizations

The time has come for history to join this complex debate. It may add further complexity: but its use of a time-scale and its capacity to explain matters should make sense of the subject. In fact, no existing civilization can be truly understood without some knowledge of the paths it has followed, the values it has inherited, and the experiences it has undergone. A civilization always involves a past, lived and still alive.

The history of a civilization, then, is a search among ancient data for those still valid today. It is not a question of telling us all there is to be known about Greek civilization or the Middle Ages in China – but only what of former times is still relevant today, in Western Europe or in modern China: everything in which there is a short-circuit between past and present, often across many centuries' gap.

Periods within civilizations

But let us begin at the beginning. Every civilization, both yesterday and today, is immediately manifest in something easily grasped: a play, an exhibition of paintings, a successful book, a philosophy, a fashion in dress, a scientific discovery, a technological advance – all of them apparently independent of one another. (At first sight, there is no link between the philosophy of Maurice Merleau-Ponty and a late painting by Picasso.)

These manifestations of a civilization, it may be noted, are always short-lived. How then can they help us to map out a past which is also present, when they seem so often to replace and destroy each other, rather than show any sort of continuity?

These spectacles are in fact subject to relentless change. The programme is continually altered: no one wants it to run for too long. This can be seen by the way in which literary, artistic and philosophical periods succeed one another. It can be said, borrowing a phrase from the economists, that there are cycles in cultural affairs as there are in economics – more or less protracted or precipitate fluctuations which in most cases violently counter those that went before. From one period to another, everything changes or seems to change, rather as stage lighting, without striking the set or changing the actors' make-up, can show them in new colours and project them into a different world. Of these periods, the Renaissance is the finest example. It had its own themes, its own colours and preferences, even its own mannerisms. It was marked by intellectual fervour, love of beauty, and free, tolerant debates in which wit was another sign of enjoyment. It was also marked by the discovery or rediscovery of the works of classical antiquity, a pursuit in which all of civilized Europe enthusiastically joined.

Similarly, there was a Romantic era (roughly from 1800 to 1850, but with both earlier and later manifestations); it coloured people's minds and feelings over a long, troubled, difficult period, in the joyless aftermath of the French Revolution and the Empire, which coincided with an economic recession throughout Europe, between 1817 and 1852. We should certainly not claim that the recession alone explained – still less, created – Romantic *Angst*: there are not only economic cycles, but also cycles in sensibility, in the arts of living and thinking, which are more or less independent of external events ... Every generation, at all events, likes to contradict its predecessor; and its successor will do the same and more. So there is likely to be a perpetual swing of the pendulum between classicism and romanticism (or baroque, as Eugenio d'Ors

called it), between cool intelligence and warm, troubled emotion –
often in striking contrast.

The resultant pattern, therefore, is a constant alternation of
mood. A civilization, like an economy, has its own rhythms. Its
history is episodic, easy to divide into sections or periods, each
virtually distinct. We refer quite happily to 'the century of Louis
XIV' or to 'the Enlightenment': we even, in French, speak of
'classic civilization' in the seventeenth century, or 'the civilization
of the eighteenth century'. To call such short periods civilizations,
according to the philosophically minded economist Joseph Chappey, is 'diabolical': it seems to him to contradict the very idea of
civilization, which (as we shall see) involves continuity. But for
the moment let us leave this contradiction aside. Unity and
diversity, after all, always coexist uneasily. We have to take them
as they come.

'Turning-points', events, heroes: all help to clarify the special role
of exceptional events and people in the history of civilizations.

Every episode, when studied closely, dissolves into a series of
actions, gestures and characters. Civilizations, in the last analysis,
are made up of people, and hence of their behaviour, their achievements, their enthusiasms, their commitment to various causes, and
also their sudden changes. But the historian has to select: among
all these actions, achievements and biographies, certain events or
people stand out and mark a 'turning-point', a new phase. The more
important the change, the more clearly significant its harbingers.

One example of a crucial event was the discovery of universal
gravitation by Sir Isaac Newton in 1687. Significant events include
the first performance of *Le Cid* in 1638 or of *Hernani* in 1830.
People stand out likewise, in so far as their work marks an epoch
or sums up an historical episode. This is the case with Joachim du
Bellay (1522–60) and his *Defence and Illustration of the French
Language*; with Gottfried Wilhelm Leibniz (1646–1716) and his
infinitesimal calculus; or with Denis Papin (1647–1714) and his
invention of the steam-engine.

But the names that really dominate the history of civilizations are those which survive a number of episodes, as a ship may ride out a series of storms. A few rare spirits mark the limits of vast periods, summing up in themselves a number of generations: Dante (1265–1321) at the end of the 'Latin' Middle Ages; Goethe (1749–1832) at the end of Europe's first 'modern' period; Newton on the threshold of classical physics; or Albert Einstein (1879–1955), herald of today's sub-atomic physics with all its enormous significance for the world.

The founders of great philosophies also belong in this exceptional category: Socrates or Plato, Confucius, Descartes or Karl Marx – each dominates more than one century. In their way, they are founders of civilizations, scarcely less important than those outstanding founders of the world's abiding religions, Buddha, Christ and Muhammad.

In fact, the measure of an event's or a person's importance in the hurly-burly of history is the time they take to be forgotten. Only those that endure and are identified with an enduring reality really count in the history of civilization. Thus may be discerned, through the screen of familiar historical events, the emerging outlines of the more continuous reality which we must now seek to discover.

Underlying structures

Looking at historical periods has produced only transient pictures: projected on the backcloth of civilizations, they appear and then vanish again. If we look for the permanent features behind these changing images, we shall find other, simpler realities which present a quite new interest. Some last for only a few seasons; others endure for several centuries; others still persist so long as to seem immutable. The appearance, of course, is illusory; for, slowly and imperceptibly, they too change and decay. Such are the realities referred to in the previous chapter: the ceaseless constraints imposed by geography, by social hierarchy, by collective psychology and by economic need – all profound forces, barely recognized at first, especially by contemporaries, to whom they always seem perfectly natural, to be taken wholly for granted if they are thought about at all. These realities are what we now call 'structures'.

Even historians may not notice them at first: their habitual chronological narratives are often too busy to see the wood for the trees. To perceive and trace underlying structures one has to cover, in spendthrift fashion, immense stretches of time. The movements on the surface discussed a moment ago, the events and the people, fade from the picture when we contemplate these vast phenomena, permanent or semi-permanent, conscious and subconscious at the same time. These are the 'foundations', the underlying *structures* of civilizations: religious beliefs, for instance, or a timeless peasantry, or attitudes to death, work, pleasure and family life.

These realities, these structures, are generally ancient and long-lived, and always distinctive and original. They it is that give civilizations their essential outline and characteristic quality. And civilizations hardly ever exchange them: they regard them as irreplaceable values. For the majority of people, of course, these enduring traits, these inherited choices, these reasons for rejecting other civilizations, are generally unconscious. To see them clearly one has to withdraw, mentally at least, from the civilization of which one is a part.

Take as a simple example, with very deep roots: the role of women in the twentieth century in a society like ours in Europe. Its peculiarities may not strike us – so 'natural' do they seem – until we make a comparison with, say, the role of Muslim women or, at the other extreme, that of women in the United States. To understand why these differences arose, we should have to go far back into the past, at least as far as the twelfth century, the age of 'courtly love', and begin to trace the Western conception of love and of the couple. We should then have to consider a series of factors: Christianity, women's access to schools and universities, European ideas about the education of children, economic conditions, the standard of living, women's work outside the home and so on.

The role of women is always a structural element in any civilization – a test: it is a long-lived reality, resistant to external pressure, and hard to change overnight. A civilization generally refuses to accept a cultural innovation that calls in question one of its own structural elements. Such refusals or unspoken enmities are relatively rare: but they always point to the heart of a civilization.

Civilizations continually borrow from their neighbours, even if they 'reinterpret' and assimilate what they have adopted. At first sight, indeed, every civilization looks rather like a railway goods yard, constantly receiving and dispatching miscellaneous deliveries.

Yet a civilization may stubbornly reject a particular import from outside. Marcel Mauss has remarked that every civilization worthy of the name has refused or rejected something. Every time, the refusal is the culmination of a long period of hesitation and experiment. Long meditated and slowly reached, the decision is always crucially important.

The classical instance is the Turkish capture of Constantinople in 1453. A modern Turkish historian claims that the city gave itself up, that it was conquered from within, before the Turkish attack. Although an exaggeration, this thesis is not unfounded. In fact, the Orthodox Church (or Byzantine civilization) preferred to submit to the Turks rather than unite with the Latins who were its only possible saviours. This was not a 'decision', taken hastily on the spot under the pressure of events. It was rather the natural outcome of a long process, as long in fact as the decadence of Byzantium, which day after day made the Greeks more and more reluctant to draw closer to the Latins across the great divide of their theological disputes.

Greco-Latin union would have been possible. The Emperor Michael Palaeologus had accepted it at the Council of Lyon in 1274. The Emperor John V, in 1369, had professed the Catholic faith in Rome. In 1439, the joint Council of Florence had once more shown that union was attainable. The most eminent Greek theologians, John Beccos, Demetrios Lydones and John Bessarion, had all written in favour of union, with a talent which their opponents could not equal. Yet, between the Turks and the Latins, the Greeks preferred the Turks. 'Because it was jealous of its independence, the Byzantine Church appealed to the enemy and surrendered to him the Empire and Christendom.' Already in 1385 the Patriarch of Constantinople had written to Pope Urban VI that the Turks offered to the Greek Church 'full liberty of action' – and that was the decisive phrase. Fernand Grenard, from whom these points are taken, added: 'The enslavement of Constantinople by Muhammad II was the triumph of the separatist Patriarch.' The West, for its part, was well aware of how much the Eastern Church disliked it. 'These schismatics,' wrote Petrarch, 'feared and hated us with all their guts.'

Another refusal which was slow to take shape was the closing of Italy and the Iberian Peninsula to the Protestant Reformation. In France, there was more hesitation: for nearly a hundred years the country was a battleground between two different forms of belief.

A further refusal, and one which was not wholly political (or unanimous), was that which so long divided the industrialized West, including North America, from the totalitarian Marxist Socialism of Eastern Europe. The Germanic and Anglo-Saxon countries said No categorically: France and Italy – and even the Iberian Peninsula – gave a more mixed and equivocal response. This, very probably, was a clash between civilizations.

One might add that, if Western Europe had taken to Communism, it would have done so in its own way, adapting it as it is currently adapting capitalism, very differently from the USA.

Just as a civilization may welcome or refuse elements from another civilization, so it may accept or reject survivals from its own past. It does so slowly, and almost always unconsciously or partly so. In this way, it gradually transforms itself. Little by little, it sifts the mass of data and attitudes offered by the remote or recent past, stressing one or setting aside another; and as a result of its choices it assumes a shape which is never wholly new but never quite the same as before.

These internal rejections may be firm or hesitant, lasting or short-lived. Only the lasting rejections are essential in the areas which are gradually being explored by psychological history, and which may be as large as a country or a civilization. Examples of such exploration include: two pioneering studies of life and death in the fifteenth and sixteenth centuries, by Alberto Tenenti; an examination of *The Idea of Happiness in Eighteenth-century France*, by R. Mauzi; and a fascinating, fascinated book by Michel Foucault on *The History of Madness in the Classical Age*, 1961. These three cases are instances of a civilization working over its own heritage – something rarely brought fully to light. The process is so slow that contemporaries never notice it. Each time, the rejection – and the occasional acceptance of alternatives – takes centuries, with prohibitions, obstacles and healing processes which are often difficult and imperfect and always very prolonged.

This is what Michel Foucault, in his own peculiar terminology, calls 'dividing oneself off' – that is, in the case of a civilization, expelling from its frontiers and from its inner life any value that it spurns. 'One might,' writes Foucault,

trace the history of the *limits*, of those obscure actions, necessarily forgotten as soon as they are performed, whereby a civilization casts aside something it regards as alien. Throughout its history, this moat which it digs around itself, this no man's land by which it preserves its isolation, is just as characteristic as its positive values. For it receives and maintains its values as continuous features of its history; but in the area which we have chosen to discuss it makes its essential choice – the *selection* [our emphasis] – which gives it its positive nature – the essential substance of which it is made.

This text deserves close attention. A civilization attains its true persona by rejecting what troubles it in the obscurity of that no man's land which may already be foreign territory. Its history is the centuries-long distillation of a collective personality, caught like any individual between its clear, conscious objective and its obscure, unconscious fate, whose influence on aims and motives is often unobserved. Clearly, such essays in retrospective psychology have been affected by the discoveries of psychoanalysis.

Michel Foucault's book studies a particular case: the distinction between reason and madness, between the sane and the mad, which was unknown in the Middle Ages, when the Fool, like any unfortunate, was more or less mysteriously held to be an emissary from God. But the mentally deranged were imprisoned, at first harshly and brutally, in the seventeenth century with its passion for social order. It regarded them as mere jetsam, to be banished from the world like delinquents or the incorrigibly idle. Then, in the nineteenth century, they were treated more fairly, even kindly, because they were recognized as ill. Yet, although attitudes changed, the central problem remained. From the classical age until today, the West has distanced itself from madness, banning its language and banishing its victims. Thus the triumph of reason has been accompanied, under the surface, by a long, silent turbulence, the almost unconscious, almost unknown counterpart to the public victory of rationalism and of classical science.

One could of course give other examples. Alberto Tenenti's book patiently traces the way in which the West distanced itself from the Christian idea of death as envisaged in the Middle Ages – a simple transition from exile on earth to real life beyond the grave. In the fifteenth century, death became 'human' – humanity's supreme ordeal, the horror of decomposing flesh. But in this new conception of death people found a new conception of life, prized anew for its own intrinsic worth. Anxiety about death abated in the following century, the sixteenth, which – at least at the beginning – was marked by *joie de vivre*.

So far, the argument has presupposed peaceful relations between civilizations, each free to make its own choice. But violence has often been the rule. Always tragic, it has often proved ultimately pointless. Successes like the Romanization of Gaul and of much of Western Europe can be explained only by the length of time the process took – and, despite what is often alleged – by the primitive level from which Rome's vassals began, by their admiration for their conquerors, and in fact by their acquiescence in their own fate. But such successes were rare: they are the exceptions that prove the rule.

When contact was violent, in fact, failure was more frequent than success. 'Colonialism' may have triumphed in the past: but today it is an obvious fiasco. And colonialism, typically, is the submergence of one civilization by another. The conquered always submit to the stronger; but their submission is merely provisional when civilizations clash.

Long periods of enforced coexistence may include concessions or agreements and important, often fruitful, cultural exchange. But the process always has its limits.

The finest example of cultural interpenetration in a climate of violence is described in Roger Bastide's outstanding book on *African Religions in Brazil* (1960). This tells the tragic story of black slaves torn from their roots in Africa and flung into the patriarchal Christian society of colonial Brazil. They reacted against it; but at the same time they adopted Christianity. A number of runaway black slaves founded independent republics – *quilombos*: that of Palmeiras, north-east of Bahia, was not conquered without a full-scale war. Although stripped of everything, blacks such as these reinstated old African religious practices and magic dances. In their *candomblés* or *macumbas* they fused African and Christian rites in a synthesis which is still alive today, and even making further headway. It is an amazing example. The vanquished surrendered – but preserved themselves too.

History and civilization

Looking back over civilizations' resistance or acquiescence in the face of change, their permanence and their slow transformation, we can perhaps offer one last definition, which may restore their

unique and particular essence: that is, their long historical continuity. Civilization is in fact the longest story of all. This is a truth
which the historian may at first not realize. It will emerge in the
course of successive observations, rather in the same way that the
view of a landscape broadens as the path ascends.

History operates in tenses, on scales and in units which frequently
vary: day by day, year by year, decade by decade, or in whole
centuries. Every time, the unit of measurement modifies the view.
It is the contrasts between the realities observed on different time-
scales that make possible history's dialectic.

For the sake of simplicity, let us say that the historian works on
at least three planes.

One, which we may call A, is that of traditional history, habitual
narrative, hurrying from one event to the next like a chronicler of
old or a reporter today. A thousand pictures are seized on the
wing, making a multi-coloured story as full of incident as an
unending serial. No sooner read than forgotten, however, this
kind of history too often leaves us unsatisfied, unable to judge or
to understand.

A second plane – B – is that of episodes, each taken as a whole:
Romanticism, the French Revolution, the Industrial Revolution,
World War II. The time-scale here may be ten, twenty or fifty
years. And facts are grouped, interpreted and explained in accordance with these phenomena, whether they be called periods, phases,
episodes or cycles. They can be regarded as events of long duration,
stripped of superfluous detail.

A third plane – C – transcends these events: it considers only
phenomena that can be measured over a century or more. At this
level, the movement of history is slow and covers vast reaches of
time: to cross it requires seven-league boots. On this scale, the
French Revolution is no more than a moment, however essential,
in the long history of the revolutionary, liberal and violent destiny
of the West. Voltaire, likewise, is only a stage in the evolution of
free thought.

In this final perspective – sociologists, who have their own imagery, might say 'on this last deep level' – civilizations can be seen as distinct from the accidents and vicissitudes that mark their development: they reveal their longevity, their permanent features, their structures – their almost abstract but yet essential diagrammatic form.

A civilization, then, is neither a given economy nor a given society, but something which can persist through a series of economies or societies, barely susceptible to gradual change. A civilization can be approached, therefore, only in the long term, taking hold of a constantly unwinding thread – something that a group of people have conserved and passed on as their most precious heritage from generation to generation, throughout and despite the storms and tumults of history.

This being so, we should hesitate before agreeing with the great Spanish historian Rafaël Altamira (1951) or with François Guizot (1855) that the history of civilizations is 'all of history'. No doubt it is: but only if seen in a particular way, using the largest time-scale that is compatible with human and historical concerns. Not, to borrow the well-known comparison made by Bernard de Fontenelle, the history of roses, however beautiful, but that of the gardener, whom the roses must think immortal. From the point of view of societies, economies and the countless incidents of short-term history, civilizations must seem immortal too.

This long-term history, history-at-a-distance – blue-water cruising on the high seas of time, rather than prudent coastal navigation never losing sight of land – this way of proceeding, call it what you will, has both advantages and drawbacks. Its advantages are that it forces one to think, to explain matters in unaccustomed terms, and to use historical explanation as a key to one's own time. Its drawbacks or dangers are that it can lapse into the facile generalizations of a philosophy of history more imaginary than researched or proved.

Historians are surely right to mistrust over-enthusiastic explorers like Oswald Spengler or Arnold Toynbee. Any history which is pressed to the point of general theory requires constant returns to practical reality – figures, maps, precise chronology and verification.

Rather than any theory of civilizations, therefore, we must study real instances if we wish to understand what civilization is. All the rules and definitions that we have outlined so far will be clarified and simplified by the examples that follow.

II. Civilizations
Outside Europe

PART I: ISLAM AND THE MUSLIM WORLD

4. History

=====

Civilizations take ages to be born, to settle, and to grow.

It is true to say that Islam arose with Muhammad in a few short years: but the statement is also misleading and hard to understand. Christianity, likewise, was born with Christ, yet also in a sense predated Him. Without Christ or Muhammad, there would have been neither Christianity nor Islam: but each of these new religions seized upon the body of a civilization already in place, in each case breathing a soul into it. Each was able to draw upon a rich inheritance – a past, a living present, and – already – a future.

Islam as a successor civilization: the Near East in new form

As Christianity inherited from the Roman Empire of which it was a prolongation, so Islam instantly took hold of the Near East, perhaps the world's oldest crossroads of civilized humanity. The consequence was immense. Muslim civilization made its own a series of ancient geopolitical obligations, urban patterns, institutions, habits, rituals and age-old approaches to faith and to life itself.

Faith: even in its religion Islam is linked with Judaism and Christianity, with the family of Abraham, and with the Old Testament and its rigorous monotheism. For Islam, Jerusalem is a holy city, and Jesus is the greatest prophet before Muhammad, who alone surpasses Him.

Life: Islam has perpetuated, down to the present day, forms of behaviour thousands of years old. In the *Arabian Nights* stories, to salute the sovereign is 'to kiss the earth between one's hands'. This was a practice current at the court of King Chosroes I of Persia (AD 531–79) and no doubt earlier still. In the sixteenth and seventeenth centuries and later, European ambassadors at Istanbul, Isphahan and Delhi tried to avoid it because they thought it humiliating for themselves and, still more, for the princes they represented. Long before, Herodotus was indignant at Egyptian manners which he found disgusting. 'In the open street, as a salutation, they half-prostrate themselves to one another; they behave like dogs, lowering their hands to their knees.' This greeting is still practised today. Nor are these the only instances. Turkish baths or hammams are in fact a survival of ancient Roman baths, which the Arab conquests brought to Persia and elsewhere. The hand of Fatima, the Muslim equivalent of 'our medals and scapularies', already adorned Carthaginian gravestones. And Emile Félix Gautier, who reports these facts, does not hesitate to recognize traditional Muslim costume in the dress of the Babylonians, as described by Herodotus more than twenty-four centuries ago. 'The Babylonians,' wrote Herodotus, 'wear first of all a linen tunic which hangs down as far as their feet.' In Algeria, Gautier comments, this would be called a *gandura*. 'Above it they wear another tunic made of wool [a jellaba]; over that, a little white cloak [a small white burnous]; and on their heads a conical cap' – a fez or tarboosh.

It is hard to know where to draw the line when inquiring what in the Islamic countries is truly Muslim and what is not. The couscous of North Africa has even been said to be of Roman or Punic origin. And the characteristically Muslim low-built house with a patio, so frequently seen in Egypt and the Maghreb, is certainly pre-Islamic: it resembles both the porticoed Greek house and 'the African house from the earliest centuries of our era'.

These are details, but their message is clear: Muslim civilization, like Western civilization, is derivative – a civilization of the second degree, to use the terminology of Alfred Weber. It was not built on a *tabula rasa*, but on the lava of that fluid, lively and motley civilization which preceded it in the Near East.

So it was not with the preaching of Muhammad, or the first decade of dazzling Muslim conquests (632–42), that the biography of Islam began. Its real origins lie deep in the immemorial history of the Near East.

The history of the Near East

United by the Assyrians, the Near East was further welded together, for many years, by the conquests of the Persian kings Cyrus the Great, Cambyses and Darius (521–485 BC). Two centuries later, the immense structure built by the Achaemenides dynasty fell to the onslaught of the Greeks and Macedonians under Alexander the Great (336–23 BC). Their victory was even more rapid than that of the Arabs ten centuries later.

Those ten centuries, broadly speaking, were an extraordinary 'colonial' period, during which the Greeks dominated an immense ill-defined area between the Mediterranean and the Indian Ocean. As colonists, they founded cities and great ports like Antioch and Alexandria, and formed vast States – the Syria of the Seleucids and the Macedonia of the Ptolemys. Although moving among their subjects, they did not mix with them: they never lived in the countryside, which remained foreign territory. In fact, the tiny Greco-Macedonian people colonized this vast tract of Asia as Europeans later colonized Africa, imposing their language and administration and imparting some of their dynamism.

The Roman conquest also extended to Asia Minor, Syria and Egypt, continuing this colonial era. Behind the Roman façade Greek civilization lived on; and it regained its dominance when the Roman Empire fell in the fifth century and Byzantium – Greek civilization again – took its place. E. F. Gautier, living in Algeria not so long ago, was obsessed by this immense colonial adventure which history one day swept aside, leaving barely a vestige behind.

As a colony, the Near East disliked its masters. From 256 BC onwards, the vast State of the Parthian Arsacidae dynasty, then that of the Persian Sassanids (from AD 224), established themselves across Iran from the edge of the Indus to the fragile frontiers of Syria. Rome and Byzantium fought exhausting wars against this powerful, organized and bellicose neighbour – seignorial, bureaucratic, with large cavalry forces and links in the Far East with India, Mongolia and China. The bows used by the Persian knights, whose arrows could pierce Roman breastplates, were probably of Mongol origin. Inspired by 'the superior religion of Zoroaster', Persia vigorously resisted 'the intruder – hellenism'. Yet this political hostility did not prevent its welcoming, on occasion, cultural influence from the West. Greek philosophers banished by Justinian took refuge in the great capital of Ctesiphon on the Tigris; and it was through Iran that Christian heretics persecuted by Byzantium reached China, where they later enjoyed singular success.

In the troubled Near East, converted to Christianity, a prey to continual and violent religious strife, and struggling against the presence of the Greeks, the first Arab conquerors (634–42) found immediate accomplices. Syria in 634 and Egypt in 639 welcomed the new arrivals. More unexpectedly, Persia rapidly succumbed in 642. The old Empire, exhausted by its long struggle with Rome and Byzantium, defended itself ineffectively – despite its horses and elephants – or failed to defend itself at all, against the cruel raids of the Arab warriors on their camels. The Near East surrendered, abandoning itself to the invaders. The Arabs found it harder to conquer North Africa, between the middle of the seventh and the beginning of the eighth centuries; but thereafter they overran Spain very rapidly in 711.

Altogether, except for the mountains of Asia Minor, which were defended and saved by Byzantium, the Arab conquerors very quickly seized the whole of the Near East, and then pushed well beyond it towards the West.

Was the speed of their success (a) the result of surprise, favouring an attack that no one expected? (b) the natural outcome of fast, destructive raids which isolated the towns and forced them to surrender one by one? or (c) the culmination of slow changes in the Near East, which was in the process of what today would be called 'decolonization'?

All three hypotheses are no doubt valid. Yet, in the history of civilizations, such short-term explanations are not enough. Neither connivance nor lassitude on the part of the vanquished can account for so lasting a defeat. Would it not make more sense to suppose that there was some deep and ancient religious and moral affinity between the conquerors and the conquered, the result of lengthy coexistence? The new religion preached by Muhammad, in fact, was forged at the heart of the Near East, in accordance with its fundamental spiritual vocation.

Islam, in the springtime of its expansion, simply revived that ancient oriental civilization which had long been so powerful – at the very least the 'second pillar' of the edifice of which the first was Arabia itself. As a civilization, it was solidly based in extremely wealthy areas, alongside which Arabia then seemed very poor.

It was the destiny of Islam to relaunch that civilization in a different orbit, and to carry it to undreamed-of heights.

Muhammad, the Koran and Islam

The immediate origins of Islam confront us at once with a man, a book and a religion.

Muhammad's decisive achievements took place between about 610 or 612 and the date of his death in 632. Arabia at that time was fragmented by rival tribes and confederations, and wide open to foreign influence and to the colonizing efforts of Persia, of Christian Ethiopia, of Syria and of Byzantine Egypt. Without Muhammad, it would never have achieved unity and, thus strengthened, sent its marauders towards the broad frontiers in the North.

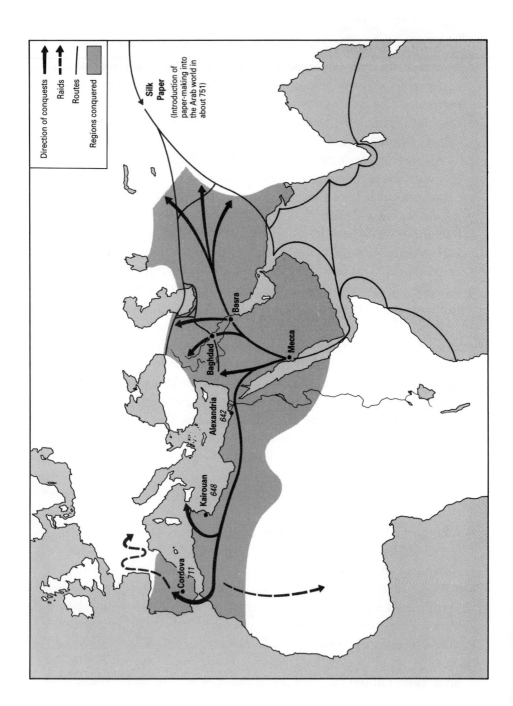

3. Arab conquests

Neither Byzantium nor the Parthians, rivals for so many centuries, had had the least fear or intimation that a serious enemy might emerge from among such impoverished neighbours. True, they staged violent raids; but the raiders came and went. There seemed no cause for alarm, especially in the frontier areas – often a no man's land – which the Persians and Greeks quarrelled over, on the edge of the 'fertile crescent'.

With the success of Muhammad, everything changed. Scholarly research has freed his biography from some of its later embellishments; but the picture which appears once the gilt is removed is all the more attractive and moving. Born in about 570, Muhammad endured many hardships in the first forty years of his life. He emerged from obscurity only in his fortieth year, between 610 and 612. 'One night in the last ten days of Ramadan, in a cave in Mount Hira,' not far from Mecca, while he was sleeping, 'the Uncreated Word was infused into the finite world, and the Book came down into the heart of the Prophet.' In a dream, a mysterious being showed him 'a roll of fabric covered with signs, and commanded him to read it. "I cannot read," said Muhammad. "Read, read," said the Angel, wrapping the fabric round Muhammad's neck. "What am I to read?" "Read, in the name of your Lord who created man.". . . "The chosen one came to himself, aware that a book had come down into his heart."' (E. Dermenghem) A small detail: the word translated here as 'read' can also mean 'preach': so it remains uncertain whether or not the Prophet could read and write.

The sacred story is well known. How Muhammad, after hearing the words of the Archangel Gabriel (his mysterious visitor) considered himself an emissary of God, the last and greatest of the prophets in the biblical tradition. How, to begin with, his only supporter was his wife Khadija, while his relations, rich merchants from Mecca, were almost immediately hostile; how at that time he was full of uncertainty and on the edge of despair, madness and suicide. There is no need to retrace step by step Muhammad's 'pilgrimage' as glimpsed through the accounts of contemporaries, through the *hadits* or sayings of the Prophet, and through the *suras* or chapters of the Koran, the posthumous collection of Muhammad's revelations. The essential point is to realize the beauty, the explosive force and the 'pure music' of this 'inimitable' text (a proof of its divine origin), and of Muhammad's preaching (often preceded by trances in which he remained unconscious for a long time). The poetry is extraordinary and powerfully rhythmic: even in translation it retains much of its force. Pre-Islamic Arabia was in that sense Homeric: poetry opened its ears and its hearts.

For years, the Prophet preached only to a small group of the faithful – some relatives, some unfortunates, some of the very poor. Alongside the merchants enriched by the caravan trade between Egypt, Syria and the Gulf, Mecca also had its labourers, artisans and slaves. One such was Bilal, the black slave whose freedom was bought by Abu Bakr, the friend and future father-in-law of the Prophet. Bilal became the first Islamic *muezzin*, whose duty was to call Muslims to prayer.

The rich, for their part, were soon alarmed by Muhammad's teachings, which at first had amused and then begun to annoy them. Under threat, some of Muhammad's disciples took refuge in Christian Ethiopia, while some sixty others fled to the oasis of Yatrib, north of Mecca. Muhammad joined them there. Yatrib became Medina, the City of the Prophet, and his flight or *hegira* marked the starting-point of the Islamic calendar (16 July 622). A minute detail may be noted in passing: Medina seems to have acquired its name before the actual *hegira*.

At that time, three-quarters of its inhabitants were peasants, with two rival Arab tribes and a number of Jews, most of whom were merchants. Muhammad's policy *vis-à-vis* the Jews, originally friendly, grew defiant and finally hostile. Islamic prayers, previously offered in the direction of Jerusalem, were now turned towards Mecca. All this took place against a background of continual strife: in order to live, the fugitive Muslims raided their neighbours and plundered the long Mecca caravan routes. Ten years fighting at last enabled the Prophet to return in triumph to

Mecca, having shown singular decisiveness, prudence and patience in the face of appalling difficulties.

A revealed religion, gradually formed from the chapters of the future Koran, and from the words and deeds of the Prophet, Islam (submission to God) is a faith of exemplary simplicity. Its 'five pillars' are: the proclamation of a single God, Allah, with Muhammad as His emissary – that is the *chahada*; prayer five times a day; fasting during the twenty-nine or thirty days of Ramadan; alms for the poor; and pilgrimage to Mecca. The *jihad* or holy war was not one of these fundamental rules, but it became highly important later.

Islam's religious symbolism presents no mysteries, although a number of points in it are controversial, opening the way to various complicated interpretations of its mysticism. From this point of view, Islamic theology resembles Christianity: both involve potentially difficult spiritual paths.

As regards prayer, the Prophet was inspired by Christian and Jewish practices. In respect of pilgrimage, however, he remained faithful to Arab and Meccan traditions. He preserved, in fact, the customs of earlier, interlinked pilgrimages – to the Kaaba in Mecca and to Mt Arafat near the city, perhaps an ancient spring feast and an ancient autumn festival, the former analogous to the Feast of the Tabernacles in the Old Testament. These age-old rites, whose deepest meaning was in any case lost in the mists of time, were transposed into a new form. 'Muhammad annexed the old institution, justifying it *a posteriori* by means of a cultural legend. He claimed that Abraham, with his son Ishmael, the ancestor of the Arabs, had in his day organized the cult of the Holy Kaaba and its attendant pilgrimages. Thus Islam acquired priority over Judaism, founded by Moses, and over Christianity, identified with Jesus.' Is it adequate to explain the invocation of Abraham as political calculation, the mere desire to assert the priority of Islam? Do religions not have their own religious logic, their own truths? This is what Youakim Moubarac argues in *Abraham in the Koran* (1958). And for Louis Massignon, 'Islam reveres in Abraham the first of the Muslims – which is true, *theologically true*.'

The essential point is to realize how much religious beliefs and practices matter in the life of Muslims, imposing their own strict discipline. Everything, including the law, derives from the Koran. Religious practice remains far more alive in Islam today than in the Christian countries. 'For 1360 years,' wrote Louis Massignon in 1955, '150,000 people from every country have made an annual pilgrimage to Arafat.' There are as many such pilgrims from a typical village in Egypt as there are Easter church-goers in a typical village in France. The advantage is clearly with Islam. But does this necessarily imply more intense faith? Christianity has had to undergo internal ordeals, often due to the civilization it brings with it. Most of these Islam has so far been spared. Is that not because it is still based, for the most part, in ancient, archaic societies where religious rites continue unchanged, like other forms of social behaviour, and like the rest of life itself?

Arabia: the problem of a barely urbanized culture

What precise role did the huge Arabian Peninsula play in the success of Muhammad and the expansion of Islam? The answer is by no means simple.

Towns were of prime importance in Islam: Muhammad lived and worked in the urban world of Mecca, in the margin of an Arabia that remained primitive. Mecca's prosperity at that time was still recent, born of its caravan links with distant, foreign cities, and confined to large-scale trade and the emerging capitalism of the Meccan merchants. It was in Syrian towns, no doubt, rather than in Arabia itself, that Muhammad first encountered Jewish and Christian circles in the days before his revelation, when he was still a convoy courier. At all events, his commandments presuppose an urban background: the call of the *muezzin*, collective prayers on Fridays, the veil for women, the dignity required of the faithful and their *imams* or prayer leaders – all these imply witnesses, crowds and the press of an urban throng.

'These strict and prudish ideals were those of the austere Hejaz merchants. There too Islam sought the decorum of the cities rather than the disorder of the fields.' (X. de Planhol) It is against this background that some of the Prophet's *hadits* must be understood. 'What I fear for my people is milk in which the devil lurks between the froth and the cream. They will eagerly drink it and return to the desert, *leaving the centres of communal prayer.*' (Our emphasis.) Another remark attributed to the Prophet concerns his seeing a ploughshare: 'That never enters the house of the faithful but it brings with it degradation.' In a word, as the Koran itself declares: 'The Arabs of the desert are the most hardened in their impurity and hypocrisy.' The centres of faith, in those early days of Islam, were therefore in the towns, in a way that recalls the beginnings of the Christian church in the West. At that time, the infidel was the pagan, the *paganus* – the peasant. True, the Arabian bedouin were unusual 'peasants'. It was still possible to encounter them, at the beginning of the twentieth century, living as they always had. It may still be possible, sometimes, in the heart of Arabia today.

An expert on Islam, Robert Montagne (1893–1954) wrote a very fine book on this *Civilization of the Desert* – a civilization which any ethnographer would undoubtedly call a culture.

It had virtually no towns, in fact; and those it had were very primitive indeed. Yatrib, at the time of the *hegira*, was not even a match for Thebes, in Boeotia, at the time of Epaminondas. Around these 'towns', in valleys with a minimum of water, there were a few settled peasants, serfs bound to the soil, but in very small numbers. The majority of Arabs were nomads, 'like swarms of bees', forming very small social groups – patriarchal families, sub-clans, clans, tribes and confederations of tribes. These labels, invented by those studying Arabian society, are based purely on number: a clan implies 100 to 300 tents, and a tribe – the biggest unit with any cohesion – means 3,000 people. On that scale it was possible to maintain, or at least to believe in, the blood relationship, which was the only link the Bedouin recognized. The tribe was the great fighting unit, comprising brothers, cousins and clients. The confederation, on the other hand, was only a fragile union whose members were scattered over vast distances.

The very hard life lived by the bedouin in the deserts and semi-deserts of Arabia was made possibly only by camel-breeding. Frugal and resistant to thirst, camels made possible long journeys from one pasture to the next. On plundering raids or *rezzous*, they carried fodder, leathern water-bottles and grain. The horses, spared until the last moment, were used in the final attacking charge.

Nomadic daily life followed the vanishing grass. With their pack-camels and their white racing she-camels, the bedouin travelled as much as a thousand kilometres from North to South and vice versa. In the North, on the edge of the fertile crescent between Syria and Mesopotamia, nomadic habits were weakened by contact with settled peasants. As well as camels, sheep were bred; and their travelling range was very limited. Once the Bedouin became sheep-farmers, they were no more than *chaouya* or shepherds – only one step above the despised lowest category, the breeders of oxen or buffaloes, firmly tied to one place.

In central and southern Arabia, camel-breeding nomads remained untainted, retaining their claims to nobility. These aristocratic tribes were continually at war: the stronger drove out the weak. The desert, teeming with more people than it could support, thereby shed its surplus population, most of which moved Westwards: Sinai and the narrow ribbon of the Nile were no barriers on the way to the Sahara and the Maghreb.

There were both geographical and historical reasons for this exodus towards the West. Geographically, the Northern deserts were cold and inhospitable after the heat of the South. The Arabs failed to conquer Asia Minor in the seventh century because their camels could not withstand the sharp cold of what are now the Anatolian plains, where the Bactrian camel was more at home. The Sahara, however, is in effect the prolongation of the Arabian Desert beyond the Red Sea. Historically, the deserts in the North and in central Asia were already occupied by nomads of their own, with two-humped camels, horses, and mounted warriors, as mobile as they were fierce. Here there were no empty spaces for easy occupation by newcomers.

Not without hesitation, bedouin Arabia supplied Islam with an exceptional fighting force. The nomads were not converted overnight: they remained combative and unpredictable. Even in Spain, at the time of the Ommayad caliphs, old quarrels between parties from Yemen and from Qais flared up again, thousands of miles from their place of origin.

When the Prophet died, moreover, the nomads who had supposedly accepted his authority rose up against Islam. The fight was long and bitter; and Muhammad's successor, caliph Omar (634–44) found no better solution to these infernal disputes than to send horsemen and cameleers on the *jihad* or holy war – thereby removing them from Arabia and transcending the quarrels between the tribes.

Thus the bedouin accomplished Islam's first conquests. They traversed huge distances, these small groups – miniature nations – with their desert convoys, their goatskin or camelskin tents, their habits and customs, their pride and their deep concern to remain pastoral people and avoid the ignoble, stifling life of settled peasants. They rained down like hailstones on those vast Western spaces which Islam was to conquer. Wherever they went, they brought their language, their folklore, their faults and their virtues. One of their greatest virtues was their passionate belief in hospitality, a shining characteristic of all Islam.

One example is the long odyssey of the Beni Hilal tribe. Having left the South of the Hejaz in the seventh century, they were in a bad way in upper Egypt in about 978, but descended on North Africa in the mid-eleventh century like a swarm of locusts. In the twelfth century, they were crushed by the Berbers at the battle of Setif in 1151, and they dispersed throughout the Maghreb. Their epic still survives in folklore today – 'from the desert of Transjordania to Biskra and Port-Etienne' in Mauritania.

Islam, soon to become so fine a civilization, owed almost all its successive victories to the power of belligerent 'cultures', primitive Arab peoples whom each time it rapidly assimilated and 'civilized'. For a century, the Arab tribes gave Islam the first of these victories. Then the rough mountain peoples of North Africa, the Berbers, helped it to conquer Spain and organize Fatimid Egypt. Finally, it used the Turko-Mongols, central Asian nomads, on and almost within its borders, whom it was able to convert. From the tenth century onwards, Turkish mercenaries formed the bulk of the armies serving the caliphs of Baghdad. They were first-rate soldiers and archers, and extraordinary horsemen.

Jahiz, the great Arab writer of the ninth century, was a little condescending towards these rough people, whom he portrayed in unforgettable terms. But once again, history repeated itself. The poor became rich, the nomads became citizens, and both set out to show that it is sometimes but a small step from servant to sovereign. Mercenaries one day, masters the next, the Seljuk Turks and then the Ottoman Turks became the new princes of Islam. 'The great lord' or 'the Grand Turk' – that was the title the West accorded to the Ottoman leader, once the capture of Constantinople in 1453 had fully confirmed Turkish power.

Perhaps it has been the destiny of Islam to attract and use the primitive peoples who surround or cross its territory, but then to fall prey to their violent power. Ultimately, order is restored and wounds are healed. The successful primitive warrior is tamed by the all-powerful urban life of Islam.

5. Geography

═══

While the areas covered by Islam are interlinked, they vary considerably, especially in outlying regions. Islam's history, in fact, has never been untroubled. In a broader context, however, these variations have their limits. Seen in its entirety, Islam is an immense and stable system, if with different facets that need to be explained.

Islam's lands and seas

Maps tell the essential story. They show the regions held and then abandoned by Islam, each time in the face of foreign, rival civilizations: against the West in Sicily, the Iberian Peninsula, Languedoc, Southern Italy and the Western Mediterranean; against Eastern Europe and Orthodox Christianity in Crete and the Balkan Peninsula; against the Hindu world in the Indo-Gangetic Plain and in North and Central Deccan.

The areas that are still Islamic today – as they have been since the beginning, or at least for a very long time – remain immense. Not always very wealthy, they stretch from Morocco and the Atlantic Sahara as far as China and the Indian Archipelago – 'from Dakar to Jakarta', to quote the subtitle of a recent book.

In this survey we should not forget the broad high seas, once more or less thoroughly exploited, but now largely deserted by the Muslim States, except for limited coastal navigation. The sea belongs to those who sail it, and today there is almost no Muslim shipping left. It was very different in the past, in the Mediterranean, the Red Sea, the Persian Gulf, the Caspian and above all in the Indian Ocean. Arab sailing dhows, their planks secured with palm-fibre ropes and no nails, used the monsoon cycle to pursue active and large-scale trade. By the ninth century they had reached Canton. In 1498, Vasco da Gama pursued and pillaged them. But neither Portugal nor, later, Holland was able to exclude them from low-cost trade in the Indian Ocean. Only at the end of the nineteenth century were they outclassed by steamships.

So the Arabs' maritime epic was long-lived. Islam owed its ancient glory not only to its horsemen but also to its seamen. Their symbol was Sindbad the Sailor. Although Sindbad described odysseys amid the marvels, miracles and catastrophes encountered in the India Ocean, it was surely in the Mediterranean that Islam's fate as a world sea-power was decided. There, the Muslims first conquered, then fought desperately, and finally were defeated.

Islam's important conquests included not only Syria, Egypt, Persia, North Africa and Spain, but also almost the whole Mediterranean. Its victory would have been permanent if, having taken Crete in 825, it had remained there. But in 961 Byzantium recaptured that vital outpost, and held on to Rhodes and Cyprus – all commanding the sea routes that led to the Aegean.

In the East, then, Islam suffered a setback. Byzantium continued to dominate the Aegean and its countless islands, as well as, on either side of the Balkan Peninsula, both the vast Black Sea and the Adriatic, that doorway to Italy which the Venetians used to make their first, modest fortune as shippers of wood, salt and wheat for the wealthy Byzantines.

The Western Mediterranean, on the other hand, succumbed to the sea power of Egypt, North Africa and Spain – all by now flying the green flag of Islam. In 825 the Andalusians conquered Crete; between 827 and 902 the Tunisians settled in Sicily, which flourished prodigiously under their rule. It became the vital heart of the 'Saracen' Mediterranean, with Palermo its finest city, on the edge of the Conca d'Oro, that great hill-girt plain which irrigation now turned into a Garden of Eden.

The Muslims also reached various places in Corsica and Sardinia, and briefly in Provence; they threatened and insulted Rome, and landed unopposed at the mouth of the Tiber. They also occupied in force the Balearic Islands, a key port of call for Western Mediterranean trade, making possible direct rather than coastal voyages between Sicily and Spain.

So the Western Mediterranean, that highway of wealth, was dominated by Islam. This breathed life and prosperity into seaports like Palermo, Alexandria (hitherto a coastal outpost of the great metropolis of Cairo) and Tunis (ten miles from the sea, as if prudently keeping its distance). Other cities grew or recovered: Bejaia (Bougie) with its nearby forests, essential for shipbuilding; Algiers and Oran, both then still modest; the lively Spanish port of Almeria; and, on the navigable part of the Guadalquivir River, flowing into the Atlantic, the flourishing city of Seville.

Islam's ascendancy lasted more than a hundred years. True, it was soon a prey to Christian piracy: the rich always tempt pillage by the poor. And in and around the tenth century, in contrast to what later became familiar, the rich were Muslims and the pirates were Christians. Amalfi, Pisa and Genoa were all hornets' nests. The situation grew dramatic with the Norman conquest of Sicily. No less than the pirate vessels, the Normans' fast ships ran down the Muslim dhows. The occupation of Sicily, in fact, was the first breach in the 'heathen' domination of the sea.

There followed a slow strangulation, a gradual constriction whose ill-effects were soon felt throughout the 'Muslim lake'. In about 1080, at the time of the Cid Campeador, and just before the arrival of the Almoravids (who came from Sudan and North Africa in 1085 to help the Muslims in Spain), an Arab poet from Sicily hesitated to accept an invitation to Spain, despite the fifty gold dinars which he was offered by Motamid, the King of Toledo. 'Do not be surprised,' he wrote, 'to see how my hair has turned white with grief; save your surprise for the fact that my eyes' pupils are still black! The sea belongs to the Christians, and our ships sail there only at enormous risk. All that the Arabs now hold is the land.' The tables had indeed been turned.

The Crusades, which soon followed (1095–1270), enabled the Italian city–states' fleets to reconquer their home waters – as well as those held by the Byzantines. The great historical episodes (the capture of Jerusalem in 1099, the foundation of the States of the Holy Land, the Latin capture of Constantinople in 1204 after the extraordinary diversion of the Fourth Crusade) should not be allowed to disguise another major event: the conquest of the Mediterranean's maritime trade routes. When in 1291, with the fall of St John of Acre, Christianity lost its last important outpost in Asia, it nevertheless retained uncontested supremacy throughout the Mediterranean.

Islam did not react until two or three centuries later. Then, the Ottoman Turks did their best to recover naval supremacy. Their victory at Préveza in 1538 seemed to promise them domination of the Mediterranean; but their crushing defeat at the Battle of Lepanto in 1571 very soon halted their resurgence, which in any case had been purely military. Against the teeming fleets of Venice, Genoa and Florence, the Turks had been able to muster only a limited number of merchant ships, most of them Greek, and plying only between Istanbul, the Black Sea and Egypt. Later, of course, came the incessant activity of the Muslim corsairs, and the exceptional ascendancy of Algiers. Even so, Islam never again acquired a merchant fleet.

Thus, in the Mediterranean, triumphs and disasters followed one another. In the Indian Ocean, life was more peaceful – until the appearance of the Portuguese there in 1498, after they had rounded the Cape of Good Hope. From then onwards, Islam's flank was turned.

The essayist Essad Bey rightly remarked: 'Islam is the desert.' But that desert or group of deserts is surrounded on the one hand by two navigable stretches of salt water, the Mediterranean and the Indian Ocean, and on the other by three land masses fairly densely populated – the Far East, Europe and Black Africa. Above all, Islam is an 'intermediary continent' linking these vast regions.

Clearly, between the Atlantic and Northern China or the Siberian forests there are different kinds of desert: the hot deserts of the South, the home of the Arabian dromedary, are very unlike the cold deserts of the North, whose camels are the true, two-humped variety. The dividing line between them runs roughly from the Caspian to the mouth of the Indus.

Every desert, of course, has somewhere its river bank or seashore, its 'sahels' with settled peasants, its steppes and its oases where the hoe and the swing-plough can prepare the ground for crops. There are even, in these ancient civilized countries, idyllic river oases like the fertile valleys of the Nile, the Tigris, the Euphrates, the Indus, the Amou Daria and the Syr Daria, with exceptionally rich soil – though often tilled so long as to be exhausted. Given the climate, these places are vulnerable, and far too easily affected by the least human error or natural misfortune. An invasion, a long war, torrential rain or over-population – with any of these, vast farming areas are likely to be literally lost: the desert will engulf and bury towns and countryside alike.

The fate of Islam, therefore, rests on precarious foundations. Its overcrowded towns swollen by commerce, its sparse agricultural areas and its intense civilization all face constant difficulties. A present-day demographic map shows this clearly. Islam consists of a few densely populated regions, separated by vast stretches of empty space. Despite ingenious irrigation plans, despite the success of dry farming, despite the tenacity of patient, hard-working peasants, and despite the use of wonderfully well-suited trees like olives and date-palms, Islam has never enjoyed stable sufficiency, still less abundance. Any abundance has always been temporary, the fruit of a passing fashion for some luxury item, or the privilege of some especially fortunate town.

Such – at first sight paradoxically – was the case with Mecca, enormously enriched by the influx of pilgrims. There, miraculously, everything seemed possible. In 1326 Ibn Batûta, the greatest of all Arab travellers, sang the praises of Mecca's affluence: the 'delicious flavours' of its 'rich viands', the excellence of its fruits, grapes, figs, peaches, dates 'the like of which is found nowhere else in the world', and its incomparable melons. He concluded: 'Altogether, every kind of merchandise from every country can be found gathered in this town.' Elsewhere, all too often, hunger was a daily companion. 'I can enclose my hunger in the recesses of my belly,' wrote one Arab poet, 'just as an expert spinner can twist her fingers and tighten the threads in her hand.' And it was one of the Prophet's followers who said of him: 'He left this life without once having satisfied his hunger for barley bread.'

The results can easily be seen. One was the prevalence of nomadic, pastoral life, as in Arabia. With variations, this was the pattern throughout the deserts where Islam was obliged to live. The constraints were rigorous. The bedouin have often been portrayed, unsparingly, as savages, despite their noble pedigree. If they failed to understand the settled peasants, the latter returned the compliment. One Islamic expert, Jacques Berque, has tried to redress the balance: 'These bedouin, so often decried, how magnificent they are!' Yes, they were splendid specimens of the human animal. For Islam, they were allies whom it was hard to tame and lead. And yet they were useful allies. Without them, Islam would have been lost.

Condemned as they were to an austere and frugal existence, they had little chance of what today would be called 'social progress', especially since it would have required them to adopt a settled life – as indeed so many Muslim States have done today, and on a gigantic scale. For good or ill, the Ottoman Empire followed this course as early as the sixteenth century, settling its colonies of nomadic *yourouks* in both Asian and European Turkey. This closed and resolutely nomadic culture had its own inevitable logic. In the terminology of Arnold Toynbee, it was a prisoner of its own 'response'.

As a civilization that lacked manpower, Islam was obliged in the past to recruit it where it could. This shortage of people was one element in its fundamental poverty. Today, paradoxically, Islam is overpopulated, as we shall see. With between 365 and 400 million people, it numbers between a seventh and an eighth of the world's population – far too many for its limited resources. Formerly, however, in the days of its glory, Islam at the most had 30 to 50 million people, in a world population of 300 to 500 million. That was not many: for if, very roughly, the proportion remains the same, Islam in those days had, relatively speaking, far more onerous tasks. It was in fact the leading power in the Old World of Europe, Africa and Asia, which before the discovery of America was a planet in itself.

This gave it crushing responsibilities: government, trade, war, military security. To discharge them, Islam had everywhere to take on people as it found them, with a degree of tolerance unknown in the populous West. It also sought them outside its own frontiers, everywhere, with a determination which made classical Islam a slave civilization *par excellence.*

This immense and continual recruitment was for a long time the indispensable basis for Muslim activities. One after another, all the neighbouring countries made their contribution to it: European Christians captured on land or sea by the Muslims themselves, or bought secondhand like the Slav prisoners of war resold by Jewish merchants at Verdun in the ninth century; African blacks, Abyssinians, Indians, poor Turks and Slavs, Caucasians. In the sixteenth century, Russians captured in raids by the Crimean Tartars were sent as slaves to Turkish Istanbul.

Such slaves often made astonishing fortunes. One example was that of the Mamelukes in Egypt, who seized power just when Louis IX's crusade came to grief, in 1250. Most of them were of Turkish, and later Caucasian origin; and although slaves, they had been trained as soldiers. They governed Egypt fairly successfully until the Ottoman conquest in 1517; but even then they did not disappear from the scene. Napoleon met them at the Battle of the Pyramids. 'The Mamelukes were parvenus,' writes a present-day historian, 'but they were not petty.' The equally famous Turkish Janissaries resembled them in more than one respect.

Every Muslim town had different districts for different races, religions and languages. In 1651, during a palace revolution at the court of the Ottoman Padishah, 'the curse of Babel fell on the Icoglans or pages and officers of the Sultan in the seraglio, and made them powerless'. Under extreme stress, they forgot the Ottoman language they had artificially learned, and 'the ears of witnesses,' wrote Paul Ricaut in 1668, 'were assailed by a tumult of different voices and tongues. Some shouted in Georgian, some in Albanian, some in Bosnian, some in Mingrelian, others in Turkish or Italian.' A fine example, but only one among many: Algiers was just as polyglot under the Turkish corsairs.

A continent as intermediary: trade-routes and towns

Not being well endowed by nature, Islam would have counted for little without the roads across its desert: they held it together and gave it life. Trade-routes were its wealth, its *raison d'être*, its civilization. For centuries, they gave it a dominant position.

Until the discovery of America, Islam dominated the Old World, determining its global destiny. It alone, as we have said, brought together the three great cultural zones of the Old World – the Far East, Europe and Black Africa. Nothing could pass between them without its consent or tacit acquiescence. It was their intermediary.

Ships, caravans and merchants: however difficult Islam's political situation frequently was, it continued to benefit from its geographical position athwart the routes that others had to take. Obviously, it was not always fully aware of this exceptional position, or fully able to exploit it. In the cold deserts of Asia, Islam was only precariously in control of a very turbulent nomad population. Muslim Turkestan, strung along the oases, was a region of outposts, and never an effective frontier. It was impossible, in fact, to exclude the Turks, the Turkomans or the Mongols from the road that led from the Aral Sea to the Black Sea and the Caspian.

The most vigorous of these nomads overran Iran and threatened Baghdad. The map on p. 86 shows the magnitude of the Mongol incursion in the thirteenth century.

For centuries, nevertheless, Islam alone sent Sudanese gold and black slaves to the Mediterranean, and silk, pepper, spices and pearls to Europe from the Far East. In Asia and Africa, it controlled trade with the Levant. Only from Alexandria, Aleppo, Beirut or Syrian Tripoli did Italian merchants take over.

Islam was therefore above all a civilization based on movement and transit. This meant long sea voyages and multiple caravan routes – between the Indian Ocean and the Mediterranean, from the Black Sea to China and India, and from the Dark Continent to North Africa.

Despite the presence of elephants in the East and of horses and donkeys everywhere, these caravans consisted mainly of camels. A pack-camel could carry a load of some six hundredweight or 300 kilograms. Since a caravan might consist of five or six thousand camels, its total capacity equalled that of a very large merchant sailing-ship.

A caravan travelled like an army, with a leader, a general staff, strict rules, compulsory staging-posts, and routine precautions against marauding nomads – with whom it was prudent to come to terms. At fixed intervals along the way, equivalent to a day's march except in the heart of the desert, there were huge buildings, the caravanserais or khans, where both people and animals could find partial lodging. These in effect were stations on the caravan line. Every European traveller described their gigantic halls and tolerable comfort. Some, like the notable khans of Aleppo, still survive today.

This caravan system could not be coordinated with maritime trade except by means of an extensive semi-capitalist organization. Islam had its merchants, some of them Muslim, some not. Chance has preserved letters from the Jewish merchants in Cairo at the time of the First Crusade (1095–9). They show knowledge of every method of credit and payment, and every form of trade association (disproving the too facile belief that these were invented later by the Italians). They also bear witness to trade over long distances. Coral travelled from North Africa to India; slaves were bought in Ethiopia; iron was brought back from India at the same time as pepper and spices. All that implied large-scale movement of money, merchandise and people.

There is nothing surprising, therefore, in the extent of the Arabs' travels, although they seemed fabulous at the time. Islam itself, which was always in movement, which lived by movement, led the way. Ibn Batûta, a Moroccan born in Tangier in 1304, travelled 'round the world' between 1325 and 1349, going to Egypt, Arabia, the Lower Volga, Afghanistan, India and China. In 1352, he went to Black Africa and the banks of the Niger, where he complained that the Sudanese, although Muslim, showed too little respect for 'the Whites'. In the gold town of Sijilmassa, he was surprised to meet a compatriot from Ceuta, the brother of a certain Al–Buchri, whom he had known in China. Islam at that time abounded in wanderers of this kind, who were unfailingly welcomed, from the Atlantic to the Pacific, by Muslim hospitality, comparable to that of the Russians.

Such travels would have been unthinkable without powerful towns. These naturally flourished in Islam, and were the motors which made possible the circulation of people, money and goods. Everything passed through them: merchandise, pack-animals, people and rare acquisitions. Of these last, on their way to Europe, an incomplete list might include: exotic plants (sugar cane, cotton), silkworms, paper, a compass, Indian (so-called Arabic) numerals, perhaps gunpowder, and – as well as a certain very famous medicine – the germs of terrible epidemic illnesses from China and India, the homes of cholera and the plague.

Broadly speaking, all these towns looked alike. Their streets were narrow and generally sloping, so as to be washed auto-matically by the rain. A *hadit* of the Prophet's prescribed that streets should be seven cubits wide, or between ten and thirteen feet, permitting two laden asses to pass each other. But this was often impossible: houses encroached on the street despite the letter of the law, and very often had an overhanging upper floor, like medieval houses in the West. This was partly because Islam forbade multi-storey houses (except in Cairo and in Mecca and its port of Jedda): building too high was held to be a mark of reprehensible pride on the owner's part.

Given the anarchic absence of municipal administration, any serious population pressure in a town led to a proliferation of these low houses, each invading vacant space, crowding its neighbours, and creating a higgledy-piggledy effect.

A French traveller by the name of Thévenot, in 1657, was astonished to note that 'there is not a single fine street in Cairo, but a multiplicity of little twisted alleys, making it obvious that all the houses were built without any kind of plan, taking up whatever space they chose and oblivious of whether they blocked the passageway or not.' Another Frenchman, Volney, a century later in 1782, described these same narrow streets.

Since they are not paved, the masses of people, camels, asses and dogs which crowd into them kick up a disagreeable dust. Frequently, people throw water in front of their doors, and the dust gives way to mud and malodorous fumes. Contrary to normal custom in the East, the houses are two or three storeys tall, topped by a paved or loamed terrace. Most of them are built of mud or badly fired brick; the rest are made from soft stone from the nearby Mt Moqattam. All of them look like prisons, because they have no windows on to the street.

A similar picture was painted of Istanbul in the nineteenth century: 'Not only carriages but even horses can hardly pass each other. The Street of the Divan, at that time the broadest in the city, was no wider than 2.5 or 3 metres at certain points.' True as a general observation. However, eleventh-century Cairo had some houses of seven to twelve storeys; and ninth-century Samarra had a grand straight avenue several kilometres long and 50 to 100 metres wide. These, perhaps, were exceptions that proved the rule.

Narrow as it was, the street in any Muslim country was always

very lively – a permanent meeting place for people who enjoyed
open-air display. It was 'the essential artery, the rendezvous for
story-tellers, signers, snake-charmers, mountebanks, healers,
charlatans, barbers and all those professionals who are so suspect in
the eyes of Islam's moralists and canon lawyers. Add to that the
children and their often violent games.' And as well as the streets,
the terraces were inter-communicating, although they were
reserved for the women.

Such teeming disorder, however, never excluded an overall
plan – especially since this was based on the very structure of the
town and the life of its inhabitants. At its centre was the Great
Mosque for the weekly sermon. 'To it and from it everything
flows, as if it were a heart' (Jacques Berque). Nearby was the
bazaar, i.e. the merchants' quarter with its streets of shops (the
souk) and its caravanserais or warehouses, as well as the public
baths which were established and maintained despite frequent
condemnations. Artisans were grouped concentrically, starting
from the Great Mosque: first, the makers and sellers of perfumes
and incense, then the shops selling fabrics and rugs, the jewellers
and food stores, and finally the humblest trades – curriers, cobblers,
blacksmiths, potters, saddlers, dyers. Their shops marked the edges
of the town.

In principle, each of these trades had its location fixed for all
time. Similarly, the *maghzen* or Prince's quarter was in principle
located on the outskirts of the city, well away from riots or
popular revolts. Next to it, and under its protection, was the
mellah or Jewish quarter. The mosaic was completed by a very
great variety of residential districts, divided by race and religion:
there were forty-five in Antioch alone. 'The town was a cluster of
different quarters, all living in fear of massacre.' So Western
colonists nowhere began racial segregation – although they
nowhere suppressed it.

This rigidity in spite of apparent disorder was increased by the
fact that towns were often confined within walls with grandiose
gateways, and surrounded by huge cemeteries on which it was

difficult to build. Present-day traffic problems have necessitated change – sometimes beyond all proportion. In a frenzy of street widening, Istanbul recently became an incredible building-site, with houses cut in two so that the doors of rooms open on to nothing, with a new main thoroughfare, its lateral tributaries suspended 'like glacial valleys', and with forests of pipework high in the air as a result of hasty excavation.

Broadly speaking, Muslim towns had neither the political liberties nor the sense of architectural order that Western cities strove for once they were sufficiently developed. But they did have all the elements of genuine town life: a conformist bourgeoisie, plus a mass of poorer people, indigent artisans and pickpockets, all living more or less off crumbs from rich men's tables. They enjoyed sophisticated pleasures, less constrained than elsewhere, which seemed to purists appallingly perverse. They were also bastions of education, with their schools attached to the mosques, their *medersas*, and their universities. Finally, they were a constant pole of attraction for people from the surrounding countryside, whom they tamed and domesticated as towns have always done since the very beginning. 'No one in the world has more need of punishment, for they are thieves, wastrels and felons,' wrote a citizen of Seville, thinking no doubt of the endless quarrels which broke out at the gates or even in the market-place with people from the country, come to sell animals, meat, hides, rancid butter, dwarf palm-trees, 'green grass' or chick-peas. He need not have worried: nine times out of ten, townspeople's vigilance or cunning won the day. Any robber was robbed in his turn, and without mercy, for town-dwellers in Islam, even more than in the West, had a very firm grip on the highly primitive peasantry outside the gates. Thus Damascus controlled the peasants near the Ghouta and the mountain people of Jebel ed Druze; Algiers controlled the corsairs and the peasants of the Fahs, the Mitija and the Kabyle Mountains. Similarly, the silk-wearing bourgeoisie of Granada contrasted with the poor, cotton-clad peasants from the mountains nearby.

Once again, however, these are the characteristics of all towns,

Muslim and Western alike. What distinguished the Muslim towns, essentially, were their early growth and their exceptional size.

The importance of towns in Islam is not surprising: they were of the essence of its civilization. Towns, roads, ships, caravans and pilgrimages were all part of a single whole, all, as Louis Massignon has aptly said, elements of *movement*, all 'lines of force' in Muslim life.

6. The Greatness and Decline of Islam

===

Islam's splendid apogee was between the eighth and the twelfth centuries AD. Everyone agrees about that. But when did its decadence begin? Its decisive decline is often said to have dated from the thirteenth century. That, however, confuses two very different things: the end of an ascendancy and the end of a civilization.

In the thirteenth century, Islam clearly lost its position of leadership. But its really dangerous decline hardly began until the eighteenth century, which in the long life of civilizations is a very short time ago. It shared the fate of many nations that are now called 'under-developed' because they missed the Industrial Revolution – the first revolution whereby the world could advance at the dizzy speed of machines. This failure did not kill Islam as a civilization. All that happened was that Europe gained two centuries of rapid material progress, leaving Islam behind.

No Muslim civilization before the eighth or ninth century

Islam became a political entity in the few years it took the Arabs to conquer an empire. But Islamic civilization was born of the union between that empire and the ancient civilizations whose territory it touched. This took a long time and many generations. To begin with, the conquering Arabs scarcely sought to convert their new subjects: quite the reverse. They contented themselves with exploiting the rich civilizations they had vanquished: Persia, Syria, Egypt, Africa (Roman Africa, which the Arabs called Ifriqya, broadly present-day Tunisia) and Spain (or Andalusia, el-Andalous). Any Christians who tried to convert to Islam were whipped. Since only non-Muslims paid taxes, why should the conquerors allow their revenue to be thus reduced? 'The population of the occupied countries maintained their own way of life without being molested, but . . . were treated like superior cattle, to be taken care of because they paid most of the taxes' (Gaston Wiet).

Such was the situation under the first four successors of Muhammad, the 'well directed caliphs' (632–60). (The word caliph or *kalifa* can be rendered as 'successor', 'lieutenant', or 'deputy ruler', as the translator prefers.) It continued under the Omayyad caliphs (660–750) who established their capital in Damascus. During these years of continual warfare, religious questions were seldom if ever brought to the fore. The struggle with Byzantium, for example, was political rather than religious.

What was more, the administration of the occupied territories remained in the hands of the 'natives', and documents continued to be written either in Greek or in Pahlavi (Sassanian Persian). Art and architecture, too, remained hellenistic in inspiration, even when it came to building mosques. Their central courts, colonnades, arcades and cupolas followed the Byzantine model. Only the minaret, designed for the muezzin's call to prayer, was truly Islamic, although it too resembled the Christian bell-tower. In this first phase of conquest, the Arabs created an Empire and a State, but not yet a civilization.

Only towards the middle of the eighth century did decisive changes come about – a vast political, social and eventually intellectual upheaval, when the caliphate passed to the Abbasid dynasty, and their black flag replaced the white flag of the Omayyads.

Then it was that the Muslim world turned back towards the East and withdrew a little from the Mediterranean, which had previously absorbed so much of its attention. Under the new caliphs the capital of Islam in effect shifted from Damascus to Baghdad, causing great discontent among those who saw their influence thus diminished, as well as among client or conquered peoples. It was the end of the reign of the 'thoroughbred' Arabs, which had lasted at most for a century – three or four brilliant generations – during which their higher caste of warriors had sunk into the delights of wealth and luxury, otherwise known as civilization, which Ibn Khaldun, an Arab nobleman from Andalusia, later described as 'evil personified'.

Then, quite naturally, the old civilized countries reasserted their supremacy, at a time of rapidly growing material prosperity on every side. In about 820 the caliph's annual revenue was perhaps five times that of the Byzantine Empire. Huge fortunes were made under a capitalist trading system, well ahead of its time, that extended as far as China and India, the Persian Gulf, Ethiopia, the Red Sea, Ifriqya and Andalusia.

'Capitalist' is not too anachronistic a word. From one end of Islam's world connections to the other, speculators unstintingly gambled on trade. One Arab author, Hariri, had a merchant declare: 'I want to send Persian saffron to China, where I hear that it fetches a high price, and then ship Chinese porcelain to Greece, Greek brocade to India, Indian iron to Aleppo, Aleppo glass to the Yemen and Yemeni striped material to Persia . . .' In Basra, settlements between merchants were made by what we should now call a clearing system.

Trade meant towns. Enormous cities were built as its headquarters. They included not only Baghdad, which from 762 until its brutal destruction by the Mongols in 1258 was a real 'city of light', the largest and richest capital in the Old World, but also – not far away on the Tigris – huge Samarra, as well as the great port of Basra, Cairo, Damascus, Tunis (a reincarnation of Carthage) and Cordoba.

Starting from the words of the Koran and of traditional poetry, all these cities made or virtually remade so-called 'classical' Arabic – a learned, artificial, literary language which became the idiom common to all Islamic countries, as Latin was to their Christian counterparts. By contrast with it, the forms of Arabic spoken in the different countries, and even Arabian Arabic itself, came more and more to seem like dialects. Classical Arabic was not only a language: it was also a literature, a philosophy, a fervent universal faith and a civilization, evolving in Baghdad and from there spreading far and wide.

The result, even before the Abbasids, was a serious crisis in the recruitment of public officials. In 700, the Omayyad caliph Abd'-el-Malik summoned the future monk Joannes Damascenus (655–749), who was then his adviser, and told him that he had decided henceforth to ban the Greek language from all public administrative documents. 'This,' wrote the Arab historian Baladhori, 'greatly displeased Sargoun [i.e. Sergius, Joannes Damascenus's other name], and when he left the Caliph he was very sad. Meeting some Greek officials, he told them: "You had better seek another profession to earn your living: your present employment has been withdrawn by God."'

It was the end of a long *modus vivendi* by which Christians and Muslims had lived in mutual tolerance. A completely new era was beginning.

Linguistic unity in the Arab world, in fact, had created an essential tool for intellectual exchanges, for business, for government and for administration. The Jewish merchants' letters mentioned earlier were written in Arabic, although using the Hebrew alphabet. Culture gained immense advantage from this linguistic asset. The son of the famous Haroun al-Rashid, Mâmûn (813–33), had large numbers of foreign and especially Greek works translated into Arabic. Knowledge of them spread all the more rapidly in so far as Islam very soon began using paper, which was so much cheaper than parchment. In Cordoba the Caliph El-Hakam II (961–76) was said to have a library of 400,000 manuscripts, with forty-four volumes of catalogues. Even if these figures are exaggerated, it is worth noting that the library of Charles V of France ('Charles the Wise', son of 'John the Good') contained only 900.

These crucial centuries saw the internal transformation of Islam. The religion of Muhammad was complicated by Byzantine-style exegesis, and supplemented by a form of mysticism that many specialists see as a resurgence of neo-Platonism. Even the driving-force of the Shi'ite schism seems to have come in part from depths outside the scope of early Arabic Islam. The Shi'ites venerated the pious Caliph Ali, assassinated by the Omayyds, and they opposed the Sunni Muslims who represented the majority and the mainstream of Islam. One of their places of pilgrimage, Karbala in Iraq, still attracts thousands of the faithful. 'Ali seemed like a second Christ, and his mother Fatima like a second Virgin Mary. The death of Ali and his sons was recounted like a Passion' (E. F. Gautier).

Even at the heart of its religion, therefore, Islam renewed itself by borrowing from ancient Eastern and Mediterranean civilizations, now rejuvenated and recruited for a common spiritual and temporal task with the help of a common language. Arabia had been only an episode. From one point of view, indeed, Muslim civilization began only when multitudes of non-Arabic peoples were converted to Islam, and when Islamic schools spread throughout the '*Ummâ*' or community of the faithful, from the Atlantic to the Pamirs. Once again, old wine was poured into new bottles.

The golden age of Islam: eighth to twelfth centuries

For four or five centuries, Islam was the most brilliant civilization in the Old World. That golden age lasted, broadly speaking, from the reign of Mâmûn, the creator of the House of Science in Baghdad (at once a library, a translation centre and an astronomical observatory), to the death of Averroës, the last of the great Muslim philosophers, which took place at Marrakesh in 1198, when he was just over seventy-two years old. But the history of the arts and of ideas is not the only key to the time of Islam's greatness.

Léon Gautier, an historian of Muslim philosophy, has pointed out that those periods when Islamic thought most flourished were

times of peace and general prosperity, when good fortune afforded the protection of an enlightened and all-powerful caliph. Such, in the East, in the eighth and ninth centuries, were the Abbasid caliphs who, from Al-Mansur to El-Mutawakkil, unceasingly encouraged for nearly a century the spread of Greek science and philosophy in the Muslim world, thanks to a vast effort of translation made by Nestorian Christians . . . Such also, in the West in the twelfth century, were the Almohad caliphs, who had the habit of holding long, speculative talks alone with their favourite doctor or philosopher. Other favourable periods were those when, on the contrary, the decadence of the Empire enabled bold thinkers to choose from among competing minor potentates a benevolent patron such as Sayf al-Dawla, Emir of Aleppo in the first half of the ninth century and protector of the philosopher Al-Farabi.

Léon Gautier, clearly, sees the problem in terms of political history. For him, civilization depends on princes and 'enlightened despots'. Yet the rapid decline of the Baghdad caliphate after a series of misfortunes, which led to unprecedented political fragmentation, by no means hindered the development of philosophy. On the contrary, it made possible a degree of intellectual freedom, if only by enabling a scholar to flee from one State or one princely protector to another nearby. This was a regular feature of Renaissance Italy and of seventeenth- and eighteenth-century Europe. Islam often enjoyed the same opportunity.

But intellectual advantages are never enough by themselves. Important material advantages both sustain and explain them.

By about AD 750, Islam had largely attained its greatest geographical extent. Further expansion was blocked by counter-attacks from outside. Constantinople, besieged in 718, was saved by the courage of the Emperor Leo III, the Isaurian, and by Greek fire; Gaul and the West were saved by Charles Martel's victory at the Battle of Tours or Poitiers in 732 or 733, and by the simultaneous uprising in the Maghreb. The result was some slight degree of stability on the frontiers of Islam, while within it, throughout the Empire, a vast economic system took root, grew and bore fruit.

This growth involved the establishment of a market economy, a money economy and a progressive 'commercialization' of agricultural goods, not all of which were consumed on the spot, the surpluses being sold in the towns and adding to their general prosperity. The date trade mobilized every year more than 100,000 pack-camels. Market halls in the towns acquired names like the 'melon house'. Melons from Merv in Transoxiana were particularly prized. In dried form they were shipped westwards in large quantities and over long distances; as fresh fruit they were sent to Baghdad by special relay stages, in leather containers packed with ice. The cultivation of sugar-cane, likewise, became an industry. Also to be noted when considering foodstuffs was the development of flour-milling. There were water-mills near Baghdad, for instance, and windmills by 947 at Seistan, while at Basra the flow of the Tigris was used to turn the wheels of floating mills.

This enterprising economy explains the development of numerous industries – iron, wood and textiles (linen, silk, cotton and wool) – as well as the enormous spread of cotton-fields in the East. Carpets from Bokhara, Armenia and Persia were already famous. Basra imported vast quantities of kermes and indigo to dye textiles red and blue. Indian indigo, which came via Kabul, was reputed to be finer than that from Upper Egypt.

All this activity had countless repercussions. The money economy shook the foundations of a society composed mainly of lords and peasants. The rich became richer, and arrogant; the poor became poorer still. The growth of irrigation techniques increased the demand for peasant slaves; and Islam's wealth enabled it to pay five or six times as much for them as any of its competitors. Social tension was the inevitable result.

Islamic prosperity was not the only factor: but it explained a great deal. In particular, it helped to foster a revolutionary climate and an uninterrupted series of urban and agrarian disturbances, often linked with nationalist movements like those that broke out in Iran. Literature from the period too easily suggests modern expressions and concepts: nationalism, capitalism, the class struggle. Take a pamphlet by Al-Ifriki, written in about the year 1000. 'No, assuredly I shall not pray to God, so long as I remain poor. Leave praying to the Sheik, the commander of armies, with his cellars full to bursting. Why should I pray? Am I powerful? Do I have a palace, horses, fine clothes, or a golden belt? To pray would be sheer hypocrisy when I don't even own the meanest plot of land.'

Since all things are interconnected, the Islamic heresies that proliferated during these hectic centuries all had, like Europe's medieval heresies, social and political roots. A dissident group appears, develops and takes different shapes under encouragement or persecution. The history of Muslim thought is intimately linked with that of such volatile cabals.

One historian, A. Mez, has used the ambiguous word 'Renaissance' to describe Islam's golden age. This suggests that its brilliance can be compared only with that of the astonishing Italian Renaissance. The comparison has in any case the advantage of stressing the fact that intellectual and material wealth were both involved in Islamic civilization, as they were in fifteenth-century Italy. Both, in fact, were based on urban societies enjoying the benefits of trade and riches. Both were the product of small, brilliant circles of exceptional people who drew deeply on the ancient civilization which they revered and revived, and who lived centuries ahead of their contemporaries. Both, however, were under external threat from barbarians more or less thinly disguised.

For Italy at the end of the fifteenth century, the barbarians were the mountain-dwellers of the Swiss cantons, the Germans to the north of the Brenner Pass, the French, the soft-shod Spaniards or the Turks (who captured Otranto in 1480). For the Islam of Avicenna or Averroës, the barbarians were the Seljuk Turks, the Berbers, the Saharan nomads or the Western Crusaders. Frequently barbarians were sought after, invited – as happened later in Italy. From the earliest days of the Baghdad Caliphate, as we have seen, there was a demand for Turkish slaves and mercenaries. These slaves were offered to buyers by their own parents, 'to secure their future'. In Spain for a very long time a few gold coins were enough to buy off Christian invaders from the North and send them back home. Then, one fine day, the battle became serious. The King of Seville, Al-Mutamid, now had to protect himself from the Christian barbarians by asking for help from other barbarians, the Almoravids of North Africa.

Paradoxical as it may seem, Islamic civilization as a whole, between 813 and 1198, was both one and many, universal and regionally diverse. First, its unity. Everywhere Islam built mosques and *medersas* whose decoration was deliberately and uniformly 'abstract'. All took the same form: a central courtyard, arcades, a basin for ritual washing, a *mihrab* or niche to show the direction for prayer, a *minbar* or pulpit in the pillared nave, and a minaret. All used the same architectural repertoire: columns with capitals, different-shaped arches (splayed, Moorish, trefoiled, multilobular, ogival, stalactitic), ribbed cupolas, mosaics, ceramics and finally the evocative calligraphic art of the arabesques.

Everywhere, likewise, Islam produced poetry on the same principles and with the same favourite phrases. It celebrated God ('the flawless rose is God'), nature, love, bravery, noble blood, the horse, the camel ('as massive as a mountain . . . Its beaten track forms a girdle round the earth'), knowledge, the forbidden pleasures of wine, and flowers of every kind. The whole Islamic world also shared the same folktales, originally from India, which we know today as *The Arabian Nights*, collected in writing in the fourteenth century after long gestation by word of mouth.

Everywhere Islamic philosophy (*falsafa*) took over that of Aristotle and the Peripatetics: it made immense efforts to place God in a cosmos which, following the Greeks, it regarded as eternal and hence excluding any notion of the Creation.

Everywhere there were the same techniques, industries, industrial objects and furniture, as can be seen from excavations like those of Madînat al-Sahra, near Cordoba. Everywhere, too, there were the same fashions, copying the tastes of Baghdad. Spain was the final destination of such cultural imports from the East, and their gradual impact can be traced across the country: the growing fashion for masquerading under surnames borrowed from famous Eastern poets, the general adoption of the burnous after the arrival of the Almoravids, the vogue for certain literary themes or certain medical prescriptions and so on.

Everywhere from Persia to Andalusia wandering entertainers performed. They came mostly from Egypt; but there were also girl dancers and singers, trained in Medina or Baghdad, and wearing yellow in the East and red in the West. All the poets spoke of them. Everywhere, finally, Muslims played chess and the very popular *kurâg*, using wooden carved figures of barded horses. It was an absorbing game: 'The Captain of Al-Mutamid, Ibn Martin, was surprised in his dwelling at Cordoba by a detachment of enemy soldiers while he was playing *kurâg*.'

Two further examples show the cohesion of Islam. One is that of a vizier, the regent of Khorassan in Persia at the beginning of the tenth century, 'sending missions to all countries to ask for copies of the customs of all the Courts and all the ministeries, in the Greek empire, in Turkestan, in China, in Iraq, in Syria, in Egypt, in Zenjan, Zabol and Kabul . . . He studied them carefully and selected those he judged best' to enforce on the court and administration of Bokhara. The other example, more strictly within the limits of the Muslim world, is that of Hakam II, the Caliph of Cordoba, who bought books written in Persia, Syria and elsewhere as soon as they appeared, and 'sent a thousand dinars in pure gold to Abulfaraj al-Isfahani to obtain the first copy of his famous anthology' (Renan).

But this cultural unity did not destroy clear and lively regional characteristics. In the tenth century when the Muslim empire split, each region recovered something of its independence, with room to breathe and reaffirm its own particular character, which it had always jealously preserved despite its borrowings from and contributions to Islam as a whole. A new geographical pattern began to take shape.

Muslim Spain, responding and adapting to successive outside influences, gradually acquired its own Spanish character – one of its many incarnations in the course of history.

Iran asserted its individuality still more strongly and vigorously. With the Baghdad Caliphate it recovered its energy and its own style. Baghdad was an Iranian city. The Abbasid period saw the great success of enamelled terracotta, whose homeland was Persia, and of another of its treasures, pottery with a metallic glaze. Persia's *iwâns* or huge porches recalled the palaces of Chosroës. The Arabic language remained dominant, but Persian – written in Arabic script – became a second great literary language, and spread very far afield, especially towards India (and, much later, throughout the Ottoman Empire). Half demotic, it had the advantage of reaching a broad public; and it also gained from the almost complete eclipse of Greek. At the end of the tenth century the poet Fidawsi wrote *The Book of the Kings* in praise of the ancient Iranians. From the eleventh century onwards Persian was increasingly used for books on popular science.

Persia was certainly a national civilization with its own powerfully individual character – but from now on *within* the vast civilization of Islam. The great exhibition of Iranian art in Paris in 1961 was illuminating in this respect. It showed how profoundly the pre-Islamic and Islamic periods differed, yet revealed continuity between them nevertheless.

This polarity between universality and regionalism existed throughout Islam. Extreme cases were Muslim India, Muslim Indonesia and Black Africa, deeply penetrated by Islam but still overwhelmingly itself.

In India the interaction of two civilizations gave rise to genuinely Indo-Islamic art, whose apogee came in the twelfth and especially the thirteenth century. In Delhi, in particular, amazing examples of it still remain. Their strangeness is explained by their eclecticism. For example the great mosque in the city, which dates from 1193, was designed by Muslims and then built by Indian masons and sculptors, who mixed Indian-style floral scrolls with Arab calligraphic decoration. In this fashion a whole new art evolved, sometimes predominantly Muslim, sometimes mainly Hindu, according to the time and the place. Eventually, by the eighteenth century each strain had so much affected the other that it became impossible to tell them apart.

At its higher levels the golden age of Muslim civilization was both an immense scientific success and an exceptional revival of ancient philosophy. These were not its only triumphs; literature was another: but they eclipse the rest.

Science and philosophy

First, science: it was here that the Saracens (as they were sometimes called at that time) made the most original contributions. These, in brief, were nothing less than trigonometry and algebra (with its significantly Arab name). In trigonometry the Muslims invented the sine and the tangent. The Greeks had measured an angle only from the chord of the arc it subtended: the sine was half the chord. The Chosranian (the adopted name of Mohammed Ibn-Musa) published in 820 an algebraic treatise which went as far as quadratic equations: translated into Latin in the sixteenth century, it became a primer for the West. Later, Muslim mathematicians resolved biquadratic equations.

Equally distinguished were Islam's mathematical geographers, its astronomical observatories and instruments (in particular, the astrolabe) and its excellent if still imperfect measurements of latitude and longitude, correcting the flagrant errors made by Ptolemy. The Muslims also deserve high marks for optics, for chemistry (the distillation of alcohol, the manufacture of elixirs and of sulphuric acid) and for pharmacy. More than half the remedies and healing aids used by the West came from Islam, including senna, rhubarb, tamarind, nux vomica, kermes, camphor, syrups, juleps, plasters, pomades, unguents and distilled water. Muslim medical skill was incontestable. The Egyptian Ibn al-Nafis – although his findings remained unused – discovered the pulmonary circulation of the blood three centuries before Michael Servetus and long before the later discoveries of William Harvey.

In the field of philosophy, what took place was rediscovery – a return, essentially, to the themes of peripatetic philosophy. The scope of this rediscovery, however, was not limited to copying and handing on, valuable as that undoubtedly was. It also involved continuing, elucidating and creating. The philosophy of Aristotle, transplanted into the Muslim world, inevitably looked like a dangerous explanation of the world and of humanity, confronting as it did a revealed religion, Islam, which was also a general explanation of the world, and an extremely rigorous one. But Aristotle obsessed and conquered all the *falasifat* (i.e. practitioners of *falsafa*, or Greek philosophy). There, again, A. Mez's comparison with the Renaissance makes sense: there was indeed such a thing as Muslim humanism, valuable and varied, which can only be sum-marized here.

It involved a long succession of thinkers at different times and places. Of these, five names stand out: Al-Kindi, Al-Farabi, Avicenna, Al-Gazali and Averroës. Avicenna and Averroës are the best-known, and the latter was the more important, owing to the immense repercussions of what was called Averroism in medieval Europe.

Al-Kindi (we know only the date of his death in 873) was born in Mesopotamia, where his father was Governor in Kûffah. Because of his birthplace, he was known as 'the philosopher of the Arabs'. Al-Farabi, born in 870, was of Turkish origin. He lived in Aleppo and died in 950 in Damascus, where he had gone with his patron Sayf al-Dawla when the city was captured. He was known as 'the second Master' – the first being Aristotle. Avicenna (properly, Ibn-Sina) was born at Afshena, near Bokhara, in 980; he died at Hamadan in 1037. Al-Gazali, born in Tūs in Persia, died there in 1111; towards the end of his life he became something of an anti-philosopher, a passionate spokesman for traditional religion. Averroës, whose real name was Ibn-Rushd, was born at Cordoba in 1126 and died at Marrakesh on 10 November 1198.

These dates and place-names show that Muslim humanism was widespread and long-lived throughout Islam – all the more so in that each of these leading figures was surrounded by colleagues, students and devoted readers.

The list also shows that the last major Muslim philosopher flourished in Spain – the last, but not the greatest, although it was he who acquainted the West with Arab philosophy and with Aristotle himself.

In this long perspective, the real question is that which Louis Gardet has put very forcefully (and, incidentally, answered in the negative): was there a truly Muslim philosophy? Which means: was there a single philosophical tradition, running from Al-Kindi to Averroës? Was such philosophy a function of the atmosphere of Islam? Was it original? As is often the case, the cautious countryman's answer 'Yes and no' is not only prudent here, but indispensable.

Yes, there was one philosophical tradition. Trapped between Greek thought on one side and the revealed truth of the Koran on the other, it was tossed to and fro between them. It owed to Greece, and to Islam's scientific bent, its clear but not exclusive rationalism. All the philosophers in question were what we should call scientists, concerned with astronomy, chemistry, mathematics and – always – medicine. Medicine it was that often won them the favour of princes and enabled them to earn a living. Avicenna wrote a medical *Canon*, or encyclopaedia. Averroës did likewise; and in Europe Muslim medecine was for a long time the *nec plus ultra*, even as late as the comedies of Molière.

Greek influence gave Muslim philosophy internal cohesion. 'The author of this book is Aristotle,' wrote Averroës in his preface to the *Physics*. 'He was the son of Nicomachus and the wisest of the Greeks. He founded and completed logic, physics and metaphysics. I say that he founded them, because none of the works written on these subjects before him is worth discussing . . . None of those who have followed him until now, that is, over some 1,500 years, has been able to add anything to his works, or find in them any significant error.' As admirers of Aristotle the Arab philosophers were forced into an interminable debate between prophetic revelation, that of the Koran, and a human philosophical explanation, that of the Greeks. The agonizing dispute between revelation and explanation required mutual concessions by both reason and faith.

Faith, revealed through Muhammad, had imparted to humanity a divine message. Could the thinker, unaided, discover the truth of the world and set his own reason in judgement over the value of dogma? In the face of this dilemma all our philosophers revealed great, perhaps excessive, dialectical skill. Avicenna, says Maxim Rodinson, 'was not a genius for nothing: he found a solution.' His solution, which was not his alone, ran roughly as follows: the prophets had revealed higher truths 'in the form of fables, symbols, allegories and images or metaphors'. Theirs was a language for the mass of the people, aimed at keeping them happy. The philosopher, by contrast, has the right to go far beyond such language. He insists on very great freedom to choose, even when there is stark and utter contradiction between the rival approaches.

For example the philosophers normally believed like the Greeks that the world was eternal. But if it had always existed, how could it have been created at a certain time, as revelation maintained? Pushing his logic to the limit, Al-Farabi declared that God could not know particular objects or beings, but only concepts or 'universals' – whereas the God of the Koran, like God in the Old Testament, 'knows all that is on land or in the sea. No leaf falls without His knowledge. No seed in the darkness of the earth, no green shoot nor dried twig exists that has not been recorded and written.' There were other contradictions. Al-Farabi did not believe in the immortality of the soul. Avicenna did: but he did not believe in the resurrection of the body, affirmed by the Koran. After death, he thought, the soul returned to its own universe, that of disembodied beings. Logically therefore there could be no individual reward or punishment, no paradise and no Hell. God, disembodied beings and souls are the ideal world, in face of which matter is incorruptible and eternal – because 'movement did not precede stillness, nor stillness movement . . . All movement is caused by previous movement . . . God has no reason to be new.'

These quotations, borrowed from Ernest Renan, may arouse curiosity, but they fall short of satisfying it. Close attention and hard work would be needed to follow the dubious logic of such explanations.

Those philosophers who since Renan have taken an interest in these now distant dilemmas have not found it easy to resolve them. Their interpretations depend on their own cast of mind, rationalist or idealist – or, which amounts to the same thing, their preference for one philosopher or another. Al-Kindi sailed on religious waters that raised no storms; Avicenna was undeniably idealistic; Averroës was a philosopher for the end of the world. Al-Gazali, the defender of the faith, made his own the stubborn dogma of early Muslim theologians: he sought to ignore or even to destroy peripatetic philosophy, for his own thought led him into very different, mystical paths. He renounced the world to take up the white woollen mantle or *sûf* worn by the sufi, adherents of mystical faith rather than rational theology. They were known as 'God's fools'.

Averroës, the Cordoba physician, became the faithful editor of and commentator on the works of Aristotle. The advantage of his work was that it gave both the full Arabic translation of the Greek text and a dissertation on it, consisting of remarks and digressions. The text and commentary were translated from Arabic into Latin in Toledo, and thereby reached Europe, where they sparked off the great philosophical revolution of the thirteenth century. So Muslim philosophy, despite what is sometimes said, did not die an immediate death under the powerful, desperate blows of Al-Gazali. In the end, however, it did die, together with Muslim science, before the end of the twelfth century. Then it was that the West took up the torch.

Stagnation or decadence: twelfth to eighteenth centuries

In the twelfth century, after quite extraordinary triumphs, 'Saracen' civilization was suddenly checked. Even in Spain scientific, philosophical and material progress barely continued after the last decades of the century. The suddenness of this change poses a number of questions.

Was it caused, as used to be argued, by the passionate and all too effective onslaughts made by Al-Gazali against philosophy and free thought? No one can take that theory very seriously. Al-Gazali was a product of his time – a symptom as much as a cause. Besides, philosophy had always had its detractors from its earliest days, as can be seen from the countless times when books were ordered to be burned – a proceeding unthinkable unless there was violent public hostility. Equally, many philosophers were publicly disgraced and condemned to exile – at least until circumstances changed; and there were also times when the *fiq*, the Koranic science of law, reigned supreme and reduced any philosopher to silence. What is more, after Al-Gazali philosophy flourished once again, and not only with Averroës.

Was it the fault of the 'Barbarians'? This is what a recent historian, S. D. Gothein, has suggested. They had been the military saviours of Islam against the threats from Asia and the West. Had they also sapped it from within?

In Spain, these dangerous rescuers had been, first, the Almoravids or Barbarians from the Sudan and the Sahara, then the Almohads from North Africa. In the Near East, Islam's saviours had been the Seljuk Turks, nomads from the cold steppes of Central Asia, or slaves from the countries of the Caucasus. In S. D. Gothein's view, decadence began 'when power was taken over by barbarian soldier slaves in almost all of the Muslim States' and 'the unity of the Mediterranean world was broken'. Unity had been the making of Islam, but it meant nothing to 'these barbarian peoples who in no way shared Mediterranean traditions'.

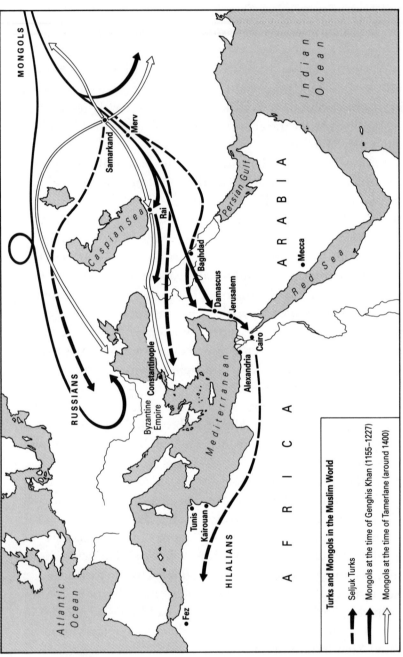

4. *Did the Mongols hasten the decline of Islam?*

Genghis Khan (the 'universal king' 1205–8) imposed his domination on the Mongol tribes (1205–8). He then conquered Northern China. Next, he turned Westwards and reached the Caucasus via the 'Ural-Caspian gateway'. In his wake, the Mongols descended on Europe and Asia: in 1241 they reached Poland and Hungary, and in 1258 they took Baghdad. Tamerlane (1336–1406) relaunched the conquest: in 1398 he took Delhi, in India; in 1401 he destroyed Baghdad.

Turks and Mongols in the Muslim World

Seljuk Turks

Mongols at the time of Genghis Khan (1155–1227)

Mongols at the time of Tamerlane (around 1400)

One might retort that these barbarians, in the West as in the East, were not much more barbaric than the great majority of the Arabs who had made the first conquests; and that, like them, they were more or less rapidly civilized by contact with the ancient Islamic countries. The Almohad Caliphs were the protectors of Averroës. In traditional accounts of the Crusades Saladin, the great Kurdish Sultan and opponent of Richard the Lion-Heart, is a rather noble figure, at least in the eyes of Christian barbarians. Finally thanks to Egypt Islam re-established its autonomy by crushing the Mongols at Ain Jalut in Syria on 3 September 1260, and by seizing Acre, the last Christian outpost in the Holy Land, in 1291.

Was the problem rather, the loss of the Mediterranean? As the eleventh century drew to a close, Europe began its reconquest of that inland sea, and Islam began to lose the benefits of it. The historian Henri Pirenne believed that in the eighth and ninth centuries the Muslim conquest of the Mediterranean had deprived the West of free movement there, and forced it back upon itself. Now Pirenne's thesis worked the other way round. The Mediterranean began to be closed to Islam, which found itself permanently handicapped, unable to expand and ill-equipped for its ordinary daily life.

It seems strange that E. F. Gautier, who in 1930 was the first to stress this sudden setback to Saracen civilization, did not seek to apply to it Henri Pirenne's theory, which at that time was widely discussed. In the present state of our knowledge, it is probably the best explanation for Islam's abrupt reverse.

Islamic civilization survived this rebuff. It may not have matched its past achievements, but it continued nevertheless. In 1922, when Paul Valéry declared 'Civilizations, we know you to be mortal,' he was surely exaggerating. The seasons of history cause the flowers and the fruit to fall, but the tree remains. At the very least, it is much harder to kill.

After the twelfth century, Islam undoubtedly saw some very

dark days. From the West it suffered the long ordeal of the Crusades (1095–1270), from which it emerged half-victorious with the recapture of Acre in 1291. But although it recovered the land, it lost control of the sea. From Asia it was half-submerged by long, cruel and savage Mongol invasions between 1202 and 1405: Turkestan, Iran and Asia Minor never fully recovered from their destructive onslaught. The capture of Baghdad in 1258 was the symbol of these misfortunes. Islam recovered from its wounds, but only partially.

At the same time, during these dark centuries – the thirteenth, fourteenth and fifteenth – Islam's particular hardships were worsened by economic difficulties on a world scale. From China to India and Europe, the Old World as a whole endured a protracted crisis. Everything and everyone suffered, and for centuries on end. In Europe, the crisis seems to have come later (from 1350 or 1357 onwards) and to have been of shorter duration (it ended between 1450 and 1510): but it was none the less real. Its most obvious manifestation was the so-called Hundred Years' War, from 1337 to 1453, accompanied by a long series of other foreign, civil and social conflicts, and by desolation and poverty. When assessing Islam's misfortunes, therefore, one has to distinguish between what were world phenomena and what was specifically Muslim.

At all events, it was in a climate of general gloom and pessimism that Ibn-Khaldun, the last great Muslim philosopher, wrote his magisterial works. An historian (and, as we should say now, a sociologist) of Andalusian origin, he was born in Tunisia in 1332. He led a busy and eventful life as a diplomat and statesman in Granada, Tlemcen, Bejaia, Fez and Syria; he died a *cadi* or judge in Cairo in 1406, a year after Tamerlane, to whom he had been sent as ambassador.

Ibn-Khaldun's major work was the *Kitab Al-Ibar* or *Book of Examples*, a vast compilation dealing in an original way with the history of the Berbers. Its Introduction alone is a masterpiece, the first systematic treatise on the methodology and sociology of

Muslim history; it was translated into French in the nineteenth century under the title of *Prolégomènes*, and into English in 1958 as *The Muqaddimah: an Introduction to History*.

With the return of better times and a recovery in the world economy, broadly in the sixteenth century, Islam once more profited from its intermediary position between East and West. The greatness of Turkey lasted until 'the so-called tulip period' in the eighteenth century. In Istanbul the 'tulip period' was when unmistakable real or stylized representations of the flower appeared constantly on pottery and in miniatures or embroidery. The tulip period is a fitting title for an age that lacked neither strength nor grace. Politically this recovery was marked by the rapid and brilliant victories of the Ottoman Turks, which began well before their conquest of Constantinople in 1453. That resounding success, moreover, was followed by others. By the sixteenth century they had made Turkey one of the great powers in the Mediterranean.

The new masters of Byzantium and of the Arabian holy places soon more or less restructured the whole of Islam. After 1517 the Ottoman Sultan, the Grand Turk, became the Caliph of all the faithful. The only areas outside Turkish control were distant Turkestan, Morocco beyond the 'Regency' of Algiers, and Shi'ite Persia, which became more nationalist than ever with the growth of the Sefavi dynasty. Mongol and Turkish Muslim mercenaries, led by Zehir–Eddin Muhammad Baber (1495–1530), a distant descendant of Tamerlane, seized the Empire of Delhi, and in 1526 founded the Empire of which Baber was the first Great Mogul. It soon dominated most of India.

In the same year, 1526, the Turks defeated Christian Hungary at the Battle of Mohacs. It was clear that Islam was enjoying a general renaissance under Turkish and Sunni influence, which everywhere entailed total victory for Muslim orthodoxy and traditional religion. Power reasserted itself; independent thinking was curbed; an iron regime was imposed.

In the Balkans and the Near East Turkish domination coincided with visible material prosperity, rapid population growth and the

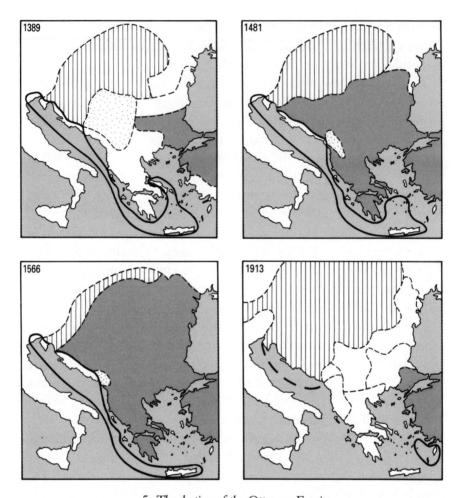

5. *The destiny of the Ottoman Empire*

In grey, Ottoman possessions. The dotted areas show Serbia. Vertical lines show Hungary. Surrounded by a thick black line, Venetian and (after 1913) Italian possessions.

establishment of flourishing towns. In 1453 Constantinople had had barely 80,000 inhabitants. In the sixteenth century, when it had become Istanbul, there were 700,000 spread among the city itself, the Greek quarter of Pera beyond the Golden Horn and Scutari (Üsküdar) on the Asian side of the Bosphorus. This capital, which like all great cities combined great luxury and appalling poverty, provided the much envied model of a civilization that under the Ottomans spread its influence far and wide, exporting for instance the pattern of its huge mosques, including the Süleymaniye, built for Süleyman the Magnificent.

Turkey's real greatness, denied for a long time in the West, is now gradually re-emerging through research by historians. The superlative Turkish archives, at last classified and catalogued, are being opened to scholars: they reveal, one by one, the workings of a multifarious, painstaking, advanced and authoritarian bureaucracy which was able to compile a detailed census, devise a coherent administrative policy, amass huge reserves of gold and silver, and systematically colonize the Balkans, the bastion of the Empire against Europe, by settling nomads there. It also imposed forced labour, and maintained an astonishing, rigorously trained army. It all seems curiously modern.

This great machine ran down eventually, but not before the end of the seventeenth century. Its last great tremor was the siege of Vienna in 1687. Thereafter, was the Turkish Empire stifled by its lack of maritime outlets? Morocco stood between it and the open space of the Atlantic; the Red Sea gave it inadequate access to the Indian Ocean; and in the Persian Gulf it faced the violent opposition of the Persians and, still more, of new arrivals from Europe with their superior fleets and their powerful commercial backers.

Or did the Turkish Empire die because it failed to adapt well and quickly to new technology?

Or, again, and more obviously still, because in the eighteenth and above all in the nineteenth century it faced the powerful rivalry of modern Russia? The victories of the Austrian cavalry during Prince Eugene's campaigns (especially from 1716 to 1718) had endangered only the edges of Turkey in Europe. With Russian intervention a young colossus had arrived to challenge a moribund or at least a tired one.

Even so, the Turkish Empire was not at first the 'sick man of Europe' that the great powers' diplomacy maltreated so shamelessly in the nineteenth century. Turkish Islam remained for a long time powerful, brilliant and formidable. So did Sefavi Persia, admired in the seventeenth century by the observant French traveller Tavernier. So did the Great Mogul, who at the beginning of the eighteenth century almost seized the whole of Deccan in the South, despite close surveillance by the British and the French.

Beware, therefore, of hasty judgements about the early decadence of Islam, which tend to anticipate history.

7. The Revival of Islam Today

═══

Islam relapsed into that inferno or purgatory of living humanity that we euphemistically call the Third World. Relapsed, because it had previously enjoyed what was undoubtedly a better relative position.

This decline, definite if more or less belated, led in the nineteenth century to humiliation, suffering and bitterness, followed by general foreign domination. The facts are well known. Only Turkey escaped that fate – hence its brilliant and brutal reaction, on the brink of disaster, under Mustapha Kemal Pasha (1920–38). This indeed served as a model for later national reactions and triumphs. Today, the liberation of Islam is very nearly complete. But it is one thing to secure independence, and quite another to keep pace with the rest of the world and look clearly towards the future. That is much more difficult.

The end of colonialism and the birth of new nationalist movements

Nothing is easier than to retrace today the chronology of colonization and then of 'decolonization' in Islam's various regions. One by one (except for the ex-Soviet Muslim Republics) they have all attained full political independence.

Soviet colonialism? Habitually, under this heading, only British, French, Belgian, German or Dutch colonies are mentioned. They certainly make up a great part of the whole. But there has also been Russian and then Soviet colonialism, of which less is usually said. To all appearances, it kept a grip on at least 30 million Muslims – more than the entire population of the Maghreb today.

Is the word colonialism appropriate here? In the years that followed the Russian Revolution of 1917, there were certainly efforts to emancipate and decentralize the Soviet Union. Concessions were made to local autonomy, and immense material progress was achieved. 'Today, all the Muslim nations of the USSR, above all in Turkestan and the Caucasus, have their own scientific, administrative, and political managerial classes, their intelligentsia. They have closed the gap between themselves and the Tartars, and no longer need to seek help from the intellectuals in Kazan' – the old, once exclusive centre of Muslim culture in Russia.

In the process, however, the natural solidarity among the various Muslim Republics has been weakened, and the idea of a vast 'Turanian' State has passed into limbo. In the Soviet federal system, culture was 'national in its form, but proletarian and socialist in its content'. The results were clearly secularization, to the detriment of Islam's religious values, and nationalism, now practically limited to the horizons of the region, with no reference to the *Umma* of fellow-Muslims, and normally making only short-term demands for 'the reform of the institutions' or 'a bigger role for administrators from the minority nationalities'.

In other words, the Muslim problems of the USSR were for the moment unrelated to the ordinary demands of Islam as expressed, vociferously, on the international stage. The Muslim Soviet Republics enjoyed a degree of independence, but were tightly bound within the USSR, with a common foreign policy, and wholly dependent on the Union for defence, finance, education and rail transport.

All this was a long way from the experience and the visions of Sultan Galiev, who from 1917 to 1923 was a senior Communist official, but then an anti-revolutionary agitator until he was sentenced to death in 1929. As a Muslim, he had dreamed of uniting all the Muslims in the Soviet Union into a single State, and using it, like a long probe pointing Eastwards, to inject the Revolution and its ideology into the heart of Asia – a continent he thought ripe for political upheaval, whereas industrial working-class Europe seemed to him no more than an 'extinct revolutionary furnace'. Would Islam have been able to set Asia alight? In centre-stage today, one would-be political heir of divided Islam is Pan-Arabism, which in public international disputes is only too ready to take over. The purely Arab world is the ambitious heart and crossroads of Islam. It is easy, therefore, to mistake the Middle East (and its North African outposts) for the whole of Islam, and to see no more than this or that region, this or that well-known figure. This happens all the time in the daily news. Clearly, the part should not be confused with the whole.

But the essential, insistent characteristic of Islam today is precisely its internal division, the insidious fragmentation of its identity and its lands. In some places, this is the result of relentless political pressures; in others, it is due to geography, which has placed Islam under the exclusive influence of other civilizations or economic systems.

In the Indian Archipelago, the 80 million Muslims who live alongside or intermingle with deep Hindu and animist traditions, and in a very individual economic structure, are in a sense already half lost. In the Indian subcontinent, Pakistan consists of two enormous areas separated by the teeming breadth of India, whose very numbers make it somewhat of a threat. In China, the 10 million Muslims are a group apart, very definitely 'lost'. In Black Africa, victorious Islam itself fell part-victim to, and was partly deformed by, various powerful animistic cults.

The Islamic faith of such peoples often serves them as an argument for nationalism and a means of resistance. But for Islam as a whole, all those countries which no longer look towards Mecca as strictly as before, which no longer flock on pilgrimages or fully subscribe to the political ideal of an effective and united Pan-Islam – these countries are undoubtedly lost or very likely to be lost. Distance, politics and the growth of atheism and secularism all play their part. Since 1917, only a few hundred Soviet pilgrims have made their way to Mecca.

Is Islam at present 'at the Garibaldi stage'? In the heart of the Muslim countries, in the Near East, Pan-Islam is coming into conflict with sharp and vehement local nationalism. The dissolution of the United Arab Republic of Egypt and Syria in September 1961 was a striking example. Pakistan, Afghanistan, Iran, Turkey, Lebanon, Syria, Iraq, Jordan, Saudi Arabia, Tunisia, Morocco, Mauritania and Yemen are all of them attached to their particular prerogatives, and often more or less openly hostile to each other, even if they sometimes achieve momentary solidarity against the outside world and its threats.

Such vehement nationalism, which drives people – and especially young people and students – to violent and dramatic gestures, too often seems out of date, in the unsympathetic eyes of Westerners. We have too many good reasons for regretting our own past nationalist excesses, for which Europe paid so dearly, not to look on new explosions of nationalism, when Europe is uniting, with a certain lack of enthusiasm and, indeed, rather unfairly, all the more so when the nationalists are attacking the West.

Unfairly? Here, very justly expressed, are the feelings of one Afghan intellectual, Najm oud-Din Bammat, writing in 1959:

Islam today has to go through a number of revolutions at once: a religious revolution like the Reformation; an intellectual and moral revolution like the eighteenth-century Enlightenment; an economic and social revolution like the European Industrial Revolution of the nineteenth century; and, in the age of the two great Eastern and Western blocs or systems, a number of small nationalist revolutions of its own. At a time when pacts are being forged on a world scale, the Muslim countries are still waiting and searching for their Garibaldis.

There is no question – far from it – of casting aspersions on the shining reputation of Garibaldi. But the wars of national unity that were so necessary in the past were followed in Europe by Armageddon.

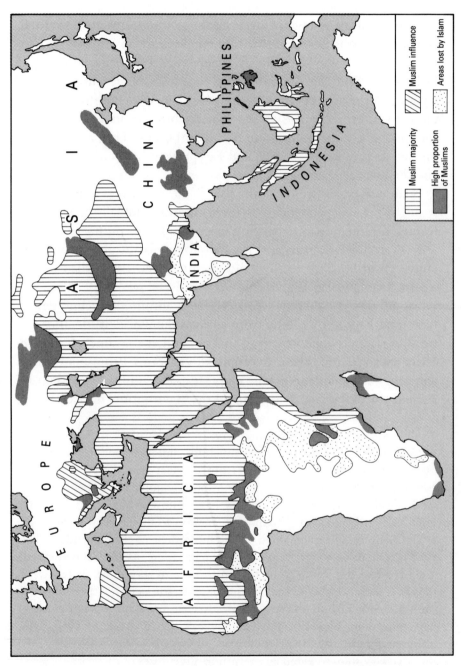

6. Muslims in the world today

(This sketch does not indicate Islam's almost total domination of India in ancient times.)

Is nationalism likely to profit Islam any more than it profited Europe? May it not lead Muslim States into an impasse, in an interdependent world economy where such fragmentation makes little sense? Still more, does it not engender dangerous conflicts? Every independent country, so long as it has some military power, tends to interpret Pan-Islam or Pan-Arabism in its own way, in the sole light of its own interests and ambitions. This, as everyone knows, is how Pakistan, Iraq and Egypt have behaved in the past; and the lists are open to all comers.

Nationalism, however, can also be a necessary stage in the struggle for independence – a form of anti-colonialism, rejecting foreign domination, and backing liberation by strength.

It should be no surprise that all forms of Arab nationalism converge in hostility to their old enemy Israel. Established in the aftermath of World War II, the State of Israel seemed to them the work of the West at its worst. Israel's admirable technological triumphs, backed by capital from all over the world, its demonstrations of strength against Egypt in 1948 and at the time of Suez in 1956, when its tiny army overran the vast Sinai Peninsula – these and other achievements arouse envy, fear and animosity, adding to ancient scores. Jacques Berque has written with some justice:

Arabs and Jews are both, if I may say so, peoples of God. Two peoples of God at once – that is really too much for diplomats and generals! The inevitable conflict arises precisely from the fact that the two sides are cousins, both descendants of Abraham, both ennobled by a belief in one God . . . In the face of the West they have followed different paths. The Jews, in the diaspora, have adapted their ways to the insistent technology of the Gentiles, but maintained all the more their community ideal. The Arabs, remaining in their own lands, have been invaded and divided, but have had the privilege or the misfortune to stay more or less what they were. Hence the present inequality of resources on either side, and the difference in both words and deeds. The most lucid Arab essayists have meditated bitterly on what they call the 'disaster' of 1948. Like Taine or Renan after 1870, they have advised their compatriots to take the necessary steps to avoid any return to adventures of that sort.

Nationalism has a role to play in the near future: all Muslim countries will have to adopt and apply strict austerity plans. They will need, in fact, plans for solidarity and social discipline; and nationalism will help all these young countries to deal with the serious economic difficulties they face. It will make it easier to accept essential innovations which clash with very ancient social, religious and family structures – age-old ancestral habits, perpetuated in Islam's traditionalism, and only too likely to spark off violent reactions.

For, at all costs, Islam has to modernize and adopt in large measure the technology of the West, on which the world now so much depends. The future hangs on the acceptance or rejection of this world civilization. Powerful traditions call for its refusal; but nationalist pride may incite people to accept what they would instinctively reject.

Islam has often been denied the flexibility needed for so drastic a change. So much so, that numerous observers claim that, owing to its 'impermeable', 'intransigent' heart, spirit and civilization, Islam will find all its efforts to modernize effectively blocked. Is this true?

In fact, Islam has already accepted some aspects of the modern world by which it feels besieged, and it could accept more. It was not without hesitation and conflict that Christianity did so in the past; yet in the end its integrity survived the process of adaptation. To regard Islam as an exceptionally intransigent religion, totally lacking flexibility, is to forget how many heresies it has nurtured. They alone bear witness to uneasiness and possible stress. The Koran itself, moreover, offers to reformers the ever-open door of the *ijtihad*. 'The Prophet,' wrote Pierre Rondot, 'is deemed to have foreseen cases where the Koran or the *sounna* (tradition) give no guidance: in which instances he recommended reasoning by analogy or *qiyas*; and if that could not be done, then one should submit all possible precedents to one's judgement and vision or *ray*. This personal effort of interpretation, the *ijtihad*, played a considerable role in the future development of Muslim thought. In our day, the reform movement explicitly intends to reopen that door.' Every religion, indeed, has its emergency exits. Islam may delay or oppose changes; but it can also be influenced and outflanked.

Economists, at grips with daily reality, continually protest against ready-made, stereotyped explanations based on the supposedly unchangeable 'facts' of Muslim life. The real difficulty, they say, is much more mundane: it is simply the scale of the transformation to be made. Islam has dropped two centuries behind the West – and the centuries in question are those which changed Europe much more than during the whole of the past between classical antiquity and the eighteenth century. How could Islam make up so much leeway in a short time? It would mean taking hold of its archaic societies and reshaping them – but with a farming system still poor and precarious, and with industries which are isolated within an economy incapable of reaching and enriching the inert mass of a rapidly growing population. Furthermore, like all societies, Islam has its plutocrats, few in number but all the more powerful for that. Beliefs and traditions often serve as pretexts whereby the privileged defend their own interests, keeping in being some societies that are truly 'medieval' as in Yemen, feudal as in Iran, or archaic as in Saudi Arabia – despite, or perhaps even because of, its oil.

These difficulties severely tested the work of the reformers: brilliant and brutal on the part of Mustapha Kemal in Turkey; accompanied by violent rhetoric from Kassem in Syria; marked by stubbornness in the case of Nasser in Egypt; or wise and capable on the part of Bourguiba in Tunisia. Whatever their nature or their style, they mostly faced similar obstacles. All their reforms had to overcome various supposed taboos inherent in Muslim civilization; and the supreme, unmistakeable test was the emancipation of women, first beginning to be proclaimed, then – more slowly – on the way to being achieved. The end of polygamy, the limitation of husbands' right to repudiate their wives unilaterally, the abolition of the veil and the admission of women to universities, employment and the vote: all these are or will be of the utmost importance.

Moves towards them prove that reform is not a lost cause, but that it needs champions and decisive battles. The struggle will be many-sided. The most serious danger would be to be tempted away from it by the attractions, the convenience or the imperatives of political situations inflamed on any excuse or none at all.

The ideal tactic would be to take only one step at a time, and each time choose the essential step. But politics is not a Cartesian theorem. Economic progress alone requires from Islam – as from everyone – a concentrated, perhaps exclusive political effort. And in the practical world this may well mean tackling problems as they arise, whether they be old or new.

Thus all these States, proud of their independence, have demanding and passionate political ambitions to be met and diverted from blind alleys. They have susceptibilities which need careful handling: Islam has as many as Europe, which is not notably thick-skinned. Islam also has its young people, its impatient students, who rather resemble the French *polytechniciens* in the 'July Revolution' of 1830. It has its soldiers, as apt for uprisings and *coups d'état* as those in Latin America before 1939. It has its power-hungry political parties, and its politicians pursuing the mirage of their own image and carried away by the sheer violence of their speeches. They have to raise their voices to be heard above the clamour of the world.

Clearly, foreign interests are present: France in North Africa, Britain in Kuwait and the sparsely populated Southern part of Arabia; the United States everywhere, calmly supplying credits and advice; the USSR, sparing or prodigal according to circumstances, and always vigilant in this vast, contested no man's land. Everywhere, finally, social revolution lies in wait, showing its colours and sharpening its demands.

History is on its side. In Turkey, where the military *coup d'état* of 27 May 1960 led many to hope for social reforms which have been long in coming. In Iran, where a first revolution came from above, at once conservative and modern-minded, made some progress despite the hostility of young people, fundamentalists, partisans of the former Minister Dr Mossadeq, and the Iranian Communist Party, the *Toudeh*. In Jordan, where a courageous king stands up to dangers on every side. In Lebanon, which in happier and wiser times sought to be the Switzerland of the Near East. In Iraq, where change was more verbal than real, but where the Kurdish problem remains a deep running sore. In Egypt, where after the secession of Syria from the United Arab Republic the country embarked on a form of social Communism whose partial success may well prove infectious. One might complete the picture by adding the uneasiness of Pakistan, disquieted by India, which now seems more bellicose than had been thought, and has its eyes on Kashmir; the ambitions of Indonesia, which has been encouraged by India's success against Goa to want to establish a protectorate over Irian, or Dutch Guinea; and the uncertainties in all of North Africa, which is waiting to see what course to follow after the denouement of the Algerian tragedy.

All these worries weigh on the policies of the Islamic States, exposing them to unexpected explosions of violence which greatly harm both them and their neighbours. Who can evaluate how much the Bizerta affair of 1961 cost France (which is rich) and Tunisia (which is poor)? In that crisis, was Bizerta the real issue, or was it mutually wounded pride? France was bitter because she thought she had done a great deal for Islam (which was obviously true); Islam was bitter because it believed that the independence it had been given was not complete. Indeed, no country is truly independent if its economy is such as to consign it at once to the Third World.

Yet the former mother countries are only partly responsible for this continued state of economic dependence. It results also from other specific causes, including Islam's past, its dearth of natural resources and its immoderate birth-rate. All these are serious handicaps; but they can be remedied.

Muslim States in the modern world

Growth is always hard-won: Islam faces the same dilemma as the rest of the Third World: to be integrated into the world economy, it must as soon as possible complete its own Industrial Revolution. The task is simple to describe: but it will be costly, requiring hard work whose results will not be immediate or very quickly affect the standard of living. The Muslim countries' time as colonies by no means prepared them for this responsibility; and that is certainly the colonial powers' most serious failing.

True, the colonists made an important contribution to the places they ruled. Very backward countries, where life had not changed for centuries, were suddenly brought into contact with highly developed civilizations. They gained something from that: modern medicine and hygiene, which greatly reduced the death-rate; more or less effective education, depending on circumstances (and here the French colonies were better than most); many material investments, in ports, roads and railways; modern agricultural arrangements, often with irrigation dams; and in some cases a sensible approach to industrialization.

That, some may say, is a lot. Yes and no. On the one hand, the colonists' contribution partially destroyed old structures; on the other, it replaced them very imperfectly. What was set up was not designed for a national economy, but for an economy linked with the mother country, dependent upon it and upon the life of the world. Hence the very uneven levels of development from one sector to another, and the need for newly independent States to reform the structure of their economies so as to meet all their national requirements. This difficulty adds one more to the many others they face, arising from the nature of their civilization and the poor quality of most of their land.

To tackle these tasks, the Muslim countries need help as well as self-help. They have to adapt to the changing policy of the privileged world – of which they are well aware and at which

they are adept. They lack neither intelligence nor political skill.
Still more, however, they have to adapt themselves and grapple
with the real world. This squaring of the circle is the hardest of
their tasks.

There is no single, simple solution. Not even that offered by oil,
which seems so great a benefactor. Petroleum is an undoubted
asset, and its benefits have raised the standard of living in all the
oil-producing countries. Nature, as we know, has accorded it
generously to the Near East. Nevertheless, the major international
oil companies, which alone could afford the huge costs of prospect-
ing and extracting, remained for a long time the chief beneficiaries
of oil: they took possession of it at source in exchange for royalties;
they refined it; they distributed it. Early attempts to retain it at
source, as Iran briefly did in 1951 and Iraq proposed in 1961, were
effectively thwarted: oil was valuable only when it was sold.
Today, ownership patterns have changed; but at present there is
no shortage of oil in the world, and with other forms of energy,
including nuclear energy, on the horizon, Islam's virtual monopoly
of fuel supplies may not last for ever.

Incidentally, foreign exploitation was not the only evil involved.
In the Muslim countries, oil royalties enriched a privileged class.
The money was not distributed fairly, but too often financed
artificial luxury on the part of a particular caste. Nor did this
luxury stimulate local production: it was wasted on foreign imports
which could never become productive at home. Saudi Arabia used
much of its oil revenue to build new cities, new roads, new
railways and new airports. That was obviously progress. But much
of it also went into the unbridled and anachronistic opulence of
the royal family and the main tribal chiefs. Such a spectacle pleased
neither the young, excited by the revolution in Egypt, nor the
middle classes, eager to play their part in public affairs.

To some observers, Middle Eastern oil looks very like the silver
of South America in the sixteenth century, which passed through
Spain without stimulating the economy there, and went on to
enrich still further the flourishing economies of the rest of Europe.

In any case, oil is and will remain the starting-point of endless conflicts in the Near East. One early example was that between General Kassem of Iraq and the eight major international oil companies whose representative on the spot was the IPC or Irak Petroleum Co. Talks went on for three years before being suspended. Fields within the concessions that were not being exploited were withdrawn from company control. Reconciliation no doubt remained possible by making concessions to Iraq, including a better than fifty-fifty division of profits. There was also the possibility of bringing in more accommodating newcomers as oil prospectors, from Japan and Italy, notably to explore under-sea resources in the Persian Gulf. But even so the oil-producing countries do not hold all the aces, and they still risk future setbacks.

All the Muslim States have set to work and achieved great things, including general growth in production. But the growth of the population continually undermines their efforts. Everything is progressing, yet everything has to be begun afresh.

The demographer Alfred Sauvy pointed this out in an article on the Near East in *Le Monde* (7 August 1956) which has lost none of its force. 'The Arab world,' he wrote (and he could have written 'the Muslim world as a whole'),

is a demographic volcano. At fifty per thousand, or six to seven children per family, the birth-rate is one of the highest in the world. Far from falling, it has actually gained from the decline of polygamy, as well as from better hygiene. And while the birth-rate reaches new heights, the death-rate is falling rapidly, owing to fewer epidemics, famines or inter-tribal wars. The present mortality rate is not precisely known, but it is certainly tending downwards, towards twenty per thousand. There is nothing exceptional in a population growth of 2.5 to 3 per cent a year. This is the case in Algeria, in Tunis and probably in Egypt. Such a rate of growth, which doubles the population in a single generation, is far in excess of that which flooded Europe in its heyday (1 to 1.5 per cent a year), and it lacks the safety-valve of emigration and colonization. The Muslim world combines the death-rate of Europe in 1880 with a birth-rate such as Europe attained only in the most flourishing periods of the Middle Ages. It is an explosive mixture.

Sauvy added, presciently: 'It would be näive to think that these countries, which have rapidly growing populations and needs, and which between them have the oil, the pipelines and the Suez Canal, will resign themselves to watching so much wealth flow across and out of their territory without demanding an important share of it for themselves.'

The result of so rapid an increase in the population of the Muslim countries is to prevent any rise in the standard of living, despite the growth of production. This is a frequent phenomenon in the Third World. Everywhere, however, positive steps have been taken to deal with it. As a result, unemployment has decreased. In Tunisia, to take only one example, 200,000 or 300,000 unemployed were found jobs without outside help or very large-scale investments: they set to work making roads, terracing farmland against erosion, building houses, or simply planting trees. One economist calculated that between 1952 and 1958 agricultural production in the Near East increased roughly as much as that in the world as a whole. Every branch of industry has made similar progress. In Egypt, the index of manufacturing industries, based on 100 in 1953, rose as follows over the same period: 1951, 95; 1952, 98; 1953, 100; 1954, 107; 1955, 117; 1956, 125; 1957, 132; 1958, 143. In Pakistan, industrial production rose from 100 in 1952 to 128 in 1954 and 215 in 1958.

So there was progress, a general increase in the national revenue and hence, it would seem, a greater chance to devote more to investment and encourage growth. So far so good: but against that ran the rising tide of population. The number of people increased still faster than the quantity of goods to be shared among them, and the income per head fell – as in every quotient whose denominator (in this case, the population) grows faster than the numerator. The more a swimmer battles against an overwhelming tide, however much progress he makes through the water, the more he is driven back over the ground. Islam, where everything is advancing, nevertheless has to watch its standard of living receding, or barely staying the same.

It should be added, however, that these calculations of income per head are only estimates. The figures for population are themselves often uncertain, with a margin of error which may be as much as 20 per cent. The national income, too, is hard to calculate exactly in the frequent absence of reliable national statistics. Equally, it is far from easy to evaluate precisely the output of scattered and primitive artisans, or of a rural economy with vast areas of subsistence farming where the peasants live on what they produce. All our figures, therefore, are no more than approximate indications. But that is already enough.

Given the growth of the population, the mere fact of maintaining the standard of living per head is a proof that the economy is vigorous and able to cope with this massive biological threat. The Muslim countries as a whole bear witness to this vigour; and if some are losing ground, their loss is small. Their people consume on average less than 2,600 calories a day (the lower limit in rich countries), but in general they are above subsistence level and everywhere (except in parts of Africa) outside the world's pitiless famine zones. They are below the line dividing wealth and poverty, but above the line dividing poverty from destitution. This, at least, is something gained.

Between these two dividing-lines, different countries occupy different positions. In terms of national revenue per head of population, measured in US dollars in the 1960s, they ranked in ascending order as follows: Libya 36; Afghanistan 50; Nigeria 64; Pakistan 66; Indonesia 88; Jordan 100; Syria 110; Iran 115; Egypt 122; Tunisia 132; Iraq 142; Morocco 159; Algeria 210; Turkey 219; Lebanon 247. The figures are modest indeed by comparison with Europe (more than 1,000) and the United States (2,200). They look substantial only when compared with those for Black Africa and elsewhere.

It may be noted that some of the best figures in the above list

are those for countries once or still associated with France –
Lebanon, Syria, Morocco, Algeria and Tunisia. French colonization as such can hardly claim credit for that, although at one time
it had its merits, essentially because it trained a range of intellectuals
and managers and bridged the gap, more effectively than
elsewhere, between different peoples and different civilizations.

Lebanon owed its relative prosperity to the spread of its trade,
its capitalism and its culture throughout Islam, Black Africa and
Latin America, as well as to its dual religious heritage, Christian
and Muslim. Algeria benefited from French and international
investments (in agriculture, dams, roads, schools, medical services,
Saharan oil) and from labour migration to France – none of them
interrupted by the long Algerian War which began in 1954.

In the struggle for development, every economy has certain
advantages or trump cards. Iraq, Iran, Saudi Arabia, and Algeria
have oil; Egypt has the fertile Nile Valley, the Suez Canal, high
quality cotton and a flourishing textile industry; Turkey and
Morocco have industrial development, very often intelligently
devised; Indonesia has rubber, oil and tin mines; Pakistan has vast
resources of wheat and jute.

These assets are invaluable: but the task remains difficult and risky.

The problems to be solved are intricate. At once economic and
social, they are so closely interrelated that it seems impossible to
tackle them one by one. Taken together, they demand a formidable
plan of campaign.

This involves, in fact:

- *Above all, better farming.* This means doing violence to archaic
  property laws, attacking the multiple problems of irrigation,
  and stopping the erosion and devastation of arable land. In a
  word, agrarian policy and technology.
- *Establishing industrial firms* (State-owned or private, in heavy
  industry or light), and if possible integrating them into the
  country's economy as a whole. They need to be based on the
  economy's global structure and to contribute to its general
  growth.

- *Solving the problem of investments* – a burning question because it involves foreign aid (which may be private international capital, brought in via Swiss banks, or Governmental assistance from the Soviet Union, the United States, France, or the European Community).
- *Creating a market*. Here, there are two problems. First, a market presupposes a certain standard of living (which is what all these measures are intended to attain); and secondly, any effective market needs to be far bigger than on a merely national scale. Hence various plans, launched with more enthusiasm than success, for a Pan-Arab market, a Maghreb market or an African market. The dreams are sensible: what is hard is to make them come true.
- *Educating and training the workforce*, all the more necessary in that automation, otherwise feasible in industries starting from scratch, would not solve the urgent, crucial problem of unemployment and surplus labour.
- *Training managers and others*: engineers, teachers and administrators. Teaching and technical training are on the agenda, and they are long-term tasks. Only great eagerness to learn, on the part of the people, will make it possible to overcome immense difficulties here.

Altogether, enormous investments are needed, and in some cases they will not pay for a very long term. As J. Berque puts it: 'Generations of people will be sacrificed to the future. Only a few have the sad privilege of realizing this. Certain young Syrian–Lebanese poets, trying to grasp this phenomenon, have invoked the myth of Thannus, the Eastern God destined for a painful death but also for rebirth. This is how they account for their people's permanent fear and present bitterness.'

A choice has to be made: in the face of such stark problems, such urgent and difficult solutions, and such huge unavoidable sacrifices, the leaders of the various States very naturally hesitate over what strategy to adopt. The world proposes at least two; and the choice to be made determines and transcends the whole future of Islam.

The options, broadly speaking, are as follows: either to maintain Western-style capitalism, half interventionist and half *laissez-faire*, with a degree of political liberalism; or to follow the Communist experiments – Soviet, Yugoslav or Chinese. Put more simply still, it means either retaining Government and society as they are, with whatever improvements are possible; or overthrowing the whole structure with a view to building afresh on a different basis. These alternatives are not, unfortunately, purely intellectual or even purely practical. They are affected by a myriad other factors, both foreign and domestic.

Everywhere, or almost everywhere, a middle class is emerging, composed partly of intellectuals, many of them young. They still resent the deep disappointment that has followed attempts to imitate the West. In politics, for example, all the Muslim States except Afghanistan and Yemen have Parliaments: but what advantage has this been to the emerging middle class? Disillusioned, and impatient for a role in public affairs, its members

turn to Communism, which they see as a means of one day taking control. Bureaucracy, and the Soviet ideal of planning, seem to promise guarantees of stability and ways of solving almost impossible economic problems. The young Muslim intelligentsia is tempted by the modern, scientific air of Marxist dialectic. Admittedly, this is only a reaction against the medieval constraints that still paralyse Islamic thinking; but it is all the more dangerous in that those who promote it have already looked in vain in the liberal, democratic thought of the West for ways into a modern, rational philosophy. Henceforward, Marxism seems to them the only possible solution (A. Benigsen).

The West is too inclined to see in the Islamic States' past dealings with the USSR only moves to obtain machines, arms and credits at low cost. There is much more to it than that. Communist experiments still fascinate young people in the Islamic countries. The West often relies on nothing but retrograde aristocracies in a *papier-mâché* theatrical decor. Here, as elsewhere, it lacks a truly global policy. The answer is not, in fact, to convince Islam that the Western model is better in itself or preferable to some other. Nor is it even to offer, more or less generously, a gold-mine of credits. Instead, it is to give developing countries an effective model of planning which suits their needs and gives them the hope and the prospect of a better future.

Muslim civilization in the twentieth century

Is Muslim civilization itself endangered by this deep crisis? The question arises in several forms.

Is there still, amid the immense fragmentation of nationalities and political rivalries, anything like a united Muslim civilization?

If so, is it not threatened by what Jacques Berque has called 'the adoption of universal fashions in technology and behaviour'? Can it, in other words, survive the impact of industrial civilization, now becoming universal, but in fact the creation of the West?

And would this risk not be all the greater if Islam were to choose as its path to modernity a Marxist creed which could destroy the religion that is so important in binding it together?

Is there still a Muslim civilization? The political divisions within Islam seem to have put paid to Pan-Islamic dreams for a long time to come. But, as in the past, Pan-Islamism is still a fact and a facet of Muslim civilization. That civilization is still unmistakably visible in daily life. From one end of Islam to the other, there are similar beliefs, morals, habits, family relationships, tastes, leisure pursuits, games, behaviour and even cooking. A European, whisked from one town to another in the Muslim countries of the Mediterranean, would be far more struck by their resemblances than by their differences. In Pakistan and the Indian Archipelago, the differences are greater, and greater still in Muslim Black Africa: there, in fact, Islamic civilization encounters its rivals, often no less powerful, and sometimes more so.

In Black Africa, Muslims are linked by little more than religion – if that. Preaching (for Egypt has launched a missionary campaign in the name of Pan-Arabism) is often done in French, in countries where that language is spoken. This implies that cultural links are more or less non-existent, or at least fragile and indirect. Nor is it certain that the religious link really works among the African masses, who in fact are transforming – *Africanizing* – Islam as freely as they do Christianity. In short, the strength of Pan-Islamism in Black Africa, when it exists at all, is political and social at most. It is not a facet of civilization as such.

Pakistan, meanwhile, is part of a civilization which has rightly been called Indo-Muslim. Its language, Urdu, mixes words of Iranian or Arabic origin with others derived from Sanskrit. It is written from right to left, like Arabic, but is otherwise quite different.

One of the surest proofs that countries are truly part of the unity of Muslim civilization remains that of language. The twentieth century has preserved 'literary' Arabic, which was always the cement of Islam: it is the common written language, used in newspapers and books. The national languages are purely oral.

And there is a further link. Islam's economic and social problems are almost all essentially identical, in so far as they arise from the clash between an archaic and traditional Muslim civilization, still largely unchanged, and a modern civilization which challenges it everywhere. In some places the problem has scarcely yet appeared; in others it is already acute: but everywhere the solutions required are very likely to be similar. This is only logical, since the starting-points are the same. Those countries that have made most headway in their reforming efforts are simply the precursors of the others.

Here again, however, 'Islam in exile' – in Black Africa, the Indian Archipelago and subcontinent, and China – differs from the rest because its future is linked with that of other civilizations.

A further question: will Islam cast off its old traditional civilization, like a worn-out garment, as it draws closer to industrialization and modern technology?

This question is not specific to Islam. What it really means is: will modern civilization, with computers, artificial intelligence, automation and nuclear technology, make the world uniform, for good or ill, and destroy individual civilizations?

Mechanization, with all that it involves, is certainly able to distort, destroy and reconstruct many aspects of a civilization. But not all. In itself, mechanization is not a civilization. To suggest that it is would be to claim that Europe today was born entirely anew at the time of the Industrial Revolution. That was certainly a brutal shock: but European civilization long predates it. The nations of Europe, indeed, make it very doubtful whether mechanization could unite or homogenize the planet. Moulded already by a single civilization, that of the Christian and humanist West; caught up almost simultaneously, more than a century ago, in the same adventure of industrialization; sharing the same techno-logy, the same science, similar institutions and all the social consequences of mechanization – these nations should surely have lost, long ago, those strong individual quirks which still enable us to speak of French civilization, or German, or English, or Mediter-ranean. Yet a Frenchman has only to cross the Channel, an English-man to set foot on the Continent, or a German to enter Italy, and each of them can see at once that industrialization does not mean standardization. And if technology cannot destroy regional differ-ences, how could it annihilate the great civilizations, founded on such powerfully different and individual religions, philosophies and human and moral values?

Would matters be different if the Muslim world embraced technology together with Marxism, whose tenets are so much opposed to the traditional spiritual values of Islam? This more precise question is frequently asked; and to answer it is neither easy nor indeed completely possible. Yet part of the answer may be suggested by what has been said already.

To be plain: Marxism is not in itself a substitute civilization. It is a social movement, a purposive form of humanism, a rationaliza-tion of human affairs. If one day it were adopted by Islam, it would lead to coexistence and sharing, as in the Soviet Union Marxism coexisted with Russian civilization, or in China with Chinese. And while it has greatly affected both these civilizations, it has not extinguished either. Nor is that part of its programme.

Y. Moubarac is undoubtedly right when he argues that in such a situation, 'Islam would find it harder to resist the grip of Marxism than Christianity has, because Muslims still make no distinction between spiritual and temporal affairs. For this reason, the spiritual is in greater danger of being submerged in the technological materialism of a Communist Muslim society.' Why is Moubarac right? Because *before* the Industrial Revolution, everywhere or almost everywhere, Christianity had had to absorb the impact of secular scientific rationalism. It had taken its time to adapt, and it had counter-reacted; but it had kept its balance and given up only what it could spare. This initiation, which had armoured it against rationalism, had armoured it against technology and Marxism too.

For Islam, in which religion determines every action in life, technology (Marxist or otherwise) is a wall of fire that has to be leapt through at a single bound, rejecting a civilization grown too old and finding fresh stimulus in the new world beyond the flames. Islam's choice will depend upon itself and upon the rest of the world, swinging like a pendulum first one way and then the other, East and West. Like the Third World as a whole, Islam seems likely to have to follow not its own inclination, but rather the bloc that has the greater weight.

PART II: AFRICA

8. The Past

Black Africa (which is really composed of many Black Africas) is almost entirely surrounded, by two deserts and two oceans: the huge Sahara in the North and the Kalahari in the South; the Atlantic on the West and the Indian Ocean on the East. These are serious barriers, especially since most of Africa's ocean outlets are poor: there are no good ports, and the rivers are not easily navigable owing to rapids, waterfalls and the silting up of estuaries.

Still, the barriers can be crossed. Very early on, the Indian Ocean was used by sailing boats taking advantage of the monsoons. European explorers conquered the Atlantic in the fifteenth century. The Kalahari only partly closes the way to the South; and the Sahara was crossed as early as classical antiquity. When the dromedary arrived from North Africa in the first centuries of the Christian era, traffic across the Sahara increased tenfold, with salt and then textiles coming Southwards, and black slaves and gold dust going North.

Altogether, however, Black Africa made only slow and imperfect contact with the outside world. Yet it would be wrong to suppose that its doors and windows remained closed and barred for centuries. Nature is powerful, but not omnipotent: history too often influences events.

★

Geography

That geography does not determine everything can be seen
immediately by looking at the frontiers or marginal zones of
Black Africa, which itself occupies only part of the continent as a
whole.

In the North, North-East and East, the Sahara characteristically
limits Black Africa, whether or not it forms an impenetrable barrier.

Black Africa, as a European Community committee puts it, is
'Africa South of the Sahara'. From the Mediterranean coast as far
as the Sudanese Sahel, the population is white; and this 'White
Africa' also includes Ethiopia, which undoubtedly has white ethnic
strains within a mixed population very different from true Black
Africans. Other factors, too, make Ethiopia a world apart: its very
individual civilization, its Christian religion (from AD 350
onwards), its mixed agriculture, based on stockbreeding and arable
farming, growing wheat and vines. In the past it successfully
resisted not only the attacks of Islam, which had managed to
encircle it, but also the efforts of European powers to cut it off
from the Indian Ocean and the Red Sea.

Prehistorians and ethnographers even believe that in the earliest
times Ethiopia was a secondary source of both arable farming and
animal husbandry, which had originated in India. Without its
intermediary role, multitudes of black peasants working the soil
with the hoe might never have discovered the unexpected
advantages of stockbreeding.

In fact, Ethiopia can be seen as the heart of a vast area of East
Africa, stretching North as far as the sixth Nile falls, East as far as the
Somali Deserts, and South as far as Kenya, if not beyond. This is
an intermediary Africa, neither black nor white but both at once,
possessing like White Africa a written language (and hence a
history): a civilization linked to the great centres in the North and
undeniably involved in the crucial interplay of Asia, the Mediter-

ranean and Europe. It may be noted, finally, that the Sahara is continued to the East of Ethiopia in Eritrea and the Somali lands – a long, dry, desolate area which marks a further boundary of Black Africa.

To the South, the accidents of history halted, and will continue to halt, the natural expansion of Black Africa. In the seventeenth century, wanting to establish a port of call on the sea passage to India, the Dutch settled in the Southern tip of the continent, in an area then virtually empty. In 1815, the British seized this strategic stronghold; and soon the Dutch colonists, the Boers or farmers, moved North and occupied the grassy plains of the veld, where they set up prosperous stock-breeding farms.

So a White Africa was gradually established in the South of the continent as well as in the North. It flourished on the wealth of its gold and diamond mines and its industries. To withstand what it saw as a rising black tide (10 million blacks, 3 million whites and 1.5 million coloured), South Africa steeled itself within a defiant racist policy (apartheid or segregation) which in 1960 led it to break with the Commonwealth. Was that a mere episode, or a definite break? It could not by itself arrest the progress of history: nor will it.

A final exception, again due to historical reasons, is the island of Madagascar, which must also be regarded as outside Black Africa. Its population consists of two elements: black Bantu from the nearby mainland, and Malaysian tribes which came in several waves from the East. Many inhabitants of Madagascar are of mixed descent, but the Western part of the island is mainly Bantu and the Eastern mainly Malaysian. According to still incomplete research, mixed inheritance predominates, with the African strain about twice as strong as the Malaysian.

Despite this ethnic diversity, Madagascar enjoys great cultural unity; and here the dominant strain is Malaysian. The language is Indonesian; so, undoubtedly, are the craft and farming techniques: 'land-clearing by fire, long-handled spades, flooded rice-fields, taro

growing, yams, bananas, dog-breeding, black pigs, poultry . . .
sperm-whaling, turtle-fishing, outrigger canoes, hunting with
spears, blow-pipes and slings, weaving of baskets and rush mats (of
which most of their furnishings consist) . . .' Madagascar's Eastern
immigrants probably came via the North rather than straight
across the India Ocean. The proof, slender but sufficient, is that
the Mascarene Islands of Mauritius, Réunion and Rodriguez were
uninhabited until the seventeenth century, whereas they would
have been natural and even necessary ports of call for anyone
sailing from the Indian Archipelago to Madagascar direct.

In other words, the history and civilization of the Indian Ocean
long dominated Madagascar, separating it from the mainland.
Today, however, proximity is linking Africa more and more with
the young Malagasy Republic.

In understanding Black Africa, geography is more important than
history. The geographical context is not all that matters, but it is
the most significant. Climate accounts for the alternation of vast
areas of grass and trees which inevitably involve different ways of
life.

In the West, equatorial rainwater collects, forming an immense
mass of virgin forests, akin to those of the Amazon and Indonesia,
on roughly the same latitudes. These forests act as 'sponges, soaked
with water; they are thick with giant trees and tangled underbrush,
dark and silent. They resist – or have resisted – attempts to clear
them; they are not propitious for human settlement or even for
travel, except by river; life there is precarious and isolated, based
on fishing and hunting.' Typically, such forests are the refuge of
the remaining African pygmies, survivors of the negrillos who
were probably Africa's earliest inhabitants.

The forest is more widespread to the North of the Equator than
to the South: it borders the Gulf of Guinea on its Northern side,
from Liberia to Cameroon. The gap in it shown on the map,
mainly wooded savanna and palm plantations, is the Southern part

7. The diversity of Africa: geography

of Benin. To the East, the equatorial forest ends at the Congo
Basin, on the edge of the East African uplands.

Around the rain forest, in roughly concentric rings, there are
tropical forests which become drier and drier the further away
they are, then wooded savanna with tall grass, clumps of trees, and
spinneys along the watercourses, then bare savanna, and finally the
steppes.

In human terms, there are two distinct areas, both subject to periods of rain and drought: one is stock-breeding country, the other not (on account of the tsetse fly).

The stock-breeding areas are among the most flourishing in Black Africa. The cattle are not used for draught purposes, since the fields are tilled with the hoe. Crops include millet, sorghum, yams, maize and rice; while for export there are cotton, groundnuts, cocoa, and palm oil – this last one of the richest resources, especially in Nigeria.

The great distinction, clearly, is between the areas with and without animal husbandry. The former, in the North and East – the outer zone – are the richest, the best balanced, and for a long time have been the most open to the outside world. They have also been an important focus for much of Africa's history.

Superimposed on these rural divisions there are also ethnic differences. Black Africans – who must never for one moment be thought of as belonging to a single ethnic group – can broadly be divided into four. There are the pygmies, a very primitive residue of the past, with a barely articulate language; on the edge of the Kalahari Desert there are small and ancient groups of Khoi-khoi or Hottentots and Saan or Bushmen; there are the Sudanese, from Dakar to Ethiopia; and from Ethiopia to South Africa there are the Bantu.

The two biggest groups are the Sudanese and the Bantu, both of them linguistic and cultural entities in their own right. The Bantu, who probably originated in the area of the Great Lakes, have maintained greater cohesion than the Sudanese. But both groups include many profoundly different peoples, owing partly to the accidents of history and partly to regional variations. In the case of the Sudanese, there has also been interbreeding with Islamic and Semitic peoples, given the immigration of Moors and Muhammadanized Berber Peuls, who had begun as herdsmen and become more and more settled. A detailed ethnic map of Africa defies any rationale not based on solid practical experience: it reveals endless conflicts, movements and migrations, some pressing forward, others retreating. Hence the mixtures and tensions that are found all over Black Africa; in both the remote and the recent past, successive waves of people either overlapped or fought with each other. There is still not complete stability. It would be fascinating to know of all these migrations, their dates, their direction and their speed. To a diligent research worker, that would not be impossible: it is rare for 'the inhabitants of a village not to know from which village the founders of their community came'.

The tensions were most acute, perhaps, in the area between the twelfth and fifteenth parallels of latitude, populated by the Sudanese. The most typical example is that of the refugee peoples known as palaeo-negritic (implying, as is quite likely, that they are the oldest ethnic group except for the pygmies). They were primitive hunter–gatherers and peasants assiduously fertilizing mountain terrain which was often very poor. By dint of very intense cultivation, they managed to sustain some fifty people in a square kilometre or so; and they usually occupied strongholds which were easy to defend. The same is true of the Dogons, the most northerly of these deeply entrenched people, as it is of all the so-called 'naked tribes' of Africa – 'the Coniagis and Bassaris of Guinea, the Bobos and Lobis of the Ivory Coast, the Nankasas of modern Ghana, the Kabrei and Sombas of Togo and Benin, and the Fabis and Angus of Nigeria'. These are all small ethnic groups, mere specks on the map.

Among the large groups, mention should be made of the Toucouleurs, the Mandingues, the Bambarras, the Hausas, the Yoruba and the Ibo – the last two of which are the two main groups in Nigeria, the richest and most densely populated country in Black Africa.

Each of these peoples has its own beliefs, its own way of life, its own social structure, and its own culture, no two of which are identical. This diversity is what makes Africa so immensely interesting. Experiences differ so markedly from one place to another that it is difficult to imagine a common future for all those concerned.

'The areas in which native Africans have taken refuge from external authority are often quite close to the most highly developed capitals.'

Variations in skin colour, which range from the deepest black of the Sudanese to the light, almost yellow pigmentation of the Hottentots and the pygmies, are only the anthropological, physiological counterparts of a much more essential diversity of societies and cultures.

The African continent suffers, and has suffered in the past, from many privations and serious general weaknesses. It would be impossible to list them all or to describe how at different times they have been better or worse. We have seen that Black Africa has had few outlets to the rest of the world – a serious handicap, because all progress in civilization is made easier by mutual contact and influence. This relative isolation explains the important gaps which were scarcely filled, if at all, before the arrival of the Europeans and the establishment of their colonies. The wheel, for example, was unknown: so were the plough and the use of pack-animals: so was writing except in Ethiopia (which is not really part of Black Africa) and the countries of the Sudan and the East coast (where writing came from Islam, which they very soon adopted).

These examples show that, very often, external influence filtered only very slowly, drop by drop, into the vast African continent South of the Sahara.

The same is true of the often discussed but still unsolved problem of how much Ancient Egypt influenced Black African societies. Glass beads have been found in Gabon, a statuette of Osiris has been discovered at Malonga in South-East Zaïre, and another South of the Zambesi. This is flimsy evidence, but it suggests the possibility of limited relationships, especially in the broad domain of art and its techniques, such as casting by the lost-wax process.

It has to be admitted, however, that exotic plants – certain kinds of rice from the Far East, maize, sugar cane and cassava – came to Africa rather late in the day. They were probably unknown there in ancient times.

There were other weaknesses. One was the shallowness of the red lateritic soil (contrasting with the bright red of rarer deposits, which were deeper and more friable); another was the climatic limit on the number of days when the land could be worked; a third was the regular shortage of meat in most people's diet.

In most African tribes, meat was eaten only at great feasts. The goats and sheep which Kikuyu farmers in Kenya fed on rough pasture around their fields were reserved for sacrifices and public ceremonies. The Kikuyu's nomadic neighbours, the pastoral Masai, lived off the produce of their flocks, but the animals were too valuable to be killed. Meat, seen as a source of strength and virility, was scarce everywhere, and was the subject of longings crudely expressed in this pygmy hunting chant:

> In the forest where no one else goes,
> Hunter, lift up your heart: glide, run and leap.
> Meat is before you, great joyous meat –
> Meat which strides like a hill,
> Meat which rejoices the heart,
> Meat which will roast on your hearth,
> Meat which your teeth will bite,
> Fine red meat, and steaming blood to drink.

Even so, the disadvantages should not be overstressed. First, Black Africa made progress in ancient times that was no less rapid than in prehistoric Europe. There were also artistic triumphs, and not only in the fine Benin bronzes of the eleventh to fifteenth centuries, or the equally fine textiles made from various vegetable fibres. Last but not least, Africa was an early pioneer in metallurgy – as early as 3000 BC in the case of iron. It is absurd – and untrue – to claim that Black Africans were introduced to iron only after the Portuguese reached Cape Bojador on the coast of the Western Sahara in AD 1434. Iron weapons were known very early on. Metalworking was perfected in what is now Zimbabwe as early as the Middle Ages. Tin-working was probably practised in Upper Nigeria 2,000 years ago. Finally – a significant detail – it has often been remarked that in Black African societies the blacksmiths form a separate, powerful and much respected caste. This is certainly the product of very ancient traditions.

The dark past

The long past of Black Africa is little known, as is that of all peoples lacking a written language. Its history has come down to us only through oral traditions, archaeological research and the accounts of occasional outside observers.

Three sets of facts, however, emerge from this dark past: the growth of cities, kingdoms and empires, all of mixed civilization and mixed blood; trade in black slaves, a very ancient practice, which reached diabolical proportions in the sixteenth century, when opening up the American continent proved too great a task for Europe alone; finally, the brutal irruption of the European powers, which in the Final Act of the Berlin Conference in 1885 completed the partitioning, with the aid of a map, of what theoretically remained 'unclaimed' in the huge African continent, still only half explored by Europeans but henceforth totally colonized.

In Black Africa, history favoured the development of higher political and cultural arrangements only where there were, on the one hand, the combined resources of tillage and animal husbandry and, on the other, contacts with the outside world – either along the edge of the Sahara or on the shores of the Indian Ocean. It was there that ancient empires and flourishing ancient cities were to be found.

Here there developed a special Africa whose past is relatively well-known, with societies and cultures organized into States, as against an elusive Africa which left far less trace on history. Referring to some natives on the Atlantic coast of the Sahara, a fifteenth-century Portuguese explorer remarked scornfully: 'They do not even have kings.' So there was one Africa with kings – whose history is not wholly unknown – and another without them, lost in oblivion.

Black Africa, then, developed along two of its outer margins, in which it was in contact with Islam. That contact was not always peaceful and agreeable. It often involved colonization – although it was through colonization that Black Africa was able to breathe the air of the outside world.

The first glimmerings appeared on Africa's Eastern coast. Centuries before the Christian era, it had been in contact with Arabia and the Indian subcontinent. But it was only with the first Muslim expansion, in the seventh century, that very firm links were formed between Arabia and Persia on the one hand and East Africa on the other. From 648 onwards, a series of market towns sprang up: Mogadishu, Sofala, Malindi, Mombasa, Brava and Zanzibar – this last founded in 739 by Arabs from the South of the Peninsula, while Kilwa was founded in the tenth century by the Shirazi, from Shiraz in Persia.

These towns were busy and prosperous on account of the trade in slaves, ivory and gold. Gold was found in large quantities up-country from Sofala, as witness Arab geographers like Masudi (916) and Ibn al Wardi (975). The goldfields and mines seem to have been in Matabeleland, between the Zambesi and the Limpopo, as well as – although some deny it – in what is now the Transvaal. The gold was found in both dust and nuggets. All this trade was linked – thanks to the monsoon – with India, which exported iron and cotton goods.

Mainly African, these towns had only a small minority of Arab or Persian colonists: they also had closer links with India than with Arabia. Their apogee was in the fifteenth century, but at that time their economy was still based on barter, not money, at least as regards trade with the African interior. The latter profited from it nevertheless. Far away as it was, it had political structures like the Kingdom of Monomotapa in what is now Zimbabwe (Monene Motapa signified 'Lord of the Mines'). Admittedly, we know less about the kingdom than its fame might suggest: it is said to have been destroyed in the seventeenth century by the Mambo or sovereign of the Rowzi.

It used to be thought that after Vasco da Gama's voyage in 1498, the establishment of the Portuguese in the Indian Ocean dealt a mortal blow to the trading towns of the Southern African coast. Today, this view is no longer held. Their hybrid civilization – half-African, half-Arab – continued to spread through the interior, although the coastal towns made no attempt to conquer it. The coastal ruins in Kenya and Tanzania, which used to be thought medieval, seem in fact to date from the seventeenth, eighteenth and even the nineteenth centuries. All, incidentally, used blue-and-white Chinese porcelain.

The Empires on the bend of the Niger bring us to another busy and fruitful contact with Islam. As we have said, trade links with the edge of the Sahara increased at the beginning of the Christian era, with the arrival of the dromedary in North Africa and on the desert trails. The growth of trade (in gold and slaves) and the increase in the number of caravans led White (chamito-Semitic) Africa into the land of the Blacks (which the Arabs called the *Bled es Sudan*).

The first of these Niger empires, Ghana, seems to have been established around AD 800 (and so was contemporary with Charlemagne). Its capital, also called Ghana and proverbial for its wealth, was at Kumbi Saleh, 340 kilometres North of Bamako in present-day Mali, on the edge of the Sahara. It may have been built by white men from the North; in any case, it soon belonged to Black people of the Soninke tribe, a branch of the Mande people, who in turn were part of the Mandingos. Attacked by the Muslims, the capital was captured and destroyed in 1077.

But because the trade in gold continued (from the goldfields of Senegal, the Benue River and the Upper Niger), another Empire soon came into being slightly to the East, benefiting the Mandingos and owing allegiance to Islam. This was the Mali Empire, which spread throughout the whole bend of the Niger. Under the reign of Kankan Musa (1307–37), who went on pilgrimage to Mecca, a number of merchants and educated people reached the banks of the Niger. Timbuktu then became an influential capital, regularly frequented by the nomadic Touaregs. Later, they seized the town and contributed to the downfall of the Empire.

A further Eastward thrust then brought prosperity to the Songhay Empire, with its capitals in Gao and Timbuktu. The Empire benefited from its links with Cyrenaica and from the exploits of Sonni Ali (1464–92), who was no doubt the strongest of all these builders of Empires. He himself was not a very orthodox Muslim, but his successor's defeat by the usurper Muhammad Askia marked the definitive victory of Islam in the new Empire.

By now, however, the glorious heyday of the Nigerian Empires was over. The Atlantic sea-route discovered by the Portuguese became the new channel for Black African gold; and although this did not kill the Saharan trade it greatly weakened it. During this general decline, a Moroccan expedition led by Spanish renegades conquered Timbuktu and destroyed the Songhay Empire in 1591. This success earned the Sultan of Morocco, Moulay Ahmed, the titles of El Mansur (the victorious) and El Dehbi (the golden). Yet the expedition was a complete disappointment for its organizers, who had hoped to conquer a fabulous El Dorado. The Sultan retained only formal and distant sway over these impoverished countries, where from 1612 to 1750 there were no fewer than 120 pashas, pawns in the hands of the Moorish garrisons which elected and, if necessary, dismissed them.

In the eighteenth century, in fact, power in the countries of the Niger was shared between the nomads and the Bambarras of Segu and Kaarta. The age of the great Empires was past. The prosperous trans-Saharan trade alone had established and maintained their brilliant and precocious supremacy. They died with it.

These great States, therefore, should not be regarded as typical: they were the exception rather than the rule. Few other States in Black Africa attained such proportions. Thus Benin, already outstanding in the eleventh century and enjoying a degree of artistic perfection in the fifteenth, was of very limited size. Essentially, it was a clearing, none too well organized, in the dense

mass of equatorial rain forest between the waters of the Gulf of
Guinea and the inland tablelands. It was in Yoruba country,
between the Niger Delta and present-day Lagos, in a region very
early built up.

Its reputation outstripped its size. It enjoyed the equivocal
advantage of fairly early contact, via the Northern trade routes,
with Cairo's artists and wealthy customers, and later with the
Portuguese. These links gave it the further benefit of becoming an
astonishing artistic centre for sculptors in ivory and workers in
bronze. Its amazing, prodigious success was not the work of its
princes. According to one Africanist, Paul Mercier, Benin owed
far more to the high density of its Yoruba population, its urban
structure, and its climatic good fortune. Being close to the Gulf of
Guinea, it had two rainy seasons (at the sun's two zeniths) and
therefore two harvests a year instead of one.

The major phenomenon of the fifteenth century, and still more of the
sixteenth, was the development of the trade in Black slaves. Despite
official bans, this continued until about 1865 in the North Atlantic
and probably still later in the South Atlantic, while it persisted
into the twentieth century along the Red Sea routes leading to the
East.

Black slave-trading was not a diabolical invention from Europe.
It was Islam, in very early contact with Black Africa, through the
countries between Niger and Dar-Fur and via its markets in East
Africa, which first practised the Black slave trade on a large scale.
Its reasons were the same, incidentally, as those which led Europe
to follow suit: it lacked manpower for many laborious tasks. But
trade in slaves has been a universal phenomenon, affecting all
primitive societies. And although Islam was then a slave society
par excellence, neither slavery nor the slave trade was its invention.

The Black slave trade has left behind very many documents (for
example in the commercial archives of both Europe and the New
World), from which one can glean statistics and series of prices.

This bookkeeping history, unpleasant in itself, is not the whole of the story: but it gives a necessary sense of scale.

In the sixteenth century, annual shipments of Black slaves to America amounted to between 1,000 and 2,000; in the eighteenth, they were between 10,000 and 20,000; and the biggest total, some 50,000, was reached in the nineteenth century just before the trade was banned. These figures are approximate, as are global estimates of the number of Black Africans transported to the New World. The most convincing are those published by P. Rinchon: about 14 million – which is more than Moreau de Jonnès thought in 1842 (12 million), but fewer than the estimate made by the demographer Carl Saunders, who perhaps went too far in approaching the 20 million mark. Saunders's figures would presuppose an average of sixty thousand slaves a year for the three and a half centuries between 1500 and 1850 – a number which seems not to tally very well with even the transport that was available.

We also have to distinguish between departures from Africa and arrivals in the New World. There were considerable losses, owing partly to the circumstances of capture and partly to the very severe conditions on the voyage. So the damage done by the European slave trade alone no doubt greatly exceeds what the above figures would suggest. The slave trade caused huge human losses to Black Africa.

These were all the more catastrophic in so far as the slave trade with Islam continued too, and even increased at the end of the eighteenth century. Caravans arriving in Cairo from Dar-Fur could bring 18,000 to 20,000 slaves in one trip. In 1830, the Sultan of Zanzibar claimed dues on 37,000 slaves a year; in 1872, 10,000 to 20,000 slaves a year left Suakin for Arabia. At first sight, the Islamic slave trade seems to have affected far more people than the European slave trade, which was limited by the length of the voyage, the smallness of the ships and the abolition of the trade itself, proclaimed several times in the nineteenth century – which proves that trading continued despite its prohibition, although against the difficulties that all smuggling has to meet.

V. L. Cameron, in 1877, reckoned that the annual outflow to Islam, via the North and the East, was some 500,000 people, and he concluded: 'Africa is bleeding from every pore.' This enormous figure can be accepted only with reservations; but the traffic was certainly very extensive and the demographic loss for Africa was appalling.

The question then arises: how far did the Black population compensate for this catastrophic deficit by increasing the birth-rate? In about AD 1500 the population of Africa was between 25 and 35 million, White Africans included. This, of course, is an historical estimate. By 1850, it was at least 100 million. So, despite the great depredations of the slave trade, there was demographic growth. It was a growing population that made possible the terrible trade in slaves. This may explain how the trade continued so long – but as a hypothesis only.

It has to be recognized, frankly, that the European slave trade stopped at the very moment when America no longer urgently needed it. European emigration to the New World took the place of the Black slave trade, in the first half of the nineteenth century towards the United States, in the second towards South America. One may add, in Europe's defence, that there had always been reactions of pity and indignation *vis-à-vis* Black slavery. Nor were these purely formal, for they culminated, eventually, in William Wilberforce's great movement, in Britain, for the liberation of the blacks and the abolition of slavery.

Without claiming that one branch of the slave trade (towards America) was more humane – or less inhuman – than the other (towards Islam), one might further point out a fact which is important for the present time: i.e. that there are still African communities in the New World. Powerful ethnic groups have developed and survived in both North and South America, whereas no such exiled African communities are still to be found in Asia or the lands of Islam.

This is not the place to condemn, still less to praise, the European colonization of Africa, but simply to note that colonization, like almost all culture-contact between civilizations, had both positive and negative cultural impact.

Colonization was ugly: it involved both atrocities and absurdities, such as the purchase of vast territories for a few rolls of cloth or a little alcohol. One is not defending such things by admitting that the shock of colonization was often decisive and even at length beneficial for the social, economic and cultural development of the colonized Black peoples themselves. For Europe, after the final act of the Congress of Berlin in 1885, the colonization of Africa was the last great overseas adventure. And if this tardy takeover was short-lived (lasting less than a century), it took place rapidly, and at a time when Europe and the world economy were in full expansion.

It was a developed and demanding industrial society, with modern means of action and communication, which met and invaded Black Africa. And Africa itself was receptive, more flexible than ethnographers even recently believed: it was able to seize the objects and practices offered by the West, and reinterpret them, giving them new meaning, and matching them whenever possible to the needs of its traditional culture.

Even in South Africa, where the Bantu world was subjected to cultural uprooting (entering another civilization) that was all the more rapid in that industrialization and urbanization were more intense there than elsewhere, educated Africans, living in Western style, nevertheless held to the traditions inherited from their past, if only as regards marriage, the family and the roles of brothers and of eldest or youngest sons. To take one example, the dowry for the bride's father is today paid in cash, but reckoned in heads of cattle in accordance with former custom.

Referring to colonialism's positive impact, we were not thinking of purely material benefits such as roads, railways, ports and dams, or those systems for exploiting the soil or the subsoil which the

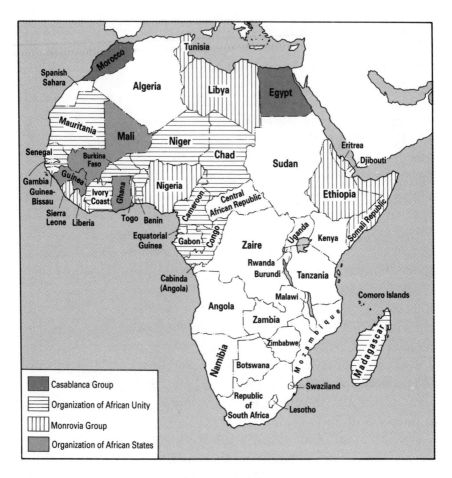

8. Africa's internal diversity

Over and above national diversity there are fragile links between groups of States.

colonists established, very much for their own ends. This legacy, important as it sometimes seems, would be of little use and short lifespan if those who received it had not also acquired, in the painful ordeal of colonization, the ability to use it rationally today. Education and a certain level of technology, of hygiene, of medicine and of public administration: these were the greatest benefits left by the colonists, and some measure of compensation

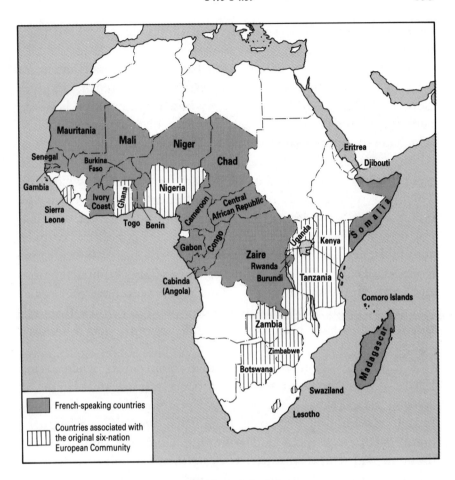

9. Africa and the West

Alongside French-speaking Africa, there is English-speaking Africa, slightly more scattered. Economic ties reflect these cultural links.

for the destruction which contact with Europe brought to old tribal, family and social customs, on which all of Africa's organization and culture were based. It will never be possible to gauge the full results of such novelties as employment for wages, a money economy, writing and individual ownership of land. Each was undoubtedly a blow to the former social regime. Yet these blows were surely a necessary part of the evolution taking place today.

On the other hand, colonization had the real disadvantage of dividing Africa into a series of territories – French, English, German, Belgian, and Portuguese – whose fragmentation has been perpetuated today in too large a cluster of independent States, which are sometimes said to have 'Balkanized' Africa.

Some of these divisions are artificial, and some are geographical. Very few have any cultural basis. But are they irreparably harmful? They may well seriously hinder the fulfilment of some visions of a united Africa, or at least of an African common market. But it is not certain whether Africa is ready, as yet, for political or even cultural unity. It is not only the old colonial administrative frontiers that divide the continent: there is also ethnic, religious and even linguistic diversity. The main weakness of today's national divisions is their failure to correspond to cultural frontiers. But could they have been expected to do so, more than a hundred years ago?

A still more serious reproach is that colonization, when giving Black Africans the useful tool of a modern international language, actually played a bad trick on them by giving them at least two: French and English. It is to be feared that everything a language brings with it, shaping and colouring education and habits of thought, will tend to thwart Africa's efforts for unity by dividing it into two camps, English-speaking and French-speaking. It seems unlikely that one will swamp the other – for example that the numerical advantage of English-speaking Africa will overcome French-speaking Africa, which is culturally stronger and which has enjoyed for far longer an effective educational system producing the political and administrative infrastructure which is the best guarantee of success.

None the less, it is regrettable for the future of African unity that this important division should have been added to all those which history and geography have already too lavishly conferred.

9. Black Africa: Today and Tomorrow

For a study of civilizations, Black Africa is a very rich source. Most of it, in recent years, has achieved independence. 'Negritude' or the search for indigenous roots, which has been called 'a form of humanism in the making', has begun to articulate specifically African values and possibilities. Africans are eagerly seeking their own history, which has to be pieced together and almost invented. All this gives Black Africa one great advantage: it is a cultural world in full and rapid evolution. To the outside observer it offers every conceivable pattern of life, from the most archaic to the most modern and urban. It also embodies every stage of culture-contact.

The awakening of Africa

All African experts seem to agree on one point: they have every confidence in Africans' immense adaptability, their great powers of assimilation and their exemplary patience. All these will be needed if they are to travel alone, and increasingly alone, the very long road that will lead them from a still rudimentary economy to a fully developed one, from a still tempting traditional life to the hard necessities of change, from a still partly tribal society to the national discipline required for modernization and industrialization. Everything has to be created – even the right mentality.

We should not forget that Black Africa is facing this long-drawn-out challenge with little organization, limited resources, and a great variety of attitudes in different regions and among different peoples.

To begin with, much of the continent is still underpopulated, lacking the superabundance of manpower which both handicaps and helps most under-developed countries. In the league table of development, Black Africa comes last. This will no doubt make possible the most spectacular progress: but it also implies the longest distance to go.

In the bedrock of its ancient cultures, Africa is not really one entity. Its traditional civilization, which already embodied many different beliefs and attitudes, acquired new religious elements from outside. It was affected above all by Islam, with its social and intellectual prestige and its admittedly mediocre Koranic schools. Islam, in fact, made great concessions to primitive religions, which it transcended but did not exclude. The second great outside influence was that of Christianity, which generally developed where trade was most intense. It too superimposed itself on a whole series of ancient beliefs and customs.

One must add to these differences a number of economic contrasts, notably the huge gulf between areas open to trade and those closed to it, or between town and country.

Such is the rather incongruous whole which is rapidly being transformed to meet a future that black statesmen and intellectuals seem to contemplate with both courage and common sense.

This transformation is undoubtedly essential; and it does not depend solely on the policies and attitudes of the newly independent African countries *vis-à-vis* the rest of the world or the problems of Africa itself – including its possible unity or its passionate disputes, as exemplified in the Conferences of Casablanca (January 1961), Monrovia (May 1961) and Lagos (February 1962).

Admittedly, policy is important: but it is only a means to an end. It changes, and can be deflected by the least puff of wind. Above all, it alone cannot fully control the enormous change of which it is a part.

Steeped as it is in primitive religion and culture, the weight of past tradition slows down the general impetus and complicates, or at least delays, the changes that need to be made.

Most of the people in Black Africa (especially in the rural areas which make up the vast majority of the continent) still owe allegiance to primitive cultures and religions which form the basis of their whole society. Traditional religion takes different forms according to regions and ethnic groups. Everywhere, however, it is animistic, in the sense of believing that all natural beings are inhabited by spirits which survive their death, and that spirits also inhabit objects (fetishism). Another common and almost universal feature is ancestor-worship. Legendary chiefs or heroes, revered at first as ancestors, are eventually assimilated into the ranks of the higher gods, often headed by the Great God of Heaven, of the Earth or of the Creation. The spirits of African ancestors or gods not only show themselves to the living, but may also return to take possession of them. This is the significance of a number of sacred dances, like those in Benin in which the gods Vodun or Orishas 'descend upon the head' of certain performers, who go into a trance as soon as the god inhabits them.

In all these cults, 'prayers and invocations are said, gifts of food and palm oil are offered, and animals are sacrificed' on the altars of gods or ancestors, who are thereby 'fed'. In return, they are expected to help and protect the living.

This religious organization is the guarantor of Africa's social organization, invariably based on the notion of kinship and the patriarchal family, in accordance with strict hierarchy which gives the patriarch absolute authority over the whole community of the family or clan (that authority normally being inherited through the male line from father to son, and more rarely through the female line).

In those societies which were formerly under the influence of the great African Empires, the social hierarchy gives certain families aristocratic superiority over the others; there are also 'castes' based on the artisan professions. Each of them has gods and ancestors whose respective power closely corresponds to that of the social groups themselves.

So strong is the link between religion and society that in the towns, where this social order is dislocated by modern life (and especially by education), either Christianity or Islam, according to circumstances, has tended very largely to replace animism, which remains the religion of the rural areas. Every town and every region affected by education, by modernization or by industry and organized labour, has therefore to grapple with the difficult problems of culture-contact.

One example is the survey made in 1958 in Porto Novo, in Benin (formerly Dahomey), by the sociologist Claude Tardits. Obviously, it cannot be valid for the whole of Africa. But it gives an idea of the problem. Porto Novo, which is Benin's capital, is an old city with awkward access to the sea and therefore somewhat superseded by the port of Cotonou. Despite this relative decline, Porto Novo remains lively, in a country which is better educated and more intellectual than its neighbours. Benin, as Emmanuel Mounier said, 'is the Latin Quarter of Black Africa'.

This does not mean that education forever guarantees the future of those known locally as '*évolués*' – those who have gone to school and, as the saying goes, 'seen the light'. (In 1954, 43,419 children, or 15 per cent of those of school age, actually attended school. For Africa, this was a record figure, but its importance should not be exaggerated.) There are high-grade and low-grade *évolués*. At the top of the social pyramid, in a population of perhaps just over 1.5 million people, only 100,000 of them city-dwellers, the genuine élite of truly cultivated people would number at the most 1,000 – three times the number of the former white colony, which was only 300 strong. And how hard it is to train even this tiny minority!

In Porto Novo itself the chief obstacle, naturally, is the inertia of a traditional society which is already diverse and divided – into at least three groups. One consists of the Gun, the descendants of Benin peasants now settled in the town. A second is the Yoruba, merchants from neighbouring Nigeria. A third is made up of 'Brazilians', Africans who have returned from Brazil, often Christians, but sometimes Islamic converts who have had astonishing adventures. Each of these groups has its own insignia, its own susceptibilities, its own ways of resisting change. Each, too, has its clans; and it is according to clan that houses are grouped, that marriages were and often still are arranged, and that religious rules and practices are maintained. On the value of religion as a social cement, a missionary at Porto Novo had this to say: 'On fetishism I will make only one remark, but it may have some value as coming from a missionary: it is a fine institution which is on the wane.' He added: 'I do not say that it is a fine religion.'

Women were the first to revolt against family tradition, so as to be able to make (as one in two of them now do) the marriage of their choice. But emancipation has still to contend with a polygamous and deeply conservative past, as witness this confession by a Benin woman: 'When my husband took other wives, he gave me the money because I was his first, and I distributed it to the others. It was I who chose my husband's other two wives, whom he took some years after we were married. My fellow-wives kneel to me and perform the services I ask of them.' Another added:

I kneel to my father-in-law, to my mother-in-law, and to the uncles and aunts and elder brothers and sisters of my husband. I do not kneel to the younger brothers and sisters, but I owe them respect. I serve all my husband's family: I run errands, I do the housework, I draw water for everyone, I go to market, I grind the pimento. When I prepare a meal, I from time to time offer a little of the food I have cooked to an aunt, an uncle or a brother of my husband's, or to my mother-in-law or my father-in-law.

Imagine, therefore, an *évolué* in the midst of such a clan, and in a city still more than half rustic. He will be torn between his new cultural habits, sometimes acquired abroad, and these rituals which have not necessarily lost all hold on him – between affection for his family and the impossibility of obeying all its laws.

What dislocates everything is the urban environment – work, school, even the sight of street life, in contrast with rural surroundings, where everything remains stubbornly unchanged. A certain dressmaker, an *évoluée*, learned her trade with the nuns in Cotonou, then married a civil servant. She was happy in her workshop and with her clients. 'After we had been married for a year my husband, who is a clerk in the administration, was sent to the North. There I had nothing to do, because the women either dress in leaves or go naked.' Finally, the husband was moved back. 'For the last year I have lived in Porto Novo ... My husband has bought me another sewing-machine.'

In line with this example one has only to think of the elegant women of the cities, or the Dakar models draped in sumptuous white. A vision of the future, like the bold modernity of the city: less poetic no doubt than the old colonial houses of Gorée on the island opposite Dakar, but more in the spirit of the times.

Town and country here are engaged in the age-old dialogue between advanced civilizations and primitive cultures. But in Africa the towns are only a minority. And the speed of African development will finally depend on their relative strength or weakness.

Although quickly established, Africa's independent governments have shown in practice unexpected stability. Since this is a general phenomenon it calls for a general explanation, interesting as individual instances may be. In fact, in the face of these governments, the governed have shown unlimited patience, much greater for instance than the deference of Louis XIV's subjects *vis-à-vis* their *Roi Soleil*. To rule, in Black Africa, necessarily means to reign. Surprising as it may seem, the exercise of power there rejuvenates and reinvigorates rather than wearying the ruler. The President of Liberia, Mr Tubman, in office since 1944, was still there in 1962, and was re-elected in 1963: an impressive record. There seems to be something about power here which shields it from European instability: perhaps it has an almost royal tinge.

At all events, on the base of the statue of the Osagyefo ('Victorious in All') of Ghana, President Kwame Nkrumah, the following
inscription is carved: 'Seek ye first the kingdom of politics, and all
these things shall be added unto you.' It corresponds to the terser
French maxim: 'Politics first.'

So power has to be seized and retained. Since it cannot be
divided and can barely be supervised, the opposition has no role.
To show itself, indeed, would be fatal. Ghana, Sierra Leone and
Guinea have shown this plainly enough. Already there are young
intellectuals, at odds with their countries' dictatorial governments,
who travel through Europe or find places in American universities:
some of them are dismissed ambassadors who think it wise not to
return home. Hence the remark by the Prime Minister of Senegal:
'Ghanocracy does not interest us' – a proof that Africa is far from
uniform, even on the political plane.

We should recognize, however, that African rulers need a great
deal of wisdom to resist very tangible temptations. If Europeans
are not to be unfair in judging governments and one-party States
which seem to them outlandish, they have to realize how small, in
Africa, is the governing class. The rulers of Black Africa are
always surrounded by the same exiguous élite, far fewer in number
than those who in the past served René of Anjou or Philip the
Fair. Liberia, for example, is run by some 2 per cent of its population, Afro-Americans of whom not all are even probably full-time
employees. The mass of the population remains inert, alienated
from the official apparatus of the State, or what the French call '*le
pays légal*'. This does not mean that the small élites are undivided:
there are endless disagreements within them, and sudden energetic
action by the authorities is not without justification.

At the same time, if governing poses few political problems, its
administrative problems are immense. If people are to be committed to modernization, they must be convinced and recruited. In
tackling this difficult task, some governments have been trapped
in their own demagogic schemes.

Effective administration needs people, managers, unswerving

devotion and discipline; building from scratch needs capital and carefully calculated investment. Above all, reason must reign supreme – which is the rarest of all situations, in every country in the world.

In Guinea-Bissau, the first of France's former possessions in Africa to choose freedom and independence when they were offered by the Government of General de Gaulle in 1958, President Sékou Touré's Socialist Government produced a three-year plan. In itself, it was not wrong-headed or mistaken: but it had been drawn up on the basis of economic criteria and statistical series – whereas traditional society is always a further element of the problem that should be taken into account. 'One after another, various State enterprises in charge of importing foreign produce collapsed: Alimag, which specialized in food; Libraport, for paper and books; Ematec, for technical supplies; Pharmaguinée, for pharmaceuticals; and all their sister firms.' Their failure was not due only to internal (and external) scandals: it was also the result of miscalculation – creating organizations which took no account of Guinea's human element. These presupposed not only honest and well-educated people, but an administrative hierarchy, managers, and a system of checks. All nationalized industries require very competent and ubiquitous managers. Here, they have to be trained.

Economic and social issues at stake

The future of the Black African States is still uncertain: it is being decided on the chessboards of Africa and the world – with vigour, and with some illusions.

Some of the players have short-term and perhaps ill-judged designs on the territory of their immediate neighbours. Africa's artificial frontiers are no justification for this: but they sometimes serve as a pretext.

Morocco has in the past laid claim to the whole of Mauritania, to the Rio de Oro, to Ifni and to part of the Algerian Sahara. Guinea-Bissau has cast envious eyes on densely populated Sierra Leone. Ghana – whose name deliberately recalls the great Empire of the past – has historical arguments for seeking to annexe Togo and the Ivory Coast. Mali – whose name is equally significant – dreams of 'federating' with Burkina Faso and Niger, and helping itself to part of the Algerian Sahara. Broader if more abstruse ambitions have included the gathering of African States into two groups, as at the time of the two rival Conferences in 1961. The Casablanca group – the extremists – comprised Morocco, Ghana, the United Arab Republic as it then was (Egypt and Syria), Guinea, the provisional Government of Algeria, and Mali. The Monrovia group – the sensible moderates – consisted of Tunisia, Libya, Mauritania, Senegal, Sierra Leone, Liberia, the Ivory Coast, Upper Volta (now Burkina Faso), Nigeria, Niger, Chad, Cameroon, the Central African Republic, Gabon, Congo Brazzaville (now Congo), Ethiopia, Somalia and Madagascar.

Even at the time, such classification looked impermanent, if only because the independence of Algeria was shortly to introduce an unpredictable new element. Much has changed since then; and the future remains undecided – including the future of African unity or the quest for it. This was the subject of the third Conference at that time, held in Lagos in February 1962, and badly prepared by the Nigerian Government. It failed: the 'Brazzaville Twelve' faced opposition from the Casablanca group, for whom the failure to invite the provisional government of Algeria provided a good pretext for intransigence.

These and subsequent manoeuvres were inevitably complex. Everyone is in principle committed to an Africa entirely free: but freedom can mean many different things. President Nkrumah wanted the last of European occupation to come to an end by 31 December 1962; but at the same time he sought to secure from this 'strong man' policy a position of leadership which the other States were not eager to grant him. This was also what held up the proposed union between Ghana and Guinea.

Even a generation later, it remains very hard to see which if any country or group of countries is likely to emerge above the others and impose unity on all of them. Leadership is as much a matter of wisdom as of brute force, and more a matter of real power than of political strength.

In size of population – which implies so much in a continent short of people – English-speaking Africa certainly predominates, owing both to a high general density and to the towns of Ghana, Sierra Leone and Nigeria. Progress is in the towns: those of Nigeria are the largest in Black Africa. In 1963, Lagos had more than 300,000 inhabitants and Ibadan more than 500,000; by 1980, Lagos had more than 4 million, and Ibadan about 1 million.

French-speaking Black Africa, at first with the exception of Guinea, quickly became associated with the European Community; English-speaking Black Africa followed suit when the Community was enlarged to include Britain.

Despite its relative demographic weakness, French-speaking Black Africa also enjoys the advantage of a well-educated middle class. Geographers add that one city in French-speaking Africa, because of its position and its power, is of world status. That is Dakar, which commands both the South Atlantic and the trans-African air route. All this of course may either change as world communications change, or in fact be confirmed.

What is really at stake, surely, is development – an evolution in terms of power, numbers, and economic progress. Except for the oil-works of Senegal and the aluminium factories of Guinea, Africa's backward economy supplies raw minerals and foodstuffs, and buys industrial products. Its future will necessarily depend on both suppliers and purchasers. In normal conditions of reciprocal trade, the possibilities for development and for annual investment remain meagre, and their growth is slow. In trying to improve matters, one is liable to turn to a credit policy, which opens the way to immediate dependence, whether one likes it or not. If the USSR supplied the rails for the Conakry–Kankan railway, which had to be maintained and repaired, this raised the question of which technicians would do the job, and what role there was for the railwaymen and their trade unions. If Senegal or Benin undertook to set up an important university faculty, they would no doubt do so on an almost totally non-fee-paying basis, along the lines they had inherited from France. But for this they would need both teachers and credits from France, as they have needed technicians and secondary-school teachers too. One thing leads to another.

So Black Africa cannot avoid seeking aid from the two great industrial blocs, and indeed from the third, China, which offers its services in a missionary spirit, but always with a large human contingent owing to its own abundance of people.

Without accepting one or other of these solutions, or all of them at once, Black Africa has no hope of completing important public works or carrying out economic plans. It is not enough even to make sacrifices as remarkable as those agreed to in Nigeria on 19 December 1961, the anniversary of its independence. These included: reduced salaries for members of the Government, no more official cars, no more paid overtime and an increase in taxes. There still remained a need for machine tools. Mali, likewise, after its break with Senegal, was saved only by the lorries supplied by the German Federal Republic to give it an outlet to Kankan, the Conakry railway and the ocean beyond.

Equally, all the machinery in the world would be useless without the skilled manpower to use it. This vital problem depends on prior conscious effort on the part of the African countries themselves.

In Guinea, under the Communist-inspired regime of Sékou Touré, a Swiss journalist reported on a conversation with some Czechoslovak technicians. 'Look,' said one of them:

the French had an advantage over us. They could give orders. Yesterday, my car's battery went flat. That was all; but at the official garage no one would listen to me, and the black mechanic immediately fiddled with the carburettor. They have a mania for getting at the most delicate parts of the engine. The result is that since then I have to walk everywhere, and it may last quite a while. A Frenchman would have blown his top. We're not allowed to. But in this heat and humidity it would have been justified and might have done some good. Africa! I really can't understand why France and Britain ever put this millstone round their necks. My contract runs for a year, and I shall be glad to get away. I shan't have trained anyone: it's quite impossible.

The moral of this small psychodrama is very simple. Education works only if the recipients really want it.

A more hopeful augury is the testimony of a young French teacher who came to the Ivory Coast in October 1961. He was delighted to find what a thirst for knowledge, what spontaneous hard work and what intelligence his second- and third-form pupils showed. They at least knew that they were Africa's future.

Art and literature

What evidence do art and literature provide about this changing world, straddled between today and tomorrow? All observers have to admit that the native African art which the West so greatly admired – masks, bronzes, ivories, wood carvings – is declining and dying before our eyes. It is already dead. Is that because, as is often said – and with some justice – the social and above all the religious framework which had always nurtured such art is itself collapsing under the violent and repeated onslaughts of urban industrial civilization?

At all events, it is undeniable that the Africa we once knew is growing ever more distant, with its songs, its dances, its artistic vision, its religions, its intoned or chanted legends, its conception of time past, of the universe, of people, of plants, of animals and of gods – a whole traditional civilization which, as we know from the example of the West itself, will be swept away if its present deterioration gathers speed.

Yet Europe has conserved more than a little of its traditional past, which it continues to cherish, sometimes unawares. What will Africa retain of its own civilization?

African art takes us back to a vanished civilization, far older than that of the present day. Young Black African literature is different. It is highly Westernized, if only because it uses European languages: there are few literary experiments in African languages, which are oral and have only lately and with difficulty been transcribed. This new literature, moreover, deals with the far end of black evolution – with what the situation is likely to be when the majority of Africans have 'seen the light'. These sturdy, lively stories in fact reflect African reality as seen by the *évolués*, and they cast extraordinary light on those aspects of it which are the most original and the least compatible with the values of other civilizations.

Take for example the *Nouveaux Contes d'Amadou Koumba*, by the already well-known West African writer Birago Diop. Their subject-matter may be the past: but their form, the linear fashion in which they are enclosed in a balanced narrative obeying literary rules, goes well beyond what Jean Duvignaud has called 'the lost paradise' of folk-tales. Their Western style alone denotes a literature 'uprooted from the communities of which it continues to dream'. There is a parallel here with the first Latin writers in Gaul. Wherever new Black literature has arisen (in Africa or in the New World, and in whichever Western language – French, English, Spanish, or Portuguese) – with Langston Hughes, Richard Wright, Aimé Césaire, Senghor (former President of Senegal), Diop, Fanou, Glissant, Ferdinand Oyono, Diolé or Camara Laye – wherever it may be, there should be no talk of betrayal, but rather of passionate attachment across the inevitable gap created by changing times.

'They have modified the very structure of their beings,' as Jean Duvignaud so aptly remarks, 'in so far as a language is a living thing and a way of life. In the process, something has died for ever – the immediacy of mythology.' That is no doubt true. But the change of language is not the only dislocation that has affected these writers. It is a complete metamorphosis, as described in *L'Enfant noir* by Camara Laye, the autobiography of a young villager, a son 'of the great family of blacksmiths', who goes to study in Paris. His mother looks on, helpless, every time he leaves.

Yes, she had had to watch this process, this mechanism that had led from the village school in Kouroussa to Conakry and from there to France; and all this time, while she had struggled, she had had to see the mechanism in motion: first this wheel, then that, then a third, and then others, many others that no one else may have seen. And what could have been done to prevent the wheels turning? One could only watch them, watch the workings of destiny: my destiny was to go!

Yes, a new civilization is emerging, as best it may, fragile or firm, from the age-old flux of a traditional living civilization which still nourishes its peoples. That is the important point. Africa is leaving behind it a civilization many centuries old; but it will not thereby lose *its* civilization. Transformed and divided as it may be, it will remain itself, deeply marked by a psychology, by tastes, by memories, and by everything that gives a land its character. Senghor has even spoken of an African 'physiology' which dictates a certain 'emotive attitude' to the world, so that 'the magic world is more real to the Black African than the visible world' – a path to knowledge, in fact. Those Black writers who appear most Westernized in their work are also those who insist most strongly on the particular psychological insight of their people.

This is confirmed by a further passage from *L'Enfant noir*, which describes the extraordinary, almost magical gifts of its hero's mother.

These wonders – and they really were prodigious – seem to me today like fabulous features of the far distant past. Yet that past was recent – only yesterday. Still, the world is moving and changing, and mine is changing more rapidly, perhaps, than any other: so much so that we seem no longer to be what we were, that we *are* no longer what we were, and that we were already not quite ourselves when these wonders took place before our eyes. Yes, the world is moving and changing: it is moving and changing so much that my own totem – I have my own totem, too – is unknown to me.

Can the break with the past be more vividly described? But the author adds:

I hesitate a little about saying what these powers of my mother's were, and I do not even want to describe all of them: I know that my account will arouse scepticism. Myself, when I remember them, I am uncertain how to take them. They seem incredible; they are incredible! But all I need is to remember what I have seen, what my eyes have seen ... I have seen these incredible things; I see them in my mind's eye as I saw them then. Are there not things everywhere which are not explained? With us, there are countless things that are not explained, and my mother lived in intimacy with them.

'Things that are not explained': they are perhaps the secret that every civilization makes its own.

PART III: THE FAR EAST

10. An Introduction to the Far East

Our intention is to consider *exclusively* the common, convergent characteristics of the Far East, with the successive aid of geography and history, and then to look at the very distant origin of its civilizations, which are still flourishing today. This last is the most important characteristic of all.

What geography shows

Simply to see the Far East in all its immensity is already to go halfway towards understanding its strange destiny and civilizations. For this first contact, travellers, journalists and geographers are the best guides. Provided, that is, that they do not explain everything in authoritarian fashion on the basis of some absolute geographical determinism, which is no more appropriate in Asia than it is in Europe, or in any country long worked upon by history and patient human effort.

The Far East is broadly speaking a tropical and sub-tropical world. It includes the 'furnace' of India, its forests and jungles; Southern China, hot and rainy; and the Indian Archipelago with its giant forests and rapidly growing plants (a metre a day in the case of certain lianas in the Botanical Gardens of Buitenzorg, in Java).

But India itself is also the Indus, the middle Ganges, central Deccan and its dry climate, sheltered by the Western Ghats – in other words arid and semi-arid areas. China, likewise, is also

Northern China, the immense open plains of loess and recent alluvial deposits, with very hard winters, as well as wooded Manchuria and the frozen deserts of the far North.

The whole of Northern China, with Peking, the imperial capital, on its South-Eastern edge, suffers from biting cold. In the winter there, peasants sleep on their stoves. A proverb runs: 'Let everyone sweep the snow from in front of his own door and pay no heed to the white frost on his neighbours' roof-tiles.' 'In winter, when it freezes,' declared a cultivated man in the eighteenth century, 'if poor relations and friends come to our door, we first boil up a big bowl of rice to give them, and we add a small saucer of pickled ginger. This is the best way to warm up old people and comfort those in need. We cook thick soups which we drink with the bowl held in both hands and our necks hunched into our shoulders: on frosty or snowy mornings, when one takes this meal, all of one's body feels warm.'

Sometimes, these cold snaps and sudden snows move down towards the tropical South. In 1189, it snowed at Hangchow, the capital of the Southern Sung dynasty, not far from the Yangtze-Kiang. 'The stalks of the bamboos snapped with a strange sound.'

At first sight, then, geography bears witness to the diversity rather than the unity of these many-faceted countries. But perhaps it is misleading to see things in these terms. The geography of South-East Asia is certainly very varied: but it is not geography which unites the area, but rather a fairly homogeneous *material* civilization which is dominant almost everywhere alongside geographical, physical and human factors. This civilization is too ancient, too deeply rooted in the distant past, and 'the product of too much individual and collective psychology to be regarded as simply a function of local physical conditions' (P. Gourou). It has an autonomous existence as a semi-independent force and an influence on its own.

All reports show that this civilization is everywhere frankly the same, and almost entirely vegetarian. This has been repeatedly affirmed by all Western travellers, in the past as in the present, as soon as they set foot in Asia.

A Spanish visitor in 1609 reported that the only meat eaten by the Japanese was game. A German doctor in about 1690 declared they knew nothing of milk and butter. They fed on *gokost*, 'the five products of the earth' (as in China, the figure 5 is sacred in Japan). These products were: rice, 'white as snow'; sake, liquor made from rice; barley, intended in principle for cattle, but used to make flour and cakes (the ears of barley in the fields, said this same doctor, were of an 'admirable red'); finally, white peas not unlike butter beans. To which were added millet, vegetables and fish, but always very, very little meat.

Twenty years earlier, in India, a French doctor watched the huge crowd of the procession which accompanied the Great Mogul Aurangzeb on his journey from Delhi to Kashmir. He was astonished by the sobriety of the soldiers, 'whose food was very simple . . . Of all these horsemen, not a tenth, not even a twentieth eat meat on the march. They are happy so long as they have their *kicheris*, a mixture of rice and other vegetables, over which they pour browned butter.'

The inhabitants of Atchin on the island of Sumatra were no more demanding. 'Their only food is rice,' said a traveller in 1620. 'The rich add a little fish and some greenstuffs. One has to be a great lord in Sumatra to have a roast or boiled chicken . . . They say that if there were 2,000 Christians on the island they would soon exhaust its stock of beef and poultry.'

China lived on the same diet. 'If the Chinese ate as much meat as we in Spain do,' wrote Father de las Cortes in 1626, 'there would not be nearly enough grazing for it.' Even the rich were content with little. 'To give themselves an appetite they garnish their meals with small pieces of pork or chicken or other meat' – what we might call titbits. A British traveller in the eighteenth century made the same point. Even in Peking, supplied with animals from Tartary, 'the people eat only very little meat, which they mix with vegetables to give it some taste. Milk, butter, and cheese . . . are little known to the Chinese.' Not that they disliked meat: far from it. If an animal – a cow, a camel, a sheep or an ass –

died from an accident or a disease, it was eaten at once. 'These people do not know the difference between clean and unclean meat,' the British traveller concluded in some disgust. In China, they ate snakes, frogs, rats, dogs, bats and so on.

These observations are confirmed by innumerable passages of Chinese literature itself, which is admirably precise about matters of daily life. A character in one novel, a spoiled young widow, 'one day wants duck, the next day fish and at other times fresh vegetables and bamboo-shoot soup. When she has nothing to do, she must have oranges, biscuits and water-lilies. She drinks a lot of rice wine; every evening, she eats fried sparrows and salted crayfish; she drinks three litres of wine made from a hundred flowers.' All of which, clearly, is debauchery, the caprice of the rich.

Chen Pan K'ia (1693–1765), poet, painter, calligrapher, and a very generous man, wanted all the people in his house to share in feast days. He wrote in his *Family Letters*: 'Every time there is fish, boiled rice, fruits and cakes, they should be shared out fairly.' The food mentioned in his letters include buckwheat girdle-cakes and thick, warm rice soups. Such was the norm. Even a very rich moneylender, the owner of a pawnshop, who is described in a medieval tale, although he pounces with delight on any *sapeke* coin he finds on the ground, lunches on 'a plate of cold rice with boiling water poured over it'.

Little, in fact, has changed in the twentieth century. In 1959, a journalist wrote: 'I know very well that Chinese cooking has always been the art of making something out of nothing; that a nation of too many people, forbidden to raise beef cattle – which is a gross waste of calories – tries to use everything that we let slip away.'

The Chinese remain vegetarians: 98 per cent of the calories they consume come from vegetable sources; they use no butter, cheese or milk, and very little meat or fish. Their carbohydrates come in part from wheat, and in the North from millet, while rice predominates in the South. Their protein comes from soya, mustard seed and various vegetable oils.

The one country that is changing its food habits, vastly increasing its fish consumption and above all turning to meat, is Japan.

The ubiquity of rice in the South-East and its export to the North are the reasons why this vegetarian diet is so widespread. The West, consuming wheat and other similar cereals, was obliged thereby to adopt, very early in its history, first the practice of leaving fields fallow and then the rotation of crops. Otherwise, the soil was rapidly exhausted and wheat produced no yield. Part of the land, therefore, automatically became grassland or pasture – all the more so because wheat growing required considerable help from animals. Rice, by contrast, can be grown in the same area every year, indefinitely. Most of the work is manual, and buffaloes are used only for light work in the mud of the paddy-fields. Everywhere, indeed, crops are tended meticulously by hand. In these circumstances, to feed on meat would be a fantastic waste. The animals would have to be fed on grain, which human beings themselves prefer to eat.

The prime result is to make possible a greater increase in population than would be possible on any carnivorous diet. Six or eight peasants can be fed from a single hectare (2.47 acres) if their diet is purely vegetarian. The food productivity of a given area used in this way is undeniably greater than if it is employed otherwise. This is what has made possible the 'teeming Asian millions'.

As in India, the population increase in China is relatively recent. It effectively began in Southern China in the eleventh and twelfth centuries, with the spread of early rice strains, making possible two harvests a year. In the thirteenth century, the population was probably 100 million. From the end of the seventeenth century it grew very rapidly. Today, it is so large that it could not adopt a different diet, even if it wished. 'The Chinese are thus shackled by determinism: their civilization has no option but to continue along the course which it has charted itself.' In the eighteenth century, the population of India also passed the 100-million mark.

Wittfogel holds that: a civilization based on rice implies a system of artificial irrigation, which in turn requires strict civic, social and political discipline. Rice links the peoples of the Far East to water: in Southern India, to tanks or reservoirs; in the Indo-Gangetic Plain, to wells or irrigation canals fed by watercourses. In China, likewise, irrigation takes many forms: in the South it relies on gentle rivers (and on the regular flooding of the Poyang and Tung Ting lakes on the edge of the Yangtze), on wells, on canals (of which the Imperial Canal, now the Grand Canal, was the model, as a means of both communication and irrigation), and on the wild rivers of the North, such as the Pei-ho or the Hoang-ho (the Yellow River), which had to be dammed and tamed – and which still frequently break their banks. Irrigation is practised everywhere, on the terraces of the Philippines or Java, in Cantonese China, in Japan; with its bamboo aqueducts and its primitive or modern pumps it entails strict working discipline and obedience – like ancient Egypt, the classical example of the constraints imposed by irrigation.

Rice-growing almost certainly began in about 2000 BC on levelled-out low-lying ground. It gradually spread to all land that could be watered; and at the same time it was improved by selecting seed which made possible early varieties of rice. From then on, K. A. Wittfogel has argued, rice-growing led to the establishment of authoritarian, bureaucratic regimes in the Far East, with hordes of state functionaries.

This thesis has been challenged, with some justice, on various points of detail. Above all, it is far too simplistic. Water supplies needed for rice, and rice itself, certainly determined many features of life in the Far East: but these constraints were only part of a far more complex structure. That should not be forgotten. Yet, at the same time, those very constraints must be remembered: they mattered, and they matter still.

Huge areas of the Far East remain wild or primitive. Here above all the civilizations of the plain predominate, based on irrigation. True, there are paddy-fields in the mountains too: but they are confined to narrow terraces, in over-populated regions where there are enough people for the immense labour involved, as for instance in Java. Regularly, where intensive cultivation succeeds, civilized people in the Far East occupy only small areas. The rest – especially mountains, isolated regions and certain islands – becomes the refuge of primitive peoples and cultures.

A book published by Georges Condominas in 1957, entitled *We Have Eaten the Forest*, takes us up-country from Saigon to the region beyond the summer resort of Dalat, and chronicles the daily life of a primitive tribe. Its members live in a forest, and every year they take more of it to grow crops. The trees are 'girdled', cut down or burnt. On the land thus cleared, 'planting is done with a dibber: a quick hole in the earth, a few seeds, and a toe to brush the earth back again'. Most of the crop is dry-grown rice. Part of the forest is eaten every year. After twenty years, the tribe returns to its starting-point, if all has gone well – i.e. if the forest, left to lie fallow, has grown again in the meantime.

This itinerant agriculture (known as *ladang* in Malay, and by various other names in the many other places where it is practised) is a primeval affair, practically without domesticated animals. It sustains a thousand different peoples, all extremely primitive. They are ill-adapted, obviously, to the present day: but they survive in isolated areas.

The West, by contrast, assimilated its own primitive peoples very early on. It had no lack of isolated, backward regions: they can still be recognized today. But it managed to reach them, convert them, link them to its cities, and exploit their resources.

No such process took place in the Far East. This immense difference explains the presence in China of so many peoples who have not been 'made into Chinese', and in India that of so many tribes outside the caste system and its taboos (and in effect outside Indian civilization).

It also explains many details of the present and the past. In 1565, at the battle of Talikoti, the 'Hindu' Kingdom of Vijayanagar in the Deccan, despite its million soldiers, was mortally defeated by the cavalry and especially the artillery of the Muslim sultans. The great and splendid city was left defenceless: its inhabitants could

not even flee, for all vehicles and all draught animals had left with
the army. But it was not the victors who pillaged the city: instead
of invading it, they were diverted into pursuing the vanquished
and cutting their throats. It was the primitive tribes around the
city, hordes of Brinjaris, Lambadis and Kurumbas, who descended
on the capital and sacked it.

A German doctor *en route* for Siam in the seventeenth century
met a Japanese merchant who a few years before, in 1682, had
been shipwrecked with others on a desert island near the coast
of Luzon in the Philippines. There had been about ten of them:
they had lived well on the abundant eggs of wild birds and the
thick banks of shellfish along the coast. After eight years of this
luxurious life they built a boat, bent sail, and finally arrived,
exhausted, on the island of Hainan in the Gulf of Tonkin. There
they learned that they had barely escaped certain death. Hainan
was half Chinese and half primitive; and they had been lucky
enough to land in the Chinese half. In the other half of the
island, the savages would have shown them no quarter. Formosa
(Taiwan) likewise, although conquered by the Chinese in 1683,
long remained divided into Chinese and non-Chinese areas, like
many islands and 'virtually watertight compartments of the
continent'.

Present-day figures for the non-Chinese peoples of China remain
impressive. While such peoples make up only 6 per cent of the
total population, they occupy 60 per cent of China's territory
(including, admittedly, such inhospitable areas as the Gobi Desert,
Turkestan and Tibet). In terms of space, in other words, they are
in the majority.

They include the Chuangs of Kwang-si, the Miaotse, the Lis,
the Thais and the Yis (largely dispersed from Yünnan to Kansu);
the Hui of Kansu, and the Yaos. *Vis-à-vis* all or most of them, the
policy of Imperial China in the past, and of Chiang Kai-shek's
China later, was strict segregation. The gates of Yi towns bore
notices: 'Yis are forbidden to meet or to walk in the streets in

groups of more than three' – 'Yis are forbidden to ride on horseback.' China today has improved their conditions and given them a certain autonomy, but not the semi-independence that the Soviets granted to their ethnic minorities. At the same time, all these backward societies (which practised slavery, as among the Yis of Liangsiang, or serfdom, *ula*, among the Tibetans) have been shaken to their foundations. Determined efforts have been made to give the most primitive among them written languages. Thus today only China concerns itself with its backward peoples (for their own good but certainly against their will).

Between the civilized areas, those occupied by primitive peoples are also the domain of wild animals. There are lions in the Punjab, wild boars on the coasts of Sumatra, crocodiles in the rivers of the Philippines and, everywhere, king of the great cats, the sabre-toothed and sometimes man-eating tiger.

Innumerable past accounts give a more colourful version of this fact. Father de las Cortes, a Spanish Jesuit shipwrecked in 1626 near Canton, spoke of the many tigers who roamed the Chinese countryside and often came into towns and villages to seize human prey.

A French doctor, François Bernier, visited the Ganges Delta in about 1600. Bengal, he reported, was certainly by far the richest and most populous part of India, 'a gift from the Ganges' as Egypt was a gift from the Nile, a great sugar- and rice-producing region. In the midst of this prosperity, however, there were uninhabited islands in the bends of the river, and they were frequented by pirates. 'These islands,' wrote Bernier, 'are peopled only by tigers, who sometimes swim from one island to another, or by gazelles, pigs, and once-domestic poultry returned to the wild. And it is because of these tigers that, when travelling between the islands in small rowing boats, as is the custom, it is dangerous in many places to set foot on land. At night, when mooring the boat to trees, one must take care to keep it some distance offshore, for some always drift in; and it is said that some tigers have been bold enough to jump into the boats and carry off the people sleeping there, even choosing (if local boatmen are to be believed) the biggest and fattest.'

Barbarism against civilization: the evidence of history

The vast civilizations of the Far East – above all, those of India and China – would have lived in peace if they had been disturbed only from primitive areas within their borders, the domain of poor 'forest-eating' farmers. But the real scourge, comparable to the biblical plagues of Egypt, came from the great deserts and steppes (to the West and North of China, to the North and West of India), which are torrid under the summer sun, and in winter buried under enormous drifts of snow.

These inhospitable lands were peopled by pastoral tribes – Turks, Turcomans, Kirghiz and Mongols. As soon as they appeared in history, they were what they would remain until their decline in the mid-seventeenth century: hordes of violent, cruel, pillaging horsemen full of daredevil courage. Only in the seventeenth century, in fact, with the aid of gunpowder, did the settled peoples defeat these savage nomads. Thereafter, they kept them at a distance: confined and cowed, they were reduced to merely sur- viving, as they have done to this day. Neither Inner and Outer Mongolia (Chinese and Soviet), nor Chinese and Soviet Turkestan, are now in themselves key countries on the chequerboard of the world. All that matter are their extent and their airfields – which are not their property.

What is the relevance of these nomads to the study of present-day civilizations? Their fantastic onslaughts undoubtedly delayed the development of the great civilizations that were their neighbours. Hermann Goetz said that of India in his classic compilation *The Epochs of Indian Civilization*, published from 1929 onwards: but his remark applies equally to China. For India was open to the world of the nomads only through the narrow Khyber Pass through the Afghan mountains, whereas China had the misfortune to be bordered by the vast Gobi Desert. The Great Wall of China, built from the third century BC onwards, was an important military barrier; but it was more symbolic than effective, and it was breached many times.

According to the Sinologist Owen Lattimore, the nomads were former peasants. The development of more advanced agriculture had forced out those less able to master it, towards the mountain country of the 'forest-eaters', and above all to the edges of the deserts and the steppes. Driven out from richer regions, all they now had were these vast but very sparse pastures. In this way, civilization had been 'the mother of barbarism': it had turned farmers into nomadic shepherds. But these barbarians kept returning from their places of refuge, because of internal crises, social revolutions and great increases of population. They came back to the farmlands – and rarely in peace. They came as raiders, triumphant conquerors: they defied and despised the settled peasants they defeated. Take as an example the *Memoirs of Zehir-Eddin Mohammed Baber* (1495–1530), the first Great Mogul of India, who in 1526 seized most of its provinces in the North:

Although Hindustan is a country full of natural charm, its inhabitants are ungracious, and dealings with them yield no pleasure, no response and no lasting relationship. Without ability, intelligence or cordiality; they know nothing of generosity or manly feeling. In their ideas as in their work they lack method, staying-power, order and principle. They have neither good horses nor tasty meat: they have no grapes, no melons, and no succulent fruit. There is no ice here, and no fresh water. In the markets one can obtain neither sophisticated food nor even good bread. Baths, candles, torches, chandeliers, schools – none of these is known . . .

Apart from the rivers and streams that flow in the ravines and valleys, they have no kind of running water in their gardens or their palaces. Their buildings lack charm, air, regularity and elegance. Country-dwellers and poor people mostly go naked. The only garment they wear is what they call a *langota*, which is nothing but a short piece of cloth hanging down some eighteen inches below their navel. Underneath this there is another piece of cloth fixed between the legs with the cord of the *langota*, which it passes through, and which serves to attach it behind. The women drape round their bodies a *lang*, one half of which they use to cover their loins, and the other half their heads.

The great advantage of Hindustan, apart from the huge size of its territory, is the great quantity of gold to be found there, either in ingots or in coin.

Thus this Muslim from Turkestan, flushed with victory, proud of his nomadic desert life, and looking down from the heights of Islam, passed judgement on the ancient civilization of India, its art, and its architecture. His disdain, although not that of a Westerner, is no more pleasant.

The details of great Mongol conquests need not concern us here, except in so far as they affected China and India, in each case striking a blow to the heart. As in the two last great waves of invasion, in the thirteenth to fourteenth and the sixteenth to seventeenth centuries. The sketch-maps on pp. 86, 192, 227 and 229 show the chronological limits and varying shape of these incursions, both towards the West and distant Europe, and towards the East, with a further drive towards the South and India, and some rebounds in the direction of China. This no doubt was because, from the beginning of the fifteenth century onwards, China was the 'sick man of Asia', attracting the raiders' greed. When Tamerlane (Timur Beg) died in 1405 he was preparing an attack on China.

Each time, in fact, that nomad aggression exploded, China and India were the victims. Nor were their capitals spared. Two pairs of dates by themselves tell the story. In 1215, the year of Philip Augustus's victory over Otto IV at Bouvines, Genghis Khan captured Peking; in 1644 it was captured again by the Manchu, with the help of the Mongols. In 1398 Tamerlane took Delhi; it was taken again by Baber in 1526.

These events were unsung catastrophes. Each time, millions of lives were lost. Until the twentieth century and its technological wars, the West produced nothing like such wholesale massacres. India, where these wars were further complicated by the clash of civilizations (the invading barbarians being converts to Islam), had an appalling history. Like China, it finally triumphed over these multiple invasions only because of its extraordinary hold on life. Moreover, it had never been completely subjugated as far as the tip of Cape Comorin; and the Deccan's economy had always been linked (sometimes by emigration) to the countries of the Indian Ocean.

For India as for China, these tidal waves of invasion meant repeated destruction and setbacks. In the long run, both absorbed their invaders, but at very great cost. Were the barbarians, then, largely responsible for the widening gap between the Far East and Europe? Is that the key element in the region's fate?

For India, this is arguably so. In the beginning (in the second millennium BC) the Aryans of the Punjab were comparable with the ancestors of the Hellenes, the Celts, the Italiots and the Germanic peoples. The counterpart of the *Iliad* and the *Odyssey* was the knightly culture of the *Mahabharatra*, recounting the wars to conquer the upper Gangetic plain. In the fifth century BC, at the time of the Buddha, Northern India was covered with aristocratic republics and small kingdoms not unlike those of Hellas, with the beginnings of commerce as in Greece. In the third century, Chandragupta and Ashoka founded the first Empire, which united Afghanistan and all of India except the southern tip of the Deccan, always beyond the conqueror's grasp. This was the period when Alexander's Graeco-Macedonian Empire was being built. From the time of Christ there began the invasion of the Scythians from the North. It culminated, from the third to eighth centuries, in the vast Gupta Empire, renewing India's endless struggle between fair- and dark-skinned peoples. Soon afterwards, as in the Western Middle Ages, there were masses of peasant serfs, and great feudal States. The parallels between India and Europe were not of course absolute, especially as regards the forms of their respective societies; but there was no overwhelming difference of degree between them until the thirteenth century and the great Mongol assault.

From then on, the gap progressively widened. And the same question arises for China: how far was its development slowed down by the Mongol conquest, completed in 1279, and by that of the Manchu between 1644 and 1683? Until at least the thirteenth century, China was ahead of the West in science and technology. From then, it was outdistanced.

It is clear, all the same, that the invaders from the steppes cannot be held completely responsible for the chequered fate of the Far East. The destruction they wrought was immense. But in time everything was repaired and healed. One might almost say: healed too well. The invasions, which in the West involved breaks with the past and the birth of new civilizations, were material disasters for China and India, but changed neither their way of thinking nor their social structures and way of life. There was never a great leap forward like that which took ancient civilization from Greece to Rome, or converted Rome to Christianity – or like that which led the Middle East to Islam.

The immobility of the Far East, its extraordinary fidelity to its own ways, was partly the result of internal factors. These in turn partly explain its lagging behind the West – which, incidentally, was entirely relative. The Far East did not really drop back: it remained where it was, but at the time when the rest of the world was visibly progressing, leaving it further and further behind.

Distant origins: the reasons for cultural immobility

It was in prehistoric times, undoubtedly, in the dawn of the first civilizations, that the die was cast. The civilizations of the Far East were entities which very early achieved remarkable maturity, but in a setting that made some of their essential structures almost impervious to change. This gave them astonishing unity and cohesion. But they also found it extremely difficult to adapt themselves, to want to evolve and to be able to. It was as if they had systematically rejected the idea of growth and progress.

What we must try to understand, forgetting our Westerners' experiences, is that the two great civilizations of the Far East are thousands of years old. In the Far East, monuments deteriorate and decay all too quickly, in so far as they are often made of fragile materials, as in China and Japan. Human society and culture, by contrast, seem indestructible. They date back, not a few centuries, but to a far more distant past. Imagine the Egypt of the Pharaohs, miraculously preserved, adapted more or less to modern life, but having kept its beliefs and some of its customs.

Hinduism, still very much alive, has been the almost unaltered basis of Indian civilization for more than a thousand years; and it in its turn has borrowed and passed on some religious ideas which date from a further thousand years back. In China, the cult of ancestors and of the gods of nature, which dates from at least the first millennium BC, has continued in Taoism, Confucianism and Buddhism, which have by no means suppressed it. It remains alive.

These ancient and tenacious religious systems are linked with social structures which are no less hardy – castes in India, family and social hierarchies in China. In both cases, perennial religion and perennial society seem to support each other. This is characteristic of primitive cultures, in which all ways of life and thought are totally and directly rooted in the supernatural. This is more disconcerting to find in civilizations like those of India and China, so highly developed in their different domains: but that only makes it all the more remarkable.

Unlike the West, which clearly separates the human from the sacred, the Far East makes no such distinction. Religion is involved with all aspects of human life: the State, philosophy, ethics and social relations. All fully partake of the sacred; and this is what gives them their perennial resistance to change.

By a curious but understandable contradiction, this involvement of the sacred in all aspects of life, including the most trivial, often disconcerts Westerners. Accustomed to place religion on a spiritual pedestal, they get the erroneous impression that in the Far East there is an absence of religious feeling, accompanied but not adequately replaced by formal rituals. What is difficult for Westerners to grasp is the importance and real meaning of these religious rites.

To perform them is to conform to the divine order which governs all human affairs. It is to live a religious life. Thus Hinduism essentially consists much more in the recognition of the values represented by the caste hierarchy than in 'belief in spiritual beings or the cult of the gods, both of which are only a fragment of the whole'.

The Chinese, likewise, are little concerned to distinguish among an infinity of gods. What matters is to perform *vis-à-vis* all of them all the obligatory rites, to do all the duties required by the cult of ancestors, and finally to meet, in family and social life, all the obligations imposed by a complicated hierarchy.

True, the spiritual contexts in India and China are very different: their religious and social systems bear no resemblance at all. If one simply contrasts the West with the Far East *en bloc*, one risks overlooking the latter's deep divisions. India is not China, needless to say. And if China, by contrast with the West, appears to be deeply imbued with religion, compared with India it seems like a rationalist country. In the distant past, in the fifth to third centuries BC, it underwent the major intellectual crisis of the Contending States, which has been likened to the vital philosophical crisis in ancient Greece that saw the birth of the scientific spirit. Confucianism, as we shall see, took up the legacy of this agnostic and rationalist upheaval, adapting it to political circumstances and enabling it to survive the great religious disputes of the third to the tenth century AD, and remodelling it into the neo-Confucianism which prevailed from the thirteenth century onwards.

In China, therefore, two strands of thought coexisted, and the immobility of society was due to political, economic and social factors as much as to religious influence; whereas in India religion played the dominant role. How, there, could one reform human society or even question it, when its organization reflected spiritual truth?

11. The China of the Past

The China of the past, with which we must begin because it has by no means entirely disappeared, took a very long time to acquire and develop its characteristic features. It then became a single entity, difficult to divide into the 'periods' beloved of historians. Over many centuries, through an interminable series of disasters and conquests, it seemed to remain unchanged and unchangeable.

Yet, however slowly this great leviathan evolved, it was never immobile. Like all civilizations, it accumulated experience, and made continual choices among its resources and possibilities. Nor, despite appearances, was it closed to the outside world. External influences reached it and made themselves felt.

Religion

Its first aspects – the most important and the hardest to understand fully – are those of its religious life. This is not easy to define. It included a number of different systems, as did Western religion; but they were not mutually exclusive. A believer might move from one form of piety to another, embracing mysticism and rationalism at the same time. Imagine a European passing from Protestantism to Catholicism, and even to atheism, without meeting the slightest intellectual or religious obstacle, and taking from each of them what he needed. 'In the most agnostic or the most conformist of the Chinese there is a latent anarchist and mystic,' wrote Marcel Granet. 'The Chinese are either superstitious or practical, or rather they are both at once.' It is this 'both at once' that a Westerner often finds hard to grasp.

These remarks, which apply even to the recent past, are worth remembering at the outset. They explain in advance one fundamental fact: that when Confucianism and Taoism took shape in China, at roughly the same time, followed much later by Buddhism, none of the three displaced the others, despite their arguments and struggles. Indeed, they were not always mutually distinct. They grafted themselves, in fact, on to a much older, more primitive and powerful religious life. It has been said that these 'Big Three' sailed on ancient religious waters. In reality, they foundered there.

The roots of China's religious life are far older than the three great spiritual disciplines that were grafted on to it. Many lively strains were present in that hybrid, and they permeated all religious practices. China's religious heritage dates back to before the first millennium BC, when the country itself was first taking shape. Nothing thereafter fundamentally changed it.

The introduction of the plough made possible much greater density of population, concentrated in villages and manors. China at that time practised both ancestor-worship and the cult of the gods of the manorial land. The obvious comparison is either with the earliest days of Greece or with the distant beginnings of Rome, each with its typical ancient cities.

Ancestor-worship placed exceptional importance on patrilinear family groupings, in which the name passed from father to son. Beyond these families, the larger group of the clan (*sing* in Chinese) consisted of all the people descended from the same ancestor and hence bearing the same tribal name. Thus for the Ki, the first ancestor was the sovereign Millet, while for the Sseu it was Yu the Great, the legendary hero who drained away the waters of the Flood.

Originally, ancestor-worship and its attendant family structure were confined to the patrician class. Later, plebeian families imitated this ancient model and began to worship their ancestors as if they were gods.

Alongside the ancestors, and little different from them, were the local gods of the manor, ranging from the gods of each house, of the hills, of the watercourses, and of the various forces of nature in different parts of the territory, right up to the gods of the manorial land, *chö*, who dominated all the others. 'A Chen prince defeated in 548 BC surrendered to his conqueror in mourning clothes, carrying in his arms the god of the Land, and preceded by his General, who bore the vases of his ancestors' temple. What he was thus offering was the manor itself' (H. Maspéro).

When China was politically united and the individual manors became subject to monarchical authority, a great god of the Royal Land – the Sovereign Land – took precedence over all the local gods. Not unnaturally, he was the god of the Dead: he 'kept them under guard in his sunless prisons, at the heart of the Nine Dark-nesses, near to the Yellow Springs'. There was also the god of the Heavens (the god of On High); there were gods of the mountains, of the Four Seas and of the Rivers (the Count of the River was the god of the terrible Yellow River, the Hoang Ho). In fact, there were as many gods as the thousands of characters in the classical Chinese alphabet.

This burgeoning polytheism embraced the immortality of the soul – either at the Yellow Springs or Hades, in the celestial realm of the God of On High, or on earth in the temple of the ancestors. The destination of the soul beyond the grave was often determined by the social position of its owner on earth. Princes, ministers and other important persons were destined for the good afterlife in Heaven, the greatest of them still attended by their servants. Ordinary mortals went to the Yellow Springs, the Nine Dark-nesses, i.e. to Hell. Those of intermediate status lived on in the tomb of their ancestors. All this was somewhat blurred at the edges, partly because everyone had several souls, and partly because the afterlife was possible only as a result of offerings and sacrifices made by the living, similar to those reserved for the gods. The

dead and the gods all eat: 'We fill with offerings the cups of wood
and cups of earthenware,' ran the ritual chant accompanying the
sacrifice of the victims. 'When their aroma has risen the Lord of
On High begins to eat.' Between the gods and the living, bargains
were regularly struck: protection was given in exchange for offerings. A god declared: 'If you make sacrifices to me, I will give you
happiness.' A prince pleaded: 'My offerings are abundant and
pure. Surely the Spirits will support me.' Another complained:
'What crime have people committed today, that Heaven sends us
trouble and affliction, a dearth of vegetables and grain! There are
no gods that I have not honoured; I have not been sparing with
victims!'

Between the fifth and third centuries BC, feudal China
disintegrated in the troubled period known as that of the 'Contending States'. Then it was, amid continual wars, that the manors
were swallowed up by more or less sizeable, more or less stable,
principalities. At length the Han Empire arose and imposed a
unifying peace. This long and violent crisis was accompanied by
intense anxiety and ideological debate among Chinese thinkers,
reacting against the formalized religion of the past. The whole
intellectual future of China was affected by this time of upheaval,
which recalls either the Greece of the fifth and fourth centuries BC
or the Italy of the Renaissance with its political and social dramas,
during which the main problem – for both the tyrants and their
subjects – was simply to live, or to survive.

Thus China in the sixth to third centuries BC had its politicians
(jurists), calculating what chance (*che*) circumstances might offer
the Prince or the State. It also had its rhetors or 'sophists',
concerned for public welfare. These sophists often belonged to the
ancient school of Mo-Ti (or Mö-Tseu), whose doctrine was known
as *mohism*.

Were the disciples of Mö-Tseu a kind of order of chivalry in
the service of the oppressed, or a sort of congregation of Preaching
Friars? These comparisons more or less indicate their activities and
their 'commitment'. And the name that later historians have given

them – 'sophists' – also reflects their passion for talking, for persuading by argument, for endlessly debating, each following a different line of thought. A whole relativist, rationalist philosophy, quite distinct from the precepts of religion, took shape in the background of these lively discussions.

Only a part of these philosophical novelties survived into the Han period. That, broadly speaking, was what became Confucianism. It was clearly rationalist, in reaction against ancient religion; but it was also a reaction against the rhetorical excesses of the sophists, the multiplicity of their doctrines and the political and social consequences they might involve. Confucianism, in fact, was a return to order in three respects – intellectual, political and social.

At the same time, it perpetuated in China a form of pseudo-rationalism which survived the religious pressures of Taoism and above all of Buddhism, which were very strong until the tenth century. In the thirteenth century, it consolidated itself as neo-Confucianism.

Confucianism was not only an attempt to explain the world in rational terms: it was also a system of political and social ethics. If it was not, as has been argued, a true religion, it was at least a philosophical attitude which could adapt itself as much to a religious frame of mind as to scepticism or even sheer agnosticism.

It owed its name to Confucius (551–479 BC according to tradition). Although he left no writings of his own, his doctrine being handed down by his disciples, he was indeed the founder of the system that became the badge of the Chinese intelligentsia of which he was a part.

Confucianism was above all, in fact, the expression of a particular caste, the educated class known as mandarins. They were the representatives of the new social and political order which gradually arose after China's feudal disintegration. In brief, they were the administrators and civil servants of this new China. Embodying as they did the authority of the State, these lettered functionaries grew more and more numerous as the first great principalities were formed and as writing became the necessary medium of discipline and government. For a long time they were allowed only subordinate posts, while the great aristocratic families monopolized senior positions; but the formation of the first great Empire, that of the Han dynasty (206 BC to AD 220), ensured the mandarins' ultimate triumph.

The development of Confucianism was closely linked with the teaching of the educated classes. The Great School founded in 124 BC by the Emperor Wu taught an already complex body of doctrine, based on reading and glossing the five classic books (Mutations, Odes, Documents, Springs and Autumns, and Rites) which were regarded as representing the Confucian tradition. In fact, they dated from both before and after his time, and their text was properly reconstituted and intelligibly commented upon by scholars only in the fourth and third centuries BC.

Each master taught only one book, always the same, and according to only one interpretation. In the Great School, therefore, there were as many teachers for each book as there were possible interpretations (fifteen, in the first century AD). Every master directly addressed only some ten or so assistants, who in turn taught the pupils. In the year AD 130, the School had 1,800 active students and 30,000 who merely attended lectures. Their studies were tested by stiff examinations. The questions were written on slips of wood, at which the candidates aimed with bow and arrow. Each had to answer whatever question the arrow struck.

In its broad outlines, this system survived until the early twentieth century. Naturally, however, the passage of time brought with it modifications, new commentaries and *summae*, virtually constituting new books. The most important of these revisions was undertaken between the eighth and the twelfth centuries by the Five Masters, founders of what became known as neo-Confucianism. The most famous of the five, Chu Hi (d. 1200), was responsible for the doctrine which until the fall of the Chinese Empire in 1912 remained the unchanging rule and official framework of Chinese philosophy.

As a doctrine for sophisticated people, Confucianism was an attempt to explain the world, respecting the general sense of tradition but rejecting popular primitive beliefs. Hence its rather lordly detachment, its contempt for superstition, and its obvious scepticism. Confucius never spoke of the gods; and although he respected the spirits, the ancestors, he preferred to keep them at a distance. 'If you cannot serve people,' he said once, 'how can you serve spirits? How can those who do not know the living expect to know the dead?'

The followers of Confucius gave a general explanation of the forces of nature, and of human relations with the supernatural world, which might be seen as a first attempt at a scientific theory of the universe. The life of the world, and its vicissitudes, they thought, were not determined by the caprices of the gods, gratified or angry, but by the interaction of impersonal forces. So they spoke of the heavens, not of the god of on high. Yet for these novel explanations, the followers of Confucius often used extremely old words and notions, of popular or even peasant origin, to which they gave new philosophical meanings. One example was *yin* and *yang*.

In popular language and literature, these two words simply implied contrast. *Yin* could be the shadow, *yang* the sun; *yin* the cold, wet season – winter, *yang* the hot, dry season – summer; *yin* feminine and passive, *yang* masculine and active. The Confucians took over these two words and used them to mean 'two concrete and complementary aspects of the universe which oppose each other in space and alternate in time'. Their mutual opposition was the source of all the energy in the universe. Their alternation was incessant. 'A time of rest called *yin* and a time of activity called *yang* never coexist: they succeed each other, endlessly, and their alternation determines everything.' This was most notable with the seasons: the *yin* of autumn and winter followed the *yang* of spring and summer; and the same went for day and night, cold and heat. In human beings, this same 'duel' produced love and hatred, anger and joy.

What produced the alternating phenomena of *yin* and *yang* was *tao*, which was the principle of alternation itself – and hence of every entity's unity and of all evolution. The proverb declared: 'One *yin* and one *yang* make the whole, *tao*.'

Unfortunately, if in nature all things follow their *tao*, their prescribed path, and if the *yang* of the heavens and the *yin* of the earth infallibly alternate to solve all the problems of nature and humanity, human beings are an exception to the rule. They are a special disturbing factor in the universe, uniquely endowed with the freedom not to follow their *tao*, and to deviate from their proper path. When they do so, their evil actions destroy the original harmony of the world.

The Confucians believed that in this way human beings precipitated all the disturbances from which they suffered, whether natural (eclipses, earthquakes, floods) or human (revolutions, public disasters, famines). The neo-Confucians, by contrast, limited the scope of human destructive power to humanity itself. Lacking virtue, human beings condemned themselves to abasement. This, as we shall see, was the principle of imperial power: sovereigns were automatically raised up or deposed according to whether or not they followed the path decreed by heaven.

Confucianism thereby established an ethic and a rule of life which tended to maintain order and hierarchy in society and the State, reacting sharply against the intellectual and social anarchy of the sophists and the jurists.

Starting from ancient religious practices, the Confucians relied, for moral serenity and control of the feelings, on a series of rites and family and social attitudes. These procedures determined everyone's lives, their rank, their rights and their duties. Following their *tao* meant above all remaining forever in the right place – or rather the place allotted to them – in the social hierarchy. 'That is the real meaning of Confucius's celebrated definition of good government: "May the prince be a prince, the subject a subject, the father a father, the son a son."'

Naturally, the obedience and respect that were due to the prince or the mandarin stemmed from their superiority. 'The prince's nature is like the wind, that of humble people is like the grass. When the wind blows, the grass always bends.' The cardinal virtue of the prince's subjects was absolute obedience, on which the community's harmony depended. Hence the importance that Confucianism continued to attach to 'ancestor-worship, purged of all religious feeling, but demanded as a cement of hierarchy', as Etienne Balazs puts it – because ancestor-worship maintained hierarchy and absolute obedience within the family itself.

Obviously, 'the virtues inculcated by the Confucians – respect, humility . . . submission and subordination to elders and betters' – powerfully reinforced the social and political authority of the educated class, i.e. their own. This formal and traditional ethic played a large part in China's continuity and social immobility.

Roughly contemporary with Confucianism, and born of the same prolonged crisis, Taoism was a mystical quest and a religion of individual salvation. In its popular form, it was bound up with the secret societies that were so important in China. Theoretically, it originated with the teaching of Lao-Tse, 'the Master', a mythical figure of the seventh century BC. But the book attributed to him, setting out his doctrine, dates only from the fourth or the third century BC.

Taoism is a mystic quest for the absolute and for immortality. Like the Confucians, the Taoists reinterpreted for their own use the general notions of *yin*, *yang*, and *tao*. For them, the *tao* was a mystical absolute, the primary life force 'from which everything derives'. To define it was hardly possible. Here is one attempt, from a text attributed to Lao-Tse:

The *tao* that people seek to express is not the *tao* itself; the name people wish to give it is not an adequate name. Without a name, it represents the origin of the universe; with a name, it is the Mother of all beings. By Non-Being, let us seize its secret; by Being, let us approach it. Non-Being and Being, issuing from a single source, differ only in their name. This single source is called Darkness. To darken that Darkness – that is the gateway to all wonders.

The perfection or holiness sought by the Taoists was mystic union with the eternal *tao*: it was 'to efface oneself alive in this original and sovereign presence which envelopes everything without itself ever being enveloped' – in the 'formlessness which engenders all forms, in the *tao* which possesses eternal life'. To do so was at the same time to achieve immortality.

That was a mystic experience, barely understandable in itself, and attainable only by asceticism and meditation. 'Listen not with the ear but with the Heart [which for the Chinese meant the Spirit]; listen not with the Heart but with the Breath . . . It is the Breath which, when empty, attains reality. Union with the *tao* can be reached only by Emptiness; this Emptiness is the fasting of the Heart.'

The aim was to achieve, by long years of meditation and purification, and by repeated good works, what an adept was said to achieve in a few days. 'After three days, he could detach himself from the outside world; after seven days, from the things around him; after nine days, from his own existence. Then . . . he attained clear insight and saw what was Unique. Having seen what was unique, he could reach the state in which there was neither present nor past, and finally that in which there was neither life nor death.'

Here, Taoism joins company with all the great mystical experiences, whether Christian, Islamic or Buddhist.

But the immortality sought by the Taoists was not only the salvation of the soul: it was also physical immortality, thanks to a series of recipes for long life, purifying and unburdening the body. These involved countless practices: breathing exercises to help the free circulation of the breath and the blood, and avoid 'obstruction, coagulation and clotting'; careful dieting, to avoid ordinary foodstuffs (especially cereals) and replace them with vegetable or mineral nostrums; finally, alchemy. This last included the gold vessel which purified all food, liquid gold (gold liquor) and above all cinnabar (red mercuric sulphide) when it had nine times been transformed into mercury and back again so as to make 'the red pill of immortality'.

After these various treatments, 'the bones turn to gold, the flesh to jade, and the body becomes incorruptible'; as light as a stalk of straw, it can rise to an apotheosis which carries the adept, now immortal, to the abode of the gods. To avoid troubling the world of the living, he pretends to die as others do, leaving behind him a stick or a sword which he has made look exactly like a corpse.

Alchemy, and the quest for elixirs of longevity, give point to the story of Chang-Chuen ('Eternal Spring'), a Taoist monk who was seventy-three (though thought to be 200) when Genghis Khan made him leave his monastery and come to him in Mongolia to bring him the recipe for a long life. When the old monk arrived, on 9 December 1221, the Emperor asked him: 'What remedy have you brought me?' The monk replied: 'None. I have with me only one *tao* to guarantee life.' He and the Emperor died within days of each other, in 1227.

There was finally a popular Taoist religion which ignored the holiness of the Masters and the complicated practices involved in the quest for a long life. The Chinese language itself distinguishes between 'the Taoist people', *tao-min*, and the true adepts, *tao-che*. The mass of the *tao-min* were content to take part in numerous services, to make abundant offerings and to perform acts of penance. They themselves could not claim immortality, but those who lived a pure life were assured of a better existence in the next world. They would not escape the Yellow Springs, but would serve as assistants to the god Earth, and would rule over the miserable throng of the dead. These details show how the people's version of Taoism had had to come to terms, as it did on other matters, with ancient beliefs.

Popular Taoism repeatedly formed extremely hierarchical churches, and a series of more or less secret sects with anarchistic and mystical tendencies. In the face of Confucianism, the traditionalist partisan of social order, Taoism was always the symbol of individualism, personal freedom and rebellion.

Buddhism, the latest arrival among the 'Big Three', was a religion imported into China by missionaries from India and Central Asia. But it too borrowed from the common pool of traditional Chinese thought and was profoundly altered in the process.

Buddhism arose in India in the sixth and fifth centuries BC. It flourished there under the Emperor Ashoka (273–236 BC). Gradually rejected, and assimilated by Hinduism, it kept some following in the North and North-West of India, among the Greek rulers surviving from Alexander's conquests, then it reached Central Asia, including Bactria (in the North of present-day Afghanistan) and the Tarim Basin (in Chinese Turkestan).

It was there, in about the second century BC, that the Chinese conquerors encountered it. Three centuries later, in the first century AD, it began to invade the Han Empire, partly along the central Asian trade-routes, but also by sea and across Yunnan in the South-West of China. Not until much later, in the third century AD, did it really spread through the whole of Chinese society, including both the élite and the masses. Its influence remained preponderant until the tenth century.

Buddhism teaches that after their death people are reborn in other bodies, for a new life which is more or less happy according to what they did in their previous lives, but which always involves suffering. The only issue out of this suffering is the way preached by Buddha: this makes it possible to attain Nirvana, that is, to melt into unconditional eternal life and to be delivered from the cycle of reincarnation. That way is difficult, because what causes people to be born again after their death is their eagerness to live. This has to be quenched by detachment and renunciation. To that end, it has to be understood that neither the Self nor what surrounds it has any real existence: they are only an illusion. Such understanding is not a reasoned conclusion, but an intuitive realization which the sage can reach only by contemplation and by spiritual exercises carried out in one lifetime or several.

The initial success of this religion, which was very alien to the Chinese spirit, was the result of a lengthy misunderstanding. It was not presented to the Chinese under its true colours. The first Buddhist adepts all came from Taoist circles; and they assumed that Buddhism was only a slight variant of their own religion. Both indeed were religions based on salvation, and their contemplative practices looked similar from the outside, although those of Buddhism were physically less painful and may have seemed more attractive. The debate might have been clarified by study of the relevant Sanskrit texts: but these came to light only slowly. They were very difficult to turn into Chinese; and when translations were eventually made, they were usually the joint work of Indian missionaries and the first Taoist converts, who naturally used the vocabulary of Taoism, thereby compounding the confusion. Thus it was that Buddhist illumination became union with the *tao*, Nirvana was translated by the Chinese word for the abode of the Immortals, and so on. This distorted form of Buddhism spread rapidly thanks to a vast network of male and female monastic communities.

As in the case of Taoism, a popular version of the religion united those of the faithful who were content to take part in its simplest rites, say prayers, give alms, avoid the five deadly sins and attend dramatic sessions in which the priest saved the souls of the ancestors by recalling them from their infernal dwelling-place. By the same means, the faithful themselves could hope to reach the Western Heaven after their death, if interceded for by the saints, saviours of the souls of the damned.

The misunderstanding was dispelled only when many translations of the Sanskrit texts became available – i.e. very late in the day, not before the sixth and seventh centuries.

In fact, Taoism and Buddhism were mutually contradictory. The one sought 'the drug of immortality', the survival of the body; the other considered the body to be a set of shackles imposed on people by their imperfections, and something which did not even really exist. For the Buddhist, the very Self was non-existent: in Nirvana all personality was dissolved. For the Taoist, in the Paradise of the Immortals, every saint would keep his own personality forever.

Only a few great Chinese thinkers were troubled by the belated discovery of these differences, and by the impossibility of 'using the Buddhist system to attain the sense of the *tao*', as one of them wrote in the seventh century. By then, Buddhism had become 'Chinese'. Favoured and persecuted by turns – and thus severely affected by the wave of repression in 845 which closed all the monasteries, Buddhism none the less perpetuated a certain number of 'duly selected beliefs, which China had admitted to its heritage without adapting them to its own usage' (Demiéville). In this way, faith in the transmigration of souls spread throughout China, even among educated Taoists, while Buddhist metaphysics deeply affected neo-Confucianism from the thirteenth century onwards.

It cannot be said, therefore, that Buddhism was destroyed by Chinese civilization. Instead, it added to it, setting its permanent seal upon it (as in countless works of art), while at the same time being indelibly steeped in its influence. This, however, has been the fate of all religions in China.

What then did religion mean to the majority of the Chinese, beyond the great neo-Confucian upheavals of the thirteenth century and later? In other words, what did that majority see in the brightly painted brick temples rising above the brown or grey of the ordinary houses with their walls of wood or clay? No particular religion, and all of them at the same time.

Each member of the faithful turned sometimes to the Buddhist priests and sometimes to the Taoists. Both officiated in the same temple; the statue of Buddha stood there, as well as the altar of the local god or the statue of Confucius, himself almost deified. Offerings were made to all of them. During the Second World War, a joint prayer was said in one Chinese temple, addressed to a list of 687 divinities – including Christ. What is interesting to note is that this pantheon of gods included some from the earliest times, and that none of the ancient religious disputes gave one form of belief any precedence over another.

At the time of Marco Polo, at the court of the Great Khan who then held in his grip both China and the Mongol Empire, a religious storm broke out which looked like destroying everything. The Khan had dismissed the Confucians (save for those he kept on as civil servants); he had persecuted the Taoists, in many cases to death; and he had encouraged the Mongol shamanists (animists), as well as, still more, the Buddhists of the Tibetan rite, welcoming at his court its lamas, miracle-workers and magicians. One Christian sect, the Nestorians, also enjoyed his favour. Shortly after Marco Polo's departure, a Western monk, Fra Giovanni di Montecorvino, even succeeded in building the first Catholic church at Cambaluc (Peking), so close to the Khan's palace that he could not fail to hear its bells. 'This extraordinary fact,' wrote Fra Giovanni, 'was known to people everywhere.' Yet neither his ambitions nor those of the Jesuits later came to fruition. Was it ever possible to convert the Chinese to one single religion? And especially to one from abroad?

Politics

Under this heading we must follow a long and complex process of evolution. Nor will it suffice simply to survey the mass of habits and rituals involved in the monumental institution of the Empire. We shall need to explain how it owed its strength to a corps of educated civil servants, the mandarins, who until the quite recent past were one of the most salient original features of Chinese society and civilization. We shall see, finally, that these institutions were justified by their achievements: the maintenance of stability in a huge society, and of political unity in an enormous domain. That unity was the *raison d'être* of the imperial monarchy.

The imperial monarchy illustrated 'Chinese continuity'. Following the lead of Chinese chroniclers and historians, one could trace the monarchy back through 4,000 years of history, with twenty-two dynasties which official chronology places end to end without indicating the slightest interval or interruption. But this neat arrangement should not be taken at face value. First of all, its steady succession was interrupted by disturbances and impostures. Secondly, there was no imperial institution until China was united by the 'First Emperor' of the Ch'in, Ch'in Shi Hwang-ti (221–206 BC), and consolidated and stabilized by the Han dynasty (206 BC to AD 220).

If one accepts this reasonable starting-point, the Chinese empire lasted from 221 BC to AD 1911–12, which saw the fall of the Manchu dynasty (also known as the Ch'ing dynasty), dating from 1644. So the Empire was long-lasting, an axis around which the history of China turned, slowly, century after century. It is easy, therefore, to understand what preoccupied Chinese philosophers and historians: they sought to emphasize the longevity and legitimacy of the monarchy, and if necessary to restore order, retrospectively, to epochs where history had neglected to supply it. All the more so in that China's imperial order was not merely human but also religious, founded on supernatural values.

Social and supernatural order, in fact, were two sides of the same coin. So the Emperor was both a temporal and a spiritual ruler: none of his actions was purely that of a layman; and in fact he supervised both natural and supernatural order in the world. As sovereign in both domains, he not only appointed civil servants, but also decided on the hierarchy in the temples, gave a name to 'this or that canonized sage' and presided over the ritual beginning of farm work, by ploughing the first furrow at the Feast of Spring.

Sinologists often stress that the Emperors of China did not rule by divine right. This is no doubt true by comparison with the Divine Right of Kings as propounded in the West in the Middle Ages and early modern times. But there is more than one similarity between the Chinese imperial monarchy and, for example, that of ancient Rome. 'Chinese political philosophy never taught anything resembling the Western doctrine of the Divine Right of Kings': but was there any need to, if the Emperor was 'truly the son of Heaven', if he ruled by virtue of a mandate from Heaven, a contract which, according to one Chinese philosopher, 'rewarded only virtue'? The role of virtue is important in explaining the disasters, to the Empire and to himself, which the Emperor could not always prevent. Floods, calamitous droughts, refusal to pay taxes, defeats by the barbarians at the frontier, peasant revolts (which were very frequent): all these troubles arose from a breach of the fundamental contract, a lack of virtue on the part of the Emperor, who thereby ceased to enjoy the mandate of Heaven. Such portents were unmistakable: they betokened a change of dynasty, failing which generations of people risked following an unworthy Emperor into sudden oblivion. Popular uprisings, at least in ancient China, were regarded as advance warnings that an Emperor was about to fall. An old proverb claimed (a little like the Western *vox populi, vox Dei*): 'Heaven sees with the eyes of the people.'

So the mandate of Heaven would legitimately pass from a family that had fallen from grace to a new dynasty which necessarily possessed virtue because it received the mandate. 'The Chinese expression *Koming*, which translates our word "revolution", and which Republican China has adopted, means literally "the withdrawal of the mandate". A ruler who has lost this indispensable protection is obliged to step down.' It was essential therefore, for the sake of imperial continuity and the unity of China, to adjust the chronology of successive dynasties so as to eliminate interregna (*jouen*) when, as we should say, usurpers ruled. As one dynasty ended, so another necessarily received the mandate of Heaven. Embarrassment begins, for the historian, when in a troubled period several rivals contest or even share power. The Chinese historian then finds it hard to say which were the true inheritors of the mandate, or of the 'continuity' (*chang-tong*) – the legitimacy, as we in the West should call it. For want of a better solution, he will then choose those who seem 'the most worthy', and give them in retrospect 'all the consideration that is owing to the Son of Heaven'.

The fact that legitimacy was accorded, by right, to whomever was strong enough to seize power (since his strength must have come from Heaven) explains the continuity of China's history despite the dramatic upheavals that punctuated it.

The public pomp of this unchanging monarchy was extra-ordinary and full of splendour: the court, the palace teeming with ministers, officials, eunuchs, courtesans and concubines, and the ceremonies brilliantly staged. When the Sung Emperor went to the southern outskirts of his capital Hang-chow to sacrifice in the temple there to his ancestors and to Heaven, the great avenue leading to the temple was levelled and sanded in advance. Soldiers lined the route, richly bedecked elephants walked before the im-perial carriage; and when the procession began, the torches which had been lit at nightfall beside the road were all put out at once. It was a grandiose spectacle, and one that stirred popular emotion. True, every ruler in the world no doubt calculates the effect of a complex, well-drilled ceremony: the 'entries' of the Kings of France into their loyal cities, for example, were equally well-attended. The displays mounted by the Chinese monarchy had similar motives, but were still more splendid and more authentic-ally religious. To gauge their effect, imagine the impact in Europe of a series of imperial dynasties maintaining the self-same style and significance from Augustus until the First World War.

This monarchy, in essence rather primitive, coexisted with a 'modern' corps of educated officials, the mandarins. The West was puzzled by them, misunderstanding their true position, and vainly seeking in the China of the Ming or the Manchu a close or distant social parallel with Europe, where alongside the monarchy stood the clergy, the nobility and the third estate. The importance of the mandarins made them look to Western eyes rather like aristocrats.

In fact, they were senior officials, few in number and recruited through complex competitive examinations. Their education, like their profession (but not their birth), made them an exclusive caste: in the thirteenth century they totalled perhaps ten thousand families. Although it was not a closed social caste, it was difficult to enter, since it was reserved for intellectuals, whose knowledge, language, concerns, ideas, and habits of mind united them in a kind of complicity and at the same time cut them off from the rest of the world.

Emphatically, they were not described as nobles, or lords, or plutocrats (which some of them were). Their closest counterparts, according to Etienne Balazs, are the 'technocrats' of our present-day industrial societies. These, representing a powerful State, are highly interventionist, concerned with efficiency and productivity, and rationalists to the core.

The mandarins resembled them: like them, they enjoyed social advantages and exceptional prestige as a result of their intellectual qualifications and examination success; like them, they were 'a tiny minority in number, but omnipotent in power, influence, position, and prestige'; like them, 'they knew only one profession – administration and government'.

A well-known passage from Mencius (Meng-tseu, d. 314 BC), on the difference between those who think and those who labour, neatly expressed the mandarins' ideal: 'The pursuits of men of quality are not those of the poor. The former work with their brains, the latter with their bodies. Those who work with their brains *govern the others*; those who work with their physical strength are governed by them. Those who are governed support the others; those who govern are supported by the rest.' Horror of manual labour was a mark of honour: the hand of an educated man, who let his nails grow to an extravagant length, could perform only one task – using the brush with which he wrote.

But what did governing imply in ancient China? Broadly speaking, as in a State today, performing all the tasks of administration and justice. The mandarins raised taxes, sat in judgement, policed society, if need be conducted military operations, drew up work schedules and built and maintained roads, canals, dams and irrigation systems. Their role, as K. A. Wittfogel has put it, was 'to correct the cruelty of Nature' – forestalling droughts and floods, laying in stocks of foodstuffs, and in brief overseeing the proper workings of a complex farming society which demanded strict discipline, especially to deal with the river system and ensure that irrigation was effective.

The mandarins represented this discipline, this stability in society, the economy, the State and civilization. They stood for order against disorder. Order, no doubt, was not an unmixed blessing. But it was 'the price to be paid for the homogeneity, longevity and vitality of Chinese civilization'. Only the iron hand of the mandarins was able to maintain the unity of a vast Empire, facing on the one hand feudal lords and on the other a peasant society which invariably lapsed into anarchy whenever it was left to fend for itself. So in the face of Taoism, which opposed all collective constraints and called for a return to nature, the mandarins preached the virtues of hierarchy, public order and Confucian ethics.

In this sense, they were largely responsible for China's social immobility. They maintained a balance between the great propertied landlords, held to their duties, and the poverty-stricken peasants, who nevertheless retained their own poverty-stricken land. The mandarins also kept an eye on any emerging capitalists, merchants, moneylenders and *nouveaux riches*. They in turn were restrained as much by the mandarins' prestige as by their surveil-lance: regularly, some day or another, the descendants of merchants who had made their fortune would let themselves be tempted by the life of letters and the attractions of power, and would take the famous examinations. This is at least one of the reasons why Chinese society did not evolve, as in the West, towards a capitalist system. It remained at the stage of paternalism and tradition.

Chinese unity meant the North plus the South. The territory of China was not really unified until the thirteenth century, when all of it suffered from disasters. The Mongol conquest (1211–79) culminated in the defeat of the Sung dynasty in the South and the capture of its capital Hang-chow, which Marco Polo visited shortly afterwards and saw in all its prosperity and beauty. The new masters of China not only pushed Chinese rule to its furthest geographical limits: they gave life and strength to this amalgam of different territories. The latter had often been joined together under the Han, the T'ang and the Sung dynasties, but it was now that the progress already accomplished reached its peak, confirming the wealth and supremacy of Southern China, and spreading prosperity throughout the Empire.

For centuries, the South had been a 'Far West', a 'semi-barbaric Mezzogiorno', with few inhabitants except occasional aboriginal tribes whom it was difficult to hold in check. From the eleventh century at the latest, however, the South awoke from its semi-colonial sleep, thanks to early varieties of rice which made possible two harvests a year. From then onwards it became the granary of China. If the first two millennia (before the eleventh century) had been dominated by the people of the Yellow River, the third (from the eleventh century to the twentieth) became more or less the preserve of the people from the Yangtze-kiang and further South as far as Canton. Hang-chow and Nanking, however, the capitals of the Blue River country, were both superseded by Peking, the capital established in the North for obvious geopolitical reasons, to act as a shield against the Northern barbarians and nomads.

The primacy of the South was soon reflected in the size of its population. By the thirteenth century, there were ten Southern Chinese for every one in the North. It also enjoyed primacy in quality and efficiency, as it still does. Over the last three centuries, the vast majority of Chinese intellectuals have been natives of Kiang-si and Che-kiang provinces, and most of the leaders of the twentieth-century revolution came from Hunan. Such is the result, today, of the shift in China's centre of gravity some ten centuries ago. Between the eleventh and the thirteenth centuries, the great Chinese hour-glass was turned upside-down, to the permanent advantage of the land of rice and to the detriment of the land of millet and wheat. But the new China was still the China of the past, which it continued and enriched. The South, so to speak, was China's America – as Manchuria became much later, in the twentieth century.

★

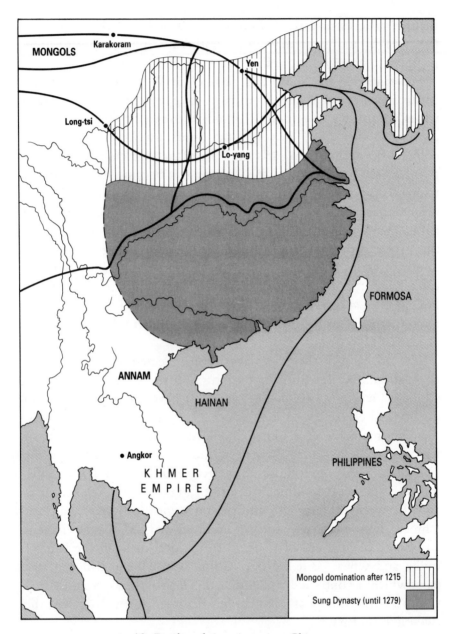

10. Roads and rivers in ancient China

Roads are shown with thick lines, rivers with thin.

Social and economic affairs

Underlying classical China's semi-immobility, her economic and social structures were semi-immobile too. They, indeed, were the foundations of that enormous house.

Like all global societies, China was a complex of different societies, all interlocked. Some were conservative, others more progressive. Any change came through slow imperceptible evolution.

The basis of Chinese society was largely agricultural and proletarian, with an enormous mass of needy peasants and impoverished city-dwellers. The world of the poor scarcely saw its masters – very rarely, the Emperor or the princes of the blood, few in numbers but extremely rich; rarely too the great landowners, but more often their hated bailiffs, at work at close quarters; and just as rarely the great and much feared State officials, who governed the country at a distance but 'with a rod of bamboo', as Father de las Cortes said. Everyone, however, sympathized with junior officials; and everyone constantly wished a violent death on usurers and moneylenders.

Such, at least, was the tenor of popular folk-tales from the Sung dynasty onwards. They described a society both patriarchal and based on slavery, both modern and peasant – very different, certainly, from the 'model' of Western societies. It was patriarchal on account of its powerful family links, the long unbreakable ligatures of ancestor-worship.

Family solidarity extended to the most distant cousins and even to childhood friends. This was not a matter of charity, but of justice. A privileged person who made his fortune was exploiting the advantages of the family unit, drawing upon the blessings of its ancestors. It was only fair that a man who had thus used up the luck of the family should share with all his relations the prosperity that he owed them.

This same society was based on slavery – or at least, if slavery was never its major feature, it was nevertheless a frequent practice. In general, slavery was the spontaneous outcome of unrelenting poverty and irremediable over-population. Its unhappy victims sold themselves when times were hard; and, throughout the Far East, parents sold their children. The practice continued in China until the law of 1908 which, almost at the end of the Manchu dynasty, forbade both slavery and the sale of children. However, it authorized parents 'in times of famine, to sign long-term work contracts which committed their children up to the age of twenty-five'.

Chinese society, with a vast majority of peasants, was not in the true sense feudal. It had no fiefs to be the subject of investiture, no peasant tenure, no peasant serfs. Many peasants owned their tiny patches of soil. But above them there were 'rural notabilities' (*chen che*), who rented out their land, sometimes acted as moneylenders, and required peasants to work for them and to pay to use an oven or a mill, usually in kind, in bushels of grain or pots of fat. At the same time, these notabilities had links with the mandarins (many of them large landowners), who as we have said represented the interests of the State, and thus tended to curb any excessive power of one class over another, and especially that of any feudal class which might be able to challenge central authority.

This complex social network kept order among the four groups of the old hierarchy: at the top, the mandarins (*che*); the peasants (*nong*); the artisans (*kong*); and the merchants (*chang*). The last two, who might have played a determining role, were held in check, like the others, by a watchful government. In any case, their influence would have depended on spurts of economic growth; and these were no more than intermittent.

Despite what many Sinophile specialists and historians maintain, China's economic achievements were modest and, to be frank, backward compared with those of the West. Not for one second, of course, could one accuse China of global inferiority *vis-à-vis* Europe. Her inferiority lay in her economic structure, her market outlets and her merchant middle class, less well developed than that of Islam or the West. First, and most crucially, there were no free cities. Nor were there entrepreneurs eager to make profits – a passion which may or may not be regrettable, but which in the West was certainly a spur to progress. As early as the thirteenth century, Chinese traders were willing to spend money on the pride and vanity of public ostentation: in this they resembled merchants in the West. But, rather more than their Western counterparts, they had a taste and a love for literature. One merchant's son could write poems of every kind. 'All the descriptions of merchants' lives that we find in folk tales from the Sung dynasty show that their aim was to make enough money to lead a comfortable life, fulfil their moral and social duties, and above all to discharge their obligations to their parents and their whole family.' And, in the case of the very rich, to enable some of their relatives to join the privileged mandarin caste.

In other words, they only half-heartedly shared the capitalist mentality of the West. Furthermore, many Chinese merchants, like the artisans, were itinerants, travelling from place to place; and this alone is a sign that the Chinese economy was not yet mature. Europe in the thirteenth century was already emerging from that phase. In the early Middle Ages, itinerant trade had been the norm, but now there were more and more business houses in place. Only poor traders had to travel with their own merchandise because they had no agents or branches and could not do business by letter. Only poor artisans, likewise, carried all their gear on their backs and wandered through towns and countryside looking for work. But in China, even in the eighteenth century, sugar craftsmen still came to the sugar-cane fields with their equipment, breaking the canes with their bare hands and making syrup and brown sugar. Industrial development, likewise, was sparse: a few rather primitive coal-mines in the North, and in the South the famous ovens for making porcelain.

Nor was there any credit system, at least until the eighteenth and (in some places) the nineteenth century. Hence the importance of the moneylender, long embedded like a painful splinter in Chinese society, and the sure sign of a backward, suffocating economy.

Finally, despite its rivers, its junks, its sampans, its rafts of logs, its free trade between provinces, its porters and its Northern camel-trains, China suffered from poor internal communications and still more limited links with the rest of the world. It was also very much over-populated.

Isolated as it was, China tended to live on its own resources. It had only two major outlets – the sea and the desert. Even these could be used only in favourable circumstances and when there was a potential trading partner at the end of the journey.

During the Mongol period (1215–1368), for about a century (1240–1340), both outlets were operative at the same time. Kublai Khan (1260–94), the friend and protector of Marco Polo and his family, made great efforts to build a fleet, so as to be free of Muslim ships and protect himself against Japanese competitors and pirates. At the same time, he kept open and free of obstacles the great Mongol road which led beyond the Caspian to the Black Sea and the prosperous colonies of the Genoese and Venetians in Kaffa and the Tana region.

Thus opened up, China was undoubtedly prosperous, supplied with silver money by Western merchants. Wonder of wonders, it also developed paper money. But that lasted only for a time.

In any case, the great national revolution, in which the Ming drove the Mongols back to the desert (1368) and purged China of these unassimilated aliens, virtually coincided with the closing of both her trading outlets. The desert was once more a barrier which the new China could not cross: the sea, in the end, proved equally disappointing. From 1405 to 1431–2, Admiral Cheng-ho mounted no fewer than seven successive sea-going expeditions, one of which consisted of sixty-two large junks with 17,800 soldiers on board.

All of these fleets left Nanking to re-establish China's protectorate on the Sunda Isles, which supplied her with gold dust, pepper and spices. They reached Ceylon and left a garrison there, then pushed on to the Persian Gulf, the Red Sea, and finally the coast of Africa, whence they brought back some marvellous giraffes which astonished the crowds.

This episode has seemed strange to Sinologists, and all the more interesting for that. A little more wind, and the Chinese ships might have rounded the Cape of Good Hope half a century before the Portuguese: they might have discovered Europe, and even America. But in 1431–2 the adventure came to an end, and it was not repeated. China, huge as it was, had to regroup its resources to face its eternal enemies in the North. In 1421 it transferred its capital from Nanking to Peking.

Later, in the seventeenth and eighteenth centuries, the Manchu emperors re-opened the desert road, taking over vast areas as far as Tibet and the Caspian, resisting the nomads and driving them off to the West. These conquests gave China peace in the North, and enabled her to go beyond Manchuria and seize part of Siberia as far as the Amur (Treaty of Nerchinsk with Russia, 1689). A further result, from the second half of the eighteenth century onwards, was the opening of the great trading fairs of Kiakhta to the South-East of Irkutsk, where furs from the Far North were exchanged for cotton, silk and tea from China. As for the seaway, the Europeans tried to open it in the sixteenth, seventeenth and eighteenth centuries. They succeeded in the nineteenth, but to their own advantage.

China expanded. By the thirteenth century there were probably 100 million Chinese (90 million in the South, 10 million in the North). The figure fell with the end of Mongol domination and the national revolution of the Ming dynasty in 1368. By 1384 the population had dropped to 60 million (a reliable estimate); but with the return of peace it seems soon to have risen to its previous level. There was a further fall, probably, at the time of the Manchu conquest (1644–83) – followed, when peace was restored, by an enormous expansion in the eighteenth century. Thereafter, the growth of the population reached dizzy heights.

This excessive wealth of manpower necessarily had drawbacks. It probably prevented technological progress. Teeming humanity made machines unnecessary, as slavery had in classical Greece and Rome. For human power could be used for anything. In 1793, a

British traveller marvelled at the sight of a ship being transferred from one level of water to another without going through a lock, but simply being lifted by human strength. Father de la Cortes in 1626 had already admired – and drawn – Chinese porters in the act of lifting an enormous tree-trunk. No task, in other words, was too heavy for human beings. And in China they came so cheap.

This over-population weighed on the life of China, immobilizing it in the iron grip of a conservative administration, and above all blocking the development of technology. There was such a thing as Chinese science, whose wealth, precociousness, ingenuity and even modernity are coming to light more and more every day. Joseph Needham, who carefully chronicled its development, remarked that its 'organic' conception of the world was precisely that to which present-day science is turning, in contrast to the Newtonian mechanistic view which prevailed until the end of the nineteenth century. Curiously, however, in China technology did not keep up with science: it marked time. The main reason, without a doubt, was the over-abundance of manpower. China had no need to devise machines to spare human labour. It was the permanent victim of the poverty resulting from endemic over-population.

12. China Yesterday and Today

The China of the past did not disappear overnight. It receded little by little, and not before the nineteenth century. Then, events moved rapidly. Ancient China was opened up by force, and suffered lengthy humiliation. It took a long time to realize how far it had fallen, and longer still to find remedies. It succeeded in the twentieth century, but only at the cost of a fabulous effort, for which history affords not the remotest precedent.

The time of imposed treaties: China as humiliated victim (1839–1949)

China was not occupied, like India, or reduced like her to the status of a colony. But Chinese territory was invaded, pillaged and regularly exploited. All the great powers took their share. And China emerged from the ordeal only when the People's Republic was established in 1949.

From the sixteenth century onwards, China was in touch with European trade. Important as that fact was, it had little effect on China – until later, when one-sided treaties began to be imposed.

In 1557 the Portuguese settled in Macao, opposite Canton; and from there they played an important role, especially between China and Japan. In the seventeenth century, the Dutch and the British seized the best pickings. Then, in the second half of the eighteenth century, the golden age of 'the China trade' began, although limited at that time to the single port of Canton.

For China, the trade was important; but it had little effect on the country as a whole. European merchants, the majority of them British, dealt with a privileged circle of Chinese traders, the *Co-hong*, who had a monopoly of buying and selling. In so far as this trade benefited both parties, it grew by leaps and bounds. It covered gold (which was cheap in China owing to the rarity and high price of silver: the ratio was 8 to 1 in China, as against 15 or more to 1 in Europe); tea, in ever greater demand in the West; and cotton and cotton goods, imported from India. This trade was financed by a belated credit system. European merchants advanced money to Chinese traders, who divided and re-loaned it in exchange for produce from the furthest corners of the Empire, forming thereby an already modern financial network. This was Europe's normal practice in overseas trade – to lend to a local merchant, in the course of each voyage, the money he needed to collect a cargo for the following visit, and thus enjoy priority in the market.

Undoubtedly, 'the China trade' dazzled Europe. Often, if not always, it made enormous profits. China benefited too, and did not resent the intrusion of foreign methods and merchandise: their economic impact was limited to a small circle and had little effect on the country as a whole.

But with the nineteenth century everything changed. Europe grew overbearing and greedy. It was strengthened, moreover, by the British conquest of India, which gave it a firm foothold in the East. As a result, Western intervention became brutal and destructive.

The Opium War of 1840 to 1842 opened five treaty ports to Westerners, including Canton and Shanghai (by the Treaty of Nanking). The T'ai-p'ing rebellion enabled the Westerners to intrude further, in 1860, and secure the opening of seven more treaty ports. The Russians then obliged China to cede them the Maritime Province, where they built Vladivostok. China's troubles, in fact, were only beginning. The first Sino-Japanese War lost her Korea; and the great powers profited from her weakness to make further inroads. The Russians settled in Manchuria. The Boxer rising in 1900, aimed against foreigners, precipitated further intervention by all the European powers, backed by the United States and Japan. The Russo-Japanese War of 1904–5 gave the Japanese some of what the Russians had already seized from China. The First World War gave Japan further advantages, this time via the Germans, notably in Shantung.

By 1919, therefore, China had lost important parts of its territory. Even within its frontiers, the West and Japan enjoyed liberties, privileges and 'concessions', the best known of which was the international concession of Shanghai. They controlled part of the railways and the customs – guarantees for the payment of interest on foreign loans; here and there they had established their own post offices, their own consular jurisdiction, their own banks, their own trading houses, their own industries and mines. In 1914 their total investments in China had amounted to $1,610 million, of which $219 million came from Japan.

Following the expedition of the eight powers after the Boxer rising, and the capture of the Imperial capital in 1901, the Legations' quarter of Peking was militarily occupied 'and surrounded by a glacis, where the Chinese were forbidden to build'. 'The Peking diplomatic corps strictly supervised, *de facto* if not *de jure*, all Chinese affairs, or at least all those controlled by the Peking Government.'

Dismantled economically, China was also subjected to a large-scale invasion by foreign culture and religion. It was submerged, physically and spiritually, at the time of the treaties imposed on it, which it rightly called 'the one-sided treaties'.

To shake off the yoke of the West, China needed first to modernize – i.e. in some degree Westernize itself. Reform and liberation were two tasks that were often mutually contradictory: yet both had to be performed. It took a lot of time and trouble, much hesitation and experiment, before the shape of the struggle ahead became clear. China was unable to learn Western ways overnight, as Japan did in the Meiji era of modernization. She had, in fact, a difficult double apprenticeship.

Thus the powerful, complex and 'traditional' (because peasant)
T'ai-p'ing rebellion of 1850 to 1864, which briefly set up a
separatist government in Nanking, was nationalist and xenophobic:
but at the same time it sought to overthrow some of China's
ancient social and political customs. During their short-lived
triumph, the T'ai-p'ing rebels abolished slavery, emancipated
women, suppressed polygamy and the binding of feet and admitted
women to public examinations and official posts. They also hoped
to achieve technological and industrial modernization, although
their efforts did not go deep. Essentially, theirs was one more of
the many agrarian revolts that had taken place in the past, usually
on the eve of a change of dynasty. In that respect, the T'ai-p'ing
uprising was an attempt to oust landowners and collectivize their
estates. It finally failed, mainly because of the help that the West
gave to the Manchu dynasty, so as to maintain Western trading
advantages. A further reason was that T'ai-p'ing plans for
modernization remained too vague, while China was in no state as
yet to accept them.

The Boxer rebellion of 1900, led by a secret society with mysterious and terrifying rituals, was motivated solely by xenophobia.
But that xenophobia was shared at the time by the whole of
China, beginning with the fearful Dowager Empress Tz'e-hsi,
who by giving the signal for action against the foreigner (probably
in complicity with the Boxers) in fact ensured that both they and
China were crushed in 1901. Tz'e-hsi, incidentally, was also a
fierce opponent of reform. She had cleverly and skilfully foiled the
enlightened attempt at modernization that had been made in 1898,
known as the 'Hundred Days'. On paper, at least, this would have
laid the foundations for a genuine revolution in China's institutions
and economy.

At the beginning of the twentieth century, in other words, the
hour of reform had not yet struck. Those seeking change had to
confront 'the organic deafness of the mandarins, whose ears were
harder to open than the Chinese ports', as Etienne Balazs put it.
They also faced indifference on the part of the people, who were

tempted only by 'the blind alley of xenophobia'. At the most, all they wanted was to learn the foreigners' 'tricks' – the secrets of their efficiency.

The double problem remained difficult to solve. The Western 'Barbarians' had to be driven out; but to achieve this China had to learn the science and technology of the West. Its very slow apprenticeship was the work of young middle-class intellectuals who met Westerners and travelled abroad, and still more that of the many poverty-stricken students attending the modern schools and universities set up by the Government in the final years of the Manchu dynasty. They helped form a series of secret societies, some frankly republican, others still monarchist, but all eager for the 'recovery' of China and for radical reform.

Thus there came into being China's first really revolutionary movement, closely linked with the name of Sun Yat-sen. Sun Yat-sen (1866–1925) was a doctor from a village in Kwang-Tung. He had been involved in a number of revolutionary movements, on account of which he had spent several years in exile outside China. In 1905, in Tokyo, he became president of a republican league which soon acquired great importance throughout China and produced a well-thought-out political programme. This movement was directly involved in the revolution of 1911 which overthrew the Manchu dynasty and installed Sun Yat-sen at the head of China's first republican government. This revolution, however, was thwarted almost at once. After fourteen days, Sun Yat-sen resigned in favour of General Yuan Shih-kai (d. 1916), who tried to re-establish the old regime with himself as its beneficiary.

So the liberal constitution of 1912 was suspended, and China sank into anarchy. The military governors of the provinces, soon to be called the Warlords, allied themselves with the rural notabilities to extort as much as possible from taxes and rents. They soon became the pitiless masters of China. Sun Yat-sen, who had once more gone into exile, founded a new party which he called the Komintang ('the party of the Revolution'). This was a play on words. The Kuomintang, founded in 1912 in the first euphoric months of the Republic, had meant 'the great party of the Nation'. The substitution of '*Koming*' (Revolution) for '*Kuomin*' (Nation) signified that the original party had not finished its work, and that the revolution had still to be pursued.

In the process, China had yet to suffer repeated misfortunes and crises, which came to an end only in 1949 with the victory of the Communists and the establishment of the People's Republic. The date has some significance: from the Opium War of 1840–42 it took China a century of effort and hardship to recover her independence and her pride. 'From now on,' declared a professor in 1951, 'we can again be proud that we are Chinese.'

During that century of expectation and struggle, the old regime began to decay, especially in its most traditional and conservative respects. It abandoned 'the hierarchy of mandarins with crystal or mother-of-pearl buttons, the ritual of Reports to the imperial throne annotated with a vermilion brush by the Son of Heaven, the audiences in brocade robes', and also the exorbitant privileges granted to the Westerners and the Japanese.

After much suffering, then, China reached one of those rare moments when a civilization renews itself by breaking apart, sacrificing some of those structural features which hitherto had been essential to it. For China, the crisis was all the more extra-ordinary in that it challenged what had been in place for thousands of years. Still, the destruction was not total: nor could it have been. In building afresh, China remained faithful to her own forms of thought and sensibility. It will certainly take a number of decades for the new Chinese civilization to assume its distinctive shape.

For the moment, all we can do is try to understand the experiments now in progress, which in fact have barely begun.

China renewed

This is not the place to praise or condemn the People's Republic of China, although one could do both. Our purpose is to note what it has done or tried to do, and then to see – or try to see – how this affects Chinese civilization, which is undergoing the greatest and most violent human experiment in all its very long history. What is being undertaken is an effort to establish order in many fields: social, economic, political, intellectual and moral.

This has meant placing things, people and classes – and if possible the outside world – in a new situation, created by Chinese will-power. Pride has its part in the process – pride as at least one link with the ancient past, when China was confident of its role at the centre of the universe.

The People's Republic of China has an enormous mass of people and resources – some real, some potential and needing to be exploited. Its economic development will depend on both.

China's population continues to grow. In 1952, it was 572 million; in 1953, 582; in 1954, 594; in 1955, 605; in 1956, 620; in 1957, 635; in 1958, 650; in 1959, 665; in 1960, 680; in 1961, 695. By 1984, it had passed one thousand million. These are not precise census figures, except for 1953 (and even there some reservations must be made): they are estimates, reasonably well founded. As in all less developed countries (and China in 1949 was the biggest such country in the world), the growth of the population, owing to a high birth-rate (in the region of 40 per 1,000) and a falling death-rate, poses appalling problems. Demographic growth on this scale limits in advance – and indeed seriously threatens – any real hope of higher living standards.

And yet China's economic growth-rate, from 1949 to 1962, was truly prodigious, unparalleled in the present or the past. Even Russia's first Five-Year Plan did not surpass China's, from 1953 to 1957 inclusive. Of course, the economy was more or less starting from scratch; and those who have lagged behind in the past have the chance to grow at relatively impressive speed. Poor to begin with, they can double their wealth without becoming rich. Later, when they have reached a certain level, they are likely to succumb to the law of diminishing returns, which spares neither capitalist nor socialist economies.

In measuring China's extraordinary development, one also has to remember that it is the fruit of inexorable will-power and effort on the part of the most populous country in the world. One might add that planning an economy is an art already demonstrated not only by earlier Soviet experience, but also by contemporary capitalism itself.

This is not the place to draw up a detailed balance-sheet. Relying on official figures for total revenue from 1952 onwards, without trying to scrutinize too closely statistics that are hard to check, one can note the following serial progression: 1952, 100; 1953, 114; 1954, 128; 1955, 128; 1956, 145; 1957, 153; 1958, 206; 1959, 249. The growth-rates in 1958 and 1959 respectively were 34 per cent and 22 per cent which is simply fabulous. Even allowing for the difficulty of working out the total revenue of so vast and various a country, economists cannot disguise either their astonishment or their admiration. This was indeed a 'Great Leap Forward'.

Non-economists may find it easier to judge the progress made by looking at figures for particular products. Steel (millions of tons): 1949, 0.16; 1952, 1.3; 1960, 18.4. Coal (millions of tons): 1949, 32; 1960, 425. Pig-iron (millions of tons): 1949, 0.25; 1960, 27.5. Electricity (milliards of kilowatt-hours): 1949, 4.2; 1960, 58. Cotton (millions of metres): 1949, 1.9; 1960, 7,600. Cereals, plus sweet potatoes and ordinary potatoes, counting their weight at a quarter of their fresh weight (tons): 1957, 185 million; 1958, 250 million; 1959, 270 million. Further data are supplied by the (triple) map of the Chinese railways, showing those that existed in 1949, those built by 1960 and those then planned. A further triple map could be drawn up for hydro-electric power-stations (old, new and planned), as also for ordinary power-stations. Nor should one forget the huge project for harnessing the Yangtze-Kiang, from the lower part of the Szechuan basin to the stretches of rapids and gorges, of which the longest is the Xiling. These great public works will provide an enormous reserve of energy, make possible major irrigation to the North, improve the course of the river, make thousands of kilometres of it navigable to deep-water ships, and in the gorges themselves encourage the establishment of ultra-modern factories.

These achievements were the result of superhuman efforts, made possible by the mobilization of China's huge society, which had not only to be pressed into political support and forced labour, but also to be remodelled.

This was not just a very effective means to an end: it was an end in itself – and a gamble. The regime deliberately staked its existence on its relentless modernization plans. And while it did not hesitate to apply draconian measures, it also began with some support from the Chinese masses, because it put an end to the dreadful corruption that had marred the previous regime in the last years of Chiang Kai-shek.

The whole of society was taken in hand: peasants, industrial workers, intellectuals and members of the Party. As for the wealthiest of the middle classes – the middlemen who had been intermediaries between Chinese and European merchants – they had fled in 1949 with the fall of Chiang Kai-shek. The industrial middle classes were reabsorbed into the system when private firms were turned into mixed enterprises (private and public) in 1956; and there remained, more or less untouched, only a limited number of middle-class businessmen, dealing with some aspects of trade but clearly in a precarious position.

Among the peasant population, reform was gradual but rapid. It began with the Agrarian Law of 30 June 1950, which ruthlessly ousted landed proprietors and rich peasants. Less well-off peasants lost part of their property; finally, each peasant was allotted a minute piece of land (just over one-third of an acre) – which in itself shows how vast a number of takers there were: of 600 million Chinese in 1954–5, more than 500 million were on the land. These innumerable scraps of land were the beginning of egalitarian ownership on a Lilliputian scale.

In October 1956 collectivization began, with the establishment of collective farms. A further step was the creation in 1958 of rural communes, each grouping together as many as 20,000 peasants, whereas a collective farm had only a few hundred. The communes were a new form of organization, and perhaps too ambitious: their role was at once political, agricultural, industrial and military. The peasant was also a soldier, and some peasants bore arms: this gave the regime the extra security of having an army on hand, ready to intervene at any time. However, on 20 November 1960, the communes seem to have been stripped of their prerogatives and responsibilities, in favour of production brigades, whose prospects looked uncertain. All that could be said was that the authorities were hesitating, not about their objective but about how to achieve it, given that food production was the only part of the economy whose growth remained slow.

The authorities similarly mobilized the industrial workers, whose numbers went on growing, and who were controlled by the trade unions in conjunction with the Party. The government asked them, like the peasants, to make superhuman efforts. After the second Five-Year Plan, it ran an active propaganda campaign to obtain further 'Great Leaps Forward' which the Plan had not envisaged. Hence spectacular feats of competition to reach productivity targets, and a host of slogans: 'More, better, quicker, cheaper'; 'One day is worth twenty years and a year is worth a millennium'; '1958 will be the first of three years of hard struggle for a thousand years ahead'.

It would be easy to quote thousands of examples of heroic effort – despite poor working conditions, low wages, insufficient food and lack of housing. One model working woman – and the title meant extra duties as well as prestige – was celebrated for rinsing her face in cold water to keep herself awake during her night shifts at the factory.

As for the intellectuals, the students and the members of the Party – was their heroism less in evidence, or were the targets assigned to them much less clear? What is certain is that the discipline imposed on them was more complex, more capricious and more cruel.

Members of the Party were never exempt from purges and

forced confessions. They had to endure such things as the campaigns against 'the three evils' and 'the five evils'. The first, in January and February 1952, attacked 'corruption, waste and bureaucracy' on the part of civil servants: it revealed a number of scandals, later deliberately exaggerated, which gave some former country-dwellers, who had become 'Party officials' in the towns the unpleasant surprise of losing jobs to which they had become all too comfortably accustomed. In the same year, the campaign against 'the five evils' (corruption, tax evasion, fraud, sale of State property and theft of economic secrets) caused enormous upheavals, including suicides and severe mass punishments. Other purges, other forced confessions and other suicides followed.

For students, whose numbers were constantly growing, there was barely a moment when the heavy hand of the authorities was not coming down on them, humiliating and disciplining them, and forcing them to do manual labour in the factories or the fields.

Teachers and other intellectuals by no means escaped persecution. They were very briefly allowed to speak their minds after the Soviet invasion of Hungary in 1956. This was the time of the so-called 'Hundred Flowers', when it was said that thoughts, like flowers, could blossom in a hundred different forms. Called upon to explain their own ideas, but hesitant to do so, the intellectuals found themselves in a strange situation – especially since what they said was at once published in the press. 'Marxism–Leninism,' declared one of them, 'is an old, outdated theory, unsuitable for China. It needs to be revised.' One teacher declined to give any opinion: 'I am afraid,' he said, 'of the present freedom. Its essential feature is that one has to talk. The pressure is painful. Let us relax for the moment. Later, we shall see what happens.' Another teacher noted: 'The people have not enough to eat, and yet some say that the standard of living has risen.' Mere heckling, one might think: a little recreation for old intellectuals who had disliked their Marxist re-education courses. But, on the contrary, it was a very serious affair. The Hundred Flowers did not last out a single springtime: they flourished 'vigorously for one short month', from 8 May to

8 June 1957. Then came repression. Many unwary people were summarily dismissed for what they had said.

All this is a reminder that China was engaged, not in an open debate, but in a life-and-death struggle. Its problem was to remodel society, to change its psychology, to purge its errors, its heritage and its possible regrets: to try to enthuse it with pride, with work and with self-satisfaction; and above all to impose obedience.

'If one constrains 650 million Chinese to think correctly, they will be brought to act correctly, according to the norms which the Chinese Communist Party judges essential to its march towards a Socialist China.' To this end the radio, the press and countless speeches engaged in incessant propaganda, unparalleled by any other 'socialist' or 'totalitarian' experiment. Its main weapon was criticism, organized daily through compulsory debates in every workplace. This was the way to find out those among the group whose attitude was satisfactory, those who could be persuaded and those implacably opposed. Everyone was called upon to attack these dissenters. 'Oral attack' (*tou-cheng*) was 'a humiliating mixture of violent criticism, combined with sarcasm, reproaches and – very rarely – mild physical chastisement.'

This ideological action was conceived as a 'long-term, complex and large-scale' campaign (Mao Tse-tung). Its rigour was adjusted to different social groups – moderate for the peasants, but very intense in factories, offices, universities, schools and units of the army. There was some resistance to indoctrination, and punishment was used to enforce it. At the beginning of the revolution, penalties were severe and brutal. Later, they grew milder but they remained extremely harsh.

In literature and art the Party had a 'cultural' commissar, in charge of discipline and the struggle against insidious bourgeois and reactionary infiltration in these fields. Every writer had to set an example, and not only in words. One author who lived in the country was praised for writing every morning in the 'collective literature' vein, and also growing a field of sweet potatoes and breeding pigs ... Writers convicted of 'Right-wing deviationism' were liable to sanctions, like the well-known novelist Ting Ling, who was sent for 're-education by work' to a desolate region in Northern Manchuria, where she had to remain for two years.

Clearly, these punishments were mild by comparison with the terrible summary executions that took place in the first few months of the Revolution – and later. Clearly, too, the resistance and sabotage mentioned in official documents were the exception, not the rule. Sincere and enthusiastic conversions were far more numerous, and many were expressed in moving ways. To embrace the ideology that now triumphed was to embrace a fatherland and a nation: it was to believe in the future and to believe in China.

The agricultural experiment was the only major failure of Communist China. A few record harvests, some exaggerated statistics and a strong dose of official optimism managed to conceal the real facts until 1958. In the West, enthusiastic books and articles helped to sustain the illusion. But the catastrophic harvests of 1959, 1960 and 1961 severely punctured that optimism – in part unfairly. The unfairness lay in the fact that these very poor harvests were mainly the result of natural causes. China has always been subject to the equal and opposite misfortunes of droughts and floods, sometimes alternating, sometimes even simultaneous. They especially affect the great provinces in the North. In 1961, they destroyed more than half of the crops. Tornadoes and floods claimed millions of victims – whereas from March to June of that same year, below Jouan, one could cross the Yellow River on foot, since drought had reduced it to a ridiculous trickle. Droughts, typhoons, floods and venomous insects – none of these ancient enemies has surrendered to the new China.

One might add that China, like all the Communist States, has paid dearly for its industrial success. It has perhaps staked too much on industrialization at the expense of agriculture. The official press, as well as blaming 'natural calamities unparalleled for a hundred years', also accuses people, speaking of sabotage. 'Some of the officials and auxiliary workers who in August 1960 were sent to the country, to help the people's communes save the harvest, failed in their duty and disobeyed the orders of the Government and the Party', often with the connivance of 'retrograde elements in the population'. We should take this 'explanation by scapegoat' with a pinch of salt. It seems likely that collectivization, in China as elsewhere, met resistance from the peasantry, usually more traditionalist than the rest of the population. Some subsequent measures on the part of the authorities may have been concessions, like the emphasis placed on small rather than large production brigades.

China's poor harvests brought much in their train. They slowed down economic growth, and made it necessary to cut back the food exports to Russia, which had helped pay for imports of Russian goods and services. They obliged China to ask the capitalist countries for deliveries of grain: 9–10 million tons from Canada, Australia, the United States, France, Burma and even Taiwan. In London, where the sea transport for this enormous cargo was organized, it was reckoned that it would cost China £80 million a year for three years. How would she pay? Probably in mercury, gold and silver.

Without a doubt, this was a heavy blow for a growing economy, and it left a question-mark hanging over China's future. This, indeed, was the dark side of an economic success which in other respects was undeniably energetic and spectacular.

Chinese civilization in the modern world

None of this great progress would have been possible without the help of what in the immensity of China does duty for nationalism – a very individual sentiment which some have called, hideously, 'culturalism'. This is in fact a form of pride which is not national, but cultural, attached not to a nation but to a civilization. It is an ancient but enduring phenomenon, and it needs to be explored. For China today, which at first sight seems so novel and revolutionary, is linked thereby to a long and proud tradition which had been deeply wounded by the sad century (1840–1949) before the Communist Revolution.

China regards herself as a great power and a great civilization. She has always believed in her superiority over the rest of the world and in the supremacy of her civilization, outside of which, in her view, there was only barbarism. In the past, her pride was very like that felt by the West. For this reason, the century of one-sided treaties had been doubly cruel. The first humiliation was for China to find herself reduced to being one nation among many: the second was to be dominated by the Barbarians with their science and their arms. Chinese nationalism today, fierce and virulent as it is, can be seen as revenge – the firm decision to become a great nation, *the* great nation, whatever the cost. Hence the eagerness to redouble revolutionary efforts, to press on unstintingly, to seize on new resources like translations of Russian Marxist–Leninist manuals. Just as in the past China lapped up the sacred texts of Buddhism and sought acquaintance with Mr De (democracy) and Miss Sai (science), so now she pursues history, sociology and ethnography.

There is no doubt that Communist China feels that she has the vocation of leading the proletarian peoples against the over-fed and over-rich nations of the world, demonstrating how to achieve a swift revolution whose lessons she will gladly and generously teach. Despite her own difficulties, China has never stopped exporting supplies and capital: between 1953 and 1959, she distributed $1,191 million to Albania, Burma, Cambodia, Ceylon, Cuba, Egypt, Guinea, Hungary, Indonesia, Mongolia, Nepal, North Korea, North Vietnam and Yemen. This list does not include the aid given to the Algerian rebels, or an agreement made with Ghana in 1961. These and other facts (for instance that 40 per cent of the credits went to non-Communist countries) show that the People's Republic intends to play an international role, perhaps beyond its present resources, but certainly below the height of its ambitions.

The occupation of Tibet in 1950, followed by the latent conflict with India; claims on the island of Formosa (Taiwan) where Chiang Kai-shek's army had taken refuge; the desire to resume normal relations with Japan and with the West, whose economy would suit China's needs far better than would that of the Soviet Union – as witness the semi-clandestine import of machine-tools via Macao and Hong Kong; finally, the wish to enter the United Nations, where her place was at that time occupied by the nationalists in Formosa: all that reflected a desire for power and influence, as did the clash and near-breach between Chinese and Soviet Marxism which broke out at the 1961 Moscow Conference. China is determined to be a great power. In 1945, she was 'unable to make a motor-scooter'; by 1962 she was on the brink of producing an atomic bomb. Through this astounding revolution, she rediscovered her original pride and her dignity as a great civilization.

This is the point made by a leading Sinologist, Etienne Balazs, whose views of the Chinese revolution in its long historical context are summarized below.

If the Chinese experiment is a convincing success, all the less developed countries are likely to try to copy it. This is what makes so crucial and so agonizing, for China's friends and enemies alike, the fundamental question: will the experiment succeed, or is it already beginning to fail?

Let us admit, frankly, that there is no point in studying figures and statistics – partly because they are manipulated for the good of the cause, and more especially because Chinese statisticians are groping and floundering in trial and error. What is surprising is not that their estimates are shaky, but rather that they are good enough for planning to go forward without too many mistakes and for the results to be calculated accurately enough to register the general trend. All in all, that trend is positive.

One can of course point to some notorious failures in the five-year plans, such as the 'pocket' blast-furnaces, inadequate grain production or the difficulties of the people's communes. But the basic and stable features of the Chinese experiment are worth considering rather than criticizing, since they seem to have been well devised:

- the most determined industrialization, with a growth-rate far higher (and long likely to remain far higher) than that of either the Soviet Union and Eastern Europe or the less developed countries (on average, 20 per cent against 7 to 10 per cent);
- clear determination to 'walk on both legs' as long as necessary – i.e. to use the industrial income for investment so as to maintain the growth-rate, and to continue in other sectors to use the resources at hand, with rural artisans supplying agricultural tools and other consumption goods for the peasant masses;
- a general austerity programme, not confined to the masses and so making it possible to impose sacrifices on them;
- great flexibility on the part of the authorities, who can acknowledge their mistakes and immediately change tack.

All this is possible only because of certain essential facts of Chinese civilization.

First, numbers. The hardships involved in the experiment, even if they include the sacrifice of certain people, or even many people, cannot compromise the success of the experiment itself. There are too many people in China, and there always have been.

But, above all, the unprecedented mobilization of more than 600 million people by 10 million officials, disciplined and devoted members of the Party. And at the head of the Party, with a few exceptions, there remains the old guard, leaders hardened by thirty years of persecution, civil war, armed resistance against Japan, patient advances and retreats in military strategy and political tactics, with unequalled experience in governing things and people.

One cannot help thinking that they are the heirs of the great bureaucratic tradition in the ancient Empire, successor of the mandarins, those educated officials accustomed to governing a great State with a very firm hand. A new intelligentsia, bold and active, has eliminated the old one, bookish and conservative; and it masters. This powerful organization, seamless from top to bottom, and able to make everyone work unceasingly, is perhaps the secret of China's unique experiment. In a very short time, the most ancient living civilization has become the youngest and most active force in all the less developed countries. But this in turn is perhaps because it has been able to rely on one of the longest-lived and most solid features of its age-old civilization: its bureaucratic tradition.

A further question is posed by China's development: the Sino-Soviet conflict. Was a real conflict expressed by the demonstrations at the 22nd Congress in 1961 and the sly digs printed by the opposing official newspapers, Moscow's *Pravda* and Peking's *The People's Daily*? Or were these superficial appearances, against which Socialist solidarity would always prevail?

To tell the truth, divorce was almost impossible: it would have had international consequences which would be very dangerous for both sides. But the antagonism was real and deep; and here too there are historical reasons.

True, the conflict had modern origins. Here were two great people who have both tried the experiment of Communism in the hope of modernization. And while one was sighing with some relief after forty years of penury and suffering, the other was gasping in a super-human effort and bowed under miserable austerity. While the *nouveau riche* was flamboyantly taking his place in the councils of nations, the poor relation had no voice there, and was banished like a leper from the international scene. One was obliged to go forward at all costs, under pain of falling back: the other had grown wary and prudent. These were certainly reasons for friction.

But the rivalry surely lay deeper, in China's prickly nationalism and her desire for revenge on the West. For Russia, Socialist or not, was still Western, still Barbarian. China claims nothing less, in her effort to efface the past, than to become the capital of the Third World. Then, once more, she will indeed be 'The Middle Kingdom'.

13. India Yesterday and Today

India is an amalgam of areas, and also of disparate experiences, which never quite succeed in forming a single whole. It is too vast for that (4 million square kilometres including Pakistan, i.e. between three and four times the size of the six founder-members of the European Community). It is also too densely populated: without Pakistan, its inhabitants in 1963 numbered more than 438 million. Twenty years later, that figure had risen to more than 730 million. It is furthermore very diverse. In the South is Deccan, a region of conservative peoples and civilizations, obstinately resisting change. In the North-West, the arid lands of the Indus are linked with Iran and, beyond the Khyber Pass, with Turkestan and all of turbulent Central Asia. This North-West frontier, vulnerable to invasion, is India's dangerous and often tragic zone. Finally (except under the British Raj), no single political power has ever succeeded in dominating the whole subcontinent, either in the past or in the present, following its violent and sanguinary partition between India and Pakistan in 1947.

Ancient India (before the British Raj)

Without going back as far as the mysterious culture of the Indus (3000 to 1400 BC), one can distinguish three Indian civilizations which emerged gradually, slowly succeeded each other, and also overlapped:

- an Indo-Aryan or Vedic civilization, from 1400 BC to the seventh century AD;
- a medieval Hindu civilization (Hinduism), which replaced its predecessor until the thirteenth century;
- an Islamic-Hindu civilization, imposed like a straitjacket by the conquering Muslims in the thirteenth to eighteenth centuries, and whose vigorous and sustained colonialism was replaced by Britain's from the eighteenth century onwards.

None of these three civilizations, it should again be stressed, united the whole subcontinent: nor did any of the great 'universal' Empires they successively supported. Until the eighteenth century, India never experienced the imposition of a single regime such as marked – and greatly simplified – China's past.

Vedic India passed through three or four main stages between 1400 BC and the seventh century AD. These two millennia were dominated by invasion and settlement by Aryan peoples from Turkestan, who entered India from the North-West and slowly spread across the plains of the Central Indus, then the Central Ganges. Their civilization affected only a part of the Indo-Gangetic Plain; but this, very early on, was the living heart of India.

This first, 'Vedic' civilization (from *Veda*, sacred knowledge) drew partly on what the newcomers brought with them and partly on innumerable borrowings from those already there. It developed extremely slowly, clashing at times with the very varied brown or black indigenous population – pygmies who were early arrivals from Africa; Proto-Mediterraneans who had come later, no doubt from Mesopotamia, and whose physical type is preserved among the Dravidians in the South; and peoples from Central Asia with Mongoloid characteristics (especially in Bengal).

These pre-Aryans were for the most part already settled on the land, as farmers and stationary stockbreeders, grouped in villages and even in towns, on the banks of the Indus, the focus of an already ancient civilization of citizens and merchants. These pre-Aryans were numerous, and remained so; even today, they make up the majority of the Indian population.

The Indo-Aryans, by contrast, mostly but not invariably had pale skins and fair hair. They were nomadic herdsmen related to the many peoples who in the second millennium invaded the plains of Iran or Asia Minor and the distant countries of Europe. These invaders of India were kin to the Hellenes, the Italiots, the Celts, the Germanic peoples and the Slavs.

Stage one, before 1000 BC: invasion

The first Aryan invasion came from Turkestan towards Iran and India. It thus came to grips, from Mesopotamia to the Indus, with an already homogeneous and flourishing civilization of towns, tall houses and settled peasants. This civilization may have become decadent by the time the invaders reached the countries of the Indus; but those countries fought for a long time to preserve their independence from the newcomers, and much delayed their advance towards the East.

The Aryans' sacred texts, written in Sanskrit, describe these interminable struggles which took place before 1000 BC in the Punjab and the Kabul River area, involving men, gods and anti-gods (the *asoura* or divine protectors of the enemy). This long phase is reflected in the oldest of the sacred books, the *Rig Veda* or *Hymnal*, embodying the mythology and beliefs of a first Vedic religion. This included at least thirty-three gods, divided among earthly gods, gods of heaven and gods of the 'intermediate space' (the atmosphere). In the midst of these 'somewhat pale' deities, two gods stood out: Varuna, upholder 'of the cosmic and moral laws and observer of the guilty, whom he catches in his snares'; and, still more important, Indra, the fair-haired victorious hero of a thousand conflicts, who having defeated the demon Vita freed the waters of the sky, which ever since have flooded and fertilized the earth. All these gods mixed with human beings, like the divinities of Olympus who mixed with the warriors confronting each other beneath the walls of Troy. All demanded sacrifices: milk, wheat, meat and a fermented drink (*soma*) obtained from a mysterious plant.

In short, then, this was a formal and pluralist religion, consisting purely of rites. The Aryans had not yet completely given up their nomadic habits in favour of a settled life which would have involved more order, even in the religious domain.

Stage two, from 1000 to 600 BC: conquest and settlement.

The invaders gradually adopted a settled life in an area slightly further or slightly extended to the East, and of which the essential crossroads was what is now Delhi. This Eastward thrust went as far as what is now Varanasi (Benares), involving gigantic battles – or battles reported as such. By about 800, the invaders had reached Bengal and perhaps Central India.

The huge geographical, social, economic and political changes that resulted explain the enormous religious innovations recorded in new sacred books, then in the *Commentaries* (*Brahmanas*) and the *Upanishads* – that *Treatise on Approaches* which opened the secret doors of religious speculation. Although retaining its original basis, religion was gradually becoming more complex. It began to show monotheistic tendencies, although the intermingling of victors and vanquished flooded it with an enormous mass of non-Aryan beliefs. These included yoga ('self-mastery'), whose practices became an important part of Vedic religion alongside the ritual sacrifices.

More and more, religious beliefs and attitudes grew gloomier. Soon it began to be thought that people's souls were subject to incessant reincarnation, constantly returning to a new earthly existence, full of endless pain. At the same time, the first social divisions (*varna*) appeared in a society that was at once 'magic', 'pseudo-feudal' and 'colonial' – a mixture in which not everything could be explained (as used to be thought) in terms of victors and vanquished. In the highest rank, the brahmins were the priests, masters of spiritual matters. Then came the warriors, kings, princes and great lords (*kshatryas*). In the third rank were smallholding peasants, stockbreeders, artisans, and merchants (*vaisyas*); and in the fourth and last rank were the *sûdras*, who originally at least were native slaves. Later, this caste system slowly solidified, with its taboos, its exclusions, its multiple bans on inter-marriage and its strict divisions between *pure* and *impure*.

Temporal and spiritual power was divided between the two highest castes. Primitive royalty soon found itself deprived of any religious monopoly − in contrast to what was the rule elsewhere, in China as much as in, for example, ancient Egypt.

The relationship between the spiritual and the political principles of the *imperium* was made fully evident in a peculiar institution . . . It was not enough for the king, the model or essence of the *kshatryas* caste, to employ brahmins for the public ritual: he had to have a permanent personal relationship with *one* brahmin, his *purohita* (literally, 'one placed forward'). We might translate this as 'chaplain'; but one must bear in mind the idea of a spiritual avant-garde or delegated authority − a 'greater self'. Not only would the gods not eat the king's offerings without a *purohita*, but the king depended on him for his own actions, which would not succeed without the *purohita*'s help. His relationship with the king was like that of thought with willpower: it was as close as marriage. The *Rig Veda* had said it already: 'He lives, he prospers in his dwelling; the earth showers him with its gifts; the people obey him of their own accord. This is the king, in whose domain the brahmin walks in front.

(Louis Dumont)

Such, at least, is what the brahminical texts declare and repeat.

This religious primacy, associated but not identified with political power, was in Louis Dumont's view the main reason why Indian society was fragmented. Since the first two castes were associated with each other, they stood in contradistinction to the rest of society; and the first three castes, likewise, shunned the mass of the *sûdras*.

The brahmins based their pre-eminence on the inordinate fear that they inspired. The complexity of the ritual made them indispensable as organizers of sacrifices: if one single detail were omitted, the god being invoked would at once slip away, and the terrible Varuna would exact his pitiless revenge. As custodians of the ritual's secrets, the priests could act as they thought fit: they could attack the old, naïve anthropomorphism of the Aryans, or disparage Indra and all the divine heroes of the old hymns. For their own use they created a supreme god, Brahma, who presided over their sacrifices. To tell the truth, he was never very popular.

Two other leading gods, however, had an enthusiastic following – Siva Rudra among the peasants, and Vishnu, identified with the hero Krishna Vasudeva, among the aristocrats. What was more, 'warriors' and 'peasants' (the second and third of the castes) readily turned towards yoga, which the brahmins adopted too, and towards other indigenous ritual practices – or, in some cases, towards free philosophical speculation, which in the sixth and fifth centuries BC gave birth to two new religions, Jainism and Buddhism.

Stage three: the early success of Jainism and Buddhism in the sixth and fifth centuries BC.

Little by little there emerged minute royal principalities, then aristocratic towns, linked together by trade. The towns, which soon became densely populated, thrived on the luxury of their princely courts and on their rich middle-class citizens. Bankers and merchants made large profits from the sea and caravan routes, which brought among other things fine textiles in cotton, linen or silk. From 600 BC onwards, iron-working was practised, as shown by the weapons found in contemporary tombs. Distant Aden was the great market city which re-exported Indian iron towards the Mediterranean.

In this busy environment, somewhat comparable to that of Greece in the same two centuries, two great religions developed, each promising salvation: Jainism and Buddhism. The latter is better known and more important than the former, because it spread outside India; but within India both had equal support. Both, equally, were 'unofficial' and 'secular', adopted by the ruling classes independently of the brahmins, and disseminated by merchants. Both founded monasteries, and both propounded rules for individual salvation. Buddhism, as we have seen, preached a form of renunciation, negating the desire to live and the sense of life, and trying to break the vicious circle of reincarnation so as to attain Nirvana. Jainism, by contrast, saw in personal suffering, and the quest for suffering, an effective route to salvation. Both religions were founded by aristocrats: Buddhism by Siddhartha Gautama, perhaps a king's son (563?–483?), known also as Sakya Muni (the sage of the Sakyas) or the Buddha (the Enlightened); and Jainism by Vardhamana Mahavira (540?–468), the 'Conqueror' of the world (Jina).

The Buddha, who came from Nepal, had his 'revelation' in about 525; and after that he spent the rest of his life preaching in the Ganges Valley. His religion, which began to be modified soon after his death, was based on his sayings, as collected and transmitted by his disciples. They contain no statement about God; but this silence is not a denial: it remains characteristic of his doctrine, like its rejection of any kind of divine 'monism' – the belief that there is only one substantial thing or kind of thing in the universe. In agreement with the dominant ideas of his time (those of the *Upanishads*), he rejected also the idea that the world and the Universal Being were real. For him, nothing was real outside our consciousness. 'You have returned to me like a lookout-bird which had left the ship and flown to all points of the compass in search of land, but found it nowhere. For the elements (Earth, Fire, Water and Air) have their basis in the consciousness. They lose it when consciousness is lost. When consciousness no longer exists, all the elements in the universe will be totally destroyed.'

In fact, the Buddha was a 'renouncer', an abstinent (*sannyasi*). The 'renouncer' was a man who left society and wandered, living on alms, in search of a spiritual absolute capable of setting him free. He was concerned not with reforming society but with securing his personal salvation. So Buddhism was a religion for the individual, the 'desocialized' person. In this respect it resembled the many heresies which regularly arose in India and which were essentially ways of withdrawing, by personal asceticism and the quest for sainthood, from the religion of the brahmins and the constraints of society with which it was so closely linked. The Buddhist abstinent, in contrast to the Christian (whose aim was to escape death), tried to escape from life and its cycle of reincarnations. 'Here, my brother monks, is the holy truth about the suppression of pain: it is the hunger for existence and pleasure that leads from reincarnation to reincarnation ... Here, my brother monks, is the holy truth about the suppression of pain: the extinction of this hunger by destroying desire, by banishing desire, by renouncing it, by leaving it no room.' Such was the price of breaking the cycle of reincarnations and attaining Nirvana.

To reach it, the righteous must follow 'the road with eight branches' (including science, which dispelled all vanity); must respect the five prohibitions (of murder, theft, adultery, drunkenness and lying); must abstain from the ten sins (including insults, gossip, envy, hatred and dogmatic error); and must practise the six transcendent virtues (loving one's neighbour, patience, moral purity, energy, alms-giving and kindness). But to achieve perfection meant going further still. It meant becoming a *bodhisattva* or saint, and then a Buddha (receiving mystical enlightenment). Only Buddhas could dissolve in Nirvana.

Stage four: during the so-called 'Empire' period, from 321 BC to AD 535, Jainism and Buddhism spread very widely, dominating philosophy and the arts, but without for one moment displacing current ritual practices, whether or not derived from Vedism.

To defend their positions, the brahmins relied more and more on the popular cults which they gathered together as if to make a rampart. This slow process led in the direction of Hinduism, a vast eclectic synthesis to which we shall return shortly.

Thus it was that a hierarchical society took shape and hardened, notably into the caste system so peculiar to India, which grew up between 300 BC and AD 700. This, then, was a relatively late phenomenon, and not to be confused with the former *varnas*, which bore more resemblance to the social classes in pre-Islamic Iran. The castes, which still exist in India today, took about a thousand years to emerge, partly from the chance mixture of races and cultures, and partly as a result of the growing multiplicity of different trades. The result was several thousand castes (of which there were still 2,400 or so in 1960). At the bottom of the heap, the victims of every prohibition, were the pariahs, the 'untouchables'.

This composite civilization profited from the establishment of universal Empires (the Mauryas dynasty, 321–181 BC, and especially the Gupta dynasty, AD 320–525) to spread beyond the strict limits of Northern India, towards Nepal, the Himalayas, Tibet, Siam and Indonesia (notably after the fall of the Gupta), and to infiltrate not only the island of Ceylon, which it 'colonized', but also the Dravidian stronghold of the Deccan. Everywhere, it imposed 'classical and sophisticated' Sanskrit, which became throughout India the vehicle of a princely civilization in contrast to the culture of the masses.

With the Mauryas Empire and the justly famous reign of Ashoka (264–226 BC), Buddhism won the day. Centuries later, however, when a new classical India took shape, it did so under the victorious insignia of Hinduism, or what is known as the Hindu 'Renaissance', since this was the time of its artistic greatness, when India mastered all that it had learned from elsewhere. This included in particular the art of Greece, brought through Alexander the Great's conquests in the Indus area, 327–325 BC. But Indian art also affirmed its own character of purity and strength; and it invented, so to speak, the Hindu temple (the *sikhara* – literally its dominant spire), which for centuries was as typical of India as the cathedrals were of the West. Built on a huge platform with broad staircases leading up to it, the temple was surrounded by chapels or by an

ambulatory. The sheer size of the sanctuary represented Mount Meru, the mythical Olympus on which the gods were believed to live.

The Hindu Renaissance was also a great literary period. It was at the court of Chandragupta I I (AD 386–414) that the 'nine precious stones' – the outstanding poets and thinkers of the time – lived and worked. There too, in particular, Kalidasa wrote *Sakuntala*, the drama which, when translated into English in 1789 and German in 1791, made such a lively impression on Herder and Goethe.

Because Hinduism inherited some very ancient traditions, one cannot precisely date its origin, whether at the end of the Gupta dynasty or at the dissolution of the rather ephemeral Harsha empire (606–47). But it certainly established itself as a whole during these Indian Middle Ages – roughly between the death of Harsha and the foundation of the Delhi sultanate in 1206. Hinduism is more than a religion or a social system: it is the core of Indian civilization, and while its origins were very ancient, it remains a living reality even in the India of Pandit Nehru and his successors.

In exploring this phenomenon, we may find that some useful light is shed by expressions drawn from the history of Europe – 'Middle Ages', 'feudal fragmentation' and so on. But if we use them, we should not take them literally. While Hinduism was as important to medieval India as Christianity was in the European Middle Ages, India bore scarcely any resemblance to Merovingian, Carolingian or even feudal Europe.

The historical context counts. Even before the end of the Gupta dynasty, trade was probably slowing down. This recession affected the merchants, the adherents and supporters of Jainism and Buddhism. Soon, both religions suffered persecution, with their devotees impaled and executed, their monasteries destroyed, and so on.

Throughout India's history, whenever its richest regions – from the Ganges to Gujarat and the edge of the Arabian Sea – were no longer flourishing under the stimulus of large-scale trade, the great

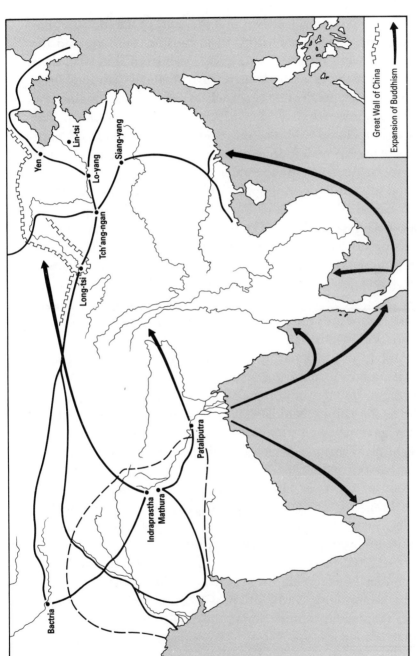

11. *China and India after Buddha (500 BC to AD 500)*

During this troubled period, Buddhism spread by sea to Indo-China and Indonesia, and by land towards the heart of Asia and China. In India, on the other hand, it declined. Pataliputra was Ashoka's capital. The Greek Empire of Bactria (ringed by a broken black line, with the towns of Mathura and Indraprastha) for a time stretched as far as Pataliputra. These hellenized regions acted as a relay for Buddhism.

Legend:
- ⌐⌐⌐ Great Wall of China
- ➤ Expansion of Buddhism

Map labels: Yen, Lin-tsi, Siang-yang, Lo-yang, Tch'ang-ngan, Long-tsi, Bactria, Indraprastha, Mathura, Pataliputra

unifying Empires crumbled. Not that the mass of the Indian population was too much troubled by their collapse: the king and the
ruling classes were always of a different caste from almost all their
subjects. It was fairly natural, then, that on these occasions India
split up into independent States, each of which then fragmented
again, into a series of warlike principalities and lordships. The
history of the Hindu 'Middle Ages', dominated by regional 'warriors', is made up of hundreds of local chronicles in which even
learned specialists can easily lose their way.

What is interesting is not to pursue the history of these States one
by one, nor to dwell on this burgeoning of local loyalties – in
Bengal, in Gujarat, or in the Deccan (the 'Indian Byzantium', as
some historians have called it, thinking of its particular fate, its
powerful resistance and its expansion by sea at the time of the Chola
Empire in 888–1267). No: the most important phenomenon for our
purpose was the development of local literature in Bengali (Bengal),
in Gujarati in the area round the Gulf of Cambay and the Kathiawar
Peninsula, and in Dravidian languages, mainly in the South. (The
word 'Dravidian', awkwardly coined in 1856 by Bishop Robert
Caldwell but now unavoidable, denotes the languages of the Deccan,
not its races. The most important of these languages is Tamil.)

In brief, the Hindu 'Middle Ages' and the slowing-down of the
economy gave renewed strength and vigour to India's human and
geographical diversity – which had always been powerful in any
case. This diversity flourished as abundantly as 'tropical vegetation';
it was one of the basic characteristics of Hinduism, and it gave
modern India the profusion of languages which it finds such a
handicap. But at the same time, despite India's diversity, religious
and cultural unity was undoubtedly taking shape.

Unity resulted from the brahmins' efforts to synthesize belief.
Hinduism, in Northern India, was a religious synthesis achieved
by the brahmins, using Vedic and post-Vedic elements, non-Aryan
elements assimilated centuries ago, and finally the multiplicity of
particular local cults, taken over by a religion which sought to
embrace everything.

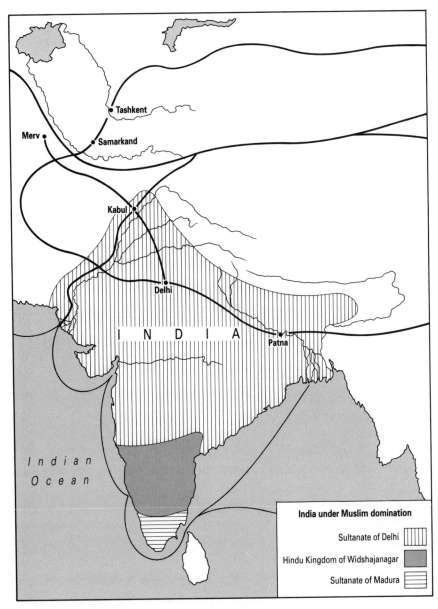

12.India in the fourteenth century

This map shows the main roads (thick black line) and the political divisions, with (in the far South) the short-lived Sultanate of Madura, set up in 1335.

During this slow process, what was happening in the South? Gradually, Southern India was replacing the North in politics, in art, and also in the development of religious ideas. Between the seventh and twelfth centuries, the Deccan was the home of the highest and most brilliant artistic achievements: the subtle, classical Pallava art of Mamalaparam, the violent and masterful art of Ellora, and the lyrical, sensual art of Konarak. We may also note that, long before these artistic triumphs, the South had produced Sankara and Ramanuja, the last really great Indian philosophers and theologians.

What Hinduism made popular, under thousands of different names, was an accessible and merciful god, willing to help and glad to be worshipped. The imagery varied, but the substance remained the same. Against Buddhism and Jainism, traditional religion had taken its revenge – although it had adopted and assimilated both sects' teaching of purity and non-violence, and even their vegetarianism. In general, however, it was simply reinterpreting in new language a set of ancient popular beliefs.

This Hinduism concluded that three great gods coexisted 'at the summit'. Brahma (who above all received 'literary homage') was the creator of the world; Vishnu was its preserver; and Shiva was its destroyer. Separate yet inseparable, they expressed in their different ways the supreme Being whose role it was to act as providence for humanity. This explained the occasions when they 'descended' to earth, as in the *avataras* of Vishnu – his numerous incarnations to preserve world peace. He might appear as a fish, a tortoise, an enormous wild boar, a man-lion or even – this was the ninth *avatara* – in the form of the Buddha, whose work was thereby integrated into the whole religious system. Shiva, the destroyer, was identified 'with death, with time: he was Hara, he who removes'. Like Vishnu, Shiva delegated his powers, often to goddesses. In Southern India, he had a wife, Minashki ('she with the eyes of a fish'), who was the daughter of a king.

It is impossible here to explore fully this rich and exuberant mythology, of which H. Zimmer's intelligent and agreeable book,

Myths and Symbols in the Art and Mythology of India (1951), gives a useful idea. Nor can we dwell further on the meticulous rituals of prayers and sacrifices, on the cult of the dead, on the cremation ceremony which remains general for the majority of Hindus (only ascetics and children being buried), or on the long and complex procedures for marriage. India was and remains extremely conservative as regards such rites.

For believers, the essential problem was personal salvation. If, favourably judged, they entered Paradise 'on the sun's rays', or if they were condemned and went to Hell, in either case the decision, whether reward or punishment, would not be long maintained. The soul would be reincarnated to continue its unhappy fate. However, by means of prayers, rituals and pilgrimages, or with the aid of talismans, people could sometimes escape from the *kharman*, the act which always has repercussions – and notably causes reincarnation. In this way, they would be 'saved': but their salvation would be negative, very different from the Buddhist progress towards spiritual freedom, which required individual purification and asceticism, and saintly renunciation.

The turbid waters of Hinduism – of Indian civilization itself – submerged Buddhism as they did Jainism. Some of its formal aspects were assimilated, but its spirit was rejected, even in Bengal, where it had put down deep roots. India felt the lack of it; the saint or 'renouncer' would always attract a following. Bowed down by the weight of a close-knit, inescapable society, the dominant religion allowed individual liberty only in the form of abnegation, of 'non-action'. In these circumstances, 'sects' naturally multiplied. They were a means of intellectual and moral liberation.

It was perhaps the void left by Buddhism which led to the massive conversions to Islam which took place in Bengal after the last persecutions the Buddhists suffered, in the twelfth century. Something similar happened in the Balkans in the fifteenth century, when Bogomil Christian heretics, so often persecuted, became converts to Islam after the arrival of the Turks.

Muslim India (1206–1757) was pioneered in the seventh century by the foundation of trading colonies on the Malabar coast, and confirmed in 711–12 by an invasion from Sind and the establishment of various inland colonies, Muslim India spread very slowly across the lands that led to the Indus and the Ganges. Later, it tried in vain to conquer the whole of the subcontinent. The Muslims fought for a long time to gain possession of the semi-desert area of Northern India. Even by the early eleventh century, in AD 1030, only the Punjab was in their hands. It took them two centuries more to found the Sultanate of Delhi (1206) and extend it to Northern India – a key stronghold which gave them everything, or almost everything.

This conquest, successful after countless setbacks, ended in wholesale military occupation. The Muslims, who were few in number and based solely in the larger towns, could not rule the country except by systematic terror. Cruelty was the norm – burnings, summary executions, crucifixions or impalements, inventive tortures. Hindu temples were destroyed to make way for mosques. On occasion there were forced conversions. If ever there were an uprising, it was instantly and savagely repressed: houses were burned, the countryside was laid waste, men were slaughtered and women were taken as slaves.

Usually, the plains were left to be run by native princes or village communities. These intermediate authorities were responsible for paying the heavy taxes which were sometimes the counterpart of a certain autonomy, as in the case of the rajahs of Rajputana.

India survived only by virtue of its patience, its superhuman power and its immense size. The levies it had to pay were so crushing that one catastrophic harvest was enough to unleash famines and epidemics capable of killing a million people at a time. Appalling poverty was the constant counterpart of the conquerors' opulence, including the splendour of the palaces and feasts in Delhi, which the sultans had made their capital, and which was a source of wonder to Muslim travellers such as the famous Ibn Batûta.

The sultans in Delhi had the good fortune to be largely spared the shock of the first Mongol invasions under Genghis Khan and his immediate successors, in the thirteenth century. They even profited from these troubles to extend their own conquests towards the South, which had hitherto resisted the establishment of Muslim rulers. The tide turned when Tamerlane invaded their territory and in 1398 successfully raided Delhi, and sacked it without mercy. Having conquered it, however, he at once withdrew with his booty and his files of prisoners – so that the Muslims were more or less able to re-establish their hold on India, although they never regained their former splendour.

It was an ailing and divided Empire that was overthrown some 130 years later, in 1526, at the Battle of Panipat, by an army of adventurers led by Baber, who claimed to be a descendant of Genghis Khan. His army was very small, but it was equipped with harquebuses and field guns, whose carriage wheels, on the field of battle, were secured with chains to resist possible mounted charges. After Baber's victory, moreover, he enlarged the army with mercenaries from Iran, from Kashmir, from Islamic countries, and later from the West.

Baber was a Sunni Muslim. His victory was therefore a victory for orthodox Islam, for those with pale skins and for gunpowder. With it was established the Empire of the Great Mogul, which in principle endured for more than three centuries, until 1857, when it was belatedly suppressed by the British after the Indian Mutiny. In reality, its lustre had died with the last of its great rulers, Aurangzeb (1658–1707), long before the British occupied Bengal in 1757.

From 1526 to the death of Aurangzeb, Muslim India attained renewed splendour, recalling the great years of the Delhi sultanate – with the same violence, the same forced coexistence, the same impositions, and the same successes.

The same violence: Islam ruled by fear, and founded its luxury on India's general poverty. Perhaps it had no alternative. On the one side were the fabulous riches admired by travellers from the West;

on the other, a series of famines, a fabulous death-rate and innumerable children abandoned or sold by their families.

The same forced coexistence: As time went by, there were more and more mutual links. Akbar (1555–1606), the greatest of the Mogul rulers, even tried to set up a less arbitrary administration and establish a new religion which would have brought Islam and Hinduism into a single system (the Din Ilahi or Divine Religion). This, however, had few converts outside the Emperor's immediate circle, and it died with him. Still, the attempt was a significant move.

In fact, the conquerors could not do without their Hindu subjects. Immense regions of India remained independent, whether they paid their taxes or not. François Bernier, a French doctor who worked for the Great Mogul, noted in 1670: 'In this same expanse of country, there are a number of nations of which the Mogul is not very much the master, since most of them have their own particular rulers and leaders, who obey him and pay tribute to him only when they are forced to, some paying very little, and others nothing at all.'

The necessities of war and of continual lesser conflicts tended to limit the Great Mogul's authority, although in principle it was absolute. His court was a vast army of 50,000 to 200,000 men gathered in Delhi: cavalry, musketeers, gunners; light field guns (the so-called 'stirrup artillery') and heavy cannon; reserves of horses and elephants – a whole crowd of soldiers, grooms and servants. Their leaders, the *omerahs*, enjoyed pensions and profits (land was granted them for life); they were adventurers, often of very humble origins, which by no means prevented their parading in the streets 'superbly dressed, sometimes on an elephant or a horse, sometimes in a palanquin or sedan chair, usually followed by a large number of horsemen and bodyguards, with a quantity of footmen marching in front and alongside to clear the way, dispel the flies and the dust with peacocks' tails, and carry toothpicks, spittoons, or drinking-water'. 'For one Muslim,' Bernier goes on, 'there are hundreds of infidels.' The whole army could not be recruited from among so-called Moguls with pale skins (who, for fear that their children might lose this privilege, preferred to marry white women from Kashmir). So soldiers had to be found among the infidels and the men with darker complexions.

The Delhi contingent always included Rajputs (natives of Rajputana), who were often led by their own rajahs. Some of the latter could if need be raise huge armies of native soldiers. They were required, sometimes, to fight against even Muslim mercenaries, or against such dangerous neighbours as the Shi'ite Persians, or against the Pathans, Muslims from Bengal, or against Hindu or Muslim princes from the Deccan, who were traditionally hostile.

All this was paid for by the Great Mogul's abundant treasury, supplied more by the trade of his vast States than by the income from his land. The treasury, in fact, was a centre for the collection and dissemination of wealth. Every time a silver coin was deposited there, it had a small hole punched in it: many coins bore several such marks.

A considerable part of non-Muslim India took part in this distribution system – or, as we might say, was in on it. Over time, coexistence was inevitable, involving compromise and limited mutual tolerance. We have already mentioned the mixed Islamic and Hindu art which developed in Delhi and other Mogul capitals. One thing is certain: it was a true hybrid, as much Indian as Muslim. On the cultural and religious plane, however, India remained itself. Despite everything, Islam did not affect it deeply. It was significant that Tulsi Das, the Brahman who became the greatest poet in the Hindi language, lived under the Mogul empire, from 1532 to 1623.

Indeed, Islam's authoritarian domination, whatever its other innumerable results, made less impact on Hindu society and the Indian economy than did the contact with the West which began at the end of the fifteenth century, increased in the sixteenth and seventeenth, and multiplied again in the general expansion of the eighteenth. Apart from gunpowder, which accounted not only for the Muslim victory in 1526 but also for the destruction of

Vizianagaram in 1565, Islam had no great advantage over the India it had conquered.

With the death of Aurangzeb in 1707, as we have seen, the Empire began to vacillate in the face of dangers from the West and the South. In 1738, the Afghans seized Delhi; and already in 1659 the Hindu Mahrattas of Central India had begun the very powerful attacks which had only briefly halted and which in the eighteenth century became triumphant.

That said, however, we should not be over-hasty in condemning the Muslim record in India. It would be unfair to isolate this colonial experiment, extremely violent and prolonged as it was, from the countless similar exploits then taking place in the world. Whatever else it did, this centuries-long occupation implanted into the teeming mass of India an enormous number of faithful Muslims, 24 per cent of the population according to the 1931 census (77 million, compared with 239 million Hindus), or roughly one Muslim for every three Hindus. Thirty years later, since the 1947 partition was very approximate, the percentage of Muslims in India was between 20 and 25 per cent, and closer to the second figure: 44 million Muslims out of a total population of 438 million, while the population of Pakistan was some 85 million, including a number of non-Muslims. So Muslim India, too, has miraculously survived, and it remains hard to isolate from the shared Indo-Muslim civilization of which it is a part.

*British India (1757–1947): an ancient economy at grips
with the modern West*

In the sixteenth century, the Portuguese had a number of warehouses in the Far East. Vasco da Gama had reached Calicut on 17 May 1498, and Goa was occupied in 1510. But Portuguese India flourished for less than a century. In the seventeenth century, British, Dutch and French factories dominated the scene.

Even before the defeat of the French in 1763, Robert Clive's victory at Plassey (Palassi, to the North of present-day Calcutta) on 23 June 1757, in effect inaugurated British India. It lasted almost two centuries, until Indian independence in 1947; and thus virtually matched the longevity of the Great Mogul's Empire. Like that Empire, it grew gradually, and was not complete until it conquered the Punjab in 1849; equally, it left outside its direct control a number of autonomous States, the Native States and Agencies, although under British rule their independence was much more theoretical than real. In fact, the whole subcontinent felt the shock of Britain's aggressive domination, backed by immense economic superiority. Until the First World War, distant Britain was about the greatest industrial, trading and banking power in the world. The British Raj profoundly affected every structural aspect of Indian life.

India became an exporter of raw materials. Exploitation, gradually spreading as more of the country was conquered, was in the hands of the East India Company, which was not dissolved until 1858; and from the earliest, highly corrupt times of Lord Clive (who was attacked in the House of Commons and committed suicide in 1774), it took the triple form of exploiting local potentates, merchants and peasants. Exploitation was pursued without shame in the rich and soon conquered provinces of Bengal, Behar and Orissa. A modicum of order and justice was not imposed until 1784, after which a more honest regime was established.

In those early years, pillage and embezzlement had already led to fearful disasters. On 18 September 1789, Lord Cornwallis, the Governor-General of India, wrote: 'I can state without hesitation that a third of the Company's lands in Hindustan are now a jungle, inhabited only by wild beasts.' It was hardly an exaggeration. True, the new rulers, who bore their share of responsibility, were also the playthings and victims of a process over which they had scant control. Many of the evils in question were the result of developing a money economy in a country like India, which despite its very long exposure to world trade, had never known such a system before. British law, and Western concepts regarding land ownership, also led to unintended catastrophes. All in all, an ancient stability, achieved with difficulty and based on India's very remote past, was now severely shaken and at risk.

As the eighteenth century drew to a close, India was a rural world of countless villages, often very poor: groups of huts such as could still be seen, in 1962, near to Madras among other places. 'Wall of dried mud, a roof of interlaced palm leaves and the only entrance a low door . . . The smoke from the fire, burning dried cow-dung, escaped as best it could through the slits in the roof.' But these villages formed close-knit, stable and self-sufficient communities, ruled by a chief or a council of elders, who in some regions even organized a regular redistribution of land. In the village there would also be artisans – blacksmiths, woodworkers, sawyers, goldsmiths – plying the same craft from father to son for centuries, and paid in kind for their services with a portion of the village crop. Some of these villages included slaves in the service of the wealthier peasants, who were responsible for feeding, housing and clothing them. The community as a whole was responsible for the taxes or forced labour demanded by the State or by the nearest lord. Part of its crops and its efforts were thus earmarked for elsewhere, for the minority India of the distant Government towns, from which nothing came back. Taxes were the sole link the town maintained with its villages, which were unable to buy from it any of the goods it imported or manufactured. Its industries' products remained luxuries, reserved for a small circle of town-dwellers, or for export. But if the pressure from these privileged persons became intolerably heavy, the villagers could decamp, looking for somewhere else to settle and hoping for a better fate.

The ancient subsistence economy of the villages lasted a long time. Since it comprised both farmers and artisans, it had little need of the outside world, except for salt and iron, and so remained almost a closed system. Its social organization was based on the castes, keeping all the villagers in their place, from the brahmin (who was at once a teacher, a priest and an astrologer), to the elders, or to the wealthier peasants who belonged to the higher castes. At the bottom of the scale, the majority were untouchables, labouring on the land.

This whole system deteriorated more and more in the eighteenth and nineteenth centuries. To raise revenue, the British used the existing tax-collectors, but they gave them ownership of the villages – which they had never had before. Thus there came into being, starting in Bengal, a number of spurious landlords, the *zamindars*. Their task was to supply the British authorities with the due amount of tax; but to secure their own commission they required more from the peasants. Soon, they ceased to live on the spot, and employed agents to do their work. The unhappy peasantry of Bengal found itself saddled with an impressive panoply of middlemen and parasites.

In places where they had not appointed *zamindars*, the British themselves collected the taxes, which were payable in cash. Any peasant short of ready money now had to resort to a usurer. Such moneylenders began to flourish all over India. In the past, they had had to be wary of peasant resistance and anger: now, they had the law and the judges on their side. If a debt was not repaid, they would seize the peasant's livestock, and then his land. Poor peasant, poor *ryot*! Since the price of land continually rose, the moneylender was well placed to become a landowner; moreover, speculative price-rises attracted investors to buy land as a guaranteed source of revenue. The result was a growing number of large-scale land-owners, normally little concerned to improve their soil, and simply living on their profits. By the end of the nineteenth century, out of 100 million peasants perhaps a third were still smallholders, and the average size of their holdings was less than ten acres, the minimum needed for survival. In the process, nine out of ten of the councils of elders (which are being revived today) had ceased to exist.

The situation was further worsened by:
● the squeezing-out of the village artisans by competition from

British and even Indian industry, and their relegation to work on the land, where the pressure was already so great; and

● the dual policy systematically pursued by British capitalists, who regarded India as (a) a market for their industrial products (they were quick to destroy the very ancient Indian cotton industry, which had developed rapidly in the eighteenth century, at a time when Indian painted or printed textiles were becoming fashionable in Europe); and (b) a market on which to buy certain raw materials, such as jute from Bengal or cotton from the dark, rich *regur* soil near Bombay, to be shipped to Britain's cotton mills in Lancashire.

Raw materials earmarked for export were carried to the ports by railways. These had been built quite early on, and during the second half of the nineteenth century they revolutionized the interior of the country. Towns arose with no other purpose than to collect and dispatch merchandise. More and more, too, Indian peasants grew cash crops – products which were not intended to feed their families or their villages. Growing crops for industry overtook the growing of food, except in the grain-fields of the Punjab, which however exported its wheat. The result, with a growing population, was a series of catastrophic famines in the last thirty years of the nineteenth century, and a general lowering of food consumption, perceptible even in the imperfect statistics which are all we have.

The world economic crisis of 1929, and the collapse of raw material prices, led to a further concentration of property in the hands of landlords and moneylenders. The size of free peasants' holdings shrank even more, and their debts grew unreasonably large. Crippled by that burden, the peasants' position *vis-à-vis* their creditors was worse than that of former serfs *vis-à-vis* their masters. Economically, the *ryots* had less and less freedom, however great their theoretical freedom under the law.

The beginnings of modern industry appeared late in the day, around the 1920s, at the same time as the first protective tariffs. The growth of local industry at that time was helped by a number of factors: an abundance of cheap labour, the emergence of modern towns with a large proletariat, easy access to raw materials and finally the activities of capitalists.

These came from three main groups. There were the Parsis, descendants of disciples of Zoroaster who had fled Persia more than a thousand years ago; they lived chiefly in the region of Bombay. There were the Marwaris, who came from a high caste in the interior of Rajputana, and who had been shielded from British competition because their regions had been so backward. Finally, there were the Jains from Gujarat.

Three industrial cities predominated: Calcutta with (150 miles to the East) the metal-working industries of the Tata group (a family of Parsis) and the mass-production of jute; Bombay, centre of the cotton industry and of automobile assembly; and Ahmadabad, 500 kilometres to the North, purely a cotton centre. These and other industries – above all, the food industries – developed chaotically during the Second World War, especially after 1942, with shortages of food and textiles which led to such fantastic price rises on the black market that for a time, given the threat from Japan, there were fears that India might be totally undermined.

In 1944, the industrialists adopted the Bombay Plan. Semi-official and over-optimistic, this foresaw large-scale investments made possible by Britain's repayment of the debts she had run up in India during the Second World War. The plan encouraged agreements with British firms and businessmen, like the Birla-Nuffield arrangements for automobile production. Even today, long after Indian independence, British capital is still invested in the many businesses controlled by the banks in Cliver Street, Calcutta.

This industrial boom only intensified the drift from the land towards the towns. 'If you are ruined,' says a Tamil proverb, 'run to town.' There was employment there, in workshops, factories and domestic service (where money wages 'were little better than nothing'). Unexpected links were forged between certain castes in the Kathiawar Peninsula and the recruitment of cooks for well-to-do households in Bombay, or between the poor on the South-West coast of the Deccan and craftsmen making hand-rolled cigarettes in Bombay factories. All this added to the general upheavals in the Hindu population, increasing its social mobility.

So, even before independence, India already had bustling modern cities, with their sordid slum quarters, the *bustees* of Calcutta, the all too famous *chawls* of Bombay or the *cheris* of Madras, with mud walls like those of the villages.

Britain rethought her policy in India after the Indian Mutiny by the sepoys or native soldiers in 1857–8. This, indeed, was an opportunity to revise Britain's whole attitude and, on 1 September 1858, to end the rule of the East India Company, replacing it in London with a large and powerful ministry, the India Office, while in Calcutta a viceroy took the place of the Company's former Governor-General.

Had the British not been too hasty, for instance, in annexing princely territory in India? From now on, they determined to respect local autonomy; and in 1881, when they restored the independence of the sultanate of Mysore, which they had previously taken over, this was a symbol of the new approach. And if, in this motley Indian world, they were no longer to rule directly, the best course was carefully to maintain the country's existing divisions, and use them – especially along the great divide between Muslims and Hindus. First and foremost, these divisions must be maintained in the army. On this subject, in 1858, Lord Elphinstone used a significant metaphor. The safeguards for British power, he said, were those steamers whose safety was ensured by the division of the hull into water-tight compartments. 'I should like to ensure the safety of our Indian Empire by building our Indian Army on the same lines.' Hindus, Muslims and Himalayan Sikhs, that is, would henceforth be kept in separate compartments, and would never again serve in the same units.

These plans were soon overtaken by events. By the 1870s, a long economic crisis in the world was affecting India, causing famine, epidemics and peasant revolts. Well-meaning people thought that the regime should be liberalized, to bring some Hindus into the administration, and perhaps even the government. In 1885, with 'the Viceroy's blessing', the National Congress Party was formed. It became, as we might say now, the loudspeaker of nationalism – although at that time the nationalists were still only a very small but active minority.

Its adherents came – and came in growing numbers – from the busy middle class that was emerging in the towns and the universities. This was not the aristocratic or princely class, nor that of the big landlords, who were deeply attached to the traditional past, and whose social conservatism very well suited the masters of India. Instead, it was a real middle class, of diverse origins, pushed to the fore by changing conditions. It included capitalists like the Parsis, the Marwaris and the Jains, but also Ishmaelite Muslims or people whose castes had a political vocation, such as the Pandits of Kashmir, who were linked to the brahmins, and who had supplied a number of statesmen in the days of the Moguls (and continued to do with the family of Jawaharlal Nehru). Mahatma Gandhi likewise came of a family which for generations had produced ministers for the princes ruling in the Kathiawar Peninsula, in Gujarat.

Drawn by Western civilization, these men had enjoyed its benefits and seen both its advantages and its dangers. Gandhi's philosophy, for example, drew on the non-violent traditions of India, the vehement pacifism of Tolstoy and Jesus Christ's Sermon on the Mount. Members of this Indian intelligentsia sailed on troubled waters, dreaming of some religious synthesis whereby Hinduism might be purged. Consciously or not, many of them were inspired by some of India's innumerable heresies. One could cite ten or twenty names, beginning with Dayanand Sarasvati (1824–83), who founded a new Hindu sect, rejected both Christianity and Islam, but admitted that he was attracted by the West, and tried to find in the *Vedas* some elements of scientific modernity, including electricity and the steam-engine. The list might end with the names of Gandhi's master spirit, Gopal Krishna Gokhale (1866–1915) and Rabindranath Tagore (1861–1941), known the world over for his poems, for which in 1913 he received the Nobel Prize, and one of which, 'Jana Gana Mana', became the modern Indian national anthem.

A long period of unrest and propaganda, with much procedural wrangling, led at last to the independence and partition of India on 15 August 1947. With the demands of one side and the caution, backsliding and hypocrisy of the other, the negotiation was unedifying (but less so than any other decolonization process!). What was reasonable one day became unreasonable the next, and concessions were always made too late. Moreover, what satisfied the Muslims (the separation of Bengal into two provinces, that in the East being joined to Assam to form an ethnic whole in 1905) annoyed the Hindus; while the Muslims were annoyed, in their turn, when in 1911 the decision was postponed. For the nationalists, uniting Hindus and Muslims (grouped in the Muslim League in 1906) remained an insoluble problem.

Another major difficulty was to make contact with the masses. This was the extraordinary achievement of Mahatma Gandhi (1869–1948). After studying law in Bombay and London, Gandhi had practised in Natal from 1893 to 1914, defending Indian immigrants in South Africa. Returning to India in 1914, he quickly made an impression on the nationalists, dominated them, and mobilized their strength. His programme was 'to make religious use of political forces'. His title, Mahatma, meant 'Noble', 'Very Reverend'. The only force, he taught, with which one could constrain another's will was the force of truth, non-violence to all living creatures and purity. The religious emphasis in his work increased its effectiveness a hundredfold. Gandhi aroused the masses. This became clear with the first boycott (on 20 September 1920) of the 1919 Constitution which Britain had just conceded, and again in December 1921, when Gandhi called for a campaign of disobedience. When such powerful silent demonstrations were followed by serious disturbances and murders, Gandhi remained true to his doctrine and stopped the protest. His second campaign eight years later, on 26 January 1930, ended in a boycott of salt (sold by the Government), followed by agreements, a new and very long protest campaign (1932–4), and at length a new Constitution, the India Act of 1937.

Indian independence was therefore ripe before the outbreak of the Second World War, which precipitated it. On 8 August 1942, Congress adopted Gandhi's motion calling on the British to quit India. In 1942 and 1943, with the Japanese advancing in Burma and threatening Assam, the situation became very serious: stations and public buildings were destroyed.

When peace returned, tension increased. On 11 June 1947, the British Parliament at last accorded Indian independence. The ties were broken. But free India was internally divided: on 15 August, it split into two 'dominions' – the Indian union and Pakistan (the latter in two separate parts). The partition was imperfect: it left in India a minority of 44 million Muslims; while the political frontier in the East gave the jute-producing areas to Pakistan and the textile works along the Hooghly River to India. Refugees flowed in both directions, in appalling conditions, and there were innumerable killings. In vain, Gandhi tried to reach some agreement with Islam; but on 30 January 1948, a Hindu fanatic, believing that any agreement would be a betrayal of Hinduism, assassinated the Mahatma. Partition took place amid civil war and untold violence. The cost was 2 or 3 million dead.

It is often said that British policy was responsible for partition. Is that fair? The allegation lends too much importance to political gestures and transparently obvious tricks. Once again, India's past determined its present and took its revenge. That past was the real culprit.

So, as soon as it became independent, India split in two. In three, if one counts the independence and secession of Burma in 1947, and in four, if one adds the secession of East Pakistan as Bangladesh in 1971. Meanwhile on 4 February 1948, Ceylon too had become an independent dominion: with its own particular civilization it had always been a world apart and had never been attached to British India.

Will India be spared a Chinese-style revolution?

Since 1947, India has made considerable industrial progress, greater than in the preceding century and a half. In doing so, she adjusted to partition more successfully than Pakistan. She established order at home; she reached agreement with France, which gave up her Indian warehouses; she occupied and liquidated the States held by princes and maharajahs, and notably Hyderabad (September 1948); she seized Goa, Damao and Diu from the Portuguese in 1961. She established her rights in Kashmir, and resisted Chinese pressure along the uncertain Himalayan frontier. The brutality with which she occupied Goa certainly disappointed India's sincere friends throughout the world, in so far as she seemed to them one of the rare countries capable of political wisdom. Yet the prestige of Pandit Nehru survived the shock: while he lived, he remained the most eminent global spokesman for the Third World.

If one adds that India's parliamentary regime works reasonably well, as has been shown by elections to the central Lok Sabha and to the fourteen state assemblies, and that the country has been divided in a reasonable fashion into those fourteen linguistic States, it becomes clear that independent India has a number of valuable successes to its credit. But this is not the really original feature that India presents to the world and to her own teeming human universe. What is truly striking is her Government's patient effort, redoubled in the third and subsequent five-year plans, to lead her people out of their appalling difficulties. The Indian population in the early 1960s was already on the way to numbering 500 million; twenty years later it was nearly three-quarters of a billion. The Government's task was to assist their economic development without violence, without bombast, relying on nature, circumstances and people, and forcing the pace of events only where this was feasible and success seemed likely.

President Nehru explained his policy very well to a French journalist on 18 April 1962. 'We are not Socialist doctrinaires,' he said.

In the long term, we simply want to lead this country to prosperity; in the short term, we want to raise the standard of living and reduce social inequality. To that end, we are acting on the economy, but leaving plenty of room for private enterprise: part of heavy industry, all small and medium-sized industry, and the whole of agriculture, are outside the public sector. In the countryside, we are encouraging cooperatives, but we have no intention of imposing collective farming. Once again, we are not Socialist doctrinaires. We are going forward step by step, and trying to solve problems peacefully. Don't forget, for example, that while we dethroned the Maharajahs we left them their palaces, their immunities and their privileges, and we gave them a lifetime civil pension which was often very generous. You see: we always try to follow a democratic path.

The proper word would perhaps be *liberal*, with all its virtues, drawbacks and ambiguities. In any case, the problem is clearly stated: India adopted the methods and points of view of the 'free world'. It needed and wanted to bring about a revolution. Will it be able to do so without adopting the Chinese model?

Its task is to put an end to, and at least alleviate, India's evident and atrocious poverty. This, distressing but all too real, is the dominant problem, the starting-point from which we have to begin.

India, unlike so many other States, has the virtue of not concealing her wounds, either from herself or from others. She has always suffered from poverty. We know this from the very earliest witnesses, who remarked on apocalyptic famines in pre-Christian times. Today, poverty is still obvious to the naked eye. India's large cities – monstrous Calcutta, enormous Bombay, even the capital New Delhi outside its very attractive districts – offer pitiful spectacles of ragged clothing, diseased bodies, hovels for dwellings and mere scraps for food.

The most obvious index of India's poverty is her appalling

surplus of labour. In the days of the Great Mogul, so many children were sold into slavery by their parents that to buy them was an act of charity. In 1923, André Chevrillon noted:

The division of labour here is pushed to the nth degree. A coachman has to drive, a groom has to open the door, a peon has to shout warnings. The European has to put up with this fuss. It would be monstrous if he went on foot or carried a parcel. A British officer cannot move without dragging in his wake a procession of people and baggage. Last year, in London, a mere corporal remarked in my presence that in India he rang for his servant to have him pick up a handkerchief . . . Just as in Rome, where the patrician had his army of servants, clients and freedmen.

A picture from the past, some of whose details date. But also applicable today. What is one to make of those ordinary middle-class homes with ten or a dozen servants? Or of those miserable men, women and children by the river in Calcutta (in 1962), 'who squat in the filth, harassed by flies but too indifferent to brush them off or even stretch out a hand to beg from passers-by'? What is one to think, following the same witness, of those roadmenders' workshops that look like scenes out of hell: 'Naked men, women in saris and children in rags, spreading almost by hand the tar which is heated in enormous pots on wood fires'? If the workshops were modernized, the number of unemployed would immediately rise. At Bangalore, in the Deccan, an ultra-modern factory makes wagons, 'but human ants reappear at the end of the production line, where the painting is done by a multitude of workmen'.

These sad pictures are among the first to be included in the dossier of modern India: they come from an India that has always existed. A few figures summarize the situation: 438 million inhabitants in 1962; a very high death-rate of 25 to 30 per 1,000; a 'natural' birth-rate of some 45 per 1,000; hence an increase of about 20 per 1,000, i.e. 8 million more people every year. These figures are discouraging. They curb in advance almost any growth of income per head, even if the gross national product is increasing, as it clearly is. In 1962, income per head stood at 280 rupees a year, when the rupee was worth one French franc, so the daily income per head was less than 100 old francs or one new franc, i.e. approximately ten new pence. In the roadmending workshops, the wage was one rupee per day.

Can the growth of population be slowed down? Only by higher living standards – but that would mean that the problem was already solved. Propaganda for birth-control, publicly advocated, and sterilization (1,500,000 voluntary sterilizations) are not enough to stem this human tide. India is not as disciplined as Japan, where the same battle – although much more effective – is still not easy.

Besides, these are not the only problems.

There is no need to be an economist to understand what was proposed by the third five-year plan (1961–5). Like the previous plans, this concentrated on a number of tangible points: fertilizers for agriculture, transport, heavy industry, mechanical industry, etc. – everything that was fairly easy to change, and quickly, in the justified hope that the results would have wider repercussions. Intervention took every possible form; and the Government turned a deaf ear to the recommendations made in April 1959 by a group of experts from the Ford Foundation, who proposed that the whole thrust of the new plan then being prepared should be confined to agriculture. They proposed to raise India's grain production, in 1959 estimated at 73 million tons, to 100 million or even 110 million. Was it wiser, as other experts thought and the Government decided, not to give up the industrial effort and the investments required for it, in the belief that the food situation was not likely to become catastrophic by 1965? Food would certainly remain a very difficult problem; but India had survived other such ordeals.

Once priorities had been decided, the usual and almost invariable conditions were laid down. An important part of the national income was set aside for the necessary investments: 5 per cent for the first plan, 11 per cent for the second, 14 per cent for the third. These huge sums unavoidably worsened the budget deficit, all the more so since there had to be massive foreign purchases, usually on unfavourable terms. So the country was obliged to invoke foreign aid, some of it private and by no means free of charge, some of it in grants or soft loans. These brought into play once more the spectacular rivalry between the United States and the USSR. Each was to supply 5 per cent of the foreign aid envisaged in India's third five-year plan. The Soviet Union concentrated its funds on large-scale projects such as the Bhilai steel-works; the United States, which in the past had given twenty times as much as its rival, spread its aid over a number of areas. But the monotonous competition between the two superpowers need not detain us here. Nor need we dwell on the detail of the industrial investments – the race to build steel-works, or the establishment of a factory making cinematograph film, built by a French firm, and making India the second biggest producer of film in the world, after the United States.

What is interesting is that the economy is taking off. After Japan, and not far behind China, India is becoming one of Asia's great industrial powers. There is reason to believe that she enjoyed some advantage from having started early, by 1920 at the latest, and been ahead of the game. Today, at last, the economy looks as if it may win the race against soaring population figures. In 1963, it was impossible to believe that by 1970 the income per head might have doubled. By 1983 it had risen from 280 rupees to 2,400 rupees. This did not mean that India had reached the promised land: but she had started on her way.

The stony road ahead is littered with obstacles – political, social and cultural. The political difficulties included the moral dictatorship of Pandit Nehru and his family, which posed formidable succession problems. The pre-eminence of the Congress Party is not in itself an institutional system, and it makes difficult the interplay of fruitful, reasonable and constructive rivals for power. In the early 1960s, the reactionary right-wing accused the Communist and Communist-leaning left of eating beef – a disappointing polemic. In 1962, the Communist-inspired left won only 10 per cent of the votes, but in the local government of Kerala, before it was somewhat arbitrarily ousted, it showed rare qualities of probity and efficiency. The Socialists for their part accused Nehru, as they did his successors, of defending 'a corrupted regime'. But these opposition parties remained marginal, and Congress remained dominant.

As regards social problems, it is always easier to talk about a fair distribution of wealth than to impose it. On the crucial issue of land ownership, the many agrarian laws passed in various States have been ineffective in practice. Legally dispossessed, the big landowners have almost everywhere recovered their advantage over the small peasants. The latter are free, which is a great step forward; but they remain very poor and ill-equipped. Part of the arable soil still lies fallow. Even the large-scale irrigation projects favour the big landowners, who keep the water for themselves when it has to be paid for or is in great demand. The peasants enjoy little of these benefits. To make matters worse, the big landowners are conservative and reluctant to accept technological progress. There, indeed, is a 'corrupted regime' and a pre-revolutionary situation.

Finally, traditional civilization still holds the mass of Indians in its tight and manifold grip. For Hindus to step out of the caste system and join the social revolution of modern life is like making the necessary transition to a wholly different universe. Hinduism, in fact, is the major obstacle and the essential difficulty standing in the way of any serious move towards modernization. Its power can be measured by the incredible amount of offerings of food which an undernourished and near-starving population will in certain circumstances bring to the temples – as, for example, in 1962, when the conjunction of the stars was held to predict the imminent end of the world. The strings of wandering cows, taking their meagre fodder where they can, the flocks of crows stealing grain and the swarms of insects that are never attacked, even if they ruin the harvest – all these are concomitants of Hinduism. The cows are sacred, and all living beings must be respected.

The worst aspect of Hinduism is undoubtedly the caste system,

which kept the population cooped up in so many separate compartments. True, there is some social mobility; and in the long term
the system will no doubt disappear. But it persists. The
untouchables – the *harijans*, who number at least 50 million, and
whom Gandhi championed – have become as other people under
the law. The Indian constitution has abolished all legal distinction
between citizens. Furthermore, it is non-religious. But there
remains a vast distance between theory and practice. In this area,
change is very slow, and is confined almost entirely to the intellectual élite. Even there it remains hesitant: is it not significant that
many political battles are still as much a matter of caste differences
as of personal rivalry? However, a middle class is growing. Its
members seek their fortune by passing through one or other of
India's forty-six or more universities. Not all succeed: there is so-
called 'educated unemployment'. But most move on to become
officials in the administration, lawyers, doctors or politicians.

This many-faceted middle class is, at least in appearance, open
to all castes. Publicly, it models its dress and behaviour on the
British. Yet, for these very same people, family life is often a
refuge where they rediscover traditional dress and diet, and can
return to former ways. And modern life, in almost all its aspects,
represents a break with religious tradition. It is against tradition,
for example, to regard the public water supply as pure and not
polluted, because it has passed through so many 'impure' places. It
is against tradition to take cod-liver oil as prescribed by the doctor,
because fish is forbidden; to agree to inter-marriage, or to announce
a wedding in the press with a note saying 'caste immaterial'; or to
house engineers, managers and workpeople in the same building,
near some new factory, without regard for the taboos that are
broken when they are lodged together.

The fact that such cases occur shows that some progress has
been made in the reform of Hinduism, and that its formalism is on
the wane. Ever since the Buddha, indeed, the liveliest religious
thinkers in India have fought against its excesses. In 1800, Ram
Mohan Roy, the founder of a new sect known as the Brahmo

Samaj, tried to reform Hinduism in this way, and to move it towards monotheism. Other reformers followed, and others still will no doubt emerge.

For India is now conscious of the obstacle that her cultural tradition puts in her way. This awareness already existed at the time of Mahatma Gandhi, who was certainly responsible, more than anyone, for 'revealing' modern India, both by the enthusiasm and by the opposition he aroused. Gandhi in fact sought to harness all the spiritual traditions of India to the cause of progress as he saw it, and to enhance national pride. This was how, with unerring instinct, he awakened the Indian masses and formed a passionate popular movement. But, at the same time, the tradition that he sought to revive meant in a number of areas preventing India's adopting certain modern ways.

This was the basic conflict which in the end divided Gandhi from his Socialist fellow-militant, Pandit Nehru. Nehru himself summed it up: 'An abyss separates those whose psychology is turned towards the future from those who lean towards the past.' Gandhi's principles fatally distanced him from any kind of social revolution. For him, the revolution should take place in people's hearts. It was not a matter of changing the existing order of things, but of persuading people, whatever their wealth or influence, to devote themselves to the service of their fellow human beings and agree, in Gandhi's words,

to be filled with the art and beauty of abnegation and voluntary poverty ... to embrace those activities which are the basis of the nation ... by spinning and weaving with their own hands ... to banish from their hearts all caste prejudice, in all its forms, to campaign for total abstinence from intoxicating drinks and from drugs ... and, in general, to cultivate the purity of one's being. These are the means of serving which enable one to live at the level of the poor

– preferably in the traditional framework of village life.

In short, Nehru concluded, discussing Gandhi's views in his book *My Life and My Prisons*: 'For him, those who wished to serve the masses should not concern themselves so much with raising the standard of living as with lowering themselves, levelling themselves, so to speak, with the masses and mixing with them on an equal footing. That, for him, was true democracy.' Despite the admiration that Nehru and his friends felt for some aspects of this individual ethic and for Gandhi himself, they thought that to use it as a collective ideal was against the logical conceptions of 'every modern democrat, socialist, and even capitalist: it would mean returning to an outdated spirit of paternalism, which was unwittingly reactionary'. Above all, they thought, it would mean failing to face the break that India must make with certain aspects of her past if she wanted to emerge from under-development and mass poverty.

That India has in fact followed Nehru rather than Gandhi can be seen from the failure of Gandhi's disciple Vinoba Bhave, who in 1947, before the death of the *bapu* or 'father', founded the Bhoodan movement. Its aim was to solve the agonizing agrarian problem by persuading landowners to make voluntary gifts of land. These gifts would then be redistributed to the poor, either individually or collectively.

To understand the meaning of this idealistic movement, it has to be remembered that Vinoba Bhave, who came from a good family, and was highly cultivated and an excellent mathematician, had in 1916 burned all his diplomas, in the presence of his mother, to commit himself to the way of life of the 'renunciators' or Hindu ascetics. He had shared, prominently (i.e. often in prison), in all Gandhi's campaigns. When starting the Bhoodan movement, he had worked out that some 62 million acres of arable land would be needed to solve the peasant problem. Ten years later, he had secured only about 5 million. In quantitative terms, his failure was clear.

It was on foot, going from village to village, covering thousands of miles, barely eating, and every day spinning cotton as preached by Gandhi, that the saintly Vinoba Bhave had conducted his campaign. But what was possible in Gandhi's day, because of

Gandhi and because times had been different, had become anachronistic in modern India. Vinoba Bhave aroused some enthusiasm; but the boos that greeted him in some peasant villages in Gujarat were the sign of a new era, a new awareness. His failure, saddening though it might seem in an edifying storybook, perhaps marked the awakening of India in search of real, reasonable, modern solutions as against a mouldering *ancien régime*.

'Today,' Nehru concluded,

India's ancient culture has outlived itself. Silently, desperately, it is struggling against a new and all-powerful adversary, the civilization of the capitalist West. It will be defeated, because the West brings with it science; and science means bread for millions of hungry people. But the West also brings an antidote for the poisons of a civilization of cut-throat snatch-as-snatch-can; and that antidote is the principle of socialism, the idea of cooperation in the service of the community and for the good of all. Which is not so far away from the old brahmanic ideal of 'service'; but which also implies the 'brahmanization' (in a lay sense, of course) of all classes and all groups, and the abolition of class distinctions. And perhaps India, when it changes costume, as is inevitable, since the old one is in rags, will have the new one cut on this pattern, so that it fits both present conditions and old habits of mind. The principles which India will espouse must be in contact with its roots in the soil.

14. The Maritime Far East

==

At first sight, it seems arbitrary to group together Indo-China, Indonesia, the Philippines, Korea and Japan. But these places, distant as they are from each other, are all close, historically, to those two great human oceans, China and India, which have never ceased to wield very far-ranging influence. That closeness has been all the greater because of the sea-routes that have made for easy access. The seas of Eastern and South-East Asia – the Sea of Japan, the Yellow Sea, the East China Sea, the Banda Sea and the Sulu Sea, for example – are many of them small and shallow, epicontinental seas, hemmed in by the nearby land. Except in the neighbourhood of the Philippines and Japan, great ocean depths are only to be found to the East and the South, beyond the strings of volcanic islands that separate these narrow seas from the Indian and Pacific Oceans. The seas, in fact, are so many 'Mediterraneans', surrounded by land and dotted with islands: they are already on a human scale.

Another feature they share is that they are swept by periodic winds – the monsoons, which regularly reverse their direction at the beginning of summer and the beginning of winter. Everywhere, too, there are typhoons, sometimes of hurricane force. But these, though often tragic, do not last for ever. Normally, ships can sail peacefully, between islands or along the coasts, with a steady wind. Navigation here means island-hopping, sheltering from any sudden storms, and not losing sight of the shore, lined with mangroves. If the sea threatens to be too rough, the anchor is dropped to a seabed which is often very near the surface. Thus secured, the Arab dhow, the Chinese junk or the Dutch cargo ship could, as a hundred accounts testify, easily ride out heavy weather. When it passed, they went on.

Such were the advantages and possibilities of these familiar, domestic seas. They teemed with sailors who felt at home there, trading and privateering in a well-established routine. If necessary, they ventured further: some Malays sailed as far as Madagascar, while Polynesians in outrigger canoes went to Hawaii, Easter Island and New Zealand. Much more often, they stayed in home waters, whose ways they knew. Both the Japanese and the Chinese were cases in point. 'The Chinese,' declared Father de las Cortes in 1626, 'do not sail on the high seas.' Ocean navigation, however, took the Arabs to distant islands, followed later by the Portuguese, the Dutch and the British.

Busy traffic very soon humanized these inland seas, linking their coasts, their civilizations and their history. Each such entity kept its own permanent characteristics; but the sea performed miracles of culture-contact, encouraging interchange and leading to mutual resemblances.

Indo-China

Indo-China is not the best example of these maritime communities. It is a large part of South-East Asia, given its name by the Danish–French geographer Conrad Malte-Brun (1755–1826). A broad peninsula, divided by high mountains, it is also crossed by very broad valleys running roughly from North to South and looking a little like the spread fingers of a hand. To the South, it shrinks into the long, narrow Malay Peninsula; to the East and West, it is flanked by the sea. Even in its broader, Northern area it has been continually traversed since prehistoric times – so much so that all the races identified by prehistorians have left traces there: aboriginal Australians, Melanesians and Mongoloids from prehistoric China.

These races are the basis of the present population, the Melanesian type being found among the still primitive mountain people.

In historic times, four main movements of population have affected Indo-China. The first, coming from China, entered by force; the second, coming by sea from India, was peaceful. The other two both came by sea: the Islamic influx which reached and occupied the Malay Peninsula, and the European (French and British) invasion, powerfully reinforced in the nineteenth century. This submerged everything, until in recent times it was in turn submerged in the bitter and prolonged conflicts of decolonization.

The ancient civilization of Indo-China is flanked, and in large part explained, by the two vast areas of China and India.

Chinese civilization arrived by force in Tonkin and Annam (Northern and Central Vietnam) some ten centuries ago. This was a long-lasting colonial conquest, at once military, administrative and religious (Confucian, Taoist and Buddhist), carried out as a Southern extension of the occupation of South China, a major event in Chinese history. The native population was either driven back or dominated. Thus there came into being that lively culture of the Annamite people, which eventually spread further in the South of Indo-China.

The Hindu influence was that of merchants, who founded ports of call and warehouses out of which they traded, often in alliance with local chieftains. Some of the latter made their fortunes through these contacts: their technical and cultural advantages enabled them to spread their influence, impose themselves, and then set up kingdoms from which arose new, partly Hindu but very mixed civilizations. They included the kingdom of Chiampa on the coast of Central Vietnam; the kingdom of the Mons at the Western extremity of South-East Asia; and, in the Mekong Delta, the kingdom of Funan, later absorbed by Chel-La, which gave birth to the Khmer empire, the dominant power in South-East Asia from the ninth to the fourteenth century. The ruined city of Angkor attests to its magnificence.

Between the eleventh and the fourteenth century, invasions and conquests by Burmese and Thai ('free') peoples led to the emergence of more indigenous kingdoms, to the detriment of the Khmers and the Mons. These kingdoms eventually gave birth to the Burmese State of Lan-Xang, whose Eastern part survives as present-day Laos, and Siam (now Thailand, 'land of the free').

The Europeans, who arrived in the nineteenth century and left in the twentieth, only provisionally occupied these countries. Nevertheless, South-East Asia was deeply marked by this forceful colonial conquest, French in the East, British in the West, with between them the independent buffer state of Siam, whose status as such was recognized in 1896. The French in 1887 formed the Indo-Chinese Union out of Tonkin, Annam, Cochin-China, Cambodia and Laos. The British added Burma to their Indian Empire, and at the far end of the Malay Peninsula imposed their rule on the Malay States, making Singapore one of the biggest ports in the Far East.

The Second World War, which saw Japanese domination spread rapidly throughout South-East Asia, destroyed at one blow these short-lived colonial structures. The Malay States, Singapore and Burma secured their independence without a struggle, thanks to a wise British policy; but the Vietnamese fought a long battle with the French. The States of Eastern Indo-China did not become fully independent until the Treaty of Geneva, on 21 July 1954.

This left the former French Indo-China divided into four. The Geneva Treaty partitioned Annam at the 17th parallel, the Northern part, with Tonkin, forming the Democratic Republic of Vietnam, the Southern part, with Cochin-China, becoming the Republic of Vietnam. The independent kingdom of Laos had already been recognized by France on 19 July 1949, and that of Cambodia on 8 November 1949. Broadly speaking, Laos and Cambodia were neutral between the two blocs, the USA and the USSR. North Vietnam belonged to the Communist world and had ties with China, which weighed heavily upon it, with the Soviet Union, and with Czechoslovakia. South Vietnam came under the control of the United States.

At the start of this qualified independence, these States had to face the fearful problems that beset all less-developed countries: modernizing industry and agriculture, improving the balance of payments, keeping pace with – and, if possible, overtaking – the ever-pressing growth of the population. Would the Socialist methods of North Vietnam succeed better than the liberal measures taken elsewhere? It was impossible to say: politics and possible conflict prevented free choice and honest comparisons. There was nothing to be deduced, for example, from the fact that North Vietnam possessed armaments – old, traditional Russian armaments – or that Cambodia's assembly plants were exporting Citroën two-horsepower cars.

None of these young States faced a simple situation. North Vietnam, energetic as it was, was the only Communist experiment in South-East Asia; and while it gained certain advantages from its exceptional position, it was somewhat uneasy at the power of absorption enjoyed by its large and very near neighbour, China. South Vietnam profited from its alliance with the United States; but it had to put up with a war on its territory as a result: the maintenance of American-style semi-colonialism was opposed by part of the population, who preferred to ally with the Communist North. The end of the Vietnam War, of course, turned this alliance into the union of North and South under Communist rule.

Equilibrium in this area was and remains precarious, like the neutral status of Laos and Cambodia, now Kampuchea. The different interests involved are so numerous and so contradictory that no one could reasonably predict how present conflicts will turn out.

Beyond these immediate issues, the old cultural problems remain. Over-population in the plains still contrasts with the half-emptiness of the mountain regions. Two historical ages confront each other. The plains, growing rice, made possible the high density of population in the deltas of the Red River (the Hong), the Mekong, the Menam (the Chao Phraya) and the Irrawaddy. It was on this form of agriculture and this mass of people that the dominant civilizations were based. The Annamites, heirs to Chinese civilization, have always occupied the low-lying areas of the Red River Delta. In the seventeenth century, they destroyed the Hindu-influenced kingdom of Champa, and in the eighteenth they seized the Mekong Delta from the Cambodians. In historical terms, these were relatively recent triumphs.

To the East, the close-knit civilizations of the plains, in Cambodia, Siam and Burma, were strongly influenced by Hinduism, and Buddhism also maintained its hold on them. Higher up, however, in the mountains of all these countries, small, primitive, semi-independent peoples, with animist religions, grew crops in burned clearings. They still survive.

In the motley world of Indo-China, Christian missionaries had some notable successes, almost always outside Buddhist and Islamic territory (the main Islamic area being, as we have seen, the Malay Peninsula). After 1954, Christian peasants from North Vietnam staged a mass exodus of 300,000 people towards the South, where the Catholics were in power in Saigon. Not unnaturally, it was among the animists that Christian propaganda was most successful. Thus, in the Union of Burma, the conversion to Protestantism of a large number of the Karens enhanced their unity and strengthened them against the central power, essentially in the hands of Burmese Buddhists.

These details are not the dominant feature of South-East Asia's complex and uncertain future; but they shed light on it – as does the existence there still of British and French schools. South-East Asia remains a crossroads: it welcomes many influences, absorbing or rejecting them in different ways according to its own different ethnic and cultural composition.

Indonesia

Beyond the Malay Peninsula, 'Asia drowns in the Pacific'. Indonesia is its prolongation Eastwards: its thousands of islands form 'the biggest archipelago in the world'. It too has always been, and still is, a meeting-point of many colours. But this diversity has not robbed it of a certain unity, which has to be constantly safeguarded and often re-established, now as in the past.

The Indonesian archipelago has always been, as it were, the centre of a vast compass rose: it has constantly felt the shock of even very distant events. This was so as early as prehistoric times. In the first centuries of the Christian era, when seamen and merchants from India came to found colonies here, as they also did in Burma, Siam or Cambodia, they brought with them Hinduism and Buddhism, which flourished side-by-side, adapting to local insular 'cultures' and acting as a support to the new kingdoms.

The first of these new kingdoms was established in Sumatra; but the most important and powerful flourished in Java. Their influence, however, was more or less limited – as was that of the civilization they brought with them. Java had high mountains, huge virgin forests and a peasant population organized in villages, with very lively traditions which were sufficient unto themselves. As a result, Indo-Javanese civilization remained a thin veneer on the surface, whether represented by its script, derived from the pali script of India, by its poems, by its fables, based in Hindu models, or by its tombs and temples, such as make up the eighth-century architectural group that covers the Borobudur Hill – 'an image of the world according to the Buddhism of the Mahayana (the Great Vehicle)'.

Between the 'kings' of the *Kraton* fortresses there were continual wars, culminating in the emergence, at the end of the thirteenth century, of a 'universal' Hindu Empire, the Empire of the Majapahit. From Java, this ruled the other islands in a vast network of vassals and dependents, with the aid of a powerful and active fleet. It dominated Singapore, the 'city of lions', on its island off the Southern coast of the Malay Peninsula; in the East it reached New Guinea, and in the North the Philippines. In 1293, it disarmed a seaborne expedition sent against it by Mongol China.

But its greatness did not last. In 1420, the Muslims took Malacca;

and from 1450 onwards their victorious invasion finished off the Empire, or what remained of it. Political self-interest and holy war combined to demolish for good the huge structure of empire. When the Portuguese arrived at the beginning of the sixteenth century, nothing remained of it but ruins and memories. Only the island of Bali preserved, alongside its own traditions, the Brahman heritage of those ancient times.

The Portuguese occupied Malacca in 1511, and the Moluccas or Spice Islands (the source of cloves) in 1512. In 1521 they landed on the vast island of Sumatra. Their invasion was assisted by the political quarrels which divided the archipelago; but their occupation of the islands was a summary affair, with no great effort to put down roots. It left more or less untouched the traditional life of the archipelago, with all its comings and goings. These included the trade by Arab boats out of Achin, the Western tip of Sumatra, where they took on spices and gold dust bound for the Red Sea; and the regular trips by junks from Southern China which, from Marco Polo's time and before (indeed, from the seventh century as regards North-East Borneo), visited the Indonesian islands to bring knick-knacks, porcelain, silk, and their heavy copper and lead coins or *sapekes*, and to take in exchange rare woods, pepper, spices and the gold dust panned by the gold-washers of Borneo and Celebes.

The Portuguese invasion was the exploitation by force of ancient trading links which extended from Java to Macao, near Canton, and beyond as far as Japan. In the seventeenth century came a much more serious incursion, that of the Dutch. By 1605 they reached Amboina in the Moluccas; by 1607 they were in Celebes. In 1619 they founded Batavia and had subjugated Java, where they practised a policy of divide-and-rule by encouraging rivalry among the sultans of the island, medieval princes whose *Kratons* − (part-court, part-castle) − dominated the heights. By 1604, when they drove the Portuguese out of Malacca, the Dutch had become the rulers of the whole Indonesian archipelago.

From then on, they dominated the two great sea-routes: the

Malacca Straits between Sumatra and the Malay coast, on the way
to the West, to Siam and India; and the Strait of Sunda between
Java and Sumatra, the channel for the powerful sailing-ships which
came straight from the Cape of Good Hope without touching
India, and sailed back to Europe on the same route with their rich
cargoes from the East. Exploitation by one set of traders had been
replaced by another which, despite some early competition from
the British, culminated in the formation of the Dutch East India
Company. Founded in 1602, this remained for a long time the
flagship of Western capitalism – until its belated failure in 1798,
which was due to its own mistakes and muddles, but also to
exceptional political circumstances. For a brief time, the Dutch
East Indies were occupied by the British; but in 1816 they were
returned to Holland, and it once again settled there methodically
and comfortably – until the Japanese invasion on 28 February
1942.

   At that point, the model structure collapsed. After Japan's defeat
in 1945, Indonesian nationalists (who had both collaborated with
the wartime invaders and fought fiercely against them), proclaimed
Indonesia independent under President Ahmed Sukarno, on 17
August 1945, in the midst of wild popular enthusiasm. 'When a
month later, on 28 September, the allied Commander-in-Chief
General Christison landed at Batavia with British and Indian troops,
he found the walls of the city covered with anti-Dutch slogans.'

   The obstinate reaction of the Dutch Government, and its efforts
to re-establish the old order or at least save some of it, sparked off
a classical decolonization crisis similar to several in France's recent
history. While the 'colonialists' succeeded easily enough in the
sparsely populated islands such as Celebes and Borneo, where
Indonesia was more or less empty, they encountered fierce opposition in Sumatra, and still more in Java. Guerrilla warfare soon
immobilized the Dutch troops and nullified their victories around
the big towns. Their vast 'policing operation', begun on 21 July
1947, raised insurmountable difficulties. They had more success
with their blockade of the rebel regions in Java, which caused

unspeakable suffering. Intervention by India, Australia, the United States and the United Nations finally produced an imperfect agreement, on 17 February 1948; but this was followed by a second 'policing operation' as ineffective as the first. On 27 December 1949, in The Hague, the Queen of the Netherlands signed away her sovereignty over the former Dutch East Indies, save for the 'Dutch' part of New Guinea. At Batavia, renamed Jakarta, the red-and-white flag of Indonesia replaced the Dutch red, white and blue.

These details, which inadequately summarize a long and dramatic conflict, are essential for understanding Indonesia today. At heart, it has not yet emerged from its recent struggles: it is still reliving them; and hostility to The Netherlands is often used as an excuse for, and a counter-irritant to, its own difficulties. That hostility was a necessary unifying force for the new Republic. The tussle for West Irian (Netherlands New Guinea until 1 May 1963, when it became part of Indonesia) had no other *raison d'être*.

Had that last piece of Indonesia been arbitrarily kept by the country's former rulers? It was a primitive island: it possessed natural resources, but to exploit them was beyond the power of either Indonesia or The Netherlands. As for its inhabitants – the Papuans – they had nothing in common with either the Indonesians or the Dutch. But who cared about that?

Indonesian civilization is an extreme mixture of races, religions, standards of living, geographical features and cultures. All the islands, including even Java, harbour primitive peoples, often still living in stone-age conditions. They also include many different races. In Java, there are three Malay groups: the Sudanese, the Madurans and the Javanese themselves. In Sumatra, there are the Malays, the strange Minangkabaus, the Bataks and the Atchinese. And this is without counting the Chinese merchants in the towns. Detested but indispensable, they act as wholesalers, retailers, lenders and usurers; and although everyone regards them as parasites, no one can do without them. Since 1948, moreover, they have enjoyed the support of mighty Communist China.

All these peoples have their own languages or dialects. But they need a common language, a lingua franca, to link their closed worlds; and since the sixteenth century (and no doubt earlier) this has been Malayo-polynesian, or more familiarly Malay. It is the basis of the Indonesian language, Bahasa Indonesia, which was the official language of the nationalists even before it became that of the new Republic. Even so, it had to be adapted to new uses, notably in the scientific field. On one occasion, a commission on terminology adopted 37,795 new expressions in a single decree.

To all intents and purposes, in fact, it is a new language. Its role in Indonesia cannot really be compared with that of Hindi in India. There, Hindi is certainly a common language, but alongside English, which has remained very much alive. Dutch has not survived in the same way in Indonesia, for a number of reasons but essentially because the Dutch (with the exception of a few belated and inadequate efforts) did not develop modern technical education or the teaching of their own language. They wanted, claims one economist, 'to establish their superiority on the basis of the natives' ignorance. The use of Dutch would have narrowed the gap between the rulers and the ruled – and that had to be avoided at all costs.'

Indonesia's linguistic diversity is mirrored by cultural diversity, and even cultural confusion. In the archipelago, the great religions had curious adventures. They never triumphed by themselves: they coexisted with popular beliefs which beleaguered or overlaid them, and they sometimes merged with one of their major rivals.

Here, for instance, is the testimony of some villagers about twenty-five kilometres out of Jogjakarta, which briefly became the capital of Java when the Dutch reoccupied Batavia. They were talking with a traveller from Europe. ' "In Java we are all Muslims," declared Karjodikromo, a peasant, without the slightest hesitation. "Then why do you speak of your gods? Muslims believe in only one God." Karjodikromo seemed embarrassed, and his father came to his rescue. "It's difficult," he said calmly. "We can't neglect the other gods. They can help us or harm us. Our rice depends on

Devi Shri, the wife of Vishnu.'' [Devi was in fact held to be the wife of Shiva.] (Tibor Mende)

In the whole country, moreover, there was not a mosque to be seen. The Muslim villagers offered fruit and refreshments on the altars of Devi Shri; and, to drive off evil spirits, put up bamboo flutes in the fields through which the wind could whistle. Equally, they were urged to cut the rice stalks silently, with the *ani-ani*, 'the little blade that the reaper hides in his hand'. Silently and quickly, so that the good spirits may not fly away.

A similar picture could be painted of Bali, that wonderful island, where the heritage of the great Indo-Javanese Empire and its Hindu beliefs has been preserved – but for how long? Here, the dead were cremated to enable their souls to ascend to the light. Yet, at the same time, a whole series of animist beliefs and practices survived, linked with the still prevalent cult of ancestor-worship.

It is not easy to maintain the unity of these diverse peoples. Hostility to the Dutch was not a panacea. Unification is difficult when the problem is to modernize a primitive, poverty-stricken economy or at the very least to instil patience into a population mostly made up of over-worked peasants. The greatest help that Dutch colonization gave the new government was that it exploited the rural population so completely that only small landowners were allowed to keep their holdings. So the young Indonesian Republic faced no large estates to redistribute, and had no need to fear agrarian unrest. All the peasants were equally poor.

They were prisoners, for the most part, of a subsistence economy. Rice was their basic food and their most important food crop, far ahead of maize, taro or sago. Buffaloes were bred solely as draught or pack animals. Little or no meat was eaten, and only small amounts of fish. Barely anything went to market: a little rice, some cloth, a homemade toy – a few such things sold in town would make just enough money for small purchases, including cheap cigarettes, 'perfumed with cloves and shaped like small elongated cones'.

Industry remained in its infancy, apart from oil installations, rubber plantations and their associated plant, and coal and tin mines, both in Sumatra (or on the islands of Bangka and Beliton in the case of tin), which were run by Anglo-American companies before Dr Sukarno nationalized them. But whether European, Chinese or national, Indonesia's industrial activities are scarcely in a position to hasten its economic growth. At the same time, since the break with The Netherlands, there have been fewer outlets for the major export products – rubber, coffee, tobacco, copra and sugar – that the Dutch developed at the expense of traditional food crops.

Even so, 75 per cent of Indonesian exports are still made up of raw materials such as rubber, oil and tin.

Although independent, therefore, the country remains in a typically colonial economic situation, dangerously dependent on fluctuations in world markets. Thus, in 1951, the end of the Korean War and the halt in the rise of raw material prices had a catastrophic effect on Indonesia's budget.

With galloping inflation and a population increasing by about a million a year, the situation in the early 1960s was continuing to get worse. Java would have starved without massive imports of rice from abroad. To which should be added the lack of qualified managers, a top-heavy administration, endemic lack of security and an ill-organized army. It is hard not to agree with a member of Indonesia's political opposition that too much time had been spent on slogans, propaganda and spectacular campaigns like that for West Irian, and not enough on systematic plans.

Plans, in fact, had become an urgent necessity. The recovery of freedom and the euphoria that it caused were certainly unlikely to encourage a huge effort on the part of the population: but that effort had to be made. Indonesia itself had to be united. What kind of unity could exist among so many scattered islands without a national navy and air force?

Java's large population gives it a central place in Indonesia's 'solar system'. In 1815 it had 5 million inhabitants, in 1945, 50 million, in 1962, 60 million – two-thirds of Indonesia's total population: it also had three-quarters of her total resources. But its population density (400 per square kilometre) was close to the practicable limit. There was no question of taking further land from the forest, which had already been reduced to the minimum: to go further would 'enter the danger zone'. A possible safety-valve was the island of Sumatra, with only thirty inhabitants per square kilometre, and with abundant land and mineral resources. But the Sumatran soil, less rich than that of Java, would need special treatment such as ordinary peasants could not provide.

Javanese centralism angers many Indonesians, encouraging active separatism and a number of movements calling for effective federation. In the late 1950s and the early 1960s, separatist insurrections multiplied, with the Republic of the Moluccas at Amboina, Dar ul Islam in Western Sumatra, Pansunda in Java, Dr Hatte's movement in the Padang region of Sumatra, and the secession of the 'Colonels' in Celebes. The last of these Colonels, Colonel Simbolon, surrendered on 27 July 1961.

There were further difficulties. The Government felt obliged to curtail the freedom of the Communist, Socialist and liberal Muslim parties. 'Sukarnism' then became the only party, with a programme of 'guided democracy'.

With freedom curbed and opponents, though pardoned, pushed aside, the 'strong man' – 'Bang Karno' (Brother Sukarno) – felt he could and should pursue spectacular policies. Hence the great conference of neutral Third World countries held in Bandung in 1955. Hence also the efforts to secure West Irian. Appeasing nationalism gave some support to a Government which in all fields and for many years to come faced only difficult and ungrateful tasks. In 1967, in fact, President Sukarno was deposed and succeeded by T. N. J. Suharto.

The Philippines

The case of the Philippines, which is not on the official French curriculum, is no exception to the general rule in South-East Asia.

These islands too have been a remarkable crossroads and meeting-point for different peoples.

Human beings were present there from at least Neolithic times; and ironworking took place a number of centuries before the Christian era. From the fifth century AD onwards, the archipelago was caught up in the Indo-Malay civilization whose main source was Java: under the opulent Majapahit Empire, that civilization pervaded the islands. Chinese traders, too, soon made their presence felt, forming an élite of merchants and mariners who imposed their authority on the peasants, serfs bound to the soil.

In the fifteenth century, Islam made its appearance on the large island of Mindanao. In the sixteenth, the archipelago was discovered by the Spaniards under Ferdinand Magellan, who died there in 1521: in 1565 they settled on Luzon, the other large island, in the North. With them, Christianity resumed its traditional battle with the infidels, the *Moros*, this time in the Far East.

Often in revolt, and in any case ill-governed by the authorities in Manila, the islands remained under Spanish rule until 1898, when an internal rebellion broke out and the United States fleet intervened. The upshot was not immediate independence, because at the end of the Spanish-American War, when the Treaty of Paris was signed on 10 December 1898, the Philippines were placed under United States tutelage, to the great indignation of the local nationalists. To calm his bad conscience, the US President William McKinley made it his task 'to teach and civilize the Filipinos as people for whom Christ died on the cross'.

Not until 1946 did the islands become independent, at least in theory.

By the early 1960s, after a fairly turbulent past, they had a very large population of 25 million inhabitants, increasing annually by 700,000, on some 300,000 square kilometres or 116,000 square miles – just over half the area of France. It was mixed population: 95 per cent of it Malay, but blended with other elements; 400,000-500,000 primitive peoples difficult to classify; 200,000 immigrant Chinese; and 70,000 Negritos.

There were then some 20 million Catholics – the only such large and close-knit Christian group in the Far East. The next biggest Christian grouping comprised 2 million Catholic dissidents or Aglypayans, so called after the founder of their sect, a former priest named Aglypya, who helped organize the 1898 rebellion; then came 500,000 Protestants. Muslims numbered some 2 million, and there were 500,000 pagans. Since 1898, English has largely replaced Spanish in the Philippines, except in a few old families; while Tagal, a Malay dialect, has come back into its own. Finally, a large number of other dialects are spoken. At least half the population, in the early 1960s, remained illiterate.

The country is poor, if not destitute, and essentially rural; and large estates continue to grow at the expense of the small peasant. What one American observer has called a 'parasito-feudal' society hinders reform and tends to thwart foreign aid. Only in Manila is there a money economy: the rest of the country relies on barter. Peasant poverty accounts for the huge Communist revolt of the *buks*, which was welcome when Japan was dominant in the Second World War, but savagely repressed by the Philippine authorities after the end of the war and the occupation. But fire continued to smoulder under the ashes: the Chinese example, and that of Fidel Castro in Cuba, still haunted people's imaginations. Even with American aid (and supervision), the country's progress was infinitely slow – so much so that the growth of the population absorbed any improvement in advance.

Korea

Between 1950 and 1953, Korea played a dramatic role, of which it was and remains the victim. The Korean War of those years was essentially a conflict between the world's major powers, an armed struggle between East and West.

During the Second World War, at Yalta in February 1945, and after it in December of the same year, the independence of Korea seemed to be taken for granted. The country had been liberated in the North by Soviet troops and in the South by American forces brought in from Japan. Their two occupation zones were separated only by the conventional dividing-line of the 38th parallel. But in spite of intervention by the United Nations, this line continued to divide Korea. In the South, an independent Republic of Korea was established on 15 August 1948; in the North, a Democratic or People's Republic on Communist lines. In 1950, Communist troops from North Korea invaded the South. There followed an armed riposte by the United States and its allies. On the North Korean side, Chinese volunteers intervened to redress the balance. In July 1953, an armistice re-established the dividing-line along the 38th parallel. But this arbitrary division of the country has not made life easier for either the North or the South.

Korea has been the victim of its peculiar strategic position, surrounded by the Japanese archipelago, Manchuria, Siberia and China. It is a prime example of the dangers that threaten small States in the neighbourhood of large ones, which think themselves justified in doing anything, in the present as in the past.

A huge peninsula of 220,000 square kilometres (85,000 square miles) stretching roughly from North to South, Korea is divided from Manchuria only by the narrow valleys of the Yalu and Tumen Rivers, which run parallel to the tall White Mountains – the barrier that maintains and perhaps originally established Korean independence. From the 43rd to the 34th parallel, the country is a stretch of land some 800 to 900 kilometres (500 to 560 miles) long, at a rough glance not unlike the Italian peninsula.

Like Italy, Korea has the misfortune to be a natural highway. China regards it as a gateway, and thinks that it must be watched over like Turkestan or North Vietnam. Japan feels at sea if it cannot by fair means or foul secure access to this peninsula to which geography has, as it were, moored its islands – on slightly too long a warp. So if ever Japan feels especially strong or especially threatened, Korea suffers in consequence. It did so more than once between Hideyoshi's abortive attempts to seize the peninsula, from

1592 to 1598, and the successful Japanese occupation of Korea from 1910 to 1945.

To cap it all, Korea was also 'the Soviet outlet when Vladivostok is blocked by ice'. The Sea of Japan freezes as far South as the 38th parallel; and as early as the beginning of the twentieth century Tsarist Russia had an interest in this key route. In the past, when the Japanese threatened the King–Emperor of Korea, he took refuge in the Russian Embassy.

A poor country, cold despite the presence of rice-fields and bamboo at least as far North as Seoul, and covered in the North with vast conifer forests, Korea has busy coasts and extensive plains only towards the West and the South. The plains supply none too adequate food for a large population of 31 million (more than 140 people per square kilometre). The Southern part of the peninsula stretches a long way seawards and is prolonged by a series of islands. The best known of them is Tsushima, in the middle of the Korea Strait. The distance between Korea and Japan is little more than 100 kilometres as the crow flies; that between Korea and the mouth of the Yangtze-Kiang is 500 kilometres.

So Korea is much affected by the sea: it is not only a nation of peasants living off the land, the forests and the mines, but also a nation of fishermen, sailors and merchants. Very early in its history it organized fruitful contacts between China and Japan; and from the Middle Ages onwards it served in particular as a link between Southern China, in touch with Arab and Persian trade, and the regions in the North. As a highway and a crossroads, it was a country of traders and emigrants.

Korea is almost an island, deliberately reclusive but also, willy-nilly, open to the outside world, by which it has been culturally enriched.

The remote history of the Three Kingdoms (from the first century BC to the seventh century AD) is that of China's cultural conquest in Korea. These three kingdoms appeared one after another in less than fifty years: that of Silla in 57 BC, that of Kokuryô in 37 BC, and the precarious kingdom of Paekche, backed by Japan, in 18 BC. They all belonged, therefore, to roughly the same epoch, but Chinese civilization came to them in turn. Buddhism was first established in Kokuryô, then in Paekche in AD 384, and finally in Silla in 527.

Silla, the most primitive of the three, bested the other two and from AD 668 to 935 held all of Korea in its grip. Thus enlarged, the kingdom enjoyed great and prosperous trade so long as the T'ang Empire continued to rule China (618–907): it lived in that reflected splendour.

After the breakdown of Silla's extended authority, Korean unity was restored by a new Unitary State, Koryô (913–1392), from which the country derived its name. Its civilization flourished, aided by the development of printing. This was a gift from China, which had invented it in the ninth century: but it was the Koreans who in 1234 invented metal type. Buddhism spread among both the educated class and the mass of the people, in the simplified form of Segn (in Chinese *Tch'an*, in Japanese *Zen*). At the same time, and more firmly, Confucianism took root and prospered. Cast-iron sculptures appeared, then dry-lacquer statues and dazzling ceramics 'in which can be detected the taste of the traditional Korean goldsmiths'.

This efflorescence was undoubtedly linked to general progress throughout the Far East. But Korea had the good fortune to be shielded from the onslaughts of the Barbarians who dominated China and who for a long time did no more than touch upon the peninsula. In the end, however, Mongol China, which had tried to burst open all the gates of Middle Kingdom and had failed against Japan, succeeded in Korea, dominating the country for more than a century, from 1259 to 1368.

When Korea recovered its independence, it came under the rule of its last dynasty, that of the Yi, which remained in power until the Japanese occupation in 1910. With the exception of some troubled years, as for instance between 1592 and 1635, when Korea was caught between Ming China and aggression from Japan, the Yi dynasty was a fruitful period of peace and independence.

The main feature of those centuries, without a doubt, was the emergence of a middle class, and the consequent rise of a civilization which drew part of its inspiration from the inexhaustible imagination of ordinary people. A change in handwriting helped this assimilation of popular culture. 'Until then, Chinese handwriting had enabled only lettered people to think and write in the spoken language. Novels previously written in Chinese now began to be written in Korean, and a whole new class of society acquired access to culture. In the eighteenth century, this enrichment resulted in an effervescence comparable to the Enlightenment in Europe' (Vadime Elisseeff).

At the summit of Korean society, however, there still remained an aristocratic, sophisticated civilization, characterized by the success of neo-Confucianism, with a rationalistic and stoic bent. It was then that there took root those family cults and that ethic on which neo-Confucianism is based. Even today, despite all their troubles, Koreans are still 'its most faithful representatives'.

Nothing can be said with confidence about the situation today. A country which nature has designed for unity, and which history has solidly united for centuries past, has been split apart by current events, turning it into two countries, eyeing each other like rivals from the same womb. The old capital of Han-Yang, commonly known as Seoul (i.e. 'the capital'), which belongs to South Korea, no longer commands the Seoul–Gen-san road. Imagine Italy cut in two and Rome deprived of the road to Ancona. The North has industry, steel, iron and electricity. The South, in the early 1960s, had only rice, large estates and the open sea.

At that time, they looked like two immobile puppets, abandoned because since 1953 no one has any longer worked or even held their strings.

15. Japan

Japan lies at the far extremity of the human world. Its Northern island, Hokkaidō (Yezo), lies in the remote, cold latitudes of the Sea of Okhost. To the East, where its best ports are found, it faces the vast and wondrous emptiness of the Pacific. To the West and South, less forbidding seas, often thick with mist, narrow a little between Korea and the Southern island of Kyushu.

As an archipelago, Japan has often been likened to the British Isles. They, however, are much closer to the nearby continent. Japan is more isolated, insular and alone. To break out of its solitude, it has had to make frequent and conscious efforts. If not, it would be naturally inward-looking. Yet a Japanese historian has pointed out that 'Everything that seems essentially Japanese in our civilization is actually derived from abroad'.

As early as the sixth century, in fact, there was what might be called 'a Chinese Japan'; and since 1868 there has been a highly successful 'Western Japan'. Nevertheless, both these key influences have merged into a 'Japanese' Japan whose insular origin is clear beyond all doubt. In this country of miniature gardens, tea ceremonies and flowering cherries, even the Buddhist religion, brought in through China, has been remodelled to suit the Japanese. And this Japanese version of Buddhism is even further removed from the original than the Chinese variant was and is.

Although apparently so malleable, Japan has turned its many borrowings into a very particular civilization of its own. It remains faithful to its old traditions: they coexist with the far-reaching

Westernization which it began to accept almost a century ago, without reservations, and indeed eagerly, as a key to greater power. This strange duality explains the remark made by a journalist in 1961: 'What is the most extraordinary thing about Japan? The Japanese.'

Japan before Chinese influence

From its earliest origins in the fifth millennium BC until the sixth century AD, when Chinese civilization made its first notable impact on the country, Japan was in the grip of a primitive but vigorous culture which developed only slowly. This early Japan is so little known that specialists freely declare there to have been no Japanese history before the arrival of Buddhism in AD 552. In fact, that distant past seems to have foreshadowed what happened later: under the impact of invasions and foreign innovations, Japan made and remade itself on lines copied from abroad.

From the fifth millennium BC until the beginning of the Christian era, little of Japan can be discerned except one favoured area, the central plain between what is now Kyôto and, to the South-East, Yamoto. Ancient documents call this region Kinki. It forms the heartland of the great island of Hondo, not far from Japan's narrow and beautiful Mediterranean, the Seto Naikai or Island Sea which links it with the Southern islands of Shikoku and Kyushu.

This central area was the scene of three great changes, one after another.

● It is almost certain that the first inhabitants of the archipelago were the primitive Aïnos, whose traces are still to be found in the Ryukyu Islands, but who today are confined to Hokkaidō and Sakhalin. The first culture that archaeologists have discovered includes elements from Korea, Manchuria, and from the far-off Lake Baïkal in Siberia; and prominent among them are primitive ceramics decorated with rope patterns impressed

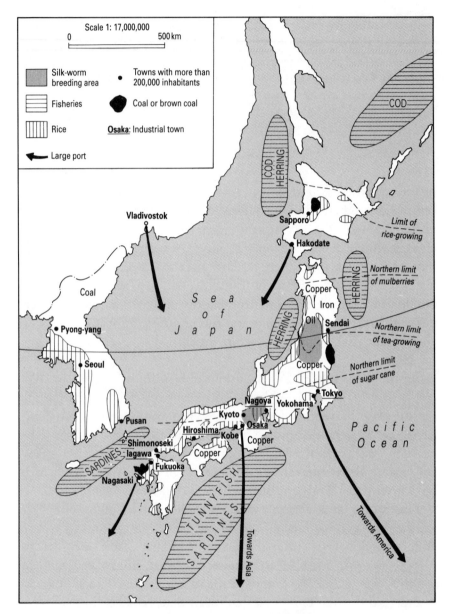

13. Japan, land of the sun and the sea

Japan is China's orient. That is the origin of its name, 'the land of the rising sun' – in Chinese 'Je-pen'.

on the clay when still wet − hence the name given to the culture, Jômon (meaning 'rope pattern'). From this mixed heritage one can deduce that people from the continent reached Japan very early on, and that at that time there began the struggle which so long pitted the Japanese against the Aïnos.

● In about the third and second centuries BC, a new invasion seems to have taken place, coming from China (especially South China) and distant Indonesia. A variety of new objects date from this epoch: the potter's wheel, bronze and bronze mirrors, bells, iron, Han Chinese coins and finally rice and the Southern type of house, open and well-aired. This is the so-called 'Yayoi Street' civilization, named after the Tokyo street in which such characteristic finds have been excavated. Among the innovations discovered, rice − replacing millet − was a revolution in itself. The idea of the King as a living god, which pervades the whole of Japanese history, may have been imported at the time by Proto-Malays coming from the South; but there can be no certainty either way.

● The second and third centuries AD were marked by the building of a number of nobles' tombs, which have been preserved to the present day. At this time, a series of clans emerged, with knightly leaders, more or less free peasants and artisans and an already large mass of serfs. The leaders claimed that they were the children of local gods. Under Korean influence, the artisans' guilds adopted the title *be* (meaning group or section), preceded by the name of their trade. The scribes became known as *fuma-be*; the weavers, *ori-be*; the saddlers, *kuratsukuri-be*; and the story-tellers, *katari-be*, who handed on the legends of heroic deeds.

There was already by now a political and religious system, whose primitive beliefs deified the various forces of nature. Profoundly conservative, Japan never abandoned this religion, which long afterwards, in the nineteenth century, came to be called Shinto (the way of the Gods). The West often calls it shintoism.

It was at this time, setting its face against the Aïnos' countries, and beginning in the Yamoto region, that Japan made its first attempt to form an Empire. The Empire traced its origins to the legendary imperial Japanese dynasty, born of the Sun-God Amaterasu: this tenacious religious tradition was still being celebrated in Shinto temples when Japan was defeated in 1945. Under the pressure of the US occupiers, the Emperor of Japan finally renounced his claim to divine descent.

The Empire took time to establish. In the eighth century, when the first Japanese chronicles were written, the country was still not completely united. It was a very slow process to link with the imperial dynasty the various regional clans (*uji*), each with its leader, its land, its peasants and its artisans – like the imperial dynasty itself. It was all the more difficult in that the clan leaders were often of foreign origin (Korean or Chinese). But the process of organization was made easier by the need to join forces against the Aïnos, the Barbarians 'from beyond the Eastern barrier'.

This system, royal and vigorously feudal, became fully formed in the sixth century, when the Koreans introduced into Japan Chinese writing, Confucianism and Buddhism. The influence of Confucian ideas was evident in the ordinances issued in 604 by Prince Shotoku, who proclaimed the rights of undivided central authority: 'The country does not have two rulers; the people do not have two masters.'

This was the beginning of the Japan known to history, with its hierarchy, its scribes, its chronicles and its embassies to the Emperors of China, the first being accredited in 607. A court aristocracy, the *kuge*, formed around the prince, the distributor of lands and 'benefices' (*shoen*), which everyone tried to transform into what the West would call 'fiefs'.

This imperial Japan soon developed under a new influence – the growing and finally all-powerful ascendancy of Chinese civilization. China even baptized the archipelago, calling it 'the land of the rising sun', in Chinese *Je-pen* (origin of our 'Japan'), and in Japanese *Nippon* (the Japanese pronunciation of the same ideograms).

Japan learns from Chinese civilization

For centuries, Chinese civilization dominated Japan. It flourished there in unexpected ways. Sometimes, what it brought was so altered as to become unrecognizable – as in the case of Buddhism, which in its Zen form became by a singular turn of fate, from the twelfth century onwards, the doctrine of the 'bloodthirsty samurai'. In other areas, Japan preserved its borrowings from China in archaic forms long forgotten by China itself. Such was the case with ancient Chinese music, lost in China but still played in Japan. In every instance, however, Chinese civilization was modified under the influence of a people, a society and a set of traditions radically different from those of China. This was all the more so in that Chinese ways often reached Japan through Korea, which did not always faithfully copy the original model.

The first Sino-Japanese civilization flourished in the golden age of ancient Japan. During this long transplanting process, Japan refused nothing from China: the classics, calligraphy, painting, architecture, institutions and law (that of the T'ang dynasty).

So Japan, like China, was divided into provinces – although far smaller than China's vast domains. When the capital, Nara ('the capital' in Korean), was built in 710, it was laid out on the Chinese model, copying the town of Lo Yang in Korea, with a chequerboard pattern and the Imperial palace at its Northern end. In 994, when the capital was transferred to Heïankyo ('capital of peace') or Kyôto ('the capital' in Japanese), it was again built on this same plan. From then on, incidentally, it ceased to move from place to place as it had in the past, when every emperor had built his own. By the time Nara was built, the court and its offices had become too sizeable to be transferred elsewhere so frequently, shifting anew with every reign. Once it had moved to Kyôto, the capital stayed there for centuries.

Chinese influence was everywhere, and the scribes' chronicles, which recounted the history of these times, were written in mandarin style and in Chinese ideograms, although in the Japanese language. Still, Japan's many borrowings from China should not mislead us: the court at Kyôto, which soaked up Chinese culture, was only the small centre of a much larger country; and the spread of that culture in the rest of Japan was patchy and slow. Kyôto was bathed in bright light: around it there were still many shadows.

On its narrow stage, however, the late tenth to the early twelfth century saw many splendours, linked it would seem with an economic boom. When this early prosperity faded, Kyôto's cultural golden age faded too, and sombre centuries followed.

What survives from that golden age includes the brilliant, precious, poetic literature of the *monogatari*, part novels, part fairy stories: one, entitled *Ochikubo monogatari*, or *The Cellar Story*, is very like *Cinderella*. More striking still were the *nikki*, poetic diaries which the ladies of the court wrote in Japanese, while the men wrote in Chinese. This very lively feminine literature re-creates for us the festivities of the court – concerts, dances, poetry contests, imperial excursions into the surrounding countryside, 'pleasures ruled by strict etiquette which made life in the palace a perpetual display, as well-drilled as a ballet'. It also reveals, unsurprisingly, a series of political and amorous intrigues, with 'the inevitable promiscuity which occurs in these insufficiently segregated quarters'.

It seems to have been an idle, futile world, 'corrupted by literature'. A lady of the court whom we know only by her nickname of Sei-Shōnagon, and who lived around the year 1000, left occasional writings which are sometimes merciless and always amusing. Their tone can be gathered from the distinction Shōnagon makes between agreeable and disagreeable things: the latter, she says, are of course more numerous than the former. They include 'a hair on one's writing-desk or a grain of sand in the ink-rod, which grates when rubbed; an insignificant person who talks a lot and laughs loudly; or, just when one wants to listen to something, a baby crying; a dog which starts to bark when it sees a man who is coming to meet one secretly at night; a man whom one has hidden, more or less, and who begins to snore. Or again, someone coming to see one in secret, puts on a tall, conspicuous hat, then when the time comes to leave, takes every precaution not to be seen, but bumps into something which falls with a loud crash' (based on R. Sieffert).

While the privileged classes lived and played in these ways, Buddhism slowly pervaded Japan in a new and democratic form. A freshly inspired clergy made contact with the 'middle classes' – artisans and small landowners. A highly simplified form of worship devoted itself exclusively to the saviour Buddha, Buddha Amida, who guaranteed to believers their access to the Heaven of the West. Rather as in China, knowledge of the ideas and beliefs of true Buddhism soon became confined to a few rare theologians and members of the élite, while popular Buddhism took everything on board, including the old beliefs of Shinto: so much so that the two religions were virtually fused into one. This was *Shingon*, in which the local gods became particular and temporary manifestations of the Buddhist gods.

Shinto sanctuaries came under the control of this new sect, known also as Dualist Shintoism. With the worship of Amida, a new Buddhist iconography arose. The magnificent 'rolls' that date from this period also show the Japanese landscape, and picture the activities of various social classes in scenes which are often full of humour.

At the same time, writing became more widespread, mainly using a simplified alphabet of only forty-seven syllables.

From the twelfth century onwards, this imperial system collapsed. It had long shown signs of weakness. While it had copied the institutions of the brilliant T'ang dynasty in China, it had not managed to establish a corps of educated civil servants which would have enabled it to break the power and ambition of the old aristocracy. Soon, the Empire gave way to the Shoguns, who ruled Japan from 1191 to 1863 – the seemingly interminable counterpart of the Middle Ages in Europe.

From the end of the eighth century until 1186 – almost four centuries – feudal clans threatened the imperial authorities. The Emperors still reigned, but they barely ruled. They were the prisoners and playthings of the all-powerful Fujiwara family, which controlled the key posts and supplied the Emperor with wives and concubines selected exclusively from among Fujiwara relatives. The family even deposed Emperors and chose their successors. As one historian has said, 'The power of the Mikado was an empty box whose key the Fujiwara jealously kept to themselves.'

The end of the Fujiwara's long reign ushered in the interminable period known as the Shogunate. This unexpected turn of events more or less institutionalized, in the person of the Shogun, the Emperor's domination by the seignorial clans, huge families that were often descended from the Emperors' numerous children, forming a kind of privileged nobility. Their reign, the Shogunate, saw different clans jockeying for power and replacing each other, but within a framework of underlying agreement. If nothing else, they were united in seeking to dominate the rest of the population. Of its castes – nobles, peasants, artisans and merchants – only the nobles were left in peace. At the bottom of the scale, the very poorest – notably the leather-workers – were untouchables, although far fewer than in India.

With the economy less prosperous, the Shogunate represented a feudal and military reaction in leaner times. It was marked also by a belligerent aristocracy. This, far away from the court, carved out for itself very extensive domains in newly colonized and still rebellious areas in the North and East of Hondo, 'beyond the barrier', where they practised large-scale horse-breeding. As against Kyôto, with its effeminate, and much hated upstart courtiers, the new regime put itself forward as an egalitarian government of soldiers, the *bakofu* or 'bivouac government', headed by a general or Shogun. It has been compared to the rule of the Mayors of the Palace in the later, decadent days of the Merovingian kings in Europe. There was, however, one difference: in Japan, the ineffectual titular ruler was never deposed. The Mikado continued to reign, but not to rule, alongside the Shogun whose investiture he performed by virtue of his divine authority, as in Europe was done for the Emperor by the Pope.

The first shoguns established themselves near the end of the Tokaido (the road from Kyôto, to Yedo, now Tokyo) at Kamakura, which became in effect the capital of Japan. It remained there until 1332; then it was moved back to a district of Kyôto, Muromachi, from 1393 to 1576. In 1598 it was finally settled in Yedo, until then a fishing port, where it stayed until 1868. Historians commonly refer to the Kamakura, Muromachi and Yedo periods, which together virtually extend throughout the long centuries of the Shogunate (1192–1868).

In all these periods, the dominant figures were the warriors, the knights, the *bushi*. As the dominant caste, they easily imposed their views, their tastes and their brutality, as well as – at the beginning especially – a certain simplicity in government, as in dress and domestic life. The *suikan* and the *hitatara*, rather plain clothes, replaced the swollen and cumbrous garments, the *noshi* or the *sokutai*, which were formally required by ancient etiquette. Hunting, jousting and horse-racing, too, replaced the stuffy pleasures of the past.

The habitual violence of the time was tamed somewhat when the Shoguns settled in Kyôto, from 1393 to 1576. The ancient city then recovered its rights and its role, with the result that the classical golden age was not wholly tarnished in the age of the knights and the soldiers.

The last years of the sixteenth century and the first years of the seventeenth marked a violent break in the midst of the Shogunate's lengthy rule. For more than two centuries, in fact, the Tokugawa revolution isolated Japan from the rest of the world, and tightened the grip of feudal habits and institutions.

In the late sixteenth century, a son of peasant stock named Hideyoshi established a dictatorship in the archipelago. Although he did not take the title of Shogun, he restored order and undertook a long and perhaps ill-justified war against Korea

(1592–8) which ended only with his death. Soon afterwards, the
Tokugawa clan obtained supremacy under the patient and skilful
Hideyori or Iyeyasu. Made Shogun by the emperor, he decided to
establish himself at Yedo, in the sensible belief that it was from that
turbulent region, and not from Kyôto, that Japan could and should
be governed. By abdicating in favour of his son, Hideyori succeeded in making the Shogunate hereditary in his family, which
thus 'reigned' until 1868.

In 1639, the Yedo government took the fateful decision to close
Japan to foreigners. From then on, only Chinese and Dutch ships
with special permits were allowed in; and the Dutch were permitted to bring only munitions, arms, spectacles and tobacco. For the
rest, the archipelago could and did live off its own resources. The
ban covered Japanese as well as other vessels: it had even begun
with them, in 1633. It had lasting results. Can it be explained?

It would appear that the rulers of Japan had become afraid of
Westerners. The first arrivals, the Portuguese, had reached
Kyūshū in 1534. Their cannons, harquebuses and enormous
ships impressed the islanders; so, still more, did the numerous
conversions to Christianity which the newcomers very quickly
secured. Might this religion not encourage revolt on the part of
the nobles and peasants, as it rather did in 1638?

At the same time, a very deep and widespread economic recession was starting, led by China but also affecting distant India.
Was Japan feeling the pinch, needing to protect itself and in
particular to halt the outflow of precious metals? Since the heroic
days of Hideyoshi, Japan's aggression against Korea and China,
whose ships it subjected to countless piratical raids, seemed to
show that the country was more and more fending for itself. The
brilliance of Ming China touched it not at all. Finally, its rulers
were anxious to immobilize an unstable society and a peasantry
too eager for freedom, though often reduced to despair. The self-
imposed blockade thus 'froze' Japan's institutions until the arrival
of Admiral Perry's 'black ships' in 1853.

Until then, Japan lived on its own, preserving its clans and its archaic aristocracy, to which essential class everything was subordinate – as witness the sustained success of *dhyâna* or *Zen*, that strange variant of Buddhism.

Yet this isolationist Japan, triple-locked as it were, was perhaps less unfortunate and deprived than might at first be thought. It was obliged to exploit its own resources, spiritual as well as material. One sign of such health and wealth was the emergence of vernacular literature in the sixteenth century, and its development during the 'Osaka century' from 1650 to 1750. Thus there arose, alongside the traditional Nôh plays, the lively part-dancing, part-singing kabuki theatre. During the Shogunate, darkness was never quite complete.

The rule of the Shoguns was feasible, of course, only under strict discipline and what amounted to a police state. The great nobles or *daimyos*, the heads of clans and districts, numbered about 270. They had at their beck and call a multitude of 'faithful servants', the samurai, who were rewarded with money or benefits in kind but never, as in the West, with grants of land in perpetuity, which would have given them a certain independence. The *ronin*, a samurai who had lost or (if it were conceivable) left his lord, was condemned either to starve or to become a brigand.

All accounts state, repeat, and proclaim that the samurai was devoted body and soul to his master, in accordance with his religious code of honour, the oral code of *Bushido*. The story of the forty-seven *ronins* whose master had killed himself by committing hara-kiri, who avenged him and then committed suicide themselves on his grave, in the winter of 1703, has been told many times. This rough code of honour was developed in the pitiless school of continual civil wars.

For it was among themselves and against each other that the Japanese mostly fought. Nothing more was heard of the Aïnos. Mongol China tried twice, in 1274 and 1281, to hurl an armada against Japan, but a 'divine wind', the *Kamize*, blew into a storm which destroyed the invading fleet. Against Korea, as we have seen, Japan's war lasted only six years. So it was among themselves that the Japanese used the lance and the sword; and continual fighting trained them to respect a hierarchy that was fixed once and for all. So much so that in the Japanese language, as late as 1868, verbs 'indicated the status of both subject and object'. For example, the use of the auxiliary *ageru* showed 'that the action expressed by the main verb was performed by an inferior for the benefit of a superior'.

The result was a country extraordinarily disciplined, divided into castes, firmly ruled, and at one and the same time ostentatious and desperately poor. This double image of wealth and splendour for some and destitution for others is vividly described in the traveller's tale of a Westphalian doctor, Herr Kämpfer, who was working for the Dutch East India Company, and whose book, published in 1690, is a masterpiece of observation. No one who has read it is likely to forget its accounts of gruelling journeys, of rivers that have to be forded under the protection of a cordon of ferrymen from bank to bank, holding hands to moderate the current and make the crossing a little less dangerous. Equally telling are Kämpfer's memories of villages with miserable hovels, and of peasants kneeling in the fields by the side of the road when sumptuous processions of great nobles go by. The roads between Kyôto and Yedo, headquarters of the Shogun, were busy with the passage of *daimyos*, whose duty it was to pay him regular visits. Their entourages were veritable armies of halberdiers, gunners and servants accompanying their master on his journey to the capital.

These rich feudal lords were required to spend six months a year in their palaces at Yedo. The façades of the buildings were adorned with rich armorial bearings, which Rodrigo Vivero had described with admiration in 1609. Set apart from the rest of the town, the palaces were grouped near that of the Shogun. Yet, beautiful as they were, in reality they were prisons. When in residence, their occupants were under surveillance; when absent, they left their families as hostages. They could hardly ever escape – no one could escape – the swarms of judges, informers and watchdogs on the roads, in the towns and in the taverns. In town, every street was isolated, as in China, by gates at each end which were shut as soon as any incident took place, such as theft, pilfering or some other crime. The culprit – real or suspected – would immediately be seized, and punishment would swiftly follow, usually involving death.

Similarly severe and detailed supervision was applied to the only trade allowed, with restrictions, after 1639 – i.e. that of the Chinese and the Dutch. (The latter had shamelessly lent their ships and their cannons to help crush uprisings by Japanese Christians in 1638.) Whenever the ships of the Dutch East India Company arrived, they were put in quarantine at the island of Deshima within the harbour of Nagasaki, and all goods, sailors, merchants, agents and officials of the Company were carefully checked. Contemporary accounts give the impression of a watchful, mistrustful regime, of a country bristling with fortresses and teeming with soldiers. Justice was harsh in the West; but here it was harsher. Every traveller was struck by the sight of gibbets and tortured bodies. One of the hills near Kyôto was called 'the mount of severed ears'.

In matters of culture and religion, feudal Japan certainly evolved. As in Korea and China, Buddhism here took various forms (one of them being Zen, another the fanatical cult of the Lotus of Good Faith, which held that Japan was the only country of the true Buddha). Zen, which also came from China, was identified from the twelfth century onwards with the samurai. Whereas rationalist neo-Confucianism was a convenient doctrine for the Shogunate, Zen became a soldier's faith, far removed from its original role as a religion of love and non-violence. But this transformation, of course, was characteristic of that time and that society.

The teachings of Zen were encapsulated in very short anecdotes, *koans*, intentionally absurd, with unexpected moral lessons. They sought at all costs to liberate the unconscious, instinctive self which was normally half asleep. 'Let go of your wits and become like a ball in a mountain torrent.' It was a strange kind of self-discipline, to set free and awaken one's instincts and then trust oneself to their impetus. In retrospect, it sounds like a psychoanalytic cure, calling for no more complexes: 'When you walk, walk; when you sit, sit. Above all, never hesitate!' Hesitate at nothing, in fact: that is the most frequent advice, obviously apt for a soldier. 'Clear all obstacles out of your path. If the Buddha is in your way, kill the Buddha. If it is your ancestor, kill your ancestor. If it is your father and mother, kill your father and mother. If it is a relation, kill your relation. Only in this way will you succeed in liberating yourself. Only in this way will you escape from your fetters and be free.'

This language, of course, is not to be taken literally. The Buddha, the ancestors and the relations merely symbolized all the constraints of a society obsessed with etiquette, where from the earliest years every girl and boy was enclosed in the straitjacket of an education that was all iron rules. Everyone was drilled to obey a code dictating how one should eat, speak and sit: it even laid down the position in which one should sleep, motionless, with one's head on a small wooden cross-piece. One must 'never lose control of one's mind or one's body', as a result of conditioning aimed at quelling the most natural reflexes, rather as the miniature garden curbed the natural growth of plants and trees. All the teachings of Zen, earmarked for soldiers, seem to have been directed against the inhibitions and constraints of what is called Japan's 'code of politeness'. As in every society, real life modified and reconciled opposites. Japan was both rigorous and flexible at the same time. Zen was its indispensable counterweight.

Modern Japan

Japan's break with the outside world lasted more than two centuries, until the Revolution which began the Meiji era in 1868, soon followed by the intense industrialization of the country. Japan's industrialization was a unique phenomenon, an 'economic miracle' that shed new light on Japanese civilization. Its speed, and above all its extraordinary success, cannot be explained only by the arguments normally advanced by economists, relevant though they are. Something more was involved.

The isolationist centuries contributed. From 1639 to 1868, despite being almost wholly cut off from the rest of the world, Japan made very great progress. By the eighteenth century, this had become obvious. The population increased: so did rice production: so did the growing of new crops. Towns grew bigger. In the eighteenth century, Yedo had at least a million inhabitants. This general quickening of the economy would not have been possible without a surplus of agricultural produce, especially rice, to put on the urban markets. It also benefited from the ease with which grain could be stored and transported, and from the possibility of supplying the towns with enough fuel in the form of charcoal.

Society itself encouraged economic development. The *daimyos*, whom a suspicious Government uprooted and forced to live in Yedo, were systematically ruined by their continual and costly journeys. When a money economy really began, in the seventeenth century, it was more vigorous than in China, though on a smaller scale; and urban luxury implied – indeed required – the expenditure of cash. This obliged the great nobles to sell part of their vast rice harvests, as well as to borrow money – made easier because the credit system, which had been known for a long time, now began to be general in Japan, in the form of various notes and bills of exchange. Nobles, like samurai, were forbidden to trade: they therefore employed nominees. So a merchant class arose and prospered, lending money to the *daimyos*, joining their entourage and, in a country where, more than elsewhere, fine feathers made fine birds, copying their dress. The merchants soon managed to place their sons and daughters in aristocratic families, infiltrating them by marriage and adoption. However, warned off by a few spectacular executions which the Government used as pretexts for confiscating sizeable fortunes, the merchants mostly kept out of sight.

They were particularly important in Osaka, then the economic hub of Japan. It was here that all the wealthy, both nobles and businessmen, met in the 'Flower Quarter', a city of pleasure within the town itself, where geishas, 'expensively educated' courtesans, played 'the role that had been fulfilled by the noble ladies of the court at Eïan' (Kyôto). Mocking, caustic stories about the Flower Quarter and its scandals, suicides and murders delighted the uncultivated public. True lovers of literature supposedly spurned these popular entertainments, preferring 'the delights of Confucian scholasticism'.

All this shows that even before 1868 Japanese life was in rapid flux. By the eighteenth century, an economic boom had resulted in an active type of pre-capitalism, ready to take off. In the nineteenth century, things began to move faster still. The Meiji era would be incomprehensible were it not for the transfers and positionings that had gone before, the preliminary accumulation of economic resources and capital, with all the social tensions that they implied.

Too many *daimyos* had been ruined by politics or luxury. Gradually, Japan began to see more and more samurai without masters, *ronins*, poverty-stricken knights. It was a little like Germany in the fifteenth century, where might was right. At all events, it was this group of the dispossessed that gave the first successful impetus to the Revolution. The arrival of the American fleet in 1853 had been 'the spark that lit the powder'. And when the Emperor Mutsu Hito seized power in 1868, he had no difficulty in overthrowing the old feudal regime and its traditional castes. All he overthrew, in fact, was a façade.

Industrialization is not simply an economic phenomenon: it always involves social changes, and these may assist or hinder the economic process itself. In the case of Japan, society was no hindrance. That fact is all the more remarkable in that, generally speaking, industrialization dislocates society. In the West, as Karl Marx observed, it produced the mass proletariat, class conflict and the Socialist movement.

Japan was a case apart. In a way that at first seems

incomprehensible, it achieved its Industrial Revolution, with all its attendant changes of activity, without any revolutionary breaks in the structure of society. 'This immense transformation was digested by a culture already changing, and it followed a path which, on reflection, may well be revealed as entirely new.'

There were perhaps several reasons. Japanese society was highly disciplined, and it maintained its traditional discipline during the new experience it underwent after 1868. Obedient, respectful of hierarchy, it had always accepted uncomplainingly that luxury was reserved for the few; it equally accepted, without always realizing the fact, that modern capitalism in Japan should be built in the midst of relationships that remained feudal. If one thinks of Russian industrialists in the eighteenth century, settled in the Urals in the midst of their serfs, a similar picture – *mutatis mutandis* – could be painted of Japan's great industrial firms. They it was who in the nineteenth century ensured the success of the operation and drew the profits, without provoking any reaction from the labouring masses.

Before the outbreak of war in 1942, fifteen families at most accounted for more than 80 per cent of Japan's capital. Colloquially, they were known as *zaïbatsu* – a term which has become classic. There were the famous Mitsui, Mitsubishi, Sumitovo and Yasuda, plus the imperial House, which according to experts was by far the richest of these very rich families. In the social hierarchy, these lords of big business were the equivalent of the *daimyos* of the past with their clans. The workpeople were their serfs, and the foremen, managers and engineers were the modern samurai. The firms remained family businesses, a mixture of feudalism and paternalism in this world where 'free enterprise and communism were both regarded as strange, foreign ideas, likely to destroy the Kodo, the imperial path of Japan'. The authorities could and still can impose their wishes on this docile, patiently frugal people, content to work for only small reward.

This explains the miraculous volte-face that took place in 1868. The Shogun handed over power to the Emperor, who in theory embodied the most traditional authority in the country: imagine, in the West, the Pope assuming lay power over people and property. And the Emperor who exerted this traditional authority decided to opt for revolution: he abolished the feudal system, ordered industries to be established, found the necessary investment and himself set up factories. After which, he quite often ceded the firms to selected private individuals, much as he might have ceded vast fiefs of a kind hitherto unknown. At the same time, he imposed on Japan an immense programme of work. It was carried out. The son of the Sun, venerated in the temples on account of his divine origin, had ordered the country to industrialize. For that, Japan had no need of some new ideology or faith: they existed already, enabling the whole country to be manoeuvred as one.

In these circumstances, it is hardly surprising that Japan could be both very modern and very traditional. 'The mystical character of the Emperor's authority served both the status quo and the revolution' – both social immobility and a completely new economy.

This is not a misleading explanation: it is confirmed by the conscious revival, in the eighteenth and still more in the nineteenth century, of the very ancient national beliefs that were organized under the name of Shinto. Shinto was the way of God, *kami*; but the meaning of *kami* in this context was closer to that of *mana*, which in the distant South Seas signified the impersonal supernatural power that resided in beings and things. Supreme *kami* belonged to Ameratsu, the goddess of the sun, who transmitted it to the long line of her sons.

The surrender of Japan after the atomic bombs were dropped on Hiroshima (6 August 1945) and Nagasaki (8 August) was followed by an unprecedented collapse. The country had only recently conquered much of South-East Asia: now it lost it all. Worse still, it lost all that had been built up since the Meiji era (1868), which had made Japan such an extraordinary anomaly in the Far East in the first part of the twentieth century.

Japan's post-1945 miracle (the second in its history), like those of Germany, France and Italy, relaid the foundations of its prosperity and gave it a level of development never attained before. It was a dizzying achievement. Japan was no longer, now, the military power it had been before 1942. But it was a great economic power.

The 1961–70 plan called for Japan's national income to be doubled by the final year, with spectacular growth in several sectors of the economy. Taking 100 as the base in 1955, industrial and mining output was intended to be 648 by the 'target year', steel production 296, machine tools 448 and chemicals 344. These calculations were not certain, of course; but they were not irresponsible: the recent past proved that.

Between the end of the nineteenth century and the Second World War, Japan's average growth rate had been 4 per cent per year; from 1946 to 1956 it was 10.6 per cent (compared with 4.3 per cent in France); from 1957 to 1959, 9.2 per cent; and from 1959 to 1962 it remained extremely high. These were record figures which only the German Federal Republic and the Soviet Union could rival, if that. The 1961–70 plan assumed an annual growth rate of 8.3 per cent.

The reasons for this progress are not far to seek. The most important, no doubt, was the fact that the US occupation authorities eventually allowed the trusts to be re-established more or less as before. The old patriarchal *zaibatsu* they dissolved for good, although a few reappeared: but very large new firms emerged, to become some of the biggest in the world. Japanese capitalism, which triumphantly achieved this unprecedented progress, was like American capitalism based on enormous units, able to use labour and capital more efficiently than the small artisan firms which – with some difficulty – survived only on account of family work or very low-paid labour.

At the same time, since the big Japanese firms were no longer self-financing, as they had been before 1941, industrial success involved the establishment, under the protection of the Bank of Japan, of a whole system of large banks and investment trusts, with much greater freedom than in France. These attracted small savers' capital with every resource of American-style publicity and propaganda. The result was a delirium of buying on the stock market, even on the part of naturally cautious peasants, which was encouraged by the fabulous profits made on the Tokyo stock exchange during the booms: it did 400 times as much business as before the war. From June 1961, however, a fall in prices curbed this excess of gambling and helped shift personal investments back to deposit accounts and savings banks.

The abundance of small savers explains the very high level of investment in Japan (in 1962, more than 20 per cent of national expenditure) and the interest which foreign and especially American capitalists have shown in Japanese firms. Their interest has so far been rather platonic, since in 1960 Japan had not yet fully liberalized its exchange controls, and profit on capital invested there was hard to get out of the country. A Swiss newspaper of 12 April 1961, envisaging the possibility of complete liberalization, declared: 'All in all, we prefer Japan to South Africa, where a great deal of European capital is stagnating. There is no doubt that the country is in full expansion, that its abundant labour force has exceptional skill, and that its leaders have not only unshakeable faith in their success, but also astonishing ability.' If foreign capital were to become seriously involved, Japan's growth rate could become even more impressive.

Can anyone identify the driving forces behind such progress? It is always difficult to analyse an economy in rapid flux. Statistics quickly grow stale and out of touch with reality. But it is certain that until recently a powerful stimulus was the superabundance of labour. Japan's economic plan estimated its population at 94 million in 1961 and 104 million in 1970 – an annual increase of a million, year in year out. By 1984, it had reached 120 million.

These increases have not hindered economic growth: the plan looked forward to a doubling of national income by 1970; and birth control was expected to slow down the rate at which the population grew. In 1962, moreover, the smaller numbers born during the war came on to the labour market, with the result that vacancies (especially for skilled workers) exceeded supply. Hence a subsequent increase in the salaries paid to engineers and teachers.

Undoubtedly, both wages and the standard of living remained at that time much lower than in the West or the United States. Given Japan's different habits and needs, however, the situation was far from catastrophic. There were certainly slums around Osaka and Tokyo (where the population was increasing by 400,000 per year, 300,000 of them immigrants). But the average food consumption was 2,100 calories a day, and the annual income in dollars between $200 and $300 – four times that in India. By 1984 it had reached $8,810. The enormous increase in fishing, where Japan was ahead of every other nation with an annual catch of 6 million tons, drawn from as far away as the Atlantic and the Caribbean; improved productivity on the land, where the US authorities had insisted on all holdings of more than six acres being sold, and where growing under glass, in winter, had made possible a second harvest and an earlier rice crop, avoiding the summer typhoons; and finally the slow attempt to exploit the resources of Yezo (Hokkaido), the cold island in the North: all contributed to great and stable growth.

The domestic market likewise supported the expansion of industry. A higher standard of living meant new purchases: washing machines, transistors, television sets, and cameras (Japan's huge factories flood the home market first). New tastes brought changes in demand – for more meat and fish, for Western-type pastries, canned and frozen goods, pharmaceutical remedies (especially tranquillizers), beer (more and more replacing rice wine) and Ceylon tea (replacing green tea, of which Japan produced 77,000 tons a year). Dress and interior decoration began to follow Western models. Admittedly, the average Japanese remained what the journalist Robert Guillain called 'bi-civilized', wearing Western clothes in the street but in the evening reverting to traditional Japanese costumes and habits. But the Japanese are clearly more and more affected and attracted by Western ways, and are succumbing to them.

Obstacles nevertheless remain. Not everything augurs well for the Japanese economy. Although it is a miracle of effort, of patient and intelligent work, it has its limits, its frailties and its dangers. Nor should one forget that the agrarian reform has produced a myriad smallholders, the poorest of them dependent upon those slightly better off, and all incapable of grouping together or yielding to truly modern and scientific methods. 'Only Socialism,' claimed one reporter, 'would succeed in that.' A likely story: agriculture has been the stumbling-block of almost all socialist experiments. Besides, all attempts at agrarian reform, at all times and in all countries, have led to great disappointments when they have tried to be rapid and radical. Agricultural habits are the most ingrained of all.

What is more, Japan has a population almost twice that of France in an area only half as large (300,000 against 550,000 square kilometres); while its arable land is only 15 per cent of the total compared with 84 per cent in France. It also has meagre natural resources. Wool, cotton, coal, iron ore and oil all have to be imported for its industries; and Japan's growth rate is such that it also requires large purchases of foreign machinery and equipment. Hence, in 1961, disturbing signs of a weakening trade balance, despite official optimism. On a reasonable estimate, it seemed that a favourable balance would not have been possible without the US occupation army's opportune expenditure in Japan. This shows how vulnerable its success still was.

The problem, for a country very much attached to its industrial prosperity, was not so much to produce as to sell. Here, Japan remained dependent on the prosperity and goodwill of its trading partners in the 'free world'. And this goodwill could not be taken for granted. The West, and especially France (which is always too hesitant in these matters) remembered the commercial dumping that Japan had practised relentlessly before 1939, and feared the powerful price competition that its industries now practised as a result of low wages. The West's reservations were made clear by its slowness to conclude even imperfect trade agreements, and its constantly calling them in question.

All this was disquieting enough to tempt Japan to become 'neutralist like Nehru', and involve itself to the hilt with the economy of China and South-East Asia. At the same time, Japanese Socialists and Communists could not help fearing that when the US presence was removed, a number of social gains would be at risk, notably the parliamentary constitution of 1951 and, still more, the trade unions, which had been slow to develop in so docile a country, all the more so since large-scale capitalism accepted them very reluctantly. These conflicting concerns explained the results in the 1961 election, which gave only a 'routine victory' to the 'moderate liberals' – i.e. big business, which according to informed observers spent more than 5,000 million yen (100 yen = roughly 1 French franc) to 'save this last chance' and defeat the Socialists.

But the problem cannot be put off for ever, if only because Japan's prosperity imposes superhuman tasks involving continual tension. Tokyo (which with its suburbs had a population of 10 million in the early 1960s) is the most populous city in the world, and is growing so fast that it is already suffocating and thinking of filling in part of its bay to build on. Osaka has already set the example, to provide space for the heavy industries attracted there by the huge reservoir of labour. These details indicate how the grandiose and the precarious coexist in Japan's fabulous growth.

But it is in politics and in the broader field of civilization that the greatest uncertainties arise. Japan did not become a parliamentary democracy overnight, by American decree. It could not have been expected to; and a number of small, significant details confirm the fact. Japan's industrialists are still paternalistic, and wary. The nationalist aggressiveness of the past is by no means extinct. Japan has its violent and fanatical right-wing political parties, invoking the country's always fervent traditionalism. The Imperial family, humiliated by the victors in the Second World War, remains in place; and anyone rising against it would still risk being lynched. The eternal Japan of the past is far from dead or forgotten.

On 12 November 1960, the Socialist leader Inegiro Asanuma, 'the Mirabeau of Japan', spoke on television. He denounced 'the felony of the so-called Japan–American security pact, the aggressive tool of Yankee imperialism.' Millions of Japanese could hear and see him on the screen. Then they saw a student, still not seventeen years old, rush forward and stab him, his hands crossed on the dagger in the hold recommended by *judoka* to keep the blow straight. Three weeks later, the student committed suicide in his cell. The crime and the suicide produced a huge wave of emotion. Japan could not help admiring someone who was willing to die for his ideas, even if his crime was unworthy and repellent. It would be a mistake to see this attitude, and others, as a reflection of religious beliefs. By comparison with other countries, Japan is not particularly religious, not particularly concerned with the after-life. In this, it is the opposite of India. What dominates Japan is a certain code – in society, in education: a code of honour and civilization: *its* civilization.

III. European Civilizations

We began our survey with non-European civilizations: Islam, Black Africa, China, India, Japan, Korea, Indo-China and Indonesia. There was an advantage in beginning at some distance from Europe, going abroad to realize more fully that Europe is not, or is no longer, the centre of the universe. Yet the contrast between Europe and non-Europe is fundamental to any serious attempt to explain the world as it is.

So we now return to ourselves, to Europe and its own impressive civilizations. We shall see them more objectively for having studied the others. And by Europe we mean not only the West and the Old World, but also the New: the Americas which derive directly from Europe, and the complex phenomenon of the Soviet Union, now the CIS, which despite what is often said has always remained European, even in its ideology.

Part I: Europe

To begin with, it may be useful to recall a few basic notions, obvious as they may seem:

That Europe is an Asian peninsula – 'a little cape': hence its double role. First, it is linked with the East by a broadening continental land mass. Once, this was difficult to cross; then, railways spanned it; now, air travel virtually ignores it. Secondly, Europe is linked, in all directions, with the seven seas. An essential part of its history is that of ships, convoys and the conquest of distant oceans. Peter the Great acted shrewdly when, on his first visit to Europe in 1697, he went to work in the shipyards of the extraordinary village of Zaandam, near Amsterdam. Already by the end of the fifteenth century, the expansion of Western Europe through the voyages of discovery decisively confirmed its double role.

That there are contrasts between East and West and between North and South: between the warm Mediterranean, the *Mare Internum* or internal sea of the South, and the cold 'Mediterraneans' of the North – the Channel, the North Sea and the Baltic. The contrasts are of every kind: in people, in diet, in tastes and in the age of the respective civilizations. Various 'isthmuses' link North and South – the Russian, the German and the French – and grow shorter as one travels Westward. To a geographer, Western Europe looks like the narrow end of a funnel whose broad end lies to the East.

That these East–West and North–South contrasts are as much

the result of history as of geography. Historically, the West looked to Rome and the East to Constantinople. The major separation, in the ninth century AD, was the decisive success of Sts Cyril and Methodius in preaching the Gospel and shaping the future of the East along Greek Orthodox lines. A later division occurred, this time between North and South, with the Protestant Reformation which, rather curiously, 'split' Christendom roughly along the ancient *limes* of the Roman Empire.

16. Geography and Freedom

The history of Europe has everywhere been marked by the stubborn growth of private 'liberties', franchises or privileges limited to certain groups, big or small. Often, these liberties conflicted with each other or were mutually exclusive.

Clearly, these liberties could exist only when Western Europe as such had taken shape and become relatively stable. Undefended, or strife-torn, it could afford no such luxury. Liberty and stability were inseparable.

Europe takes shape: fifth to thirteenth centuries

The accompanying maps, showing the major invasions of Europe, make it unnecessary to recount at length the accidents and catastrophes in the course of which the Western end of the European Peninsula gradually became a coherent whole. Europe's geographical area was defined in the course of a series of wars and invasions. It all began with the division of the Roman Empire, confirmed but not caused when it was partitioned on the death of Theodosius in 395 AD.

The Eastern Mediterranean has almost always been populated, endowed with a very old civilization, and engaged in a number of economic pursuits. From the very beginning of the Roman conquest, there was also a Western Mediterranean – a Far West, so to speak, which was primitive if not barbaric. There, by founding cities, Rome partially established a civilization which, if not always exactly Roman, was at least an imitation of the original.

Once the 395 partition had occurred, the *pars Occidentalis* underwent a series of disasters on the three frontiers surrounding it: in the North-East along the Rhine and the Danube; in the South on the Mediterranean; and in the West on the extensive 'ocean frontier' from Denmark to Gibraltar, which for a long time had been peaceful and secure. The new threats, and the reaction to them, defined and settled Europe's geographical area.

In the North-East, the double *limes* of the Rhine and the Danube could not resist the pressure of the Barbarians, fleeing from the Huns. In 405, Radagaisus led a Barbarian army into Italy as far as Tuscany. Soon afterwards, on 31 December 406, a horde of Barbarian peoples crossed the frozen Rhine near Mainz and overcame the Gallic provinces.

Once broken through, the door was not closed again until the defeat of the Huns at Châlons-sur-Marne in 451. After that, reconstruction was fairly rapid. Merovingian Gaul re-established the Rhine frontier, and it was soon shifted well to the East: the Carolingians maintained it far beyond the river, imposing their authority over the whole of Germany and pressing as far as 'Hungary', then under the Avars. Conversion to Christianity, in which the great St Boniface played a leading role, consolidated this huge Eastward advance. The West succeeded, in fact, where the caution of Augustus and Tiberius had failed.

From then onwards, Germany protected the Western world against the Asiatic East. It halted the Hungarian cavalry at Merseburg in 933, then crushed it at Augsburg in 955. The Germanic Holy Roman Empire derived its *raison d'être* from this protective role when in 962 it replaced the Carolingian Empire, which had been founded by Charlemagne on Christmas Day in the year 800.

No longer threatened, the Eastern frontier became a growth point, and was pushed Eastwards with the birth of Christian States

in Poland, Hungary and Bohemia, as a result of Germanic colonization in the eleventh to thirteenth centuries. Here, indeed, there
was relative peace until the huge Mongol invasion in about 1240,
miraculously halted on the edge of Poland and the Adriatic. Its
only victim was South-Western Russia.

In the South, a dangerous frontier was created by the first successes
of the Muslim conquest – all the more so because of successive
'defections', by North Africa (hitherto Christian), by Spain and
then by Sicily. In the West, the Mediterranean became a 'Muslim
lake'. The first effective reaction against this was the establishment
of heavy cavalry, which gave Charles Martel his victory at Poitiers
in 732. The result of that victory was the immense but short-lived
triumph of the Carolingians, whose influence was felt beyond the
Rhine, and as far as Saxony and Hungary.

But Islam was a powerful neighbour, and Christianity had to
undertake a difficult and dramatic campaign against it, inventing
its own Holy War, the Crusade. Crusading became interminable.
The First Crusade – not, obviously, the first war against Islam, but
the first that was collective, self-conscious and spectacular – was
launched in 1095. The last, which was by no means the end of the
struggle, was St Louis's expedition to Tunisia in 1270.

Although the Egyptian recapture of Acre in 1291 put an end to
these great Eastern adventures, the appeal of crusading continued
to trouble and excite emotions in the West, leading to unexpected
upsurges in the fifteenth and sixteenth centuries. In the seventeenth
century, again, there were 'the lonely Crusaders', as they were
called by Alphonse Dupront, an historian who has traced as far as
the nineteenth century this obsessive mystique. It can even be
detected as an element in the last days of colonialism.

Recent and very doubtful calculations have estimated that
between 1095 and 1291 the Crusades cost the West 4 or 5 million
men out of its small population of barely 50 million. No one can
say whether these figures are accurate. But in any case the Crusades
were a dramatic experience for Europe in the making, and its first

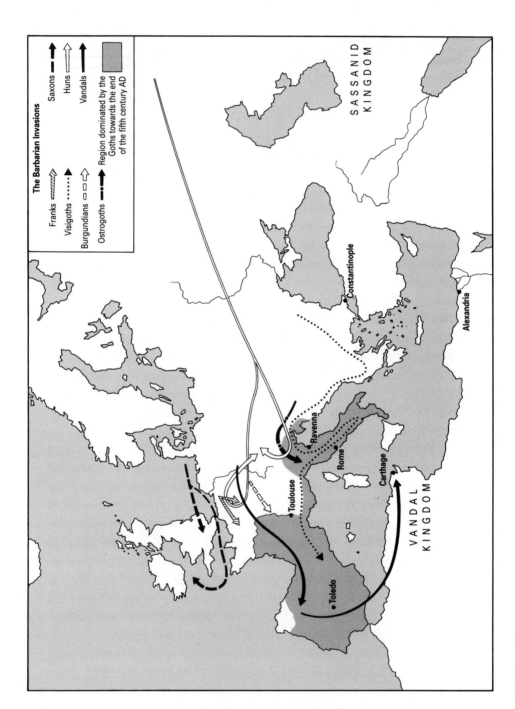

14. *The great invasions (1)*

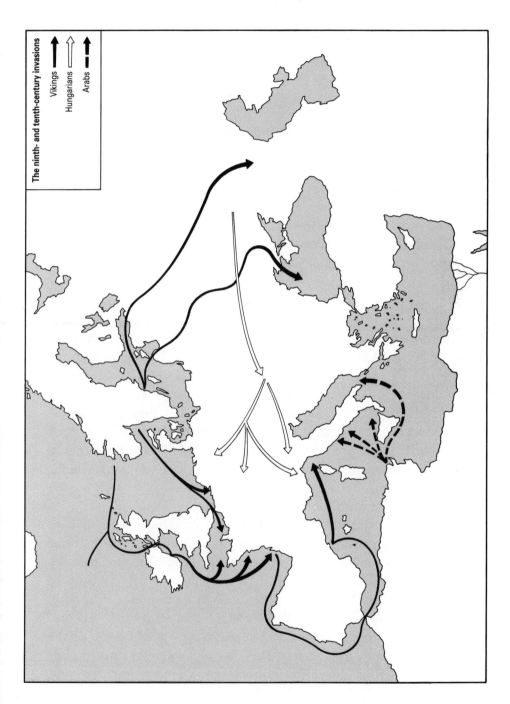

15. *The great invasions* (2)

real triumph – in at least two respects. The first was its precarious
and provisional recapture of the Holy Sepulchre; the second, its
definitive reconquest of the rich Mediterranean. The Crusades
completed the process whereby the West's Southern borders were
fixed; and for a long time, until the great maritime discoveries in
the fifteenth and sixteenth centuries, they were the most important
of all.

To the North-West and West, as far South as the Mediterranean,
Europe was taken unawares, in the eighth, ninth and tenth
centuries, by the Norse invasions – taken unawares and powerless,
hence all the more distressed. Except for The Netherlands, Ireland
and Italy, Europe was slow to develop seapower of her own. Yet
in the long run the invasions proved advantageous.

To say this is not to defend the pitiless Norse pirates. They took
a savage toll of Europe. Yet it is hard not to admire admirable
exploits: their excursions across the entire breadth of Russia, their
discovery of America – no sooner found than lost again because,
as Henri Pirenne wrote, 'Europe did not yet need it.' Economic
historians are still more indulgent to the Vikings, arguing that by
putting back into circulation the treasures that they pillaged, especially from the Church, they reactivated capital which had been
immobilized as precious metal, lying idle since the Western
economic recession following the fall of Rome. The Vikings' thefts,
it is argued, made them suppliers of money; and it was this money
that once more stimulated the economy of the West.

To understand the first European civilization, one has to
remember the disasters it suffered, imagine the appalling 'Dark
Ages' of the ninth and tenth centuries and realize the primary
poverty of a continent that had to struggle every day simply to
survive. Lacking broad outlets, reduced to a subsistence economy,
this impoverished Europe was in Marc Bloch's words 'a citadel
besieged or rather invaded'; and at that time it could not bear the
weight of very large States. They were no sooner formed than
they collapsed or crumbled. Charlemagne's Empire, rapidly built,

disintegrated not long after the death of the great Emperor in 814. The Germanic Holy Roman Empire fairly soon became a huge dilapidated mansion, and Western Europe split into countless tiny domains. The feudal system (based on the fief or, in Latin, the *feodum*) maintained units that were more theoretical than real within the various kingdoms of the West, some of which were very slowly modernized, like France, while others remained wilfully archaic, like the German Empire.

Yet this troubled world, oppressed from within and attacked from without, was already quite clearly a homogeneous civilization. Despite its diversity, it has to be called, in Lucien Febvre's words, a 'feudal civilization', which everywhere tackled the same major problems, in conditions and with solutions that were often alike. This civilization was born of many ethnic and economic strains, with repeated struggles, common beliefs, and above all the same difficulties which it tried to remedy.

Feudalism built Europe. In the eleventh and twelfth centuries, Europe achieved its first youthful vigour under a lively feudal regime – a particular and very original political, social and economic order, based on a civilization that was already at its second or third fermentation.

But how should this multi-coloured civilization be defined?

There could be no feudalism, in Europe or elsewhere, without the previous fragmentation of a larger political entity. In the present case, the entity in question was the huge Carolingian Empire – the first 'Europe', its name affirmed as such (*Europa, vel regnum Caroli*), which disappeared soon after the death of its great Emperor, whom a court poet hailed as '*pater Europae*', the Father of Europe.

Feudalism was the natural consequence of the Empire's fragmentation. In June 1940, when France was falling to the Nazis, a French officer had a dream: he wished that every unit of the army could by some miracle recover for a moment its autonomy, the right to act as it saw fit, without obeying the general orders which bound it to a High Command that was growing less and less effective and, without wishing to, was dragging everyone into the drift towards defeat. The feudal system was born of a similar reaction – but with the essential difference, among others, that the disaster which prompted it was less rapid than that of June 1940. It took several centuries for feudalism to be formed. Yet its very nature was both defensive and local. The castle on its mount, with the village or villages it protected huddled close to it: this was not an accidental or optional arrangement but a defensive weapon.

Nevertheless, feudalism was something else as well. It was a society based on relations between man and man, a chain of dependencies; it was an economy in which land was not the only but the most frequent recompense for services rendered. The lord received from the king, his suzerain, or from a lord of higher rank than himself, a fief (*feodum*) or lordship. In return, he had to supply a series of services, including assistance in four cases. 1. He had to pay his lord's ransom. 2. He had to pay when his eldest son was dubbed a knight. 3. He had to pay when his eldest daughter was married. 4. He had to pay when his suzerain went on a Crusade. In turn, the lord ceded parts or elements of his own lordship to those subordinate to him, whether minor lords or peasants. To the latter he granted land (we still refer to 'tenure' and 'tenement'), which the peasant tilled, paying a rent as money (quit-rent), as a portion of the crops (a tithe, or share-cropping), or as labour. The lord in return defended and protected the peasant.

This social pyramid, with its obligations, its rules and its allegiances, mobilizing economic, political and military strength, enabled the West to survive and to safeguard its old Christian and Roman heritage, to which it added the ideas, virtues and ideologies of the seigneurial regime (its own civilization).

Europe by then had forgotten the name of Europe. In practice, it had become a compartmentalized world, where all that mattered was the small region, the narrow, limited mother country.

Certainly, in these early days of Europe's life, there were very great advantages in each region's being able to grow at leisure in its own way, like a plant in the wild. Each was thus able to become a robust and self-aware entity, ready to defend its territory and its independence.

What is interesting is that nevertheless, despite this political compartmentalization, there was a convergence in Europe's civilization and culture. A traveller on a pilgrimage (to St James of Compostela, for instance) or going about his business, felt as much at home in Lübeck as in Paris, in London as in Bruges, in Cologne as in Burgos, Milan or Venice. Moral, religious and cultural values, and the rules of war, love, life and death were the same everywhere, from one fief to another, whatever their quarrels, their revolts or their conflicts. That is why there was indeed one single Christendom, as Marc Bloch said: there was what might be called a civilization of chivalry, of the minstrel and the troubadour, of courtly love.

The Crusades expressed that unity, because they were mass movements, collective adventures and passions, common to all the innumerable small-scale mother countries.

Liberty and rights: eleventh to eighteenth centuries

Imagine that it might be possible to assemble the sum total of our knowledge of European history from the fifth century to the present, or perhaps to the eighteenth century, and to record it (if such a recording were conceivable) in an electronic memory. Imagine that the computer was then asked to indicate the one problem which recurred most frequently, in time and space, throughout this lengthy history. Without a doubt, that problem is liberty, or rather liberties. The word liberty is the operative word.

The very fact that, in the twentieth-century conflict of ideologies, the Western world has chosen to call itself 'the free world', however mixed its motives, is both fair and appropriate in view of Europe's history during these many centuries.

The word liberty has to be understood in all its connotations, including such pejorative senses as in 'taking liberties'. All liberties, in fact, threaten each other: one limits another, and later succumbs to a further rival. This process has never been peaceful; yet it is one of the secrets that explain Europe's progress.

But the word 'liberty' has to be defined. Here, it means not so much individual liberty, the normal criterion in the 'free world' of today, but rather the liberty of groups. It is no accident that the Middle Ages spoke much more of *libertates* (liberties) than of *libertas* (liberty). In the plural, the word meant very much the same as *privilegia* (privileges) or *jura* (rights). Liberties, in fact, were the franchises or privileges protecting this or that group of people or interests, which used such protection to exploit others, often without shame.

These collective liberties were slow to develop to their full extent. Later, they were also slow to be brought within reasonable limits, or abolished. In general, they were stubbornly long-lived.

The peasants were among the first to begin to be liberated, but certainly the last to be fully free. It could even be argued that their liberation is still incomplete today. The peasant is free, in our sense of the term, only if no outside interest – seigneurial, urban or capitalist – comes between him and the land; if he is subject to no bond-service; and, finally, if his work is productive enough to feed him and leave a surplus, and if this surplus, should it reach the nearby market, does not simply make the fortune of some intermediary, but enables the peasant to buy, at the very least, what he needs.

That amounts to quite a few conditions. While European peasants in the past can be said to have enjoyed some advantages and even certain liberties, this is only by comparison with other peasants who were certainly much more downtrodden. Broadly speaking, European peasants benefited from every economic boom.

Thus it was at Europe's economic awakening, which began no earlier than the tenth century. At that time, agricultural production increased everywhere: not only in the 'new' countries of the North, where three-year crop rotation spread from the Germanic lands and from Poland, but also in the regions of the South (Italy and Southern France), where two-year rotation (one year of cereals, one year lying fallow) remained the rule.

This rise in production was linked to the increase in population and to the growth of towns. The latter was an essential precondition for greater output; but the towns benefited from it too.

From the eleventh century onwards, and as long as economic growth continued, the lot of the peasants rapidly improved. Hitherto, they had been bound to the soil as serfs. 'After having belonged to the man of the sword and to his rival the man of the Church, the land fell into the possession of the man of the plough . . . It was abandoned to any workers who sought to take it over, in exchange for a very small annual interest paid to the former owners.' This quit-rent system applied 'at a time when land was abundant and people were scarce, so that human labour was more sought after than land' (d'Avenel). There can be no doubt that over large areas (but not all) the peasants enjoyed a certain degree of freedom. 'We were free by the twelfth century,' the historian Henri Pirenne liked to say, referring to peasants in the West.

But this liberation was neither complete nor universal; nor, above all, was it definitive. A certain equilibrium existed, it is true, and was widespread. In practice, it left the land with the peasants, who were lords and masters in their own domains, and who could pass on or sell their holdings. Their money rent, moreover, was fixed quite early on, which in the long term was to their advantage, since over the centuries coinage went on losing its value, so that rents established once and for all eventually became derisory in real terms.

These advantages, however, had no very firm legal basis. The lord continued to enjoy superior rights over the land, and could recover his oppressive powers if the time, the place and the circumstances were right. The history of peasant revolts is the proof of that: the *jacquerie* in France in 1358, Wat Tyler's rebellion of workers and peasants in 1381, the sudden vast rebellion of the German peasants in 1524–5, or – in France again – the repeated peasant uprisings in the first half of the seventeenth century. Every time, these risings, these 'general strikes', were put down. Only the ever-present threat of them helped the peasants to retain part of the liberties and advantages that they had earlier acquired.

These privileges were called into question again, throughout Europe, with the capitalist economic development of the modern world. Beginning in the sixteenth century, and still more in the seventeenth, capital faced economic recession: finding no easy outlets elsewhere, it turned back to the land. A large-scale 'seigneurial' reaction – as much middle-class as aristocratic – spread outwards from the towns, large and small, into the surrounding countryside. Properties of a new type (farms, 'granges', 'metairies' – the words vary from region to region, and do not always bear their modern meanings) were established, preferably with a single tenant and at the expense, above all, of peasant smallholdings. Their owners were usually imbued with a genuine capitalist spirit: they looked for productivity and profit as moneylenders. The peasants became indebted to them, so much so that one fine day their holdings might be seized, or the land would become subject to one of the innumerable registered rents paid to the rich, contracts for which abounded in notaries' files. Everything at that time was to the peasant's disadvantage – even the tenancy contracts which called for payment in kind, in wheat, and not always in cash.

Although this reaction was detectable all over Europe, it was particularly tragic in Central and Eastern Europe – in Germany beyond the Elbe, in Poland, Bohemia and Austria, and even in the Balkans and in Muscovy. As the sixteenth century ended, there was established throughout these regions (some of them 'still barbarian') what historians more and more tend to call 'the second serfdom'. The peasants were enmeshed once more in a seigneurial regime, this time worse than that of the past. The lord was the head of the farm, the entrepreneur, the wheat merchant. To meet the growing demand for grain, he forced his peasants to increase the amount of bond-service they owed him – five days a week in

Bohemia, where peasants could till their own land only on Saturdays, while in Slovenia, where it had been ten days a year in the fifteenth century, it was six months a year by the end of the sixteenth. Bond-service was performed on the land held directly by the lord (the home farm or 'reserve'). This system, which in the East continued until the nineteenth century, was no doubt largely responsible for the extra backwardness of these areas by comparison with the West.

In the West, in fact, under a relatively liberal regime, changes favourable to the peasants began in the eighteenth century – in France, with John Law's banking system, which sparked off everything (including rural drunkenness). The French Revolution completed these developments, by freeing peasant holdings, at a stroke, from the feudal dues they laboured under. This example was copied elsewhere during the revolutionary and Napoleonic Wars.

The towns were motors that never stopped. They bore the brunt of Europe's first advance, and were rewarded by their 'liberties'.

The long decline of the West resulted, in the tenth century, in the near-ruin of the towns, which barely survived.

But when the economic tide turned, with the boom of the eleventh to thirteenth centuries, the towns enjoyed a remarkable renaissance. It was as if, in this great recovery, the towns prospered more rapidly than the lumbering territorial States. These hardly began to show any modern characteristics until the fifteenth century at the earliest: but the towns broke through the fabric of the feudal States they grew in, as early as the eleventh and twelfth centuries. Modern, and ahead of their time, they signalled the future. Indeed, they were the future already.

Of course they were not always, nor had they at first been, strictly independent. But great free cities emerged early in Italy, which was then the most advanced country in Western Europe. The same was true of The Netherlands, 'that second Italy'. Venice, Genoa, Florence, Milan, Ghent and Bruges were already 'modern' cities at a time when the kingdom of Louis IX was still typically 'medieval'.

Following these cities, governed by Dukes, Doges or Consuls, countless lesser towns fought for and won the right (by virtue of their charters) to govern themselves and look after their finances, their legal system and the land they possessed.

In general, complete liberty could be achieved only through material prosperity sufficient to enable certain specially favoured towns not merely to guarantee their economic survival but also to provide for their external defence. These were city–states. Only a few towns attained that status; but all of them relied on their trade and the work of their craft guilds to give them a certain independence and a right to private liberties.

The guilds worked both for the local market and for distant trade. There can be no doubt that the urban economy was able to prosper as it did only because it largely overflowed its local confines. In the fifteenth century the town of Lübeck – the most important of that huge trading group of cities between the Baltic and the Rhine known as the Hanseatic League – had links with the whole of the known world. The same could be said of Venice, Genoa, Florence or Barcelona.

In these privileged centres, primary capitalism triumphed as a result of distant trade. It was the beginning of the age of the Merchant Adventurers. They supplied raw materials and labour, and ensured the sale of industrial products, while the guild masters became more and more wage-earning employees, like their 'companions' in this *Verlagsystem* – an untranslatable word used by German historians to denote, very roughly, production to order. The merchants were the leading lights of the *popolo grasso* or rich bourgeoisie. Their underlings, the 'thin people', often staged rather unsuccessful revolts – in Ghent, for example, or in Florence, where the violent revolution of the Ciompi broke out in 1381.

These internal conflicts in the manufacturing towns betokened social tensions which were already class struggles: '*taquebans*' was the word used by Beaumanoir when speaking of the Flanders artisans, who staged what we should now call strikes for higher wages. Gradually, a further gulf appeared between the guild masters and the 'companions'. The latter, held back by the need to make costly and difficult 'masterpieces' in order to secure promotion, formed groupings, associations and 'lodges', and frequently travelled from one town to another. They were in fact the first working-class proletariat.

Such proletarians, however, if they were citizens, were privileged by virtue of their citizenship – at least as long as the great days of the independent or semi-independent cities lasted.

Was there, as Max Weber thought, a special typology applicable to medieval European towns – 'closed towns', as he called them? It is true that they were exclusive, refusing to give any consideration to those outside their walls. Nothing was superior to them: there was no equivalent of the efficient despotism exerted by the Chinese mandarins as agents of the State. The countryside around them was often under their control: the peasants, who could not be citizens, were obliged to sell their grain exclusively to the town markets, and were often forbidden to own looms – unless, that is, the town required their services. The system was certainly very different from that of the city–states in the ancient world, which had been politically open to the country around them: the Athenian peasant, at that time, had been a citizen with the same status as an inhabitant of the town.

No wonder the rights of citizenship were granted only grudgingly, except when the town urgently needed to increase its population. In 1345, for example, shortly after the Black Death, Venice promised citizenship to anyone who would settle there. Normally, the 'Signoria' was less generous. It recognized two types of citizenship. One, known as *de intus*, created only second-class citizens; the other, known as *de intus et de extra*, conferred full rights, and was jealously scrutinized by an aristocracy anxious to safeguard its own privileges. It took fifteen years' residence in Venice to acquire *de intus* citizenship, and twenty years for the other. Distinction was also made, on occasion, between 'new' and 'old' citizens. A decree of 1386 laid down that only 'old' Venetians had the right to trade with the German merchants based in the city.

Egoistic, vigilant and ferocious, towns were ready to defend their liberties against the rest of the world, often with very great courage and sometimes without any concern for the liberties of others. Bloodthirsty wars between cities were the forerunner of the national wars to come.

The liberty of the cities was soon threatened, however, when modern States, which had been slower to develop, grew more powerful in the fifteenth century. Then, the towns were often brought to heel by the State, which could both confer privileges and impose sanctions. Hence some serious crises, such as that of the Castile *comunidades* in 1521, or the crushing of Ghent by Charles V in 1540. There were also, inevitably, compromises, since modern monarchy needed the towns' support. They had to submit to authority, renouncing some of their privileges in order to safeguard others. In compensation for giving up certain liberties, they gained access to the new world of the modern State – greater trade, profitable loans, and also in certain countries such as France the purchase of public office. A territorial economy grew up, replacing the urban economy which had preceded it. But this territorial economy was still controlled by the towns. Alongside the State, they continued to rule the roost.

So-called 'territorial States' (i.e. modern States) were latecomers to Europe. The ancient form of kingship, based on blood links and on relations between suzerain and vassal, took a long time to disappear – or at least to be transformed. The turning-point came in the fifteenth century, and at first almost exclusively in areas where the urban revolution had been least marked. Neither Italy nor The Netherlands, and not even Germany, which had had so many free, rich and active towns, was the chosen terrain for this new type of government. Modern monarchy developed above all in Spain, France and Britain, with rulers of a new kind: John II of Aragon (the father of Ferdinand the Catholic), Louis XI and the Lancastrian Henry VII.

These territorial States were served by 'functionaries' – or, to avoid anachronism, let us say 'officers': all of them servants of the State, like the 'jurists' trained in Roman Law, and the great Secretaries of State, the 'Ministers'.

The States were aided also by the loyalty of the masses, who saw the Monarch as their natural protector against the Church and the nobles. In France, the monarchy was able to rely on popular devotion until the eighteenth century: the historian Jules Michelet called it 'a religion of love'.

The modern State arose from the new and imperious needs of war: artillery, battle fleets and larger armies, made combat ever more costly. War, the mother of all things – *bellum omnium mater* – also gave birth to the modern world.

The modern State soon recognized no authority higher than its own – neither the Holy Roman Empire, increasingly ignored by its own Princes, nor the Papacy, whose moral and political authority had once been immense. Every State wanted to be isolated, uncontrolled and *free*: reasons of State became the ultimate law. (The expression '*raison d'Etat*', now amounting to the *ultima ratio*, first appeared in a speech that Cardinal della Casa made to Charles V on the subject of an ignoble incident during the capture of Mantua in 1552.) This was a stage in the evolution of Western political systems away from traditional kingship, with its paternalist and mystical overtones, and towards the modern monarchy of the jurists.

Several writers were quick to note the emergence of States which acknowledged no higher authority – '*superiorem non recognoscentes*', in the words of the fourteenth-century jurist Bartolo de Sassofarrato. But they were well in advance of political events. In France, it was not until 1577 that Jean Bodin advanced the theory of the State's undivided sovereignty, in his *Traité de la république* – 'republic' in this case meaning nothing more specific than the Latin *res publica*, the body politic. For Bodin, the sovereign State was above all laws except Natural and Divine Law: there was nothing superior to it on the human scene.

Just as the Pope never ties his hands, as canon lawyers say, so the sovereign Prince cannot tie his own hands, even if he wishes. Hence we see, at the end of edicts and ordinances, these words: For such is our pleasure. They are there to make it clear that the laws of the sovereign Prince, while they are based on good and sufficient reasons, nevertheless depend solely on his pure and simple will.

The will of the sovereign invaded the State. '*Das Ich wird der Staat*' – 'The I becomes the State' – wrote a German historian. This is the famous dictum '*L'Etat, c'est moi*' generally attributed to Louis XIV, but also ascribed at least once to Elizabeth I of England. Although Spanish monarchs called themselves 'Catholic Kings' and the French 'Very Christian Kings', they on occasion opposed the Papacy, defending the liberties of the Gallican Church or the temporal and spiritual interests of Spain. These were signs of changing times. There had of course been precedents for such action: but now it was becoming systematic, natural, and a matter of course.

As the modern State tightened its grip, so European civilization became 'territorial' and national. Hitherto, it had been urban, maturing in many small, diverse and privileged cities. Now the Golden Century in Spain (which really extended from 1492 to 1660) and the Great Century in France were both coterminous with entire States.

At the heart of these larger civilized entities, an important role was played by the capital cities, sustained by the presence and the expenditure of the Government, and hence raised to the previously unknown rank of super-cities. Paris and Madrid acquired their lasting reputations; London virtually became England. The weight and the life of the whole State began to centre on these urban monstrosities, henceforward unrivalled instruments of luxury, machines for creating both civilization and misery.

One can easily picture the immense movement of people, capital and wealth that these great States engendered – and the redistribution of liberties that was involved, some being abolished or maintained on sufferance, others encouraged or invented afresh.

Specially privileged towns included Marseille, the *de facto* headquarters of trade with the Levant; Lorient, founded in 1666 and soon accorded the monopoly of trade with India; and Seville, which in 1503 had obtained the far greater privilege of exclusive rights to trade with America, 'the India of Castile'. In 1685, however, Seville's monopoly was transferred to Cadiz.

Certain liberties were secured because the State could not do everything or retain all its rights. In France, for example, from the death of Colbert in 1683 until the Revolution in 1789, the absolutist State gradually grew less effective; and the bourgeoisie, which bought 'offices' of state, acquired a sizeable share of political authority. It was against the King that provincial liberties were asserted. The social privileges of the clergy, the nobility and the Third Estate were encrusted in the structure of the French State. It could not get rid of them, and hence it missed the 'enlightened' reforms of the eighteenth century elsewhere.

Even those countries which at that time won political freedom did no more than hand responsibility for the State to a powerful group of privileged persons. This was the case in the United Provinces, with their middle-class businessmen; it was also the case in Britain after the Glorious Revolution of 1688. The British Parliament represented a double aristocracy, Whig and Tory, bourgeoisie and nobility – certainly not the country as a whole.

While 'liberties' and privileges were accumulating, what became of individual liberty? This question makes no sense if 'the freedom of the individual' means what it does today – everyone's freedom as a person, simply by virtue of being a person. It took a long time for the concept of that kind of freedom to become clear. At the most, therefore, one can only inquire whether individual liberty was increasing *in fact*, or not. The answer has to be both contradictory and pessimistic.

The intellectual ferment of the Renaissance, and that of the Reformation in so far as it raised the principle of individual interpretation of revealed truth, laid the bases for freedom of conscience. Renaissance humanism preached respect for the greatness of the human being as an individual: it stressed personal intelligence and ability. *Virtù*, in fifteenth-century Italy, meant not virtue but glory, effectiveness, and power. Intellectually, the ideal was *l'uomo universale* as described by Leon Battista Alberti – an all-rounder himself. In the seventeenth century, with Descartes, a whole philosophical system stemmed from *Cogito, ergo sum* (I think, therefore I exist) – *individual* thought.

The philosophical importance thus attached to the individual coincided with abandonment of traditional values. This was encouraged by the progressive establishment, in the sixteenth and seventeenth centuries, of an effective market economy, hastened by the arrival of precious metals from America and by the growth of credit facilities. Money upset and weakened the old rules governing such economic and social groups as town authorities and craft or merchant guilds, all of which at the same time lost some of their usefulness as well as their former rigidity. In daily life, therefore, the individual rediscovered a certain freedom of choice. But, at the same time, the apparatus of the modern State imposed a new order which strictly limited such freedom. The individual owed a duty to society, and had to respect privileges and those who enjoyed them.

One of Descartes's letters states the problem clearly. If, in theory, everyone is free, a self-sufficient individual, how then will society survive, and what rules will it follow? It was Princess Elizabeth, Princess Palatine, daughter of James I, who put the question; and on 15 September 1645 Descartes replied as follows.

Although every one of us is a person separate from the others, and hence endowed with interests that are in some ways distinct from those of the rest of the world, one must always reflect that one could not survive alone, and that one is in effect one of the parts of the universe, and more particularly still one of the parts of this earth and one of the parts of this State, this Society, this family to which one is linked by residence, by oath and by birth. One must always serve the interests of the whole of which one is a part, in preference to those of one's own person in particular.

In the name of these 'interests of the whole', the seventeenth century undertook a strict 'training programme', not only for the poor, but for all 'useless' elements in society – all those who did not work. True, there was a worrying rise in the numbers of the poor, owing partly to the increase in the population throughout the sixteenth century and to the economic crisis which began at the end of that century and grew worse in the seventeenth. The growing numbers of the poor were reflected in begging, vagrancy and theft, all of which led to repressive reactions. In 1532, the Paris Parlement had the capital's beggars arrested 'to force them to work in the sewers, chained together in pairs'. Compare also how the town of Troyes treated its indigent population, in 1573.

But these were transitory measures. Throughout the Middle Ages, the poor, the vagrants and the mad had been protected by the right to hospitality and alms to which they were entitled in the name of God, because Christ had sanctified poverty by one day wearing the garments of the poor – and the poor might always turn out to be God's emissaries. The whole spiritual movement personified by St Francis had exalted the mystical value of Lady Poverty, holy poverty. And in any case the unfortunate, the mad, the derelicts of society tended to wander from one town to another: most people were eager to send them on their way rather than keeping them within the city walls.

Hence a certain form of liberty, at least in the physical sense, was open to a peasant who fled from his lord to find another who was less oppressive, or to take refuge in the town. The same was true of a soldier in search of a recruiting officer, or of an immigrant leaving for better wages or for the New World and the illusion of a better life. There were also the unemployed, the inveterate vagrants, the beggars, the mental defectives, the handicapped and the thieves – kept alive without work by charity or crime, and therefore in some senses free.

All these people, protected hitherto under the shadow of the Almighty, became in the seventeenth century the enemies of a society that was urban, already capitalist, attached to order and efficiency, and shaping the State in the same spirit to the same ends. Throughout Europe (in Protestant as well as Catholic areas), the poor, the sick, the unemployed and the insane were pitilessly locked up (sometimes with their families) alongside delinquents of every kind. It was what Michel Foucault (who studied the phenomenon in connection with madness in early modern times) called 'the great imprisonment' of the poor – legalized detention organized by a painstaking administration. This also made it possible not only to put away a debauched or prodigal son or a spendthrift father, at the request of their families, but also, with a *lettre de cachet* from the king, to incarcerate a political rival.

A very large number of establishments were founded for these purposes: hospitals, charitable workshops, workhouses, *Zuchthäuser*. Whatever they might be called, they were simply draconian barracks, with forced labour as well. In France, after the decree establishing the Hôpital Général in 1656, which at the same time set in motion this whole new social policy, almost 1 per cent of the Paris population found itself locked up! The severity of this repression was not moderated until the eighteenth century.

In a world where liberty already existed only for those with privileges, the seventeenth century thus helped to impose real restraints on the elementary freedom to abscond or become a vagrant – the only freedom which until then had been allowed to the poor. At the same time, as we have seen, peasant privileges were curbed. Shortly before the 'Enlightenment', Europe plumbed the depths of misery.

There was one solitary corrective to this gloomy picture. Liberty, which so few could attain, remained in Europe that ideal towards which people's thoughts, and also their history, slowly progressed. It was a major trend in the history of Europe, as was shown by the many peasant revolts in the seventeenth century, by the no less frequent popular uprisings (in Paris in 1633, in Rouen from 1634 to 1639, in Lyon in 1623, 1629, 1633 and 1642), and by political and philosophical developments in the eighteenth century.

The French Revolution itself did not succeed in establishing complete liberty, any more than we can boast of having established it today. True, the Revolution abolished feudal privileges on the night of 4 August 1789; but peasants still had to face creditors and landlords. In 1791, by the Le Chapelier law, it equally abolished corporations; but that left workers at the mercy of their employers. It took a century before trade unions became legal in France, in 1884. Nevertheless, the 1789 Declaration of the Rights of Man and of the Citizen remains a landmark in the history of freedom, a fundamental fact in the development of European civilization.

Liberty, or the quest for equality? Napoleon believed that the French did not want liberty, but sought equality – equality before the law, the abolition of feudal rights – in a word the end of private liberties and privileges. From liberties to liberty: that phrase encapsulates one of the fundamental thrusts in the history of Europe. The still abstract, theoretical notion of liberty, which developed from the Renaissance and Reformation until the French Revolution, grew more powerful when it was spelled out in the Declaration of the Rights of Man and of the Citizen. With the advent of liberalism, it became a doctrine.

Thenceforward liberty – in the singular – became an explicit factor in world affairs and in history. It was invoked – legitimately or not – by almost all the ideologies and claims advanced in the nineteenth century by the very varied movements covered by the artificial term 'liberalism', which is highly equivocal because it has so many meanings.

In one of its definitions it denotes a political doctrine, seeking to increase the power of the legislative and the judiciary and limit that of the executive. In this sense it is opposed to authoritarianism. In another definition, liberalism is an economic doctrine with the triumphant slogan '*laissez faire, laissez passer*', seeking to prevent the State's intervening in economic relations between individuals, classes and nations. Finally, liberalism is a philosophical doctrine, calling for freedom of thought and maintaining that religious unity is not a *sine qua non* for social or national unity. This necessarily implies the idea of tolerance and of respect for others and for the human individual, as expressed in the ancient tag *Homo homini res sacra.*

So liberalism is more than 'the doctrine of a party . . . a climate of opinion'. Grappling with the many varied problems of the nineteenth century, it tackled innumerable tasks and faced innumerable obstacles. In Germany and Italy, it identified with nationalism: was not the primary liberty that had to be won that of Nation itself? In Spain and Portugal, it clashed with the monstrous power of a solidly entrenched *ancien régime*, supported by the Church. In Britain and France, by contrast, it virtually achieved its political objectives. Slowly and imperfectly, the liberal, constitutional State took shape, embodying fundamental freedom: freedom of opinion, of the press and of parliament; individual liberty; and the gradual extension of the right to vote.

At the same time, throughout the first half of the nineteenth century, liberalism served as a screen for the political emergence of a new propertied class, the business aristocracy and bourgeoisie. 'Outside a small circle, the individual whose rights liberalism defended with so much zeal was still only an abstraction, unable to benefit fully from these advantages.' This was as true in Britain, with its Conservatives and Liberals, its old and its new money, as in France at the time of the Restoration and the July Monarchy. The propertied class which called itself liberal was immediately opposed to universal suffrage and to the masses in general. Yet how could such political egoism be sustained in the face of industrial society, whose appalling realities so soon appeared? Economic liberalism, which presupposed equal competition among individuals, was no more than a pious fiction. The more time went by, the more the enormity of that fiction became obvious.

In fact, this first, 'bourgeois' form of liberalism was above all a defensive action, by no means disinterested, against the aristocratic *ancien régime* – 'a challenge to the vested interests that the traditions of half a millennium had made sacred'. In this way it came between the aristocratic society of the *ancien régime* which it had destroyed and an industrial society in which the proletariat was beginning to demand its rights. In other words, the bourgeoisie's espousal of liberty was not all that it seemed to be: it was much more like the old struggles for liberties pursued by groups that were really seeking privileges.

The revolutions of 1848 were a crucial landmark for liberty. In France, it was then that universal suffrage was established, whereas in Britain the key electoral reform took place in 1832. Henceforward, with or without the franchise, the only form of liberalism that could survive was political liberalism, in principle open to all classes of people. Alexis de Tocqueville and Herbert Spencer, each in a different way, noted this development and foretold the triumph of the masses, which both feared. But although liberalism thus gathered new strength, it soon clashed with the ever more direct and powerful thrust of Socialism, as well as with such prophets of authoritarianism – some nowadays even call it 'fascism' – as Carlyle or Napoleon III.

The political scene was flanked, therefore, on the one side by the up-and-coming revolution of Socialism in all its many varieties, and on the other by a counter-revolution which knew neither its own name nor how far it might go. Between the two, liberalism continued its life, formed its many governments, and practised its bourgeois wisdom and egotism. It recovered its fire a little, in France, only in its battles with the Church. The Liberals were henceforth aware of their limitations, and even began to doubt their own cause. In 1902–1903, the sensible *Revue de métaphysique et de morale* published a series of articles on 'The Crisis of Liberalism', concerned particularly with the monopoly of education. But the real and final crisis came a little later, between the two World Wars.

But who would dare to argue that liberalism, virtually banished now from active politics, and intellectually devalued, is really dead today? It was more than a political epoch and more than the contrivance or camouflage of a particular class. For Western civilization it was a high ideal; and, however much it may have been tarnished or betrayed, it remains part of our heritage and our language: it has become second nature. Any breach of individual liberties affronts and incenses us. Politically, too, in the face of authoritarian or technocratic States, and societies which are always coercive, a certain defiant and anarchic liberalism, invoking the individual and his rights, continues its leavening work in the West and in the world.

17. Christianity, Humanism and Scientific Thought

The spiritual and intellectual life of Europe was always subject to violent change. It favoured and created divisions and discontinuities, and indeed dramas, always with the aim of building a better world.

Yet these *coups de théâtre* should not distract attention from the tenacious continuity of Europe's thought and civilization, evident throughout all its successive phases, from the *Summa* of St Thomas Aquinas to the *Discours de la Méthode* of René Descartes, and uninterrupted by the Renaissance, the Reformation and the French Revolution itself. Even the Industrial Revolution, a decisive break with the past, did not affect all aspects of Europe's life and thought.

Christianity

All religions evolve. All in their different ways, however, are separate worlds, with their own loyalties, their own permanence, and their own frames of reference.

Western Christianity was and remains the main constituent element in European thought – including rationalist thought, which although it attacked Christianity was also derivative from it. Throughout the history of the West, Christianity has been at the heart of the civilization it inspires, even when it has allowed itself to be captured or deformed by it, and which it contains, even when efforts are made to escape. To direct one's thoughts against someone is to remain in his orbit. A European, even if he is an atheist, is still the prisoner of an ethic and a mentality which are deeply rooted in the Christian tradition. He remains, one might say, 'of Christian descent', in the same way that Montherlant used to say that he was 'of Catholic descent' although he had lost his faith.

Already widespread in the Roman Empire, Christianity became the official religion as a result of the Edict of Constantine in 313, three centuries after the birth of Christ. The Roman Empire comprised all the Mediterranean countries and, in Europe, several outside the lands of the olive and the vine. This was the region inherited at the outset by the new triumphant religion – the 'Christian vineyard', to adapt a phrase of Paul Valéry's, using a play on words ('*aire*' meaning both 'area' and 'threshing-floor') to mark Christianity's links with the land, with bread, wine, wheat, the vine and even holy oil – all characteristic of the Mediterranean starting-point from which Christian belief was later to spread so widely.

In this way, before the ordeal of the fifth-century invasions and the disasters following Islam's victories between the seventh and the eleventh centuries, Christianity had time to adapt itself in some degree to the Roman world. It established its hierarchy there; it learned to distinguish clearly between the temporal – 'the things which are Caesar's' – and the spiritual; and it overcame the ferocious dogmatic disputes which arose not only from the subtleties and the agility of the Greek language and the Greek mind, but also from the need to define the theological bases of Christianity, to give it shape, and to decide where it led.

This slow and difficult task fell to the first Councils (of Nicaea in 325, Constantinople in 381, Ephesus in 431, Chalcedon in 451 and so on), and to the Fathers of the Church. These included the Apologists, who before Constantine were embattled against paganism, and then the Dogmatics, who defined Christian doctrine as distinct from the teachings of dissident sects. St Augustine was not the last in this succession (which some believe to have continued into the eighth and even the twelfth century); but he was by far the most important to the West. A Berber, born in 354 at Thagaste (now Souk-Ahras) in Africa, he died as Bishop of Hippo (later Bône, now Annaba) in 430, while the Vandals were besieging the town. The exceptional brilliance of his works (*The City of God*, *The Confessions*), his contradictory nature, his desire to bring together faith and intelligence, classical and Christian civilization, the old wine and the new – these deliberate efforts made him in some ways a rationalist. For him, faith came first: but he nevertheless declared '*Credo ut intelligam*' – 'I believe in order to understand.' He also said '*Si fallor, sum*' – 'If I am mistaken, I exist' – and '*Si dubitat, vivit*' – 'If he doubts, he is alive.' It would be misleading to see in these remarks a very distant anticipation of Descartes's '*Cogito ergo sum*': but they clearly have affinities with it. Posterity undoubtedly concentrated its attention on St Augustine as a theologian, and on what he wrote about predestination. But Augustinianism gave Western Christianity some of its colour and its ability to adapt and debate – if only by insisting on the vital need to embrace the faith in full awareness, after deep personal reflection, and with the will to act accordingly.

It was not a hesitant or infant Church that was overtaken by the apocalyptic disasters of the barbarian invasions. In that dark fifth century, it had already taken shape like the Empire itself, as the civilization of the ancient world which it had taken over, and which it was to save, in some respects, by saving itself.

The Church saved itself in an imperilled world, but only by dint of countless heroic feats. It had to convert the new arrivals; convert those peasants who were still barely Christian or who too readily neglected the teaching of the Church; convert the inhabitants of the new regions occupied by the West. It had to maintain a hierarchy linked to Rome and to the Bishop of Rome, the Pope – at a time when feudalism was splitting the West into tiny districts and many bishoprics. It had to fight hard battles, of which the most famous was that between the Empire and the Papacy, ended but not settled by the Concordat of Worms on Investitures in 1122. Altogether, this was an immense and laborious task, a repetitive and tedious campaign of persuasion, marked by defeats and new beginnings in which everything was called in question, over and over again. But the development of monastic life, with the Benedictines and the Cistercians, led to the material and spiritual colonization of the countryside in the eleventh and twelfth centuries, while the preaching of the friars, Dominican and Franciscan, in the thirteenth century, made a powerful impact on the towns.

Every century had its challenges and battles. In the thirteenth century, there was the struggle against the Cathari; in the violent fifteenth century, the great debate between the Councils and the Papacy at the Councils of Constance and Basle. In the sixteenth century came the explosion of the Reformation, then the Counter-Reformation led by the Jesuits, the conversion of the New World and the authoritative pronouncements of the Council of Trent (1545–63). The seventeenth century saw the Jansenist challenge. The eighteenth produced a more determined struggle against adherents of a new kind of atheism, less discreet than that of the seventeenth-century 'libertines'. That battle had not been won when the century ended: it had barely been started when the French Revolution broke out.

Finally, apart from the hostility of adversaries with conscious and articulate ideologies, the Church had constantly to deal with a regular, monotonous process of de-Christianization, which was often no more than a crude lapse from civilization back to barbarism. Wherever communications were difficult, off the beaten track (for instance in the Alps or on the edges of Europe, in Mecklenburg as late as the thirteenth century, or in Lithuania and Corsica in the fifteenth and sixteenth centuries), old pagan cults sprang up again at every opportunity. In one place it might be the cult of the snake, in another that of the dead and the stars. So numerous were the superstitions, and so tenaciously rooted in folklore, that the Church often had to content itself with clothing them in light ecclesiastical garb.

In these battles, Christianity used every kind of weapon: education, preaching, temporal power, art, religious drama, miracles and the popular cult of the saints, which was sometimes so intrusive that the Church's servants themselves took fright and reacted against it. In 1633, in Lisbon, two Capuchins felt obliged to admit that 'St Anthony of Padua seems to be the God of Lisbon . . . The poor ask for alms only in his name and . . . invoke only him when they are in danger. For them, their St Anthony is everything: he is their magnetic North and, as the preacher says, the Saint of needles; if ever a woman looks for her needle, she finds it with the help of St Anthony.' The fashion for St Anthony even crossed the sea. A century later, a French traveller in Brazil reported 'prodigious devotion' to him.

Popular superstition, in fact, was always liable to undermine or compromise religious life from within, distorting the very bases of the faith. When it did so, everything had to be started again.

When St John of the Cross settled with two companions at Duruelo in Castile, where St Teresa had located the first monastery of the Reformed Carmelites, it was to lead the most frugal monastic life amid the snows of winter, but not in any cloistered sense. 'They often went out barefoot along the worst of paths to preach the Gospel to the peasants as if to savages . . .' This proves, if proof were needed, that conversion still remained necessary, even in a Christian country.

The work of Christianity thus had to be done on two different levels. One was that of intellectual life, where it had to defend itself against adversaries who were sometimes well-intentioned but never lacking in numbers. The other was that of the masses, whose hard life and isolation too easily cut them off from religious feelings and simple faith.

Christianity ebbed and flowed: it had successes and setbacks and long periods of stagnation. We can trace these only crudely, from outside, in so far as the daily experience of religion, and its reality for the average person, too often remains unknown. Very broadly, however, its general evolution is unmistakable.

From the tenth to the thirteenth century, Christianity was advancing vigorously everywhere. Churches and monasteries still stand, in many cases, as witnesses: the whole Church was carried along by a powerful movement that was also economic and social: Europe was active, full of life, and expanding rapidly. Then came the Black Death and a brutal, catastrophic decline. Everything suffered, even the progress of Christianity, during the long series of disturbances and strife that historians call the Hundred Years' War (1337–1453). Its repercussions went far beyond the main belligerents, France and Britain: they extended, in fact, to the whole of the West.

In the second half of the fifteenth century, a new religious resurgence occurred, affecting the whole of Europe, which was returning to peace but also to serious disquiet. From about 1450 to about 1500, there was what Lucien Febvre has called 'a time of trouble'. Some historians have simply labelled it 'the pre-Reformation'; but this is a misnomer, since the anxiety that was then general was in no way bound to lead to the 'Protestant', protesting attitude of the Reformation. In those countries that remained faithful to Rome, the same religious anxiety led to another kind of reform, a Catholic reform, which most historians call 'the Counter-Reformation'. Here again, the word is not particularly apt.

However that may be, the sixteenth and seventeenth centuries were a time of keen religious passions, of fierce spiritual disputes whose vehemence should not surprise us. Such for instance was the sharp quarrel between the rigour of the Jansenists and the simpler, laxer, but very human ethic of the Jesuits at the time of Saint-Cyran, of the Gentlemen of Port-Royal, of Mme de Sévigné, of Racine, and of Pascal.

With the eighteenth century, there was a great reverse. This time, material progress did not serve the cause of the Church. It went with a scientific and philosophic movement which on the contrary opposed the Church in the name of progress and reason.

★

Humanism and humanists

European thought is inconceivable except in the context of a dialogue with Christianity, even when the dialogue is sharp and the dispute violent. This context is essential to the understanding of humanism, one of the fundamental aspects of Western thought.

To begin with, a question of vocabulary: the word humanism is ambiguous, and can be hazardous unless we at once define its usage and its civic status. It is a learned expression, coined by German historians in the nineteenth century (and, to be precise, in 1808). Pierre de Nolhac, the author of *Petrarch and Humanism* 'has claimed the honour of having introduced it into the official language of the French University in 1886, in his course of lectures at the *Ecole des Hautes Etudes*'. So the word is a relative neologism, and therefore lends itself easily to personal interpretations, for good or ill. Until then, only the word 'humanists' had been used, referring to a precise group of men in the fifteenth and sixteenth centuries who had taken that name themselves.

But the word humanism did not remain restricted to these 'humanists' and to the 'spirit of the Italian and European Renaissance' that they embodied. It meant that, but also many other things — so many that it brought to present-day usage a huge wealth of connotations. An inquiry in 1930 turned up expressions such as '*new* humanism', '*Christian* humanism', '*pure* humanism' and even '*technical*' and '*scientific* humanism'. A survey today would produce similar results, proving that if the word was once a learned or technical expression, it has tended to become popular and take on new meanings, and therefore corresponds to living questions and concerns.

In historical studies, we find references to the humanism of the twelfth century (underlying scholasticism), to that of the Renaissance or the Reformation, to the humanism of the French Revolution (by which is often meant its originality and many-sidedness) and even to 'the humanism of Karl Marx or Maxim Gorky'. One can only wonder what this series of 'humanisms' has in common, apart from the need and the obvious eagerness to treat them all as a family of problems.

Perhaps we may reasonably borrow from Augustin Renaudet, the historian of Tuscan and European humanism, a broad definition which seems to cover this very general sense.

The name of humanism can be applied to an ethic based on human nobility. Turned towards both study and action, it recognizes and exalts the greatness of human genius and the power of its creations, opposing its strength to the brute force of inanimate nature. What is essential remains the individual's effort to develop in himself or herself, through strict and methodical discipline, all human faculties, so as to lose nothing of what enlarges and enhances the human being. 'Reach towards the highest form of existence,' said Goethe at the beginning of Part Two of *Faust*, 'by dint of uninterrupted effort.' Similarly, Stendhal said to Eugène Delacroix on 31 January 1850: 'Neglect nothing that can make you great.' Such an ethic based on human nobility requires of society a constant effort to embody the most highly perfected form of human relations: an immense feat, an immense cultural achievement, an ever greater knowledge of humanity and of the world. It lays the foundations of individual and collective morality; it establishes law and creates an economy; it produces a political system; it nourishes art and literature.

This eloquent definition ought to be adequate. But it does not stress powerfully enough that sense of the movement which is exaggerated, on the other hand, by Etienne Gilson's curt definition: Renaissance humanism, he declared in substance, was the Middle Ages 'not plus humanity but minus God'. The phrase is unfair and too extreme; but it does indicate the natural inclination, conscious or unconscious, of all humanist thought. Humanism frees and magnifies humanity, diminishing the role of God even if not completely forgetting it.

In a certain sense, too, humanism is always against something: against exclusive submission to God; against a wholly materialist conception of the world; against any doctrine neglecting or seeming to neglect humanity; against any system that would reduce human responsibility ... It is a perpetual series of demands – a manifestation of pride.

Calvin had no illusions. 'When we are told to rely on our own strength and ability, are we not being raised to the uppermost end of a reed which cannot bear our weight and immediately breaks, so that we fall down?' Calvin was not one of those who placed their first faith in humanity.

For the humanist, it was quite otherwise. His faith, if he had a faith, had to accommodate his confidence in humanity. And it is in the light of this inveterate tradition of European humanism that one can understand the remarks of the sociologist Edgar Morin when he left the Communist Party: 'Marxism, my friend, has studied economics and the social classes. That's marvellous, my friend. But it forgot to study humanity.'

Humanism is all drive, an embattled march towards the progressive emancipation of humanity, with constant attention to the ways in which it can modify and improve human destiny. Its history has been complex and fitful, marked by checks and reverses and by those obvious contradictions which pervade all of Europe's past.

Europe seems always to have been anxiously seeking some solution to its problems and difficulties other than those already to hand. Hence an almost morbid quest for what was new, difficult, forbidden and very often scandalous – something on which the West is a very rich source of information. For want of space, we shall limit our account to three exceptional but significant cases: Renaissance humanism, its near contemporary Reformation humanism and, much later, in the eighteenth century, the passionate humanism of the French Revolution.

Renaissance humanism was a dialogue of Rome with Rome, between pagan Rome and Christian Rome, between classical and Christian civilization. It was certainly one of the most fruitful and continuous debates that the West has ever known.

It was a matter of living, or living once more, with the classical past. The short, decisive final sentence of Machiavelli's *Dell'arte della Guerra* has often been quoted: 'This country [Italy] seems born to revive dead things.' But if these *cose morte* were so eagerly brought back to life, it was a proof that life had need of them, and that they were within reach, and not dead at all.

To tell the truth, pagan Rome never died out in the West. Ernst Curtius, in a technically meticulous study, has shown how amazingly tenacious the civilization of the Lower Empire proved to be, and how the West relied on it to an unheard-of degree for its literary themes, its ways of thought, its metaphors, and even its clichés.

It was natural for Christian Europe to accept this day-to-day contact with ancient Rome, because there was no alternative, no rival civilization to tap. Equally, Christianity had acquiesced in such coexistence before the Roman Empire fell. In the second century, St Justin had declared that any noble thought, 'wherever it comes from, is the property of Christians'. St Ambrose said: 'All truth, whoever its interpreter may be, comes from the Holy Spirit.' Only Tertullian asked: 'What have Athens and Jerusalem in common?' But his voice raised barely an echo.

Yet, while the classical heritage had entered into the life, language and habits of thought of the Western Middle Ages, classical literature and its poets, philosophers or historians had often ceased to arouse the passions or even the interest of intellectuals. While Latin remained a living language, Greek was now almost unknown. In the finest libraries, manuscripts of classical works lay forgotten in the dust. The humanists sought these texts everywhere, to re-read them, edit them and add their impassioned commentaries, so as to restore to public honour the works and the languages of classical antiquity – Greek and Latin – with which they henceforth lived.

No one, perhaps, expressed it better than Machiavelli, during his second period of exile, in 1513, in the evening of his life. He was then living among peasants and woodcutters . . .

Night falls, and I return to my dwelling. I go into the library, and as I cross the threshold I cast off my everyday clothing, covered with filth and mud, and put on the costume of the royal court . . . Thus honourably clad, I enter the classical court of the Ancients. They welcome me warmly, and I feast on the nourishment for which I was born and which is mine *par excellence.* There I have no qualms at speaking with them, and inquiring about the motives for their actions. And they, by virtue of their humanity, duly reply.

Renaissance humanism was marked by such reading, such continual conversation. Rabelais and Montaigne were humanists of this sort: their books, full of memories of their reading, are the living proof. Beside every humanist, one can recognize – with a smile of complicity or malice – the Ancient who leads him by the hand, and thereby explains or exposes him. Erasmus of Rotterdam, now known as the Prince of humanists, was called by his detractors 'Lucian'. Other 'Lucianists' included Rabelais and Bonaventure des Périers; while Machiavelli 'was' Polybius.

It is not easy to assign dates to this broad current of thought. Our artificial word 'humanism' and the term 'Renaissance' (invented, almost as artificially, by Jules Michelet and Jacob Burckhardt) tread on each other's toes. The two phenomena overlap in both time and space.

Avignon was undoubtedly the starting-point of humanism and, with it, the Renaissance. The town came to life with the return of Petrarch in 1337; and thanks to the presence of the Popes it was for a long time the most 'European' and the most luxurious city in the West. Even after the Papacy had returned to Rome in 1376, the Anti-Popes enabled it to retain its luxury and lustre. However, it was in Florence that the Renaissance fully established, later, its 'cultural hegemony', which lasted at least until the death of Lorenzo the Magnificent in 1492, and even until the city's capture by Clement VII and the Imperial forces of Charles V, in 1530. These chronological limits, 1337 and 1530, are certainly applicable to the bulk of the phenomenon which affected not only Italy, but the West as a whole. The last great humanist, Erasmus, born in Rotterdam in 1437, died in Basle in 1536. But these two long centuries cannot be fully understood unless the historical net is cast more widely, backwards beyond 1337 (an indeterminate date in any case) and forwards beyond 1530.

Backwards into the past, because the transition from the Middle Ages to the Renaissance was not the total break that used to be imagined. The Renaissance was not at the opposite pole from medieval philosophy, despite the gibes that humanists hurled at scholasticism. 'Fifty years ago,' wrote one historian, in 1942, 'the Middle Ages and the Renaissance looked as strikingly different as black and white or night and day. Then, one argument compounding another, the frontier between the two has become so confused that to distinguish between them one begins to need a compass.'

Forwards beyond 1530 or 1536, because it is not at all obvious that after the death of Erasmus (the hero of all liberal-minded people today) the civilization of the Renaissance lost its freedom and died under the cold blast of the religious wars that dominated the next century and more.

They certainly interrupted the triumphant advance of the Renaissance. But where the realities of civilization are concerned, what has lasted two centuries cannot be destroyed overnight. In the long term, the humanists won some important points. They won in the realm of education, where classical antiquity has remained an essential element almost to the present day: we are only now beginning to move away from it. But above all, since the humanists, Europe has never lost the confidence in human ability and intelligence which they proclaimed and which has remained the greatest inspiration in the life and thought of the West.

Humanism was the work of 'a few élite spirits' in relatively narrow circles – passionate Latinists, less numerous but no less passionate Hellenists, and Hebraists like Thomas Platter, the ropemaker, or Pico della Mirandola. But their influence was by no means confined to a few cities or brilliant princely courts like that of Francis I. The humanists were scattered all over Europe, and linked by copious correspondence: the marvellous Latin letters of Erasmus fill a dozen octavo volumes in the edition by P. S. and H. M. Allen and H. W. Garrod. All Europe was affected by the humanist phenomenon: Italy to begin with, but also France, Germany (without forgetting the special role of Bohemia), Hungary, Poland, The Netherlands, Britain . . . Lists of names could be quoted to prove the point (as could, in France, the establishment of 'Royal Lectors') in fact, supernumerary professors – commissioned by Francis I to teach subjects banned by the University; later, they became the nucleus of the Collège de France.

Was Renaissance humanism an attack on Christianity or not? Must the movement be seen as heading straight towards atheism and irreligion? Or should Machiavelli, Rabelais or Montaigne at least be hailed as authentic precursors of free thought?

To do so is perhaps to judge the Renaissance too much by present-day criteria. That it turned aside from the traditional teaching of scholasticism and theology is certain. Equally certainly, it relished classical literature that was wholly pagan, and the thrust of its thinking was the exaltation of humanity. But this does not necessarily mean that humanism opposed either God or the Church.

The conclusion of Lucien Febvre's detailed and closely argued study of Rabelais's work is that it was impossible, or at the very least extremely difficult, for anyone in Rabelais's day to embrace with confidence philosophic atheism. The mental equipment of the period scarcely allowed such thoughts: it lacked the key words, the conclusive arguments, and the indispensable scientific support. The Renaissance did not neglect scientific research, but it by no means gave it top priority.

In truth, no valid conclusion can be reached unless one is prepared to weigh and weigh again the thoughts and feelings of the time, rediscover the atmosphere of those distant days, and re-examine one by one the over-hasty accusations of atheism made by the polemics of contemporaries or the passion of historians. In almost every case, the judge will encounter insoluble errors and ambiguities.

The dialogue by Lorenzo Valla, *De Voluptate* (1431), which caused a scandal at the time, is a dispute in Ciceronian Latin between Epicureans and Stoics. Since the latter had been in vogue hitherto (with Petrarch, Salutato and Poggio), the dialogue sought to redress the balance a little by favouring the Epicureans. But at the end of what was a purely literary debate, the author reappeared, to reaffirm the supernatural order of Christianity.

Hypocrisy, one might imagine today. But it would be a facile rewriting of history if we refused to recognize that atheism was forged much later, on the anvil of solid materialistic science. In the sixteenth century, as a general rule, the denial of God scarcely entered into people's concerns, desires or needs.

Nor should Machiavelli be too hastily accused of being a pagan because he criticized the priests and the Church 'who have made us irreligious and evil', or because he reproached Christianity for 'having sanctified the humble and the contemplative, and having made humility the supreme virtue . . . whereas the religion of classical antiquity exalted greatness of soul'. It might be fairer to blame him for having learned too well the lesson of the terrible times he lived through, and removed ethics from politics – an operation that has yet to be reversed . . .

In the same way, let us be clear about the Academy founded by Lorenzo de' Medici. Its basis was Neo-Platonist, and it sided with Plato's idealism against Aristotelian philosophy – perhaps seeking a compromise between classical antiquity and Christianity. But the fact that Pico della Mirandola, who attended it, made a speech about the dignity of humanity – *De dignitate hominis* – in no way prevented him, at the end of his too short life, from hoping to go and preach the Gospel, 'crucifix in hand, barefoot, in the cities, towns and countryside', or from having himself buried in his robes as a Dominican of the Third Order. His was one example, among a hundred others, of what has been called 'religious humanism'. Even the case of the Paduan Pompanazzi, who for some was an obvious atheist, remains for others undecided. That of Bonaventure des Périers, the strange author of the no less strange *Cymbalum Mundi* (1537–8), was studied in a brilliant book by Lucien Febvre, published in 1942. He concluded that if the character of Mercury in these dialogues represents Christ, as seems certain, then this time Christ is under attack, and atheism has to be suspected. We should neither ignore nor exaggerate the importance of Bonaventure's book, which is a very unusual instance in the literature of its time.

Philippe Monnier, a devoted historian of the Florentine *quattrocento*, claims that the humanists, fascinated by the prestige of the Ancients, 'copied them, imitated them, repeated them, adopted their models, their examples, their gods, their spirit and their language' and that 'such a movement, pushed to its logical extreme, would tend towards nothing less than the elimination of the Christian phenomenon'. According to our logic, perhaps. Perhaps not according to that of the fifteenth and sixteenth centuries. 'It would be . . . senseless,' wrote the sociologist Alexander Rustow,

to look for such antagonism, given that the triumph of classical antiquity over the Church . . . was almost complete and was taking place within the Church itself. Did Rome not develop as a flourishing centre of the Renaissance, and were the Popes not initiators of the movement? It was Alexander VI who executed the humanists' enemy in Florence, Savonarola, burned on 20 May 1498. What was more, the classical antiquity now revived in people's minds was tolerant. Greek philosophers had attended the feasts and services of the gods, whether they believed in them or not. Why should their disciples attack a Church which showed so little hostility to them? It was Erasmus who exclaimed: 'St Socrates, pray for us!'

The Renaissance distanced itself from medieval Christianity much less in the realm of ideas than in that of life itself. It could perhaps be called a cultural, not a philosophic betrayal. Its atmosphere was one of lively enjoyment, relishing the many pleasures of the eye, the mind and the body, as if the West were emerging from a centuries-long period of Lent.

The Renaissance bears witness to a sociology, a psychology of joy. Rarely in history did people feel so powerfully that they were living in fortunate times. 'The *Memento mori* of the Middle Ages was replaced by a *Memento vivere*.' The contemplation of death and the *danses macabres* of the late fifteenth century disappeared as if by magic, as if the West had 'parted' (in Michel Foucault's sense) or separated itself in spirit from meditation about death. The change can be traced in the many successive *Artes moriendi*, tracts on how to die a good death. In them, death gradually ceased to be a calm, celestial journey to a better life: it became earthly, with all the fearful signs of bodily corruption – a human death, the supreme ordeal that humans have to face. No one any longer willingly said with St Augustine: 'We here below are travellers longing for death'; but at the same time no one any longer believed that 'this life is rather death than life, a kind of hell'. Life recovered its value and importance.

It was on earth that people had to build their kingdom; and this new conviction coloured the emergence of all 'the positive forces in modern culture: freedom of thought, mistrust of authority, the victory of intellectual education over the privilege of birth (i.e., in terms of the *quattrocento*, the victory of the concept of *humanitas* over that of *nobilitas*), enthusiasm for science, and the deliverance of the individual . . .' (Nietzsche).

The humanists were well aware of this new ferment of ideas. 'Without doubt, this is the golden age,' declared Marsilio Ficino (1433–99). In 1517, Erasmus said almost the same thing: 'We must wish the century good luck: it will be the golden age.' In his famous letter of 28 October 1518, to the Nuremburg humanist Willibad Pirkheimer, Ulrich von Hütten wrote: 'What a century! What literature! How good it is to be alive!' One dare not add the example of Rabelais's fictitious Abbaye de Thélème, because it is so very well known . . . And yet!

No one would deny that this acute awareness of humanity's vast and varied potential prepared the way, in the fullness of time, for all the revolutions of modern times, including atheism. But the humanists were much too busy organizing their own kingdom to think of contesting that of God.

From the first third of the sixteenth century, the impetus and exhilaration of the Renaissance began to be curbed. 'Sombre people' gradually filled the Western stage. Like all periods of joy, of bright sunshine, like all great periods of good fortune, real or supposed, like the century of Alexandria's brilliance, like the century of Augustus, like that of the Enlightenment, the perfection of the Renaissance was only short-lived.

Protestant humanism was the source from which the great flood of the Reformation flowed between the fifteenth and the sixteenth centuries. A key date was 31 October 1517, when Luther's Ninety-five Propositions were displayed on the doors of the Schlosskirche in Wittenburg.

The Reformation was accompanied by the appalling excesses of the Wars of Religion. These began in Germany in 1546, the year when Luther died, and ended more than a century later, in 1648. Meanwhile, they spread to other countries; and everywhere they left behind them widespread ruin. Tardy and more or less enduring compromise agreements were signed: the Peace of Augsburg in 1555, the Edict of Nantes in 1598, the Letter of Majesty in Bohemia in 1609. But the Reformation, unlike Renaissance humanism, quickly became a mass phenomenon, and thousands of men and women, to defend their faith, had to face civil war and violent repression (as in the Netherlands at the time of Philip II, or in France after the Revocation of the Edict of Nantes in 1685, and at the time of the Cévennes insurrection). The alternative was exile, either in the New World or in a country that upheld their faith, following the random principle of *Cujus regio, ejus religio.*

All this violence died down in the eighteenth century, and sometimes earlier. Protestantism survived it; and today it colours a large part of the Western world, notably Anglo-Saxon, Germanic

16. Europe's three Christianities

and Nordic countries, with its own particular variety of humanism.
It is not easy, however, to identify the precise nature of Protestant
humanism, since there is not one Protestant Church, but many,
each expressing the different views of different people. Nevertheless,
they all belong to the same family, especially when they are contrasted
with their neighbour, the Catholic West.

What interests us here is not the Reformation in itself, but the legacy it left to modern Europe. So we shall not linger over the traditional history of Reformation Protestantism. That can be studied, if necessary in the useful summary supplied by Emile Léonard.

Within a matter of twenty years, two types of Protestantism – two long 'waves' – followed each other. One was dominated by the passionate activity of Martin Luther (1483–1546); the other was led by the thoughtful and authoritarian John Calvin (1509–64). The two men were almost totally different. Luther was a peasant from the frontier regions of Eastern Germany. There was something direct, strong and natural in his rustic spiritual rebellion – what Nietzsche called a 'peasantry of the spirit', *ein Bauerstand des Geistes.* To denounce the abuses, absurdities and complications of the Church; to dispel uncertainty by staking everything on redemption by faith ('just people are saved by their faith'); to be content with spontaneous, emotional views without seeking to reduce them to meticulous order – that was the clear and simple message of the young Luther. It was romantic and revolutionary. 'God will not put up with this for long!' he cried: 'We are not living in yesterday's world, where people were hunted and herded like game!' True, Luther could not for ever sustain this attitude, which antagonized the rich and powerful. In 1525, he had to distance himself from the German peasants between the Elbe, the Rhine and the Alps, who had mounted a revolt which was partly inspired by his teachings.

Yet he remained at the opposite pole from Calvin, the city-dweller, the cool intellectual, the patient, tireless organizer, the lawyer who must always follow his logic to the end. Luther met Predestination as revealed truth: Calvin treated it as a mathematical formula and deduced the results. If the elect had always been predestined for salvation, was it not their vocation to rule the others? This was the logical conclusion that Calvin applied in Geneva in 1536–8 and 1541–64, with a firm hand but invoking the spirit of humility. It was what Oliver Cromwell did in the British Isles in the harsh days of the Puritan Revolution.

Such were the two major strands in Protestantism. They prevailed in different places, but they had points in common: the break with Rome and with the cult of the Saints, the abolition of the regular clergy, the reduction of the sacraments from seven to two (Eucharist and baptism), although with lingering disagreement about the Eucharist. Nor should one forget what for simplicity's sake (for a complete list would be long) one can call eccentric or marginal forms of Protestantism, such as the early humanist varieties (Zwingli in Zurich, Oecolampadius in Basle, Henry VIII in Britain) or the 'pietistic' Protestantism of the much persecuted Anabaptists.

The frontier between the Catholic and Protestant worlds is still a tangible feature of European civilization. Was it fixed only by the fortunes of war?

Like the rings of a tree-trunk, Europe grew in successive layers. Its oldest wood – the heart of the tree – was what had been conquered (and civilized) by the Roman Empire, when it stretched West and North as far as the Rhine and the Danube in one direction and the British Isles in the other (although here it held, insecurely, only part of the whole, mainly in the South-East). Beyond these frontiers, European civilization was a late arrival, after the fall of the Roman Empire: here, the sapwood was young and thin. Medieval Europe colonized the surrounding territory (in the best sense of the term), sending missionaries and building churches. The abbeys and bishoprics established there by distant Rome laid sturdy foundations.

Is it coincidental that this old frontier of the Roman Empire, the frontier between ancient Europe and the new, recently 'colonized' Europe is broadly speaking the same as that which divided the Catholic from the Protestant world? Of course, the Reformation had its purely religious aspects: it was one outcome of the rising tide of religion that was evident throughout Europe, making the faithful ever more aware of the abuses and disorders in the Church, and the limitations of worship that was too matter-of-fact, too much a matter of gestures rather than true devotion.

These feelings were common to Christendom as a whole. But the old Europe, no doubt more attached to the religious traditions linking it so closely with Rome, maintained that connection, while the new Europe, younger and more mixed, less firmly tied to the religious hierarchy, broke completely away. Already one can sense here something of a national reaction.

The later development of the two worlds has often lent itself to what might be called sectarian pride. The virtues of Protestantism have been credited with the rise of capitalism and of scientific thought, i.e. with that of the modern world. But the respective positions of Protestantism and Catholicism can be explained more reasonably against the background of economic and general history. In fact, it is hard to see anything in Protestantism that would make it intellectually superior – or inferior – to the Catholic world. On the other hand, it has certainly affected European culture, bringing to it a new and original contribution of its own.

To make clear what that contribution was, we must distinguish between the early, militant Protestantism of the sixteenth century and the victorious, established Protestantism of the eighteenth.

Inaugurated under the banner of liberty and revolt, the Reformation soon lapsed into the same degree of intransigence of which it accused its enemy. It built a structure as rigid as medieval Catholicism, 'in which everything was subordinated to the scale of spiritual values derived from revelation: the State, Society, education, science, economics and Law'. At the top of the scale was 'the Book', the Bible, and – as its interpreters – the Protestant Church and State. The latter (it might be a Prince or a city) enjoyed the *jus episcopale* of old.

Needless to say, this system by no means produced the religious liberty for which people had originally fought. Order, strictness and the iron hand: these were the watchwords of the early Protestant Churches, whether at Basle or at Zurich. The Reformers might be followers of Erasmus; but they had no hesitation in drowning the dreadful Anabaptists. There were similar massacres in The Netherlands. It was paradoxical. That the 'Papists' should have hunted down, hanged, butchered or drowned the unfortunates who denied the Holy Trinity or the divinity of the Son, and simultaneously attacked the Church, the State and the wealthy – that, if by no means charitable, at least had a certain logic. But on what grounds did the Reformation inflict the same persecution? One example was the *tragoedia serveta*. Michel Servet, a Spanish Protestant physician, was arrested one day in Geneva on his way out of church. Accused of pantheism and of denying the Trinity, he was tortured and burned at the behest of Calvin, who had long had him under surveillance. In 1554, Sebastian Castellio (1515–63), a 'Savoyard' humanist and apostle of liberal Reform, protested against this in a moving and indignant pamphlet addressed to the ruler of Geneva, whom he had earlier served and liked. He was indignant because no one felt more keenly the errors and crimes of the triumphalist Reformation. 'There is almost no sect,' he wrote, 'which does not regard others as heretics; with the result that, if you are thought to be right in one city or region, in the next you will be thought a heretic. So much so that if anyone today wants to live, he must have as many religions as there are cities or sects – just as anyone travelling from one country to another has to change his money from day to day, because what is valid here becomes valueless elsewhere.' Himself, Castellio determined to remain faithful to the free interpretation of Scripture. 'As for the Anabaptists,' he said, 'it is up to them to decide what they do with what they sense, think or write about the word of God.'

Castellio's remained an isolated voice. He died in poverty, surrounded by a few loyal followers. But in the seventeenth century, at the time of the disputes between the strict Calvinists and the Arminian or Socinian dissidents, his works were republished in Amsterdam, one of them bearing the significant title *The Candle of Savoy*. Indeed, Castellio the Savoyard became one of the harbingers of the new course that Protestantism finally took.

Later Protestantism favoured liberty of conscience. Dogmatic rigour gradually lessened, especially in the eighteenth century, perhaps with the waning of active pressure from Catholicism and the energetic Counter-Reformation. But Protestantism also evolved of its own accord towards greater freedom of conscience, in the same spirit as the Enlightenment, and mainly under the influence of scientific progress. As always, it is very difficult to disentangle cause and effect. Did Protestantism, by returning to its spiritual origins and to the free study of the Scriptures, help Europe towards greater independence of mind? Or was the evolution of Protestantism itself part of the general evolution of philosophical and scientific thought in Europe? Both possibilities may have been combined, each influencing the other.

It cannot be denied that Protestantism, unlike its Catholic rival, fitted into the evolution of the great liberal century. But it has to be admitted, too, that countries of Catholic tradition and training such as France were also leading spirits in that evolution.

At all events, Protestantism now inclined towards the free study of Scripture, historical criticism of sacred texts and a kind of deist rationalism. In so doing, it put an end to its internal squabbles; and that was what mattered. All the marginal sects, hitherto spurned as suspect – the Puritans in Britain, the Anabaptists in Germany and The Netherlands – now flourished and even multiplied. The Anabaptists, under the name of Mennonites, prospered in Britain, went to America, founding a colony in Providence, Rhode Island, and became a powerful Protestant sect in the United States. At the end of the seventeenth century there reappeared – descendants of the 'Inspired' of the sixteenth century – the group that called itself the Society of Friends, known more generally as the Quakers. In 1681 the Quaker William Penn founded the colony of Pennsylvania. There was a similar upsurge in Germany, with the pietism of the pastor Philip Jakob Spener, a protégé of the Elector of Brandenburg (who later, in 1701, became the first King of Prussia, Frederick I). Spener was also involved in the foundation of the influential University of Halle in 1681. In the middle of the eighteenth century, the whole of Lutheran Germany was stirred up by his disciples. But none of these movements was as powerful as, in Britain, the Methodism of John and Charles Wesley and George Whitefield.

There would be little point here in enumerating these successful sects, other than to show how freely Protestant thought flourished in a religious movement no longer subject to any strict theology. 'Theology is no longer identified with religion,' wrote a Protestant university teacher, Ferdinand Buisson, in 1914; 'one must pass so that the other may endure.' This, fundamentally, is what now distinguishes Protestant from Catholic society. The Protestant is always alone with God. He can, so to speak, work out his own religion, live it, and remain in keeping – conform – with the religious world. More than that, he can choose from among the many sects that which solves, without pain, his own personal problem. One might almost say that each of the different sects corresponds to a different social group or class.

As a result, Protestant society is untouched by the schism between lay and confessional matters that marks modern Catholic societies, where everyone has to choose between a certain mental obedience or a break with the Church – a community to which one either belongs or not. With Catholicism, spiritual conflicts are in that sense public: one is obliged to state one's position. In Protestant society such conflicts certainly exist, but they take place in private. Hence the series of differences in behaviour and attitudes which draw an imperceptible but indelible line between the Anglo-Saxons and Catholic Europe.

Europe has always been, and still is, revolutionary. All its history confirms that fact. But at the same time it has always been, and still is, endlessly counter-revolutionary. Here again, what matters is not the series of revolutionary movements in themselves, but rather their effect on the future – which we shall call 'revolutionary humanism'. By this unfamiliar phrase we mean the human content and the intellectual 'legacy' of the Revolution. Others refer to 'the revolutionary mystique' or 'the revolutionary spirit'. We refer, of course, to the French Revolution, the only one with European and world significance before the Russian Revolution of 1917.

Revolutionary movements and the Revolution

Until the Russian Revolution, the French Revolution of 1789 was always referred to – in France, at least – as 'the Revolution', implying that it was the first and only one. In fact, however, a number of revolutionary movements had occurred earlier, in a Europe that was tense, restive and unwilling to put up with the worst. But historians have been reluctant to call them 'revolutions'.

They would scarcely give that name, for example, to the numerous peasant revolts that we have already noted in various parts of Europe between the fourteenth and seventeenth centuries. And it is often in a particular sense that the word 'revolution' is used, for instance about struggles for national liberation: by the Swiss cantons, definitively freed in 1412; by the United Provinces, finally victorious in 1648; by the American colonies of Britain, the future United States, in 1774–82; by Spanish America between 1810 and 1824. It can also be applied to the emergence of the Scandinavian countries – Sweden, Norway and Denmark – securing their independence either peacefully or by brute force. All these were no doubt reactions against the modern State: but they were still more against foreigners – an important nuance.

A 'real' revolution is always against a modern State: that is essential. And it always comes from within, with a view to the State's reforming itself. Before 1789 in Europe (if we ignore the failures of the Catholic League and the Fronde), only the two English revolutions had been worthy of the name – the first involving a violent Civil War (1640–58), the second peaceful (the 'Glorious Revolution' of 1688). But the French Revolution, which overthrew from within one of the strongest States in the West, had quite different repercussions. Between 1789 and 1815 it spread throughout Europe; and the memory of it acquired, for the world as a whole, the value of a powerful symbol, seen afresh by every generation and always able to arouse new passions.

The power of that symbol is still great. Travelling in the USSR

in 1958, a French historian was surprised to find that when his
Soviet colleagues said 'the Revolution', they were referring to the
French Revolution, and not their own. The same historian, teaching at the University of São Paulo, Brazil, in 1935, echoed Albert
Mathiez by pointing out that most of the so-called 'giants' of the
1792 Convention were simply mortal men and in some cases
rather ordinary. His Brazilian students reacted at once, as if at
sacrilege, and one of them declared: 'We, you know, are waiting
for the French Revolution.'

So the 1789 revolution lives on throughout the world, even
when it might have been supplanted, as a myth, by the October
Revolution in Russia. In France, the Russian Revolution tends
totally to dominate the trade-union and revolutionary press, in so
far as it relates to the practical realities of the day. But the fervour
still aroused, even fairly recently, by 1789 can only really be
appreciated by those who remember the monstrous uproar and
excitement that greeted the Sorbonne lectures by Alphonse Aulard
(who died in 1928) and the eagerness of those who went there to
hear Albert Mathiez (d. 1932) or Georges Lefebvre (d. 1960). The
survival of the Revolution in the political and ethical thinking of
Europeans affects their arguments and attitudes, even when their
attitudes are hostile to it.

*There were two, three or four French Revolutions. Like a multi-stage
rocket today, the Revolution involved several successive explosions and
propellant thrusts*

It seemed at first to be a moderate, 'liberal revolution', although
involving some dramatic episodes like the Fall of the Bastille and
the Terror. This first Revolution developed rapidly, in four successive stages: an aristocratic revolt (the Assembly of the Notabilities
in 1788), a bourgeois revolt 'by lawyers', as has been said (the
meeting of the States General), then an urban and a peasant revolution, both of which were decisive.

A second and brutal Revolution followed, after the declaration of war against Austria on 20 April 1792. 'It was the war of 1792 that led the French revolution astray,' wrote Alphonse Aulard. It is true; and the occupation of The Netherlands after Jemappes made the conflict inevitable. We should recognize also that by turning France into a modern nation (and before the song and dance of the Federations that dramatized the fact), the Revolution affirmed and revealed its strength and prepared the subsequent explosion. This second phase, which was as violent within as without, ended with the fall of Robespierre on 27–28 July 1794 (9–10 Thermidor in the Year II).

The third Revolution (if the word is still appropriate) took place between Thermidor and Brumaire (from 28 July 1794 to 9–10 November 1799) and covered the last months of the Convention and the whole of the Directoire. The fourth Revolution included the Consulate, the Empire and the Hundred Days (1799–1815).

Napoleon certainly continued the Revolution, stabilizing and mastering it, but adding to the uncertainties of its broad future the dramatic insecurity of his own career and the fragility of an illegitimate regime which had to justify itself, come what may, by uninterrupted successes. After his defeat at Austerlitz, the Emperor Francis II, applauded by his loyal subjects, remarked to the French ambassador: 'Do you think, Sir, that your Master would be welcomed thus in Paris if he had lost a battle such as I have lost?' This sally bears comparison with the exclamation of a French royalist who was fascinated by Napoleon's glory. 'What a pity,' he said, 'that he was not a Bourbon!'

If the French Revolution had maintained its original intentions, it would have resembled 'enlightened despotism'

In this eventful history, only the second Revolution involved dramatic violence: it was an unexpected deviation from the norm. It has often been argued that, if the revolution had not drowned in blood in the spring of 1792, there could have been an almost peaceful, moderate revolution on the British model, as so many French thinkers had hoped. One such was Montesquieu, who wrote in his *Lettres persanes* in 1721: 'Existing laws should be touched only with a gingerly hand.' Another was Rousseau, who believed that an ancient nation could not survive revolutionary upsets. 'As soon as its fetters are broken,' he declared, 'it falls asunder and no longer exists.'

The beginnings of the Revolution seemed to reflect this spirit, not so much revolutionary as seeking reform. A firm king should have been able to maintain or restore that state of affairs. But neither the advice of Mirabeau nor that of Barnave could wean Louis XVI away from the privileged persons who surrounded him and made him a prisoner in his own Court. Need this ancient debate really be revived?

It was not the first time that sensible political solutions had been rejected. The plans of the enlightened reformers in France had always been blocked, since the beginning of Louis XVI's reign: hence the dismissal of Turgot in 1776. And the same stubborn reaction occurred everywhere in the Europe of enlightened despotism, in which so many worthy people had believed that all they need do was persuade the prince or the king, and that once he had become a 'philosopher' all would be well. But the sovereigns of the Enlightenment preferred half-measures. Even when Frederick II brought the Prussian aristocracy to heel, he did so with such moderation that on his death in 1787 Prussia witnessed a widespread aristocratic revival.

How could Louis XVI be expected to succeed where Frederick II had failed? When, finally, Louis invoked foreign assistance, he unleashed the adroit manoeuvres of counter-revolution and European conservatism. Overtaken by events, the Revolution developed in ways that its sponsors had not expected.

They admitted as much. 'Revolutionary is not what one is, but what one becomes,' said Carnot. 'The pressure of events may lead us to results we had not thought of,' said Saint-Just. The revolution continued for only a few months along this unexpected path, to its own cruel detriment and that of others; then the fall of Robespierre opened the way to reaction and to the pleasures of life renewed. 'Paris became sparkling again,' wrote Michelet.

A few days after Thermidor, a man who is still alive and who then was ten years old, was taken by his parents to the theatre. On the way out, he admired the long line of brilliant carriages which he had never seen before. People in servants' livery, hat in hand, said to the people coming out: 'Do you need a carriage, *Sir*?' The child hardly understood this new locution. He had it explained to him, and was told only that the death of Robespierre had brought a considerable change.

But was Michelet right to end his *History of the French Revolution* (1853) at 10 Thermidor? Logically, no: once the Thermidor reaction had ended, France returned to the moderate 'first' Revolution, whose essential achievements the Directoire and the Consulate maintained. What was rejected was the work of the terrorist Convention.

Abroad, in any case, no one believed that the Revolution was over. On 12 September 1797, the Russian ambassador in Britain wrote to his Government (in French): 'What was likely . . . has happened in Paris: the dictatorial triumvirate has arrested two directors and sixty-four members of the two Councils, without any kind of legal proceeding. They are to be sent to Madagascar. So much for France's fine constitution and her wonderful liberty! I would rather live in Morocco than in that land of alleged equality and freedom.' Why the rancour? Not everyone outside France spoke ironically of 'her wonderful liberty'. It was in the name of the Revolution that Napoleon pursued his conquests; and, everywhere that his regime was established, laws, customs and feelings were permanently affected, despite the resentment or hatred that the occupation aroused. Goethe and Hegel supported Napoleon. In the face of a reactionary Europe far behind the political and social stage that France had reached, they saw him as what Hegel called 'the soul of the world on horseback'.

The Napoleonic Wars extended to Europe what had been a

civil war in France. For a quarter of a century, to all those countries menaced by Napoleon, the Revolution was both a reality and a threat. Thus perceived, as an imminent possibility, the message of the Revolution, whether admired or abhorred, made powerful headway in the West, stirring passions and dividing opinion. And finally, with its drama, its vivid colours, its saints and martyrs, its lessons, and its aspirations – often disappointed but always revived – the Revolution looks to the twentieth century almost like Holy Writ.

The message of the French Revolution

True, to all appearances, the Revolution seems reduced to silence after 1815. It lived on, however, in people's hearts and minds, and its essential achievements were maintained.

The Restoration did not restore all the social privileges that the Revolution had abolished (and certainly not the old feudal rights). National property was not returned to its previous owners; and even if its distribution was unfair, too much having gone to the rich, the Revolution's achievements in this area were safeguarded – as was the principle of individual rights guaranteed by the Charter of 1814. When the Government of Charles X seemed to be preparing reactionary measures, there was an instant outcry, followed by the July Monarchy and the return to the tricolour flag. Revolutionary language and ideology had largely reappeared.

Already in 1828, a companion of Gracchus or François Babeuf, Philippe Buonarotti, had described in his *History of the Conspiracy for Equality, known as the Babeuf Conspiracy*, how the 'Equals' had planned a sort of 'plebeian Vendée', how they had failed and been executed – though Babeuf stabbed himself on 26 March 1797 to escape execution. It had been a 'Communist' or communal movement, faithful to Rousseau's dictum: 'You are lost if you forget that land belongs to no one and its fruits belong to everyone.' The example and the book both had immense success. Auguste Blanqui, that impenitent revolutionary whom no one, in retrospect, can fail to like, was a passionate reader of Buonarotti.

This example may help to show how it was that the Revolution could always, even now, speak more or less the language that every generation wanted to hear. After its apparent eclipse in the Second Empire, from 1875 onwards, its symbols continued to form the ideological basis of the Third Republic and of the whole revolutionary Socialist movement.

What revolutionary humanism essentially believed was that violence could be legitimate if it was used to defend law, equality, social justice or the much loved mother country. The revolutionary might be its author – or its victim, for 'to take to the streets' could as easily involve dying there, making a final protest, as emerging victorious. But to dare embrace violence – to dare to die or to kill – was acceptable only if it were the sole means of deflecting destiny, making it more human and fraternal. In a word, the Revolution meant violence in the service of an ideal. The Counter-Revolution sprang from similar roots. Its failing, in historical terms, was that it looked backward and tried to move backward. And to return to the past is possible only by wrenching things out of true – momentarily, at that. In the long term, no action can last and bear the weight of history unless it goes in history's direction and at history's pace, instead of trying in vain to slow it down.

However that may be, it remains remarkable that 1789 should have still inspired mass workers' movements even as late as the twentieth century. First, because in its earliest intentions as in its results, the French Revolution was always a prudent affair. Then, its heroic legend, full of miracles performed by demigods or 'giants', has been partly destroyed, tarnished by the demythologizing efforts of objective historians. None have done so more effectively than those on the Left, anxious to substantiate their revolutionary fervour by reference to the documents. In this way, the Revolution has lost many of its saints. But, at the same time, its message has become clearer.

Historical revisionism, in fact, has rehabilitated the 'red' period of the Terror, identified the significance of the suffering it underwent as well as that it inflicted, and brought to light, in plea of justification, the tragic aspect of its situation. Henceforward it is the 'Incorruptible' Robespierre and then that tardy hero Gracchus Babeuf who take precedence over Danton or Carnot, 'the organizer of victory'. And it is their language that reaches out to us, a powerful language, because it anticipates what was to come. Universal suffrage, the separation of Church and State, the Ventôse decree providing for some redistribution of wealth – all these ephemeral victories won by the 'second' Revolution, and repudiated after Thermidor, were instances of anticipation. It took a long time, in some cases, for them to be revived in our time and for our benefit.

At all events, it is thanks to them that the revolutionary humanism of 1789 still lives on. The hesitations and reservations that European Socialism felt, especially recently, in the face of Communism (with its different ideal and its different form of revolution) – these are signs that a certain left-wing ideology, fed on memories and on some key words, refused to identify its revolution with that of Marx or, later, the Soviets. One example is the criticism that Jean Jaurès made of Marxist ideas after the signature of the pact with Jules Guesde in 1905 which established Socialist unity 'under the auspices of the Communist Manifesto'. At the beginning of his *Socialist History of the French Revolution*, Jaurès announced that it would be 'at once materialist with Marx and mystical with Michelet' – i.e. faithful to Michelet's 'revolutionary mystique', the Revolution's living heritage. Only late in the day, and incompletely, did Western civilization in France and elsewhere manage to distance itself from that heritage and the ideals of 1789.

Scientific thought before the nineteenth century

The growth of scientific thought in Europe before the eighteenth century raises the question of the infancy of modern science – indeed, of pre-science (in the same sense as one may speak of 'pre-industry' before the Industrial Revolution). This is not the place to summarize the evolution of science, or even to try to identify the dividing line between pre-science and modern science. The problem is to discover not how, but why science developed, and only in the context of Western civilization. As Joseph Needham, the chemist and Sinologue, unambiguously put it, 'Europe did not create just any science, but world science.' And it did so almost alone. Why then did science not develop in much earlier civilizations – in China, for example, or out of Islam?

All scientific proceedings are undertaken in the context of a certain view of the world. There can be no progress, no reasoning and no fruitful hypothesis if there is no general set of references with which to locate one's position and then choose one's direction. The way in which different views of the world have succeeded one another provides the best background for studying the development of science.

The history of the sciences (and of science), if seen from a certain distance, looks like the very slow transition from one general rational explanation to another general explanation, each being treated as a theory that took account of all the scientific data currently available, until the moment when that all-embracing theory was exploded because new data violently contradicted it. So another hypothesis had to be put together as best it might; and that in its turn became the point of departure for further advance.

Since the thirteenth century, Western science has lived with only three general explanations or world systems: that of Aristotle, which although of ancient lineage entered the interpretations and speculations of the West in the thirteenth century; that of Descartes and Newton, which founded classical science and which is an original Western creation except for its decisive borrowings from the work of Archimedes; and finally the relativity theory of Albert Einstein, announced in 1905, which inaugurated contemporary science.

These vast interpretations of the world dominate science, but never of course fully encapsulate it. Their establishment poses complex problems; and so does their eventual deterioration. The moment when they no longer fit the facts usually heralds real progress, a turning-point in the general history of science.

Aristotle's system was a very ancient inheritance, from the Peripatetic School of the fourth century BC. The essentials of its teaching reached the West much later via Arabic translation, in Toledo, and the commentaries of Averroës. In Paris, this meant a veritable revolution. In 1215, the University's syllabus was changed from top to bottom; formal logic replaced the study of Latin literature, and especially of the poets. 'Philosophy is invading and abolishing everything.' Translations of Aristotle abounded, leading to an enormous mass of commentaries. There followed a very fierce dispute between the Ancients and the Moderns. In a contemporary poem, written in about 1250, the Philosopher says to the Poet: 'I have devoted myself to knowledge, while you prefer puerile things like prose, rhythm and metre. What good are they? You know grammar, but you know nothing of Science and Logic. Why do you puff yourself up so, if you are only an ignoramus?'

The world system worked out by Aristotle dominated Europe until the seventeenth and even the eighteenth century, because it did not immediately yield under the attacks of Copernicus, Kepler and Galileo.

Aristotle's theory of the cosmos is of course completely out of date. But it is a theory, elaborately although not mathematically worked out. It is neither a crude verbal extension of common sense, nor a childish fantasy: it is a doctrine which, although naturally based on the findings of common sense, nevertheless elaborates them systematically, in an extremely strict and coherent manner.

Alexandre Koyre

Undoubtedly, Aristotle stated as an axiom that there was a 'cosmos' – a single *uni*verse. But was Einstein any different? When Paul Valéry asked him: 'But what proof is there that there is unity in nature?' he answered: 'It's an act of faith' (Paul Valéry, *L'Idée* *fixe*). And Einstein said elsewhere: 'I cannot think that God plays dice with the cosmos.'

This Aristotelian unity of the world was an 'order': every being had its natural place there, and so should remain permanently at rest. Such was the settled position of the Earth at the centre of the Cosmos and its successive spheres. However, the Cosmos was disturbed by a variety of movements. Some were natural, like that of a body that falls to the ground, or a light body – flame or smoke – that rises in the sky, or like the circular movement of the stars, or rather of the celestial spheres. Some movements, on the other hand, were violent and abnormal, being imparted to a body by pushing or pulling it: they stopped when the impulsion stopped. There was one sizeable exception: that of a body thrown, a projectile. Its movement was not natural; but it was not any longer bound up with the impulsion – it was neither pushed nor pulled. The projectile must therefore be propelled by the whirling of the air it passed through. This solution came to the rescue of the system; but it was the weak point that all its critics attacked.

Unfailingly, they asked: *a quo moveantur projecta?* It was a question that raised a number of problems, including the inertia or acceleration of the fall of heavy objects; and these were matters that were already tackled by the Parisian 'nominalists' of the fourteenth century, including William of Ockham, Jean Buridan and Nicholas Oresme. Oresme, who was a mathematical genius, discovered the principle of the law of inertia, the fact that the speed of falling was proportional to the time taken to fall, etc. But his thought was not immediately followed up.

The history of the experiments and disputes which resulted in Aristotle's system being dethroned by classical Newtonian physics and science generally would be fascinating to recount, and very long. That 'great leap forward' was brought about by exceptional people all over Europe who were in touch with each other. Science, by now, was international: it transcended political or linguistic barriers and occupied the whole of the West. Progress was undoubtedly aided by the sixteenth century's economic boom, and equally by the widespread distribution of ancient Greek scientific works, made possible by printing. The works of Archimedes, for example, became known only late in the day, in the last years of the sixteenth century. And his thought was very fruitful: fore-shadowing differential and integral calculus, he put forward the useful idea of a limit. To appreciate the value of that, think of calculating π.

But progress was slow. In mathematics, the five great steps forward, as listed by an historian of science, were made with long intervals between them: the analytic geometry of Pierre de Fermat (1629) and René Descartes (1637); Fermat's higher arithmetic (around 1630–65); combinative analysis (1654); Galileo's dynamics (1591–1612) and those of Newton (1666–84); Newton's universal gravitation (1666 and 1684–7).

Nor was this true only of mathematics. In the vast subject of astronomy, although the Greeks themselves had briefly entertained the notion of an heliocentric universe, the geocentric system inherited from Ptolemy strenuously resisted change, and it took a long time for Copernicus (1473–1543) and Kepler (1571–1630) to be vindicated.

The major event, transcending all these efforts, was the establishment of a new model of the world: the abstract, geometrized universe of Descartes and, still more, of Newton, in which everything depended on one principle, that of universal gravitation, whereby bodies attract each other in proportion to their mass and in inverse ratio to the square of the distance between them (1687).

This picture of the world was also tenacious. It survived all the scientific revolutions of the nineteenth century, until a new magic explanation of the world appeared – Einstein's special (1905) and general (1916) theories of relativity. Anyone who completed his studies before 1939 will still have lived, in spirit, in the clarity and definiteness of the Newtonian universe.

Descartes was 'a free man'. That geometrized or mechanized universe was not the sole creation of any of the scholars we have cited or could have cited. Still, without yielding to misplaced nationalism, let us give René Descartes (1596–1650) the mention he deserves.

We must begin with a parenthesis. Descartes eludes biographers because he was discreet, deliberately shy and of restrained sensibility. After 1628, apart from a few visits, he lived outside France and mainly in Holland. He died in Stockholm, the guest of Queen Christina of Sweden. In Amsterdam, where he spent much of his time, he was delighted to be able to lose himself in the crowd, 'never recognized by anyone'. To reconstruct his thought and rediscover its movement is as difficult as investigating his secretive life.

His *Discours de la Méthode* (1637) has tended to simplify our picture of him. We have been tempted to notice only its peremptory rules – whereas it is in fact the preface to three works: *La Dioptrique*, *Les Météores*, and the very well-known *Géométrie*; and they should not be isolated from each other. Moreover, the *Discours* is in some ways a simplified, shortened version of the *Regulae*, which were not published until after Descartes's death. Were the *Regulae* written, as it would appear, around 1629 and taken up again in 1637, to be distilled into the *Discours de la Méthode*? Or, alternatively, do the four precepts of the Method date from the famous winter of 1619–20, as the *Discours* explicitly says? In that case, the *Regulae* would be a later, longer and more complicated version of them. The fact is that the style of thinking differs as between the books. The strict and austere *Géométrie* contrasts with the richer, more inventive mathematics offered us in Descartes's *Letters*, where he is as it were stimulated, heated by 'the challenges of his critics'. Hence a number of doubts must remain: but they in no way alter the significance of the whole. From Descartes we have the first systematic and modern critical appraisal of knowledge, a first heroic struggle against all intellectual or metaphysical illusions, all errors arising 'from poetic intuition'.

On the scientific plane, more than a few words are needed, even if we limit our study of his work to those aspects of it that concerned the future and have survived to our day, leaving aside his physics and optics, which were clearly not revolutionary, and concentrating on his geometry – the discipline in which, in his own view, he had best applied his Method.

Descartes rid himself, not without difficulty, of the 'geometrical realism' of the Greeks. His mathematics introduced pure abstraction. 'The scope of thinking, instead of being imposed in a realist way, is then determined by a network of relationships.' By this means, going further than his predecessors – notably François Vieta, whom he knew, and Buonaventura Cavalieri, whom he should have known – he advanced 'with giant strides the theory of equations. For any further progress, mathematics had to wait for Evariste Galois (1811–32)'.

The fact that Cartesian mathematics can be understood today by a student just beginning the subject should not disguise the magnitude of Descartes's achievement. Thus he evoked, alongside the 'true' (positive) and 'false' (negative) roots of an equation, its 'purely imaginary' roots. Thus his demonstration implied, although without fixing them precisely, the axes of coordinates (orthogonal or not). Thus he decomposed, or rather composed in advance, a function made up of a certain number of binomials in the form of simple equations multiplying each other, as $(x - 1)$ $(x + 4)$ $(x - 7)$, etc.

The historian Lucien Febvre was right to see Descartes as living his reason as he lived his faith, erecting a barrier against all that the sixteenth century, in its naturalism, had brought with it by way of fables, approximations, pre-logical thought, qualitative physics, and also resisting all those Renaissance 'rationalists' who had seen in Nature only 'a box of miracles or an incentive to dream'.

The key years 1780–1820 raised a final problem: crossing the threshold that led to truly modern science. Magnificent as the eighteenth century was, it was not yet on equal terms with modern science, conversant with its attitudes, its language and its methods.

This was demonstrated by one of Gaston Bachelard's finest

books, *The Formation of the Scientific Spirit* (1935). It sought to enumerate the trouble and awkwardness experienced by scientists who were trying to free themselves, not without difficulty, from common prejudice and from a certain pre-logical mentality whose power and weight seem astonishing today. This psychoanalysis of the Enlightenment obviously concentrated only on its darker side, its errors, aberrations and absurdities. But are absurdities not the eternal accompaniment of the advancing scientific spirit? May we not suffer from them in connection with the science of tomorrow?

In the eighteenth century, the biggest obstacle to progress was perhaps the compartmentalization of science into different sectors, each independent of the others. Some were advancing rapidly: mathematics, chemistry, thermodynamics, geology and economics (if that is a science). Others were lagging behind, and sometimes stationary, as were medicine and biology. At that time, the various disciplines remained separate. The language of mathematics was not commonly used; and − no less serious a failing − links with technology were spasmodic.

These difficulties were gradually resolved. In France, new ground was not fully broken until about 1820–26, when the Academy of Sciences became 'the most brilliant meeting of scholars there had ever been: Ampère, Laplace, Legendre, Biot, Poinsot, Cauchy . . .' (Louis de Broglie). There was similar brilliance all over Europe.

Why, precisely, was the threshold crossed, forging the scientific future of a civilization that then, and then only, was definitively carried away by its impetus? There is an obvious materialist explanation. The unprecedented economic growth that occurred in the eighteenth century affected the whole world, and Europe became its reigning power. Material and technological conditions increased their demands and their constraints. Little by little, a collaborative response appeared. Industrialization, the subject of the next chapter, was thus the decisive element, the *motor* of change. Which amounts to explaining one obviously Western phenomenon − science − by another, industrialization. These two seem to echo each other and they certainly go side by side. This is what Joseph Needham, already quoted, likes to affirm. Much earlier than the West, China possessed the rudiments of science, in an elegant and advanced form. But she failed to reach the decisive stage, because she never experienced the economic impetus that spurred Europe on – that 'capitalist' tension which at the end of the race, or during it, enabled Europeans to cross the decisive threshold. The beginnings of that creative tension had been felt long before, with the rise of the great medieval trading cities, and above all from the sixteenth century onwards.

All Europe's strength, material and spiritual, combined to produce this development, the fruit of a civilization plucked when it was fully ripe and with full awareness of the responsibility it entailed.

18. The Industrialization of Europe

One of Europe's key responsibilities was that of bringing about the Industrial Revolution which spread, and is still spreading, throughout the world. This formidable technological advance was Europe's own achievement, and one that was relatively recent in the history of civilizations, since it took place only two centuries ago. Until then, Europe – for all its brilliance – was in material terms underdeveloped, not by comparison with the world around it, but by contrast with what Europe itself was to become. How then did Europe succeed in crossing this industrial threshold? How did its civilization react to the results of its own achievement?

These are the questions that arise immediately. And they concern our immediate interests.

They require a preliminary look at the state of Europe before industrialization. And that economic *ancien régime* still prevails in many parts of the world that are trying to go beyond it.

The Industrial Revolution is a complex phenomenon. Nowhere did it take place in one single process. Certain sectors lagged behind for a long time, as the wool industry in Yorkshire or ironmongery around Birmingham did until the middle of the nineteenth century – to take examples only from Britain, which was the first in the field. The contrasts that are visible in South America today, for example, are normal in all countries in the process of industrialization.

Europe's example proves that, from its very beginnings, industrialization raises serious problems. Any country that undertakes to industrialize itself must envisage at the same time a change in its social structure, if it wishes to avoid the long gestation of a revolutionary ideology such as those which so much affected and afflicted Europe.

The origins of the first Industrial Revolution

There were four successive Industrial Revolutions, each of the last three building on its predecessor's achievements: that of steam, that of electricity, that of the internal combustion engine and that of nuclear energy.

The problem for us is to examine as closely as possible how this series of revolutions began. That means looking at the leading position of Britain between 1780 and 1890. Why was she the first to industrialize? How? And before 1780, what was the general situation of Europe in industrial matters?

The word 'industry', before the eighteenth century – or rather, before the nineteenth – risks evoking a false picture. At the very most, then, there was what may be called 'pre-industry'. The very first 'industrial revolution', may be said to have occurred in the twelfth century, when wind- and water-mills spread throughout Europe. But after that, for some seven centuries, there was no major technological innovation. Pre-industry, even in the eighteenth century, had only medieval sources and forms of energy. The power of a water-mill was normally in the region of 5 horsepower; that of a windmill, in windswept regions such as Holland, sometimes exceeded 10 horsepower, but its output was intermittent. Without abundant energy resources and powerful machines, industrial life was condemned to semi-immobility, despite a multiplicity of small and often very ingenious technical inventions. Such industry as there was found itself hemmed in by an archaic economic system: derisory agricultural productivity, costly and primitive transportation, and inadequate markets. Only labour was super-abundant.

And industry in any modern sense was virtually non-existent. Local artisans, working close to home, often met the essential needs of the nearby population. In a few sectors only were there firms which worked for much wider markets, or which specialized in luxury products. Such, in France, were certain 'royal' manufactures dating from the seventeenth century. Examples of this kind were fairly common in the up-to-date textile industries. It was here, indeed, that the British Industrial Revolution began.

In fact, the textile industry more than any other made possible relatively large-scale production in a still traditional artisan world. In the sixteenth and seventeenth centuries, and even in the thirteenth century in the textile cities of Italy and Flanders, rich merchants *'qui faciunt laborare'* (who commissioned work) encouraged the establishment of quite large organizations in town – a few big workshops and some retail outlets. 'Masters' (often ordinary wage-earners with two or three assistants) worked at home, as very frequently did peasant men and women outside the town involved in the same enterprise.

A sixteenth-century document describes the Segovia merchants, enriched by cloth-making, as 'real fathers of families who, in their own houses and outside, support a large number of people, in many cases up to 200 or 300, and thereby employ other hands to produce a huge diversity of the finest cloths'.

In Laval in about 1700 the linen industry employed some 5,000 workers in and around the town. With their families, they numbered 20,000, 'the richest of whom had not 100 francs in the world'. There were a further 500 master weavers who bought their thread from the tow-sellers, 'known as *cancers* because they devoured the unfortunate weavers'. Above them there were thirty wholesale merchants, the real organizers of the industry: they bleached the raw linens and sent them to distant markets. These merchant entrepreneurs represented what a typological historian calls 'commercial or merchant capitalism': they supplied the raw materials, paid the wages, stored the goods and sold them, often exporting them over long distances and usually buying, in return, other profitable products.

Since travel was so slow, these commercial transactions took a long time to complete. In the fifteenth century wool washed in Spain and sent to Florence to be worked, was then sold as fine cloth in Alexandria, Egypt, in return for oriental goods which were sold in Florence or elsewhere in Europe – all of which took three years and often more. So the operation, although usually profitable, was a long-term affair. It immobilized a lot of capital for a lengthy period, and was not without dangers. The merchant entrepreneur dominated the system, since he alone had the capital to finance it – usually in association with others, so as to spread the risk. He took both the responsibility and the profits.

Manufacturing: the word, for a long time ill-defined, in retrospect seems to fit fairly well the concentration of workmen in the same building (or in buildings close to each other), supervised by foremen. In the eighteenth century, this practice grew more widespread; and at the same time there was some division of labour in the workshops. An article in the *Encylopédie* in 1761 ascribed the superiority of the Lyon silk factories to the fact that they employed a large number of people (there were 30,000 silk workers in the town) in such a way that 'one worker does only one single thing, which he will do all his life, while another does something else; hence everyone performs his given task promptly and well'.

This organization, however, was singled out as an exception. Ordinary artisan work, with no division of labour, remained the rule, even when the first signs of the Industrial Revolution were about to appear.

Pre-industrial Europe, then, lacked neither entrepreneurs nor capital; it was not deaf to the demands of the market, including the international market; in places, it had a labour force already partly mobilized in large numbers and ready to serve the entrepreneurs. It suffered, however, like today's less developed countries, from a badly organized economy. The agricultural sector, in particular, was too weak to enable any economic boom to develop fully. The market outlets were inadequate; the competition was cut-throat; the slightest crisis ruined everything. There were frequent bankruptcies among industrialists and merchants. A trading guide dating from the mid-eighteenth century drew attention to the dangers of 'fashion' in manufacturing: 'In the provinces we find vestiges of defunct manufacturing firms; every year we see one of them collapse, while others arise, soon to fall again in their turn.'

In fact, pre-industry survived only as a result of very low wages. Did the conditions of workers improve in some regions where prosperity finally allowed wages to rise? Paradoxically, no: where that happened, industry died, or was at least in a very bad way, under the onslaught of foreign competition. This was the case with Venice in the seventeenth century and Holland in the eighteenth. In 1777, the Administrator of Picardy noted: at present, day labourers need twice as much money to live on, yet they earn no more than they did fifty years ago, when food was half as cheap; so they have no more than half of what they need.

Nothing can change, or will change, without technological innovations. But we should acknowledge at once that such innovations cannot themselves determine everything. This can be seen by looking at the special case of Britain. There, the technological innovations occurred in two key industries – textiles (above all) and the mines. Their repercussions were not always rapid; but they reached a long way into other sectors of the economy.

The British mines, and especially the Cornish tin mines, which had been worked for a long time and at ever deeper levels, were constantly plagued by the infiltration of water. It was an old problem: it had been raised in the sixteenth century by Georg Agricola in his treatise *De re metallica*. But were the large hydraulic wheels then in use capable of working powerful enough pumps, or relays of pumps? To create a vacuum, they used air pressure and could not exceed its power: each time, they raised a theoretical column of water only some ten metres tall.

The search for powerful pumps finally produced the large, heavy and very costly steam-engine invented by Thomas

Newcomen, from 1712 to 1718. When repairing one of these, the Scotsman James Watt, from the University of Edinburgh, made the discovery that led him to devise his own much simpler and more efficient machine, first conceived in 1776. So steam was in use before Watt: from the beginning of the eighteenth century it was working machines which were used much more than was once thought, as recent studies have proved. Some were even in use in France around 1750, in the Anzin coal mines near Valenciennes. More spectacular achievements – the first automobile, the first steamboat made by Beugnot and Jouffroy – came in and around 1770.

The textile industry, however, was the main driving-force, as it continued to be until the mid-nineteenth century and the advent of the railways. It led all the others, being both a producer of basic necessities and a provider of luxuries.

According to Max Weber, the textile industry's ups and downs dominate all the material past of the West. First came the age of linen (Charlemagne was dressed in something like canvas); then the age of wool; then the age of cotton – or rather a craze for cotton – in the eighteenth century. And it was for cotton that the first real factories came into being. Bound up with the Indian, African and American trade, and with the traffic in black slaves, cotton was established in or around the great colonial ports such as Liverpool and Glasgow. It profited from their energy and their accumulated capital. No wonder then that these popular industries demanded and even initiated technological improvements.

New machines appeared, each with its nickname: John Kay's flying shuttle in 1733; James Hargreaves's improved spinning-jenny in 1767; Sir Richard Arkwright's water-powered spinning mill in 1769; Samuel Crompton's spinning mule in 1773. The summit of these achievements, although in France, was undoubtedly the improved loom invented by Joseph Marie Jacquard in 1800 and first exhibited in 1801.

Here, then, is one explanation. Economic growth favours some particular sector of industry, and technology responds to the demand. Everything happens spontaneously and empirically. Technology made demands on science, which naturally and promptly responded. *Homo sapiens* joined forces with *homo faber*; from now on, they moved forward together.

Science had made obvious progress during the eighteenth century. But in general it was a deliberately theoretical affair, unaccustomed to working with technology, which was still at the artisan stage and which scarcely asked it any questions. At the end of the eighteenth century everything changed. From then on, industry itself began to make requests of pure science rather than merely of technology, that science of the hand and the craft.

The admirable James Watt (1736–1819), for instance, was not just a self-taught artisan: he had a scientific mind, and was well versed in both engineering and chemistry. A professional scientist, John Black, born in Bordeaux in 1728 of Scottish parents, was Professor of Chemistry at Edinburgh, where he did notable work on alkalis, and died in 1799. It was he who may have suggested the principle of latent heat on which Watt based his steam-engine: by keeping the cylinder warm with a jacket, he used the expansive force of the steam, which hitherto had been condensed on entering the cooled cylinder and thereby wasted.

Science made hundreds of similar contributions to the growth of industry. One such concerned the bleaching of linen. The traditional process had involved spreading the cloth in the fields and watering it, soaking it in various solutions, first alkaline and then slightly acid. This had required large spaces and much time, sometimes as long as six months. For an industry rapidly expanding, this was a bottleneck, especially since the weak acid that was used for what was called 'souring' was buttermilk, and that was not produced on an industrial scale. One improvement was to use very dilute sulphuric acid, which worked more quickly; but that had to be produced in large quantities. It was here that a real scientist, a doctor called John White, a former pupil of the University of Leyden, made his contribution. The discovery of chlorine in 1774 by the Swede Carl Scheele, its use by the Frenchman

Claude Louis Berthollet for bleaching textiles and the development
in Britain of a practical method of doing so – all brought the
process close to perfection. And that, clearly, was the result of
international scientific efforts.

Nothing, perhaps, is a better illustration of the collaboration
between science and technology than the career of Matthew
Boulton (1728–1809). Of modest origin (a 'new man'), he was a
practical and creative industrialist: he financed the work of James
Watt. But he was also a scientist, passionately devoted to chemistry.
His circle included not only Watt, but a doctor and mathematician,
William Small, the doctor and poet Erasmus Darwin (grandfather
of Charles Darwin and Francis Galton), and many others. Industrial
Britain was becoming scientific Britain, with its capitals,
significantly, in Birmingham and Manchester. London, the
headquarters of merchant capitalism, remained for a long time
outside the scope of these novelties, and only recovered its place in
British scientific life in about 1820. That fact alone is noteworthy.
It was the growth of industry that obliged science to act.

But is that a sufficient explanation? In France, applied science
was undoubtedly ahead of Britain: we have only to think of
chemists like P. J. Macquer (1718–84) or Claude Louis Berthollet
(1748–1822). So why was the progress of French industry so much
less rapid? The fact is, clearly, that the Industrial Revolution arose
from other causes too. Some (the most important) were economic;
others were social. The broader explanation – economic and social
– is indeed the best.

Long before, owing to its 'Glorious' or 'bourgeois' Revolution
in 1688, Britain had acquired political stability. Its society was
open to capitalism: the Bank of England had been founded in
1694. Its economy had benefited from many investments in
projects of general utility, such as roads and canals: in the
eighteenth century there was even a 'canal craze'.

The Industrial Revolution in Britain began, too, as part of a
general economic boom in the eighteenth century which then
affected the whole world.

But would it have been possible without the rapid increase in Britain's population that took place in the eighteenth century – of the order of 64 per cent? Similar increases occurred elsewhere in the world, in China as in Europe; but it was more marked in some countries than in others. In France, for example, it was only about 35 per cent. For Britain, the result was a superabundance of inexpensive labour.

Finally, a very important role was played by the changes in British agriculture – the enclosures and new scientific methods – which loosened the perennial straitjacket of inadequate food production.

The Industrial Revolution in Britain came in two phases: the first in the cotton industry, between 1780 and 1830, and the second in metal production. The latter, involving heavy industry, was made possible by the building of the railways. This second phase had an enormous impact; but it was financed by the profits made from the first. Cotton had led the way, and it is to cotton that we must return to form any judgement of how the Industrial Revolution began.

The fashion for cotton was then widespread in Europe, including Britain. The British had for a long time imported, for themselves and for other markets in Europe and elsewhere, the printed or painted cotton goods that came from their Indian trading-stations, known in France as *indiennes* and in Britain as chintz, from the Hindi word *chint*. The success of these fabrics led British manufacturers to imitate them. Stimulated by technological progress, the cotton industry expanded more and more. There was great demand for its products on the coasts of Africa (where a slave was known as a 'piece', *'uma peça d'India'* in the old Portuguese expression, meaning the item of printed cotton for which he was exchanged). The next big market was in Brazil, opened up and monopolized by the British in 1808, before they repeated the same procedure two years later in the whole of Spanish America. Later, British cotton goods competed directly with Indian products in Britain itself, completely wiping out their

Indian rivals. The British also exported to the Mediterranean. And between 1820 and 1860 the sale of British cotton textiles to the rest of the world continually grew. The amount of raw cotton used by British mills rose from 2 million pounds in 1760 to no less than 366 million pounds in 1850.

This immense success had many repercussions. Buttressed by the prodigious boom in cotton, Britain flooded the world market with all kinds of goods; and from it she excluded others. Her aggressive Government, willing to wage war whenever necessary, reserved for British industry this vast domain where expansion seemed to know no limits. No one could wrest this world market from Britain's stranglehold, because the rise in output was accompanied (as became the rule in the future) by an astounding decrease in costs. Between 1800 and 1850, the price of cotton goods went down more than 81 per cent, while that of wheat and most other foodstuffs fell by barely a third. Wages remained more or less stable, but because machinery had greatly reduced the human element, their incidence on costs was very much less. Not surprisingly, this first instance of mass production greatly improved the lot of the people. Michelet observed a similar phenomenon in France when discussing the cotton crisis of 1842.

The expansion of the metallurgical industry came very much later. Here, until the nineteenth century, production had depended exclusively on war. 'Cast iron in the eighteenth century meant the casting of cannons,' wrote an Englishman in 1831; but the British had scarcely any except on board ship: land warfare concerned them relatively little. In the eighteenth century, in fact, they produced less iron than Russia or France, and often imported it from Russia or Sweden. The decisive technological discovery was that of coke smelting, made in the seventeenth century; but it was not widely used, and smelting by charcoal continued for a long time.

The coming of the railways, between 1830 and 1840, altered everything. They were heavy consumers of iron, cast iron and steel. Both at home and abroad, Britain set about building them.

At the same time, the arrival of metal-hulled steamships turned British shipbuilding into an enormous heavy industry. With that, cotton ceased to be the key sector in Britain's economic life.

The spread of industrialism in Europe and beyond

In other countries, in Europe and elsewhere, industrialization came at different times and in somewhat different contexts. Nevertheless, history seems on the whole to have repeated itself every time, although it was concerned with different societies, different economies and different civilizations. Reduced to its economic essentials, in fact, every industrial revolution followed roughly the same fairly simple 'model', as economists would say.

Three stages: this was the hypothesis put forward in 1952 by the American economist Walt W. Rostow. Although debatable, it certainly clarified the discussion.

At the beginning, the key moment is take-off. As an aircraft accelerates along the runway, then lifts off, so an economy about to expand rises quite steeply from the industrial *ancien régime* that held it down. Normally, take-off occurs in a single sector, or at most in two. It was cotton in Britain and in New England (the special case of an 'American' take-off); in France, Germany, Canada, Russia and the United States it was the railways; in Sweden it was building timber and iron-ore mines. In each case, the key sector darts forward, modernizing rapidly: the speed of its growth and the modernity of its technology are precisely what distinguish this phenomenon from previous industrial expansion, which lacked both explosive force and long-term staying power. The industry that has thus shot ahead increases its output, improves its technology, organizes its marketing and then stimulates the rest of the economy.

After that the key industry, having served as a motor, settles at its cruising altitude: it has performed its task. The reserves it has helped to accumulate then move to another sector, often related to the first; and that in its turn takes off, modernizes and reaches its ideal height.

As this process extends from one sector to another, the economy as a whole attains industrial maturity. In Western Europe, after the take-off of the railways (i.e. of iron, coal and heavy industry), it was the turn of steel, modern shipbuilding, chemicals, electricity and machine tools. Much later, Russia followed the same path. In Sweden, the essential roles were played by wood pulp (for paper-making), timber and iron. Generally speaking, it was in the first years of the twentieth century that the Western world as a whole reached the threshold of maturity. Britain, which had crossed it in about 1850, now found herself more or less on a level with her partners.

At that point, these experienced and fairly well-balanced economies, which had secured adequate incomes and achieved a certain abundance, no longer saw industrial expansion as their primordial goal. Where now were they to direct their power and their possible investment? Faced with the choice – for choice had become possible – not all the industrial societies reacted in the same way. Their different responses reflected the nature of the history they had so far lived through, and partly determined their future. It will be no surprise to learn that they based their choices, consciously or not, on the nature of their different civilizations.

Time to choose: what has to be chosen is a style of life to suit a whole society. There are a number of options. One might concentrate on careful social legislation, taking as its priorities the security, well-being and leisure of the whole population. One might decide that well-being depended on widespread mass consumption, with enough goods and services of a high standard produced to supply the vast majority. Or one might, finally, use the greater power of the society or the nation in the often vain and always dangerous quest for dominance in world politics.

The turn of the century, around 1900, saw the maturity of the United States. Briefly but significantly, it then tried power politics, in the form of the 1898 war against Spain for Cuba and the Philippines. This would seem to have been a conscious gesture, in view of Theodore Roosevelt's writing at the time that 'the United States needed a war', or that it had to be given 'something to think about other than material gain'. A few years later, it made timid and ephemeral attempts to pursue a progressive social policy. But after the interruption caused by the First World War, the United States committed itself fully to the option of mass consumption, with the boom in automobiles, in building and in household gadgets.

In Western Europe, the moment of decision was delayed by two World Wars and by the need for postwar reconstruction. Broadly speaking, mass consumption made its appearance after 1950, but with the restrictions and modifications imposed by government policy and by the pressure of a powerful Socialist tradition. In France, for example, these included the series of social laws ranging from free education to the medical organization of 'social security'. Some sectors, moreover, lagged behind completely, by force of circumstances or on account of reluctance to abandon traditional ways. To take one example, the agricultural revolution, American-style, ran into countless obstacles in continental Europe. The constant problems faced in this field by the Soviet Union are well known; and the situation is also complicated in France and Italy, neither of which has yet full modernized its agriculture.

Finally, not all regions were equally involved in the process. Just as the South of the United States remained backward long after 1900, so large parts of Europe lagged behind. They included the South-West and West of France, the *mezzogiorno* in Italy, the whole Iberian Peninsula outside the industrial centres of Barcelona and Bilbao, all the Communist republics (except the USSR itself, Czechoslovakia and the German Democratic Republic), the rest of the Balkans and Turkey.

In short, there have always been these two Europes, described by a journalist in 1929 as the Europe of the car and the Europe of the cart. To take one symbol out of thousands, we need only go

near Cracow, on a road where narrow four-wheeled wagons laden
with wood, and flocks of geese with their drovers, are more
numerous than the automobiles. Yet suddenly we see the huge
installations of Nova Huta, that town of metallurgical industries
founded from nothing by Socialist Poland. Such contrasts are still
an integral part of life in Europe today.

Credit, financial capitalism, and State capitalism: a credit revolution
accompanied the Industrial Revolution, and fully profited from its
success.

Capitalism of a kind has always existed, as witness ancient
Babylon, which had bankers, merchants engaged in distant trade,
and all the instruments of credit, such as bills of exchange, promis-
sory notes, cheques, etc. In this sense, the history of capitalism
extends 'from the Hammurabi to Rockefeller'. But credit in Europe
in the sixteenth and seventeenth centuries still had a very restricted
role. It developed considerably in the eighteenth century. By then,
if only on account of trade with India and the East India
Companies, or trade with China, which helped develop Canton,
there was already a form of international capitalism, covering
most of the commercial centres in Europe. At that time, however,
financiers as such hardly concerned themselves with trade or
industry: they managed public funds in the service of the State.

With the success of industrialization, banking and finance
developed very rapidly. So much so that, alongside industrial
capitalism, financial capitalism gained the upper hand and sooner
or later controlled all the levers governing economic life. In France
and Britain, its ascendancy became clear in the 1860s. Old and
new banks extended their networks, and specialized as deposit
banks, credit banks, merchant banks, etc. To follow the modernization of banking, it would be useful to trace in France, for example,
the history of Crédit Lyonnais, founded in 1863, that of Pierpont
Morgan in the United States, or the international network of the
Rothschilds. Everywhere, banks succeeded in attracting a huge
clientele, 'all the savings-minded public'; they sought and captured

'all dormant or sterile deposits', no matter how small. And the craze for 'shares' began. Industries, railways, shipping companies were gradually caught up in this complex banking network; and the operations of financial capitalism at once became international. French banks allowed themselves to be tempted more and more by the attractions of foreign loans. Thus it was that French savers took the perilous path of loans to Russia. Yet these foreign loans were at one time an important source of income for the French economy: a favourable balance of payments offset a deficit in the balance of trade. After 1850, they also contributed to basic investments in much of Europe and elsewhere.

Today, the heyday of financial capitalism in Europe seems to have passed, despite the theoretical debates that the subject can always arouse, and despite a certain number of exceptions that prove the rule. Thus, a merchant bank like the Banque de Paris et des Pays-Bas is still a very major power, and London, Paris, Frankfurt, Amsterdam, Brussels, Zurich and Milan remain vital financial centres. But – despite disillusionment with State Socialism, and despite efforts to limit public spending, partly by privatization – State capitalism has become a leading feature of the scene.

In the 'nationalized' sectors of those economies where State control has increased, the State itself has become an industrialist and a banker. Even elsewhere, its role has grown enormously since the nineteenth century. Extensive taxation, coupled with investment in public funds such as (in France) *comptes-chèques postaux*, *caisses d'épargnes* and *bons du Trésor*, or (in Britain) National Savings, Government loans or Treasury Bonds, has put at Governments' disposal enormous sums of money. The State is the grand master of investment in the infrastructure of industry, without which there can be no policies of growth, no effective social programmes and in a word no future.

Every year, even to ensure progress as modest as ours appears to be, a large slice of the national income has to be invested. Investment multiplies its own initial impact by stimulating a whole series of economic transactions. More and more, it looks as if

States need to plan their economic development, if only in the sense of setting targets and predicting the results of concerted action. The Soviet Union's famous five-year plans have been imitated all over the world. In January 1962, President J. F. Kennedy actually announced a five-year plan for US trade! France's own indicative five-year plans have in the past provoked lively controversy. They are, in their way, a national heart-searching as well as an economic balance-sheet. One of their aims is to assist take-off in backward regions by what they call 'a policy of training'.

Looking back on the Industrial Revolution and its repercussions, we should neither omit nor exaggerate the driving force of colonialism. It did not give Europe her central, predominant place in the world; but it may well have helped her to retain it. By 'colonialism' – another debatable word – we mean all European expansion, at least since 1492.

Undeniably, expansion favoured Europe. It gave her access to new areas in which to settle her surplus population and, nearby, rich and exploitable civilizations which she did not fail to exploit. The major landmarks in this process of exploitation were: in the sixteenth century, the arrival of 'treasures' (gold and silver ingots) from America; the brutal opening-up of India after the battle of Plassey (23 June 1757), at which the British defeated the nawab of Bengal; the forced exploitation of the Chinese market after the First Opium War in 1839–42; and the partition of Africa at Berlin in 1885.

The result, in Europe, was to establish huge trading concerns in the Iberian Peninsula, the Low Countries and then the British Isles, altogether greatly strengthening some of those capitalist networks which assisted the progress of industrialization. Europe gained a large surplus from these distant lands overseas.

And that surplus played its part. It was no coincidence that Britain, so successful overseas, was the first to enjoy 'take-off'. It still remains to be established whether, as we believe, the Industrial

Revolution later consolidated colonialism, to Europe's benefit, by confirming European primacy and prestige. There is no doubt, however, that France's industrial growth was independent of her presence in Senegal, or her establishment in Algeria (1830), Cochin-China (1858–67) and Tonkin and Annam (1883).

Equally debatable is the human and moral record of colonialism as such. It is a complex question, in which guilt and responsibility are not all on one side. Colonialism had both positive and negative aspects. Only one thing is certain: the history of that type of colonialism is over: the page is turned.

Socialism and industrialism

To the credit of the West, it tried very hard to find a valid and effective social, humanitarian response to the many hardships involved in industrialization. It worked out what we might call a social form of humanism, if we had not already overworked that convenient word.

The search for decent solutions went on throughout the nineteenth century – an age at once sad, dramatic and marked by genius. It was sad, because of the ugliness of daily life; it was dramatic, on account of continual upheavals and wars; and it was marked by genius, as shown by its progress in science and technology, as well as, to a lesser degree, in social affairs.

At all events, the upshot is clear. Today, long after the nineteenth century, a sober collection of social provisions, which could still be improved, is enshrined in laws which aim to give the mass of people a better life and to disarm revolutionary demands.

This complex and imperfect achievement did not result automatically or easily from dispassionate moral or factual analysis. It arose from a very determined struggle, which in the West involved at least three phases. (We shall return to the particular case of Russia and the Soviet Union.)

The revolutionary and ideological phase was that of social

reformers or 'prophets' (as their many enemies called them). It lasted from 1815 to 1871 – i.e. from the fall of Napoléon Bonaparte until the Commune. Its true turning-point was perhaps 1848, the year of successive revolutions.

The phase of militant organized labour (trade unions and political parties) actually began before the siege of Paris, but was essentially concentrated between 1871 and 1914.

The political or governmental phase largely began after the First World War. The State began to undertake social measures after 1919 and 1929; it intensified them, with the help of greater affluence, from 1945–50 until the present day.

This chronological framework suggests that in the face of industrialization the protests and demands of working people often changed both their direction and their tone, in line with variations in material prosperity. They were vehement in times of economic hardship (1817–51; 1873–96; 1929–39), and less so in periods of economic growth (such as 1851–73, or from 1945 onwards). One historian, discussing such fluctuations in Germany, has declared: 'In 1830, the word proletariat was not yet known; by 1955 it had almost passed out of use.'

Of the three phases in question, the first (which concerned only social ideas) was perhaps the most important, because it marked a turning-point for an entire civilization. From 1815 to 1848 and 1871, this great movement of ideas, acute analyses and prophecies broadly shifted ideological interest from politics to society. From then on, the State was no longer the target of people's demands: now, it was society that had to be understood, healed and improved.

With a new programme came a new language. With words like *industrial* and *industrialist*, *industrial society* and *industrial firm*, *proletariat*, *mass*, *Socialism*, *Socialist*, *capitalist*, *capitalism*, *Communist* and *Communism*, revolutionary ideology found a new vocabulary.

It was the Count de Saint-Simon who invented the noun and adjective *industriel* (derived from the old word industry) and probably the phrase *société industrielle*, seized upon by Auguste Comte,

Herbert Spencer and many others. For Comte, the expression denoted that form of society which had supplanted military society, hitherto (in his view) the dominant mode. While military society had been warlike, industrial society, he thought, would have to be peaceful – a claim that Herbert Spencer rightly refused to make.

The word *proletariat* was included in the French Academy's Dictionary in 1828. *Mass*, in the singular and especially in the plural, became the key word, 'the terminological symptom of the changes that became explosive in the reign of Louis-Philippe'. 'I have an instinct for the masses: that is my sole political asset,' said Alphonse Lamartine in 1828. And Louis-Napoléon Bonaparte in his *Extinction of Poverty* (1844) declared: 'Today, the reign of castes is over: one can govern only with the masses.'

These 'masses' were above all the poor, exploited, urban working-class masses. Hence the idea that the present time was dominated by conflict between social classes – what Karl Marx called 'the class struggle'. This, of course, was an age-old phenomenon, present in all materially advanced societies in the past. But there is no denying that in the nineteenth century it greatly intensified, causing a good deal of heart-searching.

Socialist and *Socialism* came into general use in the 1830s. So too did *Communism*, in the vague sense of economic and social equality. Thus Auguste Blanqui, 'General of the revolutionary masses', felt able to write that 'Communism is the safeguard of the individual'. The word *capitalism* was used by Louis Blanc in his *Organization of Work* (1848–50) and by Proudhon in 1857; it appeared in the Larousse dictionary in 1867, but it was not overwhelmingly popular until the beginning of the twentieth century. The word *capitalist* was more vigorous. In 1843, Lamartine exclaimed: 'Who would recognize the Revolution as it is now? Instead of enjoying independent work and industry, we see France sold to the capital-ists!' Less successful new words included 'bourgeoisism' and 'collectism'.

Nevertheless, memories of 1789 had not lost their power. The

Jacobins, the Terror, the Committees of Public Safety – all these were words and ideas that continued to haunt people's minds, either as models or as monsters. For most reformers, 'the Revolution' remained a talisman and a source of strength. At the time of the Commune, in 1871, Raoul Rigault declared: 'We are not seeking legality: we are making Revolution.'

From the Count de Saint-Simon to Karl Marx, the working-out of 'massive philosophies' (to use Maxime Leroy's expression for philosophies inspired by the problems of the masses) was largely completed by 1848. February of that year saw the publication of the *Communist Manifesto* by Karl Marx and Friedrich Engels, which still remains the Bible of the movement.

A detailed list of the many reformers who were active in this first part of the nineteenth century would show fairly clearly the leading role of the three countries then facing industrialization – Britain, France and Germany. It would also show how important French thinking on the subject was: a question to which we shall return shortly. Finally, it would emphasize the part played by the Count de Saint-Simon. This unusual man, slightly mad but also a genius, was in a sense the ancestor of all social, Socialist, and non-Socialist ideologies, and indeed of French sociology itself (as Georges Gurvitch has said). He certainly influenced another and much greater giant, Karl Marx, who as a young man in Trier read Saint-Simon's writings and drew from them many of his own arguments and ideas.

With the exception of Saint-Simon, the social reformers can be divided into three age-groups: those born in the last three decades of the eighteenth century (Robert Owen, 1771; Charles Fourier, 1772; Etienne Cabet, 1788; and Auguste Comte, 1798); those born in the first decade of the nineteenth century (Pierre Joseph Proudhon, 1809; Victor Considérant, 1808; Louis Blanc, 1811); and the more homogeneous generation of Karl Marx (1818), Friedrich Engels (1820), and Ferdinand Lassalle (1825). This German group brought up the rear. It has been said that the death of Lassalle, killed in a duel in 1864, removed the only colleague who could rival Marx, and so ensured the success of Marxism. But it would be more accurate to ascribe its success to the authoritative power of *Das Kapital* (1867).

This is not the place to study these 'massive philosophies' one by one. All are in effect analyses of 'developing society' – *'la société en devenir'*, in Saint-Simon's elegant phrase. They are, so to speak, medications or courses of treatment. For Saint-Simon and his disciples (Barthélémy Enfantin and Michel Chevalier, who made business fortunes under the Second Empire), effort was to be concentrated on the organization of production. The French Revolution, which they disliked, had failed, they thought, because it had not organized the economy. Fourier, who also detested the Revolution, thought that the priority should be to organize consumption.

Armand Barbès and Auguste Blanqui, Louis Blanc and Pierre Joseph Proudhon, all remained faithful to the principles of 1789, the two former as men of action, the two latter in order to 'fulfil and perfect' those principles. Victor Considérant, on the other hand, rejected them, though less violently than his master Charles Fourier.

Apart from Marx, of whom more later, the most original of these thinkers was Proudhon, so attached to liberty as to be almost an anarchist, as much *vis-à-vis* the Church as against the State. What he sought was a social dialectic which could illuminate scientifically a society on the move, in all its contradictions. It was necessary to resolve them, he thought, in order to grasp the social machinery that they implied. This was scientific speculation, very far from the passions of religion or action. It was at the opposite pole from the spirit of those like Owen, Cabet and Fourier who founded the phalansteries, and was equally opposed to that of the revolutionaries and of Karl Marx, determined to build with their own hands the better world of which they were the prophets.

The primacy of French thinking in these fields, very evident in the early years of the nineteenth century, requires explanation. France was undoubtedly the country of the Revolution – the

great Revolution. She was certainly on hand for the revolutions of
1830 and 1848; and in 1871, alone and under foreign conquest, she
none the less fed the proud revolutionary flame of the Paris
Commune.

Yet, these characteristics apart, the Socialist tradition in France
was one of the results of the country's industrialization. As
elsewhere, reforming or revolutionary thought in France was the
work of intellectuals, the vast majority of whom were socially
privileged. And, again as elsewhere, these ideas acquired life and
strength only when they were taken up and acted upon by working
people. But, more than elsewhere, intellectual reactions in France
were both early and extreme – whereas industrialization there
came later than in Britain, France's take-off occurring around
1830 – 60.

This is so: but the take-off theory over-simplifies the real process.
It names an H-hour when the great industrial rocket is supposed to
lift off in one go. Is there ever so clear an economic H-hour? To
imagine so is to ignore the whole incubation period that precedes
any such sudden spurt. Recent studies have found that France's
industrial growth-rate, between 1815 and 1851, was fairly high –
about 2.5 per cent a year. Such growth was enough to increase the
move to the towns in the eighteenth century, to change existing
society and to give France, already shaken by the Revolution and
the Napoleonic Wars, that 'demolition-and-building-site' look
which so much struck contemporary witnesses.

The growth of towns alone produced a rapid worsening of their
human and material condition. From Balzac to Victor Hugo, all
observers found this worrying. Poverty, begging, robbery,
delinquency, truancy, epidemics and crime: all were increased by
the rapid crowding of working people into the unspeakable
promiscuity of the slums. And the newcomers never stopped
coming. As late as 1847, Michelet noted that the peasant 'admires
everything in the town; he wants everything; he will stay there if
he can . . . Once he has left the land, he hardly ever returns.' Yet
in 1830, a troubled year, Orléans had to support 12,500 needy

people out of a total of 40,000 inhabitants – i.e. nearly one in three. In Lille in the same year, the proportion was one in 2.21.

It would seem as if town life at that time was especially bedevilled by industry. Industry affected the town and drew people towards it, but it could not raise local standards or even provide for those it attracted. It may be that urban poverty then was no worse than poverty in the country. But in the towns, in view of everyone, there was the alarming spectacle of a population of workers who were victims of the industry that gave them work but cared little about how they lived.

So, when the beginnings of industrialization began to transform the towns, the first 'ideologists' were confronted with a society not unlike that of less developed countries today. Later, from 1851 onwards, with the economic boom and growth that accompanied the Second Empire (1852–70) the condition of working people began to improve.

From organized labour to social security: this question is too large and complex to be treated in depth here. Would it be possible, in any case? It would mean collating, on the one hand, Socialist thinking (a family of ideas evolving, complementing and contradicting each other), and on the other the demands of organized labour, in the real context of work and daily life. How were Socialist ideas treated by the tough and turbulent mass of working people?

The question is hard to answer, especially since organized labour often pursued its own policies, as in Britain, in a realistic, cautious and practical way, ignoring ideology and extremist militant politics. Then again, if the first phase had been that of social theorists, the second that of trade unions and the third that of workers' political parties, the final phase was that of the States. In some cases, they refused workers' demands (or made reluctant concessions for prudential reasons, which amounted to almost the same thing). In other cases, they met or even anticipated the claims, drawing their sting in advance.

In this process, therefore, at least four groups were involved: theorists of every kind, trade unionists with many different attitudes, politicians from among (or sympathizing with) the workers, and representatives of the State. All were very different from one another. Yet there was a general evolution in Europe, in roughly the same stages, at least in the three key countries – Britain, France and Germany – and in their neighbours – The Netherlands, Belgium, the Scandinavian countries and Switzerland. Outside these privileged areas, progress was slower, and has not always been completed, even today. Here are some of the landmarks in that progress, where it has occurred:

Before 1871:

In Britain, large numbers of trade unions were established from 1858–67 onwards. From the beginning, they campaigned for the abolition of the old laws on relations between master and servant. The first Congress of the trade unions was held in 1866. At that time, the unions included only skilled workers.

In France at this time there were few positive steps. In 1864 there was a Combination Law which allowed legitimate strikes; in 1865, the French Section of the International opened an office in Paris, following the opening of the first, in London, in the previous year; in 1868 it opened another in Lyon. The Second Empire was at once 'progressive and compressive': it improved workers' conditions, but was careful to limit their liberties.

In Germany, the situation evolved just as slowly. In 1862, Lassalle founded the Allgemeiner Deutscher Arbeiter Verein. Seven years later, the Congress of Eisenbach saw the establishment of the Workers' Social-Democrat Party, with Marxist leanings.

Before 1914:

Up to that date, immense progress was made.

In Britain, in 1881, Henry Mayers Hyndman founded the Social Democratic Federation to spread 'Socialist' ideas among the workers, who had hitherto been impervious to politics as such. At about the same time, in 1884, the trade union movement began to reach poorer, unskilled workers. Not till ten years later, however, did the London dockers stage their great historic strike. In 1893, the Independent Labour Party was established, and five years later the General Federation of Trade Unions. The electoral successes of the Labour Party were followed by an almost revolutionary development, the 'radical' Government of 1906. A series of welfare laws followed, promising a gradual transformation of Britain.

In France there were similar developments. In 1877 Jules Guesde founded the first Socialist newspaper, *L'Egalité*, and two years later the French Workers' Party, the Parti ouvrier français or POF. In 1884 the trade unions were legally recognized; from 1887 onwards, labour exchanges began to be set up. The year 1890 saw the first celebration of 1 May, Labour Day; and 1893 the first election of Jean Jaurès, Socialist deputy for Carmaux. In 1895, the Confédération Générale du Travail was established. In 1901 came the foundation of two Socialist parties – the Parti socialiste de France, led by Jules Guesde, and the Parti socialiste français, led by Jean Jaurès. In 1904 the newspaper *L'Humanité* was founded; and in 1906 the two Socialist parties were merged as the Parti socialiste unifié.

In Germany, the Socialists were harassed by Bismarck's emergency laws of 1878; but from 1883 onwards the State passed a number of welfare measures. After Bismarck's resignation in 1890, the trade unions reorganized, and soon had more than a million members. They also had great political success, with 3 million left-wing votes in the 1907 election, and 4,245,000 in 1912.

All this being so, and without exaggerating the strength of the Second International, it could be argued that in 1914 the West was not only on the brink of war, but also on the brink of Socialism. The Socialists were close to seizing power and building a Europe as modern as it is today – and perhaps more so. In a few days, a few hours, war destroyed their hopes.

It was a very great failing on the part of European Socialists that they were unable to prevent the First World War. This is freely

admitted by those historians who are most sympathetic to Socialism, and who are anxious to know who in particular should bear
the blame for this reverse. On 27 July 1914, Léon Jouhaux and his
colleague Dumoulin, Secretaries of the French CGT, met K.
Legien, Secretary of the German Trade Unions, in Brussels. Did
they meet by chance, in a café, or with no purpose other than to
admit their despair? We do not know. Nor do we know what to
make of Jean Jaurès's last actions, on the very day he was assassinated (31 July 1914). He had gone to Brussels to try, in vain, to
persuade the German Socialists to strike rather than accept mobilization for war.

   Western Europe today, in so far as it has adopted Socialist ideals,
has done so slowly and incompletely, by the ballot box, by laws
and by the establishment in France in 1945–6, and in Britain a
little later, of a social security system. Already, the European
Community, by declaring the principle that all States should bear
equal burdens in this field, has in effect opted for the eventual
adoption of similar rules throughout its member countries.

19. Unity in Europe

======

An historian of humanism, Franco Simone, has warned us to be wary of the supposed unity of Europe: a romantic illusion, he says. To reply that he is both right and wrong is simply to affirm that Europe simultaneously enjoys both unity and diversity — which on reflection seems to be the obvious truth.

The preceding chapters have described a number of things shared by the whole of Europe: its religion, its rationalist philosophy, its development of science and technology, its taste for revolution and social justice, its imperial adventures. At any moment, however, it is easy to go beyond this apparent 'harmony' and find the national diversity that underlies it. Such differences are abundant, vigorous and necessary. But they exist just as much between Brittany and Alsace, between the North and the South of France, between Piedmont and the Italian *mezzogiorno*; between Bavaria and Prussia; between Scotland and England; between Flemings and Walloons in Belgium; or among Catalonia, Castille and Andalusia. And they are not used as arguments to deny the national unity of each of the countries concerned.

Nor are these national instances of unity a contradiction of Europe's own. Every State has always tended to form its own cultural world; and the study of 'national character' has enjoyed analysing these various limited civilizations. The brilliantly clever books of Elie Faure or Count Hermann Alexander Keyserling are not in this respect completely misleading: but let us simply say that they peer too closely at the individual tiles in a mosaic which, seen from a greater distance, reveals clear overall patterns. Why must one be forced to choose, once and for all, between the detail and the whole? Neither need exclude the other: both are real.

Outstanding art and culture

Some of Europe's shared characteristics can justly be called 'brilliant'. It is they that give European civilization, on the highest plane of culture, taste and intellect, a fraternal and almost monolithic air, as if bathed in a single, unvarying light.

Does that mean that all the nations of Europe have exactly the same culture? Certainly not. But any movement that begins in one part of Europe tends to spread throughout it. Tends only: a cultural phenomenon may very well face resistance or rejection in one part of Europe or another – or, conversely, it may be so successful that, as often happens, it goes beyond Europe's frontiers, ceases to be 'European', and begins to belong to humanity in general. Nevertheless, broadly speaking, Europe is a fairly coherent cultural whole, and has long acted as such *vis-à-vis* the rest of the world.

Art enjoys multiple resonance. Artistic phenomena in Europe spill over the borders of their native countries, whether Catalonia (probably the source from which early Romanesque spread), the Ile de France, Lombardy, fifteenth-century Florence, Titian's Venice or the Paris of the Impressionists.

Regularly, every centre where princely houses, palaces or churches have been built has attracted artists from the four corners of Europe. This was shown in the fifteenth century, to take one example among a thousand, by the Dijon of the Dukes of Burgundy and of the sculptor Claus Sluter. The wanderings of Italian Renaissance artists readily explain how the style of one city was so easily contaminated by that of another. A particular fresco, begun by one artist, might be completed by a second; a particular church might have called for work by a succession of architects.

Santa Maria del Fiore, in Florence, for instance, had to wait for the bold Filippo Brunelleschi before it was crowned by its cupola.

A prince's or a rich merchant's caprice or love of luxury had a role to play: without such stimulus, it would be hard to understand how styles spread so rapidly at a time when communications were slow and less numerous than now. In the fifteenth and sixteenth centuries the Italians, like those whom Francis I of France summoned to his court, were in effect the teachers of all Europe. In the eighteenth century it was the French who carried classical art far afield: they were to be found even in Russia. And how many Versailles Europe possesses – how many gardens *à la française.*

So Europe has been swept by great waves, if not tides, which have been slow to cover all the area, but slow also to recede. One has only to think of those great successes when all Europe seemed to march in step: Romanesque, Gothic, Baroque and Classicism.

Each time, the phenomenon was surprisingly long-lived. Gothic art held sway, in general, for three centuries. To the South, it reached little further than Burgos and Milan: the true Mediterranean spirit rejected it. Yet Venice, at the beginning of the sixteenth century, was entirely Gothic – in its own unique way. Paris was still Gothic in the mid-sixteenth century. Renaissance architecture was confined to a few places: to the Louvre, which was under construction; to the Palais de Madrid, now demolished; and to Fontainebleau, where Francesco Primaticcio ('Le Primatice') had worked and where Leonardo da Vinci returned before he died. From the sixteenth century onwards, Baroque enjoyed immense success: an offshoot of both Rome and Spain, it was the art of the Counter-Reformation (so much so that at one time it was known as 'Jesuit art'). But it also spread to Protestant Europe; and it made great inroads toward the East, in Vienna, Prague and Poland.

In the eighteenth century, French architecture took much less time to establish itself. To understand how so many French towns, like Tours and Bordeaux, were remodelled, the most illuminating sight is that of the former Leningrad. St Petersburg, built in an empty space with no buildings to restrain the freedom of the architects, certainly was and still is the most beautiful of eighteenth-century cities, and the one that best expresses that century's sense of grouping, proportion and vistas.

Painting and music spread no less freely. Musical techniques or pictorial preoccupations were easily taken up into general circulation, and went the rounds of Europe.

It would be impossible to deal adequately in a few lines with the fascinating story of the rapid changes in musical instruments and techniques which accompanied successive stages in Europe's history. The instruments used in classical antiquity, from the flute to the harp, were handed down from generation to generation; next came the organ, the harpsichord, the violin (made popular especially by Italian virtuosi, although the present-day bow, which dates from the eighteenth century, was invented by a Frenchman), and then the various types of piano.

The history of musical form is obviously bound up with the development of musical instruments. In the Middle Ages, singing predominated, whether accompanied or not. Polyphony, which developed in the ninth century, used the organ as bass accompaniment to liturgical song. In the fourteenth and fifteenth centuries, the *Ars nova* of the Florentines was a vocal polyphony in which a number of instruments were introduced as if they were voices. This 'new art' reached its zenith in the *a capella* music of Palestrina (1525–94).

But vocal music gave way to instrumental music, especially with the development of bow instruments. It was the beginning of the concert, of so-called 'chamber music', written for a small number of instruments (for example, a quartet). Originally, chamber music meant secular music, or that of the court as distinct from that of the Church. In 1605, Enrico Radesca was '*musico di camera*' to Amadeus of Savoy; in 1627, Carlo Farina was '*suonatore di violino di camera*'. Chamber music was above all a form of dialogue: it was the art of conversation. Italy was its birthplace, with the concerto in which groups of instruments conferred together, followed by a solo instrument responding to the whole orchestra. Arcangelo Corelli (1653–1713) was the first to play as a soloist; Antonio Vivaldi (1678–1743) was the master of the art. Germany preferred the sonata, with two instruments or sometimes one alone. In France, the suite very freely brought together a number of dance movements.

With the symphony, finally, came large-scale orchestral music – large-scale in the number of instruments and in the number of listeners. In the eighteenth century, with the Stamitz family, the sonata form was already treated symphonically. In the next century, in the Romantic period, the tendency was to enlarge the orchestra, but also to give a more prominent role to the soloists, of whom Niccolò Paganini and Franz Liszt were characteristic examples.

Special mention must be made of Italian opera, which seems to have originated in Florence at the end of the sixteenth century. It went on to conquer Italy, Germany and Europe: Mozart, Handel and Gluck all at first wrote operas 'in the Italian manner'. Then, of course, came German opera.

Revolutions in painting – and they were virtual revolutions – also affected the whole of Europe. Even when ideas about painting seemed contradictory, the same contradictions appeared everywhere. There were perhaps two major revolutions. One was Italian, that of the Renaissance, when the pictorial space became geometric, with the laws of perspective, long before the science of Galileo and Descartes had 'geometrized' the world. The second revolution took place in France towards the end of the nineteenth century, and affected the very nature of painting itself, leading to cubism and abstract art. We have mentioned Italy and France only to identify the places where these revolutions began: in fact, if one takes the great names or the great innovators, they clearly belong to European painting as a whole. Today, indeed, we should have to say 'Western painting', since it has travelled far beyond Europe's own shores.

Philosophies, too, carry unique messages. Europe has had a

single philosophy, or something very like it, at every stage of its development. At the very least there has always been what Jean-Paul Sartre liked to call 'a dominant philosophy', reflecting the needs of society at the time – no doubt because the whole of the West, at any given moment, has had a single dominant economic and social structure. Whether or not the philosophy of Descartes was that of a rising bourgeoisie and a slowly growing capitalist world, it certainly dominated and pervaded the Europe of its day. Whether or not Marxist philosophy is that of the rising working classes and of Socialist society, or industrial society, it has clearly played a dominant role in the West and in the world, which it divided as, until only very recently, it divided Europe.

For philosophies to spread so readily, there had to be innumerable international links. Take two important periods in German philosophy: from the publication of Immanuel Kant's *Critique of Pure Reason* in 1781 to the death of Hegel in 1831; and from Edmund Husserl (1859–1938) to Martin Heidegger (1889–1976). The influence of these German thinkers cannot be understood unless one bears in mind the many translations – French, English, Italian, Spanish, Russian, etc. – that were made of each of their works. Translation is one measure of the degree to which two major movements in German philosophy were integrated into the intellectual life of Europe.

It may be noted that, in the case of existentialism, it was its reinterpretation by Jean-Paul Sartre and Maurice Merleau-Ponty that retransmitted it to the rest of the world, and especially to Latin America.

As regards the natural sciences, there can be no question: they were strictly pan-European from the time of their first success. It is difficult to give any one nation in Europe the credit for this discovery or that, because so many of them were the result of work that was going on everywhere at once, in a series of stages that successively involved all the scientists in Europe. Any example will serve to prove the point. That of the Keplerian revolution, so well described in Alexandre Koyre's 1962 study, is ideal for the purpose. Johann Kepler (1571–1630) belonged to a virtual family of kindred spirits – his predecessors (above all, Copernicus), his contemporaries (above all, Galileo) and his disciples. If we were to mark on a map their birthplaces and the centres where they worked, the whole of Europe would be covered with black dots.

Medicine, biology and chemistry showed a similar pattern. None of the sciences can be described as having been German, British, French, Italian or Polish, even for a short time. They were always European.

Developments in the social sciences, by contrast, resembled those in philosophy, in the sense that they tended to originate in particular countries and then spread rapidly to the rest of Europe. Sociology began as a predominantly French speciality; economics, especially in the twentieth century, has been mainly a British or Anglo-American achievement; geography has been both German and French (as witness Friedrich Ratzel and Vidal de la Blache). In the nineteenth century, history was dominated by Germany and by the great name of Leopold von Ranke (1795–1886): German historiography impressed all Europe with its erudition and its meticulous reconstruction of the past. Today, the situation is less simple; but European historiography – now in fact world historiography – forms a coherent whole. Within it, a French school is important, dating from the days of Henri Berr, Henri Pirenne, Lucien Febvre, Marc Bloch, Henri Hauser and Georges Lefebvre, supported by economists like François Simiand or sociologists like Maurice Halbwachs. This school seeks to synthesize all the social sciences, and it has revitalized the methods and prospects of historiography in France.

Literature in Europe shows the fewest signs of unity. Rather than European literature, there is national literature, and while there are cross-frontier links, there are also considerable contrasts. The lack of unity in this field is by no means regrettable, and indeed is natural. Literature, whether essays, novels or plays, is based on what most differentiates national civilizations: their language, their daily life, their way of reacting to sorrow, pleasure, the idea of love, or death, or war; their way of entertaining themselves, their food, their drink, their work, their beliefs. Through their literature, nations once more become characters, individuals whom one can try to analyse – even to psychoanalyse – with the help of this essential evidence.

There are, of course, clear and lasting cases of convergence: literature has its fashions. In the nineteenth century, for instance, the Romantic Movement that followed the rationalist Enlightenment affected the whole of Europe; and in its turn it was followed by social realism. There has been ceaseless interplay of 'influences' – between individuals and among groups of writers or 'schools'. Clearly, however, every literary work has its roots in a particular social and emotional milieu, and in unique personal experience. One can scarcely speak of unity in national literature. How then, *a fortiori*, can one seek unity on a European basis?

Is there not, furthermore, a major obstacle in the question of language? No translation can fully convey a literary experience. Each of the great languages of Europe, it is true, owes some of its riches to others, even if only one of them could become the lingua franca, like Latin in former times and French in the eighteenth century. The royal treatment that Voltaire received, in St Petersburg or in Paris, can be explained only by the royal status of the French language. Today, however, resort to a single language is possible for science (which has almost created a universal artificial language with its international technical terms): but it is not possible for literature – the more so in that literature is all the time growing more demotic. The 'international' French of the eighteenth century was after all the language of an élite minority.

Should the cultural unity of Europe be safeguarded, or does it need to be completed? With Europe bent on abolishing its internal frontiers, is this chequered cultural unity enough? Evidently not, because those who seek a politically united Europe are much concerned with the unifying effects that could be achieved by a well-thought-out reform of education. If qualifications were harmonized it would be possible to pursue one's studies from one university to another; and this, more than the establishment of one or more European universities (such as that now set up outside Florence), would create a European arena for study and research.

And would that not promote, of necessity, a modern form of humanism embracing all the living languages of Europe?

Economic interdependence

For centuries, Europe has been enmeshed in what has amounted to a single economy. At any given moment, its material life has been dominated by particular centres of privilege and influence.

During the later Middle Ages, Venice was the channel where everything gathered, to pass in or out. With the beginning of modern times, the centre of gravity for a time was Lisbon, then Seville – or rather, it alternated between Seville and Antwerp until the last quarter of the sixteenth century. Then, at the beginning of the seventeenth century, Amsterdam became the great trading centre until the early years of the eighteenth century, followed by London, which maintained its supremacy until 1914 and even 1939. There has always been an orchestra and a conductor.

Each time, the centre of gravity has been all the more influential, at its best, because not only European economic life has been attracted there, but also the economic life of the wider world. For Europe, on the eve of war in 1914, London was not only the great market for credit, for maritime insurance and reinsurance, but also for American wheat, Egyptian cotton, Malayan rubber, Banca and Billiton tin, South African gold, Australian wool and American and Middle Eastern oil.

Very early on, Europe became a coherent material and geographical whole, with an adaptable monetary economy and busy communications along its coasts and rivers and then via the carriageways and roads for pack animals that complemented its natural thoroughfares.

Early in Europe's history, pack animals conquered the great
barrier of the Alps, through the Brenner Pass (on the way to
Venice), the Gothard and the Simplon (on the way to Milan) and
by the Mont-Cenis. At the time, the curious term 'great carriages'
was used to describe the mule trains that carried this trade across
the mountains, enabling the Italian economy to expand towards
the North and North-West of Europe, eager for its luxury textiles
and for the products of the Levant. In Lyon, in the sixteenth
century, trade and trade fairs flourished owing to the confluence
of carriage roads, river traffic, and these 'great carriages' from the
Alps.

From the mid-nineteenth century the railways rid continental
Europe of its rigidity and inertia, and spread a civilization of
material well-being and rapid communications, boosted by busy
industrial and commercial cities.

Two examples out of this long history may illustrate Europe's
economic interdependence, although they do not explain it. One
is that of the *mude*, the fleets of Venetian merchant galleys. In the
fifteenth century they mostly plied the Mediterranean, but some
went as far as London and Bruges, while well-frequented land
routes, especially through the Brenner Pass, led from the North to
Venice, where the German merchants shared a huge warehouse,
the Fondego dei Tedeschi, near the Rialto Bridge.

The second example, in the sixteenth century, is that of the
circulation of money and bills of exchange, starting from Seville
and going the rounds of Europe. In fact, approximately the same
sums passed from hand to hand and place to place in the process of
trade and payments.

It is easy to understand, then, why the different regions of
Europe were affected almost simultaneously by the same cycles of
economic change. In the sixteenth century, a huge price rise began
in Spain as a result of the sudden influx of precious metals from
America. The same price inflation affected the whole of Western
Europe, and penetrated even as far as Moscow, then the centre of a
still primitive economy.

This does not mean that all of Europe has always developed at the same rate or attained the same level. A line could be drawn from Lübeck or Hamburg, through Prague and Vienna as far as the Adriatic, to divide the economically advanced Western part of Europe from the backward area to the East – a fact already attested by the difference in the respective situation of peasants on either side of the line. The contrast is beginning to fade; but it still exists.

Furthermore, even in prosperous Western Europe, there are richer centres – 'growth areas' – interspersed among less developed regions, some of them backward or 'under-developed'. Even today, in almost all European countries, some places are still poor by comparison with the nation as a whole, the more so since new investments tend to be attracted to the most thriving areas.

Indeed, there can be no commercial relations, and hence no economic interdependence, unless there are differences of voltage or of development, in which some regions lead the way and others follow. Development and under-development complement and depend upon each other. By way of brief illustration, take the history of banking in France. In the second half of the nineteenth century it expanded rapidly owing to the belated mobilization of savings and dormant or semi-dormant capital in parts of the French provinces and countryside. The immediate beneficiaries were banks like the Crédit Lyonnais, established in 1863, and destined to grow very powerful; but the once backward areas that had supplied the capital soon felt the recoil, as it were, stimulating their economy and linking it to the general life of the nation.

The logic of the Common Market: despite the differences between regional and national economies, economic links have long bound Europe together. Can they be organized to form a coherent and fully interdependent whole? That is the question facing the series of ventures launched since the end of the Second World War, of which the Common Market or European Community is the most successful, although it was not the first and is not the only such endeavour.

Everything began, undoubtedly, on account of Europe's miserable situation after 1945: its total collapse threatened the equilibrium of the world. Hence the first constructive steps: the United Europe Movement publicly launched in London in May 1947; the Marshall Plan (3 July 1947), conceived for a variety of reasons, some political and military, others economic, cultural and social. Europe – a certain kind of Europe – was groping forward.

For the moment, let us consider only economic problems. From this point of view, the relative failure of EFTA, the Europe of the Seven ('the shipwrecked', as one journalist called them), cleared the way and the future for what was then the 'Europe of the Six', commonly known as the Common Market but in fact grouping in the European Community three legal entities: the ECSC, set up by the Treaty of Paris in 1951, and the EEC and Euratom, established by the Treaty of Rome on 25 March 1957. Even now, the European Community does not include all Western Europe, let alone Europe as a whole. But if Europe is really to be built, the Community will grow both broader and deeper.

At the time of writing, in February 1962, a number of requests for entry were under negotiation. Since then, the Community has grown to number twelve; and further applications for membership or association are pending. So the Community may well grow to cover the whole of what is traditionally known as Europe – even if it is forbidden to stretch 'as far as the Urals'.

Through the Common Market, then, it should be possible to gauge the chances of achieving European economic union.

The formation of the EEC or Common Market resulted from the laborious negotiation of the Treaty of Rome, whose complex provisions began to come into effect from 1 January 1958. This experiment is still relatively recent, and must therefore, be judged with caution.

The undeniably rapid economic growth enjoyed by the Six during the early years of the Common Market was the double result of a favourable world climate and the beneficial effects of the first measures taken by the Community itself. The gradual opening of frontiers was clearly a stimulus, as was shown by the increase of trade among the countries concerned.

All the same, the vital part of the experiment still lies ahead. The Treaty of Rome and the subsequent decisions of the member Governments provide for a series of further steps. The question is: do the steps taken so far promise well for a future which, on paper, should involve total economic integration?

Contrary to some pessimistic forecasts, the Community's industries (including those of France which it was once feared might prove more vulnerable than their German competitors) have adapted well to the Common Market. There have been structural changes, including a tendency towards mergers which has favoured large-scale firms such as the Régie Renault or Pechiney and St-Gobain in France. There have had to be industrial shake-ups: for instance, certain less productive coal mines have had to be closed – although these painful decisions would have been necessary in any case.

Certainly, if only industry were concerned, agreements and compromises would be easy. Given modern technology, firms can be flexible *vis-à-vis* the market and *vis-à-vis* government plans. Equally, there are few difficulties with credit, which depends on the stability and mutual support of Europe's currencies. These enjoyed a long period of relative calm, so much so that the dollar gradually and fitfully ceased to be the only standard currency held in reserve alongside gold. Plans for closer monetary integration in Europe, moreover, made great strides in those years.

Such, then, is the rosy, reassuring side of the Common Market. But that is not the whole story, as recent events have shown. And there are further shadows. Some are political, and to these we shall return in a moment. Others are economic.

These economic problems concern: the geographical limits of the Common Market within Europe; its relations with the rest of the world; and the internal difficulties of agriculture.

The Common Market is clearly incomplete. It has important lacunae in the West. In the East, there was for a long time the

'Iron Curtain', behind which Comecon tried to develop its own
counterpart to the Common Market in the West. At the time of
writing the major problem was whether or not Britain would join
the Community: negotiations had begun in 1961, and they were
still in progress. Since then, Britain, Denmark and Ireland have
joined, followed by Greece, Spain and Portugal. But Britain's
entry, in particular, posed a number of problems. She had greatly
to loosen some of the ties that bound her to the Commonwealth,
in particular the preferential economic regime which was a relic of
Empire. This was difficult from an economic point of view, and
required Commonwealth agreement. Psychologically, it also
meant as it were turning the last page in the most successful
imperial history ever known.

   No less important is the problem of the Common Market's
relations with the rest of the world, and in particular with Africa
south of the Sahara. (The North African countries, with the exceptions of Libya and Egypt, remained for a long time within the
economic orbit of France.) This problem of the Community's
external relations also included that of relations with the Commonwealth – solved for the most part, with the exception of the
former Dominions, by the Lomé Convention linking African,
Caribbean and Pacific countries with the Community. Last but
not least, there was the question of the Community's relations
with the United States. In 1962, some feared that a 'colossal'
Atlantic market might swallow up the European Common
Market. Others saw Europe as the first step, the Atlantic as the
second and the world as the third. They, however, were unrealisti-
cally optimistic. All these problems, moreover, were also political;
and that in no way made them easier to solve.

   The problems of European agriculture, on the other hand, are
primarily economic, and of great importance for the Common
Market. They are also extremely complicated.

   Change was inevitable for the old peasant world of Europe – an
admirable world, deeply rooted in the past, but with a fairly
modest level of productivity, as the statistics show. The six

founder-member States of the European Community had 25 million country-dwellers (families included) out of a total population of 160 million. In the early 1960s, Sicco Mansholt, the former Dutch Minister of Agriculture who was then Vice-President of the Common Market Commission responsible for agricultural policy, estimated that 8 million of these farmers would have to find other employment if farming was to be modernized.

Modernizing agriculture meant increasing the output per person and reducing the number employed in it, not only because greater productivity implied more mechanization, but also because the total agricultural income lagged behind the general growth-rate of the European economy. In an expanding economy, growth tends to concentrate on industrial goods and services. In developed countries, an increase in income no longer leads to greater demand for food. If I have more money, I buy a car, a television set, books or clothes; I travel; I go to the theatre. But I do not eat more bread and meat or, let us hope, drink more wine or spirits.

Broadly speaking, then, if farm incomes were to increase at the same rate as those in other sectors of the economy, it was calculated in the early 1960s that by 1975 one farmer in three should leave the land so that more could be produced by a smaller number of people. The annual reduction, it was thought, should be about 4 per cent, whereas the actual rate was 2 per cent in Britain and 1.5 per cent in France. At that pace, it would take Britain twenty-two years and France twenty-seven to reach the target figure. What was more, there could be surprises. The tapering-off of Europe's boom years meant that there were fewer jobs in industry for former farmworkers; and in Italy, for example, with a peasant population originally numbering 4.5 million, those who left the land were mostly unemployed farmworkers; so, despite the drift to the towns, the structure of agriculture remained almost unchanged.

For all these reasons, European farm prices remain uncompetitive on the international market, where American and Canadian surpluses are sold at very low prices – lower sometimes than on the home market, owing to government subsidies. So the high prices of European agricultural products remain possible only as a result of protection, which isolates them from the world market.

The other serious agricultural problem for the Common Market lies in the disparities in production and prices as between different member States. Before the Community adopted its Common Agricultural Policy, France (which was more than self-sufficient, especially in cereals) could sell its surpluses abroad only at world prices. This obliged the French Government to buy them at home-market prices and sell them at a loss outside France. Thus in 1961, French wheat and barley were sold to Communist China, and chilled meat to Russia. Italy had the same problem with fruit and vegetables, and The Netherlands for dairy products. Germany, by contrast, imported many of the agricultural products it needed, but it bought them outside the Common Market, and was reluctant to lose the export opportunities that were the counterpart of these imports.

Farm prices were also different from country to country, depending both on relative productivity and on the degree of protection that governments were willing or obliged to supply. Thus, grain prices were lowest in France and highest in Germany, while milk was cheapest in The Netherlands. At what level, in a Common Agricultural Policy, were prices to be levelled out?

Finally, since agriculture had to be modernized, and since this was costly, who was to foot the sizeable bill? The solution adopted in Brussels, when the Common Agricultural Policy began to be established on 14 January 1962, was that the Community as a whole should bear the expense. This solution was unfavourable to Germany, whose economy was predominantly industrial. But the predominantly agricultural countries – France, Italy and The Netherlands – refused to move to the second stage of the Common Market's transition period unless at least the outlines of the Common Agricultural Policy were in place. The agreement took so long to reach, after 200 hours of discussion, that for a time the fate of the Community seemed to be in the balance. Which led one journalist to remark that 'Europe happily swallowed coal and steel and the atom, but it baulked at fruit and vegetables.'

The agreement provided for progress by stages: the first steps were to be taken in July 1962. But the Governments and the farmers' unions knew that the days of the old national systems were numbered and that adaptation was now unavoidable.

The movement of farm products throughout the Community was to be unrestricted, if necessary with compensatory taxes to offset remaining differences in price. This principle alone required institutional arrangements, regulation and supervision. Means already existed for the settlement of disputes. At the same time, there had to be a variable levy at the Community's external frontiers to prevent its prices being undercut by imports from abroad.

In later years, the Common Agricultural Policy was subject to countless arguments, criticisms, adjustments and compensatory arrangements: it seemed always to be undergoing reform. But it made possible a Common Market in farm produce, however much it might be flawed. With a single market in industrial products due to be perfected by the end of 1992, the Community was on the way to becoming an economic union. Will it stop at that stage? No. There remains the problem of political unity.

Political delay

Invited to build European unity, culture responds readily; the economy is more or less willing; only politics drags its feet. It has its reasons. Some are good, some less good, some false. Some are based on outdated, nineteenth-century concerns. Others are of the present; others still result from looking ahead.

The truth is that all of Europe has long been involved in the same political system, from which no State could escape without grave risks to itself. But that system did not encourage unity in

Europe: on the contrary, it divided European countries into groups of varying membership, whose basic rule was to prevent any hegemony being imposed on the whole family of nations. This was not out of pious respect for the liberty of others. Each State, in fact, pursued its own selfish ends. However, if it was too successful, it sooner or later found the others lined up against it.

Such, very broadly, was the principle of the 'European balance of power'. Has the Europe of today really given up this age-old policy?

The nineteenth century did not invent 'the balance of power' or 'the concert of Europe', although it practised them assiduously. In reality, similar constraints had been accepted for centuries. They were not the result of careful calculation by diplomatists or even by their masters, but rather, on the contrary, the outcome of a spontaneous, instinctive sense of equilibrium, of which statesmen were only partly aware.

The basic rule was always the same. When a State seemed to be too powerful (even if the impression was false, as in the case of France under Francis I, in 1519–22), its neighbours would jointly tilt the scales in the opposite direction so as to make it more moderate and better behaved. Francis I's defeat and capture at Pavia in 1525 showed that a mistake had been made: the too powerful monarch was the victor, Charles V. So the scales were tilted in the opposite direction: even the Turks were invited to add their weight.

The growing power of the States made this imperfect balancing-act ever more dangerous. Only Britain, from the safety of its island, could pursue the balance of power with impunity: not being on the seesaw, she was happy to weigh down one end or the other with money or troops, but preferably money. For a long time, she pitted her weight against the French, automatically allying with France's rivals. But when Germany became far too powerful, defeating France in 1871 because Britain and a divided Europe had failed to intervene, there came the Entente Cordiale and the Franco-Russian alliance. After 1890, above all, economic growth

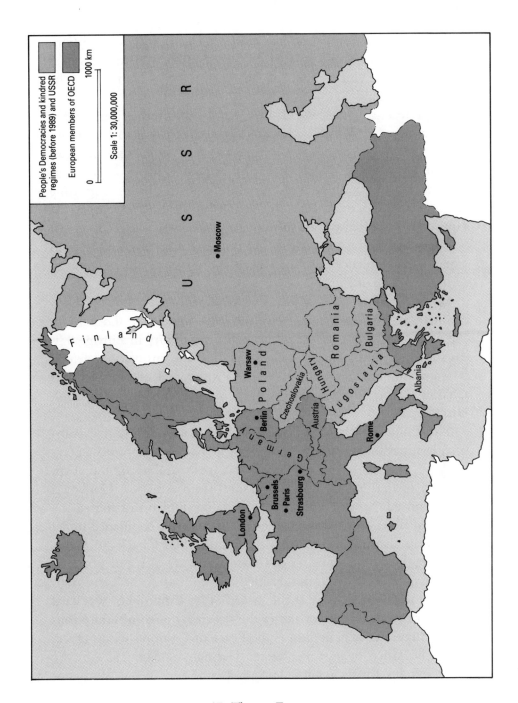

People's Democracies and kindred regimes (before 1989) and USSR

European members of OECD

Scale 1: 30,000,000

0 ⊢———⊣ 1000 km

U   S   S   R

● Moscow

Finland

Warsaw
●
P o l a n d

Berlin
●

Czechoslovakia

G e r m a n y

Austria

Hungary

R o m a n i a

B u l g a r i a

Y u g o s l a v i a

Albania

Rome
●

Brussels
●

Paris
●

Strasbourg
●

London
●

17. The two Europes

and an increased population had made Germany too powerful not to be enraged at being isolated by her enemies, yet not powerful enough to convince them of her inexorable superiority. The ultimate outcome was war.

Until recently, the world as a whole was the prisoner of a balance of power which had become global rather than European. 'East' and 'West' were two camps between which the neutrals sought a third role which was valid only if it had power on its side. It was an old system, certainly, which for a long time threatened the world with the results of its breakdown, as its failures had so often caused suffering in Europe.

Unity by force always failed. The only moral of this monotonous story is that violence has never been enough to enable anyone to seize the whole of Europe.

Without going back as far as Charlemagne, let us look for a moment at Charles V (1500–58), the least unpleasant and perhaps the most attractive of those who sought hegemony in Europe. His dream was to conquer Christendom and use his authority to defend it against the infidel Muslims and the Protestant Reformation. For Charles V, the 'Imperial idea' had its roots in the historic Spanish crusade.

The Emperor lacked nothing: he had troops, admirable commanders, passionately loyal followers; he had the support of great bankers like the Fuggers; he had incomparable diplomatists, mastery of the sea and finally 'treasure' from America. Under his reign, indeed, Spain became the warehouse which distributed the gold and silver from the American mines, partly to finance trade, but partly also to meet political necessities. Did Charles V fail in his struggle with France, as has been claimed? Yes and no. Yes, because none of his victories enabled him to master the vast extent of the country, which lay at the 'heart' of his Empire but was hard to traverse at the speed (or rather the slowness) of communications at that time. In 1529, he signed the Peace of Cambrai with France. Later, he failed against Protestant Germany (1546, 1552–5); he wore out his forces against Turkish Islam, and the Muslims not only threatened Vienna but also raided the coast of Spain as far as Gibraltar and beyond.

In other words, it was a 'concert of Europe' that defeated Charles V, using every method including even the scandalous stratagem of alliance with the Sultan.

Louis XIV imposed his will on Europe only during the lean years of the seventeenth century, when everyone fell back, as it were, on traditional strengths, which profited France with its peasant economy and its very primitive capitalism, well controlled by a strong Government, until the death of Jean Baptiste Colbert in 1683. When the world economy picked up again, probably from about 1680, France soon lost her supremacy. Already in 1672 the flooding of Holland had prevented the French army from reaching Amsterdam; in 1688 William of Orange came to the throne in Britain; and in 1692 Admiral de Tourville's fleet was utterly defeated at the battle of La Hogue off the Eastern coast of the Cherbourg peninsula. In the great War of Spanish Succession, France was unable to match all her enemies, nor to seize the Iberian Peninsula and, beyond it, the wealth of Spanish America.

Napoleon's adventures surely followed the same pattern. On the one hand, so many victories; on the other, resounding defeat at Trafalgar in 1805. While France's conquests were confined to the continent, vast as it was, Britain could deploy her strength on the open sea. It took only 100 or 150 wooden hulks to defend the Straits of Dover, which some had thought to 'stride across' in 1805; and the same applied to the Straits of Messina. So while Naples belonged to the French or to Murat, Sicily remained the refuge of the Bourbons.

Hitler's Germany, likewise, united against itself a coalition that matched the threat it represented – a coalition including the greater part of the world.

The Common Market seeks political unity. Can the political unity of Europe be achieved today, not by violence, but by the common will of the countries concerned? A plan is taking shape, and it arouses obvious enthusiasm in some quarters. But it also raises serious difficulties.

Some of these difficulties we have already noted. In particular, only Western Europe is so far uniting: the building of Europe had to begin 'with what remained of it'. Then again, unity in Europe poses problems elsewhere, in so far as it affects the economic and political equilibrium of the world. Already on 14 November 1958, a banker declared: 'In certain parts of the world there are fears that the European Union may adopt a discriminatory policy *vis-à-vis* non-member countries' – i.e. that it might follow certain options, for example preferring the tropical products of Black Africa to those of Latin America. Similar fears of 'fortress Europe' have been expressed, however unjustifiably, about the Single Market to be achieved by the end of 1992.

But the primary difficulties are internal and institutional: they are not of a kind that can be easily solved by a treaty or by compromise.

Is it possible that the Governments of 'Europe of the States', in General de Gaulle's phrase, will make concessions and sacrifice part of their sovereign rights?

As long ago as 8 August 1950, André Philip told the Council of Europe: 'For a whole year, to avoid disagreements, our Assembly has accepted every kind of compromise. The result? Nothing has been done. Public opinion will be disgusted with us very soon unless we prove that we really came here to build Europe.' On 17 August Philip threatened 'to go and build Europe elsewhere'.

Eleven years later, in Brussels, Paul-Henri Spaak, the Belgian Foreign Minister, declared, on 10 January 1962, four days before the agreement on the Common Agricultural Policy (which he could by no means predict):

Everything leads me to believe that there cannot be a united and effective Europe without supranationality. The so-called 'Europe of the States' is a narrow, inadequate idea. The longer I live, the harder I shall fight against the rule of unanimity and the veto. A few weeks ago, I was at the United Nations and saw the Soviet veto at work. More recently still, I had a similar experience at Nato: on the German question and Berlin, the opposition of one Government prevented Nato from taking a firm and constructive position. What is happening now at the Palais des Congrès on the subject of Europe's Common Agricultural Policy is very far from making me change my mind. In these discussions I look in vain for the spirit of Community. Everyone is defending the interests of his own farmers ... If the accursed rule of unanimity were abolished, the negotiations in the Council would go much faster ... We are offered a Europe of the States in the field of foreign policy. What would that do except create chaos? All the member States bar one might discuss the question of Communist China, and the one might block all decisions ... So I wonder if it would be at all a good idea to give up the spirit of supranationality in these matters.

All these arguments are good. But in a very divided group, majority voting is not necessarily a panacea that can solve all problems. A majority may be formed by wheeler-dealing, by private compromise, by what in some Assemblies are called 'conversations in the corridors'; and these may no more produce a coherent or disinterested policy than bargaining about the veto. The essential question is how far the political views of the present States in Europe can be reconciled, at least on certain deep and basic principles. If not, it will mean a return to the hazards of the 'European balance of power', but this time inside the new Community edifice.

The advocates of political unity affirm, and go on affirming, that the unity they seek will be a matter of free decisions.

No predominance, declared one German businessman in 1958: no Napoleonic or Hitlerian Europe. 'Unity thus based on force can only provoke an explosion, once the grip of the dominant nation is relaxed. Let it be said in passing that today we have an example of that before our eyes: i.e. the States grouped round the power of Russia [*sic*] in the Warsaw Pact are controlled, economically as well as politically, only in the interests of Russia [*sic*].'

That quotation, selected from hundreds of others, helps to

elucidate the problem. For many people at that time, the aim was
to regroup Europe, or 'what remained of it', against the Soviet
danger. This was clearly the American policy, that of a 'buckler'
against the USSR. When the Schuman Plan for the European
Coal and Steel Community was being debated on 15 December
1951, the French Premier Paul Reynaud was categorical: 'Let us
remember that Pentagon's abandonment of its plan to defend
Europe only at the Pyrenees is thanks to General Eisenhower, who
has never ceased repeating that the European countries, with France
in the lead, want to build Europe. Draw your own conclusions
about what would happen if the Schuman Plan were rejected.'

Against this spirit of political and even military calculation, one
can imagine another, which is more reasonable because it is more
realistic. This is how Senator André Armengaud, a Member of the
European Parliament, put the problem in a remarkable lecture he
gave in February 1960. In his eyes, Europe was flanked on the one
side by the growth of a Communist economy, born in 1917 in
'Petrograd', 'which all traditional economists had said would have
no future', and on the other by the great liberation, throughout
the world, of the peoples once colonized by Europeans. So Europe
too must organize itself in a wholly new way, not simply for
capitalist profit, which creates regimes in which the advantages are
'reserved for minorities', but in order to make the optimum use of
the labour force. In other words, start from the opposite end.

It would seem wise to see Europe not as a matter of profit for
profit's sake, but as a question of the benefits for people; and
equally to see East–West competition in terms of the best solution
for the human problems of twentieth-century society. Will such
wisdom have the chance to be heard?

It is not only a question of knowing whether European union
will be achieved and whether it is viable: we have also to ask
whether it will be accepted by the other major powers in the
world. One or another might be made uneasy by the Union's
economic claims or its possible political orientation. Will it lead
one day to a peaceful Europe, including in its prosperity a Germany

reconciled to the changes in some of its former frontiers? Or will it create an aggressive Europe? Will the new Europe agree to make its contribution to the solution of the world's development problems – on which everyone's lives depend in today's interdependent world? Or will it be unable to catch up with the future, and continue to believe that nationalistic self-interest still makes sense, and that 'European nationalism' can carry on where the nation-States of Europe were forced to leave off? In a word, will it be an inventive Europe, making for peace, or a routine Europe, still creating the kind of tensions that we know only too well?

To ask that is virtually to pose the fundamental question: what can European civilization still do for the world of tomorrow?

Need one point out that this seems to be the least of the concerns of those who are currently building Europe? Their rational debates about customs duties, prices and production levels, like the most generous of their mutual concessions, address only the spirit of calculation. They never seem to go beyond the purely and highly technical level of specialists who are experts in the remarkable projections of economic planning. No one would deny, of course, that these are indispensable.

But we misunderstand people if we give them only these sensible addition and multiplication sums, which look so wan alongside the waves of enthusiasm – and the not unintelligent 'crazes' – that have enlivened Europe in the past, and even the recent past. Can a European consciousness be achieved solely through statistics? Might it not, on the contrary, escape them and overflow them in unpredictable ways?

It is disturbing to note that Europe as a cultural ideal and objective is the last item on the current agenda. No one is concerned with a mystique or an ideology; no one pays attention to the misleadingly calm waters of Revolution or of Socialism, that still run deep; no one seems concerned by the living waters of religious faith. But Europe will not be built unless it draws upon those old forces that first formed it and still move within it: in a word, unless it calls forth the many forms of humanism that it contains.

In fact, it has no choice. It will either work with them or, inevitably, sooner or later, they will overturn it and cast it away. 'Europe of the peoples' is a fine slogan; but it remains to be achieved.

PART II: AMERICA

20. Latin America, the Other New World

America consists of two great cultural entities. The word 'America' by itself is loosely used to denote the United States (plus, sometimes, Canada, so much within the US orbit). That is the New World *par excellence*, the land of amazing futuristic achievements. The other America, the bigger of the two, seems to have accepted its relatively recent name of 'Latin America', first used in about 1865 by France, partly for her own reasons, and later adopted by Europe as a whole. This America is both one and many, highly coloured, dramatic, divided, and full of rivalry.

To begin with Latin America helps to avoid the immediate comparison with North America, which otherwise might overwhelm it in advance with the habitual weight of its immense material wealth. In this way, we can better observe Latin America as it deserves to be seen, with its deep humanism, its own particular problems and its own very evident progress. In the past, it was far ahead of the other America: it was the first rich America, and for that reason envied and coveted. In the past. Then the wheel of fortune turned. The present state of Latin America is very far from happy: it is overcast with heavy clouds. Here, the day has not yet fully dawned.

★

Geography, Nature and society: literature bears witness

More than any other region in the world, Latin America is constantly and rapidly changing. Today's pictures of it are likely to be
worthless tomorrow, or at least to look false.

If we cannot see it for ourselves, we should at least read its
admirable literature – direct, unsophisticated, naïvely and frankly
political. It offers a myriad journeys for the spirit, and its testimony
is sharper than anything to be found in reports or in sociological,
economic, geographical and historical studies (although many historical works are nevertheless excellent). Literature also reveals –
and this is invaluable – the essence of countries and societies which
are always private and often secretive, despite the warmth and
apparent openness of their welcome.

Geographically, Latin America is vast. Its still sparse population
seems shrunk, as it were, in such outsize garments. There is an
immense amount of space, an intoxicating amount.

Flying, of course, has reduced and humanized this vastness,
making distances almost disappear. So the foreign traveller is more
and more likely to overlook the fundamental fact of Latin
America's size. Already a few years ago it took no longer than six
hours to cross the Amazon basin – or, rather, to fly over it,
because travelling through it is still extremely difficult: *isto é matto*,
'that is forest', say the Brazilians. Flights over the Andes, between
Argentina and Chile, were then made by twin-engined light
aircraft which flew along the La Cumbre pass just over its little
rack-rail train, buffeted from one side to the other of the broad
valley, but *between* the mountains – beneath them, in fact. Now,
four-engined aircraft fly right over the Andes every day, and the
mountains are no more than ten or fifteen minutes of glaciers
sparkling in the sun before the plane descends towards the Chilean
coast or the empty Argentine plain. Above all, flying has become
universal: its buoyant song is now heard everywhere in Latin
America.

18. Spanish America and Portuguese America

In grey, Spanish-speaking regions; vertical lines, Portuguese-speaking regions. The two bar charts show the respective areas (above) and populations (below) of these two regions of Latin America. Spanish America has an even higher proportion of people than territory, and so is relatively more densely populated than Portuguese America.

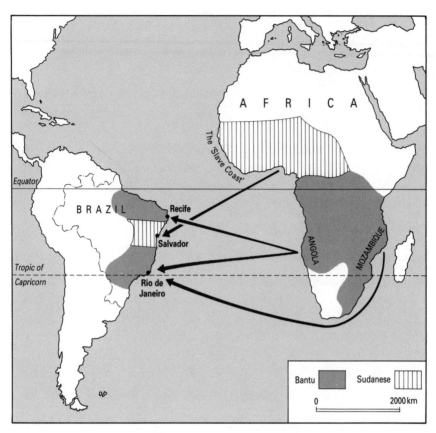

19. The origins of Latin America's black population

   But in fact only privileged travellers experience these prodigious
leaps, these luxury excursions which take them from Mexico City,
where the Nortes (the North winds) are still freezing the plants in
the gardens, to deposit them a little while later in the heat of
Yucatán or Vera Cruz, or transport them to the flower-strewn
paradise of the Pacific Coast at Acapulco. Likewise only profitable
or luxury goods are carried by air: seafood from Chile bound for
Buenos Aires; animals on the hoof, or choice cuts of meat, from
Mendoza across the Cordilleras to Santiago or to the Chilean
miners in the Northern desert.

So the shrinking of distances remains an exception, despite appearances. On the airfields of Rio de Janeiro an aircraft lands or takes off every minute. But the passengers are only a tiny fraction of the population, basically its middle class. In Latin America, the airways are not a mass transportation system like the trains, buses and private cars that have given Europe so tightly knit a communications network.

Latin America lived and still lives, as it was shaped, in an area measured by the steps of people and animals. Its pace was not set by the railways, which are few, or by the roads. Some of these latter are superb, as in the case of the Mexican *carreteras*; but they too are not numerous and are continually under construction or repair. Latin America still bears the mark of these leisurely ways.

One must realize and accept the immensity of distances in Latin America if one is to ride or travel with Martin Fierro, the gaucho of the heroic past, invented by José Hernández in 1872, or with Segundo Sombra, the last free, wandering gaucho on the Argentine pampas, invented in his turn by the brilliant Ricardo Guiraldes in 1939. Similar awareness helps one to see 'the backlands' of North-Eastern Brazil, the up-country area of drought and hunger described by Euclydes da Cunha in *Os Sertões* (1902). It also helps understanding of Lucio Mansilla's account of his negotiations with the Indians, written in instalments for *La Tribuna* in Buenos Aires, and published in 1870 as *Una excursión a los Indios ranqueles*, a marvellous picture of the vast Argentine interior and its indigenous peoples. A still better example is the work of the naturalist and novelist William Henry Hudson (1841–1922), which includes an account of Patagonia, then almost virgin territory.

Nor should we forget the magnificent travel writings of the German Alexander von Humboldt (1769–1859) and the Frenchman Auguste de Saint-Hilaire (1799–1835), who although foreigners were so much captivated by the countries they described that South American literature virtually annexed them from the start.

One of the most vivid images from these classical accounts is that of the mule trains, with their fixed routes, their almost fixed timetables, and their regular 'halts', the *ranchos* where people, animals and goods stayed overnight before continuing the trail next day. Such mule-trains have been called the first trucking service, the first railways. They were certainly the first means of crossing wide open spaces that are still vast and untamed, even today. For, as we know, if people do not settle firmly in one place, as in the West, if they uproot themselves so readily, it can only be because they see wider horizons a little further on. So even now, streams of animals still pour across the heart of the continent as they did in the sixteenth and seventeenth centuries, to wind up at traditional cattle markets like those in up-country Bahia. It is a primitive, inexpensive way of exploiting resources, a kind of cut-price capitalism, so long as the land is available at little or no cost.

So people were isolated – lost or drowned in these vast areas; the towns were far, far apart, and far from the mother countries or the colonial capitals; and some of the provinces were larger than Italy or France. What more natural, then, if all of them, especially in the past, ran their own affairs as they thought best: there was no alternative, and the first priority was survival. In both North and South America, 'American democracy' with its principle of self-government is partly a result of there being so much space. Space moderates everything and conserves everything – until it is conquered.

Until recently, the great objective was to free the peasants from the barbaric constraints of Nature. In South America, Nature produced and still produces admirable people, poor, tough and hard-working: the gauchos of the pampas, the Brazilian *caboclos*, the Mexican peasants or peons. These last were naturally rebellious, provided they had a real leader like Emilio Zapata, who fought for their cause between 1911 and 1919.

Was not the real problem, then, to free these people from the poverty which was the really barbaric constraint on their lives? All the idealistic intellectuals of the nineteenth and twentieth centuries dreamed of doing just that. Not to train people (unless it was vital) in the way that one breaks in a wild horse: but to teach them to live better, to care for their health, to read. It was an urgent task, and one as yet unfinished: there are still 'illiteracy crusades' led jointly and enthusiastically by travelling groups of teachers, doctors and health experts.

The peasants, those 'barbarian' heroes, naturally figure in many novels of the nineteenth and twentieth centuries. In the past, they were often portrayed as at grips with civilization in a sort of duel of love. This sentimental symbolism often produced sob-stories – but they too had evidential value: adjust them a little, and they could be *romans noirs*.

Martin Fierro (1872), in the Argentine pampas, is a primitive creature, but a Christian and a minstrel who sings his own songs. He gives up his outlaw life to join the Indians in the desert; but he had always had his *pundonor*, his point of honour – although it often involved a knife-blow in some *pulperia*, a fortified inn selling liquor in the middle of the desert. *Doña Bárbara* had a woman as central character. It was written in 1929 by Rómulo Gallegos, who in 1947 became a democratic President of Venezuela until he was exiled by a military coup in the following year. Bárbara's name was chosen to make its symbolism clear: dazzlingly beautiful but savage and ruthlessly unscrupulous, she has the qualities and faults that enable her to take whatever she wants, shamelessly. But have no fear: she cannot finally defeat the gentle, naïve and likeable 'doctor of laws' whom an inheritance brings to the *llanos*, those pastoral plains at the head of the rivers, up which the boats travel at a snail's pace – which at least gives the passengers time to shoot at sleeping alligators. And of course the doctor is a crack shot . . . The heroine of *La Negra Angustias* (which in 1944 won its author, Francisco Rojas Gonzales, the Mexican national literature prize) is also beautiful and naïve. But she is also – and disbelief has to be suspended to make the novel work – a cruel and pitiless bandit leader. One fine day, this innocent tigress is suddenly tamed by a modest teacher who teaches her to read. The miracle takes place. Angustias marries her teacher and espouses civilization.

Not all the novels in this vein are quite so sentimental. *La*

Vorágine, written in 1925 by the Colombian José Eustasio Rivera, is the sad story of a couple swallowed up by the Amazon jungle. But whether the books be optimistic or otherwise, it is *Nature* they blame – Nature which turns people into savages, and which is all that needs to be conquered if they are to be civilized and freed. According to the Chilean novelist Benjamin Subercaseaux, Chile's misfortune is its 'crazy geography' (*Chile o una loca geografía*, 1940).

That vision and that literature belong to the past. Today, their world is gradually slipping below the horizon – which in some respects is a matter for regret.

A literature of peasant and social protest is coming into being. Today, the literary hero *par excellence* is still the pauper, cut off from the world by Nature, distance or poverty itself, but now taken up by a new kind of literature – combative, violent, direct and highly coloured. This presents the poor as above all the victims of society, of civilization, which seems as indifferent to their suffering as untamed Nature itself. This literature marks a turning-point, the beginning of a new era. Its tone is certainly revolutionary: it bears witness to an acute awareness of South America's specific problems, and a lack of confidence in the benefits to be expected from 'civilization' by itself. Hence its sombre realism and its despair.

Los de abajo (1916), by the Mexican novelist Mariano Azuela (1873–1952), is one long cry of defiance. It hurls us into that complex mass revolution which after 1910 made modern Mexico without completing it, costing perhaps a million poverty-stricken lives. It tells the story of a handful of revolutionary soldiers who were killed (and whom the author saw die, since he was an army doctor with a group of revolutionaries): the disenchanted story of poor devils ill-equipped to fight an implacable society whose rich members were too rich and too ferocious, while its poor were too numerous and too naïve.

The very long novels of the great Brazilian writer Jorge Amado, most of them set in the Bahia region, a country of hunger, emigration and perpetual poverty, combine violence and beauty to an exceptional degree. However great their political commitment and polemical tone, they form an extraordinary and truthful report-age on an incredibly primitive peasantry and its battle with hunger, in an almost feudal countryside where people have not even the beauties of nature to console them.

Everywhere in this literature the same painful testimony recurs. The novelist Jorge Icaza takes us to his native Ecuador. On the map, it looks small. In fact, it is bigger than Italy: with the Galapagos Islands, it covers some 123,000 square miles. In 1962, it had only 2 million inhabitants, and had offered to take a further million immigrants; twenty years later, its population was over 9 million. Alfonso Pereira, the hero of Icaza's 1934 novel *Huasipungo* (translated into English in 1962), takes his family to his estate high in the mountains, far from Quito and reached by a rough mule track. He cannot stay in town, because his daughter is pregnant by an Indian she was foolish enough to trust, and only in the mountains will the illegitimate birth pass unnoticed. The journey is strange and eventful. When the mules reach the edge of the upland marshes, they get bogged down. Everyone dismounts. Then:

The three Indians wiped the frost off their faces with the back of their sleeves and prepared to take their employers on their backs. They took off their ponchos, rolled their rough, baggy trousers up to their thighs, removed their hats, and rolled their ponchos round their necks like bandits' scarves, exposing their bodies to the biting cold that came in through the holes and tears in their cotton clothes . . . Then they offered their shoulders so that the family (father, mother, and daughter) could exchange the backs of the mules for the backs of the men.

And the procession pressed on through the frosty mud . . .

A little strained as literature, but always moving. Perhaps, simply because the life it described was so hard, it dwelt on what amounted to a violent agrarian dispute and so was content to see only the poverty of the countryside. That of workers in the industrial suburbs or in remote mining regions was beyond its scope and experience. One of the rare accounts of urban poverty to be published (apart from sociological studies for specialists) is the disturbing diary of an almost illiterate black Brazilian, Carolina María de Jésus, living in a São Paolo shack-town. This daily record of her life is not a work of literature, and still less a sociological treatise, but a piece of evidence in the raw. (A French translation was published by Stock in 1962 under the title *Le Dépotoir*.)

With rare exceptions like this, what monopolizes the literature is rural poverty, which seems cut off from any kind of hope or remedy other than revolt, violence and revolution. That is no doubt one of the reasons why Fidel Castro's revolution in Cuba, so much a peasant revolution, has made such an impact throughout Latin America. Whatever its failings or its fate, it marked a moment in history. At the very least, it underlined the absolute necessity for a serious examination of Latin America's political and social problems and the solutions they require. This is something of which all Latin American intellectuals are aware, whatever their personal opinions.

Racial problems: quasi-fraternity

Nevertheless, whatever hesitancy, delays and mental reservations there may have been, Latin America has solved or at least is solving one of its most serious problems: that of race. The first and not the only difference between North and South America is surely the latter's spontaneous and growing freedom from ethnic prejudice. All is not perfect, of course, in this domain. But where in the world have people done better, or even as well? There has already been immense success.

Yet history had stacked the cards against it, by placing side by side in Latin America the three great 'races' of the world with their contrasting skin-colours: yellow (in the case of the Indians, wrongly called 'Red' Indians), black and white. All three were very vigorous: none was prepared to let the others eclipse it.

Ethnic problems would not have arisen, obviously, if pre-Columbian America had remained untouched, with its own coherent civilizations: the Aztecs (plus the Mayas), i.e. broadly speaking, the Mexicans; the brilliant series of Andean civilizations in the high mountains which the Inca Empire had more or less united under its pseudo-'Socialist' authority; and the primitive cultures that occupied the remaining vast areas of the New World.

Nor would ethnic problems have arisen if Europe at the end of the fifteenth century had been overpopulated, able to impose its law by force everywhere, instead of a small world of only some 50 million inhabitants, busily (and of necessity) producing their daily bread, and only sparingly sending a few individuals on American adventures. In *all* of the sixteenth century, only some 100,000 people left Seville for the New World. They might be able to conquer, but could they really grasp the America they invaded?

Finally, the ethnic problem would have lacked its third constituent if the coasts of the Gulf of Guinea to begin with, and then the whole African littoral, had not supplied the manpower that was missing: the black slaves without whom there would have been no sugar, no coffee and no gold dust.

Thus it is that the three races now face each other. None was powerful enough to eliminate the others, or even to try to. Obliged to live together, they have managed – despite a little inevitable friction – to accept the fact, to mix and to achieve a certain degree of mutual tolerance and esteem.

Ethnic regions remain: nothing is clearer, in any case, than the geographical demarcation of the different races, which in fact is a relic of the past.

It was the Indian civilizations that the first white conquerors encountered. The newcomers treated the Indians savagely; they might have swept them away. The effects of conquest were followed by the still greater catastrophes of exploitation and forced labour. The indigenous population decreased in alarming proportions. Everywhere that the Indians had remained primitive – nomadic, tribal, living on cassava – they were driven out, almost as soon as the Europeans arrived; they survived only in a few very remote regions where a few whites arrived late and with great difficulty, as in Amazonas.

Yet the really tightly knit Indian civilizations all managed finally to survive. Unarmed, lacking in tools (they had neither iron nor the wheel, neither gunpowder nor any domestic animals save the llama), and attacked immediately in their heartlands of Cuzco and Mexico, then Tenochtitlan, they were certainly an easy prey. They were saved only by their tenacious solidarity. Today, Mexico is proud to call itself 'Indian territory'; and on the Andean plains the old native life continues – miserably poor, but lively and deeply rooted, irreplaceable.

The blacks, on the other hand, remained where chance, the climate, the plantations, gold seams or gold dust, and urban life took them from the sixteenth century onwards and kept them when slavery was abolished. Later, they often moved to active industrial centres. Logically, therefore, they were to be found on the Atlantic coast, and where Indian labour was lacking. So they were preponderant in Northern Brazil – the heart of the country in colonial times – and they abounded in all its large modern cities. In the West Indies, they were at home everywhere.

The whites, finally, took possession of the American continent in at least two main stages. Each time, different peoples were involved.

In the course of the first conquest, they settled wherever they could live, preferably in those areas where the great Indian civilizations already existed. There they found 'subjects' to rule, and supplies ready to hand. This was the case of the Spaniards, whose great colonial cities were Mexico, Lima (which they founded) and, in the high Andes of present-day Bolivia, Potosi, also founded by them, on account of its silver mines: in 1600, it already had 150,000 inhabitants, living at an altitude of more than 13,000 feet. Spanish colonial art, mainly baroque in style, is still there, bearing witness to the splendour enjoyed by the newly rich in these colonial cities. But most of their inhabitants, remember, were Indian.

The Portuguese in Brazil, by contrast, encountered only a weak scattering of Indians. Hence the decisive importance of the blacks. The great Brazilian cities of the colonial era were in substance African: Bahia, the old capital, with its 365 churches (one for every day of the year); Recife, the great Northern sugar centre, established by the Dutch during their brief occupation (1630–53); Ouro Preto ('Black Gold'), founded in the interior owing to the gold rush; Rio de Janeiro, which became the capital in 1763. São Paulo at that time was no more than a small town with a population of adventurers; there were a few whites and many Indians, as well as those of mixed race who at the time were called 'burnt wood', or (in Portuguese) *mamelucos*.

Memories of the colonial epoch call to mind the achievements of Creole America; and to the British and the French they evoke in particular the West Indies – Santo Domingo and Jamaica, the islands of sugar and then coffee. But the picture was the same everywhere: a strange mixture of primitive, medieval, slave existence and capitalist life. Only the owner of the land, the sugar-cane mills, the silver mines or the gold fields was involved in a money economy, not his slaves or his servants. The result was strange families like those of classical antiquity, whose *paterfamilias* for a long time had the power of life or death over all members of his family or household, with the master's grand house towering above the rows of huts for the slaves. Then the towns sprang up with their luxury houses (the *sobrados*, as houses with several storeys were called in colonial Brazil), their merchants' shops, and also the slums of the poor, known in the past as *mucambos* and now as *favelas* – the equivalent of the shacktowns or oildrum cities in so many conurbations today.

After 1822 and 1823, Latin America was freed from the Spanish and Portuguese mother countries – and from the Cadiz and Lisbon merchants. But then it was exploited systematically and shamelessly by capitalists from all over Europe, and especially from London. The newly independent States were far too naïve as clients of

European industrialists and bankers. Thus, for example, London sold to Mexico in 1821 the rather outdated war supplies that had helped Britain to win the battle of Waterloo.

At the same time, however, Latin America now accepted, more than in the past, immigration from Europe, and no longer solely Spanish or Portuguese. On a small scale at first, with artists, intellectuals, engineers and businessmen, it grew rapidly from 1880 onwards, when steamships began to ply the South Atlantic. They brought huge numbers of Italians, Portuguese and Spaniards, as well as thousands and thousands of other Europeans.

Not all of South America took them in equal numbers. They brought new wealth to Southern Brazil, South of the latitude on which São Paulo stands, Brazil in the past having been centred on the North. They did the same for Argentina and Chile. Over vast areas, this immigration acted like a human bombardment, destroying the old social order – not overnight, but rapidly all the same. It began to fill the countryside. What the 'doctor of laws' in *Doña Bárbara* could not achieve, the immigrants made possible. They created modern Brazil, modern Argentina, modern Chile. Before 1939, a European visitor could in the course of his travels in Latin America find an admirably hard-working Italy in one place, and in another – in the Rio Grande do Sul, in Santa Catalina, or in Chile – a Germany still faithful to its civilization, its distant mother country and its eventful history.

It was these immigrants who did so much for the pioneer areas and young industries. It is they, again, who are to be found on the edges of the populous regions: on the Chilean 'frontier' South of Bio-Bio; in Patagonia, so recently a desert; or in the depths of the State of São Paulo, with their new coffee plantations (*cafezais*). Since these quickly exhaust the soil, the *fazendas* have to move on in search of new land, often burning the forests to provide it. All that is a familiar and fateful story, which could be retold. But it is not what essentially concerns us here. The essential point is the fraternity that exists among the races: all of them have worked together, in their different ways, to make Latin America.

They have also clashed, many times, and for social reasons. Difference of colour was and remains a social difference. True, anyone who grows rich or wields authority crosses or will cross the dividing-line, whatever the exact shade of his skin. But in Peru, for example, Indians and those of mixed race call those who rule them '*blancos*'. In other words, wealth and power have been, and usually still are, in the hands of genuine whites.

In so far, that is, as 'genuine' whites exist. For the most part – and this is important – the races are very extensively mixed. The Recife sociologist Gilberto Freyre, writing about his own North-Eastern area of Brazil, *O Nordeste*, (although the 'Nordeste' has spread over much of Brazil), has smilingly declared: 'We all have a pint of black blood in our veins.' Where mixed blood is most frequent, in Mexico (whites and Indians) and in North-East Brazil (whites and blacks), tolerance and inter-ethnic fraternity are also more noticeable than elsewhere.

Even in these areas, however, there have been problems. Mixed-race Latin America long had an inferiority complex *vis-à-vis* faraway Europe, which in turn tended far too much to encourage it. North America, too, set a notoriously bad example. Travelling to the United States, on the other hand, has been a kind of cautionary experience for many South American intellectuals with white but not pure white skins: it has taught them tolerance and given them the precious gift of self-respect at the same time as respect for their countries.

Latin America's inferiority complex and its attendant prejudices have not disappeared as if by magic. But a great wind of change has been blowing since 1919, or 1930, and even more since 1945. One might still feel drawn to Europe, but could one still owe it so much respect after the follies of the first World War, the economic disasters that followed 1929 and the horrors of the Second World War? Largely free, and largely welcoming immigrants, the Latin American countries have gradually been acquiring greater self-esteem. The change is slow, and is not yet complete, but it has been under way for a long time. In 1933, the early works of

Gilberto Freyre were published in Brazil. They no longer spoke the traditional literary language of the novel or the essay, but adopted the crisp tone of the new social sciences. This was a decisive turning point in the biggest, most human and perhaps most humanistic country in the New World. Likewise, the pro-Indian revolution that began in Mexico in 1910 not only inaugurated a series of political and agrarian revolutions. It also opened the way to hope.

The degree to which the races enjoy equality and fraternity obviously differs from place to place. Too often, past social stratification forms an obstacle. There are some countries in Latin America where almost the whole population is white, as in Argentina (with only a few remnants of the Indian peoples in the far North or the far South). There are also countries where, according to anthropologists, the mixture of races has already produced new, uniform and stable ethnic types. One example is Costa Rica.

But even if fraternity among the races is not always complete or not always possible, it is a general phenomenon, and one of the special features of this 'other America' – its distinguishing characteristic, its most attractive aspect, and something recognizably unique. Landing in Panama on the way back to his own country, a South American traveller feels a sudden thrill: all the different skin colours, the ringing voices, the cries, the songs – no doubt about it: this is already home.

The economy: civilizations on trial

Despite its carefree air, its love of pleasure, its exuberance and its noisy popular festivities, Latin America today is as full of deep suffering as it was in the past. Keyserling called it 'the continent of sadness'. Like all countries or continents that embark on genuine industrialization, it has to face a total transformation of its structure and its behaviour; and the shock, for Latin America, is especially hard.

Why? Because this is a world which is unstable, changing, uncertain and lacking economic and social order – owing to the fact that for centuries it has been continually destroyed and rebuilt. It is a world that has been buffeted, a contradictory world where the most primitive kind of human existence continues right alongside the enclaves of an ultra-modern life. Altogether, it is a world full of vitality, and therefore all the harder to define, organize and steer.

Economic fluctuations are unpredictable tidal waves. Latin America is speeding towards material wealth. This is a race it has been committed to for centuries, willy-nilly, and more often as a loser than as a winner. In doing so, it was no doubt following a world trend. But in any race it is one thing to be among the leaders, setting the pace, and quite another to be the last, making desperate strides to catch up. South America was certainly the last in this race, leaping and stumbling in ways that looked almost comic – to everyone else. It had to hurry; and if it wanted to sell it must at all costs produce sugar, or coffee, or rubber, or *charque* (dried meat), or nitrates, or cocoa, and always sell them cheap. And so, each time, it was caught off balance by successive 'cycles' in the world economy, with their sudden unexpected downturns.

This process explains South America's present economic situation as well as its past. It adapted itself to all the requirements of the world's demand for raw materials in an economy that to begin with was of a strictly colonialist type, and then after the colonial period became an economy based on dependence.

Foreign capitalists (or rather, large international firms), in alliance with the big landowners and local politicians, encouraged the production of exportable raw materials, leading the productive areas to concentrate all their efforts, manpower and resources on one single activity, to the exclusion and the detriment of everything else. The resultant growth might in the long run have borne fruit for the whole of the country, if frequent shifts in demand had not regularly wiped out these investments. When that happened, efforts had to be switched to another sector of production – and at the same time, very often, to another region.

The variety of its climates and the vastness of its territory enable South America to survive these extraordinary changes of direction which in fact, on a national basis, were an unheard-of waste of space and people: everywhere, they prevented the establishment of lasting, stable and healthy economic structures and the formation of a settled peasant society.

The first of these economic cycles was that connected with precious metals; and it began with the European conquest itself. The 'gold' cycle lasted barely longer than the middle of the sixteenth century; the 'silver' cycle, affecting above all the mines in Mexico and Potosi, ended around 1630–40. Their cost was heavy sacrifice. If the Indians had not been ruthlessly conscripted for the task, who would have accepted work in the Potosi mines and foundries, at the exhausting altitude of 13,000 feet in bitterly cold mountains lacking wood and food and even, sometimes, water? The silver ingots were taken to the Pacific, then to Callao, Lima's port, and finally to Panama; from there, by mule-train and then by boat on the Chagres River, they reached the Caribbean sea coast. After that, Spanish fleets carried them to Spain.

Who profited from this great system? Spanish merchants and 'civil servants', and (already) international businessmen such as the Genoese men of affairs or *hombres de negocios* who were accredited lenders to the King of Spain. The beneficiary was certainly not America itself, constantly losing its ingots and silver coins, its very currency, in exchange for a few fabrics, some wheat flour, jars of oil, barrels of wine and black slaves.

The Potosi silver mines began to be less productive in the seventeenth century; and with that Spanish America was almost left to its own unhappy fate.

In 1680, it was the turn of Portuguese America to experience a gold rush, based this time on the work of black slaves. This slowed down in about 1730 – at the same time as the silver mines of New Spain (present-day Mexico) began to revive. The Brazilian province of Minas Gerais ('General Mines') then lost much of its role and its population, and converted as best it could to the production of cotton.

One could trace in the same way the cycle of stockbreeding with its many variations, down to its present-day practice in Argentina; the cycle of sugar production begun on a large scale in Brazil and shifting at the end of the eighteenth century towards the Caribbean (Jamaica, Santo Domingo, Martinique); the cycle of coffee-growing, which became especially important in Brazil from the nineteenth century onwards, taking up an immense amount of space, and encroaching more and more on the interior. The Argentine Chaco, formerly known for its *quebracho*, a tannin-producing shrub, has since 1945 seen a rapid increase in cotton production.

A whole book could not do justice to the vast subject of these 'cycles' in specialized products and single cash crops. At present, rightly denounced as catastrophic, the system may well be in its final phase, to be replaced by the beginnings of real industrial production and coherent national economies. But the whole economic structure of South America has been marked by this old, unstable, irrational practice, with its abrupt changes and incessant moves from place to place: every time, provinces and towns were first animated and then deserted, or at best obliged to undertake formidable and costly reconversions.

Major crises followed these cyclical changes. Their destructive power was enough to upset the whole economy of a strong and healthy country. A single example will suffice. It has the advantage of being, sadly, up to date. It concerns Argentina in this century.

In about 1880, Argentina began to be really prosperous. In a few years, by completely transforming the old structure of its economy, it became a major exporter of grain and meat to the European market. Until then, the Argentine pampas, the enormous plain around Buenos Aires, had been a desert roamed by wild cattle, which the gauchos hunted almost exclusively for the export of leather. From that time onwards, rather like the prairie in the United States, the pampas was turned over to wheat-growing and to grazing for selected cattle stock, carefully fed and fattened.

Until 1930 (and leaving out the difficult decade from 1890 to

1900) Argentina enjoyed incredibly rapid growth: in population first of all, thanks to a large number of Italian immigrants; in production, thanks to regular exports; then in capital investment, with silos, mills and freezing plants. Out of this there soon came the normal development of light industry. Wage-earners' purchasing power, the return on capital and even the number of cars per thousand of population all reached a peak.

From 1930 onwards, the crisis began, imperceptibly at first on account of the general euphoria. Then the war, which favoured all exporters of raw materials, delayed any realization that things were going wrong. But after 1945, with the steep fall in farm prices on the world market, the whole Argentine economy declined, and this time rapidly. Official figures admit that the national income per head went down by an average of 0.4 per cent per year after 1948; but US economists believe that this figure should be at least 2 per cent – a fact made still more serious by an average fall of 3 per cent a year in the investment rate per head. Argentina's trade balance was in deficit; wages and the general standard of living had fallen considerably; so, as a result, had the possibility of sustaining fairly well developed national industries like textiles, food, leather, etc. Unemployment was increasing; the countryside was losing its population to the towns, which swelled beyond measure even when they had no work to offer. Five per cent of the country's total population – i.e. about a million people – were living in shack-towns, called in Argentina *villas miseria*. Industrialization, the sole hope of rescue, had come to a halt. Above all, there seemed no way out: the State budget was on the brink of bankruptcy.

In other words, Argentina, which before the Second World War was the richest country in South America, favoured by its climate and the quality of its soil and its people, had become not the poorest – it was too far ahead for that – but the country that was regressing the fastest. Euphoric confidence had given way to confusion. This explains the series of political crises in Buenos Aires that marked the following decades.

Argentine economists believe with some reason that the agrarian system, built from scratch by the boom in wheat and meat, was in reality harmful. On the one hand it involved a myriad tiny holdings, far too small to be economic, covering 34 per cent of the land farmed; on the other, a handful of big landowners had 42 per cent of the territory and 64 per cent of the cattle. That is undoubtedly the main obstacle in the way of national recovery, which needs agrarian reform able to ensure rational production and to rebuild a national market, without which industry can obviously not survive.

Economic incoherence is a hindrance to modern industrialization: the development of South America has generally produced unbalanced and rather incoherent economies.

What is obvious everywhere is the inadequacy of existing means of communication. They were not built rationally to serve the national economy, but arbitrarily to link production areas with seaports for the export trade, leaving between them enormous stretches of territory without the smallest road. The airways, although they exist everywhere, serve only as a partial remedy. The hero of *Huasipungo*, Alfonso Pereira, failed to appreciate the privilege of keeping his feet dry when his Indian carried him through the marshland. 'Ah,' he sighed, 'if only my father had been cleverer he would have forced all his *péones* to build roads, and then we should not have been in this plight today!'

Another anomaly is the violent contrast between under-developed areas, or those abandoned after a period of development, and those which are relatively overdeveloped. There are still a few poetic little towns in the Brazilian interior, places like Minas Velhas, living as primitive a life as a very modest medieval city, far from anywhere, with only a few patrician houses recalling better days; while the 'civilized' zone is too often confined to a strip of land along the coast, linked to the great export routes of old.

Finally, there is something missing. Nowhere in Latin America is there the equivalent of Europe's farmers, a strong and solid basis for the economy, the heirs of traditions going back for thousands of years.

Sucked into the mad mercenary world of the single cash crop, herded into vast holdings hastily funded by foreign importers, then suddenly abandoned with these domains themselves, owing to some unexpected change in demand, much of the farming population is made up of nomadic agricultural labourers. Sooner or later, many of them are drawn by unemployment towards the nearest town, either in the hope of a problematical job or in order to emigrate to another province, still in search of work. Hence the apparent paradox that in some countries where there is more than plenty of land, and where the farm population makes up 60 or 70 per cent of the total, there is a lack or at least a shortage of food crops. Why? Because on the one hand there is no breed of settled peasants, who really know how to get the best from the soil, while on the other hand ownership of the countryside is so unequally divided that this alone prevents any true settlement on the part of the peasants and any normal production. All too often, one is reminded of feudal Russia.

Alongside this archaic rural world, industry has developed in those areas – generally along the coasts – which were favoured by the recent past. Here, an accumulation of domestic or foreign capital, the presence of people who have come into fruitful contact with Europe or the United States, a certain number of scientific and technical personnel and a further contribution by immigrants, have made it possible to switch from agricultural exports to industrial production. The results are sometimes surprising: ultra-modern cities with large numbers of skyscrapers have grown like mushrooms. São Paulo, in Brazil, is a dazzling example.

As a result, Latin America has a double economy: one sector, developed and even relatively overdeveloped and over-industrialized, lives a modern life; but it coexists with huge sectors of agricultural life that are still very primitive and absolutely archaic. The dichotomy is worsening, too, in so far as all new developments are concentrated in the sector that is already developed.

One example of this is Brazil. Its development, unlike that of Argentina, began late: it was already notable, however, by 1930 or so, and after the war it expanded vigorously. In the fifteen years up to 1962, its production doubled in real terms. Even per head of population, its gross national product increased, from 1948 to 1958, by an average of 3 per cent a year. During that time, São Paulo and Rio de Janeiro mushroomed even more rapidly than the most famous fast-growing cities in the United States. Light industries and textiles led on to the establishment of some heavy industries. Statistics showed impressive economic growth.

No doubt: but that growth was mainly in the industrial field. During the same period, agricultural production grew only as fast as the population – i.e. by about 1.5 per cent a year. Cultivated land made up only 2 per cent of the total area! Almost 70 per cent of the population was living, or rather vegetating, in this meagre farm sector, covering some 50 million acres, with very low productivity. The North-East, with a third of Brazil's population, was purely agricultural, and so was exposed to real hunger, and to all the diseases associated with malnutrition.

This situation could not change quickly, because the already developed part of the country attracted so much of the available private investment, State aid and credit, and even the currency earned by exports from the North, such as cocoa, sugar, cotton and vegetable oils.

Discussing Brazil or Mexico, several observers have suggested that these countries' developed sectors are in the same position *vis-à-vis* their undeveloped sectors as the mother countries once were *vis-à-vis* their former colonies. A very great part of the country can attain neither production nor income, and hence cannot meet its minimum consumer needs: one is sacrificed to the other.

The Brazilian Government, at grips with the urgent problem of industrialization, clearly went for the solution that was most economic and most likely to produce quick results. But were these results the most lasting?

For a number of years, Brazil's industrial expansion rate showed

signs of slowing down: there was a danger of over-production, for
want of a big enough domestic market. Unemployment, inflation
and a considerable rise in the cost of living, which squeezed the
national market still more, were all signs that industrial development could no longer continue without a policy which explicitly
sought to improve the agricultural sector of the economy so as to
achieve a growth in consumption and a decent standard of living
for the mass of the people, without which modern industry would
have no firm foundations to build on.

There is a grave social problem. The need to solve it faces all
the Latin American countries undergoing industrialization, and in
much the same terms: it is all the more pressing because their
social problem is so acute. There is an ever-growing gap between
that section of society which shares in development and profits
from it, and that which remains on the outside. This is an explosive
situation.

Another explosive factor is the growth-rate of the population,
which at about 2.5 per cent is the highest in the world, compared
with 2 per cent or so in Africa and 1.3–2 per cent in Asia. A mass
of rural proletarians descends on the towns to become an urban
proletariat, often unemployed, the more depressed because
alongside it is the luxury of an industrialized society to which
almost all ways of entry are barred.

All sociologists in recent years concur in their judgement of the
immense efforts made by Latin America today. Its industries could
not have failed to be impressive, since they have benefited from
the latest advances of modern technology. Architects and engineers
in South America, whether native or foreign, have nothing for
which to envy their colleagues elsewhere. But the human side of
the story is appalling: destitution and chaos stare in at the gates of
order and luxury.

Take for example the Huachipato blast furnaces, in the far
South of Santiago, Chile. The 6,000 middle-grade employees who
work there

are technically outstanding and in good trim. What a contrast with the condition of some of the workmen's families, who are crowded ten deep in little huts on the edge of the works, which the Company lets us visit so as to reveal openly (to the inquiry team) the difficulties it faces. And the situation there is far better than in the nearby mining town of Lota. I have rarely seen a sadder sight than that of miners there spending what could be their leisure hours on the threshold of their houses, squatting in the coal-dust, while here, there and everywhere the children are swarming in the filth of the streets or around the market stalls of Lota Baja, where evil-smelling meat lies open to the flies and the dust. More children still swarm in the slums and the squalid quaysides of nearby Talcahuano ... I was told in Lota that barely a quarter of the poor children there would manage to escape from that sad community: three-quarters of them would live and die there.

(Georges Friedmann)

A similar report on the coalmines of San Geronimo, at Rio Grande do Sul (Brazil), or on the Bolivian tin mines, would be scarcely more optimistic. On the edges of the most luxurious towns in Latin America, even around São Paulo, the same proletarian poverty is to be seen. It spreads into the heart of Buenos Aires, of whose 6 million inhabitants (in 1962) 55 per cent were working-class, 60 per cent of them ex-farmworkers who had left the land. As was once the case in Europe, these rustics are unsatisfactory as factory hands: they clock in one day, but fail to reappear the next. Many firms replace 75 per cent of their workforce every year. The workers' ignorance compounds their poverty: everywhere, failure to follow the most elementary rules of diet makes undernourishment worse. There are few skilled workers in the European sense; and the few there are tend to be overpaid, forming a kind of urban middle class outside the world of ordinary workpeople, and little inclined to show solidarity with them.

Everything conspires, therefore, to isolate and ignore that poverty-stricken world and leave it to its own devices. Official labour laws are often the most liberal imaginable: but there is an enormous gap between the letter of the law and what happens in practice. Trade unions exist, but they have nothing in common with those in the industrialized countries, except for the name; they are not even organized on a national basis. In a word, the working class is poor, uneducated, disorganized, often illiterate and often a prey to an emotional and romantic form of politics (of which Peronism was an example). It finds no solid support anywhere, either materially or intellectually. All this presages a difficult future, for a long time ahead.

An intellectual élite of writers, good teachers, some rare politicians, a few cultivated doctors and some lawyers have courageously faced these new and daunting problems. Unhappily, however, the weakness of the ruling classes and the political and economic élite is another of South America's serious and permanent handicaps. The crisis of industrial growth pitilessly eroded an old, fastidious and cultivated society, which might have proved unable to cope with the modern world but was none the less extremely attractive. The misfortune is that nothing as yet has appeared which could fully take its place.

Before 1939, when Latin America was still semi-colonial, only a few actors seemed to occupy the small stage of political life and culture, at the same time as they dominated the peaceful world of business. Charming, likeable and cultivated, they owned hundreds, thousands of acres, as well as the richest of libraries. Some of them were veritable Renaissance princes, just the type to captivate a journalist, traveller or intellectual from Europe. On the eve of the Second World War, however, they already gave the impression of being a social anachronism. They bore immense responsibilities – one in charge of almost all the British capital in Brazil, another the representative of something like the Dearborn Chemical Society, another running public finance, governing a State or hoping to become President of the Republic, and yet another a General risen from the ranks. But they all seemed to rule, as it were, from the inner sanctum of their thoughts and their libraries, as if in an unreal universe. They believed in the virtues of culture, civilization and reason. They seemed to belong to the liberal and aristocratic mode of nineteenth-century Europe, in an atmosphere of benevolent despotism, or perhaps enlightened paternalism.

And at the same time, outside their charmed and firmly closed circle, there were new men, industrialists and immigrants who had made their fortune. They were beginning to achieve astonishing economic success; and only their children would acquire a certain polish.

Today, society has evolved and the wheel has come full circle. Broadly speaking, power has passed from the landlords to the industrialists and bankers; vast family properties have given way to sumptuous mansions – in Brazil on the beaches of Rio or behind Petropolis; in Mexico at Vera Cruz, Acapulco or Cuernavaca below the capital, or in the rich suburbs of Mexico City itself. The towns, meanwhile, have taken on the appearance of major cities, with luxury hotels, skyscrapers and restaurants perched at the top of their thirty storeys in the American style. Not to mention that last wonder of the world which eclipsed all the others: Brasilia, the artificial capital city in the heart of up-country Brazil. This whole new world is taking its revenge on the old.

What South America continues to lack are consistent political parties and, still more, élites, a stable middle class or *medio pelo*, as it is called in Chile (where the term ordinarily applies to cross-breed cattle). A few intellectuals are by no means enough. It needs time, calm and an economy less sharply split between very poor and very rich, before such a middle class can emerge. But it will be indispensable for social equilibrium in a world which so far remains fundamentally capitalist.

The relative lack of a middle class on which serious political parties could rely explains why governments in South America have traditionally been so unstable. Competition among the parties has been usurped by competition among men. The army has played a very important role, following the still surviving tradition of the *libertadores*, the romantic Generals who successfully championed independence at the beginning of the nineteenth century.

However, the rapidly growing political awareness that urbanization is creating, even among very ordinary people, may force Latin America to undertake the immensely difficult task of extensively reforming its present social and economic system. Without such reform, a Mexican author has argued, it will remain for ever in the ante-room of truly modern capitalism, the power-house of wealth and well-being, without being fully admitted. That in turn would lead willy-nilly to violence – which would not necessarily, by any means, open the doors to genuine Social-ism.

A Brazilian, Josué de Castro, perceptively wrote in 1962: 'There is no doubt that Brazil' – and he could have written 'Latin America' – 'needs to achieve a giant leap in social history. What we have to ensure is that the leap does not end in the abyss: so we must muster our strength to reach the other side.'

South Americans' sense of insecurity, instability and uncertainty is undoubtedly justified. Less justified, perhaps, is their pessimism. The instability they feel is more than anything that of a civilization trying to find itself and define its own nature, under the pressure of painful but powerful realities.

For a long time, the only civilization that modern Latin America knew was alien to it: a faithful copy, made by a small group of highly privileged people, of the civilization of Europe, with all its refinements. There, too, literature bears witness. How many books there are by nineteenth-century South American authors which contain no clue to suggest that they were written outside Europe! Culture, for many people at that time, was an ivory tower in which they took refuge from time to time from the life which surrounded them and which had no place in the higher realms of the spirit.

That intelligentsia closely followed European thought, with both satisfaction and passion. That is why one still encounters, throughout South America, a very lively form of revolutionary humanism, and some traces of Auguste Comte's positivism which at first sight seem strangely out of place. (The slogan *Ordem e Progresso* on the Brazilian flag was in fact a homage to Comte.)

Those times are past. South American civilization now involves the mass of an increasingly urban population: it is feeling the impact of a powerful indigenous way of life, and can no longer simply accept its inheritance from Europe without adapting it very substantially. Latin America is building a new civilization – its own.

The emergence of a mass culture throughout the world, spread and imposed by the press, radio, television and the cinema, would sooner or later have made change inevitable. What is important for Latin America is that its intellectuals have anticipated the inevitable and already given it a shape. The eclipse of Europe's prestige owing to the First World War and above all the Second World War, and a certain defiance *vis-à-vis* the might of the United States, have coincided for them with the discovery of their own riches and their own tasks. The sense of guilt about the injustices of society, of which we spoke at the beginning of this chapter, has done the rest: the people, the *caboclo*, the *peón*, the Indian and the black have at last taken their places at the common table. They have ceased to be savages whose only interest was as passive recipients of the blessings of white civilization. Now, the interest lies in their own life, their thought, their proverbs and their religion; they have become the subject of sympathy and study by sociologists, and at the same time part and parcel of the national culture which is beginning to evolve.

That is what explains the publication, unthinkable fifty years ago, and the success (120,000 copies sold in Brazil, equalled only by some of Jorge Amado's novels) of the humble diary we mentioned earlier. As one Brazilian critic remarked, this book by Carolina María de Jésus is anything but a work of art. 'It is a document written by a woman of the people, an unequivocal message of fraternity, understanding and social justice.' Nor has it only made its author relatively wealthy: the slums that it describes (which can be seen in the film *Orfeu Negro*) have partly been demolished with a view to reconstruction.

The same change is evident in the growing interest in South America's popular folklore, which if understood aright is not only picturesque but sturdy. Sometimes, admittedly, it is already a little adulterated, like the loud and charming music of the Mexican *mariachis*, fiddlers who play in mixed groups in the bars of Mexico and elsewhere, and whom tourists' attentions have already somewhat spoiled. Their name is said to derive from the 'marriage' feasts at the time of the French occupation. If the etymology is perhaps dubious, it at least indicates, surprisingly, that the French presence did not leave too bitter an after-taste in popular memory.

Of course, one must leave the tourist routes behind if one wants to find true folklore and hear those old sentimental or lugubrious Brazilian songs which as always invoke the sorrowful moon or, still more, enjoy the dances and songs that are improvised to the music of primitive instruments. Thus in a market deep in the interior of Bahia, alongside the cattle pens, humble stalls offer a choice of, say, steaming rice, a live piglet, a scraggy quarter-chicken, or for a few *tostoẽs* every kind of tropical fruit – and a blind beggar will improvise his entreaty, his thanks and even a song. Any foreigner who is thought generous – and who has had himself described for the purpose – has a right to a long piece of improvisation in which personal compliments are mixed with the traditional blessings.

In fact, all the events of daily life are grist to the mill of these popular singers. Ubatuba, a small remote port on the Atlantic coast near São Paulo, was linked to the rest of the world, in 1947, only by one old car which twice a week came down from the Serra do Mar along an absurd mule track. Then it was decided at least to give it an electricity supply; and pylons advanced on the town through the forest, one by one. This *chegada da luz* – the arrival of light – was the theme of a song improvised one night by a musician with a *violão* (a primitive instrument) – an interminable hymn to the glory of civilization.

Each country in Latin America has its own folklore, its own music, its own stories, deriving from Indian, Spanish or black traditions. Folklore also deeply colours religious life. Despite the work of Protestant missionaries, which has often been more spectacular than effective, Catholicism predominates: but it is a primitive, medieval form of Catholicism, firmly believing in miracles; the Christian story mingles with Indian myths, and magic rites from the African past are confused or combined (*candomblés*) with Roman ritual. The fact that there are few priests encourages this free interpretation, which dilutes not only the Christian faith but also the native traditions. One day, Latin America will have to put its religious house in order. One historian of Protestantism, Emile G. Léonard, who is a Protestant himself, believes that the spiritual situation is reminiscent of Europe at the time of the Reformation or shortly before it: there are keen spiritual needs on the one hand which are poorly met on the other. However, signs of change abound.

Modern literature and all of life and culture in Latin America are in fact engaged in a return to their native sources. From this point of view, the best example is Mexico, where there is a broad and powerful movement towards 'Indianity', seeking the living springs of the nation. Mexico is remaking itself. It has taken much suffering; it has involved revolution and catastrophe. But out of them has sprung a popular, populist literature, as well as a revolutionary art, prefigured by José Orozco in the vaults of Guadalajarra Cathedral, and taken up by a whole new school of painting. One might add, finally, the emergence of an indigenous cinema, one of whose early fruits was the admirable *Maria Candelaria*.

21. America *par excellence*: the United States

======

This America has always insisted that it is unique. As a civilization, it was for a long time a traveller without baggage, convinced that the future would forever grow brighter and that seizing it was simply a matter of willpower. Thomas Jefferson, one of the authors of the 1787 Constitution, declared: 'America is new in its forms and principles.' Since then it has never ceased to consider itself new every morning, and to think with Jefferson that 'the land belongs to the living'. It was certainly able to stride confidently through economic, social and political crises: its reserves and its stock of optimism never seemed on the point of running out.

That has been so, at least, until relatively recent times. A first shock was the unexpectedly severe crisis of 1929, which began in Wall Street and was all the more painful because it struck at the heart of a thriving economy, rapidly expanding and, as it were, off its guard. America then found itself facing its first material catastrophe. To recover, psychologically, it was not enough to become more prosperous than ever. For the first time, America took a long look at its past – not so much to understand itself, since the average American has no spontaneous belief in the explanatory powers of history, but rather to seek some sort of consolation.

The growth of a taste for retrospective nostalgia accompanied the slow decline of traditional faith. When competition and enterprise were rapidly growing, Americans thought about the future; when they were flourishing, they thought about the present. Now, in the age of mergers, of giant corporations and monopolies, which reduce the scope for competition and the opportunities to be seized, they turn with regret to the golden age behind them.

Thus one percipient observer, Richard Hofstadter, in 1955.

America, still so young, has grown a little older. The Vietnam War has aged it still more. It has become conscious of its history, and is approaching the moment of truth. It has realized that its former refusal to be interested in the past, its fierce individualism, its isolationism and its rejection of any restraint on individual or national freedom, were all reflections of the 'unity of cultural and political traditions on which American civilization was based'.

Could it be that the situation of the United States today has made those implicit traditions redundant? Certainly, the past is beginning to weigh on its shoulders.

A reassuring past:
opportunities and setbacks

For a long time, America believed that it was forging a new future, unshadowed by what had gone before, because the past was effaced automatically and at once. The golden rule was to avoid any ties or attachments to one's roots, and to gamble on the unexpected. The operative word was 'opportunity'. Any man worthy of the name must seize his opportunity when it came and exploit it to the hilt. In the ensuing 'competition' with others he proved himself and showed his worth.

As an entity, the United States behaved in the same way. Its past is a series of opportunities offered, seized almost at once and fully exploited – a series of 'coups' to be brought off, usually with success. Let us begin with a balance-sheet of these opportunities, from both the distant and the more recent past.

★

Colonization and independence

The first opportunity was the rather belated conquest and occupation of part of the American seaboard. To be settled is to begin to exist. The race for the whole of America was begun by the epoch-making voyage of Christopher Columbus in 1492. Spain (Castile) was the winner. Eight years later, in 1500, the Portuguese under Alvarez Cabral seized the land of the Holy Cross (Santa Cruz), in the present-day country that owes its name of Brazil to the wood used for red dye, the *pao brasil*. Then came the French. Their merchantmen and pirate ships (sometimes indistinguishable) roamed all the Atlantic coast of the New World, from Newfoundland (discovered by the beginning of the century) to the Caribbean, Florida and Brazil (held by the Portuguese, but more in theory than in practice). In 1534–5 the French reconnoitred Canada, and settled there in 1603. The British were the last to arrive. In the last years of the sixteenth century, Walter Ralegh landed on the shore of what at once became Virginia, but the settlement he founded there was short-lived; and the *Mayflower* pilgrims reached Cape Cod, in what was to be Massachusetts, in 1620.

At first sight, these parts of the New World were not a very attractive geographical package: a cheerless coast, broken up by estuaries, gulfs and inland seas like Chesapeake Bay, and also wooded and marshy, cut off in the West by the Allegheny Mountains. Altogether, it was a vast area whose different parts were cut off from each other except by slow coastal navigation. There were also later rivals from Holland and Sweden to cope with, as well as surprise attacks by the native Indians. The French, nevertheless, starting from the St Lawrence River, had seized or at least explored and then occupied the Great Lakes and the huge Mississippi Basin as far as the delta, where New Orleans was built. They had thus executed a vast pincer movement, and won the first round.

From then on, the British bridgehead was squeezed between Florida, where the Spaniards had established their outposts, and this over-mighty French Empire, with its trappers in search of furs and its active Jesuit missionaries. When the British seriously began expanding Westwards in the eighteenth century, they came up against the forts of the French garrison towns.

Where in all that lay the 'American' opportunity? Probably in the fact that the British colonies, although fairly small in relative terms, were solidly occupied, especially in the North, where Boston, Massachusetts, was springing up, and in the centre, with New York (formerly New Amsterdam) and Philadelphia, the Quakers' city.

Linked with the mother country and its trade, these cities, founded in the wilderness, had the advantage of self-government: they enjoyed a quasi-liberty like that of typical medieval cities in Europe. Unrest in Britain served their interests: it exiled across 'the herring pond' not only unruly members of Protestant sects, but also 'cavaliers' who were frowned upon by Cromwell. There were so many such newcomers that by the time the real struggle ended, in 1762, the British numbered a million, against only 63,000 French. The British or 'American' opportunity was to have achieved this overwhelming numerical superiority in the teeth of both France and Spain.

Alfred Sauvy made the point well.

Once there were a million English on this continent, against some 70,000 French, the issue was decided, even if the fortunes of war had smiled on Montcalm at Quebec in 1759. Long before Voltaire, colonization and, above all, peopling the colonies did not essentially interest the French authorities. Mistakenly, they feared that France might be depopulated; and they also faced other domestic difficulties and concerns. So much so, that (bearing in mind the countries' respective sizes) thirty people from Britain left Europe for every single person from France. What a strange discrepancy between cause and effect: if the English language and its accompanying culture dominate the world today, that is because only a few French ships every year carried to the New World a minute number of people, most of whom were illiterate.

It can be a mistake for historians to play at 'what might have been'. An American, a passionate and single-minded Francophile, amused himself one day – not without admitted regrets – by imagining what North America would have been like if it had inherited French clarity, *douceur de vivre* and gastronomy. But that dream is well beyond the bounds of what history would have made possible.

America's first great economic advance took place against a background that was mainly agricultural. But its success (much greater than that of Canada) derived also from its connection with the sea. In North and South alike, water and waterways played an important role. Barques, fishing and merchant ships, and later the magnificent racing clippers swarmed on the seas, some reaching the Caribbean and South America, some going to Europe and the Mediterranean, others penetrating as far as the Pacific. During the War of Independence from 1776 to 1782, the American 'Insurgents' came as far as the English Channel, threatening Britain's shipping and commerce; and British frigates were repeatedly defeated during America's victorious war against Britain from 1812 to 1815 – an episode eclipsed, in many general histories, by the better-known struggle against Napoleon.

These maritime ventures helped make the fortune of a number of American cities, from the seventeenth century onwards. Admittedly, Britain's mercantile laws required on the one hand that the American colonies buy from the mother country all the manufactures they needed, even if they were imported from other European countries, and on the other that they sell to Britain and her colonies almost all their agricultural produce (except for a few products like grain and fish whose import into Britain was banned). Yet in 1766 Pennsylvania bought £500,000 worth of goods from Britain while selling her only £40,000 worth. It was a paradox often noted.

'Well then, how do you settle the difference?' Benjamin Franklin was asked when he was summoned before a House of Commons committee to explain this anomaly. 'The difference,' he explained,

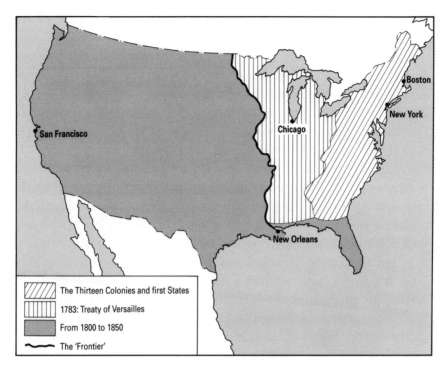

20. The expanding United States

is paid for by the goods we send to the West Indies, and which are sold in our own islands or to the French, Spaniards, Danish and Dutch; or by those which we send to other North American colonies – New England, Nova Scotia, Carolina and Georgia; or again, by those we send to the various countries of Europe . . . Everywhere we receive money, or bills of exchange, or goods, all of which enable us to pay Great Britain. Everything, added to the profits from the activity of our merchants and sailors on these round voyages, and to the transport offered by their ships, finally comes to Great Britain to right the balance.

This large-scale triangular trading system added the profits of freight service and trade among foreign countries to the commerce legally permitted by Britain – not forgetting some very active smuggling and some privateering that occasionally bore fruit. Nor should we omit fishing. America's sailors neglected none of the opportunities offered by the sea.

Towards the end of the eighteenth century, indeed, there was no question: the tonnage of American shipping was greater than that of any other country except Britain. In proportion to population, the United States was the biggest maritime nation in the world. This involved it willy-nilly in the world economy, forcing it to accept the ensuing constraints and pressures, but enabling it to enjoy the benefits too. All the precocious and ingenious devices of a society built on credit, as no other had been, derived from the fact that it was obliged to compensate for its own subordinate position and seek out the precious metal which it lacked, but which for that very reason it had to pass on as soon as possible, so as to pay its debts.

Every history of maritime good fortune tells of distant and surprising adventures. In this case there is an embarrassment of riches: the arrival of convoys of 'American' wheat in the Mediterranean or in the ports of revolutionary France; the Americans' success at the same time in blockade-running in the direction of the Spanish and Portuguese New World; the way in which they reached the Pacific via Cape Horn, and then, much later, from San Francisco. Scarcely had the former colonies won their freedom from Britain, in 1782, than they were trying to sail to China. And it was the desire for a port of call on the way to China, and for a safe haven for Pacific whalers, that led America in 1853 to send Admiral Perry's 'black ships' into the Bay of Tokyo, with the fateful consequences that everyone knows.

Nothing is more revealing than chance encounters with American ships in those days, travelling the seven seas. The *Lion*, the three-master carrying Lord McCartney to China as British Ambassador, put in at the island of St Paul in the South Atlantic in February 1793. There they found five seal-hunters (three French and two British) who were preparing to send 25,000 sealskins to sell in Canton, on board a Boston ship that was half-French and half-American and was also carrying to China a cargo of Canadian beaver furs. A few months later, the Ambassador had the pleasure of seizing this imprudent ship, in the waters off Canton, as a prize of war – because she was vaguely French, because war had been declared between France and Britain in January 1793, and because he had just heard the news.

Another tiny example: on his second journey round the world in the service of the Tsar, Otto von Kotzebue, son of the German poet and dramatist, was in a Southern Alaskan port on 26 April 1825. He met there an American two-master which had come straight from Boston to this small Russian outpost via Cape Horn, laden with foodstuffs which it was exchanging for 21,000 skins of 'sea cats', which were inferior to the precious furs of sea-otters, but which their purchaser hoped to take via the Sandwich Islands to sell in Canton. 'When the ship arrived in port in Alaska, the whole crew was drunk, including the captain; only by luck did they avoid the reefs and the shoals; but the Americans are so skilful that even when drunk they can always manage.'

This was also the heyday of whaling, the speciality of New England and the State of New York. The novelist Herman Melville (1819–91) described this rough world, where he had lived himself, its tough and dangerous life, and the prosperous little towns that depended on this one occupation – towns like New Bedford and Nantucket. Whaling declined after 1850, when mineral oil and gas replaced spermaceti oil as a source of light.

At about the same time, United States shipping found itself facing stiff competition from British iron-clad steamers. Its relative failure to recover from this blow was partly due to the fact that its attention was now turning inwards, to the frontier in the West. Conquering the continent – its own continent – pressing on Westwards, building railroads, encouraging coastal and inland navigation to provide further links: this huge task drew it away from the ocean. It was the new opportunity.

As so often in American life, when one activity is no longer essential, another presents itself. The latter becomes urgent: the former is left behind. In this case, it could be said that America exchanged the ocean, in which it now had less than a 50 per cent share, for a huge area of land which it seized in its entirety, and for itself alone.

No historical event is better known than the American colonies' seizure of their independence from Britain (1776–82). Even so, it has to be placed in context.

With the end of France's Empire in America in 1762, Britain's aid to the colonies at once became less vital and her demands upon them became more onerous. However, neither they nor Britain intended to bring about a break. The breach between them grew by itself, a result of misunderstandings, inadequate concessions and ineffectual violence. Every subsequent instance of decolonization, even today, has involved a similar succession of largely irrational events.

Was Britain wrong in not making swifter and bigger concessions? In imposing taxes to pay the huge costs of the war against France, then removing them, but leaving in place the tax on tea, with the result that the tea-chests on board two East India Company ships were thrown into Boston harbour on 16 December 1773? No taxation without representation is part of Britain's political tradition; and the British in America were not represented in Parliament at Westminster. So it was a major error.

A British historian writing in 1933, moreover, was surely right to point out that from the mid-eighteenth century onwards the centre of gravity of the British Empire began to shift from America and the Atlantic to India and the Indian Ocean. Bengal was occupied in 1757; and the rush for 'the China trade' began at about the same time. Was Britain being drawn away from the New World and towards the Far East by the eagerness of capitalism in search of still greater profit margins?

However that may be, some such series of reasons led to a spectacular war with the American colonies, and finally to Britain's humiliating defeat. The intervention of France and Spain hastened the success of the 'Insurgents'; but in 1782 the latter signed a secret peace with Britain, abandoning their allies. The result was that at the Treaty of Versailles in the following year Britain lost less than she might have feared. She also quickly realized that economic prosperity would more than make up for her political defeat. Historians may wonder, however vainly, what might have happened if the Industrial Revolution had not supervened to give Britain the makings of lasting power.

If, moreover, what interests us is the future of the United States, we should go beyond the international aspects of the story – beyond La Fayette, beyond the distant exploits of Admiral de Suffren de Saint Tropez, beyond even the plain and realistic intelligence of Benjamin Franklin. What mattered was independence itself, spelled out in the Declaration of Independence on 4 July 1776, and in the slowly matured Constitution of 1787. In those crucial years, young America found itself.

By 'young America' we mean a particular America, the first to take shape. Geographically, it was limited to the Atlantic coast and its hinterland; economically, it was above all agricultural; socially, it was dominated by the land-owning class of the Founding Fathers themselves, those 'founders of American democracy' idealized in picture-book history.

It is not disrespectful, and it may be useful, to see them for a moment as they were, from George Washington to Thomas Jefferson – men who had the will-power to draw up what they were convinced would be the best constitution in the world. It has long been said that the founding fathers based their constitution 'on the philosophy of Hobbes and the religion of Calvin'. For them too, man was 'a wolf to man' and his 'carnal spirit' was far removed from God. After the Shays Rebellion in 1787, General Knox wrote to Washington: 'The Americans after all are men – men with the turbulent passions which belong to that animal.'

The Declaration of Independence proclaimed both the right to rebel and equality before the law. But the great idea which preoccupied and motivated these landowners, businessmen, lawyers, planters, speculators and bankers – these 'aristocrats' – was to safeguard property, wealth and social privilege. America was new-born, but it already contained wealthy people, whose wealth (however modest) qualified them to lead the others. As proof, one has only to listen to the founding fathers, gathered in the Philadelphia Convention to draw up the Constitution, or to read their letters and those of their like. Their basic assumptions are very clear. Charles Pinckney, a young planter, proposed that only someone who possessed at least $100,000 should be able to be President. Alexander Hamilton called for 'the impudence of democracy' to be curbed. All of them, like Peggy Hutchinson, a Governor's daughter, regarded the masses as 'the dirty mob'. A young diplomat and statesman, Gouverneur Morris, declared: 'The crowd is beginning to think and reason. Poor reptiles! They warm themselves in the sun, and the next moment they will bite . . . The gentry is beginning to fear them.' And the lawyer and politician James Murray Mason acknowledged: 'We have been too democratic . . . Let us beware of going too far to the opposite extreme.' No one, finally, was more imbued with the sacrosanct principles of democracy than Jeremy Belknap, a New England clergyman; yet he wrote to one of his friends: 'We should uphold as a principle the fact that the Government derives from the people, but oblige the people to realize that they are not fit to govern themselves.'

That indicates the general line of thought. The order to be imposed in the name of liberty and equality was already a capitalist order, modest as the capital involved might be. Power and responsibility belonged to the rich. The others were granted the great concession of being protected against the rich, as the rich were, conversely, against them. Thereafter, it mattered little that the American Constitution was thought to be revolutionary, new, egalitarian and fair, in so far as it sought to balance against each other the impulses of the human animal, always selfish and fierce.

The 1787 Constitution is in effect a machine full of ingenious counterweights. Powers, Jefferson said, 'have to be so divided and balanced among the different bodies . . . that none of them can overstep the legal limits without being effectively countered by the others'. As for society, there was no question of abolishing privileges, and certainly not those of property, which was sacrosanct; but care would be taken to ensure that the road to privilege – i.e. wealth – was open to all. That, surely, would be easy in a vast and still 'new' country like America.

Richard Hofstadter summarized this ideal with good-humoured irony. 'The Founding Fathers believed,' he said, 'that a well-thought-out State would check interest by interest, class by class, faction by faction, and one branch of government by another, in a harmonious system of mutual frustration.'

It has to be admitted, however, that while nineteenth-century American history turned 'healthy competition' into a huge and ferocious struggle among private interests, the struggle there was more genuine and therefore fairer than in the capitalist countries of Europe. In America, profit was not reserved to a narrow, closed social class; everyone had a chance to seize opportunities in a society with more openings and advantages than elsewhere, and so one day to cross the great divide. The 'self-made man' is the classical symbol of that early America, which today may be on the way out.

Conquering the West

From the beginning, the United States saw itself as a pioneering nation. The same can be said, in fact, of all nations with a huge territory to take, to tame and to humanize – whether Russia, Brazil or Argentina. Geographical expansion is the first form of growth, and the key to all the others. This is true of an economy, a nation, a State, and indeed of a civilization.

History arranged things well. It enabled the United States to expand from the Atlantic to the Pacific, almost without hindrance. Imagine France spreading, virtually unmolested, from the Atlantic to the Urals! In 1803 the United States purchased Louisiana; in 1821 it acquired Spanish Florida; in 1846, to the possible detriment of Canada, it received Oregon from Britain; at about the same time, at the cost only of a too one-sided war, it took Texas, New Mexico and California from Mexico, enlarging its territory even further in 1853. If one thinks of the terrible invasions and catastrophes that attended the expansion of Russia, for instance, or of Europe itself, America's pioneering history – although at the expense of the Indians – looks relatively easy. In reality, the task was immense. Alone, young America would not have been able to master it.

From the beginning, a 1787 law had wisely stipulated that the territories so far unoccupied in the West should become the common property of the Union. Subsequently, as they were peopled, these lands became new States, eventually numbering forty-eight (with Alaska becoming the forty-ninth, and Hawaii the fiftieth). Colonization took many forms. It began in 1776 at the latest, and can be regarded as having ended with the distribution of the last portions of Oklahoma in 1907. Historical narratives, novels and films have made it familiar, from the covered wagons of the first emigrants and their battles with the Indians armed with bows and arrows, to the slow journeys of the last colonists, on the railroads built from coast to coast. Is there any point in returning to these hackneyed images of the heroic Far West?

What needs to be stressed, in fact, is how much the 'frontier', the territory conquered by the whites, represented a great adventure, both material and psychological. Material, in that credit, i.e. capitalism, played a key role in it, from the beginning. Psychological, in that it revealed new dimensions in Protestantism and, beyond that, in American civilization at its second and decisive stage.

Capitalism organized this great move Westward. Picture a settler who has just received his 160-acre homestead, who builds his house by fitting together its pre-cut wooden sections. At first, he tills the light soil on the hills, then gradually moves down to heavier land, and even into the valleys, sometimes clearing them of brushwood, sometimes of timber. He is a farmer, but not a peasant. Until now, he may well have followed a quite different trade. To survive, the only skill he needs is to be able to drive a team of horses; the crops, usually wheat, can be grown without elaborate preparation, and the ground need not be manured. Especially if he is the first to arrive, he will almost certainly have only one idea: to resell his property. He will have lived there for a few years, and will have spent scarcely anything, since all he needs will have been advanced to him in his remote outpost. He will have lived off canned food (already), and used coal for heating if the railroad has reached the neighbourhood. Once two or three good harvests have provided him with capital, he no longer hesitates; he sells his homestead, he takes the profits that will have accrued with the arrival of new settlers, and he moves on – further West, that is, to start over again. To go back East would be a confession of failure. (Based on Louis Girard.) So the settler was not a peasant or farmer, rooted in the soil: he was a speculator. He brought off a coup, as one historian has rightly said. He gambled; and of course he did not always win. But he went on.

A very similar case would be that of a town being built in the Middle West in about 1860. Picture it reduced to its essentials: a rudimentary railroad depot, an equally rudimentary hotel, a general store, a church, a school, a bank. The town has only just been founded, but already everyone is speculating on its growth, and hence buying good land around it and recruiting newcomers. Soon, it has electricity and a tramway; not long afterwards, the telephone. To cite Louis Girard once more, 'Travellers very often notice that electric light and trams are brought into streets which as yet have no houses. Precisely, they are told: this is so that houses will be built, so that the land will sell faster.' In Bismarck, the capital of North Dakota, founded in 1878, and dominated by German settlers, they inaugurated the capitol in 1883.

The inhabitants of Bismarck organized a grand ceremony. They invited not only the up-and-coming James Bryce (who five years later wrote *The American Commonwealth*), but also General Ulysses S. Grant, a distinguished soldier and former President. There was also Sitting Bull, a great Sioux chief who had fought valiantly against the white man: he came to enhance the prestige of the ceremony, and said a few gracious words in his native tongue. What amazed Bryce, a commonsense Scotsman, was that the future capitol was a mile away from the town. His astonishment surprised the inhabitants of Bismarck. They said: but since the city is going to grow, the Capitol has to be a long way from the present town.

The point is clear: that town, like the others, could not live only in the present. It also lived in the future – the secret of all economic success. It counted not on the money it had but on the money that was coming, whether it came or not. What was admirable was that, except during reverses like the recession of 1873, the money always came. The gambles very often paid off.

The America that conquered the West and the Far West was essentially Protestant. Protestantism was alone in facing the settlers' difficult human situation when they were so quickly scattered over such an expanse of land. There they were, without pastors, reduced simply to reading the Bible – if that. True, many of the settlers lived in a kind of medieval simplicity, and their spontaneous religious life was lively: it was sometimes fertile in inventing new beliefs, like those of the Mormons, the founders of Utah. It is to the credit of American Protestantism that it kept alive and quickened the flame of faith: that was one of its finest achievements.

To succeed, it had to adapt to its task, grow simpler, and to distance itself somewhat from the sects already in being (like the Congregationalists or the Episcopalians). It had to curtail its theological teaching and its liturgy, to rely on feelings and on the impact of spectacular meetings. The itinerant ministers of the Baptists, the Methodists and the Disciples of Christ did so remarkably well. They were not the inventors of such emotional forms of worship: Protestant reawakenings and revivals had supplied the model for them. But at least they were able to adapt Protestantism and to simplify it. The Baptists, for instance, abandoned their sectarianism, and the Methodists their Anglican heritage. The new preachers always stressed 'individual study of divinity', 'individual sovereignty' and 'works rather than faith'. The language of Christ was reduced to direct and simple communion.

Beyond their strictly religious aims, these Western preachers fashioned – without knowing it – the American way of life. This was the ideal, the model, the pattern of civilization to which immigrants in the second half of the nineteenth century, Protestant or not, found themselves obliged to adapt.

These spontaneous developments, on the part of the congregations as on that of their pastors, were the work of ordinary people, 'the only makers of churches'. They shared out the vast domain of the frontier like the conquerors they were: the Disciples founded their little churches in the West and Middle-West, the Methodists went to the North-West, the Baptists to the South-West. Altogether, what they did was comparable to the work of the Spanish missionaries who, from the sixteenth century onwards, had to spread the word of God among the immigrants who had come to the New World from Spain at the same time as they sought to convert to Christianity the mass of the Indians, thereby laying the foundations of what is now Latin America.

Industrialization and the growth of towns

The word 'industrialization' by itself is inadequate to describe the way in which the material life in the United States has been transformed between 1880 and the present day. During this century or so, a mainly agricultural country became mainly industrial, as the following figures show. This change would not have been possible without the enormous growth of towns.

There would be no point, here, in tracing the detail of this enormous change, with a mass of statistics and economic indicators. Books on economics and geography give all the necessary facts. Historically, however, it is worth noting that in New England, as in Britain, industrialization began with the expansion of textiles,

A. Value of agricultural and industrial production
(in billions of dollars)

	1880	1899	1909	1919
Agricultural	2.4	4.7	8.5	23.7
Industrial	9.3	11.4	20.6	60.4

B. Rural population (in millions and percentages)

	1880	1899	1909	1919	1950
Population	32.9	39.3	41.6	44.6	—
Percentage	65.0	51.7	45.3	36.4	15.6

and that – as in many European countries – it became firmly entrenched at the time of the railway boom, from 1865 to the crisis of 1873.

It would be more relevant to show: (a) the huge scale of America's success, which still deeply affects its human geography, as has been shown by the twentieth-century boom in the 'Deep South', on the edge of the Gulf of Mexico; (b) the advanced nature of certain achievements, harbingers of 'the life of the future'; (c) the way in which capitalism has continually revolutionized itself (a subject to be pursued in our next chapter); (d) the arrival of European labour, as vital to the building of industry and giant cities as it was to the opening-up of the West; and (e) the way in which this huge human and material development was moulded, more or less effectively, into the existing civilization that is known, for want of a better term, as 'the American way of life'. But for the moment we shall look only at the last two of these vast subjects.

Until about 1880, the United States had taken on English and Scottish immigrants, the first layer of its European population. Then came an influx of German and Irish people – the latter making America a little less British and even a little less Protestant. Yet the country was still dominated by British culture, and by Protestantism, until between 1880 and 1914, when it took on 25 million Slavs and Mediterraneans, most of them Catholic.

They were absorbed, not so much by the agricultural West as by the urban and industrial East. They changed the East, but not out of all recognition, as for example Argentina was changed, at about the same time, by a wave of Italian immigration which flooded both countryside and towns. There was nothing surprising in the contrast. The United States had towns and industries that were already flourishing; it also had immense powers of persuasion and assimilation. The absorption of the new immigrants was rapid and highly effective. 'Consider a group of Americans taken at random,' wrote André Siegfried in 1956. 'The Nordic types are far from dominant among them. One could as well believe that they come from Naples or Vienna as from London or Hamburg. Yet they are certainly Americans, and they behave and react as Americans. From this point of view, assimilation has worked.'

What had succeeded was a combination of factors: the language, the American way of life and the enormous power of attraction that the New World held for its immigrants. This last was the most important of all. Furthermore, by the quota laws of 1921–4 and the McCarran Act of 1952, the United States virtually closed the door. Since then, the arrival of new immigrants has been a mere drop in the human ocean, despite the sensational scientific achievements of a distinguished few.

Today, there is very little immigration in the South except from Mexico and Puerto Rico, and in the North except from French Canada, some of whose strays are to be found in Detroit, Boston or even New York. All such immigration, now, is a mere trickle. True, New York is the biggest 'Puerto Rican' city in the

world; but then Paris is a great 'North African' city in the same
sense and for the same reason: every large city looks for unskilled,
low-paid, menial labour, and if it fails to find it at home it looks
elsewhere.

America's new arrivals supplied its industry with the cheap
labour that helped it to start up and then to expand. They also
supplied their poor and their proletariat to the great cities, of which
New York is the unrivalled prototype. The growth of towns was
exceptional and never-ending: the whole of the Eastern seaboard,
in fact, from Boston as far South as Washington, has now become
a single built-up area – a megalopolis, in geographers' terminology:
only here and there are there trees, a few cultivated fields, or
suburbs which meet and intermingle. Princeton University stands
in the centre of one of these reserves of grass and trees, between
Philadelphia and New York City. A moment's inattention, and it
would be submerged by these familiar nearby monsters.

And yet, despite this vast transformation and this massive influx
of immigrants, American civilization has held its own. It has assimilated everything – machines, factories, the amazing growth of
the 'tertiary sector' (services), the swarms of automobiles (of which
Europe offers only a distant foretaste), and finally the arrival of
non-Protestant immigrants.

American civilization took shape in three stages: on the Atlantic
seaboard; from the Atlantic to the Pacific; and then 'vertically', by
industrialization. It was the second stage, that of the Far West and
the new forms of Protestantism, which settled, perhaps, the essential elements in the American way of life: respect for the
individual, extremely simplified religious faith, heavily concentrated on works (mutual aid, singing together, social duties,
etc.), and the supremacy of the English language, eclipsing all the
rest.

Can such a society be called religious? Yes, the opinion polls
answer: almost 100 per cent. Benjamin Franklin said as much in
1782, when America was in its infancy: 'In the United States,

atheism is unknown; unbelief is rare and secret.' Today, official language still invokes religion. Any move in foreign policy can readily be called a 'crusade', whether by Woodrow Wilson or by General Eisenhower. Equally, social differences find religious expression. At the bottom of the scale there are the Baptist communities, made up of modest people who until recently were very poor. More 'chic' is the world of the Methodists; and finally, most distinguished of all, there are the Episcopalians (i.e. those with Bishops), whose liturgical ceremonies derive from the Anglican Church. Episcopalianism, one historian has written, is also the Church of the newly rich – those who have 'kicked away the social ladder' they have climbed.

Indeed, in their own eyes, it matters little how Americans organize their beliefs. Their religious life is tolerant, pluralist, divided into different sects or denominations. There is only one Church in the old, exclusive sense of the term; and that is the Catholic Church. Members of the same family find it natural to belong to different sects, since everyone is free to believe in his or her own way, provided they believe: that is the only obligation. In Boston there is a small 'church' built in ultra-modern style. At the entrance, a plaque announces that no particular cult is celebrated on the premises, which are devoted to prayer by all believers in the world, whatever their faith. The only part of the interior which is not in shadow is a great slab like an altar, which is lit from an opening in the roof by a beam of light, reflected down by a large curtain made of pieces of mirror, reminiscent of a Calder mobile.

Wonderful tolerance, a European might think – if he were unaware that atheism and secularity on the Western model, and in particular governmental and educational secularity as in France, are rare in the United States, if not actually inconceivable. On the other hand, a certain kind of non-religion or rationalism is prevalent in some quarters, as it has been in Europe since Charles Darwin's *Origin of Species* and Ernest Renan's *Life of Jesus*. Rationalism of this kind has encouraged the growth of more and more nebulous deism.

The important fact for America's cultural cohesion is that what might have been a divisive factor, that is the Catholicism of certain immigrants, beginning with the Irish, then the Germans, Italians, Slavs and Mexicans, finally adapted – and adapted well, to American life, finding a place for everyone. On this point, the role of the first Catholic immigrants – the Irish – was decisive.

In any case, while the Catholic Church has safeguarded its world unity and its hierarchy, in America it has fully accepted the separation between Church and State, in contrast to its attitude in countries where it enjoys a majority. It has also fully accepted American nationalism. Finally, it has agreed deliberately to emphasize works as distinct from faith, thereby moving with the main current of American life. One statement among many may be quoted as an illustration: it comes from an American Archbishop: 'An honest vote and good behaviour in relation to others will do more for the glory of God and the salvation of souls than flagellation in the middle of the night or pilgrimages to Compostela.'

Like the Protestant sects, the Catholic Church (which now has 30 million American adherents) has organized its own associations, schools and universities. What is more, while the Protestant Churches have had little success in converting the poor in the cities, the Catholic Church has made notable headway in this area.

The relative failure of the Protestant Churches in the towns may be due to its rural success in the nineteenth century, as well as to the growing wealth which has made it more middle-class and lessened its fervour (despite recent signs of revival). For religion in America – and more generally American culture as a whole – is continually threatened by the drift of its adepts towards bourgeois wealth.

Religion, however, is only one of the reasons why American civilization is so coherent. Others include its rapid growth, the attraction of a society in which social differences are marked only by money, and in which – at least until very recently – the road to wealth was anyone's to take. For a European immigrant, to accept these social rules was to step out of the old European social categories and open the way to hope.

Such is the liberal side of a civilization which in other ways imposes constraints, barely allowing the individual to escape from the tacit rules of the American way of life. If the immigrants themselves have some difficulty in adjusting, if they sometimes suffer from nostalgia, their children are eager to melt into the American mass. All sociologists have noted this desire, on the part of immigrants' children, to lose the traces of their origin.

Finally, what has played the biggest role in this process has been the abundance of 'opportunities' in America: the frontier, industrialization and the growth of the great cities have all been wealth creators, and wealth assists assimilation. There is a great distance between the quarrelsome Irish immigrant of the first generation in the 1830s, living in a shack or a slum, and the 'lace-curtain Irish' of the second or third generation. The rising tide of America's prosperity has borne up its first civilization over the new waves of humanity that have swept on to its shores.

While this first civilization soon marked itself off, decisively, from its British origins, it none the less remains more Anglo-Saxon than truly European. Continental Europe has always blended Mediterranean and Nordic traditions. To quote André Siegfried once more: 'This interpenetration of the two civilizations is lacking in the United States, where the Anglo-Saxon side has absorbed everything.' This is no doubt regrettable, in that the hazards of history have made the rest of the American continent, save for Canada, a strictly Latin world, first Portuguese and Spanish, then deeply marked by Italian immigration. It is a fact that the two Americas find it hard to understand each other: they are ill-equipped to do so. And that, at the present time, could be dangerous.

22. Failures and Difficulties: From Yesterday to the Present

===

So far, we have noted opportunities and successes. There have also been difficulties and mishaps. They seem to have accumulated in more recent times, growing with each successive historical 'watershed' – in 1880, 1929 and perhaps 1953. Yet they may mislead us, and in two ways. Looked at closely, is there any human grouping that is immune from the difficulties inherent in life itself? And in so vast a civilization as that of America the distinction between good fortune and bad cannot be either clear or decisive. Every difficulty demands effort, stimulates a response and (as in mathematics) 'changes its sign'. A mishap is a warning, a test. It only rarely spells universal disaster. Heinrich Heine's well-known words, 'A new Spring will restore to you what Winter has taken', are often true for individuals, and more often still for nations. The United States has problems, and may face crises; but it remains in the best of health – more so, perhaps, than it imagines.

An old nightmare: Black America, an ineradicable colony

In the midst of America's opportunities, a major difficulty arose in its very early days, and one that could not be wished away. This was the presence of black Africans, brought to its shores from the seventeenth century onwards as the Southern plantations developed: tobacco in Virginia from 1615 onwards; rice in

Carolina from 1695, and then in Georgia; cotton in the nineteenth century in all the area to the South-West of Virginia.

History and geography bear the responsibility. The Atlantic seaboard, where the United States began, has a series of climatic zones, all close together. New York, despite its being on the same latitude as Naples, is affected by a cold current from Labrador, and has the same climate as Moscow. Only an overnight train journey, however, divides it from tropical areas and their exotic products. In the South, slavery was established almost as a matter of course, a kind of extension of the Caribbean economy that was so prosperous in the eighteenth century. The Spanish maintained it in Florida, and the French in New Orleans (from 1795 onwards, for sugar cane), as did George Washington and Thomas Jefferson in their Virginia properties.

Thus was introduced into Anglo-Saxon America a lively and wayward Africa, unstoppable by force, by prejudice or by concessions. The 1787 Constitution, however liberal in tone, did not actually abolish slavery. All it did was to provide for the elimination of the slave-trade after a delay of twenty years – which indeed it was, in 1807.

From that date, blacks were no longer brought into America legally, although clandestine shipments continued for many years, and they were being reared like cattle. In the nineteenth century, the cotton boom paradoxically worsened their condition. Hitherto, they had lived in their employers' houses: but now they were herded into great work-gangs, as on the estates of Ancient Rome. Ruling over these penniless black workpeople was a society of cultivated, well-mannered whites, a powerful colonial aristocracy. In 1852, Harriet Beecher Stowe's novel *Uncle Tom's Cabin*, revealing the plight of the blacks, unleashed a wave of sympathy in the North. Another more recent novel, Margaret Mitchell's *Gone With the Wind* (1936), spoke of the charm and the pleasures of life in the old South: but the life in question was mainly that of the privileged white owners. The tense and complex stories of William Faulkner are set in a later phase of this same Southern life, full of nostalgia for the civilized past, telling of hunting parties and conversations over the corn liquor or the moonshine. All these books reveal a dual truth, black and white – and probably contain dual lies.

In short, whereas the Indians, the first victims of colonization, virtually disappeared after their struggle against the Europeans, surviving hardly at all outside the reservations where they live as representatives of a vanished race, the blacks, without wholly meaning to, put up a stiff resistance. So the United States contains within it a colony which has not been truly liberated, despite all the official measures taken – an ethnic minority whose weight and presence nothing can remove.

In the mid-nineteenth century, the question of whether slavery should be abolished or maintained sparked off the explosion of the Civil War (1861–5); but it was only one of many issues in the fratricidal dispute between the States of the North and those of the South.

- The North was industrial, and in favour of high customs tariffs; the South, which sold cotton, preferred to buy its manufactures from Europe, where the quality was higher. It therefore called for the policy of the open door.
- The dispute had a political aspect too. Of the two parties jockeying for power, the Democrats were strongest in the South and the Republicans in the North.
- The dispute was all the more bitter because a prize was at stake. Which of the two blocs, North or South, would win the allegiance of the new States emerging in the West?
- On a practical point, finally, the crisis raised a serious problem. Could individual States that were part of the Union oppose measures adopted by its central Government? Did they have the right, if necessary, to secede?

All these reasons for rivalry crystallized round the two sides' violent disagreement on the abolition of slavery. The South began the War by attacking Fort Sumter on 12 April 1861; it ended it by capitulating on 9 April 1865, after an appalling, exhausting struggle. On 18 December 1865, the 13th Amendment to the

Constitution abolished slavery. It freed almost 5 million blacks (4,800,000 in 1870, compared with 33 million whites), or 12.7 per cent of the total population. This proportion later increased: it reached 13.1 per cent in 1880, then declined regularly as European immigrants arrived. By 1920 it was 10 per cent, and it seems to have settled at about this figure.

Countless details of daily life could easily be cited to show how hollow the political concessions made to the blacks have turned out to be. Political rights have been by-passed to keep blacks in 'their inferior position'. All the more so because many of them, before 1914, remained in the South, where habit and tradition automatically tended to keep them down. In the industrialization that began there around 1880 they found only a subordinate role, mainly as manual labourers, while better-paid posts went to 'poor whites'. It was only with the First World War that there was large-scale black migration Northwards, to Harlem in New York, to the 'black belt' in Chicago, to Detroit and elsewhere.

The black minority has followed and shared in America's economic expansion. Today it has its wealthy members, even its 'new rich'; it has universities, churches, musicians, writers and poets. But always, as it advances, true equality still retreats out of reach. 'As often happens,' wrote André Siegfried in 1956,

a systematic desire to look on the bright side could lead one to believe that the problem is now solved. A number of European visitors have made this mistake. The truth is that social discrimination continues, somewhat attenuated in the North, but hardly at all attenuated in the South. In the East and the Middle West, we shall no doubt see blacks effectively involved more and more in the life of the whites. A distinguished black may now and then be invited to a dinner or a social gathering; more and more representatives of the once persecuted race will be elected without discrimination to administrative posts. This is a long way from supposing that the barrier will soon fall or be substantially lowered. Most blacks in the United States simply feel and want to be American, without mention of race; but for the whites they remain

'American blacks' – a considerable nuance. Colour, in fact, seems to be an insurmountable obstacle to complete assimilation.

It seems, indeed, to be caught up in the hopelessly slow process whereby cultural changes take place, when they do. The prejudices involved, the antagonism, and the attitudes struck (see Faulkner's novels) are much more in tune with yesterday than with today. Segregation, lynching (now very rare), open or hidden hostility: all lag behind the movements that are making them obsolete. But those movements have at last begun. The incidents at Little Rock, Arkansas, where white schools, backed by the State Governor, had refused to accept blacks, as the new federal law required, was an early landmark. When the federal Government finally won, it was a sign of the times and the future, however great the problem and the segregationist passions it aroused. Even so, things are changing very slowly; and only the astonishing patience and political loyalty of black Americans holds out any hope that the problem will be solved peacefully.

In conclusion, should we see this problem as a misfortune, both for America in general and for black America, so put-upon and so patient? No: because in addressing the problem American humanism finds itself facing a difficulty whereby it will be judged and enhanced. No again: because the United States has been offered from Africa a very special and original cultural contribution, already being incorporated into American civilization (and especially into its music). What is more, this Africa-in-America is materially and intellectually by far the most advanced of all black communities in the world, industrious on its own account and also enjoying the momentum of American culture and civilization. Time is on its side; but if time does not remove this serious contradiction in American life, lasting intellectual and moral unease will remain. That is something that no one in his heart of hearts can desire. It is vital for America to find and to apply a satisfactory solution.

Capitalism: from the trusts to State intervention and oligopoly

Fortune or misfortune: once more one hesitates to make a judgement, this time about the history of capitalism in the United States. It too has helped as well as harmed the civilization on which it has left its indelible imprint – and by which it has been no less deeply marked in its turn. Money has been and still is king in the free democracy that America seeks to be. The reign of business is an obvious fact: it makes itself visible, if only in the giant buildings of Lower Manhattan. But American capitalism, with its free and sometimes too free interplay of supply and demand, has brought material prosperity unequalled anywhere else in the world. All other countries, whatever their political regimes, try to copy and equal it. And American idealism, whose vigour and often total unselfishness no one can deny, is in part a response to the pervasive materialism of big business, an escape from it and also a reproof. Capitalism, in the United States, has often had a guilty conscience.

More than that, it can be argued that American capitalism has gradually been made more humane, under the pressure of a society which is pragmatic rather than revolutionary, and too wealthy no doubt to nurture subversion as in Europe before 1848 or 1914.

As we have seen, America was a farming nation until about 1880. Then, all at once, it underwent the most amazing transformation, and seemed caught unawares by its sudden access of industry, wealth and power. The European Community, in the early days of the Common Market, found what it was like to enjoy rapid material progress. Everything was affected by the rising tide – including the growth of moderate, pragmatic Socialism. In America, likewise, capitalism developed only by adapting, by making more and more concessions, by offering shares in progress, so to speak. It has undergone considerable evolution, from the trusts of the late nineteenth century to the huge oligopolies which in twos or threes dominate the vast domestic market.

It is clear that capitalism, growing, checked or diverted, but always evolving, is the driving force of material life and, beyond that, of politics and civilization in the United States. In transforming itself, it has transformed America. That, in part, is the origin of the present and permanent crisis of American civilization.

To see how American capitalism has evolved, we must return for a moment to the time of the trusts (bearing in mind that 'trust' also means 'confidence' and that a trustee is an agent or proxy). Legally speaking, a trust is a union of stockholders with shares in different companies, the shareholders delegating to trustees the task of representing them. As a result, a group of trustees may bring together *de facto* a number of companies whose articles forbid them to merge. So this can be a way of evading the law. Some trusts may bring together companies active in kindred or complementary industries; and when they are powerful enough they naturally aim at establishing a monopoly – although the immense size of the United States has always made that difficult. An operation of this kind was successfully mounted by John D. Rockefeller (1839–1937) between 1870, when Standard Oil of Ohio was formed, and 1879, when the Standard Trust was effectively established. The trust went well beyond the strict limits of the original business, since it involved a series of firms extracting, transporting, refining and selling oil (especially abroad) – the sales soon being linked with the enormous spread of automobiles.

The United States Steel Corporation, founded in 1897, was also certainly a trust, and more certainly still a giant enterprise. Rockefeller, retired from Standard but not from speculation, had profited from the virtual absence of fiscal controls to amass an enormous fortune: he used it later to finance an immense amount of charitable work. Meanwhile, Rockefeller had bought some iron ore deposits near Lake Superior – he had received them, in fact, as payment by insolvent clients. Shortly afterwards, he secretly arranged for the building of a cargo fleet to carry the ore via the Great Lakes. Then, more by necessity than from choice, he made an agreement with the steel king Andrew Carnegie (1835–1919), owner of the great Pittsburg steelworks. With the help of the banker John Pierpont Morgan (1837–1913), the giant US Steel Corporation came into being, covering 60 per cent of American production. A last touch was added when the shares were floated on the stock exchange: Morgan doubled the capital, successfully doubling the value. He had speculated, with good reason, on the rapid rise of the shares.

These operations, and others that could be cited, notably in discussing the rivalry between railroad firms, illustrate a technique and a climate – that of fierce, remorseless capitalism, analogous to Machiavellian politics. Nor were Rockefeller, Carnegie and Morgan so very different, in some respects, from the determined princes of the Renaissance.

The heyday of that business boom was between the California gold rush of 1849 (or 1865, after the surrender of the South at Appomatox) and the beginning of the twentieth century. Its plutocrat princes, some hard-faced, some debonair, ruthlessly pursued their vision of America. They broke or brushed aside the obstacles that stood in their way, and made no secret of paying any necessary bribes. One of them wrote: 'If you have to pay to get a fair solution, it is simply right and proper to do so. When a man has the power to do great harm, and will only act straight if he is paid an inducement, since it saves time, then it's one's duty to go ahead and pay the judge.' The end justifies the means; whatever suits us is right . . .

This was the age of the great economic achievements, the railways, the gold rush, the settlement of the West and the new men, the new rich who exemplified the reassuring and not always accurate myth of the 'self-made man'. It was the age of unwittingly cynical capitalism. Its leaders, in the midst of their struggles and connivances, could not be expected to see themselves through our squeamish eyes. They were fighters who cared little what methods they used and thought only of their objective: size, efficiency or even the public good – all of which would certainly enhance their own wealth and status, but since 'the best man won' did they not, in all fairness, deserve their reward?

But it would be a mistake to think that these activities, or the later propaganda which made out all successful businessmen to be 'self-made men' were always greeted with approval and credulity. Far from it: the public, and even some businessmen, were acutely uneasy about monopolies and the measures that seemed to encourage them. Spontaneous and 'natural' mergers between firms, together with the long-lasting boom that followed the turn of the century, made for more and more trusts and monopolies. They seemed to spring up like mushrooms: 86 of them between 1887 and 1897; 149 between 1898 and 1900; 127 between 1901 and 1903. But very soon they began to fight each other; and the Presidential campaign of 1896 was partly a struggle between the opponents of the trusts, led by William Jennings Bryan, and their supporters, led by the successful candidate William McKinley. Then some of the trusts fell victim to their own excess of ambition, like that in the merchant marine which Pierpont Morgan had planned.

The short, sharp economic crises of 1903 and 1907 made public opinion very sensitive on the subject; and there was widespread approval when President Theodore Roosevelt broke up a railway trust in 1904. Measures such as this, and much campaigning, led to the Clayton Anti-Trust Act of 1914, named after a Democrat friend of President Woodrow Wilson.

Many observers have argued that this was merely beating the air – that it was vain to imagine that the trend towards ever bigger economic concentrations could be stopped by a law. An American Socialist leader, Daniel de Leon, actually allied himself with that movement. 'The ladder,' he wrote, 'that humanity has climbed towards civilization is progress in working methods, more and more powerful means of production. The trust is at the top of the ladder, and around it modern social storms are raging. The middle class is trying to break it, and turn back the march of civilization. The proletariat is trying to preserve it, improve it, and open it to everyone.'

That attitude is clear: leave untouched the technological progress that is America's triumph and pride, but humanize the process, and if possible share in the progress. To pursue such a policy, the only arbiter with enough size and power was the Federal State, because the trusts spanned individual States' frontiers and operated in a number of States at once. Only the Federal State was really in their league. Even so, it had to grow, to strengthen itself and impose itself as a power in the land. The trusts, or big business, had for their part to realize that there was an advantage in facing only one authority whose support they could secure, whose opposition they respected and whose decisions they accepted, willingly or not. One example, in 1962, was President John F. Kennedy's opposition to a rise in the price of steel.

Today, it has been said, with the oligopolies, the labour unions and the 'countervailing power' of the State, 'something like neo-capitalism is being established in the United States, adaptable in its developed form to twentieth century conditions, and already very different from traditional capitalism'.

This neo-capitalism is difficult to define: it has many aspects, and all of American civilization is expressed in its complex but orderly system. Could anyone ever list all its elements? Efficiency, including automation and its offshoots; mass production for an enormous homogeneous market with standardized tastes, encouraged by all-pervasive, all-powerful advertising; and in the bigger firms, a major role for public relations and human relations departments – acting as foreign ministries and ministries of the interior, whose respective duties are to justify the firms *vis-à-vis* the public and the consumers on the one hand and the workers on the other. A thousand details are important in this scheme of things: but the key to them all is economics. It is worthwhile, therefore, to look at the rules, the limits, and the success of that great motive force. To this end, let us consider a number of elements one by one: the role of the market in nineteenth-century liberal economies; the oligopolies; the labour unions; and the Federal Government.

The market (supposedly free, of course) was for liberal economists the regulator and arbiter of all economic life. Through the sacrosanct medium of competition, it put everyone and everything in the right place. The ideal economy, according to capitalist tradition, was one in which competition had full rein (and hence without monopolies), where there was no State intervention, where equilibrium was achieved automatically through the interplay of supply and demand, and where crises, unemployment and inflation were abnormal phenomena which had to be resisted. Unemployment, which had to be explained because it was present, even before the twentieth century, was even blamed on abnormal pressure by the labour unions.

To complete this traditional picture, it has to be repeated that production was always held to be beneficial. All goods produced, in fact, stimulated trade, according to the law of outlets formulated by Jean-Baptiste Say in 1803. 'Products,' he declared, 'are traded for products'; so to make a product was to give oneself a supplementary medium of exchange. This had been the doctrine of liberal economists from Adam Smith to Jeremy Bentham, David Ricardo, Jean-Baptiste Say and the great Alfred Marshall. In other words, in this competitive 'model' of economic life, everything was self-regulating, including the propensity to save or invest. And if by some mischance that propensity required regulation, it was enough to adjust the interest rate, raising or lowering it by the right amount.

However, at a certain stage in the development of capitalism, all these old rules, taught and repeated *ad nauseam*, were belied by the facts. In the twentieth century, monopolies, crypto-monopolies and oligopolies came to dominate large sectors of the economy, and the most advanced sectors at that. They distorted the sacrosanct free play of competition. The State intervened, as in the New Deal or, outside the United States, in so many five-year plans. Finally, long crises began to appear from 1929 onwards: unemployment and inflation played a large part in them, and came to be seen, after all, as regrettable but normal phenomena in economic and social life. Hence the importance of *The General Theory of Employment, Interest and Money*, published in 1936 by the British economist

John Maynard Keynes (1883–1946). This marked a break with liberal economics and its traditional competitive model. America accepted it as the law of the prophets in twentieth-century economics and often used it as a basis for political action.

The oligopolies: there is oligopoly, or imperfect competition, or incomplete monopoly, when a few large suppliers 'try to satisfy the needs of a multitude of purchasers'. In fact, as we have seen, the battle against the trusts did not put an end to natural, organic mergers between firms. In many industries, and not only in the United States, mergers resulted in the formation of giant companies. Thus, before 1939, a single enormous company, the Aluminum Company of America, dominated the aluminium market. Normally, a few giant firms shared this branch or that; there were three or four, for instance, in tobacco and cigarette manufacture.

Alongside the giants, small firms continued, living as best they could, and likely sooner or later to disappear. They were no more than survivals from the past. While it may be easy to enter an infant industry which attracts risk capital, as with oil when Rockefeller was young, or cars when Henry Ford was starting out, it is much more difficult when the industry is well-established, and when experience, economies of scale, technological progress and self-financing are the vital areas in which privileged firms hold all the cards.

Studies and statistics underline the fact: 200 large-scale enterprises control about half the fabulous material wealth of the United States. Often, they are impersonal corporations, sometimes owned by their employees. In these conglomerate empires, wages and salaries are enormous by comparison with Europe; but they are usually fixed rather than profit-related. 'Profits as such,' explained Henry Ford, 'belong to the firm itself: they protect it and allow it to grow.'

Thus were established this exceptional form of capitalism and the reign of the 'giants', against which anti-trust laws can now do so little – as was seen, for example, in the attempted Government action against the makers of Chesterfield, Lucky Strike and Camel cigarettes in 1948. Perhaps if there were only one monopoly . . . but 200! It would take radical reform, a revolution, to change matters; but no one dreams of such a thing. The oligopolies will not be divided into small-scale firms.

So the leading roles are filled and well filled. 'In the aristocracy of business, the Dukes are the Presidents of General Motors, Standard Oil of New Jersey, the Du Pont de Nemours Chemical Society and the United States Steel Corporation. The Counts, Barons, Knights and Squires follow on, in strict proportion to the assets of their different firms.' Those who enjoy such vested interests intend to keep them. 'The present generation of Americans, if it survives, will buy its steel, its copper, its brass, its automobiles, its tyres, its soap, its switches, its breakfasts, its bacon, its cigarettes, its whisky, its cash-registers and its coffins from one or other of the few firms which currently supply them' (J. K. Galbraith).

True, as has often been said, these giant firms have their advantages. They follow and brilliantly exploit technological progress, and supply high-quality goods at low prices. This is clear if one compares those industries which, when modernized, merged into large corporations and those which continued on nineteenth-century lines. For the United States was built on at least two basic structures, the old capitalism and the new. Agriculture in general, dressmaking, and the mines are examples of the old, in the sense that the firms involved are of very moderate size. In agriculture, they are often minuscule. In Missouri, a 'big' producer may market 9,000 bales of cotton. In absolute terms, that is an enormous amount; but as a proportion of total production it is very small – so small that its producer can have no influence on prices. In fact, he is at their mercy – and so are all his fellow-producers of cotton. Similarly, there is a huge difference between the 'petropoly' organized by the American oil majors, whose growth has been sensational, and the archaic situation of the 6,000 coal-mining firms, which have gone on relying on the work of ill-paid miners, and whose technological progress, such as it is, has depended on relatively recent intervention by the State.

But the market is recovering its role. Clearly, prices never take the big firms by surprise. They control them in advance; and, true to the principle of 'fair and honest' competition, they intervene in them only after having worked out what effect a decision to raise or lower them is likely to have on rival firms which could do the same to them. The result is that prices are fixed fairly high to ensure the security and the profits of the giants, which is why smaller firms still manage to live, to exist, to survive in the shadow of the big corporations, thanks to prices which they can match. This being so, and a price war being avoided, all that really remains is an advertising war, which is clearly a luxury confined to 'affluent societies'. One can hardly imagine advertising at all in a really poor society.

Nevertheless, the 200 giants (no longer controlled, it seems, by the banks, whose power suffered from the 1929 crash) do not reign undisputed or alone. The natural tendency that has concentrated sales in a few hands, at least in certain advanced sectors, has also concentrated purchases, this time in a few other hands.

So the 'economic power' of the producers comes up against the 'countervailing power' of the purchasers. In this balancing act, the advantages of monopoly can be on either side: a big supplier may face many purchasers, a big purchaser may face many suppliers, or – as is often the case – one giant may face another. In this case there has to be compromise. If the steel producers tried to fix 'arbitrary prices' in Detroit, they would have difficulty in imposing them on a clientele as important and powerful as the local automobile manufacturers.

Clearly, an oligopoly can play both roles, buying and selling, and so exert both economic power and countervailing power, either in turn or simultaneously. But for the most part there will be conflict and tension between the two.

The labour market is where countervailing power has most obviously grown. Industrial giants have seen the rise, in their own sectors, of giant unions. These too have tried to profit from the giant firms' monopoly influence on the market. Since the firms can raise their prices, they only have to be squeezed enough and they will raise wages, enabling their workforce to share their privileges. That word is no exaggeration, in view of the fact that some American labour unions are themselves rich companies, with enormous buildings, large and well-managed capital and a president and staff who are royally paid.

At the other extreme, where capitalism is still backward, the unions can hardly exert such effective pressure. Is this why so much of American agriculture remains outside the scope of active union organization?

At all events, the traditional rivalry between producers and labour unions is tending to take a very different shape in the United States today. It often looks more like a form of association – for which the consumer risks having to pay. The giants of industry have made possible the emergence of giants of labour, whose countervailing power acts as a control on wages and prices.

Nevertheless, since this control can be erratic, mistaken or rigid, and since any errors on such a scale can have appalling consequences, the role of the State has grown more and more, making it the supreme regulator, pledged to ensure the proper working of the whole machine. Since the trauma of 1929, few people contest this need, although it flatly contradicts the tradition of economic liberalism.

Obviously, the economic evolution of the United States has compelled the Federal State to intervene, with care, as a 'countervailing power'. It was no longer a question of intervening blindly, as in the anti-trust measures that followed the Clayton Act of 1914. What it now had to do was to analyse in depth the various elements in the economic situation, to predict its likely development, using all the tools of modern economic science, and to be ready at any time to act in this sector or that, whether to mop up unemployment, stimulate production, curb inflation or whatever was needed.

It is easy to see why the size of the Federal Administration has grown since the New Deal. Whereas Herbert Hoover had a staff of only thirty-seven, Harry S. Truman had 325 officials and 1,500 other employees. In the past, the White House alone was big enough for the work of the Presidency. Today, there is also an Executive Office Building – and that is already overcrowded. Little by little, power is being concentrated in the White House, and the whole country is feeling the effects. A large bureaucracy is backed by an army of expert technicians, immune from the uncertainties of the old spoils system, which often led to officials being replaced according to the results of elections. This new permanence in the bureaucracy is a revolution in itself. These days, the President is in charge of well-qualified executive personnel.

The whole great system of the Federal Administration, organized to deal with the decisive matters which can and should guide the economy, finds itself confronted at the same time by America's social problems. Can even a limited degree of economic intervention take place without intervention on social policy too?

As soon as the State takes some responsibility for economic organization, it becomes responsible for social injustice. It can no longer ignore those Americans who are not organized, who are on the fringes of the labour unions or completely outside them, like the 2 million farmworkers who have no rights and who form a rural proletariat of outcasts. Should there be a minimum wage? Should America move towards a system of social security on European lines?

If it did, there would be a social policy, in an affluent society which has solved many old problems but also created new difficulties, some of them needing urgent attention. It would certainly be a further break with the traditions of American civilization, which is ferociously individualist and which above all believes in the ability of people to 'make it' on their own. Almost all citizens of the United States dislike the idea of the State's intruding into the way society works. The question is whether, today, that can be avoided.

To illustrate the problem, and the need to make a choice, consider the reactions of Soviet citizens who took refuge in the United States after the Second World War, and whom a sociologist asked for their impressions. Generally speaking, they recognized that their material life was better; but they very much missed the free medical treatment and, still more, the equality among all patients that they had enjoyed in the Soviet Union. Even a visitor from France realizes, once in the United States, how valuable the French social security system is. For all America's wealth, it has nothing equivalent to offer. A young teacher in a big American university suddenly finds that he has an incurable disease. He can no longer work. What will become of him? He failed to take out insurance, you are told. So he and his wife and children lose house and home . . .

Many authorities believe that America should and eventually will adopt a social welfare policy. Public opinion is becoming aware of the problem. Despite special pleading by certain newspapers, Federal taxes are no longer seen as an unfair punishment imposed on the strong and able producers of wealth to benefit the lazy and incapable. Ever since the New Deal, the Federal Administration has been regarded 'as essentially beneficent', and in any case necessary.

This immense change is altering and diminishing, more and more, the role of the individual States, which used to be virtually autonomous republics. It may also profoundly transform the structure of American society and civilization – and all the more so because the United States has begun to revise its view of its role, its tasks and its responsibilities in the world.

The United States in the world

In this century, after a long tradition of general isolationism, the United States has rediscovered the world. This has presented it with a series of new and often painful problems. Instinctively, it would be glad to ignore them. But the very might of the United States inevitably involves it with the rest of the world: in foreign policy, as in domestic affairs, it has no choice. The world has become too small; and anything that America does, intentionally or not, has repercussions on a global scale.

It is very hard to realize to what degree isolationism has been a basic feature of the United States. It arose in part from a feeling that emerged very clearly as soon as America was independent – the sense of having founded a new world, entirely different from the Europe of the past, and very much better. Psychoanalysts have called this a 'revolt against the parents'. But it was encouraged also by Americans' awareness of having made their own history, independently, in the broad new expanse of the American continent and the security that distance gave them.

America, in fact, was free to concern itself only with what happened within its borders and to maintain prosperity there; free to erect protective tariffs that cut it off like a Great Wall of China with no fear of threats from any neighbour; free to expand without shame or remorse. Its own conquests by land simply enlarged its territory; others' conquests by sea were appalling colonial adventures. In the nineteenth century, the only inescapable ties it felt were with the rest of the American continent: in 1823, that solidarity was expressed in the Monroe Doctrine of 'America for the Americans'. The message – for it was indeed a message, and from James Monroe, the President of the United States – also in effect affirmed the United States' lack of involvement in European affairs. Both the positive and the negative aspects of the Monroe Doctrine were often repeated and reaffirmed in later years.

But the rest of the world could not be ignored: it was linked to America by trade, imports and exports, and by diplomatic relations. In 1898, a wave of belligerence even took the Americans to Puerto Rico, where they remain, to Cuba, which is no longer theirs, and to the distant Philippines, which they have never really left, even after Philippine independence. The world has also flocked to America, with its hordes of European, Japanese, Chinese and

other immigrants. In a natural reaction which experience proved
to be dangerous, the United States closed its doors to immigration
from 1921 to 1924. It was perhaps the most disastrous decision that
could have been made from the point of view of Europe and the
world in the unhappy, crisis-filled years after the First World War:
in effect, it removed a safety-valve.

In 1917 and 1918, the United States had played a decisive part
in the First World War. But after the Treaty of Versailles, which
it had instigated, it withdrew from active international politics,
and did not join the League of Nations. It abandoned the world to
Britain's false and fragile domination – an ancient achievement
relying on lengthy sea-routes and left in place, as we have seen, by
the war. One of America's more important reasons for intervening in the war in 1917 had no doubt been to safeguard Britain's
world position, which suited the United States, if only because it
helped guarantee the future of Anglo-Saxon civilization – *their*
civilization.

The well-meaning Woodrow Wilson had not wanted America
to turn in on itself, but he had failed to prevent it. By contrast
with that failure, can Franklin Delano Roosevelt be judged to
have succeeded in the various 'summit' meetings at Casablanca,
Teheran and Yalta which preceded his own death and the end of
the Second World War? He certainly helped to reshape a world
whose future was admittedly hard to predict. But did he not
concede too much to the needs of the moment and to principles
that were even less valid than those of Woodrow Wilson, and
often morally debatable? It was certainly in line with American
tradition to encourage the liberation of the colonial empires; but it
also meant weakening the West and, sooner or later, calling into
question the status of Latin America, which in economic matters
could be regarded as a 'colonial' dependency of the United States.
Then, at the same time, to let half of Europe fall under Soviet
domination was a very far cry from the sacrosanct principle of
self-determination. But Roosevelt believed that world peace
required small countries to cease their trouble-making. He wanted

to disarm the whole world, with the exception of the then Big Four – China, the USSR, Britain and the United States. Perhaps he was still nostalgic for isolationism: if we are obliged to concern ourselves with the rest of the world, let us at least make sure that it keeps quiet . . .

This is a view of Roosevelt and his policies that has been expressed in the United States itself. It is certainly open to question. But is fairly widely shared among non-Americans, especially in the West. These observers from outside the New World believe that the United States, without having wished it or realized it in advance, has assumed the leadership of the world. They also believe that America has often thought problems to be simple, a matter of common sense and good will, and any difficulties the outcome of prejudice or selfishness on the part of the Old World. In fact, quite a few of its policy decisions have been unfortunate, and have got out of control. They have proved that loans and good intentions are not enough as means of world leadership, and that domination by trade and money, however legitimate from America's traditional viewpoint, today arouses almost as much mistrust as the old colonial domination that it resembles. The Americans, meanwhile, have tended to believe that their failures were a proof of ingratitude or envy on the part of the peoples they had helped or sought to help.

In fact, like everyone else, they have had to serve their apprenticeship, and take the precise measure of a world they had so long ignored or tried to ignore, a world which now, for their own safety's sake, they must watch over and if possible lead. They have taken this task seriously and recognized some of their own errors. That too is an American tradition, both likeable and fruitful: to believe in what one is doing, but be ready to admit one's mistakes. The sooner one corrects one's aim, the sooner one is likely to hit the target.

An example of this was President Kennedy's initiative in gathering round him the leading intellectuals and economic and political experts of the day, to make a serious study of the problems he faced. Reporting on their discussions, a journalist wrote on 21 May 1962: 'After getting the "talents" and "brains" around him to work at full pressure, he made a synthesis of their conclusions as a guide for future policy. Uncertainties remain, here and there. Some options are still open. But the essential line he has chosen is clear. For the first time in many years, we know quite a lot about the intentions of the US President.' That should not be attributed only to the President's own efforts, or to those of the intellectuals and Harvard professors he summoned to clarify the political agenda. In reality, during the tense and dramatic years between the Marshall Plan and the Korean War, and through later dramas – Berlin, Cuba, Laos, Vietnam, the Middle East, China, Eastern Europe and the USSR – the United States and its public opinion have realized both the huge extent and the necessary limits of their world role and responsibilities. The days of isolationism are long gone.

Power entails responsibility. The emergence of the United States as a world leader – a role which it has had to assume for fear of dangerous instability – is one result of the prodigious growth in its power. To describe that power, we need quite a number of adjectives: economic, political, scientific, military and global.

The power of the United States became obvious with the end of the Second World War and the dropping of the atomic bomb on Hiroshima in 1945. It immediately posed the problem of European and world leadership in the terms of a duel between East and West. In the past, Europe had almost always been divided into two rival camps, whose membership varied according to which leading nation was the source of the danger or the threat. In the years after the Second World War, the whole world lived according to this ancient pattern, which Raymond Aron aptly called 'bi-polar'. It was not only ideology that divided the free world from the Communist bloc: indeed, as the years went by, they began to share points of resemblance. The Communist world started to organize its industry in large units, and the free world started to enlarge the role of the State.

Leadership, in the postwar world, seemed to offer two alternative power centres: either Washington or Moscow. The neutrals in the Third World, and the allies or satellites of the superpowers, were little more than spectators at the drama that so much affected them: their only role was to add their own very modest weight to the balance. The superpowers might dominate them, but they equally had to woo them, attract them and keep their loyalty.

In 1945, the United States was the winner, and was lulled by its superiority, confirmed decisively and tragically by the bombs on Hiroshima and Nagasaki. On 12 July 1953, when the Soviet Union exploded its first hydrogen bomb, equilibrium was restored. In 1957, with the launching of the first Sputnik, the Soviets won an important point, all the more important because the conquest of space meant the construction of very long-range missiles, capable of striking targets more than 6,000 miles away. In the years that followed, achievements by one side or the other alternated, maintaining a precarious balance of power. The armaments built up on either side were more and more terrifying in scope and scale, and the Cold War was intensified by the mutual fear they aroused. No less afraid and angry were the other nations of the world, following the drama with open eyes and empty hands. For, while the balance-of-power policy pursued by Washington and Moscow was neither better nor worse than that of Europe in the past, the fearful weapons it involved posed a very different threat. Humanity was in danger of destroying itself.

That struggle obsessed the United States, affecting not only its policies but also its life and thought. The year of the Soviet hydrogen bomb was a turning-point like 1929, for very different reasons but with no less impact on people's minds. The tension of the Cold War frayed their emotions, their imaginations and their hearts. It distorted everything, replacing America's normal climate of freedom with the mistrustful psychology of war. The McCarthyite panic of the 1950s was one of the symptoms; and the fever took a very long time to disperse. It seemed as if the whole world might be dragged into the same destructive state of mind.

The golden rule for world peace is surely to think with, not against; and for a whole generation both the United States and the Soviet Union obstinately thought against each other.

From both sides, denouncing each other and piling up weapons of defence that neither dared use, the Cold War exacted a heavy price.

Let us close that sorry, bygone chapter and finally consider American novels. Their rich and complex evidence will suggest an appropriate verdict on the civilization they interpret. To be complete, we ought no doubt to call as witnesses the rest of literature, from poetry to theatre and cinema, as well as art, architecture and the natural and social sciences. The flowering of American culture and intelligence includes the economists of Harvard and Chicago just as much as the artists, the toolmakers, the functionalist designers and the industrial technologists.

But in this brief summary we have to choose; and we choose the testimony of the novel for two reasons. First, because for many years it has had a great influence on European and world literature; and secondly because its development since the beginning of the twentieth century sheds light on the development of American life.

American literature was 'discovered' by Europe around 1920–25; but its reputation in Europe grew particularly in the years that followed the Second World War.

Large numbers of translations, presented and annotated by writers like Jean-Paul Sartre, André Malraux or Cesare Pavese, were eagerly welcomed; and the influence of American novelists was so obvious, not only in Britain but also in France, Italy and Germany, that one critic called that period 'the age of the American novel'. It was also the age of 'Americanism', whose traces could be detected in jazz, in dance, in clothes, and even in the art of the cartoon, of which the *New Yorker* offered splendid examples whose style was sometimes copied abroad.

In the novel, what Europeans discovered was a new kind of

writing, a narrative technique very different from their own tradition of the psychological novel. It was what has been called 'an art of bare and objective reporting', 'a photographic art', whose aim was to show, not to comment. To plunge the reader into a character's mental world, the novel made him feel directly, brutally, the sensations and emotions the character experienced, without ever trying to make sense of them. It was the method of the cinema, whose influence here was very clear.

For Europeans, the American novel was marked not only by this technique, but also by a climate of violence and brutality. It was, wrote a French critic,

literature made by and for the cinema, coloured by the habit of 'hot news' and the detective story . . . brutal, passionate, feverish and frenetic, without an ounce of refinement, literature like a blow of the fist, enjoyed despite or because of that, according to taste. It is fast and hard: there is something healthy, lively, and strong about it which at present is found nowhere else.

In reality, these words describe a certain movement in the American novel, called by the Americans 'naturalism', which developed between the two wars: its leading representatives included Ernest Hemingway, William Faulkner, John Steinbeck and John Dos Passos. These writers were all born between 1890 and 1905. By their age and their work, they belonged to an earlier generation, more and more remote from the way the American novel developed after the Second World War. This was away from naturalism and towards an older tradition – no less brilliant and original, but less familiar to the continental European public: the nineteenth-century tradition of Herman Melville (1819–91), Nathaniel Hawthorne (1804–64) and Henry James (1843–1916).

What is pertinent to our purpose is the general movement, and what it reveals about American civilization. One constant fact is worth noting: writers do not enjoy in the United States the natural, respected role that 'men of letters' tend to have in Europe. The American writer is always an isolated individual. He lives on the margin of society, and very often comes to a tragic end after a more or less brief success. 'There are no second acts in American lives,' said one of them, F. Scott Fitzgerald (1896–1940); and his remark applied to him and a number of his colleagues, few of whom lived to a successful old age. Characteristically, then, the American writer is an asocial being who is not content merely to express his revulsion or his unease at the world around him, but lives out his rebellion and constantly pays the price in pain and solitude. So the evolution of the American novel faithfully reflects that of America's social tensions.

In the nineteenth century, the spectre haunting the background of Melville's and Hawthorne's sombre works was America's Calvinist Puritanism. It gave them their obsessive theme of the tragic struggle between good and evil – even if, at the same time, they rejected the weight of that obsession. Both Melville and Hawthorne in a certain sense denounced the society they lived in; and in both cases it exacted its price.

With the beginning of the twentieth century, there was a general movement against the intransigence of Puritanism. The Puritan tradition is still powerful, notably in the social taboos which have in some respects taken over from moral taboos in the United States. But already by the end of the nineteenth century Puritanism had ceased to be the symbol of society's misdeeds. It was then that naturalist novels in the manner of Emile Zola began to appear, often with Socialist leanings. They coincided with the huge expansion of America's power in the years after 1880.

From then onwards, until the Second World War, industrial and capitalist society – the 'futurist' side of American life – became the favourite target of literary non-conformists. One of them was Sinclair Lewis, whose well-known novel *Babbitt* (1922) was a vengeful caricature of the American businessman; but there were also the voluntary exiles who lived in Paris or elsewhere in Europe between the wars: Hemingway, Fitzgerald, Dos Passos, Henry Miller and Katherine Anne Porter – the 'lost generation' as they were called by Gertrude Stein, one of their number whose

Parisian salon was a rallying-point for such Americans abroad. Other rebels included James Farrell, Faulkner, Steinbeck, Erskine Caldwell and Richard Wright. There was a whole generation, in fact, of 'left-wing intellectuals'. They were scandalized by the trial and execution of Nicola Sacco and Bartolomeo Vanzetti in 1927 (Dos Passos himself was imprisoned on that occasion), by the Spanish Civil War (see Hemingway's novel, *For Whom the Bell Tolls*), by Mussolini's aggression and by attacks on Roosevelt's New Deal. Many of them saw Socialism as a hope of salvation for the society of their day.

The Second World War and its aftermath, the beginnings of the Cold War, overthrew that belief. American novelists first rediscovered a sense of solidarity with their own country, then realized the hollowness, for them, of the Marxist dream. The new American generation was far removed from social realism. It preferred novels in which symbols, poetry, and art for art's sake reclaimed their place. It looked back to Henry James, to Melville, and also to Fitzgerald, a very individual member of the 'lost generation', who was only forty-four when he died. Had rebellion ceased to be at the heart of American literature? For a time, it seemed so, with the sharp recrudescence of nationalism after the war, as well as the emergence of a generation of university writers who enjoyed some security and so more willingly identified themselves with their own civilization. But those same years also saw the appearance of the 'beatniks', young intellectuals who completely rejected the norms of the society around them, and in this sense resembled their elders in the 'lost generation', but were otherwise utterly different. The men and women of the 1920s and 1930s, who had believed in the future of the Left, were succeeded by a group whose only refuge was art, alcohol or drugs, and whose main theme was that of solitude and 'incommunicability' in a world now signifying nothing.

But let us not forget that America lives in advance of modernity. It is still the country of the future – and that, at least, is a sign of hope and a proof of vitality. Its huge resources will surely enable it

to recover its old optimism and self-confidence. Claude Roy wrote
in his *Clefs pour l'Amérique – Keys to America*:

America is one of those places in the world where, despite everything,
humanity's *potential* continues to flourish . . . Coming back from the
United States, one is completely confident that a new kind of people can
be born, more certain of their ability, more imbued with wise, down-
to-earth, practical contentment. We may make fun of the refrigerators
and vitamins, the accumulation of gadgets . . . But I do not believe that
we have the right to make fun of a certain type of American who has
already mastered the art of living and asserted the power of humanity
over what once seemed ineluctable fate.

23. An English-speaking Universe

———

From the eighteenth century until at least 1914, London was the centre of the world. Even a brief visit still reminds one of its greatness: Buckingham Palace, St James's Palace, Downing Street, the Stock Exchange, dockland on the lower reaches of the Thames – all these continue to evoke the past. More than anywhere else in the West, the British Isles have established outposts over distant seas. Who can fail to admire such immense success? Rudyard Kipling divided his life between India, a house in South Africa, a North American ranch, Egypt, and many other places. He was right in thinking that Britain could best be understood from afar, from its warlike imperial frontiers, and especially from India. That may be why one of his French friends, arriving in Algiers one day in 1930, cabled him: 'Now that I am in Algiers, I shall at last understand France.'

Little remains of either the British or the French Empire. But to the British the idea of Empire still has special importance. Much more than in France, it accounts for a number of institutions and political reflexes. Hence the agonizing choice that Britain seemed to face when contemplating joining the European Community: should she opt for the Commonwealth or the Common Market? To choose the latter meant joining forces with continental Europe, from which she had hitherto preserved 'splendid isolation'; it appeared to imply abandoning the world dimensions of which she was justly proud, and renouncing one of her most powerful traditions.

★

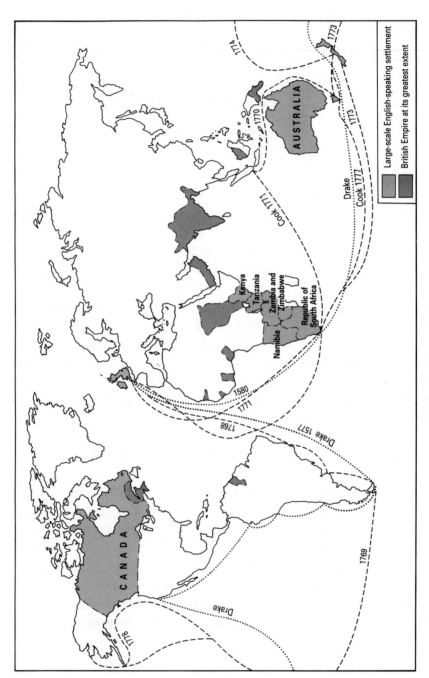

21. *The English-speaking universe*

In Canada: France and Britain

Britain lost 'America', but she kept Canada: she even helped it to extend from the Atlantic to the Pacific (*a mari usque ad mare* – from sea to sea). The essential dates in this process were: 1759, when Montcalm was defeated outside Quebec; 1782, when the British and American 'loyalists', still loyal to the King after the revolt of the American colonies, reached Ontario and the Maritime Provinces; 1855–85, when the Maritime Provinces and their British inhabitants grew more and more prosperous, their ships and sailors on the Atlantic more than rivalling those of the United States; 1867, when after many mishaps the Dominion of Canada was founded, consisting of Ontario, Quebec, Nova Scotia and New Brunswick. In 1870, Manitoba joined the Dominion; in 1871 British Columbia; and in 1873 Prince Edward Island, the seventh province. Between 1882 and 1886, the Canadian Pacific Railway was built, 'virtually along the frontier with the United States'; it made possible the colonization of the prairies, from which the 'half-breeds' (born of French Canadians and Indian women) were driven out. Even so, the Canadian pioneers were of fairly mixed stock. They advanced Westwards much like their United States counterparts, founding two further provinces – Alberta and Saskatchewan (1907). Newfoundland, finally, became the tenth province after a plebiscite in 1948.

French Canadians today make up a third of Canada's population: they number some 6 million people. Confined (so to speak) in the immense province of Quebec, they broadly occupy the Eastern outskirts of Canada, the estuary of the St Lawrence River and its lower and middle reaches. Although encircled, they are none the less deeply entrenched.

Today's French-speaking Americans are the descendants of some 60,000 peasants from Western France, divided between the Mississippi and the St Lawrence. When they were abandoned by the Treaty of Paris in 1763, they managed to hold the province of

Quebec and strike deep roots there. French Canadians are peasants, not farmers like their English-speaking compatriots. They were not tempted by the call of the West: they only slowly moved to the towns, and took a long time to be attracted away by the factories of New York or Detroit. As a people, they are lively, straightforward and cheerful.

British Canada, which established itself to the West, cut off the French Canadians from the great expeditions to the heart of the continent, and in a sense encircled them: the Maritime Provinces, the United States and Ontario actually surround Quebec and make it a kind of insular territory. French Canada accepted that fact. It clung to its land; it remained strictly faithful to its clergy – which was its salvation after 1763; and it retained its language, which essentially is eighteenth-century French. Today, it has every appearance of a closed, introverted society and civilization – peasant, conservative and with an active clergy which has defended and maintained tradition and spread a classical form of culture.

The break with France in 1763 was a wound that has still not healed: the French Canadians felt shamelessly abandoned. Thereafter, Canada lost touch with 'the old country' – past and present France. What contacts there are do not always bear fruit. For France has changed since the eighteenth century: it has experienced the Revolution, a Republican regime and secularism; it has also kindled the flame of an avant-garde, socially concerned Catholicism, which is revolutionary in its own way.

French Canada, as has been said perhaps too often, finds these innovations hard to understand: it is surprised by them, and shies away. But it too is evolving. Its Catholic, peasant civilization is changing, accepting the needs of progress; its universities are making a huge effort to modernize themselves and to come to terms with the various social sciences. And this whole movement is undoubtedly motivated by stubborn resistance to the other Canada – British Canada – and to 'Americanization'.

British Canadians make up about half (48 per cent) of Canada's population. They have virtually adopted the American way of life (which also affects French Canada). They in fact inhabit a second America. Toronto is its characteristic city, looking firmly Southwards to the United States. Its Americanization is obvious and all-pervasive: in the houses and apartments, in furniture, in cooking and in education, where children are left to their own devices at an early age, and are free to start having girlfriends and boyfriends just like their American contemporaries across the border. Still more, the world of business is organized on the active and powerful American model. In other words, Anglo-Saxon Canada would find it easy to draw even closer to its powerful neighbour after cutting its ties with distant Britain. The most recent immigrants, moreover, mainly located beyond Ontario, come from various countries outside the Anglo-Saxon world, and feel the same attraction. In the end, what preserves Canada's independence is the fact of its internal divisions, and in particular the latent tension between British and French Canadians, which has by no means been removed by economic growth and well-being.

With a population of 18 million in 1962, growing at the rate of 28 per cent a year and reaching 25 million two decades later, and with a land area of nearly 3.5 million square miles (sixteen times the size of France), Canada is an 'international power'. Its economy is rapidly expanding, partly thanks to its many natural resources and its enormous reserves of hydro-electric energy. Everywhere, American-style industry is on the increase, although some older economic activities still flourish – including forestry, with its rafts of logs floating down the great rivers.

What is more, Canada is independent. Its allegiance to the British crown is no more than theoretical, and the Governor-General who represents the monarch has only a ceremonial role, and is actually a Canadian.

These political and economic facts, however, cannot remove the tensions which, whether deliberately or not, tend to isolate French Canada. After Paris, Montreal is the biggest French city in the world; but it is visibly dominated by 'British' banks, hotels and shops, and its business life is conducted in English.

British Canada may be richer than French Canada: but economic grievances are not the main problem. The really divisive factor is the rejection of one civilization by another. It may seem surprising that Canada, alongside the United States with its prodigious example of rapid and total cultural assimilation, should still after two centuries not have fully absorbed 60,000 French people – although by now they number 6 million. Perhaps it was because the British, not always intentionally, kept them out of the conquest of the prairies and the West. This may have helped to make them turn in on themselves, a closed peasant community, *ipso facto* traditionalist, and unreceptive to influences from outside. At all events, now as in the past, the division between the two groups is visible and profound.

Might it, at a time which seems to encourage all 'national' demands, eventually take a political form? That would be another matter. Some, it is true, are already talking of independence, and even proposing future dates. There is a 'Lawrentian Alliance' which is explicitly nationalist: but it also presents itself mainly as 'a national educational movement'; and one of its members declared in 1962: 'We are not a mass movement.' In fact, 'a Canadian France' exists, stubbornly determined to live and survive: but, in the world of giants that is America, would it be possible for a mere 6 million people to organize themselves in a political and economic unit that was viable yet truly independent? That is the essential question.

Southern Africa: Dutch, British and Blacks

In South Africa, an old port of call on the sea route to India, and formerly essential for sailing vessels, the British established themselves in 1815. They replaced and dominated the Dutch, who had been there for more than a century, since 1652, just as in 1763 they had taken over from, and imposed their will on, the French Canadians. The result was unrest and serious tension, which culminated in the Boer War of 1899–1902, but also dragged on after it.

White Africa, already rent by these violent internal quarrels, and facing the arrival on the East Coast of immigrants from India (including Gandhi, in 1907), was above all involved in a potential confrontation with the black Africans themselves. In the long run, this threatened to be violent and dramatic; but even now it is still in its early days. The storm – or the solution – is yet to come.

The development of the 'frontier', in the American sense of the word, is the dominant feature of South Africa's evolution. To be understood, it has to be seen alongside many other shifting frontiers – in the United States, in Brazil, in Argentina, in Chile, in Australia and in New Zealand. What is involved here is not so much local or African history, but the history of the world.

In South Africa, the frontier came into being when the first few cautious white colonists arrived (almost at once accompanied by coloured slaves) and came into contact with the indigenous tribes – either the Bushmen of the Kalahari Desert or, to the North and East, under various tribal names, the Bantu, cattle-breeders ready enough to trade their animals for iron, copper, tobacco, or bric-à-brac. Gradually, the frontier began to move inland from the Cape, further and further from the growing township, across a land that was dry and almost empty: because the native Africans, despite thefts of cattle and occasional violent raids, were never strong enough really to endanger the small white colony.

Not until the 'Great Trek' of 1836 did the colonists make a decisive move towards the Orange Free State, Natal and the Transvaal. The reasons help to explain the nature and the problems of this first Northward and Eastward thrust. The stimulus came, not so much from the city of Cape Town itself, which for a long time was modest in size and influence, but rather from the ships that put into port there or further to the North in Saldanha Bay. Disembarking their crews, and leaving in hospital those who were ill with scurvy, they were all anxious to buy food, and especially fresh food. Wheat production in South Africa was not very profitable: it could be bought more cheaply in India, at Surat or in Bengal. Nor was wine-growing: Cape wines at that time had a well-deserved poor reputation. So the local peasants opted for the far more remunerative production of meat. They began to sell carcasses and (despite prohibitions) cattle or sheep on the hoof. Cattle-breeding was not only a less costly investment than crop-growing: it was also far more profitable. What was more, distance was no object, as it was for wheat or wine, since the animals made their own way to the port.

So, from the eighteenth century onwards, the stockbreeders pushed back the frontier and pressed further into the interior. The same movement continued in the nineteenth century, sometimes more rapidly, sometimes less, depending on the number and needs of the ships. The Franco-British wars in the eighteenth century were a great opportunity for profitable trade.

But there were also political reasons for this expansion. In 1815, Britain occupied South Africa; and in 1828 the British government of the Cape Colony issued the famous Fifteenth Ordinance making whites and coloured people equal before the law. In 1834, more-over, slavery was abolished in the British Empire, former slave-owners receiving indemnities (which they complained were too small). In 1828, it had been reckoned that for 55,000 whites in South Africa and 32,000 free blacks, there were 32,000 slaves. Their liberation, and a black African raid on the Eastern frontier in the same year, 1834, helped to trigger off the Great Trek which two years later took the Boers (farmers) or Voortrekkers into the vast grassy plateaux of the Orange Free State and the Transvaal. These set themselves up as independent Republics and were eventu-ally recognized as such by Britain in 1852 and 1854. Ten years earlier, in 1843, she had purely and simply annexed neighbouring Natal.

The vast expansion that began with the Great Trek was the major event in the history of the Afrikaners, akin to the conquest of the West in that of the United States. It scattered the white population over a very broad area, greatly increasing the likelihood of contact and conflict with indigenous black Africans, and especially with the federated Zulu tribes, which were simultaneously expanding Southwards, and were not brought to a halt until 1879.

In 1884, after a war with the Boers, Britain formally recognized the independence of the Boer Republics; but she never fully accepted it. The result was the Second Boer War.

The discovery of gold and diamonds in Witwatersrand had already led to further conflict. Cecil Rhodes, Premier of the Cape Colony, in effect representing both British imperialism and the interests of the mining companies (he was a founder of De Beers), precipitated the major clash. He encircled the Orange and Transvaal Republics by establishing chartered companies in Bechuanaland (Botswana) and Rhodesia (Zimbabwe); he fomented incidents over the foreign labour brought in to work the mines; and in 1895 he connived at the Jameson Raid, a simple act of piracy on land, which obliged him to resign as Premier in the following year.

Open war did not break out, however, until October 1899. When it did, it at once proved disastrous for the British, turning to their advantage only late in the day, partly owing to their establishment of concentration camps during the long period of guerrilla warfare that followed the main engagements. The Treaty of Vereeniging, on 31 May 1902, incorporated the Transvaal and the Orange Free State in the British Empire, but promised them eventual self-government, which they finally received in 1907. Three years later, the Union of South Africa became a dominion under the British Crown.

South Africa's essential problem is that of race relations, usually referred to under the inadequate name of Apartheid.

Since the Second World War especially, South Africa has enjoyed rapid urban and industrial growth. But this has only worsened the human conflicts that threaten it. Today's descendants of the Dutch colonists and French Calvinist refugees, who came to the Cape from the seventeenth century onwards, are for the most part landowners. Their farms are very large, with an average size of some 1,800 acres; but their productivity is generally low on account of the climate and the poor quality of the soil. Only 4 per cent of the country, besides, is under cultivation. What was needed, after the war, was to shift from extensive to intensive farming, with greater mechanization to reduce the enormous numbers of seasonal workers crowded into compounds like those used for industry and the gold mines. There was scope for greater use of fertilizers, for establishing crop rotation in place of uninterrupted single-crop maize production over vast areas, for integrating cattle with arable production and for putting an end to the most backward forms of stockbreeding. All that required time, loans, investments, and also the maintenance of large holdings, big enough to bear the necessary costs.

Many of the big landowners are blunt and sometimes headstrong people who look back nostalgically to distant days before the arrival of the British, when life was simple and 'biblical', with docile black Africans around them, born to be servants or slaves. The great majority of the landowners are descendants of the Boers and speak Afrikaans, a derivative of Dutch. English-speaking South Africans, descendants of the British, are almost as numerous: but they for the most part live in the towns and have been responsible for the industrialization whose profits they have enjoyed.

Until 1939, the British and the Afrikaners tried to keep on good terms with each other, and to deal jointly with the formidable problems of relations between black Africans and whites. But this political understanding broke down when Dr Daniel François Malan's Nationalist Party won the 1948 election and Malan pursued a policy of intolerant nationalism which sought both the 'Afrikanerization' of the British elements in South Africa and, more particularly, absolute segregation (*apartheid*) of South African blacks.

In 1961, South Africa left the Commonwealth. Britain had refused to associate herself with its dangerous racial policy, which had aroused violent condemnation throughout the world. It was surely a policy of desperation. The growth of the population and of the economy threw the situation into sharp relief. The figures were there to show it: in 1962, out of 15 million inhabitants, 10 million were black, 3 million 'European', 1.5 million 'Cape coloured' of mixed race, and 0.5 million Asian. The whites, in other words, made up 20 per cent of the total; and that proportion was only very slightly declining with the passage of time.

The policy of *apartheid vis-à-vis* black Africans and Asians (found only in Natal) was deliberately and efficiently selfish. The succession of laws which put it into effect were like a sea wall continually under repair and reinforcement at any weak points. Their aim was to exclude black Africans (and even Asians) from certain areas, forbid them to own land and confine them to 'Native Reserves' where they were supposed to be protected. This raised two immediate problems. It was almost impossible for black Africans to live on the meagre soil of the Reserves, which not only were too small, but also became unproductive when over-exploited by primitive farming methods. At the same time, white agriculture needed labour – more so even than industry, which was rapidly expanding and which had been designed for mass production by an unskilled labour force. The combined result, against which *apartheid* fought its unceasing battle, was 'the invasion of the white man's territory'. Black Africans outnumbered whites in Durban and Johannesburg; and their incomes were 17 to 40 per cent lower.

To stem the flow from the Native Reserves, the South African Government at that time tried to improve the productivity of agriculture within them, by organizing specialist training; and to bring industry into them or near them. But the latter policy meant depriving white industries of cheap labour at the same time as exposing them to new competition from the Native Reserves.

There was also, at that time, the question of the British protectorates of Bechuanaland (now Botswana), Basutoland (now Lesotho) and Swaziland. Despite the provisions of the Act setting up the Union of 1910, they were never transferred to South Africa; and, although economically close to it, they eventually became self-governing and then politically independent. Similar aspirations were expressed by Namibia, the former South-West Africa, whose SWAPO guerrilla organization fought a long battle to attain that end.

'From many points of view,' it has been said, 'the Union of South Africa is at a crossroads: in the midst of an agrarian and industrial revolution, it is also having to face a social revolution' – which is mainly racial. Now, it is looking for new ways to break the stalemate and bring together its different civilizations, European and local. A viable solution still seems a long way off.

Australia and New Zealand, or Britain at last unchallenged

In three of her overseas settlements, Britain has managed to remain alone: in the United States, at least to begin with, and in Australia and New Zealand. Her solitude has been fruitful. In Australia as in New Zealand, what we see are lively, homogeneous versions of Britain: they are neither Canada, with its two peoples, nor South Africa, with its dramatic problems. These antipodean Dominions, 'the furthest away from the mother country, are the most British of all'.

Both Australia and New Zealand are relatively recent creations, or at least recent recruits to a European, international way of life. Australia dates in this sense from 1788, or just over two centuries ago; and for a long time its beginnings were modest, with 12,000 Europeans in 1819 and 37,000 in 1821. New Zealand dates from 1840, if one ignores the establishment of Protestant missionaries there in 1814 and Catholics in 1837. So it was only a century and a half ago that the British settled in the North Island in 1840, a few years ahead of the whalers, who arrived in 1843. At that time, there were only about a thousand colonists in New Zealand.

Australia and New Zealand owe their homogeneity to the virtual extinction of the indigenous population after the coming of the whites. In Australia, the aborigines almost vanished. In New Zealand, the Maoris were at first decimated, but later somewhat recovered and revived.

Geographically, Australia and New Zealand are very different. Australia is a massive continent; New Zealand consists of islands with high mountains, flanked by stormy seas along a jagged coastline. The history of the native populations offers similar contrasts.

In Australia, very ancient human migration, in the sixth millennium BC, brought the Australoids – apparently adventurous travellers who were soon trapped in a prison where the soil, the flora and the fauna were all extremely poor. The Australasian tribes stagnated and regressed there, always on the edge of famine. They became a living museum of archaic, primeval ways, from which sociologists and ethnographers have gleaned a wealth of knowledge about primitive societies. All discussions and interpretations of totemism are based on the study of these meagre lives.

It is a hard truth that these peoples, still living in the Stone Age, could not survive contact with the whites. Their fragile society fell apart. The last aboriginal Tasmanian died in 1876. In Australia itself, the aborigines were almost all driven back into Queensland and the Northern Territory: there were some 20,000 of them.

In New Zealand, the contact was more dramatic, but finally less disastrous for the native population, the Maoris. These were Polynesians who had settled mainly in the North Island; they belonged to the old and flourishing civilization of Polynesian seafarers. They had probably arrived in New Zealand between the ninth and the fourteenth centuries AD: it marked the Southernmost extent of their wanderings, far from their own tropical countries, lands of the banana, the elephant's ear plant and the yam. New Zealand was very different from that tropical world. What delighted its European colonists was its temperate climate, unlike that of Spain, to which it was diametrically opposite on the globe.

The Maoris therefore had to adapt as best they could to the North Island. They hunted its many birds – its only fauna; they bred dogs, the only domestic animals they had brought with them; they fished, not in the stormy sea, but in lakes and rivers; and they dug up roots. They coped with the cool climate by building wooden houses and spinning linen garments. Hardened by incessant wars among their tribes, they put up fierce resistance to the Europeans.

The wars they fought were murderous for their opponents and still more for themselves. They were finally defeated in 1868. What was more, the new diseases that came in with the whites decimated them. However, at the beginning of the twentieth century the Maoris began to recover from the crisis that had nearly exterminated them. In 1896, they numbered only 42,000. By 1952, there were 120,000, by 1962, 142,000. A high birth-rate, family allowances and employment in cities like Auckland, all had helped to bring about the increase. But they were still only some 6 per cent of New Zealand's total population of 2,230,000, and seemed no threat to the unity of its civilization.

The short history of Australia and New Zealand is marked by a series of economic opportunities, regularly linked to the vicissitudes of the world's economy or its history. These opportunities were sudden, and had to be seized immediately, like a moving train that could be caught or missed.

One opportunity for Australia was Britain's need, after the American War of Independence, to find an alternative to Virginia as a place to transport its convicts. So the first colony in Australia began as a penal colony. The first shipment of prisoners reached Port Jackson (where Sydney now stands) on 18 January 1788. The transportation of criminals to New South Wales was not abolished until 1840.

Almost at once, however, alongside the settlers or small land-owners, 'squatters' began to breed merino sheep for their fine wool. The undemanding tasks of sheep-breeding suited the convicts' temperament; and, at the same time, capital from the big land-owners and brisk demand from Britain and elsewhere made the fortune of Australian wool, which even today is still supreme in the world.

Soon afterwards, from 1851 to 1861, there was a gold rush similar to that in California in 1849. It spread throughout New

South Wales undisciplined bands of 'diggers'; but it helped to people the country and encouraged economic growth. The newcomers had to be fed.

New Zealand, too, experienced successive booms – in wool, in wheat and also in gold, which was first discovered in the South Island, in 1861. The North Island was discountenanced for a time and put at a disadvantage by the gold rush: in 1865, the capital was even transferred from Auckland to Wellington (where it remains). But the New Zealand economy benefited greatly from the stimulus, since here too the gold prospectors had to be supplied and fed. From 1869 to 1879, both islands enjoyed enviable prosperity.

But this is not the place to record in detail these periods of growth and good fortune, often followed by stagnation or slump – as suffered by both New Zealand and Australia from 1929 to 1939. What matters here is to note the successful industrialization of Australia. So far, despite huge hydro-electric resources, New Zealand has not had comparable success.

What is clear in the case of both these distant European outposts is that their fortunes are linked with those of the rest of the world – and much more so than they are inclined to think. Perhaps they are misled by the ease and comfort of their lives, by a degree of well-being that seems all the more striking at a few hours' flying time from the less developed countries of the Far East, where poverty and overpopulation prevail. Australia and New Zealand are 'European' countries in their own right, and not colonies: despite their allegiance and loyalty to the Commonwealth (their biggest supplier and a vital customer), they are both independent States (Australia since 1901, New Zealand since 1907).

The constant concern of Australia and New Zealand has been to keep for themselves the great advantages that their immense area offers, to control immigration, and to maintain at all costs a high standard of living and a pragmatic social policy which works well because it is backed by abundance.

By the beginning of the twentieth century, New Zealand was

already a true modern democracy. It had an eight-hour day in
1856; the separation of Church and State in 1877; votes for women
in 1893, when land reform also broke up the biggest estates;
compulsory conciliation procedures between unions and employers
in 1894–5; and old-age pensions in 1898. There were similar
developments in Australia, where the door to immigration, closed
in 1891, opened for the new and final gold rush that in 1893 led to
the foundation of Coolgardie, deep in the desert of Western
Australia. A social policy on New Zealand lines was established
without difficulty, and under the Australian Labour Party's rule
the country became 'the workers' paradise'.

The vast sums spent on social security had obvious beneficial
effects: on wages, on the standard of living, on infant mortality
and on the expectation of life. But all this welfare had to be paid
for; and it made great inroads on public finance and the national
income. In Australia, with the growth of industry and of giant
cities like Sydney and Melbourne, with nearly 2 million inhabitants, frequent strikes could be extremely expensive. For example,
'according to the *Chamber of Commerce Journal* for October 1949,
they cost Australia 20,800,000 tons of coal between January 1942
and June 1949'. Such demands and difficulties explain why the
Labour Parties of both Australia and New Zealand have had their
reverses at the polls. But these have not led to excessive polemics,
or to extreme changes in basic policy. The practitioners have
changed, but the practice has remained broadly the same.

Is that practice, finally, reasonable? It consists broadly speaking,
in reserving the wealth of a quasi-continent for 15 million Australians (0.75 to a square mile), and that of New Zealand, with more
land than Britain, for 3.2 million inhabitants (4.5 to the square
mile). But in today's world, the 'proletariat at the gate' is growing
at threatening speed. The Second World War brought the Japanese
to the very shores of Australia, which was saved only by the US
naval victory in the Coral Sea, in May 1942. The lesson has not
been lost on the Australian Government, which has tried, not very
successfully, to welcome immigrants to increase its strength and

supply its industry. But New Zealand has continued to go its own way; and affluence there has begun to produce its usual results – a slower birthrate (29 per 1,000 in 1962) and an ageing population, with a death rate of 9.3 per 1,000. New Zealand may be a new country and an early democracy: but in terms of population it is no longer young.

Part III: The Other Europe: Muscovy, Russia, the USSR, and the CIS

The other Europe developed late too, almost as late as America, but on the continent of Europe itself and therefore cemented to the West. This other Europe was Russia, the Muscovy of early days, which became the USSR and then the CIS. What we shall look at is: its origins and its long, long past; its adoption of Marxism after the Revolution of 1917; and its situation after years of Communism – its *entelechy*, as philosophers might say.

And all the time, of course, the subject is the same. A subject whose prestige derives in part from its political Revolution, but also from the speed with which it accomplished its admittedly imperfect industrial revolution. Barely industrialized in 1917, by 1962 it had become a counter-weight to the powerful United States. That spectacular success seemed to hold out hope to the less developed countries. Could they too make a similar Great Leap Forward? Did it depend, or not, on Communism to make it possible?

24. From the Beginning to the October Revolution of 1917

It is not at all easy to summarize in a few pages, in reasonable fashion, a past as long as that of Russia, marked as it is by violent disasters on a scale almost unmatched by the many vicissitudes suffered by Western Europe.

The first difficulty is the sheer immensity of the area in which this complex and many-sided history evolved. Its 'planetary' size also makes it very diverse. The second difficulty is that the Slav peoples came only late on a scene where they were never absolutely alone. The cradle of the Slavs, the ancestors of the Russians, was in the Carpathians and what is now Poland – the only country whose Slav inheritance is really unmixed. So the actor in question is not the first to enter: but when he does he dominates the stage.

Kiev

This vast area, so long virtually denuded of people, recalls the wide open, empty spaces of the American continent. In such immensity, human beings shrink to nothing. Endless plains, giant rivers, regions monotonously unchanging, mile after mile of crushing distance, interminable carrying of boats over land from one river to another: this is Nature on an Asian scale.

To the North of an imaginary line between Kiev and Perm, huge forests continue those of Northern Europe, linking them with the mainly coniferous Siberian taiga on the far side of the Urals. This ancient mountain chain, running from North to South, is a minor barrier rather like the Vosges, but it acts as the conventional Eastern limit of Europe, the frontier between Russia-in-Europe and Russia-in-Asia.

To the South stretches the treeless expanse of the steppes (the word is of Russian origin): the black steppes with their fertile *chernozem* or 'black soil'; the grey or chestnut-coloured steppes with their tall grasses, which in the dry season grow almost as high as a rider on horseback; the white steppes with their patches of saline soil, along the banks of the Caspian Sea.

Russia is made up of these great low-lying lands between the White Sea, the Arctic Ocean, and the Baltic in the North and the Black Sea and the Caspian in the South. The Baltic and the Black Sea are the busiest and most welcoming of these seaways, and essential to Russia, whose vocation, it would seem, is to link them, using them as doors and windows through which to communicate with the West and the Mediterranean, i.e. with European civilization.

But Russia also opens out on to the troubled Asia of the steppes – the Asia of those nomads whose quarrels, wars and incursions we have already traced, threatening invasion as late as the sixteenth century. If these nomads from the East overran Iran and headed for Baghdad, that was no problem: the storm was diverted, and Russia could only profit from the result. But because there was no room for everyone under the Middle Eastern sun, many of these Asian visitors had no alternative but to move on towards the Russian steppes, from the Volga to the Don, the Dnieper, the Dniester and even further. These invasions struck at Muscovy many times.

So Russian territory acted as an enormous frontier zone between Europe, which it protected, and Asia, whose violent blows it painfully absorbed.

Russia could not really exist unless it filled the whole isthmus between the Baltic and the southern seas, and controlled any links between them. For this reason among others, Russian history begins with the Kiev principality in the ninth to thirteenth centuries AD.

The Eastern Slavs, of Aryan origin like all Slavs, brought their tribes and clans, after many adventures, as far as the towns, fields and plains of the Dnieper Basin. This migration, begun in the early years of the Christian era, was completed in about the seventh century AD. In the East, these Slavs found a number of peoples already settled: Finns who had come down from the distant Urals; survivors of the Scythians, Sarmatians and Kama River Bulgarians, all of whom had come from Central Asia; Goths from the Vistula and Niemen Rivers; Alans and Khazars (the latter subsequent converts to Judaism) from the shores of the Caspian and the Don.

This early Russia, a mixture of peoples from Europe and Asia, was that of the so-called 'Little Russians'. The intermingling of races and the prosperity of the towns – that whole burgeoning of life between Great Novgorod in the North and Kiev in the South – depended on the flourishing trade routes that stretched from the Baltic to the Black Sea and beyond. They went as far as Byzantium, whose wealth and luxury dazzled the inhabitants of Kiev, tempting them into foolhardy expeditions against it, and even to Baghdad, then just entering its heyday. From North to South along these routes came amber, furs, wax and slaves; from South to North went fabrics, rich silks, and gold coins. These last have been unearthed by archaeologists all along the trade-routes – a line of golden dots to prove how prosperous they were. Prosperity, indeed, was the key. It supported cities far too big to live off the rudimentary farmland around them: cities which joined hands across great distances, from Novgorod to Kiev, exchanging their goods, their quarrels and their princes.

The Russia of Kiev constantly had to defend itself, especially against attacks from the South. But the far Scandinavian North was always willing to supply it with useful mercenaries – servants one day, masters the next, but always warriors. These 'Normans', or rather 'Varangians' came mostly from Sweden, still rustic and primitive, but sometimes also from Denmark. They were readily attracted by the Dnieper road that linked the Russian towns and led 'toward the Greeks' across this whole wealthy area which they significantly called the Gardarikki, 'the kingdom of cities'. One family of these soldier–adventurers founded the Rurik dynasty. Its origins are obscure, but in the tenth century it dominated Kiev and the other towns. The Russia of Kiev goes under various names: one is 'the Principality'. Another is Rurikovitchi – the dynasty of Rurik.

The splendours of this early Russia can be understood if one looks at their historical context. At that time, the Western Mediterranean had long been closed by the Islamic conquest of the seventh and eighth centuries: so the overland route between Novgorod and Kiev was an alternative link between the countries of the North and the rich lands of the South. When in the eleventh and twelfth centuries Muslim supremacy at sea came to an end and the Western Mediterranean was open again, there was less reason to take the interminable land route, which involved not only river travel but also portage, carrying the merchandise from one waterway to another. The Latin occupation of Constantinople in 1204 put an end to it altogether: the sea had conquered the land.

Even before that date, the Kiev princes found it more and more difficult to defend their frontiers and to reach the Balkans and the Black Sea. An old saying alleged: 'When it comes to eating and drinking, people go to Kiev, but when Kiev has to be defended, there is suddenly no one there.' This was certainly true. The nomads from the South continually hurled their mounted warriors against the lands and cities of the Principality: after the Pechenegs came the 'Turci', and later the Kipchaks or Kumans, whom Russian chroniclers called Polovtsians.

In the eleventh century, some of the people of Kiev moved – one might almost say fled – to the North-West, settling in clearings that the peasants made in the vast forests near Rostov (Rostovlaroslavski, a small Northern town, not to be confused with today's Rostov-on-Don). There, a new Russia took shape, and a new mixture of Slavs and Finns. The latter, of Mongoloid origin, made up the bulk of the population: together, they formed the group known as the Great Russians. This new Russia, barbaric but robust, had already emerged before the lights of Kiev were extinguished. In fact, the powerful Mongol attack which overcame Kiev on 6 December 1241, destroyed a State that had long been losing ground. Five years later, a traveller saw only 200 poverty-stricken houses where the great city had once stood.

The old Russian cities were Western cities. For centuries, the Russia of Kiev was renowned for its material success and the splendour of its cities. There was no trace then of any difference or time-lag between Eastern and West Europe.

Comparative historians have nevertheless noted that the cities of the Kiev Principality differed in some respects from their contemporaries in the West. The latter were surrounded by a sprinkling of small towns, often almost villages, which shared the tasks of their big neighbour. The Russian cities were not. Nor, more especially, were they sharply cut off from the surrounding countryside. Thus, the lords of the land round Great Novgorod sat in its assembly, the Veche, whose decisions were law in the city and in its vast hinterland. They were its masters, together with the Council (*Soviet*) of leading merchants. And in Kiev, pride of place went also to the lords or boyars who made up the *druzhina* or guard of the Prince. These, then, were 'open' towns like those of antiquity, such as Athens, open to the patrician eupatrids of Attica, and not at all like the towns of the West in the Middle Ages, closed in upon themselves, jealously guarding the privileges of their citizens.

The Russian Orthodox Church

Through its conversion to Orthodox Christianity, the Kiev Principality determined Russia's future for centuries to come.

Kiev's trade routes, in fact, carried not only merchandise but also the preaching of missionaries. The Principality's Christian conversion resulted from the policy of Vladimir I also known as St Vladimir or Sunny Vladimir. For a time he had thought of adopting Judaism for himself and his subjects, but he was dazzled by the beauty of Byzantine ritual. In about 988, he officially converted the whole population: the people of Kiev were Christened *en masse* in the waters of the Dnieper. But in fact the new religion had been spreading, especially in the South and in Kiev itself, for more than a hundred years. This had been part of the general movement that had followed St Basil's decisive mission to the Khazars in 861, the conversion of the Moravians in 862, the Bulgars in 864 and the Serbs in 879. The conversion of Russia, therefore, was only one event among several. It was a further proof of the exceptional influence enjoyed by the old Byzantine Church, after the iconoclast dispute had at last been settled at the Council of Nicaea in 787 – a sign of return to health in a Church whose preaching then reached out to the heart of distant Asia.

But it took some time before Christianity thoroughly penetrated first Little Russia and then Great Russia. Its great successes came later. The cathedral of Santa Sophia in Kiev was built between 1025 and 1037, and Santa Sophia in Novgorod between 1045 and 1052, while one of the first monasteries, the Monastery of Caves, was founded in Kiev in 1051.

The fact is that town and country dwellers in Russia were attached to their pagan cults, and that these were eradicated none too rapidly and none too well. Pre-Christian beliefs and habits of mind survived in some cases into the twentieth century, especially as regards marriage, death and healing. They permanently coloured Russian Christianity, whose special contribution to Orthodox liturgy, like its cult of icons and its emphasis on Easter celebrations, has often been underlined.

The fact that the world and civilization of Russia were sucked into the orbit of Byzantium from the tenth century onwards helped to distinguish Eastern from Western Europe.

The differences between Catholics and Greek Orthodox Christians, often explained in various different ways, pose a major problem which it is more important to formulate (if possible) than to resolve. From our viewpoint, those differences are mainly historical.

Western Christianity has been subjected to particular ordeals. It was in part the heir of the Roman Empire. It had conquered that Empire, but its victory had coincided with 'Christian imperialism'. This bore fruit in the West when, after the fall of the Empire in the fifth century, Christianity inherited its tasks and its 'universal structure'. The Western Church was oecumenical: it transcended nations and States; it used its language, Latin, which everyone shared, as a way of maintaining unity. Finally, it retained the Empire's hierarchies, its centralization, and its ancient, august capital, Rome. Even more, the Church in the West confronted all the political and social problems that were so numerous and pressing in the first Dark Ages of Western civilization. It was the great community that could meet all needs, spiritual or physical: it could preach to the heathen, educate the faithful, and even clear new arable land.

The Byzantine Church, in the tenth century, was part of a solid and still surviving Empire which gave it neither the duties nor the dangers of expansion into the temporal sphere. The Byzantine Empire dominated it and confined it to its spiritual tasks. The Orthodox Church which became that of Russia was less distinct from the laity than was the Roman Church, and half indifferent to political affairs. It was ready to accept whatever national framework it was offered, and little concerned with organization or hierarchy. Its only aim was to impart the spiritual tradition it had imbibed from tenth-century Greek thought.

As the language of the liturgy, the Greek Church jealously preserved Greek, 'regarding it as an élite language of which barbarians were not worthy'. In Slav countries, therefore, the liturgical language was Slavonic, into which Sts Cyril and Methodius (between 858 and 862) had translated the sacred texts, for use by the various Slav peoples they had undertaken to convert. They had had to invent an alphabet for it, since the Thessalonian Slavonic into which they were turning the Scriptures was only a spoken language. Hence the importance of liturgical Slavonic, that first written language, in the cultural history of the Slav peoples.

The difference between the spiritual traditions of the two Churches can be seen in several ways. Thus, for instance, the word for 'truth', in Greek and still more in Slavonic, means 'that which is eternal and constant, really existing, outside the created world' as our reason perceives it. So the word *pravda* means both 'truth' and 'justice', as distinguished from *istina* or 'earthly truth'. 'The Indo-European root *var* has given the Slav languages the word *vera*, meaning "faith"' – not truth. In Latin, on the other hand, the word *veritas* (*verité* in French, *verità* in Italian, *verdad* in Spanish), in its legal, philosophical or scientific sense always means 'a certainty, a reality for our reason'. Likewise the word *sacrament*, in the West, involves the religious hierarchy which alone can administer it; whereas in the East it means above all a 'mystery' – 'that which transcends our senses and comes from on high' directly from God.

Certain liturgical details also reveal profound differences. The Holy Week before Easter is marked in the West by mourning, concerned with the passion, suffering and death of Christ the man. In the East, it is full of joy, with songs that celebrate the resurrection of Christ as Son of God. Russian crucifixes, too, show Christ at peace in death rather than the suffering Saviour more familiar in the West.

This may well be because Christianity in the West was confronted from the start with human, collective, social and even legal problems, while religious thought in the East remained more circumscribed, more individual and purely spiritual, easily becoming mystical. Some see in this the origin of the general cultural differences that Alexis Khomiakov described in terms of 'mystical Orthodox and rationalist Westerners'. Is Western Christianity thus partly responsible for the characteristically European spirit of rationalism, which so quickly developed into free-thinking criticism, and against which Christianity defended itself before finally adapting to it?

Russian Orthodoxy, by contrast, has not faced such perilous battles, at least until recent years. But it had to choose, in the seventeenth century, between a purified official religion (purged, for instance, of the habit of making the sign of the cross with two fingers of the right hand, contrary to Greek Orthodox practice) and a popular, conventional, moralizing religion which soon became mutely rebellious. The popular reformers were excommunicated, and there was Schism, *Raskol*. From then on there was a continual campaign against the Raskolniki. And these, of course, were only internal struggles. Attacks from outside, by free-thinkers, scarcely began before the last century of Tsarist Russia. Then after the Revolution of 1917, the Orthodox Church had to fight for its life, for its very existence, by surreptitious actions and the acceptance of compromise. Has it won from this all-out combat some hope of renewal? Is it willing to try new paths, parallel to Social Democracy, such as twentieth-century Catholicism has deliberately explored over the past fifty or more years?

Greater Russia

The second Russia, the Russia of the forests, reached maturity when it too spanned the isthmus between the Northern and Southern seas. This was when Ivan the Terrible (or rather 'Grozny', the Fearsome, 1530–84) managed to subdue Kazan (1551) and then Astrakhan (1556), and control the great Volga River, from its sources all the way to the Caspian Sea.

He secured this double success by use of the cannon and the harquebus. The invaders from Asia, whose horses had carried them 'into the flank of the West', finally fell back when faced with gunpowder. Ivan could not reach the Black Sea, which had been in the hands of the Turks since the fifteenth century, and

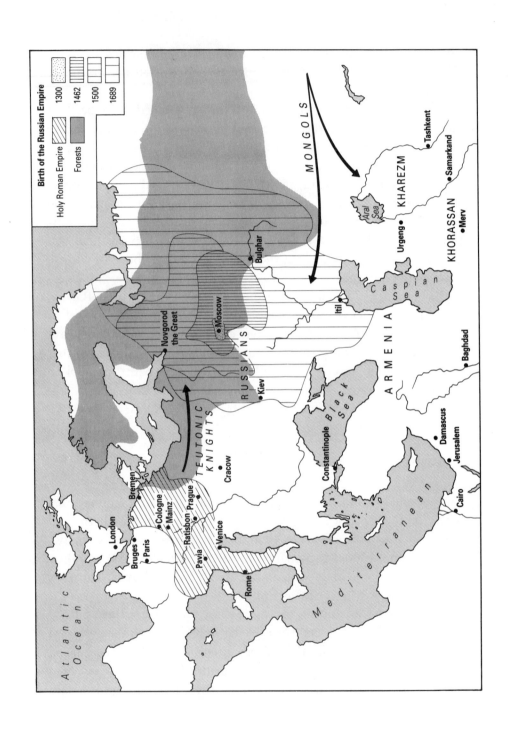

Birth of the Russian Empire

Holy Roman Empire

Forests

1300
1462
1500
1669

MONGOLS

KHAREZM

Tashkent

Samarkand

KHORASSAN

Merv

Urgeng

Aral Sea

Caspian Sea

Itil

Bulghar

ARMENIA

Baghdad

Moscow

Novgorod the Great

RUSSIANS

Kiev

Black Sea

Constantinople

Damascus

Jerusalem

Cairo

TEUTONIC KNIGHTS

Cracow

Bremen

Cologne

Mainz

Ratisbon

Prague

London

Bruges

Paris

Pavia

Venice

Rome

Atlantic Ocean

Mediterranean

which they kept jealously and powerfully defended. But the Caspian, which he did reach, was on the way to Persia and India.

So a new Russia slowly took shape and triumphed, starting from another latitude and in difficult circumstances, very different from the favourable conditions in which the Russia of Kiev had begun life. Here, by contrast, there were poverty, serfdom and feudal fragmentation.

Even before the fall of Kiev in 1241, the whole of Southern Russia – the steppes – had been occupied by the Mongols – the Tatars, as the Russians called them. They had then formed a great independent Mongol State, adding to its vast homeland in the steppes those Northern Russian States and cities that recognized its authority. This State, the Khanate of the Golden Horde, had its capital at Sarai on the banks of the lower Volga.

The establishment and maintenance of the Khanate depended not only on its army, but also on its tax-gatherers and its wealth. This lasted a long time, at least as long as the 'Mongol route' to India and China remained open, until about 1340. It was used mainly by Italian merchants, chiefly from Venice and Genoa. After its closure, although the Golden Horde survived in the South, it gradually lost its hold on the forest country in the North.

It was there that the Principality of Moscow had grown up, in

22. The expansion of Russia

At the beginning of the eleventh century Kiev, on the Dnieper, dominated the Southern part of what is now Russia (some sixty principalities). Its princes became converts to the Greek Orthodox Church. Kiev was an important staging-post between the Slav countries and Byzantium, between the West and the Far East. At the end of the twelfth century, it lost its importance, and then was overrun by the Mongols. In the fourteenth century Moscow, sheltered by its forests, for a time escaped invasion. Daniel, a son of Alexander Nevsky (Prince of Novgorod the Great), guided the first steps of the Muscovite State. Ivan the Great (1462–1505) was the first great enlarger of Russian territory. Under his rule, Muscovite warriors crossed the Urals and established a foothold in Siberia. Peter the Great (1672–1725) was the legendary founder of Russian power, conqueror of the Swedes and the Turks, great reformer and the founder of St Petersburg (1703). The towns of Bulghar and Itil were destroyed by the Mongols in the thirteenth century.

the midst of obscure struggles among many small feudal domains. Founded in the thirteenth century, it gradually 'reassembled' Russian territory (rather as the Capetian kings had recovered French territory to add to the Ile-de-France), and finally threw off the Tatar yoke in 1480. With that, the 'Tsar' of Moscow replaced the Khan of the Golden Horde. The remains of the Horde, mainly the Tartars of the Crimea, between the Volga and the Black Sea, survived until the eighteenth century, owing to support from the Ottoman Turks, whose more or less docile vassals they were.

But this whole process had taken three centuries; and during this time, while Russians and Tatars had very often fought and opposed each other, they had even more frequently been at peace, trading with each other and sometimes helping each other too. The leaders of the Golden Horde had in general favoured and supported the rise of Moscow. Being late, lax converts to Islam, they were largely tolerant, letting the peoples they conquered believe and worship as they wished. At Sarai, there was actually an Orthodox church.

Between rulers and ruled, moreover, many marriages took place – so much so that there was talk in Muscovy of a 'semi-oriental' aristocracy. In the fifteenth century, too, when the decline of Tatar power was already evident, many Muslims settled in Russian States, became Christian converts, and entered the service of the princes, arousing jealousy on the part of native Russians. Several great families, such as the Godunovs and the Saburovs, are of Tatar origin.

The Mongols imposed their prestige on the Muscovite princes for a long time. They came from a more civilized society, a better organized State (on which the Muscovites modelled their own), and a money economy unrivalled in the North. The Russian language today still retains some characteristic words of Mongol origin: *kazna*, the fisc; *tamojna*, the customs; *iam*, a postal station; *dengui*, money; *kaznachei*, a treasurer. This more advanced civilization left a certain Asian imprint on manners and customs in Muscovy, which behaved a little like a barbarian society subjugated and enlightened by its betters. The situation was a little like the coexistence of Christians and their brilliant Muslim invaders in Spain, but with less violent mutual clashes. The Tsar of Moscow began to dominate the Muslim Khan, incidentally, in about 1480 – at the very time when the Spanish Reconquista was about to culminate in the taking of Granada in 1492.

Moscow's predominance was the outcome of countless minor struggles with its neighbouring principalities. It was not assured until the reign of Ivan III (1462–1505), whom some Russian historians have compared and even preferred to Peter the Great. In 1469, soon after coming to the throne, Ivan married Sophia, the heiress of the Palaeologi, the last Greek Emperors of Constantinople. So Moscow, shortly after the fall of Constantinople (Czarigrad), captured by the Turks in 1453, could have become the Third Rome, 'dominating and saving the world'. But this long-term and largely honorific success (the title of 'Tsar', perhaps a corruption of 'Caesar' being adopted by Moscow hereditary princes only in 1492) was less important than victory over the Lithuanians, the Golden Horde (whose tutelage was thrown off in 1480) and the great trading city of Novgorod.

The struggle with Novgorod was long, hard-fought and dramatic. In 1475, Moscow waged a 'cold war' and entered the city peacefully; in 1477–8, Ivan had the bell of the Veche removed; in 1480, he exiled a hundred noble families; in 1487, he drove 7,000 inhabitants out of the city. It was the end of what had been called Gospodin Velikyi Novgorod – My Lord Novgorod the Great.

As much as the idea of being a Third Rome, or the adoption of the new title 'Tsar', what made clear Moscow's ascendancy was the arrival there of Italian artists: Ridolfo Fioravanti, nicknamed 'Aristotle', from Bologna; Marco Ruffio and Pietro Solario, builders of palaces and churches. 'It was then that the Kremlin took its present shape.' The cannon-maker who gave Ivan III's army its powerful artillery was also an Italian, Paolo Debossis. So, almost a century before Ivan the Terrible and the decisive victories in Kazan and Astrakhan, Muscovite power was making its first forceful mark, and this already involved, undoubtedly, renewed contact with the West.

All these successes and innovations demanded an immense effort by the State. Ivan Peresvetov, an ideologue from the time of Ivan the Terrible, worked out a political theory based on terror. And we know that the *oprichina*, the police system set up by Ivan the Terrible, enabled him 'to crush the opposition of the princes and the boyars and strengthen the centralization of the Russian State'.

Russia turned more and more towards Europe. That was the crucial fact in its history in modern times, until 1917 and even beyond. By this policy, which it pursued with tenacity, Russia acquired modern technology, which itself was rapidly improving. The industrial age gave it an early revenge on Asia, which had threatened it for so many centuries. Later, it also stole a march on Europe.

Did Asia play some part in the rise of Russia? Two historians, the Kulischer brothers, believe that it did. In their view, the peoples of Asia, over the centuries, have tilted this way and that: sometimes towards Europe and the Mediterranean, sometimes towards the Far East and especially China. Russia's situation, they believe, has been partly determined by this process, which from the fifteenth century onwards led the nomads to move Eastward. This relieved the Asian pressure on Southern Russia. Tatar Islam lost some of its strength in its Far Eastern adventure; and when the balance tilted back again towards Europe in the eighteenth century, it was too late. The Westward advance of the Kirghiz and Bakshir nomads, caused by pressure from the Chinese in the seventeenth and eighteenth centuries, was halted by a solidly built barrier, which even the semi-Asiatic revolt by Pugachev in 1773–4 was unable to break.

This no doubt over-simple explanation needs to be corrected. Clearly, while there was less pressure from Asia, Russia was also better able to resist it, on account of the superior technology it had acquired from the West and 'begun to deploy. The Russian economy was improving too, if only because of contact with more and more active European trade in the Baltic outlets. Nothing is more typical, either, than the temporary Russian occupation of the Baltic port of Narva in the sixteenth century. That outlet was shut again almost immediately, but it was not long before Russia had its revenge.

The dialogue between Muscovy and the West, which as we have seen began at least as early as the reign of Ivan III, continued and intensified. A traveller from Germany, Baron von Herbestein, was held to have 'discovered' Moscow in 1517, rather as Christopher Columbus 'discovered' America. At all events, more and more people – merchants, adventurers of every kind, vendors of advice or plans, architects and painters – went to this other New World. This was long before Peter the Great, as a child, made friends with the foreigners in the suburb of Sloboda, whom he later appointed as counsellors. In 1571, the Duke of Alba, then Governor of the Spanish Low Countries, warned the German Reichstag that all Christendom was in danger from the smuggling of arms to Muscovy, which might well become its enemy. Twenty years earlier, in 1553, the English navigator Richard Chancellor, having lost his other ships in a storm, reached St-Nicholas-of-Archangel on the White Sea. From there the Muscovy Company, founded by London merchants, traded for a number of years across the breadth of the country as far as Persia.

Closer ties between Russia and the West, already adumbrated, multiplied and loomed larger, like a close-up in the cinema, with the bold, brutally hasty measures taken by Peter the Great (1689–1725) and the long, outwardly glorious reign of Catherine II, Catherine the Great (1762–96). As a result, the frontiers and the external shape of modern Russia *vis-à-vis* Europe were greatly changed. In the eighteenth century, in fact, it continually sought to dominate and extend its own territory, if necessary at others' expense. The main link with the West was organized from St Petersburg (later Leningrad), the new capital built from scratch on the Neva, starting in 1703. With more and more British and Dutch ships calling there, its trade continually grew. Russia was becoming more and more European. Most European countries assisted in the process, but especially the Balts and the Germans. Russia's neighbours had the front seats.

The definitive conquest of the South (begun but not completed by Peter the Great) and the colonization of the Crimea in 1792 took place in a relative vacuum. Hence the 'Potemkin villages' – collapsible façades – which Catherine the Great's favourite, General G. A. Potemkin, had erected and dismantled in the course of her famous journey to the South. Here, there was still no proper link with the Black Sea; it was not fully established until the beginning of the nineteenth century and the development of Odessa by the Duke de Richelieu. It was 1803 before the first wheat from the Ukraine reached the ports of the Western Mediterranean, to the alarm of landowners in Italy and later in France.

Altogether, then, both in general and in the detail of its many endeavours, the history of Russia in the eighteenth and nineteenth centuries is one of all-absorbing 'culture contact', with its illusions, its errors, its absurdities and snobbery, but also its positive results. 'Scratch a Russian and you will find a Muscovite': the saying may have come from Russia, but it was very popular in the West. But why should the Muscovite not remain a Muscovite, with his own tastes, his own peculiarities and his own qualms? In Moscow today, one can visit the Ostankino Palace (now also a museum), which Prince Sheremetyev had had built by his serfs in the eighteenth century in the purest classical style. Visitors are often surprised at the freshness of the internal painting, with its gilt, its decorations and *trompe-l'œil* ceilings, much of it scarcely retouched. The guide explains that the whole building, whose thick walls seem to be of masonry, is in fact made of wood, which resists humidity. The prince had declared, not without reason, that nothing equalled the comfort of Russia's wooden houses, to which he had always been accustomed. So he had kept to wood but dressed it *à la française*.

That was rather typical of eighteenth-century Russia, which called in countless Westerners to help it, even to build its industry

– or what industry there was at that time. Crowds of engineers, architects, painters, artisans, musicians, singing teachers and governesses descended on a country eager to learn and ready to tolerate anything in order to do so. The mass of buildings in a city like St Petersburg; or – a small symbolic detail – Voltaire's library, still intact; or, still more, the enormous numbers of documents in French in the public archives: all these bear eloquent witness to the great apprenticeship which the Russian intelligentsia underwent, and with rather good grace at that.

France, in fact, played a privileged part in this cultural process. In return, it was somewhat dazzled by 'the Russian mirage'. The autocratic Catherine was thought liberal in France because she had *The Marriage of Figaro* staged in Russia before it was authorized by Louis XVI. We should be less gullible, In reality, Catherine II's Government was socially retrograde: it consolidated the power of the nobility and worsened the condition of the serfs.

Only aristocratic culture was readily influenced by Paris and Versailles. It contained small seeds of revolution, and spread to intellectuals and students, who could hardly fail to watch with envy the events of 1789, which shook the old Europe even if they failed to transform it. But it was against the Russian colossus that the French Revolution (or Napoleon's Empire, which was its sequel) came to grief – a fact that deserves to be remembered.

In the background, out of sight but sometimes surfacing, revolution nevertheless ran like a thread throughout the history of modern Russia, from the sixteenth century to the explosion of October 1917.

After the brilliance of the Kiev Principality, which itself concealed many disturbances and social tensions, in the Middle Ages Russia remained backward. Feudalism took root there just when it was waning in the West. From the fifteenth century to the twentieth, Russia became more and more European: but only a small part of the population was involved in the process: a few great aristocrats, some landowners, intellectuals and politicians. What was more, the growth of trade with the West, in Russia as in Central Europe, turned the aristocracy into wheat producers and merchants. A 'second wave of serfdom' was the obvious result, from the Elbe to the Volga. Peasants' liberties lost their meaning. Until then, serfs had had the right, unless they were in debt, to change masters every year on St George's Day. Now they lost it. A ukase by Ivan IV (Ivan the Terrible) in 1581 forbade any further move. At the same time, rent and forced labour weighed ever more heavily on their shoulders.

Admittedly, they could and did still flee to Siberia or to the great rivers of the South. They could even cross the frontier and join the outlaw Cossacks. In this way, the Moscow region lost half its peasants, eager for liberty and adventure. But as soon as the Government established in these distant regions either its own control or that of a nominee, the liberty they had won in practice was contested in law. It was the old, old story of Russian liberties, perpetually won and perpetually lost again. Was it not always the lord's right to seize a fugitive? The Code of 1649 even abolished any time-limit on that right.

Undoubtedly there were huge, widespread and fearsome revolts. In 1669, for example, 200,000 rebels – Cossacks, peasants and natives of Asia – seized Astrakhan, Saratov and Samara; overrunning the lower Volga, they killed landowners and members of the prosperous middle class. Their leader Stenka Razin was not captured until 1671, when he was executed and quartered in Moscow, on Red Square. A century later, in the same regions, Pugachev's uprising had equally massive initial success. Cossacks from the Don and the Ural Rivers, Bakshirs, Khirgiz, serfs from seignorial domaines and from the great iron and copper foundries in the Ural Mountains, all joined the revolt, known as the Pugachevina. The rebels advanced as far as Nijni–Novgorod, hanging landowners as they went and promising everyone land and liberty. They took Kazan, but did not immediately march on Moscow. Pugachev was captured and beheaded in 1775. Order seemed to have been restored.

These facts are very well known. Soviet historians have been glad to make much of them, and with good reason. The more time passed, the worse the plight of Russian peasants became. For when the 'second wave of serfdom' began, there was also 'a second wave of aristocracy'. The boyars of the time of Ivan the Terrible were no longer the boyars of the Kiev Principality, similar to lords of the manor in the West, masters of their own land. Ivan had systematically crushed these independent noblemen: he had executed them by the thousand; he had confiscated their estates and given them to his own men, the *oprichniki* – noble officials who held their lands, or as we might say their 'benefices', only for their lifetime. This being so, the very retrograde reform carried out by Peter the Great was the Entailment Law of 1714, which gave these officials and their heirs, in perpetuity, full possession of the lands they held. So the 'second aristocracy' was confirmed in its privileges, with its ranks fixed for good by the imperial court. Menchikov, Peter the Great's favourite, thus received 100,000 serfs. This showed the double face of Russia in all its contradictions: modernity *vis-à-vis* Europe, medieval backwardness at home.

From that time onwards, a kind of pact united Tsarism with aristocracy that surrounded and served it, always submissive and fearful in face of the master's caprice. The peasants suffered in consequence: they were trapped in insoluble difficulties. Even mass emancipation, in 1858, 1861 and 1864, did little to help. Half the collective constraints imposed on the village, the *mir*, remained in place. Lands recovered from the lords could be bought back. What was more, the landowners still kept part of their domains. The question was not dealt with until 1917, when there was the greatest agrarian explosion in Russian history, a profound and practical reason for the Revolution. Even then, it found no permanent solution: for no sooner had the peasants thrown off their old fetters than collectivization began. Peasants in Russia had a very brief experience of owning their own land.

The explosive rural situation had created revolutionary tension throughout Russian life. It explained the immense and immediate response to the French Revolution of 1789, commented on day after day in all the newspapers, not only in St Petersburg and Moscow, but as far away as Tobolsk in Siberia. The Revolution in France was followed passionately by liberal aristocrats, by bourgeois merchants and by intellectuals and publicists, many of them of humble stock. (See the short study by Michael Strange, *The French Revolution and Russian Society*, which appeared in French translation in Moscow in 1960.) The Declaration of the Rights of Man, the news of riots in France, the spread of the Terror 'touched immediately on the most burning questions in a regime of autocracy and serfdom': they expressed the feelings which, according to one contemporary, could be read in Russia 'in the face of every peasant'.

Other tensions arose alongside this essential peasant problem as industrialization began in the mid-nineteenth century. It was a time when, in the reign of Nicholas I (1825–55), but certainly not at his bidding, Russian literature took giant strides, with Pushkin (1799–1837), Lermontov (1814–41), Gogol (1809–52), Turgenev (1818–83), Dostoyevsky (1821–81) and Tolstoy (1828–1910). All in all, this was an immense period of Russian self-discovery.

New types of revolution or revolutionary unrest soon began and proliferated. There was the limited movement of the 'Decabrists' or 'Decembrists' in 1825; there was the shooting in front of the Winter Palace in 1905; there were the Nihilists in the 1860s; there was the foundation in Minsk in 1898, of the Russian Social-Democratic Party, the first Marxist party; there were the Slavophiles (sometimes chauvinist revolutionaries); there were extreme 'Occidentalists'. Above all it was students, together with intellectuals, young people generally and exiles, who bore the torch of the revolution that was to come. All of Russian history had been kindling its flame.

25. The USSR after 1917

Since we have already glanced at the political, economic, and social antecedents of the Russian Revolution of 1917 and its aftermath, this chapter will be concerned with the more general problems of Soviet civilization: How was Marxism involved in the Russian Revolution? What influence does it have on the Soviet Union in a human sense, quite apart from the plans and statistics, important as they are? Amid all the vicissitudes, constraints and shocks, what are we to make of the present and future of Soviet, now CIS, civilization?

From Marx to Lenin

Karl Marx's thought fairly quickly caught the attention of intellectual and revolutionary circles in Russia, which were favourable to the West and therefore at odds with the Slavophile traditionalists. Thus Marxism very soon won converts among economists and historians at the University of St Petersburg – partly, it was said, in opposition to its conservative counterpart in Moscow.

Marxism was the fruit of collaboration between Marx (1818–83), the key figure, and Friedrich Engels (1820–95) who worked with him for forty years and survived him for twelve. With its elaborate doctrine, it marked an essential turning-point in revolutionary thought and action in the nineteenth and twentieth centuries, arguing that revolution was a natural and inevitable outcome of modern industrialized capitalist society. It seemed to offer an overall view of the world which closely linked social analysis and economic explanation.

Marx's dialectic (the search for truth through contradictions or statement and counter-statement) was inspired by Hegel, although it spurned his philosophy. For Hegel, things of the spirit dominated the material world ('mind over matter'), and consciousness was humanity's essential trait. For Marx, by contrast, the material world dominated things of the spirit. 'The Hegelian system,' he wrote, 'stood on its head; we have set it on its feet'. This did not prevent Marx's dialectic taking over the terms or successive stages of Hegel's: (1) the thesis or statement; (2) the antithesis or negation; (3) the synthesis or negation of the negation, i.e. the statement of an evolving truth taking account of both thesis and antithesis, and reconciling them.

This way of reasoning was always in the background of Marx's arguments. As the Russian revolutionary Alexander Herzen put it, 'Dialectic is the algebra of revolution.' It was certainly the language of Karl Marx, a device for identifying and defining contradictions, once they were 'scientifically' recognized, and then overcoming them. Marxism has been defined as dialectical materialism. The phrase is not inaccurate, although Marx himself never used it and, as Lenin remarked, he emphasized the dialectic far more than the materialism. Following Lenin, others made the same remark about historical materialism, a rather unhappy expression devised by Engels: Marx, it was said, had emphasized the history far more than the materialism. He undoubtedly drew the dialectical arguments for his revolutionary doctrine from an historical analysis of society. That was one of the major innovations in his work.

Western society in the mid-nineteenth century seemed to him to be suffering from a major contradiction, dialectical analysis of which was the basis of Marxist thought. To summarize it briefly: work, for humanity, was a way of being freed from Nature, of mastering it. By working, people became aware of their own nature, which was to be part of a society, as workers among other things. In society, which meant both work and freedom, there was both 'human naturalism' and 'natural humanism'. This was the thesis, the statement about the value and purpose of human work.

Then came the antithesis, the negation. In the society that Marx was studying, work did not free people: it enslaved them. They were not allowed to own the means of production (the land or the factory) and its profits. They were obliged to sell their work, to part with it while others enjoyed its fruits. Modern society had made work a means of enslavement.

So what was the synthesis, the negation of the negation, the way out of that contradiction? When capitalist society (which entailed the selling of people's labour) reached the stage of industrialization, with mass production and mass manpower, it led to the formation of a growing class of wage-slaves, the proletariat. This automatically sharpened the class struggle or class war, and therefore soon provoked revolution.

Industrial capitalism, Marx believed, was the last stage of a long historical process that had brought human society from slavery to feudalism and then to capitalism, first commercial and finally industrial. The world of the nineteenth century had thus simultaneously reached the stage of industrialization and that of revolution, which would abolish private property. The next step would be communism.

But communism would not replace capitalist society overnight. ('Capitalist', incidentally, was a word that Marx used, at least from 1846 onwards: 'capitalism', although very useful, he did not.) As he explained in 1875, there would be 'an inferior stage of communism' during which the new society would emerge as best it could from the old. This stage was known as Socialism: its slogan was 'To each according to his work'. The next and higher stage was Communism proper. It was rather like the promised land. With it, society could proclaim on its banners: 'From each according to his ability (at the production stage), to each (at the consumption stage) according to his needs.' Manifestly, Marx's dialectic was optimistic: it was an 'ascendant' philosophy, as Georges Gurvitch has written.

To Russian revolutionaries, however, Marx's message may well have seemed pessimistic. For the moment, after all, he had concluded that revolution in Russia was theoretically impossible, although he had second thoughts on the subject around 1880, when revolutionary unrest there was once more in the news. In Russia, he thought, the industrial proletariat had not yet fully developed: it would take years for the new conditions created by capitalism's productive power to operate to the full. Only then would there be 'a period of social revolution'. As yet, the time was not ripe.

Marx and Engels pondered, explored and debated this problem, using Britain as an example. When the first volume of *Das Kapital* was published in 1867, Britain was already in the midst of her Industrial Revolution – or, more precisely, in the midst of the difficulties it had caused without as yet providing ways of overcoming them. Marx and Engels also considered the examples of France and Germany, the latter by now only slightly behind the former and rapidly gaining ground. All such examples, of course, were very far removed from conditions in Tsarist Russia.

That being so, how could one expect a social revolution in the name of Marxist principles in Russia at the end of the nineteenth century, where industrialization had made very little headway and where the peasants made up 80 per cent of the population, and industrial workers only 5 per cent?

Lenin was well aware of this contradiction, from the time when he published *The Development of Capitalism in Russia* in 1899, and still more just before and after the Revolution of 1905. Admittedly, as a disciple of Marx, Lenin was the prisoner of doctrines he admired and in which he felt at home. He had very few ideas not already to be found in Marx's writings. On the other hand, although his real talent was for planning revolutionary action, he was far more original, even as a thinker, than is often said.

He came, in fact, from the minor Russian aristocracy, as his voice and accent showed. He was not, therefore, simply a 'representative of the Russian people', its simplicity and its 'practical intelligence'. Nor was he solely a man of action. In fact, when he was accorded 'the honour of cleaning the Second International's Augean Stable', it was because he had already produced original and concrete analyses of its problems and searching criticisms of its practice. When he went into action, it was always after passionate and lucid thought. Wherever he differed from Marx, therefore, it was where disagreement was to be expected: on revolutionary strategy and tactics, which he saw in a Russian context and in terms of relations between the 'proletariat' and the 'Revolutionary Party'.

In a word, Lenin gave politics systematic priority over economic and social matters, and the 'Party' priority over the proletarian mass. He was in favour, one might almost say, of 'politics first'. For Marx, revolution was the result of social explosions that were almost natural events, occurring in their own good time under the pressure of industrialization and the class struggle. The proletariat, herded into the towns as a result of industrialization, was explosive and revolutionary by its very nature. Alongside it, part of the bourgeoisie had been the forcing-house of the new ideologies; but now it had already fulfilled its revolutionary role. On occasion, perhaps, the help of the democratic and liberal middle classes might still be useful: but for a long time Marx and Engels were very hesitant to use it. And after 1848, not without reason, they especially mistrusted the reactionary potential of the French peasants, whom they saw as 'false proletarians' deeply attached to their parcels of land.

Debates about what form revolutionary action should take continued long after Marx's death in 1883. Rosa Luxemburg (1870–1919), from Germany, shared Marx's views. For her, only the industrial proletariat was to be trusted: it must be the sole driving force of revolution, since all the other classes were its enemies. The 'Party', therefore, must belong to the proletariat, which must watch it closely from within and control it. That, she believed, was the only way to prevent its being bureaucratized.

Lenin took a different tack. Like some reformists, he doubted whether the proletariat ('under imperialism') was naturally and spontaneously revolutionary: and in any case spontaneity horrified him. The time had come, he thought, to emphasize the Party and possible alliances which might rally to the proletariat's cause any other oppressed social groups, whoever they might be. In 1902, in *What is to be Done?*, he maintained that, without the leadership of a centralized party of professional revolutionaries, the proletariat would opt not for revolution, but for reformism and trade-unionism, dreaming perhaps of a utopian working-class aristocracy. Was it not the case that in Britain at that time, the up-and-coming Labour Party was having to oppose the Trade Unions' hesitant conservatism, as in France, where the unions were more anti-Socialist than is often thought. Contradicting Rosa Luxemburg and some others, Lenin added that the age of national wars was not yet over, and that there had to be alliances with the liberal bourgeoisie. Furthermore, and still in disagreement with Rosa Luxemburg and 'Luxemburgism', he called for a programme of agrarian reform, and refused in any case to regard the peasants as re-actionary. On that crucial point, he was surely influenced by Russia's revolutionary Socialists. Like them, he saw the enslaved peasantry as the essential driving-force of revolution, and did not intend to ignore its immense explosive power. In the event, it ensured success for the 1917 Revolution. As regards Russia, Lenin had been right.

This is not the place to examine in detail the ideological dis-cussions and declarations that marked and in some cases influenced the development of the Soviet Union after 1917. Suffice it to say that there was a cultural shift, from Marxism to Leninism. The latter was a revised form of Marxism 'reinterpreted', as anthropo-logists might say, to adapt it to the under-industrialized, still mainly agrarian Russia of the Tsars at the beginning of the twentieth century – so near in time still, and yet so far. 'The proletariat,' declared Lucien Goldmann, 'was too small in numbers, and therefore too unimportant, economically, socially and politically, to spark off by itself a revolution which would at once have ranged the rest of society against it.'

The Russian Social-Democratic Party, later the Communist Party, was founded in 1898 by the second generation of Russian Marxists (Lenin, Julius Martov and Fyodor Ilich Dan) with the agreement of the first generation (Georgy Plekhanov, Pavel Axelrod, Vera Zassulich, Lev Deutsch), who while abroad had formed the Group for the Liberation of Work (Grouppa Osvobojdeniya Trouda).

During the Social-Democratic Party's second congress, in 1903 in London, a deep split occurred. On one side were the Bolsheviks (Russian for 'the majority', although in this case it was by one vote); on the other were the Mensheviks ('the minority'), including Plekhanov himself. Why the dispute? Because of Article 1 in the Party's statutes, into which Lenin had introduced measures that went by the name of 'democratic centralism'. They provided for:

- a preponderant role for 'professional revolutionaries', i.e. technicians;
- strict, indeed iron discipline by the Party;
- wider and dictatorial power for the Central Committee over the whole of the Party, and especially its grass-roots organizations;
- if need be, a small Bureau to take over all the Party's powers.

Was that clear enough? It made the Party an autonomous war machine, which the Mensheviks accused of dictatorship and disregard for democratic principles. (Trotsky predicted that Lenin's measures would end in the dictatorship of one man, the Chairman of the Central Committee.)

All the same, there is plenty of evidence that this tactical approach was made necessary by the state of social and industrial development in Russia at the time. In 1905, Lenin attacked the argument advanced by a small number of Socialists who believed, he said, 'that a Socialist (i.e. proletarian) revolution was possible, as if the productive forces of the country were sufficiently developed for such a revolution to take place'. More revealing still is the last-minute argument between Lenin and Georgy Plekhanov, the founder of Russian Marxism, on the eve of the seizure of power by the revolutionaries in 1917. Lenin denied planning to take power: if he took it, he said, it would simply be in the hope of support from the Socialist revolution that was about to break out in the advanced capitalist countries – a hope which the Russian Revolution would soon have to abandon, condemned as it quickly was to stand alone. Plekhanov, reverting to basic Marxist arguments – the weakness of the industrial proletariat, the backwardness of Russian capitalism, the huge majority of the peasant population – warned Lenin that if he seized power he would be forced, whether he liked it or not, to impose dictatorship and terrorist methods of government. Lenin retorted that to talk like that was to insult him. But he seized power, and he unleashed the agrarian revolution, just like Mao Tse-tung thirty years later.

Even so, these problems continued to worry him. When in 1921, with the New Economic Policy (NEP), he for a short time put the machine into reverse, his public statements characteristically echoed the same line of thought that had run through earlier polemics. 'We were mistaken,' he declared. 'We acted as if one could build Socialism in a country where capitalism scarcely existed. Before we can achieve a Socialist society, we must rebuild capitalism.' In the event, the New Economic Policy barely survived Lenin's death. From 1928–9 onwards, Stalin espoused industrialization, which was pursued with whatever means lay to hand. Its difficulties and its achievements are a matter of history.

But let us return to 1883, the date of Marx's death, to illustrate the debate more clearly. Georgy Plekhanov, imagining a case in which the revolutionaries seized power 'by accident' or 'by conspiracy', wrote that 'in those circumstances all they would be able to build would be a Socialism like the Empire of the Incas', i.e. with an authoritarian regime. In saying this, Plekhanov was echoing a remark of Marx's own. Discussing a similar eventuality, Marx had spoken of 'convent Socialism' or the 'Socialism of the barracks'.

To recall these words and these debates, as has often been done, is not to condemn the events of October 1917 and their consequences in the name of some 'pure Marxism' which history has somehow swept aside or scorned. The point is that, by chance, the Socialist revolution occurred in the least industrialized country in Europe at the time. So it was impossible for it to take place in accordance with the Marxist scenario of a seizure of power by the proletariat. Power was seized by the Communist Party (as the Social-Democratic Party became) – i.e. by a tiny minority of the vast Russian population, perhaps some 100,000 people all told. This highly organized minority took advantage of the appalling stampede of 10 or 12 million peasants, escaping from the army and flooding back to their villages. On the way, some of them fought and killed each other; when they arrived home, they began to commandeer the estates of aristocrats, the rich bourgeoisie, the Church, the convents, the Crown and the State.

Lenin is said to have asked: 'If Tsarism could last for centuries thanks to 130,000 aristocratic feudal landowners with police powers in their regions, why should I not be able to hold out for a few decades with a party of 130,000 devoted militants?' He is also said to have remarked, in Napoleonic fashion: 'We'll attack, and then we'll see.'

'To hold out for a few decades' until Russia had reached a degree of development and industrialization that might have allowed a 'reasonable' revolution: that, for years, seemed to be the crucial problem. It was also the motivation for an implacable dictatorship which was never the 'dictatorship of the proletariat' but that of the communist leaders – in the name of a proletariat that did not yet exist. 'Under Stalin, the dictatorship of the leaders even became that of one single man.' The historical example that those sombre and dramatic years in the life of Russia cannot fail to evoke is that of the Committee of Public Safety in 1793–4: but in this case dictatorship did not so quickly fail. The reason was undoubtedly the iron discipline of a single Party which prevented any lasting rebellion: quite the reverse of what happened in Paris in 1794.

★

Marxism and Soviet civilization

For many years the USSR had lived under a political dictatorship, without freedom of the press, freedom of speech, freedom of association or freedom to strike, with a single, disciplined, 'monolithic' Party in which underlying conflicts only came to the surface now and then as dramatic personal confrontations. After the death of Stalin in 1953 there was a certain liberalization – or rather, humanization, since 'liberalization' was then for Communists a dirty word. It was a slow process, but apparently irreversible. And was not the reason for this 'de-Stalinization', as some called it, the fact that the dramatic, emergency days of the Committee of Public Safety were long past? The USSR had not emerged from all its internal difficulties, by any means, but it had joined the ranks of the major industrialized countries, the privileged nations. It had won its place by the sweat of its brow, but it was there. At the same time it had built, whether knowingly or not, some of the structures necessary to a mass civilization. For the first time, perhaps, it had the chance to choose its own road, its own revolution, internally at least – since its role in world politics as a leader of the other Communist countries placed other constraints upon it, from the outside.

Even by then, Marxism had already changed. Fifty years of effort and conflict on all fronts had been a long ordeal. No wonder that during that time Marxism–Leninism, as a State doctrine, while maintaining its cherished themes and doctrines, evolved a great deal. It would have been a wonder had it not.

Official speeches went on repeating the sacrosanct clichés: the class struggle, *praxis*, slavery, feudalism, capitalism, relative pauperization, dialectical materialism, the material base or the coming of a wonderfully happy classless society. But that did not mean that the whole massive ideology of Marxism, like all ideologies and religions, had not by virtue of its own position been obliged to come to terms with real life. In any case, the revolutionaries, like the Russian intelligentsia of the turn of the century before them, had always held that an idea was valid only if it took shape in practical life, in praxis. As a system of tightly knit ideas, Marxism could therefore be valid only if it were embodied in the actual experience of millions of people. And if it 'became concrete' in this way, bringing itself 'up-to-date', experience was bound to rub off on it. Its disciples claimed that 'Marxism was a conception of the world that overtook itself'. Sympathetic observers made the same point. 'Twentieth-century Communism,' they said, 'underwent transformations comparable to those of Christianity in the first to the fourth century.'

One would have to be a casuist to count all the changes, infidelities and heresies of which Marxism accused itself and Marxists accused each other. To catalogue them would not be without interest, so long as no particular detail were allowed to take precedence, however significant it might seem. A catalogue of that sort would make sense only against the practical background that would explain it and be explained by it. Nor is it the clearest or most important way of appraising the Soviet experiment.

In fact, if the years since 1917 seem a long time to those who have lived through their vicissitudes, they are still not long enough to reveal how deeply or otherwise that brutal break with the past, and the ordeals and further revolutions that followed it, have affected the nation's underlying ideological, social and cultural evolution. We should need to distinguish what in all that experience was an aberration (especially but not exclusively in the early transitional years before 1930) and what was not. Only then could we hope to determine what relationship there has been between an ideology imposed by force and a society sucked into an experiment which it had not chosen and which it neither fully accepted nor even fully understood.

How far, for example, was the re-establishment of widely differing wage-rates, already planned by Lenin, an accident, a decision expressing Stalin's all-powerful will, a social necessity or an inevitable economic trend? The result, in any case, was a social hierarchy, with obvious privileges for those in its higher ranks. A Soviet university teacher remarked with a laugh: 'We are the Soviet bourgeoisie.' Of course, such a hierarchy can re-establish a class system only if its privileges, which go with office, can be passed on to the next generation, so that the children gain advantages (education, money or jobs) from their parents' social position. This tendency is natural in every society with a strong family life, and Communism in the Soviet Union has in no way destroyed it. Stalin even strengthened it.

A further basic problem has been agriculture. Soviet attempts to organize it on collective lines were failures, and were resisted by the peasantry, with long memories of their maltreatment by Stalin. But this peasant discontent, so often echoed in muffled form by Russian novels, is surely also a normal and almost inevitable reaction on the part of any traditional culture suddenly torn from its ancient habits by rapid economic modernization. The problem would seem to arise in all countries seeking to modernize at speed, irrespective of the solutions adopted.

It is by no means clear, meanwhile, that the last word has been spoken in the more or less tense dialogue between Soviet ideology and the Orthodox Church – if, indeed, there is such a thing as a last word. In the face of 'religious alienation', the regime adopted militant materialism, aggressive rationalism – not denying God but vehemently affirming human concerns. The Second World War helped to revive orthodox belief, and led to a compromise between the Church and Stalin, who re-established the Patriarchate of Moscow, abolished by Peter the Great. Stalin even made reference, in a speech on 7 November 1951, to Alexander Nevsky, prince and saint of the Orthodox Church. No doubt the majority of the practising faithful are of the older generation. But what are the real attitudes of most people when it comes to baptism, marriage and funerals? The pomp and circumstance with which the State tried to surround civil weddings may be a proof that it had a fight on its hands, or at least had to fill a vacuum.

Finally, with successive generations, the dramas of the past have begun to recede in people's memories. Marxism–Leninism has now moved into the background, rather as Western Cartesian thinking, though still pervasive, has become less conscious as a philosophy. This need not imply that the ultimate ideals of Communism have been totally abandoned: but they are no longer burning issues, to be discussed every moment of the day. Even in the 1960s, out of 220 million Soviet citizens, only 9 million were members of the Party. Marxism–Leninism was their trademark, their watchword, their everyday language. But what about everybody else?

The biggest change that Communism brought to life in the USSR, however, was rapid industrialization, and the hope of successfully completing it by building on its successes, overcoming its difficulties and repairing its failures.

In human terms, the change cost Soviet citizens dear. The leaders of the Revolution in 1917 did not inherit an industrial infrastructure ready-made, 'supplied in advance by capitalism'. They had to build it; and this in part explains the particular nature of Stalinist dictatorship. It took on the basic task 'that elsewhere was performed by nineteenth-century capitalism'. The cruelties of Stalin's regime are not wholly to be explained either as the whims of a power-mad dictator or as the stern necessities of Socialism or Communism. They were also in part a response to underdevelopment, a ruthless State policy devised to invest human labour in the race to industrialize a backward and mainly agrarian country.

How far that goal was attained will be debated by specialists for a long time to come. Statistics are a fertile ground for controversy. Their language is international, so peoples compare themselves with each other like children comparing their height. It is important of course, to use the same units of measurement. Official figures, for example, show industrial production in France to have increased by 7.7 per cent a year between 1953 and 1959 (1953 = 100, 1959 = 156), by 8.3 per cent in Germany (1953 = 100, 1959 = 169), and by 11.3 per cent in the USSR (1953 = 100, 1959 = 190). But these official statistics are not directly comparable. The

West calculates its indices in net value, the Soviets in gross value. The Soviet economist Strulinin showed that industrial production in 1956, calculated in gross value, was 22.9 times that in 1928, but only 14.7 times that if calculated net. With discrepancies on that scale, it was easy to imagine how long the USSR's critics and its apologists could be locked in debate.

However, while the Soviet Union's economic goals remained beyond its grasp, in the 1960s they were not entirely out of sight. Immense progress had been made, with quite extraordinary achievements in a number of places, not excluding Siberia.

Great social changes followed the 1917 Revolution. In all the Soviet Republics, industrialization began to change people's lives; and this fact in its turn affected the life of the Union. Everywhere, new structures began to emerge.

A first major change was the influx of peasants into the towns. The USSR imposed the growth-rate of an American boom on a people traditionally stolid and in 1917 still essentially peasant. Everywhere, tension arose between pace and peace, between the ubiquitous pressure for change and the stolidity which often became stubborn resistance to it. In the Central Asian Republics, the coexistence of Americanism and orientalism was more extraordinary still.

The figures show the scale of the change. In 1917, 80 per cent of the Russian population were peasants, and only 5 per cent were industrial workers. By 1962, the peasants were barely in the majority, with 52 per cent, while the proportion of industrial workers and managers had risen to 35 per cent. Over the same period, the number of bureaucrats had been multiplied by 10, and the number of intellectuals by at least 100. Altogether, there had been a huge drift from the land and into the cities.

The results could be seen almost everywhere. With the exception of the former capital, Leningrad, which retained the metropolitan air it had always had, cities old and new, including Moscow (which had become a sort of gigantic Chicago), took on a peasant appearance. Their life became curiously rural. Intellectuals and students were no exception. 'A new race was created in Russia', invading every sphere of life, from the humblest job to heights of scientific research – the summit of the social scale. Stalin's double programme of industrialization in the cities and collectivization on the land created urban jobs and rural jobless, forcing peasants to seek work in the towns whether they liked it or not – all this in only a few years.

In 1947, peasants were still recognizable in the towns they had invaded: they wore rustic clothes; they moved slowly; they shouted as they scrambled on to buses and trams. Already by 1956 a change was visible. The peasants had become more urbanized, and with a higher standard of living they were better dressed. By 1958, one no longer saw women and children walking barefoot; behaviour in theatres and cinemas was exemplary; peasant boorishness was on the wane. And yet people's rural origins, still so recent, showed in a myriad tiny ways. That is perhaps why in Leningrad, by contrast, everything seemed more urbane, the women more elegant, the language spoken more correct. Thanks also to its physical appearance, admirably restored after 1945, the place gives the impression of an old European city, quick, attractive and cultivated, linked by its busy port to the wider world. It has not been swamped by the countryside. Yet perhaps, despite its industrial suburbs, it still remains a little cut off from the extraordinary bustle of life – that very feature that makes Moscow so clearly a capital.

The influx of labour from the countryside quickly outnumbered the skilled workers of the past. Peasants filled the factories, ignorant, ill-trained, clumsy and, like all peasants, suspicious of machinery. Turned overnight into factory-hands, they at first achieved only low productivity. So, to make up the lack of production, more of them were drafted in.

There was a similar influx of peasants, or at least of their children, into the schools and universities. In 1917, at least 75 per cent of the population was illiterate. By the 1960s, it was claimed, illiteracy had been totally eradicated. This would certainly explain the growing numbers of libraries, reading-rooms and popular editions of Russian classics (although not of Dostoyevsky or Sergey Yesenin until 1955). These, as well as selected foreign translations, were often printed in enormous numbers – on occasion, as many as 10 million. True, the price of books, on mediocre paper, was derisory. Was this why the classics were so popular? Or was it because contemporary authors seemed lame, and the press was dull and difficult? At all events, radio, television and records were also extensively devoted to further education.

What O. Rosenfeld has called 'this cultural revolution' in itself encouraged a genuine social revolution – an immense desire for emancipation, a hunger to learn and rise in the social scale. 'Crazy over-ambition', a harsh observer might say. Let us call it rather an eagerness for culture, the key to both money and prestige. Whatever their motive, there were more and more students at universities and technical schools, or taking correspondence courses and evening classes. Often, the children of peasants had the best results. In this way, the USSR was training the intellectual élite it needed – engineers, research workers, officers, professors – out of its inexhaustible human resources. What happened in France after Jules Ferry's educational reforms, and then with free education in secondary schools and universities, was organized by the Soviet authorities at vertiginous speed – and therefore not always without mishaps. It still seems astonishing, for instance, that from 1947 to 1956, secondary education in the Soviet Union was fee-paying, not free.

By the 1960s, however, the level of education was generally said to have fallen.

Once made, that statement calls for qualification. The Russian spoken today, it is true, is no longer the refined language of the past. The education so widely offered is utilitarian, mass-producing the specialists needed by modern society, from the school-teacher to the engineer or even the university professor. 'Semi-intellectuals', said one observer, not normally so unkind.

Unkind or not, was the remark fair? Was this mass semi-culture simply a normal feature in a new country, as is often suggested, or

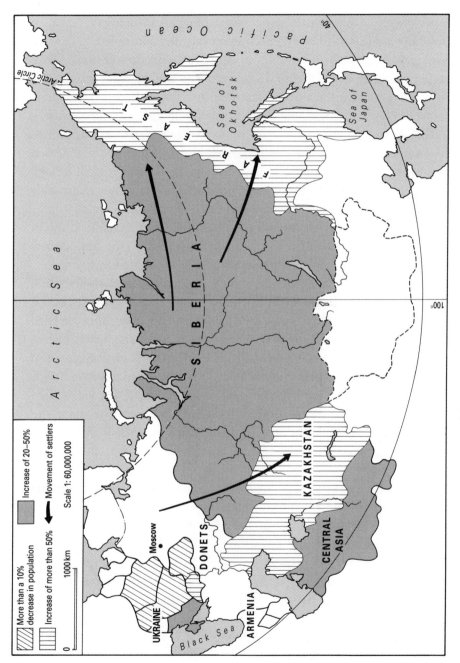

23. *Emigration within the USSR*

more simply still characteristic of an emerging mass civilization? In all the highly industrialized countries in the world, in Europe or America, universal education tends to produce more specialists, and a lower level of general culture. Yet the number of people forming a true intellectual élite has not diminished: at the very worst, it has remained the same. Instead of the very small intellectual élite and the very large mass of illiterates that traditional civilizations maintained, modern civilizations present a more complex picture: a small élite, a very small number of illiterates and a mass of people for whom education is mainly vocational, not a form of higher intellectual training.

In fact, at this higher level, Soviet or CIS intellectuals, scholars and teachers are in our view (and taking account of ideological differences) comparable with those in Europe or the United States. They are also the heirs of the same culture. For a Parisian intellectual, for example, to go from French universities to the Moscow Academy of Sciences is to feel at home, to enjoy immediate mutual comprehension in any discussion or jest. The first impression is that the USSR's total isolation since the Revolution – the physical isolation that cut it off from uninterrupted relations with Europe – had no effect at this academic level. At first sight, this seems surprising. But on second thoughts, one recalls that at the beginning of the twentieth century Europe and Russia were steeped in the same civilization. And in the life of a civilization, the time since then is relatively short. Despite all the fantastic upheavals that have shaken so many social and political structures in the former Soviet Union, it still largely belongs to the same civilization as that of Russia in 1917, i.e. our own.

True, literature and the arts seem to contradict this assertion.

Indeed, if we look in them, as usual, for the best portrait of the society that supports them, in the case of the Soviet Union that portrait looks decidedly pale. But were the pious official works, so absurdly unrealistic, to be regarded as truly representative of Soviet writers and artists, and even of Soviet society and daily life? They were of course the fruit of exceptional circumstance.

Their unconvincing tone was absent from the works of Marx, Engels and even Lenin. It emerged only at the beginning of Stalin's ascendancy, around 1930. Then, the authorities attacked any intellectuals who questioned or rejected Stalin's iron discipline and the mobilization of 'the artistic and literary front' in pursuit of the five-year plan. The first victim was the Association of Proletarian Writers, the RAPP: it was dissolved in 1932, together with similar organizations for music and the fine arts. In their place a single body was formed, under the direct control of the Communist Party.

At the same time, artists and writers were ordered to become 'engineers of human souls'. In 1934 Andrei Zhdanov, the Party Secretary, defined their dogma, 'the method of Socialist Realism'. What artists and writers must do was to describe with 'veracity' the 'historically concrete character' of Socialist reality, and in particular the conditions of production, thus contributing to 'the ideological transformation and the education of workers in the spirit of Socialism'. Their duty, as Zhdanov himself put it, was to be 'tendentious', to produce 'edifying' works, in which people were clearly divided into 'positive heroes', the true Communists, and 'negative characters' – all the rest. The avant-garde movements that had flourished in all the arts at the beginning of the Revolution, and which in the Soviet Union continued to be called 'left-wing art', were now condemned as 'formalist' and suppressed. A number of writers and theatre directors were arrested, and mysteriously disappeared. Most writers took refuge in silence or semi-silence. Mikhail Sholokhov, the author of *Quiet Flows the Don*, whose first three volumes were published between 1925 and 1933, and the fourth in 1940, wrote nothing more until the death of Stalin.

After the Second World War, to counteract the influence of 'the corrupt West', the 'Zhdanov line' was even more strongly enforced. Literature, theatre and the cinema were all kept under close surveillance; the slightest deviation was denounced and punished. In 1948, the great composers Sergei Prokofiev, Dmitri Shostakovich and Aram Khachaturian were violently attacked for writing 'hermetic' music and misusing dissonance.

In other words, throughout Stalin's dictatorship, artists were brought to heel like the rest of the Soviet population. All the products of that period were conformist and mediocre.

Did the death of Stalin change everything? Yes and no. There was certainly an immediate reaction, and a sudden slackening of tension: but the liberal explosion was thought dangerous, and at that time it was very soon damped down.

The end of 1953 and the following year saw a profusion of plays satirizing the faults of Soviet society; and an article by a young critic on 'sincerity in literature', published in the magazine *Novy Mir*, ridiculed the official distinction between 'positive' and 'negative' characters. Although the authors of these squibs were punished for their boldness, de-Stalinization and the attack on the 'cult of personality' encouraged further outspokenness. Hundreds of thousands of deportees returned, and assurance was given that severe sanctions would no longer be applied. This sparked off intense intellectual excitement, and what might be called a literary changing of the guard: those writers who had made their names under Stalin now fell silent, and those of his former victims who were still alive reappeared in print. So great was the effervescence that the authorities were worried. In 1957, they were advised and warned to avoid 'revisionism' and systematically blackening Soviet reality in the guise of a refusal to 'embellish and varnish it'. This reaction was a clear expression of the policy pursued by Nikita Khrushchev.

He certainly condemned Stalin's methods. Even defeated political opponents were no longer executed or subjected to physical violence; and there was some liberalization in cultural matters and relations with other countries. But to open the floodgates to a violently critical campaign, at the very moment when the revelation of Stalin's crimes had deeply shaken a generation of his young and faithful admirers, would have looked like endangering the regime and the USSR's position as leader of the world's Communist countries, as well as perhaps weakening its international power. So the Government reacted – forcefully.

Was the public, then, concerned by that struggle? Huge popular audiences enjoyed the classic plays of the Russian or foreign repertoire; they liked folklore, 'pure, stylized or adapted'; they flocked to classical operas that were a revelation to people until recently still peasants. Hence the success of *Faust*, *La Traviata* or *Carmen*, rivalling the Red Army dancers or Tchaikovsky's ballet *Swan Lake*. But it would still be a mistake to believe that in these matters there was a sharp distinction between 'lowbrows' and 'highbrows', the general public and the intellectual élite. The freedom of expression that Soviet writers and artists were seeking was in fact a crucial problem, then and in the future.

The problems that beset art and literature hardly affected mathematics and the natural sciences. These, for the most part, were in a very flourishing state. There were many reasons for this. The sciences, as an intellectual discipline, have usually been subject to little detailed control. Very often, they have no relevance to political or ideological debates, and can avoid them. At the same time, the Russians have always been exceptional mathematicians. Furthermore, the Government has not been sparing with either cash or encouragement; and there is something inspiring about building a new world or imagining others as yet undreamed of. Finally, it has to be admitted that in the field of research there is something to be said for authoritarianism. In the capitalist countries, research tends to be dispersed among the different branches of industry, and is partly determined by industry's needs. In the USSR, it has been concentrated on Government priorities. Industry has lost out; so, still more, have consumer comforts, for so long disdained. But research has benefited, as has the organization of scientific teams. And today, success in research depends more on teams than on brilliant individuals. So there may be homage due to the Academy of Sciences of the USSR.

What conclusion can we draw? That in the years after the Second World War, the Soviet Union was still emerging from immense difficulties; and that it had the potential for great material success. Some things it had already achieved. But the establishment of a new structure was far from completed. It was haunted by tragic memories, as well as, paradoxically, by its own world reputation. At a time when it could almost be free to choose its own future, it had to take account of what international repercussions its choice might have.

This somewhat limited its freedom – a limitation that continued long after de-Stalinization. It also limited its own 'superstructures' of art and literature, those means of 'escape' without which no civilization can fully explore itself or express itself. Let us hope that before long the arts will spring into sudden life, like the apple trees in Bolshoi Square in Moscow in the first warm sunshine in May.

The Congress of October 1961

The dramatic 22nd Congress of the Communist Party, in October 1961, threw a fantastic light on the then situation of the USSR. There is no point now, of course, in recalling the dramatic clash of personalities, the lists of condemnations, of excommunications, of the 'living dead' or the 'walking corpses'. Nor is there any need to analyse in detail a turmoil that so much recalls a Dostoyevsky novel – perhaps the tormented and tormenting characters of *The Brothers Karamazov*.

What mattered, and what was first clearly shown at that time, was Soviet civilization itself, confronted with its difficult tasks and choices, in both domestic and foreign affairs. The future depends on how they are tackled. There are three major problems. The first concerns the non-Russian nationalities, the people of other races and civilizations within the union of federated Republics. The second is the economic and material situation (but is it only material?) of ex-Soviet civilization as a whole. The third is the fate of international Communism, which already in 1961 was ceasing to be monolithic and becoming 'polycentric', a kind of 'Communism of the States'.

As regards the first problem, what is at stake is the Union itself. The USSR, as its name implied, regarded itself as a federation of Republics, or States that were in principle independent, but bound together. In the CIS, can their mutual relations be improved in such a way as to produce a powerful and unified civilization?

The Union was first formed by the Empire of the Tsars; and even before 1917 it had already suffered many misadventures. Divided, restored, consolidated, then called in question again, it continued to pose a difficult problem with no perfect solution. While clearly autonomous, none of the Republics was truly independent, since its defence, its policing and its communications were under control by the central authorities, represented by delegates on the Central Committee of each Republic. There was local nationalism – 'chauvinism' – and it was condemned. Clashes occurred. Georgia had to be brought back in the Union in 1921; forty years later, de-Stalinization offended its fidelity to its most famous son. The Baltic States, freed in 1918, annexed in 1940 and reoccupied in 1945, had had privileged status under the Tsars: but the Soviet Union long refused to renew it. There was a crisis in Kirgizia in 1949–51, when the Soviet authorities banned the national epic poem, *Ma as*. And in 1958 the Supreme Soviet announced its intention to recognize Azei as the only language of Azerbaijan.

Local interests and cultures, traditional languages and historical memories, fidelity or otherwise to Communism, and the immigration or intrusion of Russians or Ukrainians into other Republics: all these gave rise to problems, and sometimes to tensions, of a colonial type. To take one example, after the reclamation of virgin land in Kazakhstan, there were more Russians there than Kazakhs.

The only policy of which the USSR was capable came as no surprise: it sought to maintain and safeguard the life and 'harmony' of the Union. This it did by making reasonable and even very generous concessions to the non-Russian Republics – especially since they represented, all told, only a very small part of the USSR's strength. This was the policy that emerged at the 20th

Congress of the Party in 1956. The result was a series of measures to give them greater autonomy – an avowed return to Lenin's nationality policy. To a Westerner, all this was reminiscent of the traditional problems of colonization and decolonization – but with one importance difference. In the case of the USSR, the 'colonies' and the 'mother country' were geographically and physically in direct contact. On the agenda of the 21st Congress of the Communist Party there was explicit mention of the word 'assimilation' – a highly charged and evocative term. Was it possible? And would the USSR be able to achieve it, when the West had so often failed?

In 1959, the Secretary of the Kazakhstan Communist Party declared: 'Lenin's thesis that nations can merge by growing economically and doing more and more together has been confirmed by experience.' This is perfectly possible. There have been examples of successful assimilation in the past. A common policy, mutual concessions and the need to live together can be powerful influences; so can the building of new structures, political, economic and social, which both sides share as a result of so many years' experience of Communism. Nevertheless, civilizations are tenacious. This can be seen in the matter of language alone: the Republics of the USSR defended theirs with stubborn success. They were not prepared to renounce their local civilizations. At the time of writing, the debate was still going on – as it is today. It may well have been that the fight against illiteracy, and the spread of education, actually helped to intensify national awareness among the peoples of Central Asia.

Prosperity or 'bourgeois' civilization: the announcement of a twenty-year plan to lead the USSR to the delights of Communist society did not seem a vain project in 1962.

So long as such and such a condition was met, said the experts, the USSR should be able to make its 'Great Leap Forward' into prosperity. They never agreed on what the conditions were. But the Soviet public passionately wanted peace and longed for material progress, which it believed was possible. That is why in the

1960s so many younger people eagerly took part in the active running of the country. An immense change seemed to be imminent, whatever form it might take and whatever label it might later receive.

In 1962, Soviet life was dominated by the hope of rapidly advancing towards the final stages of the Industrial Revolution. The Khrushchev revolution seemed to open the way to such progress, since the seven-year plan of 1958 had stressed the new industries by a 'sophisticated' consumer society – electronics, electro-mechanics, nuclear energy, plastics, chemicals. All of these were industries which, even before they called forth a new generation of consumers, required and would have to train 'a new type of working class' – white-coated technicians, technologists, scientific and industrial research workers, and so on. The pressure of these new social forces would sooner or later make the democratization of the USSR inevitable and irreversible, concluded the sociologist from whom we gleaned these details.

But that pressure, of course, had to make its way through both the live and the inert counter-pressures of Communist society and the Party itself. It was logical, moreover, for the Party to try to control and apportion any new prosperity and comfort, so as to make the success its own.

That might have been possible, but only if the USSR could have proved that its years of Communism had radically changed it: that, if the Russia of 1917 was still part of Western civilization, the Soviet Union could achieve prosperity along lines different from the 'bourgeois' West, where it had been the best way of staving off revolution.

On this point, at the time of writing, it was impossible to make predictions. The future remained entirely open. It did, however, still seem possible that the former USSR might invent its own solution, copying neither the American nor the European model.

International Communism? There too, the future remained open, with few hints of what was to come. Western commentators on the October 1961 Congress tended to see it as marking the end of the monolithic International Communist Party. It seemed to them that the USSR was consciously abandoning its leadership and the sacrifices that implied, in order to concentrate on its own 'Great Leap Forward' and become the only Communist country to achieve Communist perfection, thanks to material prosperity. It seemed, in a word, as if the USSR was accepting 'bicentrism' for itself and China, or even polycentrism – 'Communism of the States', leaving everyone to their own problems and their own fate.

It seemed rash to be so categorical. Even in the great Communist family, politics follows its ordinary rules. Anger, quarrels, even threats, are often followed by reconciliation and compromise (which is not only an Anglo-American idea). Soviet mistrust of China is nothing new: it has roots in centuries of history, and also in the nineteenth-century conflicts in which Russia was one of the great powers that shared the spoils of China's wealth. But Soviet mistrust of the United States was no less deep-rooted at the time of the Cold War. The same reasons that obliged the United States to emerge from isolationism make it impossible for the USSR, like it or not, to concern itself only with its own economic problems. It has to see its internal policy in the context of international reality.

Nevertheless, in the 1960s, there seemed to be signs of differentiation among the various Communist parties in the world, gravitating round the USSR like planets around a sun, and many of them quite unlike each other.

In outer orbit were the national Communist parties. Some were in the hostile environment of prosperous Western countries like France or Italy, or even virtually non-existent, as in the Anglo-Saxon countries or West Germany. Others, at that time, were living underground lives in Western countries politically hostile to them but economically weak: this was the case in Spain, Portugal and Latin America. Others again were fighting their political battles in the open, in less developed countries still fascinated by the Soviet and Chinese experiments, and still living on hope.

Closer, but none the less distant, were the satellite Communist countries. Those of the 'glacis' facing the West had protected Soviet territory, like buffer states, since the Second World War: Eastern Germany, Poland, Hungary, Czechoslovakia, Romania and Bulgaria. In all of them, great economic and social changes were under way. All except Bulgaria, perhaps, were rapidly industrializing; both Eastern Germany and Czechoslovakia, moreover, had inherited viable industrial economies from pre-Communist days. Outside the 'glacis', finally, were Albania's eccentric Communist system and the equally individual Yugoslavia.

The position of these countries at that time was complex. On the one hand, they could not stray far from the Soviet Union; on the other, some of the structural reforms on which they staked their future (agrarian reform, the break-up of huge estates in Poland and Hungary, and industrialization) would not have been possible, or would certainly have been much harder, without the brutal intrusion of Communism. In fact, their relations with the USSR and with Communism itself differed from country to country, more or less confident, free and fruitful according to their various economies and the different civilizations from which they sprang.

Finally, in the far distance, weighed down by its difficulties but upheld by its pride, there was Communist China, the largest less-developed country in the world. It was certainly the least docile and the most dangerous of the USSR's partners.

This rapid sketch-map reflects not only political positions as they then were, but also economic situations which change less rapidly. These do not determine the future, but they influence it in advance. The former USSR, whose decades of effort put it in some ways in the lead, may well have to suffer the solitude its efforts have earned.

Index